Politics

Palgrave Foundations

A series of introductory texts across a wide range of subject areas to meet the needs of today's lecturers and students

Foundations texts provide complete yet concise coverage of core topics and skills based on detailed research of course requirements suitable for both independent study and class use – the firm foundations for future study.

Published

A History of English Literature (second edition)
Biology
British Politics (second edition)
Chemistry (fourth edition)
Communication Studies
Contemporary Europe (third edition)
Economics
Economics for Business
European Union Politics
Foundations of Marketing
Global Politics
Modern British History
Nineteenth-Century Britain
Philosophy
Physics (third edition)
Politics (third edition)
Theatre Studies

Politics

Third Edition

ANDREW HEYWOOD

palgrave
macmillan

First edition 1997
Second edition 2002
Third edition 2007

First published 1997 by
PALGRAVE MACMILLAN

Palgrave Macmillan in the UK is an imprint of Macmillan Publishers Limited,
registered in England, company number 785998, of Houndmills, Basingstoke,
Hampshire RG21 6XS.

Palgrave Macmillan in the US is a division of St Martin's Press LLC,
175 Fifth Avenue, New York, NY 10010.

Palgrave Macmillan is the global academic imprint of the above companies
and has companies and representatives throughout the world.

Palgrave® and Macmillan® are registered trademarks in the United States,
the United Kingdom, Europe and other countries.

ISBN-13: 978 0–230–52557–3   hardback
ISBN-10: 0–230–52557–1   hardback
ISBN-13: 978 0–230–52497–2   paperback
ISBN-10: 0–230–52497–4   paperback

This book is printed on paper suitable for recycling and made from fully
managed and sustained forest sources. Logging, pulping and manufacturing
processes are expected to conform to the environmental regulations of the
country of origin.

A catalogue record for this book is available from the British Library.

A catalog record for this book is available from the Library of Congress.

13   12   11   10
16   15   14   13   12   11

Printed and bound in China

For Mark and Robin

Contents

PART 1

Theories of Politics

PART 3

Political Interaction

PART 4

Machinery of Government

List of boxes

Concepts

Focus

Political figures

Preface

THIS book provides a comprehensive and up-to-date introduction to the study of politics. It is designed to be of use to students taking courses in any field of the discipline, as well as general readers with an interest in the subject.

Politics stubbornly (and splendidly) refuses to stand still. The idea that history is 'speeding up' was not just a symptom of *fin de siècle* anxiety; in a sense, history *is* speeding up. For instance, the final decades of the twentieth century saw the collapse of communism, the end of the Cold War, the emergence of a global economy, a technological revolution in production and communications and the rise of political Islam. Indeed, we appear to be living in a kind of 'post-world'; ideas such as postmodernism, postmaterialism, post-Fordism, post-socialism and postindustrialism vie with one another to demonstrate how much and which bits of the familiar world have now disappeared. And yet not all is flux and confusion. The pace of change may have increased, but certain aspects of social existence and important features of the political landscape have proved to be remarkably resilient to change. Therefore, while this book gives full weight to modern developments such as globalization, the growth of feminism and green politics, the upsurge of ethnic nationalism and the emergence of new social movements, conventional approaches to the discipline are not neglected, and the contribution of classical thinkers such as Plato, Aristotle, Marx and Mill is not ignored.

This third edition features wider discussion of a number of topics as well as additional boxed material. A new chapter has been added on the mass media and political communication, reflecting the extent to which politics and the media are, in the contemporary world, inextricably entwined. There is also extended coverage of developments such as the post-Cold War world order and the 'war on terror', the rise of identity politics and multiculturalism, and of state transformation in a global era. Throughout the book, greater attention has been given to the increasingly important global dimension of politics. The book nevertheless continues to adopt a holistic approach that tries to bring out what is distinctive about political analysis as a whole, and also highlights concerns that are shared by all who are interested in the subject. In an attempt to bridge the political philosophy/political science divide, links are drawn between normative and empirical theory, and a genuinely international perspective is adopted in preference to a country-by-country or system-by-system one.

The book is organized around five central themes. Part 1 on the theories of politics examines the conceptual and methodological issues that underpin the study of politics, and thus serves as an introduction to theories and ideas that are addressed throughout the book. Part 2 on nations and globalization discusses the role and significance of the nation-state, particularly in the light of internationalization and the emergence of global politics. Part 3 on political interaction looks at links between the political and nonpolitical worlds and at channels of communication between government and the governed. Part 4 on the machinery of government considers the institutional and political processes that affect both the nature of government and its style of operation. Part 5 on policy and performance analyses how policy is made and how the performance of political systems can be judged, thus linking back to the theoretical and ideological issues examined in Part 1.

Each chapter starts with an outline of its major themes and a series of questions that indicate the central topics that are addressed in the chapter. At the end of each chapter there is a summary, a list of questions for discussion, and suggestions for further reading. Additional material is provided throughout the text in the form of glossary panels and boxed information. Brief biographies are provided of key political thinkers and significant political figures, together with a discussion of their theoretical role or importance. Concept boxes offer a fuller discussion of important political terms and concepts, particularly those with meanings that are complex or contested. Focus boxes give either further insight into particular theories or approaches, or an overview of relevant debates and arguments. These boxes are comprehensively cross-referenced, emphasizing the interlocking character of the discipline. A glossary containing definitions of all the significant terms and concepts in the text is included at the end of the book. The bibliographical details of the references in the text (except for works only referred to in the boxes) are given in the bibliography at the end of the book, in addition to details of other relevant works. The companion website to the third edition can be found at www.palgrave.com/foundations/heywood. The website contains useful website addresses, chapter notes, questions (with answers) and supplementary material.

I would like to express my sincere gratitude to the academic reviewers who commented on earlier drafts of this work, namely John Greenaway, Wyn Grant, Chris Brown and Gerry Stoker. Their advice and criticism was both constructive and insightful, and undoubtedly improved the book at a number of points. Discussions with colleagues and friends, particularly Karon and Doug Woodward, also helped to sharpen the ideas and arguments developed here. My publishers, Steven Kennedy and Suzannah Burywood have been a constant source of support and encouragement, leavened, I am glad to say, by patience when necessary. My most heartfelt thanks, however, go, as ever, to my wife Jean. Not only did she take sole responsibility for the preparation of the typescript of this book, but she also offered advice on both style and content, which was especially useful when I was in danger of lapsing into incoherence. This book is dedicated to my sons, Mark and Robin.

Andrew Heywood, *2007*

Acknowledgements

The author and publishers wish to thank the following for permission to use copyright material:

Associated Press, p. 374; David Fukuyama, p. 31; Donna Coveney/MIT, p. 234; Duckworth, p. 211; The E. F. Schumacher Society, p. 195; Empics, pp. 55, 57, 62, 65, 79, 81, 253, 289, 385, 416; Getty Images, pp. 6, 7, 12, 47, 49, 52, 77, 111, 116, 129, 166, 175, 186, 213, 216, 226, 250, 327, 336, 344, 373; Harvard University News Office, pp. 60, 100, 146; The Macmillan Archive, p. 190; Martha Stewart, p. 210; Naomi Klein, p. 309; People's History Museum, p. 208; Polity Press, p. 253; Roger-Viollet, pp. 152, 227; Topham Picturepoint, pp. 48, 168, 191, 199, 310; Ullstein Bild, pp. 9, 58, 90, 220, 223; The Walker Art Gallery, National Museums Liverpool, p. 63; Yale University Office of Public Affairs, p. 298.

Every effort has been made to trace all the copyright holders, but if any have been inadvertently overlooked the publishers will be pleased to make the necessary arrangement at the first opportunity.

Theories of Politics

What is Politics?

CHAPTER 1

'Man is by nature a political animal.'
ARISTOTLE, *Politics*, 1

Politics is exciting because people disagree. They disagree about how they should live. Who should get what? How should power and other resources be distributed? Should society be based on cooperation or conflict? And so on. They also disagree about how such matters should be resolved. How should collective decisions be made? Who should have a say? How much influence should each person have? And so forth. For Aristotle, this made politics the 'master science': that is, nothing less than the activity through which human beings attempt to improve their lives and create the Good Society. Politics is, above all, a social activity. It is always a dialogue, and never a monologue. Solitary individuals such as Robinson Crusoe may be able to develop a simple economy, produce art, and so on, but they cannot engage in politics. Politics emerges only with the arrival of a Man (or Woman) Friday. Nevertheless, the disagreement that lies at the heart of politics also extends to the nature of the subject and how it should be studied. People disagree about both what it is that makes social interaction 'political', and how political activity can best be analysed and explained.

The central issues examined in this chapter are as follows:

Key issues

▶ What are the defining features of politics as an activity?
▶ How has 'politics' been understood by various thinkers and traditions?
▶ Does politics take place within all social institutions, or only in some?
▶ What approaches to the study of politics as an academic discipline have been adopted?
▶ Can the study of politics be scientific?
▶ What roles do concepts, models and theories play in political analysis?

■ Defining politics

Politics, in its broadest sense, is the activity through which people make, preserve and amend the general rules under which they live. Although politics is also an academic subject (sometimes indicated by the use of 'Politics' with a capital P), it is then clearly the study of this activity. Politics is thus inextricably linked to the phenomena of **conflict** and **cooperation**. On the one hand, the existence of rival opinions, different wants, competing needs and opposing interests guarantees disagreement about the rules under which people live. On the other hand, people recognize that, in order to influence these rules or ensure that they are upheld, they must work with others – hence Hannah Arendt's (see p. 9) definition of political power as 'acting in concert'. This is why the heart of politics is often portrayed as a process of conflict resolution, in which rival views or competing interests are reconciled with one another. However, politics in this broad sense is better thought of as a search for conflict resolution than as its achievement, as not all conflicts are, or can be, resolved. Nevertheless, the inescapable presence of diversity (we are not all alike) and scarcity (there is never enough to go around) ensures that politics is an inevitable feature of the human condition.

Any attempt to clarify the meaning of 'politics' must nevertheless address two major problems. The first is the mass of associations that the word has when used in everyday language; in other words, politics is a 'loaded' term. Whereas most people think of, say, economics, geography, history and biology simply as academic subjects, few people come to politics without preconceptions. Many, for instance, automatically assume that students and teachers of politics must in some way be biased, finding it difficult to believe that the subject can be approached in an impartial and dispassionate manner. To make matters worse, politics is usually thought of as a 'dirty' word: it conjures up images of trouble, disruption and even violence on the one hand, and deceit, manipulation and lies on the other. There is nothing new about such associations. As long ago as 1775, Samuel Johnson dismissed politics as 'nothing more than a means of rising in the world', while in the nineteenth century the US historian Henry Adams summed up politics as 'the systematic organization of hatreds'. Any attempt to define politics therefore entails trying to disentangle the term from such associations. Not uncommonly, this has meant attempting to rescue the term from its unsavoury reputation by establishing that politics is a valuable, even laudable, activity.

The second and more intractable difficulty is that even respected authorities cannot agree what the subject is about. Politics is defined in such different ways: as the exercise of power, the exercise of authority, the making of collective decisions, the allocation of scarce resources, the practice of deception and manipulation, and so on. The virtue of the definition advanced in this text, 'the making, preserving and amending of general social rules', is that it is sufficiently broad to encompass most, if not all, of the competing definitions. However, problems arise when the definition is unpacked, or when the meaning is refined. For instance, does 'politics' refer to a particular way in which rules are made, preserved or amended (that is, peacefully, by debate), or to all such processes? Similarly, is politics practised in all social contexts and institutions, or only in certain ones (that is, government and public life)?

From this perspective, politics may be treated as an 'essentially contested' concept (see p. 19), in the sense that the term has a number of acceptable or legitimate mean-

Conflict: Competition between opposing forces, reflecting a diversity of opinions, preferences, needs or interests.

Cooperation: Working together; achieving goals through collective action.

ings. On the other hand, these different views may simply consist of contrasting conceptions of the same, if necessarily vague, concept. Whether we are dealing with rival concepts or alternative conceptions, the debate about 'what is politics?' is worth pursuing because it exposes some of the deepest intellectual and ideological disagreements in the academic study of the subject. The different views of politics examined here are as follows:

- politics as the art of government
- politics as public affairs
- politics as compromise and consensus
- politics as power and the distribution of resources.

Politics as the art of government

'Politics is not a science ... but an art', Chancellor Bismarck is reputed to have told the German Reichstag. The art Bismarck had in mind was the art of government, the exercise of control within society through the making and enforcement of collective decisions. This is perhaps the classical definition of politics, developed from the original meaning of the term in Ancient Greece.

The word 'politics' is derived from **polis**, meaning literally city-state. Ancient Greek society was divided into a collection of independent city-states, each of which possessed its own system of government. The largest and most influential of these city-states was Athens, often portrayed as the cradle of democratic government. In this light, politics can be understood to refer to the affairs of the *polis* – in effect, 'what concerns the *polis*'. The modern form of this definition is therefore 'what concerns the state' (see p. 91). This view of politics is clearly evident in the everyday use of the term: people are said to be 'in politics' when they hold public office, or to be 'entering politics' when they seek to do so. It is also a definition that academic political science has helped to perpetuate.

In many ways, the notion that politics amounts to 'what concerns the state' is the traditional view of the discipline, reflected in the tendency for academic study to focus upon the personnel and machinery of government. To study politics is in essence to study government, or, more broadly, to study the exercise of authority. This view is advanced in the writings of the influential US political scientist David Easton (1979, 1981), who defined politics as the 'authoritative allocation of values'. By this he meant that politics encompasses the various processes through which government responds to pressures from the larger society, in particular by allocating benefits, rewards or penalties. 'Authoritative values' are therefore ones that are widely accepted in society, and are considered binding by the mass of citizens. In this view, politics is associated with 'policy' (see p. 426): that is, with formal or authoritative decisions that establish a plan of action for the community.

However, what is striking about this definition is that it offers a highly restricted view of politics. Politics is what takes place within a **polity**, a system of social organization centred upon the machinery of government. Politics is therefore practised in cabinet rooms, legislative chambers, government departments and the like, and it is engaged in by a limited and specific group of people, notably politicians, civil servants and lobbyists. This means that most people, most institutions and most social activities can be regarded as being 'outside' politics. Businesses, schools and other educational institutions, community groups, families and so on are in this sense 'nonpolitical',

Concept

Authority

Authority can most simply be defined as 'legitimate power'. Whereas power is the *ability* to influence the behaviour of others, authority is the *right* to do so. Authority is therefore based on an acknowledged duty to obey rather than on any form of coercion or manipulation. In this sense, authority is power cloaked in legitimacy or rightfulness. Weber (see p. 220) distinguished between three kinds of authority, based on the different grounds upon which obedience can be established: *traditional* authority is rooted in history; *charismatic* authority stems from personality; and *legal–rational* authority is grounded in a set of impersonal rules (see the section on legitimizing power, pp. 219–22).

Polis: (*Greek*) City-state; classically understood to imply the highest or most desirable form of social organization.

Polity: A society organized through the exercise of political authority; for Aristotle, rule by the many in the interests of all.

Niccolò Machiavelli (1469–1527)

Italian politician and author. The son of a civil lawyer, Machiavelli's knowledge of public life was gained from a sometimes precarious existence in politically unstable Florence. He served as Second Chancellor (1498–1512), and was despatched on missions to France, Germany and throughout Italy. After a brief period of imprisonment and the restoration of Medici rule, Machiavelli embarked on a literary career. His major work, *The Prince*, published in 1531, drew heavily upon his first-hand observations of the statecraft of Cesare Borgia and the power politics that dominated his period. It was written as a guide for the future prince of a united Italy. The adjective 'Machiavellian' subsequently came to mean 'cunning and duplicitous'.

because they are not engaged in 'running the country'. By the same token, to portray politics as an essentially state-bound activity is to ignore the increasingly important international or global influences upon modern life, such as the impact of trans-national technology and multinational corporations. In this sense, this definition of politics is a hangover from the days when the nation-state (see p. 123) could still be regarded as an independent actor in world affairs. Moreover, there is a growing recognition that the task of managing complex societies is no longer simply carried out by government but involves a wide range of public and private sector bodies. This is reflected in the idea that government is being replaced by 'governance'.

This definition can, however, be narrowed still further. This is evident in the tendency to treat politics as the equivalent of party politics. In other words, the realm of 'the political' is restricted to those state actors who are consciously motivated by ideological beliefs, and who seek to advance them through membership of a formal organization such as a political party. This is the sense in which politicians are described as 'political', whereas civil servants are seen as 'nonpolitical', as long as, of course, they act in a neutral and professional fashion. Similarly, judges are taken to be 'nonpolitical' figures while they interpret the law impartially and in accordance with the available evidence, but they may be accused of being 'political' if their judgement is influenced by personal preferences or some other form of bias.

Concept

Governance

Governance is a broader term than government (see p. 26). Although it still has no settled or agreed definition, it refers, in its widest sense, to the various ways through which social life is coordinated. Government can therefore be seen as one of the institutions involved in governance; it is possible to have 'governance without government' (Rhodes, 1996). The principal modes of governance are markets, hierarchies and networks. The wider use of the term reflects a blurring of the state/society distinction, resulting from changes such as the development of new forms of public management, the growth of public–private partnerships, the increasing importance of policy networks (see p. 432), and the greater impact of both supranational and subnational organizations ('multi-level governance'). While some associate governance with a shift away from command and control mechanisms to a reliance on consultation and bargaining, others argue that it implies a preference for 'less government' and the free market.

Aristotle (384–322 BCE)

Greek philosopher. Aristotle was a student of Plato (see p. 12) and tutor of the young Alexander the Great. He established his own school of philosophy in Athens in 335 BCE; this was called the 'peripatetic school' after his tendency to walk up and down as he talked. His 22 surviving treatises, compiled as lecture notes, range over logic, physics, metaphysics, astronomy, meteorology, biology, ethics and politics. In the Middle Ages, Aristotle's work became the foundation of Islamic philosophy, and it was later incorporated into Christian theology. His best known political work is *Politics*, a study of the ideal constitution.

Power

Power, in its broadest sense, is the ability to achieve a desired outcome, and it is sometimes referred to in terms of the 'power *to*' do something. This includes everything from the ability to keep oneself alive to the ability of government to promote economic growth. In politics, however, power is usually thought of as a relationship: that is, as the ability to influence the behaviour of others in a manner not of their choosing. It Is referred to In terms of having 'power *over*' people. More narrowly, power may be associated with the ability to punish or reward, bringing it close to force or manipulation, in contrast to 'influence', which also encompasses rational persuasion (see the faces of power focus box, p. 11). A distinction has also been drawn between 'hard' power and 'soft' power (see p. 142).

The link between politics and the affairs of the state also helps to explain why negative or pejorative images have so often been attached to politics. This is because, in the popular mind, politics is closely associated with the activities of politicians. Put brutally, politicians are often seen as power-seeking hypocrites who conceal personal ambition behind the rhetoric of public service and ideological conviction. Indeed, this perception has become more common in the modern period as intensified media exposure has more effectively brought to light examples of corruption and dishonesty, giving rise to the phenomenon of **anti-politics**. This rejection of the personnel and machinery of conventional political life is rooted in a view of politics as a self-serving, two-faced and unprincipled activity, clearly evident in the use of derogatory phrases such as 'office politics' and 'politicking'. Such an image of politics is sometimes traced back to the writings of Niccolo Machiavelli, who, in *The Prince* ([1531] 1961), developed a strictly realistic account of politics that drew attention to the use by political leaders of cunning, cruelty and manipulation.

Such a negative view of politics reflects the essentially liberal perception that, as individuals are self-interested, political power is corrupting, because it encourages those 'in power' to exploit their position for personal advantage and at the expense of others. This is famously expressed in Lord Acton's (1834–1902) aphorism: 'power tends to corrupt, and absolute power corrupts absolutely'. Nevertheless, few who view politics in this way doubt that political activity is an inevitable and permanent feature of social existence. However venal politicians may be, there is a general, if grudging, acceptance that they are always with us. Without some kind of mechanism for allocating authoritative values, society would simply disintegrate into a civil war of each against all, as the early social-contract theorists argued (see p. 93). The task is therefore not to abolish politicians and bring politics to an end, but rather to ensure that politics is conducted within a framework of checks and constraints that ensure that governmental power is not abused.

Politics as public affairs

A second and broader conception of politics moves it beyond the narrow realm of government to what is thought of as 'public life' or 'public affairs'. In other words, the distinction between 'the political' and 'the nonpolitical' coincides with the division between an essentially *public* sphere of life and what can be thought of as a *private* sphere. Such a view of politics is often traced back to the work of the famous Greek

Anti-politics: Disillusionment with formal and established political processes, reflected in nonparticipation, support for antisystem parties, or the use of direct action.

Concept

Civil society

The term 'civil society' has been defined in a variety of ways. Originally, it meant a 'political community', a society governed by law, under the authority of a state. More commonly, it is distinguished from the state, and the term is used to describe institutions that are 'private' in that they are independent from government and organized by individuals in pursuit of their own ends. 'Civil society' therefore refers to a realm of autonomous groups and associations: businesses, interest groups, clubs, families and so on. Hegel (see p. 90), however, distinguished between the family and civil society, viewing the latter as a sphere of egoism and selfishness. The term 'global civil society' refers to transnational organizations, such as NGOs (see p. 297) and social movements (see p. 308) that are 'private', non-profit-making, self-governing and voluntary.

philosopher Aristotle. In *Politics*, Aristotle declared that 'man is by nature a political animal', by which he meant that it is only within a political community that human beings can live 'the good life'. From this viewpoint, then, politics is an ethical activity concerned with creating a 'just society'; it is what Aristotle called the 'master science'.

However, where should the line between 'public' life and 'private' life be drawn? The traditional distinction between the public realm and the private realm conforms to the division between the state and civil society. The institutions of the state (the apparatus of government, the courts, the police, the army, the social-security system and so forth) can be regarded as 'public' in the sense that they are responsible for the collective organization of community life. Moreover, they are funded at the public's expense, out of taxation. In contrast, civil society consists of what Edmund Burke (see p. 49) called the 'little platoons', institutions such as the family and kinship groups, private businesses, trade unions, clubs, community groups and so on that are 'private' in the sense that they are set up and funded by individual citizens to satisfy their own interests, rather than those of the larger society. On the basis of this 'public/private' division, politics is restricted to the activities of the state itself and the responsibilities that are properly exercised by public bodies. Those areas of life that individuals can and do manage for themselves (the economic, social, domestic, personal, cultural and artistic spheres, and so on) are therefore clearly 'nonpolitical'.

An alternative 'public/private' divide is sometimes defined in terms of a further and more subtle distinction, namely that between 'the political' and 'the personal' (see Figure 1.1). Although civil society can be distinguished from the state, it nevertheless contains a range of institutions that are thought of as 'public' in the wider sense that they are open institutions, operating in public, to which the public has access. One of the crucial implications of this is that it broadens our notion of the political, transferring the economy in particular from the private to the public realm. A form of politics can thus be found in the workplace. Nevertheless, although this view regards institutions such as businesses, community groups, clubs and trade unions as 'public', it remains a restricted view of politics. According to this perspective, politics does not, and should not, infringe upon 'personal' affairs and institutions. Feminist thinkers in particular have pointed out that this implies that politics effectively stops at the front door; it does not take place in the family, in domestic life, or in personal relationships. This view is illustrated, for example, by the tendency of politicians to draw a clear distinction between their professional conduct and their personal or domestic behaviour. By classifying, say, cheating on their partners or treating their children badly as 'personal' matters, they are able to deny the political significance of such behaviour on the grounds that it does not touch on their conduct of public affairs.

Public	Private
The state: apparatus of government	Civil society, autonomous bodies: businesses, trade unions, clubs, families, and so on

Public	Private
Public realm: politics, commerce, work, art, culture, and so on	Personal realm: family and domestic life

Fig. 1.1 Two views of the public/private divide

Hannah Arendt (1906–75)

German political theorist and philosopher. Hannah Arendt was brought up in a middle-class Jewish family. She fled Germany in 1933 to escape from Nazism, and finally settled in the USA, where her major work was produced. Her wide-ranging, even idiosyncratic, writing was influenced by the existentialism of Heidegger (1889–1976) and Jaspers (1883–1969); she described it as 'thinking without barriers'. Her major works include *The Origins of Totalitarianism* (1951), which drew parallels between Nazi Germany and Stalinist Russia, her major philosophical work *The Human Condition* (1958), *On Revolution* (1963) and *Eichmann in Jerusalem* (1963). The final work stimulated particular controversy because it stressed the 'banality of evil', by portraying Eichmann as a Nazi functionary rather than as a raving ideologue.

The view of politics as an essentially 'public' activity has generated both positive and negative images. In a tradition dating back to Aristotle, politics has been seen as a noble and enlightened activity precisely because of its 'public' character. This position was firmly endorsed by Hannah Arendt, who argued in *The Human Condition* (1958) that politics is the most important form of human activity because it involves interaction amongst free and equal citizens. It thus gives meaning to life and affirms the uniqueness of each individual. Theorists such as Jean-Jacques Rousseau (see p. 79) and John Stuart Mill (see p. 48) who portrayed political participation as a good in itself have drawn similar conclusions. Rousseau argued that only through the direct and continuous participation of all citizens in political life can the state be bound to the common good, or what he called the 'general will' (see p. 79). In Mill's view, involvement in 'public' affairs is educational in that it promotes the personal, moral and intellectual development of the individual.

In sharp contrast, however, politics as public activity has also been portrayed as a form of unwanted interference. Liberal theorists in particular have exhibited a preference for civil society over the state, on the grounds that 'private' life is a realm of choice, personal freedom and individual responsibility. This is most clearly demonstrated by attempts to narrow the realm of 'the political', commonly expressed as the wish to 'keep politics out of' private activities such as business, sport and family life. From this point of view, politics is unwholesome quite simply because it prevents people acting as they choose. For example, it may interfere with how firms conduct their business, or with how and with whom we play sports, or with how we bring up our children.

Politics as compromise and consensus

The third conception of politics relates not so much to the arena within which politics is conducted as to the way in which decisions are made. Specifically, politics is seen as a particular means of resolving conflict: that is, by compromise, conciliation and negotiation, rather than through force and naked power. This is what is implied when politics is portrayed as 'the art of the possible'. Such a definition is inherent in the everyday use of the term. For instance, the description of a solution to a problem

Consensus

The term 'consensus' means agreement, but it usually refers to an agreement of a particular kind. It implies, first, a broad agreement, the terms of which are accepted by a wide range of individuals or groups. Second, it implies an agreement about fundamental or underlying principles, as opposed to a precise or exact agreement. In other words, a consensus permits disagreement on matters of emphasis or detail. The term 'consensus politics' is used in two senses. A *procedural* consensus is a willingness to make decisions through consultation and bargaining, either between political parties or between government and major interests. A *substantive* consensus is an overlap of the ideological positions of two or more political parties, reflected in agreement about fundamental policy goals. Examples are the UK's post-1945 social-democratic consensus, and Germany's social-market consensus.

as a 'political' solution implies peaceful debate and arbitration, as opposed to what is often called a 'military' solution. Once again, this view of politics has been traced back to the writings of Aristotle and, in particular, to his belief that what he called 'polity' is the ideal system of government, as it is 'mixed' in the sense that it combines both aristocratic and democratic features. One of the leading modern exponents of this view is Bernard Crick. In his classic study *In Defence of Politics*, Crick offered the following definition:

> Politics [is] the activity by which differing interests within a given unit of rule are conciliated by giving them a share in power in proportion to their importance to the welfare and the survival of the whole community. (Crick, [1962] 2000:21)

In this view, the key to politics is therefore a wide dispersal of power. Accepting that conflict is inevitable, Crick argued that when social groups and interests possess power they must be conciliated; they cannot merely be crushed. This is why he portrayed politics as 'that solution to the problem of order which chooses conciliation rather than violence and coercion' (p. 30). Such a view of politics reflects a deep commitment to liberal–rationalist principles. It is based on resolute faith in the efficacy of debate and discussion, as well as on the belief that society is characterized by consensus rather than by irreconcilable conflict. In other words, the disagreements that exist *can* be resolved without resort to intimidation and violence. Critics, however, point out that Crick's conception of politics is heavily biased towards the form of politics that takes place in western pluralist democracies: in effect, he equated politics with electoral choice and party competition. As a result, his model has little to tell us about, say, one-party states or military regimes.

This view of politics has an unmistakeably positive character. Politics is certainly no utopian solution (compromise means that concessions are made by all sides, leaving no one perfectly satisfied), but it is undoubtedly preferable to the alternatives: bloodshed and brutality. In this sense, politics can be seen as a civilized and civilizing force. People should be encouraged to respect politics as an activity, and should be prepared to engage in the political life of their own community. Nevertheless, a failure to understand that politics as a process of compromise and reconciliation is neccessarily frustrating and difficult (because in involves listening carefully to the opinions of others) may have contributed to a growing popular disenchantment with democratic politics across much of the developed world. As Stoker (2006:10) put it, 'Politics is designed to disappoint'; its outcomes are 'often messy, ambiguous and never final'.

Politics as power

The fourth definition of politics is both the broadest and the most radical. Rather than confining politics to a particular sphere (the government, the state or the 'public' realm) this view sees politics at work in all social activities and in every corner of human existence. As Adrian Leftwich proclaimed in *What is Politics? The Activity and Its Study* (2004), 'politics is at the heart of *all* collective social activity, formal and informal, public and private, in *all* human groups, institutions and societies'. In this sense, politics takes place at every level of social interaction; it can be found within families and amongst small groups of friends just as much as amongst nations and on the global stage. However, what is it that is distinctive about political activity? What marks off politics from any other form of social behaviour?

Focus on . . .

'Faces' of power

Power can be said to be exercised whenever A gets B to do something that B would not otherwise have done. However, A can influence B in various ways. This allows us to distinguish between different dimensions or 'faces' of power:

▶ **Power as decision-making:** This face of power consists of conscious actions that in some way influence the content of decisions. The classic account of this form of power is found in Robert Dahl's *Who Governs? Democracy and Power in an American City* (1961), which made judgements about who had power by analysing decisions in the light of the known preferences of the actors involved. Such decisions can nevertheless be influenced in a variety of ways. In *Three Faces of Power* (1989), Keith Boulding distinguished between the use of force or intimidation (the stick), productive exchanges involving mutual gain (the deal), and the creation of obligations, loyalty and commitment (the kiss).

▶ **Power as agenda setting:** The second face of power, as suggested by Bachrach and Baratz (1962), is the ability to prevent decisions being made: that is, in effect, 'non-decision-making'. This involves the ability to set or control the political agenda, thereby preventing issues or proposals from being aired in the first place. For instance, private businesses may exert power both by campaigning to defeat proposed consumer-protection legislation (first face), and by lobbying parties and politicians to prevent the question of consumer rights being publicly discussed (second face).

▶ **Power as thought control:** The third face of power is the ability to influence another by shaping what he or she thinks, wants, or needs. This is power expressed as ideological indoctrination or psychological control. This is what Lukes (2004) called the radical view of power, and it overlaps with the notion of 'soft' power (see p. 142). An example of this would be the ability of advertising to shape consumer tastes, often by cultivating associations with a 'brand'. In political life, the exercise of this form of power is seen in the use of propaganda and, more generally, in the impact of ideology (see p. 45).

At its broadest, politics concerns the production, distribution and use of resources in the course of social existence. Politics is, in essence, power: the ability to achieve a desired outcome, through whatever means. This notion was neatly summed up in the title of Harold Lasswell's book *Politics: Who Gets What, When, How?* (1936). From this perspective, politics is about diversity and conflict, but the essential ingredient is the existence of scarcity: the simple fact that, while human needs and desires are infinite, the resources available to satisfy them are always limited. Politics can therefore be seen as a struggle over scarce resources, and power can be seen as the means through which this struggle is conducted.

Advocates of this view of power include feminists and Marxists. Modern feminists have shown particular interest in the idea of 'the political'. This arises from the fact that conventional definitions of politics effectively exclude women from political life. Women have traditionally been confined to a 'private' sphere of

Plato (427–347 BCE)

Greek philosopher. Plato was born of an aristocratic family. He became a follower of Socrates, who is the principal figure in his ethical and philosophical dialogues. After Socrates' death in 399 BCE, Plato founded his own academy in order to train the new Athenian ruling class. Plato taught that the material world consists of imperfect copies of abstract and eternal 'ideas'. His political philosophy, expounded in *The Republic* and *The Laws*, is an attempt to describe the ideal state in terms of a theory of justice. Both works are decidedly authoritarian and pay no attention to individual liberty, believing that power should be vested in the hands of an educated elite, the philosopher kings. He was therefore a firm critic of democracy. Plato's work has exerted wide influence on Christianity and on European culture in general.

existence, centred on the family and domestic responsibilities. In contrast, men have always dominated conventional politics and other areas of 'public' life. Radical feminists have therefore attacked the 'public/private' divide, proclaiming instead that 'the personal is the political'. This slogan neatly encapsulates the radical-feminist belief that what goes on in domestic, family and personal life is intensely political, and indeed that it is the basis of all other political struggles. Clearly, a more radical notion of politics underlies this position. This view was summed up by Kate Millett in *Sexual Politics* (1969:23), in which she defined politics as 'power-structured relationships, arrangements whereby one group of persons is controlled by another'. Feminists can therefore be said to be concerned with 'the politics of everyday life'. In their view, relationships within the family, between husbands and wives, and between parents and children, are every bit as political as relationships between employers and workers, or between governments and citizens.

Marxists have used the term 'politics' in two senses. On one level, Marx (see p. 55) used 'politics' in a conventional sense to refer to the apparatus of the state. In the *Communist Manifesto* ([1848] 1967) he thus referred to political power as 'merely the organized power of one class for oppressing another'. For Marx, politics, together with law and culture, are part of a 'superstructure' that is distinct from the economic 'base' that is the real foundation of social life. However, he did not see the economic 'base' and the legal and political 'superstructure' as entirely separate. He believed that the 'superstructure' arose out of, and reflected, the economic 'base'. At a deeper level, political power, in this view, is therefore rooted in the class system; as Lenin (see p. 81) put it, 'politics is the most concentrated form of economics'. As opposed to believing that politics can be confined to the state and a narrow public sphere, Marxists can be said to believe that 'the economic is political'. From this perspective, civil society, characterized as Marxists believe it to be by class struggle, is the very heart of politics.

Views such as these portray politics in largely negative terms. Politics is, quite simply, about oppression and subjugation. Radical feminists hold that society is patriarchal, in that women are systematically subordinated and subjected to male power. Marxists traditionally argued that politics in a capitalist society is characterized by the exploitation of the proletariat by the bourgeoisie. On the other hand, these negative implications are balanced against the fact that politics is also seen as the means through which injustice and domination can be challenged. Marx, for instance, predicted that class exploitation would be overthrown by a proletarian revolution, and radical feminists proclaim the need for gender relations to be reordered through a sexual revolution. However, it is also clear that when politics is portrayed as power and domination it need not be seen as an inevitable feature of social existence. Feminists look to an end of 'sexual politics' achieved through the construction of a nonsexist society, in which people will be valued according to personal worth rather than on the basis of gender. Marxists believe that 'class politics' will end with the establishment of a classless communist society. This, in turn, will eventually lead to the 'withering away' of the state, bringing politics in the conventional sense also to an end.

Studying politics

Approaches to the study of politics

Disagreement about the nature of political activity is matched by controversy about the nature of politics as an academic discipline. One of the most ancient spheres of intellectual enquiry, politics was originally seen as an arm of philosophy, history or law. Its central purpose was to uncover the principles upon which human society should be based. From the late nineteenth century onwards, however, this philosophical emphasis was gradually displaced by an attempt to turn politics into a scientific discipline. The high point of this development was reached in the 1950s and 1960s with an open rejection of the earlier tradition as meaningless metaphysics. Since then, however, enthusiasm for a strict science of politics has waned, and there has been a renewed recognition of the enduring importance of political values and normative theories. If the 'traditional' search for universal values acceptable to everyone has largely been abandoned, so has been the insistence that science (see p. 16) alone provides a means of disclosing truth. The resulting discipline is today more fertile and more exciting, precisely because it embraces a range of theoretical approaches and a variety of schools of analysis.

The philosophical tradition

The origins of political analysis date back to Ancient Greece and a tradition usually referred to as 'political philosophy'. This involved a preoccupation with essentially ethical, prescriptive or **normative** questions, reflecting a concern with what 'should', 'ought' or 'must' be brought about, rather than with what 'is'. Plato and Aristotle are usually identified as the founding fathers of this tradition. Their ideas resurfaced in the writings of medieval theorists such as Augustine (354–430) and Aquinas (1225–74). The central theme of Plato's work, for instance, was an attempt to describe the nature of the ideal society, which in his view took the form of a benign dictatorship dominated by a class of philosopher kings.

Such writings have formed the basis of what is called the 'traditional' approach to politics. This involves the analytical study of ideas and doctrines that have been central to political thought. Most commonly, it has taken the form of a history of political thought that focuses on a collection of 'major' thinkers (that spans, for instance, Plato to Marx) and a canon of 'classic' texts. This approach has the character of literary analysis: it is interested primarily in examining what major thinkers said, how they developed or justified their views, and the intellectual context within which they worked. Although such analysis may be carried out critically and scrupulously, it cannot be **objective** in any scientific sense, as it deals with normative ques-

Normative: The prescription of values and standards of conduct; what 'should be' rather than what 'is'.

Objective: External to the observer, demonstrable; untainted by feelings, values or bias.

tions such as 'why should I obey the state?', 'how should rewards be distributed?' and 'what should the limits of individual freedom be?'.

The empirical tradition

Although it was less prominent than normative theorizing, a descriptive or empirical tradition can be traced back to the earliest days of political thought. It can be seen in Aristotle's attempt to classify constitutions (see pp. 27–8), in Machiavelli's realistic account of statecraft, and in Montesquieu's (see p. 336) sociological theory of government and law. In many ways, such writings constitute the basis of what is now called comparative government, and they gave rise to an essentially institutional approach to the discipline. In the USA and the UK in particular this developed into the dominant tradition of analysis. The empirical approach to political analysis is characterized by the attempt to offer a dispassionate and impartial account of political reality. The approach is 'descriptive' in that it seeks to analyse and explain, whereas the normative approach is 'prescriptive' in the sense that it makes judgements and offers recommendations.

Descriptive political analysis acquired its philosophical underpinning from the doctrine of empiricism, which spread from the seventeenth century onwards through the work of theorists such as John Locke (see p. 47) and David Hume (1711–76). The doctrine of empiricism advanced the belief that experience is the only basis of knowledge, and that therefore all hypotheses and theories should be tested by a process of observation. By the nineteenth century, such ideas had developed into what became known as positivism, an intellectual movement particularly associated with the writings of Auguste Comte (1798–1857). This doctrine proclaimed that the social sciences, and, for that matter, all forms of philosophical enquiry, should adhere strictly to the methods of the natural sciences. Once science was perceived to be the only reliable means of disclosing truth, the pressure to develop a science of politics became irresistible.

The scientific tradition

The first theorist to attempt to describe politics in scientific terms was Karl Marx. Using his so-called materialist conception of history (see p. 55), Marx strove to uncover the driving force of historical development. This enabled him to make predictions about the future based upon 'laws' that had the same status in terms of proof as laws in the natural sciences. The vogue for scientific analysis was also taken up in the nineteenth century by mainstream analysis. In the 1870s, 'political science' courses were introduced in the universities of Oxford, Paris and Columbia, and by 1906 the *American Political Science Review* was being published. However, enthusiasm for a science of politics peaked in the 1950s and 1960s with the emergence, most strongly in the USA, of a form of political analysis that drew heavily upon **behaviouralism**. For the first time, this gave politics reliably scientific credentials, because it provided what had previously been lacking: objective and quantifiable data against which hypotheses could be tested. Political analysts such as David Easton proclaimed that politics could adopt the methodology of the natural sciences, and this gave rise to a proliferation of studies in areas best suited to the use of quantitative research methods, such as voting behaviour, the behaviour of legislators, and the behaviour of municipal politicians and lobbyists.

Behaviouralism, however, came under growing pressure from the 1960s onwards. In the first place, it was claimed that behaviouralism had significantly constrained

Behaviouralism: The belief that social theories should be constructed only on the basis of observable behaviour, providing quantifiable data for research.

the scope of political analysis, preventing it from going beyond what was directly observable. Although behavioural analysis undoubtedly produced, and continues to produce, invaluable insights in fields such as voting studies, a narrow obsession with quantifiable data threatens to reduce the discipline of politics to little else. More worryingly, it inclined a generation of political scientists to turn their backs upon the entire tradition of normative political thought. Concepts such as 'liberty', 'equality', 'justice' and 'rights' were sometimes discarded as being meaningless because they were not **empirically** verifiable entities. Dissatisfaction with behaviouralism grew as interest in normative questions revived in the 1970s, as reflected in the writings of theorists such as John Rawls (see p. 60) and Robert Nozick (see p. 100).

Moreover, the scientific credentials of behaviouralism started to be called into question. The basis of the assertion that behaviouralism is objective and reliable is the claim that it is 'value-free': that is, that it is not contaminated by ethical or normative beliefs. However, if the focus of analysis is observable behaviour, it is difficult to do much more than describe the existing political arrangements, which implicitly means that the *status quo* is legitimized. This conservative value bias was demonstrated by the fact that 'democracy' was, in effect, redefined in terms of observable behaviour. Thus, instead of meaning 'popular self-government' (literally, government *by* the people), democracy came to stand for a struggle between competing elites to win power through the mechanism of popular election. In other words, democracy came to mean what goes on in the so-called democratic political systems of the developed West.

Recent developments

Amongst recent theoretical approaches to politics is what is called formal political theory, variously known as 'political economy', 'public-choice theory' (see p. 300) and 'rational-choice theory'. This approach to analysis draws heavily upon the example of economic theory in building up models based upon procedural rules, usually about the rationally self-interested behaviour of the individuals involved. Most firmly established in the USA, and associated in particular with the so-called Virginia School, formal political theory provides at least a useful analytical device, which may provide insights into the actions of voters, lobbyists, bureaucrats and politicians, as well as into the behaviour of states within the international system. This approach has had its broadest impact on political analysis in the form of what is called institutional public-choice theory. The use of such techniques by writers such as Anthony Downs, Mancur Olson and William Niskanen, in fields such as party competition, interest-group behaviour and the policy influence of bureaucrats, is discussed in later chapters. The approach has also been applied in the form of game theory, which has been developed more from the field of mathematics than from economics. It entails the use of first principles to analyse puzzles about individual behaviour. The best known example in game theory is the 'prisoners' dilemma' (see Figure 1.2).

By no means, however, has the rational-choice approach to political analysis been universally accepted. While its supporters claim that it introduces greater rigour into the discussion of political phenomena, critics have questioned its basic assumptions. It may, for instance, overestimate human rationality in that it ignores the fact that people seldom possess a clear set of preferred goals and rarely make decisions in the light of full and accurate knowledge. Furthermore, in proceeding from an abstract model of the individual, rational-choice theory pays insufficient attention to social and historical factors, failing to recognize, amongst other things, that human self- interestedness

Empirical: Based on observation and experiment; empirical knowledge is derived from sense data and experience.

Science, scientism

Science (from the Latin *scientia*, meaning 'knowledge') is a field of study that aims to develop reliable explanations of phenomena through repeatable experiments, observation and deduction. The 'scientific method', by which hypotheses are verified (proved true) by testing them against the available evidence, is therefore seen as a means of disclosing value-free and objective truth. Karl Popper (1902–94), however, suggested that science can only falsify hypotheses, since 'facts' may always be disproved by later experiments. Scientism is the belief that the scientific method is the only source of reliable knowledge, and so should be applied to fields such as philosophy, history and politics, as well as the natural sciences. Doctrines such as Marxism, utilitarianism (see p. 427) and racialism (see p. 120) are scientist in this sense.

Focus on . . .

The prisoners' dilemma

Two criminals, held in separate cells, are faced with the choice of 'squealing' or 'not squealing' on one another. If only one of them confesses, but he provides evidence to convict the other, he will be released without charge, while his partner will take the whole blame and be jailed for ten years. If both criminals confess, they will each be jailed for six years. If both refuse to confess, they will only be convicted of a minor crime, and they will each receive a one-year sentence. The options are shown in Figure 1.2.

In view of the dilemma confronting them it is likely that both criminals will confess, fearing that if they do not the other will 'squeal' and they will receive the maximum sentence. Ironically, the game shows that rational behaviour can result in the least favourable outcome (in which the prisoners jointly serve a total of 12 years in jail). In effect, they are punished for their failure to cooperate or trust one another. However, if the game is repeated several times, it is possible that the criminals will learn that self-interest is advanced by cooperation, which will encourage both to refuse to confess.

Prisoner B

	Confesses	Does not confess
Confesses	A: B: 6, 6	A: B: 0, 10
Does not confess	A: B: 10, 0	A: B: 1, 1

Fig. 1.2 Options in prisoners' dilemma — **Prisoner A**

may be socially conditioned, and not merely innate. As a result, a variety of approaches have come to be adopted for the study of politics as an academic discipline.

This has made modern political analysis both richer and more diverse. To traditional normative, institutional and behavioural approaches have been added not only rational-choice theory but also a wide range of more recent ideas and themes. Feminism has, particularly since the 1970s, raised awareness of the significance of gender differences and patriarchal structures, questioning, in the process, established notions of 'the political'. What is called 'new institutionalism' has shifted attention away from the formal, structural aspects of **institutions** to, for instance, their significance within a larger context, their actual behaviour and the outcomes of the policy process. Green politics has challenged the anthropocentric (human-centred) emphasis of established political and social theory and championed holistic approaches to political and social understanding. Critical theory, which is rooted in the neo-Marxism (see p. 96) of the Frankfurt School, established in 1923, has extended the notion of critique to all social practices drawing on a wide range of influences, including Freud and Weber (see p. 220). Postmodernism (see p. 67) has questioned the idea of absolute and universal truth and helped to spawn, amongst other things, **discourse** theory. Finally, a general but profoundly important shift is that political philosophy and political science are now less likely to be seen as distinct modes of enquiry, and still less as rivals. Instead, they have come to be accepted simply as contrasting ways of disclosing political knowledge.

Can the study of politics be scientific?

Although it is widely accepted that the study of politics should be scientific in the broad sense of being rigorous and critical, some have argued, as has been pointed out, that it can be scientific in a stricter sense: that is, that it can use the methodology of the natural sciences. This claim has been advanced by Marxists and by positivist social scientists, and it was central to the 'behavioural revolution' of the 1950s. The attraction of a science of politics is clear. It promises an impartial and reliable means of distinguishing 'truth' from 'falsehood', thereby giving us access to objective knowledge about the political world. The key to achieving this is to distinguish between 'facts' (empirical evidence) and 'values' (normative or ethical beliefs). Facts are objective in the sense that they can be demonstrated reliably and consistently; they can be proved. Values, by contrast, are inherently subjective, a matter of opinion.

However, any attempt to construct a science of politics must confront three difficulties. The first of these is the problem of data. For better or worse, human beings are not tadpoles that can be taken into a laboratory or cells that can be observed under a microscope. We cannot get 'inside' a human being, or carry out repeatable experiments on human behaviour. What we can learn about individual behaviour is therefore limited and superficial. In the absence of exact data, we have no reliable means of testing our hypotheses. The only way round the problem is to ignore the thinking subject altogether by subscribing to the doctrine of **determinism**. One example would be behaviourism (as opposed to behaviouralism), the school of psychology associated with John B. Watson (1878–1958) and B. F. Skinner (1904–90). This holds that human behaviour can ultimately be explained in terms of conditioned reactions or reflexes. Another example is 'dialectical materialism', the crude form of Marxism that dominated intellectual enquiry in the USSR.

Second, there are difficulties that stem from the existence of hidden values. The idea that models and theories of politics are entirely value-free is difficult to sustain when examined closely. Facts and values are so closely intertwined that it is often impossible to prise them apart. This is because theories are invariably constructed on the basis of assumptions about human nature, human society, the role of the state and so on that have hidden political and ideological implications. A conservative value **bias**, for example, can be identified in behaviouralism, rational-choice theories and systems theory (see pp. 19–20). Similarly, feminist political theories are rooted in assumptions about the nature and significance of gender divisions.

Third, there is the myth of neutrality in the social sciences. Whereas natural scientists may be able to approach their studies in an objective and impartial manner, holding no presuppositions about what they are going to discover, this is difficult and perhaps impossible to achieve in politics. However politics is defined, it addresses questions relating to the structure and functioning of the society in which

Discourse: Human interaction, especially communication; discourse may disclose or illustrate power relationships.

Determinism: The belief that human actions and choices are entirely conditioned by external factors; determinism implies that free will is a myth.

Bias: Sympathies or prejudices that (often unconsciously) affect human judgement; bias implies distortion (see p. 238, the 'political bias' concept box).

Concept

Ideal type

An ideal type (sometimes 'pure type') is a mental construct in which an attempt is made to draw out meaning from an otherwise almost infinitely complex reality through the presentation of a logical extreme. Ideal types were first used in economics, for instance, in the notion of perfect competition. Championed in the social sciences by Max Weber, ideal types are explanatory tools, not approximations of reality; they neither 'exhaust reality' nor offer an ethical ideal. Weberian examples include types of authority (see p. 5) and bureaucracy (see p. 383).

we live and have grown up. Family background, social experience, economic position, personal sympathies and so on thus build into each and every one of us a set of preconceptions about politics and the world around us. This means that scientific objectivity, in the sense of absolute impartiality or neutrality (see p. 329), must always remain an unachievable goal in political analysis, however rigorous our research methods may be. Perhaps the greatest threat to the accumulation of reliable knowledge thus comes not from bias as such, but from the failure to acknowledge bias, reflected in bogus claims to political neutrality.

Concepts, models and theories

Concepts, models and theories are the tools of political analysis. However, as with most things in politics, the analytical tools must be used with care. First, let us consider concepts. A concept is a general idea about something, usually expressed in a single word or a short phrase. A concept is more than a proper noun or the name of a thing. There is, for example, a difference between talking about a cat (a particular and unique cat) and having a concept of a 'cat' (the idea of a cat). The concept of a cat is not a 'thing' but an 'idea', an idea composed of the various attributes that give a cat its distinctive character: 'a furry mammal', 'small', 'domesticated', 'catches rats and mice', and so on. The concept of 'equality' is thus a principle or ideal. This is different from using the term to say that a runner has 'equalled' a world record, or that an inheritance is to be shared 'equally' between two brothers. In the same way, the concept of 'presidency' refers not to any specific president, but rather to a set of ideas about the organization of executive power.

What, then, is the value of concepts? Concepts are the tools with which we think, criticize, argue, explain and analyse. Merely perceiving the external world does not in itself give us knowledge about it. In order to make sense of the world we must, in a sense, impose meaning upon it, and this we do through the construction of concepts. Quite simply, to treat a cat as a cat, we must first have a concept of what it is. Concepts also help us to classify objects by recognizing that they have similar forms or similar properties. A cat, for instance, is a member of the class of 'cats'. Concepts are therefore 'general': they can relate to a number of objects, indeed to any object that complies with the characteristics of the general idea itself. It is no exaggeration to say that our knowledge of the political world is built up through developing and refining concepts that help us make sense of that world. Concepts, in that sense, are the building blocks of human knowledge.

Nevertheless, concepts can also be slippery customers. In the first place, the political reality we seek to understand is constantly shifting and is highly complex. There is always the danger that concepts such as 'democracy', 'human rights' and 'capitalism' will be more rounded and coherent than the unshapely realities they seek to describe. Max Weber tried to overcome this problem by recognizing particular concepts as 'ideal types'. This view implies that the concepts we use are constructed by singling out certain basic or central features of the phenomenon in question, which means that other features are downgraded or ignored altogether. The concept of 'revolution' can be regarded as an ideal type in this sense, in that it draws attention to a process of fundamental and usually violent political change. It thus helps us make sense of, say, the 1789 French Revolution and the eastern European revolutions of 1989–91 by highlighting important parallels between them. The concept must nevertheless be used with care because it can also conceal vital differences, and

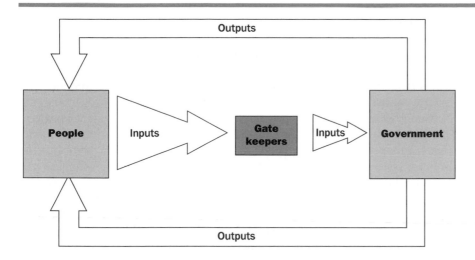

Fig. 1.3 The political system

thereby distort understanding – in this case, for example, about the ideological and social character of revolution. For this reason, it is better to think of concepts or ideal types not as being 'true' or 'false', but merely as more or less 'useful'.

A further problem is that political concepts are often the subject of deep ideological controversy. Politics is, in part, a struggle over the legitimate meaning of terms and concepts. Enemies may argue, fight and even go to war, all claiming to be 'defending freedom', 'upholding democracy' or 'having justice on their side'. The problem is that words such as 'freedom', 'democracy' and 'justice' have different meanings to different people. How can we establish what is 'true' democracy, 'true' freedom or 'true' justice? The simple answer is that we cannot. Just as with the attempt to define 'politics' above, we have to accept that there are competing versions of many political concepts. Such concepts are best regarded as 'essentially contested' concepts (Gallie, 1955/56), in that controversy about them runs so deep that no neutral or settled definition can ever be developed. In effect, a single term can represent a number of rival concepts, none of which can be accepted as its 'true' meaning. For example, it is equally legitimate to define politics as what concerns the state, as the conduct of public life, as debate and conciliation, and as the distribution of power and resources.

Models and theories are broader than concepts; they comprise a range of ideas rather than a single idea. A **model** is usually thought of as a representation of something, usually on a smaller scale, as in the case of a doll's house or a toy aeroplane. In this sense, the purpose of the model is to resemble the original object as faithfully as possible. However, conceptual models need not in any way resemble an object. It would be absurd, for instance, to insist that a computer model of the economy should bear a physical resemblance to the economy itself. Rather, conceptual models are analytical tools; their value is that they are devices through which meaning can be imposed upon what would otherwise be a bewildering and disorganized collection of facts. The simple point is that facts do not speak for themselves: they must be interpreted, and they must be organized. Models assist in the accomplishment of this task because they include a network of relationships that highlight the meaning and significance of relevant empirical data. The best way of understanding this is through an example. One of the most influential models in political analysis is the model of the political system developed by David Easton (1979, 1981). This can be represented diagrammatically (see Figure 1.3).

Model: A theoretical representation of empirical data that aims to advance understanding by highlighting significant relationships and interactions.

Concept

Paradigm

A paradigm is, in a general sense, a pattern or model that highlights relevant features of a particular phenomenon, rather in the manner of an ideal type. As used by Kuhn (1962), however, it refers to an intellectual framework comprising interrelated values, theories and assumptions, within which the search for knowledge is conducted. 'Normal' science is therefore conducted within the established intellectual framework; in 'revolutionary' science, an attempt is made to replace the old paradigm with a new one. The radical implication of this theory is that 'truth' and 'falsehood' cannot be finally established. They are only provisional judgements operating within an accepted paradigm that will, eventually, be replaced.

This ambitious model sets out to explain the entire political process, as well as the function of major political actors, through the application of what is called systems analysis. A system is an organized or complex whole, a set of interrelated and inter-dependent parts that form a collective entity. In the case of the political system, a linkage exists between what Easton calls 'inputs' and 'outputs'. Inputs into the political system consist of demands and supports from the general public. Demands can range from pressure for higher living standards, improved employment prospects, and more generous welfare payments to greater protection for minority and individual rights. Supports, on the other hand, are ways in which the public contributes to the political system by paying taxes, offering compliance, and being willing to participate in public life. Outputs consist of the decisions and actions of government, including the making of policy, the passing of laws, the imposition of taxes, and the allocation of public funds. Clearly, these outputs generate 'feedback', which in turn shapes further demands and supports. The key insight offered by Easton's model is that the political system tends towards long-term equilibrium or political stability, as its survival depends on outputs being brought into line with inputs.

However, it is vital to remember that conceptual models are at best simplifications of the reality they seek to explain. They are merely devices for drawing out understanding; they are not reliable knowledge. In the case of Easton's model, for example, political parties and interest groups are portrayed as 'gatekeepers', the central function of which is to regulate the flow of inputs into the political system. Although this may be one of their significant functions, parties and interest groups also manage public perceptions, and thereby help to shape the nature of public demands. In short, these are in reality more interesting and more complex institutions than the systems model suggests. In the same way, Easton's model is more effective in explaining how and why political systems respond to popular pressures than it is in explaining why they employ repression and coercion, as, to some degree, all do.

The terms **theory** and model are often used interchangeably in politics. Theories and models are both conceptual constructs used as tools of political analysis. However, strictly speaking, a theory is a proposition. It offers a systematic explanation of a body of empirical data. In contrast, a model is merely an explanatory device; it is more like a hypothesis that has yet to be tested. In that sense, in politics, while theories can be said to be more or less 'true', models can only be said to be more or less 'useful'. Clearly, however, theories and models are often interlinked: broad political theories may be explained in terms of a series of models. For example, the theory of pluralism (discussed in Chapters 4 and 5) encompasses a model of the state, a model of electoral competition, a model of group politics, and so on.

However, virtually all conceptual devices, theories and models contain hidden values or implicit assumptions. This is why it is difficult to construct theories that are purely empirical; values and normative beliefs invariably intrude. In the case of concepts, this is demonstrated by people's tendency to use terms as either 'hurrah! words' (for example 'democracy', 'freedom' and 'justice') or 'boo! words' (for example 'conflict', 'anarchy', 'ideology', and even 'politics'). Models and theories are also 'loaded' in the sense that they contain a range of biases. It is difficult, for example, to accept the claim that rational-choice theories (examined above) are value-neutral. As they are based on the assumption that human beings are basically egoistical and self-regarding, it is perhaps not surprising that they have often pointed to policy conclusions that are politically conservative. In the same way, class theories of politics, advanced by Marxists, are based on broader theories about

Theory: A systematic explanation of empirical data, usually (unlike a hypothesis) presented as reliable knowledge.

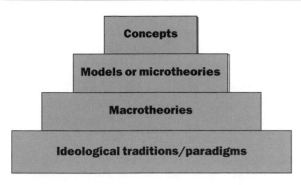

Examples: power, social class, rights, law

Examples: systems analysis, public choice, game theory

Examples: pluralism, elitism, functionalism

Examples: liberalism, Marxism, feminism

Fig. 1.4   Levels of conceptual analysis

history and society and, indeed, they ultimately rest upon the validity of an entire social philosophy.

There is therefore a sense in which analytical devices, such as models and microtheories, are constructed on the basis of broader macrotheories. These major theoretical tools of political analysis are those that address the issues of power and the role of the state: pluralism (see p. 82), elitism (see p. 84), class analysis, and so on. These theories are examined in Chapters 4 and 5. At a still deeper level, however, many of these macrotheories reflect the assumptions and beliefs of one or other of the major ideological traditions. These traditions operate rather like what Thomas Kuhn in *The Structure of Scientific Revolutions* (1962) called paradigms. A paradigm is a related set of principles, doctrines and theories that help to structure the process of intellectual enquiry. In effect, a paradigm constitutes the framework within which the search for knowledge is conducted. In economics, this can be seen in the replacement of Keynesianism by monetarism (and perhaps the subsequent shift back to neo-Keynesianism); in transport policy it is shown in the rise of Green ideas.

According to Kuhn, the natural sciences are dominated at any time by a single paradigm; science develops through a series of 'revolutions' in which an old paradigm is replaced by a new one. Political and social enquiry is, however, different, in that it is a battleground of contending and competing paradigms. These paradigms take the form of broad social philosophies, usually called political ideologies: liberalism, conservatism, socialism, fascism, feminism and so on. Each presents its own account of social existence; each offers a particular view of the world. To portray these ideologies as theoretical paradigms is not, of course, to say that most, if not all, political analysis is narrowly ideological in the sense that it advances the interests of a particular group or class. Rather, it merely acknowledges that political analysis is usually carried out on the basis of a particular ideological tradition. Much of academic political science, for example, has been constructed according to liberal–rationalist assumptions, and thus bears the imprint of its liberal heritage.

The various levels of conceptual analysis are shown diagrammatically in Figure 1.4.

Summary

◆ Politics is the activity through which people make, preserve and amend the general rules under which they live. As such, it is an essentially social activity, inextricably linked, on the one hand, to the existence of diversity and conflict, and on the other to a willingness to cooperate and act collectively. Politics is better seen as a search for conflict resolution than as its achievement, as not all conflicts are, or can be, resolved.

◆ Politics has been understood differently by different thinkers and within different traditions. Politics has been viewed as the art of government or as 'what concerns the state', as the conduct and management of public affairs, as the resolution of conflict through debate and compromise, and as the production, distribution and use of resources in the course of social existence.

◆ There is considerable debate about the realm of 'the political'. Conventionally, politics has narrowly been seen as embracing institutions and actors operating in a 'public' sphere concerned with the collective organization of social existence. However, when politics is understood in terms of power-structured relationships, it may be seen to operate in the 'private' sphere as well.

◆ A variety of approaches have been adopted to the study of politics as an academic discipline. These include political philosophy or the analysis of normative theory, an empirical tradition particularly concerned with the study of institutions and structures, attempts to introduce scientific rigour through behavioural analysis, and a variety of modern approaches including the use of rational-choice theory.

◆ The study of politics is scientific to the extent that it is possible to gain objective knowledge about the political world by distinguishing between facts and values. This task is nevertheless hampered by the difficulty of gaining access to reliable data, by values that are implicit in political models and theories, and by biases that operate within all students of politics.

◆ Concepts, models and theories are the tools of political analysis, providing the building blocks of knowledge. However, they are only analytical devices. Although they help to advance understanding, they are more rounded and coherent than the unshapely and complex realities they seek to describe. Ultimately, all political and social enquiry is conducted within a particular intellectual framework or ideological paradigm.

■ Questions for discussion

▶ If politics is essentially social, why is not all social activity political?

▶ Why has politics so often carried negative associations?

▶ How could you defend politics as a worthwhile and ennobling activity?

▶ Is politics inevitable? Could politics ever be brought to an end?

▶ Why has the idea of a science of politics been so attractive?

▶ Is it possible to study politics objectively and without bias?

■ Further reading

Ball, A. and B. Guy Peters, *Modern Politics and Government* (7th edn.) (Basingstoke: Palgrave Macmillan, 2005). A popular short introduction to politics that covers a wide variety of themes and issues.

Crick, B., *In Defence of Politics* (rev. edn.) (Harmondsworth and New York: Penguin, 2000). A thoughtful and stimulating attempt to justify politics (understood in a distinctively liberal sense) against its enemies.

Hay, C., *Political Analysis: A Critical Introduction* (Basingstoke and New York: Palgrave Macmillan, 2002). A coherent and accessible introduction to some of the key issues in political science.

Heywood, A., *Key Concepts in Politics* (Basingstoke and New York: Palgrave Macmillan, 2000). A clear and accessible guide to the major ideas and concepts encountered in political analysis.

Leftwich, A. (ed.), *What is Politics? The Activity and Its Study* (Cambridge: Polity Press, 2004). A very useful collection of essays examining different concepts of politics as well as contrasting views of the discipline.

Marsh, D. and G. Stoker (eds), *Theory and Methods in Political Science* (2nd edn.) (Basingstoke and New York: Palgrave Macmillan, 2002). An accessible, yet comprehensive and sophisticated, exploration of the nature and scope of the discipline of political science.

Stoker, G., *Why Politics Matters: Making Democracy Work* (Basingstoke and New York: Palgrave Macmillan, 2006). A stimulating analysis of why democratic politics is doomed to disappoint and how civic participation can be revived.

Governments, Systems and Regimes

CHAPTER 2

'That government is best which governs not at all.'

HENRY DAVID THOREAU, *Civil Disobedience* (1849)

Classifying the various forms of government has been one of the principal concerns of political analysis through the ages. This process can be traced back to the fourth century BCE, when Aristotle made the first recorded attempt to describe the political regimes then in existence, using terms such as 'democracy', 'oligarchy' and 'tyranny' that are still commonly employed today. From the eighteenth century onwards, governments were increasingly classified as monarchies or republics, or as autocratic or constitutional regimes. During the twentieth century, these distinctions were further sharpened. The 'three worlds' classification of political systems, which was particularly fashionable during the Cold War period, created an image of world politics dominated by a struggle between democracy and totalitarianism. However, in the light of modern developments, such as the collapse of communism, the rise of East Asia, and the emergence of political Islam, all such classifications appear outdated. Nevertheless, it is not entirely clear what these shifts mean. Some interpret them as indications of the triumph of western liberal democracy; others see evidence of the modern world becoming politically more diffuse and fragmented.

The central issues examined in this chapter are as follows:

Contents

Key issues

▶ What is the difference between governments, political systems and regimes?

▶ What is the purpose of classifying systems of government?

▶ On what basis have, and should, regimes be classified?

▶ What are the major regimes of the modern world?

▶ Has western liberal democracy triumphed worldwide?

Concept

Government

In its broadest sense, to govern means to rule or control others. Government can therefore be taken to include any mechanism through which ordered rule is maintained, its central features being the ability to make collective decisions and the capacity to enforce them. A form of government can thus be identified in almost all social institutions: families, schools, businesses, trade unions and so on. However, 'government', as opposed to 'governance' (see p. 6), is more commonly understood to refer to the formal and institutional processes that operate at the national level to maintain public order and facilitate collective action. The core functions of government are thus to make law (legislation), implement law (execution) and interpret law (adjudication). In some cases, the political executive (see p. 358) alone is referred to as 'the Government', making it equivalent to 'the Administration' in presidential systems.

Political system: A network of relationships through which government generates 'outputs' (policies) in response to 'inputs' (demands or support) from the general public.

Government gridlock: Paralysis resulting from institutional rivalry within government or the attempt to respond to conflicting public demands.

■ Traditional systems of classification

Before we examine how different systems of rule have been classified, it is necessary for us to reflect on both *what* is being classified, and *why* such classifications have been undertaken. First, what is 'government', and how do governments differ from 'political systems' or 'regimes'? 'Government' refers to the institutional processes through which collective and usually binding decisions are made; its various institutions constitute the subject matter of Part 4 of this book. A **political system** or regime, on the other hand, is a broader term that encompasses not only the mechanisms of government and the institutions of the state, but also the structures and processes through which these interact with the larger society.

A political system is, in effect, a subsystem of the larger social system. It is a 'system' in that there are interrelationships within a complex whole, and 'political' in that these interrelationships relate to the distribution of power, wealth and resources in society. Political regimes can thus be characterized as effectively by the organization of economic life as they are by the governmental processes through which they operate. A regime is therefore a 'system of rule' that endures despite the fact that governments come and go. Whereas governments can be changed by elections, through dynastic succession, as a result of *coups d'état* (see p. 411), and so on, regimes can be changed only by military intervention from without or by some kind of revolutionary upheaval from within.

Why classify political systems?

The interest in classifying political systems stems from two sources. First, classification is an essential aid to the *understanding* of politics and government. As in most social sciences, understanding in politics is acquired largely through a process of comparison, particularly as experimental methods are generally inapplicable. It is not possible, for instance, to devise experiments to test whether, say, US government would be less susceptible to institutional **government gridlock** if it abandoned the separation of powers (see p. 339), or whether communism could have survived in the USSR had reforms been instigated a generation earlier. In consequence, we look to comparison to throw into relief what we are studying. Through the highlighting of similarities and differences between what might otherwise be bewildering collections of facts, comparison helps us to distinguish between what is significant and meaningful, and what is not. In this process, we are able both to develop theories, hypotheses and concepts, and, to some extent, to test them. As Alexis de Tocqueville (see p. 227) put it, 'without comparisons to make, the mind does not know how to proceed'. The attempt to classify systems of rule is therefore merely a device for making the process of comparison more methodical and systematic.

The second purpose of classification is to facilitate *evaluation* rather than analysis. Since Aristotle (see p. 7), those who have sought to understand political regimes have often been as keen to 'improve' government as to understand it. In other words, descriptive understanding is closely tied up with normative judgements: questions about what *is* are linked to questions about what *should* be. In its extreme form, this process may involve a search for an 'ideal' system of rule, or even a utopia, and this can be seen in works such as Plato's (see p. 12) *Republic*, Thomas More's *Utopia* ([1516] 1965), and Peter Kropotkin's *Fields, Factories and Workshops* (1912). In a more modest form, this type of classification allows for qualitative judgements to be made in relation to political structures and governmental forms. Only a comparative approach, for instance, enables us to consider questions such as 'should the transition to liberal democracy in Russia and other former communist states be welcomed and encouraged?', 'should India abandon federalism in favour of either a unitary system or regional independence?', and 'should the UK adopt a "written" constitution?'

All systems of classification have their drawbacks, however. In the first place, as with all analytical devices, there is a danger of simplification. The classification of regimes under the same heading draws attention to the similarities that they share, but there is a risk that the differences that divide them will be ignored or disguised. A related problem is a possible failure to see that a phenomenon may have different meanings in different contexts. For instance, in Japan and throughout East Asia, 'the state' may be different in kind and significance from 'the state' as generally understood in the context of the West. Comparative analysis is therefore hampered by the constant danger of **ethnocentrism**. Second, value biases tend to intrude into the classification process. This can be seen in the tendency to classify communist and fascist regimes as 'totalitarian', implying that western liberal democracies were fighting the *same* enemy in the Cold War as they had done in the Second World War. Finally, all systems of classification have the drawback that they are necessarily state-bound: they treat individual countries as coherent or independent entities in their own right. Although this approach is by no means invalid, it is now widely viewed as incomplete in the light of the phenomenon of globalization (see p. 143).

Classical typologies

Without doubt, the most influential system of classification was that devised by Aristotle in the fourth century BCE, which was based on his analysis of the 158 Greek city-states then in existence. This system dominated thinking on the subject for roughly the next 2500 years. Aristotle held that governments could be categorized on the basis of two questions: 'who rules?', and 'who benefits from rule?'. Government, he believed, could be placed in the hands of a single individual, a small group, or the many. In each case, however, government could be conducted either in the selfish interests of the rulers or for the benefit of the entire community. He thus identified the six forms of government shown in Figure 2.1.

Aristotle's purpose was to evaluate forms of government on normative grounds in the hope of identifying the 'ideal' constitution. In his view, tyranny, oligarchy and democracy were all debased or perverted forms of rule in which a single person, a small group and the masses, respectively, governed in their own interests and there-

Who rules?

		One person	The few	The many
Who benefits?	Rulers	Tyranny	Oligarchy	Democracy
	All	Monarchy	Aristocracy	Polity

Fig. 2.1 Aristotle's six forms of government

Concept

Utopia, utopianism

A utopia (from the Greek *outopia*, meaning 'nowhere', or the Greek *eutopia*, meaning 'good place') is literally an ideal or perfect society. Although utopias of various kinds can be envisaged, most are characterized by the abolition of want, the absence of conflict, and the avoidance of violence and oppression. Utopianism is a style of political theorizing that develops a critique of the existing order by constructing a model of an ideal or perfect alternative. Good examples are anarchism and Marxism. Utopian theories are usually based on assumptions about the unlimited possibilities of human self-development. Utopianism is often used as a pejorative term to imply deluded or fanciful thinking, and a belief in an unrealistic and unachievable goal.

Ethnocentrism:
The application of values and theories drawn from one's own culture to other groups and peoples; ethnocentrism implies bias or distortion (see p. 429).

Concept

Absolutism

Absolutism is the theory or practice of absolute government, most commonly associated with an absolute monarchy (see p. 366). Government is 'absolute' in the sense that it possesses unfettered power: government cannot be constrained by a body external to itself. The absolutist principle nevertheless resides in the *claim* to an unlimited right to rule (as in Divine Right), rather than in the *exercise* of unchallengeable power. Rationalist theories of absolute power generally advance the belief that only absolute government can guarantee order and social stability. Absolutism should, however, be distinguished from autocracy and dictatorship (see p. 405). As it is based on a principled claim, whether religious or rational, it does not invest government with arbitrary and unlimited power.

Demagogue: A political leader whose control over the masses is based on the ability to whip up hysterical enthusiasm.

Republicanism: The principle that political authority stems ultimately from the consent of the people; the rejection of monarchical and dynastic principles.

fore at the expense of others. In contrast, monarchy, aristocracy and polity were to be preferred, because in these forms of government the individual, small group and the masses, respectively, governed in the interests of all. Aristotle declared tyranny to be the worst of all possible constitutions, as it reduced citizens to the status of slaves. Monarchy and aristocracy were, on the other hand, impractical, because they were based on a God-like willingness to place the good of the community before the rulers' own interests. Polity (rule by the many in the interests of all) was accepted as the most practicable of constitutions. Nevertheless, in a tradition that endured through to the twentieth century, Aristotle criticized popular rule on the grounds that the masses would resent the wealth of the few, and too easily fall under the sway of a **demagogue**. He therefore advocated a 'mixed' constitution that combined elements of both democracy and aristocracy, and left the government in the hands of the 'middle classes', those who were neither rich nor poor.

The Aristotelian system was later developed by thinkers such as Thomas Hobbes (see p. 327) and Jean Bodin (1530–96). Their particular concern was with the principle of sovereignty (see p. 131), viewed as the basis for all stable political regimes. Sovereignty was taken to mean the 'most high and perpetual' power, a power that alone could guarantee orderly rule. Bodin's *The Six Books of the Commonweal* ([1576] 1962) offered a wider-ranging account of the locus of sovereignty in political regimes, both contemporary and classical. He concluded that absolutism was the most defensible of regimes, as it established a sovereign who makes law but is not bound by those laws. The overriding merit of vesting sovereignty in a single individual was that it would then be indivisible: sovereignty would be expressed in a single voice that could claim final authority. Bodin nevertheless argued that absolute monarchs were constrained by the existence of higher law in the form of the will of God or natural law. On the other hand, in *Leviathan* ([1651] 1968), Hobbes portrayed sovereignty as a monopoly of coercive power, implying that the sovereign was entirely unconstrained.

These ideas were later revised by early liberals such as John Locke (see p. 47) and Montesquieu (see p. 336), who championed the cause of constitutional government. Locke, in *Two Treatises of Government* ([1690] 1965), argued that sovereignty resided with the people, not the monarch, and he advocated a system of limited government to provide protection for natural rights, notably the rights to life, liberty and property. In his epic *The Spirit of the Laws* ([1734] 1949), Montesquieu attempted to develop a 'scientific' study of human society, designed to uncover the constitutional circumstances that would best protect individual liberty. A severe critic of absolutism and an admirer of the English parliamentary tradition, he proposed a system of checks and balances in the form of a 'separation of powers' between the executive, legislative and judicial institutions. This principle was incorporated into the US constitution (1787), and it later came to be seen as one of the defining features of liberal democratic government.

The 'classical' classification of regimes, stemming from the writings of Aristotle, was rendered increasingly redundant by the development of modern constitutional systems from the late eighteenth century onwards. In their different ways, the constitutional **republicanism** established in the USA following the American War of Independence of 1775–83, the democratic radicalism unleashed in France by the 1789 French Revolution, and the form of parliamentary government that gradually emerged in the UK created political realities that were substantially more complex than early thinkers had envisaged. Traditional systems of classification were therefore displaced by a growing emphasis on the constitutional and institutional features of political rule. In many ways, this built on Montesquieu's work in that particular attention was paid to the relationships between the various branches of government. Thus monarchies were distinguished from republics, parliamentary systems (see p. 337) were distinguished from presidential ones (see p. 362), and unitary systems were distinguished from federal ones (see p. 167).

The 'three worlds' typology

During the twentieth century, historical developments once again altered the basis of political classification. The appearance in the interwar period of new forms of authoritarianism (see p. 38), particularly in Stalinist Russia, Fascist Italy and Nazi Germany, encouraged the view that the world was divided into two kinds of regime: democratic states and totalitarian states. The stark contrast between democracy and totalitarianism dominated attempts at regime classification through much of the 1950s and 1960s, despite the fact that the fascist and Nazi regimes had collapsed at the end of the Second World War. Nevertheless, there was a growing awareness that this approach was shaped by the antagonisms of the Cold War, and that it could perhaps be seen as a species of Cold War ideology, and this stimulated the search for a more value-neutral and ideologically impartial system of classification. This led to the growing popularity of the so-called 'three worlds' approach – the belief that the political world could be divided into three distinct blocs:

- a capitalist 'first world'
- a communist 'second world'
- a developing 'third world'.

The three-worlds classification had economic, ideological, political and strategic dimensions. Industrialized western regimes were 'first' in economic terms, in that their populations enjoyed the highest levels of mass affluence. In 1983, these countries generated 63 per cent of the world's **gross domestic product** (GDP) while having only 15 per cent of the world's population (World Bank, 1985). Communist regimes were 'second', insofar as they were largely industrialized and capable of satisfying the population's basic material needs. These countries produced 19 per cent of the world's GDP with 33 per cent of the world's population. The less developed countries of Africa, Asia and Latin America were 'third' in the sense that they were economically dependent and often suffered from widespread poverty. They produced 18 per cent of the world's GDP with 52 per cent of the world's population.

The first and second worlds were further divided by fierce ideological rivalry. The first world was wedded to 'capitalist' principles, such as the desirability of private enterprise, material incentives, and the free market; the second world was committed to 'communist' values such as social equality, collective endeavour, and the need for centralized planning. Such ideological differences had clear political manifestations. First-world regimes practised liberal-democratic politics based on a competitive struggle for power at election time. Second-world regimes were one-party states, dominated by 'ruling' communist parties. Third-world regimes were typically authoritarian, and governed by traditional monarchs, dictators or simply the army. The three-worlds classification was underpinned by a bipolar world order, in which a USA-dominated West confronted a USSR-dominated East. This order was sustained by the emergence of two rival military camps in the form of NATO and the Warsaw

Concept

Totalitarianism

Totalitarianism is an all-encompassing system of political rule that is typically established by pervasive ideological manipulation and open terror and brutality. Totalitarianism differs from both autocracy and authoritarianism in that it seeks 'total power' through the politicization of every aspect of social and personal existence. Autocratic and authoritarian regimes have the more modest goal of a monopoly of political power, usually achieved by excluding the masses from politics. Totalitarianism thus implies the outright abolition of **civil society**: the abolition of 'the private'. Totalitarian regimes are sometimes identified through a 'six-point syndrome' (Friedrich and Brzezinski, 1963):

- an official ideology
- a one-party state, usually led by an all-powerful leader
- a system of terroristic policing
- a monopoly of the means of mass communication
- a monopoly of the means of armed combat
- state control of all aspects of economic life.

Civil society: The realm of autonomous groups and associations; a private sphere independent from public authority (see p. 8).

Gross domestic product: The total financial value of final goods and services produced in an economy over one year.

Liberal democracy

Liberal democracy is a form of democratic rule that balances the principle of limited government against the ideal of popular consent. Its 'liberal' features are reflected in a network of internal and external checks on government that are designed to guarantee liberty and afford citizens protection against the state. Its 'democratic' character is based on a system of regular and competitive elections, conducted on the basis of universal suffrage and political equality (see p. 73). Although it may be used to describe a political principle, the term 'liberal democracy' is more commonly used to describe a particular type of regime. The defining features of this type of regime are as follows:

- constitutional government based on formal, usually legal, rules
- guarantees of civil liberties and individual rights
- institutionalized fragmentation and a system of checks and balances
- regular elections that respect the principle of 'one person, one vote; one vote, one value'
- party competition and political pluralism
- the independence of organized groups and interests from government
- a private-enterprise economy organized along market lines.

Pact. Not infrequently, the 'nonaligned' third world was the battleground upon which this geopolitical struggle was conducted, a fact that did much to ensure its continued political and economic subordination.

Since the 1970s, however, this system of classification has been increasingly difficult to sustain. New patterns of economic development have brought material affluence to parts of the third world, notably the oil-rich states of the Middle East and the newly industrialized states of East Asia, South East Asia, and, to some extent, Latin America. In contrast, poverty has, if anything, become more deeply entrenched in parts of sub-Saharan Africa, which now constitutes a kind of 'fourth world'. Moreover, the advance of democratization (see p. 32) in Asia, Latin America and Africa, especially during the 1980s and 1990s, has meant that third-world regimes are no longer uniformly authoritarian. Indeed, the phrase 'third world' is widely resented as being demeaning, because it implies entrenched disadvantage. The term 'developing world' is usually seen as preferable.

Without doubt, however, the most catastrophic single blow to the three-worlds model resulted from the eastern European revolutions of 1989–91. These led to the collapse of orthodox communist regimes in the USSR and elsewhere, and unleashed a process of political liberalization and market reform. Indeed, Francis Fukuyama went as far as to proclaim that this development amounted to the 'end of history' (Fukuyama, 1989). He meant by this that ideological debate had effectively ended with the worldwide triumph of western liberal democracy. Quite simply, second-world and third-world regimes were collapsing as a result of the recognition that only the capitalist first world offered the prospect of economic prosperity and political stability.

Regimes of the modern world

Since the late 1980s, the regime-classification industry has been in a limbo. Older categories, particularly the 'three worlds' division, were certainly redundant, but the political contours of the new world were far from clear. Moreover, the 'end of history' scenario was only fleetingly attractive, having been sustained by the wave of

Francis Fukuyama (born 1952)

US social analyst and political commentator. Fukuyama was born in Chicago, USA, the son of a Protestant preacher. He was a member of the Policy Planning Staff of the US State Department before becoming an academic; he is currently at Johns Hopkins University. A staunch Republican, he came to international prominence as a result of his article 'The End of History?' (1989), which he later developed into *The End of History* *and the Last Man* (1992). These claimed that the history of ideas had ended with the recognition of liberal democracy as 'the final form of human government'. In *Trust* (1996) and *The Great Disruption* (1999), Fukuyama discussed the relationship between economic development and social cohesion. In *After the Neocons* (2006) he developed a critique of US foreign policy in the post-9/11 period.

democratization in the late 1980s and early 2000s, and drawing impetus in particular from the collapse of communism. In some senses, this liberal-democratic triumphalism reflected the persistence of a western-centric viewpoint, and it may, anyway, have been a hangover from the days of the Cold War. The image of a 'world of liberal democracies' suggested the superiority of a specifically western model of development, based perhaps especially on the USA, and it implied that values such as individualism, rights and choice are universally applicable. One result of this was a failure to recognize the significance, for instance, of Islamic and Confucian political forms, which tended to be dismissed as mere aberrations, or simply as evidence of resistance to the otherwise unchallenged advance of liberal democracy.

However, one of the difficulties of establishing a new system of classification is that there is no consensus about the criteria upon which such a system should be based. No system of classification relies on a single all-important factor. Nevertheless, particular systems have tended to prioritize different sets of criteria. Among the parameters most commonly used are the following:

- Who rules? Is political participation confined to an elite body or privileged group, or does it encompass the entire population?
- How is compliance achieved? Is government obeyed as a result of the exercise or threat of force, or through bargaining and compromise?
- Is government power centralized or fragmented? What kinds of check and balance operate in the political system?
- How is government power acquired and transferred? Is a regime open and competitive, or is it monolithic?
- What is the balance between the state and the individual? What is the distribution of rights and responsibilities between government and citizens?
- What is the level of material development? How materially affluent is the society, and how equally is wealth distributed?
- How is economic life organized? Is the economy geared to the market or to planning, and what economic role does government play?
- How stable is a regime? Has the regime survived over time, and does it have the capacity to respond to new demands and challenges?

A *constitutional–institutional* approach to classification that was influenced by 'classical' typologies was adopted in the nineteenth and early twentieth centuries.

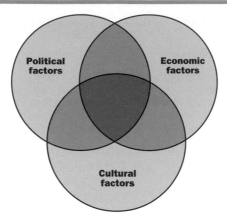

Fig. 2.2   Key regime features

This approach highlighted, for instance, differences between codified and uncodified constitutions, parliamentary and presidential systems, and federal and unitary systems. A *structural–functional* approach, however, was developed out of systems theory, which became increasingly prominent in the 1950s and 1960s. This approach was concerned less with institutional arrangements than with how political systems work in practice, and especially with how they translate 'inputs' into 'outputs'. The 'three worlds' approach was *economic–ideological* in orientation, as it paid special attention to a systems level of material development and its broader ideological orientation. The approach adopted here, however, is in some ways different from each of these three. It attempts to take account of three key features of a regime: its political, economic and cultural aspects. The assumption in this approach is that regimes are characterized not so much by particular political, economic or cultural factors as by the way in which these interlock in practice (see Figure 2.2).

The significance of this approach is that it emphasizes the degree to which formal political and economic arrangements may operate differently depending on their cultural context. For instance, multiparty elections and a market economy may have very different implications in western liberal societies than they do in non-western ones. Nevertheless, in view of the profound political upheavals of the late twentieth century, it would be foolish to suggest that any system of classification can be anything but provisional. Indeed, regimes are themselves fluid, and the regime-classification industry is constantly struggling to keep up to date with an ever-changing political reality. Nevertheless, five regime types can be identified in the modern world:

- western polyarchies
- new democracies
- East Asian regimes
- Islamic regimes
- military regimes.

Western polyarchies

Western polyarchies are broadly equivalent to regimes categorized as 'liberal democracies' or even simply 'democracies'. Their heartlands are therefore North America, western Europe and Australasia. Huntington (see p. 138) argued that such regimes are a product of the first two 'waves' of democratization: the first occurred between 1828 and 1926 and involved countries such as the USA, France and the UK; the second occurred between 1943 and 1962 and involved ones such as West Germany, Italy, Japan and India. Although polyarchies have in large part evolved through moves towards democratization and **liberalization**, the term 'polyarchy' is preferable to 'liberal democracy' for two reasons. First, liberal democracy is sometimes treated as a political ideal, and is thus invested with broader normative implications. Second, the use of 'polyarchy' acknowledges that these regimes fall short, in important ways, of the goal of democracy.

The term 'polyarchy' was first used to describe a system of rule by Dahl (p. 298) and Lindblom in *Politics, Economics, and Welfare* (1953), and it was later elaborated in Dahl's *Polyarchy: Participation and Opposition* (1971). In the view of these authors, polyarchical regimes are distinguished by the combination of two general features. In the first place, there is a relatively high tolerance of opposition that is sufficient at least to check the arbitrary inclinations of government. This is guaranteed in practice by a competitive party system, by institutionally guaranteed and protected civil liberties, and by a vigorous and healthy civil society. The second feature of polyarchy is that the opportunities for participating in politics should be sufficiently widespread to guarantee a reliable level of popular responsiveness. The crucial factor here is the existence of regular and competitive elections operating as a device through which the people can control and, if necessary, displace their rulers. In this sense, there is a close resemblance between polyarchy and the form of democratic elitism described by Joseph Schumpeter (see p. 253) in *Capitalism, Socialism and Democracy* (1942). Both Lindblom (1977) and Dahl (1985) nevertheless acknowledged the impact on polyarchies of the disproportional power of major corporations. For this reason, they have sometimes preferred the notion of 'deformed polyarchy'.

Thus defined, the term 'polyarchy' may be used to describe a large and growing number of regimes throughout the world. All states that hold multiparty elections have polyarchical features. Nevertheless, western polyarchies have a more distinctive and particular character. They are marked not only by representative democracy and a capitalist economic organization, but also by a cultural and ideological orientation that is largely derived from western liberalism. The most crucial aspect of this inheritance is the widespread acceptance of liberal individualism. Individualism (see p. 196), often seen as the most distinctive of western values, stresses the uniqueness of each human individual, and suggests that society should be organized so as to best meet the needs and interests of the individuals who compose it. The political culture of western polyarchies is influenced by liberal individualism in a variety of ways. It generates, for example, a heightened sensitivity to individual rights (perhaps placed above duties), the general perception that choice and competition (in both political and economic life) are healthy, and a tendency to fear government and regard the state as at least a potential threat to liberty.

Western polyarchies are not all alike, however. Some of them are biased in favour of centralization and majority rule, and others tend towards fragmentation and pluralism. Lijphart (1990, 1999) highlighted this fact in distinguishing between 'majority' democracies and 'consensus' democracies. Majority democracies are organized along parliamentary lines according to the so-called **Westminster model**. The clearest example of this is the UK system, but the model has also, in certain respects, been adopted by New Zealand, Australia, Canada, Israel and India. Majoritarian tendencies are associated with any, or all, of the following features:

Concept

Polyarchy

Polyarchy (literally 'rule by many') refers generally to the institutions and political processes of modern representative democracy. As a regime type, a polyarchy can be distinguished from all nondemocratic systems and from small-scale democratic ones based on the classical or Athenian model of direct participation. Polyarchy can be understood as a rough or crude approximation of democracy, in that it operates through institutions that force rulers to take account of the interests and wishes of the electorate. Its central features are as follows (Dahl, 1989: 211):

- Government is in the hands of elected officials.
- Elections are free and fair.
- Practically all adults have the right to vote.
- The right to run for office is unrestricted.
- There is free expression and a right to criticize and protest.
- Citizens have access to alternative sources of information.
- Groups and associations enjoy at least relative independence from government.

Liberalization: The introduction of internal and external checks on government power and/or shifts towards private enterprise and the market.

Westminster model: A system of government in which the executive is drawn from, and (in theory) accountable to, the assembly or parliament.

Concept

The West

The term the West has two overlapping meanings. In a general sense, the term refers to the cultural and philosophical inheritance of Europe, which has often been exported through migration or colonialism. The roots of this inheritance lie in Judeo-Christian religion and the learning of 'classical' Greece and Rome, shaped in the modern period by the ideas and values of liberalism. The term the East refers to Asia in general and the Orient in particular. In a narrower sense that was fashionable during the Cold War, 'the West' meant the USA-dominated capitalist bloc, as opposed to the USSR-dominated East. Although eastern Europe no longer belongs to the East in this sense, it has always been unclear whether Russia belongs to the West in the broader sense.

- single-party government
- a lack of separation of powers between the executive and the assembly
- an assembly that is either unicameral or weakly bicameral
- a two-party system
- a single-member plurality or first-past-the-post electoral system (see p. 257)
- unitary and centralized government
- an uncodified constitution and a sovereign assembly.

In contrast, other western polyarchies are characterized by a diffusion of power throughout the governmental and party systems. The US model of pluralist democracy is based very largely on institutional fragmentation enshrined in the provisions of the constitution itself. Elsewhere, particularly in continental Europe, consensus is underpinned by the party system and a tendency towards bargaining and power sharing. In states such as Belgium, Austria and Switzerland, a system of **consociational democracy** has developed that is particularly appropriate to societies that are divided by deep religious, ideological, regional, cultural or other differences. Consensual or pluralistic tendencies are often associated with the following features:

- coalition government (see p. 288)
- a separation of powers between the executive and the assembly
- an effective bicameral system
- a multiparty system
- proportional representation (see p. 258)
- federalism (see p. 167) or devolution
- a codified constitution and a bill of rights.

On another level, of course, each polyarchical regime, and, indeed, every regime, is unique, and therefore exceptional. US **exceptionalism**, for instance, is often linked to the absence of a feudal past and the experience of settlement and frontier expansion. This may explain the USA's deeply individualist political culture, which, uniquely amongst western polyarchies, does not accommodate a socialist party or movement of any note. The USA is also the most overtly religious of western regimes, and it is the only one, for instance, in which Christian fundamentalism has developed into a major political force.

India is a still more difficult case. It is certainly not part of the West in cultural, philosophical or religious terms. In contrast to the 'developed' polyarchies of Europe and North America, it also has a largely rural population and a literacy rate of barely 50 per cent. Nevertheless, India has functioned as an effective polyarchy since it became independent in 1947, even surviving Indira Gandhi's 'state of emergency' in the late 1970s. Political stability in India was undoubtedly promoted by the cross-caste appeal of the Congress Party and the mystique of the Nehru–Gandhi dynasty. However, the decline of the former and the end of the latter has perhaps transformed modern India into something approaching a consociational democracy.

New democracies

A third wave of democratization began, according to Huntington (1991), in 1974. It witnessed the overthrow of right-wing dictatorships in Greece, Portugal and Spain,

Consociational democracy: A form of democracy that operates through power-sharing and a close association amongst a number of parties or political formations.

Exceptionalism: The features of a political system that are unique or particular to it, and thus restrict the application of broader categories.

Communism

Communism, in its simplest sense, is the communal organization of social existence on the basis of the collective ownership of property. As a theoretical ideal, it is most commonly associated with the writings of Marx, for whom communism meant a classless society in which wealth was owned in common, production was geared to human need, and the state had 'withered away', allowing for spontaneous harmony and self-realization. The term is also used to describe societies founded on Marxist principles crucially adapted by Leninism and Stalinism. The key features of 'orthodox' communism as a regime type are as follows:

- Marxism–Leninism is the 'official' ideology.
- A communist party that is organized on the principles of 'democratic centralism' enjoys a monopoly of political power.
- The communist party 'rules' in the sense that it dominates the state machine, creating a fused state–party apparatus.
- The communist party plays a 'leading and guiding role' in society, controlling all institutions, including the economic, educational, cultural and recreational institutions.
- Economic life is based on state collectivization, and it is organized through a central planning system (see p. 192).

the retreat of the generals in Latin America, and, most significantly, the collapse of communism. By 2003, 63 per cent of states, accounting for about 70 per cent of the world's population, exhibited some of the key features of liberal-democratic governance. Most prominently, this process has been characterized by the adoption of multiparty elections and market-based economic reforms. Nevertheless, many of these states are 'countries in transition', best classified as **new democracies** or **semi-democracies**. The process of democratic transition has been both complex and difficult, highlighting the fact that democracy should not simply be viewed as the 'default position' for human societies. New democracies not only lack developed democratic political cultures but they also have to handle the strains produced by the external forces of globalization (see p. 143) as well as rapid internal change. The most dramatic evidence of their vulnerability is the reemergence of the armed forces into politics, as occurred, for example, in military coups in Pakistan in 1979 and in Thailand in 2006. However, particular problems are faced by postcommunist states in bringing about democratization.

One feature of postcommunist regimes is the need to deal with the politico-cultural consequences of communist rule, especially the ramifications of Stalinist totalitarianism. The ruthless censorship and suppression of opposition that underpinned the communist parties' monopoly of power guaranteed that a civic culture emphasizing participation, bargaining and consensus failed to develop. In Russia this has produced a weak and fragmented party system that is apparently incapable of articulating or aggregating the major interests of Russian society. As a result, communist parties or former communist parties have often continued to provide a point of stability. In Romania and Bulgaria, for example, the institutions of the communist past have survived into the postcommunist era, while in states such as Hungary, Poland and Russia communist parties, now embracing, if with differing degrees of conviction, the principles of social democracy, have made an electoral comeback.

A second set of problems stem from the process of economic transition. The 'shock therapy' transition from central planning to *laissez-faire* capitalism, advocated by the International Monetary Fund, unleashed deep insecurity because of

New democracies: Regimes in which the process of democratic consolidation is incomplete; democracy is not yet the 'only game in town' (Przeworski, 1991).

Semi-democracy: A regime in which democratic and authoritarian features operate alongside one another in a stable combination.

Confucianism

Confucianism is a system of ethics formulated by Confucius (551–479 BCE) and his disciples that was primarily outlined in *The Analects*. Confucian thought has concerned itself with the twin themes of human relations and the cultivation of the self. The emphasis on *ren* (humanity or love) has usually been interpreted as implying support for traditional ideas and values, notably filial piety, respect, loyalty and benevolence. The stress on *junzi* (the virtuous person) suggests a capacity for human development and potential for perfection realized in particular through education. Confucianism has been seen, with Taoism and Buddhism, as one of the three major Chinese systems of thought, although many take Confucian ideas to be coextensive with Chinese civilization itself.

the growth of unemployment and inflation, and it significantly increased social inequality. Since the heady days of the early 1990s, the pace of economic liberalization has sometimes been greatly reduced as a consequence of a backlash against market reforms, often expressed in growing support for communist or nationalist parties. A final set of problems result from the weakness of state power, particularly when the state is confronted by centrifugal forces effectively suppressed during the communist era. This has been most clearly demonstrated by the reemergence of ethnic and nationalist tensions. The collapse of communism in the USSR was accompanied by the breakup of the old Soviet empire and the construction of 15 new independent states, several of which (including Russia) continue to be afflicted by ethnic conflict. Czechoslovakia ceased to exist in 1992 with the creation of the Czech Republic and Slovakia. Ethnic conflict has been most dramatic in Yugoslavia, where it precipitated full-scale war between Serbia and Croatia in 1991, and led to civil war in Bosnia in 1992–96.

Important differences between postcommunist states can also be identified. The most crucial of these is that between the more industrially advanced and westernized countries of 'central' Europe, such as the Czech Republic, Hungary and Poland, and the more backward, 'eastern' states such as Romania, Bulgaria and, in certain respects, Russia. In the former group, market reform has proceeded swiftly and relatively smoothly; in the latter, it has either been grudging and incomplete or it has given rise to deeper political tensions. This was reflected in early membership of the EU for the Czech Republic, Hungary, Poland, Slovakia, Slovenia and the Baltic states (Estonia, Latvia and Lithuania), achieved in 2004. However, Bulgaria and Romania joined the EU in 2007, with other Balkan postcommunist states, including Croatia, Albania, Bosnia-Herzegovina and Serbia, still waiting to join. Another distinction is between the states upon which communism was 'imposed' by the Soviet Red Army at the end of the Second World War and those that were once part of the USSR. With the exception of the Baltic states, the former Soviet republics are marked both by their longer history of communist rule and by the fact that they were part of the Russian empire in Tsarist times as well as the Soviet period. There is, of course, a strong argument as well for Russian exceptionalism. This may be based on Russia's imperial past and the tendency for Russian nationalism to have an authoritarian and expansionist character, or on the fact that, since the time of Peter the Great, Russia has been divided by competing western and Slavic identities, and so is unclear about both its cultural inheritance and its political destiny.

East Asian regimes

The rise of East Asia in the late twentieth century may ultimately prove to be a more important world-historical event than the collapse of communism. Certainly, the balance of the world's economy shifted markedly from the West to the East in this period. In the final two decades of the twentieth century, economic growth rates on the western rim of the Pacific Basin were between two and four times higher than those in the 'developed' economies of Europe and North America. However, the notion that there is a distinctively East Asian political form is a less familiar one. The widespread assumption has been that modernization means westernization. Translated into political terms, this means that industrial capitalism is always accompanied by liberal democracy. Those who advance this position cite, for example, the success of Japan's 1946 constitution, bequeathed by the departing USA, and the introduction of multiparty elections in countries such as Thailand, South Korea and Taiwan in the 1980s and 1990s. However, this interpretation fails to take account of the degree to which polyarchical institutions operate differently in an Asian context from the way they do in a western one. Most importantly, it ignores the difference between cultures influenced by Confucian ideas and values and ones shaped by liberal individualism. This has led to the idea that there are a specific set of **Asian values** that are distinct from western ones.

East Asian regimes tend to have similar characteristics. First, they are orientated more around economic goals than around political ones. Their overriding priority is to boost growth and deliver prosperity, rather than to enlarge individual freedom in the western sense of civil liberty. This essentially practical concern is evident in the 'tiger' economies of East and South East Asia (those of South Korea, Taiwan, Hong Kong, Singapore and Malaysia), but it has also been demonstrated in the construction of a thriving market economy in China since the late 1970s, despite the survival there of monopolistic communist rule. Second, there is broad support for 'strong' government. Powerful 'ruling' parties tend to be tolerated, and there is general respect for the state. Although, with low taxes and relatively low public spending (usually below 30 per cent of GDP), there is little room for the western model of the welfare state, there is nevertheless general acceptance that the state as a 'father figure' should guide the decisions of private as well as public bodies, and draw up strategies for national development. This characteristic is accompanied, third, by a general disposition to respect leaders because of the Confucian stress on loyalty, discipline and duty. From a western viewpoint, this invests East Asian regimes with an implicit, and sometimes explicit, authoritarianism. Finally, great emphasis is placed on community and social cohesion, embodied in the central role accorded to the family. The resulting emphasis on what the Japanese call 'group think' tends to restrict the scope for the assimilation of ideas such as individualism and human rights, at least as these are understood in the West.

There is also differentiation between East Asian regimes. The most significant difference is that, although China's acceptance of capitalism has blurred the distinction between it and other East Asian regimes, profound political contrasts survive. China, in political terms at least, and North Korea, in both political and economic terms, are unreconstituted communist regimes, in which a monopolistic communist party still dominates the state machine. China's 'market Stalinism' contrasts sharply with the entrenched and successful electoral democracy of, for instance, Japan. Moreover, whereas other East Asian regimes are now industrialized and increasingly urbanized, China, despite its dramatic economic growth, remains predominantly agricultural. To some extent, this also explains different modes of economic development. In Japan and 'tiger' economies such as Taiwan and Singapore, growth is now based largely on technological innovation and an emphasis on education and training, whereas China continues, in certain respects, to rely on her massive rural population to provide cheap and plentiful labour. A final range of differences stem from cultural contrasts between overwhelmingly Chinese states such as Taiwan and China, and Japan and ethnically mixed states such as Singapore and Malaysia. For example, plans to introduce Confucian principles in Singapore schools were dropped for fear of offending the Malay and Indian populations. Similarly, Malaysian development has been based on a deliberate attempt to reduce Chinese influence and emphasize the distinctively Islamic character of Malay culture.

Concept

Theocracy

Theocracy (literally 'rule by God') is the principle that religious authority should prevail over political authority. A theocracy is therefore a regime in which government posts are filled on the basis of the person's position in the religious hierarchy. This contrasts with a secular state, in which political and religious positions are kept strictly separate. Theocratic rule is illiberal in two senses. First, it violates the distinction between private and public realms, in that it takes religious rules and precepts to be the guiding principles of both personal life and political conduct. Secondly, it invests political authority with potentially unlimited power, because, as temporal power is derived from spiritual wisdom in this type of regime, it cannot be based on popular consent or be properly constrained within a constitutional framework.

Asian values: Values that supposedly reflect the history, culture and religious backgrounds of Asian societies; examples include social harmony, respect for authority and a belief in the family.

■ Concept

Authoritarianism

Authoritarianism is a belief in, or practice of, government 'from above', in which authority is exercised regardless of popular consent. Authoritarianism thus differs from authority. The latter rests on legitimacy (see p. 219), and in that sense it arises 'from below'. Authoritarian regimes therefore emphasize the claims of authority over those of individual liberty. However, authoritarianism is usually distinguished from totalitarianism. The practice of government 'from above' associated with monarchical absolutism, traditional dictatorships, and most forms of military rule is concerned with the repression of opposition and political liberty, rather than with the more radical goal of obliterating the distinction between the state and civil society. Authoritarian regimes may thus tolerate a significant range of economic, religious and other freedoms.

Islamic regimes

The rise of Islam as a political force has had a profound effect on politics in North Africa, the Middle East, and parts of Asia. In some cases, militant Islamic groups have challenged existing regimes, often articulating the interests of an urban poor since the 1970s disillusionment with Marxism–Leninism. In other cases, however, regimes have been constructed or reconstructed on Islamic lines. Since its inception in 1932, Saudi Arabia has been an Islamic state. The Iranian revolution of 1979 led to the establishment of an Islamic republic under Ayatollah Khomeini (1900–89), an example later followed in the Sudan and Pakistan. In countries such as Gaddafi's Libya, more idiosyncratic and disputed interpretations of Islam have been translated into political practice.

Islam is not, however, and never has been, simply a religion. Rather, it is a complete way of life, defining correct moral, political and economic behaviour for individuals and nations alike. The 'way of Islam' is based on the teachings of the Prophet Muhammad (570–632) as revealed in the Koran, regarded by all Moslems as the revealed word of God, and the Sunna, or 'beaten path', the traditional customs observed by a devout Moslem that are said to be based on the Prophet's own life. Political Islam thus aims at the construction of a theocracy in which political and other affairs are structured according to 'higher' religious principles. Nevertheless, political Islam has assumed clearly contrasting forms, ranging from fundamentalist to pluralist extremes.

The fundamentalist version of Islam is most commonly associated with Iran. Until his death in 1989, Khomeini presided over a system of institutionalized clerical rule, operating through the Islamic Revolutionary Council, a body of 15 senior clerics. Although a popularly elected parliament has been established in the form of the Islamic Consultative Assembly, all legislation is ratified by the Council for the Protection of the Constitution, which ensures conformity to Islamic principles. **Shari'a** law continues to be strictly enforced throughout Iran as both a legal and a moral code. The forces of revolutionary fundamentalism nevertheless reasserted themselves through the Taliban regime in Afghanistan, 1997–2001, which was characterized by the imposition of strict theocratic rule and the exclusion of women from education, the economy and public life in general. Fundamentalism (see p. 66) is no less significant in Saudi Arabia, where it has similarly absolutist implications, although the temper of the essentially conservative Sunni regime in Saudi Arabia differs markedly from the revolutionary populism (see p. 378) of Shi'ite Iran.

Moslems themselves, however, have often objected to the classification of any Islamic regime as 'fundamentalist', on the grounds that this perpetuates long-established western prejudices against an 'exotic' or 'repressive' East, serving as examples of 'orientalism' (Said, 1978). Evidence that Islam is compatible with a form of political pluralism can be found in Malaysia. Although Islam is the official state religion of Malaysia, with the Paramount Ruler serving as both religious leader and head of state, a form of 'guided' democracy operates through the dominance of the United Malays National Organization (UMNO), operating through a broad coalition, the Barisan Nasional, and within a multiparty framework. The UMNO has, since 1981, pursued a narrowly Islamic and pro-Malay strategy fused with an explicitly Japanese model of economic development. Authoritarian tendencies have nevertheless reemerged since 1988, when the independence of the judiciary effectively collapsed following a wave of political arrests and the imposition of press

Shari'a: Islamic law, believed to be based on divine revelation, and derived from the Koran, the Hadith (the teachings of Muhammad), and other sources.

censorship. Turkey also offers an interesting example of the relationship between Islam and democracy. Although the republic of Turkey, founded in 1923 by Mustafa Kamal Ataturk (1881–19) was firmly rooted in secularism. Islamic political parties have been gaining strength since the 1990s. The Welfare Party briefly led a coalition government in 1996, before being broken up by the army, and the Justice and Development party (AKP), from which it emerged, won a landslide victory in the 2002 general election. Nevertheless, the AKP is committed to political pluralism and enthusuastically supports early membership of the EU.

Military regimes

Whereas most regimes are shaped by a combination of political, economic, cultural and ideological factors, some survive through the exercise, above all, of military power and systematic repression. In this sense, military regimes belong to a broader category of authoritarianism. Military authoritarianism has been most common in Latin America, the Middle East, Africa and South East Asia, but it also emerged in the post-1945 period in Spain, Portugal and Greece. The key feature of a military regime is that the leading posts in the government are filled on the basis of the person's position within the military chain of command. Normal political and constitutional arrangements are usually suspended, and institutions through which opposition can be expressed, such as elected assemblies and a free press, are either weakened or abolished.

Although all forms of military rule are deeply repressive, this classification encompasses a number of regime types. In some military regimes, the armed forces assume direct control of government. The classical form of this is the military **junta**, most commonly found in Latin America. This operates as a form of collectivemilitary government centred on a command council of officers who usually represent the three armed services: the army, navy and air force. Junta regimes are often characterized by rivalry between the services and between leading figures, theconsequence being that formal positions of power tend to change hands relatively frequently.

The second form of military regime is a military-backed personalized dictatorship (see p. 405). In these cases, a single individual gains pre-eminence within the junta or regime, often being bolstered by a cult of personality (see p. 375) designed to manufacture charismatic authority. Examples are Colonel Papadopoulos in Greece in 1974–80, General Pinochet in Chile after the 1973 military coup, and General Abacha in Nigeria, 1993–98. In the final form of military regime, the loyalty of the armed forces is the decisive factor that upholds the regime, but the military leaders content themselves with 'pulling the strings' behind the scenes. This, for example, occurred in post-1945 Brazil, as the armed forces generally recognized that the legitimacy of the regime would be strengthened by the maintenance of a distinction between political and military offices and personnel. Such a distinction, however, may fuel an appetite for constitutional and representative politics, and reduce the scope for direct military intervention, thereby, over time, encouraging polyarchical tendencies. The character of military regimes is discussed at greater length in Chapter 18.

◼ Summary

◆ Government is any mechanism through which ordered rule is maintained, its central feature being its ability to make collective decisions and enforce them. A

Junta: Literally, a council; a (usually military) clique that seizes power through a revolution or *coup d'état*.

political system, or regime, however, encompasses not only the mechanisms of government and institutions of the state, but also the structures and processes through which these interact with the larger society.

◆ The classification of political systems serves two purposes. First, it aids understanding by making comparison possible and helping to highlight similarities and differences between otherwise shapeless collections of facts. Second, it helps us to evaluate the effectiveness or success of different political systems.

◆ Regimes have been classified on a variety of bases. 'Classical' typologies, stemming from Aristotle, concentrated on constitutional arrangements and institutional structures, while the 'three worlds' approach highlighted material and ideological differences between the systems found in 'first world' capitalist, 'second world' communist and 'third world' developing states.

◆ The collapse of communism and advance of democratization has made it much more difficult to identify the political contours of the modern world, making conventional systems of classification redundant. It is nevertheless still possible to distinguish between regimes on the basis of how their political, economic and cultural characteristics interlock in practice, even though all systems of classification are provisional.

◆ 'End of history' theorists have proclaimed that history has ended, or is destined to end, with the worldwide triumph of western liberal democracy. Indeed, the most common form of regime in the modern world is now some form of democracy. However, there is evidence that regime types have become both more complex and more diverse. Significant differences can be identified among western polyarchies, new democracies, East Asian regimes, Islamic regimes and military regimes.

▮ Questions for discussion

▶ Does Aristotle's system of political classification have any relevance to the modern world?

▶ Is there any longer such a thing as the 'third world'?

▶ To what extent have postcommunist regimes discarded their communist past?

▶ Why have liberal-democratic structures proved to be so effective and successful?

▶ How democratic are western polyarchies?

▶ Do Confucianism and Islam constitute viable alternatives to western liberalism as a basis for a modern regime?

▮ Further reading

Brooker, P., *Non-Democratic Regimes; Theory, Government and Politics* (Basingstoke: Macmillan, and New York: St Martin's Press, 2000). A useful and wide-ranging survey of the different forms of non-democratic regime.

Hadenius, A. (ed.), *Democracy's Victory and Crisis* (New York and Cambridge: Cambridge University Press, 1997). An excellent reader that examines the global resurgence of democracy and reflects on its implications.

Hague, R. and M. Harrop, *Comparative Government and Politics: An Introduction*, 6th edn (Basingstoke: Palgrave Macmillan, 2004) (US edn: *Political Science: A Comparative Introduction*, 3rd edn (New York: Palgrave Macmillan). A succinct and stimulating introduction to comparative politics that adopts a genuinely international approach.

Lijphart, A., *Patterns of Democracy: Government Forms and Performance in Thirty-Six Countries* (New Haven, CT: Yale University Press, 1999). An updated version of a classic and highly influential attempt to distinguish between forms of democratic rule.

Political Ideologies

'The philosophers have only interpreted the world in various ways: the point is to change it.'

KARL MARX, *Theses on Feuerbach* (1845)

No one sees the world as it is. All of us look at the world through a veil of theories, presuppositions and assumptions. In this sense, observation and interpretation are inextricably bound together: when we look at the world we are also engaged in imposing meaning upon it. This has important implications for the study of politics. In particular, it highlights the need to uncover the presuppositions and assumptions that we bring to political enquiry. At their deepest level, these assumptions are rooted in broad political creeds or traditions that are usually termed 'political ideologies'. Each of these 'isms' (liberalism, socialism, conservatism, feminism, fascism, and so on) constitutes a distinctive intellectual framework or paradigm, and each offers its own account of political reality – its own world view. However, there is deep disagreement both about the nature of ideology and about the role, for good or ill, that it plays in political life.

The central issues examined in this chapter are as follows:

Key issues

▶ What is political ideology?

▶ What are the characteristic themes, theories and principles of each of the major ideologies?

▶ What rival traditions or internal tensions does each ideology encompass?

▶ How have the major ideologies changed over time?

▶ How can the rise and fall of ideologies be explained?

▶ Has ideology come to an end? Could ideology come to an end?

Contents

◼ What is political ideology?

Ideology is one of the most controversial concepts encountered in political analysis. Although the term now tends to be used in a neutral sense, to refer to a developed social philosophy or world view, it has in the past had heavily negative or pejorative connotations. During its sometimes tortuous career, the concept of ideology has commonly been used as a political weapon to condemn or criticize rival creeds or doctrines.

The term 'ideology' was coined in 1796 by the French philosopher Destutt de Tracy (1754–1836). He used it to refer to a new 'science of ideas' (literally an idea-ology) that set out to uncover the origins of conscious thought and ideas. De Tracy's hope was that ideology would eventually enjoy the same status as established sciences such as zoology and biology. However, a more enduring meaning was assigned to the term in the nineteenth century in the writings of Karl Marx (see p. 55). For Marx, ideology amounted to the ideas of the 'ruling class', ideas that therefore uphold the class system and perpetuate exploitation. In their early work *The German Ideology*, Marx and Engels wrote the following:

The ideas of the ruling class are in every epoch the ruling ideas, i.e. the class which is the ruling *material* force in society, is at the same time the ruling *intellectual* force. The class which has the means of mental production at its disposal, has control at the same time over the means of mental production. (Marx and Engels, [1846] 1970:64)

The defining feature of ideology in the Marxist sense is that it is false: it mystifies and confuses subordinate classes by concealing from them the contradictions upon which all class societies are based. As far as capitalism is concerned, the ideology of the property-owning bourgeoisie (bourgeois ideology) fosters delusion or 'false consciousness' amongst the exploited proletariat, preventing them from recognizing the fact of their own exploitation. Nevertheless, Marx did not believe that all political views had an ideological character. He held that his own work, which attempted to uncover the process of class exploitation and oppression, was scientific. In his view, a clear distinction could be drawn between science and ideology, between truth and falsehood. This distinction tended, however, to be blurred in the writings of later Marxists such as Lenin (see p. 81) and Gramsci (see p. 208). These referred not only to 'bourgeois ideology' but also to 'socialist ideology' or 'proletarian ideology', terms that Marx would have considered absurd.

Alternative uses of the term have also been developed by liberals and conservatives. The emergence of totalitarian dictatorships in the interwar period encouraged writers such as Karl Popper (1902–94), J. L. Talmon and Hannah Arendt (see p. 9) to view ideology as an instrument of social control to ensure compliance and subordination. Relying heavily on the examples of fascism and communism, this Cold War liberal use of the term treated ideology as a 'closed' system of thought, which, by claiming a monopoly of truth, refuses to tolerate opposing ideas and rival beliefs. In contrast, liberalism, based as it is on a fundamental commitment to individual freedom, and doctrines such as conservatism and democratic socialism that broadly subscribe to liberal principles are clearly not ideologies. These doctrines are 'open' in the sense that they permit, and even insist upon, free debate, opposition and criticism.

A distinctively conservative use of the term 'ideology' has been developed by thinkers such as Michael Oakeshott (see p. 211). This view reflects a characteristically conservative scepticism about the value of **rationalism** that is born out of the belief

Rationalism: The belief that the world can be understood and explained through the exercise of human reason, based on assumptions about its rational structure.

that the world is largely beyond the capacity of the human mind to fathom. As Oakeshott put it, in political activity 'men sail a boundless and bottomless sea'. From this perspective, ideologies are seen as abstract 'systems of thought': that is, as sets of ideas that distort political reality because they claim to explain what is, frankly, incomprehensible. This is why conservatives have traditionally dismissed the notion that they subscribe to an ideology, preferring instead to describe conservatism as a disposition, or an 'attitude of mind', and placing their faith in **pragmatism**, tradition (see p. 221) and history.

The drawback of each of these usages, however, is that, as they are negative or pejorative, they restrict the application of the term. Certain political doctrines, in other words, are excluded from the category of 'ideologies'. Marx, for instance, insisted that his ideas were scientific, not ideological, liberals have denied that liberalism should be viewed as an ideology, and conservatives have traditionally claimed to embrace a pragmatic rather than ideological style of politics. Moreover, each of these definitions is loaded with the values and orientation of a particular political doctrine. An inclusive definition of 'ideology' (one that applies to all political traditions) must therefore be neutral: it must reject the notion that ideologies are 'good' or 'bad', true or false, or liberating or oppressive. This is the virtue of the modern, social-scientific meaning of the term, which treats ideology as an action-orientated belief system, an interrelated set of ideas that in some way guides or inspires political action.

Liberalism

Any account of political ideologies must start with liberalism. This is because liberalism is, in effect, the ideology of the industrialized West, and is sometimes portrayed as a **meta-ideology** that is capable of embracing a broad range of rival values and beliefs. Although liberalism did not emerge as a developed political creed until the early nineteenth century, distinctively liberal theories and principles had gradually been developed during the previous 300 years. Liberalism was the product of the breakdown of feudalism and the growth, in its place, of a market or capitalist society. Early liberalism certainly reflected the aspirations of a rising industrial middle class, and liberalism and capitalism have been closely linked (some have argued intrinsically linked) ever since. In its earliest form, liberalism was a political doctrine. It attacked absolutism (see p. 28) and feudal privilege, instead advocating constitutional and, later, representative government. By the early nineteenth century, a distinctively liberal economic creed had developed that extolled the virtues of *laissez-faire* capitalism (see p. 189) and condemned all forms of government intervention. This became the centrepiece of classical, or nineteenth-century, liberalism. From the late nineteenth century onwards, however, a form of social liberalism emerged that looked more favourably on welfare reform and economic intervention. Such an emphasis became the characteristic theme of modern, or twentieth-century, liberalism.

Elements of liberalism

• **Individualism:** Individualism (see p. 196) is the core principle of liberal ideology. It reflects a belief in the supreme importance of the human individual as opposed to any social group or collective body. Human beings are seen, first and foremost, as individuals. This implies both that they are of equal moral worth and

Concept

Ideology

From a social-scientific viewpoint, an ideology is a more or less coherent set of ideas that provides a basis for organized political action, whether this is intended to preserve, modify or overthrow the existing system of power relationships. All ideologies therefore (a) offer an account of the existing order, usually in the form of a 'world view', (b) provide a model of a desired future, a vision of the Good Society, and (c) outline how political change can and should be brought about. Ideologies are not, however, hermetically sealed systems of thought: rather, they are fluid sets of ideas that overlap with one another at a number of points. At a 'fundamental' level, ideologies resemble political philosophies; at an 'operative' level, they take the form of broad political movements (Seliger, 1976).

Pragmatism: A theory or practice that places primary emphasis on practical circumstances and goals; pragmatism implies a distrust of abstract ideas.

Meta-ideology: A higher or second-order ideology that lays down the grounds on which ideological debate can take place.

that they possess separate and unique identities. The liberal goal is therefore to construct a society within which individuals can flourish and develop, each pursuing 'the good' as he or she defines it, to the best of his or her abilities. This has contributed to the view that liberalism is morally neutral, in the sense that it lays down a set of rules that allow individuals to make their own moral decisions.

- **Freedom**: Individual freedom (see p. 324), or liberty (the two terms are interchangeable), is the core value of liberalism; it is given priority over, say, equality, justice or authority. This arises naturally from a belief in the individual and the desire to ensure that each person is able to act as he or she pleases or chooses. Nevertheless, liberals advocate 'freedom under the law', as they recognize that one person's liberty may be a threat to the liberty of others; liberty may become licence. They therefore endorse the ideal that individuals should enjoy the maximum possible liberty consistent with a like liberty for all.

- **Reason**: Liberals believe that the world has a rational structure, and that this can be uncovered through the exercise of human reason and by critical enquiry. This inclines them to place their faith in the ability of individuals to make wise judgements on their own behalf, being, in most cases, the best judges of their own interests. It also encourages liberals to believe in **progress** and the capacity of human beings to resolve their differences through debate and argument rather than bloodshed and war.

- **Equality**: Individualism implies a belief in foundational equality: that is, the belief that individuals are 'born equal', at least in terms of moral worth. This is reflected in a liberal commitment to equal rights and entitlements, notably in the form of legal equality ('equality before the law') and political equality ('one person, one vote; one vote, one value'). However, as individuals do not possess the same levels of talent or willingness to work, liberals do not endorse social equality or an equality of outcome. Rather, they favour equality of opportunity (a 'level playing field') that gives all individuals an equal chance to realize their unequal potential. Liberals therefore support the principle of **meritocracy**, with merit reflecting, crudely, talent plus hard work.

- **Toleration**: Liberals believe that toleration (that is, forbearance: the willingness of people to allow others to think, speak and act in ways of which they disapprove) is both a guarantee of individual liberty and a means of social enrichment. They believe that pluralism (see p. 82), in the form of moral, cultural and political diversity, is positively healthy: it promotes debate and intellectual progress by ensuring that all beliefs are tested in a free market of ideas. Liberals, moreover, tend to believe that there is a balance or natural harmony between rival views and interests, and thus usually discount the idea of irreconcilable conflict.

Progress: Moving forwards; the belief that history is characterized by human advancement based on the accumulation of knowledge and wisdom.

Meritocracy: Rule by the talented; the principle that rewards and positions should be distributed on the basis of ability.

- **Consent**: In the liberal view, authority and social relationships should always be based on consent or willing agreement. Government must therefore be based on the 'consent of the governed'. This is a doctrine that encourages liberals to favour representation (see p. 248) and democracy. Similarly, social bodies and associations are formed through contracts willingly entered into by individuals intent on pursuing their own self-interest. In this sense, authority arises 'from below' and is always grounded in legitimacy (see p. 219).

- **Constitutionalism**: Although liberals see government as a vital guarantee of order and stability in society, they are constantly aware of the danger that government may become a tyranny against the individual ('power tends to corrupt' (Lord Acton)).

John Locke (1632–1704)

English philosopher and politician. Locke was born in Somerset in the UK. He studied medicine at Oxford University before becoming secretary to Anthony Ashley Cooper, First Earl of Shaftsbury, in 1661. Locke's political views were developed against the backdrop of the English Revolution, and they are often seen as providing a justification for the 'Glorious Revolution' of 1688, which ended absolutist rule and established a constitutional monarchy in Britain under William of Orange. Locke was a key thinker in the development of early liberalism, placing particular emphasis upon 'natural' or God-given rights, identified as the rights to life, liberty and property. As he was an exponent of representative government and toleration, his views had a considerable impact upon the American Revolution. Locke's most important political works are *A Letter Concerning Toleration* (1689) and *Two Treatises of Government* ([1690] 1965).

They therefore believe in limited government. This goal can be attained through the fragmentation of government power, by the creation of checks and balances amongst the various institutions of government, and through the establishment of a codified or 'written' constitution embodying a bill of rights that defines the relationship between the state and the individual.

Classical liberalism

The central theme of classical liberalism is a commitment to an extreme form of individualism. Human beings are seen as egoistical, self-seeking and largely self-reliant creatures. In what C. B. Macpherson (1962) termed 'possessive individualism', they are taken to be the proprietors of their own persons and capacities, owing nothing to society or to other individuals. This **atomist** view of society is underpinned by a belief in 'negative' liberty, meaning noninterference, or the absence of external constraints upon the individual. This implies a deeply unsympathetic attitude towards the state and all forms of government intervention.

In Tom Paine's (see p. 250) words, the state is a 'necessary evil'. It is 'necessary' in that, at the very least, it establishes order and security and ensures that contracts are enforced. However, it is 'evil' in that it imposes a collective will upon society, thus limiting the freedom and responsibilities of the individual. The classical liberal ideal is therefore the establishment of a minimal or 'nightwatchman' state, with a role that is limited to the protection of citizens from the encroachments of fellow citizens. In the form of **economic liberalism**, this position is underpinned by a deep faith in the mechanisms of the free market and the belief that the economy works best when left alone by government. *Laissez-faire* capitalism is thus seen as guaranteeing prosperity, upholding individual liberty, and, as this allows individuals to rise and fall according to merit, ensuring social justice.

Modern liberalism

Modern liberalism is characterized by a more sympathetic attitude towards state intervention. Indeed, in the USA, the term 'liberal' is invariably taken to imply support for **'big' government** rather than 'minimal' government. This shift was born out of the recognition that industrial capitalism had merely generated new forms of

Atomism: The belief that society is made up of a collection of largely self-sufficient individuals who owe little or nothing to one another.

Economic liberalism: A belief in the market as a self-regulating mechanism tending naturally to deliver general prosperity and opportunities for all.

Big government: Interventionist government, usually understood to imply economic management and social regulation.

John Stuart Mill (1806–73)

UK philosopher, economist and politician. Mill was subject to an intense and austere regime of education by his father, the utilitarian theorist James Mill (1773–1836). This resulted in a mental collapse at the age of 20, after which he developed a more human philosophy influenced by Coleridge and the German Idealists. His major writings, including *On Liberty* (1859), *Considerations on Representative Government* (1861) and *The Subjection of Women* (1869), had a powerful influence on the development of liberal thought. In many ways, Mill's varied and complex work straddled the divide between classical and modern liberalism. His distrust of state intervention was firmly rooted in nineteenth-century principles, but his emphasis upon the quality of individual life (reflected in a commitment to 'individuality'), as well as his sympathy for causes such as female suffrage and workers' cooperatives, clearly looked forward to twentieth-century developments.

injustice and left the mass of the population subject to the vagaries of the market. Influenced by the work of J. S. Mill, the so-called New Liberals (figures such as T. H. Green (1836–82), L. T. Hobhouse (1864–1929) and J. A. Hobson (1858–1940)) championed a broader, 'positive' view of freedom. From this perspective, freedom does not just mean being left alone, which might imply nothing more than the freedom to starve. Rather, it is linked to personal development and the flourishing of the individual: that is, the ability of the individual to gain fulfilment and achieve self-realization.

This view provided the basis for social or welfare liberalism. This is characterized by the recognition that state intervention, particularly in the form of social welfare (see p. 439), can enlarge liberty by safeguarding individuals from the social evils that blight individual existence. These evils were identified in the UK by the 1942 Beveridge Report as the 'five giants': want, ignorance, idleness, squalor and disease. In the same way, modern liberals abandoned their belief in *laissez-faire* capitalism, largely as a result of J. M. Keynes' (see p. 190) insight that growth and prosperity could be maintained only through a system of managed or regulated capitalism, with key economic responsibilities being placed in the hands of the state. Nevertheless, modern liberals' support for collective provision and government intervention has always been conditional. Their concern has been with the plight of the weak and vulnerable, those who are literally not able to help themselves. Their goal is to raise individuals to the point where they are able, once again, to take responsibility for their own circumstances and make their own moral choices. The most influential modern attempt to reconcile the principles of liberalism with the politics of welfare and **redistribution** was undertaken by John Rawls (see p. 60).

Redistribution: A narrowing of material inequalities brought about through a combination of progressive taxation and welfare provision.

Ancien régime: (*French*) Literally, old order; usually linked with the absolutist structures that predated the French Revolution.

 # Conservatism

Conservative ideas and doctrines first emerged in the late eighteenth century and early nineteenth century. They arose as a reaction against the growing pace of economic and political change, which was in many ways symbolized by the French Revolution. In this sense, conservatism harked back to the ***ancien régime***. In trying to resist the pressures unleashed by the growth of liberalism, socialism and nationalism, conservatism stood in defence of an increasingly embattled traditional social order. However, from the outset, divisions in conservative thought were apparent. In

Edmund Burke (1729–97)

Dublin-born UK statesman and political theorist who is often seen as the father of the Anglo-American conservative tradition. Burke's enduring reputation is based on a series of works, notably *Reflections on the Revolution in France* ([1790] 1968), that were critical of the French Revolution. Though sympathetic to the American Revolution, Burke was deeply critical of the attempt to recast French politics in accordance with abstract principles such as liberty, equality and fraternity, arguing that wisdom resided largely in experience, tradition and history. Nevertheless, he held that the French monarchy was in part responsible for its own fate since it had obstinately refused to 'change in order to conserve'. Burke had a gloomy view of government, recognizing that it could prevent evil but rarely promote good. He regarded market forces as 'natural law'.

continental Europe, a form of conservatism emerged that was characterized by the work of thinkers such as Joseph de Maistre (1753–1821). This conservatism was starkly autocratic and reactionary, rejecting out of hand any idea of reform. A more cautious, more flexible, and ultimately more successful form of conservatism nevertheless developed in the UK and the USA that was characterized by Edmund Burke's belief in 'change in order to conserve'. This stance enabled conservatives in the nineteenth century to embrace the cause of social reform under the paternalistic banner of 'One Nation'. The high point of this tradition in the UK came in the 1950s as the Conservative Party came to accept the postwar settlement and espouse its own version of Keynesian social democracy. However, such ideas increasingly came under pressure from the 1970s onwards as a result of the emergence of the New Right. The New Right's radically antistatist and antipaternalist brand of conservatism draws heavily on classical liberal themes and values.

Elements of conservatism

- **Tradition:** The central theme of conservative thought, 'the desire to conserve', is closely linked to the perceived virtues of tradition, respect for established customs, and institutions that have endured through time. In this view, tradition reflects the accumulated wisdom of the past, and institutions and practices that have been 'tested by time', and it should be preserved for the benefit of the living and for generations yet to come. Tradition also has the virtue of promoting stability and security, giving individuals a sense of social and historical belonging.

- **Pragmatism:** Conservatives have traditionally emphasized the limitations of human rationality, which arise from the infinite complexity of the world in which we live. Abstract principles and systems of thought are therefore distrusted, and instead faith is placed in experience, history and, above all, pragmatism: the belief that action should be shaped by practical circumstances and practical goals, that is, by 'what works'. Conservatives have thus preferred to describe their own beliefs as an 'attitude of mind' or an 'approach to life', rather than as an ideology, although they reject the idea that this amounts to unprincipled opportunism.

- **Human imperfection:** The conservative view of human nature is broadly pessimistic. In this view, human beings are limited, dependent, and security-seeking creatures, drawn to the familiar and the tried and tested, and needing to live in stable and orderly communities. In addition, individuals are morally corrupt: they are tainted by selfishness, greed and the thirst for power. The roots of crime and disorder therefore reside within the human individual rather than in society. The maintenance of order (see p. 413) therefore requires a strong state, the enforcement of strict laws, and stiff penalties.

• **Organicism:** Instead of seeing society as an artefact that is a product of human ingenuity, conservatives have traditionally viewed society as an organic whole, or living entity. Society is thus structured by natural necessity, with its various institutions, or the 'fabric of society' (families, local communities, the nation and so on), contributing to the health and stability of society. The whole is more than a collection of its individual parts. Shared (often 'traditional') values and a common culture are also seen as being vital to the maintenance of the community (see p. 178) and social cohesion.

• **Hierarchy:** In the conservative view, gradations of social position and status are natural and inevitable in an organic society. These reflect the differing roles and responsibilities of, for example, employers and workers, teachers and pupils, and parents and children. Nevertheless, in this view, hierarchy and inequality do not give rise to conflict, because society is bound together by mutual obligations and reciprocal duties. Indeed, as a person's 'station in life' is determined largely by luck and the accident of birth, the prosperous and privileged acquire a particular responsibility of care for the less fortunate.

• **Authority:** Conservatives hold that, to some degree, authority is always exercised 'from above', providing leadership (see p. 372), guidance and support for those who lack the knowledge, experience or education to act wisely in their own interests (an example being the authority of parents over children). Although the idea of a **natural aristocracy** was once influential, authority and leadership are now more commonly seen as resulting from experience and training. The virtue of authority is that it is a source of social cohesion, giving people a clear sense of who they are and what is expected of them. Freedom must therefore coexist with responsibility; it therefore consists largely of a willing acceptance of obligations and duties.

• **Property:** Conservatives see property ownership as being vital because it gives people security and a measure of independence from government, and it encourages them to respect the law and the property of others. Property is also an exteriorization of people's personalities, in that they 'see' themselves in what they own: their houses, their cars, and so on. However, property ownership involves duties as well as rights. In this view, we are, in a sense, merely custodians of property that has either been inherited from past generations ('the family silver'), or may be of value to future ones.

Paternalistic conservatism

The **paternalistic** strand in conservative thought is entirely consistent with principles such as organicism, hierarchy and duty, and it can therefore be seen as an outgrowth of traditional conservatism. Often traced back to the early writings of Benjamin Disraeli (1804–81), paternalism draws upon a combination of prudence and principle. In warning of the danger of the UK being divided into 'two nations: the Rich and the Poor', Disraeli articulated a widespread fear of social revolution. This warning amounted to an

Natural aristocracy: The idea that talent and leadership are innate or inbred qualities that cannot be acquired through effort or self-advancement.

Paternalism: An attitude or policy that demonstrates care or concern for those unable to help themselves, as in the (supposed) relationship between a father and a child.

appeal to the self-interest of the privileged, who needed to recognize that 'reform from above' was preferable to 'revolution from below'. This message was underpinned by an appeal to the principles of duty and social obligation rooted in neofeudal ideas such as *noblesse oblige*. In effect, in this view, duty is the price of privilege; the powerful and propertied inherit a responsibility to look after the less well-off in the broader interests of social cohesion and unity. The resulting one-nation principle, the cornerstone of what can properly be termed a **Tory** position, reflects not so much the ideal of social equality as the vision of organic balance, a cohesive and stable hierarchy.

The one-nation tradition embodies not only a disposition towards social reform, but also an essentially pragmatic attitude towards economic policy. This is clearly seen in the 'middle way' approach adopted in the 1950s by UK Conservatives. This approach eschewed the two ideological models of economic organization: *laissez-faire* capitalism on the one hand, and state socialism and central planning on the other. The former was rejected on the grounds that it results in a free for all, which makes social cohesion impossible, and penalizes the weak and vulnerable. The latter was dismissed because it produces a state monolith and crushes all forms of independence and enterprise. The solution therefore lies in a blend of market competition and government regulation – 'private enterprise without selfishness' (H. Macmillan).

Very similar conclusions were drawn after 1945 by continental European conservatives, who embraced the principles of **Christian democracy**, most rigorously developed in the 'social market' philosophy (see p. 188) of the German Christian Democrats (CDU). This philosophy embraces a *market* strategy insofar as it highlights the virtues of private enterprise and competition, but it is *social* in that it believes that the prosperity so gained should be employed for the broader benefit of society. Such a position draws from Catholic social theory, which advances an organic view of society that stresses social harmony. Christian democracy thus highlights the importance of intermediate institutions, such as churches, unions and business groups, bound together by the notion of 'social partnership'. The paternalistic strand of modern conservatism thought is often linked to the idea of 'compassionate conservatism'.

The New Right

The New Right represents a departure in conservative thought that amounted to a kind of counter-revolution against both the post-1945 drift towards state intervention and the spread of liberal or progressive social values. New Right ideas can be traced back to the 1970s and the conjunction between the apparent failure of Keynesian social democracy, signalled by the end of the postwar boom, and growing concern about social breakdown and the decline of authority. Such ideas had their greatest impact in the UK and the USA, where they were articulated in the 1980s in the form of Thatcherism and Reaganism, respectively. They have also had a wider, even worldwide, influence in bringing about a general shift from state- to market-orientated forms of organization. However, the New Right does not so much constitute a coherent and systematic philosophy as attempt to marry two distinct traditions, usually termed 'neoliberalism' and 'neoconservatism'. Although there is political and ideological tension between these two, they can be combined in support of the goal of a strong but minimal state: in Andrew Gamble's (1981) words, 'the free economy and the strong state'.

Noblesse oblige: (*French*) Literally, the obligations of the nobility; in general terms, the responsibility to guide or protect those less fortunate or less privileged.

Toryism: An ideological stance within conservatism characterized by a belief in hierarchy, an emphasis on tradition, and support for duty and organicism.

Christian democracy: An ideological tendency within European conservatism, characterized by commitment to social market principles and qualified interventionism.

Friedrich von Hayek (1899–1992)

Austrian economist and political philosopher. An academic who taught at the London School of Economics and the Universities of Chicago, Freiburg and Salzburg, Hayek was awarded the Nobel Prize for Economics in 1974. As an exponent of the so-called Austrian School, he was a firm believer in individualism and market order, and an implacable critic of socialism. *The Road to Serfdom* (1948) was a pioneering work that attacked economic interventionism; later works such as *The Constitution of Liberty* (1960) and *Law, Legislation and Liberty* (1979) developed themes in political philosophy. Hayek's writings had a considerable impact on the emergent New Right.

Neoliberalism

Neoliberalism is an updated version of classical political economy that was developed in the writings of free-market economists such as Friedrich Hayek and Milton Friedman (see p. 191) and philosophers such as Robert Nozick (see p. 100). The central pillars of neoliberalism are the market and the individual. The principal neoliberal goal is to 'roll back the frontiers of the state', in the belief that unregulated market capitalism will deliver efficiency, growth and widespread prosperity. In this view, the 'dead hand' of the state saps initiative and discourages enterprise; government, however well intentioned, invariably has a damaging effect upon human affairs. This is reflected in the liberal New Right's concern with the politics of ownership, and its preference for private enterprise over state enterprise or nationalization: in short, 'private, good; public, bad'. Such ideas are associated with a form of rugged individualism, expressed in Margaret Thatcher's famous assertion that 'there is no such thing as society, only individuals and their families'. The **'nanny state'** is seen to breed a culture of dependence and to undermine freedom, which is understood as freedom of choice in the marketplace. Instead, faith is placed in self-help, individual responsibility and entrepreneurialism. Such ideas are widely seen to be advanced through the process of globalization (see p. 143), viewed by some as neoliberal globalization.

Neoconservatism

Nanny state: A state with extensive social responsibilities; the term implies that welfare programmes are unwarranted and demeaning to the individual.

Permissiveness: The willingness to allow people to make their own moral choices; permissiveness suggests that there are no authoritative values.

Neoconservatism reasserts nineteenth-century conservative social principles. The conservative New Right wishes, above all, to restore authority and return to traditional values, notably those linked to the family, religion and the nation. Authority is seen as guaranteeing social stability, on the basis that it generates discipline and respect, while shared values and a common culture are believed to generate social cohesion and make civilized existence possible. The enemies of neoconservatism are therefore **permissiveness**, the cult of the self and 'doing one's own thing', thought of as the values of the 1960s. Indeed, many of those who style themselves neoconservatives in the USA are former liberals who grew disillusioned with the progressive reforms of the Kennedy–Johnson era. Another aspect of neoconservatism is the tendency to view the emergence of multicultural and multireligious societies with concern, on the basis that they are conflict-ridden and inherently unstable. This position also tends to be linked to an insular form of nationalism that is sceptical about both multiculturalism (see p. 119) and the growing influence of supranational bodies such as the UN and the EU. Neoconservatism has also developed into a distinctive appraoch to foreign policy, particularly in the USA. This aspect of neo-conservative politics is discussed in Chapter 7.

◼ Socialism

Although socialist ideas can be traced back to the Levellers and Diggers of the seventeenth century, or to Thomas More's *Utopia* ([1516] 1965), or even Plato's *Republic*, socialism did not take shape as a political creed until the early nineteenth century. It developed as a reaction against the emergence of industrial capitalism. Socialism first articulated the interests of artisans and craftsmen threatened by the spread of factory production, but it was soon being linked to the growing industrial working class, the 'factory fodder' of early industrialization. In its earliest forms, socialism tended to have a fundamentalist (see p. 66), utopian and revolutionary character. Its goal was to abolish a capitalist economy based on market exchange, and replace it with a qualitatively different socialist society, usually to be constructed on the principle of common ownership. The most influential representative of this brand of socialism was Karl Marx, whose ideas provided the foundations for twentieth-century communism (see p. 35).

From the late nineteenth century onwards, however, a reformist socialist tradition emerged that reflected the gradual integration of the working classes into capitalist society through an improvement in working conditions and wages and the growth of trade unions and socialist political parties. This brand of socialism proclaimed the possibility of a peaceful, gradual and legal transition to socialism, brought about through the adoption of the 'parliamentary road'. Reformist socialism drew upon two sources. The first was a humanist tradition of ethical socialism, linked to thinkers such as Robert Owen (1771–1858), Charles Fourier (1772–1837) and William Morris (1854–96). The second was a form of **revisionist** Marxism developed primarily by Eduard Bernstein (see p. 59).

During much of the twentieth century, the socialist movement was thus divided into two rival camps. Revolutionary socialists, following the example of Lenin (see p. 81) and the Bolsheviks, called themselves communists, while reformist socialists, who practised a form of constitutional politics, embraced what increasingly came to be called social democracy. This rivalry focused not only on the most appropriate means of achieving socialism, but also on the nature of the socialist goal itself. Social democrats turned their backs upon fundamentalist principles such as common ownership and planning, and recast socialism in terms of welfare, redistribution and economic management. Both forms of socialism, however, experienced crises in the late twentieth century that encouraged some to proclaim the 'death of socialism' and the emergence of a postsocialist society. The most dramatic event in this process was the collapse of communism brought about by the eastern European revolutions of 1989–91, but there was also a continued retreat of social democracy from traditional principles, making it, some would argue, indistinguishable from modern liberalism.

Revisionism: The modification of original or established beliefs; revisionism can imply the abandonment of principle or a loss of conviction.

Elements of socialism

• **Community:** The core of socialism is the vision of human beings as social creatures linked by the existence of a common humanity. As the poet John Donne put it, 'no man is an Island entire of itself; every man is a piece of the Continent, a part of the main'. This refers to the importance of community (see p. 178), and it highlights the degree to which individual identity is fashioned by social interaction and membership of social groups and collective bodies. Socialists are inclined to emphasize nurture over nature, and to explain individual behaviour mainly in terms of social factors rather than innate qualities.

• **Fraternity:** As human beings share a common humanity, they are bound together by a sense of comradeship or fraternity (literally meaning 'brotherhood', but broadened in this context to embrace all humans). This encourages socialists to prefer cooperation to competition, and to favour collectivism over individualism (see p. 196). In this view, cooperation enables people to harness their collective energies and strengthens the bonds of community, while competition pits individuals against each other, breeding resentment, conflict and hostility.

• **Social equality:** Equality (see p. 440) is the central value of socialism. Socialism is sometimes portrayed as a form of egalitarianism, the belief in the primacy of equality over other values. In particular, socialists emphasize the importance of social equality, an equality of outcome as opposed to equality of opportunity. They believe that a measure of social equality is the essential guarantee of social stability and cohesion, encouraging individuals to identify with their fellow human beings. It also provides the basis for the exercise of legal and political rights.

• **Need:** Sympathy for equality also reflects the socialist belief that material benefits should be distributed on the basis of need, rather than simply on the basis of merit or work. The classic formulation of this principle is found in Marx's communist principle of distribution: 'from each according to his ability, to each according to his need'. This reflects the belief that the satisfaction of basic needs (hunger, thirst, shelter, health, personal security and so on) is a prerequisite for a worthwhile human existence and participation in social life. Clearly, however, distribution according to need requires people to be motivated by moral incentives, rather than just material ones.

• **Social class:** Socialism has often been associated with a form of class politics. First, socialists have tended to analyse society in terms of the distribution of income or wealth, and they have thus seen social class (see p. 197) as a significant (usually the most signifi-cant) social cleavage. Second, socialism has traditionally been associated with the interests of an oppressed and exploited working class (however defined), and it has traditionally regarded the working class as an agent of social change, even social revolution (see p. 224). Nevertheless, class divisions are remediable: the socialist goal is either the eradication of economic and social inequalities or their substantial reduction.

• **Common ownership:** The relationship between socialism and common ownership has been deeply controversial. Some see it as the *end* of socialism itself, and others see it instead as simply a *means* of generating broader equality. The socialist case for common ownership (in the form of either Soviet-style state collectivization, or selective nationalization (a 'mixed economy')) is that it is a means of harnessing material resources to the common good, with private property being seen to pro-

Karl Marx (1818–83)

German philosopher, economist and political thinker, usually portrayed as the father of twentieth-century communism. After a brief career as a university teacher, Marx took up journalism and became increasingly involved with the socialist movement. He moved to Paris in 1843. He finally settled in London after being expelled from Prussia, and worked for the rest of his life as an active revolutionary and writer supported by his friend and lifelong collaborator Friedrich Engels. In 1864 Marx helped to found the First International, which collapsed in 1871 because of growing antagonism between Marx's supporters and anarchists led by Bakunin. Although much of his voluminous writings remained unpublished at his death, Marx's classic work was the three-volume *Capital* ([1867, 1885, 1894] 1970). His best-known and most accessible work is the *Communist Manifesto* ([1848] 1967).

mote selfishness, acquisitiveness and social division. Modern socialism, however, has moved away from this narrow concern with the politics of ownership.

Marxism

As a theoretical system, Marxism has constituted the principal alternative to the liberal rationalism that has dominated western culture and intellectual enquiry in the modern period. As a political force, in the form of the international communist movement, Marxism has also been seen as the major enemy of western capitalism, at least in the period 1917–91. This highlights a central difficulty in dealing with Marxism: the difference between Marxism as a social philosophy derived from the classic writings of Karl Marx and Friedrich Engels (1820–95), and the phenomenon of twentieth-century communism, which in many ways departed from and revised classical principles. Thus the collapse of communism at the end of the twentieth century need not betoken the death of Marxism as a political ideology; indeed, it may give Marxism, now divorced from the vestiges of Leninism and Stalinism, a fresh lease of life.

To some extent, the problem stems from the wide range and complex nature of Marx's own writings, which have allowed him to be interpreted by some as an economic determinist, but by others as a humanist socialist. A distinction has also been drawn between the character of his early writings and that of his late writings. This is often portrayed as the distinction between the 'young Marx' and the 'mature Marx'. What is clear, however, is that Marx believed that he had developed a new brand of socialism that was scientific, in the sense that it was concerned primarily with disclosing the nature of social and historical development rather than with advancing an essentially ethical critique of capitalism. Marx's ideas and theories reached a wider audience after his death, largely through the writings of his lifelong collaborator Engels, the German socialist leader Karl Kautsky (1854–1938), and the Russian theoretician Georgi Plekhanov (1856–1918). A form of orthodox Marxism, usually termed **dialectical materialism** (a term coined by Plekhanov, not Marx), came into existence that was later used as the basis for Soviet communism. This 'vulgar' Marxism undoubtedly placed a heavier stress on mechanistic theories and historical determinism than did Marx's own writings.

Dialectical materialism: The crude and deterministic form of Marxism that dominated intellectual life in orthodox communist states.

Elements of Marxism

- **Historical materialism:** The cornerstone of Marxist philosophy is what Engels called 'the materialist conception of history'. This highlighted the importance of economic life and the conditions under which people produce and reproduce their means of subsistence. Marx held that the economic 'base', consisting essentially of the 'mode of production', or economic system, conditions or determines the ideological and political 'superstructure'. This suggests that social and historical development can be explained in terms of economic and class factors. Later Marxists portrayed this as a mechanical relationship, implying that immutable economic 'laws' drive history forwards regardless of the human agent.

- **Dialectical change:** Following Hegel (see p. 90), Marx believed that the driving force of historical change was the dialectic, a process of interaction between competing forces that results in a higher stage of development. In its materialist version, this model implies that historical change is a consequence of internal contradictions within a 'mode of production' reflected in class antagonism. Orthodox Marxism ('dialectical materialism') portrayed the dialectic as an impersonal force shaping both natural and human processes.

- **Alienation: Alienation** was a central principle of Marx's early writings. It is the process whereby, under capitalism, labour is reduced to being a mere commodity, and work becomes a depersonalized activity. In this view, workers are alienated from the product of their labour, from the process of labour, from fellow workers, and, ultimately, from themselves as creative and social beings. Unalienated labour is thus an essential source of human fulfilment and self-realization.

- **Class struggle:** The central contradiction within a capitalist society arises from the existence of private property. This creates a division between the bourgeoisie or capitalist class, the owners of the 'means of production', and the proletariat, who do not own property and thus subsist through selling their labour (literally 'wage slaves'). The bourgeoisie is a 'ruling class'. It not only has economic power through the ownership of wealth, but also exercises political power through the agency of the state and possesses ideological power because its ideas are the 'ruling ideas' of the age.

Alienation: A state or process of depersonalization; separation from one's genuine or essential nature.

Class consciousness: A Marxist term, denoting an accurate awareness of class interests and a willingness to pursue them; a class-conscious class is a class for-itself (see p. 225).

- **Surplus value:** The relationship between the bourgeoisie and the proletariat is one of irreconcilable conflict, reflecting the fact that the proletariat is necessarily and systematically exploited under capitalism. Marx believed that all value derives from the labour expended in the production of goods. This means that the quest for profit forces capitalist enterprises to extract 'surplus value' from their workers by paying them less than the value of their labour. Capitalism is therefore inherently unstable, because the proletariat cannot be permanently reconciled to exploitation and oppression.

- **Proletarian revolution:** Marx believed that capitalism was doomed, and that the proletariat was its 'grave digger'. According to his analysis, capitalism would pass through a series of increasingly serious crises of overproduction. This would bring the proletariat to revolutionary **class consciousness**. Marx proclaimed that proletarian revolution was inevitable, and predicted that it would occur through a spontaneous uprising aimed at seizing control of the means of production. In his later years, however, he speculated about the possibility of a peaceful transition to socialism.

Joseph Stalin (1879–1953)

USSR political leader 1924–53. Stalin (an adopted name, meaning 'man of steel') was the son of a shoemaker. He was expelled from his seminary for revolutionary activities, and joined the Bolsheviks in 1903. He became the general secretary of the Communist Party in 1922. After winning the struggle for power following Lenin's death, he established an increasingly brutal totalitarian dictatorship that was supported by an elaborate cult of personality. His ideological heritage is closely linked to the doctrine of 'Socialism in One Country', which justified industrialization and collectivization in terms of the need to resist capitalist encirclement, and the need to eliminate the *kulaks* (rich peasants) as a class. Stalin thus fused a quasi-Marxist notion of class war with an appeal to Russian nationalism.

• **Communism**: Marx predicted that proletarian revolution would usher in a transitionary 'socialist' period during which a 'dictatorship of the proletariat' would be required to contain a counter-revolution mounted by the dispossessed bourgeoisie. However, as class antagonism faded and a fully communist society came into existence, this proletarian state would simply 'wither away'. A communist (see p. 35) society would be classless in the sense that wealth would be owned in common by all, and the system of 'commodity production' would be replaced by one of 'production for use' geared to the satisfaction of genuine human needs. With this, the 'prehistory of man' would come to an end, allowing human beings for the first time to shape their own destinies and realize their full potential ('the free development of each is the precondition for the free development of all' (Marx)).

Orthodox communism

Marxism in practice is inextricably linked to the experience of Soviet communism, and especially to the contribution of the first two Soviet leaders, V. I. Lenin (see p. 81) and Joseph Stalin. Indeed, twentieth-century communism is best understood as a form of Marxism–Leninism: that is, as orthodox Marxism modified by a set of Leninist theories and doctrines. Lenin's central contribution to Marxism was his theory of the revolutionary or vanguard party. This reflected Lenin's fear that the proletariat, deluded by bourgeois ideas and beliefs, would not realize its revolutionary potential because it could not develop beyond 'trade-union consciousness': a desire to improve working and living conditions rather than to overthrow capitalism. A revolutionary party, armed with Marxism, was therefore needed to serve as the 'vanguard of the working class'. This was to be a party of a new kind: not a mass party, but a tightly knit party of professional and dedicated revolutionaries capable of exercising ideological leadership. Its organization was to be based on the principle of democratic centralism, a belief in freedom of debate married to unity of action. Thus, when Lenin's Bolsheviks seized power in Russia in 1917, they did so as a vanguard party, claiming to act in the interests of the proletarian class.

The USSR was, however, more profoundly affected by Stalin's 'second revolution' in the 1930s than it had been by the 1917 Bolshevik Revolution. In reshaping Soviet society, Stalin created a model of orthodox communism that was followed in the post-1945 period by states such as China, North Korea and Cuba, and throughout eastern Europe. What can be called economic Stalinism was initiated with the launch in 1928 of the first Five Year Plan, which brought about the swift and total

Herbert Marcuse (1898–1979)

German political philosopher and social theorist, and cofounder of the Frankfurt School. A refugee from Hitler's Germany, Marcuse lived in the USA from 1934. He developed a form of neo-Marxism that drew heavily upon Hegel and Freud. Marcuse came to prominence in the 1960s as a leading thinker of the New Left and a 'guru' of the student movement. Marcuse portrayed advanced industrial society as an all-encompassing system of repression that subdued argument and debate, and absorbed opposition. His hopes rested not with the proletariat, but with marginalized groups such as students, ethnic minorities, women, and the countries of the Third World. His most important works include *Reason and Revolution* (1941), *Eros and Civilization* (1958) and *One-Dimensional Man: Studies in the Ideology of Advanced Industrial Society* (1964).

eradication of private enterprise. This was followed in 1929 by the collectivization of agriculture. All resources were brought under the control of the state, and a system of central planning dominated by the State Planning Committee (Gosplan) was established. Stalin's political changes were no less dramatic. During the 1930s Stalin transformed the USSR into a personal dictatorship through a series of purges that eradicated all vestiges of opposition and debate from the Communist Party, the state bureaucracy and the military. In effect, Stalin turned the USSR into a totalitarian dictatorship, operating through systematic intimidation, repression and terror.

Although the more brutal features of orthodox communism did not survive Stalin's death in 1953, the core principles of the Leninist party (hierarchical organization and discipline) and of economic Stalinism (state collectivization and central planning) stubbornly resisted pressure for reform. This was highlighted by Gorbachev's **perestroika** reform process (1985–91), which merely succeeded in exposing the failings of the planning system, and in releasing long-suppressed political forces. These eventually consigned Soviet communism to what Trotsky (see p. 385) had, in very different circumstances, called 'the dustbin of history'. However, political Stalinism survives in China, despite the embrace of market reforms, and North Korea remains a thoroughgoing orthodox communist regime.

Modern Marxism

A more complex and subtle form of Marxism developed in western Europe. By contrast with the mechanistic and avowedly scientific notions of Soviet Marxism, western Marxism tended to be influenced by Hegelian ideas and by the stress upon 'Man the creator' found in Marx's early writings. In other words, human beings were seen as makers of history, and not simply as puppets controlled by impersonal material forces. By insisting that there was an interplay between economics and politics, between the material circumstances of life and the capacity of human beings to shape their own destinies, western Marxists were able to break free from the rigid 'base–superstructure' straitjacket. Their ideas have therefore sometimes been termed neo-Marxist (see p. 96). This indicates an unwillingness to treat the class struggle as the beginning and end of social analysis.

The Hungarian Marxist Georg Lukács (1885–1971) was one of the first to present Marxism as a humanistic philosophy. He emphasized the process of 'reification', through which capitalism dehumanizes workers by reducing them to passive objects

Perestroika: (*Russian*) Literally, restructuring; a slogan that refers to the attempt to liberalize and democratize the Soviet system within a communist framework.

Eduard Bernstein (1850–1932)

German socialist politician and theorist. An early member of the German SPD, Bernstein became one of the leading advocates of revisionism, the attempt to revise and modernize orthodox Marxism. Influenced by British Fabianism and the philosophy of Kant (see p. 129), Bernstein developed a largely empirical critique that emphasized the absence of class war, and proclaimed the possibility of a peaceful transition to socialism. This is described in *Evolutionary Socialism* ([1898] 1962). He left the SPD over his opposition to the First World War, although he subsequently returned. Bernstein is often seen as one of the founding figures of modern social democracy.

or marketable commodities. In his *Prison Notebooks*, written in 1929–35, Antonio Gramsci (see p. 208) emphasized the degree to which capitalism was maintained not merely by economic domination, but also by political and cultural factors. He called this ideological 'hegemony'. A more overtly Hegelian brand of Marxism was developed by the so-called Frankfurt School, the leading members of which were Theodor Adorno (1903–69), Max Horkheimer (1895–1973) and Herbert Marcuse. Frankfurt theorists developed what was called 'critical theory', a blend of Marxist political economy, Hegelian philosophy and Freudian psychology, which had a considerable impact upon the New Left in the 1960s. A later generation of Frankfurt members included Jürgen Habermas (see p. 223).

Social democracy

Social democracy lacks the theoretical coherence of, say, classical liberalism or fundamentalist socialism. Whereas the former is ideologically committed to the market, and the latter champions the cause of common ownership, social democracy stands for a balance between the market and the state, a balance between the individual and the community. At the heart of social democracy there is a compromise between, on the one hand, an acceptance of capitalism as the only reliable mechanism for generating wealth and, on the other, a desire to distribute wealth in accordance with moral, rather than market, principles. For socialists, this conversion to the market was a difficult, and at times painful, process that was dictated more by practical circumstances and electoral advantage than by ideological conviction. In the early twentieth century, this process could be seen at work in the reformist drift of, for example, the German Social Democratic Party (Sozialdemokratische Partei Deutschlands (SPD)), especially under the influence of revisionist Marxists such as Eduard Bernstein. At its 1959 Bad Godesburg congress, the SPD formally abandoned Marxism and accepted the principle 'competition where possible, planning where necessary'. A similar process took place within ethical or 'utopian' socialist parties that had never been anchored in the certainties of Marxism. For example, the UK Labour Party, committed from the outset to a belief in 'the inevitability of gradualism', had, by the 1950s, recast its socialism in terms of equality rather than nationalization (Crosland, 1956).

The chief characteristic of modern social democratic thought is a concern for the underdog in society, the weak and vulnerable. There is a sense, however, in which social democracy cannot simply be confined to the socialist tradition. It may draw

John Rawls (1921–2002)

US academic and political philosopher. His major work, *A Theory of Justice* (1970), is regarded as the most important work of political philosophy written in English since the Second World War. It has influenced modern liberals and social democrats alike. Rawls proposed a theory of 'justice as fairness' that is based on the belief that social inequality can be justified only if it is of benefit to the least advantaged (in that it provides them with an incentive to work). This presumption in favour of equality is rooted in Rawls's belief that most people deprived of knowledge about their own talents and abilities would choose to live in an egalitarian society, rather than an inegalitarian one. As, for most people, the fear of being poor will outweigh the desire to be rich, redistribution and welfare can be defended on grounds of fairness. The universalist presumptions of his early work were modified to a certain degree in *Political Liberalism* (1993).

on a socialist belief in compassion and a common humanity, a liberal commitment to positive freedom and equal opportunities, or, for that matter, a conservative sense of paternal duty and care. Whatever its source, it has usually been articulated on the basis of principles such as welfarism, redistribution and social justice. In the form of Keynesian social democracy, which was widely accepted in the early period after the Second World War, it was associated with a clear desire to 'humanize' capitalism through state intervention. It was believed that Keynesian economic policies would secure full employment, a mixed economy would help government to regulate economic activity, and comprehensive welfare provision funded via progressive taxation would narrow the gap between rich and poor. However, declining economic growth and the emergence in advanced industrial societies at least of a 'contented majority' (Galbraith, 1992), have brought about a further process of revision.

To some extent, the socialist character of social democracy has long been questioned. Some socialists, for instance, used 'social democracy' as a term of abuse, implying unprincipled compromise or even betrayal. Others, such as Anthony Crosland (1918–77), argued that socialists had to come to terms with changing historical realities, and were thus happy to draw on the ideas of liberal theorists such as John Rawls. Since the 1980s, however, social democracy more obviously moved into retreat. This occurred for a variety of reasons. In the first place, changes in the class structure, and particularly the growth of professional and clerical occupations, meant that social-democratic policies orientated around the interests of the traditional working class were no longer electorally viable. Second, globalization appeared to render all specifically national forms of economic management, such as Keynesianism, redundant. Third, nationalized industries and economic planning proved to be inefficient, at least in developed states. Fourth, the collapse of communism undermined the intellectual and ideological credibility not just of state collectivization but of all 'top-down' socialist models. In this context it became increasingly fashionable for politicians and political thinkers to embrace the idea of an ideological 'third way'.

Third way

The term 'third way' is imprecise and subject to a variety of interpretations. This occurs because third-way politics draws on various ideological traditions, including modern liberalism, one-nation conservatism and modernized social democracy. Different third-way projects have also developed in different countries, including those associated with the New Democrats and Bill Clinton in the USA and New Labour and Tony Blair in the UK, as well as those that have emerged in countries such as Germany, the Netherlands, Italy and New Zealand. Certain characteristic third-way themes can nevertheless be identified. The first of these is the belief that socialism, at least in the form of 'top-down' state intervention, is dead: there is no alternative to what Clause 4 of the UK Labour Party's constitution, rewritten in 1995, refers to as 'a dynamic market economy'. With this goes a general acceptance of globalization and the belief that capitalism has mutated into a 'knowledge economy', which places a premium on information technology, individual skills and both labour and business flexibility. The second feature of third-way politics is that, by contrast with neoliberalism, government is recognized as having a vital economic and social role. However, this role is a more focused one, concentrating on the promotion of international competitiveness by building up education and skills, and the strengthening of communities and civil society to contain the pressure generated by market capitalism. In this sense, the third-way stance is a form of liberal communitarianism (see p. 179); its 'new individualism' calls for a balance between rights and **entrepreneurialism**, on the one hand, and social duty and moral responsibility on the other.

The final feature of third-way politics is that it has broken with socialist egalitarianism (which is seen as a form of 'levelling') and embraces instead the liberal ideas of equality of opportunity and meritocracy. Third-way politicians typically endorse welfare reform. They reject both the neoliberal emphasis on 'standing on your own two feet' and the social-democratic commitment to 'cradle to grave' welfare in favour of an essentially modern liberal belief in 'help people to help themselves', or as Clinton put it, giving people 'a hand up, not a hand out'. This has led to support for what has been called a 'workfare state', in which government support in terms of benefits or education is conditional on individuals seeking work and becoming self-reliant. Critics of the third way, on the other hand, argue either that it is contradictory, in that it simultaneously endorses the dynamism of the market and warns against its tendency to social disintegration, or that, far from being a centre-left project, it amounts to a shift to the right. It has, for instance, been condemned for accepting the framework of neoliberalism, particularly by endorsing global capitalism, and for supporting creeping authoritarianism in echoing communitarian calls for the strengthening of the family and in backing 'tough' law and order policies.

> ### Concept
>
> ### Third way
>
> The 'third way' encapsulates the idea of an alternative to both capitalism and socialism. It draws attention to an ideological position that has attracted political thinkers from various traditions, including fascism, social democracy and, most recently, post-socialism. In its modern form, the 'third way' is an alternative to old-style social democracy and neoliberalism. The former is rejected because it is wedded to statist structures that are inappropriate to the modern knowledge-based and market-orientated economy. The latter is rejected because it generates a free-for-all that undermines the moral foundations of society. The key third-way values are opportunity, responsibility and community. Although the third way is sometime portrayed as 'new' or modernized social democracy, opponents suggest that it has entirely disengaged from the socialist tradition by embracing market and private-sector solutions.

▉ Other ideological traditions

Fascism

Whereas liberalism, conservatism and socialism are nineteenth-century ideologies, fascism is a child of the twentieth century. Some would say that it is specifically an interwar phenomenon. Although fascist beliefs can be traced back to the late nineteenth century, they were fused together and shaped by the First World War and its aftermath, and in particular by the potent mixture of war and revolution that characterized the period. The two principal manifestations of fascism were Mussolini's Fascist dictatorship in Italy in 1922–43, and Hitler's Nazi dictatorship in Germany in

Entrepreneurialism: Values or practices associated with commercial risk-taking and profit-orientated business activity.

Adolf Hitler (1889–1945)

German Nazi dictator. Hitler was the son of an Austrian customs official. He joined the German Worker's Party (later the Nationalsozialistische Deutsche Arbeiterpartei (NSDAP), or Nazi Party) in 1919, becoming its leader in 1921. He was appointed Chancellor of Germany in 1933, and declared himself Führer (Leader) the following year, by which time he had established a one-party dictatorship. The central feature of Hitler's world view, outlined in *Mein Kampf* ([1925] 1969), was his attempt to fuse expansionist German nationalism and virulent anti-Semitism into a theory of history in which there was an endless battle between the Germans and the Jews, who represented, respectively, the forces of good and evil. Hitler's policies contributed decisively to both the outbreak of the Second World War and the Holocaust.

1933–45. Forms of neofascism and neo-Nazism also resurfaced in the final years of the twentieth century that took advantage of the combination of economic crisis and political instability that followed the collapse of communism.

In many respects, fascism constituted a revolt against the ideas and values that had dominated western political thought since the French Revolution: in the words of the Italian Fascist slogan, '1789 is dead'. Values such as rationalism, progress, freedom and equality were thus overturned in the name of struggle, leadership, power, heroism and war. In this sense, fascism has an 'anticharacter'. It is defined largely by what it opposes: it is a form of anticapitalism, antiliberalism, anti-individualism, anticommunism, and so on. A core theme that nevertheless runs throughout fascism is the image of an organically unified national community. This is reflected in a belief in 'strength through unity'. The individual, in a literal sense, is nothing; individual identity must be absorbed entirely into that of the community or social group. The fascist ideal is that of the 'new man', a hero, motivated by duty, honour and self-sacrifice, prepared to dedicate his life to the glory of his nation or race, and to give unquestioning obedience to a supreme leader.

Not all fascists, however, think alike. Italian Fascism was essentially an extreme form of statism (see p. 102) that was based on unquestioning respect and absolute loyalty towards a 'totalitarian' state. As the Fascist philosopher Gentile (1875–1944) put it, 'everything for the state; nothing against the state; nothing outside the state'. German National Socialism, on the other hand, was constructed largely on the basis of racialism (see p. 120). Its two core theories were Aryanism (the belief that the German people constitute a 'master race' and are destined for world domination), and a virulent form of anti-Semitism (see p. 121) that portrayed the Jews as inherently evil, and aimed at their eradication. This latter belief found expression in the 'Final Solution'.

Anarchism

Anarchism is unusual amongst political ideologies in that no anarchist party has ever succeeded in winning power, at least at national level. Nevertheless, anarchist movements were powerful in, for example, Spain, France, Russia and Mexico through to the early twentieth century, and anarchist ideas continue to fertilize political debate by challenging the conventional belief that law, government and the state are either wholesome or indispensable. The central theme within anarchism is the belief that

Mary Wollstonecraft (1759–97)

UK social theorist and feminist. Deeply influenced by the democratic radicalism of Rousseau, Wollstonecraft developed the first systematic feminist critique some 50 years before the emergence of the female-suffrage movement. Her most important work, *A Vindication of the Rights of Women* ([1792] 1985), was influenced by Lockian liberalism, and it stressed the equal rights of women, especially the right to education, on the basis of the notion of 'personhood'.

However, the work developed a more complex analysis of womanhood itself that is relevant to the concerns of contemporary feminism. Wollstonecraft was married to the anarchist William Godwin, and she was the mother of Mary Shelley, the author of *Frankenstein*.

political authority in all its forms, and especially in the form of the state, is both evil and unnecessary (anarchy literally means 'without rule'). Nevertheless, the anarchist preference for a stateless society in which free individuals manage their own affairs through voluntary agreement and cooperation has been developed on the basis of two rival traditions: liberal individualism, and socialist communitarianism. Anarchism can thus be thought of as a point of intersection between liberalism and socialism: a form of both 'ultraliberalism' and 'ultrasocialism'.

The liberal case against the state is based on individualism and the desire to maximize liberty and choice. Unlike liberals, individualist anarchists such as William Godwin (1756–1836) believed that free and rational human beings would be able to manage their affairs peacefully and spontaneously, government being merely a form of unwanted coercion. Modern individualists have usually looked to the market to explain how society would be regulated in the absence of state authority, developing a form of anarchocapitalism, an extreme form of free-market economics. The more widely recognized anarchist tradition, however, draws upon socialist ideas such as community, cooperation, equality and common ownership. Collectivist anarchists therefore stress the human capacity for social solidarity that arises from our sociable, gregarious and essentially cooperative natures. On this basis, the French anarchist Pierre-Joseph Proudhon (see p. 166), for instance, developed what he called mutualism, the belief that small communities of independent peasants, craftsmen and artisans could manage their lives using a system of fair and equitable exchange, avoiding the injustices and exploitation of capitalism. Other anarchists, such as the Russian Peter Kropotkin (1842–1921), advanced a form of anarcho-communism, the central principles of which were common ownership, decentralization and self-management. Modern thinkers influenced by anarchism include Noam Chomsky (see p. 234) and the US libertarian and social ecologist Murray Bookchin (1921–2006).

Feminism

Although feminist aspirations have been expressed in societies dating back to Ancient China, they were not underpinned by a developed political theory until the publication of Mary Wollstonecraft's *A Vindication of the Rights of Women* ([1792] 1985). Indeed, it was not until the emergence of the women's suffrage movement in the 1840s and 1850s that feminist ideas reached a wider audience, in the form of so-

Concept

Ecology, ecologism

Ecology (from the Greek *oikos* and *logos*, and meaning 'study of the home') is the study of the relationship between living organisms and their environment. It thus draws attention to the network of relationships that sustain all forms of life, and highlights the interconnectedness of nature. Ecology (a term first used by Ernst Haeckel in 1873) can be regarded as a science, a descriptive principle, or even a moral value. Ecologism is a political doctrine or ideology that is constructed on the basis of ecological assumptions, notably about the essential link between humankind and the natural world: humans are part of nature, not its 'masters'. Ecologism is sometimes distinguished from environmentalism, in that the former implies the adoption of a biocentric or ecocentric perspective, while the latter is concerned with protecting nature, ultimately for human benefit.

called 'first-wave feminism'. The achievement of female suffrage in most western countries in the early twentieth century deprived the women's movement of its central goal and organizing principle. 'Second-wave feminism', however, emerged in the 1960s. This expressed the more radical, and sometimes revolutionary, demands of the growing Women's Liberation Movement (WLM). Feminist theories and doctrines are diverse, but their unifying feature is a common desire to enhance, through whatever means, the social role of women. The underlying themes of feminism are therefore, first, that society is characterized by sexual or gender inequality and, second, that this structure of male power can and should be overturned.

At least three contrasting feminist traditions can be identified. Liberal feminists, such as Wollstonecraft and Betty Friedan (see p. 310), have tended to understand female subordination in terms of the unequal distribution of rights and opportunities in society. This 'equal-rights feminism' is essentially reformist. It is concerned more with the reform of the 'public' sphere, that is, with enhancing the legal and political status of women and improving their educational and career prospects, than with reordering 'private' or domestic life. In contrast, socialist feminists typically highlight the links between female subordination and the capitalist mode of production, drawing attention to the economic significance of women being confined to a family or domestic life where they, for example, relieve male workers of the burden of domestic labour, rear and help to educate the next generation of capitalist workers, and act as a reserve army of labour.

However, the distinctive flavour of second-wave feminism results mainly from the emergence of a feminist critique that is not rooted in conventional political doctrines, namely radical feminism. Radical feminists believe that gender divisions are the most fundamental and politically significant cleavages in society. In their view, all societies, historical and contemporary, are characterized by patriarchy (see p. 98), the institution whereby, as Kate Millett (1969) put it, 'that half of the population which is female is controlled by that half which is male'. Radical feminists therefore proclaim the need for a sexual revolution, a revolution that will, in particular, restructure personal, domestic and family life. The characteristic slogan of radical feminism is thus 'the personal is the political'. Only in its extreme form, however, does radical feminism portray men as 'the enemy', and proclaim the need for women to withdraw from male society, a stance sometimes expressed in the form of political lesbianism.

Environmentalism

Although environmentalism is usually seen as a new ideology that is linked to the emergence of the ecological, or Green, movement in the late twentieth century, its roots can be traced back to the nineteenth-century revolt against industrialization. Environmentalism therefore reflects concern about the damage done to the natural world by the increasing pace of economic development (exacerbated in the second half of the twentieth century by the advent of nuclear technology, acid rain, ozone depletion, global warming and so on), and anxiety about the declining quality of human existence and, ultimately, the survival of the human species. Such concerns are sometimes expressed through the vehicle of conventional ideologies. For instance, ecosocialism explains environmental destruction in terms of capitalism's rapacious desire for profit. Ecoconservatism links the cause of conservation to the desire to preserve traditional values and established institutions. And ecofeminism

Fig. 3.1 As ecologists argue, human-centredness poses a threat to both nature and, ultimately, human survival (Middlesbrough, UK).

locates the origins of the ecological crisis in the system of male power, reflecting the fact that men are less sensitive than women to natural processes and the natural world.

However, what gives environmentalism its radical edge is the fact that it offers an alternative to the **anthropocentric** or human-centred stance adopted by all other ideologies; it does not see the natural world simply as a convenient resource available to satisfy human needs. By highlighting the importance of ecology, environmentalism or, as some of its proponents would prefer to call it, ecologism develops an ecocentric world view that portrays the human species as merely part of nature. One of the most influential theories in this field is the Gaia hypothesis, advanced by James Lovelock (1979, 2006). This portrays the planet Earth as a living organism that is primarily concerned with its own survival. Others have expressed sympathy for Eastern religions that emphasize the oneness of life, such as Taoism and Zen Buddhism (Capra, 1983). 'Shallow' ecologists, or 'light Greens', such as those in some environmental pressure groups, believe that an appeal to self-interest and common sense will persuade humankind to adopt ecologically sound policies and lifestyles. 'Deep' ecologists, or 'dark Greens', on the other hand, insist that nothing short of a fundamental reordering of political priorities, and a willingness to place the interests of the ecosystem before those of any individual species, will ultimately secure planetary and human survival. Members of both groups can be found in the 'antiparty' Green parties that have sprung up in Germany, Austria and elsewhere in Europe since the 1970s.

Religious fundamentalism

Religion and politics overlap at a number of points, not least in the development of the major ideological traditions. Ethical socialism, for instance, has been grounded in a variety of religious creeds, giving rise to forms of Christian socialism, Islamic socialism and so on. Protestantism helped to shape the ideas of self-striving and individual responsibility that gained political expression in classical liberalism. Religious fundamentalism, however, is different, in that it views politics (and indeed all aspects of personal and social existence) as being secondary to the 'revealed truth'

Anthropocentrism: The belief that human needs and interests are of overriding moral and philosophical importance; the opposite of ecocentrism.

> **Concept**
>
> ## Fundamentalism
>
> Fundamentalism (from the Latin *fundamentum*, meaning 'base') is a style of thought in which certain principles are recognized as essential 'truths' that have unchallengeable and overriding authority, regardless of their content. Substantive fundamentalisms therefore have little or nothing in common, except that their supporters tend to evince an earnestness or fervour born out of doctrinal certainty. Although it is usually associated with religion and the literal truth of sacred texts, fundamentalism can also be found in political creeds. Even liberal scepticism can be said to incorporate the fundamental belief that all theories should be doubted (except for itself). Although the term is often used pejoratively to imply inflexibility, dogmatism and authoritarianism, fundamentalism may also give expression to selflessness and a devotion to principle.

of religious doctrine. From this perspective, political and social life should be organized on the basis of what are seen as essential or original religious principles, commonly supported by a belief in the literal truth of sacred texts. As it is possible to develop such principles into a comprehensive world view, religious fundamentalism can be treated as an ideology in its own right.

Where does religious fundamentalism come from, and what explains its resurgence at the end of the twentieth century? Two contrasting explanations have been advanced. One views fundamentalism as essentially an aberration, a symptom of the adjustment that societies make as they become accustomed to a modern and secularized culture. The second suggests that fundamentalism is of enduring significance, and believes that it is a consequence of the failure of **secularism** to satisfy the abiding human desire for 'higher' or spiritual truth.

Forms of religious fundamentalism have arisen in various parts of the world. The significance of Christian fundamentalism, for example, has increased in the USA since the 1970s as a result of the emergence of the 'New Christian Right', which campaigns against abortion, and for the introduction of prayers in US schools and a return to traditional family values. In Israel, Jewish fundamentalism, long represented by a collection of small religious parties, has grown in importance as a result of attempts to prevent parts of what are seen as the Jewish homeland being seceded to an emerging Palestinian state. Hindu fundamentalism in India has developed to resist the spread of western secularism, and to combat the influence of rival creeds such as Sikhism and Islam.

The most politically significant of modern fundamentalisms is undoubtedly Islamic fundamentalism. The idea that intense and militant faith in Islamic beliefs should constitute the overriding principles of social life and politics first emerged in the writings of thinkers such as Sayyid Qutb (1906–66) and activities of the Muslim Brotherhood. Their goal was the establishment of an Islamic state based on the principles of *shari'a* law. Political Islam was brought to prominence by the Iranian revolution of 1979, which led to the founding of the world's first Islamic state, under Ayatollah Khomeini (1900–89). It has subsequently spread throughout the Middle East, across North Africa, and into parts of Asia. Although the Shi'ite fundamentalism of Iran has generated the fiercest commitment and devotion, Islam in general has been a vehicle for expressing anti-westernism, through both antipathy towards the neocolonialism of western powers, and attempts to resist the spread of permissiveness and materialism. This was clearly reflected in the Taliban regime in Afghanistan,

Secularism: The belief that religion should not intrude into secular (worldly) affairs, usually reflected in a desire to separate church from state.

Concept

Postmodernism, postmodernity

Postmodernism is a controversial and confusing term that was first used to describe experimental movements in western arts, architecture and cultural development in general. As a tool of social and political analysis, postmodernism highlights the shift away from societies structured by industrialization and class solidarity to increasingly fragmented and pluralistic information societies (that is, to postmodernity) in which individuals are transformed from producers to consumers, and individualism replaces class, religious and ethnic loyalties. From this perspective, conventional political ideologies such as Marxism and liberalism tend to be rejected as irrelevant 'meta-narratives' that developed out of the process of modernization. Postmodernists argue that there is no such thing as certainty; the idea of absolute and universal truth must be discarded as an arrogant pretence. In this sense, postmodernism is an example of 'anti-foundationalism'. Emphasis is thus placed on the importance of discourse, debate and democracy.

1997–2001, and also in the growth of *jihadist* groups such as al-Qaeda, for whom the spiritual quest has come to be synonymous with militant politics, armed struggle and possibly martyrdom.

The end of ideology?

Much of the debate about ideology in the late twentieth century focused on predictions of its demise, or at least of its fading relevance. This came to be known as the 'end of ideology' debate. It was initiated in the 1950s, stimulated by the collapse of fascism at the end of the Second World War and the decline of communism in the developed West. In *The End of Ideology?: On the Exhaustion of Political Ideas in the 1950s* (1960), the US sociologist Daniel Bell declared that the stock of political ideas had been exhausted. In his view, ethical and ideological questions had become irrelevant because in most western societies parties competed for power simply by promising higher levels of economic growth and material affluence. In short, economics had triumphed over politics. However, the process to which Bell drew attention was not so much an end of ideology as the emergence of a broad ideological consensus (see p. 10) amongst major parties that led to the suspension of ideological debate. The ideology that prevailed in the 1950s and 1960s was a form of welfare capitalism, which in the UK and elsewhere took the form of a Keynesian–welfarist consensus.

A more recent contribution to this debate was made by Francis Fukuyama (see p. 31) in his essay 'The End of History?' (1989). Fukuyama did not suggest that political ideology had become irrelevant, but rather that a single ideology, liberal democracy, had triumphed over all its rivals, and that this triumph was final. This essay was written against the background of the collapse of communism in eastern Europe, which Fukuyama interpreted as indicating the demise of Marxism–Leninism as an ideology of world-historical importance. Anthony Giddens (1994), by contrast, argued that conventional ideologies of both left and right have become increasingly redundant in a society characterized by globalization, the decline of tradition and the expansion of **social reflexivity**. An alternative way of interpreting these developments, however, is offered by postmodernism, which suggests that the major ideologies, or 'grand narratives', were essentially products of a period of modernization that has now passed. On the other hand, the very assertion of an end of ideology, an end of history,

Jihad: Conventionally translated as 'holy war' but, more correctly, as 'holy struggle' or 'effort'; intense and all-consuming devotion to Islamic goals.

Social reflexivity: Interaction between people who enjoy a high level of autonomy within a context of reciprocity and interdependence.

or an end of modernity can be seen as ideological in itself. Rather than heralding the final demise of ideology, such assertions may merely demonstrate that ideological debate is alive and well, and that the evolution of ideology is a continuing and perhaps unending process.

◼ Summary

◆ Ideology is a controversial political term that has often carried pejorative implications. In the social-scientific sense, a political ideology is a more or less coherent set of ideas that provides a basis for organized political action. Its central features are an account of existing power relationships, a model of a desired future, and an outline of how political change can and should be brought about.

◆ Ideologies link political theory with political practice. On one level, ideologies resemble political philosophies, in that they constitute a collection of values, theories and doctrines: that is, a distinctive world view. On another level, however, they take the form of broad political movements, and are articulated through the activities of political leaders, parties and groups.

◆ Every ideology can be associated with a characteristic set of principles and ideas. Although these ideas 'hang together' in the sense that they interlock in distinctive ways, they are systematic or coherent only in a relative sense. All ideologies thus embody a range of rival traditions and internal tensions. Conflict within ideologies is thus sometimes more passionate than that between ideologies.

◆ Ideologies are by no means hermetically sealed and unchanging systems of thought. They overlap with one another at a number of points, and they sometimes have shared concerns and a common vocabulary. They are also always subject to political or intellectual renewal, both because they interact with, and influence the development of, other ideologies, and because they change over time as they are applied to changing historical circumstances.

◆ The significance of particular ideologies rises and falls in relation to the ideology's relevance to political, social and economic circumstances, and its capacity for theoretical innovation. Ideological conflict in the twentieth century forced major ideologies such as liberalism, conservatism and socialism to re-examine their traditional principles, and it fostered the growth of new ideologies, such as feminism, ecologism and religious fundamentalism.

◆ Debate about the end of ideology has taken a number of forms. In the early post-Second-World-War period, it was linked to the declining appeal of fascism and communism and the view that economic issues had displaced ideological ones. The 'end of history' thesis suggests that liberal democracy has triumphed worldwide. Postmodernism implies that conventional ideologies are irrelevant, as they were intrinsically a product of an earlier period of modernization.

◼ Questions for discussion

▶ Why has the concept of ideology so often carried negative associations?

▶ Is it any longer possible to distinguish between liberalism and socialism?

▶ To what extent do New Right ideas conflict with those of traditional conservatism?

▶ Is the 'third way' a meaningful and coherent ideological stance?

▶ Has Marxism a future?

▶ What circumstances are most conducive to the rise of fascism?

▶ Do anarchists demand the impossible?

▶ Why have feminism, ecologism and fundamentalism grown in significance? Do they have the potential to displace conventional political creeds?

▶ Is it possible to dispense with ideology?

Further reading

Freedman, M., *Ideology: A Very Short Introduction* (Oxford: Oxford University Press, 2003). A brief (as promised) but authoritative guide to the nature of ideology and its place in the modern world.

Heywood, A., *Political Ideologies: An Introduction* 4th edn (Basingstoke and New York: Palgrave Macmillan, 2007). An accessible, up-to-date and comprehensive guide to the major ideological traditions.

Good introductions to particular ideologies include the following: Arblaster (1984) on liberalism, O'Sullivan (1976) on conservatism, Wright (1987) on socialism, Giddens (2001) on the 'third way', Marshall (1991) on anarchism, Laqueur (1979) on fascism, Bryson (1992) on feminism, Dobson (1990) on ecologism, and Marty and Appleby (1993) on religious fundamentalism.

Democracy

> 'Democracy is the worst form of government except all the other forms that have been tried from time to time.'
>
> WINSTON CHURCHILL, *Speech,* UK House of Commons (1947)

The mass conversion of politicians and political thinkers to the cause of democracy has been one of the most dramatic, and significant, events in political history. Even in Ancient Greece, often thought of as the cradle of the democratic idea, democracy tended to be viewed in negative terms. Thinkers such as Plato and Aristotle, for example, viewed democracy as a system of rule by the masses at the expense of wisdom and property. Well into the nineteenth century, the term continued to have pejorative implications, suggesting a system of 'mob rule'. Now, however, we are all democrats. Liberals, conservatives, socialists, communists, anarchists and even fascists are eager to proclaim the virtues of democracy and to demonstrate their own democratic credentials. Indeed, as the major ideological systems faltered and collapsed in the late twentieth century, the flame of democracy appeared to burn yet more strongly. As the attractions of socialism have faded, and the merits of capitalism have been called into question, democracy emerged as perhaps the only stable and enduring principle in the postmodern political landscape.

The central issues examined in this chapter are as follows:

Key issues

▶ How has the term 'democracy' been used?

▶ Around what issues has the debate about the nature of democracy revolved?

▶ What models of democratic rule have been advanced?

▶ What are the strengths and weaknesses of each of these models?

▶ How do democratic systems operate in practice?

▶ Does democracy actually ensure rule by the people?

◼ Defining democracy

The origins of the term democracy can be traced back to Ancient Greece. Like other words ending in 'cracy' (for example, autocracy, aristocracy and bureaucracy), democracy is derived from the Greek word *kratos*, meaning power, or rule. Democracy thus means 'rule by the *demos*' (the *demos* referring to 'the people', although the Greeks originally used this to mean 'the poor' or 'the many'). However, the simple notion of 'rule by the people' does not get us very far. The problem with democracy has been its very popularity, a popularity that has threatened the term's undoing as a meaningful political concept. In being almost universally regarded as a 'good thing', democracy has come to be used as little more than a 'hurrah! word', implying approval of a particular set of ideas or system of rule. In Bernard Crick's (1993) words, 'democracy is perhaps the most promiscuous word in the world of public affairs'. A term that can mean anything to anyone is in danger of meaning nothing at all. Amongst the meanings that have been attached to the word 'democracy' are the following:

- a system of rule by the poor and disadvantaged
- a form of government in which the people rule themselves directly and continuously, without the need for professional politicians or public officials
- a society based on equal opportunity and individual merit, rather than hierarchy and privilege
- a system of welfare and redistribution aimed at narrowing social inequalities
- a system of decision-making based on the principle of majority rule
- a system of rule that secures the rights and interests of minorities by placing checks upon the power of the majority
- a means of filling public offices through a competitive struggle for the popular vote
- a system of government that serves the interests of the people regardless of their participation in political life.

Perhaps a more helpful starting point from which to consider the nature of democracy is Abraham Lincoln's Gettysburg Address, delivered in 1864 at the height of the American Civil War. Lincoln extolled the virtues of what he called 'government of the people, by the people, and for the people'. What this makes clear is that democracy links government to the people, but that this link can be forged in a number of ways: government *of*, *by* and *for* the people. The precise nature of democratic rule has been the subject of fierce ideological and political debate. The next main section of this chapter looks at various models of democracy. This section, however, explores the terms of the 'democracy debate'. These boil down to the attempt to answer three central questions:

- Who are the people?
- In what sense should the people rule?
- How far should popular rule extend?

Who are the people?

One of the core features of democracy is the principle of political equality, the notion that political power should be distributed as widely and as evenly as possible.

However, within what body or group should this power be distributed? In short, who constitutes 'the people'? On the face of it, the answer is simple: 'the *demos*', or 'the people', surely refers to *all* the people, that is, the entire population of the country. In practice, however, every democratic system has restricted political participation, sometime severely.

As noted above, early Greek writers usually used *demos* to refer to 'the many': that is, the disadvantaged and usually propertyless masses. Democracy therefore implied not political equality, but a bias towards the poor. In Greek city-states, political participation was restricted to a tiny proportion of the population, male citizens over the age of 20, thereby excluding all women, slaves and foreigners. Strict restrictions on voting also existed in most western states until well into the twentieth century, usually in the form of a property qualification or the exclusion of women. Universal suffrage was not established in the UK until 1928, when women gained full voting rights. In the USA it was not achieved until the early 1960s, when African-American people in many Southern states were able to vote for the first time, and in Switzerland it was established in 1971 when women were eventually enfranchised. Nevertheless, an important restriction continues to be practised in all democratic systems in the form of the exclusion of children from political participation, although the age of majority ranges from 21 down to as low as 15 (as in Iranian presidential elections). Technical restrictions are also often placed on, for example, the certifiably insane and imprisoned criminals.

Although 'the people' is now accepted as meaning virtually all adult citizens, the term can be construed in a number of different ways. The people, for instance, can be viewed as a single, cohesive body, bound together by a common or collective interest: in this sense, the people are one and indivisible. Such a view tends to generate a model of democracy that, like Rousseau's (see p. 79) theory, examined in the next main section, focuses upon the 'general will' or collective will, rather than the 'private will' of each individual. Alternatively, as division and disagreement exist within all communities, 'the people' may in practice be taken to mean 'the majority'. In this case, democracy comes to mean the strict application of the principle of **majority rule**. This can nevertheless mean that democracy degenerates into 'the tyranny of the majority'. Finally, there is the issue of the body of people within which democratic politics should operate. Where should be the location or 'site' of democracy? Although, thanks to the potency of political nationalism, 'the people' are usually defined in national terms, the ideas of local democracy and, in the light of globalization (see p. 143), **cosmopolitan democracy** have also received attention.

How should the people rule?

Most conceptions of democracy are based on the principle of 'government *by* the people'. This implies that, in effect, people govern themselves – that they participate in making the crucial decisions that structure their lives and determine the fate of their society. This participation can take a number of forms, however. In the case of direct democracy, popular participation entails direct and continuous involvement in decision-making, through devices such as referendums, mass meetings, or even interactive television. The alternative and more common form of democratic participation is the act of voting, which is the central feature of what is usually called representative democracy. When citizens vote, they do not so much make the decisions

---

Concept

Political equality

In broad terms, political equality means an equal distribution of political power and influence. Political equality can thus be thought of as the core principle of democracy, in that it ensures that, however 'the people' is defined, each individual member carries the same weight: all voices are equally loud. This can be understood in two ways. In liberal-democratic theory, political equality implies an equal distribution of political rights: the right to vote, the right to stand for election and so on. This is often summed up as the principle 'one person, one vote; one vote, one value'. In contrast, socialists, amongst others, link political influence to factors such as the control of economic resources and access to the means of mass communication. From this perspective, political equality implies not merely equal voting rights, but also a significant level of social equality.

Majority rule: The rule that the will of the majority or numerically strongest overrides the will of the minority, implying that the latter should accept the views of the former.

Cosmopolitan democracy: A form of democracy that operates at supranational levels of governance and is based on the idea of transnational or global citizenship.

Focus on . . .

Direct democracy and representative democracy

Direct democracy (sometimes 'participatory democracy') is based on the direct, unmediated and continuous participation of citizens in the tasks of government. Direct democracy thus obliterates the distinction between government and the governed and between the state and civil society; it is a system of popular self-government. It was achieved in ancient Athens through a form of government by mass meeting; its most common modern manifestation is the use of the referendum (see p. 250). The merits of direct democracy include the following:

- It heightens the control that citizens can exercise over their own destinies, as it is the only pure form of democracy.
- It creates a better-informed and more politically sophisticated citizenry, and thus it has educational benefits.
- It enables the public to express their own views and interests without having to rely on self-serving politicians.
- It ensures that rule is legitimate in the sense that people are more likely to accept decisions that they have made themselves.

Representative democracy is a limited and indirect form of democracy. It is limited in that popular participation in government is infrequent and brief, being restricted to the act of voting every few years. It is indirect in that the public do not exercise power themselves; they merely select those who will rule on their behalf. This form of rule is democratic only insofar as representation (see p. 248) establishes a reliable and effective link between the government and the governed. This is sometimes expressed in the notion of an electoral mandate (see p. 252). The strengths of representative democracy include the following:

- It offers a practicable form of democracy (direct popular participation is achievable only in small communities).
- It relieves ordinary citizens of the burden of decision-making, thus making possible a division of labour in politics.
- It allows government to be placed in the hands of those with better education, expert knowledge and greater experience.
- It maintains stability by distancing ordinary citizens from politics, thereby encouraging them to accept compromise.

that structure their own lives as choose who will make those decisions on their behalf. What gives voting its democratic character, however, is that, provided that the election is competitive, it empowers the public to 'kick the rascals out', and it thus makes politicians publicly accountable.

There are also models of democracy that are built on the principle of 'government *for* the people', and that allow little scope for public participation of any kind, direct or indirect. The most grotesque example of this was found in the so-called **totalitarian democracies** that developed under fascist dictators such as Mussolini and Hitler. The democratic credentials of such regimes were based on the claim that the 'leader', and the leader alone, articulated the genuine interests of the people, thus implying that a 'true' democracy can be equated with an absolute dictatorship. In such cases,

Totalitarian democracy:
An absolute dictatorship that masquerades as a democracy, typically based on the leader's claim to a monopoly of ideological wisdom.

popular rule meant nothing more than ritualized submission to the will of an all-powerful leader, orchestrated through rallies, marches and demonstrations. This was sometimes portrayed as plebiscitary democracy. Although totalitarian democracies have proved to be a travesty of the conventional notion of democratic rule, they demonstrate the tension that can exist between 'government *by* the people' (or popular participation), and 'government *for* the people' (rule in the public interest). Advocates of representative democracy, for example, have wished to confine popular participation in politics to the act of voting, precisely because they fear that the general public lack the wisdom, education and experience to rule wisely on their own behalf.

How far should popular rule extend?

Now that we have decided who the people are, and how they should rule, it is necessary to consider how far their rule should extend. What is the proper realm of democracy? What issues is it right for the people to decide, and what should be left to individual citizens? In many respects, such questions reopen the debate about the proper relationship between the public realm and the private realm that was discussed in Chapter 1. Models of democracy that have been constructed on the basis of liberal individualism have usually proposed that democracy be restricted to political life, with politics being narrowly defined. From this perspective, the purpose of democracy is to establish, through some process of popular participation, a framework of laws within which individuals can conduct their own affairs and pursue their private interests. Democratic solutions, then, are appropriate only for matters that specifically relate to the community; used in other circumstances, democracy amounts to an infringement of liberty. Not uncommonly, this fear of democracy is reflected in a rejection of direct or participatory forms of democracy.

However, an alternative view of democracy is often developed by, for example, socialists and radical democrats. In **radical democracy**, democracy is seen not as a means of laying down a framework within which individuals can go about their own business, but rather as a general principle that is applicable to all areas of social existence. People are seen as having a basic right to participate in the making of *any* decisions that affect their lives, with democracy simply being the collective process through which this is done. This position is evident in socialist demands for the collectivization of wealth and the introduction of workers' self-management, both of which are seen as ways of democratizing economic life. Instead of endorsing mere political democracy, socialists have therefore called for 'social democracy' or 'industrial democracy'. Feminists, similarly, have demanded the democratization of family life, understood as the right of all to participate in the making of decisions in the domestic or private sphere. From this perspective, democracy is regarded as a friend of liberty, not as its enemy. Only when such principles are ignored can oppression and exploitation flourish.

Models of democracy

All too frequently, democracy is treated as a single, unambiguous phenomenon. It is often assumed that what passes for democracy in most western societies (a system of regular and competitive elections based on a universal franchise) is the only, or the only legitimate, form of democracy. Sometimes this notion of democracy is qualified

Concept

Plebiscitary democracy

Plebiscitary democracy is a form of democratic rule that operates through an unmediated link between the rulers and the ruled, established by plebiscites (or referendums). These allow the public to express their views on political issues directly. This is thus a species of direct, or participatory, democracy. However, this type of democracy is often criticized because of the scope it offers for demagoguery (rule by political leaders who manipulate the masses through oratory, and appeal to their prejudices and passions). This type of democracy amounts to little more than a system of mass acclamation that gives dictatorship a populist (see p. 378) gloss. There is, nevertheless, a distinction between plebiscitary democracy and the use of referendums to supplement a system of representative democracy.

Radical democracy: A form of democracy that favours decentralization and participation, the widest possible dispersal of political power.

by the addition of the term 'liberal', turning it into liberal democracy (see p. 30). In reality, however, there are a number of rival theories or models of democracy, each offering its own version of popular rule. This highlights not merely the variety of democratic forms and mechanisms, but also, more fundamentally, the very different grounds on which democratic rule can be justified. Even liberal democracy is a misleading term, as competing liberal views of democratic organization can be identified. Four contrasting models of democracy can be identified as follows:

- classical democracy
- protective democracy
- developmental democracy
- people's democracy.

Classical democracy

The classical model of democracy is based on the *polis*, or city-state, of Ancient Greece, and particularly on the system of rule that developed in the largest and most powerful Greek city-state, Athens. The form of direct democracy that operated in Athens during the fourth and fifth centuries BCE is often portrayed as the only pure or ideal system of popular participation. Nevertheless, although the model had considerable impact on later thinkers such as Rousseau (see p. 79) and Marx (see p. 55), Athenian democracy developed a very particular kind of direct popular rule, one that has only a very limited application in the modern world. Athenian democracy amounted to a form of government by mass meeting. All major decisions were made by the Assembly, or *Ecclesia*, to which all citizens belonged. This met at least 40 times a year. When full-time public officials were needed, they were chosen on a basis of lot or rota to ensure that they constituted a microcosm of the larger citizenry, and terms of office were typically short to achieve the broadest possible participation. A Council consisting of 500 citizens acted as the executive or steering committee of the Assembly, and a 50-strong Committee, in turn, made proposals to the Council. The President of the Committee held office for only a single day, and no Athenian could hold this honour more than once in his lifetime. The only concession made to the need for training and experience was in the case of the ten military generals, who, unlike other public officials, were eligible for reelection.

What made Athenian democracy so remarkable was the level of political activity of its citizens. Not only did they participate in regular meetings of the Assembly but they were, in large numbers, prepared to shoulder the responsibility of public office and decision-making. The most influential contemporaneous critic of this form of democracy was the philosopher Plato (see p. 12). Plato attacked the principle of political equality on the grounds that the mass of the people possess neither the wisdom nor the experience to rule wisely on their own behalf. His solution, advanced in *The Republic*, was that government be placed in the hands of a class of philosopher kings, the Guardians, whose rule would amount to a kind of enlightened dictatorship. On a practical level, however, the principal drawback of Athenian democracy was that it could operate only by excluding the mass of the population from political activity. Participation was restricted to Athenian-born males who were over 20 years of age. Slaves (the majority of the population), women and foreigners had no political rights whatsoever. Indeed, Athenian citizens were able to devote so much of their lives to politics only because slavery relieved them of the need to engage in

Jeremy Bentham (1748–1832)

UK philosopher, legal reformer and founder of utilitarianism. Bentham developed a moral and philosophical system that was based on the idea that human beings are rationally self-interested creatures or **utility** maximizers, which he believed provided a scientific basis for legal and political reforms. Using the 'greatest happiness' principle, his followers, the Philosophic Radicals, were responsible for many of the reforms in social administration, law,

government and economics in the UK in the nineteenth century. A supporter of *laissez-faire* economics, in later life Bentham also became a firm advocate of political democracy. His utilitarian creed was developed in *Fragments on Government* ([1776] 1948), and more fully in *Principles of Morals and Legislation* (1789).

arduous labour, and the confinement of women to the private realm freed them from domestic responsibilities. In this light, in fact, the Athenian *polis* could be seen as the very antithesis of the democratic ideal. Nevertheless, the classical model of direct and continuous popular participation in political life has been kept alive in certain parts of the world, notably in the township meetings of New England in the USA and in the communal assemblies that operate in the smaller Swiss cantons. It is also the basis for the wider use of referendums, particularly in relation to constitutional issues, and for new experiments in democracy such as people's panels and electronic democracy.

Protective democracy

When democratic ideas were revived in the seventeenth and eighteenth centuries, they appeared in a form that was very different from the classical democracy of Ancient Greece. In particular, democracy was seen less as a mechanism through which the public could participate in political life, and more as a device through which citizens could protect themselves from the encroachments of government, hence protective democracy. This view appealed particularly to early liberal thinkers whose concern was, above all, to create the widest realm of individual liberty. The desire to protect the individual from over-mighty government was expressed in perhaps the earliest of all democratic sentiments, Aristotle's response to Plato: '*quis custodiet custodes?*' ('who will guard the Guardians?').

This same concern with unchecked power was taken up in the seventeenth century by John Locke (see p. 47), who argued that the right to vote was based on the existence of **natural rights** and, in particular, on the right to property. If government, through taxation, possessed the power to expropriate property, citizens were entitled to protect themselves by controlling the composition of the tax-setting body: the legislature. In other words, democracy came to mean a system of 'government by consent' operating through a representative assembly. However, Locke himself was not a democrat by modern standards, as he believed that only property owners should vote, on the basis that only they had natural rights that could be infringed by government. The more radical notion of universal suffrage was advanced from the late eighteenth century onwards by utilitarian theorists such as Jeremy Bentham and James Mill (1773–1836). The utilitarian (see p. 427) case for democracy is also based on the need to protect or advance individual interests. Bentham came to believe that, since all individuals seek pleasure and the avoidance

Utility: Use value; satisfaction derived from material consumption.

Natural rights: God-given rights that are fundamental to human beings and are therefore inalienable (they cannot be taken away).

of pain, a universal franchise (conceived in his day as manhood suffrage) was the only way of promoting 'the greatest happiness for the greatest number'.

However, to justify democracy on protective grounds is to provide only a qualified endorsement of democratic rule. In short, protective democracy is but a limited and indirect form of democracy. In practice, the **consent** of the governed is exercised through voting in regular and competitive elections. This thereby ensures the accountability of those who govern. Political equality is thus understood in strictly technical terms to mean equal voting rights. Moreover, this is above all a system of constitutional democracy that operates within a set of formal or informal rules that check the exercise of government power. If the right to vote is a means of defending individual liberty, liberty must also be guaranteed by a strictly enforced separation of powers via the creation of a separate executive, legislature and judiciary, and by the maintenance of basic rights and freedoms, such as freedom of expression, freedom of movement, and freedom from arbitrary arrest. Ultimately, protective democracy aims to give citizens the widest possible scope to live their lives as they choose. It is therefore compatible with *laissez-faire* capitalism (see p. 189) and the belief that individuals should be entirely responsible for their economic and social circumstances. Protective democracy has therefore particularly appealed to classical liberals and, in modern politics, to supporters of the New Right.

Developmental democracy

Although early democratic theory focused on the need to protect individual rights and interests, it soon developed an alternative focus: a concern with the development of the human individual and the community. This gave rise to quite new models of democratic rule that can broadly be referred to as systems of developmental democracy. The most novel, and radical, such model was developed by Jean-Jacques Rousseau. In many respects, Rousseau's ideas mark a departure from the dominant, liberal conception of democracy, and they came to have an impact on the Marxist and anarchist traditions as well as, later, on the New Left. For Rousseau, democracy was ultimately a means through which human beings could achieve freedom (see p. 324) or autonomy, in the sense of 'obedience to a law one prescribes to oneself'. In other words, citizens are 'free' only when they participate directly and continuously in shaping the life of their community. This is an idea that moves well beyond the conventional notion of electoral democracy and offers support for the more radical ideal of direct democracy. Indeed, Rousseau was a strenuous critic of the practice of elections used in England, arguing in *The Social Contract* ([1762] 1913) as follows:

> The English people believes itself to be free, it is gravely mistaken; it is only free when it elects its member of parliament; as soon as they are elected, the people are enslaved; it is nothing. In the brief moment of its freedom, the English people makes such use of its freedom that it deserves to lose it.

Consent: Assent or permission; in politics, usually an agreement to be governed or ruled.

General will: The genuine interests of a collective body, equivalent to the common good; the will of all provided each person acts selflessly.

However, what gives Rousseau's model its novel character is his insistence that freedom ultimately means obedience to the **general will**. Rousseau believed the general will to be the 'true' will of each citizen, in contrast to his or her 'private' or selfish will. By obeying the general will, citizens are therefore doing nothing more than obeying their own 'true' natures, the general will being what individuals would will if they were to act selflessly. In Rousseau's view, such a system of radical developmental democracy required not merely political equality but a relatively high level of

Jean-Jacques Rousseau (1712–78)

Geneva-born French moral and political philosopher, perhaps the principal intellectual influence upon the French Revolution. Rousseau was entirely self-taught. He moved to Paris in 1742, and became an intimate of leading members of the French Enlightenment, especially Diderot. His writings, ranging over education, the arts, science, literature and philosophy, reflect a deep belief in the goodness of 'natural man' and the corruption of 'social man'. Rousseau's political teaching, summarized in *Émile* (1762) and developed in *The Social Contract* ([1762] 1913), advocates a radical form of democracy that has influenced liberal, socialist, anarchist and, some would argue, fascist thought. His autobiography, *Confessions* (1770), examines his life with remarkable candour and demonstrates a willingness to expose his faults and weaknesses.

economic equality. Although not a supporter of common ownership, Rousseau nevertheless proposed that 'no citizen shall be rich enough to buy another and none so poor as to be forced to sell himself' ([1762] 1913:96).

Rousseau's theories have helped to shape the modern idea of participatory democracy taken up by New Left thinkers in the 1960s and 1970s. This extols the virtues of a 'participatory society', a society in which each and every citizen is able to achieve self-development by participating in the decisions that shape his or her life. This goal can be achieved only through the promotion of openness, accountability (see p. 418) and decentralization within all the key institutions of society: within the family, the workplace and the local community just as much as within 'political' institutions such as parties, interest groups and legislative bodies. At the heart of this model is the notion of 'grass-roots democracy': that is, the belief that political power should be exercised at the lowest possible level. Nevertheless, Rousseau's own theories have been criticized for distinguishing between citizens' 'true' wills and their 'felt' or subjective wills. The danger of this is that, if the general will cannot be established by simply asking citizens what they want (because they may be blinded by selfishness), there is scope for the general will to be defined from above, perhaps by a dictator claiming to act in the 'true' interests of society. Rousseau is therefore sometimes seen as the architect of so-called totalitarian democracy (Talmon, 1952).

However, a more modest form of developmental democracy has also been advanced that is compatible with the liberal model of representative government. This view of developmental democracy is rooted in the writings of John Stuart Mill (see p. 48). For Mill, the central virtue of democracy was that it promotes the 'highest and harmonious' development of individual capacities. By participating in political life, citizens enhance their understanding, strengthen their sensibilities, and achieve a higher level of personal development. In short, democracy is essentially an educational experience. As a result, Mill proposed the broadening of popular participation, arguing that the franchise should be extended to all but those who are illiterate. In the process, he suggested (radically, for his time) that suffrage should also be extended to women. In addition, he advocated strong and independent local authorities in the belief that this would broaden the opportunities available for holding public office.

On the other hand, Mill, in common with all liberals, was also aware of the dangers of democracy. Indeed, Mill's views are out of step with mainstream liberal thought in that he rejected the idea of formal political equality. Following Plato, Mill did not

Concept

Parliamentary democracy

Parliamentary democracy is a form of democratic rule that operates through a popularly elected deliberative assembly, which establishes an indirect link between government and the governed. Democracy, in this sense, essentially means responsible and representative government. Parliamentary democracy thus balances popular participation against elite rule: government is accountable not directly to the public but to the public's elected representatives. The attraction of such a system is that representatives are, by virtue of their education and the opportunities that they have to deliberate and debate, supposedly better able than citizens themselves to define the citizens' best interests. In the classical form of parliamentary democracy, associated with J. S. Mill and Burke (see p. 49), parliamentarians are required to think for themselves on behalf of their constituents. Modern party politics, however, has fused the ideas of parliamentary democracy and mandate democracy (see p. 252).

Deliberative democracy: A form of democracy that emphasizes the need for discourse and debate to help define the public interest.

believe that all political opinions are of equal value. Consequently, he proposed a system of plural voting: unskilled workers would have a single vote, skilled workers two votes, and graduates and members of the learned professions five or six votes. However, his principal reservation about democracy was derived from the more typical liberal fear of what Alexis de Tocqueville (see p. 227) famously described as 'the tyranny of the majority'. In other words, democracy always contains the threat that individual liberty and minority rights may be crushed in the name of the people. Mill's particular concern was that democracy would undermine debate, criticism and intellectual life in general by encouraging people to accept the will of the majority, thereby promoting uniformity and dull conformism. Quite simply, the majority is not always right; wisdom cannot be determined by the simple device of a show of hands. Mill's ideas therefore support the idea of **deliberative democracy** or parliamentary democracy.

People's democracy

The term 'people's democracy' is derived from the orthodox communist regimes that sprang up on the Soviet model in the aftermath of the Second World War. It is here used, however, to refer broadly to the various democratic models that the Marxist tradition has generated. Although they differ, these models offer a clear contrast to the more familiar liberal democratic ones. Marxists have tended to be dismissive of liberal or parliamentary democracy, seeing it as a form of 'bourgeois' or 'capitalist' democracy. Nevertheless, Marxists were drawn to the concept or ideal of democracy because of its clear egalitarian implications. The term was used in particular to designate the goal of social equality brought about through the common ownership of wealth ('social democracy' in its original sense), in contrast to 'political' democracy, which establishes only a facade of equality.

Marx believed that the overthrow of capitalism would be a trigger that would allow genuine democracy to flourish. In his view, a fully communist society would come into existence only after a transitionary period characterized by 'the revolutionary dictatorship of the proletariat'. In effect, a system of 'bourgeois' democracy would be replaced by a very different system of 'proletarian' democracy. Although Marx refused to describe in detail how this transitionary society would be organized, its broad shape can be discerned from his admiration for the Paris Commune of 1871, which was a short-lived experiment in what approximated to direct democracy. Marx predicted, however, that, as class antagonisms faded and a fully communist society came into existence, the proletarian state would simply 'wither away'. Not only would this bring an end to the need for government, law and even politics, but it would also, effectively, make democracy redundant.

The form of democracy that was developed in twentieth-century communist states, however, owed more to the ideas of V. I. Lenin than it did to those of Marx. Although Lenin's 1917 slogan 'All power to the Soviets' (the workers' and soldiers' and sailors' councils) had kept alive the notion of commune democracy, in reality power in Soviet Russia quickly fell into the hands of the Bolshevik party (soon renamed the Communist Party). In Lenin's view, this party was nothing less than 'the vanguard of the working class'. Armed with Marxism, the party claimed that it was able to perceive the genuine interests of the proletariat and thus guide it to the realization of its revolutionary potential. This theory became the cornerstone of 'Leninist democracy' in the USSR, and it was accepted by all other orthodox

Vladimir Ilyich Lenin (1870–1924)

Russian Marxist theorist and active revolutionary. As leader of the Bolsheviks, Lenin masterminded the 1917 Russian Bolshevik Revolution, and became the first leader of the USSR. His contributions to Marxism were his theory of the revolutionary or vanguard party, outlined in *What is to be Done?* ([1902] 1968), his analysis of colonialism as an economic phenomenon, described in *Imperialism, the Highest Stage of Capitalism* ([1916] 1970), and his firm commitment to the 'insurrectionary road to socialism', developed in *State and Revolution* (1917). Lenin's reputation is inevitably tied up with the subsequent course of Soviet history; he is seen by some as the father of Stalinist oppression, but by others as a critic of bureaucracy and a defender of debate and argument.

communist regimes as one of the core features of Marxism–Leninism. However, the weakness of this model is that Lenin failed to build into it any mechanism for checking the power of the Communist Party (and particularly its leaders) and for ensuring that it remained sensitive and accountable to the proletarian class. To rephrase Aristotle, 'who will guard the Communist Party?'.

Democracy in practice: rival views

Although there continues to be controversy about which is the most desirable form of democracy, much of contemporary debate revolves around how democracy works in practice and what 'democratization' (see p. 32) implies. This reflects the fact that there is broad, even worldwide, acceptance of a particular model of democracy, generally termed liberal democracy. Despite the existence of competing tendencies within this broad category, certain central features are clear:

- Liberal democracy is an indirect and representative form of democracy in that political office is gained through success in regular elections that are conducted on the basis of formal political equality.

- Liberal democracy is based on competition and electoral choice. These are achieved through political pluralism, tolerance of a wide range of contending beliefs, and the existence of conflicting social philosophies and rival political movements and parties.

- In liberal democracy, there is a clear distinction between the state and civil society. This distinction is maintained through the existence of autonomous groups and interests, and the market or capitalist organization of economic life.

Nevertheless, there is a considerable amount of disagreement about the meaning and significance of liberal democracy. Does it, for instance, ensure a genuine and healthy dispersal of political power? Do democratic processes genuinely promote long-term benefits, or are they self-defeating? Can political equality coexist with economic inequality? In short, this form of democracy is interpreted in different ways by different theorists. The most important of these interpretations are advanced by:

- pluralism
- elitism

Concept

Pluralism

The term pluralism is used in two senses, one broad the other narrow. In its broader sense, pluralism is a belief in, or a commitment to, diversity or multiplicity (the existence of many things). As a descriptive term, pluralism may be used to denote the existence of party competition (political pluralism), a multiplicity of ethical values (moral pluralism), or a variety of cultural norms (cultural pluralism). As a normative term, it suggests that diversity is healthy and desirable, usually because it safeguards individual liberty and promotes debate, argument and understanding. More narrowly, pluralism is a theory of the distribution of political power. It holds that power is widely and evenly dispersed in society rather than concentrated in the hands of an elite or a ruling class. In this form, pluralism is usually seen as a theory of 'group politics' in which individuals are represented largely through their membership of organized groups, and all such groups have access to the policy process.

- corporatism
- the New Right
- Marxism.

Pluralist view

Pluralist ideas can be traced back to early liberal political philosophy, and notably to the ideas of Locke and Montesquieu (see p. 336). Their first systematic development, however, is found in the contributions of James Madison (see p. 344) to *The Federalist Papers* (Hamilton, Jay and Madison, [1787–89] 1961). In considering the transformation of America from a loose confederation of states into the federal USA, Madison's particular fear was the 'problem of factions'. In common with most liberals, Madison argued that unchecked democratic rule might simply lead to majoritarianism, to the crushing of individual rights and to the expropriation of property in the name of the people. What made Madison's work notable, however, was his stress upon the multiplicity of interests and groups in society, and his insistence that, unless each such group possessed a political voice, stability and order would be impossible. He therefore proposed a system of divided government based on the separation of powers, bicameralism (see p. 345) and federalism (see p. 167), that offered a variety of access points to competing groups and interests. The resulting system of rule by multiple minorities is often referred to as 'Madisonian democracy'. Insofar as it recognizes both the existence of diversity or multiplicity in society, and the fact that such multiplicity is desirable, Madison's model is the first developed statement of pluralist principles.

The most influential modern exponent of pluralist theory is Robert Dahl (see p. 298). As described in *Who Governs? Democracy and Power in an American City* (1961), Dahl carried out an empirical study of the distribution of power in New Haven, Connecticut, USA. He concluded that, although the politically privileged and economically powerful exerted greater power than ordinary citizens, no ruling or permanent elite was able to dominate the political process. His conclusion was that 'New Haven is an example of a democratic system, warts and all'. Dahl recognized that modern democratic systems differ markedly from the classical democracies of Ancient Greece. With Charles Lindblom, he coined the term 'polyarchy' (see p. 33) to mean rule by the many, as distinct from rule by all citizens. The key feature of such a system of pluralist democracy is that competition between parties at election time, and the ability of interest or pressure groups to articulate their views freely, establishes a reliable link between the government and the governed, and creates a channel of communication between the two. While this may fall a long way short of the ideal of popular self-government, its supporters nevertheless argue that it ensures a sufficient level of accountability and popular responsiveness for it to be regarded as democratic.

However, the relationship between pluralism and democracy may not be a secure one. For instance, one of the purposes of the Madisonian system was, arguably, to constrain democracy in the hope of safeguarding property. In other words, the system of rule by multiple minorities may simply have been a device to prevent the majority (the propertyless masses) from exercising political power. A further problem is the danger of what has been called 'pluralist stagnation'. This occurs as organized groups and economic interests become so powerful that they create a log jam, resulting in the problem of government 'overload'. In such circumstances, a pluralist system may simply become ungovernable. Finally, there is the problem identified by

Dahl in later works such as *A Preface to Economic Democracy* (1985), notably that the unequal ownership of economic resources tends to concentrate political power in the hands of the few, and deprive it from the many. This line of argument runs parallel to the conventional Marxist critique of pluralist democracy, and has given rise to neopluralism (see p. 94).

Elitist view

Elitism developed as a critique of egalitarian ideas such as democracy and socialism. It draws attention to the fact of elite rule, either as an inevitable and desirable feature of social existence, or as a remediable and regrettable one. Classical elitists, such as Vilfredo Pareto (1848–1923), Gaetano Mosca (1857–1941) and Robert Michels (1876–1936), tended to take the former position. For them, democracy was no more than a foolish delusion, because political power is always exercised by a privileged minority: an elite. For example, in *The Ruling Class* ([1896] 1939), Mosca proclaimed that, in all societies, 'two classes of people appear – a class that rules and a class that is ruled'. In his view, the resources or attributes that are necessary for rule are always unequally distributed, and, further, a cohesive minority will always be able to manipulate and control the masses, even in a parliamentary democracy.

Pareto suggested that the qualities needed to rule are those of one of two psychological types: 'foxes' (who rule by cunning and are able to manipulate the consent of the masses), and 'lions' (whose domination is typically achieved through coercion and violence). Michels, however, developed an alternative line of argument based on the tendency within all organizations, however democratic they might appear, for power to be concentrated in the hands of a small group of dominant figures who can organize and make decisions, rather than being in the hands of an apathetic rank and file. He termed this 'the iron law of oligarchy' (see p. 280). This notion of bureaucratic power was later developed by James Burnham, who, in *The Managerial Revolution* (1941), argued that a 'managerial class' dominated all industrial societies, both capitalist and communist, by virtue of its technical and scientific knowledge and its administrative skills.

Whereas classical elitists strove to prove that democracy was always a myth, modern elitist theorists have tended to highlight how far particular political systems fall short of the democratic ideal. An example of this can be found in C. Wright Mills' influential account of the power structure in the USA. In contrast to the pluralist notion of a wide and broadly democratic dispersal of power, Mills, in *The Power Elite* (1956), offered a portrait of a USA dominated by a nexus of leading groups. In his view, this 'power elite' comprised a triumvirate of big business (particularly defence-related industries), the US military, and political cliques surrounding the President. Drawing on a combination of economic power, bureaucratic control, and access to the highest levels of the executive branch of government, the power elite is able to shape key 'history-making' decisions, especially in the fields of defence and foreign policy, as well as strategic economic policy. The power-elite model suggests that liberal democracy in the USA is largely a sham. Electoral pressures tend to be absorbed by the 'middle levels of power' (Congress, state governments and so on), and groups such as organized labour, small businesses and consumer lobbyists are able to exert influence only at the margins of the policy process. Elitists have, moreover, argued that empirical studies have supported pluralist conclusions only because Dahl and others have ignored the importance of non-decision-making as a manifestation of power (see p. 11).

Concept

Pluralist democracy

The term pluralist democracy is sometimes used interchangeably with liberal democracy to indicate a democratic system based on electoral competition between a number of political parties. More specifically, it refers to a form of democracy that operates through the capacity of organized groups and interests to articulate popular demands and ensure government responsiveness. As such, it can be seen as an alternative to parliamentary democracy and to any form of majoritarianism. The conditions for a healthy pluralist democracy include the following:

- There is a wide dispersal of political power amongst competing groups, and, specifically, elite groups are absent.
- There is a high degree of internal responsiveness, with group leaders being accountable to members.
- There is a neutral governmental machine that is sufficiently fragmented to offer groups a number of points of access.

Concept

Elite, elitism

The term elite originally meant, and can still mean, the highest, the best, or the excellent. Used in a neutral or empirical sense, however, it refers to a minority in whose hands power, wealth or privilege is concentrated, justifiably or otherwise. Elitism is a belief in, or practice of, rule by an elite or minority. *Normative* elitism suggests that elite rule is desirable: political power should be vested in the hands of a wise or enlightened minority. *Classical* elitism (developed by Mosca, Pareto and Michels) claimed to be empirical (although normative beliefs often intruded), and it saw elite rule as being inevitable, an unchangeable fact of social existence. *Modern* elitism has also developed an empirical analysis, but it is more critical and discriminating about the causes of elite rule. Modern elitists, such as C. Wright Mills (1916–62), have often been concerned to highlight elite rule in the hope of both explaining it and challenging it.

Certain elite theorists have nevertheless argued that a measure of democratic accountability is consistent with elite rule. Whereas the power-elite model portrays the elite as a cohesive body, bound together by common or overlapping interests, competitive elitism (sometimes called democratic elitism) highlights the significance of elite rivalry (see Figure 4.1). In other words, the elite, consisting of the leading figures from a number of competing groups and interests, is fractured. This view is often associated with Joseph Schumpeter's (see p. 253) 'realistic' model of democracy outlined in *Capitalism, Socialism and Democracy* (1942: 269):

> The democratic method is that institutional arrangement for arriving at political decisions in which individuals acquire the power to decide by means of a competitive struggle for the people's vote.

The electorate can decide which elite rules, but cannot change the fact that power is always exercised by an elite. This model of competitive elitism was developed by Anthony Downs (1957) into the 'economic theory of democracy'. In effect, electoral competition creates a political market in which politicians act as entrepreneurs bent upon achieving government power, and individual voters behave like consumers, voting for the party with the policies that most closely reflect their own preferences. Downs argued that a system of open and competitive elections guarantees democratic rule because it places government in the hands of the party whose philosophy, values and policies correspond most closely to the preferences of the largest group of voters. As Schumpeter put it, 'democracy is the rule of the politician'.

As a model of democratic politics, competitive elitism at least has the virtue that it corresponds closely to the workings of the liberal-democratic political system. Indeed, it emerged more as an attempt to *describe* how the democratic process works than through a desire to *prescribe* certain values and principles – political equality, popular participation, freedom or whatever. Democracy, then, is seen simply as a political method: as a means of making political decisions by reference to a competitive struggle for the popular vote. To the extent that the model is accurate, its virtue is that it allows considerable scope for political leadership by placing decision-making in the hands of the best-informed, most-skilled, and most politically committed members of society. On the other hand, although competition for power undoubtedly creates a measure of accountability, competitive elitism must at best be considered a weak form of democracy. Not only can one elite only be removed by replacing it with another, but the role allotted to the general public (that of deciding every few years which elite will rule on its behalf) is likely to engender apathy, lack of interest, and even alienation.

Corporatist view

The origins of corporatism (see p. 299) date back to the attempt in Fascist Italy to construct a so-called 'corporate state' by integrating both managers and workers into the processes of government. Corporatist theorists, however, have drawn attention to parallel developments in the world's major industrialized states. In the form of **neocorporatism**, or liberal corporatism, this gave rise to the spectre of 'tripartite government', in which government is conducted through organizations that allow state officials, employers' groups and unions to deal directly with one another. To a large extent, this tendency to integrate economic interests into government (which was common in the post-1945 period, and particularly prominent in, for example,

Neocorporatism: A tendency found in western polyarchies for organized interests to be granted privileged and institutionalized access to policy formulation.

Power elite model: single, coherent elite

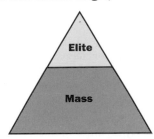

Competitive elite model: fractured elite

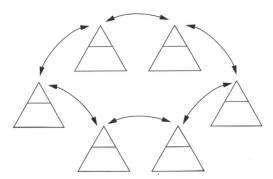

Fig. 4.1 Elite models

Sweden, Norway, the Netherlands and Austria) was a consequence of the drift towards economic management and intervention. As government sought to manage economic life and deliver an increasingly broad range of public services, it recognized the need for institutional arrangements designed to secure the cooperation and support of major economic interests. Where attempts have been made to shift economic policy away from state intervention and towards the free market (as in the UK since 1979), the impact of corporatism has markedly diminished.

The significance of corporatism in terms of democratic processes is clearly considerable. There are those who, like the British guild socialists, argue that corporatism makes possible a form of functional representation, in that individuals' views and interests are articulated more by the groups to which they belong than through the mechanism of competitive elections. What is called 'corporate pluralism' thus portrays tripartism as a mechanism through which the major groups and interests in society compete to shape government policy. Most commentators, however, see corporatism very much as a threat to democracy. In the first place, corporatism only advantages groups that are accorded privileged access to government. 'Insider' groups therefore possess a political voice, while 'outsider' groups are denied one. Second, corporatism can work to the benefit of the state rather than major economic interests, in that the **peak associations** that the government chooses to deal with can be used to exert discipline over their members and to filter out radical demands. Finally, corporatism threatens to subvert the processes of electoral or parliamentary democracy. Policy is made through negotiations between government officials and leaders of powerful economic interests rather than through the deliberations of a representative assembly. Interest-group leaders may thus exert considerable political

Peak association: A group recognized by government as representing the general or collective interests of businesses or workers.

power, even though they are in no way publicly accountable and their influence is not subject to public scrutiny.

New Right view

The emergence of the New Right from the 1970s onwards has generated a very particular critique of democratic politics. This has focused upon the danger of what has been called 'democratic overload': the paralysis of a political system that is subject to unrestrained group and electoral pressures. One aspect of this critique has highlighted the unsavoury face of corporatism. New Right theorists are keen advocates of the free market, believing that economies work best when left alone by government. The danger of corporatism from this perspective is that it empowers sectional groups and economic interests, enabling them to make demands on government for increased pay, public investment, subsidies, state protection and so on. In effect, corporatism allows well-placed interest groups to dominate and dictate to government. The result of this, according to the New Right, is an irresistible drift towards state intervention and economic stagnation (Olson, 1982).

Government 'overload' can also be seen to be a consequence of the electoral process. This was what Brittan (1977) referred to as 'the economic consequences of democracy'. In this view, electoral politics amounts to a self-defeating process in which politicians are encouraged to compete for power by offering increasingly unrealistic promises to the electorate. Both voters and politicians are held to blame here. Voters are attracted by promises of higher public spending because they calculate that the cost (an increased tax burden) will be spread over the entire population. Politicians, consumed by the desire to win power, attempt to outbid one another by making ever more generous spending pledges to the electorate. According to Brittan, the economic consequences of unrestrained democracy are high levels of inflation fuelled by public borrowing, and a tax burden that destroys enterprise and undermines growth. As characterized by Marquand (1988), the New Right view is that 'democracy is to adults what chocolate is to children: endlessly tempting; harmless in small doses; sickening in excess'. New Right theorists therefore tend to see democracy in strictly protective terms, regarding it essentially as a defence against arbitrary government rather than a means of bringing about social transformation.

Marxist view

As pointed out in relation to people's democracy, the Marxist view of democratic politics is rooted in class analysis. In this view, political power cannot be understood narrowly in terms of electoral rights, or in terms of the ability of groups to articulate their interests by lobbying and campaigning. Rather, at a deeper level, political power reflects the distribution of economic power and, in particular, the unequal ownership of productive wealth. The Marxist critique of liberal democracy thus focuses upon the inherent tension between democracy and capitalism: that is, between the political equality that liberal democracy proclaims and the social inequality that a capitalist economy inevitably generates. Liberal democracies are thus seen as 'capitalist' or 'bourgeois' democracies that are manipulated and controlled by the entrenched power of a **ruling class**.

Marxism thus offers a distinctive critique of pluralist democracy. Power cannot be widely and evenly dispersed in society as long as class power is unequally distributed.

Ruling class: A Marxist term, denoting a class that dominates other classes and society at large by virtue of its ownership of productive wealth.

Indeed, in many respects, the Marxist view parallels the elitist critique of pluralism. Both views suggest that power is ultimately concentrated in the hands of the few, the main difference being whether the few is conceived of as a 'power elite' or as a 'ruling class'. However, significant differences can also be identified. In the first place, whereas elitists suggest that power can be derived from a variety of sources (education, social status, bureaucratic position, political connections, wealth, and so on), Marxists emphasize the decisive importance of economic factors, notably the ownership and control of the means of production. Moreover, elitists are less clear about the significance of elite rule, acknowledging, for example, that when competition exists within a fractured elite policy may, to some extent, be shaped by democratic pressures. Marxists, in contrast, tend to argue that the ruling class is bent on pursuing its own economic interests, and that it makes concessions to other classes only in order to stabilize capitalism and perpetuate a system of unequal class power.

Modern Marxists, however, have been less willing to dismiss electoral democracy as nothing more than a sham. **Eurocommunists**, for example, abandoned the idea of revolution, embracing instead the notion of a peaceful, legal and democratic 'road to socialism'. Neo-Marxists such as Jürgen Habermas (see p. 223) and Claus Offe (1984) have nevertheless drawn attention to the contradictions, and perhaps inherent instability, of capitalist democracy. In this view, on the one hand, the democratic process forces government to respond to popular demands, leading to an inexorable rise of public spending and a progressive expansion of the state's responsibilities, especially in economic and social life. On the other hand, the long-term survival of capitalism is threatened by a fiscal crisis in which high taxes become a disincentive to enterprise, and ever-rising government borrowing leads to permanently high inflation. Forced either to resist democratic pressures or to risk economic collapse, capitalist democracy would, Habermas (1973) argued, find it increasingly difficult to maintain legitimacy. These issues are discussed at greater length in Chapter 10.

■ Summary

◆ The very popularity of democracy has threatened its use as a meaningful political term, and perhaps reduced it to a mere 'hurrah! word'. The meanings of the term have ranged from a system of rule by the masses and a form of government based on direct and popular continuous popular participation to rule by the majority and a system of party competition that operates through regular and popular elections.

◆ Debates about the nature of democracy have tended to focus on three central issues. First, who are the people, or how far should political power be distributed? Second, should the people in effect rule themselves, or should government be left in the hands of politicians and parties that claim to represent them? Third, what matters is it appropriate to decide collectively through the use of democratic processes?

◆ There are a number of rival models of democracy, each offering its own version of popular rule. These include: classical democracy, which is based on the principle of popular self-government; protective democracy, which is rooted in the individualist assumptions of liberalism; developmental democracy, which is concerned with broadening the scope for popular participation; and people's democracy, which pays particular attention to the distribution of class power.

Eurocommunism: A form of deradicalized communism that attempted to blend Marxism with liberal-democratic principles.

◆ Classical democracy, which is based on the political system in Athens in Ancient Greece, is defended on the grounds that it alone guarantees government *by* the people. Protective democracy gives citizens the greatest scope to live their lives as they choose. Developmental democracy has the virtue that, in extending participation, it widens liberty and fosters personal growth. People's democracy aims to achieve economic emancipation, rather than merely the extension of political rights.

◆ In practice, there is broad acceptance of a particular model of democracy, generally termed liberal democracy. Its central features are that it is an indirect and representative form of democracy that is based on regular elections. It operates through party competition and electoral choice, and it observes a clear distinction between the state and civil society, thus allowing for the existence of autonomous groups and private property.

◆ There is considerable controversy about how liberal-democratic systems work in practice. Pluralists praise their capacity to guarantee popular responsiveness and public accountability. Elitists highlight the tendency for political power to be concentrated in the hands of a privileged minority. Corporatists draw attention to the incorporation of groups into government. The New Right focuses on the dangers of 'democratic overload'. And Marxists point to tensions between democracy and capitalism.

Questions for discussion

▶ Why has democracy come to be so universally well regarded?

▶ Is direct democracy in any way applicable to modern circumstances?

▶ What are the principal virtues of democracy?

▶ What are the drawbacks or dangers of democracy?

▶ Which model of democracy is most attractive, and why?

▶ Do modern forms of representative democracy deserve to be described as democratic?

▶ What are the major threats to democracy in modern society?

Further reading

Arblaster, A., *Democracy*, 2nd edn (Milton Keynes: Open University Press; Minneapolis: University of Minnesota Press, 1994). A succinct and thoughtful introduction to the theory of democracy.

Dahl, R., *Democracy and its Critics* (New Haven, CT: Yale University Press, 1989) A wide-ranging and thorough discussion of the democratic ideal and democratic practices.

Gill, G., *The Dynamics of Democratization: Elite, Civil Society and the Transition Process* (Basingstoke: Palgrave Macmillan, 2000). A clear and accessible overview of the scale, scope and character of democratization in the contemporary world.

Held, D., *Models of Democracy*, 3rd edn (Oxford: Polity, 2006). A rigorous and stimulating examination of rival models of democracy and the present state of democratic theory.

Macpherson, C. B., *The Life and Times of Liberal Democracy* (Oxford: Oxford University Press, 1977). A short, lucid and perceptive discussion of important themes in liberal-democratic theory.

The State

> 'The purpose of the State is always the same: to limit the individual, to tame him, to subordinate him, to subjugate him.'
>
> MAX STIRNER, *The Ego and His Own* (1845)

Contents

The shadow of the state falls upon almost every human activity. From education to economic management, from social welfare to sanitation, and from domestic order to external defence, the state shapes and controls, and where it does not shape or control it regulates, supervises, authorises or proscribes. Even those aspects of life usually thought of as personal or private (marriage, divorce, abortion, religious worship and so on) are ultimately subject to the authority of the state. It is not surprising, therefore, that politics is often understood as the study of the state, the analysis of its institutional organizations, the evaluation of its impact on society, and so on. Ideological debate and party politics, certainly, tend to revolve around the proper function or role of the state: what should be done by the state and what should be left to private individuals and associations? The nature of state power has thus become one of the central concerns of political analysis. This debate (the so-called 'state debate') touches on some of the deepest and most abiding divisions in political theory.

The central issues examined in this chapter are as follows:

Key issues

▶ What is the state, and how can it be distinguished from government?

▶ How has state power been analysed and explained?

▶ Is the state a force for good or a force for evil?

▶ What roles have been assigned to the state? How have responsibilities been apportioned between the state and civil society?

▶ How has the role and power of the state been affected by globalization?

Georg Wilhelm Friedrich Hegel (1770–1831)

German philosopher. Hegel was the founder of modern idealism and developed the notion that consciousness and material objects are in fact unified. In *Phenomenology of Spirit* (1807) he sought to develop a rational system that would substitute for traditional Christianity by interpreting the entire process of human history, and indeed the universe itself, in terms of the progress of absolute Mind towards self-realization. In his view, history is, in essence, a march of the human spirit towards a determinant endpoint. His major political work,

Philosophy of Right (1821), portrayed the state as an ethical ideal and the highest expression of human freedom. Hegel's work had considerable impact upon Marx and other so-called 'young Hegelians', as well as on later Marxist, such as the Frankfurt School. It also shaped the ideas of liberals such as T. H. Green (1836–82), and influenced fascist thought.

■ What is the state?

The term 'state' has been used to refer to a bewildering range of things: a collection of institutions, a territorial unit, a philosophical idea, an instrument of coercion or oppression, and so on. This confusion stems, in part, from the fact that the state has been understood in three very different ways, from an idealist perspective, a functionalist perspective and an organizational perspective. The *idealist* approach to the state is most clearly reflected in the writings of G. W. F. Hegel. Hegel identified three 'moments' of social existence: the family, civil society, and the state. Within the family, he argued, a 'particular altruism' operates that encourages people to set aside their own interests for the good of their children or elderly relatives. In contrast, civil society was seen as a sphere of 'universal egoism' in which individuals place their own interests before those of others. Hegel conceived of the state as an ethical community underpinned by mutual sympathy – 'universal altruism'. The drawback of idealism, however, is that it fosters an uncritical reverence for the state and, by defining the state in ethical terms, fails to distinguish clearly between institutions that are part of the state and those that are outside the state.

Functionalist approaches to the state focus on the role or purpose of state institutions. The central function of the state is invariably seen as the maintenance of social order (see p. 413), the state being defined as that set of institutions that uphold order and deliver social stability. Such an approach has, for example, been adopted by modern Marxists, who have been inclined to see the state as a mechanism through which class conflict is ameliorated to ensure the long-term survival of the capitalist system. The weakness of the functionalist view of the state, however, is that it tends to associate *any* institution that maintains order (such as the family, mass media, trade unions and the church) with the state itself. This is why, unless there is a statement to the contrary, an organizational approach to the definition of the state (see below) is adopted throughout this book

The *organizational* view defines the state as the apparatus of government in its broadest sense: that is, as that set of institutions that are recognizably 'public' in that they are responsible for the collective organization of social existence and are funded at the public's expense. The virtue of this definition is that it distinguishes clearly between the state and civil society (see p. 8). The state comprises the various institutions of government: the bureaucracy, the military, the police, the courts, the social-security system and so on; it can be identified with the entire 'body politic'. This makes it possible to identify the origins of the modern state in the emergence in fifteenth-century and sixteenth-century Europe of a system of centralized rule that succeeded in subordinating all other institutions and groups, spiritual and temporal. The modern notion of sovereign statehood was, indeed, formalized in the Treaty of Westphalia 1648. Moreover, the organizational approach allows us to talk about 'rolling forward' or 'rolling back' the state, in the sense of expanding or contracting the responsibilities of the state, and enlarging or diminishing its institutional machinery.

In this light, it is possible to identify five key features of the state:

- The state is *sovereign*. It exercises absolute and unrestricted power in that it stands above all other associations and groups in society. Thomas Hobbes (see p. 327) conveyed this idea by portraying the state as a 'leviathan', a gigantic monster, usually represented as a sea creature.

- State institutions are recognizably '*public*', in contrast to the 'private' institutions of civil society. Public bodies are responsible for making and enforcing collective decisions, while private bodies, such as families, private businesses and trade unions, exist to satisfy individual interests.

- The state is an exercise in *legitimation*. The decisions of the state are usually (although not necessarily) accepted as binding on the members of society because, it is claimed, they are made in the public interest or for common good; the state supposedly reflects the permanent interests of society.

- The state is an instrument of *domination*. State authority is backed up by coercion; the state must have the capacity to ensure that its laws are obeyed and that transgressors are punished. A monopoly of 'legitimate violence' (Max Weber) is therefore the practical expression of state sovereignty.

- The state is a *territorial* association. The jurisdiction of the state is geographically defined, and it encompasses all those who live within the state's borders, whether they are citizens or noncitizens. On the international stage, the state is therefore regarded (at least in theory) as an autonomous entity.

Not only is the state separate from civil society, but it is also internally differentiated, containing various branches or sections. The state apparatus thus embraces the political executive or government, in the narrow sense, possibly an assembly or parliament, the judiciary, the bureaucracy, the military, the police, local and regional institutions, and so on. The most important distinction, however, is that between the 'state' and the 'government', two terms that are often used interchangeably. This distinction is not just of academic interest. It goes to the very heart of the idea of limited and **constitutional government**. In short, government power can be held in check only when the government of the day is prevented from encroaching upon the absolute and unlimited authority of the state.

The principal differences between government and the state are the following:

- The state is more *extensive* than government. The state is an inclusive association that encompasses all the institutions of the public realm and embraces all the members of the community (in their capacity as citizens). Government is *part* of the state.

- The state is a continuing, even *permanent*, entity. Government is *temporary*: governments come and go, and systems of government can be reformed and remodelled.

Concept

The state

The state is a political association that establishes sovereign (see p. 131) jurisdiction within defined territorial borders, and exercises authority through a set of permanent institutions. These institutions are those that are recognizably 'public' in that they are responsible for the collective organization of communal life, and are funded at the public's expense. The state thus embraces the various institutions of government, but it also extends to the courts, nationalized industries, social-security system, and so forth; it can be identified with the entire 'body politic'. For the German sociologist Max Weber (see p. 220), the state was defined by its monopoly of the means of 'legitimate violence'. Debate over the nature of state power and the role of the state is, arguably, the central theme in political thought.

Constitutional government: A system of government that operates within a set of legal and institutional constraints that both limit its power and protect individual liberty.

- Government is the *means* through which the authority of the state is brought into operation. In making and implementing state policy, government is 'the brains' of the state, and it perpetuates the state's existence.

- The state exercises *impersonal* authority. The personnel of state bodies is recruited and trained in a bureaucratic manner and is (usually) expected to be politically neutral, enabling state bodies to resist the ideological enthusiasms of the government of the day.

- The state, in theory at least, represents the permanent interests of society: that is, the *common* good or general will. Government, on the other hand, represents the *partisan* sympathies of those who happen to be in power at a particular time.

Rival theories of the state

Reaching an agreement about what we mean by 'the state' provides a basis upon which to examine a deeper problem: what is the nature of state power, and what interests does the state represent? From this perspective, the state is an 'essentially contested' concept. There are a number of rival theories of the state, each of which offers a different account of its origins, development and impact on society. Indeed, controversy about the nature of state power has increasingly dominated modern political analysis and goes to the heart of ideological and theoretical disagreements in the discipline. These relate to questions about whether, for example, the state is autonomous and independent of society, or whether it is essentially a product of society, a reflection of the broader distribution of power or resources. Moreover, does the state serve the common or collective good, or is it biased in favour of privileged groups or a dominant class? Similarly, is the state a positive or constructive force, with responsibilities that should be enlarged, or is it a negative or destructive entity that must be constrained or, perhaps, smashed altogether? Four contrasting theories of the state can be identified as follows:

- the pluralist state
- the capitalist state
- the leviathan state
- the patriarchal state.

The pluralist state

The pluralist theory of the state has a very clear liberal lineage. It stems from the belief that the state acts as an 'umpire' or 'referee' in society. This view has also dominated mainstream political analysis, accounting for a tendency, at least within Anglo-American thought, to discount the state and state organizations and focus instead on 'government'. Indeed, it is not uncommon in this tradition for 'the state' to be dismissed as an abstraction, with institutions such as the courts, the civil service and the military being seen as independent actors in their own right, rather than as elements of a broader state machine. Nevertheless, this approach is possible only because it is based on underlying, and often unacknowledged, assumptions about state neutrality. The state can be ignored only because it is seen as an impartial arbiter or referee that can be bent to the will of the government of the day.

Focus on . . .

Social-contract theory

A social contract is a voluntary agreement made amongst individuals through which an organized society, or state, is brought into existence. Used as a theoretical device by thinkers such as Hobbes, Locke and Rousseau (see p. 79), the social contract has been revived by modern theorists such as John Rawls (see p. 60). The social contract is seldom regarded as a historical act. Rather, it is used as a means of demonstrating the value of government and the grounds of political obligation; social-contract theorists wish individuals to act *as if* they had concluded the contract themselves. In its classic form, social-contract theory has three elements:

- The image of a hypothetical stateless society (a 'state of nature') is established. Unconstrained freedom means that life is 'solitary, poor, nasty, brutish and short' (Hobbes).
- Individuals therefore seek to escape from the state of nature by entering into a social contract, recognizing that only a sovereign power can secure order and stability.
- The social contract obliges citizens to respect and obey the state, ultimately in gratitude for the stability and security that only a system of political rule can deliver.

The origins of this theory of the state can be traced back to the writings of seventeenth-century social-contract theorists such as Thomas Hobbes and John Locke (see p. 47). The principal concern of such thinkers was to examine the grounds of **political obligation**, the grounds upon which the individual is obliged to obey and respect the state. They argued that the state had arisen out of a voluntary agreement, or social contract, made by individuals who recognized that only the establishment of a sovereign power could safeguard them from the insecurity, disorder and brutality of the **state of nature**. Without a state, individuals abuse, exploit and enslave one another; with a state, order and civilized existence are guaranteed and liberty is protected. As Locke put it, 'where there is no law there is no freedom'.

In liberal theory, the state is thus seen as a neutral arbiter amongst the competing groups and individuals in society; it is an 'umpire' or 'referee' that is capable of protecting each citizen from the encroachments of fellow citizens. The neutrality of the state reflects the fact that the state acts in the interests of *all* citizens, and therefore represents the common good or public interest. In Hobbes' view, stability and order could be secured only through the establishment of an absolute and unlimited state, with power that could be neither challenged nor questioned. In other words, he held that citizens are confronted by a stark choice between absolutism (see p. 28) and **anarchy**. Locke, on the other hand, developed a more typically liberal defence of the limited state. In his view, the purpose of the state is very specific: it is restricted to the defence of a set of 'natural' or God-given individual rights, namely 'life, liberty and property'. This establishes a clear distinction between the responsibilities of the state (essentially the maintenance of domestic order and the protection of property) and the responsibilities of individual citizens (usually seen as the realm of civil society). Moreover, since the state may threaten natural rights as easily as it may

Political obligation: The duty of the citizen towards the state; the basis of the state's right to rule.

State of nature: A society devoid of political authority and of formal (legal) checks on the individual; usually employed as a theoretical device.

Anarchy: Literally, without rule; anarchy is often used pejoratively to suggest instability or even chaos.

Concept

Neopluralism

Neopluralism is a style of social theorizing that remains faithful to pluralist values while recognizing the need to revise or update classical pluralism in the light of, for example, elite, Marxist and New Right theories. Although neopluralism embraces a broad range of perspectives and positions, certain central themes can be identified. First, it attempts to take account of modernizing trends, such as the emergence of postindustrial and postcapitalist society. Second, while capitalism is certainly preferred to socialism, free-market economic doctrines are usually regarded as obsolete. Third, western democracies are seen as 'deformed polyarchies', in which major corporations exert disproportionate influence.

uphold them, citizens must enjoy some form of protection against the state, which Locke believed could be delivered only through the mechanisms of constitutional and representative government.

These ideas were developed in the twentieth century into the pluralist theory of the state. As a theory of society, pluralism (see p. 82) asserts that, within liberal democracies, power is widely and evenly dispersed. As a theory of the state, pluralism holds that the state is neutral insofar as it is susceptible to the influence of various groups and interests and all social classes. The state is not biased in favour of any particular interest or group, and it does not have an interest of its own that is separate from those of society. As Schwarzmantel (1994:52) put it, the state is 'the servant of society and not its master'. The state can thus be portrayed as a 'pincushion' that passively absorbs pressures and forces exerted upon it. Two key assumptions underlie this view. The first is that the state is effectively subordinate to government. Nonelected state bodies (the civil service, the judiciary, the police, the military and so on) are strictly impartial and are subject to the authority of their political masters. The state apparatus is therefore thought to conform to the principles of public service and political accountability (see p. 418). The second assumption is that the democratic process is meaningful and effective. In other words, party competition and interest-group activity ensure that the government of the day remains sensitive and responsive to public opinion. Ultimately, therefore, the state is only a weather vane that is blown in whatever direction the public at large dictates.

Modern pluralists, however, have often adopted a more critical view of the state, termed the neopluralist theory of the state. Theorists such as Robert Dahl (see p. 298), Charles Lindblom and J. K. Galbraith (see p. 199) have come to accept that modern industrialized states are both more complex and less responsive to popular pressures than classical pluralism suggested. Neopluralists, for instance, have ack-nowledged that business enjoys a 'privileged position' in relation to government that other groups clearly cannot rival. In *Politics and Markets* (1977) Lindblom pointed out that, as the major investor and largest employer in society, business is bound to exercise considerable sway over any government, whatever its ideological leanings or manifesto commitments. Moreover, neopluralists have accepted that the state can and does forge its own sectional interests. In this way, a state elite, composed of senior civil servants, judges, police chiefs, military leaders and so on, may be seen to pursue either the bureaucratic interests of their sector of the state or the interests of client groups. Indeed, if the state is regarded as a political actor in its own right, it can be viewed as a powerful (perhaps the most powerful) interest group in society. This line of argument encouraged Eric Nordlinger (1981) to develop a state-centred model of liberal democracy, based on 'the autonomy of the democratic state'.

The capitalist state

The Marxist notion of a capitalist state offers a clear alternative to the pluralist image of the state as a neutral arbiter or umpire. Marxists have typically argued that the state cannot be understood separately from the economic structure of society. This view has usually been understood in terms of the classic formulation that the state is nothing but an instrument of class oppression: the state emerges out of, and in a sense reflects, the class system. Nevertheless, a rich debate has taken place within Marxist theory in recent years that has moved the Marxist theory of the state a long way from this classic formulation. In many ways, the scope to revise Marxist attitudes towards the state stems from ambiguities that can be found in Marx's own writings.

Marx did not develop a systematic or coherent theory of the state. In a general sense, he believed that the state is part of a 'superstructure' that is determined or conditioned by the economic 'base', which can be seen as the real foundation of social life. However, the precise relationship between the base and the superstructure, and in this case that between the state and the capitalist mode of production, is unclear. Two theories of the state can be identified in Marx's writings. The first is expressed in his often-quoted dictum from *The Communist Manifesto* ([1848] 1967): 'The executive of the modern state is but a committee for managing the common affairs of the whole bourgeoisie'. From this perspective, the state is clearly dependent upon society and entirely dependent upon its economically dominant class, which in capitalism is the **bourgeoisie**. Lenin thus described the state starkly as 'an instrument for the oppression of the exploited class'.

A second, more complex and subtle, theory of the state can nevertheless be found in Marx's analysis of the revolutionary events in France between 1848 and 1851, *The Eighteenth Brumaire of Louis Bonaparte* ([1852] 1963). Marx suggested that the state could enjoy what has come to be seen as 'relative autonomy' from the class system, the Napoleonic state being capable of imposing its will upon society, acting as an 'appalling parasitic body'. If the state did articulate the interests of any class, it was not those of the bourgeoisie, but those of the most populous class in French society, the smallholding peasantry. Although Marx did not develop this view in detail, it is clear that, from this perspective, the autonomy of the state is only *relative*, in that the state appears to mediate between conflicting classes, and so maintains the class system itself in existence.

Both these theories differ markedly from the liberal and, later, pluralist models of state power. In particular, they emphasize that the state cannot be understood except in a context of unequal class power, and that the state arises out of, and reflects, capitalist society, by acting either as an instrument of oppression wielded by the dominant class, or, more subtly, as a mechanism through which class antagonisms are ameliorated. Nevertheless, Marx's attitude towards the state was not entirely negative. He argued that the state could be used constructively during the transition from capitalism to communism in the form of the 'revolutionary dictatorship of the proletariat'. The overthrow of capitalism would see the destruction of the bourgeois state and the creation of an alternative, proletarian one.

In describing the state as a proletarian 'dictatorship', Marx utilized the first theory of the state, seeing the state as an instrument through which the economically dominant class (by then the proletariat) could repress and subdue other classes. All states, from this perspective, are class dictatorships. The 'dictatorship of the proletariat' was seen as a means of safeguarding the gains of the revolution by preventing counter-revolution mounted by the dispossessed bourgeoisie. Nevertheless, Marx did not see the state as a necessary or enduring social formation. He predicted that, as class antagonisms faded, the state would 'wither away', meaning that a fully communist society would also be stateless. Since the state emerged out of the class system, once the class system had been abolished, the state, quite simply, loses its reason for existence.

Marx's ambivalent heritage has provided modern Marxists, or neo-Marxists, with considerable scope to further the analysis of state power. This was also encouraged by the writings of the Italian Marxist Antonio Gramsci (see p. 208), who emphasized

Bourgeoisie: A Marxist term, denoting the ruling class of a capitalist society, the owners of productive wealth.

Concept

Neo-Marxism

Neo-Marxism (sometimes termed modern Marxism) refers to attempts to revise or recast the classical ideas of Marx while remaining faithful to certain Marxist principles or aspects of Marxist methodology. Neo-Marxists typically refuse to accept that Marxism enjoys a monopoly of the truth, and have thus looked to Hegelian philosophy, anarchism, liberalism, feminism, and even rational-choice theory. Two central themes can nevertheless be identified. First, neo-Marxists have tried to provide an alternative to the mechanistic and deterministic ideas of orthodox Marxism, refusing to accept the primacy of economics, or assign the proletariat a privileged role. Second, they have been concerned to explain the failure of Marx's predictions, looking, in particular, to the analysis of ideology and state power.

the degree to which the domination of the ruling class is achieved by ideological manipulation, rather than just open coercion. In this view, bourgeois domination is maintained largely through 'hegemony' (see p. 207): that is, intellectual leadership or cultural control, with the state playing an important role in the process. In the 1960s and early 1970s, Marxist theorizing about the state was dominated by the rival positions adopted by Ralph Miliband and Nicos Poulantzas (1936–79). Although this debate moved through a number of phases as each author revised his position, at the heart of it lay contrasting instrumentalist and structuralist views of the state.

In *The State in Capitalist Society* (1969) Miliband portrayed the state as an agent or *instrument* of the ruling class, stressing the extent to which the state elite is disproportionately drawn from the ranks of the privileged and propertied. The bias of the state in favour of capitalism is therefore derived from the overlap of social backgrounds between, on the one hand, civil servants and other public officials, and, on the other, bankers, business leaders and captains of industry. Both groups, in other words, tend to be representatives of the capitalist class. Poulantzas, in *Political Power and Social Classes* (1968), dismissed this sociological approach, and emphasized instead the degree to which the *structure* of economic and social power exerts a constraint upon state autonomy. This view suggests that the state cannot but act to perpetuate the social system in which it operates. In the case of the capitalist state, its role is to serve the long-term interests of capitalism, even though these actions may be resisted by sections of the capitalist class itself. Examples of this are the extension of democratic rights and welfare reforms, both of which are concessions to the working class that nevertheless bind them to the capitalist system.

Developments within modern Marxism have brought about a significant convergence between pluralist and Marxist theories. Just as pluralists have increasingly recognized the importance of corporate power, neo-Marxists have been forced to abandon the idea that the state is merely a reflection of the class system. For one thing, neo-Marxists have recognized that, in modern circumstances, the classical two-class model (based on the bourgeoisie and the proletariat) is simplistic and often unhelpful. Following Poulantzas, neo-Marxists usually recognize that there are significant divisions within the ruling class (between financial and manufacturing capital, for instance) and that the emergence of electoral democracy has empowered interests and groups outside the ruling class. In addition, they have increasingly seen the state as the terrain upon which the struggle amongst interests, groups and classes is conducted. This is particularly clear in the case of Bob Jessop's (1982) 'strategic relational approach' to the state. Jessop saw the state not so much as a means of perpetuating capitalism through the dilution of class tensions, but as 'the crystallization of political strategies': that is, as an assemblage of institutions through which competing groups and interests struggle for domination or hegemony. In this view, the state is therefore not an 'instrument' wielded by a dominant group or ruling class. Rather, it is a dynamic entity that reflects the balance of power within society at any given time, and thus reflects the outcome of an ongoing hegemonic struggle.

The leviathan state

The image of the state as a 'leviathan' (in effect, a self-serving monster intent on expansion and aggrandizement) is one associated in modern politics with the New Right. Such a view is rooted in early or classical liberalism and, in particular, a commitment to a radical form of individualism (see p. 196). The New Right, or at least its neoliberal wing, is distinguished by a strong antipathy towards state intervention in economic and social life, born out of the belief that the state is a parasitic growth that threatens both individual liberty and economic security. In this view, the state, instead of being, as pluralists suggest, an impartial umpire or arbiter, is an overbearing 'nanny', desperate to interfere or meddle in every aspect of human existence. The central feature of this view is that the state pursues interests that are separate from those of society (setting it apart from Marxism), and that those interests demand an unrelenting growth in the role or responsibilities of the state itself. New Right thinkers therefore argue that the twentieth-century tendency towards state intervention reflected not popular pressure for economic and social security, or the need to stabilize capitalism by ameliorating class tensions, but rather the internal dynamics of the state.

New Right theorists explain the expansionist dynamics of state power by reference to both demand-side and supply-side pressures. Demand-side pressures are ones that emanate from society itself, usually through the mechanism of electoral democracy. As discussed in Chapter 4, the New Right argue that electoral competition encourages politicians to 'outbid' one another by making promises of increased spending and more generous government programmes, regardless of the long-term damage that such policies inflict on the economy in the form of increased taxes, higher inflation and the 'crowding out' of investment. Supply-side pressures, on the other hand, are ones that are internal to the state. These can therefore be explained in terms of the institutions and personnel of the state apparatus. In its most influential form, this argument is known as the government oversupply thesis.

The oversupply thesis has usually been associated with public-choice theorists (see p. 300), who examine how public decisions are made on the assumption that the individuals involved act in a rationally self-interested fashion. Niskanen (1971), for example, argued that, as budgetary control in legislatures such as the US Congress is typically weak, the task of budget-making is shaped largely by the interests of government agencies and senior bureaucrats. Insofar as this implies that government is dominated by the state (the state elite being able to shape the thinking of elected politicians), there are parallels between the public-choice model and the Marxist view discussed above. Where these two views diverge, however, is in relation to the interests that the state apparatus serves. While Marxists argue that the state reflects broader class and other social interests, the New Right portrays the state as an independent or autonomous entity that pursues its own interests. In this view, bureaucratic self-interest invariably supports 'big' government and state intervention, because this leads to an enlargement of the bureaucracy itself, which helps to ensure job security, improve pay, open up promotion prospects, and enhance the status of public officials. This image of self-seeking bureaucrats is plainly at odds with the pluralist notion of a state machine imbued with an ethic of public service and firmly subject to political control.

The patriarchal state

Modern thinking about the patriarchal state must, finally, take account of the implications of feminist theory. However, this is not to say that there is a systematic feminist theory of the state. As emphasized in Chapter 3, feminist theory encompasses a range of traditions and perspectives, and has thus generated a range of very different attitudes towards state power. Moreover, feminists have usually not

Concept

Patriarchy

Patriarchy literally means 'rule by the father', the domination of the husband–father within the family, and the subordination of his wife and his children. However, the term is usually used in the more, general sense of 'rule by men', drawing attention to the totality of oppression and exploitation to which women are subject. The use of the term patriarchy thus implies that the system of male power in society at large both reflects and stems from the dominance of the father in the family. Patriarchy is a key concept in radical feminist analysis, in that it emphasizes that gender inequality is systematic, institutionalized and pervasive. Socialist feminists, in contrast, highlight links between gender inequality and private property, seeing patriarchy and capitalism as parallel systems of domination.

Radical feminism: A form of feminism that holds gender divisions to be the most politically significant of social cleavages, and believes that they are rooted in the structure of domestic life.

regarded the nature of state power as a central political issue, preferring instead to concentrate on the deeper structure of male power centred upon institutions such as the family and the economic system. Some feminists, indeed, may question conventional definitions of the state, arguing, for instance, that the idea that the state exercises a monopoly of legitimate violence is compromised by the routine use of violence and intimidation in family and domestic life. Nevertheless, sometimes implicitly and sometimes explicitly, feminists have helped to enrich the state debate by developing novel and challenging perspectives on state power.

Liberal feminists, who believe that sexual or gender (see p. 201) equality can be brought about through incremental reform, have tended to accept an essentially pluralist view of the state. They recognize that, if women are denied legal and political equality, and especially the right to vote, the state is biased in favour of men. However, their faith in the state's basic neutrality is reflected in the belief that any such bias can, and will, be overcome by a process of reform. In this sense, liberal feminists believe that all groups (including women) have potentially equal access to state power, and that this can be used impartially to promote justice and the common good. Liberal feminists have therefore usually viewed the state in positive terms, seeing state intervention as a means of redressing gender inequality and enhancing the role of women. This can be seen in campaigns for equal-pay legislation, the legalization of abortion, the provision of child-care facilities, the extension of welfare benefits, and so on. Nevertheless, a more critical and negative view of the state has been developed by **radical feminists**, who argue that state power reflects a deeper structure of oppression in the form of patriarchy.

There are a number of similarities between Marxist and radical-feminist views of state power. Both groups, for example, deny that the state is an autonomous entity bent upon the pursuit of its own interests. Instead, the state is understood, and its biases are explained, by reference to a 'deep structure' of power in society at large. Whereas Marxists place the state in an economic context, radical feminists place it in a context of gender inequality, and insist that it is essentially an institution of male power. In common with Marxism, distinctive instrumentalist and structuralist versions of this feminist position have been developed. The *instrumentalist* argument views the state as little more than an 'agent' or 'tool' used by men to defend their own interests and uphold the structures of patriarchy. This line of argument draws on the core feminist belief that patriarchy is upheld by the division of society into distinct 'public' and 'private' spheres of life. The subordination of women has traditionally been accomplished through their confinement to a 'private' sphere of family and domestic responsibilities, turning them into housewives and mothers, and through their exclusion from a 'public' realm centred upon politics and the economy. Quite simply, in this view, the state is run *by* men, and it is run *for* men.

Whereas instrumentalist arguments focus upon the personnel of the state, and particularly the state elite, *structuralist* arguments tend to emphasize the degree to which state institutions are embedded in a wider patriarchal system. Modern radical feminists have paid particular attention to the emergence of the welfare state, seeing it as the expression of a new kind of patriarchal power. Welfare (see p. 439) may uphold patriarchy by bringing about a transition from private dependence (in which women as 'home makers' are dependent on men as 'breadwinners') to a system of public dependence in which women are increasingly controlled by the institutions of the extended state. For instance, women have become increasingly dependent on the state as clients or customers of state services (such as child-care institutions, nursery education and social work) and as employees, particularly in the so-called 'caring' professions (such as nursing, social work and education). Further, the extension of state responsibilities into traditionally female realms such as child rearing and caring has often merely created new forms of subordination. In particular, it has tended to reinforce the role of women as a **reserve army of labour**, with employers increasingly looking to women to provide a flexible, low-paid and usually submissive workforce.

The role of the state

Contrasting interpretations of state power have clear implications for the desirable role or responsibilities of the state. What should states do? What functions or responsibilities should the state fulfil, and which ones should be left in the hands of private individuals? In many respects, these are the questions around which electoral politics and party competition revolve. With the exception of anarchists, who dismiss the state as fundamentally evil and unnecessary, all political thinkers have regarded the state as, in some sense, worthwhile. Even revolutionary socialists, inspired by the Leninist slogan 'smash the state', have accepted the need for a temporary proletarian state to preside over the transition from capitalism to communism, in the form of the 'dictatorship of the proletariat'. Nevertheless, there is profound disagreement about the exact role the state should play, and therefore about the proper balance between the state and civil society. Among the different state forms that have developed are the following:

- the minimal state
- the developmental state
- the social-democratic state
- the collectivized state
- the totalitarian state.

Minimal states

The minimal state is the ideal of classical liberals, whose aim is to ensure that individuals enjoy the widest possible realm of freedom. This view is rooted in social-contract theory, but it nevertheless advances an essentially 'negative' view of the state. From this perspective, the value of the state is that it has the capacity to constrain human behaviour and thus to prevent individuals encroaching upon the **rights** and liberties of others. The state is merely a protective body, its core function being to provide a framework of peace and social order within which citizens can conduct their lives as they think best. In Locke's famous simile, the state acts as a night-watchman, whose services are called upon only when orderly existence is threatened. This nevertheless leaves the 'minimal' or 'nightwatchman' state with three core functions. First and foremost, the state exists to maintain domestic order. Second, it ensures that contracts or voluntary agreements made between private citizens are enforced, and third it provides protection against external attack. The institutional apparatus of a minimal state is thus limited to a police force, a court system and a military of some kind. Economic, social, cultural, moral and other responsibilities belong to the individual, and are therefore firmly part of civil society.

Reserve army of labour: An available supply of labour easily shed in times of recession; the 'army' enjoys no security and exercises little market power.

Rights: Legal or moral entitlements to act or be treated in a particular way; civil rights differ from human rights.

Robert Nozick (1938–2002)

US academic and political philosopher. Nozick's major work *Anarchy, State and Utopia* (1974) is widely seen as one of the most important contemporary works of political philosophy, and it has had a profound influence upon New Right theories and beliefs. He developed a form of libertarianism that was close to Locke's and clearly influenced by nineteenth-century US individualists such as Spooner (1808–87) and Tucker (1854–1939). He argued that property rights should be strictly upheld, provided that wealth has been justly acquired in the first place or has been justly transferred from one person to another. This position means support for minimal government and minimal taxation, and undermines the case for welfare and redistribution. Nozick's rights-based theory of justice was developed in response to the ideas of John Rawls (see p. 60). In later life, Nozick modified his extreme libertarianism.

The cause of the minimal state has been taken up in modern political debate by the New Right. Drawing on early liberal ideas, and particularly on free-market or classical economic theories, the New Right has proclaimed the need to 'roll back the frontiers of the state'. In the writings of Robert Nozick this amounts to a restatement of Lockean liberalism based on a defence of individual rights, especially property rights. In the case of free-market economists such as Friedrich von Hayek (see p. 52) and Milton Friedman (see p. 191) state intervention is seen as a 'dead hand' that reduces competition, efficiency and productivity. From the New Right perspective, the state's economic role should be confined to two functions: the maintenance of a stable means of exchange or 'sound money' (low or zero inflation), and the promotion of competition through controls on monopoly power, price fixing and so on.

Developmental states

The best historical examples of minimal states were those in countries such as the UK and the USA during the period of early industrialization in the nineteenth century. As a general rule, however, the later a country industrializes, the more extensive will be its state's economic role. In Japan and Germany, for instance, the state assumed a more active 'developmental' role from the outset. A developmental state is one that intervenes in economic life with the specific purpose of promoting industrial growth and economic development. This does not amount to an attempt to replace the market with a 'socialist' system of planning (see p. 192) and control, but rather to an attempt to construct a partnership between the state and major economic interests, often underpinned by conservative and nationalist priorities.

The classic example of a developmental state is Japan. During the Meiji Period in 1868–1912 the Japanese state forged a close relationship with the *zaibutsu*, the great family-run business empires that dominated the Japanese economy up to the Second World War. Since 1945 the developmental role of the Japanese state has been assumed by the Japanese Ministry of International Trade and Industry (MITI), which, together with the Bank of Japan, helps to shape private investment decisions and steer the Japanese economy towards international competitiveness. A similar model of developmental intervention has existed in France, where governments of both left and right have tended to recognize the need for economic planning, and the state bureaucracy has seen itself as the custodian of the national interest. In countries such as Austria and, to some extent, Germany, economic development has been achieved through the construction of a 'partnership state', in which an emphasis is placed on the maintenance of a close relationship between the state and major economic interests, notably big business and organized labour. More recently, economic globalization (see p. 143) has fostered the emergence of 'competition states', examples of which are found amongst the **tiger economies** of East Asia. Their role is to develop strategies for national prosperity in a context of intensifying transnational competition.

Social-democratic states

Whereas developmental states practise interventionism in order to stimulate economic progress, social-democratic states intervene with a view to bringing about broader social restructuring, usually in accordance with principles such as fairness, equality (see p. 440) and **social justice**. In countries such as Austria and Sweden, state intervention has been guided by both developmental and social-democratic priorities. Nevertheless, developmentalism and social democracy do not always go hand in hand. As Marquand (1988) pointed out, although the UK state was significantly extended in the period immediately after the Second World War along social-democratic lines, it failed to evolve into a developmental state. The key to understanding the social-democratic state is that there is a shift from a 'negative' view of the state, which sees it as little more than a necessary evil, to a 'positive' view of the state, in which it is seen as a means of enlarging liberty and promoting justice. The social-democratic state is thus the ideal of both modern liberals and democratic socialists.

Rather than merely laying down the conditions of orderly existence, the social-democratic state is an active participant, helping in particular to rectify the imbalances and injustices of a market economy. It therefore tends to focus less upon the generation of wealth and more upon what is seen as the equitable or just distribution of wealth. In practice, this boils down to an attempt to eradicate poverty and reduce social inequality. The twin features of a social-democratic state are therefore Keynesianism and social welfare. The aim of Keynesian economic policies is to 'manage' or 'regulate' capitalism with a view to promoting growth and maintaining full employment. Although this may entail an element of planning, the classic Keynesian strategy involves 'demand management' through adjustments in fiscal policy: that is, in the levels of public spending and taxation. The adoption of welfare policies has led to the emergence of so-called welfare states, whose responsibilities have extended to the promotion of social well-being amongst their citizens. In this sense, the social-democratic state is an 'enabling state', dedicated to the principle of individual empowerment.

Collectivized states

While developmental and social-democratic states intervene in economic life with a view to guiding or supporting a largely private economy, collectivized states bring the entirety of economic life under state control. The best examples of such states were in orthodox communist countries such as the USSR and throughout eastern Europe. These sought to abolish private enterprise altogether, and set up centrally planned economies administered by a network of economic ministries and planning

Tiger economies: Fast-growing and export-orientated economies modelled on Japan: for example, South Korea, Taiwan and Singapore.

Social justice: A morally justifiable distribution of material rewards; social justice is often seen to imply a bias in favour of equality.

Concept

Statism

Statism (or, in French, *étatisme*) is the belief that state intervention is the most appropriate means of resolving political problems or bringing about economic and social development. This view is underpinned by a deep and perhaps unquestioning faith in the state as a mechanism through which collective action can be organized and common goals can be achieved. The state is thus seen as an ethical ideal (Hegel), or as serving the 'general will' or public interest. Statism is most clearly reflected in government policies that regulate and control economic life. These range from selective nationalization and economic management (sometimes called *dirigisme*, from the French *diriger*, to direct) to corporatism (see p. 299) (in both liberal and fascist forms), and Soviet-style state collectivization.

committees. So-called 'command economies' were therefore established that were organized through a system of 'directive' planning that was ultimately controlled by the highest organs of the communist party. The justification for state **collectivization** stems from a fundamental socialist preference for common ownership over private property. However, the use of the state to attain this goal suggests a more positive attitude to state power than that outlined in the classical writings of Marx and Engels (1820–95).

Marx and Engels by no means ruled out nationalization, and Engels in particular recognized that, during the 'dictatorship of the proletariat', state control would be extended to include factories, the banks, transportation and so on. Nevertheless, they envisaged that the proletarian state would be strictly temporary, and that it would 'wither away' as class antagonisms abated. In contrast, the collectivized state in the USSR became permanent and increasingly powerful and bureaucratic. Under Stalin (see p. 57), socialism was effectively equated with statism, the advance of socialism being reflected in the widening responsibilities and powers of the state apparatus. Indeed, after Khrushchev announced in 1962 that the dictatorship of the proletariat had ended, the state was formally identified with the interests of 'the whole Soviet peoples'.

Totalitarian states

The most extreme and extensive form of interventionism is found in totalitarian states. The essence of totalitarianism (see p. 29) is the construction of an all-embracing state, the influence of which penetrates every aspect of human existence. The state brings not only the economy but education, culture, religion, family life and so on under direct state control. The best examples of totalitarian states are Hitler's Germany and Stalin's USSR, although modern regimes such as Saddam Hussein's Iraq arguably have similar characteristics. The central pillars of such regimes are a comprehensive process of surveillance and terroristic policing, and a pervasive system of ideological manipulation and control. In this sense, totalitarian states effectively extinguish civil society and abolish the 'private' sphere of life altogether. This is a goal that only fascists, who wish to dissolve individual identity within the social whole, are prepared openly to endorse. It is sometimes argued that Mussolini's notion of a totalitarian state was derived from Hegel's belief in the state as an 'ethical community' reflecting the altruism and mutual sympathy of its members. From this perspective, the advance of human civilization can clearly be linked to the aggrandisement of the state and the widening of its responsibilities.

■ The state in a global era

The state and globalization

The rise of globalization (see p. 143) has stimulated a major debate about the power and significance of the state in a globalized world. Three contrasting positions can be identified. In the first place, some theorists have boldly proclaimed the emergence of 'post-sovereign governance' (Scholte, 2005), suggesting that the rise of globalization is inevitably marked by the decline of the state as a meaningful actor. Power shifts away from the state and towards global marketplaces and transnational corporations

Collectivization: The abolition of private property in favour of a system of common or public ownership.

(TNCs) (see p. 149) in particular. In the most extreme version of this argument, advanced by so-called hyperglobalists, the state is seen to be so 'hollowed out' as to have become, in effect, redundant. Others, nevertheless, deny that globalization has altered the core feature of world politics, which is that, as in earlier eras, sovereign states are the primary determinants of what happens within their borders, and remain the principal actors on the world stage. In this view, globalization and the state are not separate or, still less, opposing forces: rather, and to a surprising degree, globalization has been created by states and thus exists to serve their interests. Between these two views, however, there is a third position, which acknowledges that globalization has brought about qualitative changes in the role and significance of the state, and in the nature of sovereignty, but emphasizes that these have transformed the state, rather than simply reduced or increased its power.

Developments such as the rise of international migration and the spread of cultural globalization have tended to make state borders increasingly 'permeable'. However, most of the discussion about the changing nature and power of the state has concerned the impact of economic globalization. The central feature of economic globalization is the rise of **'supraterritoriality'**, the process through which economic activity increasingly takes place within a 'borderless world' (Ohmae, 1989). This is particularly clear in relation to financial markets that have become genuinely globalized in that capital flows around the world seemingly instantaneously, meaning, for example, that no state can be insulated from the impact of financial crises in other parts of the world. It is also evident in the changing balance between the power of territorial states and of 'deterritorialized' transnational corporations (see p. 149), which can switch investment and production to other parts of the world if state policy is not conducive to profit maximization and the pursuit of corporate interests. Globalization, furthermore, has been closely associated with a trend towards regionalization, reflected in the growing prominence of regional trading blocs such as the European Union (EU) and the North American Free Trade Agreement (NAFTA).

If borders have become permeable and old geographical certainties have been shaken, state sovereignty, at least in its traditional sense, cannot survive. This is the sense in which governance in the twenty-first century has assumed a genuinely post-sovereign character. It is difficult, in particular, to see how **economic sovereignty** can be reconciled with a globalized economy. Sovereign control over economic life was only possible in a world of discrete national economies, and to the extent that these have been, or are being, incorporated into a single globalized economy, economic sovereignty becomes meaningless. However, the rhetoric of a 'borderless' global economy can be taken too far. For example, there has been, if anything, a growing recognition that market-based economies can only operate successfully within a context of legal and social order that only the state can guarantee (Fukuyama, 2005). Moreover, although states, when acting separately, may have a diminished capacity to control transnational economic activity, they retain the facility to do so through macro frameworks of economic regulation constructed via international organizations and processes, such as the G7/G8, the World Trade Organization (WTO) and the International Monetary Fund (IMF).

The power and significance of the state has also been affected by the process of **political globalization**. However, its impact has been complex and, in some ways, contradictory. On the one hand, international bodies such as the United Nations, the EU, NATO and the WTO have undermined the capacity of states to operate as self-governing political units. It is clear, for instance, that membership of the EU threatens

Supraterritoriality: The reconfiguration of geography that has occurred through the declining importance of state borders, geographical distance and territorial location.

Economic sovereignty: The absolute authority which the state exercises over economic life conducted within its borders, involving independent control of fiscal and monetary policies and control over trade and capital flows.

Political globalization: The growing importance of international bodies and organizations, which exercise jurisdiction within an international area comprising several states.

state power, because a growing range of decisions (for example, on monetary policy, agricultural and fisheries policy, defence and foreign affairs) are made by European institutions rather than by member states. This has created the phenomenon of **multi-level governance**. 'Pure' national governance has always been a myth (Sørensen, 2004). Nevertheless, the range and importance of decisions that are made at supra-national level has undoubtedly increased, forcing states either to exert influence in and through regional or global bodies, or to operate within frameworks established by them. The WTO, for example, acts as the judge and jury of global trade disputes and serves as a forum for negotiating trade deals between and amongst its members. On the other hand, political globalization opens up opportunities for the state as well as diminishes them. This occurs through the 'pooling' of sovereignty. For example, the EU Council of Ministers, the most powerful policy-making body in the Union, is very much a creature of its member states and provides a forum that allows national politicians to make decisions on a supranational level. By 'pooling' sovereignty, member states of the EU arguably gain access to a larger and more meaningful form of sovereignty. The 'pooled' sovereignty of the EU may thus be greater than the combined national sovereignties of its various member states.

State transformation

The state is a historical institution: it emerged in response to a particular set of cir-cumstances in sixteenth-century Europe, and it has continued to evolve in the light of changing circumstances. Having developed into a nation-state (see p. 123) in the nineteenth century, during the twentieth century, and especially the post-1945 period, the state acquired wider economic and social responsibilities, leading to the emergence of the social-democratic state, or the **welfare state**. However, the period since the 1980s has witnessed, more or less quickly in different countries, a general 'rolling back' of the state through the adoption of policies such as deregulation, pri-vatization and the introduction of market reforms in the public services. Although these trends were hastened by ideological forces, notably with the rise of the pro-market and anti-state ideas of the New Right, they were also dictated by broader and more irresistible forces. Amongst these were the pressures generated by increased global competition and the need to develop more efficient and responsive means of developing public policy and delivering public services. For many, this reflected a shift from government to 'governance' (see p. 6). As societies became more complex and fluid, new methods of governing had to be devised that relied less on hierarchi-cal state institutions and more on networks and the market, thus blurring the dis-tinction between the state and society. The 'governance turn' in politics has been characterized by what has been called the 'reinvention' of government, reflected in particular in a move away from direct service provision by the state to the adoption of an 'enabling' or 'regulating' role.

Such developments have led, some argue, to the emergence of a new form of state, portrayed variously as the 'competition' state, the 'market' state or the 'postmodern' state. Philip Bobbitt (2002) went as far as to argue that the transition from the nation-state to what he termed the market state heralded a profound shift in world politics, in that it marked the end of the 'long war' between liberalism, fascism and communism to define the constitutional form of the nation-state. The core feature of the market state is a shift away from 'top-down' economic management, based on the existence of discrete national economies, to an acceptance of the market as the only reliable

Multi-level governance: A complex policy process in which authority is distributed horizontally and vertically across subnational, national and supranational levels of government.

Welfare state: A state that takes primary responsibility for the social welfare of its citizens, discharged through a range of social-security, health, education and other services (albeit different in different societies).

principle of economic organization. Instead of trying to 'tame' capitalism, market states 'go with the flow'. Whereas states were previously judged on their effectiveness in promoting growth and prosperity, alleviating poverty and narrowing social inequality, market states base their legitimacy on their capacity to maximize the opportunities available to citizens and their ability to ensure effective and unimpeded market competition. The speed with which this has happened differs in different parts of the world, as states embrace the market-state model with greater or less enthusiasm and try to adapt it to their political cultures and economic needs. A particular form of market state has developed in the Asian 'tiger' economies, sometimes classified as the **competition state**. Competition states are distinguished by the recognition of the need to strengthen education and training as the principal way of guaranteeing economic success in the new technology-dependent, or 'weightless', economy.

The nature and significance of the state in the developing world is very different, however. In cases such as South Korea, Taiwan and, despite continuing high levels of poverty and illiteracy, India, developing-world states have successfully pursued strategies of economic modernization. Others, nevertheless, have been distinguished by their weakness, sometimes being described as 'weak states', 'quasi states', 'failed states', or, at times, 'rogue states'. Most of the weakest states in the world are concentrated in sub-Saharan Africa, classic examples being Somalia, Sierra Leone, Liberia and the Congo. These states are weak in that they fail the most basic test of state power: they are unable to maintain domestic order and personal security, meaning that civil strife and even civil war become almost routine. The weakness of such states stems primarily from the experience of colonialism (see p. 122), which, when it ended (mainly in the post-1945 period), bequeathed formal political independence to societies that lacked an appropriate level of political, economic, social and educational development to function effectively as separate entities. Robert Cooper (2004) dubbed these states 'pre-modern' states, in that they live in a world of post-imperial chaos, in which such state structures as exist are unable to establish (as Weber put it) a legitimate monopoly on the use of force, thus leading to **warlordism**, widespread criminality and social dislocation.

> ### Concept
>
> #### Weak state
>
> A weak state is a state that lacks the capacity for effective action across a range of state functions. Such states typically have inefficient and corrupt administrative structures that are incapable of maintaining social order and personal security. They generally suffer from low levels of legitimacy, usually due to the strength of local and ethnic allegiances. Finally, they have a negligible impact on economic life, often being dependent on external economic interests. However, states may be classified as 'weak' for a variety of other reasons. Weak states may be defined militarily, in terms of their ability to influence neighbouring states or, more importantly, resist external aggression. States may also be considered to be economically weak, in that they have only a limited role in regulating economic and social life. (The USA may be weak in the second sense, but certainly not in the first.)

Summary

◆ The state is a political association that exercises sovereign jurisdiction within defined territorial borders. In contrast to government, which is merely one of its parts, the state encompasses all public bodies and exercises impersonal authority on the basis of the assumption that it represents the permanent interests of society rather than the partisan sympathies of any group of politicians.

◆ There are a number of rival theories of the state. Pluralists hold that the state is a neutral body that arbitrates between the competing interests of society. Marxists argue that the state maintains the class system by either oppressing subordinate classes or ameliorating class conflict. The New Right portrays the state as a self-serving monster that is intent on expansion and aggrandisement. Radical feminists point to patriarchal biases within the state that support a system of male power.

◆ Those who support the state see it either as a means of defending the individual from the encroachments of fellow citizens or as a mechanism through which

Competition state: A state which pursues strategies to ensure long-term competitiveness in a globalized economy.

Warlordism: A condition in which locally-based militarized bands via for power in the absence of a sovereign state.

collective action can be organized. Critics, however, tend to suggest that the state reflects either the interests of dominant social groups, or interests that are separate from, and antithetical to, society.

◆ States have fulfilled very different roles. Minimal states merely lay down the conditions for orderly existence. Developmental states attempt to promote growth and economic development. Social-democratic states aim to rectify the imbalances and injustices of a market economy. Collectivized states exert control over the entirety of economic life. Totalitarian states bring about all-encompassing politicization and, in effect, extinguish civil society.

◆ Modern states have been profoundly affected by the rise of economic and political globalization, although there is debate about the extent to which this has weakened state power. Emergent market states are concerned less with the provision of 'economic goods' and more with maximizing the opportunities available to citizens. Nevertheless, some weak postcolonial states barely function as states, having a negligible capacity to maintain order.

◼ Questions for discussion

▶ Would life in a state of nature really be 'nasty, brutish and short'?

▶ Does government control the state, or does the state control government?

▶ Can the state be viewed as a neutral body in relation to competing social interests?

▶ Does the nature and background of the state elite inevitably breed bias?

▶ What is the proper relationship between the state and civil society?

▶ Does globalization mean that the state has become irrelevant?

▶ Has the nation-state been transformed into a market state?

◼ Further reading

Hay, C., M. Lister and D. Marsh, *The State: Theories and Issues* (Basingstoke and New York: Palgrave Macmillan, 2006). An accessible, comprehensive and contemporary introduction to the theoretical perspectives on the state and to key issues and controversies.

Jessop, B., *State Theory: Putting Capitalist States in Their Place* (Oxford: Polity Press, 1990). A demanding but worthwhile collection of essays through which Jessop develops his own approach to state theory.

Pierre, J. and B. Guy Peters, *Governance, Politics and the State* (Basingstoke: Palgrave Macmillan, 2000). A useful discussion of the phenomenon of governance and of its implications for the role and nature of the state.

Schwarzmantel, J., *The State in Contemporary Society: An Introduction* (London and New York: Harvester Wheatsheaf, 1994). A clear and useful introduction to the study of politics that focuses on rival views of the liberal-democratic state.

Sørensen, G., *The Transformation of the State: Beyond the Myth of Retreat* (Basingstoke and New York: Palgrave Macmillan, 2004). A systematic analysis of the contemporary state that assesses the nature and extent of its transformation in a global era.

PART 2

Nations and Globalization

· · · · · · · ·

Nations and Nationalism

CHAPTER 6

'Nationalism is an infantile disease. It is the measles of mankind.'
ALBERT EINSTEIN, *Letter* (1921)

For the last 200 years the nation has been regarded as the most appropriate (and perhaps the only proper) unit of political rule. Indeed, international law is largely based on the assumption that nations, like individuals, have inviolable rights, notably the right to political independence and self-determination. Nowhere, however, is the importance of the nation more dramatically demonstrated than in the potency of nationalism as a political creed. In many ways, nationalism has dwarfed the more precise and systematic political ideologies examined in Chapter 3. It has contributed to the outbreak of wars and revolutions. It has caused the birth of new states, the disintegration of empires and the redrawing of borders; and it has been used to reshape existing regimes as well as to bolster them. Nevertheless, there are reasons to believe that the age of the nation may be drawing to a close. The nation-state, the goal that generations of nationalists have strived to achieve, is increasingly beset by pressures, both internal and external.

The central issues examined in this chapter are as follows:

Key issues

▶ What is a nation?

▶ How do cultural nationalism and political nationalism differ?

▶ How can the emergence and growth of nationalism be explained?

▶ What political forms has nationalism assumed? What causes has it articulated?

▶ What are the attractions or strengths of the nation-state?

▶ Does the nation-state have a future?

Concept

Nation

Nations (from the Latin *nasci*, meaning 'to be born') are complex phenomena that are shaped by a collection of cultural, political and psychological factors. *Culturally*, a nation is a group of people bound together by a common language, religion, history and traditions, although nations exhibit various levels of cultural heterogeneity. *Politically*, a nation is a group of people who regard themselves as a natural political community. Although this is classically expressed in the form of a desire to establish or maintain statehood, it can also take the form of civic consciousness. *Psychologically*, a nation is a group of people distinguished by a shared loyalty or affection in the form of patriotism (see p. 119). However, such an attachment is not a necessary condition for membership of a nation; even those who lack national pride may still recognize that they 'belong' to the nation.

Ethnic group: A group of people who share a common cultural and historical identity, typically linked to a belief in common descent.

What is a nation?

Many of the controversies surrounding the phenomenon of nationalism can be traced back to rival views about what constitutes a nation. So widely accepted is the idea of the nation that its distinctive features are seldom examined or questioned; the nation is simply taken for granted. Nevertheless, confusion abounds. The term 'nation' tends to be used with little precision, and is often used interchangeably with terms such as state, country, ethnic group and race. The United Nations, for instance, is clearly misnamed, as it is an organization of states, not one of national populations. What, then, are the characteristic features of the nation? What distinguishes a nation from any other social group or other sources of collective identity?

The difficulty of defining the term 'nation' springs from the fact that all nations comprise a mixture of objective and subjective features, a blend of cultural and political characteristics. In *objective* terms, nations are cultural entities: groups of people who speak the same language, have the same religion, are bound by a shared past, and so on. Such factors undoubtedly shape the politics of nationalism. The nationalism of the Québecois in Canada, for instance, is based largely on language differences between French-speaking Quebec and the predominantly English-speaking rest of Canada. Nationalist tensions in India invariably arise from religious divisions, examples being the struggle of Sikhs in Punjab for a separate homeland (Khalistan), and the campaign by Muslims in Kashmir for the incorporation of Kashmir into Pakistan. Nevertheless, it is impossible to define a nation using objective factors alone. All nations encompass a measure of cultural, ethnic and racial diversity. The Swiss nation has proved to be enduring and viable despite the use of three major languages (French, German and Italian), as well as a variety of local dialects. Divisions between Catholics and Protestants that have given rise to rival nationalisms in Northern Ireland have been largely irrelevant in mainland UK, and of only marginal significance in countries such as Germany.

This emphasizes the fact that, ultimately, nations can only be defined *subjectively* by their members. In the final analysis, the nation is a psycho-political construct. What sets a nation apart from any other group or collectivity is that its members regard themselves as a nation. What does this mean? A nation, in this sense, perceives itself to be a distinctive political community. This is what distinguishes a nation from an **ethnic group**. An ethnic group undoubtedly possesses a communal identity and a sense of cultural pride, but, unlike a nation, it lacks collective political aspirations. These aspirations have traditionally taken the form of the quest for, or the desire to maintain, political independence or statehood. On a more modest level, however, they may consist of a desire to achieve a measure of autonomy, perhaps as part of a federation or confederation of states.

The complexity does not end there, however. Nationalism is a difficult political phenomenon, partly because various nationalist traditions view the concept of a nation in different ways. Two contrasting concepts have been particularly influential. One portrays the nation as primarily a cultural community, and emphasizes the importance of ethnic ties and loyalties. The other sees it essentially as a political community, and highlights the significance of civil bonds and allegiances. These rival views not only offer alternative accounts of the origins of nations, but have also been linked to very different forms of nationalism.

Johann Gottfried Herder (1744–1803)

German poet, critic and philosopher, often portrayed as the 'father' of cultural nationalism. A teacher and Lutheran clergyman, Herder travelled throughout Europe before settling in 1776 in Weimar as the clerical head of the Grand Duchy. Although influenced in his early life by thinkers such as Kant (see p. 129), Rousseau (see p. 79) and Montesquieu (see p. 336), he became a leading intellectual opponent of the Enlightenment and a crucial influence on the growth in Germany of the romantic movement. Herder's emphasis on the nation as an organic group characterized by a distinctive language, culture and 'spirit' helped both to found cultural history, and to give rise to a particular form of nationalism that emphasized the intrinsic value of national culture.

Nations as cultural communities

The idea that a nation is essentially an ethnic or cultural entity has been described as the 'primary' concept of the nation (Lafont, 1968). Its roots can be traced back to late eighteenth-century Germany and the writings of figures such as Herder and Fichte (1762–1814). For Herder, the innate character of each national group was ultimately determined by its natural environment, climate and physical geography, which shaped the lifestyle, working habits, attitudes and creative propensities of a people. Above all, he emphasized the importance of language, which he believed was the embodiment of a people's distinctive traditions and historical memories. In his view, each nation thus possesses a **Volksgeist**, which reveals itself in songs, myths and legends, and provides a nation with its source of creativity. Herder's nationalism therefore amounts to a form of culturalism that emphasizes an awareness and appreciation of national traditions and collective memories instead of an overtly political quest for statehood. Such ideas had a profound impact on the awakening of national consciousness in nineteenth-century Germany, reflected in the rediscovery of ancient myths and legends in, for example, the folk tales of the Grimm brothers and the operas of Richard Wagner (1813–83).

The implication of Herder's culturalism is that nations are 'natural' or organic entities that can be traced back to ancient times and will, by the same token, continue to exist as long as human society survives. A similar view has been advanced by modern social psychologists, who point to the tendency of people to form groups in order to gain a sense of security, identity and belonging. From this perspective, the division of humankind into nations reflects nothing more than the natural human propensity to draw close to people who share a culture, background and lifestyle that is similar to their own. Such psychological insights, however, do not explain nationalism as a historical phenomenon: that is, as one that arose at a particular time and place, specifically in early nineteenth-century Europe.

In *Nations and Nationalism* (1983) Ernest Gellner emphasized the degree to which nationalism is linked to modernization and, in particular, to the process of industrialization. Gellner stressed that, while premodern or 'agroliterate' societies were structured by a network of feudal bonds and loyalties, emerging industrial societies promoted social mobility, self-striving and competition, and so required a new source of cultural cohesion. This was provided by nationalism. Nationalism

Volksgeist: (*German*) Literally, the spirit of the people; the organic identity of a people reflected in their culture and particularly their language.

Concept

Cultural nationalism

Cultural nationalism is a form of nationalism that places primary emphasis on the regeneration of the nation as a distinctive civilization, rather than as a discrete political community. Not uncommonly, cultural nationalists view the state as a peripheral, if not alien, entity. Whereas political nationalism is 'rational', and usually principled, cultural nationalism is 'mystical', in that it is based on a romantic belief in the nation as a unique, historical and organic whole, animated by its own 'spirit'. Typically, it is a 'bottom-up' form of nationalism that draws more on 'popular' rituals, traditions and legends than on elite, or 'higher', culture. Though often antimodern in character, cultural nationalism may also serve as an agent of modernization by enabling a people to 'recreate' itself.

therefore developed to meet the needs of particular social conditions and circumstances. On the other hand, Gellner's theory suggests that nationalism is now ineradicable, as a return to premodern loyalties and identities is unthinkable. However, in *The Ethnic Origins of Nations* (1986) Anthony Smith challenged the idea of a link between nationalism and modernization by highlighting the continuity between modern nations and premodern ethnic communities, which he called 'ethnies'. In this view, nations are historically embedded: they are rooted in a common cultural heritage and language that may long predate the achievement of statehood or even the quest for national independence. Smith nevertheless acknowledged that, although ethnicity is the precursor of nationalism, modern nations came into existence only when established ethnies were linked to the emerging doctrine of political sovereignty (see p. 131). This conjunction occurred in Europe in the late eighteenth century and early nineteenth century, and in Asia and Africa in the twentieth century.

Regardless of the origins of nations, certain forms of nationalism have a distinctively cultural, rather than political, character. Cultural nationalism commonly takes the form of national self-affirmation; it is a means through which a people can acquire a clearer sense of its own identity through the heightening of national pride and self-respect. This is demonstrated by Welsh nationalism, which focuses much more on attempts to preserve the Welsh language and Welsh culture in general than on the search for political independence. Black nationalism in the USA, the West Indies and many parts of Europe also has a strong cultural character. Its emphasis is on the development of a distinctively black consciousness and sense of national pride, which, in the work of Marcus Garvey (see p. 175) and Malcolm X (1926–65), was linked to the rediscovery of Africa as a spiritual and cultural 'homeland'. A similar process can be seen at work in modern Australia and, to some extent, New Zealand. The republican movement in Australia, for example, reflects the desire to redefine the nation as a political and cultural unit separate from the UK. This is a process of self-affirmation that draws heavily upon the Anzac myth, the relationship with indigenous peoples, and the rediscovery of a settler folk culture.

The German historian Friedrich Meinecke (1907) went one step further and distinguished between 'cultural nations' and 'political nations'. 'Cultural' nations are characterized by a high level of ethnic homogeneity; in effect, national and ethnic identities overlap. Meinecke identified the Greeks, the Germans, the Russians, the English and the Irish as examples of cultural nations, but the description could equally apply to ethnic groups such as the Kurds, the Tamils and the Chechens. Such nations can be regarded as 'organic', in that they have been fashioned by natural or historical forces, rather than by political ones. The strength of cultural nations is that, bound together by a powerful and historical sense of national unity, they tend to be stable and cohesive. On the other hand, cultural nations tend to view themselves as exclusive groups. Membership of the nation is seen to derive not from a political allegiance, voluntarily undertaken, but from an ethnic identity that has somehow been inherited. Cultural nations thus tend to view themselves as extended kinship groups distinguished by common descent. In this sense, it is not possible to 'become' a German, a Russian or a Kurd simply by adopting the language and beliefs of the people. Such exclusivity has tended to breed insular and regressive forms of nationalism, and to weaken the distinction between nation and race (see p. 200).

Nations as political communities

The view that nations are essentially political entities emphasizes civic loyalties and political allegiances rather than cultural identity. The nation is thus a group of people who are bound together primarily by shared citizenship, regardless of their cultural, ethnic and other loyalties. This view of the nation is often traced back to the writings of Jean-Jacques Rousseau (see p. 79), sometimes seen as the 'father' of modern nationalism. Although Rousseau did not specifically address the nation question, or discuss the phenomenon of nationalism, his stress on popular sovereignty, expressed in the idea of the 'general will' (in effect, the common good of society), was the seed from which nationalist doctrines sprang during the French Revolution of 1789. In proclaiming that government should be based upon the general will, Rousseau developed a powerful critique of monarchical power and aristocratic privilege. During the French Revolution, this principle of radical democracy was reflected in the assertion that the French people were 'citizens' possessed of inalienable rights and liberties, no longer merely 'subjects' of the crown. Sovereign power thus resided with the 'French nation'. The form of nationalism that emerged from the French Revolution therefore embodied a vision of a people or nation governing itself, and was inextricably linked to the principles of liberty, equality and fraternity.

The idea that nations are political, not ethnic, communities has been supported by a number of theories of nationalism. Eric Hobsbawm (1983), for instance, highlighted the degree to which nations are 'invented traditions'. Rather than accepting that modern nations have developed out of long-established ethnic communities, Hobsbawm argued that a belief in historical continuity and cultural purity was invariably a myth, and, what is more, a myth created by nationalism itself. In this view, nationalism creates nations, not the other way round. A widespread consciousness of nationhood (sometimes called popular nationalism) did not, for example, develop until the late nineteenth century, perhaps fashioned by the invention of national anthems and national flags, and the extension of primary education. Certainly, the idea of a 'mother tongue' passed down from generation to generation and embodying a national culture is highly questionable. In reality, languages live and grow as each generation adapts the language to its own distinctive needs and circumstances. Moreover, it can be argued that the notion of a 'national' language is an absurdity, given the fact that, until the nineteenth century, the majority of people had no knowledge of the written form of their language and usually spoke a regional dialect that had little in common with the language of the educated elite.

Benedict Anderson (1983) also portrayed the modern nation as an artefact, in his case as an 'imagined community'. Anderson pointed out that nations exist more as mental images than as genuine communities that require a level of face-to-face interaction to sustain the notion of a common identity. Within nations, individuals only ever meet a tiny proportion of those with whom they supposedly share a national identity. If nations exist, they exist as imagined artifices, constructed for us through education, the mass media and a process of political socialization (see p. 233). Whereas in Rousseau's view a nation is animated by ideas of democracy and political freedom, the notion that nations are 'invented' or 'imagined' communities has more in common with the Marxist belief that nationalism is a species of bourgeois ideology. From the perspective of orthodox Marxism, nationalism is a device through which the ruling class counters the threat of social revolution by ensuring that national loyalty is stronger than class solidarity, thus binding the working class to the existing power structure.

Whether nations spring out of a desire for liberty and democracy or are merely cunning inventions of political elites or a ruling class, certain nations have an unmistakably political character. Following Meinecke, these nations can be classified as 'political nations'. A 'political' nation is one in which citizenship has greater political significance than ethnic identity; not uncommonly, political nations contain a number of ethnic groups, and so are marked by cultural heterogeneity. The UK, the USA and France have often been seen as classic examples of political nations. The UK is a union of what, in effect, are four 'cultural' nations: the English, the Scottish, the Welsh and the Northern Irish (although the latter may comprise two nations, the Protestant Unionists and the Catholic Republicans). Insofar as there is a distinctively British national identity, this is based on political factors such as a common allegiance to the Crown, respect for the Westminster Parliament, and a belief in the historic rights and liberties of the British people. As a 'land of immigrants', the USA has a distinctively multiethnic and multicultural character, which makes it impossible for it to construct a national identity on the basis of shared cultural and historical ties. Instead, a sense of American nationhood has been consciously developed through the educational system, and through the cultivation of respect for a set of common values, notably those outlined in the Declaration of Independence and the US Constitution. Similarly French national identity is closely linked to the traditions and principles of the 1789 French Revolution.

What such nations have in common is that, in theory, they were founded upon a voluntary acceptance of a common set of principles or goals, as opposed to an existing cultural identity. It is sometimes argued that the style of nationalism that develops in such societies is typically tolerant and democratic. If a nation is primarily a political entity, it is an inclusive group, in that membership is not restricted to those who fulfil particular language, religious, ethnic or suchlike criteria. Classic examples are the USA, with its image as a 'melting pot' nation, and the 'new' South Africa, seen as a 'rainbow society'. On the other hand, political nations may at times fail to experience the organic unity and sense of historical rootedness that is found in cultural nations. This may, for instance, account for the relative weakness of specifically British nationalism in the UK, by comparison with Scottish and Welsh nationalism and the insular form of English nationalism that is sometimes called 'little Englander' nationalism.

Developing world states have encountered particular problems in their struggle to achieve a national identity. Such nations can be described as 'political' in two senses. First, in many cases, they have achieved statehood only after a struggle against colonial rule (see p. 122). In this case, the nation's national identity is deeply influenced by the unifying quest for national liberation and freedom. Third world nationalism therefore tends to have a strong anticolonial character. Second, these nations have often been shaped by territorial boundaries inherited from their former colonial rulers. This has particularly been the case in Africa. African 'nations' often encompass a wide range of ethnic, religious and regional groups that are bound together by little more than a shared colonial past. In contrast to the creation of classic European cultural nations, which sought statehood on the basis of a preexisting national identity, an attempt has been made in Africa to 'build' nations on the foundations of existing states. However, the resulting mismatch of political and ethnic identities has bred recurrent tensions, as has been seen in Nigeria, Sudan,

Rwanda and Burundi, for example. However, such conflicts are by no means simply manifestations of ancient 'tribalism'. To a large extent they are a consequence of the divide-and-rule policies used in the colonial past.

◼ Varieties of nationalism

Immense controversy surrounds the political character of nationalism. On the one hand, nationalism can appear to be a progressive and liberating force, offering the prospect of national unity or independence. On the other, it can be an irrational and reactionary creed that allows political leaders to conduct policies of military expansion and war in the name of the nation. Indeed, nationalism shows every sign of suffering from the political equivalent of multiple-personality syndrome. At various times, nationalism has been progressive and reactionary, democratic and authoritarian, liberating and oppressive, and left-wing and right-wing. For this reason, it is perhaps better to view nationalism not as a single or coherent political phenomenon, but as a series of 'nationalisms': that is, as a complex of traditions that share but one characteristic – each, in its own particular way, acknowledges the central political importance of the nation.

This confusion derives in part from the controversies examined above about how the concept of a nation should be understood, and about whether cultural or political criteria are decisive in defining the nation. However, the character of nationalism is also moulded by the circumstances in which nationalist aspirations arise, and by the political causes to which it is attached. Thus, when nationalism is a reaction against the experience of foreign domination or colonial rule, it tends to be a liberating force linked to the goals of liberty, justice and democracy. When nationalism is a product of social dislocation and demographic change, it often has an insular and exclusive character, and can become a vehicle for racism (see p. 120) and **xenophobia**. Finally, nationalism is shaped by the political ideals of those who espouse it. In their different ways, liberals, conservatives, socialists, fascists and even communists have been attracted to nationalism (of the major ideologies, perhaps only anarchism is entirely at odds with nationalism). In this sense, nationalism is a cross-cutting ideology. The principal political manifestations of nationalism are the following:

- liberal nationalism
- conservative nationalism
- expansionist nationalism
- anticolonial nationalism.

Liberal nationalism

Liberal nationalism can be seen as the classic form of European liberalism; it dates back to the French Revolution, and embodies many of its values. Indeed, in continental Europe in the mid-nineteenth century, to be a nationalist meant to be a liberal, and *vice versa*. The 1848 Revolutions, for example, fused the struggle for national independence and unification with the demand for limited and constitutional government. Nowhere was this more evident than in the 'Risorgimento' (rebirth) nationalism of the Italian nationalist movement, especially as expressed by the 'prophet' of Italian unification, Guiseppe Mazzini (see p. 116). Similar principles

Xenophobia: A fear or hatred of foreigners; pathological ethnocentrism.

Guiseppe Mazzini (1805–72)

Italian nationalist and apostle of liberal republicanism. Mazzini was born in Genoa, Italy, and was the son of a doctor. He came into contact with revolutionary politics as a member of the patriotic secret society, the Carbonari. This led to his arrest and exile to France and, after his expulsion from France, to Britain. He returned briefly to Italy during the 1848 Revolutions, helping to liberate Milan and becoming head of the short-lived Roman Republic. A committed republican,

Mazzini's influence thereafter faded as other nationalist leaders, including Garibaldi (1807–82), looked to the House of Savoy to bring about Italian unification. Although he never officially returned to Italy, Mazzini's liberal nationalism had a profound influence throughout Europe, and on immigrant groups in the USA.

were espoused by Simon Bolivar (1783–1830), who led the Latin-American independence movement in the early nineteenth century, and helped to expel the Spanish from Hispanic America. Perhaps the clearest expression of liberal nationalism is found in US President Woodrow Wilson's 'Fourteen Points'. Drawn up in 1918, these were proposed as the basis for the reconstruction of Europe after the First World War, and provided a blueprint for the sweeping territorial changes that were implemented by the Treaty of Versailles (1919).

In common with all forms of nationalism, liberal nationalism is based on the fundamental assumption that humankind is naturally divided into a collection of nations, each possessed of a separate identity. Nations are therefore genuine or organic communities, not the artificial creation of political leaders or ruling classes. The characteristic theme of liberal nationalism, however, is that it links the idea of the nation with a belief in popular sovereignty, ultimately derived from Rousseau. This fusion was brought about because the multinational empires against which nineteenth-century European nationalists fought were also autocratic and oppressive. Mazzini, for example, wished not only to unite the Italian states, but also to throw off the influence of autocratic Austria. The central theme of this form of nationalism is therefore a commitment to the principle of **national self-determination**. Its goal is the construction of a nation-state (see p. 123): that is, a state within which the boundaries of government coincide as far as possible with those of nationality. In J. S. Mill's ([1861] 1951:392) words:

> When the sentiment of nationality exists in any force, there is a *prima facie* case for uniting all members of the nationality under one government, and a government to themselves apart. This is merely saying that the question of government should be decided by the governed.

Liberal nationalism is above all a principled form of nationalism. It does not uphold the interests of one nation against other nations. Instead, it proclaims that each and every nation has a right to freedom and self-determination. In this sense, all nations are equal. The ultimate goal of liberal nationalism, then, is the construction of a world of sovereign nation-states. Mazzini thus formed the clandestine organization Young Italy to promote the idea of a united Italy, but he also founded Young Europe in the hope of spreading nationalist ideas throughout the continent. Similarly, at the Paris Peace Conference that drew up the Treaty of Versailles, Woodrow Wilson advanced the principle of self-determination not simply because the breakup of European empires served US national interests, but because he believed that the

National self-determination:
The principle that the nation is a sovereign entity; self-determination implies both national independence and democratic rule.

Poles, the Czechs, the Yugoslavs and the Hungarians all had the same right to political independence that the Americans already enjoyed.

From this perspective, nationalism is not only a means of enlarging political freedom, but also a mechanism for securing a peaceful and stable world order. Wilson, for instance, believed that the First World War had been a consequence of an 'old order' that was dominated by autocratic and militaristic empires bent on expansionism and war. In his view, democratic nation-states, however, would be essentially peaceful, because, possessing both cultural and political unity, they lacked the incentive to wage war or subjugate other nations. In this light, nationalism is not seen as a source of distrust, suspicion and rivalry. Rather, it is a force capable of promoting unity within each nation and brotherhood amongst nations on the basis of mutual respect for national rights and characteristics.

There is a sense, nevertheless, in which liberalism looks beyond the nation. This occurs for two reasons. The first is that a commitment to individualism implies that liberals believe that all human beings (regardless of factors such as race, creed, social background and nationality) are of equal moral worth. Liberalism therefore subscribes to universalism, in that it accepts that individuals everywhere have the same status and entitlements. This is commonly expressed nowadays in the notion of **human rights**. In setting the individual above the nation, liberals establish a basis for violating national sovereignty, as in the international campaign to pressurize the 'white' South African regime to abandon apartheid. The second reason is that liberals fear that a world of sovereign nation-states may degenerate into an international 'state of nature'. Just as unlimited freedom allows individuals to abuse and enslave one another, national sovereignty may be used as a cloak for expansionism and conquest. Freedom must always be subject to the law, and this applies equally to individuals and to nations. Liberals have, as a result, been in the forefront of campaigns to establish a system of international law (see p. 154) supervised by supranational bodies such as the League of Nations, the United Nations and the European Union. In this view, nationalism must therefore never be allowed to become insular and exclusive, but, instead, must be balanced against a competing emphasis upon cosmopolitanism (see p. 217).

Criticisms of liberal nationalism tend to fall into two categories. In the first category, liberal nationalists may be accused of being naive and romantic. They see the progressive and liberating face of nationalism; theirs is a tolerant and rational nationalism. However, they perhaps ignore the darker face of nationalism: that is, the irrational bonds of **tribalism** that distinguish 'us' from a foreign and threatening 'them'. Liberals see nationalism as a universal principle, but they have less understanding of the emotional power of nationalism, which, in time of war, can persuade people to fight, kill and die for 'their' country, almost regardless of the justice of their nation's cause. Such a stance is expressed in the assertion: 'my country, right or wrong'.

Second, the goal of liberal nationalism (the construction of a world of nation-states) may be fundamentally misguided. The mistake of Wilsonian nationalism, on the basis of which large parts of the map of Europe were redrawn, was that it assumed that nations live in convenient and discrete geographical areas, and that states can be constructed to coincide with these areas. In practice, all so-called 'nation-states' comprise a number of linguistic, religious, ethnic and regional groups, some of which may consider themselves to be 'nations'. This has nowhere been more clearly demonstrated than in the former Yugoslavia, a country viewed by the peacemakers at Versailles as 'the land of the Slavs'. However, it in fact consisted

Human rights: Rights to which people are entitled by virtue of being human; universal and fundamental rights (see p. 326).

Tribalism: Group behaviour characterized by insularity and exclusivity, typically fuelled by hostility towards rival groups.

of a patchwork of ethnic communities, religions, languages and differing histories. Moreover, as the disintegration of Yugoslavia in the early 1990s demonstrated, each of its constituent republics was itself an ethnic patchwork. Indeed, as the Nazis and later the Bosnian Serbs recognized, the only certain way of achieving a politically unified and culturally homogeneous nation-state is through a programme of **ethnic cleansing**.

Conservative nationalism

Historically, conservative nationalism developed rather later than liberal nationalism. Until the latter half of the nineteenth century, conservative politicians treated nationalism as a subversive, if not revolutionary, creed. As the century progressed, however, the link between conservatism and nationalism became increasingly apparent, for instance, in Disraeli's 'One Nation' ideal, in Bismarck's willingness to recruit German nationalism to the cause of Prussian aggrandisement, and in Tsar Alexander III's endorsement of pan-Slavic nationalism. In modern politics, nationalism has become an article of faith for most, if not all, conservatives. In the UK this was demonstrated most graphically by Margaret Thatcher's triumphalist reaction to victory in the Falklands War of 1982, and it is evident in the engrained 'Euroscepticism' of the Conservative right, particularly in relation to its recurrent bogey: a 'federal Europe'. A similar form of nationalism was rekindled in the USA through the adoption of a more assertive foreign policy, by Reagan in the invasion of Grenada and the bombing of Libya, and by Bush in the invasion of Panama and the 1991 Gulf War.

Conservative nationalism is concerned less with the principled nationalism of universal self-determination and more with the promise of social cohesion and public order embodied in the sentiment of national patriotism. Above all, conservatives see the nation as an organic entity emerging out of a basic desire of humans to gravitate towards those who have the same views, habits, lifestyles and appearance as themselves. In short, human beings seek security and identity through membership of a national community. From this perspective, patriotic loyalty and a consciousness of nationhood is rooted largely in the idea of a shared past, turning nationalism into a defence of values and institutions that have been endorsed by history. Nationalism thus becomes a form of traditionalism. This gives conservative nationalism a distinctively nostalgic and backward-looking character. In the USA, this is accomplished through an emphasis on the Pilgrim Fathers, the War of Independence, the Philadelphia Convention and so on. In the case of British nationalism (or, more accurately, English nationalism), national patriotism draws on symbols closely associated with the institution of monarchy. The UK national anthem is *God Save the Queen*, and the Royal Family play a prominent role in national celebrations such as Armistice Day, and on state occasions such as the opening of Parliament.

Conservative nationalism tends to develop in established nation-states rather than in ones that are in the process of nation building. It is typically inspired by the perception that the nation is somehow under threat, either from within or from without. The traditional 'enemy within' has been class antagonism and the ultimate danger of social revolution. In this respect, conservatives have seen nationalism as the antidote to socialism: when patriotic loyalties are stronger than class solidarity, the working class is, effectively, integrated into the nation. Calls for national unity and the belief that unabashed patriotism is a civic virtue are therefore recurrent

Ethnic cleansing: The forcible expulsion or extermination of 'alien' peoples; often used as a euphemism for genocide.

themes in conservative thought. The 'enemies without' that threaten national identity include immigration and supranationalism.

In this view, immigration poses a threat because it tends to weaken an established national culture and ethnic identity, thereby provoking hostility and conflict. This fear was expressed in the UK in the 1960s by Enoch Powell, who warned that further Commonwealth immigration would lead to racial conflict and violence. A similar theme was taken up in 1979 by Margaret Thatcher in her reference to the danger of the UK being 'swamped' by immigrants. Anti-immigration campaigns waged by the British National Party, Le Pen's National Front in France, and far-right groups in Germany such as the Republicans also draw their inspiration from conservative nationalism. National identity, and with it our source of security and belonging, is threatened in the same way by the growth of supranational bodies and by the globalization of culture. Resistance in the UK and in other EU member states to a single European currency reflects not merely concern about the loss of economic sovereignty, but also a belief that a national currency is vital to the maintenance of a distinctive national identity.

Although conservative nationalism has been linked to military adventure and expansion, its distinctive character is that it is inward-looking and insular. If conservative governments have used foreign policy as a device to stoke up public fervour, this is an act of political opportunism rather than because conservative nationalism is relentlessly aggressive or inherently militaristic. This leads to the criticism that conservative nationalism is essentially a form of elite manipulation or ruling-class ideology. From this perspective, the 'nation' is invented and certainly defined by political leaders and ruling elites with a view to manufacturing consent and engineering political passivity. In crude terms, when in trouble, all governments play the 'nationalism card'. A more serious criticism of conservative nationalism, however, is that it promotes intolerance and bigotry. Insular nationalism draws upon a narrowly cultural concept of the nation: that is, the belief that a nation is an exclusive ethnic community, broadly similar to an extended family. A very clear line is therefore drawn between those who are members of the nation and those who are alien to it. By insisting upon the maintenance of cultural purity and established traditions, conservatives may portray immigrants, or foreigners in general, as a threat, and so promote, or at least legitimize, racialism and xenophobia.

Expansionist nationalism

The third form of nationalism has an aggressive, militaristic and expansionist character. In many ways, this form of nationalism is the antithesis of the principled belief in equal rights and self-determination that is the core of liberal nationalism. The aggressive face of nationalism first appeared in the late nineteenth century as European powers indulged in 'the scramble for Africa' in the name of national glory and their 'place in the sun'. Nineteenth-century European imperialism (see p. 132) differed from the colonial expansion of earlier periods in that it was fuelled by a climate of popular nationalism in which national prestige was increasingly linked to the possession of an empire, and each colonial victory was greeted by demonstrations of popular enthusiasm, or **jingoism**. To a large extent, both world wars of the twentieth century resulted from this expansionist form of nationalism. When the First World War broke out in August 1914, following a prolonged arms race and a succession of international crises, the prospect of conquest and military glory provoked spontaneous

Concept

Patriotism

Patriotism (from the Latin *patria*, meaning 'fatherland') is a sentiment, a psychological attachment to one's nation (a 'love of one's country'). The terms nationalism and patriotism are often confused. Nationalism has a doctrinal character and embodies the belief that the nation is in some way the central principle of political organization. Patriotism provides the affective basis for that belief. Patriotism thus underpins all forms of nationalism; it is difficult to conceive of a national group demanding, say, political independence without possessing at least a measure of patriotic loyalty or national consciousness. However, not all patriots are nationalists. Not all of those who identify with, or even love, their nation see it as a means through which political demands can be articulated.

Jingoism: A mood of public enthusiasm and celebration provoked by military expansion or imperial conquest.

Concept

Racialism, racism

The terms racialism and racism are often used interchangeably, although the latter has become more common in modern usage. Racialism includes any belief or doctrine that draws political or social conclusions from the idea that humankind is divided into biologically distinct races. Racialist theories are thus based on two assumptions. First, genetic differences justify humankind being treated as a collection of races (race effectively implying species). Second, cultural, intellectual and moral differences amongst humankind derive from these more fundamental genetic differences. In political terms, racialism is manifest in calls for racial segregation (apartheid), and in doctrines of 'blood' superiority and inferiority (for example, Aryanism and anti-Semitism). Racism may be used more narrowly to refer to prejudice or hostility towards people on the grounds of their racial origins, whether or not this is linked to a developed racial theory.

public rejoicing in all the major capitals of Europe. The Second World War was largely a result of the nationalist-inspired programmes of imperial expansion pursued by Japan, Italy and Germany. The most destructive modern example of this form of nationalism in Europe has been the quest by the Bosnian Serbs to construct a 'Greater Serbia'.

In its extreme form, such nationalism arises from a sentiment of intense, even hysterical nationalist enthusiasm, sometimes referred to as integral nationalism. The term integral nationalism was coined by the French nationalist Charles Maurras (1868–1952), leader of the right-wing Action Française. The centrepiece of Maurras' politics was an assertion of the overriding importance of the nation: the nation is everything and the individual is nothing. The nation thus has an existence and meaning beyond the life of any single individual, and individual existence has meaning only when it is dedicated to the unity and survival of the nation. Such fanatical patriotism has a particularly strong appeal for the alienated, isolated and powerless, for whom nationalism becomes a vehicle through which pride and self-respect can be regained. However, integral nationalism breaks the link previously established between nationalism and democracy. An 'integral' nation is an exclusive ethnic community, bound together by primordial loyalties rather than voluntary political allegiances. National unity does not demand free debate and an open and competitive struggle for power; it requires discipline and obedience to a single, supreme leader. This led Maurras to portray democracy as a source of weakness and corruption, and to call instead for the reestablishment of monarchical absolutism.

This militant and intense form of nationalism is invariably associated with chauvinistic beliefs and doctrines. Derived from the name of Nicolas Chauvin, a French soldier noted for his fanatical devotion to Napoleon and the cause of France, chauvinism is an irrational belief in the superiority or dominance of one's own group or people. National chauvinism therefore rejects the idea that all nations are equal in favour of the belief that nations have particular characteristics and qualities, and so have very different destinies. Some nations are suited to rule; others are suited to be ruled. Typically, this form of nationalism is articulated through doctrines of ethnic or racial superiority, thereby fusing nationalism and racialism. The chauvinist's own nation is seen to be unique and special, in some way a 'chosen people'. For early German nationalists such as Fichte and Jahn, only the Germans were a true *Volk* (an organic people). They alone had maintained blood purity and avoided the contamination of their language. For Maurras, France was an unequalled marvel, a repository of all Christian and classical virtues.

No less important in this type of nationalism, however, is the image of another nation or race as a threat or enemy. In the face of the enemy, the nation draws together and gains an intensified sense of its own identity and importance, achieving a kind of 'negative integration'. Chauvinistic nationalism therefore establishes a clear distinction between 'them' and 'us'. There has to be a 'them' to deride or hate in order for a sense of 'us' to be forged. The world is thus divided, usually by means of racial categories, into an 'in group' and an 'out group'. The 'out group' acts as a scapegoat for all the misfortunes and frustrations suffered by the 'in group'. This was most graphically demonstrated by the virulent anti-Semitism that was the basis of German Nazism. Hitler's *Mein Kampf* ([1925] 1969) portrayed history as a Manichean struggle between the Aryans and the Jews, respectively representing the forces of light and darkness, or good and evil.

A recurrent theme of expansionist nationalism is the idea of national rebirth or regeneration. This form of nationalism commonly draws upon myths of past great-ness or national glory. Mussolini and the Italian Fascists looked back to the days of Imperial Rome. In portraying their regime as the 'Third Reich', the German Nazis harked back both to Bismarck's 'Second Reich' and Charlemagne's Holy Roman Empire, the 'First Reich'. Such myths plainly give expansionist nationalism a back-ward-looking character, but they also look to the future in that they mark out the nation's destiny. If nationalism is a vehicle for reestablishing greatness and regaining national glory, it invariably has a militaristic and expansionist character. In short, war is the testing ground of the nation. At the heart of integral nationalism there often lies an imperial project: a quest for expansion or a search for colonies. This can be seen in forms of **pan-nationalism.** However, Nazi Germany is again the best-known example. Hitler's writings mapped out a three-stage programme of expansion. First, the Nazis sought to establish a 'Greater Germany' by bringing ethnic Germans in Austria, Czechoslovakia and Poland within an expanded Reich. Second, they intended to achieve *Lebensraum* (living space) by establishing a German-dominated empire stretching into Russia. Third, Hitler dreamed of ultimate Aryan world domination.

Anticolonial nationalism

The developing world has spawned various forms of nationalism, all of which have in some way drawn inspiration from the struggle against colonial rule. The irony of this form of nationalism is that it has turned doctrines and principles first developed through the process of 'nation building' in Europe against the European powers themselves. Colonialism, in other words, succeeded in turning nationalism into a political creed of global significance. In Africa and Asia, it helped to forge a sense of nationhood shaped by the desire for 'national liberation'. Indeed, during the twentieth century, the political geography of much of the world was transformed by anticolonialism. Independence movements that sprang up in the interwar period gained new impetus after the conclusion of the Second World War. The over-stretched empires of Britain, France, the Netherlands and Portugal crumbled in the face of rising nationalism.

India had been promised independence during the Second World War, which was eventually granted in 1947. China achieved genuine unity and independence only after the 1949 communist revolution, having fought an eight-year war against the occupying Japanese. A republic of Indonesia was proclaimed in 1949 after a three-year war against the Netherlands. A military uprising forced the French to withdraw from Vietnam in 1954, even though final liberation, with the unification of North and South Vietnam, was not achieved until 1975, after 14 further years of war against the USA. Nationalist struggles in South East Asia inspired similar movements in Africa, with liberation movements emerging under leaders such as Nkrumah in Ghana, Dr Azikiwe in Nigeria, Julius Nyerere in Tanganyika (later Tanzania), and Hastings Banda in Nyasaland (later Malawi). The pace of decolon-ization in Africa accelerated from the late 1950s onwards. Nigeria gained independ-ence from the UK in 1960 and, after a prolonged war fought against the French, Algeria gained independence in 1962. Kenya became independent in 1963, as did Tanzania and Malawi the next year. Africa's last remaining colony, South-West Africa, finally became independent Namibia in 1990.

Early forms of anticolonialism drew heavily on 'classical' European nationalism and were inspired by the idea of national self-determination. However, emergent

Concept

Anti-Semitism

Semites are by tradition the descendants of Shem, son of Noah. They include most of the peoples of the Middle East. Anti-Semitism is prejudice or hatred towards Jews. In its earliest systematic form, anti-Semitism had a *religious* character. It reflected the hostility of the Christians towards the Jews, based on the alleged complicity of the Jews in the murder of Jesus and their refusal to acknowledge him as the son of God. *Economic* anti-Semitism developed from the Middle Ages onwards, and expressed distaste for Jews in their capacity as moneylenders and traders. Jews were thus excluded from membership of craft guilds and prevented from owning land. The nineteenth century saw the birth of *racial* anti-Semitism in the work of Wagner and H. S. Chamberlain (1855–1929), which condemned the Jewish peoples as fundamentally evil and destructive. These ideas provided the ideological basis for German Nazism and found their most grotesque expression in the Holocaust.

Pan-nationalism: A style of nationalism dedicated to unifying a disparate people through either expansionism or political solidarity ('pan' means all or every).

Concept

Colonialism

Colonialism is the theory or practice of establishing control over a foreign territory and turning it into a 'colony'. Colonialism is thus a particular form of imperialism (see p. 132). Colonialism is usually distinguished by settlement and by economic domination. As typically practised in Africa and South East Asia, colonial government was exercised by a settler community from a 'mother country' who were ethnically distinct from the 'native' population. In French colonialism, colonies were thought of as part of the mother country, meaning that colonial peoples were granted formal rights of citizenship. In contrast, neocolonialism is essentially an economic phenomenon based on the export of capital from an advanced country to a less developed one, as seen, for example, in so-called US 'dollar imperialism' in Latin America.

African and Asian nations were in a very different position from the newly created European states of the nineteenth century. For African and Asian nations, the quest for political independence was inextricably linked to a desire for social development and for an end to their subordination to the industrialized states of Europe and the USA. The goal of 'national liberation' therefore had an economic as well as a political dimension. This helps to explain why anticolonial movements typically looked not to liberalism but to socialism, and particularly to Marxism–Leninism, as a vehicle for expressing their nationalist ambitions. On the surface, nationalism and socialism appear to be incompatible political creeds. Socialists have traditionally preached internationalism (see p. 130), since they regard humanity as a single entity, and argue that the division of humankind into separate nations breeds only suspicion and hostility. Marxists in particular have stressed that the bonds of class solidarity are stronger and more genuine than the ties of nationality, or, as Marx put it in the *Communist Manifesto* ([1848] 1967:102): 'Working men have no country'.

The appeal of socialism to the developing world is based on the fact that the values of community and cooperation that socialism embodies are deeply established in the cultures of traditional, preindustrial societies. In this sense, nationalism and socialism are linked insofar as both emphasize social solidarity and collective action. By this standard, nationalism may simply be a weaker form of socialism, the former applying the 'social' principle to the nation, the latter extending it to cover the whole of humanity. More specifically, socialism, and especially Marxism, provide an analysis of inequality and exploitation through which the colonial experience can be understood and colonial rule challenged. In the same way as the oppressed and exploited proletariat saw that they could achieve liberation through the revolutionary overthrow of capitalism, third-world nationalists saw 'armed struggle' as a means of achieving both political and economic emancipation, thus fusing the goals of political independence and social revolution. In countries such as China, North Korea, Vietnam and Cambodia, anticolonial movements openly embraced Marxism–Leninism. On achieving power, they moved to seize foreign assets and nationalize economic resources, creating Soviet-style planned economies. African and Middle Eastern states have developed a less ideological form of nationalistic socialism, which has been practised, for example, in Algeria, Libya, Zambia, Iraq and South Yemen. The 'socialism' proclaimed in these countries has usually taken the form of an appeal to a unifying national cause or interest, typically championed by a powerful 'charismatic' leader.

However, nationalists in the developing world have not always been content to express their nationalism in a language of socialism or Marxism borrowed from the West. Especially since the 1970s, Marxism–Leninism has often been displaced by forms of religious fundamentalism (see p. 66), and particularly Islamic fundamentalism. This has given the developing world a specifically nonwestern, indeed an antiwestern, voice. In theory at least, Islam attempts to foster a transnational political identity that unites all those who acknowledge the 'way of Islam' and the teachings of the Prophet Muhammad within an 'Islamic nation'. However, the Iranian revolution of 1979, which brought Ayatollah Khomeini (1900–89) to power, demonstrated the potency of Islamic fundamentalism as a creed of national and spiritual renewal. The establishment of an 'Islamic republic' was designed to purge Iran of the corrupting influence of western materialism in general and of the 'Great Satan' (the USA) in particular through a return to the traditional values and principles embodied in the *Shari'a*, or divine Islamic law. By no means, however, does Islamic nationalism have a unified character. In Sudan and Pakistan, for example, Islamification has essentially been used as a tool of statecraft to consolidate the power of ruling elites. Nevertheless, in Egypt and Algeria revolutionary Islamic movements have emerged that call for moral renewal and political purification in the name of the urban poor.

■ A future for the nation-state?

As the twentieth century progressed, claims were increasingly made that the age of nationalism was over. This was not because nationalism had been superseded by 'higher' supernational allegiances, but because its task had been completed: the world had become a world of nation-states. In effect, the nation had been accepted as the sole legitimate unit of political rule. Certainly, since 1789, the world had been fundamentally remodelled on nationalist lines. In 1910, only 15 of the 192 states recognized in 2006 as full members of the United Nations existed. Well into the twentieth century, most of the peoples of the world were still colonial subjects of one of the European empires. Only three of the current 65 states in the Middle East and Africa existed before 1910, and no fewer than 107 states have come into being since 1959. These changes have been fuelled largely by the quest for national independence, with these new states invariably assuming the mantle of the nation-state.

History undoubtedly seems to be on the side of the nation-state. The three major geopolitical upheavals of the twentieth century (the First World War, the Second World War and the collapse of communism in eastern Europe) each gave considerable impetus to the concept of the nation as a principle of political organization. Since 1991 at least 18 new states have come into existence in Europe alone (14 of them as a result of the disintegration of the USSR), and all of them have claimed to be nation-states. The great strength of the nation-state is that it offers the prospect of both cultural cohesion and political unity. When a people who share a common cultural or ethnic identity gain the right to self-government, community and citizenship coincide. This is why nationalists believe that the forces that have created a world of independent nation-states are natural and irresistible, and that no other social group could constitute a meaningful political community. They believe that the nation-state is ultimately the only viable political unit. This view implies, for instance, that supranational bodies such as the European Union will never be able to rival the capacity of national governments to establish legitimacy and command popular allegiance. Clear limits should therefore be placed on the process of European integration because people with different languages, cultures and histories will never come to think of themselves as members of a united political community.

Nevertheless, just as the principle of the nation-state has achieved its widest support, other, very powerful forces have emerged that threaten to make the nation-state redundant. A combination of internal pressures and external threats has produced what is commonly referred to as a 'crisis of the nation-state'. Internally, nation-states have been subject to centrifugal pressures, generated by an upsurge in ethnic, regional and multicultural politics. This heightened concern with ethnicity and culture may, indeed, reflect the fact that, in a context of economic and cultural globalization (see p. 143), nations are no longer able to provide a meaningful collective identity or sense of social belonging. Given that all nation-states embody a measure of cultural diversity, the politics of ethnic assertiveness cannot but present a challenge to the principle of the nation, leading some to suggest that nationalism is

> ◆ **Concept**
>
> **Nation-state**
>
> The nation-state is a form of political organization, and a political ideal. In the first case, it is an autonomous political community bound together by the overlapping bonds of citizenship and nationality. It is thus an alternative to multinational empires and city-states. In the latter case, the nation-state is a principle, or ideal type (see p. 18), reflected in Mazzini's goal: 'every nation a state, only one state for the entire nation'. As such, the nation-state principle embodies the belief that nations are 'natural' political communities, whose strength derives from overlapping civic and cultural bonds. There are two contrasting views of the nation-state. For liberals and most socialists, the nation-state is largely fashioned out of civic loyalties and allegiances. For conservatives and integral nationalists, it is based on ethnic or organic unity.

in the process of being replaced by multiculturalism (see p. 215). Unlike nations, ethnic, regional or cultural groups are not viable political entities in their own right, and have thus sometimes looked to forms of federalism (see p. 167) and confederalism to provide an alternative to political nationalism. For example, within the framework provided by the European Union, the Belgian regions of Flanders and Wallonia have achieved such a degree of self-government that Belgium remains a nation-state only in a strictly formal sense. The nature of such centrifugal forces is discussed more fully in Chapter 8.

External threats to the nation-state have a variety of forms. First, advances in the technology of warfare, and especially the advent of the nuclear age, have brought about demands that world peace be policed by supranational and international bodies. This led to the creation of the League of Nations and later the United Nations. Second, economic life has been progressively globalized. Markets are now world markets, businesses have increasingly become transnational corporations (see p. 149, and capital is moved around the globe in the flick of an eyelid. Is there a future for the nation-state in a world in which no national government can control its economic destiny? Third, the nation-state may be the enemy of the natural environment and a threat to the global ecological balance. Nations are concerned primarily with their own strategic and economic interests, and most pay little attention to the ecological consequences of their actions. The folly of this was demonstrated by the Chernobyl nuclear accident in the Ukraine in 1986, which released a wave of nuclear radiation across Northern Europe that will cause an estimated 2000 cancer-related deaths over 50 years in Europe.

Finally, distinctive national cultures and traditions, the source of cohesion that distinguishes nation-states from other forms of political organization, have been weakened by the emergence of a transnational and even global culture. This has been facilitated by international tourism and the dramatic growth in communications technologies, from satellite television to the 'information superhighway'. When US films and television programmes are watched throughout the world, Indian and Chinese cuisine is as popular in Europe as native dishes, and people can communicate as easily with the other side of the world as with their neighbouring town, is the nation-state any longer a meaningful entity? These and related issues are discussed in greater depth in Chapter 7.

■ Summary

◆ Nations are defined by a combination of cultural and political factors. Culturally, they are groups of people who are bound together by a common language, religion, history and traditions. Ultimately, however, nations define themselves through the existence of a shared civic consciousness, classically expressed as the desire to achieve or maintain statehood.

◆ Distinctive cultural and political forms of nationalism can be identified. Cultural nationalism emphasizes the regeneration of the nation as a distinctive civilization on the basis of a belief in the nation as a unique, historical and organic whole. Political nationalism, on the other hand, recognizes the nation as a discrete political community, and is thus linked with ideas such as sovereignty and self-determination.

◆ Some political thinkers portray nationalism as a modern phenomenon associated with industrialization and the rise of democracy, while others trace it back to premodern ethnic loyalties and identities. The character of nationalism has varied considerably, and has been influenced by both the historical circumstances in which it has arisen and the political causes to which it has been attached.

◆ There have been a number of contrasting manifestations of political nationalism. Liberal nationalism is based on a belief in a universal right to self-determination. Conservative nationalism values the capacity of national patriotism to deliver social cohesion and political unity. Expansionist nationalism is a vehicle for aggression and imperial conquest. Anticolonial nationalism is associated with the struggle for national liberation, often fused with the quest for social development.

◆ The most widely recognized form of political organization worldwide is the nation-state, which is often seen as the sole legitimate unit of political rule. Its strength is that it offers the prospect of both cultural cohesion and political unity, thus allowing those who share a common cultural or ethnic identity to exercise the right to independence and self-government.

◆ The nation-state now confronts a number of challenges. Nation-states have been subject to centrifugal pressures generated by the growth in ethnic politics. Externally, they have confronted challenges from the growing power of supranational bodies, the advance of economic and cultural globalization, and the need to find international solutions to the environmental crisis.

Questions for discussion

▶ Where do nations come from? Are they natural or artificial formations?

▶ Why have national pride and patriotic loyalty been valued?

▶ Does cultural nationalism merely imprison a nation in its past?

▶ Why has nationalism proved to be such a potent political force?

▶ Does nationalism inevitably breed insularity and conflict?

▶ Is the nation-state the sole legitimate unit of political rule?

▶ Is a postnationalist world possible?

Further reading

Brown, D., *Contemporary Nationalism: Civic, Ethnocultural and Multicultural Politics* (London and New York: Routledge, 2000). A clear and illuminating framework for understanding nationalist politics.

Gellner, E., *Nations and Nationalism* (Ithaca, NY: Cornell University Press, 1983). A highly influential account of the emergence and character of nationalism.

Hearn, J., *Rethinking Nationalism: A Critical Introduction* (Basingstoke and New York: Palgrave Macmillan, 2006). A comprehensive account of approaches to understanding nationalism that draws on sociology, politics, anthropology and history, and develop its own critique.

Hobsbawm, E., *Nations and Nationalism Since 1780*, 2nd edn (Cambridge: Cambridge University Press, 1993). An analysis of the phenomenon of nationalism from a modern Marxist perspective.

Spencer, P. and H. Wollman (eds) *Nations and Nationalism: A Reader* (Edinburgh: Edinburgh University Press, 2005). A wide-ranging and stimulating collection of mainstream and less mainstream writings on nationalism.

CHAPTER 7

Global Politics

'War, in our scientific age, means, sooner or later, universal death.'

BERTRAND RUSSELL, *Unpopular Essays*, (1950)

The late twentieth century brought with it recognition that the world had become, in Marshall McLuhan's words, a 'global village'. The phenomenon of globalization has completely altered our understanding of politics and of the nature of political interaction. The traditional view of politics was state-centric: the state was treated as the principal political actor, and attention was focused on the national level of government activity. It therefore followed that there was a clear distinction between domestic politics and foreign politics: that is, between what took place within a nation-state and what took place outside its borders. The latter, indeed, became the subject matter of a new and separate discipline, international relations. However, globalization has weakened, and perhaps destroyed, the distinction between 'the domestic' and 'the foreign', leading, some have argued, to the emergence of a world society. Although nation-states continue to be the most significant actors on the world stage, the growing impact of supranational bodies and of transnational groups and organizations is impossible to deny.

The central issues examined in this chapter are as follows:

Key issues

▶ How has international or world politics been analysed and explained?

▶ How has world order been affected by the end of the Cold War and the advent of the 'war on terror'?

▶ What is globalization? What are its implications for the nation-state?

▶ Is globalization a beneficial or a destructive force?

▶ What are the prospects for supranational regional bodies?

▶ Could the idea of a world government ever become a reality?

Contents

◼ Understanding world politics

The recognition that there is an international dimension to politics is as old as the discipline itself, going back to accounts of conflict and war between the city-states of Ancient Greece. However, the modern international system did not come into existence until the emergence of centralized states in the sixteenth and seventeenth centuries. This process was completed by the Treaty of Westphalia (1648), which brought the Thirty Years War to an end with a formal recognition by the European powers of the sovereign independence of each state. The European state system was subsequently extended when the USA was recognized, after its defeat of Spain in 1898, as a great power, and when Japan was also so recognised after its victory over Russia in 1904–05. Imperialism (see p. 132), and especially the European 'scramble for colonies' in Africa and Asia in the late nineteenth century, gave the international system a truly global dimension.

The twentieth century thus witnessed the emergence of world politics in the sense that patterns of conflict and cooperation amongst states and international organizations extended across the globe. This was most chillingly seen in the First World War (1914–18), the Second World War (1939–45), and the Cold War (see p. 133). As the twentieth century drew to a close, however, there was a growing recognition that the very parameters of political life had changed. This more radically called into question the conventional distinction between a domestic realm and an international realm of politics. These complex and multifaceted changes have increasingly been referred to as 'globalization' (see p. 143).

In order to analyse these and other developments, however, it is necessary to examine the various perspectives from which international and world politics have traditionally been examined. The major theoretical 'schools' of international politics are the following:

- idealism
- realism
- pluralism
- Marxism.

Idealism

The defining characteristic of idealism is that it views international politics from the perspective of moral values and legal norms. It is concerned less with empirical analysis (that is, with how international actors behave) than with normative judgements (that is, with how they *should* behave). For this reason, idealism is sometimes seen as a species of utopianism (see p. 27). A broad range of idealist theories have been developed. In the Middle Ages, for instance, Thomas Aquinas (1224–74) discussed the nature of a 'just war', attempting to place the international actions of rulers in a moral context. He argued that war could be justified only if three conditions were met. First, it had to be declared by a ruler who had the authority to do so. Second, the cause that the war was fought in had to be just in the sense that it avenged a wrong. Third, the intention of just belligerence had to be to achieve good or avoid evil, not to give vent to greed or cruelty. Immanuel Kant developed what amounted to an early vision of world government. In his view, morality and reason combined to

Immanuel Kant (1724–1804)

German philosopher. Kant spent his entire life in Königsberg (which was then in East Prussia), becoming professor of logic and metaphysics at the University of Königsberg in 1770. His 'critical' philosophy holds that knowledge is not merely an aggregate of sense impressions; it depends on the conceptual apparatus of human understanding. Kant's political thought was shaped by the central importance of morality. He believed that the law of reason dictated categorical imperatives, the most important of which was the obligation to treat others as 'ends', and never only as 'means'. Kant's (1970) most important works include *Critique of Pure Reason* (1781), *Critique of Practical Reason* (1788) and *Critique of Judgement* (1790).

dictate that there should be no war, the future of humankind being based on the prospect of 'universal and lasting peace'.

Most forms of idealism are underpinned by internationalism: that is, the belief that human affairs should be organized according to universal, and not merely national, principles. This, in turn, is usually reflected in the assumption that human affairs, on both the domestic and international levels, are characterized by harmony and cooperation. One of the most influential forms of idealism has been found in liberalism. Although liberals have traditionally accepted the nation as the principal unit of political organization, they have also stressed the importance of interdependence and free trade, arguing quite simply that 'war does not pay'. Such internationalism is also reflected in a faith in collective security (see p. 158) and international law (see p. 159), which is embodied in organizations such as the League of Nations and the United Nations. President Woodrow Wilson of the USA, for example, argued that the First World War had resulted from the 'old politics' of militarism and expansionism pursued by multinational empires. In his view, the best antidote to war was the construction of a world of democratic nation-states that were prepared to cooperate in areas of common interest and had no incentive to embark upon conquest or plunder.

After years of ridicule and denigration at the hands of realist theorists, idealism was revived in the late twentieth century. What has usually been called **neo-idealism** reflects disenchantment with the amoral power politics of the superpower era. An early example of this was the attempt by President Carter in the 1970s to restore a moral dimension to US foreign policy by emphasizing that economic and military aid depended on the human-rights records of recipient regimes. The theme of international cooperation and common security was taken up more boldly in the late 1980s by the Soviet president Mikhail Gorbachev, who spoke of a 'common European house', and proclaimed that the doctrine of human rights transcended the ideological rivalry between communism and capitalism.

In many respects, the prospect of nuclear annihilation (the product of years of escalating military spending by both East and West) gave greater impetus to idealist theories. This was reflected in the emergence of the peace movement, which embraced a broadly internationalist philosophy that was often linked to pacifism, a principled rejection of war and all forms of violence as fundamentally evil. The neo-idealist position has also been advanced in relation to the notion of a 'world society', which is usually associated with the Australian diplomat and scholar John Burton

Neo-idealism: A perspective on international politics that emphasizes the practical value of morality and, in particular, respect for human rights and national independence.

Concept

Internationalism

Internationalism is the theory or practice of politics based on transnational or global cooperation. It is rooted in universalist assumptions about human nature that put it at odds with political nationalism, the latter emphasizing the degree to which political identity is shaped by nationality. The major internationalist traditions are drawn from liberalism and socialism. *Liberal* internationalism is based on individualism. This is reflected, for example, in the belief that universal human rights ultimately have a 'higher' status than the sovereign authority of the nation. *Socialist* internationalism is grounded in a belief in international class solidarity (proletarian internationalism), underpinned by assumptions about a common humanity. Feminism and environmentalism have also advanced distinctive internationalist positions.

Power politics: An approach to politics based on the assumption that the pursuit of power is the principal human goal; the term is sometimes used descriptively.

Balance of power: A pattern of interaction amongst states that tends to curb aggression and expansionism by rendering them impracticable.

Great power: A state deemed to rank amongst the most powerful in a hierarchical state system, reflected in its influence over minor states.

(1972). The world-society perspective rejects as obsolete the notion of sovereign nation-states, emphasizing instead a pattern of complexity and interdependence that Burton portrayed through the image of a cobweb. Such a view suggests that the power politics of old has largely given way to noncoercive and cooperative means of solving international conflicts.

Realism

The realist tradition, sometimes called 'political realism', can claim to be the oldest theory of international politics. It can be traced back to Thucydides' account of the Peloponnesian War (431 BCE), and to Sun Tzu's classic work on strategy, *The Art of War*, written at roughly the same time in China. Other significant figures in the realist tradition are Machiavelli (see p. 6) and Thomas Hobbes (see p. 327). However, realism only became the dominant international perspective during the twentieth century, receiving its impetus from the First World War and Second World War. Whereas idealism emphasizes that international relations should be guided by morality, realism is grounded in an emphasis on **power politics** and the pursuit of national interests. Its central assumption is that the state is the principal actor on the international or world stage, and, being sovereign, is able to act as an autonomous entity. Moreover, the rise of nationalism and the emergence of modern nation-states (see p. 123) transformed the state into a cohesive political community, within which all other loyalties and ties are subordinate to those to the nation.

Realist scholars, such as E. H. Carr (1939) and Hans Morgenthau (1948), were particularly scathing about the idealist belief in internationalism and natural harmony. Carr, in fact, argued that a naive faith in international law and collective security in the interwar period prevented statesmen on both sides of the Atlantic from understanding, and so acting to contain, German expansion. Realists emphasize that, in contrast, as there is no higher authority than the sovereign state, international politics is conducted in a 'state of nature', and is thus characterized by anarchy, not harmony. An anarchic international system is one in which each state is forced to help itself and give priority to its own national interest, defined, most basically, as state survival and territorial defence.

This is why realists place such a heavy emphasis on the role of power in international affairs, and why they tend to understand power in terms of military capacity or force. By no means, however, does international anarchy mean relentless conflict and unending war. Instead, realists insist that the pattern of conflict and cooperation within the state system conforms largely to the requirements of a **balance of power**. This view recognizes that, in pursuit of national security, states enter into alliances that, if balanced against one another, may ensure prolonged periods of peace and international stability. However, this type of international system is inherently dynamic, and when the balance of power breaks down, war is the probable result.

Realists have always acknowledged that the international order is not a classic 'state of nature', because power, wealth and resources are not equally distributed amongst states. Major actors have traditionally been accorded the status of **great powers** (during the Cold War, superpowers). The resulting hierarchy of states imposes a measure of order on the international system, reflecting the control that great powers exercise over subordinate ones through trading blocs, 'spheres of influence', and outright colonization (see p. 122). During the Cold War period this led to the creation of a bipolar world order in which rivalry between the US and Soviet power

Sovereignty

Sovereignty, in its simplest sense, is the principle of absolute and unlimited power. However, distinctions are commonly made between legal and political sovereignty, and between internal and external notions of sovereignty. *Legal* sovereignty refers to supreme legal authority: that is, an unchallengeable right to demand compliance, as defined by law. *Political* sovereignty, in contrast, refers to unlimited political power: that is, the ability to command obedience, which is typically ensured by a monopoly of coercive force. *Internal* sovereignty is the notion of a supreme power/authority within the state, located in the body that makes decisions that are binding on all citizens, groups and institutions within the state's territorial boundaries. *External* sovereignty relates to a state's place in the international order and its capacity to act as an independent and autonomous entity.

blocs extended over much of the globe. Realists have been prepared to argue, however, that bipolarity helped to maintain peace as escalating military spending led to an effective system of nuclear deterrents, especially once the condition of mutually assured destruction (MAD) was recognized in the 1960s. A stable hierarchy based on accepted rules and recognized processes thus kept anarchy at bay, and encouraged realists to adopt the modified idea of what Hedley Bull (1977) termed an 'anarchical society'.

During the 1980s, **neo-realism** (sometimes called 'new' or structural realism) developed under the influence of Waltz (1979) and others. While neo-realists continue to acknowledge the central importance of power, they tend to explain events in terms of the structure of the international system rather than the goals and make-up of individual states.

Realism and neo-realism have attracted fierce criticism, however. The central objection is that, in divorcing politics from morality, the realist perspective legitimizes military escalation and the hegemonic ambitions of great powers. This view suggests that power politics has not so much maintained peace as kept the world on the verge of nuclear catastrophe. A second critique of realism is advanced by feminist theorists, who contend that power-seeking behaviour and an obsession with national security and military might reflect the worldwide dominance of male politicians whose priorities are essentially aggressive and competitive. The central empirical weakness of realist theories is that, in focusing attention on the state as the dominant international actor, they have ignored the pluralistic tendencies that reshaped the face of international politics in the late twentieth century. 'Classical' realism has thus largely given way to neo-realism.

Pluralism

The pluralist perspective on international politics emerged, particularly in the USA, in the 1960s and 1970s, and it built on a bedrock of liberal ideas and values. In its traditional sense, pluralism (see p. 82) is a sociopolitical theory that emphasizes the diffusion of power amongst a number of competing bodies or groups. As a theory of international politics, it highlights the permeability of the state, and provides an alternative to the state-centrism of the realist model. The limitations of the state-centric approach were illustrated by John Burton's (1972) simile of the billiard table. This suggests that realism assumes that states, like billiard balls, are impermeable and self-contained units, which influence each other through external pressure.

Neo-realism: A perspective on international politics that modifies the power-politics model by highlighting the structural constraints of the international system.

Concept

Imperialism

Imperialism is, broadly, the policy of extending the power or rule of a state beyond its boundaries. In its earliest usage, imperialism was an ideology that supported military expansion and imperial acquisition, usually by drawing on nationalist and racialist doctrines. The term is now more commonly used to describe the system of political domination or economic exploitation that the pursuit of such goals helped to establish. In the Marxist tradition, imperialism is seen as an economic phenomenon that typically results from the pressure to export capital. Neo-Marxists, however, draw attention to a more subtle form of imperialism, termed neocolonialism, through which industrialized powers control foreign territory by economic domination while respecting the territory's formal political independence. Realist theorists, however, view imperialism more as a political phenomenon, seeing it as the pursuit by states of power and strategic advantage through expansion and conquest.

Sovereign states interacting in a system of international anarchy are thus seen to behave like a collection of billiard balls moving over the table and colliding with other balls. According to pluralists, this simile distorts international politics in that it both ignores the degree to which influence is increasingly exerted by transnational actors such as multinational corporations (MNCs) and nongovernmental organizations (NGOs), and fails to recognize the interdependence of states, especially in relation to economic affairs.

The resulting pluralist perspective therefore offers a mixed-actors model that, while not ignoring national governments, emphasizes that international politics is shaped by a much broader range of interests and groups. At the very least, the emphasis on external sovereignty that is central to realism has to be replaced, in this view, by the more modest notion of autonomy. This enables bodies such as Greenpeace, the Palestine Liberation Organization, Coca-Cola, and the Papacy to be recognized as international actors in precisely the same sense as, say, the French and Argentine states. Indeed, given its emphasis on the diffusion of power, the pluralist model calls the very notion of an autonomous actor into question, emphasizing that all actors (governmental and nongovernmental) operate within a framework of checks and constraints that inhibit independent movement. This view allowed, for example, Allison (1971), in analysing the 1962 Cuban missile crisis, to make the point that decisions are more commonly shaped by the bureaucratic-political context than by any 'rational' pursuit of national interest.

Finally, one of the important implications of the pluralist approach to international politics is that it highlights a shift away from power politics and national aggrandisement. This reflects not so much an idealist faith in abstract principles as the recognition that, when power is widely distributed, competition tends to be self-defeating. As a result, pluralists tend to argue that, in an increasingly interdependent world, the tendency towards cooperation and integration (perhaps most clearly manifested in Europe) will ultimately prove to be irresistible.

Marxism

Marxism offers a perspective on international politics that contrasts sharply with conventional paradigms. What makes the Marxist approach distinctive is its stress on economic power and the role played by international capital. Although Marx (see p. 55) was concerned primarily with analysing the structures of national capitalism, and particularly the antagonistic relationship between the bourgeoisie and the proletariat, an internationalist perspective was implicit in his work. This was evident in Marx's recognition that class loyalties cut across national divisions, which enabled him to proclaim, at the end of the *Communist Manifesto* ([1848] 1967), 'workers of the world, unite!'. In other words, whereas liberal and realist theories hold that power is organized *vertically*, reflecting the division of the world into independent states, Marxism advances a theory of *horizontal* organization based on international class. However, the implications of viewing capitalism as an international system were not fully explored until Lenin's *Imperialism: The Highest Stage of Capitalism* ([1917] 1970). Lenin (see p. 81) argued that imperial expansion reflected domestic capitalism's quest to maintain profit levels through the export of surplus capital, and that this, in turn, brought major capitalist powers into conflict with one another, the resulting war (the First World War) being essentially an imperialist war in the sense that it was fought for the control of colonies in Africa, Asia and elsewhere.

Modern Marxists or neo-Marxists (see p. 96), however, recognize the limitations of the classical Marxist–Leninist model. These include the fact that early twentieth-century imperialism did not prove to be the 'highest' (that is, the final) stage of capitalism, and the narrowness of the assumption that state policy is merely a reflection of capitalist interests. Indeed, insofar as they acknowledge the 'relative autonomy' of the state, neo-Marxists have drawn close to a pluralist belief that a variety of bodies (subnational, national and international) exert influence on the world stage. The distinctive feature of the neo-Marxist perspective, however, is that, whereas classical Marxism emphasized rivalry between separate national capitalisms, neo-Marxism focuses attention on the development, during the twentieth century, of a global capitalist system.

In neo-Marxist analysis, the central feature of this system is the organization of class interests on an international basis through the emergence of transnational corporations (see p. 149). In this view, these corporations have not merely displaced sovereign states as the dominant actors on the world stage; they also, like states themselves and international organizations, operate within structural constraints that ensure the long-term interests of global capitalism. According to neo-Marxists, this global structure of production and exchange is highly ordered in the sense that it has divided the world into 'core' and 'peripheral' areas (see p. 176). Core areas such as the developed North benefit from technological innovation and high and sustained levels of investment, while peripheral areas such as the less developed South provide a source of cheap labour, and are often dependent on cash crops. Such global inequalities mirror those found at a regional level within national economies. Whereas regional core areas are integrated into the global economy, peripheral regions are effectively marginalized, often becoming a breeding ground for ethnic nationalism. Economic globalization thus goes hand in hand with national disintegration.

Twenty-first-century world order

From bipolarity to unipolarity

On 9 November 1989, jubilant East German demonstrators stormed the Berlin Wall and started to dismantle what had become the chief symbol of the Cold War era. By the spring of 1990, during the Kuwait crisis that saw the construction of a broad international alliance to confront Iraqi aggression, President Bush of the USA proclaimed the emergence of a 'new world order'. In November 1990, representatives of the Warsaw Pact and NATO, the military faces of East–West confrontation, met in Paris formally to declare the end of hostilities, officially closing the book on the Cold War. However, how did the Cold War start in the first place? What did the end of the Cold War bring: did anyone win the Cold War? And what were the implications of the end of the Cold war for world order?

The debate about the origins of the Cold War is closely linked to the rivalries and ideological perceptions that helped to fuel the Cold War itself. The traditional, or 'orthodox', explanation lays the blame firmly at the door of the USSR. It sees the Soviet stranglehold over eastern Europe as an expression of long-standing Russian imperial ambitions, given renewed impetus by the Marxist–Leninist doctrine of worldwide class struggle. A 'revisionist' interpretation of the Cold War was nevertheless developed that attracted growing support during the Vietnam War from academics such as Gabriel

Concept

Cold war

A 'cold' war (the term was coined by Walter Lippman in 1944) is a state of protracted and extreme tension between countries or rival alliances that stops short of all-out war. The term is most commonly associated with a period of political, economic, cultural and military rivalry between the 'capitalist' western bloc and the 'communist' eastern bloc, and thus between the US and Soviet superpowers. This period is usually seen as having started in 1947 with the establishment of the so-called 'Truman Doctrine', although some trace it back to the 1945 Potsdam Conference, or even to western intervention against the Bolsheviks during the 1918–21 Russian Civil War. Although the 'war' was 'cold' in the sense that the adversaries avoided direct confrontation, covert operations and proxy warfare were a feature of the period. Renewed superpower tension associated with the US military buildup under Reagan is often referred to as the Second Cold War (1981–90).

Kolko (1988). This view portrayed Soviet policy as defensive, rather than aggressive, motivated essentially by the desire for a buffer zone between itself and a hostile West, and a wish to see a permanently weakened Germany. It also drew attention to the **expansionist** policies of the USA. According to this view, the goal of US policy was to establish a *Pax Americana* that would keep the markets of the world open to US capitalism. A number of 'post-revisionist' explanations have nevertheless developed. These often acknowledge the hegemonic ambitions of both superpowers, arguing that the Cold War was the inevitable consequence of a power vacuum that was a product of the defeat of Germany and Japan as well as the exhaustion of the UK (Yergin, 1980). In this sense, as realist theorists would point out, the emergence of two **superpowers** implied inevitable rivalry and tension, meaning that the **bipolar** world order was destined to be characterized by hostility, even though that hostility was to be contained by a balance of power.

Debate about the end of the Cold War is mired in as much ideological controversy as is debate about its origins. One version credits Ronald Reagan with having brought the Cold War to an end by instigating a renewed US military buildup in the early 1980s, thereby sparking off the 'Second Cold War'. The result of this was that the USSR was drawn into an arms race that its already fragile economy could not sustain. In a broader form, this explanation has been elaborated, by Fukuyama (1992) amongst others, into the triumphalist 'end of history' thesis. This thesis suggests that the West, and particularly the USA, 'won' the Cold War ultimately because only US-style liberal democracy offers a viable economic and political system.

Other versions, however, place heavier stress on the structural weaknesses of the Soviet economy. From this perspective, the inefficiency of the central-planning system, and the failure to introduce reforms at an earlier stage, undermined the legitimacy of the Soviet and eastern European communist regimes, which could not satisfy the growing demand for western-style consumer goods and western-style political freedoms. The Gorbachev reforms, initiated in 1985, merely brought about the collapse of an inefficient yet still functioning economic system, and, in relaxing the grip of the Communist Party, unleashed centrifugal forces that by the end of 1991 had brought about the destruction of the USSR itself.

The end of the Cold War is often seen as a major point of transition in world history, having profound implications for world order in particular. In bringing an end to the division of Germany and Berlin through the construction of a united Germany in 1990, it, in a sense, brought an end to the Second World War. On a larger scale, it can be seen to mark the end of the 'short' twentieth century, which had been characterized by the ideological battle between capitalism and communism. In the view of Philip Bobbitt (2002), it was the culmination of the 'long war of the nation-state', which had lasted from 1914 to 1990. This 'war' had been a struggle between fascism, communism and liberal parliamentarianism to determine the constitutional structure of the nation-state, and parliamentarianism had finally vanquished its two rivals. On a still larger scale, Robert Cooper (2004) argued that 1989 marked the end of the European state system that had come into existence during the 1648 Peace of Westphalia, at the end of the Thirty Years War. From the perspective of world order, the end of the Cold War is often seen as the '**unipolar**' moment', the end of an era of superpower bipolarity and the birth of a world in which the USA stood as the sole superpower, a '**hyperpower**' or 'global hegemon'. However, the implications of a unipolar world order only emerged over a period of time.

The birth of the post-Cold-War world was accompanied by a wave of optimism and idealism, highlighted by expectations of a 'new' world order. Whereas the Cold

Expansionism: A policy of military aggression designed to secure territorial gains, a phenomenon closely linked to imperialism.

Superpower: A power greater than a traditional 'great power', characterized by its global reach, its preponderant military capacity and its span of ideological leadership.

Bipolarity: The tendency of the international system to revolve around two poles (major power blocs); bipolarity implies equilibrium and stability.

Unipolarity: An international system in which there is one preeminent state; the existence of a single great power.

Hyperpower: A power that commands much greater power than any of its potential rivals, and so dominates world politics.

Focus on . . .

Humanitarian intervention

Humanitarian intervention is military intervention that is carried out in pursuit of humanitarian rather than strategic objectives. The growth in humanitarian intervention reflects the wider acceptance of universalist doctrines such as human rights (see p. 326) and the fact that democratic support for warfare can increasingly be mobilized only on the basis of a moral cause. Supporters of humanitarian intervention see it as evidence of the inability of states in a global age to restrict their moral responsibilities to their own people.

Humanitarian intervention has been seen as justified in the following circumstances:

- in the case of gross abuses of human rights (such as the expulsion or extermination of large numbers of defenceless people)
- when such abuses threaten the security of neighbouring states
- when the absence of democracy weakens the principle of national self-determination
- when diplomatic means have been exhausted and the human cost of intervention is less than that of non-intervention.

Critics of humanitarian intervention, however, make the following points:

- Any violation of state sovereignty weakens the established rules of world order.
- Aggression has almost always been legitimized by humanitarian justification (examples include Mussolini and Hitler).
- Military intervention invariably leaves matters worse, not better, or draws intervening powers into long-term involvement.

War had been based on ideological conflict and a balance of terror, the end of super-power rivalry opened up the possibility of a 'liberal peace', founded on a common recognition of international norms and standards of morality. Central to this emerging world order was the recognition of the need to settle disputes peacefully, to resist aggression and expansionism, to control and reduce military arsenals, and to ensure the just treatment of domestic populations through respect for human rights (see p. 326). What is more, the post-Cold-War world order appeared to pass its first series of major tests with ease. Iraq's annexation of Kuwait in August 1990 led to the construction of a broad western and Islamic alliance that, through the Gulf War of 1991, brought about the expulsion of Iraqi forces. The advent of a new moral consciousness in foreign affairs was also evident in the wider use of 'humanitarian intervention', notably in NATO's campaign of aerial bombing which removed Serb forces from Kosovo in 1999.

However, alternative interpretations of the post-Cold-War world order were not slow in emerging. Some, indeed, heralded the emergence not of a new world order, but of a new world *dis*order. One reason for this was the release of stresses and tensions that the Cold War had helped to keep under control. By maintaining the image of an external threat (be it international communism or capitalist encirclement), the Cold War had served to promote internal cohesion and give societies a sense of purpose and identity. However, the collapse of the external threat helped to unleash centrifugal pressures, which usually took the form of ethnic, racial and regional conflicts. This has occurred in many parts of the world, but particularly in eastern Europe, as demonstrated by the prolonged bloodshed in the 1990s amongst Serbs, Croatians and Muslims in the former Yugoslavia, and by the war between Russia and the secessionist republic of Chechnya that broke out in 1994. Far from establishing a world order based on respect for justice and human rights, the international community stood by in former Yugoslavia and, until the Kosovo crisis, allowed Serbia to wage a war of expansion and perpetrate **genocidal** policies reminiscent of those used in the Second World War. Other commentators, especially from the realist school, sounded warnings about the implications of a unipolar world order. Whereas the bipolar Cold War system tended towards balance and stability, albeit ensured by the condition **mutually assured destruction**, or MAD, a unipolar system creates conditions of unchecked power and, arguably, inherent instability. Not only does a single hegemonic state breed resentment and hostility amongst other states, but the global hegemon can also, potentially, disregard the multilateral constraints that normally restrict a state's freedom of manoeuvre. This was seen in the **unilateralist** tendency of US foreign policy following the election of George W. Bush in 2000, evidenced by the decision to withdraw from a range of international arms-control treaties, animosity towards the International Criminal Court and a continued refusal to sign the Kyoto Protocol on global climate change. However, the events of 11 September 2001 – or 9/11, as it quickly became known – significantly altered the direction of US foreign policy and with it the balance of world order.

The 'war on terror'

On 11 September 2001, a coordinated series of terrorist attacks were launched against the USA using four hijacked passenger aeroplanes. Two aeroplanes crashed into the twin towers of the World Trade Center in New York, causing their collapse; the third crashed into the Pentagon, the headquarters of the Department of Defense, in Washington; and the fourth, believed to be headed towards the White House, crashed in a field near Pittsburgh. In total, about 3,000 people were killed in these assaults. In a videotape released in October 2001, responsibility for the attacks was admitted by Osama bin Laden, head of the al-Qaeda organization, who praised his followers as the 'vanguards of Islam'. Immediately after the attacks, President Bush declared that they constituted an act of war, dubbing the conflict the 'war on terror'. For many, 9/11 was a defining moment in world history, the point at which the true nature of the post-Cold-War era was revealed and the beginning of a period of unprecedented global strife and instability. On the other hand, it is possible to exaggerate the impact of 9/11. As Robert Kagan (2004) put it, 'America did not change on September 11. It only became more itself'.

A variety of theories have been advanced to explain the advent of global terrorism (see p. 406) and the nature of the 'war on terror'. The most influential and widely discussed of these is Samuel Huntington's (see p. 138) theory of a 'clash of civilizations'. Huntington (1996) argued that twenty-first-century conflict would not primarily be ideological or economic but rather cultural: it would be conflict between nations and groups from 'different civilizations'. Huntington argued that the major civilizations (western, Chinese, Japanese, Hindu, Islamic, Buddhist, Latin American and Orthodox Christian) would become, in reaction to globalization, the principal actors in world affairs. Such an analysis contrasted starkly with the 'naïve'

Genocide: An attempt to eradicate a people, identified by their nationality, race, ethnicity or religion, through acts including mass murder, forced resettlements, deliberately induced starvation, and forced sterilization.

Mutually assured destruction: A condition in which two states each possess sufficient nuclear capacity to destroy the other regardless of which one attacks first; each has an invulnerable second-strike capacity.

Unilateralism: One-sidedness; a policy determined by the interests and objectives of a single state, unconstrained by other states or bodies.

Focus on . . .

The 'war on terror'

The 'war on terror' (or the 'war on terrorism'), known in US policy circles as the Global War on Terror, or GWOT, refers to the efforts by the USA and its key allies to root out and destroy the groups and forces deemed to be responsible for global terrorism. Launched in the aftermath of 9/11, it supposedly mapped out a strategy for a 'long war' that addresses the principal security threats to twenty-first-century world order. It aims, in particular, to counter the historically new combination of threats posed by non-state actors and especially terrorist groups, so-called 'rogue' states, weapons of mass destruction and the militant theories of radicalized Islam. Critics of the 'war on terror' have argued both that its inherent vagueness legitimizes an almost unlimited range of foreign and domestic policy interventions, and that, in building up a climate of fear and apprehension, it allows the USA and other governments to manipulate public opinion and manufacture consent for (possibly) imperialist and illiberal actions. Others have questioned whether it is possible to have a 'war' against an abstract noun.

expectations of 'end of history' theorists that politico-cultural divisions would narrow and ultimately evaporate as all parts of the world converged around support for liberal-democratic values and systems. Huntington particularly warned about the likelihood of conflict between China (wedded to distinctive Sinic cultural values despite rapid economic growth) and the West, and between the West and Islam. Huntington's thesis has nevertheless been widely criticized. The most common criticism is that it fails to recognize the extent to which globalization and other forces have already blurred cultural differences in many parts of the world. For instance, the notions of an 'Islamic civilization' or a 'western civilization' fail to take account of either the extent of political, cultural and social division within each 'civilization', or the extent to which Islam and the West have influenced, and continue to influence, each other. Moreover, the link between cultural difference and political antagonism is, at best, questionable, as most wars take place between states from the same, not different, civilizations. Finally, conflict between civilizations may be more an expression of perceived economic and political injustice than of cultural rivalry. The rise of militant Islam, for instance, may be better explained by tensions and crises in the Middle East in general and the Arab world in particular, linked to the inheritance of colonialism, the Israeli–Palestinian conflict, the survival of unpopular but often oil-rich autocratic regimes, and urban poverty and unemployment, rather than by cultural incompatibility between western and Islamic value systems.

Alternative explanations highlight the significance of changes in world order. According to Robert Cooper (2004) the East–West confrontation of the old world order has given way to a world divided into three parts. In the 'premodern' world, by which he meant those post-colonial states that have benefited neither from political stability nor from economic development, order and chaos reigns. Examples of such states include Somalia, Afghanistan and Liberia, sometimes seen as 'weak states' (see p. 105), 'failed states' or **rogue states**. Elsewhere, in the 'modern' world, states continue to be effective and are fiercely protective of their own sovereignty. Such a

Rogue state: A state whose foreign policy poses a threat to neighbouring or other states, through its aggressive intent, build-up of weapons, or association with terrorism.

Samuel P. Huntington (born 1927)

US academic and political commentator. Huntington has made influential contributions in three fields: military politics, strategy and civil–military relations; US and comparative politics; and political development and the politics of less developed societies. In *The Third Wave* (1991) he coined the notion of 'waves of democratization' and linked the process of democratization after 1975 to two earlier waves, in 1828–1926 and 1943–62. His most widely discussed work, *The Clash* *of Civilizations and the Making of World Order* (1996), advanced the controversial thesis that in the twenty-first century conflict between the world's major civilizations would lead to warfare and international disorder.

world still operates on the basis of a balance of power, as the interests and ambitions of one state are only constrained by the capacities of other states. In the 'postmodern' world, which Cooper associates primarily with Europe and the European Union, states have evolved beyond power politics and have abandoned war as a means of maintaining security in favour of multilateral agreements, international law and supranational governance. This view of the new world order, however, embodies a range of challenges and new security threats. Not the least of these arises from the proliferation of **weapons of mass destruction** (WMD), which in the premodern world can easily get into the hands of 'rogue' states or nonstate actors such as terrorist organizations. Particular concern has been expressed about nuclear proliferation, with the so-called 'nuclear club' already having expanded from five (the USA, Russia, the UK, France and China) to nine, with the acquisition of nuclear weapons by India, Pakistan, Israel and North Korea. Although Europe may be a 'zone of safety', outside Europe there is a 'zone of danger and chaos', in which the instabilities of the premodern world threaten to spill over into the modern and even the postmodern worlds.

Such an analysis overlaps at significant points with the neoconservative – or 'neocon' – ideas that had a particular impact on the Bush administration in the USA in the years following 9/11, and which were reflected in the so-called Bush Doctrine, outlined in June 2002. The central thrust of neoconservatism as an approach to foreign policy-making (as opposed to its domestic views, which are discussed in Chapter 3), was to develop strategies to enable the USA to take advantage of its unprecedented position of power and influence in the world following its 'triumph' in the Cold War. This meant, above all, preserving and reinforcing the USA's 'benevolent global hegemony' (Kristol and Kagan, 2004). US hegemony would be preserved through a kind of 'new' imperialism, which had three key features. First, the USA had to build up its military strength and achieve a position of 'strength beyond challenge', both to deter its rivals and to extend its global reach. This started once Bush was elected but was dramatically stepped up after 9/11. By 2007, US military spending accounted for about half of the world's military spending. Second, neoconservatism is based on a form of Wilsonian internationalism, in that it aims to spread US-style democracy throughout the world. This aim reflects the belief that democracy is the best antidote to war and expansionism, and also has the advantage that democratic regimes are more likely to open their markets to, and offer investment opportunities for, US businesses. Third, neoconservatives favour an assertive,

Weapons of mass destruction: Weapons capable of destroying large areas or killing large segments of the population; non-conventional weapons, in particular nuclear, biological, chemical and radiological weapons.

Focus on . . .

Preemptive attack

A preemptive attack (or preemptive war) is military action that is designed to forestall or prevent likely future aggression. It is therefore a form of self-defence by anticipation; it involves 'getting your retaliation in first'. As such, it is an alternative to strategies such as deterrence, containment and 'constructive engagement' as a means of dealing with potential aggressors. It has attracted particular attention since the 1990s in relation to threats from 'rogue' states and terrorism. The attraction of a preemptive attack is that military action can take place before a potential aggressor gets too strong (for example, before they acquire weapons of mass destruction), meaning that the overall cost of military conflict is reduced. Moreover, alternative strategies may constitute appeasement, and help to embolden an unchallenged potential aggressor. However, its drawbacks include the possibility that the calculations of future actions or threats, on which pre-emptive attacks are based, may be flawed. In addition, being based on anticipated rather than actual aggression, it may be difficult to establish or maintain domestic or international support for such attacks.

interventionist foreign policy that sets out to promote liberal-democratic governance through a process of 'regime change', achieved by military means if necessary. However, the most controversial aspect of the new approach to regime change was that it would be pursued through a strategy of preemptive attack.

After 9/11, the USA's approach to the 'war on terror' started quickly to take shape, in line with the Bush Doctrine. Its opening act was the US-led military assault on Afghanistan that toppled the Taliban regime within a matter of weeks. In January 2002, President Bush identified Iraq, Iran and North Korea as part of an 'axis of evil', later expanding this to include Cuba, Syria and Libya (subsequently removed form the list), but it was becoming clear that 'regime change' in Saddam Hussein's Iraq was the administration's next objective. This led to the 2003 Iraq War, fought by the USA and a 'coalition of the willing'. Although the immediate objective of this campaign – the overthrow of Saddam and the replacement of his Ba'athist regime – was speedily accomplished, the Iraq War proved to be problematical and more protracted than anticipated. In both Afghanistan and Iraq, despite early, dramatic successes, the USA and its allies found themselves fighting counter-insurgency wars against enemies whose use of the tactics of guerrilla warfare, terrorism and suicide bombings highlighted the limitations of preponderant US military power. The task of restructuring Iraq, in order to provide the basis for the hoped-for democratic reconstruction of the larger Arab world, has proved to be immensely difficult. Communal rivalry in particular between Shi'ite Arabs, often supported by Iran, and Sunni Arabs, linked to the deposed Ba'athist regime and militant Islamists, some of whom were attracted into Iraq from abroad, threatened the country with the prospect of civil war and eventual partition. Following Bush's reelection in 2004, the USA started, in some respects, to edge away from neocon foreign policy strategies. This process was significantly accelerated after Bush's Republican Party lost control of Congress in November 2006.

Critics of the Bush administration's approach to the 'war on terror' have made a number of allegations. In some cases, these highlighted tactical failings, the most notable of which were the insufficient number of troops initially deployed in Iraq and the absence of an exit strategy if the USA's objectives proved to be more difficult to achieve than anticipated. Other criticisms, however, focus more on the strategic approach to the 'war on terror'. Three problems have received particular attention. First, the USA has, arguably, overestimated the efficacy of military power. Not only have, as in the Vietnam War, guerrilla warfare tactics proved to be highly effective against a much more powerful and better-resourced enemy, but the use of military means has weakened the USA's 'soft' power (see p. 142) and damaged its reputation across much of the Middle East, and, if anything, alienated moderate Muslim opinion. In that sense, the USA has threatened to create the very 'arc of extremism' that it set out to destroy. Second, the strategy of imposing 'democracy from above' has proved to be naïve at best, failing in particular to recognize that stable democratic institutions usually rest upon the existence of a democratic culture and are supported by a certain level of socioeconomic development. Democratization (see p. 32) can also 'go wrong', when it leads to the election of militant Islamists who do not share the USA's vision of a reconstructed Iraq. Third, lack of progress with the 'Palestinian question' continues to poison the politics of the Middle East. The neocons have tended to support Israel as an article of faith, but this has embittered public opinion against the USA and the West across the Arab world and, in the process, strengthened support for militant Islam.

A final range of criticisms are ideological and structural rather than strategic or merely tactical. Commentators such as Noam Chomsky (see p. 234) have long challenged the idea that the USA is a disinterested world power. In their view, US foreign policy has long been dictated by imperialist ambitions aimed at safeguarding US interests and maintaining the USA's mastery of the global economy. Its huge military might and growing propensity for unilateralism make it, in effect, a 'rogue superpower'. From this perspective, the 'war on terror' is an ideological sham in two senses. In the first place, it conceals the USA's deeper ambitions: to extend political influence over the Middle East so as to guarantee reliable supplies of oil and, more generally, to reconstruct the region in the hope of providing wider opportunities for US business. Second, some have argued that, in exaggerating the threat of global terrorism, the 'war on terror' creates the ideological 'other', missing since the end of the Cold War, which helps to consolidate US capitalism by creating a climate of fear and apprehension.

Rise of multipolarity?

The 'unipolar moment' in world politics may, nevertheless, only be a transitionary phase in a longer process of the restructuring of world order. Unipolarity, anyway, may be inherently unstable, both because it breeds resentment and, over time, resistance towards the 'number one' power, and because the role of global hegemon may ultimately be unsustainable. In this sense, the USA may succumb to a tendency, common amongst earlier great powers (including Imperial Rome, with which the 'American empire' is sometimes compared) to **imperial over-reach** (Kennedy, 1989). Thus, although the USA may account for around 50 per cent of global defence spending, its proportion of global GDP is below 50 per cent and declining in relative terms. Moreover, economic growth in the USA may be particularly fragile because of its 'double deficit': government spending far outstrips taxation and imports significantly exceed exports. Finally, the rise of new powers and other shifts in interna-

Imperial over-reach: The tendency for imperial expansion to be unsustainable as wider military responsibilities outstrip the growth of the domestic economy.

tional politics, often associated with globalization, highlight clear **multipolar** trends in world order, with the emergence of five or possibly more major world actors. The key factors leading to the development of a multipolar world order are the following:

- the rise of China, India and other new powers
- the growing power of nonstate and usually transnational actors
- the changing nature of power and of power relations.

Of all the powers that may rival the USA the most significant is undoubtedly China. Indeed, many predict that the twenty-first century will become the 'Chinese century', just as the twentieth century was the 'American century'. The basis for China's great power status is its rapid economic progress since the introduction of market reforms in the mid-1970s, leading the World Bank to forecast that, if current growth rates persist, China will have the world's largest economy by 2020. Its huge population gives it a seemingly inexhaustible supply of cheap labour, making China, increasingly, the manufacturing heart of the global economy. In addition, China has a growing military capacity, being second only to the USA in terms of arms expenditure (albeit with a sevenfold difference between the two). It is highly likely, therefore, that Sino–US relations will define global politics in at least the first half of the twenty-first century, with a return to some form of bipolarity and growing tension, particularly over the issue of Taiwan (Carpenter, 2006). Other rising powers include India, which despite continuing serious problems of poverty and illiteracy has sustained growth rates in the early twenty-first century only just below those of China; Brazil, which benefits from a wealth of natural resources and the largest population in Latin America; and Russia, whose revival in the twenty-first century has largely been based on extensive fuel reserves. Japan and a German-dominated EU are also likely to be significant actors, particularly if economic reform enables them to reclaim competitive advantage in an increasingly globalized economy.

One of the most significant implications of globalization is that power in world politics is no longer simply exercised by and through states but is increasingly wielded by a variety of non-state actors. Multipolar trends, then, are not simply evident in the growth of new powers, but can also be found in a wider diffusion of power beyond the control of any state. These rising nonstate actors come in various guises. For example, the global economy is increasingly dominated by transnational corporations, or TNCs (see p. 149), which now account for about 50 per cent of world manufacturing production and over 70 per cent of world trade, and which are able to elude political control because of the ease with which they can relocate investment and production. Similarly, international nongovernmental organizations, or NGOs (see p. 297), have proliferated since the 1980s, coming to exercise powerful influence within international organizations such as the EU and the UN. NGOs are also, at times, able to counterbalance the power of TNCs, and may also rival states through their capacity for popular mobilization and their ability to command moral as well as expert authority. Other non-state actors that exert growing influence within an increasingly interconnected world include politico-military movements such as Hamas, Hizbullah and al-Qaeda, and a range of criminal organizations that operate in impoverished and postcommunist states in particular, which are responsible, for example, for much of the world's drug-trafficking and people-trafficking.

As well as power being reapportioned amongst the states of the world, and between states and nonstate actors, there are reasons for thinking that the nature of

Multipolarity: An international system in which there are three or more power centres, creating a bias in favour of fluidity and, perhaps, instability.

◆ Concept

Hard/soft power

Power (see p. 7) is the ability to achieve a desired outcome. However, in world politics an increasingly common distinction is made between 'hard' and 'soft' power. *Hard* power refers to the ability of one international actor (usually but not necessarily a state) to influence another through the use of threats or rewards, typically involving the use of military 'sticks' or economic 'carrots'. *Soft* power is the ability to influence other actors by persuading them to follow or agree to norms and aspirations that produce the desired behaviour. It relies on attraction rather than coercion. Soft power is often seen as more important in a world of global interdependence and freer flows of communication and information. Although hard and soft power often operate in tandem, soft power can reduce the need for hard power, and it can operate in the absence of hard power (for example, the Vatican, the Dalai Lama, Canada and Sweden).

Multilateralism: A system of coordinated relations between three or more states based on principles of conduct laid down by treaties and international organizations.

power is changing in ways that make its concentration in a small number of hands increasingly difficult to sustain. This has happened in two main ways. First, due to new technology and in a world of global communications and rising literacy rates and educational standards, 'soft' power is becoming as important as 'hard' power in influencing political outcomes. Military power, the traditional currency of world politics, has certainly not become irrelevant, but its use is greatly undermined when it is not matched by 'hearts and minds' strategies. For instance, as pointed out earlier, the use of 'shock and awe' tactics by the US military, and other demonstrations of US coercive power, have proved, in some senses, to be counter-productive, in that they strengthening hostility towards the USA and its allies both in Iraq and across the larger Arab and Muslim worlds. Second, new technology has, in a number of ways, altered power balances both within society and between societies, often empowering the traditionally powerless. This can be seen, most obviously, in the case of nuclear weapons and other weapons of mass destruction, which enable relatively weak states, such as North Korea, to withstand pressure from much more powerful states, notably the USA. Al-Qaeda's influence on world politics since 9/11 has also been out of all proportion to its organizational and economic strength, because modern technology, in the form of bombs and aeroplanes, has given its terrorist activities a global reach. Advances in communications technology, particularly the use of mobile phones and the internet, have also improved the tactical effectiveness of loosely organized groups, ranging from terrorist bands to protest groups and social movements (see p. 308). Finally, public opinion around the world, and thus the behaviour of governments, is affected by the near-ubiquitous spread of television and the wider use of satellite technology. This ensures, for instance, that pictures of devastation and human suffering, whether caused by warfare, famine or natural disaster, are shared across the globe almost instantly.

If twenty-first-century world order is to have a multipolar, rather than a unipolar or bipolar, character, what does this imply about prospects for war, peace and global stability? There are two quite different models of a multipolar world order. The first highlights a tendency towards instability and chaos, as a wider diffusion of power amongst world actors allows each greater freedom to pursue its own ends unchecked by more powerful rivals. This could result in a world of shifting alliances and coalitions, formed either to deter aggression or to take advantage of less powerful actors or groups. Arguably, both the First and Second World Wars were caused by multipolar world orders in which ambitious powers felt able to pursue expansionist goals precisely because power balances remained fluid. The alternative, and more optimistic, model of multipolar world order is rooted in **multilateralism**. This, though, requires an acceptance by all, or at least most, parties that the game of global politics should be played by certain rules, and that these rules should be formulated through broad agreement. The prospects of multilateralist multipolarity, as opposed to 'anarchical' multipolarity, coming into existence depend on three factors. The first is a widespread recognition amongst global actors of the implications of 'anarchical' multipolarity in a world of nuclear proliferation and widespread access to other weapons of mass destruction. Second, world order will be affected by the further unfolding of globalization, which, as discussed in the next section, may either strengthen a sense of interconnectedness and mutual dependence or create new rifts and divisions. Finally, the prospects for multilateralism are closely bound up with the success of the institutions of regional and global governance in establishing legitimacy and in maintaining legal frameworks for the peaceful resolution of disputes between and amongst states and other actors. The prospects for this are examined in the final part of this chapter.

Dynamics of globalization

Globalizing tendencies

Globalization is a slippery and elusive concept. Despite intensifying interest in the phenomenon of globalization since the 1980s the term is still used to refer, variously, to a process, a policy, a marketing strategy, a predicament or even an ideology. The problem with globalization is that it is not so much an 'it' as a 'them': it is not a single process but a complex of processes, sometimes overlapping and interlocking processes but also, at times, contradictory and oppositional ones. It is difficult therefore to reduce globalization to a single theme. Perhaps the best attempt to do this was in Kenichi Ohmae's (1989) idea of a 'borderless world'. This not only refers to the tendency of traditional political borders, based on national and state boundaries, to become permeable; it also implies that divisions between people previously separated by time and space have become less significant and are sometimes entirely irrelevant. Scholte (2005) therefore argued that globalization is linked to the growth of 'supraterritorial' relations between people, a reconfiguration of social space in which territory matters less because an increasing range of connections have a 'transworld' or 'transborder' character. For instance, huge flows of electronic money now surge around the world at the flick of a computer switch, ensuring that currency

Concept

Globalization

Globalization is the emergence of a complex web of interconnectedness that means that our lives are increasingly shaped by events that occur, and decisions that are made, at a great distance from us. The central feature of globalization is therefore that geographical distance is of declining relevance, and that territorial boundaries, such as those between nation-states, are becoming less significant. By no means, however, does globalization imply that 'the local' and 'the national' are subordinate to 'the global'. Rather, it highlights the *deepening* as well as the *broadening* of the political process, in the sense that local, national and global events (or perhaps local, regional, national, international and global events) constantly interact. The resulting systemic interdependences are shown in Figure 7.1.

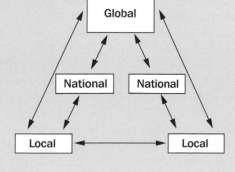

Fig. 7.1 System interdependences

and other financial markets react almost immediately to economic events anywhere in the world. Similarly, cable and satellite technology allow telephone messages and television programmes to be transmitted around the world almost instantaneously.

The interconnectedness that globalization has spawned is multidimensional. The popular image of globalization is that it is a top-down process, the establishment of a single global system that imprints itself on all parts of the world. In this view, globalization is linked to **homogenization** as cultural, social, economic and political diversity are destroyed in a world in which we all watch the same television programmes, buy the same commodities, eat the same food, support the same sports stars and follow the antics of the same celebrities. Nevertheless, globalization often goes hand in hand with localization, regionalization and multiculturalism (see p. 215). This occurs for a variety of reasons. In the first place, the declining capacity of the nation-state to organize economic and political life in a meaningful way allows power to be sucked downwards as well as squeezed upwards. Thus, as allegiances based on the nation and political nationalism fade, they are often replaced by ones linked to local community or region, or religious and ethnic identity. Religious fundamentalism (see p. 66) can, for instance, be seen as a response to globalization. Second, the fear or threat of homogenization, especially when it is perceived as a form of imperialism, provokes cultural and political resistance. This can lead to a resurgence of interest in declining languages and minority cultures as well as to a backlash against globalization, most obviously through the emergence of new 'anti-capitalist' and anti-free-trade social movements. Third, rather than simply bringing about a global monoculture, globalization has in some ways fashioned more complex patterns of social and cultural diversity in developing and developed states alike. In developing states western consumer goods and images have been absorbed into more traditional cultural practices through a process of **indigenization**. Developed states, also, have not escaped the wider impact of cultural exchange, being, in return for Coca-Cola, McDonald's and MTV, increasingly influenced by non-western religions, medicines and therapeutic practices, and art, music and literature.

Distinctive forms of globalization can also be identified. The most significant of these are:

- Economic globalization
- Cultural globalization
- Political globalization

Economic globalization is reflected in the idea that no national economy is now an island: all economies have, to a greater or lesser extent, been absorbed into an interlocking global economy. The OECD (1995) thus defined globalization as 'a shift from a world of distinct national economies to a global economy in which production is internationalized and financial capital flows freely and instantly between countries'. The collapse of communism gave powerful impetus to economic globalization, in that it paved the way for the absorption into the global capitalist system of the last significant block of states that had remained outside it. Economic globalization, for that matter, also helped to precipitate the collapse of communism in that lower trade barriers, an end to exchange controls and freer movement of investment capital from the 1980s onwards had helped to widen the economic gap between the capitalist West and an economically stagnant communist East. One of the key implications of economic globalization is the reduced capacity of national governments to

Homogenization: The tendency for all parts or elements (in this case countries) to become similar or identical.

Indigenization: The process through which alien goods and practices are absorbed by being adapted to local needs and circumstances.

manage their economies and, in particular, to resist their restructuring along free-market lines.

Cultural globalization is the process whereby information, commodities a. images that have been produced in one part of the world enter into a global flow that tends to 'flatten out' cultural differences between nations, regions and individuals. This has sometimes been portrayed as a process of **McDonaldization**. Driven in part by the growth of transnational companies and the emergence of global commodities, cultural globalization is also fuelled by the so-called information revolution, the spread of satellite communication, telecommunications networks, information technology and the internet, and global media corporations. However, as pointed out earlier, culture both serves and constrains the forces of globalization. In addition to the ubiquity of Hollywood movies, Nike running shoes and Starbucks coffee houses, selling goods across the world requires a sensitivity to indigenous cultures and social practices.

Political globalization is evident in the growing importance of international organizations. These are organizations that are transnational in that they exercise jurisdiction not within a single state, but within an international area comprising several states. Most such organizations have emerged in the post-1945 period: examples include the United Nations, NATO, the European Economic Community and its various successors, the EC and the EU, the World Bank, the International Monetary Fund (IMF), the Organization for Economic Cooperation and Development (OECD) and the World Trade Organization (WTO). When they conform to the principles of intergovernmentalism (see p. 153), international organizations provide a mechanism that enables states, at least in theory, to take concerted action without sacrificing national sovereignty (see p. 131). Supranational bodies, on the other hand, are able to impose their will on nation-states. The inter-state emphasis of political globalization sets it apart from the rival conceptions of economic and cultural globalization, which highlight the role of nonstate and market-based actors. Moreover, insofar as it reflects an idealist commitment to internationalism and some form of world government, political globalization lags markedly behind economic and cultural globalization. Whereas a global state remains a very distant prospect, global civil society, based on the activities of transnational corporations (see p. 149), nongovernmental organizations (see p. 297) and international pressure groups, has become very much a reality.

Globalization: theories and debates

Globalization has become a deeply controversial issue. While most governments and mainstream political parties are anxious to position themselves to take advantage of the benefits of the new globalized economy, an antiglobalization movement has emerged, most strongly in developed states but also, to some extent, in developing ones. In some respects, divisions over globalization have replaced more traditional left–right divisions, based upon the ideological struggle between capitalism and socialism. There is, nevertheless, a sense in which the pro- versus antiglobalization debate is nothing more than a reworking of the older and more familiar ideological divide. This is because the interconnectedness that lies at the heart of globalization is, as yet, invariably linked to the extension of market exchange and commercial practices. Globalization thus has a pronounced neoliberal or free-market ideological character. Capitalism, in short, remains the issue. Supporters of globalization, some-

McDonaldization: The process whereby global commodities and commercial and marketing practices associated with the fast-food industry have come to dominate more and more economic sectors.

times called globalists, usually argue that capitalism tends towards general prosperity and widening opportunities, in which case global capitalism will allow these benefits to be enjoyed by more people in more countries. Opponents of globalization, on the other hand, tend to associate capitalism with inequality and exploitation, in which case global capitalism will simply generate new forms of misery and injustice. In one important respect, however, the globalization debate is new: it is conducted within a postsocialist framework that no longer recognizes that there are viable alternatives to market structures and capitalist organizations. The choice is therefore between neoliberal globalization and regulated globalization, rather than between global capitalism and any qualitatively different alternative.

A first set of debates is between believers and sceptics over whether globalization is actually happening and, by extension, about the forces that are driving it. The believers, who include both supporters and opponents of the process, argue that globalization draws attention to a profound, even revolutionary, set of economic, cultural, technological and political shifts that have intensified since the 1980s. Chief amongst these are much higher levels of world trade and, in particular, a dramatic increase in financial and currency transactions; the advent of new information and communication technologies that provide instant access to images and messages across the globe; and the emergence of global commodities that are available almost anywhere in the world. In its most extreme version, **hyperglobalism**, this view subscribes to a form of technological determinism. Nevertheless, there is evidence of a slowdown in the pace of globalization since the 1990s, which has been further strengthened by the impact of the events of September 11, 2001 on, for instance, the global economy and inter-state security measures.

On the other hand, the sceptics, often subscribing to a traditional or 'old' left analysis of capitalism, argue either that there is little that is new about globalization or that its impact has been exaggerated for political reasons. Karl Marx (see p. 55), now reborn as a theorist of globalization rather than a proponent of class struggle, drew attention to the international character of capitalist organization as early as the mid-nineteenth century. J. A. Hobson (1858–1940) and V. I. Lenin (see p. 81) each highlighted intrinsic links between capitalism and imperialism in the early twentieth century. Moreover, despite the undoubted growth in world trade from the late nineteenth century onwards, the sceptics point out that the overwhelming bulk of economic activity still takes place within, not across, national boundaries. National economies, in other words, are not as irrelevant as globalization theorists usually suggest. From this perspective, globalization is often seen less as a revolutionary economic or technological force and more as an ideological device used by politicians and theorists who support neoliberal economics and wish to advance corporate interests (Hirst and Thompson, 1999). The globalization thesis has two major advantages in this respect. First, it portrays certain tendencies – namely, the shift towards labour flexibility and weaker trade unions, controls on public spending and particularly welfare budgets, and a scaling-down of business regulation – as inevitable and therefore irresistible. Second, it suggests that such shifts are part of an impersonal process, and not one linked to an agent, such as a big business, whose interests might be seen to drive, and be served by, globalizing tendencies.

The most intense debate about globalization nevertheless concerns its implications for equality and poverty. Critics of globalization have drawn attention to the emergence of new and deeply entrenched patterns of inequality: globalization is thus a game of winners and losers. The winners are invariably identified as multinational

Hyperglobalism: The view that new, globalized economic and cultural patterns are inevitable, driven by new information and communications technology.

Focus on . . .

The North–South divide

The idea of a 'North–South divide' was popularized through the work of the so-called Brandt Reports: *North–South: A Programme for Survival* (1980) and *Common Crisis: North–South Cooperation for World Recovery* (1983). Although the division of the world into a 'North' and a 'South' is based on the tendency for industrial development to be concentrated in the northern hemisphere, and for poverty and disadvantage to be concentrated in the southern hemisphere (apart from Australasia), the terms are essentially conceptual rather than geographical. The concept of the North–South divide drew attention to the way in which aid, third-world debt and the practices of TNCs help to perpetuate structural inequalities between the high-wage, high-investment industrialized North and the low-wage, low-investment, predominantly rural South. The Brandt Reports also highlighted the interdependence of the North and the South, emphasizing that the long-term prosperity of the North is dependent on the development of the South.

corporations and industrially advanced states generally, but particularly the United States; the losers, in contrast, are in the developing world, where wages are low, regulation is weak or non-existent, and where production is increasingly orientated around global markets rather than domestic needs. Whereas the US and other western economies have grown strongly since the 1980s on the basis of globalization and technological advance, absolute living standards have fallen in the poorest parts of the world, notably in sub-Saharan Africa, where 40 per cent of people live below the poverty line. Wallerstein (1984), drawing on the Marxist view of capitalism as essentially exploitative, highlighted the structural condition of uneven political and economic development that led to growing inequality between 'core' and 'peripheral' parts (see p. 176) of the economic **world-system**. Global tensions have come to be seen less in terms of East versus West and more in terms of a North–South divide.

Globalists, however, point out that the rich may have got richer but the poor are now also, in most cases, less poor. From the perspective of liberal pluralism, the emergence of a global economy is to be welcomed because free trade (see p. 157) allows each country to specialize in the production of those goods and services that it is best suited to produce. This leads to international specialization and mutual benefits. For instance, the transfer of production from developed to developing states benefits the former because production costs, and therefore prices, are kept low, but also benefits the latter because wage levels tend to rise, albeit from a low base, which will stimulate the domestic economy and foster enterprise. In this view, the only parts of the world that fail to benefit from globalization are those that remain outside it.

Globalization has also been criticized because of its tendency towards risk, uncertainty and instability. Globalists certainly acknowledge the dynamism that is inherent in any competitive market order, but, following the principles of classical economics, point out that markets tend towards long-term equilibrium, supply eventually coming into line with demand. In this view, the uncertainty and insecurity that are associated with the emergence of a global economy are likely to decline as more stable patterns of economic activity take shape. Nevertheless, globalization has been associated with increased risk and uncertainty in at least three deeper ways. In

World-system theory: The theory that the world economy is best understood as an interlocking capitalist system which exemplifies, at an international level, many of the features that characterize national capitalism.

the first place, economic decision-making is increasingly influenced by global financial markets that are inherently unstable. This is because much of their activity is speculative, and they are driven by short-term economic considerations. The fate of companies, industries, national economies and even regions of the world is therefore subject to the whims of financial markets. The financial crisis in Mexico in 1995 and the Asian financial crisis of 1997–99 may only be early indications of a crisis-prone and more unpredictable world economy. George Soros (1998) argued that such crises threatened the open society, and can be prevented only by far greater regulation, aimed at bringing speculative financial flows under control.

A second form of uncertainty is summed up in Ulrich Beck's (1992) idea of a 'risk society'. A risk society is one that is characterized by rising individualism and an associated weakening of tradition, community and established institutions. Uncertainty, in this respect, goes beyond an increase in the pace and a reduction in the predictability of economic and social change, in that it has a personal, even psychic dimension: when all fixed points are undermined, people's basic values and even sense of identity are called into question. As Marx put it in the *Communist Manifesto* ([1848] 1967), 'All that is solid melts into air'. A third form of instability is the alleged tendency of globalization towards environmental crisis and destruction. Ecosocialists explain this by reference to capitalism's blind concern with profit and its insensitivity towards ecological issues. Radical ecologists, for their part, believe that globalization is merely an extension of industrialism, an economic system that is characterized by large-scale production, the accumulation of capital and relentless growth. By spreading materialism and entrenching absolute faith in science and technology, industrialism undermines human values and deadens ecological sensibilities. Reformist ecologists call for global environmental protection. However, as the faltering process of implementing the 1997 Kyoto Protocol on climate change demonstrates, concerted state action in this area is difficult to achieve because of the economic sacrifices involved.

The most significant political debate associated with globalization concerns its impact on democracy. Supporters of globalization argued that it is a major factor underpinning the trend towards democratization (see p. 32). In its most optimistic version, advanced by Fukuyama (1989, 1992), this view suggests that globalization will lead to the 'end of history', in that the extension of market capitalism will lead to a universal acceptance of liberal democratic principles and structures. Economic freedom is inevitably associated with political freedom, because the complex and diverse pressures unleashed by market economies can be contained only within open and democratic societies. Globalization can nevertheless be seen to have undermined democracy in two important ways. First, it has concentrated economic power, and therefore political power, in the hands of transnational corporations (TNCs). TNCs now dominate most of the world's markets. Notable examples include General Motors, Ford, Esso, Shell, BP, McDonald's, AT&T, and the News Corporation. General Motors, to take just one instance, has an annual revenue that is almost equal to the combined GDP of Ireland, New Zealand, Uruguay, Sri Lanka, Kenya, Namibia, Nicaragua and Chad. Such economic and financial power is also allied to the ability to manipulate consumer tastes and entrench materialist values through the development of brands (Klein, 2000). However, it is the capacity of TNCs to relocate capital and production elsewhere in the world that gives them a decisive advantage over national governments and enables them, effectively, to escape democratic control. Developing-world states are particularly vulnerable in this respect, as they provide TNCs with a source of cheap labour and low production costs without being able to oblige them to make long-term investments or shift decision-making power from the 'home' country to the 'host' one.

Second, democracy is threatened by the fact that the pace of economic globalization far outstrips that of political globalization. Whereas economic activity increasingly pays little attention to national borders, politics continues to operate largely within them, the international organizations that do exist being too weak to call global capitalism to account. This has led to calls for a cosmopolitan conception of democracy (Held, 1995). The extension of democratic forms and processes across territorial borders would require not merely the strengthening of organizations such as the European Union and the United Nations, but also the reduction of **democratic deficits** from which these bodies currently suffer. Moreover, the institutions of global economic governance (see p. 6), such as the IMF, the World Bank, the OECD and the G7, need to develop some independence from the interests of MNCs and give greater attention to issues such as human rights, economic justice and environmental protection.

Regionalization

One view of globalization suggests that it is biased in favour of cooperation and harmony, in which case more and more parts of the world will be integrated into patterns of economic and political interdependence. However, an alternative view is that globalizing trends generate new forms of tension and conflict. In the light of the declining effectiveness of national governments, these tensions are usually evident in the growth of **regionalization**. As the territorial nation-state is seen to be less effective in delivering security, stability and prosperity, these goals are increasingly achieved through collaboration with neighbouring and geographically proximate states. The relationship between globalization and regionalization is nevertheless unclear. Regionalization may merely be a step on the road to globalization: the growth of economic interdependence is likely, initially, to have a regional character, regional organizations being able to manage the relationship between nation-states and global forces. On the other hand, regionalization may be a counter-global trend, a form of resistance to globalization. The most ominous historical precedent for the latter interpretation was the erosion and destruction of the open international economic order in the late nineteenth century through the spread of economic nationalism. Growing **protectionism** and economic rivalry contributed significantly to the intensifying international tensions that eventually led to the First World War. As the nation is no longer an effective means for protecting or advancing economic or other interests, this role may in future fall to the region.

Regionalization has been fuelled by significant strategic and economic factors. Regional defence organizations emerged in the early post-1945 period and gave expression to the new strategic tensions that were generated by the Cold War. NATO and the Warsaw Pact were the most prominent such organizations, although other bodies, such as the South-East Asian Treaty Organization (SEATO), were also formed. Nevertheless, until the collapse of communism in 1989–91, NATO and the Warsaw Pact did little more than ensure a military standoff between the US-dominated West and the Soviet-dominated East. However, the end of the Cold War led to profound changes in the role and purpose of NATO, as the sole remaining

Focus on . . .

Regional economic blocs

- **North American Free Trade Agreement (NAFTA):** This was signed in 1993 by Canada, Mexico and the USA. NAFTA was formed in part as a response to the growing pace of European integration, and is intended to provide the basis for a wider economic partnership covering the whole western hemisphere.

- **European Union:** This was formed in 1993, developing out of the European Economic Community (founded in 1957). The EU has expanded from 6 to 27 members, and now includes many former communist states. It is the most advanced example of regional integration at an economic and political level (see pp. 151–6).

- **Asia-Pacific Economic Cooperation (APEC):** This informal forum was created in 1989 and has expanded from 12 member states to 21 (including Australia, China, Russia, Japan and the USA); collectively these states account for 40 per cent of the world's population and over 50 per cent of global GDP.

- **Association of South-East Asian Nations (ASEAN):** This was established in 1967 by Brunei, Indonesia, Malaysia, Philippines, Singapore and Thailand, with Vietnam, Laos, Myanmar and Cambodia joining subsequently. ASEAN has attempted to promote a free-trade zone that would help South-East Asian states maintain their economic independence.

- **Mercosur:** The Mercosur agreement links Argentina, Brazil, Venezuela Paraguay and Uruguay with Chile, Colombia , Ecuador, Peru and Bolivia as associate members. It is Latin America's largest trade bloc, and operates as a free-trade union.

- **Free Trade Area of the Americas (FTAA):** This is an agreement made at the 1994 Miami Summit of the Americas to build a free-trade area to extend across the Americas, as a proposed extension to NAFTA. The FTAA has 34 provisional members, but it is dominated by the USA and Canada.

regional defence organization of any significance. In the absence of the Soviet threat that it was set up to contain, NATO appeared to be simply redundant. Nevertheless, rather than disbanding, NATO expanded eastward, with the Czech Republic, Hungary and Poland joining in 1999 and the Baltic states, Slovenia, Slovakia, Bulgaria and Romania joining in 2004. Moreover, its security-protecting role seems to have been replaced by an emphasis upon humanitarian intervention and peacekeeping, as in Bosnia and Kosovo in the 1990s. In 2003, NATO took its operations outside Europe for the first time when it assumed command of the international peacekeeping force in Afghanistan.

The most significant impetus towards international regionalization is undoubtedly economic, however. International trade can both foster a harmonization of interests and provoke deep suspicions and resentment. Although countries always wish to penetrate the markets of other countries, they have an equally strong incentive to protect their own markets from foreign competition. The cause of free trade hastraditionally been embraced by economically dominant powers (the UK in the nineteenth century and the USA since the mid-twentieth century), which wished to encourage weaker states to open up their markets while they themselves had little to fear from foreign competition. This, nevertheless, can fuel protectionism, as less developed states seek to protect themselves from what they perceive as unfair competition: for instance, the rise of economic nationalism in late nineteenth-century Europe was in part a reaction against the UK's industrial preeminence. If national protectionism, or 'protectionism in one country', is no longer regarded as a viable option, regionally based economic cooperation is increasingly attractive as a means of both facilitating international trade and providing protection against intensifying global competition.

Some regional trading blocs, such as the EEC, developed in the aftermath of the Second World War, but most of them have come into existence since 1990 and have been a response to economic globalization, notable examples including NAFTA, APEC, and the proposed FTAA. Already, more than one-third of world trade takes place within four regions: North and South America, Europe, Asia and Oceania, and Africa and the Middle East. The implications of economic regionalization clearly depend on whether such trading blocs become inward-looking 'economic fortresses' that resist globalization, or develop into outward-looking bodies that help to manage the integration of their regions into the global economy while also fostering internal cooperation. This will also be influenced by the success of the institutions of global economic governance, especially the WTO and the IMF, in promoting trade liberalization.

The European Union

The 'European idea' (broadly, the belief that, regardless of historical, cultural and linguistic differences, Europe constitutes a single political community) was born long before 1945. Before the Reformation in the sixteenth century, common allegiance to Rome invested the Papacy with supranational authority over much of Europe. Even after the European state system came into existence, thinkers as different as Rousseau (see p. 75), Saint-Simon (1760–1825) and Mazzini (see p. 116) championed the cause of European cooperation, and in some cases advocated the establishment of Europe-wide political institutions. However, until the second half of the twentieth century such aspirations proved to be hopelessly utopian. Since the Second World War, Europe has undergone a historically unprecedented process of integration, aimed, some argue, at the creation of what Winston Churchill in 1946 called a 'United States of Europe'. Indeed, it is sometimes suggested that European integration provides a model of political organization that will eventually be accepted worldwide as the deficiencies of the nation-state become increasingly apparent.

It is clear that this process was precipitated by a set of powerful, and possibly irresistible, historical circumstances in post-1945 Europe. The most significant of these were the following:

- the need for economic reconstruction in war-torn Europe through cooperation and the creation of a larger market
- the desire to preserve peace by permanently resolving the bitter Franco-German rivalry that caused the Franco-Prussian War (1870–71), and led to war in 1914 and 1939
- the recognition that the '**German problem**' could be tackled only by integrating Germany into a wider Europe

German problem: The structural unstability in the European state system caused by the emergence of a powerful and united Germany.

Jean Monnet (1888–1979)

French economist and administrator. Monnet was largely self-taught. He found employment during the First World War coordinating Franco-British war supplies, and he was later appointed Deputy Secretary-General of the League of Nations. He was the originator of Winston Churchill's offer of union between the UK and France in 1940, which was abandoned once Pétain's Vichy regime had been installed. Monnet took charge of the French modernization programme under de Gaulle in 1945, and in 1950 he produced the Schuman Plan, from which the European Coal and Steel Community and the European Economic Community were subsequently developed. Although Monnet rejected intergovernmentalism in favour of supranational government, he was not a formal advocate of European federalism.

- the desire to safeguard Europe from the threat of Soviet expansionism and to mark out for Europe an independent role and identity in a bipolar world order
- the wish of the USA to establish a prosperous and united Europe, both as a market for US goods and as a bulwark against the spread of communism
- the widespread acceptance, especially in continental Europe, that the sovereign nation-state was the enemy of peace and prosperity.

To some extent, the drift towards European integration was fuelled by an idealist commitment to internationalism and the belief that international organizations embody a moral authority higher than that commanded by nation-states. This was evident in the 'federalist' (see p. 167) dream of an integrated Europe that was espoused by, for example, Jean Monnet and Robert Schuman (1886–1963). Early dreams of a 'federal' Europe in which the sovereignty of the European nations would be 'pooled' came to nothing, however. Instead, a **functionalist** road to unity was followed. This is why the European project tended to focus on the means of promoting economic cooperation, seen by states as the least controversial but most necessary form of integration. The European Coal and Steel Community (ECSC) was founded in 1952 on the initiative of Jean Monnet, adviser to the French foreign minister, Robert Schuman. Under the Treaty of Rome (1957), the European Economic Community came into existence. This was committed to the establishment of a common European market and the broader goal of an 'ever closer union among the peoples of Europe'. Subsequently, **neofunctionalism** has been the most influential theory of European, and indeed regional, integration.

The ECSC, EEC and Euratom were formally merged in 1967, forming what became known as the European Community (EC). Although the community of the original 'Six' (France, Germany, Italy, the Netherlands, Belgium and Luxembourg) was expanded in 1973 with the inclusion of the UK, Ireland and Denmark, the 1970s was a period of stagnation. The integration process was relaunched, however, as a result of the signing in 1986 of the Single European Act (SEA), which envisaged an unrestricted flow of goods, services and people throughout Europe (a 'single market'), to be introduced by 1993. The Treaty of European Union (Maastricht treaty), which was negotiated in 1991, ratified in 1992 and became effective in 1993, marked the creation of the European Union (EU). This committed the EU's 15 members (Greece, Portugal, Spain, Austria, Finland and Sweden having joined) to both political union and monetary union. The centrepiece of this proposal was the

Functionalism: The theory that government is primarily resposive to human needs; functionalism is associated with incremental steps towards regional integration, within specific areas of policy-making, at a pace controlled by member states.

Neofunctionalism: A revision of functionalism that recognizes that regional integration in one area generates pressures for further integration in the form of 'spillover'.

establishment of a single European currency, the euro, which took place in 1999, with notes and coins being circulated in 2002. In 2004 the EU began its most radical phase of enlargement, as ten countries of central amd eastern Europe and the Mediterranean joined, bringing about the reunification of Europe after decades of division by the Iron Curtain. Bulgaria and Romania joined in 2007, with negotiations for membership underway with Croatia, Macedonia and Turkey, and with Albania, Bosnia-Herzegovina, Montenegro and Serbia all potential candidate countries.

The EU is a very difficult political organization to categorize. In strict terms, it is no longer a confederation of independent states operating on the basis of inter-governmentalism (as the EEC and EC were at their inception). The sovereignty of member states was enshrined in the so-called 'Luxembourg compromise' of 1966. This accepted the general practice of unanimous voting in the Council of Ministers, and granted each member state an outright **veto** on matters threatening vital national interests. As a result of the SEA and the TEU, however, the practice of **qualified majority voting**, which allows even the largest state to be outvoted, was applied to a wider range of policy areas, thereby narrowing the scope of the national veto. This trend has been compounded by the fact that EU law is binding on all member states and that the power of certain EU bodies has expanded at the expense of national governments. The result is a political body that has both inter-governmental and supranational features, the former evident in the Council of Ministers and the latter primarily in the European Commission and the Court of Justice. The EU may not yet have created a federal Europe, but because of the superiority of European law over the national law of the member states, it is perhaps accurate to talk of a 'federalizing' Europe. An attempt was made to codify the EU's various constitutional rules, particularly in the light of enlargement, through the introduction of the Constitutional Treaty, commonly known as the EU Constitution. Despite its formal approval by heads of state or government in 2004, it failed to be ratified because of referendum defeats in the Netherlands and France in 2005.

Although the European Union remains a difficult organization to categorize, it is without doubt the world's most advanced experiment in regional integration. Indeed, as an economic, monetary and, to a significant extent, political union brought about through voluntary cooperation amongst states, it is a unique political body. The transition from Community to Union, achieved via the TEU, not only extended intergovernmental cooperation into areas such as foreign and security policy, home affairs and justice, and immigration and policing, but also established the notion of EU citizenship through the right to live, work and be politically active in any member state. This level of integration has been possible because of the powerful, and, some would argue, exceptional combination of pressures in post-1945 Europe that helped to shift public attitudes away from nationalism and towards cooperation, and to convince elites that national interests are ultimately better served by concerted action rather than independence. Where such prerequisites were weak, as in the case of the UK, often dubbed Europe's 'awkward partner', participation in the integration process has tended to be either reluctant or faltering (the UK rejected an invitation to join the EEC in 1957, and negotiated an opt-out from monetary union in 1991).

Nevertheless, although the EU has done much to realize the Treaty of Rome's goal of establishing 'an ever closer union', moving well beyond Charles de Gaulle's and Margaret Thatcher's vision of Europe as a confederation of independent states, it stops far short of realizing the early federalists' dream of a European 'superstate'.

Concept

Inter-governmentalism, supranationalism

Intergovernmentalism is any form of interaction between states that takes place on the basis of sovereign independence. This includes treaties and alliances as well as leagues and confederations, such as the League of Nations and the EEC. Sovereignty is preserved through a process of unanimous decision-making that gives each state a veto, at least over matters of vital national importance.

Supranationalism is the existence of an authority that is 'higher' than that of the nation-state and capable of imposing its will on it. It can therefore be found in international federations, where sovereignty is shared between central and peripheral bodies. The European Union thus encompasses a mixture of both intergovernmental and supranational elements.

Veto: The formal power to block a decision or action through the refusal of consent.

Qualified majority voting: A system of voting in which different majorities are needed on different issues, with states' votes weighted (roughly) according to size.

Subsidiarity

Subsidiarity (from the Latin *subsidiarii*, meaning a contingent of supplementary troops) is, broadly, the devolution of decision-making from the centre to lower levels. However, it is understood in two crucially different ways. In federal states such as Germany, subsidiarity is understood as a *political* principle that implies decentralization and popular participation, with local and provincial institutions thus being supported. This is expressed in the TEU in the form of the commitment that decisions should be 'taken as closely as possible to the citizen'. However, subsidiarity is also interpreted, usually by anti-federalists, as a *constitutional* principle that defends national sovereignty against the encroachment of EU institutions. This is expressed in the TEU in the commitment that the competence of the European Union should be restricted to those actions that 'cannot be sufficiently achieved by the member states'.

Focus on . . .

How the European Union works

▶ **European Commission:** This is the executive-bureaucratic arm of the EU. It is headed by 27 commissioners (one from each of the member states) and a president (José Manuel Barroso's term of office as president began in 2004). It proposes legislation, is a watchdog that ensures that EU treaties are respected, and is broadly responsible for policy implementation.

▶ **Council of Ministers:** This is the decision-making branch of the EU, and comprises ministers from the 27 states who are accountable to their own assemblies and governments. The presidency of the Council of Ministers rotates amongst member states every six months. Important decisions are made by unanimous agreement, and others are reached through qualified majority voting or by a simple majority.

▶ **European Council:** Informally called the European Summit, this is a senior forum in which heads of government, accompanied by foreign ministers and two commissioners, discuss the overall direction of the Union's work. The Council meets periodically and provides strategic leadership for the EU.

▶ **European Parliament:** The EP is composed of 785 Members of the European Parliament (MEPs) (78 from the UK), who are directly elected every five years. The European Parliament is a scrutinizing assembly, not a legislature. Its major powers (to reject the European Union's budget and dismiss the European Commission) are too far-reaching to exercise.

▶ **European Court of Justice:** The ECJ interprets, and adjudicates on, European Union law. There are 27 judges, one from each member state, and eight advocates general, who advise the court. As EU law has primacy over the national law of EU member states, the court can 'disapply' domestic laws. A Court of First Instance handles certain cases brought by individuals and companies.

This has been ensured partly by respect for the principle of subsidiarity, embodied in the TEU, and by the pragmatic approach to integration adopted by key states such as France and Germany. Decision-making within the 'New Europe' is increasingly made on the basis of multilevel governance, in which the policy process has interconnected subnational, national, intergovernmental and supranational levels, the balance between them shifting in relation to different issues and policy areas. This image of complex policy-making is more helpful than the sometimes sterile notion of a battle between national sovereignty and EU domination.

Despite the progress it has made, the EU is confronted by a number of testing problems. Perhaps the oldest of these is the Common Agricultural Policy (CAP), which ensures that the bulk of EU funds are still used to subsidize uncompetitive farming. Although the need to reform the CAP is widely accepted, this entails tackling powerful farming lobbies in states such as France and Germany, and throughout southern Europe. A second problem is the so-called 'democratic deficit'. This is usually understood to mean the EU's lack of democratic accountability, which is reflected in the weakness of its only directly elected body, the European Parliament. Third, there are challenges that have been brought about by the process of enlargement. The most ambitious expectations of integration emerged when the organiza-

Focus on . . .

European integration: for and against

The arguments in favour of European integration include the following:

- In fostering cosmopolitanism (see p. 217) it encourages European peoples to escape from narrow and insular nationalism.

- Economic, monetary and political union creates a level of interdependence amongst states that makes war or major conflict in Europe unthinkable.

- The establishment of a continent-wide market underpins prosperity and growth and gives Europe security within the global economy.

- 'Pooling' sovereignty is the only way in which European states can exercise major and independent influence on the world stage.

- Political union and economic union go hand in hand, in that a single market has to be regulated by a common set of rules and decisions.

- European citizenship offers individuals a wider and, sometimes, stronger set of rights, freedoms and opportunities.

The arguments against European integration include the following:

- The erosion of national sovereignty means that decision-making fails to take account of distinctive national needs and interests.

- Historically embedded national identities are being weakened, sometimes provoking hostility and a nationalist backlash.

- National, language and cultural differences make it impossible for EU bodies to establish genuine political allegiances.

- The democratic deficit can never be overcome because of the distance between EU institutions and European populations.

- Integration has been driven largely by political elites and corporate interests, which have attempted to manipulate European populations into supporting the New Europe.

- Integration primarily benefits large and economically powerful states and will eventually lead to a German-dominated Europe.

tion was at its most compact, consisting of the original 'Six'. Subsequent enlargement, particularly the enlargement into eastern Europe since 2004, has created tensions between the 'widening' and 'deepening' European agendas. As a larger number of states and interests become involved in the EU policy process, decision-making becomes more difficult and threatens to become impossible. This created pressure for the introduction of a EU Constitution, but the failure to ratify the Constitution has left the EU facing the prospect of institutional sclerosis. Fourth, the EU's ability to remain economically robust is now firmly linked to the success of the single currency project, which, amongst other things, requires that common interest rates suit states that may confront different economic conditions. Finally, the EU's greater independence and assertiveness on the world stage may lead to a realignment in its relations with other major powers. This is, for example, evident in US disquiet about the creation of a European rapid reaction force and its implications for the status and position of NATO.

Global governance

Towards world government?

The logic behind the idea of world government is the same as that which underlies the classic liberal justification for the state – social-contract theory (see p. 93). Just as the only means of ensuring order and stability amongst individuals with different interests is to establish a sovereign state, the only way of preventing international conflict between states each pursuing its national interest is to create a supreme world power. However, quite apart from the practical problems of its construction, world government has at least three major drawbacks. First, once again in line with liberal thinking, world government creates the prospect of unchecked – and uncheckable – power. A world government may, then, become a world tyranny. Second, it is questionable whether the notion of global citizenship that would need to underpin such a government could ever be meaningful, in view of the cultural, language, religious and other differences that divide the peoples of the world. Third, in the light of the (geographical and institutional) distance between government and the people, it is difficult to see how effective democratic accountability could operate within a system of world government.

Nevertheless, the two world wars of the twentieth century, and in particular the advent of industrialized warfare, created irresistable pressure to establish institutions that could facilitate international cooperation. Over time, these have developed into a form of global governance. This constitutes not a single world government, but a collection of institutions through which a system of 'multi-multilateralism' can operate (Fukuyama, 2006). The earliest experiment in global governance was the ill-fated League of Nations, formed in 1919. The League of Nations unfortunately never lived up to its name. Despite the efforts of President Wilson of the USA, Congress blocked US membership of the League. Germany, defeated in the First World War, was admitted only in 1926, and resigned once Hitler assumed power in 1933. The USSR, shunned at first, became a member only in 1934, after Germany and Japan had departed.

Towards the end of the Second World War the idea of global governance gained renewed impetus. In 1944, 44 states that were fighting the Axis powers met at Bretton Woods, New Hampshire, in the USA to devise new rules and institutions to govern the postwar international trading and monetary systems. The aim of the 'Bretton Woods system' was to build a stable and cooperative international monetary system that would promote stable financial conditions and prevent a return to the **autarkic** and protectionist policies that had poisoned international relations in the interwar period. Three institutions were set up to regulate the global economy: the International Monetary Fund (IMF), the General Agreement on Tariffs and Trade (GATT), and the World Bank. Although this new monetary system was committed to establishing an open international economy, it also accepted the important role played by states in managing economic affairs, reflected in the theories of John Maynard Keynes (see p. 190), who led the UK delegation. In that sense, the Bretton Woods system conformed more to the ideas of **mercantilism** than to the commercial liberalism preached by classical economics. At the heart of the Bretton Woods agree-

Autarky: Literally, self-rule; usually understood as economic self-sufficiency brought about either by colonial expansion or by a withdrawal from international trade.

Mercantilism: A school of economic thought that emphasized the state's role in managing international trade and delivering prosperity.

Focus on . . .

Global economic governance

- **The International Monetary Fund (IMF):** The IMF was set up to oversee the global rules governing money in general and, in particular, maintain currency stability through a system of fixed exchange rates. Since 1971, the IMF has embraced a neoliberal economic model, and requires countries to carry out stringent market-based reforms as a condition for receiving assistance. The IMF has grown from its original 29 members to 184 members. Its headquarters are in Washington.

- **The World Bank:** The World Bank (formerly the International Bank for Reconstruction and Development) was designed to reduce the element of risk in foreign lending, thereby underpinning economic stability. Since the 1980s the Bank has geared its lending to 'structural adjustment', the reorientation of economies around market principles and their integration into the global economy. The World Bank's headquarters are in Washington.

- **World Trade Organization (WTO):** The WTO was established in 1995, replacing the General Agreement on Tariffs and Trade (GATT). Created by the 'Uruguay round' of negotiations (1986–95), the WTO has wider and stronger powers than those of GATT. The WTO's mission is to 'liberalize' world trade and create an 'open' global trading system. However, the 'Doha round', which started in 2001, broke down in 2006 because of disagreements between developed and developing states. The WTO had 149 members in 2005, with a further 30 countries applying to join. Its headquarters are in Geneva.

Concept

Free trade

Free trade is a system of trading between states not restricted by tariffs or other forms of protectionism. Free trade is usually seen to have economic and political advantages. Economically, it allows states to specialize in the production of goods and services that they are best suited to produce, leading to specialization and mutual benefits. Politically, free trade promotes interdependence and cosmopolitanism (see p. 117), making conflict and war less likely and perhaps impossible. Critics of free trade point out that it widens economic inequalities by giving dominant powers access to the markets of weak states while having little to fear themselves from foreign competition; that it gears economies to global markets rather than local needs; and that it places profit before considerations of community stability, workers' rights and environmental damage. The issue of free trade is central to debates about the desirability and impact of globalization.

---

ment was the proposal to establish a system of fixed exchange rates, based on the belief that floating rates are inherently unstable and make national economic planning impossible.

However, the Bretton Woods system collapsed in the early 1970s as the USA's decision to allow the dollar to float destroyed the fixed exchange rate regime and left the IMF without its central role. This occurred as the USA, the linchpin of the post-war monetary system and the principal guarantor of fixed exchange rates, was facing increasing economic difficulties. The advent of floating exchange rates initiated a major policy and ideological shift. In policy terms, it gave rise to the '**Washington consensus**'. In ideological terms, the IMF, GATT and the World Bank were converted during the 1970s to the idea of an international economic order based on free-market and free-trade principles. The replacement of GATT by the World Trade Organization (WTO) in 1995 strengthened the free trade agenda and helped to accelerate the pace of economic globalization. The WTO is seen by some as a global economic government in the making. Its supporters argue that in dismantling tariffs and other barriers to trade it is promoting worldwide development and prosperity. Opponents, however, criticize it for being a mouthpiece for corporate interests and for being insensitive to environmental and social concerns. However, since the 1980s the IMF has been more active in supporting developing states in debt crises and in helping to prevent financial crises. There is also evidence from the impasse over the 'Doha round' of negotiations that developing states, often allied to China, are starting to exert greater influence within the WTO.

Washington consensus:
A policy package that sought to reduce intervention in the market through measures of deregulation, privatization and fiscal constraint.

Collective security

The idea of collective security, simply stated, is that aggression can best be resisted by united action taken by a number of states. The theory of collective security is based on the assumption that war and international conflict are rooted in the insecurity and uncertainty of power politics. It suggests that states, as long as they pledge themselves to defend one another, have the capacity either to deter aggression in the first place, or to punish the transgressor if international order has been breached. Successful collective security depends on three conditions. First, the states must be roughly equal, or at least there must be no preponderant power. Second, *all* states must be willing to bear the cost and responsibility of defending one another. Third, there must be an international body that has the moral authority and military capacity to take effective action.

The United Nations

The United Nations, constructed at the San Francisco Conference (April–June 1945) in the dying days of the Second World War, is the most advanced experiment in global governance to date. It has attempted to avoid the manifest failures of the League of Nations, which stood by powerless as Germany, Japan and Italy pursued their expansionist ambitions in the 1930s. The UN was born out of a mixture of realism and idealism. On the one hand, there were clear advantages to extending the anti-Axis alliance of the USA, the USSR and the UK into the postwar period. On the other, there were high expectations, expressed most clearly by Franklin D. Roosevelt, that this period would be marked by a rejection of the power politics of the past, paving the way for an era of peace and international cooperation.

The UN charter laid down the highest standards of international conduct for nations wishing to join the organization. These included the renunciation of the use of force (except in self-defence), the settlement of international disputes by peaceful means, cooperation to ensure respect for human rights and fundamental freedoms, and the recognition of national sovereignty and the right to self-determination. At the heart of this approach lies a commitment to the principle of collective security and the belief that collective action can provide an alternative to the 'old politics', which were based on the pursuit of national interest and the maintenance of a balance of power. Nevertheless, although the UN (unlike the League of Nations) has undoubtedly established itself as a genuinely world body, and is regarded by most as an indispensable part of the international political scene, it is difficult to argue that it has, or perhaps could ever, live up to the expectations of its founders.

The structure of the UN centres around the General Assembly, which consists of all the member states, each of which has a single vote. The General Assembly can debate and pass resolutions on any matter covered by the charter. Important decisions must be carried by a two-thirds majority, but these decisions are recommendations rather than being enforceable international law. The General Assembly is a propaganda arena as opposed to an effective parliament, and it tends to be dominated by the large numbers of developing states. The most significant UN body is the Security Council, which is charged with the maintenance of international peace and security, and is thus responsible for the UN's role as negotiator, observer, peace keeper and, ultimately, peace enforcer. The council has 15 members. The 'Big Five' (the USA, Russia, China, the UK and France) are permanent 'veto powers', meaning that they can cancel decisions made by other members of the council. The other ten members are nonpermanent members that are elected for two years by the General Assembly. The makeup of the Security Council has attracted growing criticism, however. The existing membership essentially reflects the post-Second-World-War balance of power, and does not take account of the growing stature of Japan, India, Germany and Brazil, with states such as Nigeria, Egypt and South Africa also pushing for permanent representation.

The International Court of Justice (sometimes known as the World Court) is the judicial arm of the UN. It consists of a panel of 15 judges elected for nine-year terms by a majority of the members of both the Security Council and General Assembly. Its weaknesses are that it can arbitrate only when states choose to refer their disputes to the court, and only about a third of UN member states are prepared to acknowledge its jurisdiction in any area. The Secretariat is the executive branch of the UN, and it is headed by the UN Secretary General (since January 2007, Ban Ki-Moon). In security matters, the Secretary General works closely with the Security Council. As the closest thing to a 'president of the world', he or she can do much to influence the status and direction of the organization. Although the UN is best known for its high-profile peace-keeping operations, its reputation is shaped by the work of a number of specialist agencies coordinated by the Economic and Social Council of the General Assembly. These include the World Health Organization (WHO), the United Nations Children's Fund (UNICEF), the United Nations Educational, Scientific and Cultural Organization (UNESCO), and the United Nations High Commission for Refugees (UNHCR).

The capacity of the UN to develop into a form of world government is severely limited by the fact that it is essentially a creature of its members: it can do no more than its member states, and particularly the permanent members of the Security Council, permit. As a result, its role has been confined essentially to providing mechanisms that facilitate the peaceful resolution of international conflicts. Even in this respect, however, its record has been patchy. There have been undoubted successes, for example in negotiating a ceasefire between India and Pakistan in 1959, maintaining peace in 1960 in the Belgian Congo (now Zaire), and mediating between the Dutch and the Indonesians over West Irian (New Guinea) in 1962. However, for much of its history, the UN was virtually paralysed by superpower rivalry. The Cold War ensured that, on most issues, the USA and the USSR adopted opposing positions, which prevented the Security Council from taking decisive action. The UN's intervention in Korea in 1950 was possible only because the USSR temporarily withdrew from the Council (in protest against the exclusion of communist China), and in any case this merely fuelled fears that the UN was western-dominated. As the world drew close to nuclear war during the Cuban Missile Crisis of 1962, the UN was a powerless spectator. It was unable to prevent the Soviet invasions of Hungary (1956), Czechoslovakia (1968) and Afghanistan (1979), and it had only a very limited influence on the succession of Arab–Israeli wars in 1948, 1956, 1967 and 1973.

The end of the Cold War was the beginning, many hoped, of a new chapter for the UN. For so long marginalized by superpower antagonism, the UN suddenly assumed a new prominence as the instrument through which 'one world' could be brought about. The UN's intervention in 1990–91 to expel Iraq from Kuwait seemed to demonstrate a renewed capacity to fulfil its obligation of deterring aggression and maintaining peace, as did the USA's decision not to pursue fleeing Iraqi troops into Iraq for fear of acting outside the authority of the UN. However, these early hopes were quickly disappointed. UN peacekeepers were little more than spectators during the genocidal slaughter in Rwanda in 1994, and were reluctant to intervene in the Sudanese province of Darfur a decade later. UN-backed US intervention in Somalia led to humiliation and withdrawal in 1995, with warlord conflict continuing unabated. Recurrent fighting in the former Yugoslavia demonstrated the ineffectiveness of UN-negotiated ceasefires and UN-backed sanctions against Serbia. Most significantly, the USA and its 'coalition of the willing' went ahead with their invasion of Iraq in 2003, despite opposition from leading members of the Security Council of the UN, leaving Kofi Annan to describe the invasion as a violation of international law. Why did this happen?

Quite simply, the UN has been one of the casualties of the insecurity and shifting balances that the breakdown of the 'old' world order has precipitated. Instead of stepping into centre stage as a proto-world-government, the UN has been forced to

Concept

International law

International law is a system of rules that are binding on states, and thus define the relationships between states. Law is a set of public and enforceable rules. In the absence of a world legislature, international law draws on a number of sources: treaties, custom, general principles (such as respect for territorial integrity), and legal scholarship accumulated by the international courts. Idealists have traditionally placed heavy emphasis on international law, seeing it as a means of establishing order through respect for moral principles, which thus makes possible the peaceful resolution of international conflicts. Realists, on the other hand, have questioned the status of international law, arguing that, as it is not enforceable, it constitutes not 'law', but merely a set of moral principles.

confront a range of new problems and conflicts. These include the reluctance of states whose security is no longer threatened by East–West rivalry to commit resources to the cause of collective security or for the defence of states on the other side of the globe. This 'new isolationism' helped to prevent EU member states from taking concerted action in Bosnia, and it also discouraged the USA from getting involved at an earlier stage. Moreover, a unipolar world order threatens to sideline the UN just as effectively as did Cold War bipolarity. The unilateralist tendency in US foreign policy has been expressed not only in criticism of the disproportional burden of financial responsibilities that fall on its shoulders, but also in resentment at attempts by the UN to restrict the USA from pursuing what it perceives as legitimate security goals. Finally, the international political focus has itself shifted. The UN's role used to be to keep the peace in a world dominated by the conflict between communism and capitalism. Now it is being forced to find a new role in a world structured by the dynamics of global capitalism, in which conflict increasingly arises from imbalances in the distribution of wealth and resources. In this respect, the UN's lack of economic influence is a particular weakness, especially in the light of the growing power of the WTO, the IMF and the G7, the organization of the world's dominant economic powers. Nevertheless, in view of the UN's unique role and moral authority, even its strongest critics are willing to accept that if it did not exist it would need to be invented.

Summary

◆ International politics has been analysed in a number of ways. Idealism adopts a perspective that is based on moral values and legal norms. Realism emphasizes the importance of power politics. Neorealism highlights the structural constraints of the international system. Pluralism advances a mixed-actor model, and it stresses a growing diffusion of power. Marxism draws attention to economic inequalities within the global capitalist system.

◆ World order in the twenty-first century has been interpreted in various ways. A bipolar world order has given way to a unipolar world order based on the USA as a hyperpower. This new world order has largely been defined by the 'war on terror', as the USA has sought to combat the forces perceived to underpin the threat of global terrorism. However, the rise of new powers, the growing influence of nonstate actors and the changing nature of power is leading to a new form of multipolarism.

◆ Globalization is a complex web of interconnectedness that means that our lives are increasingly shaped by decisions and actions taken at a distance from ourselves. Economic globalization reflects the increase in transnational flows of capital and goods, destroying the idea of economic sovereignty. Cultural globalization is a homogenizing force; although globalization is by no means an entirely 'top-down' process.

◆ Globalization is a highly controversial set of processes. There is debate both about whether it is happening and about the forces fuelling it. Supporters of globalization argue that it encourages democratization, promotes prosperity and development, and widens choice and opportunity. Opponents hold it responsible for growing inequality, the ability of corporations to escape democratic control, and environmental blight.

◆ Trends towards regional integration may counterbalance globalization, with some arguing that regionalism has the capacity to displace nationalism. The European Union is the most advanced experiment in regional integration, being an example of a political union as well as an economic union. However, while it has moved towards 'pooling' sovereignty, it is, as yet, far from being a European 'superstate'.

◆ The argument for world government is basically that, if there is no global state, the international system will operate as a 'state of nature'. However, the capacity of the United Nations to play this role is restricted because of the unwillingness of states to commit resources to the cause of collective security, the unequal distribution of responsibilities in the new international system, and the difficulty of finding a new role for the UN in a world that is no longer structured by East–West rivalry.

Questions for discussion

▶ Which perspective on world politics offers the greatest insight into contemporary developments?

▶ Is the 'war on terror' evidence of the emergence of a clash of civilizations?

▶ Is a multipolar world order necessarily unstable?

▶ Is globalization a myth or a reality?

▶ Does a globalized economy mean opportunity for all or greater insecurity and deeper inequality?

▶ Is the European Union exceptional, or will it become a model for regional integration?

▶ What role could, or should, the United Nations adopt in the new international system?

▶ Is world government an attractive prospect?

Further reading

Baylis, J. and S. Smith (eds), *The Globalization of World Politics: An Introduction to Intenational Relations* (Oxford: Oxford University Press, 2005). A highly comprehensive introduction to world politics that takes full account of the impact of globalization.

Burchill, S. et al., *Theories of International Relations*, 3rd edn (Basingstoke: Palgrave Macmillan, 2005). A concise and informative introduction to the range of theoretical traditions in the field of international relations.

Chomsky, N., *Hegemony and Survival: America's Quest for Global Dominance* (New York: Owl Books, 2004). A trenchant critique of US foreign policy in the post-Cold-War era, highlighting the USA's pursuit of an 'imperial grand strategy'.

Held, D. and A. McGrew (eds), *The Global Transformation: An Introduction to the Globalization Debate* (Cambridge and Malden, MA: Polity Press, 2000). A full and wide-ranging text that examines the key issues in the globalization debate.

Hettne, B., A. Inotai and O. Sunkel (eds) *Globalism and the New Regionalism* (Basingstoke: Palgrave Macmillan, 1999). The first volume of a five-volume study of the relationship between regionalization and globalization.

McCormick, J., *Understanding the European Union: A Concise Introduction*, 3rd edn (Basingstoke and New York: Palgrave Macmillan, 2005). A concise, lively and readable introduction to the workings and development of the EU and the implications of European integration.

Scholte, J. A., *Globalization: A Critical Introduction*, 2nd edn (Basingstoke and New York: Palgrave Macmillan, 2005). The most comprehensive and accessible of the many introductions to globalization.

Subnational Politics

CHAPTER 8

> 'All politics is local.'
>
> Favourite saying of former Speaker of the US House of Representatives
> THOMAS (TIP) O'NEILL JR

Although nation-states are treated as discrete and unified entities as far as international politics is concerned, each nation-state incorporates a range of internal divisions and levels of power. Most significantly, there are territory-based divisions between central or national government and various forms of provincial, state and local government. These divisions are crucially shaped by a state's constitutional structure: that is, by whether it has a federal or unitary system of government. Each system establishes a particular territorial distribution of government power, thus providing a framework within which centre–periphery relationships can be conducted. All modern states have also been subject to contrasting pressures, if to different degrees. On the one hand, economic, international and other factors have led to a seemingly remorseless trend towards centralization. On the other hand, especially in the late twentieth century, centrifugal tendencies have increased with the rise of ethnic, regional and community politics.

The central issues examined in this chapter are as follows:

Contents

Key issues

▶ What are the respective benefits of centralization and decentralization?

▶ How do federal and unitary systems differ, and how successfully does each type of system reconcile territorial and other differences?

▶ Why has there been a tendency towards greater centralization?

▶ What factors explain the rise of ethnic politics? How serious a threat does it pose to the nation-state?

▶ To what extent is there scope in modern societies for community to replace the nation as the central focus of politics?

■ Centralization or decentralization?

All modern states are divided on a territorial basis between central (national) and peripheral (regional, provincial or local) institutions. The nature of such divisions varies enormously, however. These differences include the constitutional framework within which centre–periphery relationships are conducted, the distribution of functions and responsibilities between the levels of government, the means by which their personnel are appointed and recruited, the political, economic, administrative and other powers that the centre can use to control the periphery, and the independence that peripheral bodies enjoy. What is clear, however, is that neither central nor peripheral bodies can be dispensed with altogether.

In the absence of central government, a state would simply not be able to function as an actor on the international or world stage. It would possess no machinery for entering into strategic alliances, negotiating trade agreements, gaining representation at international summit meetings, or becoming a member of supranational bodies. This is why central government is invariably responsible for a state's external relations, as demonstrated by its control of foreign, diplomatic and defence policy. Moreover, some form of central government is necessary to mediate between peripheral bodies to ensure cooperation in areas of mutual interest. In most cases, this means that central government assumes overall control of the state's economic life, and supervises matters such as internal trade, transport and communications. There are, however, powerful reasons for further strengthening central government at the expense of peripheral institutions.

The case for **centralization** includes the following:

• **National unity:** Central government alone articulates the interests of the whole rather than the various parts: that is, the interests of the nation rather than those of sectional, ethnic or regional groups. A strong centre ensures that the government addresses the common interests of the entire community; a weak centre leads to rivalry and disharmony.

• **Uniformity:** Central government alone can establish uniform laws and public services that help people to move more easily from one part of the country to another. Geographical mobility is likely to be restricted when there are differing tax regimes and differing legal, educational and social-security systems throughout a country.

• **Equality:** Decentralization has the disadvantage that it forces peripheral institutions to rely on the resources available in their locality or region. Only central government can rectify inequalities that arise from the fact that the areas with the greatest social needs are invariably those with the least potential for raising revenue.

• **Prosperity:** Economic development and centralization invariably go hand in hand. Only central government, for instance, can manage a single currency, control tax and spending policies with a view to ensuring sustainable growth, and, if necessary, provide an infrastructure in the form of roads, railways, airports and so on.

On the other hand, there are limits to the amount of centralization that is possible or desirable. Indeed, the notion of a modern state comprising tens or even hundreds of millions of citizens being entirely governed from the centre is simply absurd. For

---

Centralization: The concentration of political power or government authority at the national level.

example, if all the services and functions of modern government were to be administered from the centre, the result would be hopeless inefficiency and bureaucratic chaos, reflecting what economists call the 'diseconomies of scale'. In general, the responsibilities vested in peripheral institutions are those that are 'domestic' in the sense that they primarily address the needs of the domestic population: for example, education, health, social welfare, and planning. The pressure to shift other responsibilities and decision-making power from central to peripheral bodies is, however, considerable.

The case for **decentralization** includes the following:

• **Participation:** Local or regional government is certainly more effective than central government in providing opportunities for citizens to participate in the political life of their community. The benefits of widening the scope of political participation include the fact that it helps to create a better educated and more informed citizenry.

• **Responsiveness:** Peripheral institutions are usually 'closer' to the people and more sensitive to their needs. This both strengthens democratic accountability and ensures that government responds not merely to the overall interests of society, but also to the specific needs of particular communities.

• **Legitimacy:** Physical distance from government affects the acceptability or rightness of its decisions. Decisions made at a 'local' level are more likely to be seen as intelligible and therefore legitimate (see p. 219). In contrast, central government may appear remote, both geographically and politically.

• **Liberty:** As power tends to corrupt, centralization threatens to turn government into a tyranny against the individual. Decentralization protects liberty by dispersing government power, thereby creating a network of checks and balances. Peripheral bodies check central government as well as each other.

Centre–periphery relationships

The balance between centralization and decentralization within a state is shaped by a wide range of historical, cultural, geographical, economic and political factors. The most prominent of these is the constitutional structure of the state, particularly the location of sovereignty (see p. 131) in the political system. Although modified by other factors, the constitutional structure provides, as a minimum, the framework within which centre–periphery relationships are conducted. The two most common forms of territorial organization found in the modern world are the federal and unitary systems. A third form, confederation, has generally proved to be unsustainable. As **confederations** establish only the loosest and most decentralized type of political union by vesting sovereign power in peripheral bodies, it is not surprising that their principal advocates have been anarchists such as Pierre-Joseph Proudhon (see p. 166). The confederal principle is, in fact, most commonly applied in the form of intergovernmentalism (see p. 153) as embodied in international organizations such as the North Atlantic Treaty Organization (NATO), the United Nations (UN), the Organization of African Unity (OAU) and the Commonwealth of Nations. Examples of confederations at the nation-state level are, however, far rarer. The USA was originally a confederation, first in the form of the Continental Congresses

Decentralization: The expansion of local autonomy through the transfer of powers and responsibilities away from national bodies.

Confederation: A qualified union of states in which each state retains its independence, typically guaranteed by unanimous decision-making.

Pierre-Joseph Proudhon (1809–65)

French anarchist. A largely self-educated printer, Proudhon was drawn into radical politics in Lyons before settling in Paris in 1847. As a member of the 1848 Constituent Assembly, Proudhon famously voted against the constitution 'because it was a constitution'. He was later imprisoned for three years, after which, disillusioned with active politics, he concentrated on writing and theorizing. His best-known work, *What is Property?* ([1840] 1970), developed the first systematic argument for anarchism, based on the 'mutualist' principle; it also contained the famous dictum 'property is theft'. In *The Federal Principle* (1863), Proudhon modified his anarchism by acknowledging the need for a minimal state to 'set things in motion' (although by 'federal' he meant a political compact between self-governing communities – in effect, confederalism).

(1774–81), and then under the Articles of Confederation (1781–89). The most important modern example of a confederal state is the Commonwealth of Independent States (CIS), which in 1991 formally replaced the USSR. The CIS was established by 11 of the 15 former Soviet republics (only Georgia and the three Baltic states refused to join). However, it lacks executive authority, and therefore constitutes little more than an occasional forum for debate and arbitration. Indeed, the evidence is that, in the absence of an effective central body, confederations either, as in the USA, transform themselves into federal states, or succumb to centrifugal pressures and disintegrate altogether, as has more or less occurred in the case of the CIS.

Federal systems

Federal systems of government have been more common than confederal systems. Over a third of the world's population is governed by states that have some kind of federal structure. These states include the USA, Brazil, Pakistan, Australia, Mexico, Switzerland, Nigeria, Malaysia and Canada. Although no two federal structures are identical, the central feature of each is a sharing of sovereignty between central and peripheral institutions. This ensures, at least in theory, that neither level of government can encroach on the powers of the other (see Figure 8.1). In this sense, a

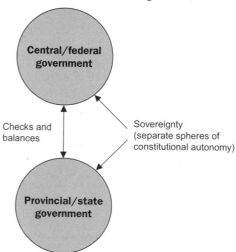

Fig. 8.1   Federal states

federation is an intermediate form of political organization that lies somewhere between a confederation (which vests sovereign power in peripheral bodies) and a unitary state (in which power is located in central institutions). Federal systems are based upon a compromise between unity and regional diversity, between the need for an effective central power and the need for checks or constraints on that power.

Why federalism?

When a list of federal states (or states exhibiting federal-type features) is examined, certain common characteristics can be observed. This suggests that the federal principle is more applicable to some states than to others. In the first place, historical similarities can be identified. For example, federations have often been formed by the coming together of a number of established political communities that nevertheless wish to preserve their separate identities and, to some extent, their autonomy. This clearly applied in the case of the world's first federal state, the USA. Although the 13 former British colonies in America quickly recognized the inadequacy of confederal organization, each possessed a distinctive political identity and set of traditions that it was determined to preserve within the new, more centralized, constitutional framework. Indeed, charter colonies such as Rhode Island and Connecticut had become accustomed to such a degree of independence from the British Crown that their colonial charters served, in the early years at least, as state constitutions.

The reluctance of the former colonies to establish a strong national government was demonstrated at the Philadelphia Constitutional Convention of 1787, which drafted the US constitution, and by the ensuing debate over ratification. The 'nationalist' position, which supported ratification, was advanced in the so-called *Federalist Papers*, published between 1787 and 1789. These were written by Alexander Hamilton, James Madison (see p. 344) and John Jay (1745–1829), who published collectively under the name Publius. They emphasized the importance of establishing a strong centralized government while at the same time preserving state and individual freedoms. Ratification was finally achieved in 1789, but only through the adoption of the Bill of Rights and, in particular, the Tenth Amendment, which guaranteed that powers not delegated to the federal government would be 'reserved to the states respectively, or to the people'. This provided a constitutional basis for US federalism. A similar process occurred in Germany. Although unification in 1871 reflected the growing might of Prussia, a federal structure helped to allay the fears of central control of the other 38 Germanic states that had long enjoyed political independence. This tradition of regional autonomy, briefly interrupted during the Nazi period, was formalized in the constitution of the Federal Republic of Germany, adopted in 1949, which granted each of the 11 *Länder* (provinces or states) its own constitution. Their number was increased to 16 as a result of the reunification of Germany in 1990.

A second factor influencing the formation of federations is the existence of an external threat or a desire to play a more effective role in international affairs. Small, strategically vulnerable states, for instance, have a powerful incentive to enter broader political unions. One of the weaknesses of the US Articles of Confederation was thus that they failed to give the newly independent US states a clear diplomatic voice, making it difficult for them to negotiate treaties, enter into alliances, and so on. The willingness of the German states in the nineteenth century to enter into a federal union and accept effective 'Prussification' owed a great deal to the intensifying rivalry of the great powers, and in particular the threat posed by both Austria and

Concept

Federalism

Federalism (from the Latin *foedus*, meaning 'pact', or 'covenant') usually refers to legal and political structures that distribute power territorially within a state. Nevertheless, in accordance with its original meaning, it has been taken to imply reciprocity or mutuality (Proudhon), or, in the writings of Alexander Hamilton and James Madison (see p. 344), to be part of a broader ideology of pluralism. As a political form, however, federalism requires the existence of two distinct levels of government, neither of which is legally or politically subordinate to the other. Its central feature is therefore the notion of shared sovereignty. On the basis of this definition, 'classical' federations are few in number: the USA, Switzerland, Belgium, Canada and Australia. However, many more states have federal-type features.

Alexander Hamilton (1755–1805)

US statesman, and co-author with James Madison and John Jay of the *Federalist Papers* (Hamilton, Jay and Madison, [1787–89] 1961). Hamilton was born in the West Indies. He fought in the American Revolution, becoming George Washington's aide-de-camp (1777–81). After studying law, Hamilton was returned to Congress in 1782, served as the USA's first Secretary of the Treasury (1789–95), and founded and led the Federalist Party until his death in a duel with his rival Aaron Burr. Hamilton's federalism was characterized by a deep distrust of democracy, support for an active central government, and the desire to boost manufacturing industry through national fiscal and economic policies. 'Hamiltonianism' thus came to represent the idea of a powerful national government with a strong executive authority able to support the emerging national economy.

France. Similarly, the drift towards the construction of a federal Europe, which began with the establishment of the European Coal and Steel Community (ECSC) in 1952 and the European Economic Community (EEC) in 1957, was in part brought about by a fear of Soviet aggression and by a perceived loss of European influence in the emerging bipolar world order.

A third factor is geographical size. It is no coincidence that many of the territorially largest states in the world have opted to introduce federal systems. This was true of the USA, and it also applied to Canada (federated in 1867), Brazil (1891), Australia (1901), Mexico (1917) and India (1947). Geographically large states tend to be culturally diverse and often possess strong regional traditions. This creates greater pressure for decentralization and the dispersal of power than can usually be accommodated within a unitary system. The final factor encouraging the adoption of federalism is cultural and ethnic heterogeneity. Federalism, in short, has often been an institutional response to societal divisions and diversities. Canada's ten provinces, for instance, reflect not only long-established regional traditions but also language and cultural differences between English-speaking and French-speaking parts of the country. India's 25 self-governing states were defined primarily by language but, in the case of states such as Punjab and Kashmir, also take religious differences into account. Nigeria's 19-state federal constitution similarly recognizes major tribal and religious differences, particularly between the north and south-east of the country.

Features of federalism

Each federal system is unique in the sense that the relationship between federal (national) government and state (regional) government is determined not just by constitutional rules, but also by a complex of political, historical, geographical, cultural and social circumstances. In some respects, for example, the party system is as significant a determinant of federal–state relationships as are the constitutionally allocated powers of each level of government. Thus the federal structure of the USSR, which unlike the USA granted each of its 15 republics the right of secession, was entirely bogus given the highly centralized nature of the 'ruling' Communist Party, to say nothing of the rigidly hierarchical central-planning system. A similar situation can be found in Mexico, where the dominant Institutional Revolutionary Party (PRI) has effectively counteracted a federal system that was consciously modelled on the US example. In the USA, Canada, Australia and India, on the other hand, decentralized party systems have safeguarded the powers of state and regional governments.

There is a further contrast between federal regimes that operate a 'separation of powers' (see p. 339) between the **executive** and **legislative** branches of government (typified by the US presidential system), and parliamentary systems in which executive and legislative power is 'fused'. The former tend to ensure that government power is diffused both territorially and functionally, meaning that there are multiple points of contact between the two levels of government. This leads to the complex patterns of interpenetration between federal and state levels of government that are found in the US and Swiss systems. Parliamentary systems, however, often produce what is called 'executive federalism', most notably in Canada and Australia. In such cases the federal balance is determined largely by the relationship between the executives of each level of government.

Nevertheless, certain features are common to most, if not all, federal systems:

- **Two relatively autonomous levels of government**: Both central government (the federal level) and regional government (the state level) possess a range of powers that the other cannot encroach upon. These include at least a measure of legislative and executive authority and the capacity to raise revenue and thus enjoy a degree of fiscal independence. However, the specific fields of jurisdiction of each level of government and the capacity of each to influence the other vary considerably. In Germany and Austria, for instance, a system of 'administrative' federalism operates in which central government is the key policy-maker, and provincial government is charged with the responsibility for the details of policy implementation.

- **Written constitution**: The responsibilities and powers of each level of government are defined in a codified or **written constitution**. The relationship between the centre and the periphery is therefore conducted within a formal legal framework. The autonomy of each level is usually guaranteed by the fact that neither is able to amend the constitution unilaterally: for example, amendments of the US constitution require the support of two-thirds of both houses of Congress and three-quarters of the 50 state legislatures. In Australia and Switzerland, for example, amendments to the constitution must also be ratified through the use of referendums (see p. 250).

- **Constitutional arbiter**: The formal provisions of the constitution are interpreted by a supreme court, which thereby arbitrates in the case of disputes between federal and state levels of government. In determining the respective fields of jurisdiction of each level, the judiciary in a federal system is able to determine how federalism works in practice, inevitably drawing the judiciary into the policy process. The centralization that occurred in all federal systems in the twentieth century was invariably sanctioned by the courts.

- **Linking institutions**: In order to foster cooperation and understanding between federal and state levels of government, the regions and provinces must be given a voice in the processes of central policy-making. This is usually achieved through a bicameral legislature, in which the second chamber or upper house represents the interests of the states. The 76 members of the Australian Senate, for example, comprise 12 from each of the six states, two from the Australian Territory, and two from the Northern Territory. An exception here is the weak federal arrangements in Malaysia, which allow the majority of members of the Senate (Dewan Negara) to be appointed by the monarch.

Executive: The branch of government that is responsible for implementing or carrying out law and policy (see p. 358).

Legislature: The branch of government that is empowered to make law through the formal enactment of legislation.

Written constitution: A single authoritative document that allocates duties, powers and functions amongst the institutions of government, and so constitutes 'higher' law.

Assessment of federalism

One of the chief strengths of federal systems is that, unlike unitary systems, they give regional and local interests a constitutionally guaranteed political voice. The states or provinces exercise a range of autonomous powers and enjoy some measure of representation in central government, usually, as pointed out above, through the second chamber of the federal legislature. On the other hand, federalism was not able to stem the general twentieth-century tendency towards centralization. Despite guarantees of state and provincial rights in federal systems, the powers of central government have expanded, largely as a result of the growth of economic and social intervention, and central government's own greater revenue-raising capacities.

The US system, for instance, initially operated according to the principles of 'dual federalism', in which federal and state governments occupied separate and seemingly indestructible spheres of policy power. From the late nineteenth century onwards, this gave way to a system of 'cooperative federalism' that was based on the growth of 'grants in aid' from the federal government to the states and localities. State and local government therefore became increasingly dependent on the flow of federal funds, especially after the upsurge in economic and social programmes that occurred under the New Deal in the 1930s. From the mid-1960s, however, cooperative federalism, based on a partnership of sorts between federal government and the states, was replaced by what has been called 'coercive federalism'. This is a system through which federal government has increasingly brought about the compliance of the states by passing laws that preempt their powers and imposing restrictions on the states and localities in the form of mandates.

A second advantage of federalism is that, in diffusing government power, it creates a network of checks and balances that help to protect individual liberty. In James Madison's words, 'ambition must be made to counteract ambition'. Despite a worldwide tendency towards centralization, federal systems such as those in the USA, Australia and Canada have usually been more effective in constraining national politicians than have been unitary systems. However, structures intended to create healthy tension within a system of government may also generate frustration and paralysis. One of the weaknesses of federal systems is that, by constraining central authority, they make the implementation of bold economic or social programmes more difficult. F. D. Roosevelt's New Deal in the USA, for example, was significantly weakened by Supreme Court decisions that were intended to prevent federal government from encroaching on the responsibilities of the states. In the 1980s, Ronald Reagan deliberately used federalism as a weapon against 'big' government, and specifically against the growing welfare budget. Under the slogan 'new federalism', Reagan attempted to staunch social spending by transferring responsibility for welfare from federal government to the less prosperous state governments. In contrast, the dominant pattern of cooperative federalism in Germany has facilitated, rather than thwarted, the construction of a comprehensive and well-funded welfare system.

Finally, federalism has provided an institutional mechanism through which fractured societies have maintained unity and coherence. In this respect, the federal solution may be appropriate only to a limited number of ethnically diverse and regionally divided societies, but in these cases it may be absolutely vital. The genius of US federalism, for instance, was perhaps less that it provided the basis for unity amongst the 13 original states, and more that it invested the USA with an institutional mechanism that enabled it to absorb the strains that immigration exerted from the mid-nineteenth century onwards. The danger of federalism, however, is that by breeding governmental division it may strengthen centrifugal pressures and ultimately lead to disintegration. Some have argued, as a result, that federal systems are inherently unstable, tending either towards the guaranteed unity that only a unitary system can offer, or towards greater decentralization and ultimate collapse.

Federalism in Canada, for example, can be deemed a failure if its purpose was to construct a political union within which both French-speaking and English-speaking populations can live in harmony. In response to the growth of **separatism** in pre-dominantly francophone Quebec, Canada has engaged since the late 1980s in a fruit-less search for a constitutional formula that would reconcile Quebec to membership of the Canadian federation. The Meech Lake Accord of 1987, which attempted to meet demands for greater autonomy by granting Quebec 'special status' within the federation, failed three years later when Manitoba and Newfoundland rejected the principle of 'asymmetrical federalism'. The Charlottetown Agreement of 1992 offered another formula, but this was rejected in a national referendum, partly because Quebec believed that it did not go far enough in granting autonomy, and partly because many anglophone Canadians feared that it threatened the integrity of the Canadian state. Nevertheless, the option of an entirely independent Quebec, backed strongly by the separatist Parti Québecois, was also narrowly rejected by the people of Quebec in a referendum at the end of 1995.

Unitary systems

The vast majority of contemporary states have unitary systems of government. These vest sovereign power in a single, national institution. In the UK, this institution is Parliament, which possesses, at least in theory, unrivalled and unchallengeable legislative authority. Parliament can make or unmake any law it wishes; its powers are not checked by a codified or written constitution; there are no rival UK legis-latures that can challenge its authority; and its laws outrank all other forms of English and Scottish law. Since constitutional supremacy is vested with the centre in a unitary system, any system of peripheral or local government exists at the pleasure of the centre (see Figure 8.2). At first sight, this creates the spectre of unchecked centralization. Local institutions can be reshaped, reorganized and even abolished at will; their powers and responsibilities can be contracted as easily as they can be expanded. However, in practice, the relationship between the centre and the periphery

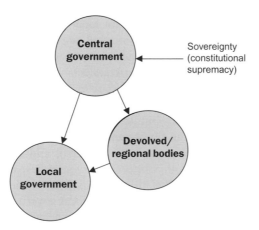

Fig. 8.2   Unitary states

Separatism: The quest to secede from a political formation with a view to establishing an independent state.

---

in unitary systems is as complex as it is in federal systems, political, cultural and historical factors being as significant as more formal constitutional ones. Two distinct institutional forms of peripheral authority nevertheless exist in unitary states: local government and devolved assemblies. Each of these gives centre–periphery relationships a distinctive shape.

Local government

Local government, in its simplest sense, is government that is specific to a particular locality, for example a village, district, town, city or county. More particularly, it is a form of government that has no share in sovereignty, and is thus entirely subordinate to central authority or, in a federal system, to state or regional authority. This level of government is in fact universal, being found in federal and confederal systems as well as in unitary ones. In the USA, for instance, there are over 86 000 units of local government that employ 11 000 000 people, compared with a total of fewer than 8 000 000 staff at federal and state levels. However, what makes local government particularly important in unitary systems is that in most cases it is the only form of government outside the centre.

It would nevertheless be a mistake to assume that the constitutional subordination of local government means that it is politically irrelevant. The very ubiquity of local government reflects the fact that it is both administratively necessary and, because it is 'close' to the people, easily intelligible. Moreover, elected local politicians have a measure of democratic legitimacy (see p. 219) that enables them to extend their formal powers and responsibilities. This often means that central–local relationships are conducted through a process of bargaining and negotiation rather than by diktat from above. The balance between the centre and the periphery is further influenced by factors such as the political culture (particularly by established traditions of local autonomy and regional diversity) and the nature of the party system. For instance, the growing tendency for local politics to be 'politicized', in the sense that national parties have increasingly dominated local politics, has usually brought with it greater centralization. In the absence of the kind of constitutional framework that federalism provides, the preservation of local autonomy relies, to a crucial extent, on self-restraint by the centre. This tends to mean that the degree of decentralization in unitary systems varies significantly, both over time and from country to country. This can be illustrated by the contrasting experiences of the UK and France.

The UK traditionally possessed a relatively decentralized local government system, with local authorities exercising significant discretion within a legal framework laid down by Parliament. Indeed, respect for **local democracy** was long seen as a feature of the UK's unwritten constitution. Following J. S. Mill (see p. 48), constitutional authorities usually praised local government as both a check on central power and a means through which popular participation, and thus political education, could be broadened. The expansion of the state's economic and social role in the post-1945 period, however, meant that local authorities were increasingly charged with responsibility for delivering public services on behalf of central government. This partnership approach to local–central relationships was abruptly abandoned by the Conservative governments of the 1980s and 1990s, which saw local government, in common with other intermediary agencies, as an obstacle to the implementation of their radical market-orientated policies.

The introduction in 1984 of 'rate capping' robbed local government of its most important power: the ability to control local tax levels and so determine its own spend-

Local democracy: A principle that embodies both the idea of local autonomy and the goal of popular responsiveness.

ing policies. Local authorities that challenged the centre, such as the Greater London Council and the metropolitan county councils, were abolished, their functions being devolved to smaller district and borough councils and a variety of newly crated **quangos**. The responsibilities of local government were also restricted through, for example, the introduction of a national curriculum for schools and legislation that permitted schools to opt out from local authority control. The ultimate aim of these policies was fundamentally to remodel local government by creating 'enabling' councils, whose role is not to provide services themselves, but to supervise the provision of services by private bodies through a system of contracting-out and privatization. Such policies have widely been interpreted as an attack on local democracy. On the one hand, power has been transferred from local to central government, and on the other, local authorities have been subjected to intensified market pressures from members of the local community in their new roles as 'customers' and 'clients'.

Very different policies were adopted in France during the same period. In a conscious attempt to transform the character of French society, and in particular the tradition of centralization that the Fifth Republic inherited from the Jacobins and Napoleon, President Mitterrand embarked on a programme of political decentralization that was implemented by the Minister for the Interior and Decentralization, Gaston Defferre, between 1982 and 1986. Traditionally, central–local relationships in France were dominated by a system of strict administrative control that operated largely through prefects (appointed by, and directly accountable to, the Ministry of the Interior), who were the chief executives of France's 96 *départements*. The established French system therefore worked very much as a hierarchical chain of command. As well as revitalizing regional government, the Defferre reforms extended both the responsibilities and the powers of local government. In particular, the executive powers of the prefects were transferred to locally elected presidents, and the prefects were replaced by Commissaires de la République, who are concerned essentially with economic planning. In addition, local authorities were absolved of the need to seek prior approval for administrative and spending decisions, these now being subject only to *a posteriori* legal and financial control. The net result of these reforms has been to give France a more decentralized state structure than it has had at any time since the 1789 revolution.

Devolution

Devolution, at least in its legislative form, establishes the greatest possible measure of decentralization in a unitary system of government, short, that is, of its transformation into a federal system. Devolved assemblies have usually been created in response to increasing centrifugal tensions within a state, and as an attempt, in particular, to conciliate growing regional and sometimes nationalist pressures. Despite their lack of entrenched powers, once devolved assemblies have acquired a political identity of their own, and possess a measure of democratic legitimacy, they are very difficult to weaken and, in normal circumstances, impossible to abolish. Northern Ireland's Stormont Parliament was an exception. The Stormont Parliament was suspended in 1972 and replaced by direct rule from the Westminster Parliament, but only when it became apparent that its domination by predominantly Protestant Unionist parties prevented it from stemming the rising tide of communal violence in Northern Ireland that threatened to develop into civil war.

One of the oldest traditions of devolved government in Europe is found in Spain. Although it has been a unitary state since the 1570s, Spain is divided into 50

Concept

Devolution

Devolution is the transfer of power from central government to subordinate regional institutions (to 'devolve' means to pass powers or duties down from a higher authority to a lower one). Devolved bodies thus constitute an intermediate level of government between central and local governments. However, devolution differs from federalism in that, although their territorial jurisdiction may be similar, devolved bodies have no share in sovereignty; their responsibilities and powers are derived from, and are conferred by, the centre. In its weakest form, that of *administrative* devolution, devolution implies only that regional institutions implement policies decided elsewhere. In the form of *legislative* devolution (sometimes called 'home rule'), devolution involves the establishment of elected regional assemblies invested with policy-making responsibilities and a measure of fiscal independence.

Quango: An acronym for quasi-autonomous non-governmental organization: a public body staffed by appointees rather than by politicians or civil servants (see p. 392).

Concept

Ethnicity

Ethnicity is the sentiment of loyalty towards a distinctive population, cultural group or territorial area. The term is complex because it has both racial and cultural overtones. The members of ethnic groups are often seen, correctly or incorrectly, to have descended from common ancestors, and the groups are thus thought of as extended kinship groups, united by blood. More commonly, ethnicity is understood as a form of cultural identity, albeit one that operates at a deep and emotional level. An 'ethnic' culture encompasses values, traditions and practices but, crucially, it also gives a people a common identity and sense of distinctiveness, usually by focusing on their origins and descent. Some see nations (see p. 110) simply as extended ethnic groups; others stress that, while ethnic groups are essentially cultural and exclusive (you cannot 'join' an ethnic group), nations are more inclusive, and are, ultimately, politically defined.

Ethnic nationalism: A form of nationalism that is fuelled primarily by a keen sense of ethnic distinctiveness and the desire to preserve it.

provinces, each of which exercises a measure of regional self-government. As part of the transition to democratic government following the death of General Franco in 1975, the devolution process was extended in 1979 with the creation of 17 autonomous communities. This new tier of regional government is based on elected assemblies invested with broad control of domestic policy. Although this reform was designed to meet long-standing demands for Catalan autonomy in the Basque area, it merely provoked a fresh wave of terrorism perpetrated by the separatist movement ETA (Euskadi Ta Askatasuna). The French government has also used devolution as a means of responding to the persistence of regional identities, and, at least in Brittany and Occitania, to the emergence of forms of **ethnic nationalism**. A key element in the Defferre reforms in France was the transition from administrative devolution to legislative devolution. As part of a strategy of 'functional regionalism', 22 regional public bodies were created in 1972 to enhance the administrative coordination of local investment and planning decisions. These, however, lacked a democratic basis and enjoyed only limited powers. In 1982, they were transformed into fully fledged regional governments, each with a directly elected council. In an attempt to stem separatism and a growing tide of terrorism, Corsica was granted the special status of a Collective Territory, which effectively made the island self-governing. The tendency towards decentralization in Europe has, however, also been fuelled by developments within the EU, and especially by the emergence since the late 1980s of the idea of 'Europe of the Regions'. Regional and provincial levels of government have benefited from the direct distribution of aid from the European Regional Development Fund, and have responded both by seeking direct representation in Brussels and by strengthening their involvement in economic planning and infrastructure development.

The UK, traditionally one of the most centralized unitary states, was slower in embracing devolution. The revival of Scottish and Welsh nationalism in the late 1960s had put devolution on the political agenda and even led to thwarted devolution proposals by the minority Labour government in 1978 and again in 1979, but devolved bodies were not established until 1999. The Scottish Parliament is the largest and most powerful of the new bodies, having tax-varying powers (the ability to raise or lower income tax by three pence in the pound) and primary legislative authority in domestic policy areas. Control of constitutional issues, defence, foreign affairs, national security and relations with the EU nevertheless continue to be reserved to the Westminster Parliament. The Welsh Assembly is an example of an administrative devolution, in that it has no control over taxation and only subordinate, or 'secondary', legislative power. The Northern Ireland Assembly was established as a result of the ongoing 'peace process' as part of the Good Friday Agreement; it has some primary legislative power but no control over taxation, although its powers will expand in accordance with the principle of 'rolling' devolution if power-sharing proves to be successful. Supporters of devolution argue that, in granting a measure of 'home rule' to Scotland and Wales in particular, the centrifugal pressures generated by separatist nationalism will abate, helping to consolidate the multinational UK state. Critics, on the other hand, warn, or, in the case of the Scottish National Party (SNP) and Plaid Cymru, hope that devolution will lead to the final breakup of the UK.

Devolution in the UK nevertheless already has a 'quasi-federal' character in that, although the Scottish, Welsh and Northern Irish bodies lack constitutional entrenchment, they enjoy democratic legitimacy and therefore political entrench-

Marcus Garvey (1887–1940)

Jamaican political thinker and activist, and an early advocate of black nationalism. Garvey was the founder in 1914 of the Universal Negro Improvement Association (UNIA). He left Jamaica for New York in 1916, where his message of black pride and economic self-sufficiency gained him a growing following, particularly in ghettos such as Harlem. Although his black business enterprises failed, and his call for a return to Africa was largely ignored, Garvey's emphasis on establishing black pride and his vision of Africa as a 'homeland' provided the basis for the later Black Power movement. Rastafarianism is also based largely on his ideas. Garvey was imprisoned for mail fraud in 1923, and was later deported, eventually dying in obscurity in London.

ment by virtue of being popular assemblies set up as a result of referendums. Moreover, the asymmetrical nature of UK devolution creates dynamic pressures that may lead to a ratcheting-up of the powers of devolved bodies: the Welsh and Northern Ireland assemblies will aspire to the powers of the Scottish Parliament, and the Scottish Parliament will, in turn, have an incentive to maintain its superior status. Most importantly, to the extent that the new legislatures come to serve as a focus of political and patriotic loyalty, devolution may further weaken the fragile sense of 'Britishness' that underpins the territorial coherence of the UK state, perhaps making pressures for federalism and, some have warned, state collapse irresistible.

Ethnic and community politics

The rise of ethnic politics

The cause of political decentralization and, in extreme cases, the phenomenon of state collapse have increasingly been fuelled by the emergence of a new style of politics: the politics of ethnic loyalty and regional identity. In some respects, the rise of ethnic politics in the late twentieth century paralleled the emergence of nationalist politics in the nineteenth century, and may have similarly wide-ranging consequences. Whereas nationalism brought about a period of nation building and the destruction of multinational empires, ethnic politics may call the long-term survival of the nation itself into question. Nationalism, in other words, may be displaced by multiculturalism (see p. 215). What accounts for the rise of this new style of politics, and what is its political character?

The growing importance of ethnic consciousness in the West is strictly a post-Second-World-War phenomenon; indeed, it can be traced back to the 1960s. The renewed importance of ethnicity in politics, however, came as a surprise to most commentators. This was because it had widely been assumed that modernity would bring about the dilution of ethnic distinctiveness, as the spread of liberal-democratic values would mean the abandonment of atavistic rivalries and communal solidarities. However, in the late 1960s and early 1970s secessionist groups and forms of ethnic nationalism sprang up in many parts of western Europe and North America. This was most evident in Quebec in Canada, Scotland and Wales in the UK, Catalonia

Focus on . . .

The core–periphery model

The core-periphery model is an explanatory framework that aims to demonstrate how and why regional imbalances in economic development occur. It can be applied either to regional imbalances within a state (as a theory of internal colonialism), or to imbalances in the global economy (as a theory of world order). However, it often acknowledges overlaps between the two. 'Core' areas, for instance, are ones that are better integrated into the global economy. The core–periphery model emphasizes a system of unequal exchange, in which the core region prospers and develops specifically through the exploitation of the periphery, pushing it into underdevelopment. The core is thus characterized by relatively high wages, advanced technology and a diversified production mix; and the periphery is characterized by low wages, more rudimentary technology and a simple production mix.

and the Basque area in Spain, Corsica in France, and Flanders in Belgium. It created pressure for political decentralization, and sometimes precipitated major constitutional upheavals. In Italy the process did not get under way until the 1990s, with the rise of the Northern League in Lombardy. There have been similar manifestations of ethnic assertiveness amongst the Native Americans in Canada and the USA, the aboriginal peoples in Australia, and the Maoris in New Zealand. In the latter two cases, at least, this has brought about a major reassessment of national identity.

In many ways, the forerunner of, and possibly prototype for, this new style of politics was found in the emergence of black nationalism. The origins of the black-consciousness movement date back to the early twentieth century and the emergence of a 'back to Africa' movement inspired by activists such as Marcus Garvey (see p. 175). Black politics, however, gained greater prominence in the 1960s with an upsurge in both the reformist and revolutionary wings of the movement. In its reformist guise, the movement took the form of a struggle for civil rights that reached national prominence in the USA under the leadership of Martin Luther King (1929–68) and the National Association for the Advancement of Colored People (NAACP). The strategy of protest and nonviolent civil disobedience was nevertheless rejected by the emerging Black Power movement, which supported black separatism and, under the leadership of the Black Panther Party, founded in 1966, promoted the use of physical force and armed confrontation. Of more enduring significance in US politics, however, have been the Black Muslims, who advocate a separatist creed based on the idea that black Americans are descended from an ancient Muslim tribe. Founded in 1929, the Black Muslims were led for over 40 years by Elijah Muhammad (1897–1975), and they counted amongst their most prominent activists in the 1960s the militant black leader Malcolm X (1925–65). Renamed the Nation of Islam, the movement continues to exert influence in the USA under the leadership of Louis Farrakhan.

Black nationalism clearly highlights one of the sources of ethnic politics: the desire to challenge economic and social marginalization, and sometimes racial oppression. In this sense, ethnic politics has been a vehicle for political liberation, its enemy being structural disadvantage and ingrained inequality. For blacks in North

America and western Europe, the establishment of an ethnic identity has provided a means of confronting a dominant white culture that has traditionally emphasized their inferiority and demanded subservience. Resurgent regional loyalties have often sprung from a system of 'internal colonialism' in which 'peripheral' geographical areas are exploited by a 'core' or 'centre' (see p. 176). Thus nationalist sentiment in Scotland and Wales is derived in part from the economic subordination of these regions to England, and particularly south-east England. This is reflected in their traditional dependence upon 'heavy' industry, their higher unemployment levels, and their lower wage and salary levels. Very much the same can be said about areas such as Brittany in France and Catalonia and the Basque area in Spain. The tendency in such cases is for ethnic nationalism to have a left-wing character, and it is usually articulated by parties and movements that have a broadly socialist philosophy.

On the other hand, when regional loyalties have intensified in 'core' areas confronted by the growing prominence of 'peripheral' ones, ethnic politics has often assumed a more right-wing character. This has occurred, for instance, in Flanders in Belgium, when economic development in predominantly French-speaking Wallonia has precipitated growing support for neofascist movements. In the 1990s, the openly racist Flemish bloc, which calls for the mass deportation of immigrants, made electoral advances in industrial areas and especially in Antwerp. Similarly, the free-market philosophy of the Northern League in Lombardy in Italy in part reflects the desire of the economically advanced Italian North (so-called Padania) to disengage itself from the more rural and less prosperous South.

Nevertheless, structural inequalities and internal colonialism cannot in themselves explain the emergence of ethnic and regional politics. Why, for instance, did ethnic and regional identities become so important in the late twentieth century when the injustices that they sought to redress dated back generations, if not centuries? The answer to this may lie in the phenomenon of postmodernism (see p. 67). Just as Gellner (1983) argued that nationalism arose to provide a source of cultural cohesion in modern, industrialized societies, ethnic consciousness may be a necessary integrative force in emerging postmodern ones. The problem of postmodernism is that it promotes diversity and weakens traditional social identities. For example, increased social mobility and the spread of market individualism have undermined both class solidarity and established political loyalties. At the same time, the capacity of the nation to establish a strong and stable social identity has been weakened by globalization (see p. 143) in its economic, cultural and political forms. In such circumstances, ethnicity may replace nationality as the principal source of social integration, its virtue being that, whereas nations are bound together by 'civil' loyalties and ties, ethnic and regional groups are able to generate a deeper sense of 'organic' identity.

The rise of ethnic consciousness has by no means occurred only in the West. Although ethnic rivalry (often portrayed as 'tribalism') is sometimes seen as an endemic feature of African and Asian politics, it is better understood as a phenomenon linked to colonialism. For example, the struggle against colonial rule helped to heighten ethnic consciousness, which tended to be mobilized as a weapon of anti-colonialism. However, the divide-and-rule policies of the colonial period often bequeathed to many newly independent 'nations' a legacy of bitterness and resentment. In many cases, this was subsequently exacerbated by the attempt of majority ethnic groups to consolidate their dominance under the guise of 'nation building'. Such tensions, for instance, resulted in the Biafran War in Nigeria in the 1960s,

Concept

Community

A community, in everyday language, is a collection of people in a given location: that is, a village, town, city, or even country. As a social or political principle, however, the term community suggests a social group that possesses a strong collective identity based on the bonds of comradeship, loyalty and duty. Ferdinand Tönnies (1855–1936) distinguished between *Gemeinschaft*, or 'community', typically found in traditional societies and characterized by natural affection and mutual respect, and *Gesellschaft*, or 'association': that is, the looser, artificial and contractual relationships typically found in urban and industrialized societies. Emile Durkheim (1858–1917) emphasized the degree to which community is based on the maintenance of social and moral codes. If these are weakened, this induces 'anomie': that is, feelings of isolation, loneliness and meaninglessness.

the long-running civil war in Southern Sudan, and a resort to terrorism by the predominantly Christian Tamils in Sri Lanka. The worst recent example of ethnic bloodshed, however, occurred in Rwanda in 1994, where an estimated 1 000 000 Tutsis and moderate Hutus were slaughtered in an uprising by militant Hutus.

The collapse of communism in eastern Europe has also created the spectre of ethnic rivalry and regional conflict. In the former USSR, Czechoslovakia and Yugoslavia, for example, this has led to state collapse and the creation of a series of new nation-states. The causes have been complex. In the first place, although communist regimes sought to resolve the 'nationalities problem' through the construction of 'socialist man', the evidence is that they merely fossilized ethnic and national loyalties by driving them underground. Second, ethnic and religious nationalism were undoubtedly vehicles for expressing anticommunism or anti-Sovietism. Third, the political instability and economic uncertainty that the collapse of communism precipitated were a perfect breeding ground for a form of politics that offered an 'organic' sense of collective identity. Nevertheless, these newly created nations are themselves subject to deep ethnic rivalries and tensions. This has been demonstrated by the rebellion of the Chechens in Russia, and the fragmentation of the former Yugoslav republic of Bosnia into 'ethnically pure' Muslim, Serb and Croat areas.

A politics of community?

Whereas ethnic politics has emerged from below as a populist (see p. 378) movement, community politics has usually been a concern of political elites. In other words, it has often been the preserve of politicians and academics, who have interpreted social breakdown and fragmentation as being part of a broader 'decline of community'. This theme has become increasingly prominent in western politics since the 1960s, reaching the point in the 1990s at which so-called 'communitarianism' (see p. 179) threatened to become an all-embracing political philosophy, making the old left/right political divide redundant. At the heart of the communitarian message is the assertion, first, that a sense of community is vital to a healthy society and, second, that in the modern period the bonds of community have been progressively weakened.

A concern with community politics and a rediscovery of 'the local' has advanced in line with the progress of globalization, which was discussed in Chapter 7. In this sense, globalization and localization may be linked responses to the decline of the nation state. Insofar as the cause of community has an ideological heritage, this lies in the traditional anarchist emphasis on self-management and cooperation. Classical anarchists such as Proudhon, Peter Kropotkin (1842–1921) and Gustav Landauer (1870–1934) extolled the virtues of small, decentralized communities, or **communes**, in which human beings can organize their lives spontaneously and resolve differences through face-to-face interaction. Similar goals also inspired the establishment of the kibbutz system in Israel. In the view of contemporary anarchists such as Murray Bookchin (1989), the need for such an emphasis on community is more pressing than it was in the nineteenth century, because of the bleak and depersonalized nature of modern city life. Bookchin's stress upon 'affinity groups' as the fundamental unit of the new society has increasingly influenced town planners, who have moved away from the idea of sprawling estates and large-scale developments, and have started to favour the construction of 'urban villages'. A similar message was

Commune: A small-scale collective organization based on the sharing of wealth and power, possibly extending also to personal and domestic arrangements.

preached by the German economist and environmental theorist Fritz Schumacher (see p. 195), whose pioneering *Small is Beautiful: A Study of Economics as if People Mattered* (1973) advocated a shift towards 'human scale' economic and social organization, based on smaller working units, communal ownership, and regional workplaces utilizing local labour and resources.

The idea of community has also been taken up by academics such as Michael Sandel (1982) and Alisdair MacIntyre (1981), who have used it to highlight the failings of liberal individualism. Communitarians have argued that, in conceiving of the individual as logically prior to and 'outside' the community, liberalism has merely legitimized selfish and egoistical behaviour and downgraded the importance of the idea of the public good. Through the writings of Amitai Etzioni (1995), such views influenced the Clinton administration in the USA as well as the UK Labour and Conservative parties. Etzioni argued that social fragmentation and breakdown has largely been a result of individuals' obsession with rights and their refusal to acknowledge reciprocal duties and moral responsibilities. This is demonstrated by the so-called 'parenting deficit': that is, the abandonment of the burdens of parenthood by fathers and mothers who are more concerned about their own lifestyles and careers. However, critics point out that, in extolling duties over rights, communitarianism may represent a shift towards authority and away from individual liberty. Moreover, the concern with community commonly has conservative implications, since it tends to be associated with attempts to strengthen existing social institutions such as the family. In this form, communitarianism seeks to legitimize the *status quo* and, in the case of the family, to consolidate women's traditional role as housewives, mothers and carers.

Summary

◆ Centralization and decentralisation both have advantages. The virtues of centralization include the following. It allows the state to be an international actor, it enables economic life to be more efficiently organized, it helps to promote national unity, and it allows for regional inequalities to be countered. The attraction of decentralization is that it broadens the scope of political participation, brings government 'closer' to the people, makes political decisions more intelligible, and fosters checks and balances within government.

◆ The most common forms of territorial organization are federal and unitary systems. Federalism is based on the notion of shared sovereignty, in which power is distributed between the central and peripheral levels of government. Unitary systems, however, vest sovereign power in a single, national institution, which allows the centre to determine the territorial organization of the state.

◆ Other factors affecting territorial divisions include the party system and political culture, the economic system and level of material development, the geographical size of the state, and the level of cultural, ethnic and religious diversity. There has been a tendency towards centralization in most, if not all, systems. This reflects, in particular, the fact that central government alone has the resources and strategic position to manage economic life and deliver comprehensive social welfare.

Concept

Communitarianism

Communitarianism is the belief that the self or person is constituted through the community, in the sense that individuals are shaped by the communities to which they belong and thus owe them a debt of respect and consideration; there are no 'unencumbered selves'. Although it is clearly at odds with liberal individualism, communitarianism has a variety of political forms. *Left-wing* communitarianism holds that community demands unrestricted freedom and social equality (the view of anarchism). *Centrist* communitarianism holds that community is grounded in an acknowledgement of reciprocal rights and responsibilities (the perspective of Tory paternalism and social democracy). *Right-wing* communitarianism holds that community requires respect for authority and established values (the view of the New Right).

◆ Political decentralization has been fuelled by the strengthening of ethnic consciousness and regional identities. The rise of ethnic politics is linked to the capacity of ethnicity to generate a sense of 'organic' identity that is stronger than the 'civic' loyalties and ties that have been typically associated with national consciousness. To some extent, the rise of ethnic nationalism reflects the impact of globalization.

◆ Growing concern has been expressed about the loss of community and the need to rediscover the 'local'. Communitarianism has been associated with demands for radical decentralization and self-management, with the notion of reciprocal rights and responsibilities, and with calls for respect for authority and the strengthening of traditional values and culture.

Questions for discussion

▶ Where should the balance between centralization and decentralization lie?

▶ Is the federal principle applicable only to certain states or to all states?

▶ What are the respective merits of federalism and devolution?

▶ Is the tendency towards centralization in modern states resistible?

▶ Does the rise of ethnic politics spell the demise of civil nationalism?

▶ Are attempts to strengthen community always implicitly conservative?

Further reading

Bookchin, M., *Remaking Society* (Montreal: Black Rose, 1989). A stimulating discussion from a leading modern anarchist of the need for decentralization and sustainable communities.

Denters, B. and L. E. Rose (eds), *Comparing Local Governance: Trends and Developments* (Basingstoke and New York: Palgrave Macmillan, 2005). A useful examination of the nature and extent of transformation of local governance, which looks across Europe as well as at New Zealand, Austalia and the USA.

Fenton, S., *Ethnicity* (Cambridge: Polity, 2003). A detailed examination of ethnicity from a sociological perspective and informed by social anthropological literature.

Menton, A. and M. A. Schain, *Comparative Federalism* (Oxford: Oxford University Press, 2006). A comparative examination of the workings and development of federalism in the USA and the EU.

Wachendorfer-Schmidt, U. (ed.), *Federalism and Political Performance* (London and New York: Routledge, 2000). An evaluation of the workings of federalism that also compares performance in federal and unitary states.

PART 3

Political Interaction

The Economy and Society

'It's the Economy, Stupid.'

> Reminder on the wall of Bill Clinton's office during the 1992 US presidential election campaign

At almost every level, politics is intertwined with the economy and with society. Ideological argument and debate have traditionally revolved around the battle between two rival economic philosophies: capitalism and socialism. Voting behaviour and party systems are shaped largely by social divisions and cleavages. Parties compete for power by promising to increase economic growth, reduce inflation, tackle poverty and so on. As President Clinton recognized, election results are often determined by the state of the economy: governments win elections when the economy booms, but are likely to be defeated during recessions or slumps. Indeed, orthodox Marxists go further and suggest that politics is merely a part of a 'superstructure' determined or conditioned by the economic 'base', the political process being nothing more than a *reflection* of the class system. Although few people (including Marxists) now hold such a simplistic view, no one would deny that socioeconomic factors are critical in political analysis. Quite simply, politics cannot be understood except within an economic and social context.

The central issues examined in this chapter are as follows:

Key issues

▶ How, and to what extent, does the economy condition politics?

▶ What are the major economic systems in the world today? What are their respective strengths and weaknesses?

▶ How far can, and should, government control the economy?

▶ What are the key economic and social cleavages in modern societies?

▶ To what extent do class, race and gender structure political life?

Economic systems

An economic system is a form of organization through which goods and services are produced, distributed and exchanged. Marxists refer to economic systems as 'modes of production'. A recurrent difficulty, however, is confusion between such systems of economic organization and the ideas and doctrines through which they have been defended. Capitalism, for instance, is sometimes treated not merely as an economic system, but also as an ideology in its own right, specifically one that defends private property, emphasizes the virtues of competition, and suggests that general prosperity will result from the pursuit of self-interest. This confusion is yet more marked in the case of socialism. The term socialism is used to refer both to a distinctive set of values, theories and beliefs, and to a system of economic organization through which these values will supposedly be realized. Although this chapter considers some of the strengths and weaknesses of economic systems (how they have been defended and why they have been criticized), its central concern is with socioeconomic organization rather than normative political theory. A fuller account of relevant ideological disputes is found in Chapter 3.

For almost 200 years, debate about economic organization has revolved around a clash between two rival systems: capitalism and socialism. So fundamental did the choice appear that it structured the political spectrum itself, reducing political views to the question of where one stood on economic organization. Left-wing beliefs were thought to favour socialism; right-wing ones reflected sympathy for capitalism. The fact that the rival systems appeared to be so fundamentally divergent helped to underpin this dichotomy.

The central features that were usually associated with a capitalist economy were the following:

- There is generalized commodity production, a commodity being a good or service produced for *exchange* – it has a market value.
- Productive wealth (the 'means of production') is held predominantly in *private* hands.
- Economic life is organized according to *market* principles: the forces of demand and supply.
- Material *self-interest* and profit maximization provide the motivation for enterprise and hard work.

In contrast, socialist economies were thought to be based on the following principles:

- There is a system of production for *use*, geared, at least in theory, to the satisfaction of human needs.
- There is predominantly *public* or common ownership of productive wealth, certainly including the 'commanding heights' of the economy.
- Economic organization is based on *planning*, a supposedly rational process of resource allocation.
- Work is based on *cooperative* effort that results from a desire for general well-being.

In practice, however, economic systems were always more complex and difficult to categorize. In the first place, it was a mistake to suggest that there was ever a single, universally accepted model of either capitalism or socialism. In practice, societies

Concept

Market

A market is a system of commercial exchange that brings buyers wishing to acquire a good or service into contact with sellers offering the same for purchase. In all but the most simple markets, money is used as a convenient means of exchange, rather than barter. Markets are impersonal mechanisms in that they are regulated by price fluctuations that reflect the balance of supply and demand, so-called market forces.

Supporters of the market argue that it has the following advantages:

- It promotes efficiency through the discipline of the profit motive.
- It encourages innovation in the form of new products and better production processes.
- It allows producers and consumers to pursue their own interests and enjoy freedom of choice.
- It tends towards equilibrium through the coordination of an almost infinite number of individual preferences and decisions.

Critics, however, point out that the market has serious disadvantages:

- It generates insecurity because people's lives are shaped by forces they cannot control.
- It widens material inequality and generates poverty.
- It increases the level of greed and selfishness, and ignores the broader needs of society.
- It promotes instability through periodic booms and slumps.

constructed their own models of capitalism and socialism depending upon their particular economic and political circumstances, and their cultural and historical inheritance. It thus makes more sense to discuss capitalisms and socialisms. Further, the simplistic 'capitalism versus socialism' model of economic organization distorted the truth by overemphasizing (often as a result of Cold War rivalry) the differences between the two models.

The abrupt abandonment of central planning following the eastern European revolutions of 1989–91 not only brought an end to the system of **state socialism**, but also destroyed the illusion that there was ever a 'pure' socialist system or a 'pure' capitalist one. No capitalist system is entirely free of 'socialist' impurities such as labour laws and at least a safety-net level of welfare, and there has never been a socialist system that did not have 'capitalist' impurities such as a market in labour and some form of 'black' economy. There have, moreover, been attempts to construct economic systems that conform to neither capitalist nor socialist models: these are usually referred to as 'third ways'. Corporatism in Fascist Italy, Perónism in Argentina, and Swedish social democracy have all been described in this way. Environmentalists, for their part, have developed their own critique, arguing that capitalism and socialism are essentially similar, both being production-orientated and growth-obsessed economic systems. A Green economy would require a radical shift in economic priorities towards ones rooted in sustainability and ecological balance.

Capitalisms of the world

Capitalist economic forms first emerged in sixteenth-century and seventeenth-century Europe, developing from within predominantly feudal societies. Feudalism was characterized by agrarian-based production geared to the needs of landed estates, fixed social hierarchies, and a rigid pattern of obligations and duties. Capitalist practices initially took root in the form of commercial agriculture that was orientated towards the market, and relied increasingly on waged labour instead of bonded serfs. The market mechanism, the heart of the emerging capitalist system,

State socialism: A form of socialism in which the state controls and directs economic life, acting, in theory, in the interests of the people.

Adam Smith (1723–90)

Scottish economist and philosopher, usually seen as the founder of the 'Dismal Science'. After holding the chair of logic and then moral philosophy at Glasgow University, Smith became tutor to the Duke of Buccleuch, which enabled him to visit France and Geneva and to develop his economic theories. *The Theory of Moral Sentiments* (1759) developed a theory of motivation that tried to reconcile human self-interestedness with an unregulated social order. Smith's most famous work, *The Wealth of Nations* ([1776] 1930), was the first systematic attempt to explain the workings of the economy in market terms, emphasizing the importance of the division of labour. Though he is often seen as a free-market theorist, Smith was nevertheless also aware of the limitations of the market.

certainly intensified pressure for technological innovation and brought about a substantial expansion in productive capacity.

The pressure to expand output and increase productivity was reflected in the so-called 'agricultural revolution', which saw the enclosure of overgrazed common land and the increased use of fertilizers and scientific methods of production. By the mid-eighteenth century, first in the UK but soon in the USA and across Europe, an industrial revolution was beginning. Industrialization entirely transformed society through the advent of machine-based factory production and the gradual shift of populations from the land to the expanding towns and cities. Indeed, so closely were capitalism and industrialization linked that industrial capitalism is generally taken to be capitalism's classical form. However, three types of capitalist system can be identified in the modern world:

- enterprise capitalism
- social capitalism
- collective capitalism.

Enterprise capitalism

Enterprise capitalism is widely seen, particularly in the Anglo-American world, as 'pure' capitalism: that is, as an ideal towards which other capitalisms are inevitably drawn. It is nevertheless apparent that this model has been rejected in most parts of the world except for the USA (the home of enterprise capitalism) and, despite its early post-1945 flirtation with Keynesian social democracy, the UK. Enterprise capitalism is based on the ideas of classical economists such as Adam Smith and David Ricardo (1772–1823) updated by modern theorists such as Milton Friedman (see p. 191) and Friedrich von Hayek (see p. 52). Its central feature is faith in the untrammelled workings of market competition, born out of the belief that the market is a self-regulating mechanism (or, as Adam Smith put it, an 'invisible hand'). This idea is expressed in Adam Smith's famous words: 'it is not from the benevolence of the butcher, the brewer, or the baker, that we expect our dinner, but from their regard to their own interest'. In the USA such free-market principles have helped to keep public ownership to a minimum, and ensure that welfare provision operates as little more than a safety net. US businesses are typically profit-driven, and a premium is placed on high productivity and labour flexibility. Trade unions are usually weak, reflecting the fear that strong labour organizations are an obstacle to profit maximization. The emphasis on growth and enterprise of this form of capitalism stems, in part, from the fact that productive wealth is owned largely by financial institutions, such as insurance companies and pension funds, that demand a high rate of return on their investments.

The undoubted economic power of the USA bears testament to the vigour of enterprise capitalism. Despite clear evidence of relative decline (whereas the USA accounted for half of the world's manufacturing output in 1945, this had fallen to one-fifth by 1990), the average productivity of the USA is still higher than Germany's and Japan's. The USA clearly enjoys natural advantages that enable it to benefit from the application of market principles, notably a continent-wide domestic market, a wealth of natural resources, and a ruggedly individualist popular culture, seen as a 'frontier ideology'. However, its success cannot be put down to the market alone. For instance, the USA possesses, in the main, a strong and clear sense of national purpose, and it has a network of regulatory bodies that constrain the worst excesses of competitive behaviour.

The principles of enterprise capitalism have been extended far beyond the USA through the impact of **economic globalization**. Globalization (which is discussed in more detail in Chapter 7) has promoted **marketization** in a variety of ways. For example, intensified international competition has encouraged governments to deregulate their economies and reduce tax levels in the hope of attracting 'inward' investment and preventing multinational corporations from relocating elsewhere. Strong downward pressure has also been exerted on public spending, and particularly welfare budgets, by the fact that the control of inflation has displaced the maintenance of full employment as the principal goal of economic policy. Moreover, the need to promote product and labour flexibility has often led to trade-union activity being controlled by legislation or other measures. Such pressures have helped to shape what is sometimes called the 'new' political economy, a depoliticized form of economic management in which direct state intervention is scaled down and the market is placed at the centre of economic life (the impact of this on the state is examined in Chapter 5). However, this 'new' political economy has at least two other features. The first of these is an emphasis on technological innovation and development, particularly the wider use of information and communication technology. Technological advance, especially in the USA, gave rise in the 1990s to the spectre of 'turbo-capitalism'. The second feature is that governments have increasingly targeted investment in human capital, in the belief that improved levels of education and training will both improve the supply-side features of the economy and enable citizens to become more flexible and self-reliant.

Enterprise capitalism also has serious disadvantages, however. Perhaps the most significant of these is a tendency towards wide material inequalities and social fragmentation. This is demonstrated in the USA by levels of absolute poverty that are not found, for example, in Europe, and in the growth of a poorly educated and welfare-dependent underclass. The tensions that such problems generate may be contained by growth levels that keep alive the prospect of social mobility. In societies such as that in the UK, however, which lack the cultural and economic resources of the USA, enterprise capitalism may generate such deep social tensions as to be unsustainable in the long run. A further problem is that enterprise capitalism's 'turbo' features may have less to do with the dynamism of the market or technological innovation than with the willingness of consumers to spend and borrow and the willingness of businesses to invest. This economic model may therefore be particularly vulnerable to the vagaries of financial markets and to shifts in consumer or business confidence.

Economic globalization: The incorporation of national economies in a single 'borderless' global economy, through transnational production and capital flows.

Marketization: The extension of market relationships, based on commercial exchange and material self-interest, across the economy and, possibly, society.

◆ **Concept**

Social market

The idea of a 'social-market economy' emerged in Germany in the 1950s. It was advanced by economists such as Alfred Muller-Armack and taken up by Christian Democrat politicians, notably Ludwig Erhard. A social market is an economy that is structured by market principles and largely free from government interference, operating in a society in which cohesion is maintained through a comprehensive welfare system and effective public services. The market is thus not an end in itself so much as a means of generating wealth in order to achieve broader social ends. A stress on partnership, cooperation and subsidiarity (see p. 154) distinguishes a social market from a free market. The social-market strategy allows Germany to achieve a policy consensus that binds together conservative and socialist opinion, and has been imitated by many EU member states.

Social capitalism

Social capitalism refers to the form of capitalism that has developed in much of central and western Europe. Germany is its natural home, but the principles of social capitalism have been adopted in various forms in Austria, the Benelux countries, Sweden, France and much of Scandinavia. This economic form has drawn more heavily on the flexible and pragmatic ideas of economists such as Friedrich List (1789–1846) than on the strict market principles of classical political economy as formulated by Smith and Ricardo. A leading advocate of the *Zollverein* (the German customs union), List nevertheless emphasized the economic importance of politics and political power, arguing, for instance, that state intervention should be used to protect infant industries from the rigours of foreign competition. The central theme of this model is the idea of a social market: that is, an attempt to marry the disciplines of market competition with the need for social cohesion and solidarity.

In Germany this system is founded on a link between industrial and financial capital in the form of a close relationship between business corporations and regionally based banks, which are often also major shareholders in the corporations. This has been the pivot around which Germany's economy has revolved since the Second World War, and it has orientated the economy towards long-term investment rather than short-term profitability. Business organization in what has been called Rhine–Alpine capitalism also differs from Anglo-American capitalism in that it is based on social partnership. Trade unions enjoy representation through works councils, and participate in annual rounds of wage negotiation that are usually industry-wide. This relationship is underpinned by comprehensive and well-funded welfare provisions that provide workers and other vulnerable groups with social guarantees. In this way, a form of 'stakeholder capitalism' has developed that takes into account the interests of workers and those of the wider community. This contrasts with the 'shareholder capitalism' found in the USA and the UK (Hutton, 1995).

The strengths of social capitalism are clearly demonstrated by the 'economic miracle' that transformed war-torn Germany into Europe's leading economic power by the 1960s. High and stable levels of capital investment, together with a strong emphasis on education and training, particularly in vocational and craft skills, enabled Germany to achieve the highest productivity levels in Europe. However, the virtues of the social-market model are by no means universally accepted. One of its drawbacks is that, because it places such a heavy stress on consultation, negotiation and consensus, it tends to encourage inflexibility and make it difficult for businesses to adapt to changing market conditions (for example, economic globalization and intensified competition from Eastern Europe, Latin America and East Asia). Further strain is imposed by the relatively high levels of social expenditure required to maintain high-quality welfare provision. These push up taxes and so burden both employers and employees. Whereas the supporters of the social market insist that the social and the market are intrinsically linked, its critics argue that social capitalism is nothing more than a contradiction in terms. In their view, the price of financing ever-expanding social programmes is a decline in international competitiveness and a weakening of the wealth-creating base of the economy.

Collective capitalism

The third form of capitalism is based on the example of post-1945 Japan. It is a model that the East Asian 'tigers' (South Korea, Taiwan, Singapore, and so on) have eagerly adopted, and, more recently, it has influenced emergent Chinese capitalism. The distinctive character of collective capitalism is its emphasis on cooperative long-term relationships. This allows the economy to be directed not by an impersonal price mechanism, but through what have been called 'relational markets'. An example of this is the pattern of interlocking share ownership that ensures that there is a close relationship between industry and finance in Japan. Some 40 per cent of the shares traded on the Tokyo stock exchange are held by industrial groups that create a nexus of sister firms, the *kigyo shudan*. The *keiretsu*, networks of cross-shareholdings that bind industrial concerns to their various subcontractors, make up a further 30 per cent of the Tokyo stock market's shares. This stability of ownership provides Japanese firms with an abundance of capital, which enables them to adopt strategies based on long-term investment rather than on short-term or medium-term profit.

The firms themselves provide the social core of Japanese life. Workers (particularly male workers in larger businesses) are 'members' of firms in a way that does not occur in the USA or even social-market Europe. In return for their loyalty, commitment and hard work, workers have traditionally expected lifetime employment, pensions, social protection, and access to leisure and recreational opportunities. Particular stress is placed on teamwork and the building up of a collective identity, which is underpinned by relatively narrow income differentials between managers and workers. This emphasis on labour and the importance of collaborative effort has led to the Japanese system being dubbed 'peoplism'. The final element in this economic mix is the government. Although East Asian levels of public spending and taxation are relatively low by international standards (often below 30 per cent of GNP), the state plays a vital role in 'guiding' investment, research and trading decisions. The model here is undoubtedly the Ministry of International Trade and Industry (MITI), which (if less overtly than in the 1950s and 1960s) continues to oversee the Japanese economy through a system of 'indicative' planning (see p. 192).

In many respects, the pre-Second-World-War Japanese economy exhibited many of the features of enterprise capitalism, including an obsession with profit maximization and a tendency towards short-termism. Economic restructuring, however, which had commenced before the war and was stepped up afterwards, proved to be spectacularly successful. The Japanese 'economic miracle' has created an industrial power that, if current investment rates are maintained, will become the largest economy in the world by 2005. However, Japanese success may soon be eclipsed by the rising might of China, the growth rates of which exceed even those of the East Asian 'tigers'. Nevertheless, a price has had to be paid for this success. Behind the public face of cooperation and collaboration, the Japanese economic model places heavy demands on workers and their families. Long hours and highly disciplined working conditions can mean that individualism is stifled and work becomes the centrepiece of human existence. Similarly, the dominance of the 'community' firm in Japanese society has kept alive a neofeudal sense of obligation, with the recognition of duty being placed above respect for rights. Critics therefore argue that collective capitalism is invariably underpinned by authoritarianism (see p. 38), the most obvious example of authoritarian capitalism being found in China's blend of burgeoning capitalism and entrenched one-party communist rule. China's mixture of market economics and Stalinist political control has nevertheless been remarkably effective in delivering sustained economic growth, benefiting from a huge supply of cheap labour and massive investment in the economic infrastructure.

Managed or unmanaged capitalism?

As this review of the world's capitalisms makes clear, the central issue in economic policy is the proper balance between politics and economics, and thus between the

Concept

Laissez-faire

Laissez-faire (in French meaning literally 'leave to do') is the principle of nonintervention of government in economic affairs. It is the heart of the doctrine that the economy works best when left alone by government. The phrase originated with the Physiocrats of eighteenth-century France, who devised the maxim '*laissez faire est laissez passer*' (leave the individual alone, and let commodities circulate freely). Classical economists such as David Ricardo and Alfred Marshall (1842–1924) took up the theme from Adam Smith. The central assumption of *laissez-faire* is that an unregulated market economy tends naturally towards equilibrium. This is usually explained by the theory of 'perfect competition'. From this perspective, government intervention is seen as damaging unless it is restricted to actions that promote market competition, such as checks on monopolies and the maintenance of stable prices.

John Maynard Keynes (1883–1946)

UK economist. Keynes' reputation was established by his critique of the Treaty of Versailles, outlined in *The Economic Consequences of the Peace* (1919). His major work, *The General Theory of Employment, Interest and Money* ([1936] 1965), departed significantly from neoclassical economic theories, and went a long way towards establishing the discipline now known as macroeconomics. By challenging *laissez-faire* principles, he provided the theoretical basis for the policy of demand management, which was widely adopted by western governments in the early post-Second-World-War period. Keynesian theories have had a profound effect upon both modern liberalism and social democracy.

state and the market. Does a capitalist economy work best when it is left alone by government, or can stable growth and general prosperity be achieved only through a system of economic management? In practice, this question boils down to an evaluation of two rival economic strategies: Keynesianism and monetarism. The centrepiece of Keynes' challenge to classical political economy, advanced in *The General Theory of Employment, Interest and Money* ([1936] 1965), was the rejection of the idea of a natural economic order based on a self-regulating market. He argued that *laissez-faire* policies (see p. 189) that established a strict distinction between government and the economy had merely resulted in instability and unemployment, most clearly demonstrated by the Great Depression of the 1930s.

In Keynes' view, capitalist economies had spiralled downwards into deepening depression during the 1930s because, as unemployment grew, market forces brought about cuts in wages that further reduced the demand for goods and services. Keynes argued against free-market orthodoxy by stating that the level of economic activity is geared to 'aggregate demand': that is, the total level of demand in the economy, which government has the capacity to manage through its tax and spending policies. When unemployment rises, government should 'reflate' the economy either by increasing public spending or by cutting taxes. The resulting budget deficit, Keynes suggested, would be sustainable because the growth thus brought about would boost tax revenues and reduce the need for government borrowing. Moreover, any such stimulus to the economy would be magnified by the **multiplier effect**.

The advent of Keynesian demand management in the early post-Second-World-War period revolutionized economic policy and appeared to provide governments with a reliable means of delivering sustained growth and ever-widening prosperity. For many, Keynesianism was the key to the 'long boom' of the 1950s and 1960s, the most sustained period of economic growth the world has ever seen. The intellectual credibility of Keynesianism, however, was damaged by the emergence in the 1970s of 'stagflation' (a simultaneous rise in both unemployment and inflation), a condition that Keynes's theories had not anticipated and could not explain. Politically, Keynesian ideas were undermined by their association with the 'tax and spend' policies that, free-market economists claimed, had sapped enterprise and initiative and undermined growth by creating permanently high inflation (a general increase in the price level). In such circumstances, pre-Keynesian monetarist ideas gained a new lease of life, particularly on the political right.

Multiplier effect: The mechanism through which a change in aggregate demand has an increased effect on national income as it circulates through the economy.

Milton Friedman (1912–2006)

US academic and economist. Professor of economics at the University of Chicago from 1948 and founder of the so-called Chicago School, Friedman also worked as a *Newsweek* columnist and a US presidential advisor. He was awarded the Nobel prize for economics in 1976. A leading exponent of monetarism and free-market economics, Friedman was a powerful critic of Keynesian theory and 'tax and spend' government policies, helping to shift

economic priorities during the 1970s and 1980s in the USA, and the UK in particular. His major works, *Capitalism and Freedom* (1962) and, with his wife Rose, *Free to Choose* (1980), have had a considerable impact on the economic thinking of the New Right.

The rise of **monetarism**, particularly as a result of the work of economists such as Friedrich von Hayek (see p. 52) and Milton Friedman, signalled a shift in economic priorities away from the reduction of unemployment, and towards the control of inflation. In a move led in the 1980s by the Thatcher government in the UK and the Reagan administration in the USA, the principal economic responsibility of government came to be seen as ensuring 'sound money'. The job of government was to squeeze inflation out of the system and leave matters such as growth, employment and productivity to the natural vigour of the market. Monetarism suggests that, in Friedman's words, 'inflation is always and everywhere a monetary phenomenon'. The implication of monetarism is that Keynesian policies designed to boost output and reduce unemployment merely fuel inflation by encouraging the government to borrow, and so 'print money'. The alternative is to shift attention away from demand-side policies that encourage consumers to consume, and towards supply-side ones that encourage producers to produce. For monetarists, this invariably means deregulation and tax cuts.

To a large extent, however, modern economics has moved beyond the simplistic nostrums of Keynesianism and monetarism, and developed more sophisticated economic strategies, even a 'new' political economy. Monetarism, at the very least, succeeded in convincing Keynesians of the importance of inflation and of the significance of the economy's supply side. 'Crude' Keynesianism has been superseded as a result of economic globalization, 1950s-style and 1960s-style economic management having been based on the existence of discrete national economies. On the other hand, the idea of an unregulated market economy has also been difficult to sustain, particularly in the light of the tendency for this type of economy to bring about low investment, short-termism, and social fragmentation or breakdown. As Francis Fukuyama (1996) pointed out, wealth creation of any kind depends on **social capital** in the form of trust, and not just on impersonal market forces. A 'new Keynesianism' has therefore emerged that rejects top-down economic management but also acknowledges the fact that the workings of the market are hampered by uncertainty, inequality and differential levels of knowledge.

Monetarism: The theory that inflation is caused by an increase in the supply of money; 'too much money chases too few goods'.

Social capital: Cultural and moral resources that help to promote social cohesion, political stability and prosperity (see p. 210).

Varieties of socialism

Modern socialists have increasingly been prepared to accept that capitalism is the only reliable means of generating wealth. They have, as a result, looked not to

---

Concept

Planning

Planning is a system of economic organization that relies on a rational allocation of resources in accordance with clearly defined goals that are realized through the partial or complete coordination of production, distribution and exchange. However, in practice, planning systems differ markedly. State socialist regimes developed a system of *directive* planning orientated around output targets set for all economic enterprises, and administered centrally through a hierarchy of party–state institutions. So-called *indicative* planning has been used in, for example, France, the Netherlands and Japan to supplement or guide the workings of the capitalist economy using the tools of economic management rather than state direction.

The strengths of planning include the following:

- It places the economy in human hands, rather than leaving it to the impersonal and sometimes capricious whims of the market.
- It gears the economy towards the satisfaction of human needs rather than the maximization of private profit.
- It is less susceptible than the market is to instability and crises.
- It can ensure a high level of material equality.

Opponents nevertheless point out the following:

- Planning cannot cope with the complexity of a modern industrialized economy.
- It is implicitly or explicitly authoritarian in that it allows central agencies to control the economy.
- It imposes elite opinions upon the masses instead of responding to consumer demand.
- It fails to reward or encourage enterprise, and tends towards bureaucratic stagnation.

---

abolish capitalism, but to reform or 'humanize' it. This has usually entailed embracing Keynesian or social-market ideas. Traditionally, however, socialists have looked to construct an alternative to market capitalism, seeing socialism as a qualitatively different economic formation from capitalism. Such attempts have been based on the assumption that socialism is superior to capitalism, both morally and productively. Although socialist literature abounds with economic models (ranging from the technocratic industrialism of Saint-Simon (1760–1825) to the decentralized self-management of Peter Kropotkin (1842–1921)), the most influential of these have been developed within the Marxist tradition. What socialist models have in common, however, is the belief that the market mechanism can and should be replaced by some form of economic planning.

Unfortunately, Marx (see p. 55) did not lay down a blueprint for the economic organization of the future socialist society, restricting himself instead to a number of broad principles. Certainly, he envisaged that private property would be abolished and replaced by a system of collective or social ownership, which would allow the economy to serve the material needs of society rather than the dictates of an all-powerful market. Nevertheless, in supporting broad popular participation at every level in society, and in predicting that the state would 'wither away' as full communism was established, Marx set himself apart from the state collectivization and central planning that was to characterize Soviet economics in the twentieth century.

Two very different models of a socialist economy have been developed:

- state socialism
- market socialism.

State socialism

Following the Bolshevik Revolution of 1917, the USSR became the first society to adopt an explicitly socialist model of economic organization. This model was not fully developed until Stalin's (see p. 57) so-called 'second revolution' in the 1930s, significant aspects of market organization having continued under Lenin's New Economic Policy in the 1920s. The model that was later exported to eastern Europe and which dominated orthodox communism in the period after the Second World War can therefore be dubbed economic Stalinism. This system was based on state collectivization, which brought all economic resources under the control of the party–state apparatus. In the USSR, a system of 'directive planning' placed overall control of economic policy in the hands of the highest organs of the Communist Party, which supervised the drawing up of output targets (in the form of Five Year Plans) by a network of planning agencies and committees.

The spectacular collapse of the state socialist model in eastern Europe and the USSR in the revolutions of 1989–91 has been widely used to demonstrate the inherent flaws of central planning, and has gone a long way towards discrediting the very idea of planning. However, this is to ignore the undoubted achievements of Soviet-style planning. For example, the central-planning system was remarkably successful in building up 'heavy' industries, and provided the USSR by 1941 with a sufficiently strong industrial base to enable it to withstand the Nazi invasion. Moreover, although planning failed dismally in its attempt to produce western-style consumer goods, it nevertheless helped the USSR and much of eastern Europe to eradicate homelessness, unemployment and absolute poverty, problems that continue to blight the inner cities in some advanced capitalist countries. Despite chronic economic backwardness, Cuba, for instance, achieved a literacy rate of over 98 per cent and a system of primary healthcare that compares favourably with those in many western countries.

However, the drawbacks of central planning are difficult to disguise. Perhaps the most fundamental of these is its inherent inefficiency, which results from the fact that, however competent and committed the planners may be, they are confronted by a range and complexity of information that is simply beyond their capacity to handle (Hayek, 1948). It is estimated, for example, that planners in even a relatively small central-planning system are confronted by a range of options that exceed the number of atoms in the universe. A further explanation of the poor economic performance of the communist system is that the social safeguards built into central planning, together with its relatively egalitarian system of distribution, did little to encourage enterprise or promote efficiency. Quite simply, although all Soviet workers had a job, it was more difficult to ensure that they actually worked. Finally, central planning was associated with the emergence of new social divisions based on political or bureaucratic position. In Milovan Djilas' (1957) phrase, a 'new class' of party–state bureaucrats emerged who enjoyed a status and privileges equivalent to those of the capitalist class in western societies. In the eyes of its left-wing critics, Soviet planning amounted to little more than a system of **state capitalism**.

Market socialism

As an alternative to the heavily centralized Soviet economic model, attempts were made to reconcile the principles of socialism with the dynamics of market competition. Such a model was introduced in Yugoslavia following the split between President Tito of Yugoslavia and Stalin in 1949, and it was also taken up in Hungary

State capitalism: A system of state ownership that replicates capitalist class relationships by concentrating economic power in the hands of a party–state elite.

after the USSR suppressed the political uprising of 1956. Similar ideas were applied in the USSR during Mikhail Gorbachev's *perestroika* programme of 'economic restructuring' in 1985–90. *Perestroika* developed as a rolling programme that initially permitted the development of cooperatives and single-proprietor businesses to supplement the central-planning system, but eventually allowed Soviet enterprises to disengage themselves from the planning system altogether and become self-financing and self-managing.

The attraction of **market socialism** is that it appears to compensate for many of the most serious defects of central planning. Not only does a market environment provide a guarantee of consumer responsiveness and efficiency, but the dangers of bureaucratic power are also kept at bay. However, this is not to say that a socialist market is entirely unplanned and unregulated. Indeed, most attempts to propose a 'feasible' or 'viable' form of socialism (Nove, 1983; Breitenbach, Burden and Coates, 1990), acknowledge the continuing need for a framework of planning, albeit one that uses collaborative and interactive procedures. At the same time, although self-management encourages cooperation and ensures a high level of material equality, it cannot be denied that the market imposes harsh disciplines. Failed businesses collapse and unprofitable industries decline, but this, in the long run, is the price that has to be paid for a vibrant and prosperous economy.

Neither the Yugoslav nor Hungarian economies, however, despite their early promise, proved to be more successful or enduring than the Soviet central-planning system. One of the chief weaknesses of market socialism is that self-management conflicts with market disciplines, as it dictates that enterprises respond first and foremost to the interests of their workforces. Free-market economists have therefore usually argued that only hierarchically organized private businesses can achieve optimal efficiency, because only they are capable of responding consistently to the dictates of the market, in that they place profit maximization above all other considerations.

Is there an economic 'third way'?

The idea of an economic 'third way' (see p. 61) that provides an alternative to both capitalism and socialism has attracted political thinkers from various traditions. For instance, this has been a recurrent theme in fascist thought, first outlined by Mussolini in relation to corporatism (see p. 299), and later embraced by, for example, Moseley in the UK and Perón in Argentina. Fascist corporatism, in contrast to its liberal variant, is based on the belief that business and labour are bound together in an organic and spiritually unified whole. In practice, however, corporatism in Italy amounted to little more than an instrument through which the fascist state smashed independent trade unions and tried to intimidate major business interests. A very different 'third way', Keynesian social democracy, was found in its most developed form in post-1945 Sweden. The Swedish economic model attempted to combine elements of both socialism and capitalism. Productive wealth was concentrated largely in private hands, but social justice was maintained through the most comprehensive welfare system and highest tax regime found anywhere in the world. In this sense, the social-democratic 'third way' could be seen as a left-wing version of social capitalism. As in the case of the social-market model, however, doubts have been raised about the viability of continued high levels of social expenditure in an increasingly competitive global economy. This was reflected in Sweden in the 1980s and 1990s in

Market socialism: An economy in which self-managing enterprises operate within a context of market competition, supposedly delivering efficiency without exploitation.

E. F. Schumacher (1911–77)

German-born UK economist and environmental theorist. 'Fritz' Schumacher moved to the UK in 1930 as an Oxford Rhodes scholar. He went on to gain practical experience in business, farming and journalism before re-entering academic life. He was an economic advisor to the British Control Commission in Germany (1946–50) and the UK National Coal Board (1950–70). His seminal *Small is Beautiful:*

A Study of Economics as if People Mattered (1973) championed the cause of human-scale production, and advanced a 'Buddhist' economic philosophy (economics 'as if people mattered') that stresses the importance of morality and 'right livelihood'. Schumacher founded the Intermediate Technology Development Group to help spread his ideas.

growing sensitivity to the pressure of international competition and a tendency to retreat from welfarist priorities. It is also notable that 'third way' ideological thinking since the 1990s has been based on a clearly post-socialist model. This is discussed in more detail in Chapter 3.

An entirely different approach to economic organization has been advanced by environmental theorists. From their perspective, capitalism and socialism are merely different manifestations of the same 'super-ideology' of **industrialism**. In other words, they are seen, essentially, as alternative ways of exploiting nature in order to satisfy the material interests of humankind. Environmentalists argue not only that this obsession with economic growth has led to the despoiling of the natural environment, but also that it has, by damaging the fragile ecosystem on which all life depends, threatened the survival of the human species itself. The Green alternative is to recast economic priorities on the basis of sustainability: that is, the capacity of a system (in this case the planet Earth) to maintain its health and continue in existence. Although ecosocialists have held capitalism's relentless pursuit of profit to be responsible for environmental destruction, the record of state socialist regimes in achieving 'sustainable growth' is hardly inspiring. The principle of sustainability perhaps suggests that questions about the ownership and organization of wealth are secondary to the more fundamental issue of the relationship between humankind and the natural world. In order to abandon the view that nature is essentially a resource available to satisfy human needs, it is necessary for an entirely different value system to be constructed, placing ecology before economics and morality before materialism. Such ideas were developed by E. F. Schumacher (1973) into the notion of 'Buddhist economics'.

■ Social structure and divisions

To suggest, as textbooks tend to do, that politics takes place in a social context fails to convey just how intimately politics and social life are related. Politics is by its very nature a social activity, and it is viewed by some as nothing more than the process through which the conflicts of society are articulated and perhaps resolved. In this sense, society is no mere ' context', but the very stuff and substance of politics itself. However, the concepts of 'the social' and 'the political' also mark out distinct (if intrinsically connected) spheres of activity. What do we mean by 'society'? In its

Industrialism: An economic theory or system based on large-scale factory production and the relentless accumulation of capital.

Concept

Individualism, collectivism

Individualism is a belief in the primacy of the individual over any social group or collective body, which suggests that the individual is central to any political theory or social explanation. This view has been closely associated with classical liberalism and, in the modern period, the New Right. From this perspective, all statements about society should be made in relation to the individuals who compose it; strictly speaking, 'there is no such thing as society' (Margaret Thatcher). This view is usually underpinned by the belief that human beings are naturally self-interested and largely self-reliant, owing nothing to society for their talents and skills.

Collectivism stresses the capacity of human beings for collective action, highlighting their willingness and ability to achieve goals by working together rather than through self-striving. It draws from the belief that there is a social core to human nature, implying that social groups (including 'society' itself) are meaningful political entities. This view can be seen, for instance, in the socialist stress on class analysis and the feminist use of gender categories, as well as in all nationalist and racialist doctrines. Collectivism is sometimes linked to statism (see p. 102), although this relationship is by no means essential.

most general sense, a society is a collection of people who occupy the same territorial area. However, not every group of people constitutes a society. Societies are characterized by regular patterns of social interaction. This suggests the existence of some kind of social *structure*: that is, a usually stable set of interrelationships amongst a number of elements. Moreover, 'social' relationships involve mutual awareness and at least a measure of cooperation. For instance, strictly speaking, warring tribes do not constitute a 'society', even though they may live in close proximity to one another and interact regularly. Societies are also usually characterized by social *divisions*, in which groups and individuals occupy very different positions, reflecting an unequal distribution of status, wealth and/or power within the society. The nature of these divisions or cleavages, and the political significance of particular divisions (class, race, gender, age, religion and so on), of course, differ from society to society.

In all cases, though, society can be seen to shape politics in a number of important ways:

- The distribution of wealth and other resources in society conditions the nature of state power (as discussed in Chapter 5).

- Society influences public opinion and the political culture (as discussed in Chapter 10).

- Social divisions and conflicts help to bring about political change in the form of reforms and revolutions (also as discussed in Chapter 10).

- The social structure shapes political behaviour, that is, who votes, how they vote, who joins parties, and so on (as discussed in Chapters 11–13).

The nature of society, however, is one of the most contentious areas of political and ideological debate, being no less controversial, in fact, than the attempt to define the content of human nature. For example, whereas Marxists and others hold that society is characterized by irreconcilable conflict, liberals tend to emphasize that harmony exists amongst competing interests and groups. Similarly, while liberals are inclined to view society as an artefact fashioned by individuals to satisfy their various needs, conservatives have traditionally portrayed it as organic, ultimately shaped by the forces of natural necessity. Perhaps the most important debate, however, concerns the relationship between the individual and society, and whether or not there

Concept

Social class

A class is, broadly, a group of people who share a similar social and economic position. For Marxists, class is linked to economic power, which is defined by the individual's relationship to the means of production. From this perspective, class divisions are thus divisions between 'capital' and 'labour': that is, between the owners of productive wealth (the bourgeoisie) and those who live off the sale of their labour power (the proletariat). Non-Marxist definitions of class are usually based on income and status differences between occupational groups. An example is the distinction between 'middle' class, white-collar (or nonmanual) workers and 'working' class, blue-collar (or manual) workers. A more sophisticated marketing-based distinction is sometimes made between professionals (class A), managers (B), clerical workers (C1), skilled manual workers (C2), semiskilled and unskilled workers (D), and those who are unemployed, unavailable for work, or unable to work (E).

is such an entity as 'society'. At the heart of this question lies the rivalry between two contrasting modes of social understanding: individualism and collectivism.

Social class

Since the advent of modern industrial societies, class has generally been viewed as the deepest and most politically significant of social divisions. Only in more traditional societies have fixed social hierarchies and preindustrial systems of stratification continued to have an impact. For example, although the caste system in India has declined in importance, the Harijan (known in the past, in English, as the 'untouchables') remain a significant political force. Class divisions reflect economic and social differences in society, and are thus based on an unequal distribution of wealth, income and/or social status. A social class is therefore a group of people who have similar economic and social positions, and are united by a common economic interest. However, any analysis of the relationship between class and politics is bedevilled by a number of problems. These include the difficulty of identifying class divisions and of establishing the relationships between or among classes. Also, has the influence of class declined, and if so, why? Underlying these questions, though, is disagreement about precisely how social class should be defined.

The rise and fall of class politics

The leading proponents of the theory of class politics have come from the Marxist tradition. Marxists regard class as the most fundamental, and politically the most

Concept

Status

Status is a person's position within a hierarchical order. It is characterized by the person's role, rights and duties in relation to the other members of that order. As status is a compound of factors such as honour, prestige, standing and power, it is more difficult to determine than an essentially economic category such as class. Also, because it is a measure of social respect (that is, a measure of whether someone is 'higher' or 'lower' on a social scale), it is more subjective. While traditional societies typically possess clear and fixed status hierarchies, these are more fluid in modern industrial societies in which status often correlates, if imprecisely, with wealth and occupation. Status hierarchies nevertheless continue to operate in relation to factors such as family background, education, gender, and race and ethnicity.

Concept

Fordism, post-Fordism

Fordism and post-Fordism are terms that are used to explain the economic, political and cultural transformation of modern society by reference to the changing form and organization of production. Fordism refers to the large-scale mass-production methods pioneered by Henry Ford in Detroit in the USA. Using techniques widely imitated until the 1960s, Ford relied on mechanization and highly regimented production-line labour processes to produce standardized, relatively cheap products. Fordist societies were structured largely by solidaristic class loyalties. Post-Fordism emerged as the result of the introduction of more flexible microelectronics-based machinery that gave individual workers greater autonomy and made possible innovations such as subcontracting and batch production. Post-Fordism has been linked to decentralization in the workplace, social and political fragmentation, and a greater emphasis on choice and individuality.

significant, social division. As Marx put it at the beginning of the *Communist Manifesto* ([1848] 1967), 'the history of all hitherto existing societies is the history of class struggle'. This reflected his belief that politics, together with aspects of life such as the law, culture, the arts, and religion, is part of a 'superstructure' that is determined or conditioned by the economic 'base'. Crudely, this implied that the political process is nothing more than the working out of class tensions or conflicts. These, in turn, are rooted in the mode of production and, in the final analysis, in the institution of private property.

In this view, in a capitalist system, a 'ruling' class of property owners (the bourgeoisie) dominates and exploits a class of wage slaves (the proletariat). This gave rise to a two-class model of industrial capitalism that emphasized conflict and progressive polarization. In Marx's view, classes were the key actors on the political stage, and they had the ability to make history. The proletariat, he argued, was destined to be the 'grave digger' of capitalism. It would fulfil this destiny once it had achieved 'class consciousness' (see p. 225) and become aware of its genuine class interests, thus specifically recognizing the fact of its own exploitation. The proletariat would therefore be transformed from a 'class *in*-itself' (an economically defined category) to a 'class *for*-itself' (a revolutionary force). This, Marx believed, would be a consequence of the deepening crises of capitalism and the declining material conditions, or immiseration, of the working class.

The Marxist two-class model has, however, been discredited by the failure of Marx's predictions to materialize, and by declining evidence of class struggle, at least in advanced capitalist societies. Even by the end of the nineteenth century it was clear that the class structure of industrial societies was becoming increasingly complex, and that it varies from system to system, as well as over time. Max Weber (see p. 220) was one of the first to take stock of this shift, developing a theory of stratification that acknowledged economic or class differences but also took account of the importance of political parties and social status. In drawing attention to status as a 'social estimation of honour' expressed in the lifestyle of a group, Weber helped to prepare the ground for the modern notion of occupational class, widely used by social and political scientists. Modern Marxists have also attempted to refine the crude two-class model. While still emphasizing the importance of wealth ownership, they have been prepared to accept that an 'intermediate' class of managers and technicians has emerged, and that there are internal divisions within both the bourgeoisie and the proletariat. Rivalry, for instance, exists between finance and industrial capital, between big business and small employers, and between workers with supervisory responsibilities and ones who are merely supervised.

For some, however, the late twentieth century was characterized by the final eclipse of class politics. By the 1960s, neo-Marxists such as Herbert Marcuse (see p. 58) were lamenting the deradicalization of the urban proletariat, and looked instead to the revolutionary potential of students, women, ethnic minorities and the third world. The traditional link between socialism and the working class was formally abandoned in works such as André Gorz's *Farewell to the Working Class* (1982). In the same period, studies of electoral behaviour drew attention to the process of class dealignment (see p. 267), a weakening of the relationship between social class and party support. It appeared that voting was becoming an increasingly issue-based activity that reflects an individual's calculation of his or her material self-interest rather than any sense of class solidarity.

Most commentators agree that behind the declining political significance of

John Kenneth Galbraith (1908–2006)

Canadian economist and social theorist. Following wartime service as the Director of the US Strategic Bombing Survey, Galbraith became a professor of economics at Harvard University. He served as the American Ambassador to India in 1961–63. Galbraith was closely identified with the Democratic Party, and was perhaps the leading modern exponent of Keynesian economics (he was certainly its most innovative advocate). He became one of the USA's most eminent social commentators. His major works include *The Affluent Society* (1958), *The New Industrial State* (1967), and *The Culture of Contentment* (1992). In *The Affluent Society* (1958) he highlighted the contrast between private affluence and public squalor, arguing that economic resources are often used in the wasteful gratification of trivial wants. *The New Industrial State* (1967) advanced a critique of corporate power in the USA.

class lies the phenomenon of deindustrialization and the rise of the 'knowledge economy' or 'information society' (see p. 237). **Deindustrialization** is the decline of traditional labour-intensive industries such as the coal, steel and shipbuilding industries. These tended to be characterized by a solidaristic culture rooted in clear political loyalties and, usually, strong union organization. In contrast, the expanding service sectors of economies foster more individualistic and instrumentalist attitudes. In *The Second Industrial Divide: Possibilities for Prosperity* (1984), Piore and Sabel suggested that these changes are part of a transition from a 'Fordist' to a 'post-Fordist' era. The eclipse of the system of mass production and mass consumption, the chief characteristics of Fordism, has produced more pluralized class formations. In the political realm, this has been reflected in the decline of class-based political parties, and in the emergence of new social movements that articulate concern about, for example, feminism, world peace, animal rights and environmental protection.

Who are the underclass?

Reports of the death of class have nevertheless been exaggerated. When issued by socialists, they reflect bitter disillusionment, but when issued by liberals and conservatives, they are little more than wishful thinking. Modern industrial, or even post-Fordist, societies are classless neither in the Marxist sense of collectively owned wealth, nor in the liberal sense of genuine equality of opportunity. For example, in the UK in 2002, the richest 1 per cent owned 35 per cent of marketable wealth, excluding dwellings, and the top 50 per cent owned 98 per cent of wealth, while 12 000 000 people (22 per cent of the population) lived in households with a total income of less than 50 per cent of the national average (*Social Trends*, 2005). What has happened, however, is that new patterns of deprivation and disadvantage have emerged in place of the class divisions of old.

One of the most influential attempts to discuss this shift and its political implications is found in J. K. Galbraith's *The Culture of Contentment* (1992). Galbraith pointed to the emergence in modern societies, at least amongst the politically active, of a 'contented majority' whose material affluence and economic security encourages them to be politically conservative. This contented majority, for instance, provides an electoral base for the anti-welfarist and tax-cutting policies that have become fashionable since the 1970s. The concentration of poverty and disadvantage amongst a minority of the population is reflected in the development of a so-called 'two-thirds, one-third' society, or, as refined by Will Hutton (1995) for the UK, a

Deindustrialization: A contraction of the economy's manufacturing base, reflected in the decline of 'heavy' industries.

◆ **Concept**

Race

Race refers to physical or genetic differences amongst humankind that supposedly distinguish one group of people from another on biological grounds such as skin and hair colour, physique, and facial features. A race is thus a group of people who share a common ancestry and 'one blood'. The term is, however, controversial, both scientifically and politically. Scientific evidence suggests that there is no such thing as 'race' in the sense of a species-type difference between peoples. Politically, racial categorization is commonly based on cultural stereotypes, and is simplistic at best and pernicious at worst. The term ethnicity (see p. 168) is sometimes preferred because it refers to cultural and social differences that are not necessarily rooted in biology.

'three-fifths, two-fifths' society. Debate about the nature of social inequality has therefore increasingly focused on what is fashionably called the 'underclass'.

The term underclass is both poorly defined and politically controversial. In its broadest sense it refers to those who suffer from multiple deprivation (unemployment or low pay, poor housing, inadequate education and so on) and are socially marginalized: 'the excluded'. Right-wing commentators such as Charles Murray (1984), however, explain the emergence of the underclass largely in terms of welfare dependence and personal inadequacy. From this perspective, welfare is seen as the cause of disadvantage, not its cure. In this view, a 'culture of dependence' has developed amongst those classified as unemployed, disadvantaged or handicapped, weakening individual initiative and robbing them of self-respect and personal responsibility. Murray further argued that, as welfare relieves women of dependence upon 'breadwinning' men, it is a major cause of family breakdown, producing an underclass increasingly made up of single mothers and fatherless children. In *The Bell Curve: Intelligence and Class Structure in American Life* (1995), written with Richard Herrnstein, Murray went further still, linking social deprivation to what he alleged to be the innate inferiority of American blacks in particular.

Left-wing commentators, on the other hand, tend to define the underclass in terms of structural disadvantage and the changing balance of the global economy. From their point of view, the chief problem is long-term unemployment, and the apparent incapacity of many modern economies, faced by technological change and stiffer international competition, to provide jobs for large numbers of their citizens. For Galbraith the underclass is a 'functional underclass', which results from the need in all industrial countries for a pool of low-paid workers to do the jobs that the more fortunate reject as distasteful or demeaning. As this need is often met by ethnic minorities and immigrant labour, the underclass is not uncommonly doubly disadvantaged, suffering from both social exclusion and racial prejudice.

Race

Racial and ethnic divisions are a significant feature of many modern societies. There is nothing new, however, in the link between race and politics. The first explicitly racialist (see p. 120) political theories were developed in the nineteenth century against the background of European imperialism. Works such as Gobineau's *Essay on the Inequality of Human Races* (Gobineau, [1855] 1970) and H. S. Chamberlain's *The Foundations of the Nineteenth Century* ([1899] 1913) attempted to provide a pseudoscientific justification for the dominance of the 'white' races of Europe and North America over the 'black', 'brown' and 'yellow' peoples of Africa and Asia. Anti-Semitic (see p. 121) political parties and movements emerged in countries such as Germany, Austria and Russia in the late nineteenth century. The most grotesque twentieth-century manifestation of such racialism was found in German Nazism, which, through the so-called 'Final Solution', attempted to carry out the extermination of European Jewry. Apartheid (Afrikaans for 'apartness') in South Africa consisted of the strict segregation of whites and non-whites between the election of the Nationalist party in 1948 and the establishment of a nonracial democracy under the leadership of the African National Congress (ANC) in 1994. Elsewhere, racialism has been kept alive through campaigns against immigration, organized, for example, by the British National Party (BNP) and Le Pen's National Front (FN) in France.

Very different forms of racial or ethnic politics have developed out of the struggle against colonialism in particular, and as a result of racial discrimination and disadvantage in general. Ethnic minorities in many western societies are poorly represented within political elites and suffer from higher levels of unemployment and social deprivation than do indigenous or white populations. For instance, 31.9 per cent of black Americans live below the government's poverty line, compared with 8.8 per cent of American whites (Peele *et al.*, 1994:260). This conjunction of racial and social disadvantage has generated various styles of political activism.

The 1960s witnessed the emergence in the USA of both a civil-rights movement that, under the leadership of Martin Luther King (1929–68), practised nonviolent protest, and a militant Black Power movement that advocated revolutionary struggle and, in the case of Malcolm X (1926–65) and the Black Muslims, preached racial segregation. Other organizations have attempted to mobilize anti-racism and counter the rise of fascist movements through marches, protests and other demonstrations. In the UK, this task has been undertaken by the Anti-Nazi League, which was formed in the 1970s to combat the National Front and was reformed in the 1990s to confront the BNP. SOS Racisme emerged in France in the 1980s to offer similar resistance against the FN. Such action is commonly undertaken by organizations outside the conventional party system, because mainstream parties have generally feared that, by openly confronting racism, they risk weakening their electoral base. The goal of establishing ethnic and racial harmony is usually now advanced through the idea of multiculturalism (see p. 215), which is examined in Chapter 10.

Gender

Social divisions based on gender or sex have traditionally attracted less attention than those rooted in, for example, social class. Researchers and academics, who were overwhelmingly male, either failed to recognize the underrepresentation of women within their own ranks and in all dominant positions in society, or merely assumed that this was natural and inevitable. The rise of 'second wave' feminism in the 1960s did much to redress this oversight, and to establish a clearer awareness of the political significance of gender. Despite the steps taken since the 1960s to reduce gender-based inequality, it is estimated by the United Nations that women worldwide contribute 66 per cent of the hours worked, earn about 10 per cent of the world's income, and own only 1 per cent of the world's property. In the UK, fewer than 4 per cent of the members of the boards of major companies are women. Even though women gained the right to vote in 1918, only 20 per cent (127) of Members of Parliament were women in 2006.

In more traditional societies, such as Japan, still-powerful informal (and sometimes formal) rules mean that women have to leave employment and return to the home on getting married, becoming pregnant, or reaching the age of 30. In Islamic states women are required to wear the veil and conform to other dress codes. They are sometimes subject to enforced seclusion in the home, and may be excluded altogether from political life. Even in progressive Scandinavia, where women have made the most significant breakthroughs in political representation, women constitute only one-quarter to one-third of the members of the national assemblies.

In the eyes of radical feminists, such as Kate Millett (1970) and Mary Daly (1978), gender divisions are the deepest and most politically significant of all social cleavages.

Concept

Gender

Although the terms 'gender' and 'sex' are often used interchangeably in everyday language, the distinction between them is crucial to social and political theory. In this context, the term 'gender' is used to refer to social and cultural distinctions between males and females, while the term 'sex' is used to highlight biological, and therefore ineradicable, differences between men and women. Gender is therefore a social construct, usually based on stereotypes of 'feminine' and 'masculine' behaviour. Feminist theories typically highlight the distinction in order to demonstrate that physical or biological differences (sexual differences) need not mean that women and men must have different social roles and positions (gender differences). In short, the quest for gender equality reflects the belief that sexual differences have no social or political significance. Antifeminist positions are often rooted in a denial of the distinction between gender and sex, implying, quite simply, that 'biology is destiny'.

All contemporary and historical societies are seen to be characterized by patriarchy (see p. 98): that is, the dominance of men and subordination of women, usually rooted in the rule of the husband–father within the family. From this perspective, nothing short of a 'sexual revolution' that would fundamentally transform cultural and personal relationships as well as economic and political structures could bring an end to gender inequality.

Most women's political organizations, however, have adopted a liberal or reformist stance. They have set out to tackle eradicable inequalities in public life, such as the underrepresentation of women in senior political, managerial and professional posts, and the injustices that flow from anti-abortion legislation and inadequate childcare and welfare support for women. This reflects their belief that such goals can be achieved through a gradual process of incremental reform rather than through a 'sex war' between women and men. The most advanced such organizations have developed in the USA: the National Organisation for Women (NOW) (founded in 1966), the National Women's Political Caucus (NWPC), and Emily's List. Their tactics have included an attempt to exploit the so-called gender gap (the difference in voting behaviour between women and men) to get more women elected to Congress and the state legislatures. Although their record in this respect has been modest, they have nevertheless increased the prominence of women's rights issues. For example, they have succeeded in the 1980s and 1990s in resisting a shift towards a pro-life position by the Supreme Court.

■ Summary

◆ Economics influences politics at almost every level. Parties compete for power by outbidding each other with promises to increase growth, reduce inflation and so on. Voting behaviour is shaped largely by class divisions and social cleavages. Election results are invariably influenced by the state of the economy. Ideological divisions have also traditionally revolved around questions about ownership and economic organization.

◆ Traditionally, capitalism and socialism were seen as clearly distinct economic forms. Capitalism was characterized by general commodity production, the private ownership of wealth, and the market organization of economic life. Socialism featured a system of public or common ownership that was based on planning, and it was supposedly geared to the satisfaction of human needs rather than market demand.

◆ Neither capitalism nor socialism has ever existed in its 'pure' form, however. The capitalist systems of the world include those that emphasize enterprise and market individualism, those that recognize the importance of social justice, and those that are based on collaborative long-term relationships. Socialist systems have either practised state collectivism or attempted to find an accommodation with the market in the form of managed or regulated capitalism.

◆ All market systems are regulated to some extent. Supporters of regulation argue that economic management is essential to counter an inevitable tendency towards market instability, which can lead to slumps and soaring unemployment. Opponents, however, warn that economic management can upset the fragile balance of the market, undermine competition and efficiency, and result in uncontrollable inflation.

◆ The structure of society, and particularly its divisions, influences politics in a number of ways. The distribution of wealth conditions the nature of state power. Society influences public opinion and the political culture. Social conflict helps to generate change through either reform or revolution. The social structure shapes all forms of political behaviour and participation.

◆ Class, race and gender divisions are the most politically significant of the social cleavages in modern society. Class politics may have been diluted by the emergence of post-Fordism, but still persist, in particular because of the influence of the 'underclass'. The growth of the civil-rights and women's movements has ensured that once-ignored race and gender divisions are now recognized as being as significant as class-based ones.

Questions for discussion

▶ Why do political questions so often boil down to economic issues? Is this healthy?

▶ What type of capitalist system is likely to be the most viable in the twenty-first century?

▶ Are free-market economies inherently unstable and prone to inequality?

▶ Are socialist economic models any longer of relevance?

▶ What would be the features of an ecologically sustainable economy?

▶ Has class conflict in modern societies been resolved or merely suppressed?

▶ To what extent has the recognition of racial and gender divisions produced meaningful political change?

Further reading

Hall, P. and D. Soskice (eds), *Varieties of Capitalism: The Institutional Foundations of Comparative Advantage* (Oxford: Oxford University Press, 2001). A stimulating examination of differences among national economies and of the impact of economic globalization.

Hampden-Turner, C. and F. Trompenaars, *The Seven Cultures of Capitalism* (New York: Doubleday, 1993). A fascinating and authoritative overview of the diverse range of capitalist forms.

O'Brien, R. and M. Williams, *Global Political Economy*, 2nd edn (Basingstoke and New York: Palgrave Macmillan, 2007).

Rush, M., *Politics and Society: An Introduction to Political Sociology* (Hemel Hempstead: Harvester Wheatsheaf, 1992). A comprehensive introduction to the relationship between political and social institutions, and between social and political behaviour.

For references on societal divisions, see the following: Saunders (1990) on social class, Fenton (2003) on race and ethnicity, and McDowell and Pringle (1992) on gender divisions.

Political Culture, Identity and Legitimacy

CHAPTER 10

> 'The strongest is never strong enough unless he turns right into might and obedience into duty.'
>
> JEAN-JACQUES ROUSSEAU, *Social Contract* (1862)

Much of politics takes place in our heads: that is, it is shaped by our ideas, values and assumptions about how society should be organized, and our expectations, hopes and fears about government. At the end of the day, what we believe about the society in which we live may be more important than the reality of its power structure and the actual distribution of resources and opportunities within it. Perception may not only be more important than reality; in practical terms, perception may *be* reality. This highlights the vital role played by what is called political culture. People's beliefs, symbols and values structure both their attitude to the political process, and, crucially, their view of the regime in which they live – most particularly, whether or not they regard their regime as rightful or legitimate. Legitimacy is thus the key to political stability, and it is nothing less than the source of a regime's survival and success.

The central issues examined in this chapter are as follows:

Key issues

▶ How do individuals and groups acquire their political attitudes and values?

▶ Do democratic regimes depend on the existence of a distinctive 'civic culture'?

▶ Are modern societies characterized by free competition between values and ideas, or by a 'dominant' culture?

▶ How do regimes maintain legitimacy?

▶ Are modern societies facing a crisis of legitimation?

▶ What happens when legitimacy collapses? Why do revolutions occur?

Political culture

Political thinkers through the ages have acknowledged the importance of attitudes, values and beliefs. However, these past thinkers did not see them as part of a 'political culture'. Burke (see p. 49), for instance, wrote about custom and tradition, Marx (see p. 55) about ideology, and Herder (see p. 111) about national spirit. All of them nevertheless agreed about the vital role that values and beliefs play in promoting the stability and survival of a regime. Interest amongst political scientists in the idea of political culture emerged in the 1950s and 1960s as new techniques of behavioural analysis displaced more traditional, institutional approaches to the subject. The classic work in this respect was Almond and Verba's *The Civic Culture* (1963), which used opinion surveys to analyse political attitudes and democracy in five countries: the USA, the UK, West Germany, Italy and Mexico. This work was stimulated in part by a desire to explain the collapse of representative government in interwar Italy, Germany and elsewhere, and the failure of democracy in many newly independent developing states after 1945. Although interest in political culture faded in the 1970s and 1980s, the debate has been revitalized since the 1990s as a result of efforts in eastern Europe to construct democracy out of the ashes of communism, and growing anxiety in mature democracies, such as the USA, about the apparent decline of social capital and civic engagement. However, there is also debate about whether or not political culture is shaped by the ideas and interests of elite groups. This, in turn, is linked to rival views of the mass media and the extent to which government can now manipulate political communication.

Civic culture or ideological hegemony?

Debate about the nature of political culture has often focused on the idea of civic culture, usually associated with the writings of Almond and Verba (1963, 1980). Almond and Verba set out to identify the political culture that most effectively upheld democratic politics. They identified three general types of political culture: participant culture, subject culture and parochial culture.

A *participant* political culture is one in which citizens pay close attention to politics and regard popular participation as both desirable and effective. A *subject* political culture is characterized by more passivity amongst citizens, and the recognition that they have only a very limited capacity to influence government. A *parochial* political culture is marked by the absence of a sense of citizenship, with people identifying with their locality rather than the nation, and having neither the desire nor the ability to participate in politics. Although Almond and Verba accepted that a participant culture came closest to the democratic ideal, they argued that the 'civic culture' is a blend of all three in that it reconciles the participation of citizens in the political process with the vital necessity for government to govern. Democratic stability, in their view, is underpinned by a political culture that is characterized by a blend of activity and passivity on the part of citizens, and a balance between obligation and performance on the part of government.

In their initial study (1963), Almond and Verba concluded that the UK came closest to the civic culture, exhibiting both participant and subject features. In other words, while the British thought that they could influence government, they were also willing to obey authority. The USA also scored highly, its relative weakness

---

Political culture

Culture, in its broadest sense, is the way of life of a people. Sociologists and anthropologists tend to distinguish between 'culture' and 'nature', the former encompassing that which is passed on from one generation to the next by learning, rather than through biological inheritance. Political scientists, however, use the term in a narrower sense to refer to a people's psychological orientation, political culture being the 'pattern of orientations' to political objects such as parties, government, the constitution, expressed in beliefs, symbols and values. Political culture differs from public opinion in that it is fashioned out of long-term values rather than simply people's reactions to specific policies and problems.

being that, as participant attitudes predominated over subject ones, Americans were not particularly law-abiding. The difficulty of building or rebuilding a civic culture was underlined by the examples of both West Germany and Italy. A decade and a half after the collapse of fascism, neither country appeared to have a strong participant culture; while the subject culture was dominant in Germany, parochial attitudes remained firmly entrenched in Italy. Almond and Verba's later study (1980) highlighted a number of shifts, notably declining national pride and confidence in the UK and the USA, which contrasted with a rise in civic propensities in Germany.

The civic-culture approach to the study of political attitudes and values has, however, been widely criticized. In the first place, its model of the psychological dispositions that make for a stable democracy is highly questionable. In particular, the emphasis on passivity and the recognition that deference to authority is healthy has been criticized by those who argue that political participation is the very stuff of democratic government. Almond and Verba suggested a 'sleeping dogs' theory of democratic culture that implies that low participation indicates broad satisfaction with government, which politicians, in turn, will be anxious to maintain. On the other hand, when less than half the adult population bothers to vote, as regularly occurs in the USA, this could simply reflect widespread alienation and ingrained disadvantage.

Second, the civic-culture thesis rests on the unproven assumption that political attitudes and values shape behaviour, and not the other way round. In short, a civic culture may be more a consequence of democracy than its cause. If this is the case, political culture may provide an index of the health of democracy, but it cannot be seen as a means of promoting stable democratic rule. Finally, Almond and Verba's approach tends to treat political culture as homogeneous: that is, as little more than a cipher for national culture or national character. In so doing, it pays little attention to political subcultures and tends to disguise fragmentation and social conflict. In contrast, radical approaches to political culture tend to highlight the significance of social divisions, such as those based on class, race and gender (see Chapter 9).

A very different view of the role and nature of political culture has been developed within the Marxist tradition. Although Marx portrayed capitalism as a system of class exploitation and oppression operating through the ownership of the means of production, he also acknowledged the power of ideas, values and beliefs. As Marx and Engels put it in *The German Ideology* ([1846]1970:64), 'the ideas of the ruling class are in every epoch the ruling ideas, i.e. the class which is the ruling *material* force of society, is at the same time the ruling *intellectual* force'. In Marx's view, ideas and culture are part of a 'superstructure' that is conditioned or determined by the economic 'base', the mode of production.

These ideas have provided Marxism with two theories of culture. The first suggests that culture is essentially class-specific: as members of a class share the same experiences and have a common economic position and interests, they are likely to have broadly similar ideas, values and beliefs. In Marx's words, 'it is not the consciousness of men that determines their existence, but their social existence that determines their consciousness'. Proletarian culture and ideas can therefore be expected to differ markedly from bourgeois ones. The second theory of culture emphasizes the degree to which the ideas of the ruling class (what Marx referred to as 'ideology') pervade society and become the 'ruling ideas' of the age. In this view, political culture, or even civic culture, is thus nothing more than **bourgeois ideology**. What is important about this view is that it sees culture, values and beliefs as a form of power. From the Marxist perspective, the function of ideology is to reconcile

---

Concept

Hegemony

Hegemony (from the Greek *hegemonia*, meaning 'leader') is, in its simplest sense, the ascendancy or domination of one element of a system over others (an example being the predominance of a state within a league or confederation). In Marxist theory, the term is used in a more technical and specific sense. In the writings of Antonio Gramsci (see p. 208), hegemony refers to the ability of a dominant class to exercise power by winning the *consent* of those it subjugates, as an alternative to the use of *coercion*. As a noncoercive form of class rule, hegemony is typically understood as a cultural or ideological process that operates through the dissemination of bourgeois values and beliefs throughout society. However, it also has a political and economic dimension: consent can be manipulated by pay increases or by political or social reform.

Bourgeois ideology: A Marxist term, denoting ideas and theories that serve the interests of the bourgeoisie by disguising the contradictions of capitalist society.

Antonio Gramsci (1891–1937)

Italian Marxist and social theorist. The son of a minor public official. Gramsci joined the Socialist Party in 1913, becoming in 1921 the General Secretary of the newly formed Italian Communist Party. Although an elected member of parliament, he was imprisoned by Mussolini in 1926. He remained in prison until his death. His *Prison Notebooks* (Gramsci, 1971), written in 1929–35, tried to counterbalance the emphasis within orthodox Marxism on 'scientific' determinism by stressing the importance of the political and intellectual struggle. Although proponents of Eurocommunism have claimed him as an influence, he remained throughout his life a Leninist and a revolutionary.

subordinate classes to their exploitation and oppression by propagating myths, delusions and falsehoods (in Engels' words, 'false consciousness'). Later Marxists have understood this process in terms of bourgeois 'hegemony' (see p. 201).

Modern Marxists have been quick to acknowledge that in no sense do the 'ruling ideas' of the bourgeoisie monopolize intellectual and cultural life in a capitalist society, excluding all rival views. Rather, they accept that cultural, ideological and political competition does exist, but stress that this competition is unequal. Quite simply, ideas and values that uphold the capitalist order have an overwhelming advantage over ideas and values that question or challenge it. Such ideological hegemony may, in fact, be successful precisely because it operates behind the illusion of free speech, open competition and political pluralism – what Herbert Marcuse (see p. 58) termed 'repressive tolerance'.

The most influential twentieth-century exponent of this view was Antonio Gramsci. Gramsci drew attention to the degree to which the class system is upheld not simply by unequal economic and political power, but also by bourgeois hegemony. This consists of the spiritual and cultural supremacy of the ruling class, brought about through the spread of bourgeois values and beliefs via 'civil society': the media (see p. 232), the churches, youth movements, trade unions and so forth. What makes this process so insidious is that it extends beyond formal learning and education into the very common sense of the age. The significance of Gramsci's analysis is that, in order for socialism to be achieved, a 'battle of ideas' has to be waged through which proletarian principles, values and theories displace, or at least challenge, bourgeois ideas.

The Marxist view of culture as ideological power rests on the distinction between subjective or *felt* interests (what people think they want) and objective or *real* interests (what people would want if they could make independent and informed choices). This draws attention to what Stephen Lukes (2004) called a radical view of power (see p. 11): 'A exercises power over B when A affects B in a manner contrary to B's interests'. Such a view of political culture has, however, attracted considerable criticism. Some have argued that it is unwarrantedly patronizing to suggest that the values and beliefs of ordinary people have been foisted upon them by manipulation and indoctrination. The acceptance of capitalist values and beliefs by the working classes may, for instance, merely reflect their perception that capitalism works.

The dominant-ideology model of political culture may also overstate the degree of homogeneity in the values and beliefs of modern societies. While a 'ruling' ideology may provide a dominant class with self-belief and a sense of purpose, it is less clear, as Abercrombie, Hill and Turner (1980) argued, that subordinate classes have been successfully integrated into this value system. Finally, the Marxist view, which purports to establish a link between unequal class power and cultural and ideological bias, may do nothing more than describe a tendency found in all societies for powerful groups to propagate self-serving ideas. Whether this constitutes a dominant value *system*, in which a coherent and consistent message is disseminated through the mass media, schools, the churches and so on, is rather more questionable.

Decline of social capital?

The process of political and economic reconstruction in former communist states has stimulated renewed interest in the issue of political culture since the 1990s. This is because pervasive state control over a number of generations had evidently destroyed or suppressed the social connections and sense of civic responsibility that usually sustain democratic politics. In other words, there was a perceived need to rebuild civil society (see p. 8), in the sense of a realm of autonomous groups and associations, including businesses, interest groups, clubs and so on. Indeed, such ideas can be traced back to Alexis de Tocqueville (see p. 227), who, in the nineteenth century, had explained the USA's egalitarian institutions and democratic practices by reference to the American's propensity for participation and civic association. No sooner had this revived concern with political culture arisen in relation to postcommunist states than it was being applied to perceived problems in mature democracies.

Robert Putnam (1993), for example, argued that variations in the quality of local government in different regions of Italy were determined by the presence, or absence, of traditions of civic engagement, reflected in differing levels of voter turnout, newspaper readership, and membership of choral societies and football clubs. In *Bowling Alone* (2000) Putnam drew attention to the USA's declining 'social capital' (see p. 210), and argued that other industrialized countries are likely to follow US trends. He highlighted the emergence of a 'post-civic' generation. This was demonstrated by a 25–50 per cent drop in the number of voluntary clubs and associations since 1965, and by sharp declines in attendance at public, town and school meetings, as well as in the membership of, and work done for, political parties. Putnam's view, which is influenced by communitarianism (see p. 179), explains declining social capital in a variety of ways. These include the spread of suburbanization and therefore of longer journeys to work; the rise of two-career families and their impact on the quantity and quality of parenting; and the tendency of television to privatize leisure time, misshape social perceptions and reduce achievement levels in children. From an alternative social-democratic perspective, however, the decline of civic engagement is explained by the triumph of consumer capitalism and the spread of materialist and individualist values.

Conservative thinkers have long supported their own view of social capital in the form of tradition (see p. 221) and in particular 'traditional values'. These are values and beliefs that have supposedly been passed down from earlier generations and so constitute a kind of cultural bedrock. Conservative politicians regularly call for such values to be 'strengthened' or 'defended', believing that they are the key to social cohesion and political stability. In the UK in the 1980s, for example, Margaret Thatcher called for the resurrection of what she called 'Victorian values', while John

Robert D. Putnam (born 1940)

US political scientist and social commentator. Putnam's work has revived interest in political culture and focused attention on the importance of 'social capital': the level of trust and cooperation in a society, what develops 'the "i" into the "we"' His most influential work, *Bowling Alone: The Collapse and Revival of American Community* (2000), used the image of a man bowling alone, rather than in a team, to illustrate the decline of community activity and political engagement in the USA. Amongst the causes of this decline, Putnam identifies the growing influence of television, changes in family structure, and the growth of geographical mobility.

Major's ill-starred 'Back to Basics' initiative attempted much the same in the 1990s. In the USA Ronald Reagan embraced the notion of the 'frontier ideology', harking back to the conquest of the American West and the virtues of self-reliance, hard work and adventurousness that he believed it exemplified. Not uncommonly, such values are linked to the family, the church and the nation: that is, to long-established institutions that supposedly embody the virtues of continuity and endurance.

In his essay 'Rationalism in Politics' (Oakeshott, 1962), Michael Oakeshott developed a further defence of continuity and tradition. Oakeshott argued that traditional values and established customs should be upheld and respected on account of their familiarity, which engenders a sense of reassurance, stability and security. This suggests that there is a general human disposition to favour tradition over innovation, the established over the new. To be a conservative, Oakeshott suggested, is 'to prefer the familiar to the unknown, to prefer the tried to the untried, fact to mystery, the actual to the possible, the limited to the unbound, the near to the distant, the sufficient to the super abundant, the convenient to the perfect, present laughter to utopian bliss' (Oakeshott, 1962:169).

The defence of traditional values and established beliefs has been one of the central themes of neoconservatism, advanced in the USA by social theorists such as Daniel Bell (1976) and Irving Kristol (1983), who have warned against the destruction of spiritual values brought about by both market pressures and the spread of permissiveness. The problem with this position, however, is that it assumes there is an authoritative moral system upon which order and stability can be based. The

Concept

Social capital

Capital refers to assets that are used in the production of goods and services. The concept of 'social capital' was developed in the 1970s to highlight the social and cultural factors that underpin wealth creation. The term has since been used to refer to social connectiveness as represented by networks, norms and trust that promote civic engagement. Social capital is thus a precondition for successful communities and good governance (see p. 6). In common with economic assets, social capital can decline or rise, usually through education and a stress on active citizenship. The alleged decline in social capital in modern society has been linked, variously, to the 'parenting deficit', the rise of individualism and the increase in social and geographical mobility. Critics of the term argue either that social capital is a consequence and not a cause of democratic government, or that it ignores the role of economic well-being in fostering civic allegiance.

Michael Oakeshott (1901–90)

UK political philosopher. Oakeshott was a professor of political science at the London School of Economics from 1951 until his retirement in 1968. His collection of essays *Rationalism in Politics and Other Essays* (1962) and his more systematic work of political philosophy *On Human Conduct* (1975) are often seen as major contributions to conservative traditionalism. By highlighting the importance of civil association and insisting upon the limited province of politics, he also developed themes closely associated with liberal thought. Though often seen as an advocate of a non-ideological style of politics, Oakeshott influenced many of the thinkers of the New Right.

simple fact is that in modern multicultural and multireligious societies it is doubtful whether any set of values can be regarded as authoritative. To define certain values as 'traditional', 'established' or 'majority' values may simply be an attempt to impose a particular moral system on the rest of society. Indeed, empirical evidence appears to support the view that political culture is becoming increasingly fragmented, and that modern societies are characterized by growing moral and cultural diversity.

An alternative view of the social capital debate suggests not that there has been a decline of civic engagement or social connectedness, but that the forms these have taken have changed. According to Inglehart (1977, 1990), such shifts are linked to the spread of affluence and to the growth, particularly amongst young people, of 'post-material' values. As new generations have grown up since the 1960s accustomed, in advanced industrial countries at least, to economic security and material well-being, 'traditional' ideas about subjects such as sex, marriage and personal conduct have been displaced by more 'liberal' or 'permissive' ones. At the same time, traditional political attitudes and allegiances have been weakened and sometimes replaced by growing interest in issues such as feminism, nuclear disarmament, animal rights and environmental protection. Thus party membership and electoral turn-out may have declined but there has been a growth of interest in single-issue protest politics and campaigning groups. Post-Fordist (see p. 198) theorists argue that such cultural changes are irresistible, because they are linked to a wholesale shift in economic and political organization that is bringing about a decline in deference and a rise of individualism.

Concept

Postmaterialism

Postmaterialism is a theory that explains the nature of political concerns and values In terms of levels of economic development. It is loosely based on Abraham Maslow's (1908–70) 'hierarchy of needs', which places esteem and self-actualization above material or economic needs. Postmaterialism assumes that conditions of material scarcity breed egoistical and acquisitive values, meaning that politics is dominated by economic issues. However, in conditions of widespread prosperity, individuals express more interest in 'postmaterial' or 'quality of life' issues. These are typically concerned with morality, political justice and personal fulfilment, and include feminism, world peace, racial harmony, ecology and animal rights. Postmaterialism has been used to explain developments such as class dealignment and the rise of new social movements.

■ Identity politics and multiculturalism

Rise of identity politics

One of the prominent features of modern politics has been a growing recognition of the significance of cultural differences within society, often portrayed as 'identity politics' or the 'politics of difference'. There is, of course, nothing new about the recognition of differences within society. Chapter 9, for instance, examines links between politics and social cleavages such as social class (see p. 197), race (see p. 200) and gender (see p. 201). However, whereas 'social cleavage' implies splits or divisions, encouraging us to treat social groups or collective bodies as entities in their own right, 'identity' links the personal to the social, in seeing the individual as 'embedded' in a particular cultural, social, institutional and ideological context. Identity refers to a sense of separate and unique selfhood, but it also acknowledges that how people see themselves is shaped by a web of social and other relationships that distinguish them from other people. Identity may also be multiple (based on factors such as gender, ethnicity, religion, citizenship and so on), and, in western societies in particular, it is increasingly based on the ability to choose, meaning that political activism assumes the character of a lifestyle choice. Nevertheless, in any of these senses, identity implies difference: an awareness of difference sharpens or clarifies our sense of identity. Such thinking has led to what is called the 'politics of recognition', which is based on the idea that identity should be fully and formally acknowledged, and that difference should be embraced, even celebrated. In this sense, the rise of identity politics reflects a shift away from **universalism** and towards **particularism**.

The foundations for identity politics, and for the ideas of multiculturalism (see p. 215) with which it is commonly associated, were laid by the postcolonial theories that emerged from the collapse of the European empires in the early post-1945 period. The significance of postcolonialism was that it sought to challenge and overturn the cultural dimension of imperial rule by establishing the legitimacy of non-western – and sometimes anti-western – political ideas and traditions. For example, Franz Fanon (1926–61), the Martinique-born French revolutionary theorist, developed a theory of imperialism that gave particular emphasis to the psychological dimension of colonial subjugation. For Fanon (1968), decolonization was not merely a political process, but one through which a new 'species' of man is created. He argued that only the cathartic experience of violence is powerful enough to bring about this psycho-political regeneration. Edward Said (see p. 213) developed a critique of **Eurocentrism** through his notion of 'orientalism' (Said, 1978). Orientalism highlights the extent to which western cultural and political hegemony over the rest of the world, but over the Orient in particular, had been maintained through elaborate stereotypical fictions that belittled and demeaned non-western people and culture. Examples of this would include notions such as the 'mysterious East', 'inscrutable Chinese' and 'lustful Turks'. Further impetus to the emergence of identity politics was given by the rise of the black consciousness movement in the 1960s, primarily in the USA. During this phase it was largely concerned with establishing black pride, often through reestablishing a distinctive African identity, as was advocated by thinkers and activists such as Marcus Garvey (see p. 175). It was also shaped by the growing political assertiveness, sometimes expressed through ethnic national-

Universalism: The theory that there is a common core to human identity shared by people everywhere.

Particularism: The theory that identity is rooted in particular rather than general characteristics, highlighting the importance of factors such as locality, culture and ethnicity (see p. 174).

Eurocentrism: A culturally biased approach to understanding that takes European, and generally western, ideas, values and assumptions to be 'natural'.

Edward Said (1935–2003)

A Jerusalem-born US academic and literary critic, Said was a leading literary critic, a prominent advocate of the Palestinian cause and a founding figure of postcolonial theory. He developed, from the 1970s onwards, a humanist critique of the western Enlightenment that uncovered its links to colonialism and highlighted 'narratives of oppression', cultural and ideological biases that disempowered colonized peoples by representing them as the non-western 'other'. He is best known for the notion of 'orientalism', which operated through a 'subtle and persistent Eurocentric prejudice against Arabo-Islamic peoples and culture.' His key texts include *Orientalism* (1978) and *Culture and Imperialism* (1993).

ism, of cultural groups in various parts of the world. This is examined in Chapter 8 in relation to the rise of ethnic politics.

Nevertheless, the most powerful factor underpinning the global significance of identity politics has been the growth of international migration, particularly since the 1950s. This has given an increasing number of societies a distinctively multicultural character, with examples of still highly homogeneous countries, such as Japan, becoming rarer. Ethnic minority communities developed in many European countries as a result of the end of empire and of deliberate attempts by governments to recruit workers from abroad to help in the process of postwar reconstruction. In the UK, for instance, immigrants came mainly from its former colonies in the West Indies and South Asia; in the case of France, they came largely from Algeria, Morocco and Tunisia; and in the case of West Germany they were usually so-called *Gastarbeiter* (guestworkers), recruited principally from Turkey or Yugoslavia. Immigration into the USA since the 1970s has come mainly from Mexico and other Latin American countries. If current immigration and population growth rates within Latino (or Hispanic) communities continue, it is estimated that by 2050 almost a quarter of the US population will be Latinos.

Since the 1980s, there has been a significant intensification of cross-border migration across the globe, creating what some have seen as a 'hyper-mobile planet'. This has happened for two main reasons. First, there have been a growing number of refugees (reaching a peak of about 18 million in 1993), which resulted from war, ethnic conflict and political upheaval in areas ranging from Algeria, Rwanda and Uganda, to Bangladesh and Afghanistan. The collapse of communism in eastern Europe, 1989–91, contributed to this both by creating, almost overnight, a new group of migrants and by sparking a series of ethnic conflicts, especially in the former Yugoslavia. Second, economic globalization has intensified pressures for international migration in a variety of ways. These include the development of a 'dual' labour market, through the growth of a stratum of low-paid, low-skilled and low-status jobs that indigenous populations are increasingly unwilling to fill. This has led to a position in which, for instance, roughly one-third of the total population of the Gulf states, and two-thirds of their working populations, are (predominantly female) non-nationals, largely from South and Southeast Asia. Such trends have significantly strained national identity in many countries, and contributed to the development of so-called 'transnational communities' (see p. 214).

> **Concept**
>
> ### Transnational community
>
> A transnational community is a community whose cultural identity, political allegiances and psychological orientations cut across or transcend national borders. Such communities challenge the doctrine of nationalism, which clearly links politico-cultural identity to a specific territory or 'homeland'. Transnational communities can therefore be thought of as 'deterritorialized nations' or 'global tribes'. However, not every **diasporic** community is a transnational community, in the sense that its members retain an allegiance to their country of origin, as well as interest and perhaps active engagement in its politics and development. The strength of these allegiances depends on factors such as the circumstances of migration and the length of stay in the new country. Nevertheless, transnational communities typically have multiple attachments, as allegiances to a country of origin do not preclude the formation of attachments to a country of settlement, creating a form of differentiated citizenship.

Models of multiculturalism

As a growing number of countries have come to accept as an irreversible fact that their populations have a multi-ethnic, multi-religious or multicultural character, various attempts have been made to reconcile cultural diversity and identity-related difference with civic and political cohesion. However, how is political stability to be maintained in societies in which the monocultural bonds of political nationalism have been fatally undermined? Some, indeed, view this as the central political challenge of the twenty-first century. Attempts to balance diversity against cohesion are usually dubbed multiculturalism. Multiculturalism is a broad and often ill-defined term, which may simply stress the range of cultural diversity found in many modern societies. Although such diversity may be linked to age, social class, gender or sexuality, multiculturalism is usually associated with cultural differentiation that is based on race, ethnicity or language. Multiculturalism not only recognizes the fact of cultural diversity, but also holds that such differences should be respected and publicly affirmed.

Although the USA, as an immigrant society, has long been a multicultural society, the cause of multiculturalism in this sense was not taken up until the rise of the black consciousness movement in the 1960s and the advent of '**affirmative action**'. Australia has been officially committed multiculturalism since the early 1970s, in recognition of its increasing 'Asianization'. In New Zealand it is linked to a recognition of the role of Maori culture in forging a distinctive national identity. In Canada, the country that has demonstrated the greatest official commitment to multiculturalism, it is associated with attempts to achieve reconciliation between French-speaking Quebec and the English-speaking majority population, and an acknowledgement of the rights of the indigenous Inuit peoples. In the UK, multiculturalism recognizes the existence of significant black and Asian communities and abandons the demand that they **assimilate** into white society. In Germany, this applies to Turkish groups.

The central theme within all forms of multiculturalism is that individual identity is culturally embedded, in the sense that people largely derive their understanding of the world and their framework of moral beliefs from the culture in which they live and develop. Distinctive cultures therefore deserve to be protected or strengthened, particularly when they belong to minority or vulnerable groups. This leads to the idea of minority or multicultural rights, sometimes seen as 'special' rights. Will Kymlicka (1995) identified three kinds of minority rights: self-government rights, polyethnic rights and representation rights. Self-government rights belong, Kymlicka argued, to

Diaspora: Literally, dispersion (from the Hebrew); implies displacement or dispersal by force, but is also used to refer to the communities that have arisen as a result of such dispersal.

Affirmative action: Reverse or 'positive' discrimination which accords preferential treatment to groups on the basis of their past disadvantage.

Assimilation: The process through which immigrant communities loose their cultural distinctiveness by adjusting to the values, allegiances and lifestyles of the 'host' society.

what he called national minorities, peoples who are territorially concentrated, possess a shared language and are characterized by a 'meaningful way of life across the full range of human activities'. Examples would include the Native Americans, the Inuits in Canada, the Maoris in New Zealand and the Aborigines in Australia. In these cases, he argued, the right to self-government should involve the devolution of political power, usually through federalism (see p. 167), although it may extend to the right of secession and, therefore, to sovereign independence. Polyethnic rights are rights that help ethnic groups and religious minorities, which have developed through immigration, to express and maintain their cultural distinctiveness. They would, for instance, provide the basis for legal exemptions, such as the exemption of Jews and Muslims from animal slaughtering laws, the exemption of Sikh men from wearing motorcycle helmets, and the exemption of Muslim girls from school dress codes. Special representation rights attempt to redress the underrepresentation of minority or disadvantaged groups in education and in senior positions in political and public life. Such rights, which in the USA take the form of affirmative action, imply the practice of reverse or 'positive' discrimination, which attempts to compensate for past discrimination or continuing cultural subordination. Their justification is not only that they ensure full and equal participation, but also that they are the only means of guaranteeing that public policy reflects the interests of all groups and peoples, and not merely those of traditionally dominant groups.

However, there is no settled view of how multicultural societies should operate, nor of how far multiculturalism should go in positively endorsing communal diversity. There are three main models of multiculturalism:

- liberal multiculturalism
- pluralist multiculturalism
- cosmopolitan multiculturalism.

Liberal multiculturalism is rooted in a commitment to freedom and toleration: the ability to choose one's own moral beliefs, cultural practices and way of life, regardless of whether these are disapproved of by others. Kymlicka (1995) has, for example, sought to reconcile liberalism with multiculturalism by advancing the idea of multicultural citizenship, based on the belief that cultures are valuable and distinctive and provide a context in which individuals are provided with meaning, orientation, identity and belonging. However, the liberal model of multiculturalism only provides a qualified endorsement of communal diversity, highlighting the dangers that may also be implicit in identity politics. This applies in three main ways. In the first place, the liberal model of multiculturalism is based on support for toleration, and toleration is not morally neutral. Toleration reflects a willingness to accept views or actions with which one is in disagreement. According to liberals, it is valuable for the individual, for whom it guarantees the right to choose one's own moral beliefs and cultural practices, but it also contributes to the vigour and health of society by ensuring that ideas and practices are tested against rival ideas and practices. However, toleration extends only to views, values and social practices that are themselves tolerant; that is, to ones that are compatible with personal freedom and autonomy. Liberal multiculturalists may therefore be unwilling to endorse practices such as female circumcision, forced (and possibly arranged) marriages and female dress codes, however much the groups concerned may believe that these are crucial to the maintenance of their cultural identity.

Concept

Multiculturalism

Multiculturalism is used as both a descriptive and a normative term. As a descriptive term it refers to cultural diversity arising from the existence within a society of two or more groups whose beliefs and practices generate a distinctive sense of collective identity. Multiculturalism is invariably reserved for communal diversity that arises from racial, ethnic or language differences. As a normative term, multiculturalism implies a positive endorsement of communal diversity, based either on the right of different cultural groups to respect and recognition, or on the alleged benefits to the larger society of moral and cultural diversity. Multiculturalism, in this sense, acknowledges the importance of beliefs, values and ways of life in establishing self-understanding and a sense of self-worth for individuals and groups alike. Critics of multiculturalism argue that multicultural societies are inherently conflict-ridden and unstable, and view normative multiculturalism as an example of political correctness.

Isaiah Berlin (1909–97)

UK historian of ideas and philosopher. Berlin was born in Riga, Latvia, and came to Britain in 1921. He developed a form of liberal pluralism that was grounded in a lifelong commitment to empiricism and influenced by the ideas of counter-Enlightenment thinkers, including Vico (1668–1744), Herder (see p. 111) and Alexander Herzen (1812–70). Basic to Berlin's philosophical stance was a belief in moral pluralism, the idea that conflicts of values are intrinsic to human life. His best-known political writing is *Four Essays on Liberty* (1958), in which he extolled the virtues of 'negative' freedom over 'positive' freedom. Berlin's writings constitute a defence of western liberalism against totalitarianism.

Second, liberals make important distinctions between 'private' and 'public' life, seeing the former as a realm of freedom in which people should, as far as possible, be able to express their language, religious and cultural identity, while emphasizing that the latter should be based on at least a bedrock of shared civic allegiances. This form of multiculturalism is, then, compatible with **civic nationalism**. Citizenship can thus be 'differentiated', in that it encompasses civic loyalties, focused on the state, as well as cultural loyalties towards a particular group or tradition. In the clearly 'republican' multiculturalism that is practised in France, this has led to a ban on the wearing of the *hijab*, or Muslim headscarves, in schools, and, since 2003, to a ban on all forms of overt religious affiliation in French schools, despite the fact that these practices are entirely lawful in private life. Third, liberal multiculturalists view liberal democracy as the sole legitimate political system, its virtue being that it alone ensures government based upon consent and provides guarantees for personal freedom and toleration. Liberal multiculturalists would therefore oppose calls, for instance, for the establishment of an Islamic state based on *Shari'a* law, and may even be willing to prohibit groups and movements that campaign for such political ends.

Pluralist multiculturalism provides firmer foundations for a theory of cultural diversity because it is based on the idea of **value pluralism**. Developed in particular in the writings of Isaiah Berlin, this holds that people are bound to disagree about the ultimate ends of life. As values conflict, the human predicament is inevitably characterized by moral conflict. In this view, liberal or western beliefs, such as support for personal freedom, democracy and secularization, have no greater moral authority than rival beliefs. This leads to a form of live-and-let-live multiculturalism, or what is sometimes seen as the politics of *in*difference. However, as Berlin remained a liberal to the extent that he believed that only within a society that respects individual liberty can value pluralism be contained, he failed to demonstrate how liberal and illiberal cultural beliefs could coexist harmoniously within the same society. An alternative basis for pluralist multiculturalism has been advanced by Bhikhu Parekh (2006). In Parekh's view, cultural diversity is, at heart, a reflection of the dialectic, or interplay, between human nature and culture. Although human beings are natural creatures, who possess a common species-derived physical and mental structure, they are also culturally constituted in the sense that their attitudes, behaviour and ways of life are shaped by the groups to which they belong. A recognition of the complexity of human nature, and the fact that any culture can express only part of what it means to be truly human, provides, Parekh argued, a viable basis for the

Civic nationalism: A form of nationalism that is based on common citizenship, rooted in support for a unifying set of political values, rather than a common culture.

Value pluralism: The theory that there is no single, overriding conception of the 'good life', but rather a number of competing and equally legitimate conceptions.

politics of recognition. Beyond pluralist multiculturalism, a form of 'particularist' multiculturalism can be identified. This places less emphasis on how a multiplicity of values and lifestyles can coexist within the same society, and more emphasis on the maintenance of cultural distinctiveness. The value of cultural distinctiveness is, not uncommonly, emphasized by a negative perception of western values and lifestyles, which are often seen to be implicitly or explicitly oppressive, tainted by their association with imperialism (see p. 132) and racialism (see p. 120).

Cosmopolitan multiculturalism endorses cultural diversity and identity politics, but views them more as transitional states in a larger reconstruction of political sensibilities and priorities. This form of multiculturalism celebrates diversity on the grounds of what each culture can learn from other cultures, and because of the prospects for personal self-development offered by a world of wider cultural opportunities and lifestyle choices. Culture is, in this view, fluid and responsive to changing political and social circumstances; it is not fixed and historically embedded, as pluralist and particularist multiculturalists would argue. This can lead to a kind of pick-and-mix multiculturalism, which portrays society as a 'melting pot', as opposed to a 'cultural mosaic' of separate ethnic or religious groups. From the individual's perspective, the exploration of different cultural options and ways of life is positively endorsed, if not encouraged. In some senses, this model stands clearly apart from pluralist and even, to some extent, liberal multiculturalism, in that it positively embraces the ideas of multiple identity and **hybridity**. Hybridity is embraced because people, regardless of their cultural origins, share the same planet and are confronted by very similar challenges and experiences. This form of multiculturalism is thus rooted in cosmopolitanism and **global consciousness**. It is the kind of multiculturalism that is usually supported by many in the anti-globalization movement.

Drawbacks of multiculturalism

Enthusiasm for multiculturalism is by no means universal, however. While some rejoice in the creation of multicultural societies, celebrating diversity and rejoicing in the end of political nationalism, others warn that they endanger freedom and threaten political instability, possibility threatening social breakdown and violence. The first set of criticisms derive from liberal individualism. Although some have attempted to reconcile liberalism with multiculturalism, individualists warn against the core assumption of multiculturalism, which is that that personal identity is embedded in group or social identity. Multiculturalism is, therefore (like nationalism and even racialism), just another form of collectivism, and like all forms of collectivism it subordinates the rights and needs of the individual to those of the social group, thereby endangering freedom and personal self-development. Amartya Sen (2006) developed a particularly sustained attack on the 'solitarist' theory on which he believes multiculturalism is based, which holds that human identity is formed by membership of a *single* social group. This leads not only to the 'miniaturization' of humanity, but also makes violence more likely, as people identify only with their own mono-group and fail to recognize the rights and integrity of members of other groups. According to Sen, such solitaristic thinking is also evident in ideas that emphasize the incompatibility of cultural traditions, such as the notion of the 'clash of civilizations' (Huntington, 1996). Even liberals sympathetic to multiculturalism condemn pluralist and especially particularist multiculturalism for endorsing as legitimate political ideas that are anti-democratic and oppressive.

Concept

Cosmopolitanism

Cosmopolitanism is literally a belief in a *cosmopolis*, or 'world state'. It thus implies the obliteration of national identities and the establishment of a common political allegiance uniting all human beings. However, the term is usually used to refer to the more modest goal of peace and harmony amongst nations, founded upon mutual understanding, toleration and, above all, interdependence. Thus the nineteenth-century 'Manchester liberals', Richard Cobden (1804–65) and John Bright (1811–89), endorsed cosmopolitanism in advocating free trade (see p. 157) on the grounds that it would promote international understanding and economic interdependence, ultimately making war impossible. The cosmopolitan ideal is also promoted by supranational bodies that aim to foster cooperation amongst nations rather than to replace the nation-state.

Hybridity: A condition of social and cultural mixing; the term has been derived from crossbreeding between genetically unalike plants or animals.

Global consciousness: An awareness of global interconnectedness, reflected (usually) in transnational moral responsibilities and universalist ethics.

The second range of concerns are usually advanced by conservative and nationalist thinkers, who argue that shared values and a common culture are the necessary preconditions for a stable and successful society. Multiculturalism, from this perspective, is inherently flawed: multicultural societies are inevitably fractured and conflict-ridden societies, in which suspicion, hostility and even violence come to be accepted facts of life. The basis for such a view is that human beings are limited and dependent creatures, who are naturally drawn to others similar to themselves, and therefore fear or distrust people who are in some way different. The multiculturalist image of 'unity in diversity' is thus a myth, a sham exposed by the simple facts of social psychology. In this view, immigration should be severely restricted and an emphasis should be placed on the assimilation of minority ethnic communities to strengthen national identity rather than on particularist identities. A further aspect of this critique is that multiculturalism often alienates majority or 'host' communities, whose culture is demeaned because they are linked to colonialism, and which lose out as a result of so-called 'special' rights and 'positive' discrimination.

However, the record of multicultural societies suggests that there is nothing natural or inevitable about inter-ethnic conflict or hostility. There is, rather, evidence of a potential for such conflict which gains expression in particular political, economic and social circumstances. The capacity of political factors to fuel ethnic hostility was dramatically demonstrated by the breakup of Yugoslavia in the 1990s. Serbs, Croats, Slovenes, Bosnians, Macedonians and others had lived alongside one another in conditions of relative peace and harmony since the Second World War. However, the collapse of communism was accompanied by an upsurge in ethnic assertiveness and nationalist rivalry, the most dramatic feature of which was the civil war in Bosnia (1992–95). This proved to be the most violent European war in the second half of the twentieth century and witnessed a brutal programme of 'ethnic cleansing' carried out by Bosnian Serbs against Muslims. Ethnic strife has also often been associated with economic and social pressures, such as growing unemployment and widening income differentials. Indeed, economically based tensions may be becoming more acute due to globalization. This has happened in two main ways. First, as Amy Chua (2003) argued, in many developing states the increased concentration of wealth in the hands of those in a position to exploit the benefits of global markets has often allowed small ethnic minorities to acquire hugely disproportional economic power. Examples of such 'market dominant' economic minorities include the Chinese in much of Southeast Asia, the Indians in East Africa and, though in a less extreme form, the Ipos in West Africa. In such circumstances, widening economic divisions have provoked growing hostility and racial prejudice. Second, economic and ethnic tensions have tended to overlap in developed states where ethnic minorities usually occupy a subservient rather than a dominant role in the economy, often being confined to marginal, low-status and low-income occupations. Such circumstances, usually linked to discrimination and other forms of structural disadvantage, have led to civil unrest and even rioting amongst ethnic minority youths, as, for example, in the UK in 1981, in Los Angeles in 1992, in Queensland, Australia, in 2004, and across much of France in 2005.

A final range of criticisms have been advanced by progressive theorists, who argue that multiculturalism fails adequately to address the interests of disadvantaged groups or sections of society. Concerns, for instance, have been raised about the extent to which multiculturalism encourages groups to seek advancement through cultural or ethnic assertiveness, rather than through the struggle for social justice. In that sense, the flaw of multiculturalism is its failure to address issues of class disadvantage: the real issue confronting minority groups is not their lack of cultural recognition, but their lack of economic power and social status. As Brian Barry (2002) argued, by virtue of its emphasis on cultural distinctiveness, multiculturalism serves to divide, and therefore to weaken, people who have a common economic interest in alleviating poverty and promoting social reform. Another feature of this is the possibility of declining support for welfare systems designed to alleviate poverty, as social responsibility across society is undermined as citizens become more aware of what divides them than of what unites them. Finally, multiculturalism has been criticized because it helps to preserve and legitimize patriarchal and traditional beliefs that systematically disadvantage certain groups within minority ethnic communities themselves. In particular, it is difficult to reconcile the interests of women, and gays and lesbians, with many forms of multiculturalism.

Legitimacy and political stability

The issue of legitimacy, the rightfulness of a regime or system of rule, is linked to the oldest and one of the most fundamental of political debates, the problem of political obligation. Why should citizens feel obliged to acknowledge the authority of government? Do they have a duty to respect the state and obey its laws? In modern political debate, however, legitimacy is usually understood less in terms of moral obligations and more in terms of political behaviour and beliefs. In other words, it addresses not the question of why people *should* obey the state, in an abstract sense, but the question of why they *do* obey a particular state or system of rule. What are the conditions or processes that encourage them to see authority as rightful, and therefore underpin the stability of a regime? This reflects a shift from philosophy to sociology, but it also highlights the contested nature of the concept of legitimacy.

Legitimizing power

The classic contribution to the understanding of legitimacy as a sociological phenomenon was provided by Max Weber. Weber was concerned to categorize particular 'systems of domination', and to identify in each case the basis on which

---

Concept

Legitimacy

The term legitimacy (from the Latin *legitimare*, meaning 'to declare lawful') broadly means rightfulness. Legitimacy therefore confers on an order or command an authoritative or binding character, thus transforming power into authority (see p. 5). It differs from legality in that the latter does not necessarily guarantee that a government is respected or that its citizens acknowledge a duty of obedience. Political philosophers treat legitimacy as a moral or rational principle, the grounds on which governments may demand obedience from citizens. The *claim* to legitimacy is thus more important than the *fact* of obedience. Political scientists, however, usually see legitimacy in sociological terms: that is, as a willingness to comply with a system of rule regardless of how this is achieved. Following Weber, this view takes legitimacy to mean a *belief* in legitimacy – that is, a belief in the 'right to rule'.

Max Weber (1864–1920)

German political economist and sociologist. Following a breakdown in 1898, Weber withdrew from academic teaching, but he continued to write and research until the end of his life. He was one of the founders of modern sociology, and he championed a scientific and value-free approach to scholarship. He also highlighted the importance to social action of meaning and consciousness. Weber's interests ranged from social stratification, law, power and organization to religion. His most influential works include *The Protestant Ethic and the Spirit of Capitalism* (1902), *The Sociology of Religion* (1920) and *Economy and Society* (1922).

legitimacy was established. He did this by constructing three ideal types (see p. 18) or conceptual models, which he hoped would help to make sense of the highly complex nature of political rule. These ideal types amount to three kinds of authority:

- traditional authority
- charismatic authority
- legal–rational authority.

Each of these is characterized by a particular source of political legitimacy and thus different reasons that people may have for obeying a regime. In the process, Weber sought to understand the transformation of society itself, contrasting the systems of domination found in relatively simple traditional societies with those typically found in industrial and highly bureaucratic ones.

Weber's first type of political legitimacy is based on long-established customs and traditions. In effect, *traditional* authority is regarded as legitimate because it has 'always existed': it has been sanctified by history because earlier generations had accepted it. Typically, it operates according to a body of concrete rules: that is, fixed and unquestioned customs that do not need to be justified because they reflect the way things have always been. The most obvious examples of traditional authority are found amongst tribes or small groups in the form of patriarchalism (the domination of the father within the family or the 'master' over his servants) and gerontocracy (the rule of the aged, normally reflected in the authority of village 'elders'). Traditional authority is closely linked to hereditary systems of power and privilege, as reflected, for example, in the survival of dynastic rule in Saudi Arabia, Kuwait and Morocco. Although it is of marginal significance in advanced industrial societies, the survival of monarchy (see p. 366), albeit in a constitutional form, in the UK, Belgium, the Netherlands and Spain, for example, helps to shape political culture by keeping alive values such as deference, respect and duty.

Weber's second form of legitimate domination is *charismatic* authority. This form of authority is based on the power of an individual's personality: that is, on his or her 'charisma'. Owing nothing to a person's status, social position or office, charismatic authority operates entirely through the capacity of a leader to make a direct and personal appeal to followers as a kind of hero or saint. Although modern political

Concept

Tradition

The term tradition encompasses anything handed down or transmitted from the past to the present (long-standing customs and practices, institutions, social or political systems, values and beliefs, and so on). Strictly speaking, tradition differs from reaction in that it denotes continuity with the past, rather than an attempt to 'turn the clock back' and re-establish the past. This continuity is usually understood to link the generations, although the line between the traditional and the merely fashionable is often indistinct. The term tradition has also been used to contrast 'traditional' societies and 'modern' societies, the former generally being seen to be structured on the basis of status (see p. 197) and by supposedly organic hierarchies, and the latter on the basis of contractual agreement and by democratic processes.

leaders such as de Gaulle, Kennedy and Thatcher undoubtedly extended their authority through their personal qualities and capacity to inspire loyalty, this did not amount to charismatic legitimacy, because their authority was essentially based on the formal powers of the offices they held. Napoleon, Mussolini, Hitler, Ayatollah Khomeini, Fidel Castro and Colonel Gaddafi are more appropriate examples.

However, charismatic authority is not simply a gift or a natural propensity; systems of personal rule are invariably underpinned by 'cults of personality' (see p. 372), the undoubted purpose of which is to 'manufacture' charisma. Nevertheless, when legitimacy is constructed largely or entirely through the power of a leader's personality, there are usually two consequences. The first is that, as charismatic authority is not based on formal rules or procedures, it often has no limits. The leader is a Messiah, who is infallible and unquestionable; the masses become followers or disciples, who are required only to submit and obey. Second, so closely is authority linked to a specific individual, that it is difficult for a system of personal rule to outlive its founding figure. This certainly applied in the case of the regimes of Napoleon, Mussolini and Hitler.

Weber's third type of political legitimacy, *legal–rational* authority, links authority to a clearly and legally defined set of rules. In Weber's view, legal–rational authority is the typical form of authority operating in most modern states. The power of a president, prime minister or government official is determined in the final analysis by formal, constitutional rules, which constrain or limit what an office holder is able to do. The advantage of this form of authority over both traditional and charismatic authority is that, as it is attached to an office rather than a person, it is far less likely to be abused or to give rise to injustice. Legal–rational authority therefore maintains

Concept

Charisma

Charisma was originally a theological term meaning the 'gift of grace'. This was the source of the power that Jesus exerted over his disciples, and the power attributed to saints in Catholic theology. As a sociopolitical phenomenon, however, charisma refers to charm or personal power: the capacity to establish leadership (see p. 372) through psychological control over others. Charismatic authority therefore has a near-mystical character and includes the ability to inspire loyalty, emotional dependence and even devotion. Although it is usually seen as a 'natural' capacity, all political leaders cultivate their charismatic qualities through propaganda, practised oratory, presentational skills and so on. Weber distinguished between *individual* charisma (linked to a person) and the charisma of *office* (linked to a position).

limited government and, in addition, promotes efficiency through a rational division of labour. However, Weber also recognised a darker side to this type of political legitimacy. The price of greater efficiency would, he feared, be a more depersonalized and inhuman social environment typified by the relentless spread of bureaucratic (see p. 383) forms of organization.

Although Weber's classification of types of legitimacy is still seen as relevant, it also has its limitations. One of these is that, in focusing on the legitimacy of a political regime or system of rule, it tells us little about the circumstances in which political authority is challenged as a result of unpopular policies or a discredited leader or government. More significantly, as Beetham (1991) pointed out, to see legitimacy, as Weber did, as nothing more than a 'belief in legitimacy' is to ignore how it is brought about. This may leave the determination of legitimacy largely in the hands of the powerful, who may be able to 'manufacture' rightfulness through public-relations campaigns and the like.

Beetham suggested that power can only be said to be legitimate if three conditions are fulfilled. First, power must be exercised according to established rules, whether these are embodied in formal legal codes or in informal conventions. Second, these rules must be justified in terms of the shared beliefs of the government and the governed. Third, legitimacy must be demonstrated by an expression of consent on the part of the governed. This highlights two key features of the legitimation process. The first is the existence of elections and party competition, a system through which popular consent can be exercised (which is discussed in Chapters 12 and 13). The second is the existence of constitutional rules that broadly reflect how people feel they should be governed (which are examined in Chapter 15).

Legitimation crises

An alternative to the Weberian approach to legitimacy has been developed by neo-Marxist (see p. 96) theorists. While orthodox Marxists were inclined to dismiss legitimacy as bogus, seeing it as nothing more than a bourgeois myth, modern Marxists, following Gramsci, have acknowledged that capitalism is in part upheld by its ability to secure political support. Neo-Marxists such as Jürgen Habermas (see p. 223) and Claus Offe (1984) have therefore focused attention not merely on the class system but also on the machinery through which legitimacy is maintained (the democratic process, party competition, welfare and social reform, and so on). Nevertheless, they have also highlighted what they see as the inherent difficulty of legitimizing a political system that is based on unequal class power. In *Legitimation Crisis* (1973) Habermas identified a series of 'crisis tendencies' within capitalist societies that make it difficult for them to maintain political stability through consent alone. At the heart of this tension, he argued, lie contradictions and conflicts between the logic of capitalist accumulation on the one hand, and the popular pressures that democratic politics unleashes on the other.

From this perspective, capitalist economies are seen to be bent on remorseless expansion, dictated by the pursuit of profit. However, the extension of political and social rights in an attempt to build legitimacy within such systems has stimulated countervailing pressures. In particular, the democratic process has led to escalating demands for social welfare as well as for increased popular participation and social equality. The resulting expansion of the state's responsibilities into economic and social life, and the inexorable rise of taxation and public spending, nevertheless con-

Jürgen Habermas (born 1929)

German philosopher and social theorist. After growing up during the Nazi period, Habermas was politicized by the Nuremburg trials and the growing awareness after the war of the concentration and death camps. Drawn to study with Adorno (1903–69) and Horkheimer (1895–1973), he became the leading exponent of the 'second generation' of the Frankfurt School of critical theory. Habermas's work ranges over epistemology, the dynamics of advanced capitalism, the nature of rationality, and the relationship between social science and philosophy. During the 1970s he moved further away from orthodox Marxism, developing critical theory into what became a theory of 'communicative action'. His main works include *Theory and Practice* (1974), *Towards a Rational Society* (1970), and *The Theory of Communicative Competence* (1984, 1988).

strain capitalist accumulation by restricting profit levels and discouraging enterprise. In Habermas's view, capitalist democracies cannot permanently satisfy both popular demands for social security and welfare rights and the requirements of a market economy based on private profit. Forced either to resist popular pressures or to risk economic collapse, such societies would find it increasingly difficult, and eventually impossible, to maintain legitimacy.

A very similar problem was identified in the 1970s in the form of what was called government 'overload'. Writers such as Anthony King (1975) and Richard Rose (1980) argued that governments were finding it increasingly difficult to govern because they were subject to over-demand. This had come about both because politicians and political parties were encouraged to outbid one another in the attempt to get into power, and because pressure groups were able to besiege government with unrelenting and incompatible demands. Government's capacity to deliver was further undermined by a general drift towards corporatism (see p. 299) that created growing interdependence between government agencies and organized groups. However, whereas neo-Marxists believed that the 'crisis tendencies' identified in the 1970s were beyond the capacity of capitalist democracies to control, overload theorists tended to call for a significant shift of political and ideological priorities in the form of the abandonment of a 'big' government approach.

In many ways, the politics of the 1980s and 1990s can be seen as a response to this legitimation or overload crisis. The call for a change in priorities came most loudly from the New Right. Theorists such as Samuel Brittan (1977) highlighted the **fiscal crisis of the welfare state** and spoke about the 'economic contradictions of democracy'. In the 1990s, governments such as Reagan's in the USA and Thatcher's in the UK sought to lower popular expectations of government. They did this by trying to shift responsibilities from the state to the individual. Welfare, for instance, was portrayed as largely a matter of individual responsibility, individuals being encouraged to provide for themselves by hard work, savings, private pensions, medical insurance and so on. Unemployment was no longer seen by the government as the responsibility of government; there was a 'natural rate' of unemployment that could only be pushed up by greedy workers 'pricing themselves out of jobs'.

More radically, the New Right attempted to challenge and eventually displace the theories and values that had previously legitimized the progressive expansion of the state's responsibilities. In this sense, the New Right amounted to a 'hegemonic pro-

Fiscal crisis of the welfare state: The crisis in state finances that occurs when expanding social expenditure coincides with recession and declining tax revenues.

ject' that tried to establish a rival set of pro-individual and pro-market values and theories. This constituted a public philosophy that extolled rugged individualism, and denigrated the 'nanny state'. The success of this project is demonstrated by the fact that socialist parties in states as different as the UK, France, Spain, Australia and New Zealand have accommodated themselves to broadly similar goals and values. As this has happened, a political culture that once emphasized social justice, welfare rights and public responsibilities has given way to one in which choice, enterprise, competition and individual responsibility have become more prominent.

Why do revolutions occur?

If legitimacy helps to ensure political stability and the survival of a regime, when legitimacy collapses the result is likely to be either a resort to repression (see p. 411), or far-reaching political change. Change is one of the most important features of political life. Many of those engaged in politics would certainly agree with Marx's assertion in *Theses on Feuerbach* ([1845] 1968) that 'The philosophers have only *interpreted* the world, in various ways; the point, however, is to *change* it'. However, attitudes to change amongst political thinkers have differed enormously. While conservatives have usually evinced a 'desire to conserve' and resisted change in the name of continuity and tradition, liberals and socialists have typically welcomed change as a manifestation of progress. Deeply embodied in the belief in progress is a faith in human reason and the capacity of people to move history forwards and create a better society through the accumulation of wisdom and knowledge.

Whether change marks progress or decay, growth or decline, it is the product of one of two processes: evolution or revolution. Evolutionary change is usually thought of as reform, gradual and incremental improvements *within* a social or political system. Reform therefore represents change within continuity, the reorganization or restructuring of, for instance, an institution, rather than its abolition or replacement. Revolution, on the other hand, is root-and-branch change. Revolutions recast the political order entirely, typically bringing about an abrupt and often violent break with the past. There has been considerable debate both about the nature of revolution and about the historical, social and political circumstances in which revolutions are most likely to occur.

Marxist theories of revolution

Marxists have used the term 'revolution' in a very specific way. Although they recognize that revolutions are crucial political events that involve the replacement of a government or the establishment of an entirely new regime, they interpret these changes as a reflection of a deeper social transformation. From this point of view, the essence of revolution is a fundamental *social* change: that is, the destruction of one economic system or 'mode of production' and its replacement by another. A Marxist may therefore reject the idea that the American Revolution (1776) brought about revolutionary change, because, although it brought independence to the former British colonies and led to the creation of a constitutional republic, it left the system of ownership and the social structure intact. Most Marxists nevertheless interpret the English, American and French Revolutions as 'bourgeois' revolutions, in that they marked a more gradual transition from a feudal mode of production to a capitalist one. Revolutions, from this perspective, are not simply abrupt and dramatic periods of political upheaval, but longer and more profound periods of social transformation. There is a sense, for example, in which the Russian Revolution started in 1917, but continued until the collapse of the USSR in 1991, its goal of 'building communism' still not having been completed.

In Marxist theory, revolution emerges out of contradictions that exist at a socio-economic level. Revolution reflects, at heart, the conflict between the oppressor and the oppressed, the exploiter and the exploited. All class societies are thus doomed. Marx believed that revolution would mark the point at which the class struggle would develop into open conflict, leading one class to overthrow and displace another. Just as the French Revolution was interpreted as a 'bourgeois' revolution, the Russian Revolution was later seen as a 'proletarian' revolution that set in motion a process that would culminate in the establishment of socialism and eventually full communism. In Marx's view, the epoch of social revolution began when the class system, the 'relations of production', became a 'fetter' upon the further development of productive techniques and innovation, the so-called 'forces of production'. He believed that this would heighten class antagonism, bringing the exploited class (in capitalism, the proletariat) to 'class consciousness'. As the proletariat achieved class consciousness, it would become a revolutionary force and would rise spontaneously in revolt.

For Marx, revolutionary change was part of an inevitable process that would drive history through a series of epochs to the eventual achievement of a classless society, a society in which there are no internal contradictions. However, revolutions have not come about as Marx forecast. Revolution has not occurred, as he predicted it would, in the advanced capitalist countries of western and central Europe. Instead of the class system becoming a fetter constraining the further development of productive forces, capitalism has exhibited a seemingly endless appetite for technological innovation, generating continual, if at times erratic, improvements in living standards. The proletariat has, in consequence, been rendered politically passive. Where Marxist revolutions have occurred in the twentieth century they have conformed to a very different pattern.

The 1917 Bolshevik Russian Revolution, led by Lenin (see p. 81), advanced the Marxist theory of revolution in two important senses. First, while classical Marxists portrayed revolution as an inevitable breakdown of class society that would occur when objective conditions were ripe, Lenin grasped the point that revolutions have to be *made*. The Bolsheviks seized power in October 1917 even though the supposed 'bourgeois' revolution had occurred only in February 1917, and the proletariat was still small and politically unsophisticated. Second, Lenin recognized the need for political leadership in the form of a 'vanguard party', a role that was taken by the Bolsheviks (later renamed the Communist Party). In a strict sense, therefore, the Russian Revolution was more a *coup d'état* than a popular revolution. In October 1917, unlike in the February Revolution that led to the fall of the Tsar, power was seized not by the masses but by a tightly knit band of revolutionaries acting in their name. Many have therefore argued that the communist regimes set up in the twentieth century under the banner of Marxism–Leninism were perversions of the Marxist revolutionary ideal.

A further important shift in Marxist theory was the displacement of the proletariat by the peasantry as the 'revolutionary class'. Lenin had hinted at this in 1917 in talking about an alliance between the urban proletariat and the peasantry, but it was more clearly established by the Chinese Revolution (1949) under the leadership of Mao Zedong. In a pattern later adopted by Marxists in Latin America, Africa and elsewhere in Asia, the Chinese Revolution was a peasant revolution carried out in the

Concept

Class consciousness

Class consciousness is a subjective awareness of a class's objective situation and interests. It thus highlights the crucial Marxist distinction between a 'class *in*-itself' and a 'class *for*-itself'. The latter supposedly exemplifies the solidarity of a class actively engaged in pursuing its common (and genuine) interests. Class consciousness is therefore the opposite of 'false consciousness', deluded understanding that conceals the fact of exploitation from subordinate classes, thus breeding political passivity. Marx believed that class consciousness would develop inevitably as a result of intensifying class conflict; Lenin argued that the proletariat needed to be brought to class consciousness through the leadership and guidance of a 'vanguard' or revolutionary party.

Mao Zedong (Mao Tse-tung) (1893–1976)

Chinese Marxist theorist and leader of the People's Republic of China, 1949–76. Mao was the son of a peasant farmer in Hunan. He initially worked as a librarian and teacher. In 1921 he helped to found the Chinese Communist Party, and in 1935 became its leader. As a political theorist, Mao adapted Marxism–Leninism to the needs of an overwhelmingly agricultural and still traditional society. His legacy is often associated with the Cultural Revolution (1966–70), a radical egalitarian movement that denounced elitism and 'capitalist roaders', and resulted in widespread social disruption, repression and death. Maoism is usually understood as an anti-bureaucratic form of Marxism that places its faith in the radical zeal of the masses.

countryside rather than in large urban areas. Rather than serving as a philosophy of social revolution, Marxism–Leninism tended in practice to be employed more as an ideology of modernization and industrialization that was particularly attractive to developing countries.

Non-Marxist theories of revolution

A variety of non-Marxist theories of revolution have been advanced. These each agree with the Marxist view in highlighting the importance of social conflict, but they disagree with Marxism in two crucial respects. First, they are not prepared to interpret political events as merely a reflection of deeper economic or social developments. Revolution is understood more as a transformation of the *political* system than as a transformation of the *social* system. Second, revolution is seen not as an inevitable process (that is, as the working-out of the logic of history), but rather as a consequence of a particular set of political and social circumstances. However, there is considerable debate about what circumstances and which set of sociopolitical factors help to bring revolutions about.

One of the most influential theories of revolution has been developed on the basis of the **systems theory** approach to politics. This approach implies that a political system will tend towards long-term stability as the 'outputs' of government are brought into line with the 'inputs' or pressures placed upon it. In this light, revolutions can be understood as a form of 'disequilibrium' in the political system that is brought about by economic, social, cultural or international changes to which the system itself is incapable of responding. For example, in *Revolutionary Change* (1966) Chalmers Johnson argued that revolutions occur in conditions of 'multiple disfunction', when the political system breaks down under the pressure of competing demands for change. The autocratic Tsarist regime in Russia, for example, proved to be incapable of responding to the mixture of pressures created by early industrialization and the dislocation and demoralization caused by the First World War. Similarly, it can be argued that, in the late twentieth century, orthodox communist regimes in the USSR and eastern Europe were unable to deal with the strains generated by the growth of an urbanized, better educated and more politically sophisticated population. However, systems analysis tends to ignore the important subjective or psychological factors that help to precipitate revolution.

A second theory of revolution has been developed out of the lessons of social psychology, but was perhaps first used by Alexis de Tocqueville in an attempt

Systems theory: The theory that treats the political system as a self-regulating mechanism responding to 'inputs' (demands and support) by issuing authoritative decisions or 'outputs' (policies).

Alexis de Tocqueville (1805–59)

French politician, political theorist and historian. Following the July Revolution of 1830 in France, Tocqueville visited the USA, ostensibly to study its penal system. This resulted in his epic *Democracy in America* (1835–40), which developed an ambivalent critique of US democracy with its equality of opportunity but warned against the 'tyranny of the majority'. His political career was ended by Louis Napoleon's coup in 1849, leaving him free to devote his time to historical work such as *The Old Regime and the French Revolution* ([1856] 1947). A friend and correspondent of J. S. Mill, de Tocqueville's writings reflect a highly ambiguous attitude to the advance of political democracy. His ideas have influenced both liberal and conservative theorists, as well as academic sociologists.

to explain the outbreak of the 1789 French Revolution. These ideas have been developed into a model of a 'revolution of rising expectations'. In *The Old Regime and the French Revolution* ([1856] 1947), de Tocqueville pointed out that revolution rarely results from absolute poverty and gross deprivation, conditions that are more commonly associated with despair, resignation and political inertia. Rather, revolutions tend to break out when a government relaxes its grip after a long period of oppressive rule. As de Tocqueville put it, 'the most perilous moment for a bad government is when it seeks to mend its ways' (p. 227). This occurred, for instance, in France when Louis XVI summoned the Estates General in 1788, and, arguably, also occurred throughout eastern Europe as a result of the Gorbachev reforms in the late 1980s. Instead of satisfying the demand for political change, reform can heighten popular expectations and generate revolutionary fervour.

The classic statement of this theory of revolution is found in Ted Gurr's *Why Men Rebel* (1970). In Gurr's view, rebellion is the result of 'relative deprivation', brought about by the gap between what people expect to receive (their 'value expectations') and what they actually get (their 'value capability'). The greatest likelihood of revolution therefore occurs when a period of economic and social development that has produced rising expectations is abruptly reversed. This creates a gap between expectations and capabilities that can lead to revolution. In *When Men Revolt and Why* (1971), James Davies explained this in terms of the J-curve theory of revolutions. The shape of the letter 'J' represents a period of rising expectations that is suddenly brought to a halt. The notion of relative deprivation is significant, because it draws attention to the fact that people's perception of their position is more important than their objective circumstances. What is crucial is how people evaluate their condition relative either to the recent past, or to what other people have. For example, popular discontent and instability in eastern Europe in the late 1980s was undoubtedly fuelled, in part, by the perceived affluence and political liberty enjoyed by populations in the capitalist West.

A third theory of revolution focuses not on pressures operating within the political system but on the strengths and weaknesses of the state itself. There is a sense in which a state can withstand any amount of internal pressure as long as it possesses the coercive power to maintain control and the political will to employ it. In this sense the consequence of a loss of legitimacy is either revolution or repression. Certainly, regimes such as Hitler's Germany, Stalin's USSR and Saddam Hussein's Iraq each survived as long as they did through their ability to crush internal opposition by the use of terror and repression. In such regimes political change is more likely to result from a rebellion within the political or military elite than from a popular revolution.

In a comparative analysis of the French Revolution, Russian Revolution and Chinese Revolution, Theda Skocpol (1979) advanced a social-structural explanation of revolutions, which highlights the international weakness and domestic ineffectiveness of regimes that succumb to breakdown. War and invasion, for instance, have often been decisive in precipitating revolutionary situations: this occurred in China in 1911 and 1949, and in Russia in 1905 and 1917. In domestic politics, states become vulnerable to revolution when they are no longer able to count upon the loyalty of their armed forces, or no longer possess the resolve and determination to exercise widespread repression. This is demonstrated by the comparison between the brutal but successful suppression of the Chinese student rebellion in Tiananmen Square in June 1989 and the swift and largely bloodless collapse of communist regimes in eastern Europe in the autumn and winter of the same year. A decisive factor in the latter case was the unwillingness of the USSR under Gorbachev either to sanction repression or to step in and suppress nascent revolutions, as it had earlier done in East Germany (1949), Hungary (1956) and Czechoslovakia (1968).

▊ Summary

◆ A political culture is a people's psychological orientation in relation to political objects such as parties, government and the constitution, expressed in their political attitudes, beliefs, symbols and values. Political culture differs from public opinion in that it is fashioned out of long-term values rather than reactions to specific policies, problems or personalities.

◆ Individuals and groups acquire their political attitudes and values through a process of political socialization. This may be seen either as a process of indoctrination that takes place throughout a person's life, or as the transmission of values from one generation to the next, largely accomplished during childhood. The major agents of socialization are the family, education, religion, the mass media and government.

◆ Considerable debate has surrounded the idea of civic culture. It has been used to identify psychological orientations, such as participation and respect for government, that help to sustain stable democratic rule. A civic culture may, however, be a consequence rather than a cause of democracy. It may overstate the value of deference, and underestimate the extent of cultural heterogeneity. Radicals and Marxists claim that a 'dominant' culture is imposed from above in the interests of privileged groups.

◆ Modern societies are sometimes believed to be suffering from a decline in social capital, reflected in lower levels of civic engagement. This has been understood as a consequence of social and cultural change, as a result of rising individualism, or as a reflection of growing inequality.

◆ Legitimacy maintains political stability because it establishes a regime's right to rule, and so underpins the regime's authority over its people. Legitimacy may be based on traditional, charismatic or legal–rational authority. Legal–rational authority is the most common basis of legitimacy in modern societies, being linked to the establishment of rule-governed behaviour through constitutionalism and electoral democracy.

◆ Structural imbalances in modern society may make it increasingly difficult to maintain legitimacy. Legitimation crises may arise from the conflict between the pressure for social and economic interventionism generated by democracy on the one hand, and the market economy's need for incentives, enterprise and price stability on the other.

◆ Revolutions are popular uprisings that consist of extra-legal mass action aimed at changing the political system. Revolutions have been explained in a variety of ways. They have been portrayed as a symptom of a supposedly deeper social transformation, as a sign of disequilibrium in the political system, as a consequence of the thwarting of rising expectations, and as a result of the declining effectiveness of the state.

Questions for discussion

▶ Is a civic culture a cause or a consequence of effective democratic rule?

▶ Has civic engagement declined or has it merely assumed new forms?

▶ Can multiculturalism be reconciled with any form of nationalism?

▶ Do societies need to be protected against cultural diversity, or should diversity be celebrated?

▶ What conditions are required for the maintenance of legitimacy in modern societies?

▶ Are capitalist systems inevitably prone to legitimation crises?

▶ Are revolutions best thought of as social phenomena or as political phenomena?

Further reading

Almond, G. A. and S. Verba (eds), *The Civic Culture Revisited* (Boston, MA: Little, Brown, 1989). An updated version of the author's classic 1963 analysis of the conditions required for democratic stability.

Bauman, Z., *Identity* (Cambridge: Polity, 2004). A thought-provoking exploration of the notion of identity in conditions of 'liquid modernity'.

Cohen, A., *Theories of Revolution: An Introduction* (London: Nelson, 1975). A clear and accessible analysis of various approaches to the understanding of revolution.

Halpern, D., *Social Capital* (Cambridge: Polity, 2005) An accessible and authoritative introduction to the increasing literature on social capital.

Parekh, B., *Rethinking Multiculturalism: Cultural Diversity and Political Theory*, 2nd edn (Basingstoke and New York: Palgrave Macmillan, 2006). A comprehensive defence of the pluralist perspective on cultural diversity that discusses practical problems of multicultural societies.

Putnam, R., *Bowling Alone: The Collapse and Revival of American Community* (New York: Simon & Schuster, 2000). A highly influential analysis of the decline of civil engagement and social participation in the USA.

Mass Media and Political Communication

> 'Mankind, in general, judge more by their eyes than their hands; for all can see the appearance, but few can touch the reality.'
>
> NICCOLÒ MACHIAVELLI, *The Prince* (1531)

Communication lies at the heart of politics. Rulers, even in authoritarian states, must communicate with their people in order to build up at least a semblance of legitimacy. In democratic states, sophisticated and complex processes of communication operate through activities such as campaigning, polling, focus-group consultation and the general politics of persuasion. Indeed, democracy itself may be seen as a form of political communication, in that it involves the ongoing negotiation of popular consent between government and the people. However, political communication is rarely unmediated. Our knowledge and understanding of politics very seldom comes from politicians directly, but, instead, comes from what we read in newspapers and magazines, see on television, hear on the radio, and, increasingly, find out about through the 'new' media, especially the internet. The mass media, though, constitute much more than a channel of communication. They are part of the political process, affecting, and not merely reflecting, the distribution of power in society at large.

The central issues examined in this chapter are as follows:

Key issues

▶ What theories have been developed about the relationship between politics and the mass media?

▶ Do the mass media strengthen democracy, or undermine it?

▶ How has the growing importance of the media affected the processes of governance?

▶ To what extent are the mass media responsible for promoting globalization?

▶ How, and how successfully, have governments used the mass media as a propaganda machine?

▶ Is the politics of 'spin' inevitable in a media age?

Concept

Mass media

The media comprise those societal institutions that are concerned with the production and distribution of all forms of knowledge, information and entertainment. The 'mass' character of the mass media is derived from the fact that the media channel communication towards a large and undifferentiated audience using relatively advanced technology. Grammatically and politically, the mass media are plural. Different messages may be put out by the 'broadcast' media (television and radio) and the 'print' media (newspapers and magazines). Similarly, tabloid and broadsheet newspapers may exhibit different sympathies. The advent of the so-called 'new' media (cable and satellite telecommunications, the Internet and so on) has, arguably, transformed the notion of mass media by dramatically increasing both media output and audience fragmentation.

Theories of the mass media

The mass media have been recognized as politically significant since the advent of mass literacy and the popular press in the late nineteenth century. However, it is widely accepted that, through a combination of social and technological changes, the media have become increasingly more powerful political actors and, in some respects, more deeply enmeshed in the political process. Three developments are particularly noteworthy. First, the impact of the so-called 'primary' agents of political socialization (see p. 233), such as the family and social class, has declined. Whereas once people acquired, in late childhood and adolescence in particular, a framework of political sympathies and leanings that adult experience tended to modify or deepen, but seldom radically transformed, this has been weakened in modern society by greater social and geographical mobility and by the spread of individualist and consumerist values. This, in turn, widens the scope for the media's political influence, as they are the principal mechanism through which information about issues and policies, and therefore political choices, are presented to the public.

Second, the development of a mass television audience from the 1950s onwards, and more recently the proliferation of channels and media output associated with the 'new' media, has massively increased the mass media's penetration of people's everyday lives. This means that the public now relies on the mass media more heavily than ever before: for instance, television is a much more important source of news and current-affairs information than political meetings; many more people watch televised sport than participate in it; and even shopping is increasingly being carried out through shopping channels and the internet. Particular interest has focused on the burgeoning political significance of the internet, with, by 2006, one billion people worldwide having access to it. Although the highest internet penetration is in North America (62 per cent), Oceania/Australia (51 per cent) and Europe (36 per cent), the highest usage growth is in Africa, the Middle East and Latin America.

Third, the media have become more powerful economic actors. Not only are major media corporations major global players, but also a series of mergers has tended to incorporate the formerly discrete domains of publishing, television, film, music, computers and telecommunications into a single massive 'infotainment' industry (Scammel, 2000). Media businesses such as Microsoft, AOL–Time Warner, Disney and News Corporation have accumulated so much economic and market power that no government can afford to ignore them.

Few commentators doubt the media's ability to shape political attitudes and values or, at least, to structure political and electoral choice by influencing public perceptions about the nature and importance of issues and problems, thereby. However, there is considerable debate about the political significance of this influence. A series of rival theories offer contrasting views of the media's political impact. The most important of these are the following:

- the pluralist model
- the dominant-ideology model
- the market model
- the elite-values model.

Pluralist model

Pluralism (see p. 82) highlights diversity and multiplicity generally. The pluralist model of the mass media portrays the media as an ideological marketplace in which a wide range of political views are debated and discussed. While not rejecting the idea that the media can affect political views and sympathies, this nevertheless suggests that their impact is essentially neutral, in that they tend to reflect the balance of forces within society at large.

The pluralist view nevertheless portrays the media in strongly positive terms. In ensuring an 'informed citizenry', the mass media both enhance the quality of democracy and guarantee that government power is checked. This 'watchdog' role was classically demonstrated in the 1974 *Washington Post* investigation into the Watergate scandal, which led to the resignation of Richard Nixon as US president. Some, moreover, argue that the advent of the 'new' media, and particularly the internet, has strengthened pluralism and political competition by giving protest groups, including 'anti-capitalist' activists, a relatively cheap and highly effective means of disseminating information and organizing campaigns. However, the pluralist model suffers from significant deficiencies. For example, weak and unorganized groups are excluded from access to mainstream publishing and broadcasting, meaning that the media's ideological marketplace tends to be relatively narrow and generally pro-establishment in character. In addition, private ownership and formal independence from government may not be sufficient to guarantee the media's oppositional character in the light of the increasingly symbiotic relationship between government and journalists and broadcasters.

Dominant-ideology model

The dominant-ideology model portrays the mass media as a politically conservative force that is aligned to the interests of economic and social elites, and serves to promote compliance or political passivity amongst the masses. In its Marxist version, associated with theorists such as Gramsci (see p. 208), it suggests that the media propagate bourgeois ideas and maintain capitalist hegemony, acting in the interests of major corporations and media moguls. Ownership, in other words, ultimately determines the political and other views that the mass media disseminate, and ownership is increasingly concentrated in the hands of a small number of global media corporations. The six largest media corporations are AOL-Time Warner, News Corporation, Viacom, Disney, Vivendi Universal and Bertelsmann AG. From this perspective, the media play an important role in promoting globalization (see p. 143), in that their tendency to spread ideas, images and values that are compatible with western consumerism (see p. 241) helps to open up new markets and extend business penetration worldwide.

One of the most influential and sophisticated versions of the dominant-ideology model was developed by Noam Chomsky (see p. 234) and Ed Herman in *Manufacturing Consent* (1994), in the form of the 'propaganda model'. They identified five 'filters' through which news and political coverage are distorted by the structures of the media itself. These filters are as follows:

- the business interests of owner companies
- a sensitivity to the views and concerns of advertisers and sponsors

Concept

Political socialization

Political socialization is the process through which individuals acquire political beliefs and values, and by which these are transmitted from one generation to the next. Families and schools are usually viewed as 'primary' agents of political socialization, while the workplace, peer groups and the mass media are viewed as 'secondary' agents of political socialization. Interest in political socialization peaked during the so-called behavioural revolution, as external stimuli was seen to explain (and possibly determine) political attitudes or behaviour. Critics nevertheless argue that socialization is based on a simplistic model of human psychology and the learning process, ignoring, in particular, the role of the thinking subject.

Noam Chomsky (born 1928)

US linguistic theorist and radical intellectual. Chomsky was born in Philadelphia, the son of eastern European immigrant parents. He first achieved distinction as a scholar in the field of linguistic studies. His *Syntactic Structures* (1957) revolutionized the discipline with the theory of 'transformational grammar', which proposed that humans have an innate capacity to acquire language. Radicalized during the Vietnam War, Chomsky subsequently became the leading radical critic of US foreign policy, developing his views in an extensive range of works including *American Power and the New Mandarins* (1969), and *New Military Humanism* (1999) and *Hegemony and Survival* (2004). In works such as (with Edward Herman) *Manufacturing Consent* (1988) he developed a radical critique of the mass media and examined how popular support for imperialist aggression is mobilized.

- the sourcing of news and information from 'agents of power' such as governments and business-backed think-tanks
- 'flak' or pressure applied to journalists including threats of legal action
- an unquestioning belief in the benefits of market competition and consumer capitalism.

Chomsky's analysis emphasizes the degree to which the mass media can subvert democracy, helping, for example, to mobilize popular support in the USA for imperialist foreign policy goals. The dominant-ideology model is nevertheless also subject to criticism. Objections to it include that it underestimates the extent to which the press and broadcasters, particularly public service broadcasters, pay attention to progressive social, racial and development issues. Moreover, the assumption that media output shapes political attitudes is determinist and neglects the role played by people's own values in filtering, and possibly resisting, media messages.

Elite-values model

The elite-values model shifts attention away from the ownership of media corporations to the mechanism through which media output is controlled. This view suggests that editors, journalists and broadcasters enjoy significant professional independence, and that even the most interventionist of media moguls are able only to set a broad political agenda but not to control day-to-day editorial decision-making. The media's political bias therefore reflects the values of groups that are disproportionally represented amongst its senior professionals. However, there are a number of versions of this model, depending on the characteristics that are considered to be politically significant.

One version of the elite-valuies model holds that the anti-socialist and politically conservative views of most mainstream newspapers, magazines and television stations derive from the fact that their senior professionals are well paid and generally from middle-class backgrounds. A quite different version is sometimes advanced by conservatives, who believe that the media reflect the views of university-educated, liberal intellectuals, whose values and concerns are quite different from those of the mass of the population. In its feminist version, this model highlights the predominance of males amongst senior journalists and broadcasters, implying that this both explains the inadequate attention given to women's views and issues by the mass media and accounts for the confrontational style of interviewing and political discussion sometimes adopted by broadcasters and journalists. Although the elite-values model helps to explain why the range of political views expressed by the mass media is often more restricted than pluralists suggest, it also has its limitations. Chief amongst these is that it fails to take full enough account of the pressures that bear upon senior media professionals: these, for example, include the views and interests of owners and commercial considerations, notably 'ratings' figures.

Market model

The market model of the mass media differs from the other models in that it dispenses with the idea of media bias: it holds that newspapers and television reflect, rather than shape, the views of the general public. This occurs because, regardless of the personal views of media owners and senior professionals, private media outlets are first and foremost businesses concerned with profit maximization and thus with extending market share. The media therefore give people 'what they want', and cannot afford to alienate existing or potential viewers or readers by presenting political viewpoints with which they may disagree. Such considerations may be less pressing in relation to public service broadcasters, such as the BBC, which are more insulated from commercial and advertiser pressures, but even here the tyranny of 'ratings' is increasingly evident.

Nevertheless, although this model dispenses with the idea that at least the privately owned mass media should be seen as part of the political process, it helps to explain some significant trends in political life. One of these may be growing popular disenchantment with politics resulting from the trivialization of political coverage. Fearful of losing 'market share', television companies in particular have reduced their coverage of serious political debate, and thus abandoned their responsibility for educating and informing citizens, in favour of 'infotainment'.

◼ Media, democracy and governance

Custodians of democracy?

The impact that the mass media have on democracy is one of the most widely debated aspects of the relationship between the media and politics. For many, the existence of a **free press** is one of the key features of democratic governance. However, how do the mass media act as custodians of democracy? And why have some questioned the mass media's democratic credentials, even arguing that they may undermine it? The mass media can be said to promote democracy in four key ways:

- by fostering public debate and political engagement
- by acting as a 'public watchdog' to check abuses of power
- by redistributing power and political influence
- by providing a mechanism through which democracy can operate.

Free press: Newspapers (and, by extension, other media outlets) that are free from censorship and political interference by government and, usually, are privately owned.

The capacity to provide a civic forum in which meaningful and serious political debate can take place is often viewed as the key democratic role of the mass media. The virtue of this is that better-informed citizens with more independent and considered views will be more politically engaged. The mass media are therefore agents of political education. Indeed, the mass media may have largely replaced formal representative institutions, such as assemblies, parliaments and local councils, as arenas for the dialogue, debate and deliberation that are the very stuff of democratic politics. This has happened because the mass media are, arguably, better suited to this role than are traditional representative bodies. In addition to offering the public perhaps its only meaningful opportunity to watch politicians in action (through, for example, interviews with politicians and televised assembly debates), the mass media provide a forum for the expression of a much wider range of viewpoints and opinions than is possible within representative institutions composed only of elected politicians. Thus, academics and scientists, business leaders and trade union bosses, and representatives of interest groups and lobbyists of all kinds are able to express views and engage in public debate through the mechanism of mass media. This, moreover, extends to the public itself, which is able to express its views through, for instance, radio phone-in programmes, 'vox pop' television shows, 'chat rooms', and internet blogs and so on. Not only do the mass media substantially widen the range of views and opinions expressed in political debate, but they also present debate and discussion in a way that is lively and engaging for the general public, devoid of the formality, even stuffiness, that characterizes the exchanges that take place in assemblies and council chambers around the world.

The 'watchdog' role of the mass media is, in a sense, a subset of the political debate argument. The role of the media, from this perspective, is to ensure that public accountability takes place, by scrutinizing the activities of government and exposing abuses of power. Once again, in carrying out this role the mass media is supplementing and, to some extent, replacing the work of formal representative institutions. Media professionals such as journalists and television presenters are particularly suited to this role because they are 'outside' politics and have no interest other than to expose incompetence, corruption or simply muddled thinking whenever and wherever it can be found. By contrast, if public accountability is left solely in the hands of professional politicians it may be constrained by the fact that those who attempt to expose ineptitude or wrongdoing wish themselves, at some stage, to hold government power. This may not only taint their motives, but it may also discourage them from criticizing processes and practices that they may wish to take advantage of in the future. However, the media can only perform this role effectively if they are properly independent, and not dominated by government. Democratic governance therefore requires either that the publicly financed media are accountable to an independent commission, or that there is an appropriate level of competition from 'free' or privately financed media.

Third, the mass media promotes democracy by widening the distribution of power and political influence in society. This is largely accomplished through the 'new' media's capacity to significantly enlarge access to information and opportunities for information exchange. Earlier advances in communications technology, notably the invention of printing in the fifteenth century and the spread of television, early-generation computers and satellites in the post-1945 period (sometimes dubbed the 'first' and the 'second' communication revolutions), tended to strengthen government more than they did the general public. Communications technology both ensured that governments knew more than their citizens did, and helped them control the flow of information to the public, giving them the ability to 'manage' public opinion. However, the so-called 'third' communication revolution, brought about since the 1990s especially by the spread of satellite and cable television, mobile phones, the internet and digital technology generally, has helped to create what has been called an 'information society'. Easier and far wider access to news and information means that, for the first time, citizens and citizen groups are privy to a quantity and quality of information that may rival that of government. This has generally empowered nonstate actors at the expense of national governments and traditional political elites. Nongovernmental organizations (see p. 297), interest groups (see p. 296) and think-tanks have thus become more effective in challenging the positions and actions of government and, sometimes, even displace government as an authoritative source of views and information about specialist subjects ranging from the environment and global poverty to public health and civil liberties. In addition, the 'new' media have facilitated political participation and helped to give the politics of protest and popular mobilization greater organizational effectiveness. Armed with mobile phones and through the use of the internet, anti-globalization, or 'anti-capitalist', protesters have thus been able to disrupt the activities and affect the actions of bodies such as the World Trade Organization and the G8.

Fourth, the media's democratic potential is embodied in the possibilities that new technology offers for expanding citizen participation, through what is called electronic democracy, 'cyber democracy' or 'e-democracy'. From this perspective, the problems that afflict many mature democracies, such as declining attendance at political meetings and falling electoral turnout, may be less a reflection of growing disenchantment with democracy and politics in general, and more an indication of the failure of the democratic process to keep up to date with how citizens in an information society wish to participate in politics and express their views. Electronic democracy, which operates through interactive television, the internet and on-line voting, appears to have at least three advantages. It overcomes the problem of size because people no longer need to assemble in large numbers to engage in political activity; it massively enlarges citizens' access to information and makes possible a truly free exchange of ideas and views; and it enables citizens to express their views easily and conveniently without having to leave home. Electronic democracy has nevertheless attracted criticism. Some of these criticisms focus on practical disadvantages, such as the greater likelihood of electoral fraud and malpractice in a system that is based on electronic, not physical, participation. Other criticisms go deeper, however, and suggest that turning the democratic process into a series of push-button referendums while citizens sit alone in their own living rooms further erodes the public dimension of political participation and reduces democratic citizenship to a series of consumer choices.

However, there are three deeper reservations about the capacity of the mass media to deliver effective democratic governance. The first of these, as advanced by dominant-ideology and elite-values theorists, is that far from providing citizens with a wide and balanced range of political views, the content of the mass media is tainted by clear political biases. Whether political bias stems from the opinions and values of editors, journalists and broadcasters, or from a more general alignment between the interests of the mass media and those of economic and social elites, it is difficult to see how the mass media's duty to provide objective information and remain faithful

Concept

Information society

An information society is a society in which the creation, distribution and manipulation of information are core economic and cultural activities, underpinned, in particular, by the wider use of computerized processes and the internet. Information societies are portrayed as successors to industrial societies, as information and knowledge are seen to replace physical capital as the principal source of wealth. In an 'information age', or 'cyber age', the principal responsibility of government is to improve education and training, both to strengthen international competitiveness and to widen opportunities for the individual. Information societies also tend to be globalized, thanks to the borderless nature of modern communications. They may nevertheless be associated with new patterns of inequality (the 'information rich' and the 'information poor'), and individuals and organizations may suffer from 'information overload'.

Political bias

Political bias refers to an expression of political views that systematically favour the values or interests of one group over another. Bias is sometimes linked to the expression of opinions, rather than facts, in which case the opposite of bias is 'objectivity'. If facts and opinions are seen to be inextricably linked, the opposite of bias is 'balance'. Bias, however, may take various forms (McQuail, 1992). *Partisan* bias is explicit and deliberately promoted (editorial comment in newspapers). *Propaganda* bias is deliberate and intentional but unacknowledged (generalizations, such as 'lazy' students or 'militant' Muslims). *Unwitting* bias occurs through a process of selection and prioritization based on seemingly professional considerations (use of 'newsworthiness' to decide media coverage). *Ideological* bias is hidden and unintended, and operates on the basis of assumptions and value judgements that are embedded in a particular belief system (private property, electoral choice and secularism portrayed as 'normal' features of political life).

to public-service principles can be discharged reliably and consistently in practice. Particular emphasis has, in this respect, been placed on the implications of media ownership, and the fact that the views and interests of major corporations or powerful media moguls cannot but, at some level, influence media output. Insofar as the mass media affects the political agenda, this agenda is likely to be politically conservative and at least compatible with the interests of dominant groups in society. Second, the mass media is not subject to public accountability; the mass media is the classic example of 'power without responsibility' (Curran and Seaton, 2003). However well-informed, knowledgeable and stimulating the views of journalists and broadcasters may be, and however eager they may be to portray themselves as the 'voice of the people', media professionals – unlike elected politicians – 'represent' no one other than themselves, and have no meaningful basis for claiming to articulate public opinion. Third, there are reasons for doubting the independence of the media from government. As discussed in the final section of this chapter, all too often a symbiotic relationship develops between media professionals and the political elite which constrains both the mass media's political views and its capacity to act as an effective 'watchdog'.

Mass media and governance

Apart from its impact (for good or ill) on democracy, the prominence of the mass media in an 'information age' has affected the processes of governance (see p. 6) in a variety of ways. The most significant of these include the transformation of political leadership, and with it a reapportionment of government power; changes to the political culture (see p. 206) that, some have warned, are leading to a growing disenchantment with politics and making societies more difficult to govern; and alterations to the behaviour of governments and the nature of policy-making.

The chief way in which the mass media has transformed political leadership is through growing interest in the personal lives and private conduct of senior political figures, at the expense of serious and 'sober' policy and ideological debate. This, in part, stems from the media's, and particularly television's, obsession with image rather than issues, and with personality rather than policies. In the UK and other parliamentary systems it is evident in a tendency towards the 'presidentialization', or 'Americanization', of politics. Such trends reflect not so much conscious bias on the part of the media as an attempt to 'sell' politics to a mass audience that is deemed to be little interested in issues and policies. This also accounts for the tendency to treat elections as 'horse races', the public's attention being focused less on policy significance of the outcome and more on who is going to win. These two tendencies invariably coincide, turning elections into 'beauty contests' between leading politicians, each of whom serves as the 'brand image' of their party. Leaders are therefore judged largely on the basis of their 'televisual' skills (relaxed manner, sense of humour, ability to demonstrate the 'popular touch', and so on), rather than their mastery of political issues and capacity for serious political debate. However, has exposing leading politicians to the unrelenting glare of media attention merely given them celebrity status, or has media attention affected the location of power within the governmental system?

There can be little doubt that the advent of the 'media age' has changed the behaviour of political leaders, as well as affected the career prospects of individual politicians. For example, presentational factors, such as personal appearance, hairstyle, dress sense and so on, have become more important in determining political preferment or advancement. However, such developments have not merely changed the 'face' of modern politics; they have reordered power relationships both within the political executive and between the executive and the assembly. The growth of 'political celebrity' gives presidents, prime ministers and other party leaders the ability to make personalized appeals to the voters, creating the phenomenon of **spatial leadership**. This allows leaders to appeal 'over the heads' of their senior colleagues, parties and government institutions, directly to the public. Furthermore, the messages they give and the policy and ideological stances they adopt are increasingly determined by leading politicians personally, supported, it appears, by an ever-expanding band of public relations consultants, 'spin doctors', media managers, pollsters and publicity directors. One of the consequences of this is that junior politicians may have an additional reason for deferring to their leaders: their fear of damaging their leader's image and reputation. If the leader is damaged, especially by splits and internal criticism, all members of his or her party or government suffer. Political power thus comes to be structured on the basis of the publicity and media attention received by individual politicians. The greater the media attention, the greater the political leverage. However, media attention is far from an unqualified benefit for political leaders. Although their triumphs and successes can be publicly trumpeted, their flaws, failings and transgressions can also be ruthlessly exposed. Indeed, the ultimate vulnerability of contemporary political leaders may well be that negative media coverage may turn them into 'electoral liabilities', encouraging their parties and colleagues to remove them in order to 'save the party', or their own political careers.

The second way in which the media has affected governance is through its impact on the political culture. The media is sometimes charged with having created a climate of corrosive cynicism amongst the public, leading to growing popular disenchantment with politics generally and a lack of trust in governments and politicians of all complexions (Lloyd, 2004). This may, in turn, be linked to trends that have afflicted mature democracies in particular, such as declining voter turnout and falling party membership. The UK is often seen as the most advanced example of such a media-driven 'culture of contempt', but similar tendencies are evident elsewhere, notably in the USA, Australia and Canada. Why has this happened? A critical stance towards politicians in general and governments in particular is, of course, vital to the maintenance of democratic governance. However, the distinction between legitimate criticism and systematic and relentless negativity may, in practice, be difficult to uphold. This occurs, in part, because increasingly intense commercial pressures have forced the media to make their coverage of politics 'sexy' and attention-grabbing. The media, after all, is a business, and this places inevitable pressure on the coverage of news and current affairs. Facts are absorbed more and more quickly into a swirl of comment and interpretation, blurring, seemingly altogether, the distinction between what happens and what it means. Similarly, routine political debate and policy analysis receive less and less attention, as the media focus instead on – or 'hype' – scandals of various kinds and allegations of incompetence, policy failure or simple inertia. Leading politicians have, as a result, come to live in a kind of ongoing reality-television programme, whose sole purpose appears to be to embarrass and denigrate them at every possible turn. The public, for their part, tend to view politicians as untrustworthy and deceitful, according them the same level of respect they would accord any other reality-television-programme participant.

Spatial leadership: The tendency of political leaders to distance themselves from their parties and governments by presenting themselves as 'outsiders' or developing their own political stance or ideological position.

The final way in which the mass media has influenced governance is through its impact on the policy-making process. This has happened in at least two ways. The first is that, just like everyone else in society, government is bombarded by a much greater quantity of information arriving almost immediately. Knowing too much can sometimes be as dangerous as knowing too little. An example of this can be found in the USA's inability to predict and prevent the September 11 terrorist attacks in 2001. The problem the USA faced was not that it lacked information about al-Qaeda, its plans and movements, but that the sheer quantity of national-security intelligence available made effective analysis almost impossible. Moreover, as news and information spreads around the globe at a faster pace, governments are forced to react to events more quickly and often before they have been fully discussed and digested. An age of '24/7 news' inevitably becomes one of '24/7 government'. Politicians are encouraged, even forced, to take a stance on issues simply to avoid being criticized for inertia or inactivity, leaving little time for the analysis of policy options and their implications. Second, greater reliance on the mass media means that it is often the media, and not government, that sets the political agenda and dictates the direction of policy-making. For example, the fact that television pictures of the Asian tsunami in December 2004 were broadcast almost immediately across the globe, creating an outpouring of public sympathy for its victims and leading to unprecedented levels of private charitable donations, forced governments around the world, within days, to substantially increase their scale of aid and support.

Media globalization

An aspect of the media's influence that has attracted growing political attention is its role in strengthening globalization. Radio and television started this process, as it became increasingly difficult to insulate the populations of one country from news, information and images broadcast from other countries. An example of this was the extent to which the communist regimes of eastern Europe were destabilized by the growing penetration of pro-western and therefore pro-capitalist radio and television broadcasts from western Europe and the USA, contributing to the revolutions of 1989–91. The 'new' media, and especially satellite television, mobile phones and the internet, have dramatically intensified this process, both because of their dramatic spread and because of their inherently transnational characters. China and Singapore are amongst the few countries still trying to censor the internet, with such attempts likely to become less and less successful over time. Insofar as the mass media facilitates, or even fuels, globalization, it has contributed to a far-reaching range of political developments, including the growth of a globalized capitalist economy, the declining (or at least changing) role of the state, and the emergence of what some see as a homogenized global culture.

The role of the mass media in promoting **cultural globalization** has been an area of particular controversy. The power of the mass media, allied to the growth of transnational corporations (see p. 149) and trends such as mass tourism, is often held to be responsible for the development of a single global system that imprints itself on all parts of the world; this results, in effect, in a global monoculture. The most prominent feature of this process has been the worldwide advance of consumerism and of the materialistic values and appetites that underpin burgeoning global capitalism. Benjamin Barber (1995) dubbed this emerging world 'McWorld', to capture the idea that mass communications and modern commerce, tied together

Cultural globalization: The process whereby information, commodities and images produced in one part of the world enter into a global flow that tends to 'flatten out' cultural differences between nations and regions.

by technology, had created a world in which people everywhere are mesmerized by 'fast music, fast computers, fast food – with MTV, McIntosh and McDonalds pressing nations into one commercially homogeneous theme park'. In this view of cultural globalization, the rich diversity of global cultures, religions, traditions and lifestyles is being subverted by a process of 'westernization' or 'Americanization', made possible by what has been called 'media imperialism'. The western, or more specifically, American character of cultural globalization stems not only from the fact that the West is the home of consumer capitalism, but also from the tendency of global media content to derive disproportionately from the West, and particularly from the USA. This is reflected in the rise of English as the global language, and in the global dominance of Hollywood films and US-produced television programmes.

However, this image of cultural homogenization fuelled by the global mass media fails to capture what is in practice a complex and often contradictory process. Alongside the media's tendency to 'flatten out' cultural differences, there are also strong tendencies towards diversity and pluralization. This has occurred in a number of ways and for a variety of reasons. In the first place, as Barber (1995) argued, the rise of McWorld has been symbiotically linked to the emergence of countervailing forces, the most notable of which is militant Islam, or what Barber called 'Jihad'. The second development is that the 'new' media, and especially computerized printing techniques, satellite television and the internet, have substantially reduced the cost of mass communication as well as widened access to it. An example of this is the success of the Qatar-based television station Al Jazeera, launched in 1996, in providing a forum for the expression of non-western views and opinions across the Arab world and beyond, providing a rival to, for instance, CNN, Voice of America and the BBC. Third, cultural exchange facilitated through the mass media is by no means a 'top-down' or one-way process; instead, all societies, including economically and politically powerful ones, have become more varied and diverse as a result of the emergence of a globalized cultural marketplace. In return for Coca Cola, McDonald's and MTV, developed states have increasingly been 'penetrated' by Bollywood films, Chinese martial arts epics, 'world music' and non-western religions and therapeutic practices.

Political communication

Propaganda machines

The notion that government and the mass media are always opposing forces, the latter exposing the failings and flaws of the former (either for the public's benefit or for commercial advantage), is highly misleading. Instead, the media have often been controlled, directly or indirectly, by government and used as a form of propaganda machine. The classic example of a propaganda machine was that constructed under Joseph Goebbels in Nazi Germany. The Nazis set out to 'coordinate' German society through an elaborate process of ideological indoctrination. For example, youth organizations were set up in the form of the Hitler Youth and the League of German Maidens; the school curriculum was entirely revised and all teachers coerced to join the Nazi Teachers' League; and the German Labour Front replaced free trade unions, providing workers with recreational facilities through the 'Strength through Joy' organization. As chief propagandist of the Nazi Party, Goebbels created in 1933

Concept

Consumerism

Consumerism is a psychic and social phenomenon whereby personal happiness is equated with the consumption of material possessions. It is often associated with the emergence of a 'consumer society' or 'consumer capitalism'. A consumer society is one that is organized around the consumption, rather than the production, of goods and services. Whereas 'productionist' societies emphasize the value of discipline, duty and hard work, consumerist societies emphasize materialism, hedonism and instant (rather than delayed) gratification. Consumerism can be defended on the grounds that it simply reflects natural acquisitiveness – the more people consume, the happier they are. Critics nevertheless view it as a manipulative process, which operates through pervasive advertising and marketing and serves the interests of capitalism by deluding people into believing that material acquisition (or 'shopping') will boost their personal esteem and social status, usually through its association with a 'brand image'.

Concept

Propaganda

Propaganda (derived from the activities of the arm of the Catholic church which sought to spread the faith and recruit members – *de propaganda fide*) is information (or *dis*information) disseminated in a deliberate attempt to shape opinions and, possibly, stimulate political action. Propaganda is a pejorative term, implying both untruth or distortion, and a (usually crude) desire to manipulate and control public opinion. Pervasive propaganda based on a monopoly of the means of mass communication is often seen as one of the defining features of totalitarianism (see p. 29), with the Nazi propaganda machine providing the classic example. Propaganda differs from political bias in that it is systematic and deliberate, whereas the latter may be partial and unconscious. A distinction is sometimes drawn between 'black' propaganda (blatant lies), 'grey' propaganda (distortions and half truths) and 'white' propaganda (the truth).

Censorship: A policy or act of control over what can be said, written, published or performed in order to suppress what is considered to be morally or politically unacceptable.

Glasnost: (Russian) Literally 'openness' or 'transparency'; the liberalization of controls over political expression and the media.

a new department, the Reich Ministry of Information and Propaganda, which inundated Germany with an unending flood of propaganda. Little in the field of mass communication and entertainment escaped the **censorship** of Goebbels' ministry. It supervised all the writing, music, theatre, dance, painting, sculpture, film and radio. Goebbels placed particular stress on radio broadcasting and encouraged the manufacture of a cheap 'people's' radio set, which resulted in huge and ever-growing audiences for his propaganda through the radio. He began the world's first regular television service in 1935, which, although restricted to closed-circuit showing in Berlin, kept going until near the end of the Second World War.

Media propaganda was also a significant feature of communist regimes. The Soviet Union, for example, not only operated a system of strict censorship over the mass media, but also fostered a journalistic culture (the 'internal censor') that demanded total support of the ideology and policies of the Communist Party, or CPSU. Both the print and broadcast media were used as propaganda tools by the Soviet authorities, with media content unwaveringly mirroring the policies of the state at each stage in the history of the Soviet Union (Oates, 2005). Particular emphasis was placed on boosting newspaper readership, with the party daily *Pravda* (Truth) having a circulation of nearly 11 million by 1980, and its fellow newspaper, *Izvestaya* (News), having a circulation of 7 million. However, the introduction of **'glasnost'** by Mikhail Gorbachev when he became CPSU General Secretary in 1985 initiated changes in the Soviet media that were to have far-reaching, and ultimately unstoppable, political implications. The high point of the media's influence came in August 1991, when journalists and broadcasters defied the coup that had toppled Gorbachev and was intended to reinstate authoritarian rule. In so doing, they contributed both to the collapse of the coup and, later in the year, to the downfall of the Soviet regime itself. Russia's record of media freedom in the postcommunist era has nevertheless been patchy. Despite the formal abolition of censorship in 1990 and the inclusion of freedom from censorship in the 1993 Russian Constitution (Article 29), the Russian media, and television in particular, continue to be dominated by state interests. Television channels such as Channel 1, NTV and RTR were criticized during the parliamentary elections of 2003 and the presidential election of 2004 for their bias towards President Putin and the government-backed United Russia party, as well as for conducting campaigns of 'black' propaganda against opposition figures and parties.

Criticisms of the use of the media as a propaganda machine are not restricted to totalitarian regimes and new democracies, however. For instance, controversy was sparked in Italy by Silvio Berlusconi's periods as prime minister in 1994 and 2001–6. Berlusconi, who is Italy's richest person, owns Mediaset, which controls three of Italy's six privately owned television channels. In 1993 he founded the Forza Italia political movement, in part to further his own political ambitions. The success of Forza Italia was certainly linked to widespread disenchantment with Italy's sclerotic party system, but the movement undoubtedly also benefited from the consistently positive coverage it received in the Berlusconi-owned media. During his second period in power, however, Berlusconi was frequently criticized for trying to extend his media control beyond the Mediaset channels, bringing pressure to bear also on the publicly owned RAI television channels. This, his critics alleged, gave Berlusconi control of almost all television sources of information in Italy, ensuring favourable coverage for Berlusconi personally and for the centre-right views of Forza Italia. Berlusconi's supporters, on the other hand, argued that he was not so much imposing his own bias as countering centre-left political bias that was deeply embedded in the publicly-owned television sector. Although the Italian example is unusual because of Berlusconi's joint role as media mogul and political leader, attempts by democratic politicians to exert influence over the media are by no means uncommon. Indeed, they have become routine in an emerging age of 'spin' and news management.

Politics of spin

In addition to political biases that operate in and through the mass media, growing concern has been expressed about the closer relationship in modern politics between government and the media, and about how each uses the other for its own purposes. This has led to a transformation in the style and substance of political communication in democratic regimes, affecting both public opinion and, more widely, the political culture. Governments of whatever complexion have always had an unreliable relationship with truth. Politicians are concerned primarily with winning and retaining power, and are thus ever sensitive to the need to maintain public support. The desire to accentuate the positive and conceal the negative is therefore irresistible. In a liberal-democratic context, in which the existence of free media rules out 'official' propaganda and crude ideological manipulation, governments have come to shape the news agenda by new techniques for the control and dissemination of information, often described as 'news management' or 'political marketing'. The favourable presentation of information and policies, or what has come to be called '**spin**', has thus become a major preoccupation of modern governments.

The art of 'spin', practised by so-called 'spin-doctors', has many facets. These include the following:

- the careful 'vetting' of information and arguments before release to the media
- the control of sources of information to ensure that only an official 'line' is presented
- the use of unattributable briefings or 'leaks'
- the feeding of stories only to sympathetic media sources
- the release of information close to media deadlines to prevent checking or the identification of counter-arguments
- the release of 'bad' news at times when other, more important events dominate the news agenda.

News management of this kind is most advanced in the USA, where it has become common for election strategists and campaign managers to take up senior White House posts if their candidate wins the presidency. The Clinton administration was widely seen to have taken 'spin' and the skills of policy presentation to new and more sophisticated levels. The Blair government in the UK also devoted particular attention to the 'packaging' of politics, leading some to criticize it for being concerned more with style than with substance. Amongst the developments that have occurred under Blair were the centralizing of government communications under the control of the prime minister's press office, a 'carrot and stick' approach to journalists, who were rewarded with information for sympathetic coverage but penalized for criticism, and the politicization of departmental information offices through the imposition of control from Downing Street. Government spending on public relatiuons, marketing and advertising also rose threefold between 1998 and 2006.

Spin: The presentation of information so as to elicit a desired response, or being 'economical with the truth'.

It would be a mistake, however, to assume that the media have been reluctant or passive players in the development of news management. The mass media need government as much as government needs the mass media. Government has always been an important source of news and information, but its role has become even more vital as the expansion in media outlets – television channels, web sites, magazines and newspapers – has created greater pressure for the acquisition of 'newsworthy' stories. In some cases, publishers, editors and journalists conspire with 'spin-doctors' to manage the news for mutual benefit. This has been alleged in the UK in relation to the Blair government and the Murdoch press, as, for instance, the government's unwillingness to press ahead with privacy legislation coincided with the conversion of, first, the *Sun*, the UK's largest selling tabloid, and then *The Times* into Labour-supporting newspapers.

In addition to undermining the rigour and independence of political reporting, the advent of media-orientated government has a range of other implications. Some, for example, argue that it strengthens democracy by allowing government to deal with the public more directly and respond more effectively to popular views and concerns. Others, however, see it as a threat to the democratic process, in that it widens the scope for manipulation and dishonesty, and weakens the role of representative institutions such as assemblies or parliaments. Moreover, it may engender apathy and undermine interest in conventional forms of political activity, in particular voting and party membership. This occurs because 'spin', style and presentation become themselves the focus of media attention, strengthening the image of government as a vast publicity machine that is disengaged from the lives and concerns of ordinary people.

◼ Summary

◆ There are rival theories of the media's political impact. Pluralists portray the media as an ideological marketplace that enhances debate and electoral choice. However, others highlight systematic media bias, stemming either from links between the media and economic and social elites, or from the personal views of the editor, broadcasters and journalists. The market model suggests that the media output simply reflects the views of the general public.

◆ The media play a key democratic role in four senses. They promote political education by providing a public forum for meaningful and serious debate; act as a public watchdog, exposing abuses of power; tend, through the 'new' media in particular, to widen access to information and facilitate political activism; and serve as a mechanism through which democracy takes place. Concerns have nevertheless been raised about the political views of the media, their lack of democratic accountability and their over-close links to government.

◆ The mass media has affected governance in various ways. These include that they have transformed political leadership and, in the process, reapportioned government power. They have also changed the political culture, and, some have warned, contributed to declining respect for politicians and politics in general. Finally, the growing influence of the media is evident in a policy-making process that has to react more rapidly and make sense of a vast amount of information.

◆ The role of the media in promoting globalization has provoked particular controversy. Some have warned against 'media imperialism', drawing attention to the media's role in spreading a global culture of consumerism and in strengthening 'westernization or 'Americanization'. However, cultural exchange facilitated by the mass media is by no means always a 'top-down' or one-way process.

◆ Governments have sometimes used the media as a propaganda machine. This involves direct control over all kinds of media output to ensure that only 'official' views and ideas are distributed. Classic examples of this can be found in Nazi Germany and in communist regimes, but there has been a growing tendency for democratic regimes to engage in news management and the politics of 'spin', providing evidence of a symbiotic relationship that tends to develop between government and the media.

Questions for discussion

▶ What is new about the 'new' media?

▶ Do the mass media reflect public opinion or shape it?

▶ Is a free media vital for democratic rule?

▶ How has the mass media changed the nature of political leadership? Are leaders stronger or weaker as a result?

▶ Is the mass media an agent of cultural homogenization?

▶ Do all governments use propaganda, or only some?

▶ Are modern governments more concerned with political marketing than with political performance?

Further reading

Axford, B. and R. Huggins (eds), *The New Media and Politics* (London and Thousand Oaks, CA: Sage, 2001). A useful and wide-ranging collection of essays that considers how, and how far, the 'new' media have transformed politics.

Bartle, J. and D. Griffiths (eds), *Political Communications Transformed: From Morrison to Mandelson* (Basingstoke: Palgrave Macmillan, 2001). A collection of articles analysing the transformed relationship between the media, political parties and voters in the UK.

Gunther, R. and A. Mughan (eds), *Democracy and the Media: A Comparative Perspective* (Cambridge and New York: Cambridge University Press, 2000). A systematic assessment of the impact of the media on politics and of politics on the media, drawing on patterns in a broad range of states.

Meyer, T. and L. Hinchman, *Media Democracy: How the Media Colonize Politics* (Cambridge and New York: Polity, 2002). A stimulating analysis of the 'mediatization' of politics, combining political theory and media theory approaches.

Philo, G. (ed.), *Message Received* (London: Longman, 1999). A radical analysis of the mass media based on research from the Glasgow Media Group.

Street, J., *Mass Media, Politics and Democracy* (Basingstoke and New York: Palgrave Macmillan, 2001). A readable and wide-ranging overview of all aspects of the relationship between the media and politics.

Representation, Elections and Voting

If Voting Changed Anything They'd Abolish It

Title of a book by KEN LIVINGSTONE (1987)

Elections are often thought of as the heart of the political process. Perhaps no questions in politics are as crucial as do we elect the politicians who rule over us, and under what rules are these elections held? Elections are seen as nothing less than democracy in practice. They are a means through which the people can control their government, ultimately by 'kicking the rascals out'. Central to this notion is the principle of representation. Put simply, this portrays politicians as servants of the people, and invests them with a responsibility to act for or on behalf of those who elect them. When democracy, in the classical sense of direct and continuous popular participation, is regarded as hopelessly impractical, representation may be the closest we can come to achieving government by the people. There is nevertheless considerable disagreement about how representation can be achieved in practice, and about how politicians should be elected and what election results actually mean.

The central issues examined in this chapter are as follows:

Key issues

▶ What is representation? How can one person 'represent' another?

▶ How can representation be achieved in practice?

▶ What do elections do? What are their functions?

▶ How do electoral systems differ? What are their strengths and weaknesses?

▶ What do election results mean?

▶ Why do people vote as they do? How can electoral behaviour be explained?

Concept

Representation

The term represent means, in everyday language, to 'portray' or 'make present', as when a picture is said to represent a scene or a person. As a political principle, representation is a relationship through which an individual or group stands for, or acts on behalf of, a larger body of people. Representation differs from democracy in that, while the former acknowledges a distinction between government and the governed, the latter, at least in its classical form, aspires to abolish this distinction and establish popular *self*-government. Representative democracy (see p. 74) may nevertheless constitute a limited and indirect form of democratic rule, provided that the representation links government and the governed in such a way that the people's views are articulated or their interests are secured.

Representation

The issue of representation has generated deep and recurrent political controversy. Even the absolute monarchs of old were expected to rule by seeking the advice of the 'estates of the realm' (the major landed interests, the clergy, and so on). In this sense, the English Civil War of the seventeenth century, fought between King and Parliament, broke out as a result of an attempt to deny representation to key groups and interests. Similarly, debate about the spread of democracy in the nineteenth and twentieth centuries centred largely upon the question of who should be represented. Should representation be restricted to those who have the competence, education and perhaps leisure to act wisely and think seriously about politics (variously seen as men, the propertied, or particular racial or ethnic groups), or should representation be extended to all adult citizens?

Such questions have now largely been resolved through the widespread acceptance of the principle of political equality (see p. 73), at least in the formal sense of universal suffrage and 'one person, one vote'. Plural voting, for example, was abolished in the UK in 1949, women were enfranchised in Switzerland in 1971, and racial criteria for voting were swept away in South Africa in 1994. However, this approach to representation is simplistic in that it equates representation with elections and voting, politicians being seen as 'representatives' merely because they have been elected. This ignores more difficult questions about *how* one person can be said to represent another, and *what* it is that he or she represents. Is it the views of the represented, their best interests, the groups from which they come, or what?

Theories of representation

There is no single, agreed theory of representation. Rather, there are a number of competing theories, each of which is based on particular ideological and political assumptions. For example, does representative government imply that government 'knows better' than the people, that government has somehow 'been instructed' by the people what to do and how to behave, or that the government 'looks like' the people in that it broadly reflects their characteristics or features? Such questions are not of academic interest alone. Particular models of representation dictate very different behaviour on the part of representatives. For instance, should elected politicians be bound by policies and positions outlined during an election and endorsed by the voters, or is it their job to lead public opinion and thereby help to define the public interest? Moreover, it is not uncommon for more than one principle of representation to operate within the same political system, suggesting, perhaps, that no single model is sufficient in itself to secure representative government.

Four principal models of representation have been advanced:

- trusteeship
- delegation
- the mandate
- resemblance.

Trustee model

A trustee is a person who is vested with formal responsibility for another's property or affairs. The classic expression of representation as trusteeship is found in Edmund Burke's (see p. 49) speech to the electors of Bristol in 1774:

You choose a member indeed; but when you have chosen him he is *not* member of Bristol, but he is a member of parliament . . . Your representative owes you, not his industry only, but his judgement; and he betrays, instead of serving you, if he sacrifices it to your opinion (Burke, 1975: 157).

For Burke, the essence of representation was to serve one's constituents by the exercise of 'mature judgement' and 'enlightened conscience'. In short, representation is a moral duty: those with the good fortune to possess education and understanding should act in the interests of those who are less fortunate. This view had strongly elitist implications, since it stresses that, once elected, representatives should think for themselves and exercise independent judgement on the grounds that the mass of people do not know their own best interests. A similar view was advanced by J. S. Mill (see p. 48) in the form of the liberal theory of representation. This was based on the assumption that, although all individuals have a right to be represented, not all political opinions are of equal value. Mill therefore proposed a system of plural voting in which four or five votes would be allocated to holders of learned diplomas or degrees, two or three to skilled or managerial workers, and a single vote to ordinary workers. He also argued that rational voters would support politicians who could act wisely on their behalf, rather than ones who merely reflected the voters' own views. Trustee representation thus portrays professional politicians as representatives insofar as they are members of an educated elite. It is based on the belief that knowledge and understanding are unequally distributed in society, in the sense that not all citizens know what is best for them.

This Burkian notion of representation has also attracted severe criticism, however. For instance, it appears to have clearly antidemocratic implications. If politicians should think for themselves because the public is ignorant, poorly educated or deluded, then surely it is a mistake to allow the public to elect their representatives in the first place. Second, the link between representation and education is questionable. Whereas education may certainly be of value in aiding the understanding of intricate political and economic problems, it is far less clear that it helps politicians to make correct moral judgements about the interests of others. There is little evidence, for example, to support Burke's and Mill's belief that education breeds **altruism** and gives people a broader sense of social responsibility. Finally, there is the fear traditionally expressed by radical democrats such as Thomas Paine (see p. 250) that, if politicians are allowed to exercise their own judgement, they will simply use that latitude to pursue their own selfish interests. In this way, representation could simply become a substitute for democracy. In his pamphlet *Common Sense* ([1776] 1987:68), Paine came close to the rival ideal of delegate representation in insisting that 'the elected should never form to themselves an interest separate from the electors'.

Delegate model

A delegate is a person who is chosen to act for another on the basis of clear guidance or instructions. In other words, a delegate is expected to act as a conduit conveying the views of others, while having little or no capacity to exercise his or her own judgement or preferences. Examples include sales representatives and ambassadors,

Altruism: A concern for the welfare of others, based on either enlightened self-interest or a recognition of a common humanity.

Thomas Paine (1737–1809)

UK-born writer and revolutionary. Paine was brought up in a Quaker family and spent his early years as an undistinguished artisan. He went to America in 1774 and fought for the colonists in the War of Independence. He returned to England in 1789, but, after being indicted for treason, fled to France as a supporter of the republican cause, where he narrowly escaped the guillotine during the Terror. Paine's radicalism fused a commitment to political liberty with a deep faith in popular sovereignty, providing inspiration for both liberal republicanism and socialist egalitarianism. He was an important figure in revolutionary politics in the USA, the UK and France. His most important writings include *Common Sense* ([1776] 1987), *The Rights of Man* (1791/92) and *The Age of Reason* (1794).

Focus on . . .

Referendums: for and against

A referendum is a vote in which the electorate can express a view on a particular issue of public policy. It differs from an election in that the latter Is essentially a means of filling a public office and does not provide a direct or reliable method of influencing the content of policy. The referendum is therefore a device of direct democracy (see p. 74). It is typically used not to replace representative institutions, but to supplement them. Referendums may be either advisory or binding; they may also raise issues for discussion (initiatives), or be used to decide policy questions (propositions or plebiscites).

Amongst the advantages of referendums are the following:

- They check the power of elected governments, ensuring that they stay in line with public opinion.
- They promote political participation, thus helping to create a more educated and better informed electorate.
- They strengthen legitimacy by providing the public with a way of expressing their views about specific issues.
- They provide a means either of settling major constitutional questions, or of gauging public opinion on issues not raised in elections because major parties agree on them.

The disadvantages of referendums include the following:

- They leave political decisions in the hands of those who have the least education and experience, and are most susceptible to media and other influences.
- They provide, at best, only a snapshot of public opinion at one point in time.
- They allow politicians to manipulate the political agenda and absolve themselves of responsibility for making difficult decisions.
- They tend to simplify and distort political issues, reducing them to questions that have a yes/no answer.

neither of whom are, strictly speaking, authorized to think for themselves. Similarly, a trade-union official who attends a conference with instructions on how to vote and what to say is acting as a delegate, not as a Burkian representative. Those who favour this model of representation as delegation usually support mechanisms that ensure that politicians are bound as closely as possible to the views of the represented. These include what Paine referred to as 'frequent interchange' between representatives and their constituents in the form of regular elections and short terms in office. In addition, radical democrats have advocated the use of **initiatives** and the right of **recall** as means of giving the public more control over politicians. Although delegation stops short of direct democracy, its supporters nevertheless usually favour the use of referendums to supplement the representative process.

The virtue of what has been called 'delegated representation' is that it provides broader opportunities for popular participation and serves to check the self-serving inclinations of professional politicians. It thus comes as close as is possible in representative government to realizing the ideal of **popular sovereignty**. Its disadvantages are nevertheless also clear. In the first place, in ensuring that representatives are bound to the interests of their constituents, it tends to breed narrowness and foster conflict. This is precisely what Burke feared would occur if members of the legislature acted as ambassadors who took instructions from their constituents rather than as representatives of the nation. As he put it, 'Parliament is a deliberative assembly of one nation, with one interest, that of the whole'. A second drawback is that, because professional politicians are not trusted to exercise their own judgement, delegation limits the scope for leadership (see p. 372) and statesmanship. Politicians are forced to reflect the views of their constituents or even pander to them, and are thus not able to mobilize the people by providing vision and inspiration.

Mandate model

Both the trustee model and the delegate model were developed before the emergence of modern political parties, and therefore view representatives as essentially independent actors. However, individual candidates are now rarely elected on the basis of their personal qualities and talents; more commonly, they are seen as foot soldiers for a party, and are supported because of its public image or programme of policies. New theories of representation have therefore emerged. The most influential of these is the so-called doctrine of the mandate. This is based on the idea that, in winning an election, a party gains a popular mandate that authorizes it to carry out whatever policies or programmes it outlined during the election campaign. As it is the party, rather than individual politicians, that is the agency of representation, the mandate model provides a clear justification for party unity and party discipline. In effect, politicians serve their constituents not by thinking for themselves or acting as a channel to convey their views, but by remaining loyal to their party and its policies.

The strength of the mandate doctrine is that it takes account of the undoubted practical importance of party labels and party policies. Moreover, it provides a means of imposing some kind of meaning on election results, as well as a way of keeping politicians to their word. Nevertheless, the doctrine has also stimulated fierce criticism. First, it is based on a highly questionable model of voting behaviour, insofar as it suggests that voters select parties on the grounds of policies and issues. Voters are not always the rational and well-informed creatures that this model suggests. They can be influenced by a range of 'irrational' factors, such as the personalities of leaders, the images of parties, habitual allegiances and social conditioning.

Initiative: A type of referendum through which the public is able to raise legislative proposals.

Recall: A process whereby the electorate can call unsatisfactory public officials to account and ultimately remove them.

Popular sovereignty: The principle that there is no higher authority than the will of the people (the basis of the classical concept of democracy).

Concept

Mandate

A mandate is an instruction or command from a higher body that demands compliance. The idea of a popular mandate arises from the claim on behalf of a winning party in an election that its manifesto promises have been endorsed, giving it authority to translate these into a programme of government. The doctrine of the mandate thus guarantees responsible party government, in that the party in power can only act within the mandate it has received. This is a 'policy mandate'. The more flexible notion of a 'governing mandate', or, for an individual leader, a 'personal mandate', has sometimes been advanced, but it is difficult to see how this in any way restricts politicians once they are in power.

Second, even if voters are influenced by policies, it is likely that they will be attracted by certain **manifesto** commitments, but be less interested in, or perhaps opposed to, others. A vote for a party cannot therefore be taken to be an endorsement of its entire manifesto, or indeed of any single election promise. Third, the doctrine imposes a straitjacket. It limits government policies to those positions and proposals that the party took up during the election, and leaves no scope to adjust policies in the light of changing circumstances. What guidance do mandates offer in the event of, say, international or economic crises? Finally (as will be discussed in the next main section of this chapter) the doctrine of the mandate can be applied only in the case of majoritarian electoral systems, and its use even there may appear absurd if the winning party fails to gain 50 per cent of the popular vote.

Resemblance model

The final theory of representation is based less on the manner in which representatives are selected than on whether they typify or resemble the group they claim to represent. This notion is embodied in the idea of a 'representative cross-section', as used by market researchers and opinion pollsters. By this standard, a representative government would constitute a microcosm of the larger society, containing members drawn from all groups and sections in society (in terms of social class, gender, religion, ethnicity, age and so on), and in numbers that are proportional to the size of the groups in society at large. The idea of characteristic representation, or as it has been called 'microcosmic representation', has traditionally been endorsed by socialist and radical thinkers. They argue that the 'under-representation' of groups such as the working class, women and racial minorities at senior levels in key institutions ensures that their interests are marginalized or ignored altogether.

The resemblance model suggests that only people who come from a particular group, and have shared the experiences of that group, can fully identify with its interests. This is the difference between 'putting oneself in the shoes of another' and having direct and personal experience of what other people go through. A 'New Man' or a 'pro-feminist' male may, for instance, sympathize with women's interests and support the principle of sexual equality, but will never take women's problems as seriously as women do themselves, because they are not *his* problems. On the other hand, the idea that representatives should resemble the represented undoubtedly causes a number of difficulties.

One of these is that this model portrays representation in exclusive or narrow terms, believing that only a woman can represent women, only a black person can represent other black people, only a member of the working class can represent the working classes, and so on. If all representatives simply advanced the interests of the groups from which they come, the result would be social division and conflict, with no one being able to defend the common good or advance a broader public interest. Moreover, a government that is a microcosm of society would reflect that society's weaknesses as well as its strengths. What would be the advantage, for example, of government resembling society if the majority of the population are apathetic, ill informed and poorly educated? Finally, the microcosmic ideal can be achieved only by imposing powerful constraints upon electoral choice and individual freedom. In the name of representation, political parties may be forced to select quotas of female and minority candidates, constituencies may be set aside for candidates from particular backgrounds, or, more dramatically, the electorate might have to be classified

Manifesto: A document outlining (in more or less detail) the policies or programme a party proposes to pursue if elected to power.

Joseph Schumpeter (1883–1950)

Moravian-born US economist and sociologist. Following an early academic career and a brief spell as Minister of Finance in post-First-World-War Austria, Schumpeter became professor of economics at Harvard University in 1932. His economic thought, developed in *Theory of Economic Development* (1912) and *Business Cycles* (1939), centred on the long-term dynamics of the capitalist system and in particular the role of 'risk-loving' entrepreneurs. In *Capitalism, Socialism and Democracy* (1942), Schumpeter drew on economic, sociological and political theories to advance the famous contention that western capitalism was, impelled by its very success, evolving into a form of socialism.

on the basis of class, gender, race and so on, and only be allowed to vote for candidates from their own group.

Elections

Although controversy continues to rage about the nature of representation, there is one point of universal agreement: the representative process is intrinsically linked to elections and voting. **Elections** may not in themselves be a sufficient condition for political representation, but there is little doubt that they are a necessary condition. Indeed, some thinkers have gone further and portrayed elections as the very heart of democracy. This was the view developed by Joseph Schumpeter in *Capitalism, Socialism and Democracy* (1942), which portrayed democracy as an 'institutional arrangement', as a means of filling public office by a competitive struggle for the people's vote. As he put it, 'democracy means only that the people have the opportunity of accepting or refusing the men [*sic*] who are to rule them'. In interpreting democracy as nothing more than a political method, Schumpeter in effect identified it with elections, and specifically with competitive elections. While few modern democratic theorists are prepared to reduce democracy simply to competitive elections, most nevertheless follow Schumpeter in understanding democratic government in terms of the rules and mechanisms that guide the conduct of elections. This focuses attention on the very different forms that elections can take.

Fig. 12.1 Elections as democracy in practice – people queing to vote in South Africa's first all-race election in 1994.

Election: A device for filling an office or post through choices made by a designated body of people: the electorate.

First, which offices or posts are subject to the elective principle? Although elections are widely used to fill those public offices whose holders have policy-making responsibilities (the legislature and executive in particular), key political institutions are sometimes treated as exceptions. This applies, for instance, to the second chambers of legislature in states such as the UK and Canada, and where constitutional monarchs still serve as heads of state. Second, who is entitled to vote, how widely is the franchise drawn? As pointed out above, restrictions on the right to vote based on factors such as property ownership, education, gender and racial origin have been abandoned in most countries. Nevertheless, there may be informal restrictions, as in the practice in most US states of leaving electoral registration entirely in the hands of the citizen, with the result that non-registration and non-voting are widespread. On the other hand, in Australia, Belgium and Italy, for instance, voting is compulsory.

Third, how are votes cast? Although public voting was the norm in the USSR until 1989, and it is still widely practised in small organizations in the form of a show of hands, modern political elections are generally held on the basis of a secret ballot (sometimes called an 'Australian ballot', as it was first used in South Australia in 1856). The secret ballot is usually seen as the guarantee of a 'fair' election, in that it keeps the dangers of corruption and intimidation at bay. Nevertheless, electoral fairness cannot simply be reduced to the issue of how people vote. It is also affected by the voters' access to reliable and balanced information, the range of choice they are offered, the circumstances under which campaigning is carried out, and, finally, how scrupulously the vote is counted.

Fourth, are elections competitive or non-competitive? This is usually seen as the most crucial of distinctions, as only about half of the countries that use elections offer their electorates a genuine choice of both candidates and parties. Single-candidate elections, for example, were the rule in orthodox communist states. This meant that public office was effectively filled through a nomination process dominated by the communist party. Electoral competition is a highly complex and often controversial issue. It concerns not merely the right of people to stand for election and the ability of political parties to nominate candidates and campaign legally, but also broader factors that affect party performance, such as their sources of funding and their access to the media. From this point of view, the nature of the party system may be as crucial to the maintenance of genuine competition as are rules about who can stand and who can vote. Finally, how is the election conducted? As will be discussed later, there are a bewildering variety of electoral systems, each of which has its own particular political and constitutional implications.

Functions of elections

Because of the different kinds of elections, and the variety of electoral systems, generalization about the roles or functions of elections is always difficult. Nevertheless, the advance of democratization (see p. 32) in the 1980s and 1990s, stimulated in part by the collapse of communism, has usually been associated with the adoption of liberal-democratic electoral systems, characterized by universal suffrage, the secret ballot and electoral competition. The significance of such systems is, however, more difficult to determine. As Harrop and Miller (1987) explained, there are two contrasting views of the function of competitive elections.

The conventional view is that elections are a mechanism through which politicians can be called to account and forced to introduce policies that somehow reflect public opinion. This emphasizes the *bottom-up* functions of elections: political recruitment, representation, making government, influencing policy and so on. On the other hand, a radical view of elections, developed by theorists such as Ginsberg (1982), portrays them as a means through which governments and political elites can exercise control over their populations, making them more quiescent, malleable, and, ultimately, governable. This view emphasizes *top-down* functions: building legitimacy, shaping public opinion and strengthening elites. In reality, however, elections have no single character; they are neither simply mechanisms of public accountability nor a means of ensuring political control. Like all channels of political communication, elections are a 'two-way street' that provides the government and the people, the elite and the masses, with the opportunity to influence one another. The central functions of elections include the following:

• **Recruiting politicians**: In democratic states, elections are the principal source of political recruitment, taking account also of the processes through which parties nominate candidates. Politicians thus tend to possess talents and skills that are related to electioneering, such as charisma (see p. 221), oratorical skills and good looks, not necessarily those that suit them to carrying out constituency duties, serving on committees, running government departments and so on. Elections are typically not used to fill posts that require specialist knowledge or experience, such as those in the civil service or judiciary.

• **Making governments**: Elections make governments directly only in states such as the USA, France and Venezuela in which the political executive is directly elected. In the more common parliamentary systems, elections influence the formation of governments, most strongly when the electoral system tends to give a single party a clear parliamentary majority. The use of proportional representation (see p. 256) may mean that governments are formed through post-election deals, and that governments can be made and unmade without the need for an election.

• **Providing representation**: When they are fair and competitive, elections are a means through which demands are channelled from the public to the government. Short of the use of initiatives and the recall, however, the electorate has no effective means of ensuring that mandates are carried out, apart from its capacity to inflict punishment at the next election. Moreover, elected governments nowhere constitute a microcosm of the larger society.

• **Influencing policy**: Elections certainly deter governments from pursuing radical and deeply unpopular policies, but only in exceptional cases, when a single issue dominates the election campaign, can they be said to influence policy directly. It can also be argued that the range of policy options outlined in elections is typically so narrow that the result can be of only marginal policy significance. Others suggest that government policy is in any case shaped more by practical dictates such as the state of the economy than it is by electoral considerations.

• **Educating voters**: The process of campaigning provides the electorate with an abundance of information, about parties, candidates, policies, the current government's record, the political system, and so on. However, this leads to education only if the information that is provided, and the way it is provided, engages public interest and stimulates debate, as opposed to apathy and alienation. As candidates and parties seek to persuade rather than to educate, they also have a strong incentive to provide incomplete and distorted information.

Proportional representation

The principle of proportional representation is the principle that parties should be represented in an assembly or parliament in direct proportion to their overall electoral strength, their percentage of seats equalling their percentage of votes. The term is generally used to refer not to a single method of election but to a variety of electoral mechanisms, those able to secure proportional outcomes, or at least a high and reliable degree of proportionality. The best known PR systems are the party-list system, the single-transferable-vote system and the additional member system, although the dividing line between proportional and majoritarian systems is sometimes unclear. Commonly used in continental Europe, PR systems are concerned more with the representation of parties than of individual candidates, and may be particularly suitable for divided or plural societies.

- **Building legitimacy:** One reason why even authoritarian regimes bother to hold elections, even if they are noncompetitive, is that elections help to foster legitimacy (see p. 219) by providing justification for a system of rule. This happens because the ritual involved in campaigning somehow confers on an election a ceremonial status and importance. Most importantly, by encouraging citizens to participate in politics, even in the limited form of voting, elections mobilize active consent.

- **Strengthening elites:** Elections can also be a vehicle through which elites can manipulate and control the masses. This possibility encouraged Proudhon (see p. 166) to warn that 'universal suffrage is counter-revolution'. Political discontent and opposition can be neutralized by elections that channel them in a constitutional direction, and allow governments to come and go while the regime itself survives. Elections are particularly effective in this respect because, at the same time, they give citizens the impression that they are exercising power over the government.

Electoral systems: debates and controversies

An electoral system is a set of rules that governs the conduct of elections. Not only do these rules vary across the world, but they are also, in many countries, the subject of fierce political debate and argument. These rules vary in a number of ways:

- Voters may be asked to choose between candidates or between parties.

- Voters may either select a single candidate, or vote preferentially, ranking the candidates they wish to support in order.

- The electorate may or may not be grouped into electoral units or constituencies.

- Constituencies may return a single member or a number of members.

- The level of support needed to elect a candidate varies from a plurality (the largest single number of votes or a 'relative' majority) to an overall or 'absolute' majority or a quota of some kind.

For general purposes, however, the systems available can be divided into two broad categories on the basis of how they convert votes into seats. On the one hand, there are *majoritarian* systems, in which larger parties typically win a higher proportion of seats than the proportion of votes they gain in the election. This increases the chances of a single party gaining a parliamentary majority and being able to govern on its own. In the UK, for example, single-party government is very firmly established despite the fact that no party has achieved an electoral majority since 1935. On the other hand, there are *proportional* systems, which guarantee an equal, or at least more equal, relationship between the seats won by a party and the votes gained in the election. In a pure system of proportional representation (PR), a party that gains 45 per cent of the votes would win exactly 45 per cent of the seats. PR systems therefore make single-party majority rule less likely, and are commonly associated with multi-party systems and coalition government. The electoral systems described in the following Focus boxes range from the most majoritarian type of system to the purest type of proportional system.

Although in some countries the electoral system provokes little debate or interest, in others it is an issue of pressing political and constitutional significance. France, for instance, has changed its electoral system so many times that any statement about it runs the risk of being out of date. The second ballot was abandoned for parliamentary elections in 1985, when France switched to a regional-list system, but it was reintroduced for the 1993 election. In the UK, although the majoritarian 'first past the post' system continues to be used for general elections, a number of more proportional

Focus on . . .

Electoral systems: single-member plurality system (SMP) ('first past the post')

Used: The UK (House of Commons), the USA, Canada and India, for example.
Type: Majoritarian.

Features:

- The country is divided into single-member constituencies, usually of equal size.
- Voters select a single candidate, usually marking his or her name with a cross on the ballot paper.
- The winning candidate needs only to achieve a plurality of votes (the 'first past the post' rule).

Advantages:

- The system establishes a clear link between representatives and constituents, ensuring that constituency duties are carried out.
- It offers the electorate a clear choice of potential parties of government.
- It allows governments to be formed that have a clear mandate from the electorate, albeit often on the basis of plurality support amongst the electorate.
- It keeps extremism at bay by making it more difficult for small radical parties to gain seats and credibility.
- It makes for strong and effective government in that a single party usually has majority control of the assembly.
- It produces stable government in that single-party governments rarely collapse as a result of disunity and internal friction.

Disadvantages:

- The system 'wastes' many (perhaps most) votes, those cast for losing candidates and those cast for winning ones over the plurality mark.
- It distorts electoral preferences by 'under-representing' small parties and ones with geographically evenly distributed support (the 'third-party effect').
- It offers only limited choice because of its duopolistic (two-major-parties) tendencies.
- It undermines the legitimacy of government in that governments often enjoy only minority support, producing a system of plurality rule.
- It creates instability because a change in government can lead to a radical shift of policies and direction.
- It leads to unaccountable government in that the legislature is usually subordinate to the executive, because the majority of its members are supporters of the governing party.
- It discourages the selection of a socially broad spread of candidates in favour of those who are attractive to a large body of voters.

systems have since 1999 been introduced for elections to the devolved bodies in Scotland, Wales and Northern Ireland, the Greater London Assembly and the European Parliament. The confusing thing about the electoral reform debate is that the shifts that have occurred reflect no consistent pattern. In 1994, while New Zealand adopted proportional representation in place of the FPTP system, Italy moved in the opposite direction, replacing the party list with the less proportional additional member system, before, in 2005, returning to the list system.

Electoral systems attract attention in part because they have a crucial impact on party performance, and particularly on their prospects of winning (or at least sharing) power. It would be foolish, then, to deny that attitudes towards the electoral system are shaped largely by party advantage. President Mitterrand's twists and turns in France in the 1980s and 1990s were dictated mainly by his desire to strengthen Socialist representation in the National Assembly. Similarly, the UK Labour Party's interest in electoral reform since the 1980s has waxed and waned according to whether it appeared that the party could win under FPTP rules. The party's conversion to PR for devolved bodies and its commitment in 1997 to holding a referendum on electoral reform for the House of Commons were, in part, a consequence of spending 18 years in opposition. It is notable that Labour's landslide victories in 1997 and 2001 coincided with declining interest in the party in changing Westminster elections. However, other less

Focus on . . .

Electoral systems: second ballot system

Used: Traditionally in France (although changes in France's electoral system have been common). **Type**: Majoritarian.

Features:
- There are single-candidate constituencies and single-choice voting, as in the first-past-the-post (FPTP) system.
- To win on the first ballot, a candidate needs an overall majority of the votes cast.
- If no candidate gains a first-ballot majority, a second, run-off ballot is held between the leading two candidates.

Advantages:
- The system broadens electoral choice: voters can vote with their hearts for their preferred candidate in the first ballot, and with their heads for the least-bad candidate in the second.
- As candidates can win only with majority support, they are encouraged to make their appeal as broad as possible.
- Strong and stable government is possible, as with FPTP systems.

Disadvantages:
- As the system is little more proportional than the FPTP system, it distorts preferences and is unfair to 'third' parties.
- Run-off candidates are encouraged to abandon their principles in search of short-term popularity or as a result of deals with defeated candidates.
- The holding of a second ballot may strain the electorate's patience and interest in politics.

Focus on . . .

Electoral systems: alternative vote system (AV); supplementary vote (SV)

Used: Australia (House of Representatives (AV)), and the UK (London mayor (SV)).
Type: Majoritarian.

Features:
- There are single-member constituencies.
- There is preferential voting. In AV voters rank the candidates in order of preference: 1 for their first preference, 2 for their second preference, and so on. In SV there is only a single 'supplementary' vote.
- Winning candidates must gain 50 per cent of all the votes cast.
- Votes are counted according to the first preferences. If no candidate reaches 50 per cent, the bottom candidate is eliminated and his or her votes are redistributed according to the second (or subsequent) preferences. This continues until one candidate has a majority. In SV all candidates drop out except the top two.

Advantages:
- Fewer votes are 'wasted' than in the FPTP system.
- Unlike the second-ballot system, the outcome cannot be influenced by deals made between candidates.
- Although winning candidates must secure at least 50 per cent support, single-party majority government is not ruled out.

Disadvantages:
- The system is not much more proportional than the FPTP system, and so is still biased in favour of large parties.
- The outcome may be determined by the preferences of those who support small, possibly extremist, parties.
- Winning candidates may enjoy little first-preference support, and have only the virtue of being the least unpopular candidate available.

cynical and more substantial considerations need to be taken into account. The problem, though, is that there is no such thing as a 'best electoral system'.

The electoral reform debate is, at heart, a debate about the desirable nature of government and the principles that underpin 'good' government. Is representative government, for instance, more important than effective government? Is a bias in favour of compromise and consensus preferable to one that favours conviction and principle? These are normative questions that do not permit objective answers. Moreover, in view of the complex role they play, elections can be judged according to a diverse range of criteria, which not uncommonly contradict one another. Electoral systems therefore merit only a qualified endorsement, reflecting a balance of advantages over disadvantages and their strength relative to other systems. These criteria fall into two general categories: those related to the quality of representation, and those linked to the effectiveness of government.

Majoritarian systems are usually thought to be at their weakest when they are evaluated in terms of their representative functions. To a greater or lesser extent, each majoritarian system distorts popular preferences in the sense that party representation is not commensurate with electoral strength. This is most glaringly apparent in their 'unfairness' to small parties and parties with evenly distributed geographical support, and their 'over-fairness' in relation to large parties and ones with geographically concentrated support. For example, in 2001 in the UK, the Labour Party gained 63 per cent of the parliamentary seats with 41 per cent of the vote, the Conservative Party won 25 per cent of the seats with 31 per cent of the vote, and the Liberal Democrats gained merely 8 per cent representation with 18 per cent of the vote. Such biases are impossible to justify in representative terms, especially since the unfortunate 'third' parties are often centrist parties, and not the extremist parties of popular image.

Two-party systems and single-party government are thus 'manufactured' by the majoritarian bias of the electoral system, and do not reflect the distribution of popular preferences. Moreover, the fact that parties can come to power with barely two-fifths of the popular vote (in 2005 in the UK, for example, the Labour Party gained a House of Commons majority with 35.3 per cent of the vote) strains the legitimacy of the entire political system, and creates circumstances in which radical, ideologically driven parties can remain in power for prolonged periods under little pressure to broaden their appeal. The Conservatives in the UK were thus able to implement a programme of market-orientated reforms in the 1980s and 1990s while never gaining more than 43 per cent of support in elections. When the majority of voters oppose the party in power, it is difficult to claim that that party has a popular mandate for anything.

Looked at in this light, proportional electoral systems seem to be manifestly more representative. Nevertheless, it may be naive simply to equate electoral fairness with proportionality. For instance, much of the criticism of PR systems stems from the fact that they make coalition government (see p. 288) much more likely. Although it can be argued that, unlike single-party governments, coalitions enjoy the support of at least 50 per cent of the electors, their policies are typically thrashed out in post-election deals, and thus are not endorsed by *any* set of electors. An additional danger is that parties within a coalition government may not exert influence in line with their electoral strength. The classic example of this is when small centre parties (such as the Free Democrats in Germany) can dictate to larger parties (for example, the CDU or the SPD in Germany) by threatening to switch their support to another party. Then, in effect, 'the tail wags the dog'.

The defence of majoritarian systems is more commonly based on government functions, and specifically on the capacity of such systems to deliver stable and effective rule. In other words, a lack of proportionality may simply be the price that is paid for strong government. In these systems, the bias in favour of single-party rule means that the electorate can usually choose between two parties, each of which has the capacity to deliver on its election promises by translating its manifesto commitments into a programme of government. Supported by a cohesive majority in the assembly, such governments are usually able to survive for a full term in office. In contrast, coalition governments are weak and unstable, in the sense that they are endlessly engaged in a process of reconciling opposing views, and are always liable to collapse as a result of internal splits and divisions. The classic example here is post-1945 Italy, which up to 2001 had had no fewer than 59 governments.

Supporters of PR argue, on the other hand, that having a strong government, in the sense of a government that is able to push through policies, is by no means an unqualified virtue, tending as it does to restrict scrutiny and parliamentary account-ability. Instead, they suggest that 'strong' government should be understood in terms of popular support and the willingness of citizens to obey and respect the government. Broadly based coalitions may possess these qualities in greater abundance than do single-party governments. By the same token, 'stable' government could mean a consistent development of government policies over a number of govern-ments, rather than a government with the ability to survive for a single electoral term. This is more likely to be achieved by coalition governments (in which one or

Focus on . . .

Electoral systems: additional member system (AMS)

Used: Germany, Italy, Russia (State Duma), New Zealand, and the UK (Scottish Parliament and Welsh Assembly). **Type**: Proportional.

Features:

- A proportion of seats (50 per cent in Germany, but more in Italy, Scotland and Wales, for instance) are filled by the FPTP system using single-member constituencies.
- The remaining seats are filled using a party list (as explained in the party-list system box).
- Electors cast two votes: one for a candidate in the constituency election, and the other for a party.

Advantages:

- The hybrid nature of this system balances the need for constituency representation against the need for electoral fairness. The party-list process ensures that the whole assembly is proportionally representative.
- Although the system is broadly proportional in terms of its outcome, it keeps alive the possibility of single-party government.
- It allows electors to choose a constituency representative from one party and yet support another party to form a government.
- It takes account of the fact that representing constituents and holding ministerial office are very different jobs that require very different talents and experience.

Disadvantages:

- The retention of single-member constituencies prevents the achievement of high levels of proportionality.
- The system creates two classes of representative, one burdened by insecurity and constituency duties, the other having higher status and the prospect of holding ministerial office.
- Constituency representation suffers because of the size of constituencies (generally twice as large as in FPTP systems).
- Parties become more centralized and powerful under this system, as they decide not only who has the security of being on the list and who has to fight constituencies, but also where on the list candidates are placed.

more parties may remain in power over a number of governments, albeit reshuffled) than by single-party governments, in which more sweeping changes in personnel and priorities are unavoidable when power changes hands.

The electoral reform debate, however, constantly risks overestimating the import-ance of electoral systems. In practice, elections are only one amongst a variety of factors that shape the political process, and may not be the most crucial. Indeed, the impact of particular electoral systems is conditioned largely by other circumstances, namely the political culture, the nature of the party system, and the economic and social context within which politics is conducted. Generalizations about the nature of coalition government are always highly suspect, for instance. Whereas coalitions in

Focus on . . .

Electoral systems: single-transferable-vote system (STV)

Used: The Republic of Ireland and the UK (Northern Ireland Assembly). **Type**: Proportional.

Features:
- There are multimember constituencies, each of which returns up to five members.
- Parties may put forward as many candidates as there are seats to fill.
- Electors vote preferentially, as in the alternative vote system.
- Candidates are elected if they achieve a quota. This is the minimum number of votes needed to elect the stipulated number of candidates, calculated according to the Droop formula:

$$\text{quota} = \frac{\text{total number of votes cast}}{(\text{number of seats to be filled} + 1)} + 1$$

For example, if 100 000 votes are cast in a constituency that elects four members, the quota is $100\,000/(4 + 1) + 1 = 20\,001$.
- The votes are counted according to first preferences. If not all the seats are filled, the bottom candidate is eliminated. His or her votes are redistributed according to second preferences, and so on, until all the seats have been filled.

Advantages:
- The system is capable of achieving highly proportional outcomes.
- Competition amongst candidates from the same party means that they can be judged on their records and on where they stand on issues that cut across party lines.
- The availability of several members means that constituents can choose who to take their grievances to.

Disadvantages:
- The degree of proportionality achieved varies, largely on the basis of the party system.
- Strong and stable single-party government is unlikely.
- Intra-party competition may be divisive, and may allow members to evade their constituency responsibilities.

Italy have typically been weak and short-lived, in Germany they have usually produced stable and effective government. Similarly, although majoritarian systems can produce significant shifts in policy as one government follows another, board policy consensuses are also not uncommon. In the 1950s and 1960s, despite an alternation in power between the Conservative and the Labour parties, UK government policy displayed a remarkable consistency of policy direction, rooted in a cross-party commitment to Keynesian social democracy. Furthermore, it is far from clear what damage electoral systems can cause. Despite Italy's famed political instability, often blamed on its now-abandoned party-list electoral system, in the post-Second-World-War period the north of the country at least experienced steady economic growth, making Italy, by the 1990s, the third most prosperous state in the EU.

Focus on . . .

Electoral systems: party-list system

Used: Israel, and in countries throughout Europe, including Belgium, Luxembourg and Switzerland, and the European Parliament. **Type**: Proportional.

Features:
- Either the entire country is treated as a single constituency, or, in the case of regional party lists, there are a number of large multimember constituencies.
- Parties compile lists of candidates to place before the electorate, in descending order of preference.
- Electors vote for parties, not for candidates.
- Parties are allocated seats in direct proportion to the votes they gain in the election. They fill these seats from their party list.
- A 'threshold' may be imposed (5 per cent in Germany) to exclude small, possibly extremist, parties from representation.

Advantages:
- This is the only potentially pure system of proportional representation, and is therefore fair to all parties.
- The system promotes unity by encouraging electors to identify with their nation or region rather than with a constituency.
- The system makes it easier for women and minority candidates to be elected, provided, of course, they feature on the party list.
- The representation of a large number of small parties ensures that there is an emphasis upon negotiation, bargaining and consensus.

Disadvantages:
- The existence of many small parties can lead to weak and unstable government.
- The link between representatives and constituencies is entirely broken.
- Unpopular candidates who are well placed on a party list cannot be removed from office.
- Parties become heavily centralized, because leaders draw up party lists, and junior members have an incentive to be loyal in the hope of moving up the list.

Public interest

The public interest consists of the general or collective interests of a community: that is, that which is good for society as a whole. Two contrasting notions of the public interest can be identified. *Strong* versions distinguish clearly between public and private interests, between the interests of the public as a collective body and the selfish or personal interests of each individual. In the view of Rousseau and many socialists the interests of the public are 'higher' than, or morally superior to, those of the individual. *Weak* versions recognize only private interests, and therefore see the public interest as nothing more than a collection of private interests, those that all individuals recognize as good for themselves. Liberal individualists often dismissed the very idea of a 'public' interest as absurd.

What do elections mean?

The importance of elections cannot be doubted. At the very least, they provide the public with its clearest formal opportunity to influence the political process, and also help, directly or indirectly, to determine who will hold government power. From this perspective, elections are about results – in other words, who wins and who loses. This view is encouraged by media coverage, which, with the aid of opinion polls, increasingly turns elections into horseraces. Nevertheless, politicians are not backward in claiming that elections have a broader and more profound meaning. Elections are, in this sense, seen as nothing less than a visible manifestation of the public interest; in short, 'the public has spoken'. Political commentators also express their opinions, proclaiming, for instance, that elections reflect a 'shift in the popular mood'. The problem, however, is that all such claims and interpretations have a strongly arbitrary character; any attempt to invest an election with 'meaning' is fraught with dangers. The people may have spoken, but it is frustratingly difficult to know what they have said.

Many of these problems stem from the difficult notion of the 'public interest'. If such a thing as a 'public' interest exists, it surely reflects the common or collective interests of *all* citizens. This is precisely what Rousseau (see p. 79) implied in the idea of the 'general will', which he understood to mean the will of all citizens, provided each of them acts selflessly. The difficulty with this view is obvious. Quite simply, individuals do not in practice act selflessly in accordance with a general or collective will; there is no such thing as an indivisible public interest. All generalizations about 'the public' or 'the electorate' must therefore be treated with grave suspicion. There is no electorate as such, only a collection of electors who each possess particular interests, sympathies, allegiances and so on. At best, election results reflect the preferences of a majority, or perhaps a plurality, of voters. However, even then there are perhaps insuperable problems in deciding what these votes 'mean'.

The difficulty in interpreting election results lies in the perhaps impossible task of knowing why voters vote as they do. As is made clear in the next section, generations of political scientists have grappled with the question of electoral behaviour but have failed to develop a universally accepted theory of voting. Voting, on the surface a very simple act, is shaped by a complex of factors, conscious and unconscious, rational and irrational, selfish and selfless. All theories are therefore partial and must be qualified by a range of other considerations. This can be seen in relation to the so-called economic theory of democracy, advanced by Anthony Downs (1957). This theory suggests that the act of voting reflects an expression of self-interest on the part of voters, who select parties in much the same way as consumers select goods or services for purchase. On this basis, the winning party in an election can reasonably claim that its policies most closely correspond to the interests of the largest group of voters.

On the other hand, it can be argued that, rather than 'buying' policies, voters are typically poorly informed about political issues and are influenced by a range of 'irrational' factors such as habit, social conditioning, the image of the parties, and the personalities of their leaders. Moreover, the ability of parties to attract votes may have less to do with the 'goods' they put up for purchase than with the way those goods are 'sold' through advertising, political campaigning, propaganda and so on. To the extent that this is true, election results may reflect not so much the interests of the mass of voters as the resources and finances available to the competing parties.

A further, and some would argue more intractable, problem is that no elective mechanism may be able reliably to give expression to the multifarious preferences of voters. This is a problem that the US economist Kenneth Arrow described in terms of his 'impossibility theorem'. In *Social Choice and Individual Values* (1951) Arrow drew attention to the problem of 'transitivity' that occurs when voters are allowed to express a range of preferences for candidates or policy options rather than merely cast a single vote. The drawback of casting but a single vote is not only that it is a crude all-or-nothing device, but also that no single candidate or option may gain majority support. For instance, candidate *A* may gain 40 per cent of the vote, candidate *B* 34 per cent, and candidate *C* 26 per cent. The situation could nevertheless become more confused if second preferences were taken into account.

Let us assume, for the sake of argument, that the second preferences of all candidate *A*'s supporters go to candidate *C*, the second preferences of candidate *B* favour candidate *A*, and the second preferences of candidate *C* go to candidate *B*. This creates a situation in which each candidate can claim to be preferred by a majority of voters. The first and second preferences for candidate *A* add up to 74 per cent (40 per cent plus *B*'s 34 per cent). Candidate *B* can claim 60 per cent support (34 per cent plus *C*'s 26 per cent), and candidate *C* can claim 66 per cent support (26 per cent plus *A*'s 40 per cent). This problem of 'cyclical majorities' draws attention to the fact that it may not be possible to establish a reliable link between individual preferences and collective choices. In other words, election results cannot speak for themselves, and politicians and political commentators who claim to find meaning in them are, to some extent, acting arbitrarily. Nevertheless, the latitude that this allows politicians is not unlimited, because they know that they will be called to account at the next election. In this light, perhaps the most significant function of elections is to set limits to arbitrary government by ensuring that politicians who claim to speak *for* the public must ultimately be judged *by* the public.

Voting behaviour

The growth of academic interest in voting behaviour coincided with the rise of behavioural political science. As the most widespread and quantifiable form of political behaviour, voting quickly became the focus for new techniques of sample surveying and statistical analysis. *The American Voter* (Campbell *et al.*, 1960), the product of painstaking research by the University of Michigan, became the leading work in the field and stimulated a wealth of similar studies, such as Butler and Stokes' *Political Change in Britain* (1969). At the high point of the behavioural revolution it was thought that voting held the key to disclosing all the mysteries of the political system, perhaps allowing for laws of mass political psychology to be developed. Even though these lofty hopes have not been fulfilled, psephology (the scientific study of voting behaviour) still commands a central position in political analysis. This is because voting provides one of the richest sources of information about the interaction between individuals, society and politics. By investigating the mysteries of voting behaviour, we are thus able to learn important lessons about the nature of the political system, and gain insight into the process of social and political change.

Voting behaviour is clearly shaped by short-term and long-term influences. Short-term influences are specific to a particular election and do not allow conclusions to be drawn about voting patterns in general. The chief short-term influence

Partisan dealignment

Partisan dealignment is a decline in the extent to which people align themselves with a party by identifying with it. As party loyalties weaken, electoral behaviour is likely to become more volatile, leading to greater uncertainty and perhaps the rise of new parties or the decline of old ones. What is seen as the 'normal' support of parties falls, and a growing number of electors become 'floating' or 'swing' voters. The principal reasons for partisan dealignment are the expansion of education, an increase in geographical and social mobility, and growing reliance on television as a source of political information. Some argue that partisan dealignment reflects growing disenchantment with conventional politics, and the failure of the party system to respond to the needs of a postindustrial society.

is the state of the economy, which reflects the fact that there is usually a link between a government's popularity and economic variables such as unemployment, inflation and disposable income. Optimism about one's own material circumstances (the so-called 'feel-good' factor) appears to be particularly crucial here. Indeed, it is often alleged that governments attempt to create pre-election booms in the hope of improving their chances of gaining reelection. The chances that political and business cycles can be brought into conjunction are clearly strengthened by flexible-term elections that allow the government to choose when to 'go to the country'.

Another short-term influence on voting is the personality and public standing of party leaders. This is particularly important, because media exposure portrays leaders as the brand image of their party. This means that a party may try to rekindle popular support by replacing a leader who is perceived to be an electoral liability, as the Conservatives in the UK did with Margaret Thatcher in 1990, and the Australian Labor Party did with Bob Hawke in 1991. Another factor is the style and effectiveness of the parties' electoral campaigning. The length of the campaign can vary from about three weeks for flexible-term elections to up to two years in the case of fixed-term elections, such as those for the US president. Opinion polls are usually thought to be significant in this respect, either giving a candidate's or party's campaign momentum, or instilling disillusionment or even complacency amongst voters.

A final short-term influence, the mass media (see p. 232), may also be of long-term significance if biased or partisan coverage reflects structural, and therefore continuing, factors such as press ownership. However, the pattern of media coverage may change from election to election. For instance, under Tony Blair's leadership the UK Labour Party made concerted attempts to court the Murdoch press in particular, helping to explain the party's return to power in 1997. All such considerations, nevertheless, operate within a context of psychological, sociological, economic and ideological influences upon voting. These are best examined in relation to rival models of voting. The most significant of these are the following:

- the party-identification model
- the sociological model
- the rational-choice model
- the dominant-ideology model.

Theories of voting

Party-identification model

The earliest theory of voting behaviour, the party-identification model, is based on the sense of psychological attachment that people have to parties. Electors are seen as people who *identify* with a party, in the sense of being long-term supporters who regard the party as 'their' party. Voting is therefore a manifestation of partisanship, not a product of calculation influenced by factors such as policies, personalities, campaigning and media coverage. This model places heavy stress on early political socialization, seeing the family as the principal means through which political loyalties are forged. These are then, in most cases, reinforced by group membership and later social experiences.

In this model, attitudes towards policies and leaders, as well as perceptions about group and personal interests, tend to be developed on the basis of party identification. Events are thus interpreted to fit with pre-existing loyalties and attachments. This partisan alignment tends to create stability and continuity, especially in terms of habitual patterns of voting behaviour, often sustained over a lifetime. From this point of view it should be possible to calculate the 'normal' vote of a party by reference to partisanship levels. Deviations from this 'normal' level presumably reflect the impact of short-term factors. One of the weaknesses of this model is the growing evidence from a number of countries of partisan dealignment. This indicates a general fall in party identification and a decline in habitual voting patterns. In the USA, partisan dealignment is reflected in a decline in the number of registered Democrats and Republicans and a rise in the number of Independents (up from 6 per cent in 1952 to 12 per cent in 1992). In the UK, it is demonstrated by a decline in the strength of allegiance to the Conservative Party and the Labour Party, 'very strong' identification with either party having fallen from 43 per cent in 1966 to 15 per cent in 2005.

Sociological model

The sociological model links voting behaviour to group membership, suggesting that electors tend to adopt a voting pattern that reflects the economic and social position of the group to which they belong. Rather than developing a psychological attachment to a party on the basis of family influence, this model highlights the importance of a social alignment, reflecting the various divisions and tensions within society. The most significant of these divisions are class, gender, ethnicity, religion and region. Although the impact of socialization is not irrelevant to this model, social-base explanations allow for rationality insofar as group interests may help to shape party allegiances. This has perhaps been clearest in relation to social class.

Not uncommonly, party systems have been seen to reflect the class system, with the middle classes providing the electoral base for right-wing parties, and the working classes providing the electoral base for left-wing parties. The Labour–Conservative two-party system in the UK was traditionally understood in precisely this light. Peter Pulzer (1967:98) was able to declare, famously, 'class is the basis of British party politics; all else is embellishment and detail'. The sociological model, however, has been attacked on the grounds that, in focusing on social groups, it ignores the individual and the role of personal self-interest. Moreover, there is growing empirical evidence that the link between sociological factors and party support has weakened in modern societies. In particular, attention has been paid to the phenomenon of class dealignment. Evidence of class dealignment can be found in most western societies. For example, absolute class voting (the proportion of voters who support their 'natural' class party) fell in the UK from 66 per cent in 1966 to 47 per cent in 1983. In 1997 the Labour Party, for the first time, received more votes from non-manual workers than from manual workers.

Rational-choice model

Rational-choice models of voting shift attention onto the individual and away from socialization and the behaviour of social groups. In this view, voting is seen as a rational act, in the sense that individual electors are believed to decide their party preference on the basis of personal self-interest. Rather than being habitual, a manifestation of broader attachments and allegiances, voting is seen as essentially instrumental: that is, as a means to an end. Rational-choice models differ in that some, like V. O. Key (1966), see voting as a retrospective comment on the party in

Concept

Class dealignment

Class dealignment is the weakening of the relationship between social class and party support. Social class (see p. 197) may nevertheless remain a significant (perhaps the most significant) factor influencing electoral choice. The impact of dealignment has been to undermine traditional class-based parties, notably working class parties of the left, often bringing about a realignment of the party system. Explanations of class dealignment usually focus on changes in the social structure that have weakened the solidaristic character of class identity. These include the embourgeoisement of the working class brought about by growing affluence, the shift from manufacturing to service industries, and the growing importance of sectoral cleavages based on the public-sector/private-sector divide.

power and how its performance has influenced citizen's choice, while others, such as Himmelveit, Humphreys and Jaeger (1985), portray voters as active in the sense that they behave like consumers expressing a choice amongst the available policy options.

The latter view stresses the importance of what is called '**issue voting**', and suggests that parties can significantly influence their electoral performance by revising and reshaping their policies. It is generally accepted that this has been one of the consequences of partisan and class dealignment. This hasalso been encouraged by the pluralism and individualism that postmodernism (see p. 67) has fostered. The weakness of rational-choice theories is that they abstract the individual voter from his or her social and cultural context. In other words, to some extent, the ability to evaluate issues and calculate self-interest (the essence of instrumental voting) is structured by broader party attachments and group loyalties.

Dominant-ideology model

Radical theories of voting tend to highlight the degree to which individual choices are shaped by a process of ideological manipulation and control. In some respects, such theories resemble the sociological model in that voting is seen to reflect a person's position in a social hierarchy. Where these theories differ from the sociological model, however, is in emphasizing that how groups and individuals interpret their position depends on how it has been presented to them through education, by the government, and, above all, by the mass media. The influence of the media on political debate and party competition is examined in more detail in Chapter 11.

In contrast to the earlier view that the mass media merely reinforce pre-existing preferences, this suggests that the media are able to distort the flow of political communications, both by setting the agenda for debate and by structuring preferences and sympathies. The consequence of this is that, if voters' attitudes conform to the tenets of a dominant ideology, parties will not be able to afford to develop policies that fall outside that ideology. In this way, far from challenging the existing distribution of power and resources in society, the electoral process tends to uphold it. The weakness of the dominant-ideology model is that, by overstating the process of social conditioning, it takes individual calculation and personal autonomy out of the picture altogether.

▉ Summary

◆ Representation is a relationship in which an individual or group stands for, or acts on behalf of, a larger body of people. This may be achieved through the exercise of wisdom by an educated elite, through guidance or instructions given to a delegate, through the winning of a popular mandate, or through representatives being drawn from the groups they represent.

◆ In modern politics, representation is invariably linked with elections. Elections may not be a sufficient condition for political representation, but are certainly a necessary condition. For elections to serve representative purposes, however, they must be competitive, free and fair, and conducted on the basis of universal adult suffrage.

◆ Elections have a variety of functions. On the one hand, they have 'bottom-up' functions, such as political recruitment, representation, making government and

Issue voting: Voting behaviour that is shaped by party policies and (usually) a calculation of personal self-interest.

influencing policy. On the other hand, radical theorists emphasize their 'top-down' functions, which include that they build legitimacy, shape public opinion, and help to strengthen elites.

◆ Electoral systems are often classified as either majoritarian systems or proportional systems. In majoritarian systems, large parties typically win a higher proportion of seats than votes, thereby increasing the chances of single-party government. In proportional systems, there is an equal, or at least more equal, relationship between the percentages of seats and votes won, increasing the likelihood of coalition government.

◆ Majoritarian systems are usually defended on the grounds that they offer the electorate a clear choice of potential governments, invest winning parties with a policy mandate, and help to promote strong and stable government. In contrast, proportional systems are defended on the grounds that they usually give government a broader electoral base, promote consensus and cooperation amongst a number of parties, and establish a healthy balance between the executive and the assembly.

◆ The meaning of elections is closely linked to the factors that shape voting behaviour. Amongst the various theories of voting are models that highlight the importance of party identification and habitual attachments, ones that emphasize the importance of group membership and social alignment, ones that are based on rational choice and calculations of self-interest, and ones that suggest that individual choices are shaped by ideological manipulation and control.

Questions for discussion

▶ Is representation merely a substitute for democracy?

▶ What conditions best promote representative government?

▶ Are elections more significant in calling politicians to account, or in ensuring the survival of a regime?

▶ Is there inevitably a tradeoff between electoral fairness and strong and stable government?

▶ How successful are elections in defining the public interest?

▶ To what extent is voting behaviour a rational and issue-based activity?

Further reading

Birch, A. H., *The Concepts and Theories of Democracy*, 2nd edn (London: Routledge, 2000). A clear and thorough discussion of the concept of representation and the theory of representative democracy.

Farrell, D. M., *Electoral Systems: A Comparative Introduction* (Basingstoke: Palgrave, 2001). A clear introduction to the six principal types of election system currently used.

Gallagher, M. and P. Mitchell (eds), *The Politics of Electoral Systems* (Oxford: Oxford University Press, 2005). An analysis of the operation of electoral systems in 22 states, which highlights the complex relationship between electoral systems and the larger political process.

Harrop, M. and W. L. Miller, *Elections and Voters: A Comparative Introduction* (Basingstoke: Palgrave Macmillan, 1987). An accessible and very informative analysis of the role of elections and debates about voting behaviour.

Katz, R., *Democracy and Elections* (Oxford and New York: Oxford University Press, 1997). A useful review of the issues linked to democracy and elections.

LeDuc, L., R. Niemi and P. Norris (eds), *Comparing Democracies: Elections and Voting in Global Perspective* (London: Sage, 1996). A good examination of the nature and health of electoral democracy and the significance of electoral systems.

Parties and Party Systems

> 'In politics, shared hatreds are almost always the basis of friendships.'
>
> ALEXIS DE TOCQUEVILLE, *Democracy in America* (1835)

So fundamental are political parties to the operation of modern politics that their role and significance are often taken for granted. It is forgotten, for instance, that parties are a relatively recent invention. As political machines organized to win elections and wield government power, parties came into existence only in the early nineteenth century. Now, however, they are virtually ubiquitous. The only parts of the world in which they do not exist are those where they are suppressed by dictatorship or military rule. Quite simply, the political party is the major organizing principle of modern politics. Whether they are the great tools of democracy or sources of tyranny and repression, political parties are the vital link between the state and civil society, between the institutions of government and the groups and interests that operate within society. Nevertheless, parties and party systems have increasingly come under attack. They have been blamed for failing to articulate the new and more diverse aspirations that have emerged in modern societies, and for failing to solve, or perhaps even address, many of their most serious problems.

The central issues examined in this chapter are as following:

Contents

Key issues

▶ What is a political party? How can parties be classified?

▶ What are the major functions of political parties?

▶ How are parties organized, and where is power located within them?

▶ What kinds of party system are there?

▶ How does the party system shape the broader political process?

▶ Are parties in decline, and is this decline terminal?

Political party

A political party is a group of people that is organized for the purpose of winning government power, by electoral or other means. Parties are often confused with interest groups (see p. 296) or social movements (see p. 308).

Four characteristics usually distinguish parties from other groups:

- Parties aim to exercise government power by winning political office (small parties may nevertheless use elections more to gain a platform than to win power).
- Parties are organized bodies with a formal 'card carrying' membership. This distinguishes them from broader and more diffuse social movements.
- Parties typically adopt a broad issue focus, addressing each of the major areas of government policy (small parties, however, may have a single-issue focus, thus resembling interest groups).
- To varying degrees, parties are united by shared political preferences and a general ideological identity.

Party politics

Political parties are found in the vast majority of countries and in most political systems. Parties may be authoritarian or democratic; they may seek power through elections or through revolution; and they may espouse ideologies of the left, right or centre, or, indeed, disavow political ideas altogether. However, parties of some kind exist from Brazil to Burundi and from Norway to New Zealand. The development of political parties and the acquisition of a party system came to be recognized as a mark of political modernization. By the late 1950s some 80 per cent of the world's states were ruled by political parties. During the 1960s and early 1970s, however, a decline set in with the spread of military rule in the developing world. Political parties were accused of being divisive, and of failing to solve overriding problems of poverty and ethnic and tribal rivalry. They also proved to be inconvenient for economic and military elites. The upsurge of democratization (see p. 32) in the 1980s and 1990s nevertheless led to a renewed flourishing of parties. In Asia, Africa and Latin America the relaxation or collapse of military rule was invariably accompanied by the re-emergence of parties. In former communist states one-party rule was replaced by the establishment of competitive party systems.

It would be a mistake, however, to assume that parties have always been with us. Political parties are part of the structures of mass politics, ushered in by the advent of representative government and the progressive extension of the franchise during the

Faction, factionalism

Originally, the terms faction and party were used interchangeably. Faction is now more commonly used to mean a section or group within a larger formation, usually a political party. Although factions may be stable and enduring, and may possess formal organization and membership, their aims and organizational status are compatible with those of their host party. If they are not, the group is seen as a 'party within a party'. A distinction is sometimes drawn between factions and tendencies, the latter being looser and more informal groups, distinguished only by a common policy or ideological disposition. Factionalism refers either to the proliferation of factions or to the bitterness of factional rivalry. The term faction is often used pejoratively; the term factionalism is always pejorative, implying debilitating infighting.

nineteenth century. Until then, what were called 'factions' or 'parties' were little more than groups of like-minded politicians, usually formed around a key leader or family. So-called 'court' parties, for instance, often developed within autocratic monarchies as a result of the struggle for influence amongst notables and advisers. Thus, when Edmund Burke (see p. 49) in the late eighteenth century described a party as 'a body of men united . . . upon some particular principle upon which they all agree', he was thinking about fluid and informal groupings such as the Whigs and the Tories, and not about the organized and increasingly disciplined machines into which they were to develop.

Parties of the modern kind first emerged in the USA. Despite the abhorrence of parties felt by the 'founding fathers' who created the US constitution, the Federalist Party (later the Whigs and, from 1860, the Republican Party) appeared as a mass-based party during the US presidential election of 1800. Many conservative and liberal parties started life as legislative factions. Only later, forced to appeal to an ever-widening electorate, did they develop an extraparliamentary machinery of constituency branches, local agents and so on. In contrast, socialist parties and parties representing religious, ethnic and language groups were invariably born as social movements or interest groups operating outside government. Subsequently, they developed into fully fledged parliamentary parties in the hope of winning formal representation and shaping public policy. By the beginning of the twentieth century, parties and party systems had, in effect, become the political manifestation of the social and other cleavages that animated society at large. However, the resulting party forms varied considerably.

Types of party

A variety of classifications have been used for political parties. The most important of these are the following:

- cadre and mass parties
- representative and integrative parties
- constitutional and revolutionary parties
- left-wing and right-wing parties.

The most common distinction is that between cadre parties and mass parties. The term *cadre* party originally meant a 'party of notables', dominated by an informal group of leaders who saw little point in building up a mass organization. Such parties invariably developed out of parliamentary factions or cliques at a time when the franchise was limited. However, the term cadre is now more commonly used (as in communist parties) to denote trained and professional party members who are expected to exhibit a high level of political commitment and doctrinal discipline. In this sense, the Communist Party of the Soviet Union (CPSU), the Nazi Party in Germany, and the Fascist Party in Italy were cadre parties, as are the Chinese Communist Party (CCP) and, in certain respects, the Indian Congress Party in the modern period. The distinguishing feature of cadre parties is their reliance on a politically active elite (usually subject to quasi-military discipline) that is capable of offering ideological leadership to the masses. Although strict political criteria are laid down for party membership, careerism and simple convenience are often powerful motives for joining such parties, as both the CPSU and the Nazis found out.

A *mass* party, on the other hand, places a heavy emphasis on broadening membership and constructing a wide electoral base. Although the extension of the franchise forced liberal and conservative parties to seek a mass appeal, the earliest examples of mass parties were European socialist parties, such as the German Social Democratic Party (SPD) and the UK Labour Party, which constructed organizations specifically designed to mobilize working-class support. The key feature of such parties is that they place heavier stress on recruitment and organization than on ideology and political conviction. Although such parties often have formally democratic organizations, except for a minority of activists membership usually entails little in the way of participation and only general agreement about principles and goals.

Most modern parties fall into the category of what Otto Kirchheimer (1966) termed 'catch-all parties'. These are parties that drastically reduce their ideological baggage in order to appeal to the largest possible number of voters. Kirchheimer particularly had in mind the Christian Democratic Union (CDU) in Germany, but the best examples of catch-all parties are found in the USA in the form of the Republicans and the Democrats. Modern de-ideologized socialist parties such as the German Social Democrats and the Labour Party in the UK also fit this description. These parties differ from the classic model of a mass party in that they emphasize leadership and unity, and downgrade the role of individual party members in trying to build up broad coalitions of support rather than relying on a particular social class or sectional group.

The second party distinction, advanced by Sigmund Neumann (1956), is that between so-called parties of representation and parties of integration. *Representative* parties see their primary function as being the securing of votes in elections. They thus attempt to reflect, rather than shape, public opinion. In this respect, representative parties adopt a catch-all strategy and therefore place pragmatism before principle and market research before popular mobilization. The prevalence of such parties in modern politics gave considerable force to arguments based on **rational choice** models of political behaviour, like those of Joseph Schumpeter (see p. 253) and Anthony Downs, which portray politicians as power-seeking creatures who are willing to adopt whatever policies are likely to bring them electoral success.

Integrative parties, in contrast, adopt proactive, rather than reactive, political strategies; they wish to mobilize, educate and inspire the masses, rather than merely respond to their concerns. Although Neumann saw the typical mobilizing party as an ideologically disciplined cadre party, mass parties may also exhibit mobilizing tendencies. For example, until they became discouraged by electoral failure, socialist parties set out to 'win over' the electorate to a belief in the benefits of public ownership, full employment, redistribution, social welfare and so on. This approach was also, rather ironically, adopted by the UK Conservatives under Margaret Thatcher in the 1980s. Abandoning the party's traditional distaste for ideology (see p. 45) and abstract principle, Thatcher embraced 'conviction politics' in pursuing a mobilizing strategy based on firm support for cutting taxes, encouraging enterprise, promoting individual responsibility, tackling trade-union power and so forth.

The third type of classification distinguishes between constitutional parties and revolutionary parties. *Constitutional* parties acknowledge the rights and entitlements of other parties and thus operate within a framework of rules and constraints. In particular, they acknowledge that there is a division between the party and the state, between the party in power (the government of the day) and state institutions (the bureaucracy, judiciary, police and so on) that enjoy formal independence and

Rational choice: An approach to politics based on the assumption that individuals are rationally self-interested actors; an 'economic' theory of politics.

political neutrality. Above all, constitutional parties acknowledge and respect the rules of electoral competition. They recognize that they can be voted out of power as easily as they can be voted into it. Mainstream parties in liberal democracies all have such a constitutional character.

Revolutionary parties, on the other hand, are antisystem or anticonstitutional parties, either of the left or of the right. Such parties aim to seize power and over-throw the existing constitutional structure using tactics that range from outright insurrection and popular revolution to the quasi-legalism practised by the Nazis and the Fascists. In some cases revolutionary parties are formally banned by being clas-sified as 'extremist' or 'antidemocratic', as has been the case in post-Second-World-War Germany. When such parties win power, however, they invariably become 'ruling' or regime parties, suppressing rival parties and establishing a permanent rela-tionship with the state machinery. In one-party systems, whether established under the banner of communism, fascism, nationalism or whatever, the distinction between the party and the state has been so weakened that the 'ruling' party has in effect substituted itself for the government, creating a fused 'party–state' apparatus. It was common in the USSR, for instance, for the General Secretary of the CPSU to act as the chief executive or head of government without bothering to assume a formal state post.

The final way of distinguishing between parties is on the basis of ideological orientation, specifically between those parties labelled left-wing and those labelled right-wing (see p. 276). *Left-wing* parties (progressive, socialist and communist parties) are characterized by a commitment to change, in the form of either social reform or wholesale economic transformation. These have traditionally drawn their support from the ranks of the poor and disadvantaged (in urban societies, the working classes). *Right-wing* parties (conservative and fascist parties in particular) generally uphold the existing social order and are, in that sense, a force for continu-ity. Their supporters usually include business interests and the materially contented middle classes. However, this notion of a neat left–right party divide is at best simplis-tic and at worst deeply misleading. Not only are both the left and the right often divided along reformist/revolutionary and constitutional/insurrectionary lines, but also all parties, especially constitutional ones, tend to be 'broad churches' in the sense that they encompass their own left and right wings. Moreover, electoral com-petition has the effect of blurring ideological identities, once-cherished principles commonly being discarded in the search for votes. The definitions of left and right have also changed over time and often differ from one political system to the next. Finally, the shift away from old class polarities and the emergence of new political issues such as environment, animal rights and feminism has perhaps rendered the conventional ideas of left and right redundant (Giddens, 1994).

Functions of parties

Although political parties are defined by a central function (the filling of political office and the wielding of government power), their impact on the political system is substantially broader and more complex. It goes without saying that there are dangers in generalizing about the functions of parties. Constitutional parties operating in a context of electoral competition tend to be portrayed as bastions of democracy; indeed, the existence of such parties is often seen as the litmus test of a healthy democratic system. On the other hand, regime parties that enjoy a monopoly of

Focus on . . .

The political spectrum

The left–right political spectrum is a shorthand method of describing political ideas and beliefs, summarizing the ideological positions of politicians, parties and movements. Its origins date back to the French Revolution and the positions that groups adopted at the first meeting of the French Estates-General in 1789. The terms left and right do not have exact meanings, however. In a narrow sense, the *linear* political spectrum (see Figure 13.1) summarizes different attitudes to the economy and the role of the state: left-wing views support intervention and collectivism, right-wing ones favour the market and individualism. This supposedly reflects deeper ideological or value differences, as follows:

Left	Right
Liberty	Authority
Equality	Hierarchy
Fraternity	Order
Rights	Duties
Progress	Tradition
Reform	Reaction
Internationalism	Nationalism

An alternative, *horseshoe-shaped* political spectrum (see Figure 13.2) was devised in the post-Second-World-War period to highlight the totalitarian and monistic (antipluralist) tendencies of both fascism and communism, by contrast with the alleged tolerance and openness of mainstream creeds. Those, like Hans Eysenck (1964), who have developed a *two-dimensional* political spectrum (see Figure 13.3) have tried to compensate for the crudeness and inconsistencies of the conventional left–right spectrum by adding a vertical authoritarian–libertarian one. This enables positions on economic organization to be disentangled from those related to civil liberty.

political power are more commonly portrayed as instruments of manipulation and political control. A number of general functions of parties can nevertheless be identified. The main functions are as follows:

- representation
- elite formation and recruitment
- goal formulation
- interest articulation and aggregation
- socialization and mobilization
- organization of government.

Representation

Representation (see p. 248) is often seen as the primary function of parties. It refers to the capacity of parties to respond to and articulate the views of both members and the voters. In the language of systems theory, political parties are major 'inputting' devices that ensure that government heeds the needs and wishes of the larger society. Clearly, this is a function that is best carried out, some would say only carried out, in

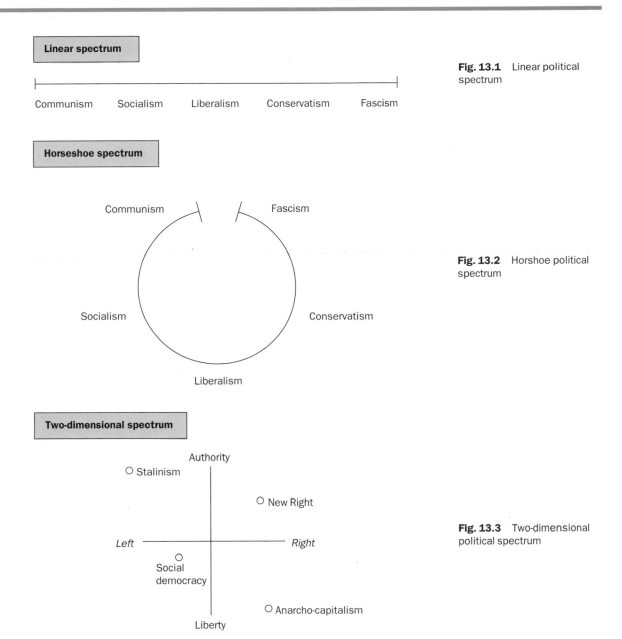

Fig. 13.1   Linear political spectrum

Fig. 13.2   Horshoe political spectrum

Fig. 13.3   Two-dimensional political spectrum

an open and competitive system that forces parties to respond to popular preferences. Rational-choice theorists, such as Anthony Downs (1957), explain this process by suggesting that the political market parallels the economic market, in that politicians act essentially as entrepreneurs seeking votes, meaning that parties behave very much like businesses. Power thus ultimately resides with the consumers, the voters. This 'economic model' can, however, be criticized on the grounds that parties seek to 'shape' or mobilize public opinion as well as respond to it, that the image of voters as well-informed, rational and issue-orientated consumers is questionable, and that the range of consumer (or electoral) choice is often narrow.

Concept

Primary election

A primary election is an intraparty election in which candidates are selected to contest a subsequent 'official' election. During the twentieth century, primaries became the principal nominating device used in the USA, also being used to choose convention delegates and party leaders. Most US states hold 'closed' primaries in which participation is restricted to registered supporters of the party (not the same as a party member); 'open' primaries allow all voters to participate regardless of party affiliation. The significance of primaries is that they give rank-and-file voters more of a voice in party affairs and lead to a more candidate-orientated and less party-orientated style of politics. Success in the primaries allows a candidate to seize control of the party machine, instead of leaving matters to the party itself.

Elite formation and recruitment

Parties of all kinds are responsible for providing states with their political leaders. One of the rare exceptions to this rule was General de Gaulle, who offered himself to France in 1944 as a 'saviour figure' standing above party divisions. Parties such as the Union for the New Republic (UNR) were his creation, as opposed to him being theirs. Much more commonly, politicians achieve office by virtue of their party post: contestants in a presidential election are usually party leaders, while in parliamentary systems the leader of the largest party in the assembly normally becomes prime minister. Cabinet and other ministerial posts are usually filled by senior party figures, though exceptions are found in presidential systems like the USA's, which allow non-party ministers to be appointed.

In most cases, parties therefore provide a training ground for politicians, equipping them with skills, knowledge and experience, and offering them some form of career structure, albeit one that depends on the fortunes of the party. On the other hand, the stranglehold that parties exert over government offices can be criticized for ensuring that political leaders are drawn from a relatively small pool of talent: the senior figures in a handful of major parties. In the USA, however, this stranglehold has been weakened by the widespread use of primary elections, which reduce the control that a party has over the process of candidate selection and nomination.

Goal formulation

Political parties have traditionally been one of the means through which societies set collective goals and, in some cases, ensure that they are carried out. Parties play this role because, in the process of seeking power, they formulate programmes of government (through conferences, conventions, election manifestos and so on) with a view to attracting popular support. Not only does this mean that parties are a major source of policy initiation, it also encourages them to formulate coherent sets of policy options that give the electorate a choice amongst realistic and achievable goals.

This function is most clearly carried out by parties in parliamentary systems that are able to claim a mandate (see p. 252) to implement their policies if they are elected to power. However, it can also occur in presidential systems with usually non-programmic parties, as in the case of the Republicans' 'Contract with America' in the US congressional elections of 1994. Nevertheless, the tendency towards de-ideologized catch-all parties, and the fact that electoral campaigns increasingly stress personality and image over policies and issues, has generally reduced the impact that parties have on policy formulation. Party programmes, moreover, are almost certain to be modified by pressure from the civil service and interest groups, as well as in the light of domestic and international circumstances. Policy implementation, on the other hand, is usually carried out by bureaucracies rather than parties, except in one-party systems like those in orthodox communist states, where the 'ruling' party supervises the state apparatus at every level.

Interest articulation and aggregation

In the process of developing collective goals, parties also help to articulate and aggregate the various interests found in society. Parties, indeed, often develop as vehicles through which business, labour, religious, ethnic or other groups advance or defend their various interests. The UK Labour Party, for instance, was created by the trade-union movement with the aim of achieving working-class political representation. Other parties have, effectively, recruited interests and groups in order to broaden their electoral base, as the US parties did in the late nineteenth and early twentieth centuries with immigrant groups.

The fact that national parties invariably articulate the demands of a multitude of groups forces them to aggregate these interests by drawing them together into a coherent whole, balancing competing interests against each other. Constitutional parties are clearly forced to do this by the pressures of electoral competition, but even monopolistic parties articulate and aggregate interests through their close relationship with the state and the economy, especially in centrally planned systems. However, not even in competitive party systems are all interests articulated, those of most vulnerable to exclusion.

Socialization and mobilization

Through internal debate and discussion, as well as campaigning and electoral competition, parties are important agents of political education and socialization. The issues that parties choose to focus on help to set the political agenda, and the values and attitudes that they articulate become part of the larger political culture (see p. 206). In the case of monopolistic parties, the propagation of an 'official' ideology (be it Marxism–Leninism, National Socialism, or simply the ideas of a charismatic leader) is consciously acknowledged to be a central, if not its supreme, function.

Mainstream parties in competitive systems play no less significant a role in encouraging groups to play by the rules of the democratic game, thus mobilizing support for the regime itself. For example, the emergence of socialist parties in the late nineteenth and early twentieth centuries was an important means of integrating the working class into industrial society. Nevertheless, the capacity of parties to mobilize and socialize has been brought into doubt by evidence in many countries of partisan dealignment (see p. 266) and growing disenchantment with conventional pro-system parties. The problem that parties have is that, to some extent, they themselves are socialized (some would say corrupted) by the experience of government, making them, it appears, less effective in engaging partisan sympathies and attracting emotional attachments.

Organization of government

It is often argued that complex modern societies would be ungovernable in the absence of political parties. In the first place, parties help with the formation of governments, in parliamentary systems to the extent that it is possible to talk of 'party government' (see p. 285). Parties also give governments a degree of stability and coherence, especially if the members of the government are drawn from a single party and are therefore united by common sympathies and attachments. Even governments that are formed from a coalition of parties are more likely to foster unity and agreement than ones that consist of separate individuals each with his or her own priorities.

Parties, furthermore, facilitate cooperation between the two major branches of government: the assembly and the executive. In parliamentary systems this is effectively guaranteed by the fact the government is formed from the party or parties that have majority control of the assembly. However, even in presidential systems the chief executive can wield some influence, if not control, through an appeal to party unity. Finally, parties provide, in competitive systems at least, a vital source of opposition and criticism, both inside and outside government. As well as broadening political debate and educating the electorate, this helps to ensure that

Focus on . . .

The iron law of oligarchy

Oligarchy is government or domination by the few. The iron law of oligarchy, formulated by Michels ([1911] 1962), suggests that there is an inevitable tendency for political organizations, and by implication all organizations, to be oligarchic. Participatory or democratic structures cannot check oligarchic tendencies; they can only disguise them.

Michels advanced a number of arguments in support of his law:

- Elite groups result from the need for specialization. Elite members have greater *expertise* and better organizational skills than those possessed by ordinary members.
- Leaders form *cohesive* groups because they recognize that this improves their chances of remaining in power.
- Rank-and-file members of an organization tend to be *apathetic*, and are therefore generally disposed to accept subordination and venerate leaders.

government policy is more thoroughly scrutinized and therefore more likely to be workable.

Party organization: where does power lie?

Because of the crucial role that political parties play, considerable attention has been focused on where power lies within parties. The organization and structure of parties thus provides vital clues about the distribution of power within society as a whole. Can parties function as democratic bodies that broaden participation and access to power? Or do they simply entrench the dominance of leaders and elites?

One of the earliest attempts to investigate internal party democracy was undertaken in Mosei Ostrogorski's *Democracy and the Organization of Political Parties* (1902), which argued that the representation of individual interests had lost out to the growing influence of the party machine and control exerted by a caucus of senior party figures. This view was more memorably expressed by Robert Michel in *Political Parties* ([1911] 1962) in the form of the 'iron law of oligarchy', or, as Michels put it, 'he who says organization says oligarchy'. Michels (1876–1936), a prominent elite theorist, wished to analyse the power structure of the German SPD; he argued that, despite the party's formally democratic organization, power was concentrated in the hands of a small group of party leaders.

For Michels, the 'law' explained the inevitable failure of democratic socialism and, indeed, exploded the myth of political democracy. Critics, however, point out that Michels' observations are generalizations made on the basis of a single political party at a particular moment in time, and also rest on questionable psychological theories. In practice, party elites have often proved to be more faction-ridden, and mass memberships less deferential and quiescent, than Michels suggested.

Attempts have been made to strengthen the democratic and participatory features of parties through reform. One of the clearest examples of this occurred in the USA in the 1970s and 1980s. US parties differ in many respects from their European counterparts. Being loose coalitions of sometimes conflicting interests held together by little more than the need to contest presidential elections, they are highly decentralized and generally nonprogrammic. Traditionally, state-based or city-based party bosses (a legacy of the **machine politics** of the early twentieth century) acted as power brokers and exercised a decisive influence at nominating conventions. Following protests and clashes at the 1968 Democratic national convention in Chicago, however, a reform movement sprang up aimed at weakening the power of local party leaders and strengthening the role of rank-and-file members.

This was accomplished largely through the wider use of nominating primaries and **caucuses**. These, first with the Democrats and later with the Republicans, attracted a growing number of issue and candidate activists into party politics, leading to the nomination of more ideological candidates such as George McGovern for the Democrats in 1972 and Ronald Reagan for the Republicans in 1980. Such tendencies have nevertheless generated concern, particularly amongst Democrats, who feared that more open and participatory structures simply result in the nomination of unelectable 'outsider' candidates. Both the main US parties have responded to this by modernizing and strengthening their committee structures, especially at national, congressional and senatorial levels. Although this has been portrayed as a process of 'party renewal', it is evidence of the parties' desire to provide better electoral support for individual candidates, rather than of the emergence of European-style, party-focused elections.

Similar moves towards democratization were also apparent in the UK Labour Party in the early 1980s. Growing resentment amongst constituency activists about the 'betrayal of socialism' by parliamentary leaders broke out into open conflict after the party's 1979 election defeat. Reformers, spearheaded by Tony Benn, succeeded in strengthening the extraparliamentary party by introducing the mandatory reselection of Members of Parliament (MPs) and an **electoral college** to elect the leader and deputy leader. However, in response to successive electoral defeats, the Labour Party shifted back towards centralized leadership. The re-emergence of a top-down authority structure could be seen in the 1987–89 policy review, initiated by the then Labour leader Neil Kinnock, the weakening of trade-union influence by the introduction of 'one member, one vote' (OMOV) under the leadership of John Smith in 1993, and in Tony Blair's success in rewriting Clause 4 of Labour's constitution (which committed the party to public ownership) in 1995, and in ensuring, after 1997, that the party governed as 'new' Labour. What is interesting about this process is that the oligarchic tendencies appeared to stem not from the dynamics of organization, but from the party's need for unity and the restoration of electoral credibility.

The existence of factions and tendencies is as important as formal organization in determining the location of power within a party. While all parties, even those with an apparently monolithic character, embrace some measure of political and ideological rivalry, the degree to which this rivalry is reflected in conflict between organized and coherent groups is crucial in determining the degree of authority of party leaders. In some cases, factions can break away from parties in the manner that in Europe communist parties often emerged out of socialist parties in the years following the 1917 Russian Revolution. Factionalism is often linked to the weight that parties place on political ideas and ideological direction. Whereas pragmatic right-wing parties usually merely have to balance or conciliate rival tendencies, more ideological parties of the left often have to deal with open disagreement and institutionalized rivalry. Together with their inclination to endorse internal democracy, this has generally made socialist parties more difficult to lead than liberal or conservative ones.

Concept

Party democracy

Party democracy is a form of popular rule that operates through the agency of a party as a democratic institution. There are two views about how this can be achieved. In the first (intraparty democracy) parties are democratic agents in that power within them is dispersed widely and evenly. This implies, for instance, that there should be broad participation in the election of leaders and selection of candidates, and a prominent role for conferences and conventions in policy formulation. In the second model, democracy dictates that policy making power should be concentrated in the hands of party members who are elected and therefore publicly accountable. In this view, a wide and even dispersal of power within the party may lead to the tyranny of non-elected constituency activists.

Machine politics: A style of politics in which party 'bosses' control a mass organization through patronage and the distribution of favours.

Caucus: A meeting of party members held to nominate election candidates or to discuss legislative proposals in advance of formal proceedings.

Electoral college: An indirect electoral mechanism; a body of electors charged with responsibility for filling a party or public office.

Perhaps a more significant consideration, however, is the extent to which parties have a secure hold on power. Factionalism is, in a sense, a luxury that only long-time parties of government can afford. This is why monopolistic communist parties were able to keep factionalism at bay only by exercising ruthless discipline enforced through the strictures of **democratic centralism**. It also explains the deeply factional nature of 'dominant' parties such as the Liberal Democratic Party (LDP) in Japan and the Italian Christian Democratic Party (Democrazia Christiana (DC)). The UK Conservative Party is an example of a party with an ethos that once stressed, above all, deference and loyalty, but which became increasingly factionalized in the 1980s and 1990s through a combination of its more ideological character and prolonged electoral success after 1979. Bottom-up pressures thus gave the party a more democratic character than its formal leader-dominated structure suggested was possible. The most conspicuous casualty of this process was Margaret Thatcher, who was rejected as party leader in 1990 despite having won three successive general elections. The same phenomenon was also apparent in John Major's embattled leadership in the 1992–97 period.

◼ Party systems

Political parties are important not only because of the range of functions they carry out (representation, elite recruitment, aggregation of interests, and so on), but also because the complex interrelationships between and among parties are crucial in structuring the way political systems work in practice. This network of relationships is called a party system. The most familiar way of distinguishing between different types of party system is by reference to the number of parties competing for power. On this basis, Duverger (1954) distinguished between 'one-party', 'two-party' and 'multiparty' systems. Although such a typology is commonly used, party systems cannot simply be reduced to a 'numbers game'.

As important as the number of parties competing for power is their relative size, as reflected in their electoral and legislative strength. As Sartori (1976) pointed out, what is vital is to establish the 'relevance' of parties in relation to the formation of governments, and in particular whether their size gives them the prospect of winning, or at least sharing, government power. This approach is often reflected in the distinction made between 'major', or government-orientated, parties and more peripheral, 'minor' ones (although neither category can be defined with mathematical accuracy). A third consideration is how these 'relevant' parties relate to one another. Is the party system characterized by cooperation and consensus, or by conflict and polarization? This is closely linked to the ideological complexion of the party system and the traditions and history of the parties that compose it.

The mere presence of parties does not, however, guarantee the existence of a party system. The pattern of relationships amongst parties constitutes a system only if it is characterized by stability and a degree of orderliness. Where neither stability nor order exists, a party system may be in the process of emerging, or a transition from one type of party system to another may be occurring. For instance, this can be said of post-communist Russia. The collapse of communist rule in 1991 and the initial banning of the CPSU was always going to make the emergence of a competitive party system a difficult, perhaps tortuous, business. Russia's problem has been a proliferation of parties and political groupings, none of which has come close to establishing a mass member-

Democratic centralism: The Leninist principle of party organization, based on a supposed balance between freedom of discussion and strict unity of action.

ship or a nationwide organization. No fewer than 43 parties contested the December 1995 parliamentary elections, with the largest of these, the Russian Communist Party, gaining just 22 per cent of the vote. However, some have argued that, in an age of partisan dealignment and volatile voting patterns, party systems are generally losing their 'systematic' character, making it more difficult to distinguish one system from another. Moreover, where subnational bodies exert significant influence, different party systems may operate at different levels within the political system.

The major party systems found in modern politics are nevertheless as follows:

- one-party systems
- two-party systems
- dominant-party systems
- multiparty systems

One-party systems

Strictly speaking, the term one-party system is contradictory since 'system' implies interaction amongst a number of entities. The term is nevertheless helpful in distinguishing between political systems in which a single party enjoys a monopoly of power through the exclusion of all other parties (by political or constitutional means) and ones characterized by a competitive struggle amongst a number of parties. Because monopolistic parties effectively function as permanent governments, with no mechanism (short of a coup or revolution) through which they can be removed from power, they invariably develop an entrenched relationship with the state machine. This allows such states to be classified as 'one-party states', their machinery being seen as a fused 'party–state' apparatus. Two rather different types of one-party system can be identified, however.

The first type has been found in state socialist regimes where 'ruling' communist parties have directed and controlled virtually all the institutions and aspects of society. Such parties are subject to strict ideological discipline, in accordance with the tenets of Marxism–Leninism, and they have highly structured internal organizations in line with the principles of democratic centralism. These are cadre parties in the sense that membership is restricted on political and ideological grounds. Some 5 per cent of the Chinese population are members of the Chinese Communist Party, and around 9 per cent of the Soviet population belonged to the CPSU. In this type of party, the party core consists of well-paid full-time officials, the *apparatchiki*, who run the party *apparat*, or apparatus, and exercise supervision over both the state machine and social institutions.

A central device through which communist parties control the state, economy and society, and ensure the subordination of 'lower' organs to 'higher' ones, is the *nomenklatura* system. This is a system of vetted appointments in which, effectively, all senior posts are filled by party-approved candidates. The justification for both the party's monopoly of power and its supervision of state and social institutions lies in the Leninist claim that the party acts as the 'vanguard of the proletariat' in providing the working masses with the ideological leadership and guidance needed to ensure that they fulfil their revolutionary destiny. **Vanguardism** has, however, been criticized for being deeply elitist and providing the seed from which Stalinism later grew. Trotsky (1937), on the other hand, offered an alternative interpretation by suggesting that, far from the 'ruling' party dominating Soviet development, its formal

Vanguardism: The Leninist belief in the need for a party to lead and guide the proletariat towards the fulfilment of its revolutionary destiny.

monopoly of power merely concealed the burgeoning influence of the state bureaucracy.

The second type of one-party system is associated with anticolonial nationalism and state consolidation in the developing world. In Ghana, Tanzania and Zimbawe, for example, the 'ruling' party developed out of an independence movement that proclaimed the overriding need for nation-building and economic development. In Zimbabwe, one-party rule developed only in 1986 (six years after independence) through the merger of the two major parties, ZANU and ZAPU, both former guerrilla groups. In other cases such parties have developed as little more than vehicles through which a national leader has tried to consolidate power, as with General Ershad's People's Party in Bangladesh in the 1980s and President Mobutu's Popular Movement of the Revolution in Zaire, 1965–97.

One-party systems in Africa and Asia have usually been built around the dominant role of a charismatic leader and drawn whatever ideological identity they have possessed from the views of that leader. Kwame Nkrumah, the leader of the Convention People's Party (CPP) in Ghana until his overthrow in 1966, is often seen as the model such leader, but other examples have been Julius Nyerere in Tanzania and Robert Mugabe in Zimbabwe. Not uncommonly, these parties are weakly organized (very different from the tight discipline found in communist one-party states), and they play, at best, only a peripheral role in the process of policy-making. Their monopolistic position nevertheless helps to entrench authoritarianism (see p. 38) and to keep alive the danger of corruption.

Two-party systems

A two-party system is duopolistic in that it is dominated by two 'major' parties that have a roughly equal prospect of winning government power. In its classical form, a two-party system can be identified by three criteria:

- Although a number of 'minor' parties may exist, only two parties enjoy sufficient electoral and legislative strength to have a realistic prospect of winning government power.
- The larger party is able to rule alone (usually on the basis of a legislative majority); the other provides the opposition.
- Power alternates between these parties; both are 'electable', the opposition serving as a 'government in the wings'.

The UK and the USA are the most frequently cited examples of states with two-party systems, though others have included Canada, Australia and New Zealand. Archetypal examples of two-party politics are nevertheless rare. The UK, for instance, often portrayed as the model two-party system, has conformed to its three defining criteria only for particular (and, some would argue, untypical) periods of its history. Even the apparent Labour–Conservative two-partyism of the early post-Second-World-War period (power alternating four times between 1945 and 1970) was punctuated by 13 years of continuous Conservative rule (1951–64), a period during which time Labour's electability was called into question. Moreover, despite persistent major party domination of the House of Commons in the UK, it is more doubtful that a two-party system has existed 'in the country' since 1974. This is suggested by the decline of combined Labour–Conservative support (down from over 95 per cent in the early 1950s to consistently below 75 per cent since 1974).

Even the seemingly incontrovertible two-partyism of the US, which, for instance, sees the Republicans and Democrats usually holding between them all the seats in the House of Representatives and the Senate, can be questioned. On the one hand, the presidential system allows one party to capture the White House (the presidency) while the other controls one or both houses of Congress, as, for instance, occurred between 1984 and 2000, meaning that it may not be possible to identify a clear government–opposition divide. On the other hand, 'third' party candidates are sometimes of significance. Ross Perot's 16 per cent of the vote in the 1992 presidential election not only highlighted the decline of the Republican and Democratic parties, but also, arguably, proved decisive in securing victory for Clinton.

Two-party politics was once portrayed as the surest way of reconciling responsiveness with order, representative government with effective government. Its key advantage is that it makes possible a system of party government, supposedly characterized by stability, choice and accountability. The two major parties are able to offer the electorate a straightforward choice between rival programmes and alternative governments. Voters can support a party knowing that, if it wins the election, it will have the capacity to carry out its manifesto promises without having to negotiate or compromise with coalition partners. This is sometimes seen as one of the attractions of majoritarian electoral systems that exaggerate support for large parties. Two-party systems have also been praised for delivering strong but accountable government based on relentless competition between the governing and opposition parties. Although government can govern, it can never relax or become complacent because it is constantly confronted by an opposition that acts as a government in waiting. Two-partyism, moreover, creates a bias in favour of moderation, as the two contenders for power have to battle for 'floating' votes in the centre ground. This was, for example, reflected in the so-called social-democratic consensus that prevailed in the UK in the 1950s and 1960s.

However, two-party politics and party government have not been so well regarded since the 1970s. Instead of guaranteeing moderation, two-party systems such as the UK's have displayed a periodic tendency towards adversary politics (see p. 350). This is reflected in ideological polarization and an emphasis on conflict and argument rather than consensus and compromise. In the UK in the early 1980s this was best demonstrated by the movement to the right by a 'Thatcherized' Conservative Party and the movement to the left by a radicalized Labour Party, although a new, post-Thatcherite consensus soon emerged. Adversarial two-partyism has often been explained by reference to the class nature of party support (party conflict being seen, ultimately, as a reflection of the class struggle), or as a consequence of party democratization and the influence of ideologically committed grass-roots activists.

A further problem with the two-party system is that two evenly matched parties are encouraged to compete for votes by outdoing each other's electoral promises, perhaps causing spiralling public spending and fuelling inflation. This amounts to irresponsible party government, in that parties come to power on the basis of election manifestos that they have no capacity to fulfil. A final weakness of two-party systems is the obvious restrictions they impose in terms of electoral and ideological choice. While a choice between just two programmes of government was perhaps sufficient in an era of partisan alignment and class solidarity, it has become quite inadequate in a period of greater individualism and social diversity.

Concept

Party government

Party government is a system through which single parties are able to form governments and carry through policy programmes. In competitive systems, party government exists nowhere in pristine form; it is therefore sensible to talk about *more* party government or *less* party government, but not about whether it exists.

The key features of party government are the following:
- The major parties possess a clear programmic character and thus offer the electorate a meaningful choice between potential governments.
- The governing party is able to claim a popular mandate and enjoys sufficient ideological cohesion and organizational unity to delivery on its manifesto commitments.
- Responsibility is maintained by the government's accountability to the electorate through its mandate, and by the existence of a credible opposition acting as a balancing force.

Dominant-party systems

Dominant-party systems should not be confused with one-party systems, although they may at times exhibit similar characteristics. A dominant-party system is competitive in the sense that a number of parties compete for power in regular and popular elections, but is dominated by a single major party that consequently enjoys prolonged periods in power. This apparently neat definition, however, runs into problems, notably in relation to determining how 'prolonged' a governing period must be for a party to be considered 'dominant'. Japan is usually cited as the classic example of a dominant-party system. Until its fall in 1993 the Liberal Democratic Party had been in power continuously for 38 years, having failed to gain an overall majority in the House of Representatives (the lower chamber of the Japanese Diet) only in 1976, 1979 and 1983. LDP dominance was underpinned by the Japanese 'economic miracle'. It also reflected the powerful appeal of the party's neo-Confucian principles of duty and obligation in the still-traditional Japanese countryside, and the strong links that the party had forged with business elites. Although the LDP continues to be Japan's largest party, it increasingly has to rely on other parties to form governments.

The Congress Party in India enjoyed an unbroken spell of 30 years in power commencing with the achievement of independence in 1947. Until 1989 it had endured only three years in opposition, following Indiri Gandhi's 1975–77 state of emergency. The African National Congress (ANC) has similarly been the dominant party in South Africa since the ending of apartheid in 1993, its position being based on its preeminent role in the long struggle against white rule. The best European examples of a dominant-party system are Sweden, where the Social Democratic Labour Party (SAP) held power for 65 of the previous 74 yeas until its defeat in 2006, and Italy, where the Christian Democratic Party (DC) dominated every one of the country's 52 post-Second-World-War governments until the party's effective collapse amidst mounting allegations of corruption in 1992–94.

The most prominent feature of a dominant-party system is the tendency for the political focus to shift from competition between parties to factional conflict within the dominant party itself. The DC in Italy, for example, functioned as little more than a coalition of privileged groups and interests in Italian society, the party acting as a broker to these various factions. The most powerful of these groups were the Catholic Church (which exercised influence through organizations such as Catholic Action), the farming community and industrial interests. Each of these was able to cultivate voting loyalty and exert influence upon DC's members in the Italian parliament.

Factions are also an integral institution in the Japanese political process. A perennial struggle for power has taken place within the LDP as various subgroups have coalesced around rising or powerful individuals. Such factionalism is maintained at the local level by the ability of faction leaders to provide political favours for their followers, and at the parliamentary level through the allocation of senior government and party offices. Although the resulting infighting may be seen as a means of guaranteeing argument and debate in a system in which small parties are usually marginalized, in Japan factionalism tends to revolve more around personal differences than it does around policy or ideological divisions. One example of this was the conflict between the Fukuda and Tanaka factions during the 1970s and 1980s, which continued long after the two principals had left the scene.

Whereas other competitive party systems have their supporters, or at least apologists, few are prepared to come to the defence of the dominant-party system. Apart from a tendency towards stability and predictability, dominant-partyism is usually seen as a regrettable and unhealthy phenomenon. In the first place, it tends to erode the important constitutional distinction between the state and the party in power. When governments cease to come and go, an insidious process of politicization takes place through which state officials and institutions adjust to the ideological and political priorities of the dominant party. For example, about one-quarter of the LDP's Diet members are former civil servants; this creates the kind of party-state nexus that is usually associated with one-party systems.

Second, an extended period in power can engender complacency, arrogance and even corruption in the dominant party. The course of Italian and Japanese politics has, for example, regularly been interrupted by scandals, usually involving allegations of financial corruption. Indeed, the decline of both the LDP and the DC in the 1990s was closely linked to such allegations. When parties cease to 'fear the ballot box' they are likely to become unresponsive and ideologically entrenched. Prolonged Conservative rule in the UK since 1979, for instance, has resulted in a party seemingly incapable of breaking loose from its Thatcherite heritage, and, in particular, unable either to abandon its **Euroscepticism** or to question the dogma of the market.

Third, a dominant-party system is characterized by weak and ineffective opposition. Criticism and protest can more easily be ignored if they stem from parties that are no longer regarded as genuine rivals for power. Finally, the existence of a 'permanent' party of government may corrode the democratic spirit by encouraging the electorate to fear change and to stick with the 'natural' party of government. Dominant-party systems may, then, be psychologically self-perpetuating. A genuinely democratic political culture arguably requires a general public that has a healthy distrust of all parties and, most importantly, a willingness to remove governments that have failed.

Multiparty systems

A multiparty system is characterized by competition amongst more than two parties, reducing the chances of single-party government and increasing the likelihood of coalitions. However, it is difficult to define multiparty systems in terms of the number of major parties, as such systems sometimes operate through coalitions including smaller parties that are specifically designed to exclude larger parties from government. This is precisely what happened to the French Communist Party (Parti Communiste Français or PCF) in the 1950s, and to the Italian Communist Party (PCI) throughout its existence. If the likelihood of coalition government is the index of multipartyism, this classification contains a number of subcategories.

Germany, for example, appeared until the 1990s to have a 'two-and-a-half-party' system, in that the CDU and SDP had electoral strengths roughly equivalent to those of the Conservative and Labour parties in the UK. However, they were forced into coalitions with the small Free Democrat Party by the workings of the additional member electoral system (see p. 237). Italian multipartyism traditionally involves a larger number of relatively small parties. Thus even the DC rarely came close to achieving 40 per cent of the vote. Sartori (1976) distinguished between two types of multiparty system, which he termed the moderate and polarized pluralist systems. In this categorization moderate pluralism exists in countries such as Belgium, the

Euroscepticism: Opposition to further European integration, based, usually, on its implications for sovereignty and national identity.

Concept

Coalition

A coalition is a grouping of rival political actors brought together either through the perception of a common threat, or through the recognition that their goals cannot be achieved by working separately. Electoral coalitions are alliances through which parties agree not to compete against one another, with a view to maximizing their representation. Legislative coalitions are agreements between two or more parties to support a particular bill or programme. Coalition governments are formal agreements between two or more parties that involve a cross-party distribution of ministerial portfolios. They are usually motivated by the need to ensure majority control of the assembly. A 'grand coalition' or 'national government' comprises all the major parties, but are usually formed only at times of national crisis or economic emergency.

Netherlands and Norway, where ideological differences between major parties are slight, and where there is a general inclination to form coalitions and move towards the middle ground. Polarized pluralism, on the other hand, exists when more marked ideological differences separate major parties, some of which adopt an anti-system stance. The existence of electorally strong communist parties, as in France, Italy and Spain until the 1990s, or of significant fascist movements, such as the Movimento Sociale Italiano (MSI) (reborn in 1995 as the 'post-Fascist' Alleanza Nazionale), provided evidence of polarized pluralism.

The strength of multiparty systems is that they create internal checks and balances within government and exhibit a bias in favour of debate, conciliation and compromise. The process of coalition formation and the dynamics of coalition maintenance ensure a broad responsiveness that cannot but take account of competing views and contending interests. Thus, in Germany, the liberal Free Democrats act as a moderating influence upon both the conservative CDU and the socialist SPD. Where SPD–Green coalitions have been formed in the *Länder* (provinces), the Green presence has helped to push environmental issues up the political agenda. Similarly, the multiparty features of the Swedish system, which make coalition government more common than not, have encouraged the SAP to build a broad welfare consensus, and to pursue moderate policies that do not alienate business interests. The conviction politics and ideological radicalism that were, for example, exemplified by Thatcherism in the UK in the 1980s and 1990s would therefore be quite unthinkable in a multiparty system.

The principal criticisms of multiparty systems relate to the pitfalls and difficulties of coalition formation. The post-election negotiations and horsetrading that take place when no single party is strong enough to govern alone can take weeks, or (as in Israel and Italy) sometimes months, to complete. More seriously, coalition governments may be fractured and unstable, paying greater attention to squabbles amongst coalition partners than to the tasks of government. Italy is usually cited as the classic example of this, its post-1945 governments having lasted on average only ten months. It would nevertheless be a mistake to suggest that coalitions are always associated with instability, as the record of stable and effective coalition government in Germany and Sweden clearly demonstrates. In some respects, in fact, the Italian experience is peculiar, owing as much to the country's political culture and the ideological complexion of its party system as to the dynamics of multipartyism.

A final problem is that the tendency towards moderation and compromise may mean that multiparty systems are so dominated by the political centre that they are unable to offer clear ideological alternatives. Coalition politics tends, naturally, to be characterized by negotiation and conciliation, a search for common ground, rather than by conviction and the politics of principle. This process can be criticized as being implicitly corrupt, in that parties are encouraged to abandon policies and principles in their quest for power. It can also lead to the over-representation of centrist parties and centrist interests, especially when, as in Germany, a small centre party is the only viable coalition partner for larger conservative and socialist ones. Indeed, this is sometimes seen as one of the drawbacks of proportional representation electoral systems, which, by ensuring that the legislative size of parties reflects their electoral strength, are biased in favour of multiparty politics and coalition government.

Thomas Jefferson (1743–1826)

US political philosopher and statesman. A wealthy Virginian planter who was Governor of Virginia 1779–81, Jefferson served as the first US Secretary of State, 1789–94. He was the third president of the USA, 1801–90. Jefferson was the principal author of the Declaration of Independence, and wrote a vast number of addresses and letters. He developed a democratic form of agrarianism that sought to blend a belief in rule by a natural aristocracy with a commitment to limited government and *laissez-faire*. He also demonstrated sympathy for social reform, favouring the extension of public education, the abolition of slavery, and greater economic equality.

■ The decline of parties?

Criticism of political parties is certainly not new. Indeed, the emergence of political parties was usually greeted with grave suspicion and distrust. For instance, in common with other 'founding fathers' who wrote the US constitution, Thomas Jefferson was fiercely critical of parties and factions, believing that they would promote conflict and destroy the underlying unity of society. The view that there is an indivisible public or national interest has also been used in the modern period by one-party systems to justify the suppression of rival parties, and by military rulers to explain the suppression of all political parties. A further concern, expressed by liberals such as J. S. Mill (see p. 48), was that, as collective bodies, parties necessarily suppress freedom of thought and the politics of individual conscience. Modern concern about parties, however, stems from evidence of their decline as agents of representation and as an effective link between government and the people.

Evidence of a 'crisis of party politics' can be found in a decline of both party membership and partisanship, reflected in partisan dealignment. For example, since the high point of party membership in the UK in the early 1950s, the Labour Party has lost approximately two-thirds of its members, and the Conservatives over half. A seemingly inexorable rise in the age of party members is as significant, the average age of Conservative Party members in 1998 being 63. Dramatic electoral swings against governing parties have intensified such concerns. Notable examples of this include the slump of the French Socialists in 1993 from 282 seats to just 70, and the virtual annihilation the same year of the Canadian Progressive Conservatives, who were swept out of office retaining only two seats. Falling voter turnout also illustrates the declining capacity of parties to mobilize electoral support. For instance, turnout in the 2001 UK general election fell from 71 per cent (itself a post-1945 low) to 59 per cent.

Alongside these changes, there is evidence of what has been called 'antipolitics': that is, the rise of political movements and organizations the only common feature of which appears to be antipathy towards conventional centres of power and opposition to established parties of government. This has been reflected in the emergence of new political movements the principle attraction of which is that they are untainted by having held power. Good examples have been the 19 per cent support that billionaire Ross Perot gained in his independent bid for the US presidency in 1992, and the dramatic success of media mogul Silvio Berlesconi's newly created Forza Italia in 1994. The rise of new social movements (see p. 308), such as the women's movement, peace movement and environmental movement, is also part of the same phenomenon. Even when they articulate their views through party organization, as in the case of Green parties, these movements tend to assume the mantle of **antiparty parties**.

How can the decline of parties be explained? One of the problems that parties suffer from is their real or perceived oligarchical character. Parties are seen as bureaucratized political machines, whose grass-roots members are either inactive or engaged in dull and routine tasks (attending meetings, sitting on committees, and so on). In contrast, single-issue protest groups have been more successful in attracting membership and support, particularly from amongst the young, partly because they are more loosely organized and locally based, and partly because they place a heavier emphasis on participation and activism. The public image of parties has been further tarnished by their links to government and to professional politicians. As political 'insiders', parties are tainted by the power, ambition and corruption that is often associated with high office. In other words, parties are not seen as being '*of* the people'; too often, they appear to be consumed by political infighting and the scramble for power, so becoming divorced from the concerns of ordinary people.

An alternative way of explaining party decline is to see it as a symptom of the fact that complex, modern societies are increasingly difficult to govern. Disillusionment and cynicism grow as parties seek power by proclaiming their capacity to solve problems and improve conditions, but fail to deliver once in government. This reflects the mounting difficulties that confront any party of government in the form of the expanding power of interest groups and an increasingly globalized economy. A final explanation is that parties may be declining because the social identities and traditional loyalties that gave rise to them in the first place have started to fade. This can certainly be seen in the decline of class politics, linked to the phenomenon of post-Fordism (see p. 198). In addition, with the decline of old social, religious and other solidarities, new aspirations and sensibilities have come onto the political agenda, notably those associated with postmaterialism (see p. 211). Whereas broad, programmic parties once succeeded in articulating the goals of major sections of the electorate, issues such as gender equality, nuclear power, animal rights and pollution may require new and different political formations to articulate them. Single-issue groups and social movements may thus be in the process of replacing parties as the crucial link between government and society.

▊ Summary

◆ A political party is a group of people organized for the purpose of winning government power, and usually displays some measure of ideological cohesion. The principal classifications of parties have distinguished between cadre and mass or, later, catch-all parties, parties of representation and parties of integration, constitutional or 'mainstream' parties and revolutionary or anti-system ones, and left-wing parties and right-wing parties.

◆ Parties have a number of functions in the political system. These include their role as a mechanism of representation, the formation of political elites and recruitment

Antiparty parties: Parties that set out to subvert traditional party politics by rejecting parliamentary compromise and emphasizing popular mobilization.

into politics, the formulation of social goals and government policy, the articulation and aggregation of interests, the mobilization and socialization of the electorate, and the organization of governmental processes and institutional relationships.

◆ The organization and structure of parties crucially influence the distribution of power within society at large. Party democracy can be promoted either by a wide dispersal of power within the party, or by the concentration of power in the hands of the party's elected and publicly accountable members. Oligarchic tendencies may be an inevitable consequence of organization, or they may arise from the need for party unity and electoral credibility.

◆ A party system is a network of relationships through which parties interact and influence the political process. In one-party systems a 'ruling' party effectively functions as a permanent government. In two-party systems power alternates between two 'major' parties. In dominant-party systems a single 'major' party retains power for a prolonged period. In multiparty systems no party is large enough to rule alone, leading to a system of coalition government.

◆ Party systems shape the broader political process in various ways. They influence the range and nature of choice available to the electorate, and affect the cohesion and stability of governments. They structure the relationship between the executive and the assembly, establish a bias in favour of either conflict or consensus, and shape the general character of the political culture.

◆ Evidence of a crisis in party politics can be found in the decline in party membership and partisanship, as well as in the rise of 'antiparty' groups and movements. This can be explained by the perception that parties are tainted by power, ambition and corruption, and that they have suffered as a result of general disillusionment caused by the growing inability of governments to deliver on their promises. They are also seen to have failed to articulate the aspirations and sensibilities associated with postmaterialism or generated by postmodernism.

▮ Questions for discussion

▶ Are all modern political parties essentially catch-all parties?

▶ Could government function in contemporary circumstances without political parties?

▶ In what ways, and to what extent, do parties promote democracy?

▶ Why do political parties so often tend to be leader-dominated?

▶ By what criteria should party systems be judged?

▶ How have modern parties adjusted to the decline of class politics and the weakening of traditional loyalties?

▮ Further reading

Castles, F. and R. Wildmann (eds), *The Future of Party Government*, vol. 1 (Berlin: Gruyter, 1986). An analysis of the conditions of party government and the problems associated with it.

Graham, B. D., *Representation and Party Politics: A Comparative Perspective* (Oxford: Blackwell, 1993). A wide-ranging discussion of the relationship between parties, representation and democracy.

Mair, P., *The West European Party System* (Oxford: Oxford University Press, 1990). A comprehensive account of parties and party systems in western Europe.

Sartori, G., *Parties and Party Systems: A Framework for Analysis* (Cambridge: Cambridge University Press, 1976). A classic if challenging analysis of the role of parties and the nature of party systems.

Wolinetz, S. (ed.), *Political Parties* (Aldershot and Brookfield, VT: Ashgate, 1997). A comprehensive set of articles that examine all aspects of the workings and significance of political parties.

Groups, Interests and Movements

CHAPTER 14

> 'Ten persons who speak make more noise than ten thousand who are silent.'
>
> NAPOLEON 1, *Maxims*

Patterns of political interaction were transformed in the twentieth century by the growing prominence of organized groups and interests. Indeed, in the 1950s and 1960s, at the high point of enthusiasm about 'group politics', it was widely asserted that business interests, trade unions, farm lobbies and the like had displaced assemblies and parties as the key political actors. The interest-group universe was further expanded, particularly from the 1960s onwards, by the growth of single-issue protest groups taking up causes ranging from consumer protection to animal rights and from sexual equality to environmental protection. Such groups were often associated with broader social movements (the women's movement, the civil-rights movement, the Green movement, and so on) and were characterized by the adoption of new styles of activism and campaigning, sometimes termed 'new politics'. Considerable debate nevertheless surrounds the nature and significance of groups, interests and movements, especially in relation to their impact on the democratic process.

The central issues examined in this chapter are as follows:

Key issues

▶ What are interest groups, and what different forms do they take?

▶ What have been the major theories of group politics?

▶ Do groups help or hinder democracy and effective government?

▶ How do interest groups exert influence?

▶ What determines the success or failure of interest groups?

▶ Why have new social movements emerged, and what is their broader significance?

Group politics

Interest groups, like political parties, constitute one of the major linkages between government and the governed in modern societies. In some respects, their origins parallel those of parties. They were the children of a new age of representative government and came into existence to articulate the increasingly complex divisions and cleavages of an emerging industrial society. While political parties, concerned with winning elections, sought to build coalitions of support and broaden their appeal, interest groups usually staked out a more distinct and clear-cut position, in accordance with the particular aspirations or values of the people they represented.

It is difficult to identify the earliest such group. Some groups predated the age of representative government, for example, the Abolition Society, which was founded in Britain in 1787 to oppose the slave trade. The Anti-Corn Law League, established in 1839, is often seen as the model for later UK groups, in that it was set up with the specific purpose of exerting pressure on government. After visiting the USA in the 1830s, Alexis de Tocqueville (see p. 227) reported that what he called **association** had already become a 'powerful instrument of action'. Young Italy, set up in 1831 by the Italian patriot Guiseppe Mazzini (see p. 116), became the model for sister national-ist organizations that later sprang up throughout Europe. Similarly, the Society for Women's Rights, founded in France in 1866, stimulated the formation of a world-wide women's suffrage movement. By the end of the nineteenth century powerful farming and business interests operated in most industrial societies, alongside a growing trade-union movement. However, most of the interest groups currently in existence are of much more recent origin. They are, in the main, a product of the explosion in pressure and protest politics that has occurred since the 1960s. As such they may be part of a broader process that has seen the decline of political parties and a growing emphasis on organized groups and social movements (see p. 308) as agents of mobilization and representation.

Types of group

The task of defining and classifying groups is fraught with danger, given the imprecise nature of groups and their multiplicity of forms. Are we, for instance, concerned with groups or with **interests**? In other words, do we only recognize groups as associations that have a certain level of cohesion and organization, or merely as collections of people who happen to share the same interest but may lack conscious-ness of the fact? Similarly, are interest groups only concerned with selfish and material interests, or may they also pursue broader causes or public goals? There is also the difficult issue of the relationship between interest groups and government. Are interest groups always autonomous, exerting influence from outside, or may they operate in and through government, perhaps even being part of the govern-ment machine itself?

This confusion is compounded by the lack of agreed terminology amongst political scientists active in this field. For instance, whereas the term 'interest group' is used in the USA and elsewhere to describe all organized groups, it tends to be used in the UK to refer only to those groups that advance or defend the interests of their members. The term 'pressure group' is therefore usually preferred in the UK, 'interest group' tending to be used as a subcategory of the broader classification.

Association: A group formed by voluntary action, reflecting a recognition of shared interests or common concerns.

Interest: That which benefits an individual or group; interests (unlike wants or preferences) are usually understood to be objective or 'real'.

Groups can nevertheless be classified into three types:

- communal groups
- institutional groups
- associational groups.

Communal groups

The chief characteristic of communal groups is that they are embedded in the social fabric, in the sense that membership is based on birth, rather than recruitment. Examples of such groups are families, tribes, castes and ethnic groups. Unlike conventional interest groups, to which members *choose* to belong, and which possess a formal structure and organization, communal groups are founded on the basis of a shared heritage and traditional bonds and loyalties. Such groups still play a major role in the politics of developing states. In Africa, for instance, ethnic, tribal and kinship ties are often the most important basis of interest articulation. Communal groups also continue to survive and exert influence in advanced industrial states, as the resurgence of ethnic nationalism and the significance of Catholic groups in countries like Italy and Ireland demonstrate.

Institutional groups

Institutional groups are groups that are part of the machinery of government and attempt to exert influence in and through that machinery. They differ from interest groups in that they enjoy no measure of autonomy or independence. Bureaucracies and the military are the clearest examples of institutional groups, and, not uncommonly, each of these contains a number of competing interests. In the case of authoritarian or totalitarian states, which typically suppress autonomous groups and movements, rivalry amongst institutional groups may become the principal form of interest articulation. The highly centralized Stalinist system in the USSR, for instance, was driven largely by entrenched bureaucratic and economic interests, in particular those centred around heavy industry. Similarly, the apparently monolithic character of the Hitler state in Germany (1933–45), concealed a reality of bureaucratic infighting as Nazi leaders built up sprawling empires in an endless struggle for power.

Institutional groups are not only of significance in non-democratic regimes. Some go so far as to argue that the bureaucratic elites and vested interests that develop in the ministries, departments and agencies of democratic systems in effect shape the policy process: they serve to constrain, some would say dictate to, elected politicians and elected governments. Such groups certainly also form alliances with conventional interest groups, as in the case of the celebrated 'military–industrial complex'. The significance of the bureaucracy and the military, and the importance of the interests that operate in and through them, are discussed in Chapters 17 and 18.

Associational groups

Associational groups are ones that are formed by people who come together to pursue shared, but limited, goals. Groups as associations are characterized by voluntary action and the existence of common interests, aspirations or attitudes. The most obvious examples of associational groups are thus what are usually thought of as interest groups or pressure groups. However, the distinction between these and communal groups may sometimes be blurred. For example, when class

Concept

Interest group

An interest group (or pressure group) is an organized association that aims to influence the policies or actions of government. Interest groups differ from political parties (see p. 272) in that they seek to exert influence from outside, rather than to win or exercise government power. Further, interest groups typically have a narrow issue focus, in that they are usually concerned with a specific cause or the interests of a particular group, and seldom have the broader programmic or ideological features that are generally associated with political parties. Interest groups are distinguished from social movements by their greater degree of formal organization. Nevertheless, not all interest groups have members in the formal sense: hence the preference of some commentators for the looser term 'organized interests'.

loyalties are strong and solidaristic, membership of an associational group such as a trade union may be more an expression of social identity than an instrumental act aimed at furthering a particular goal. Although associational groups are becoming increasingly important in developing states, they are usually seen as a feature of industrial societies. Industrialization both generates social differentiation, in the form of a complex web of competing interests, and, in a capitalist setting at least, encourages the growth of self-seeking and individualized patterns of behaviour in place of ones shaped by custom and tradition. When their primary function is to deal with government and other public bodies, such groups are usually called interest groups.

Interest groups appear in a variety of shapes and sizes. They are concerned with an enormous array of issues and causes, and use tactics that range from serving on public bodies and helping to administer government programmes to organizing campaigns of civil disobedience (see p. 307) and popular protest. However, anti-constitutional and paramilitary groups are excluded from this classification. Groups such as the Black Panthers and the Irish Republican Army (IRA) cannot be categorized as interest groups because they seek fundamentally to restructure the political system, not merely to influence it, and use the tactics of terrorism (see p. 406) and **direct action** instead of pressure politics. Structure must, however, be imposed on the apparently shapeless interest-group universe by the attempt to identify the different types of group. The two most common classifications are:

- sectional and promotional groups
- insider and outsider groups.

Sectional groups (sometimes called protective or functional groups) exist to advance or protect the (usually material) interests of their members. Trade unions, business corporations, trade associations and professional bodies are the prime examples of this type of group. Their 'sectional' character is derived from the fact that they represent a section of society: workers, employers, consumers, an ethnic or religious group, and so on. Strictly speaking, however, only groups engaged in the production, distribution and exchange of goods and services can be seen as 'functional' groups. In the USA, sectional groups are often classified as '*private* interest groups', to stress that their principal concern is the betterment and well-being of their members, not of society in general.

In contrast, *promotional* groups (sometimes termed cause or attitude groups) are set up to advance shared values, ideals or principles. These causes are many. They include 'pro-choice' and 'pro-life' lobbies on abortion, campaigns in favour of civil liberties or against sex and violence on television, protests about pollution and animal cruelty or in defence of traditional or religious values. In the USA, promotional groups are dubbed '*public* interest groups', to emphasize that they promote collective, rather than selective, benefits. When involved in international politics, these groups are often call nongovernmental organizations, or NGOs (see p. 297). Promotional groups are therefore by the fact that they aim to help groups other than their own members. Save the Whale, for instance, is an organization *for* whales, not one *of* whales. Some organizations, of course, have both sectional and promotional features. The National Association for the Advancement of Coloured People (NAACP) addresses the sectional interests of American black people (by opposing discrimination and promoting employment opportunities), but is also concerned with causes such as social justice and racial harmony.

Direct action: Political action taken outside the constitutional and legal framework; direct action may range from passive resistance to terrorism.

The alternative system of classification is based on the status that groups have in relation to government and the strategies they adopt in order to exert pressure. *Insider* groups enjoy regular privileged and usually institutionalized access to government through routine consultation or representation on government bodies. In many cases there is an overlap between sectional and insider classifications. This reflects the ability of key economic interests, such as business groups and trade unions, to exert powerful sanctions if their views are ignored by government. Government may also be inclined to consult groups that possess specialist knowledge and information that assists in the formulation of workable policy. Insider status, however, is not always an advantage, since it is conferred only upon groups with objectives that are broadly compatible with those of the government and which have a demonstrable capacity to ensure that their members abide by agreed decisions.

Outsider groups, on the other hand, are either not consulted by government or consulted only irregularly and not usually by a senior level. In many cases outsider status is an indication of weakness, in that, lacking formal access to government, these groups are forced to 'go public' in the hope of exercising indirect influence on the policy process. Ironically, then, there is often an inverse relationship between the public profile of an interest group and the political influence it exerts. Radical protest groups in fields such as environmental protection and animal rights may have little choice about being outsiders. Not only are their goals frequently out of step with the priorities of government, but their members and supporters are often attracted by the fact that such groups are untainted by close links with government. In that sense, groups may choose to remain outsiders, both to preserve their ideological purity and independence, and to protect their decentralized power structures.

Models of group politics

Some commentators believe that the pattern and significance of group politics are derived entirely from factors that are specific to each political system. The role of groups thus reflects a particular political culture, party system, set of institutional arrangements, and so on. This means that general conclusions cannot be drawn about the nature of group politics. On the other hand, the understanding of group politics is often shaped by broader assumptions about both the nature of the political process and the distribution of power in society. These assumptions are closely linked to the rival theories of the state examined in Chapter 5. The most influential of these as models of interest-group politics are the following:

- pluralism
- corporatism
- the New Right.

Pluralist model

Pluralist theories offer the most positive image of group politics. They stress the capacity of groups to both defend the individual from government and promote democratic responsiveness. The core theme of pluralism (see p. 82) is that political power is fragmented and widely dispersed. Decisions are made through a complex process of bargaining and interaction that ensures that the views and interests of a large number of groups are taken into account. One of the earliest and most influential attempts to develop a pluralist 'group theory' was undertaken by Arthur Bentley in *The Process of*

> **Concept**
>
> **Nongovernmental organization**
>
> A nongovernmental organization, or NGO, is a private, noncommercial group or body which seeks to achieve its ends through nonviolent means. NGOs are usually active in international politics and may be accorded formal consultation rights by bodies such as the UN or EU. They are sometimes termed international NGOs, or INGOs. Operational NGOs are often distinguised from advocacy NGOs. *Operational* NGOs are ones whose primary purpose is the design and implementation of projects, usually either development-related or relief-related. *Advocacy* NGOs exist to promote or defend a particular cause, and are more concerned with expertise and specialist knowledge than with operational capacity. NGOs are sometimes seen as the cornerstone of an emerging global civil society. Many regard them also as a counterweight to transnational corporations, or TNCs (see p. 149).

Robert Dahl (born 1915)

US political scientist. Appointed professor of political science at Yale University in 1946, Dahl subsequently became one of the USA's most eminent political analysts. In 1953 (with Charles Lindblom) he coined the term 'polyarchy' (rule by the many) to distinguish modern societies from classical democracy. Dahl's early writings reflect the impact of positivist and behaviouralist doctrines, and he developed in the 1950s and early 1960s a conventional pluralist position. From the late 1960s, however, together with Lindblom and Galbraith (see p. 193), he developed a radicalized form of liberalism, neopluralism, that revealed an increasing concern with the power of major capitalist corporations. His major works include *A Preface to Democratic Theory* (1956), *Who Governs?* (1961) and *Dilemmas of Pluralist Democracy* (1982).

Government ([1908] 1948). Bentley's emphasis on organized groups as the fundamental building blocks of the political process is neatly summed up in his famous dictum: 'when the groups are adequately stated, everything is stated'. David Truman's *The Governmental Process* (1951) is usually seen to have continued this tradition, even if his conclusions were more narrowly focused on the US political process.

Enthusiasm for groups as agents of interest articulation and aggregation was strengthened by the spread of behaviouralism in the 1950s and early 1960s. Systems analysis, for example, portrayed interest groups as 'gatekeepers' that filtered the multiple demands made of government into manageable sets of claims. At the same time, community power studies carried out by analysts such as Robert Dahl (1961) and Nelson Polsby (1963) claimed to find empirical support for the pluralist assertion that no single local elite is able to dominate community decision-making.

From the pluralist perspective, group politics is the very stuff of the democratic process. Indeed, it became common in the 1960s to argue that a form of pluralist democracy (see p. 83) had superseded more conventional electoral democracy, in that groups and organized interests had replaced political parties as the principal link between government and the governed. The central assumptions of this theory are that all groups and interests have the potential to organize and gain access to government, that they are internally responsive in the sense that leaders broadly articulate the interests or values of their members, and that their political influence is roughly in line with their size and the intensity of their support. One way in which this was demonstrated was by evidence that political power is fragmented in such a way that no group or interest can achieve dominance for any period of time. As Dahl (1956:145) put it, 'all the active and legitimate groups in the population can make themselves heard at some crucial stage in the process of decision'. The alternative idea of 'countervailing powers', developed in Galbraith's early writings, suggests that a dynamic equilibrium naturally emerges amongst competing groups, as the success of, say, business merely encourages opponents, such as labour or consumers, to organize to counter that success. Group politics is thus characterized by a rough balance of power.

This highly optimistic view of group politics has been heavily criticized by elitists and Marxists. Elitists challenge the empirical claims of pluralism by suggesting that they recognize only one 'face' of power: the ability to influence decision-making (see p. 84). In contrast to the notion that power is widely and evenly distributed, elite theorists draw attention to the existence of a 'power elite', comprising the heads of business corporations, political leaders and military chiefs (Mills, 1956). Marxists, for their part, have traditionally emphasized that political power is closely linked to the ownership of productive wealth, which suggests the existence of a capitalist 'ruling class'. For neo-Marxists such as Ralph Miliband (1969) this is reflected in 'unequal competition' between business and labour groups, the former enjoying a control of economic resources, a public status, and a level of access to government that the latter cannot match. The rise of globalization (see p. 143) has renewed such arguments, leading some to suggest that the increased mobility of capital and a free-trade international system has resulted in the 'corporate takeover' of government (Hertz, 2001). In the face of such criticism, a more critical or qualified form of pluralism, neopluralism (see p. 94), emerged. This has perhaps been most clearly expressed in Charles Lindblom's *Politics and Markets* (1977), which highlighted the privileged position that business groups enjoy in western polyarchies, while acknowledging that this seriously compromises the claim that such societies are democratic.

Corporatist model

Corporatist models of group politics differ from pluralism in that they attempt to trace the implications of the closer links that have developed in industrialized societies between groups and the state. Corporatism is a social theory that emphasizes the privileged position that certain groups enjoy in relation to government, enabling them to influence the formulation and implementation of public policy. Some commentators regard corporatism as a state-specific phenomenon, shaped by particular historical and political circumstances. They thus associate it with countries such as Austria, Sweden, the Netherlands and, to some extent, Germany and Japan, in which the government has customarily practised a form of economic management.

Others, however, see corporatism as a general phenomenon that stems from tendencies implicit in economic and social development, and thus believe that it is manifest, in some form or other, in all advanced industrial states. Even the USA, usually portrayed as the model of pluralist democracy, has invested its regulatory agencies with quasi-legislative powers, thereby fostering the development of formal bonds between government and major interests. From this perspective, corporatist tendencies may merely reflect the symbiotic relationship that exists between groups and government. Groups seek 'insider' status because it gives them access to policy formulation, which enables them better to defend the interests of their members. Government, on the other hand, needs groups, both as a source of knowledge and information, and because the compliance of major interests is essential if policy is to be workable. In increasingly differentiated and complex industrial societies the need for consultation and bargaining continues to grow, with the result that, perhaps inevitably, institutional mechanisms emerge to facilitate it.

The drift towards corporatism in advanced capitalist states, particularly pronounced in the 1960s and 1970s, provoked deep misgivings about the role and power of interest groups. In the first place, corporatism considerably cut down the number and range of groups that enjoyed access to government. Corporatism invariably privileges economic or functional groups, because it leads to a form of **tripartitism** that binds government to business and organized labour. However, it may leave consumer or promotional groups out in the cold, and institutionalized access is likely to be restricted to so-called 'peak' associations that speak on behalf of a range of organizations and groups. In Austria this role is carried out by the Chamber of Commerce and the Trade Union Federation, in the UK by the Confederation of British Industry (CBI) and the Trade Union Congress (TUC), and in the USA by

Tripartitism: The construction of bodies that represent government, business and the unions, designed to institutionalize group consultation.

the National Association of Manufacturers and the American Federation of Labor–Congress of Industrial Organizations (AFL–CIO).

A second problem is that, in contrast to the pluralist model, corporatism portrays interest groups as hierarchically ordered and dominated by leaders who are not directly accountable to members. Indeed, it is sometimes argued that the price that group leaders pay for privileged access to government is a willingness to deliver the compliance of their members. From this point of view, 'government by consultation' may simply be a sham concealing the fact that corporatism acts as a mechanism of social control. Third, concern has been expressed about the threat that corporatism poses to representative democracy. Whereas pluralism suggests that group politics supplements the representative process, corporatism creates the spectre of decisions being made outside the reach of democratic control and through a process of bargaining in no way subject to public scrutiny. Finally, corporatism has been linked to the problem of government 'overload', in which government may effectively be 'captured' by consulted groups and thus be unable to resist their demands. This critique has been advanced most systematically by the New Right.

New Right model

The antipathy of the New Right towards interest groups is derived, ideologically, from the individualism that lies at the heart of neoliberal economics. Social groups and collective bodies of all kinds are therefore viewed with suspicion. This is clearly reflected in the New Right's preference for a market economy driven by self-reliance and entrepreneuralism. However, the New Right has expressed particular concern about the alleged link between corporatism and escalating public spending and the associated problems of over-government. New Right anticorporatism has been influenced by public-choice theory, notably Mancur Olson's *The Logic of Collective Action: Public Goods and the Theory of Groups* (1968). Olson argued that people join interest groups only to secure 'public goods': that is, goods that are to some extent indivisible in that individuals who do not contribute to their provision cannot be prevented from enjoying them.

A pay increase is thus a public good in that workers who are not union members, or who choose not to strike in furtherance of the pay claim, benefit equally with union members and those who did strike. This creates opportunities for individuals to become 'free riders', reaping benefits without incurring the various costs that group membership may entail. This analysis is significant because it implies that there is no guarantee that the existence of a common interest will lead to the formation of an organization to advance or defend that interest. The pluralist assumption that all groups have some kind of political voice therefore becomes highly questionable. Olson also argued that group politics may often empower small groups at the expense of large ones. A larger membership encourages free riding because individuals may calculate that the group's effectiveness will be little impaired by their failure to participate.

This analysis was further developed in Olson's later work, *The Rise and Decline of Nations* (1982), which advanced a trenchant critique of interest-group activity, seeing it as a major determinant of the prosperity or economic failure of particular states. The UK and Australia, for example, were seen as suffering from 'institutional sclerosis'. This occurred as strong networks of interest groups emerged that were typically dominated by coalitions of narrow, sectional interests, including trade unions, business organizations and professional associations. The message that there is an inverse relationship between strong and well-organized interest groups, on the one hand, and

Focus on . . .

Interest groups: for and against

Arguments in favour of interest groups include the following:

- They strengthen *representation* by articulating interests and advancing views that are ignored by political parties, and by providing a means of influencing government between elections.

- They promote *debate* and discussion, thus creating a better-informed and more educated electorate, and improving the quality of public policy.

- They broaden the scope of political *participation,* both by providing an alternative to conventional party politics and by offering opportunities for grass-roots activism.

- They *check* government power and, in the process, defend liberty by ensuring that the state is balanced against a vigorous and healthy civil society.

- They help to maintain political *stability* by providing a channel of communication between government and the people, bringing outputs into line with inputs.

The arguments against interest groups include the following:

- They entrench political *inequality* by strengthening the voice of the wealthy and privileged, those who have access to financial, educational, organizational or other resources.

- They are socially and politically *divisive,* in that they are concerned with the particular, not the general, and advance minority interests against those of society as a whole.

- They exercise *non-legitimate* power, in that their leaders, unlike politicians, are not publicly accountable and their influence bypasses the representative process.

- They tend to make the policy process *closed* and more secretive by exerting influence through negotiations and deals that are in no way subject to public scrutiny.

- They make societies *ungovernable,* in that they create an array of vested interests that are able to block government initiatives and make policy unworkable.

economic growth and national prosperity on the other had a powerful impact on New Right policies and priorities. The clearest demonstration of this was the backlash against corporatism in the 1980s, spearheaded in the USA by Reagan and in the UK by Thatcher. In the USA, this took the form of an attempt to deregulate the economy by weakening regulatory agencies; in the UK, it was evident in the marginalization and later abolition of corporatist bodies such as the National Economic Development Council (NEDC or Neddy) and a determined assault on trade union power.

Patterns of group politics

How important are interest groups?

It is widely accepted that interest group activity is closely linked to economic and social development. Whereas agrarian or traditional societies tend to be dominated by a small number of interests, advanced industrial ones are complex and highly differentiated. Interest groups thus come to assume a central importance in mediating between the state and a more fragmented society, especially as the spread of education extends political awareness and organizational skills. This occurred, for example, in the USSR, where by the 1970s, despite the persistence of formal political monolithicism, most commentators had come to accept the existence of what was seen as 'institutional pluralism'. However, the roles and significance of organized interests vary from system to system, from state to state, and over time. The principal factors determining group influence are the following:

- the political culture
- the institutional structure
- the nature of the party system
- the nature and style of public policy.

The political culture is crucial for two reasons. First, it determines whether interest groups are viewed as legitimate or non-legitimate actors, whether their formation and influence is permitted and encouraged, or otherwise. Second, it affects the willingness of people to form or join organized interests or to engage in group politics. At one extreme, regimes can practise **monism**, suppressing all forms of voluntary associational activity in order to ensure a single, unchallengeable centre of state power. This typically occurs in military regimes and one-party states. Although no contemporary or historical state has succeeded in stamping out all forms of group or factional activity, monistic regimes at least push group activity underground or ensure that it is expressed through the party–state apparatus and is thus entangled with the political and ideological goals of the regime.

Pluralist regimes, on the other hand, not only permit group politics, but encourage and even, in some cases, require it. Groups may be asked to participate in policy formulation or to be represented on public bodies or quangos (see p. 392). One of the reasons for the generally high level of group activity found in the USA, for instance, is the recognition in US political culture of the right of private groups to be heard. This is enshrined in constitutional guarantees of free speech, freedom of the press, freedom of assembly, and so forth. In Japan, the absence of clear distinctions between the public and private realms has created a political culture in which, in predemocratic and democratic periods alike, a close relationship between government and business has been taken for granted.

In contrast, in some European states, organized interests are regarded with suspicion. This has traditionally been the case in France, where, influenced by Jacobin ideology, groups have been seen to both undermine the 'general will' of the people and challenge the strength and unity of the French state. At its high point in 1975, for instance, only 24 per cent of the French workforce belonged to a union, a figure that had fallen to 13 per cent by 1989. However, French political culture also embodies a tradition of direct action, demonstrated by the use by French farmers of road blocks and even lorry hijacks, and by the rebellion of students and trade unionists during the political troubles of May 1968.

The institutional structure of government is clearly significant in terms of interest-group activity in that it establishes points of access to the policy process. Unitary and centralized political systems, such as the UK's, tend to narrow the scope of group politics and concentrate it around the executive branch of government. Although

Monism: A belief in only one theory or value; monism is reflected politically in enforced obedience to a unitary power and is thus implicitly totalitarian.

this does not condemn groups to a marginal existence, it places heavy emphasis on 'insider' status and broadens the capacity of the government of the day to choose whether or not to respond to group pressure. This was most clearly demonstrated in the UK under Thatcher in the 1980s in the downgrading of corporatist bodies and the consigning of trade unions to the political wilderness. Interest-group activity in France is similarly focused on direct consultation with the administration, particularly since the strengthening of presidential government and the weakening of the National Assembly in the Fifth Republic of 1958.

US government, on the other hand, is fragmented and decentralized. This reflects the impact of bicameralism, the separation of powers, federalism and judicial review. The range of 'access points' that this offers interest groups makes the US system peculiarly vulnerable to group pressures. Groups know, for instance, that battles lost in Congress can be refought in the courts, at the state or local level, and so on. Although this undoubtedly acts as a stimulus to group formation, and enlarges the number of influential groups, it may also be self-defeating, in that the activities of groups can end up cancelling each other out. Organized interests may thus act only as 'veto groups'.

The relationship between political parties and interest groups is always complex. In some senses, they are clearly rivals. While parties seek to aggregate interests and form political programmes typically based on broad ideological goals, interest groups are concerned with a narrower and more specific range of issues and objectives. Nevertheless, interest groups often seek to exert influence in and through parties, in some cases even spawning parties in an attempt to gain direct access to power. Many socialist parties, such as the UK Labour Party, were effectively created by the trade unions, and institutional and financial links, albeit modified, endure to this day.

The pattern of interest-group politics is also influenced by the party system. Dominant-party systems tend, quite naturally, to narrow the focus of group politics, concentrating it on the governing party. Major industrial and commercial interests in Italy and Japan therefore tried to exert pressure through 'ruling' parties such as the Christian Democrats and the Liberal-Democratic Party, which, in the process, did much to entrench the factional tendencies within these parties. Multiparty systems, on the other hand, are fertile ground for interest-group activity, because they broaden the scope of access. The legislative influence of interest groups is perhaps greatest in party systems like the USA's, in which political parties are weak in terms of both organization and discipline. This was demonstrated in the late 1970s by the capacity of business interests effectively to destroy President Carter's energy programme, despite the existence of Democrat majorities in both the House of Representatives and the Senate.

Finally, the level of group activity fluctuates in relation to shifts in public policy, particularly the degree to which the state intervenes in economic and social life. As a general rule, **interventionism** goes hand in hand with corporatism, although there is a debate about which is the cause and which is the effect. Do interventionist policies force government into a closer relationship with organized interests in the hope of gaining information, advice and cooperation? Or do groups exploit their access to government to extract subsidies, supports and other benefits for their members? Whatever the answer is, it is clear that, amongst western states, the integration of organized interests, particularly functional interests, into public life has been taken furthest where social-democratic policies have been pursued.

The Swedish system is the classic example of this. Interest groups constitute an integral part of the Swedish political scene at every level. There are close, if not

Interventionism: Government policies designed to regulate or manage economic life; more broadly, a policy of engagement or involvement.

institutional, links between the trade unions and the Social Democratic Labour Party (SAP). The legislative process in the Riksdag is geared to wide consultation with affected interests, and state officials recognize 'peak' associations such as the Swedish Trade Union Confederation and the Employers' Confederation as 'social partners'. A similar pattern of corporate representation has developed in the Austrian 'chamber' system, which provides statutory representation for major interests such as commerce, agriculture and labour. In Germany, key economic groups such as the Federation of German Employers' Associations, the Federation of German Industry and the German Trades Union Federation are so closely involved in policy formulation that the system has been described as one of 'polyarchic elitism'.

How do groups exert influence?

Interest groups have at their disposal a broad range of tactics and political strategies. Indeed, it is almost unthinkable that a group should confine itself to a single strategy or try to exert influence through just one channel of influence. The methods that groups use vary according to a number of factors. These include the issue with which the group is concerned and how policy in that area is shaped. For instance, in the UK, since most policies relating to civil liberties and political rights are developed by the Home Office, a group such as Liberty (formerly the National Council for Civil Liberties) is compelled to seek 'insider' status, which it does by emphasizing its specialist knowledge and political respectability. Similarly, the nature of the group and the resources at its disposal are crucial determinants of its political strategy. These resources include the following:

- public sympathy for the group and its goals
- the size of its membership or activist base
- its financial strength and organizational capabilities
- its ability to use sanctions that in some way inconvenience or disrupt government
- personal or institutional links it may have to political parties or government bodies.

Business groups are more likely than, say, trade unions or consumer groups to employ professional lobbyists or mount expensive public-relations campaigns, because, quite simply, they have the financial capacity to do so. The methods used by interest groups are shaped by the channel of access through which influence is exerted. The principal channels of access available are:

- the bureaucracy
- the assembly
- the courts
- political parties
- the mass media
- supranational bodies.

In all states, interest-group activity tends to centre on the bureaucracy as the key institution in the process of policy formulation. Access via this channel is largely confined to major economic and functional groups, such as large corporations, employers' associations, trade unions, farming interests and key professions. In Austria, the Netherlands and the Scandinavian states, for example, corporatist institutions have been developed specifically to facilitate group consultation, usually giving 'peak' employers' and employees' associations a measure of formal representation. More commonly, the consultative process is informal yet institutionalized, taking place through meetings and regular contacts that are rarely publicized and are beyond the scope of public scrutiny.

The crucial relationship here is usually that between senior bureaucrats and leading business or industrial interests. The advantages that business groups enjoy in this respect include the key role they play in the economy as producers, investors and employers, the overlap in social background and political outlets between business leaders and ministers and senior officials, and the widely held public belief that business interests coincide with the national interest ('what is good for General Motors is good for America'). This relationship is often consolidated by a 'revolving door' through which bureaucrats, on retirement, move into well-paid jobs in private business. In Japan this practice is so clearly established that it is known as *amakudari*, literally meaning 'descent from heaven'. Two factors that have further strengthened big business' control over ministers and bureaucrats are the greater ease with which corporations can relocate production and investment in a global economy, and the advent of the 'new' public management in which governments become increasingly dependent on the private sector for investment in, and sometimes the delivery of, public services (Monbiot, 2001).

Influence exerted through the assembly, often called lobbying, is another important form of interest-group activity. One manifestation of this is the growth in the number of professional lobbyists, over 11 000 of whom were registered in Washington DC in 1990. The significance of the assembly or legislature in this respect depends on two factors: first, the role it plays in the political system and the degree to which it can shape policy, and second, the strength and discipline of the party system. Interest-group activity surrounding the US Congress is usually seen as the most intense in the world. This reflects the strength of Congress in terms of its constitutional independence and powerful committee system, and the fact that its decentralized party system allows individual representatives to be easily recruited by groups and causes. Much of this influence is exerted through financial contributions made to election campaigns by political action committees (PACs). However, since the 1990s and as a result of tighter campaign finance laws, 'hard money' donated by PACs has tended to be displaced by 'soft money' (indirect and unregulated donations).

Policy networks (see p. 432) have also developed through institutionalized contacts between legislators (particularly key figures on legislative committees) and 'affected' groups and interests. In the USA these form two 'legs' (executive agencies being the third leg) of the so-called 'iron triangles' that dominate much of domestic policy-making. Lobbying activities focused on the assembly are less extensive and less significant in states like Canada and the UK in which party discipline is strong and parliaments are usually subject to executive control. Nevertheless, a US-style lobbying industry developed in the UK in the 1980s, with a trebling of the amount of money spent on professional lobbying, usually by parliamentary consultancies. This was in part a consequence of the dismantling of corporatism in the UK. However, it created growing concern about a decline in standards in public life in general, and especially amongst MPs, which resulted in the creation of the Nolan Committee on standards in public life in 1995.

In systems in which the courts are unable to challenge legislation and rarely check executive actions, interest-group activity focused on the judiciary is of only limited significance. This applies in states like the UK and New Zealand, despite a general

Concept

Lobby

The term lobby is derived from the areas in parliaments or assemblies where the public may petition legislators, or politicians meet to discuss political business. In modern usage the term is both a verb and a noun. The verb to lobby means to make direct representations to a policy-maker, using argument or persuasion. Broadly, a lobby (noun) is equivalent to an interest group, in that both aim to influence public policy, as with the farm lobby, the environmental lobby and the roads lobby. Narrowly, following US practice, a lobbyist is a 'professional persuader': that is, a person hired to represent the arguments of interest-group clients. Professional lobbying has been criticized for amounting to the 'buying' of political influence.

tendency in the 1980s and 1990s towards judicial activism, which encouraged civil liberties and environmentalist groups in particular to fight campaigns through the courts. Where codified constitutions invest judges with the formal power of judicial review, however, as in Australia and the USA, the court system attracts far greater attention from interest groups. The classic example of this in the USA was the landmark *Brown* v. *Board of Education* Supreme Court ruling in 1954, which rejected the constitutionality of segregation laws. The NAACP had lobbied the US legal community for several years in an attempt to shift attitudes on issues such as race and segregation, and helped to sponsor the case. Similarly, in the 1980s and 1990s, the energies of the US pro-life (anti-abortion) lobby were largely directed at the Supreme Court, specifically in an attempt to overturn the 1974 *Roe* v. *Wade* judgment, which established the constitutionality of abortion.

Interest-group pressure is often also exerted through political parties. In some cases, parties and groups are so closely linked by historical, ideological and even institutional ties that they are best thought of as simply two wings of the same social movement. The UK and Australian Labour parties began in this way, and still function, if to a lesser extent, as part of a broader labour movement. Agrarian parties such as the Centre parties in Sweden and Norway are still part of a broad farmers' movement, and even Christian Democratic parties in central Europe can be seen as part of a broad Catholic movement. In other cases, however, the relationship between parties and groups is more pragmatic and instrumental.

The principal means through which groups influence parties is via campaign finance, and the benefits they hope to achieve are clear: 'he who pays the piper plays the tune'. Throughout the world, conservative or right-wing parties and candidates are funded largely by business contributions, while support for socialist or left-wing ones traditionally came mainly from organized labour. For example, George W. Bush's bid for reelection in 2004 was not only the most expensive campaign in US history, but also was financed largely by prominent corporate and industrial interests. However, groups may also have good reasons for avoiding too close an association with parties. For one thing, if 'their' party is in opposition, the government of the day may be less sympathetic to their interests; for another, open partisanship may restrict their ability to recruit members from amongst supporters of other parties. As a result, groups such as Shelter and the Child Poverty Action Group in the UK have assiduously guarded their nonpartisan status. There are, in addition, examples of political parties that have sought to 'divorce' themselves from interest groups. In the 1990s, the UK Labour Party thus reduced the influence of affiliated trade unions at every level in the party in an attempt to destroy the image that the Labour Party is merely a puppet of the union movement. However, as this was being achieved, the party was also engaged in a 'charm offensive' to attract business backers, the success of which helped to consolidate its shift to the ideological middle ground.

Very different methods are employed by groups that seek to influence government indirectly via the mass media (see p. 232) and public opinion campaigns. Tactics here range from petitions, protests and demonstrations to civil disobedience and even the tactical use of violence. Interest groups use such methods for one of two reasons. They may either reflect the group's outsider status and its inability to gain direct access to policy-makers, or they may follow from the nature of the group's activist base or the character of its ideological goals. The traditional practitioners of this form of politics were trade unions, which utilized their 'industrial muscle' in the form of strikes, pickets and marches.

However, the spectacular rise of promotional and cause groups since the 1960s has seen the emergence of new styles of activist politics practised by peace campaigners, environmental lobbyists, animal rights groups, anti-roads protesters, and so on. A common aim of these groups is to attract media attention and stimulate public awareness and sympathy. Greenpeace and Friends of the Earth, for example, have been particularly imaginative in devising protests against nuclear testing, air and water pollution, deforestation, and the use of nonrenewable energy sources. The nature and significance of such activities in relation to new social movements are examined in the next main section of the chapter.

Finally, since the closing decades of the twentieth century, interest-group activity has increasingly adjusted to the impact of globalization and the strengthening of supranational bodies. Amongst the groups best suited to take advantage of such shifts are charities and environmental campaigners (such as Greenpeace and Friends of the Earth) that already possess transnational structures and an international membership. Since its creation in 1971, Greenpeace, for example, has established offices in over 30 countries and built up an annual income of $50 000 000. Many of these organizations gained formal representation as nongovernmental organizations (NGOs) at the 1992 UN Conference on Environment and Development (commonly known as the Earth Summit) in Brazil. The better-funded NGOs now have permanent offices in Washington DC and Brussels, which monitor the work of the UN and EU respectively, and conduct regular lobbying campaigns.

Sectional interest groups in EU member states have also adjusted to the fact that, in a number of policy areas, key decisions are increasingly made by EU institutions rather than national ones. This particularly applies in relation to agriculture, trade agreements, competition policy and social and workers' rights. The most financially powerful and best-organized groups operating at the EU level are undoubtedly business interests. Their influence is exerted in various ways: through direct lobbying by large corporations, national trade bodies and 'peak' associations, and through the activities of a new range of EU 'peak' associations such as the European Round Table of Industrialists and the Union of Industrial and Employers' Confederations of Europe (UNICE). To some extent, however, the UK trade-union movement, and the Trades Union Congress (TUC) in particular, has been able to compensate for its marginalization at the national level by conducting its campaigns in favour of workers' and social rights through EU institutions.

Social movements

Interest in social movements has been revived by the emergence of so-called 'new' social movements since the 1960s: the women's movement, the environmental or Green movement, the peace movement, and so on. However, social movements can be traced back to the early nineteenth century. The earliest were the labour movement, which campaigned for improved conditions for the growing working class, various national movements, usually struggling for independence from multinational European empires, and, in central Europe in particular, a Catholic movement that fought for emancipation through the granting of legal and political rights to Catholics. In the twentieth century it was also common for fascist and right-wing authoritarian groups to be seen as movements rather than as conventional political parties.

Concept

Civil disobedience

Civil disobedience is law-breaking that is justified by reference to 'higher' religious, moral or political principles. Civil disobedience is an overt and public act; it aims to break a law in order to 'make a point', not to get away with it. Indeed, its moral force is based largely on the willing acceptance of the penalties that follow from law-breaking. This both emphasizes the conscientious or principled nature of the act and provides evidence of the depth of feeling or commitment that lies behind it. The moral character of civil disobedience is normally demonstrated by the strict avoidance of violence, as exemplified by Gandhi's (1869–1948) notion of *satyagraha* (literally 'insistence on truth'), nonviolent resistance. Other advocates of civil disobedience have included D. H. Thoreau (1817–62) and Martin Luther King (1929–68).

Concept

Social movement

A social movement is a particular form of collective behaviour in which the motive to act springs largely from the attitudes and aspirations of members, typically acting within a loose organizational framework. Being part of a social movement requires a level of commitment and political activism rather than formal or card-carrying membership; above all, movements *move*. A movement is different from spontaneous mass action (such as an uprising or rebellion) in that it implies a level of intended and planned action in pursuit of a recognized social goal. Not uncommonly, social movements embrace interest groups and may even spawn political parties: trade unions and socialist parties, for instance, can be seen as part of a broader labour movement.

New social movements

What is 'new' about the social movements that emerged in the final decades of the twentieth century? In the first place, whereas their more traditional counterparts were movements of the oppressed or disadvantaged, contemporary social movements have more commonly attracted the young, the better-educated and the relatively affluent. This is linked to the second difference: new movements typically have a postmaterial (see p. 211) orientation, being more concerned with 'quality of life' issues than with social advancement. Although the women's movement, for example, addresses material concerns such as equal pay and equal opportunities, it draws from a broader set of values associated with gender equality and opposition to patriarchy. Third, while traditional movements had little in common and seldom worked in tandem, new social movements subscribe to a common, if not always clearly defined, ideology.

In broad terms, their ideological stance is linked to the New Left: it challenges prevailing social goals and political styles, and embraces libertarian aspirations such as personal fulfilment and self-expression. It is therefore not surprising that there is a significant membership overlap, as well as mutual sympathy, amongst the women's, environmental, animal rights, peace, anti-roads, 'anti-capitalist' or anti-globalization and other movements.

A final difference between traditional and new social movements is that the latter tend to have organizational structures that stress decentralization and participatory decision-making and have also developed new forms of political activism. They thus practise what is sometimes called the 'new politics', which turns away from 'estab-

Concept

New Left

The New Left comprises the thinkers and intellectual movements (prominent in the 1960s and early 1970s) that sought to revitalize socialist thought by developing a radical critique of advanced industrial society. The New Left rejected both 'old' left alternatives: Soviet-style state socialism and de-radicalized western social democracy. Influenced by the humanist writings of the 'young' Marx, anarchism and radical forms of phenomenology and existentalism, New Left theories were often diffuse. Common themes nevertheless included a fundamental rejection of conventional society ('the system') as oppressive, a commitment to personal autonomy and self-fulfilment in the form of 'liberation', disillusionment with the role of the working class as the revolutionary agent, and a preference for decentralization and participatory democracy.

Naomi Klein (born 1970)

Canadian journalist, author and anticorporate activist. Klein's *No Logo: Taking Aim at the Brand Bullies* (2000) is a wide-ranging critique of lifestyle branding and labour abuses, and discusses emerging forms of resistance to globalization and corporate domination. It has been described as 'the book that became part of the movement' but has had wider significance in provoking reflection on the nature of consumer capitalism and the tyranny of brand culture. Klein is a frequent and influential media commentator. She lives in Toronto but travels throughout North America, Asia, Latin America and Europe tracking the rise of anticorporate activism and supporting movements campaigning against the negative effects of globalization. Her writings also include *Fences and Windows* (2002).

lished' parties, interest groups and representative processes towards a more innovative and theatrical form of protest politics. The most dramatic examples of this have been the so-called 'Battle of Seattle' in 1999, in which mass demonstrations against the World Trade Organization degenerated into violent clashes between the police and groups of protesters, and other similar 'anti-capitalist' or anti-globalization' protests, for example, in Prague in 2000 and in Genoa in 2001. Such demonstrations involve a disparate range of environmental, development, ethnic nationalist, anarchist and revolutionary socialist groups, with the internet and mobile phones providing the principal means of communications. The ideas of the emergent anti-globalization movement have been articulated in the writing of authors such as Noam Chomsky (see p. 234) and Naomi Klein (2000).

The emergence of a new generation of social movements practising new styles of activism has significantly shifted views about the nature and significance of movements themselves. The experience of totalitarianism (see p. 29) in the period between the two world wars encouraged **mass society** theorists such as Erich Fromm (1900–80) and Hannah Arendt (see p. 9) to see movements in distinctly negative terms. From the mass society perspective, social movements reflect a 'flight from freedom' (Fromm, 1941), an attempt by alienated individuals to achieve security and identity through fanatical commitment to a cause and obedience to a (usually fascist) leader. In contrast, new social movements are usually interpreted as rational and instrumental actors, whose use of informal and unconventional means merely reflects the resources available to them (McCarthy and Zald, 1973). The emergence of new social movements is widely seen as evidence of the fact that power in **postindustrial societies** is increasingly dispersed and fragmented. The class-based politics of old has thus been replaced by a new politics based on what Laclau and Mouffe (1985) called 'democratic pluralism'. Not only do new movements offer new and rival centres of power, but they also diffuse power more effectively by resisting bureaucratization and developing more spontaneous, affective and decentralized forms of organization.

Nevertheless, the impact of social movements is more difficult to assess than that of political parties or interest groups. This is because of the broader nature of their goals, and because, to some extent, they exert influence through less tangible cultural strategies. However, it is clear that in cases like the women's movement and the environmental movement profound political changes have been achieved through shifts in cultural values and moral attitudes brought about over a number of years. For

Mass society: A society characterized by atomism and cultural and political rootlessness; the concept highlights pessimistic trends in modern societies.

Postindustrial society: A society no longer dependent on manufacturing industry, but more reliant on knowledge and communication; an 'information society'.

Betty Friedan (1921–2006)

US feminist and political activist, sometimes seen as the 'mother' of women's liberation. Betty Friedan's *The Feminine Mystique* (1963) is often credited with having stimulated the emergence of 'second wave' feminism. In it, she examined 'the problem with no name': the sense of frustration and despair afflicting suburban American women. In 1966, she helped to found the National Organization of Women (NOW), becoming its first president. In *The Second Stage* (1983) Friedan drew attention to the danger that the pursuit of 'personhood' might encourage women to deny the importance of children, the home, and the family. Her later writings include *The Fountain of Age* (1993).

example, the Women's Liberation Movement (WLM) emerged in the 1960s as a collection of groups and organizations mobilized by the emerging ideas of 'second wave' feminism, as expressed in the writings of such as Betty Friedan, Germaine Greer (born 1939) and Kate Millett (born 1934). Despite the achievement by the women's movement of advances in specific areas, such as equal pay and the legalization of abortion, perhaps its most significant achievement is an increasing general awareness of gender issues and the eroding of support for patriarchal attitudes and institutions. This is a cultural change that has had a deep, if unquantifiable, impact on public policy at many levels.

The environmental movement has brought about similar politico-cultural shifts. Not only have governments been confronted by interest-group campaigns mounted by the likes of Greenpeace, Friends of the Earth and the Worldwide Fund for Nature, but they have also been influenced by broader anxieties about the environment that extend well beyond those expressed by the formal membership of such organizations. Since the 1970s these concerns have also been articulated by Green parties. Typically, these parties have embraced the idea of 'new politics', styling themselves as 'anti-system' parties, and placing a heavy emphasis on decentralization and popular activism. The impact of the environmental movement has also extended to conventional or 'grey' parties, many of which have responded to new popular sensibilities by trying to establish their Green credentials. By contrast, the 'anti-capitalist' movement, or, more accurately, the loose coalition of groups that has been brought together by resistance to globalization and its associated consumerist values and free-trade practices, has as yet been less successful. Although international summit meetings have become much more difficult to arrange, there is little sign of governments or mainstream parties revising their support for free trade (see p. 157) and economic deregulation.

■ Summary

◆ An interest or pressure group is an organized association that aims to influence the policies or actions of government. Sectional groups advance or protect the (usually material) interests of their members, while promotional ones are concerned with shared values, ideals or principles. Whereas insider groups enjoy privileged access to policy formulation, outsider groups lack access to government and so are forced to 'go public'.

◆ Group politics has been understood in a number of ways. Pluralism emphasizes the dispersal of power and the ability of groups to guarantee democratic account-ability. Corporatism highlights the privileged position that certain groups enjoy in relation to government. The New Right draws attention to the threat that groups pose in terms of over-government and economic inefficiency.

◆ Organized groups benefit the political system by strengthening representation, promoting debate and discussion, broadening political participation, and acting as a check on government power. They may nevertheless pose a threat in that they entrench political inequality, are socially and politically divisive, exercise nonlegitimate and unaccountable power, and make the policy process more closed and secretive.

◆ Interest groups exert influence through a variety of channels, including the bureaucracy, the assembly, the courts, the mass media, the parties and international bodies. The level of influence that groups have in a particular system, however, relates to how accommodating that system is to group activity in general, and to what access points it offers groups in terms of the distribution of policy-making power.

◆ Interest groups have at their disposal a wide range of tactics and political strategies. Their resources may include public sympathy for the group and its goals, the size of its membership or activist base, its financial strength and organizational capabilities, its ability to use sanctions against government, and its personal or institutional links with political parties or government bodies.

◆ A social movement is a collective body in which there is a high level of commit-ment and political activism not necessarily based on a formal organization. New social movements are distinguished by their capacity to attract the young, better-educated and relatively affluent, their generally postmaterial orientation, and their commitment to new forms of political activism, sometimes called the 'new politics'.

Questions for discussion

▶ Why is it sometimes difficult to distinguish between interest groups and political parties?

▶ Are organized groups the principal means through which interests are articulated in modern societies?

▶ Does corporatism work more to the benefit of groups, or more to the benefit of government?

▶ Do interest groups help to promote democracy or to undermine it?

▶ Why are some interest groups more powerful than others?

▶ To what extent have new social movements had an impact on public policy?

Further reading

Cigler, C. and B. Loomis (eds), *Interest Group Politics* (Washington, DC: Congressional Quar-terly Press, 1998). An examination of various aspects of group politics in the USA.

Jordan, G., *Interest Group Politics: Enhancing Participation?* (Basingstoke and New York: Pal-grave Macmillan, 2006). An assessment of how interest groups are formed and maintained, which also considers their implications for participation and democracy.

Smith, M., *Pressure Groups* (Manchester: Baseline Books, 1995). An introduction to the role and workings of pressure groups in the UK.

Tarrow, S., *Power in Movement: Social Movements and Contentious Politics* (Cambridge and New York: Cambridge University Press, 1998). A useful introduction to the nature and significance of social movements.

Wilson, G., *Interest Groups* (Oxford: Blackwell, 1990). A clear and concise discussion of the role of groups in liberal democracies.

Machinery of Government

Constitutions, the Law and Judiciaries

CHAPTER 15

'Government without a Constitution is Power without Right.'

THOMAS PAINE, *The Rights of Man* (1795)

Contents

In the 1950s and 1960s the study of constitutions and constitutional issues became distinctly unfashionable. Political analysts turned instead to what were seen as deeper political realities, such as political culture and the distribution of economic and social power. To be interested in constitutions was to perpetuate an outdated, legalistic and, frankly, boring approach to politics, to focus on how a political system portrays itself, rather than on how it actually works. Since the 1970s, however, constitutional questions have moved to the centre of the political stage. Developed and developing states have adopted new constitutions, and political conflict has increasingly been expressed in terms of calls for constitutional reform. This, in turn, has had major implications for the role of law and the position of judges. Although in theory the courts and the judiciary are strictly separate from politics, in practice, in many parts of the world, they have developed into key political institutions that have a growing capacity to shape public policy.

The central issues examined in this chapter are as follows:

Key issues

▶ What is a constitution, and what forms can it take?

▶ What is the purpose of a constitution?

▶ To what extent do constitutions shape political practice?

▶ What is the relationship between law and politics?

▶ What is the political significance of the courts?

▶ Can judges keep out of politics? Should judges keep out of politics?

Constitutions

Traditionally, constitutions were seen as important for two reason. First, they were believed to provide a description of government itself, a neat introduction to key institutions and their roles. Second, they were regarded as the linchpin of liberal democracy, even its defining feature. Sadly, neither view is correct. While constitutions may *aim* to lay down a framework in which government and political activity are conducted, none has been entirely successful in this respect. Inaccuracies, distortions and omissions can be found in all constitutions. Similarly, although the idea of constitutionalism (see p. 321) is closely linked to liberal values and aspirations, there is nothing to prevent a constitution being undemocratic or authoritarian. In the case of communist states and some developing states, constitutions have indeed been profoundly illiberal. Why then bother with constitutions? Why begin an account of the machinery of government with a discussion of constitutions? The reason is that the objective of constitutions is to lay down certain meta-rules for the political system. In effect, these are rules that govern the government itself. Just as government establishes ordered rule in society at large, the purpose of a constitution is to bring stability, predictability and order to the actions of government.

The idea of a code of rules providing guidance for the conduct of government has an ancient lineage. These codes traditionally drew on the idea of a higher moral power, usually religious in character, to which worldly affairs were supposed to conform. Egyptian pharaohs acknowledged the authority of *Ma'at* or 'justice', Chinese emperors were subject to *Ti'en* or 'heaven', Jewish kings conformed to the Mosaic Law, and Islamic caliphs paid respect to *Shari'a* law. Not uncommonly, 'higher' principles were also enacted in ordinary law, as seen, for example, in the distinction in the Athenian constitution between the *nomos* (laws that could be changed only by a special procedure) and the *psephismata* (decrees that could be passed by a resolution of the assembly). However, such ancient codes did not amount to constitutions in the modern sense, in that they generally failed to lay down specific provisions relating to the authority and responsibilities of the various institutions, and rarely established authoritative mechanisms through which provisions could be enforced and breaches of the fundamental law punished.

Constitutions are thus best thought of as a relatively recent development. Although the evolution of the British constitution is sometimes traced back to the Bill of Rights of 1689 and the Act of Settlement of 1701, or even to the Magna Carta (1215), it is more helpful to think of constitutions as late eighteenth-century creations. The 'age of constitutions' was initiated by the enactment of the first 'written' constitutions: the US constitution in 1787 and the French Declaration of the Rights of Man and the Citizen in 1789. The examples of the USA and revolutionary France not only provided in form and substance a model for later constitution-makers to follow, but also shed light on why and how constitutions come about.

The enactment of a constitution marks a major breach in political continuity, usually resulting from an upheaval such as a war, revolution or national independence. Constitutions are above all a means of establishing a new political order following the rejection, collapse or failure of an old order. In this light, the revival of interests in constitutions since the 1970s (with new constitutions being adopted in countries such as Portugal, Spain, Canada, Sweden and the Netherlands, and the issue of constitutional reform becoming more prominent in, for example, the UK, India and Australia) indicates growing disenchantment, even disillusionment, with existing political systems. In general, it can be said that political conflicts assume a constitutional dimension only when those demanding change seek to redraw, and not merely readjust, the rules of the political game. Constitutional change is therefore about the reapportionment of both power and political authority.

Classifying constitutions

Constitutions can be classified in many different ways. These include the following:

- the form of the constitution and *status* of its rules (whether the constitution is written or unwritten, or codified or uncodified)
- the ease with which the constitution can be *changed* (whether it is rigid or flexible)
- the degree to which the constitution is *observed* in practice (whether it is an effective, nominal or facade constitution)
- the *content* of the constitution and the institutional structure that it establishes (whether it is, for example, monarchical or republican, federal or unitary, or presidential or parliamentary).

Traditionally, considerable emphasis has been placed on the distinction between written and unwritten constitutions. *Written* constitutions are, in theory, constitutions that are enshrined in laws, while *unwritten* constitutions are supposedly embodied in custom and tradition (see p. 221). The former are human artefacts in the sense that they have been 'created', while the latter have been seen as organic entities that have evolved through history. This system of classification, however, has now largely been abandoned. In the first place, an overwhelming majority of states now possess basic written documents that lay down major constitutional provisions. Only three liberal democracies (Israel, New Zealand and the UK) continue to have unwritten constitutions, together with a handful of nondemocratic states such as Bhutan, Saudi Arabia and Oman. Moreover, the classification has always been misleading. No constitution is entirely written in the sense that all its rules are formal and legally enforceable. Few constitutions, for instance, specify the roles of, or even mention, political parties and interest groups. Similarly, no constitution is entirely unwritten in the sense that none of its provisions have any legal substance, all of them being conventions, customs or traditions.

Every constitution, then, is a blend of written and unwritten rules, although the balance between these varies significantly. In countries such as France and Germany in which constitutional documents act as state codes, specifying in considerable detail the powers and responsibilities of political institutions, the emphasis is clearly on written rules. The US constitution (the world's first written constitution) is, however, a document of only 7000 words that confines itself, in the main, to broad principles and so lays down only a loose framework for government. US institutions of undoubted constitutional significance, such as congressional committees, primary elections (see p. 278) and the bureaucracy, have simply evolved over time. Other constitutions, although not entirely unwritten, place considerable stress on conventions. For example, the ability of UK ministers to exercise the powers of the Royal Prerogative (technically, the monarch's powers) and their responsibility, individually and collectively, to Parliament is based entirely on convention.

Convention

A convention, in everyday language, is either a formal political meeting or an agreement reached through debate and negotiation. A constitutional convention, however, is a rule of conduct or behaviour that is based not on law but on custom and precedent. These nonlegal rules are upheld either by a sense of constitutional propriety (what is 'correct') or by practical circumstances (what is 'workable'). Conventions of this sort exist in all constitutional systems, and they usually provide guidance where formal rules are unclear or incomplete. In 'unwritten' constitutions, they are particularly significant, because they define the procedures, powers and duties of the major institutions, thus compensating for the absence of a codified document. Typically, they modify the effect of powers laid down in strict law.

Common law: Law based on custom and precedent; law that is supposedly 'common' to all.

The worldwide trend, however, is to favour the adoption of written and formal rules. Not only has the number of unwritten constitutions diminished, but also, within them, there has been a growing reliance on legal rules. Although respect for the Torah, the Jewish book of holy law, encouraged the Israelis to establish an independent state in 1948 without an authoritative constitutional document, within two years the Knesset had voted to adopt such a constitution by evolution over an unspecified period of time. The publication in the UK of documents such as Questions on Procedure for Ministers has given detailed formal substance to practices that were previously covered by ill-defined conventions. The passage in New Zealand of the Constitution Act 1986 (which consolidated previously scattered laws and principles), and the adoption in 1990 of a bill of rights (see p. 323), has been interpreted by many commentators as indicating that New Zealand should no longer be classified amongst the ranks of states with unwritten constitutions.

More helpful (and more accurate) than the written/unwritten distinction is the contrast between codified and uncodified constitutions. A *codified* constitution is one in which key constitutional provisions are collected together within a single legal document, popularly known as a 'written constitution' or 'the constitution'. As pointed out above, most constitutions can be so classified, even though they may differ in the degree to which constitutional detail is specified and the extent to which other provisions are unwritten. The significance of codification is, nevertheless, considerable.

First, in a codified constitution, the document itself is authoritative in the sense that it constitutes 'higher' law, indeed, the highest law of the land. The constitution binds all political institutions, including those that enact ordinary law. The existence of a codified constitution thus establishes a hierarchy of laws. In unitary states, a two-tier legal system exists, in which the constitution stands above statute law made by the national legislature. In federal states, there is a third tier in the form of 'lower' state or provincial laws. Second, the status of the codified document is ensured by the fact that at least certain of its provisions are entrenched, in the sense that it is difficult to amend or abolish them. The procedure for establishing the constitution and for subsequently revising it must therefore be in some way more complex and difficult than the procedure for enacting ordinary statute laws. Finally, the logic of codification dictates that, as the constitution sets out the duties, powers and functions of government institutions in terms of 'higher' law, it must be justiciable, meaning that all political bodies must be subject to the authority of the courts, and in particular a supreme or constitutional court. This substantially enhances the importance of judges, or at least senior judges, who become, in effect, the final arbiters of the constitution, and thereby acquire the power of judicial review (see p. 330).

Uncodified constitutions, although few in number, have very different characteristics. The British constitution, which is properly thought of as an uncodified but partly written constitution, draws on a variety of sources. Chief amongst these are statute law, which is made by Parliament, **common law**, conventions, and various works of authority that clarify and explain the constitution's unwritten elements. The absence of a codified document implies, most importantly, that the legislature enjoys sovereign or unchallengeable authority. It has the right to make or unmake any law whatsoever, no body having the right to override or set aside its laws. By virtue of their legislative supremacy, bodies such as the UK Parliament and the Knesset in Israel are able to function as the ultimate arbiters of the constitution: the constitution means what they say it means.

Focus on . . .

A codified constitution: strengths and weaknesses

The strengths of a codified or written constitution include the following:

- Major principles and key constitutional provisions are *entrenched*, safeguarding them from interference by the government of the day.
- The power of the legislature is *constrained*, cutting its sovereignty down to size.
- Nonpolitical judges are able to *police* the constitution to ensure that its provisions are upheld by other public bodies.
- Individual *liberty* is more securely protected, and authoritarianism is kept at bay.
- The codified document has an *educational* value, in that it highlights the central values and overall goals of the political system.

The drawbacks or weaknesses of codification include the following:

- A codified constitution is more *rigid*, and may therefore be less responsive and adaptable than an uncodified one.
- Government power may be more effectively *constrained* by regular elections than by a constitutional document.
- With a codified constitution, constitutional supremacy resides with *nonelected* judges rather than with publicly accountable politicians.
- Constitutional provisions enshrined in custom and convention may be more widely *respected* because they have been endorsed by history and not 'invented'.
- Constitutional documents are inevitably *biased*, because they endorse one set of values or principles in preference to others, meaning that they may precipitate more conflicts than they resolve.

In the UK in particular, this has stimulated deep controversy and widespread criticism. Parliamentary sovereignty (see p. 325) has been held responsible for what Lord Hailsham (1976) termed **elective dictatorship**: that is, the ability of a government to act in any way it pleases as long as it maintains majority control of the House of Commons. The concentration of power in the hands of the executive to which this leads, and the consequent threat that it poses to individual rights and liberties, has encouraged some to argue that the UK has no constitution at all. If governments can, once elected, act in whatever way they wish, they are surely at liberty to enlarge their own powers at will, and are thereby unconstrained by constitutional rules of any kind. In Griffith's (1991) phrase, the constitution in the UK is 'what happens'. Such concerns fuelled in the 1980s and 1990s a growing campaign in the UK for radical constitutional reform, which, together with the Labour Party's long period in opposition (1979–97), eventually converted the party to the reformist cause. From 1997 onwards, the Blair government reshaped important aspects of the UK's constitutional landscape. Devolution (see p. 173) was introduced in Scotland, Wales and Northern Ireland, referendums and proportional electoral systems were more widely used, the European Convention of Human Rights was incorporated into UK

Elective dictatorship: A constitutional imbalance in which executive power is checked only by the need to win subsequent elections.

law through the Human Rights Act (1998), hereditary peers were removed from the House of Lords, and freedom of information legislation was passed. Although this programme stops short of codification, some have argued that it has brought about a shift from parliamentary sovereignty to popular sovereignty (Hazell, 1999).

An alternative form of classification distinguishes between *rigid* and *flexible* constitutions. What procedures exist for amending a constitution? How easily does the constitution adapt to changing circumstances? On the face of it, codified constitutions are likely to be relatively inflexible because their provisions are in some way entrenched in 'higher' law. By the same token, uncodified ones appear to be flexible and adaptable, because laws of constitutional significance can be changed through the ordinary legislative process and conventions are, by their nature, based on conduct and practice. However, there is no simple relationship between written constitutions and rigidity, or unwritten ones and flexibility.

Various degrees of flexibility are possible, and, surprisingly, the flexibility of a constitution is not directly proportional to the formality of its procedures and rules. Whereas the US constitution has endured, albeit with amendments, since 1787, France has had, over the same period, no fewer than 17 constitutions. Similarly, amendment procedures may be more or less complex or difficult. In Australia, Denmark, Ireland and Spain, for example, referendums (see p. 250) are used to obtain the public's approval for constitutional amendments or ratify ones endorsed by the legislature. In other cases, special majorities must be achieved in the legislature, as in the requirement in Germany's Basic Law that amendments must have two-thirds support in both the Bundestag and the Bundesrat. In the USA, in addition to two-thirds majorities in both houses of Congress, constitutional amendments must be ratified by three-quarters of the states. This requirement has meant that a mere 26 constitutional amendments have been passed, with ten of these (the so-called Bill of Rights) having been introduced in the first two years of the constitution's existence.

The seeming rigidity this produces is, however, misleading. Although the words of the US constitution and other codified documents may change little, their meanings are subject to constant revision and updating through the process of judicial interpretation and reinterpretation. The role of the judiciary in this respect is examined in the final main section of this chapter. Just as written provisions can allow for flexibility, unwritten ones can, at times, be rigid. While in the UK the conventions of ministerial responsibility have proved to be so adaptable they can almost be reshaped at the convenience of the government of the day, other conventions are so deeply engrained in the political culture and in popular expectations that their abandonment or modification is virtually unthinkable. This certainly applies in the case of conventions that restrict the political role of the monarchy and prevent monarchs challenging the authority of Parliament.

A third system of classification takes account of the relationship between constitutional rules and principles, on the one hand, and the practice of government (the 'working' constitution) on the other. As early as 1867, Walter Bagehot in *The English Constitution* ([1867] 1963) distinguished between the 'dignified' parts of the constitution (the monarchy and the House of the Lords), which promoted popular allegiance but exercised little effective power, and its 'efficient' parts (the cabinet and the House of Commons). An *effective* constitution is one that fulfils two criteria. First, in major respects at least, the practical affairs of government correspond to the provisions of the constitution. Second, this occurs because the constitution has the capacity, through whatever means, to limit governmental behaviour.

An effective constitution therefore requires not merely the existence of constitutional rules, but also the capacity of those rules to constrain government and establish constitutionalism. As we shall see below, however, all constitutions are violated to a greater or lesser extent; the real issue is thus the significance and regularity of such violations. Some constitutions can be classified as *nominal*, in that their texts or principles may accurately describe governmental behaviour but fail to limit it. For instance, communist states such as the USSR had constitutions that, amongst other things, acknowledged the monopoly of power of the country's communist party, but the constitutions were politically irrelevant because the judiciary, charged with interpreting the constitution, was kept under firm party control. Other states have sham or facade constitutions. These differ substantially from political practice and tend to fulfil, at best, only a propaganda role. This is particularly the case in dictatorial or authoritarian states, where the commitment to individual rights and liberties extends little further than the content of the state's constitutional documents.

Constitutions have also been classified in terms of their content and, specifically, by the institutional structure they underpin. This enables a number of distinctions to be made. For example, constitutions have traditionally been categorized as either *monarchical* or *republican*. In theory, the former invest constitutional supremacy in a dynastic ruler, while in the latter political authority is derived from the people. However, the emergence of constitutional monarchies (see p. 366), in which power has effectively been transferred to representative institutions, has meant that, apart from in the surviving absolute monarchies in states such as Nepal and Saudi Arabia, this distinction is no longer of central importance. More widely used, though, is the distinction between *unitary* and *federal* constitutions (discussed more fully in Chapter 8): that is, the difference between constitutions that concentrate sovereignty in a single national body and ones that divide it between two levels of government.

Yet another approach is to differentiate between what are seen as *parliamentary* constitutions and *presidential* constitutions. The key here is the relationship between the executive and the assembly. In parliamentary systems the executive is derived from and accountable to the assembly, while in presidential ones the two branches of government function independently on the basis of a separation of powers (see p. 339). These different systems are examined in Chapters 15 and 16. Finally, *pluralist* constitutions can be contrasted with *monopolistic* ones. The former are characteristic of liberal democracies in that they ensure that political power is dispersed, usually through guarantees of participatory rights and party competition. The latter are more commonly found in communist or authoritarian states where the unquestionable authority of a 'ruling' party or supreme leader is formally entrenched, thus demonstrating that a constitution and liberal constitutionalism do not necessarily go hand in hand.

The purpose of a constitution

Not only do the vast majority of states have constitutions, but also most institutions and organized groups have rules that have some kind of constitutional effect. This applies in the case of international bodies such as the United Nations and the European Union, and is also true of regional and provincial government, political parties, interest groups, corporations, churches, clubs and so on. The popularity of these constitutional rules draws attention to the fact that constitutions somehow play a vital role in the running of organizations. Why is it difficult, and perhaps impossible,

> ◆ **Concept**
>
> ### Constitutionalism
>
> Constitutionalism, in a narrow sense, is the practice of limited government ensured by the existence of a constitution. Thus constitutionalism can, in this sense, be said to exist when government institutions and political processes are effectively constrained by constitutional rules. More broadly, constitutionalism is a set of political values and aspirations that reflect the desire to protect liberty through the establishment of internal and external checks on government power. In this sense, constitutionalism is a species of political liberalism. It is typically expressed in the form of support for constitutional provisions that achieve this goal: for example a codified constitution, a bill of rights, a separation of powers, bicameralism, and federalism or decentralization.

for states and other organized bodies to function without a constitution? The difficulty with answering this question is that constitutions do not have a single or simple purpose. Rather, they have a number of functions and are used in a variety of ways. The most important of these are the following:

- to empower states
- to establish unifying values and goals
- to provide government stability
- to protect freedom
- to legitimize regimes.

Empowering states

Although the popular image of constitutions is that they limit government power, a more basic function is that they mark out the existence of states and make claims concerning their sphere of independent authority. The creation of new states (whether through the overthrow of colonialism, the fragmentation of larger states, or an amalgamation of smaller ones) is invariably accompanied by the enactment of a constitution. Indeed, it can be argued that such states exist only once they have a constitition, since without one they lack formal jurisdiction over a particular territory or a governing apparatus that can effectively exercise that jurisdiction.

The state of India can thus be said to have come into existence in the period between the granting of independence in 1947 and the adoption of its federal constitution in 1950: during this time, a UK-appointed Governor General continued to exercise supervision. In the same way, the American Declaration of Independence in 1776 initiated the process through which the USA achieved statehood, but this was not completed until the US constitution was ratified in 1789. The need for empowerment also applies to subnational and supranational bodies. In federal systems, for example, constituent provinces or states have their own constitutions in order to guarantee their sphere of authority relative to that of central government. The 'constitution' of the EU, which comprises treaties and agreements such as the Treaty of Rome (1957), the Single European Act (1986) and the Treaty on European Union (or Maastricht Treaty) (1992), authorizes EU bodies to intervene in various ways in the affairs of EU member states.

Establishing values and goals

In addition to laying down a framework for government, constitutions invariably embody a broader set of political values, ideals and goals. This is why constitutions cannot be neutral; they are always entangled, more or less explicitly, with ideological priorities. The creators of constitutions therefore seek to invest their regime with a set of unifying values, a sense of ideological purpose, and a vocabulary that can be used in the conduct of politics. In many cases these aims are accomplished explicitly in preambles to constitutional documents, which often function as statements of national ideals. These ideals can vary from a commitment to democracy, freedom or the welfare state to a belief in socialism, federalism or Islam. The 1977 Soviet constitution thus proclaimed the USSR to be a 'developed socialist society', while Germany's Basic Law states a determination to 'serve the peace of the world'.

In other cases, however, these values and ideological priorities are largely implicit. Charles Beard (1913), for example, argued that the provisions of the US constitution were shaped essentially by economic interests, in particular the desire to defend property against the rising power of the propertyless masses. Similarly, it can be argued that, while the Fourteenth Amendment and Fifteenth Amendment to the US constitution acknowledge the significance of racial divisions, the constitution effectively conceals divisions that arise from social class or gender. In the case of the British constitution, the doctrine of parliamentary sovereignty has been interpreted as a means of discouraging, or even discrediting, forms of extraparliamentary political action.

Providing government stability

In allocating duties, powers and functions amongst the various institutions of government, constitutions act as 'organizational charts', 'definitional guides', or 'institutional blueprints'. As such, they formalize and regulate the relationships between political bodies and provide a mechanism through which conflicts can be adjudicated and resolved. The Indian constitution, for instance, contains a highly detailed description of institutional powers and relationships in a lengthy document containing almost 400 articles. Despite varying in their degree of specificity and their effectiveness, all constitutions fulfil the vital function of introducing a measure of stability, order and predictability to the workings of government. From this point of view the opposite of constitutional government is random, capricious or arbitrary government. This is precisely why constitutions go hand in hand with organization. Complex patterns of social interaction can be maintained only if all concerned know the 'rules of the game' and therefore who can be expected to do what.

Protecting freedom

In liberal democracies it is often taken for granted that the central purpose of a constitution is to constrain government with a view to protecting individual liberty. This is why constitutions tend to be viewed as devices for establishing and maintaining **limited government**. Certainly, constitutions lay down the relationship between the state and the individual, marking out the respective spheres of government authority and personal freedom (see p. 324). They do this largely by defining civil rights and liberties, often through the means of a bill of rights. The impact of liberal constitutionalism has ensured that in many cases 'classic' or traditional civil liberties (see p. 407), such as freedom of expression, freedom of religious worship, freedom of assembly and freedom of movement, are recognized as 'fundamental' in that they are constitutionally guaranteed. These so-called **negative rights** have a liberal character in that, because the state is thus prevented from encroaching upon the individual, they mark out a sphere of government *in*activity.

A growing number of states have, in addition, entrenched a range of economic, social and cultural rights, such as the right to healthcare, the right to education and even the right to work. These **positive rights**, however, have caused controversy, because they are linked to the expansion, not contraction, of government, and because their provision is dependent upon the economic and social resources available to the state in question. Can these rights and freedoms be thought of as 'fundamental' when there is no practical way of guaranteeing their delivery? In the Indian constitution this is acknowledged through the qualification that the right to work, for example, is secured 'within the limits of economic capacity and development'.

Limited government: Government operating within constraints, usually imposed by law, a constitution or institutional checks and balances.

Negative rights: Rights that mark out a realm of unconstrained action, and thus check the responsibilities of government.

Positive rights: Rights that make demands of government in terms of the provision of resources and support, and thus extend its responsibilities.

Concept

Freedom

The term freedom (or liberty) means, in its broadest sense, the ability to think or act as one wishes. A distinction is nevertheless often made between 'negative' and 'positive' liberty: that is, between being free *from* something and being free *to* do something (Berlin, 1958). *Negative* freedom means noninterference: the absence of external constraints on the individual. The individual is thus 'at liberty' to act as he or she wishes. *Positive* freedom is linked to the achievement of some identifiable goal or benefit, usually personal development, self-realization or self-mastery. The 'freedom from' and 'freedom to' distinction is misleading, however, because every example of freedom can be described in both ways. For instance, being free *from* ignorance means being free *to* gain an education.

Legitimizing regimes

The final function of a constitution is to help build legitimacy (see p. 219). This explains the widespread use of constitutions, even by states with constitutions that are merely nominal or a complete façade. This legitimation process has two dimensions. In the first place, the existence of a constitution is almost a prerequisite for a state's membership of the international community and for its recognition by other states. More significant, however, is the ability to use a constitution to build legitimacy within a state through the promotion of respect and compliance amongst the domestic population. This is possible because a constitution both symbolizes and disseminates the values of the ruling elite, and invests the governmental system with a cloak of legality. To make the constitution more effective in this respect, attempts are often made to promote veneration for the constitution itself, either as a document of historical importance or as a symbol of national purpose and identity.

Do constitutions matter?

The value of a constitution is often taken for granted. The existence of a constitution, so the assumption goes, provides benefits such as political stability, limited government and guaranteed rights and liberties. Nowhere is this faith in a constitution more developed than in the USA, where it amounts, in Louis Hartz's (1955) words, to 'the cult of constitution worship'. Of course this faith has been severely tested, not least by allegations during the Watergate crisis that President Richard Nixon had helped to cover up illegal acts by senior White House officials during the 1972 election campaign. Nevertheless, Nixon's resignation in 1974 enabled his successor, Gerald Ford, to declare that 'our constitution works', reiterating the classic sentiment of constitutionalism: 'we have a government of laws, not of men'. However, the mere existence of a constitution does not ensure that a government is constitutional. Indeed, there is little evidence that a constitution is a major guarantee against tyranny, still less that it offers a 'ticket to Utopia'.

Constitutions 'work' in certain circumstances. In other words, they serve their various purposes only when they are supported by a range of other cultural, political, economic and social conditions. In particular, constitutions must correspond to and be supported by the political culture; successful constitutions are as much a product of the political culture as they are its creator. This is why so many of the model liberal-democratic constitutions bequeathed to developing states by departing colonial rulers failed to take root. Constitutional rules guaranteeing individual rights and political competition may be entirely irrelevant in societies with deeply entrenched collectivist values and traditions, especially when such societies are struggling to achieve basic economic and social development.

In the same way, the various Soviet constitutions not only enshrined 'socialist' values that were foreign to the mass of the people, but also failed to develop popular support for such values during the 74 years of the USSR's existence. In the USA, as a result of widespread and institutionalized racism, the constitutional guarantees of civil and voting rights for American black people enacted after the Civil War were often not upheld in Southern states until the 1960s. On the other hand, the 1947 Japanese constitution, despite the fact that it was imposed by the occupying USA and emphasised individual rights in place of the more traditional Japanese stress on duty, has proved to be remarkably successful, providing a stable framework for postwar reconstruction and political development. As in postwar Germany, however, the

Japanese constitution has had the advantage of being sustained by an 'economic miracle'.

A second key factor is whether or not a constitution is respected by rulers and accords with the interests and values of dominant groups. Germany's Weimar constitution, for example, despite the fact that it enshrined an impressive array of rights and liberties, was easily set aside in the 1930s as Hitler constructed his Nazi dictatorship. Not only did the competitive democracy of the Weimar regime conflict with the ambitions of the Nazis and conservative elites in business and the military, but it was also poorly supported by a population facing economic crisis and little accustomed to representative government. In India under Indira Gandhi during 1975–77, and in Pakistan under General Zia ul-Haq during 1977–81, major provisions of the constitutions were abrogated by the declaration of 'states of emergency'. In these cases the support of the military leadership proved to be far more crucial than respect for constitutional niceties. The UK's uncodified constitution is often said to provide unusual scope for abuse because it relies so heavily on the self-restraint of the government of the day. This became particularly apparent as the Conservative governments of the 1980s and 1990s exploited the flexibility inherent in parliamentary sovereignty to alter the constitutional roles of institutions such as the civil service, local government and the trade unions, and, some argued, substantially undermined civil liberties.

The final factor is the adaptability of a constitution and its ability to *remain* relevant despite changing political circumstances. No constitution reflects political realities, and few set out specifically to do so. Generally, successful constitutions are sufficiently flexible to accommodate change within a broad and enduringly relevant framework; those that are infinitely flexible are, strictly speaking, not constitutions at all. The US constitution is particularly interesting in this respect. Its 'genius' has been its concentration on broad principles and the scope it therefore provides to rectify its own deficiencies. US government has thus been able to evolve in response to new challenges and new demands. The formal amendment process, for example, allowed US institutions to be democratized, and in the twentieth century judicial interpretation made possible the growth of presidential powers, a shift of authority from state to federal government, and, in certain respects, a widening of individual rights.

Such changes, however, can be said to have occurred *within* the constitution, in that core principles such as the separation of powers, federalism and individual liberty have continued to be respected, albeit in renewed form. The same is true of the reforms the Blair government introduced in the UK's uncodified constitution after 1997. In contrast, the constitution of the Fourth French Republic proved to be unworkable, because the emphasis it placed upon the National Assembly tended to produce a succession of weak and unstable governments. As the constitution offered no solution to this impasse, the result was a new constitution in 1958, inaugurating the Fifth Republic, which broadened presidential power according to a blueprint devised by General de Gaulle.

The law

Law, morality and politics

The relationship between **law** and morality is one of the thorniest problems in political theory. On the surface, law and morality are very different things. Law is a distinctive

---

Concept

Parliamentary sovereignty

Parliamentary sovereignty refers to the absolute and unlimited authority of a parliament or legislature, reflected in its ability to make, amend or repeal any law it wishes. Parliamentary sovereignty is usually seen as the central principle of the British constitution, and results from the absence of a codified constitution, the supremacy of statute law over other forms of law, the absence of rival legislatures, and the convention that no parliament can bind its successors. Supporters commended the principle for investing constitutional supremacy in a representative institution rather than an artificial body of rules or a nonelected body of judges. Critics point out that the principle is implicitly authoritarian, leading to 'elective dictatorship' when the parliament is executive-dominated.

Law: A set of public and enforceable rules that apply throughout a political community; law is usually recognized as binding.

Human rights

Human rights are rights to which people are entitled by virtue of being human; they are a modern and secular version of natural rights. Human rights are 'universal' in the sense that they belong to all humans rather than to members of any particular state, race, religion, gender or other group. They are also 'fundamental', in that they are inalienable; unlike civil rights, they do not depend on the freedoms and status accorded citizens in particular societies. Supporters of the doctrine of human rights portray them as universally applicable moral principles that stand above the traditional ideological divide. Opponents, on the other hand, argue that it is nonsense to suggest that individuals have rights that are separate from the traditions, cultures and societies to which they belong.

form of social control, backed up by the means of enforcement; it defines what *can* and what *cannot* be done. Morality, on the other hand, is concerned with ethical questions and the difference between 'right' and 'wrong'; it prescribes what *should* and what *should not* be done. Moreover, while law has an objective character, in that it is a social fact, morality is usually treated as a subjective entity: that is, as a matter of opinion or personal judgement. Nevertheless, natural law theories that date back to Plato (see p. 12) and Aristotle (see p. 7) suggest that law is, or should be, rooted in a moral system of some kind. In the early modern period, such theories were often based on the idea of God-given 'natural rights'. This assertion of a link between law and morality became fashionable again as the twentieth century progressed, and it was usually associated with the ideas of civil liberties or human rights.

However, the rise in the nineteenth century of the 'science of positive law' offered a very different view of the relationship between law and morality. Its purpose was quite simply to free the understanding of law from moral, religious and mystical assumptions. John Austin (1790–1859) developed the theory of 'legal positivism', which defined law not in terms of its conformity to higher moral or religious principles, but in terms of the fact that it was established and enforced: the law is the law because it is obeyed. This approach was refined by H. L. A. Hart in *The Concept of Law* (1961). Hart suggested that law stemmed from the union of 'primary' and 'secondary' rules, each of which had a particular function. Primary rules regulate social behaviour and can be thought of as the 'content' of the legal system: criminal law is an example. Secondary rules, on the other hand, are rules that confer powers upon the institutions of government. They lay down how primary rules are made, enforced and adjudicated, thus determining their validity.

Rule of law

The rule of law is the principle that the law should 'rule' in the sense that it establishes a framework to which all conduct and behaviour conform, applying equally to all the members of society, be they private citizens or government officials. The rule of law is thus a core liberal-democratic principle, embodying ideas such as constitutionalism and limited government. In continental Europe it has often been enshrined in the German concept of the *Rechtsstaat*, a state based on law. In the USA the rule of law is closely linked to the status of the constitution as 'higher' law and to the doctrine of 'due process'. In the UK it is seen to be rooted in common law and to provide an alternative to a codified constitution (Dicey, [1885] 1939).

Thomas Hobbes (1588–1679)

English political philosopher. Hobbes was the son of a minor clergyman who subsequently abandoned his family. He became tutor to the exiled Prince of Wales Charles Stewart, and lived under the patronage of the Cavendish family. Writing at a time of uncertainty and civil strife, precipitated by the English Revolution, Hobbes developed the first comprehensive theory of nature and human behaviour since Aristotle. His classic work, *Leviathan* (1651), discussed the grounds of political obligation and undoubtedly reflected the impact of the Civil War. It provided a defence for absolutist government but, by appealing to reasoned argument in the form of the social contract, also disappointed advocates of **divine right**.

In view of the crucial role that law plays in regulating social behaviour, no one can doubt that it has immense political significance. Nevertheless, questions about the actual and desirable relationship between law and politics – reflecting on the nature of law, and its function and proper extent – have provoked deep controversy. Much of our understanding of law derives from liberal theory. This portrays law as the essential guarantee of civilized and orderly existence, drawing heavily on social-contract theory (see p. 93). In the absence of the state and a system of law – that is, in the 'state of nature' – each individual is at liberty to abuse or threaten every other individual. The role of law, then, is to protect each member of society from his or her fellow members, thereby preventing their rights and liberties from being encroached upon.

As this protection extends throughout society and to every one of its members, law has, liberals insist, a neutral character. Law is therefore 'above' politics, and a strict separation between law and politics must be maintained to prevent the law favouring the state over the individual, the rich over the poor, men over women, whites over blacks, and so on. This is why liberals place such a heavy emphasis on the universal authority of law, embodied in the principle of the rule of law. This view of law also has significant implications for the judiciary, whose task it is to interpret law and adjudicate between parties to a dispute. Notably, judges must be independent, in the sense that they are 'above' or 'outside' the machinery of government and not subject to political influence.

However, if the central purpose of law is to protect liberty, this also implies that the proper sphere of law should be limited. In other words, law should be endorsed only as long as it enlarges, rather than contracts, freedom. One of the clearest liberal statements of this principle was made by John Stuart Mill (see p. 48), who, in *On Liberty* ([1859] 1982:73), asserted that, 'Over himself, over his own body and mind the individual is sovereign'. Mill was prepared to accept the legitimacy of law only when it was designed 'to prevent harm to others'. This is understood by moral philosophers as the 'harm principle'. By this standard, paternalistic laws aimed at preventing self-harm, such as those prohibiting addictive drugs or enforcing the use of seat-belts in cars, or ones that supposedly promote moral behaviour, such as laws against suicide or prostitution, are entirely unfounded.

An alternative view of law has been developed by conservative theorists. This draws more heavily on the idea that law is linked to order, even to the extent that

Divine right: The doctrine that earthly rulers are chosen by God and thus wield unchallengeable authority; a defence for monarchical absolutism.

'law and order' become a single, fused concept. This position draws from two sources. The first is a deeply pessimistic, even Hobbesian, view of human nature. In *Leviathan* ([1651] 1968:49) Thomas Hobbes described the principal human inclination as 'a perpetual and restless desire for power after power, that ceaseth only in death'. In this light, the roots of social disorder can be seen to reside in the individual human being, a view sometimes linked to the Christian doctrine of 'original sin'. Order can therefore be maintained only by strict laws, firm enforcement and harsh penalties. For Hobbes, law was the only means of preventing a descent into chaos and barbarity.

The second source of this conservative view of the importance of law is the belief that social stability depends on the existence of shared values and a common culture. A classic statement of this position was advanced in Patrick Devlin's *The Enforcement of Morals* (1968), which argued that society has the right to enforce 'public morality' through the instrument of law. This position goes clearly beyond Mill's **libertarianism** in implying, for example, that society has the right to protect itself against what have been seen as 'nonconsensus' practices, such as homosexuality and drug taking. In the 1980s and 1990s the New Right took up a very similar position in extolling the virtues of 'traditional morality' and 'family values', believing also that these should be upheld through the authority of law.

■ The judiciary

The judiciary is the branch of government that is empowered to decide legal disputes. The central function of judges is therefore to adjudicate on the meaning of law, in the sense that they interpret or 'construct' law. The significance of this role varies from state to state and from system to system. However, it is particularly important in states with codified constitutions, where it extends to the interpretation of the constitution itself, and so allows judges to arbitrate in disputes between major institutions of government or in ones between the state and the individual.

The significance of the judiciary has also been enhanced by the growing importance of international law (see p. 159). The International Court of Justice in the Hague (formally known as the World Court) is the judicial arm of the United Nations. It provides a forum in which disputes between states can be settled, although, as international law respects the principle of sovereignty (see p. 131), this requires the consent of all parties. The International Criminal Court (ICC) has revived the idea established by the 1945–46 Nuremberg trials of **war crimes** or 'crimes against humanity'. The ICC has indicted and arrested a number of people for mass crimes including, in 2001, the former Yugoslav president, Sloban Milosevic. In addition, there are international courts with regional jurisdiction, such as the EU's European Court of Justice in Luxembourg and the European Court of Human Rights in Strasbourg.

One of the chief characteristics of the judiciary – in liberal-democratic systems, its defining characteristic – is that judges are strictly independent and nonpolitical actors. Indeed, the ability of judges to be 'above' politics is normally seen as the vital guarantee of a separation between law and politics. However, this image of the judiciary is always misleading. The judiciary is best thought of as a political, not merely a legal, institution. As central figures in the legal process, judges play a vital role in such undeniably political activities as conflict resolution and the maintenance

Libertarianism: The belief that the realm of individual liberty should be maximized, usually associated with attempts to minimize the scope of public authority.

War crimes: Acts that violate international conventions on the conduct of war, usually involving either aggressive warfare or atrocities carried out against civilians or prisoners of war.

of state authority. Although judges are clearly political in the sense that their judgements have an undeniable political impact, debate about the political significance of the judiciary revolves around two more controversial questions. First, are judges political in that their actions are shaped by political considerations or pressures? Second, do judges make policy in the sense that they encroach upon the proper responsibilities of politicians?

Are judges political?

Certain political systems make no pretence of judicial neutrality or impartiality. For example, in orthodox communist regimes, the principle of 'socialist legality' dictated that judges interpret law in accordance with Marxism–Leninism, subject to the ideological authority of the state's communist party. Judges thus became mere functionaries who carried out the political and ideological objectives of the regime itself. This was most graphically demonstrated by the 'show trials' of the 1930s in the USSR. The German courts during the Nazi period were similarly used as instruments of ideological repression and political persecution. In other states, however, judges have been expected to observe strict political neutrality. In states that subscribe to any form of liberal constitutionalism the authority of law is linked to its nonpolitical character, which, in turn, is based on the assumption that the law is interpreted by independent and impartial judges.

Judges may be political in two senses: they may be subject to external bias or to internal bias. External bias is derived from the influence that political bodies, such as parties, the assembly and government, are able to exert on the judiciary. Internal bias stems from the prejudices and sympathies of judges themselves, particularly from those that intrude into the process of judicial decision-making. External bias is supposedly kept at bay by respect for the principle of **judicial independence**. In most liberal democracies the independence of the judiciary is protected by their security of tenure (the fact that they cannot be sacked), and through restrictions on the criticism of judges and court decisions. However, in practice, the independence of judges may be compromised because of the close involvement of political bodies in the process of judicial recruitment and promotion.

Judges in the USA supposedly hold office for life on condition of 'good behaviour'. Supreme Court judges, however, are appointed by the US president, and these appointments are subject to confirmation by the Senate. This process has, since F. D. Roosevelt's battles with the court in the 1930s, led to a pattern of overt political appointment. Presidents select justices on the basis of party affiliation and ideological disposition, and, as occurred to Robert Bork in the 1980s, the Senate may reject them on the same grounds. The liberal tendencies of the Warren Court (1954–69), and the more conservative inclinations of the Burger Court (1969–86) and subsequently the Rehnquist Court (1986–2005), were thus brought about largely through external political pressure. UK judges are also appointed by the government of the day, senior judges being appointed by the prime minister on the advice of the Lord Chancellor. Despite conventions stipulating that such appointments should be impartial, political considerations often intrude, as in the 1980 appointment to Master of the Rolls of Lord Donaldson, a former Conservative councillor and a known supporter of legal restrictions on trade union activity.

The Conseil Constitutionnel (Constitutional Court) in France, which is empowered to examine the constitutionality of laws and can thus restrain both the

Concept

Neutrality

Neutrality is the absence of any form of partisanship or commitment; it consists of a refusal to 'take sides'. In international relations, neutrality is a legal condition through which a state declares its noninvolvement in a conflict or war, and indicates its intention to refrain from supporting or aiding either side. As a principle of individual conduct, applied to the likes of judges, civil servants, the military and other public officials, it implies, strictly speaking, the absence of political sympathies and ideological leanings. Neutral actors are thus political eunuchs. In practice, the less exacting requirement of impartiality is usually applied. This allows that political sympathies may be held as long as these do not intrude into, or conflict with, professional or public responsibilities.

Judicial independence: The constitutional principle that there should be a strict separation between the judiciary and other branches of government; an application of the separation of powers.

Concept

Judicial review

The power of judicial review is the power of the judiciary to 'review' and possibly invalidate laws, decrees and the actions of other branches of government, notably the legislature and the executive. In its classical sense, the principle of judicial review stems from the existence of a codified constitution and allows the courts to strike down as 'unconstitutional' actions that are deemed to be incompatible with the constitution. A more modest form of judicial review, found in uncodified systems, is restricted to the review of executive actions in the light of ordinary law using the principle of *ultra vires* (beyond the powers) to determine whether the executive has acted outside its powers. Seen by many as a cornerstone institution of liberal constitutionalism, as it ensures a 'government of laws', judicial review also goes beyond the separation of powers in establishing, for better or worse, the supremacy of the judiciary.

assembly and the executive, is subject to particularly marked political influence. Its members have, in the main, been politicians with long experience rather than professional judges. The French president and the presidents of the National Assembly and the Senate each select one-third of the members of the court, party affiliation often being a significant factor. In Japan the Supreme Court is effectively appointed by the cabinet, with the high judges being selected by the emperor on the nomination of the cabinet. Prolonged Liberal-Democratic Party domination in the post-Second-World-War period meant, however, that the LDP packed the court with its own supporters, ensuring that it remained firmly subordinate to the Diet. One of the consequences of this was that, despite widespread **gerrymandering** in favour of the LDP in rural districts, the Supreme Court was never prepared to nullify election results, even when, as in 1983, elections were declared to be unconstitutional because of the disproportionate allocation of seats (Eccleston, 1989).

Judicial independence is not the only issue; bias may creep in through the values and culture of the judiciary as easily as through external pressure. From this perspective the key factor is not so much *how* judges are recruited, but *who* is recruited. A long-standing socialist critique of the judiciary holds that it articulates the dominant values of society, and so acts to defend the existing political and social order. This tendency is underpinned by the social exclusivity of judges and by the peculiar status and respect that the judicial profession is normally accorded. Griffith (1991) argued that this conservative bias is particularly prominent in the British higher judiciary, and that it stems from the remarkable homogeneity of senior judges, who are overwhelmingly male, white, upper-middle-class, and public-school and 'Oxbridge' educated. Similar arguments have been used to suggest that judges are biased against women, racial minorities, and, indeed, any group poorly represented within its ranks.

Although the US Supreme Court has included a nominal black judge since the 1950s and now contains two female judges, its membership has generally been dominated by white Anglo-Saxon Protestants drawn from the USA's middle and upper middle classes. On the other hand, in states such as Australia attempts have been made to counter such tendencies by making the judiciary more socially representative. For instance, since the 1980s, Australian judges have been recruited from the ranks of academics as well as lawyers. Nevertheless, even critics of the judiciary recognize that there is a limit to the extent to which judges can be made socially representative. To achieve a judiciary that is a microcosm of the larger society, it would be necessary for criteria such as experience and professional competence to be entirely ignored in the appointment of judges.

Do judges make policy?

The images of judges as simple appliers of law has always been a myth. Judges cannot apply the so-called 'letter of the law', because no law, legal term or principle has a single, self-evident meaning. In practice, judges *impose* meaning on law through a process of 'construction' that forces them to choose amongst a number of possible meanings or interpretations. In this sense, *all* law is judge-made law. Clearly, however, the range of discretion available to judges in this respect, and the significance of the laws that they invest with meaning, vary considerably. Two factors are crucial here. The first is the clarity and detail with which law is specified. Generally, broadly framed laws or constitutional principles allow greater scope for judicial interpretation. The second factor is the existence of a codified or 'written' constitution. The

Gerrymandering: The manipulation of electoral boundaries so as to achieve political advantage for a party or candidate.

existence of such a document significantly enhances the status of the judiciary, investing it with the power of judicial review.

Although sometimes seen to have arisen from English law as early as *Dr. Bonham's Case* in 1610, judicial review is best understood as a US development that resulted from the establishment of the world's first written constitution. The US constitution makes no mention of judicial review, but, arguably, embodies the logic that made its emergence inevitable. As the constitution laid down legal standards for the behaviour of government institutions, these clearly needed to be supervised or policed, and the judiciary (more specifically, the Supreme Court) was the only institution equipped for this purpose. The power of judicial review was first exercised in Chief Justice John Marshall's decision in *Marbury* v. *Madison* (1803). In this, the Supreme Court declared that the Judiciary Act of 1789 was incompatible with the 'superior paramount law' of the US constitution. This made the Supreme Court, as Robert Dahl (1956) put it, 'a political institution, an institution, that is to say, for arriving at decisions on controversial questions of national policy'.

The Supreme Court's significance as a policy-maker has been evident throughout US history. In the late nineteenth century and early twentieth century, for example, Supreme Courts wedded to *laissez-faire* principles used the doctrine of 'due process' to strike down welfare and social legislation: in particular, the court blocked much of Roosevelt's New Deal programme in the early 1930s. It was only after the so-called 'court revolution' of 1937, following the appointment of pro-New-Deal judges such as Hugo Black and William O'Douglas, that the shift to economic and social intervention gained judicial endorsement. During the 1950s and 1960s the court, under Chief Justice Earl Warren, made landmark liberal decisions such as *Brown* v. *Board of Education* (1954), which rejected segregation in schools as unconstitutional, and *Baker* v. *Carr* (1962), which required that legislative constituencies in the USA be of uniform size.

In many cases, the Supreme Court was ahead of Congress and the presidency, often paving the way for later legislation, as in the case of the civil rights reforms of the mid 1960s. Similarly, the Supreme Court upheld the constitutionality of abortion in *Roe* v. *Wade* (1973), at a time when elective institutions refused to address such a deeply controversial issue. Although the **judicial activism** of this period subsequently subsided, reflecting the impact of the conservative appointments of Republican presidents such as Nixon, Reagan and George Bush Sr, the court continued to exert influence, for instance, in allowing the gradual reintroduction of capital punishment and growing restrictions on the right to abortion. Nevertheless, perhaps the most politically significant of Supreme Court judgments came in December 2000, when the Court overturned a ruling of the Florida Supreme Court and resolved the disputed presidential election in favour of George W. Bush. Some have argued that in doing so the Court effectively substituted itself for the American people.

However, it would be a mistake to imply that US-style constitutional judicial review guarantees the supremacy of the judiciary. In the first place, judicial review is effective only as long as judges remain scrupulously independent from other institutions of government. As pointed out above, this is seldom the case in practice. It is notable, for example, that in deciding the outcome of the 2000 presidential election the Supreme Court was divided on party lines, with Republican appointees being in the majority. Moreover, although judges can interpret laws and even the constitution, they do not decide or influence their wording. Court rulings can thus be super-

Judicial activism: The willingness of judges to arbitrate in political disputes, as opposed to merely saying what the law means.

seded by constitutional amendments, as when the Sixteenth Amendment of the US constitution reversed an earlier Supreme Court ruling declaring federal income tax to be unconstitutional. Perhaps the greatest weakness of judges and courts, however, is their lack of the means of enforcement and thus their reliance on other branches of government. This was demonstrated in 1958, when President Eisenhower had to despatch federal troops to Little Rock, Arkansas, to force its schools to comply with the court's 1954 desegregation ruling, which had until that point been disregarded.

If judges are policy-makers, they must therefore operate as part of the broader machinery of government and within constraints established by the political culture and public opinion. The difficulties the judiciary may encounter in fulfilling its role as guardian of the constitution were demonstrated by the battle between Indira Gandhi and the Indian courts in the 1970s. Despite its written constitution, the balance between US-style judicial review and Westminster-style parliamentary sovereignty in India has never been fully resolved. Amid mounting criticism of Prime Minister Gandhi's autocratic leadership style, the Indian High Court in June 1975 declared her guilty of electoral malpractice and disqualified her from political office for five years. Although the Indian Supreme Court suspended the disqualification pending an appeal, within days Gandhi declared a 'state of emergency', allowing for the arrest of hundreds of her political opponents and for the introduction of stiff censorship. Even though the judiciary was able to restore its authority after the lifting of the emergency in March 1977, it has subsequently practised greater self-restraint and has been reluctant to challenge the government of the day so openly again.

The view that judges are policy-makers is less persuasive in the absence of a codified constitution. Where the constitution is unwritten, judges lack a legal standard against which to measure the constitutionality of political acts and government decisions. The UK Parliament is therefore sovereign, and the judiciary is subordinate to it. Before the Glorious Revolution of 1688 in the UK, judges were prepared to set aside acts of Parliament when they violated common law principles, as occurred in *Dr. Bonham's Case* (1610). The revolution, however, established the supremacy of statute law (law made by Parliament), a principle that has never subsequently been challenged by the courts.

The power of judicial review can nevertheless be applied in a narrower sense in the case of executive powers that are derived from enabling legislation. In such cases, the principle of *ultra vires* can be used to declare actions of ministers, for instance, unlawful. Indeed, since the 1980s there has been a marked upsurge in judicial activism in the UK, highlighting the growing political significance of judges. In 1984, for example, the House of Lords upheld a judgment of the Court of Appeal that declared the Greater London Council's system of subsidies to London Transport (the 'fares fair' scheme) to be illegal. Between 1992 and 1996, the UK Home Secretary Michael Howard was defeated by the courts on no fewer than ten occasions. This growing activism reflects both the spread of a 'human rights culture' within the UK judiciary and growing anxiety about the misuse of executive power that flows from the absence of effective constitutional checks and balances in the UK. The Human Rights Act (1988), which came into force in 2000, has bolstered this trend. Evidence of this was found in a series of defeats in the courts for the Blair government over anti-terrorism measures that were deemed to infringe individual rights or civil liberties.

Summary

◆ A constitution is a set of rules that seek to establish the duties, powers and functions of the institutions of government and define the relationship between the state and the individual. Constitutions can be classified on the basis of the status of their rules, how easily their rules can be changed, the degree to which their rules are observed in practice, and the content of their rules and the institutional structure that they establish.

◆ Constitutions do not serve a single or simple purpose. Amongst their functions are that they empower states by defining a sphere of independent authority, establish a set of values, ideals and goals for a society, bring stability, order and predictability to the workings of government, protect individuals from the state, and legitimize regimes in the eyes of other states and their people.

◆ There is an imperfect relationship between the content of a constitution and political practice. Constitutions 'work' in certain conditions, notably when they correspond to, and are supported by, the political culture, when they are respected by rulers and accord with the interests and values of dominant groups, and when they are adaptable and can remain relevant in changing political circumstances.

◆ Questions about the actual and desirable relationship between law and politics are deeply controversial. Liberal theory, sensitive to civil liberties and human rights, tends to emphasize the limited province of law operating simply as a means of guaranteeing orderly existence. The conservative view, however, emphasizes the link between law and social stability, acknowledging that law has an important role to play in enforcing public morality.

◆ The separation of law from politics is accomplished through attempts to make the judiciary independent and impartial. Judicial independence, however, is threatened by the close involvement of political bodies in the process of judicial recruitment and promotion. Judicial impartiality is compromised by the fact that nowhere are judges representatives of the larger society. In western polyarchies, for instance, they are overwhelmingly male, white, materially privileged and relatively old.

◆ As judges impose meaning on law, they cannot but be involved in the policy process. The extent of their influence varies according to the clarity and detail with which the law is specified and the scope available for judicial interpretation, and according to the existence or otherwise of a codified or written constitution, which invests in judges the power of judicial review.

Questions for discussion

▶ How useful is a constitution as a guide to political practice?

▶ What factors determine the level of respect that rulers show for their constitution?

▶ Do codified constitutions and bills of rights merely lead to the tyranny of the judiciary?

▶ On what grounds (if any) is it justifiable to break the law?

► Is it desirable that law be separate from politics, and if so, why?

► How scrupulously is judicial independence maintained in practice?

► Does it matter that the social composition of the judiciary does not reflect that of society at large?

Further reading

Alexander, L. (ed.), *Constitutionalism: Philosophical Foundations* (Cambridge and New York: Cambridge University Press, 1998). Stimulating reflections on theories and ideas that underpin constitutionalism.

Bogdanor, V. (ed.), *Constitutions in Democratic Politics* (Aldershot: Gower, 1988). A good collection of essays that considers the nature of constitutionalism and the issue of constitutional reform.

Davis, R., *Electing Justice: Fixing the Supreme Court Nomination Process* (Oxford and New York: Oxford University Press, 2005). An interesting discussion of the role of interest groups, the press and the public in the nomination of Supreme Court justices.

Griffiths, J. A. G., *The Politics of the Judiciary* (London: Fontana, 1997). A critical analysis of the political role of judges from a UK standpoint.

Lane, J.-E., *Constitutions and Political Theory* (Manchester: Manchester University Press, 1996). A thorough and coherent discussion of key debates related to constitutions and constitutionalism.

Assemblies

> 'A Parliament is nothing less than a big meeting of more or less idle people.'
>
> WALTER BAGEHOT, *The English Constitution* (1867)

Assemblies (sometimes called parliaments or legislatures) occupy a key position in the machinery of government. Traditionally, they have been treated with special respect and status as the public, even democratic, face of government. In written constitutions, for instance, they are usually accorded pride of place, being described before executives and judiciaries. Assemblies are respected because they are composed of lay politicians who claim to represent the people rather than of trained or expert government officials. Moreover, they act as national debating chambers, public forums in which government policies and the major issues of the day can be openly discussed and analysed. In most cases they are also invested with formal law-making power, giving them some capacity to shape or at least influence public policy. Nevertheless, it is widely alleged that the twentieth century witnessed a progressive weakening of parliamentary power in the form of a decline of assemblies. Although some may still play an important role in the policy process, many assemblies have been reduced to mere 'talking shops' that do little more than rubber-stamp decisions that have effectively been made elsewhere.

The central issues examined in this chapter are as follows:

Key issues

▶ What is an assembly?

▶ How do parliamentary systems of government differ from presidential ones?

▶ What are the main functions of assemblies?

▶ How are assemblies organized, and how do their internal structures differ?

▶ What are the principal determinants of parliamentary power?

▶ Why have assemblies declined? Does this decline matter?

Charles-Louis de Secondat Montesquieu (1689–1775)

French political philosopher. Montesquieu came from an aristocratic family and became an advocate before establishing his literary reputation with the publication of *Persian Letters* (1721). After settling in Paris in 1726, he travelled throughout Europe studying political and social institutions. Montesquieu's masterpiece, *The Spirit of the Laws* ([1748] 1949), is a long and rambling comparative examination of political and legal issues. He championed a form of parliamentary liberalism that was based on the writings of Locke (see p. 47) and, to some extent, a misreading of English political experience. Montesquieu emphasized the need to resist tyranny by fragmenting government power, particularly through the device of the separation of powers.

Role of assemblies

In practice, a bewildering variety of terms are used to describe political bodies with very similar functions: congress (USA), national assembly (France), house of representatives (Japan), parliament (Singapore), congress of deputies (Spain), and so on. Students of comparative politics usually classify such bodies as assemblies, legislatures or parliaments. An assembly, in its simplest sense, is a collection or gathering of people, as in, for example, a school assembly. As a political term, assembly has come to be associated with representation and popular government, an assembly, certainly in the French tradition, being viewed as a surrogate for the people. For this reason, the term is sometimes reserved for the lower, popularly elected chamber in a bicameral system (as in, for instance, Pakistan and France), or for the single chamber in a unicameral system (as in Egypt and Turkey). In this book, however, the term assembly is used to refer to both houses or chambers, and is used interchangeably with the terms legislature and parliament.

To see these bodies as legislatures is to classify them according to their primary function as law-making bodies. From this point of view, three distinct branches of government can be identified:

- Legislatures *make* law; they enact legislation.
- Executives *implement* law; they execute the law.
- Judiciaries *interpret* law; they adjudicate on the meaning of the law.

This division of government into legislative, executive and judicial institutions has been sustained by the doctrine of the separation of powers (see p. 339), and has been the traditional basis on which to analyse government since the time of Montesquieu. This view is seriously misleading, however. Institutions that are formally classified as legislatures rarely monopolize law-making power. For instance, executives (see p. 358) possess some ability to make law, through devices such as decrees or orders, and usually also have the capacity to influence, if not shape, the formal legislative process. Furthermore, the enactment of law is only one of the functions of legislatures, and not necessarily their most important one.

The term parliament (from the French *parler*, meaning 'to speak') is sometimes preferred because it avoids the limitations of the term assembly and the confusion of

Concept

Parliamentary government

A parliamentary system of government (see Figure 16.1) is one in which the government governs in and through the assembly or parliament, thereby 'fusing' the legislative and executive branches. Although they are formally distinct, the assembly and the executive (usually seen as the government) are bound together in a way that violates the doctrine of the separation of powers, setting parliamentary systems clearly apart from presidential ones (see p. 362).

The chief features of a parliamentary system are as follows:

- Governments are formed as a result of assembly elections, based on the strength of party representation; there is no separately elected executive.
- The personnel of government are drawn from the assembly, usually from the leaders of the party or parties that have majority control.
- The government is responsible to the assembly in the sense that it rests on the assembly's confidence and can be removed (generally by the lower chamber) if it loses that confidence.
- The government can, in most cases, 'dissolve' the assembly, meaning that electoral terms are usually flexible within a maximum limit.
- Parliamentary executives are generally collective is that they accept at least the formal principle of cabinet government.
- As the head of government (usually a prime minister) is a parliamentary officer, there is a separate head of state: a constitutional monarch or a non-executive president.

the term legislature. It nevertheless suggests that these bodies have a very particular character. It implies that their defining feature is that they are consultative or deliberative bodies. Regardless of their legislative powers and representative features, parliaments are above all debating chambers: that is, forums in which policies and political issues can be openly discussed and scrutinized.

Parliamentary systems and presidential systems

One of the key features of any political system is the relationship between the assembly and the government: that is, the relationship between legislative and executive authority. In exceptional cases, a form of 'assembly government' may develop in which executive and legislative power is vested in the assembly, there being no separate executive body. Such a system, for example, emerged briefly under Robespierre and the Jacobins during the French Revolution, influenced by the radical democracy of Rousseau (see p. 79). In other cases, notably in orthodox communist regimes, both the legislative and the executive bodies have been subordinate to the unchallengeable authority of a 'ruling' party. However, assembly–executive relations more commonly conform to one of two institutional arrangements: parliamentary and presidential systems of government.

Most liberal democracies have adopted some form of parliamentary government (see Figure 16.1). These are often Westminster-style systems, in that they are based on the model of the UK Parliament. Often portrayed as the 'mother of parliaments', the origins of the Westminster Parliament can be traced back to the thirteenth century, when knights and burgesses were incorporated into the king's court. During the fourteenth century, separate chambers (the House of Commons and the House of Lords) were created to represent the knights and burgesses on the one hand, and the barons and churchmen on the other. Parliament's supremacy over the king was nevertheless not established until the Glorious Revolution of 1688, and its capacity to call government to account not recognized until the gradual emergence of a democratic franchise during the nineteenth century.

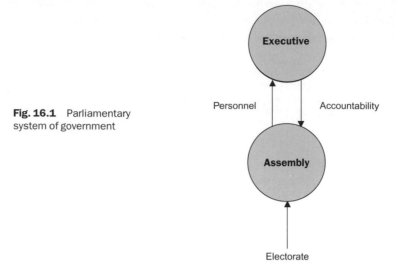

Fig. 16.1 Parliamentary system of government

Similar parliamentary systems came into existence in states such as Germany, Sweden, India, Japan, New Zealand and Australia. The central feature of these systems is a fusion of legislative and executive power: government is parliamentary in that it is drawn from and accountable to the assembly or parliament. The strength of this system is that it supposedly delivers effective but **responsible government**. Government is effective in that it rests on the confidence of the assembly and so can, in most cases, ensure that its legislative programme is passed. In short, governments can get things done. However, responsible government is maintained because the government can govern only as long as it retains the confidence of the assembly. In theory, the assembly has the upper hand because it has the ultimate power: the ability to remove the government.

Unfortunately, however, parliamentary systems often fail to live up to these high expectations. Certainly, there are examples such as Sweden in which, supported by strong norms of consultation and partnership, the assembly (the Riksdag) exerts a strong policy influence without threatening to immobilize the workings of government. However, parliamentary government is often associated with the problem of executive domination. This is the case in the UK, where a combination of strict party discipline and a disproportional electoral system (the simple plurality system) normally allows government to control Parliament through a cohesive and reliable majority in the House of Commons. This encouraged Lord Hailsham (1976) to dub UK government an 'elective dictatorship'. Ironically, therefore, parliamentary systems may allow parliaments to become little more than 'talking shops', and may reduce their members to mere 'lobby fodder'.

Parliamentary systems have also been linked with weak government and political instability. This usually occurs when the party system is fractured, and it is often associated with highly proportional electoral systems. In the French Fourth Republic during 1945–58, for instance, 25 governments came and went in little over 12 years. During this period no French government could command a stable majority in the National Assembly, in which both the Communists on the left and the Gaullists on the right were implacably opposed to the regime itself. Similar problems afflicted post-Second-World-War Italian politics. A polarized multiparty system led to the

Responsible government: A government that is answerable or accountable to an elected assembly and, through it, to the people.

establishment of no fewer than 59 governments between 1945 and 2001. Such apparent **immobilism** may, however, be misleading. In Italy, for example, changes in government typically involve a reshuffling of ministerial personnel, not a political upheaval, and only occasionally result in general elections.

The principal alternative to a parliamentary system is a presidential system of government (see Figure 17.1). Presidential systems are based on the strict application of the doctrine of the separation of powers (see Figure 16.2). This ensures that the assemblies and executives are formally independent from one another and separately elected. The classic example of this is found in the USA, where the so-called 'founding fathers' were particularly anxious to prevent the emergence of an over-strong executive, fearing that the presidency might assume the mantle of the British monarchy. The resulting system therefore incorporated a network of **checks and balances**. Congress, the US presidency and the Supreme Court are separate institutions, in the sense that no overlap of personnel is permitted, but nevertheless possess the ability to constrain one another's power. Thus, while Congress has the ability to make law, the president can veto it, but Congress can, in turn, override this veto with a two-thirds majority in both houses. In the same way, although the president has the power to make senior executive and judicial appointments, these are subject to confirmation by the upper house, the Senate.

Outside the USA, US-style presidential systems have been confined largely to Latin America. However, a 'hybrid' or semi-presidential system was established in France during the Fifth Republic. In this system there is a 'dual executive' in which a separately elected president works in conjunction with a prime minister and cabinet drawn from and responsible to the National Assembly. How such a system works in practice depends on a delicate balance between, on the one hand, the personal authority and popularity of the president and, on the other, the political complexion of the National Assembly. A similar semi-presidential system operates in Finland, in which the president is concerned largely with foreign affairs and leaves the burden of domestic responsibilities in the hands of the cabinet.

The principal virtue of presidential systems is that, by separating legislative power from executive power, they create internal tensions that help to protect individual rights and liberties. As Hobbes (see p. 327) put it, 'liberty is power cut into pieces'. In the USA, for instance, the danger of executive domination is protected against by the range of powers vested in the Congress. For instance, Congress has the right to declare war and raise taxes, the Senate must ratify treaties and confirm presidential appoint-

> ## Concept
>
> ### Separation of powers
>
> The doctrine of the separation of powers proposes that each of the three functions of government (legislation, execution and adjudication) should be entrusted to a separate branch of government (the legislature, the executive and the judiciary, respectively) (see Figure 16.2) Its purpose is to fragment government power in such a way as to defend liberty and keep tyranny at bay. In its formal sense, it demands *independence*, in that there should be no overlap of personnel between the branches. However, it also implies *interdependence*, in the form of shared powers to ensure that there are checks and balances. The separation of powers is applied most strictly in the USA, where it is the basis of the constitution, but the principle is respected in some form in all liberal democracies, notably in the principle of judicial independence.

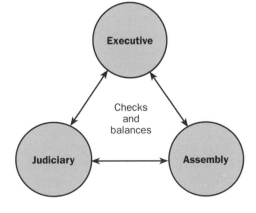

Fig. 16.2 Separation of powers

> **Immobilism:** Political paralysis stemming from the absence of a strong executive, caused by multiple divisions in the assembly and (probably) society.
>
> **Checks and balances:** Internal tensions within the governmental system that result from institutional fragmentation.

ments, and the two houses can combine to charge and impeach the president. Such fragmentation, however, may also have drawbacks.

In particular, presidential systems may be ineffective and cumbersome because they offer an 'invitation to struggle' to the executive and legislative branches of government. Critics of the US system, for example, argue that, since it allows the president to propose and Congress to dispose, it is nothing more than a recipe for institutional deadlock, or 'government gridlock'. This may be more likely when the White House (the presidency) and Capitol Hill (Congress) are controlled by rival parties, but can also occur, as the Carter administration of 1977–81 demonstrated, when both branches are controlled by the same party. A similar problem occurs in France in the form of **cohabitation** when the president is forced to work with a hostile prime minister and National Assembly.

Functions of assemblies

To simply classify assemblies as legislatures, debating chambers or representative bodies obscures their true significance. Although the role of the assembly varies from state to state and from system to system, in every case it fulfils a complex of functions. Above all, assemblies provide a link between government and the people, a channel of communication that can both support government and help to uphold the regime, and force government to respond to public demands and anxieties. The principal functions of assemblies are:

- legislation
- representation
- scrutiny
- political recruitment
- legitimacy.

Legislation

Legislation is often seen as the key function of assemblies, as is clearly implied by their common classification as legislatures. Assemblies or parliaments are typically vested with legislative power in the hope that the laws thus made will be seen to be authoritative and binding. This applies for two reasons. First, an assembly is a forum in which proposed laws can be openly discussed and debated. Second, assemblies are constituted so as to suggest that the people (or, in pre-democratic days, the major interests in society) make the laws themselves. However, the idea that assemblies possess the formal legislative authority is often deeply misleading. As pointed out above, assemblies rarely monopolize legislative authority. Constitutional law is usually placed beyond the competence of the assembly. In Ireland, for example, the constitution is amended by referendums, and in Belgium by special constitutional conventions. Executive officers, such as the French president, are often able to make law by decree, or, like the US president, can veto laws when they have been passed. The European Parliament is not a legislature at all, European law being enacted largely by the Council of Ministers. Even in the UK, where Parliament is invested with legal sovereignty (see p. 131), ministers routinely make law through statutory instruments that are subject to little effective parliamentary scrutiny.

Cohabitation: An arrangement in a semi-presidential system in which the president works with a government and assembly controlled by a rival party or parties.

More significantly, parliaments exercise little *positive* legislative power. Legislative proposals and programmes emanate, in the main, from the executive, which has the organizational coherence and access to specialist advice and information necessary for policy formulation. British MPs, for instance, still have a residual capacity to initiate legislation in the form of private member's bills, but these are debated only if the government is prepared to make time for them alongside its own legislative programme. Approximately 80 per cent of the legislation considered by the US Congress, the most independent and strongest assembly in the developed world, now stems from presidential initiatives. The *negative* legislative power of assemblies – that is, their ability to reject or amend proposed laws – is also limited. In cases such as the 'Second Chamber' of the Dutch States-General, up to half of all legislative measures are significantly redrafted as a result of parliamentary consultations. However, in the UK, government defeats in the House of Commons are rare, even exceptional, events. All too often, legislation is passed *through* assemblies, rather than *by* assemblies.

Representation

Assemblies play an important representative role in providing a link between government and the people. In the eighteenth century this was expressed by the slogan adopted by the 13 American colonies that rebelled against British rule: 'no taxation without representation'. The extension of the franchise and the eventual achievement of universal adult suffrage turned assemblies into popular forums, bodies that 'stood for' the people themselves. For this reason, the power of an assembly within the political system is usually seen as an important index of democratic government. However, it is less clear how this representative function is carried out in practice.

Representation (see p. 248) is a complex principle that has a number of contrasting implications. For example, Westminster-style parliamentary systems based on British traditions have often portrayed representatives as trustees whose prime responsibility is to exercise their own judgement and wisdom on behalf of their constituents. However, this Burkian notion of representatives as independent actors conflicts sharply with the strict party discipline now found in most assemblies, particularly those in parliamentary systems. The alternative theory of representation, the doctrine of the mandate (see p. 252), views parties, not assemblies, as the central mechanism through which representation takes place.

In other states, the idea of constituency representation takes pride of place. This applies particularly to the US Congress, as a result of its relatively weak party system and the unusually short, two-year terms of Representatives. The primary concern of both Representatives and Senators is to 'bring home the bacon'. Congress is therefore commonly dominated by what is called 'pork barrel' politics, a style of politics characterized by measures designed to bring benefits to particular constituencies that are pushed through by a form of cooperation amongst individual legislators known as 'log rolling'. However, it is the very effectiveness of Congress in its representative function that makes it an unsuitable policy-maker; it is better able to block the president's programme than to propose a coherent alternative of its own.

In the USSR and other communist states, in the absence of electoral choice and party competition, representation was often based on the degree to which assemblies resembled the larger society. The Supreme Soviet thus came far closer to being a microcosm of Soviet society (in terms of gender, nationality, occupation and so on) than assemblies in the developed West have ever done. Finally, assemblies are often mechanisms of interest representation. This is particularly the case when they

Concept

Responsibility

Responsibility can be understood in two contrasting ways. First, it means to act in a sensible, reasonable or morally correct fashion, often in the face of pressure to behave otherwise. A government may thus claim to be 'responsible' when it resists electoral pressures and risks unpopularity by pursuing policies designed to meet long-term public interests. Second, responsibility means accountability (see p. 418) or answerability. This implies the existence of a higher authority to which an individual or body is subject, and by which it can be controlled. Government is 'responsible' in this sense if its actions are open to scrutiny and criticism by an assembly that has the ability to remove it from power. This sense of the term also has an important moral dimension: it implies that the government is willing to accept blame and bear an appropriate penalty.

are seen to exert a significant degree of policy influence, and party systems are sufficiently relaxed to offer interest groups a point of access. Once again, the USA provides the prime example, with over $1.2 billion being contributed to finance congressional elections in 1999–2000, mainly from business sources.

Scrutiny and oversight

While the legislative and representative roles of assemblies have declined in significance, greater emphasis has been placed on the ability of assemblies to constrain or check executive power. Assemblies have increasingly become scrutinizing bodies, the principal role of which is to deliver responsible or accountable government. Most assemblies have developed institutional mechanisms designed to facilitate this role. Parliamentary systems, for example, usually subject ministers to regular oral or written questioning, the classic example being Question Time in the UK House of Commons. This allows the prime minister to be cross-examined once a week, and subjects other senior ministers to similar scrutiny about once a month. Germany and Finland use the practice of 'interpellation', a process of oral questioning followed by a vote to establish the confidence of the assembly in the answers given. Since questioning and debate on the floor of a chamber inevitably tend to be generalized, much of the scrutinizing work of assemblies is carried out by committees set up for this purpose. The powerful standing committees of the US Congress have served as a model for many other assemblies in this respect.

However, assemblies are not always effective in calling executives to account. In the National People's Congress in China, for example, control by a monopolistic party has turned the assembly into a mere propaganda weapon, with government policy nearly always being approved by unanimous votes. Party discipline also constrains parliamentary scrutiny elsewhere. For instance, it can be argued that, in Westminster-style systems, the principal function of the assembly is to uphold and support government, since the majority of the members of the assembly belong to the governing party. The job of scrutiny thus passes to the opposition parties, which, as long as the government retains majority control, have no power to remove it.

A further key factor is the ability of the assembly to extract information from the executive. Knowledge is power; without full and accurate information, meaningful scrutiny is impossible. In the USA, France, the Netherlands, Canada and Australia, for instance, formal freedom of information acts have been passed to establish a general right of public access to government information and records. Finally, oversight of the executive requires that parliamentary representatives be well resourced and have access to research services and expert advice. Here the contrast is dramatic, ranging from the lavish funding and large personal staffs provided for the members of the US Congress to the less well paid, inadequately resourced and sometimes overworked UK MPs.

Recruitment and training

Assemblies often act as major channels of recruitment, providing a pool of talent from which leading decision-makers emerge. This applies less in authoritarian states, where rubber-stamp assemblies seldom attract serious politicians, and less in presidential systems, in which a separation of powers prevents executive office from being filled by current members of the assembly. However, although the trend of late has been for US presidents to have been former state governors, presidents such as

Kennedy and Nixon first cut their teeth as members of Congress. In parliamentary systems, however, service in the assembly is a required career path for ministers and prime ministers, who then continue to hold their assembly seats alongside their executive offices. In many developed and developing states, assemblies recruit and train the next generation of political leaders, thus giving them experience of political debate and policy analysis.

On the other hand, assemblies can also be inadequate in this respect. Parliamentarians certainly gain experience of politics as **rhetoric**, or what is derogatorily known as 'speechifying', but they have few opportunities to acquire the bureaucratic and managerial skills required to run government departments and oversee the process of policy formulation. Moreover, it is sometimes argued that assemblies 'corrupt' politicians by socializing them into norms and values that distance them from the needs of their constituents and the instincts of grass-roots party workers. Parliamentary socialists, for example, may thus come to subscribe more passionately to the ideals of parliamentarianism than they do to the principles of socialism (Miliband, 1972).

Legitimacy

The final function of assemblies is to promote the legitimacy (see p. 219) of a regime by encouraging the public to see the system of rule as 'rightful'. This is why most authoritarian and even totalitarian states tolerate assemblies, though, of course, ones that have no legislative independence or policy-making power. The ability of assemblies to mobilize consent depends largely on their ability to function as popular conventions, endorsing laws and policies in the name of the public as well as in their interest. In addition to having propaganda value, assemblies may also perform more creditable educational functions. Parliamentary debates can help to inform and instruct citizens about the affairs of government and the major issues of the day. Thus reactions in the UK to the Argentine invasion of the Falklands in 1982 were clearly influenced by the rare Saturday sitting of the House of Commons, and what the US public knew of the Iran–Contra affair in 1988 was based largely on the hearings of the Senate Committee on Intelligence.

To a growing extent, however, the propaganda/educational role of assemblies has been taken over by the mass media (see p. 232). The rise of the electronic media in the form of radio and particularly television has given government direct access to literally millions of voters instead of it having, as before, to rely on the reporting of parliamentary debates and discussions. As a result, the status that assemblies enjoy increasingly depends less on their constitutional position and more on the media attention they receive. This helps to explain why assemblies have been increasingly anxious for their proceedings to receive television coverage. The public impact of US congressional committees has long been enhanced by the televising of their hearings. In the case of the UK, television cameras were not allowed into the House of Commons until 1989, shortly after they were first introduced in the Soviet parliament.

Structure of assemblies

Assemblies differ in a number of respects. For example, their members may be elected, appointed or even selected by inheritance, or any combination of these meth-

Rhetoric: The art of using language to persuade or influence; rhetoric can imply high-sounding but essentially vacuous speech.

James Madison (1751–1836)

US statesman and political philosopher. A Virginian delegate to the Constitutional Convention of 1787, Madison was a strong proponent of US nationalism and a keen advocate of ratification. He later served as Jefferson's Secretary of State (1801–89) and was the fourth president of the USA (1809–17). Usually regarded as a leading supporter of pluralism and divided government, Madison urged the adoption of federalism, bicameralism and the separation of powers. However, when in government, he was prepared to strengthen the power of national government. His best known political writings are his contributions, with Alexander Hamilton (see p. 168) and John Jay, to *The Federalist Papers* (Hamilton, Jay and Madison, [1787–89] 1961).

ods. When members are elected, this may be on the basis of population (in the form of equal-sized constituencies), or through regions or states. The franchise may be restricted or universal, and various electoral systems may be used (see pp. 257–63). The sizes of assemblies also vary considerably. The tiny republic of Nauru, in the West Central Pacific, has an assembly of 18 members, each of whom represents approximately 440 people. At the other extreme there is the almost 3000-member National Peoples' Congress in China, in which one member represents over 350 000 people. However, the principal structural differences between assemblies are whether they comprise one chamber or two, and the nature and role of their committee systems.

One chamber or two?

Although Yugoslavia once experimented with a five-chamber assembly, and from 1984 to 1994 South Africa had a three-chamber assembly, the vast majority of assemblies have either one or two chambers. Single-chamber, or unicameral, assemblies have been common in much of Africa, in communist states such as China, and in postcommunist states that have maintained an earlier tradition of unicameralism. Indeed, there was a clear trend towards unicameralism in the post-Second-World-War period. For instance, in 1948 Israel established a single-chamber parliament (the Knesset), and second chambers were abolished in New Zealand in 1950, Denmark in 1954, and Sweden in 1970. Such developments support the view that unicameral assemblies are more streamlined and effective than bicameral ones, especially in terms of responding to the needs of small and relatively cohesive societies. In the famous remark of the Abbé Siéyès in 1789: 'if the second Chamber agrees with the first it is unnecessary; if it disagrees it is pernicious'. Nevertheless, about half the world's states retain two-chamber, or bicameral, assemblies.

In terms of strengthening checks and balances within assemblies and between executives and assemblies, **bicameralism** has usually been seen as a central principle of liberal constitutionalism (see p. 321). This was the case in the debates amongst the 'founding fathers' who drew up the US constitution in 1787. Whereas earlier second chambers, such as the UK House of Lords, had developed as vehicles through which powerful economic and social interests could be represented in government, delegates such as James Madison saw the US Senate as a means of fragmenting legislative power and as a safeguard against executive domination.

Bicameralism: The fragmentation of legislative power, established through the existence of two (co-equal) chambers i the assembly; a device of limited government.

Focus on . . .

Bicameralism: strengths and weaknesses

The chief benefits of bicameralism are the following:

- Second chambers check the power of first chambers and prevent majoritarian rule.
- Bicameral assemblies more effectively check the power of the executive, because there are two chambers to expose the failings of government.
- Two-chamber assemblies widen the basis of representation, allowing each house to articulate a different range of interests and respond to different groups of voters.
- The existence of a second chamber can ensure that legislation is more thoroughly scrutinized, as it can relieve the legislative burden of the first chamber and rectify its mistakes and oversights.
- Second chambers can act as a constitutional safeguard, delaying the passage of controversial legislation and allowing time for discussion and public debate.

The drawbacks of bicameralism include the following:

- Unicameral assemblies are more efficient, because the existence of a second chamber can make the legislative process unnecessarily complex and difficult.
- Second chambers often act as a check on democratic rule, particularly when their members are non-elected or indirectly elected.
- Bicameral assemblies are a recipe for institutional conflict in the legislature, as well as for government gridlock.
- Bicameral assemblies may narrow access to policy-making by placing final legislative decisions in the hands of joint committees.
- Second chambers introduce a conservative political bias by upholding existing constitutional arrangements and, sometimes, the interests of social elites.

The representative advantages of bicameralism are particularly important in federal states (see p. 167), where the sharing of sovereignty creates a constant danger of irreconcilable conflict between the centre and the periphery. All of the world's 16 federal states thus have bicameral legislatures, and in 14 of them the second chamber represents the provinces or component states. These may enjoy equal representation, as in Australia, Switzerland and the USA, or they may be represented according to the size of their populations, as in Austria and Germany. Second chambers in some nonfederal states are also used to resolve regional differences. In France most members of the second chamber, and in the Netherlands all members, are elected indirectly via local government.

Most second chambers are constitutionally and politically subordinate to first chambers, which are usually seen as the locus of popular authority. This is particularly the case in parliamentary systems, in which government is generally responsible to and drawn, largely or wholly, from the lower house. In Norway, the Netherlands and Fiji all **bills**, and in India, Canada and the UK money bills, must be introduced in the first chamber. Second chambers may also be denied veto powers. The Japanese first chamber, the House of Representatives, is thus able, by a two-thirds majority, to override the House of Counsellors. The UK House of Lords only has the power to

Bill: Proposed legislation in the form of a draft statute; if passed, a bill becomes an act.

delay non-financial legislation for a single year, although it can still veto the sacking of judges and the postponement of parliamentary elections.

Not uncommonly, such weaker versions of bicameralism reflect the restricted representative basis of the upper house. Indirect elections are used in Germany, Austria and India, for example, and a combination of election and appointment is used in Belgium, Malaysia and Ireland. The Canadian Senate and the UK House of Lords are wholly nominated; indeed, until their right of attendance was removed in 1999, the majority of the members of the House of Lords were hereditary peers. A stronger version of bicameralism is found in assemblies with two chambers that have broadly equal powers. The Italian Chamber of Deputies and the Italian Senate, for example, are both elected by universal adult suffrage, and are legislatively co-equal. An electoral college representing both chambers elects the president, and the prime minister and council of ministers are collectively responsible to the whole assembly. The US Congress is perhaps the only example of an assembly that has a dominant upper chamber. Although all tax legislation must be introduced in the House of Representatives, the Senate alone exercises ratification and confirmation powers.

One of the greatest drawbacks of legislative fragmentation is the possibility of conflict between the two chambers. When the houses have broadly equal powers, a device is needed to resolve differences and prevent institutional immobilism. The most common mechanism is that used in the US Congress, in which a special joint congressional committee, composed of senior figures from both chambers, is authorized to produce a compromise agreement. In Germany, although the lower chamber (the Bundestag) is in most cases legislatively dominant, the upper chamber (the Bundesrat) enjoys considerable veto powers in relation to constitutional questions and matters related to the *Länder*. When disputes occur, they are referred to a joint Bundestag–Bundesrat conciliation committee, the members of which are drawn from the two chambers in equal proportions. A further criticism of bicameralism is that it tends to entrench a conservative political bias. To the extent that second chambers defend the constitutional structure by making it more difficult to pass radical or controversial measures, this tendency is usually seen as laudable. However, when second chambers are able to block or delay legislation approved by democratically elected first chambers, they may merely help to insulate political and social elites from popular pressure. Ironically, the opposite can also be the case. The US Senate is now as liberal, or more liberal, than the House of Representatives, and in the UK in the 1980s the House of Lords was a more effective check on the Thatcher government than was the House of Commons.

Committee systems

Almost all assemblies have a committee system of some sort. Indeed, the trend towards the use of committees, in assemblies and elsewhere, is often seen as one of the distinctive features of modern politics. Committee systems have increasingly been portrayed as the power houses of assemblies, the very hub of the legislative process; whereas parliamentary chambers are for talking, committees are for working. As Woodrow Wilson ([1885] 1961) put it: 'Congressional government is committee government. Congress in session is Congress on public exhibition. Congress in its committee-rooms is Congress at work'. It is therefore not surprising that assemblies are often classified according to their committees. In crude terms, strong assemblies have strong committees, and weak assemblies have weak committees.

Focus on . . .

Committees: advantages and disadvantages

A committee is a small work group composed of members drawn from a larger body and charged with specific responsibilities. Whereas *ad hoc* committees are set up for a particular purpose and disbanded when that task is complete, permanent or standing committees have enduring responsibilities and an institutionalized role. Committee structures have become increasingly prominent in legislative and executive branches of government, as deliberative and consultative forums and also as decision-making bodies.

Amongst the advantages of committees are the following:

- They allow a range of views, opinions and interests to be represented.
- They provide the opportunity for fuller, longer and more detailed debate.
- They encourage decisions to be made more efficiently and speedily by restricting the range of opposing opinions.
- They make possible a division of labour that encourages the accumulation of expertise and specialist knowledge.

However, committees have been criticized for the following reasons:

- They can easily be manipulated by those who set up and staff them.
- They encourage centralization by allowing a chairperson to dominate proceedings behind a mask of consultation.
- They narrow the range of views and interests that are taken into account in decision-making.
- They divorce their members from the larger body, creating a form of sham representation.

Assembly committees usually have one of three functions. First, they may carry out detailed consideration of legislative measures and financial proposals. They thus not only help to relieve the legislative burden on chambers, but also engage in more thorough and exacting examination than is possible on the floor of a house. This task is usually carried out by standing committees, which may be broad and flexible, as in the UK and France, or permanent and highly specialized, as in Germany and the USA. Second, committees may be set up to scrutinize government administration and oversee the exercise of executive power. Such committees must be permanent and specialized, because, to be effective, they have to rival the executive in terms of detailed knowledge and expertise. In the US Congress, for example, legislative and scrutinising responsibilities are vested in standing committees, whereas, in the UK Parliament and the French National Assembly, separate select or supervisory committees are set up. Third, *ad hoc* committees may investigate matters of public concern. Some of the most important examples of investigatory committees have been found in the USA, notably the Irvin Committee on Watergate, and the House Un-American Activities Committee, which became a vehicle for **McCarthyism** in the 1950s.

If powerful committees mean a powerful assembly, what makes committees powerful? It is generally agreed that the US Congress has the most powerful com-

McCarthyism: The use of witch hunts and unscrupulous investigations, as practised in the 1950s against 'communists' by US Senator Joseph McCarthy.

mittees found anywhere in the world, and these provide a model that many other assemblies have tried to adopt. Their power certainly stems from their specialist responsibilities, permanent membership and lavish support in terms of funding and access to advice. This allows them to match the expertise of the bureaucracy. Moreover, their role in the legislative process is crucial. Whereas in the UK, France and Japan bills reach committees having been debated and approved in principle by the floor of the house, in Congress committee scrutiny comes first. This means that many bills are completely redrafted, and others never see the light of day.

Most importantly, however, Congress has a relatively weak party system, which allows its committees considerable independence from the presidency. Where stricter party discipline operates, as in Australia, New Zealand and the UK, committees are effectively neutered by the fact that the majority of their members owe an overriding loyalty to the government of the day. Germany is an exception in this respect. Although Germany has an effective party system, it also possesses strong legislative committees, largely as a consequence of the need for coalition governments to conciliate the assembly in order to maintain the support of two or more parties.

In an attempt to strengthen Parliament in the UK against the executive, a system of departmental select committees was established in 1979. These were consciously modelled on the US example, and the system sought to promote open government (see p. 436) by allowing for the examination of government papers and the cross-examination of ministers and senior civil servants. It was hoped that these committees would become effective watchdogs that would be capable of influencing government policy. However, the experiment has proved disappointing, for a number of reasons. First, the hoped-for less partisan character of committees has failed to materialize, as the government has ensured that party disciplines intrude into the work of committees. Second, the select committees are inadequately resourced and have limited powers. Although they can send for 'persons, papers and records', they cannot force particular civil servants or ministers to attend, nor can they ensure that their questions are fully answered. Third, no alternative career structure has developed around the committees; MPs still look to advance their careers through jobs in government, and so tend to be more sensitive to party pressures than parliamentary ones.

▌ Performance of assemblies

Do assemblies make policy?

The difficulty with assessing the performance of assemblies is that they carry out such a wide range of functions. Should they be judged on the quality of the legislation they pass, their effectiveness in mobilizing consent, the degree to which they represent public opinion, or what? The greatest political concern, however, relates to the policy impact of assemblies: that is, their capacity to shape or at least influence what governments actually do. Do assemblies have power in the sense that they affect the content of public policy, or are they merely talking shops that draw attention away from where the real business of government happens? The key issue here is the nature of assembly–executive relations and the distribution of power between the two major branches of government. On this basis, the assemblies of the world can be classified into three broad categories:

- policy-making assemblies, which enjoy significant autonomy and have an active impact on policy
- policy-influencing assemblies, which can transform policy but only by reacting to executive initiatives
- executive-dominated assemblies, which exert marginal influence or merely rubber-stamp executive decisions.

Policy-making assemblies are rare. To exert a positive influence on the policy process, an assembly has to fulfil three criteria. First, it must command significant constitutional authority and respect. Second, it must enjoy meaningful political independence from the executive, and, third, it must possess sufficient organizational coherence to undertake concerted action. As far as the UK Parliament is concerned, these conditions were perhaps fulfilled only during its so-called 'golden age', the period between the Great Reform Act of 1832 and the Second Reform Act of 1867. In this period Parliament, its authority enhanced by the extension of the franchise but not yet hampered by the emergence of effective party discipline, changed governments, forced the removal of individual ministers, rejected government legislation, and initiated significant measures.

In the modern period, the best (and, some would argue, the only) example of a policy-making assembly is the US Congress. Congress is perhaps unique in that it enjoys an unusual combination of advantages. The separation of powers invests Congress with constitutional independence and an impressive range of autonomous powers. Relatively weak party cohesion deprives the president of the usual means of exerting legislative control, and Congress may anyway be controlled by the opposition party. A powerful committee system guarantees the organizational effectiveness of Congress. Finally, Congress has had the staffing and informational resources to operate without depending on the executive branch for assistance.

Nevertheless, despite these advantages, Congress has lost some of its influence during the modern period. Since the time of the New Deal, the US public, and for that matter Congress itself, has increasingly looked to the White House (the presidency) for political leadership (see p. 372). The main burden of Congress's work is therefore to examine the president's legislative programme. This has weakened Congress's role as a policy initiator, and has led to a situation in which 'the president proposes and Congress disposes'. Indeed, growing anxiety about the subordination of Congress was expressed in the 1960s in fears about the emergence of a so-called 'imperial presidency'. In the aftermath of the Watergate scandal, however, a resurgent Congress adopted a more assertive attitude towards presidential power, and initiated a series of reforms in the committee and seniority systems. The most striking example of Congress seizing control of public policy occurred after the 1994 elections, when the Republican Congress, led by the Speaker of the House Newt Gingrich, pushed through a radical programme of tax and spending cuts under the slogan 'Contract with America'. Nevertheless, when the Republicans controlled the White House and both houses of Congress during 2002–6, few checks were imposed on presidential power, particularly over foreign issues.

The collapse of communism in the USSR and the emergence of a postcommunist regime also underlined, albeit briefly, the importance of parliamentary power. Following the collapse of the USSR, President Yeltsin was confronted by a parliament largely unsympathetic to the liberal reforms that his administration attempted to advance. Yeltsin was forced to sack key ministers and to slow down and even reverse

Focus on . . .

Adversary politics: for and against

Adversary politics is a style of politics characterized by an antagonistic relationship between major parties that turns political life into an ongoing electoral battle. Parliamentary debate thus becomes a 'continuous polemic' before what is seen as the 'bar of public opinion'.

Adversarialism has been defended on the following grounds:

- It offers voters clear alternatives, thus promoting electoral choice and democratic accountability.
- It checks government power by ensuring that there is opposition and scrutiny.

Its dangers nevertheless include the following:

- It discourages sober and rational debate, and precludes compromise.
- It fosters polarization, which, as governments change, gives rise to political instability.

major economic reforms. However, this period of genuine parliamentary government came to a spectacular end when hardliners rebelled against Yeltsin's decision to dissolve parliament. This led in October 1993 to the military seizure of the Russian parliament (the White House) and the imposition of presidential rule. Under the new constitution, which Yeltsin imposed in 1993, the parliament was replaced by the Federal Assembly, composed of the State Duma (lower chamber) and the Federation Council (upper chamber). Although the Assembly has developed a significant legislative role, its representation and scrutiny functions remain weak.

In parliamentary systems, assemblies have generally played a policy-influencing, rather than a policy-making, role. Where exceptions have occurred, as in the Italian assembly and the National Assembly of the Fourth French Republic, this has usually been a consequence of weak coalition government (see p. 288) and a fragmented party system. More commonly, assembly–executive relations are structured by party divisions. This is most clearly the case when majoritarian or weakly proportional electoral systems invest a single party with majority control of the assembly, as has traditionally occurred in the UK, New Zealand and Australia. In such cases, the central dynamic of the parliamentary system is an antagonistic relationship between the government and the opposition, usually termed 'adversary politics'. Government governs in the sense that it is responsible for formulating and later implementing a legislative programme, while the assembly plays an essentially reactive role.

The scope that the assembly has to influence policy in these circumstances depends largely on two factors: the strength in the assembly of the governing party, and the party's ability to maintain internal unity. The Blair government dominated the UK House of Commons because of the landslide parliamentary majorities it won in 1997 and 2001, and because the Labour Party had succeeded in resolving its deepest ideological divisions before it returned to power. Nevertheless, governments in parliamentary systems must remain constantly sensitive to the morale of their backbenchers. Margaret Thatcher, for example, discovered this to her cost in November 1990 when she was abruptly removed as Conservative party leader and therefore prime minister, despite still commanding a substantial Commons majority. Other assemblies that exert a strong influence on policy are the German Bundestag and the Swedish Riksdag. However, in both these cases parliamentary influence stems less from adversary politics than from ingrained habits of negotiation and compromise fostered both by the political culture and by long experience of coalition government.

Parliamentary systems that have become accustomed to prolonged domination by a single party often have assemblies that are weak or executive-dominated. A deliberate attempt was made in the Fifth French Republic to weaken parliamentary power so as to avoid the conflict and obstructionism that had undermined the Fourth Republic. A system of rationalized parliamentarianism came into existence. This allowed the French president to dominate government largely through party control, but also through his power to dissolve the National Assembly in order to gain a new majority, as de Gaulle did in 1962 and 1968, and Mitterrand did in 1981 and 1988. De Gaulle also reduced the National Assembly's powers of political control, and limited its legislative competence by creating the Conseil Constitutionnel to ensure that its laws conform to the constitution. However, the end of Gaullist domination in 1981 created opportunities for a greater degree of parliamentary influence, particularly when the Socialists lost control of the assembly and Mitterrand was forced into cohabitation with a Gaullist government under Jacques Chirac. The same applied after 1997 when President Chirac was confronted by a Socialist-led government under Jospin.

The Japanese Diet (Kokkai) is another example of a traditionally subordinate assembly. Until the 1980s the Diet was required to do little more than ratify the decisions of the executive: this was a consequence of the unbroken domination of the Liberal Democratic Party after 1955. Rival parties were eternal outsiders, and factional divisions within the LDP were generally played out away from the Diet. However, the progressive decline in the sizes of LDP majorities led by the 1970s to a less adversarial and more conciliatory attitude towards parliamentary opposition. For instance, the membership of standing committees was broadened to include minority parties as the LDP started to relax its grip on the parliamentary process. A full system of parliamentary scrutiny and oversight finally emerged in Japan following the LDP's defeat in the 1993 election.

Less ambiguous examples of marginal assemblies have been found in communist regimes and developing states. In the former, tight control by 'ruling' communist parties and the practice of noncompetitive elections ensured that assemblies did little more than provide formal approval for the government's programme. When this control was relaxed, the consequences were often devastating for the regime. The sweeping victories for Solidarity in the 1989 parliamentary elections in Poland, for example, led directly to the fall of a communist government that had been in power since 1945. In the developing states of Africa and Asia, assemblies have played a largely integrative, rather than policy-influencing, role. Their central function has been to strengthen legitimacy and so assist in the process of nation building. It is a backhanded compliment to assemblies that the establishment of military rule has usually been accompanied by their suspension or abolition. This occurred in Chile, Pakistan and the Philippines in the 1970s, and in Turkey and Nigeria in the 1980s.

Why are assemblies in decline?

There is nothing new about the 'decline of assemblies' debate. Since the late nineteenth century anxiety has been expressed about the strengthening of executives, and particularly bureaucracies, at the expense of assemblies. This anxiety has been heightened by the fact that, since the days of Locke and Montesquieu, assemblies have been seen as the principal vehicles for delivering responsible and representative government. The notion that good government requires a strong assembly is questionable, however. Assembly power can certainly become 'excessive', especially when it leads to immobilism and policy stalemate. The model of the US Congress, for instance, has as many critics as it has admirers. There is nevertheless general agreement that, during the twentieth century, the power and status of assemblies changed, and usually for the worse. Whether this amounts to a general 'decline of assemblies', or rather a shift in their purpose or function, is another matter. The principal factors that have brought about these changes are the following:

- the emergence of disciplined political parties
- the growth of 'big' government
- the organizational weaknesses of assemblies
- the rise of interest-group and media power.

Disciplined political parties

The emergence from the late nineteenth century onwards of mass-membership parties weakened assemblies in a number of respects. In the first place, the transition from loose factions (see p. 272) to disciplined party groupings undermined the ability of individual members to represent constituents as trustees by exercising their own judgement and conscience. Parties rather than assemblies thus became the principal agents of representation, operating through the doctrine of the mandate. Party loyalty also weakened assemblies in terms of their function as debating chambers. However articulate, impassioned or persuasive parliamentary oratory may be, it has little or no impact on voting in party-dominated assemblies, which means that debate becomes sterile or ritualized. As Richard Cobden (1804–65) commented about the UK House of Commons, 'In this House I have heard many a speech that moved men to tears – but never one that turned a vote'. More important, however, is the tendency of party unity to facilitate executive domination. In parliamentary systems in particular, loyalty to party means, for the majority of parliamentarians, loyalty to the government of the day, which comprises, after all, the leading members of their own party. Far from checking or even embarrassing the executive, many assemblies have therefore come to function as its willing accomplices or doughty defenders.

'Big' government

The growth in the role of government, especially in the areas of social welfare and economic management, has usually been associated with a redistribution of power from assemblies to executives. This occurs for three reasons. First, it leads to an increase in the size and status of bureaucracies, which are responsible for administering government policy and overseeing an ever-widening range of public services. Second, it places greater emphasis on the process of policy initiation and formulation. Although individual assembly members can initiate policy in specific areas, the task of developing broad and coherent government programmes is quite beyond them. During the twentieth century most assemblies therefore adjusted to the loss of positive legislative power by accepting that their central role was to scrutinize and criticize, rather than to make policy. Third, 'big' government has meant that government policy is increasingly complex and intricate. This, in turn, has placed a higher premium on expertise, a quality more abundantly possessed by 'professional' bureaucrats than by 'amateur' politicians.

Lack of leadership

By virtue of their function as representative forums and debating chambers, assemblies suffer from a number of organizational weaknesses. In particular, they usually comprise several hundred members, who enjoy formal equality in the sense that they can all vote and contribute to debates. Although advantageous in other respects, the egalitarian and fragmented character of assemblies weakens their capacity to provide leadership and take concerted action. This problem has become more acute in an age in which the public looks to government to solve social problems and deliver sustained prosperity, and in which states have no choice but to participate in international affairs and global politics. Party-organized assemblies are certainly better able to adopt clear and coherent domestic and foreign policies, but in these cases leadership tends to be provided *by* parties and only *through* assemblies. In general, it has been political executives rather than assemblies that have been able to respond to this need for leadership, by virtue of their greater organizational coherence and the fact that they are headed by a single individual, usually a president or prime minister.

Interest group and media power

Not only have power and public attention shifted from assemblies to executives, but they have also been lost to interests and groups external to government. The rise of interest groups has threatened assemblies in two important respects. The first is that the groups have provided the public with an alternative mechanism of representation. Often set up specifically for this purpose, interest groups tend to be more effective than assemblies in taking up popular grievances and giving expression to the concerns and aspirations of particular groups. Single-issue groups, for instance, now engage in, and promote, the kind of public debate that previously took place only in parliamentary chambers. The second factor is that, while assemblies have increasingly been excluded from the process of policy formulation, organized interests have become more prominent both as representatives of 'affected groups' and as sources of expert advice and information. The mass media, and particularly television and new forms of electronic communication, have also helped to make assemblies appear redundant. This has occurred because newspapers and television have displaced assemblies as the major forums for political debate, and because political leaders increasingly wish to deal with the public via the media rather than indirectly through assemblies.

The rise of assemblies?

Many argue that the above analysis paints an over-gloomy picture. To some extent, the 'decline of assemblies' is too sweeping a notion, since it conceals the perhaps more important fact that the role of assemblies in the political process has fundamentally changed. Whereas their decline as legislatures and as policy-shaping bodies can hardly be doubted, many agree with Blondel (1973) that, if anything, they have become more important as 'communicating mechanisms'. The willingness of a growing number of assemblies to open up their proceedings to television cameras has certainly helped to raise their public profiles and strengthen them as arenas of debate and agencies of oversight. In other words, the mass media can upgrade assemblies as well as downgrade them. Similarly, there is a trend towards the professionalization of assembly work. Following the example of the US Congress, this has seen the adoption and strengthening of specialized committees and an improvement in the staff and resources available to individual assembly members.

More broadly, there is evidence in the UK and elsewhere of assemblies becoming more critical and independent as a result of the decline of parties as tightly disciplined blocs. Not only may better-informed voters expect more of individual assembly members, but also better-educated and better-resourced members may be less willing to defer to a party line and act as 'lobby fodder'. If nothing else, general recognition that the legitimacy and stability of a political system is linked to the perceived effectiveness of its assembly guarantees that, whenever assembly power is weakened, voices will be raised in protest. Ultimately, however, the desirable balance between the assembly and the executive boils down to a normative judgement about the need for representation and accountability on the one hand, and for leadership and strong government on the other.

■ Summary

◆ The terms 'assembly', 'legislature' and 'parliament' are usually used interchangeably. The term 'assembly' suggests that the body is a surrogate for the people, as it is composed of lay politicians who claim to represent the people rather than of trained or expert government officials. The term 'legislature' is misleading, because assemblies never monopolize law-making power. The term 'parliament' draws attention to the importance within assemblies of debate and deliberation.

◆ A parliamentary system is one in which government governs in and through the assembly or parliament, the executive being drawn from, and accountable to, the assembly. A presidential system is based on a separation of powers between the assembly and the executive. This establishes a relationship characterized by a combination of independence and interdependence between the two branches.

◆ Assemblies provide a link between government and the people: that is, a channel of communication that can support government and uphold the regime, and force government to respond to popular demands. The chief functions of an assembly are to enact legislation, act as a representative body, oversee and scrutinize the executive, recruit and train politicians, and assist in maintaining the political system's legitimacy.

◆ Assemblies generally comprise either one or two chambers. The attraction of bicameralism is that it strengthens checks and balances and broadens representation, which is particularly useful in federal systems. Its disadvantage is that, in this type of system, there is a tendency towards immobilism and government gridlock. Committee systems are increasingly important in the legislative process; strong assemblies usually have strong committees, weak ones have weak committees.

◆ Assemblies rarely make policy. More usually, they influence policy or are executive-dominated. The amount of power an assembly has is determined by a variety of factors. These include the extent of the assembly's constitutional authority, its degree of political independence from the executive, the nature of the party system, and the assembly's level of organizational coherence.

◆ The decline of assemblies provokes anxiety because it is linked to the health of responsible and representative government. Assemblies have declined because of the emergence of disciplined political parties, the growth in the role of government, the executive's greater capacity to formulate policy and provide leadership, and the increasing strength of interest groups and the mass media.

Questions for discussion

▶ Does the widespread adoption of parliamentary government reflect the system's success and efficiency?

▶ Why is the separation of powers considered to be such an important liberal-democratic principle?

▶ What conditions are most conducive for the promotion of responsible government?

▶ Are two chambers always better than one?

▶ In complex modern societies, are assemblies doomed to lose out to executives?

▶ Does the decline of assemblies necessarily weaken representation and account-ability?

Further reading

Davidson, R. and W. Oleszek, *Congress and Its Members* (Washington, DC: Congressional Quarterly, 1999). A useful discussion of the role of the US Congress and shifts in congressional power.

Lijphart, A. (ed.), *Parliamentary Versus Presidential Government* (Oxford: Oxford University Press, 1992). A wide-ranging collection of essays that reflect on the merits of parliamentarianism and presidentialism.

Olson, D., *Legislative Institutions: A Comparative View* (Armonk, NY: M. E. Sharpe, 1994). A good and accessible comparative introduction to assemblies.

Russell, M., *Reforming the House of Lords: Lessons from Overseas* (Oxford and New York: Oxford University Press, 2000). An accessible introduction to second chambers that pays particular attention to the reform process in the UK.

Strøm, K., W. Müller and T. Bergman (eds), *Delegation and Accountability in Parliamentary Democracies* (Oxford: Oxford University Press, 2006). A comprehensive account of the institutions of democratic delegation in western European parliamentary democracies.

Political Executives

'A ruler must learn to be other than good.'

NICCOLÒ MACHIAVELLI, *The Prince* (1513)

The executive is the irreducible core of government. Political systems can operate without constitutions, assemblies, judiciaries, and even parties, but they cannot survive without an executive branch to formulate government policy and ensure that it is implemented. Such is the potential power of executives that much of political development has taken the form of attempts to check or constrain them, either by forcing them to operate within a constitutional framework, or by making them accountable to a popular assembly or democratic electorate. Political executives, and particularly chief executives, are certainly the face of politics with which the general public is most familiar. This is because the executive is the source of political leadership. This role has been greatly enhanced by the widening responsibilities of the state in both the domestic and international realms, and the media's tendency to portray politics in terms of personalities. However, the hopes and expectations focused on executives may also prove to be their undoing. In many political systems leaders are finding it increasingly difficult to 'deliver the goods'. This problem is linked to growing disenchantment with politics in general and with politicians in particular.

The central issues examined in this chapter are as follows:

Key issues

▶ What is the executive branch of government? What does it comprise?

▶ What are the principal functions of political executives?

▶ How do presidential executives differ from parliamentary executives?

▶ Where does power lie in political executives?

▶ How should political leadership be understood and explained?

▶ Is there a crisis of leadership in modern politics?

◆ **Concept**

Executive

In its broadest sense, the executive is the branch of government responsible for the implementation of laws and policies made by the legislature. The executive branch extends from the head of government to the members of enforcement agencies such as the police and the military, and includes both ministers and civil servants. More commonly, the term is now used in a narrower sense to describe the smaller body of decision-makers who take overall responsibility for the direction and coordination of government policy. This core of senior figures is often called the *political* executive (roughly equivalent to 'the government of the day', or, in presidential systems, 'the administration'), as opposed to the *official* executive, or bureaucracy (p. 383). The term 'core' executive (see p. 372) is sometimes used to refer to those actors and bodies that are at the apex of government power.

■ Role of the executive

Who's who in the executive?

The executive is, technically, the branch of government that is responsible for the execution or implementation of policy. In practice, however, its responsibilities tend to be substantially broader as well as more complex. This complexity also extends to the composition of the executive. Members of executives have been categorized in one of two ways. First, a distinction is often drawn between the 'political' executive and the 'bureaucratic' executive. This highlights the differences between politicians and civil servants, and, more broadly, between politics and administration (see p. 387). Second, various levels of status and responsibility have been identified within executives. Whereas assemblies tend to respect at least the formal equality of their members, executive branches are typically pyramidal, organized according to a clear leadership structure.

The distinction between political and bureaucratic or official posts is most clear-cut in the case of parliamentary executives, where differences in recruitment, responsibility, status and political orientation can be identified. In parliamentary systems, the political executive comprises elected politicians, ministers drawn from and accountable to the assembly: their job is to make policy, in accordance with the political and ideological priorities of their party, and to oversee its implementation. The official executive comprises appointed and professional civil servants whose job it is to offer advice and administer policy, subject to the requirements of political neutrality (see p. 329) and loyalty to their ministers.

Nevertheless, in parliamentary systems (see p. 337) such as those in Australia, Canada, India and the UK, the political/bureaucratic distinction is blurred by the fact that senior civil servants often make a substantial contribution to policy-making and because use is commonly made of temporary, politically committed advisers. The overlap is usually even greater in presidential executives. In the USA, for example, the president is the only elected politician in the executive. Cabinet members are, in effect, appointed officials, and all the senior and many middle-ranking civil servants are politically partisan and temporary. In communist executives, for example in China and the USSR of old, the distinction is rendered virtually redundant by the all-pervasive reach of the 'ruling' communist party. Chinese bureaucrats are thus 'political' in the sense that they are in all cases ideologically committed supporters, and usually members, of the Chinese Communist Party.

In comparison with political/bureaucratic distinctions, hierarchical divisions within executive branches are easier to identify. In the first place, executives tend to be centralized around the leadership of a single individual. As Montesquieu (see p. 336) put it, 'this branch of government, having need of dispatch, is better administered by one than by many'. Two separate posts can nevertheless be identified, although they may be held by the same person. On the one hand, there is the head of state, an office of formal authority and largely symbolic importance. On the other, there is the head of government, or the chief executive, a post that carries policy-making and political responsibilities. Whereas executive presidents, as in the USA, Russia and France, 'wear two hats', the posts in parliamentary systems are usually separate. A prime minister serves as the chief executive, and the post of head of state is usually held by a non-partisan figurehead.

Focus on . . .

Heads of state

The head of state is the personal embodiment of the state's power and authority. As the leading representative of the state, the head of state enjoys the highest status in the land. However, he or she is often a figure of essentially symbolic or formal significance, with real power residing in the hands of the head of government (a post that may or may not be held by the same person). Heads of state exercise a range of ceremonial powers and responsibilities, such as awarding honours, assenting to legislation and treaties, and receiving visiting heads of state. Their power to appoint the head of government (which is significant in parliamentary systems) may nevertheless allow some scope for residual political influence. The head of state is usually either a president or monarch (see p. 366).

Beneath the chief executive, a range of ministers or secretaries have responsibility for developing or implementing policy in specific areas. There is often a hierarchy amongst these departmental bosses, imposed either by the importance of their policy areas (economics and foreign ministers generally hold leading positions) or by their entitlement to sit in the **cabinet** or in senior committees. As discussed further below, cabinets have responsibilities that range from the sharing of policy-making power in a form of collective leadership to the offering of advice and the broader coordination of executive policy. At a lower level are the massed ranks of bureaucrats and administrators (discussed in Chapter 17) who, at least in theory, are concerned less with policy formulation than with policy implementation. Finally, there are enforcement agencies, such as the police force and armed forces (examined in Chapter 18), and an array of quasi-governmental bodies, popularly known as quangos (see p. 392). These are part of the executive insofar as they help to put government policy into effect, but they are staffed by personnel who enjoy at least formal independence from the government itself.

Functions of political executives

At its most simple, the task of the political executive is to provide leadership (see p. 372). In this sense, the executive functions as the 'commanding heights' of the state apparatus, the core of the state itself. This role extends over a variety of areas, and this means that the members of the political executive have to carry out several functions, sometimes simultaneously. The most important of the areas are the following:

- ceremonial duties
- control of policy-making
- popular political leadership
- bureaucratic management
- crisis response.

Cabinet: A group of senior ministers that meets formally and regularly, and is chaired by the chief executive; cabinets may make policy or be consultative.

Ceremonial leadership

Heads of state (see p. 359), chief executives and, to a lesser extent, senior ministers or secretaries 'stand for' the state. In giving state authority personal form, they represent the larger society and symbolize, accurately or otherwise, its unity. This role is largely formal and ceremonial, and covers, for example, state occasions, foreign visits, international conferences, and the ratification of treaties and legislation. Nonexecutive presidents and constitutional monarchs are sometimes charged with these essentially ceremonial responsibilities, allowing other executive officers to get on with the day-to-day business of government. The role is nevertheless of broader significance for two reasons. First, it provides a focus for unity and political loyalty, and so helps to build legitimacy (see p. 219). Second, it allows those at the top of the executive to portray themselves as 'national leaders', which is vital to the maintenance of public support and electoral credibility.

Policy-making leadership

The key function of the political executive is to direct and control the policy process. In short, the executive is expected to 'govern'. This role was substantially expanded during the twentieth century in response to the broadening responsibilities of government. The political executive is looked to, in particular, to develop coherent economic and social programmes that meet the needs of more complex and politically sophisticated societies, and to control the state's various external relationships in an increasingly interdependent world. One important consequence of this has been the growth of the executive's legislative powers, and its encroachment on the traditional responsibilities of the assembly.

Not only do political executives usually initiate legislative programmes and help, by persuasion or direction, to make the legislative process work, but, in many cases, they also exercise a wide range of law-making powers, using decrees, orders and other instruments. However, it is misleading to imply that the political executive always dominates the policy process. Much policy, for instance, is initiated by political parties and interest groups. Moreover, by virtue of their expertise and specialist knowledge, bureaucrats or civil servants may play a crucial role in policy formulation, at best leaving the political executive to establish the overall direction of government policy.

Popular leadership

The popularity of the political executive, more than any other part of the political system, is crucial to the character and stability of the regime as a whole. At a policy level, it is the ability of the executive to mobilize support that ensures the compliance and cooperation of the general public. Quite simply, without support from the public, or from key groups in society, policy implementation becomes difficult, perhaps impossible. More importantly, the political executive's popularity is linked to the legitimacy of the broader regime. The unpopularity of a particular government or administration does not in itself weaken support for the political system, but it may do so in the absence of a mechanism for removing and replacing that government. This goes some way towards explaining the widespread use of regular and competitive elections. Of course, this is not to say that unpopular and immovable executives always spell systemic breakdown. Such regimes can survive, but only by resorting to authoritarianism (see p. 38), meaning that popular compliance is brought about through repression and ideological manipulation.

Bureaucratic leadership

Its task of overseeing the implementation of policy means that the political executive has major bureaucratic and administrative responsibilities. In this sense, chief executives, ministers and secretaries constitute a 'top management' charged with running the machinery of government. This work is organized largely along departmental lines, senior ministers having responsibility for particular policy areas and for the bureaucrats engaged to administer those areas. At a higher level, there is a need for policy coordination, which is usually accomplished through some kind of cabinet system.

However, doubts have been expressed about the effectiveness of this bureaucratic leadership. First, as political executives are staffed by politicians, they often lack the competence, managerial experience and administrative knowledge to control a sprawling bureaucratic machine effectively. Second, particular government departments can develop their own interests, especially when they forge alliances with powerful client groups. Third, the bureaucracy as a whole can develop interests that are separate from those of the political executive, encouraging it to resist the control of its notional political masters. These issues are examined in greater detail in Chapter 18 in relation to bureaucratic power.

Crisis leadership

A crucial advantage that the political executive has over the assembly is its ability to take swift and decisive action. When crises break out in either domestic or international politics it is invariably the executive that responds, by virtue of its hierarchical structure and the scope it provides for personal leadership. It is therefore common for assemblies to grant political executives near-dictatorial powers in times of war, and for executives to seize 'emergency powers' when confronted by domestic crises such as natural disasters, terrorist threats, industrial unrest and civil disorder. Clearly, however, the power to declare 'states of emergency' and to impose effective executive rule is subject to abuse. Not uncommonly, governments have used these powers to weaken or eradicate political opposition under the guise of constitutionalism.

Power in the executive: who leads?

As already noted, the roles and responsibilities of the political executive have been substantially enhanced by the emergence of democratic politics, growing government intervention, and political and economic globalization. During the twentieth century political executives acquired ever-wider policy-making and legislative responsibilities, took command of sprawling bureaucratic machines, and increasingly became the focus of popular politics and media attention. These developments have, in turn, profoundly affected the internal organization of the executive branch of government, and the distribution of power within it. By common consent, the main beneficiary of this process has been the chief executive. Heads of government now commonly have institutional responsibilities, a political status, and a public profile that sets them clearly apart from their cabinet or ministerial colleagues. Nevertheless, this image of growing centralization and the rise of personal power conflicts sharply with evidence of leadership failure, and the growing incapacity of chief executives to carry out what people have elected them to do. The complex

Presidential government

A presidential system of government (see Figure 17.1) is characterized by a constitutional and political separation of powers (see p. 339) between the legislative and executive branches of government. Executive power is thus vested in an independently elected president who is not directly accountable to or removable by the assembly.

The principal features of a presidential system are the following:

- The executive and the legislature are separately elected, and each is invested with a range of independent constitutional powers.
- There is a formal separation of the personnel of the legislative and the executive branches (except in semi-presidential systems).
- The executive is not constitutionally responsible to the legislative and cannot be removed by it (except, possibly, through **impeachment**).
- The president or executive cannot 'dissolve' the legislative, meaning that the electoral terms of both branches are fixed.
- Executive authority is concentrated in the hands of the president, the cabinet and ministers being merely advisers responsible to the president.
- The roles of head of state and head of government (chief executive) are combined in the office of the presidency – the president wears 'two hats'.

dynamics of executive power can be examined more closely by looking at the roles of presidents, prime ministers and cabinets.

In each of these three cases, however, three dimensions of power must be borne in mind:

- the *formal* dimension of power: the constitutional roles and responsibilities of executive officers and the institutional frameworks in which they operate
- the *informal* dimension of power: the role of personality, political skills and experience, and the impact of factors such as parties and the mass media
- the *external* dimension of power: the political, economic and diplomatic context of government, and the broader pressures that bear on the executive branch.

Presidents

A president is a formal head of state, a title that is held in other states by a monarch or emperor. An important distinction, however, must be made between constitutional presidents and executive presidents. Constitutional or nonexecutive presidents, found in India, Israel and Germany, for example, are a feature of parliamentary systems and have responsibilities confined largely to ceremonial duties. In these circumstances the president is a mere figurehead, and executive power is wielded by a prime minister and/or a cabinet. This section is concerned with executive presidents, who combine the formal responsibilities of a head of state with the political power of a chief executive. Presidencies of this kind constitute the basis of what is called presidential government (see Figure 17.1), as opposed to parliamentary government (see Figure 16.1).

Presidential executives may be either limited or unlimited. Limited presidential executives operate within constraints imposed by a constitution, political democracy, party competition, and some form of separation of powers (see p. 339). Above all, the powers of the president are counterbalanced by those of a popularly accountable assembly. The best-known example of limited presidentialism is found in the

Impeachment: A formal process for the removal of a public official in the event of personal or professional wrongdoing.

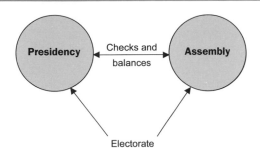

Fig. 17.1 Presidential system of government (limited presidentialism)

USA, but **semi-presidential systems** like those in France and Finland also conform to this model. In unlimited presidential executives, on the other hand, the president is invested with near-unchecked powers, meaning that these regimes are effectively dictatorships (see p. 405). They are commonly found in one-party states that rest heavily on the support of the military. Unlimited executives can be found, for example, in Libya, Iraq and Indonesia.

US-style presidential government has spawned imitations throughout the world, mainly in Latin America and, more recently, in postcommunist states such as Poland, Hungary, the Czech Republic and Russia, although apart from Russia, most postcommunist presidencies operate within what are effectively parliamentary systems. In investing executive power in a presidency, the architects of the US constitution were aware that they were, in effect, creating an 'elective kingship'. Wishing to avoid the abuse of power they believed had occurred under the British Crown, they established an intricate separation of powers between the legislative, executive and judicial branches. This was more accurately described by Richard Neustadt ([1964] 1980) as 'separated institutions sharing powers'. Thus, although the president was designated head of state, chief executive, commander-in-chief of the armed forces and chief diplomat, and was granted wide-ranging powers of patronage and the right to veto legislation, Congress was invested with strong counterbalancing powers. In particular, Congress could declare war and override presidential vetoes, and the Senate was empowered to approve appointments and ratify treaties. Indeed, until the early twentieth century the presidency remained a generally secondary institution; such policy leadership as was required was provided by Congress.

The status of the US presidency was then transformed by two key developments. First, a national economy developed that required the government to abandon its traditional *laissez-faire* policies and adopt a more interventionist approach to economic and social life. Second, the USA was forced to drop its policy of isolationism and accept a world role, assuming after the Second World War a superpower status in a bipolar (and now, arguably, unipolar) world system. Since President Franklin Roosevelt's New Deal in the 1930s, US presidents have played the role of chief legislator, and since 1945 have worn the mantle of the leader of the 'free world'. Alarmed by the ease with which President Johnson and President Nixon escalated the Vietnam War without war being formally declared by Congress, Arthur Schlesinger (1974) went so far as to proclaim the emergence of an 'imperial presidency', a presidency that had broken free from its constitutional bounds and threatened to dominate the two other branches of government.

Presidential power is nevertheless often fragile and insubstantial. Neustadt's classic text *Presidential Power* ([1964] 1980) remains correct: the chief power of the US president is the 'power to persuade': that is, the ability to bargain, encourage, and

Semi-presidential system: A system of government in which a separately elected president presides over a government drawn from, and accountable to, the assembly.

even cajole, but not dictate. The ability of US presidents to get their way depends on four crucial relationships, specifically those with:

- Congress
- the federal bureaucracy
- the Supreme Court
- the mass media.

The president's relationship with Congress is undoubtedly the most crucial. The success of particular presidents, for instance, is often quantified in terms of their 'success rate' with Congress: that is, the proportion of their legislative programme that survives congressional scrutiny. Following the Vietnam War and the Watergate scandal, however, presidents have had to confront more assertive Congresses, intent on reclaiming some of their lost powers. An early example of this was the passage of the War Powers Act 1974, which meant that congressional support was required for the dispatching of US troops abroad. More significantly, the USA's relatively weak party system deprives the president of the major lever of legislative control available to parliamentary executives: an appeal to party unity. This means, as President Jimmy Carter discovered in the 1970s, that presidents can be rebuffed by Congress even when both houses are dominated by their own party.

Presidents may be weaker still when they are confronted by a Congress that is controlled by the opposition party. This was the problem that President Clinton experienced after the election of a Republican Congress in 1994. George W. Bush's influence over Congress was also severely restricted when the Democrats gained control over the Senate in early 2001, following the defection of a Republican Senator. The difficulty confronting the president is that, regardless of party affiliation, both Representatives and Senators are concerned primarily with the 'folks back home'. Indeed, the interest that this forces them to take in domestic affairs has encouraged commentators to speak of the 'two presidencies'. These are the 'domestic' presidency, which is typically characterized by policy failure and gridlock, and from which most presidents retreat, and the 'foreign' presidency, to which they gravitate in the hope of demonstrating their leadership credentials. Even President Clinton, elected to office on a promise to focus 'like a laser beam' on the economy, could not avoid, in Rose's (1987) words, 'going international'. This trend was further strengthened by the terrorist attacks on New York and Washington on September 11, 2001.

In theory, the federal bureaucracy exists to serve the president, but in practice it often acts as an embarrassing constraint. Although presidents make, directly or indirectly, about 4000 appointments at senior and middle-ranking levels in their administrations, this is tiny in proportion to the total number of professional bureaucrats in the US, who number over 2 000 000. Moreover, it is widely argued that these bureaucrats frequently respond to interests at odds with the priorities of the administration. As Secretary of the Navy under Woodrow Wilson, F. D. Roosevelt described influencing the Navy Department as like punching a feather mattress: 'you punch and punch but it remains the same'. In his famous comment on his successor, General Eisenhower, President Truman referred to a similar problem:

He'll sit here and he'll say 'Do this! Do that!' and nothing will happen. Poor Ike – it won't be a bit like the Army.

Similar difficulties exist in relation to the Supreme Court. Since the 1950s the Court has played a significant role in US political life, forcing presidents to shape the political agenda, in part, by exercising influence over it. Although presidents appoint justices to the Supreme Court, these appointments may be rejected by the Senate (as Nixon discovered twice and Reagan once), and, once they have been appointed, judges cannot be controlled because of their security of tenure. Much of the New Deal programme in the 1930s was blocked by the Supreme Court, until F. D. Roosevelt was able to shift its ideological balance through the 'court revolution' of 1937. Eisenhower, in turn, appointed Earl Warren as Chief Justice, only later discovering his taste for judicial activism and his liberal interpretation of the constitution.

The final key relationship is that between the US president and the mass media. The media are vital to presidents who need to appeal directly to the US public 'over the heads of Congress'. In this respect, presidents like Ronald Reagan, a former actor and journalist, have been remarkably successful in 'managing' media coverage and ensuring favourable comment. Nevertheless, presidents who live by the media may also die by it. The mass media are often portrayed as the USA's fourth branch of government, which prizes both its political independence and its reputation for seeking truth. *The Washington Post*'s exposure of the Watergate scandal eventually led to the resignation of President Nixon in 1974, and relentless coverage of the Whitewater affair seriously weakened the Clinton administration in the early 1990s.

The potential within presidential systems for institutional conflict was realized in early postcommunist Russia as the Russian parliament came increasingly under the control of hardliners intent on resisting President Yeltsin's 'shock therapy' reform package. Ultimately, Yeltsin's presidency survived only because of the support of the military in crushing the parliament's rebellion in October 1993, which led to the imposition of presidential rule. The possibility of the emergence in Russia of an unlimited presidential executive was, however, offset by Yeltsin's need to balance the volatile and conflicting pressures within the Russian political system. Caught between radical reformers, conservative hardliners and die-hard nationalists, Yeltsin struggled to hold on to electoral credibility and maintain the effectiveness of his government. Russia's tradition of strong executive leadership was nevertheless reasserted after 2000 by President Putin. Putin established a hegemonic presidency based on what he called a 'dictatorship of law', his popularity bolstered through waging war against Chechnya and resisting regional separatism.

A different form of presidential government is found in semi-presidential systems, such as those in France, Austria, Finland and Portugal. These are hybrid systems. They comprise, as in presidential systems, a separately elected president invested with a range of executive powers and, as in parliamentary systems, a government, usually featuring a prime minister and a cabinet, drawn from and accountable to the assembly. In Finland and Austria, for example, such systems operate largely through a division of executive responsibilities, allowing the president to concentrate on foreign affairs and broader constitutional issues, while the prime minister and cabinet take charge of domestic policy.

However, the system constructed in the Fifth French Republic, and completed with the introduction of a separately elected president in 1962, is significantly more complex. On the one hand, in addition to carrying out the roles that the US president plays as head of state, chief executive and dispenser of appointments, French presidents enjoy a fixed seven-year term in office, and can also bring the legislature to heel by using their power to dissolve the National Assembly. On the other hand,

Focus on . . .

The monarchy debate

A monarchy is a system of the rule dominated by one person (it literally means 'rule by one person'). In general usage, however, it is the institution through which the post of head of state is filled through inheritance or dynastic succession. In absolute monarchies the monarch claims, if seldom exercises, a monopoly of political power (examples being Saudi Arabia, Nepal and Morocco). In constitutional monarchies the monarch fulfils an essentially ceremonial function largely devoid of political significance (for example, in Spain, the Netherlands and the UK).

The advantages of a constitutional monarchy are as follows:

• It provides a solution to the need for a nonpartisan head of state who is 'above' party politics.
• The monarch embodies traditional authority, and so serves as a symbol of patriotic loyalty and national unity.
• The monarch constitutes a repository of experience and wisdom, especially in relation to constitutional matters, available to elected governments.

The disadvantages of a constitutional monarchy include the following:

• It violates democratic principles in that political authority is not based on popular consent and is in no way publicly accountable.
• The monarch symbolizes (and possibly supports) conservative values such as hierarchy, deference and respect for inherited wealth and social position.
• The monarchy binds nations to outmoded ways and symbols of the past, thus impeding progress.

they are seriously constrained by the need for their governments to maintain parliamentary and public support. Thus presidents such as de Gaulle in 1958–69, Pompidou in 1969–74, and Giscard d'Estaing in 1974–81 derived their strength largely from the control that Gaullist forces exercised in the National Assembly. However, the right to call a general election does not necessarily guarantee party control of the National Assembly, as the Socialist President Mitterrand discovered in 1986, and again in 1993, when he was forced into cohabitation with Gaullist governments. Similarly, despite the fact that he possessed the formal powers of an elected monarch, de Gaulle's presidency ended in resignation in 1969 after the student riots of May 1968 and a financial crisis. The fragility of presidential power was also demonstrated by the pressures on President Chirac, particularly during the period of Jospin's Socialist-led government (1997–2002).

Prime ministers

Most of the political executives in the modern world can be classified as parliamentary executives. The structure and form of executive power found in parliamentary systems differs significantly from that in presidential ones. Parliamentary executives have three essential features. First, since executive power is derived from the assembly and closely linked to party politics, a separate head of state, in the form of a constitutional monarch or nonexecutive president, is required to fulfil ceremonial duties and act as a focus of patriotic loyalty. Second, the political executive is drawn from the assembly, which means that the separation of the personnel between the legislature and executive found in presidential systems does not occur in parliamentary systems. Third, the executive is directly responsible to the assembly, or at least to its lower chamber, in the sense that it survives in government only as long as it retains the confidence of the assembly.

The external dynamics of executive power in parliamentary systems thus contrast sharply with those found in presidential ones. In short, parliamentary executives are forced to govern in and through assemblies, while presidential executives tend to rely on a personal mandate and an independent set of constitutional powers. This undoubtedly also affects the internal dynamics of power. In particular, it creates a greater pressure in parliamentary executives for collective decision-making and collaboration, often reflected in the higher status of the cabinet in these systems. However, many commentators have argued that the growth of prime-ministerial power has effectively turned prime ministers into quasi-presidents.

Prime ministers (sometimes seen as chancellors, as in Germany, minister-presidents as in the Netherlands, or referred to by a local title like the Irish Taoiseach) are heads of government whose power is derived from their leadership of the majority party, or coalition of parties, in the assembly. The range of formal powers with which the office of prime minister is invested are typically modest in comparison with those of executive presidents. The most important of these is the control of patronage – the ability to hire and fire, promote and demote, ministers. In the Netherlands and Australia, for example, even this power is exercised by the assembly or the majority party. As the job of prime minister can have only a loose constitutional description, it is no exaggeration to say that the post is what its holder chooses to make of it or, more accurately, is able to make of it.

In practice, this boils down to two key sets of prime-ministerial relationships. The first set are with the cabinet, individual ministers and government departments; the second are with his or her party and, through it, the assembly and the public. The support of the cabinet is particularly crucial to prime ministers who are designated *primus inter pares* (first among equals), such as those in the UK, India and Australia. This status forces prime ministers to operate through a system of collective cabinet government (see p. 370). Their power is therefore a reflection of the degree to which, by patronage, cabinet management and the control of the machinery of government, they can ensure that ministers serve *under* them. In contrast, German chancellors are personally empowered by Article 65 of the Basic Law to decide the general lines of government policy. However, the same article also constrains their power by stipulating that ministers enjoy autonomy in relation to their departments.

There is no doubt that the key to prime-ministerial power and influence lies in his or her position as party leader. Indeed, the modern premiership is largely a product of the emergence of disciplined political parties. Not only is the post of prime minister allocated on the basis of party leadership, it also provides its holder with a means of controlling the assembly and a base from which the image of a national leader can be constructed. The degree of party unity, the parliamentary strength of the prime minister's party (in particular, whether it rules alone or as a member of a coalition), and the authority vested in the assembly or at least its first chamber, are therefore important determinants of prime-ministerial power. Factional rivalry within the LDP, for instance, ensured that, for much of the post-Second-World-War period, the tenure of Japanese prime ministers was short (five prime ministers came and went between 1974 and 1982) and cabinets were frequently reconstructed. Similarly,

Focus on . . .

Prime-ministerial government: virtues and vices

Prime-ministerial government has two key features. First, the office of prime minister is the central link between the legislative and executive branches of government, its holder being drawn from and accountable to the assembly, and also serving as chief executive and head of the bureaucracy. Second, prime-ministerial government reflects the centralization of executive power in the hands of the prime minister and the effective subordination of both the cabinet and departmental ministers. In this, it parallels presidentialism.

Prime-ministerial government has been criticized for the following reasons:

- It strengthens centralization by weakening the constraints formerly exerted by the cabinet and government departments.
- It narrows policy debate and weakens scrutiny by excluding criticisms and alternative viewpoints.

However, it can be defended on the following grounds:

- It reflects the personal mandate that prime ministers acquire in general elections.
- It gives government policy clearer direction by checking the centrifugal pressures embodied in departmentalism (see p. 390) and the 'nudge and fudge' of collective decision-making.

Italy's fragmented party system usually forces prime ministers to play the role of a broker within what tend to be fragile coalition governments. German chancellors, for their part, are restricted by the independence of the *Länder*, the power of the second chamber (the Bundesrat), and the authority of the Constitutional Court, as well as by the autonomy of the Bundesbank.

There is nevertheless agreement that, despite their differing constitutional and political positions, prime-ministerial power has grown in recent years. This results in part from the tendency of the broadcast media in particular to focus on personalities, meaning that prime ministers become a kind of 'brand image' of their parties. The growth of international summitry and foreign visits also provides prime ministers with opportunities to cultivate an image of statesmanship, and gives them scope to portray themselves as national leaders. In some cases, this has led to the allegation that prime ministers have effectively emancipated themselves from cabinet constraints and established a form of prime-ministerial government. For instance, in India an imperial style of premiership developed under Indira Gandhi and her son Rajiv that reached its peak during the state of emergency, 1975–77. This was possible because of the secure majorities that the Congress party enjoyed in parliament, the ruthless control exerted over the apparatus of central government, and the sway that the Gandhi dynasty continued to exert over important sections of the Indian public.

Allegations of prime-ministerial government have often been made in the UK. The unusual level of power wielded by prime ministers stems from various sources, including the following:

- the level and range of their patronage
- their control of the cabinet system, especially their ability to set up and staff cabinet committees
- their ability to dominate the assembly as leaders of the largest party, especially when that party has majority control of the lower chamber
- their position as head of the civil service, and the control this gives them over the bureaucratic machine
- their direct access to the media, which enables them to make personalized appeals to the voters.

Prime ministers stand at the apex of the administrative and political arms of government, meaning that the cabinet has been turned into a US-style advisory body that no longer exercises policy-making responsibility. The prime-ministerial government thesis appeared to have become a reality in the UK during the 1980s as Margaret Thatcher effectively recast the nature and authority of the office. In many respects, Tony Blair's premiership after 1997 built on these foundations. What distinguished Thatcher's premiership was the fact that she saw herself as a 'conviction prime minister', her role being to provide ideological leadership and policy coherence, orientated around ideas that came to be called **Thatcherism**. Blair, similarly, strongly associated his leadership of the Labour Party with the advance of the 'modernizing' project that saw the party rebranded as 'new' Labour, and 'third way' ideological priorities displace old-style socialist ones. For Michael Foley (2000), this development merely exposed the degree to which an 'authentically British presidency' had come into existence. The features of **presidentialism** that parliamentary executives have come to exhibit include the following:

- **spatial leadership:** the tendency of prime ministers to distance themselves from their parties and governments by presenting themselves as 'outsiders' or developing their own ideological stance
- **populist outreach:** the attempt by prime ministers to engage directly with the public by claiming to articulate their deepest hopes and fears
- **personalized election campaigns:** the new media's obsession with personality and the trend to portray leaders as the 'brand image' of their parties or governments
- **personal mandates:** the trend of prime ministers to claim electoral authority and to view themselves as the ideological consciences of their parties or governments
- **special advisors:** the trend for prime ministers to rely on hand-picked political advisors rather than cabinets, ministers or senior civil servants.

Thatcherism: The free-market/strong-state ideological stance adopted by Margaret Thatcher; the UK version of the New Right political project.

Presidentialism: Personalized leadership that is disengaged from parties or other government bodies, in the manner of an executive president.

Although prime ministers who command cohesive parliamentary majorities can wield power that would be the envy of many a president, they are also subject to important constraints. By no means, for instance, do prime ministers have a free hand in terms of hiring and firing. The need to maintain party unity by ensuring that the various factions and ideological wings of the party are represented in the cabinet, and the pressure in countries such as Canada to maintain regional and linguistic representation, act as important checks on prime-ministerial power. Ultimately, prime ministers are only as powerful as their cabinets, parties and broader political circumstances allow them to be. This can be seen in India, where, following the excesses of the emergency in the 1970s, prime ministers such as Desai, Singh and Rao, leading coalition or minority governments, reduced the size of the prime minister's staff, were willing to respect the autonomy of government departments, and interfered less in the affairs of state governments.

It is also interesting that the power wielded by Margaret Thatcher in the UK may have been less a consequence of her indomitable character and ideological resolution than a reflection of the unusually favourable circumstances that confronted her. Chief amongst these were the weak and divided nature of the Labour opposition, the Falklands victory of 1982, the revival of the world economy in the mid 1980s, and, partly as a result of these, the ability of the Conservatives to win three successive elections under her leadership. However, the fragility of prime-ministerial power was underlined by her removal as leader in November 1990.

The relative weakness of John Major's premiership, particularly in the 1992–97 period, stemmed less from his personal inadequacies and more from the greater difficulties his government had to face. These included the UK's slow recovery from the recession of the early 1990s, the diminishing Conservative parliamentary majority after 1992, the party's deepening rift over Europe, and the fact that the government had to confront a more electorally credible and more effectively led Labour opposition. Tony Blair, by contrast, benefited not only from his large majorities and the electoral decline of the Conservative Party, but also from the fact that, after 18 years in opposition, the Labour Pary was more responsive to demands for strong leadership and unity.

Cabinets

Virtually all political executives feature a cabinet of some sort. In France the cabinet is known as the Council of Ministers, and in the USSR it was called the Politburo. A cabinet is a committee of senior ministers who represent the various government departments or ministries. This term is not to be confused with *cabinet*, as used in France and the EU to denote small groups of policy advisers who support individual ministers. The widespread use of cabinets reflects the political and administrative need for collective procedures within the political executive. In the first place, cabinets enable government to present a collective face to assemblies and the public. Without a cabinet, government could appear to be a personal tool wielded by a single individual. Second, cabinets are an administrative device designed to ensure the effective coordination of government policy. In short, in the absence of a cabinet, government would consist of rival bureaucratic empires each bent on self-aggrandisement, rather as occurred in the Hitler state in Nazi Germany.

The precise role and political importance of cabinets vary from system to system and state to state. In presidential systems such as the USA's the cabinet exists to serve the president by acting as a policy adviser rather than a policy-maker. Indeed, in the second half of the twentieth century, executive growth in the USA occurred largely at a non-cabinet level, in the form of the construction of the Executive Office of the President (discussed in Chapter 17). In contrast, the cabinet, in theory at least, is the apex of the executive in states that respect the principle of cabinet government, such as the UK, most Commonwealth countries, and several European ones, including Italy, Sweden and Norway.

It is nevertheless difficult in practice to find examples of collective executives that operate through a cabinet or equivalent body. In theory, a form of collective leader-

Focus on . . .

Cabinet government: advantages and disadvantages

Cabinet government is characterized by two central features. First, the cabinet constitutes the principal link between the legislative and executive branches of government; its members are drawn from and accountable to the parliament, but also serve as the political heads of the various government departments. Second, the cabinet is the senior executive organ, and policy-making responsibility is shared within it, the prime minister being 'first' in name only. This system is usually underpinned by collective responsibility – all the cabinet ministers are required to 'sing the same song' and support official government policy.

The virtues of cabinet government are the following:

- It encourages full and frank policy debate within the democracy of cabinet meetings, subjecting proposals to effective scrutiny.
- It guarantees the unity and cohesion of government, since the cabinet makes decisions collectively and collectively stands by them.

However, cabinet government has been criticized for the following reasons:

- It acts as a cloak for prime-ministerial power because it forces dissenting ministers to support agreed government policy in public.
- It means that government policy becomes incoherent and inconsistent, as decisions are based on compromises between competing ministers and departmental interests.

ship operated in the USSR, reflecting the Marxist–Leninist belief that the Communist Party, rather than a single leader, was the leading and guiding force in Soviet society. In practice, Communist Party general secretaries from Stalin onwards so dominated the Politburo and its equivalent state body, the Presidium of the Council of Ministers, that all general secretaries were able to remain in office until they died, with the exception of Khrushchev, the victim of a party coup in 1964, and Gorbachev. In Germany, and commonly throughout continental Europe, a tradition of departmental specialization discourages ministers from seeing themselves as 'team players' and so counters any tendency towards cabinet government. Even in the UK system, supposedly the archetypal example of cabinet government, it is difficult to see the cabinet as a decision-making body, and still less as a democratic forum.

Not only has the rise of prime-ministerial power subverted the collective nature of UK government, but the growth in the range and complexity of government policy has also ensured that most decisions are effectively made elsewhere, and thus reach the cabinet in a prepackaged form. This highlights the important contribution that government departments make to policy formulation, as well as the impact of cabinet committees and, indeed, subcommittees. In the UK and elsewhere, the full cabinet is merely the hub of a cabinet *system*, comprising committees of subject specialists able to examine policy proposals in greater detail and depth than is possible in the cabinet itself. This system weakens the cabinet both because it strengthens the levers of control that are available to the prime minister, who sets up and staffs committees, and because full cabinets usually lack the time and expertise to challenge proposals that emanate from committees. The complex relationships that

Concept

Core executive

The core executive is a network of institutions and people who play key roles in the overall direction and coordination of government policy. It usually encompasses the prime minister, senior policy advisers, leading cabinet members, cabinet committees, and staff in strategically important government departments. The core executive model has a number of advantages. First, it gets away from the simplistic 'prime minister versus cabinet' debate, by acknowledging that these bodies operate within an institutional context. Second, it recognizes the extent to which policy influence is exerted through the building up of alliances and coalitions of support. Third, it allows for the influence of wider factors, such as economic and diplomatic developments, as these affect the resources available to core-executive actors. Finally, the model explains fluctuations in the location of executive power, as relationships and the distribution of resources change over time.

result from this have been explained by some commentators in terms of the idea of a 'core executive' (Rhodes and Dunleavy, 1995).

On the other hand, it would be a mistake to dismiss cabinets as merely 'dignified' institutions. Many prime ministers, for example, have paid a high price for ignoring the collective element within modern government. German chancellors are generally considered to be even stronger than UK prime ministers because they can be removed only by a vote of 'constructive no confidence'. This means that the Bundestag can remove a government only by approving an alternative one, not merely by withdrawing support from the existing one (as occurs in the UK). Nevertheless, Chancellor Schmidt was forced to resign in 1982 when the small Free Democratic Party withdrew from his Social-Democrat-led coalition cabinet to join forces with the Christian Democrats, led by Helmut Kohl. Coalitions certainly add to the difficulties of cabinet management, as Italian prime ministers have regularly discovered, but a single-party cabinet can also cause problems for chief executives.

Margaret Thatcher's resignation in 1990 was, to a significant degree, a consequence of her declining support within the cabinet. Indeed, in her own version of the events of November 1990, Thatcher claimed to have been ousted by a cabinet coup through the withdrawal of ministerial support once she had failed to secure re-election as party leader on the first ballot (Thatcher, 1993). Bob Hawke's removal as Australian prime minister in 1991 reinforces the lesson that parliamentary leaders cannot long survive without cabinet support. Having resisted a leadership bid by his deputy, Paul Keating, in the early summer, Hawke tried to rebuild his authority by sacking his federal treasurer, John Kerin, in the December, only to be toppled by Keating's second challenge.

The politics of leadership

In some respects, the subject of political leadership appears to be outdated. The division of society into leaders and followers is rooted in a predemocratic culture of

Concept

Leadership

Leadership can be understood either as a pattern of behaviour or as a personal quality. As a pattern of behaviour, leadership is the influence exerted by an individual or group over a larger body to organize or direct its efforts towards the achievement of desired goals. As a personal attribute, leadership refers to the character traits that enable the leader to exert influence over others; leadership is thus effectively equated with charisma (see p. 221).

Among the virtues of leadership are the following:

• It mobilizes and inspires people who would otherwise be inert and directionless.
• It promotes unity and encourages members of a group to pull in the same direction.
• It strengthens organizations by establishing a hierarchy of responsibilities and roles.

The dangers of leadership include the following:

• It concentrates power, and can thus lead to corruption and tyranny: hence the democratic demand that leadership be checked by accountability.
• It engenders subservience and deference, thereby discouraging people from taking responsibility for their own lives.
• It narrows debate and argument, because of its emphasis on ideas flowing down from the top, rather than up from the bottom.

Friedrich Nietzsche (1844–1900)

German philosopher. Nietzsche was a professor of Greek at Basel by the age of 25. He abandoned theology for philology, and became increasingly interested in the ideas of Schopenhauer (1788–1860) and the music of Wagner (1813–83). Growing illness and insanity after 1889 brought him under the control of his sister Elizabeth, who edited and distorted his writings. Nietzsche's complex and ambitious work stressed the importance of will, especially the 'will to power', and it anticipated

modern existentialism in emphasizing that people create their own worlds and make their own values. He attacked conventional values based on God, truth and morality and sought to replace these with new values and a new ideal of the human person. His best known writings include *Thus Spake Zarathustra* (1883/84), *Beyond Good and Evil* (1886) and *On the Genealogy of Morals* (1887).

deference and respect in which leaders 'knew best' and the public needed to be led, mobilized or guided. Democratic politics may not have removed the need for leaders, but it has certainly placed powerful constraints on leadership, notably by making leaders publicly accountable and establishing an institutional mechanism through which they can be removed. In other respects, however, the politics of leadership has become increasingly significant, helping to contribute to the establishment of a separate discipline of political psychology, whose major concerns include a study of the psychological makeup and motivations of political leaders (Kressel, 1993).

This growing focus on leadership has occurred for a number of reasons. For instance, to some extent, democracy itself has enhanced the importance of personality by forcing political leaders, in effect, to 'project themselves' in the hope of gaining electoral support. This tendency has undoubtedly been strengthened by modern means of mass communication (especially television), which tend to emphasize personalities rather than policies, and provide leaders with powerful weapons with which to manipulate their public images. Furthermore, as society becomes more complex and fragmented, people may increasingly look to the personal vision of individual leaders to give coherence and meaning to the world in which they live. Ironically, then, leadership may never have been so important but also so difficult to deliver.

Theories of leadership

The question of political leadership is surrounded by controversy. To what extent is leadership compatible with freedom and democracy? Does leadership inspire and motivate, or does it subdue and repress? Are strong leaders to be admired or feared? At the heart of these disagreements lie differing views about the nature of political leadership. What does the phenomenon of leadership consist of? Where does leadership come from? Four contrasting theories of leadership can be identified:

- leadership as a *personal* gift
- leadership as a *sociological* phenomenon
- leadership as an *organizational* necessity
- leadership as a *political* skill.

Fig. 17.2 President Nelson Mandela and the Dalai Lama in Cape Town, South Africa, in 1996

The traditional view of leadership sees it as a rare but natural gift. As Aristotle (see p. 7) put it, 'men are marked out from the moment of birth to rule or be ruled'. From this perspective, leadership is strictly an individual quality, manifest in the personalities of what were traditionally thought of as 'men of destiny'. The most extreme version of this theory is found in the fascist 'leader principle' (*Führerprinzip*). This is based on the idea of a single, supreme leader (always male), who alone is capable of leading the masses to their destiny. Such an idea was in part derived from Friedrich Nietzsche's notion (see p. 373) of the *Übermensch* (the 'overman' or 'superman'), who rises above the 'herd instinct' of conventional morality and so achieves self-mastery. In a more modest form, this theory of leadership is embodied in the idea of charisma, generally understood to mean the power of personality. The classic examples of charismatic leaders are usually seen as forceful personalities (such as Hitler, Castro, Nasser and Thatcher), although the more modest, but no less effective, 'fireside chats' of F. D. Roosevelt and the practised televisual skills of almost all modern leaders also exemplify charismatic qualities. However, unfortunately, leaders who exhibit genuine moral authority, such as Nelson Mandela and the Dalai Lama (see Figure 17.2), are rare.

Modern political psychology adopts a similar view of leadership, in that it analyses it in terms of human personality. One of the earliest attempts to do this was the collaboration in the late 1920s between Sigmund Freud (1856–1939) and William C. Bullitt on a controversial psychological study of President Woodrow Wilson (Freud and Bullitt, 1967). Harold Lasswell's ground-breaking *Psychopathology and Politics* (1930) suggested that leaders are motivated largely by private, almost pathological, conflicts, which are then rationalized in terms of actions taken in the public interest. A widely discussed modern analysis of political leadership has been advanced by James Barber (1988). Focusing on what he called 'presidential character', Barber categorized US presidents according to two key variables: first, whether they were 'active' or 'passive' in terms of the energy they put into their jobs, and, second, whether they were 'positive' or 'negative' in terms of how they felt about political office. He therefore identified four character types:

- active-positive
- active-negative
- passive-positive
- passive-negative.

Examples of active-positive presidents would include Kennedy, George Bush Sr and Clinton. Active-negative presidents would include Harding and Reagan. Nixon is an example of a passive-positive president, while Coolidge and Eisenhower were passive-negative. Nevertheless, the limitations of Barber's analysis are demonstrated by the way that George W. Bush was transformed from a passive-positive president into a much more assertive and active one by the terrorist attacks on the USA on 11 September, 2001.

An alternative view of leadership sees it as a sociological, rather than psychological, phenomenon. From this perspective, in other words, leaders are 'created' by particular sociohistorical forces. They do not so much impose their will on the world as act as a vehicle through which historical forces are exerted. This is certainly the approach adopted by Marxists, who believe that historical development is structured largely by economic factors, reflected in a process of class struggle. The personalities of individual leaders are thus less important than the broader class interests they articulate. Marx nevertheless acknowledged that **Bonapartism** was an exception. This was a phenomenon based on Louis Bonaparte's *coup d'état* in France in 1851, through which a personal dictatorship was established in conditions in which the bourgeoisie had lost power, but the proletariat was not sufficiently developed to seize it. Even in this case, however, Marx insisted that the Bonapartist dictatorship reflected the interests of the numerically strongest class in France, the smallholding peasantry. Similarly, in analysing Stalinism in the USSR, Trotsky (see p. 385) emphasized the degree to which Stalin's power was rooted in the dominance of the state bureaucracy (Trotsky, 1937). Sociological factors have also provided the basis for the very different idea that political leadership is largely a product of collective behaviour. In his seminal *The Crowd* ([1895] 1960), Gustav Le Bon analysed the dynamics of crowd psychology, arguing that leaders are impelled by the collective behaviour of the masses, not the other way round.

The third theory of leadership sees it in largely technical terms as a rational or bureaucratic device. In this view, leadership is essentially an organizational necessity that arises from the need for coherence, unity and direction within any complex institution. Leadership therefore goes hand in hand with bureaucracy (see p. 383). Modern large-scale organizations require specialization and a division of labour,

Concept

Cult of personality

A cult of personality (or cult of leadership) is a propaganda device through which a political leader is portrayed as a heroic or God-like figure. By treating the leader as the source of all political wisdom and an unfailing judge of the national interest, the cult implies that any form of criticism or opposition amounts to treachery or lunacy. Cults of personality have typically been developed in totalitarian regimes (first by Stalin) through the exploitation of the possibilities of modern means of mass communication, and the use of state repression to cultivate a form of ritualized idolatrization. However, the point at which routine propaganda (found in all systems) becomes a fully fledged 'cult' may be unclear in practice.

Bonapartism: A style of government that fuses personal leadership with conservative nationalism; for Marxists, it reflects the relative autonomy of the state.

which, in turn, give rise to a hierarchy of offices and responsibilities. This bureaucratic leadership conforms to what Weber (see p. 220) called legal-rational authority, in that it is essentially impersonal and based on formal, usually written, rules. The rise of constitutional government has undoubtedly invested political leadership with a strongly bureaucratic character by ensuring that power is vested in a political office rather than the individual office holder. This nevertheless conflicts with democratic pressures that force political leaders to cultivate charisma and emphasize personal qualities in order to win and retain power.

The final theory of leadership portrays it very much as an artefact: that is, as a political skill that can be learned and practised. Political leadership in this sense is akin to the art of manipulation, a perhaps inevitable feature of democratic politics in an age of mass communications. This can be seen most graphically in the cults of personality that have been constructed to support the dictatorial leaderships of figures such as Mao Zedong, Colonel Gaddafi and Saddam Hussein. Indeed, many of the classic examples of charismatic leadership can in practice be seen as forms of manufactured leadership. Stalin, for example, bolstered his own popularity by building up an elaborate cult of Lenin in the 1920s; he erected statues, renamed streets and towns, and placed Lenin's embalmed body in a mausoleum in Red Square. During the 1930s, having carefully linked himself to Lenin's heritage, Stalin transferred this cult to himself.

Similarly, Hitler's performances at the Nuremburg rallies were carefully stage-managed by Albert Speer. His every word and gesture were carefully rehearsed and choreographed; the whole event was designed to build up emotional tension that would be released by Hitler's appearance. Modern democratic politicians have no less strong a need to project themselves and their personal vision, though the skills appropriate to the television age are modest and refined compared with those suitable for mass rallies and public demonstrations. Leadership nevertheless remains an artefact; its emphasis has simply shifted towards televisual skills, the use of 'sound bites', and a reliance upon media advisers or 'spin doctors'.

Styles of leadership

A style of leadership refers to the strategies and behavioural patterns through which a leader seeks to achieve his or her goals. Quite simply, leaders are not all alike: leadership can be exercised in a number of different ways. The factors that shape the adoption of a particular leadership strategy or style are, of course, numerous. Amongst the most obvious are the personality and goals of the leader, the institutional framework within which he or she operates, the political mechanisms by which power is won and retained, the means of mass communication available, and the nature of the broader political culture. Three distinctive styles of leadership have been identified (Burns, 1978):

- *laissez-faire* leadership
- transactional leadership
- transformational leadership.

The chief feature of *laissez-faire* leadership is the reluctance of the leader to interfere in matters outside his or her personal responsibility. Such leaders have a 'hands off' approach to cabinet and departmental management. An example of such leadership could be found in the Reagan White House, and the relatively slight interest that Reagan took in the day-to-day workings of his administration. George W. Bush, similarly, was strongly inclined to delegate responsibilities to key advisers, but the so-called 'war on terrorism', launched in 2001, has forced him to adopt a more forthright leadership style. A *laissez-faire* style is not irreconcilable with ideological leadership, but it certainly requires that ideological goals constitute only a broadly stated strategic vision. The strengths of this approach to leadership are that, because subordinates are given greater responsibility, it can foster harmony and teamwork, and it can allow leaders to concentrate on political and electoral matters by relieving them of their managerial burdens. On the other hand, it can also lead to the weak coordination of government policy, with ministers and officials being allowed too much scope to pursue their own interests and initiatives. The Iran–Contra affair, for example, demonstrated how little President Reagan knew about the activities of the Central Intelligence Agency officers and White House officials for whom he was supposedly responsible.

In contrast, transactional leadership is a more 'hands-on' style of leadership. Transactional leaders adopt a positive role in relation to policy-making and government management, but are motivated by essentially pragmatic goals and considerations. Prominent amongst these are likely to be the maintenance of party unity and government cohesion, and the strengthening of public support and electoral credibility. Such leaders act as brokers who are concerned to uphold the collegiate face of government by negotiating compromises and balancing rival individuals, factions and interests against one another. In the USA, Lyndon Johnson and George Bush Sr could be seen as transactional leaders, as could Harold Wilson and John Major in the UK. This is above all a managerial, even technocratic, style of leadership, its advantage being that it is fiercely practical and allows scope for tactical flexibility. Its central drawback, however, is that such leaders may be seen as opportunistic wheeler-dealers who are devoid of firm principles or deep convictions. This was illustrated by George Bush's damaging admission during the 1992 US presidential election that he did not understand what he called 'the vision thing'.

In the third style of leadership, transformational leadership, the leader is not so much a coordinator or manager as an inspirer or visionary. Not only are such leaders motivated by strong ideological convictions, but they also have the personal resolution and political will to put them into practice. Instead of seeking compromise and consensus, transformational leaders attempt to mobilize support from within government, their parties and the general public for the realization of their personal vision. Howard Gardner (1996) suggested that a leader is 'an individual who creates a story'. The effectiveness of such a leader hinges on the degree to which the leader in question 'embodies' the story, and the extent to which the story resonates with the broader public.

General de Gaulle, for instance, recast the nature of political leadership in France as much by presenting himself as a 'father figure' and 'national leader' as by establishing a presidential system in the form of the Fifth Republic. A very similar style was adopted in the UK by Margaret Thatcher, whose avowed aim when coming into office was to run a 'conviction government'. The continued use of terms such as Gaullism and Thatcherism bears witness to the enduring impact of these leaders' ideological visions. Tony Blair in the UK also adopted a transformational stance, first in recasting the Labour Party as 'new' Labour, then in ensuring that his government pursued 'third way' rather than old-style socialist priorities, and finally in

Concept

Populism

Populism (from the Latin *populus*, meaning 'the people') has been used to describe both distinctive political movements and a particular tradition of political thought. Movements or parties described as populist have been characterized by their claim to support the common people in the face of 'corrupt' economic or political elites. As a political tradition, populism reflects the belief that the instincts and wishes of the people provide the principal legitimate guide to political action. Populist politicians therefore make a direct appeal to the people and claim to give expression to their deepest hopes and fears, all intermediary institutions being distrusted. Although populism may be linked with any cause or ideology, it is often seen to be implicitly authoritarian, 'populist' democracy being the enemy of 'pluralist' democracy (see p. 83).

cultivating a reputation as a world statesman. Not uncommonly, transformational leadership is linked to populism, reflecting the desire of such leaders to demonstrate that they are articulating the concerns and interests of 'the people'. Although the strength of transformational leadership is that it provides a basis for pushing through radical programmes of social, economic or political reform, it may also encourage a drift towards authoritarianism and lead to ideological rigidity. It is thus possible to see Thatcher herself as one of the casualties of Thatcherism, in that in 1990 she paid the price for her domineering leadership style and her unwillingness to change policy priorities even when these had become electorally unpopular.

Regardless of the leadership style they adopt, there are reasons to believe that modern political leaders face greater challenges than their predecessors did. This is important, because attitudes towards leaders, and the perceived effectiveness of leadership, do much to influence people's general view of the political process. The first difficulty that leaders face is that modern societies have perhaps become so complex and enmeshed with global influences that politicians find it almost impossible to get things done. Leaders are therefore doomed to disappoint, to fail to live up to expectations. Second, leaders suffer because old ideological and moral certainties are breaking down, and this makes it more difficult to construct compelling narratives that have wide popular resonance.

Third, modern societies are becoming more diverse and fragmented. Political leaders are therefore finding it increasingly difficult to construct a political appeal based on a common culture and a set of shared values. Fourth and finally, a cultural gap has perhaps developed between the political and the nonpolitical worlds. Political leaders are increasingly career politicians whose lifestyles, sensibilities and even language are remote from the concerns of private citizens. Far from being seen as providing inspiration and articulating popular hopes and aspirations, modern leaders tend to be viewed as self-serving and out of touch. To the extent that this is true, people become alienated from conventional politics, and perhaps look elsewhere for a source of political leadership.

■ Summary

◆ The executive branch of government is responsible for the execution or implementation of policy. The political executive comprises a core of senior figures and is roughly equivalent to 'the government of the day' or 'the administration'. The bureaucratic executive consists of public officials or civil servants. However, the political/bureaucratic distinction is often blurred by the complexities of the policy making process.

◆ Political executives act as the 'commanding heights' of the state apparatus and carry out a number of leadership roles. These include representing the state on ceremonial occasions, offering policy-making leadership in relation to strategic priorities, mobilizing popular support for the government or administration, overseeing the bureaucratic machine, and taking the initiative in the event of domestic or international crises.

◆ Presidential executives concentrate executive power in the hands of a president who combines the roles of head of state and head of government, but confronts an assembly that enjoys constitutional and political independence. Prime ministers in parliamentary systems operate through two key sets of relationships: the first is with their cabinets, ministers and departments, and the second is with their parties and the assembly from which their power stems.

◆ The power of chief executives has been enhanced by the tendency of the media and electoral politics to focus on personality and image, by the opportunities to display statesmanship provided by international affairs and summitry, and by the need for political and ideological leadership within an increasingly large and complex executive branch. Their power is nevertheless checked by the importance of government and party unity, the need to maintain support in the assembly, and the difficulty of controlling the sprawling bureaucratic machine.

◆ Political leadership has been understood in various ways. It has been interpreted as a personal gift based on individual qualities such as charisma, as a sociological phenomenon in which leaders express particular sociohistorical forces, as an organizational necessity rooted in the need for coherence and unity of direction, and as a political skill that can be learned by leaders intent on manipulating their colleagues and the masses.

◆ Leaders have adopted very different strategies to achieve their goals. *Laissez-faire* leadership attempts to foster harmony and teamwork by broadening the responsibilities of subordinates. Transactional leadership allows leaders to act as brokers and balance rival factions and interests against each other. Transformational leadership places a heavy emphasis on the mobilization of support through the leader's capacity to inspire and to advance a personal vision.

Questions for discussion

▶ In what circumstances may heads of state play a significant political role?

▶ Is the only power that a chief executive possesses the power to persuade?

▶ Are presidents or prime ministers more powerful?

▶ Is collective cabinet government a principle worth preserving?

▶ Should strong leaders be admired or feared?

▶ Are cults of personality a feature of all political systems, not just dictatorial ones?

▶ Do we get the political leaders we deserve?

Further reading

Gardner, H., *Leading Minds* (London: HarperCollins, 1996). A fascinating exploration of the nature of leadership and the skills and strategies deployed by leaders.

Poguntke, T. and P. Webb., *The Presidentialization of Politics: A Comparative Study of Modern Democracies* (Oxford: Oxford University Press). A major examination of the 'presidential logic of governance', which also considers cross-national differences.

Rhodes, R. and P. Dunleavey (eds), *Prime Minister, Cabinet and Core Executives* (Basingstoke:

Palgrave Macmillan, 1995). A collection of articles that analyse the location of executive power in the UK.

Rose, R., *The Postmodern Presidency: The White House Meets the World*, 2nd edn (New York: Chartham House, 1991). A stimulating analysis that examines the 'no win' theory of presidential power.

Wright, V., B. Guy Peters, and R. Rhodes (eds), *Administering the Summit: Administration of the Core Executive in Developing Countries* (Basingstoke: Palgrave Macmillan, 2000). A useful comparative introduction to the role of prime ministers and the configurations of core executives.

Bureaucracies

CHAPTER 18

> 'Bureaucracy is a giant mechanism operated by pygmies.'
>
> HONORÉ DE BALZAC, *Epigrams*

To many, the term bureaucracy suggests inefficiency and pointless and time-consuming formalities: in short, 'red tape'. In the field of politics, bureaucracy refers to the administrative machinery of the state: that is, the massed ranks of civil servants and public officials who are charged with the execution of government business. Others follow Max Weber in seeing bureaucracy as a distinctive form of organization found not just in government but in all spheres of modern society. What cannot be doubted, however, is that, as government has grown and the breadth of its responsibilities has expanded, bureaucracy has come to play an increasingly important role in political life. No longer can civil servants be dismissed as mere administrators or policy implementors; instead, they are key figures in the policy process, and even sometimes *run* their countries. A reality of 'rule by the officials' may lie behind the facade of representation and democratic accountability. The organization and control of bureaucratic power is therefore one of the most pressing problems in modern politics, and one that no political system has found easy to solve.

The central issues examined in this chapter are as follows:

Key issues

▶ What is bureaucracy?

▶ What are the major theories of bureaucracy?

▶ What are the functions of bureaucracies?

▶ How are bureaucracies organized? How should they be organized?

▶ Why are bureaucrats so powerful, and why has bureaucratic power expanded?

▶ How, and how successfully, are bureaucracies controlled?

Theories of bureaucracy

The question of bureaucracy engenders deep political passions. In the modern period these have invariably been negative. Liberals criticize bureaucracy for its lack of openness and accountability. Socialists, particularly Marxists, condemn it as an instrument of class subordination; and the New Right, for its part, portrays bureaucrats as self-serving and inherently inefficient. Underlying these contrasting views is deeper disagreement about the very nature of bureaucracy. Quite simply, the term bureaucracy has been used in so many different ways that the attempt to develop an overall definition may have to be abandoned altogether. Albrow (1970:84–105) identified no fewer than seven modern concepts of bureaucracy:

- bureaucracy as rational organization
- bureaucracy as organizational inefficiency
- bureaucracy as rule by officials
- bureaucracy as public administration
- bureaucracy as administration by officials
- bureaucracy as organization
- bureaucracy as modern society.

To some extent, these contrasting concepts and usages reflect the fact that bureaucracy has been viewed differently by different academic disciplines. Students of government, for example, traditionally understood bureaucracy in a literal sense to mean 'rule by the bureau': that is, rule by appointed officials. In *Considerations on Representative Government* ([1861] 1951), J. S. Mill (see p. 48) therefore contrasted bureaucracy with representative forms of government – in other words, rule by elected and accountable politicians. In the field of sociology, bureaucracy has typically been understood as a particular type of organization, as a system of administration rather than a system of government. Bureaucracy in this sense can be found not only in democratic and authoritarian states but also in business corporations, trade unions, political parties and so on. Economists, on the other hand, sometimes view bureaucracies as specifically 'public' organizations. They are thus characterized by the fact that being funded through the tax system they are neither disciplined by the profit motive nor responsive to market pressures. In order to make sense of these various usages, three contrasting theories of bureaucracy will be examined:

- bureaucracy as a rational-administrative machine
- bureaucracy as a conservative power bloc
- bureaucracy as a source of government oversupply.

Rational-administrative model

The academic study of bureaucracy has been dominated by the work of Max Weber (see p. 220). For Weber, bureaucracy was an 'ideal type' (see p. 18) of rule based on a system of rational rules, as opposed to either tradition or charisma. He identified a set of principles that supposedly characterize bureaucratic organization. The most important of these are the following:

- Jurisdictional areas are fixed and official, and ordered by laws or rules.

- There is a firmly ordered hierarchy, which ensures that lower offices are supervised by specified higher ones within a chain of command.

- Business is managed on the basis of written documents and a filing system.

- The authority of officials is impersonal and stems entirely from the post they hold, not from personal status.

- Bureaucratic rules are strict enough to minimize the scope of personal discretion.

- Appointment and advancement within a bureaucracy are based on professional criteria, such as training, expertise and administrative competence.

The central feature of bureaucracy from the Weberian perspective is its rationality, because bureaucratization reflects the advance of a reliable, predictable and, above all, efficient means of social organization. For Weber, bureaucracy was nothing less than the characteristic form of organization found in modern society, and, in his view, its expansion was irreversible. Not only was this a result of the technical superiority of bureaucracy over other forms of administration, but it was also a consequence of significant economic, political and cultural developments. The development of bureaucratization was closely linked to the emergence of capitalist economies – in particular, to the greater pressure for economic efficiency and the emergence of larger-scale business units. The development of the modern state, and the extension of its responsibilities into the social and economic spheres, also led to the growth of powerful government bureaucracies.

In Weber's view, the growth of bureaucratization was further stimulated by the pressures of democratization, which weakened ideas such as tradition (see p. 221), privilege and duty, and replaced them with a belief in open competition and meritocracy. He believed that the process of 'rationalization' would ensure that all industrial societies, whether nominally capitalist or communist, would increasingly resemble each other as they adopted bureaucratic forms of administration. This version of what is called the **convergence thesis** was subsequently developed by James Burnham (1905–87) in *The Managerial Revolution* (1941). This seminal text of **managerialism** suggested that, regardless of their ideological differences, all industrial societies are governed by a class of managers, technocrats and state officials whose power is vested in their technical and administrative skills.

Weber was nevertheless aware that bureaucracy was a mixed blessing. In the first place, organizational efficiency would be purchased at the expense of democratic participation. Bureaucratization would strengthen hierarchical tendencies, albeit ones based on merit, meaning that command would be exercised from above by senior officials rather than from below by the masses. This would destroy the socialist dream of a dictatorship of the proletariat, which, Weber (accurately, as it turned out) predicted, would develop into a 'dictatorship of the official'. In this respect, Weber drew conclusions similar to those of his friend Robert Michels (1878–1936), who developed the iron law of oligarchy (see p. 280) on the basis of his study of political parties.

However, Weber was less pessimistic than Michels about the prospects for liberal democracy. Although he recognized the tendency of bureaucrats to seek the perpetuation of bureaucracy and to exceed its administrative function, he believed that this could at least be resisted through the use of liberal devices such as electoral competition and institutional fragmentation. The other potential danger that Weber highlighted was that the domination of the bureaucratic ideal could bring about

---

Concept

Bureaucracy

Bureaucracy (literally 'rule by officials') is, in everyday language, a pejorative term meaning pointless administrative routine, or 'red tape'. In the social sciences the concept of bureaucracy is used in a more specific and neutral sense, but refers to phenomena as different as rule by nonelected officials, the administrative machinery of government, and a rational mode of organization. Despite disagreement about its location and character, it is generally accepted that abstract organization and rule-governed professional administration are features of bureaucracy. There are fewer difficulties with the use of the term bureaucracy in the field of comparative government. Here it refers to the administrative machinery of the state, bureaucrats being nonelected state officials or civil servants.

Convergence thesis: The theory that politico-economic factors dictate that capitalist and socialist states will become increasingly similar.

Managerialism: The theory that in modern society class divisions have been replaced by ones based on managerial position and bureaucratic power; technocracy (rule by experts or specialists).

a 'pigeon-holing of the spirit' as the social environment became increasingly depersonalized and mechanical. Reason and bureaucracy could therefore become an 'iron cage' confining human passions and individual freedom.

Power-bloc model

The view of bureaucracy as a power bloc stems largely from socialist analysis, and particularly from Marxism. Although Marx (see p. 55) developed no systematic theory of bureaucracy in the manner of Weber, the outlines of a theory are discernible in his writings. Rather than seeing bureaucracy as a consequence of the emergence of a complex industrial society, Marx linked it to the specific requirements of capitalism. He was thus concerned less with bureaucratization as a broader social phenomenon, and more with the class role played by the state bureaucracy. In particular, he saw the bureaucracy as a mechanism through which bourgeois interests are upheld and the capitalist system defended.

This analysis of class biases running through the state bureaucracy has been extended by neo-Marxists such as Ralph Miliband (1969). Particular attention has been paid to the capacity of senior civil servants to act as a conservative veto group that dilutes, even blocks, the radical initiatives of socialist ministers and socialist governments. As Miliband put it, top civil servants 'are conservative in the sense that they are, within their allotted sphere, the conscious or unconscious allies of existing economic and social elites' (p. 84). This happens for a number of reasons. Most obviously, despite the formal requirements of political neutrality (see p. 329), top civil servants share the same educational and social background as industrialists and business managers, and are therefore likely to share their ideas, prejudices and general outlook. The possibility that rising civil servants may harbour radical or socialist sympathies is also countered by recruitment and promotion procedures designed to ensure their ideological 'soundness'.

Miliband believed that the most important factor reinforcing the conservative outlook of higher civil servants is their ever-increasing closeness to the world of corporate capitalism. This has been a consequence of growing state intervention in economic life, ensuring an ongoing relationship between business groups and civil servants, who invariably come to define the 'national interest' in terms of the long-term interests of private capitalism. In turn, this relationship is reinforced by the interchange of personnel between government and business (often seen as a 'revolving door'), through which the state bureaucracy recruits from the private sector, and civil servants are offered lucrative employment opportunities when they retire. The implication of this analysis is that, if senior bureaucrats are wedded to the interests of capitalism, a major obstacle stands in the way of any attempt to achieve socialism through constitutional means.

One of the flaws of the Marxist theory of bureaucracy is that it pays little attention to the problem of bureaucratization in socialist systems. For Marx and Engels, this problem was effectively discounted by the assumption that the bureaucracy, with the state, would 'wither away' as a classless, communist society came into existence. This left Marxism open to criticism by social scientists such as Weber and Michels, who argued that bureaucracy is a broader social phenomenon, and one that the socialist emphasis on common ownership and planning could only strengthen. The experience of twentieth-century communism made it impossible for Marxist thinkers to continue ignoring this problem.

Leon Trotsky (1879–1940)

Russian Marxist political thinker and revolutionary. An early critic of Lenin's theory of the party and leader of the 1905 St Petersburg Soviet, Trotsky joined the Bolsheviks in 1917, becoming Commissar for Foreign Affairs and later Commissar for War. Isolated and out-manoeuvred after Lenin's death in 1924, he was banished from the USSR in 1929, and assassinated in Mexico in 1940 on the instructions of Stalin. Trotsky's theoretical contribution to Marxism consists of his theory of 'permanent revolution', his consistent support for internationalism, and his analysis of Stalinism as a form of 'bureaucratic degeneration'. His major writings include *Results and Prospects* (1906), *History of the Russian Revolution* (1931) and *The Revolution Betrayed* (1937).

The most influential Marxist analysis of postcapitalist bureaucracy was developed by Leon Trotsky. In *The Revolution Betrayed* (1937) Trotsky highlighted the problem of 'bureaucratic degeneration'. In his view, a combination of Russian backwardness and the proletariat's lack of political sophistication had created conditions in which the state bureaucracy could expand and block further advances towards socialism. The Stalinist dictatorship was thus merely the political expression of these dominant bureaucratic interests, entirely cut off from those of the masses. While Trotsky saw the bureaucracy as a social stratum that could be removed by a political revolution, the Yugoslav dissident (and former colleague of Marshal Tito) Milovan Djilas (1911–95) portrayed it as a 'new class'. For Djilas (1957) the power of the bureaucracy in orthodox communist regimes stemmed from its control of productive wealth, and this meant that communist social systems increasingly resembled a form of state capitalism.

Bureaucratic oversupply model

The idea that critics of bureaucracy come exclusively from the left was overturned by the emergence of rational choice and public choice (see p. 300) theories. These had a considerable impact on the New Right, and in particular helped to shape its views about the nature of the state and the emergence of 'big' government. Central to this model of bureaucracy is a concern with the interests and motivations of bureaucrats themselves. Rational choice theory is based on the same assumptions about human nature as those in neoclassical economics: that is, that individuals are rationally self-seeking creatures or utility maximizers. Public choice theory, particularly prominent in the USA and associated with the Virginia school of political analysis, applies this economic model of decision-making to the public sector.

In *Bureaucracy and Representative Government* (1971) William Niskanen argued that senior bureaucrats, regardless of their image as public servants, are primarily motivated by career self-interest and thus seek an expansion of the agency in which they work and an increase in its budget. This is because bureaucratic growth guarantees job security, expands promotion prospects, improves salaries, and brings top officials greater power, patronage and prestige. Bureaucracies thus contain a powerful inner dynamic, leading to the growth of government itself and the expansion of public responsibilities. For the New Right, the ability of appointed officials to dictate policy priorities to elected politicians goes a long way towards explaining how state growth has occurred under governments of very different ideological complexions. Similarly, the image of bureaucrats as nature's social democrats has important implications for New Right governments intent on rolling back the frontiers of the state. They believe that, quite simply, unless bureaucratic power can be checked or circumvented, any attempt to pursue free-market policies is doomed to failure.

This New Right critique also focuses attention on the non-market character of state bureaucracies, and draws an unflattering comparison between private-sector and public-sector bodies. In this view, private-sector bodies such as business corporations are structured by a combination of internal and external factors. The principal internal influence on a business is the quest for profit maximization, which impels the firm towards greater efficiency through the exertion of a constant downward pressure on costs. Externally, businesses operate in a competitive market environment, which forces them to respond to consumer pressures through product innovation and price adjustments.

In contrast, bureaucracies are not disciplined by the profit motive. If costs exceed revenue, the taxpayer is always there to pick up the bill. Similarly, state bureaucracies are usually monopolies, and are therefore in no way forced to respond to market pressures. The result is that bureaucracies (in common with all public-sector bodies) are inherently wasteful and inefficient. Moreover, the service they provide is invariably of poor quality and does not meet consumer needs or wishes. This 'private, good; public, bad' philosophy of the New Right dictates not only that state bureaucracies should be scaled down, but also that, when this is not possible, private-sector management techniques should be introduced.

Critics of public choice theory usually argue that it is flawed because it abstracts the individual from his or her social environment. A conservative value bias, so the argument goes, is built into the theory by the assumption that human beings are always rationally self-interested. Others, however, have used a public choice approach but reached very different conclusions. Dunleavy (1991), for example, argued that, if individual bureaucrats are rational actors, they are more likely to favour bureau-shaping strategies than, as conventional public-choice theory suggests, budget-maximizing ones.

Budget-maximizing priorities certainly go hand in hand with state growth, especially in the absence of market disciplines. However, it is difficult to undertake collective action to achieve this end, and senior officials tend to be more interested in work-related benefits than in narrowly financial benefits. Dunleavy suggested that bureaucrats are likely to assign their highest priority to providing themselves with congenial work and an amenable and attractive working environment. This is both because senior civil servants are especially concerned with the interest and importance of their work tasks, and because public-sector employment provides them with relatively modest opportunities to improve their salaries, job security and promotion prospects. Clearly, top officials concerned about bureau shaping would operate in a very different way from the empire builders of New Right demonology.

Role of bureaucracies

Functions of bureaucracies

On the face of it, bureaucracies fulfil a single, but vital, function. Their primary concern is with the execution and enforcement of the laws made by the legislature and the policies decided by the political executive. Indeed, while other functions of government (such as representation, policy-making and interest articulation) are carried out by a variety of institutions, policy implementation is solely the responsibility of civil servants, albeit working under their political masters. Moreover, the Weberian model of bureaucracies as rational and objective machines appears to divorce the administrative world from the political world. In this view, bureaucrats are seen simply as cogs in a machine, as reliable and efficient administrators operating within a fixed hierarchy and according to clearly defined rules. The reality is very different. Despite their formal subordination and impartiality, bureaucrats exert considerable influence on the policy process, and thus fulfil a number of key functions in any political system. The most important of these functions are the following:

- carrying out administration
- offering policy advice
- articulating and aggregating interests
- maintaining political stability.

Administration

The core function of the bureaucracy is to implement or execute law and policy: it is thus charged with administering government business. This is why the bureaucracy is sometimes referred to as 'the administration', while the political executive is termed 'the government'. This distinction implies that a clear line can be drawn between the policy-making role of politicians and the policy-implementing role of bureaucrats. Certainly, the vast majority of the world's civil servants are engaged almost exclusively in administrative responsibilities that range from the implementation of welfare and social-security programmes to the regulation of the economy, the granting of licences, and the provision of information and advice to citizens at home and abroad. The sizes of bureaucracies are therefore closely linked to the broader responsibilities of government. Civil service employment in the UK expanded in proportion to the role of government throughout the twentieth century. It reached a peak of 735 000 in the 1970s, but then contracted to 499 000 by 1996 owing to the pursuit of neoliberal policies from the 1980s onwards. The federal bureaucracy in the USA expanded significantly as a result of the New Deal and has now grown to over 2.5 million strong; and the USSR's central planning system eventually required 20 million state officials to administer it.

Nevertheless, the image of bureaucrats as mere functionaries who apply rules and carry out orders issued by others can be misleading. In the first place, since much administrative detail is of necessity left to officials, civil servants may be allowed significant discretion in deciding precisely how to implement policy. Second, the degree of political control exercised over the bureaucracy varies greatly from state to state. Whereas state officials in China are subject to strict and continuous party supervision, in France and Japan their high status and reputation for expertise guarantee them a considerable degree of autonomy. Third, in their capacity as policy advisers, senior civil servants at least have the ability to shape the policies that they are later required to administer.

Policy advice

The political significance of the bureaucracy stems largely from its role as the chief source of the policy information and advice available to government. This policy

Concept

Administration

The term administration is used in a number of ways. It can be used to refer collectively to the senior personnel in the executive branch, as in the 'Clinton administration'. More generally, it means the task of coordinating and executing policy. The term administration implies assisting or serving others (its root being 'to minister unto'). In this sense, all civil servants are involved in administration. More narrowly, administration means dealing with information and maintaining control. In this sense, it refers to the managerial duties of senior officials, as opposed to the day-to-day job of execution. Public administration refers either to the mechanisms and institutions through which public policy is put into effect, or to the academic discipline that studies these mechanisms.

role helps to distinguish top-level civil servants, who have daily contact with politicians and are expected to act as policy advisers, from middle-ranking and junior-ranking civil servants, who deal with more routine administrative matters. Debate about the political significance of bureaucracies therefore tends to concentrate on this elite group of senior officials. In theory, a strict distinction can be drawn between the policy responsibilities of bureaucrats and those of politicians. Policy (see p. 426) is supposedly *made* by politicians; bureaucrats simply offer *advice*. The policy role of civil servants therefore boils down to two functions: outlining the policy options available to ministers, and reviewing policy proposals in terms of their likely impact and consequences. The policy influence of senior officials is further restricted by the fact that they are either required to be politically neutral, as in the UK, Japan and Australia, or are subject to a system of political appointment, as in the USA.

However, there are reasons to believe that the policy role of civil servants is politically more significant than is suggested above. For instance, there is no clear distinction between making policy and offering policy advice. Quite simply, decisions are made on the basis of the information available, and this means that the content of decisions is invariably structured by the advice offered. Moreover, as the principal source of the advice available to politicians, bureaucrats effectively control the flow of information: politicians know what civil servants tell them. Information can thus be concealed or at least 'shaped' to reflect the preferences of the civil service. The principal source of bureaucratic power is nevertheless the expertise and specialist knowledge that accumulates within the bureaucracy. As the responsibilities of government expand and policy becomes more complex, 'amateur' politicians almost inevitably come to depend on their 'professional' bureaucratic advisers.

Articulating interests

Although by no means one of their formal functions, bureaucracies often help to articulate and sometimes aggregate interests. Bureaucracies are brought into contact with interest groups through their task of policy implementation and their involvement in policy formulation and advice. This has increased as a result of corporatist (see p. 299) tendencies that have blurred the divisions between organized interests and government agencies. Groups such as doctors, teachers, farmers and business corporations thus become 'client groups', serviced by their respective agencies, and also serve as an invaluable source of information and advice. This **clientelism** may benefit the political system insofar as it helps to maintain consensus. By virtue of having access to policy formulation, it is more likely that organized interests will cooperate with government policy. On the other hand, clientelism may also interfere with the public responsibilities and duties of civil servants. This, for instance, occurs when US regulatory agencies end up being controlled by the industries they supposedly regulate. When group interests coincide with those of the bureaucracy, a policy nexus may develop that democratic politicians find impossible to break down.

Political stability

The final function of bureaucracies is to provide a focus of stability and continuity within political systems. This is sometimes seen as particularly important in developing states, where the existence of a body of trained career officials may provide the only guarantee that government is conducted in an orderly and reliable fashion. This stability depends very largely on the status of bureaucrats as permanent and professional public servants: while ministers and governments come and go, the

Clientelism: A relationship through which government agencies come to serve the interests of the client groups they are responsible for regulating or supervising.

bureaucracy is always there. The Northcote–Trevelyan reforms of 1870 that created the modern UK civil service were based on the principles of impartial selection, political neutrality, permanence and anonymity. Even in the USA, where senior officials are appointed politically through a so-called 'spoils system', the mass of federal bureaucrats are career civil servants.

However, continuity can also have its disadvantages. In the absence of effective public scrutiny and accountability, it can undoubtedly lead to corruption, a problem that is found in many developing states, where it is compounded by widespread poverty and disadvantage. In other cases, permanence may breed in civil servants either a tendency towards arrogance and insularity, or a bias in favour of conservatism. Career civil servants can come to believe that they are more capable of defining the common good or general will than are elected politicians. They may therefore feel justified in resisting radical or reformist political tendencies, seeing themselves as custodians of the state's interest.

Organization of bureaucracies

One of the limitations of Weber's theory of bureaucracy is that it suggests that the drive for efficiency and rationality will lead to the adoption of essentially similar bureaucratic structures the world over. Weber's 'ideal type' thus ignores the various ways in which bureaucracies can be organized, as well as differences that arise from the political, social and cultural contexts in which bureaucracies operate. The organization of bureaucracies is important for two reasons. It influences the administrative efficiency of government, and affects the degree to which public accountability and political control can be achieved. The issue of organization has, however, assumed a deeper significance as pressure has built up, especially from the 1980s onwards, to reduce public spending. This partly reflects the spread of New Right ideas but is also one of the consequences of economic globalization. Many states have therefore looked to rationalize their administrative machinery, a process that has sometimes been portrayed as 'reinventing government'. This process nevertheless has major political, and even constitutional, implications.

All state bureaucracies are in some way organized on the basis of purpose or function. This is achieved through the construction of departments, ministries and agencies charged with responsibility for particular policy areas: education, housing, defence, drug control, taxation and so forth. Of course, the number of such departments and agencies varies over time and from state to state, as do the ways in which functional responsibilities are divided or combined. For example, after the 11 September, 2001 attacks on the USA, President Bush established the White House Office of Homeland Security. This is a super-department that combines the departments of immigration, customs and domestic security, and is designed to ensure a fully coordinated response to the threat of terrorism.

The most significant feature of these functionally defined bureaucracies is the degree of centralization or decentralization within them. The systems found in the remaining communist regimes, such as China, which are subject to strict party control and supervision at every level, are amongst the most centralized bureaucratic systems in the world. Nevertheless, the sizes and complexity of communist bureaucracies have also provided considerable scope for bureau and departmental independence. Despite the formal 'leadership' of the CPSU, the Soviet bureaucracy, for example, functioned as a labyrinthine mechanism for interest articulation and aggregation,

---

Concept

Corruption

Corruption, in a general sense, is a condition of depravity or moral defilement. Power is thus said to corrupt in that it breeds an appetite for domination and an insensitivity to the sufferings of others. More specifically, corruption is a quasi-legal term meaning a failure to carry out 'proper' or public responsibilities because of the pursuit of private gain. In most cases, corruption has a material or narrowly financial character, its most common political manifestations being bribery or 'sleaze'. The level of corruption in an institution or system is conditioned by a variety of factors, including the effectiveness of external checks, the level of administrative discipline, the strength of internal codes and norms, and the general level of economic development.

Departmentalism

Departmentalism refers to centrifugal pressures within a bureaucratic structure that strengthen the identity of individual departments and agencies. Agencies are thus able to pursue their own separate interests and resist both political control and broader administrative disciplines. The distinctive culture of a government agency is shaped by factors such as its policy responsibilities, the collective interests of its body of officials, and the interests of the client groups that it serves. Attempts to counter departmentalism by transferring officials from agency to agency, or by imposing stricter political control, risk diminishing levels of expertise and specialization. Such attempts may also be undermined by the tendency of ministers and senior officials to 'go native': that is, to be absorbed into the culture of their department.

amounting to a form of 'institutional pluralism' (Hough, 1977). The UK civil service has traditionally been centralized. It has a common recruitment and promotion policy, and a single career and salary structure. In some ways, the Fulton Report of 1966 furthered the ideal of a unified civil service by abolishing the division between the clerical, executive and administrative grades, which had amounted to a form of class system. However, by shifting emphasis away from 'generalists' in senior positions, it placed greater stress on subject expertise and specialist knowledge, so strengthening 'departmentalism'. Moreover, in establishing the Civil Service Department (subsequently abolished) to take responsibility for recruitment, promotions and conditions of work, it also facilitated bureaucratic autonomy.

The most centralized liberal-democratic bureaucracy has traditionally been that in France. Whereas bureaucracies in states such as the UK and Germany have developed through a process of reform and adaptation, the French system was constructed on the basis of the Napoleonic model of administration. This emphasized the importance of a highly centralized and hierarchically structured body of technical experts, wedded to the long-term interests of the French state. The Conseil d'État (Council of State) is the supreme administrative body in France; it advises on legislative and administrative matters and acts as the highest administrative court. The École Nationale d'Administration and the École Polytechnique function as training schools for civil servants, giving the so-called *grands corps* (senior administrators and technical experts) unrivalled prestige. To some extent, however, the Napoleonic model of strict discipline and uniformity has never been fully realized. Divisions tend to exist between generalists and specialists, between the *grand corps* and junior civil servants, and between rival bureaux and departments, particularly between the finance ministry and the major spending ministries.

The USA, in contrast, is an example of a decentralized bureaucracy. The federal bureaucracy operates under the formal authority of the president as chief administrator. However, it is so diffuse and unwieldy that all presidents struggle to coordinate and direct its activities. One reason for this fragmentation is that the responsibilities of the federal government overlap with those of state and local governments, whose cooperation is required to ensure effective implementation. A second reason is the impact of the separation of powers (see p. 339). While executive departments and agencies operate under presidential authority via their cabinet secretaries or directors, a bewildering array of independent regulatory commissions have been created, and are funded, by Congress. Although presidents appoint the members of these commissions, they cannot dismiss them or interfere with their responsibilities as laid down by Congress. A third reason is that there is tension between permanent civil servants, who are appointed through competitive public examination and placed on one of the General Schedule grades, and the much smaller number of political appointees in so-called Schedule C posts. While the latter can be expected to make loyalty to the administration their priority, the former may be more committed to the growth of their bureaux or the continuance of their services and programmes.

The conventional structure of government bureaucracies has come under particular scrutiny and pressure since the 1970s. In extreme cases, this has led to attempts to restructure the administrative state. The Clinton administration, for instance, was deeply impressed by the ideas developed in Osborne and Gaebler's *Reinventing Government* (1992). This suggested that the job of government is to 'steer' not to 'row': in other words, government works best when it concerns itself with policy-making and leaves the delivery of services or policy implementation to other bodies acting as agents of the state. In theory, such an approach need not necessarily be linked to the contraction of state responsibilities, but its most enthusiastic advocates have undoubtedly come from the New Right, which has embraced this analysis as part of its broader attack on 'big' government.

These ideas have been influential in the USA and a number of other western countries. The construction of an 'enabling state', even a 'skeletal state', has been taken furthest in New Zealand but they have also affected the UK, through the civil service reforms introduced by Thatcher and Major, and further developed by Blair. These ideas have provided the basis for the 'new public management'. A significant step down this road was taken in 1988 with the launching of the Next Steps initiative, which began dismantling a unified national administration by restricting ministries to their 'core' policy functions and handing over responsibility for implementation to executive agencies, as occurs in Sweden. By 1996, 70 per cent of the UK's civil servants were working in executive agencies, with a growing body of work being contracted out to private bodies.

Attempts to compensate for alleged inefficiency and unresponsiveness in public administration have also led to the wider use of performance targets and quality measurement. The Blair government, since 1997, has attempted to extend a culture of target setting and performance review across the UK public sector, linking target fulfilment to funding and being willing publicly to expose 'under-performance'. Such innovations have also been accompanied by a substantial increase in the role of quangos (see p. 392) in the administration of services such as health, education, urban development and regulation. In 1996, there were an estimated 5207 quasi-governmental bodies in the UK, spending over £60 billion a year (35 per cent of total public spending) and employing 60 000 staff. However, the most radical attempt to 'roll back the state' in the UK has been made through the policy of **privatization**, which, from the 1980s onwards, saw industries such as telecommunications, electricity, gas, water and local transport transferred from public to private ownership. Public–private partnerships have also given private bodies a greater role in public-service funding and delivery.

As governments struggle to keep public spending under control, such developments, especially the divorce between policy advice and policy implementation, are likely to become more common. However, the drive to streamline administration, promote efficiency and cut costs carries political costs. The most obvious of these is the weakening of public accountability and the emergence of a 'democratic deficit'. One of the strengths of a unified civil service is that it supports the doctrine of ministerial responsibility (see p. 396), which ensures that appointed officials are ultimately answerable to elected politicians and, through them, to the public. The creation of semi-independent executive agencies and, above all, quangos tends to mean that ministers no longer take responsibility for day-to-day administrative or operational matters. Supporters of reorganization, on the other hand, argue that this can be counterbalanced by the improvement of delivery standards through the use of charters and other performance targets.

A second problem is that the introduction of management techniques, structures and, increasingly, personnel from the private sector may weaken the public-service ethos that state bureaucracies have striven over the years to develop. The civil-service culture in states as different as Japan, India, France and the UK may be criticized for its aloofness, even arrogance, but it is at least linked to ideas such as public service and the national interest, rather than private gain and entrepreneurialism.

New public management

New public management (NPM) stands broadly for the use of private sector management techniques in government and for the transfer of government functions to private bodies. The philosophy of NPM is that government should 'steer' (decide policy) while private bodies should 'row' (deliver services), and that public bodies should be imbued with the 'entrepreneurial spirit'. Examples of the latter include holding managers directly accountable for results, setting explicit targets to assess results, allocating resources according to results, and the use of short-term contracts and open recruitment strategies. NPM represents a general shift from hierarchies to markets, and from government to governance (see p. 6). Its supporters associate it with the '3 Es': economy, efficiency and effectiveness. Critics argue that it undermines the public service ethos and weakens accountability; that it spawns new regulatory or inspection bodies; or that the 'private, good; public, bad' philosophy is basically flawed.

Privatization: The transfer of state assets from the public to the private sector, reflecting contraction of the state's responsibilities.

Focus on . . .

Quangos: advantages and disadvantages

Quango is an acronym for quasi-autonomous nongovernmental organization. This is a notoriously loose and confusing term. In its most general sense, quango refers to any body carrying out government functions that is staffed by appointees rather than by ministers or civil servants. Quangos thus include bodies with executive functions of various kinds, as well as advisory committees and tribunals. The quasi-autonomous status of quangos means that they are part of 'arm's-length' government; their nongovernmental character means that they are part of the 'nonelected state'.

The benefits of quangos include the following:

- They allow government to call on the experience, expertise and specialist knowledge of outside advisers.
- They reduce the burden of work of 'official' government departments and agencies.

Quangos have been criticized for the following reasons:

- They expand the range of ministerial patronage and so contribute to the centralization of political power.
- They weaken democratic accountability by reducing the ability of representative institutions to oversee the workings of government.
- They foster **balkanization** by making public administration more disjointed and less systematic.

Amongst other things, public service culture has helped to keep corruption at bay in most of the world's pluralist democracies. A third disadvantage is that, although this type of reorganization tends to be associated with the rolling back of the state, it may in practice lead to greater centralization and government control. This occurs because, as government relinquishes direct responsibility for the delivery of services, it is forced to set up a range of bodies to carry out funding and regulatory functions. This, in turn, allows politicians to exert influence through patronage and the setting of performance targets, powers that formerly came within the jurisdiction of professional bureaucrats (Jenkins, 1995). Finally, there are problems linked to the law of unintended outcomes. Thus, attempts to promote economy, efficiency and effectiveness may, in practice, be counter-productive. For example, as the USSR demonstrated, 'hyper-rational' planning systems based on targets can actually misdirect resources and lead to stultification.

■ Bureaucratic power: out of control?

Sources of bureaucratic power

Balkanization:
The fragmentation of a political unit into a patchwork of antagonistic entities (as has often occurred in the Balkans).

Despite their constitutional image as loyal and supportive public servants, bureaucrats have widely been seen as powerful and influential figures who collectively constitute a 'fourth branch of government'. Theorists as different as Weber, Burnham and Trotsky have drawn attention to the phenomenon of bureaucratic power and the degree to which politicians are subordinate to it. Japanese civil servants, especially those in the prestigious Japanese Ministry of International Trade and Industry, are generally viewed as the 'permanent politicians' who masterminded the Japanese 'economic miracle' of the 1950s and 1960s. Kellner and Crowther-Hunt (1980) dubbed the UK's civil service 'Britain's ruling class'. Similarly, there is a perception that the driving force in the EU behind monetary and political union is the Brussels-based administrative staff of the European Commission, the so-called eurocrats.

Concern about bureaucratic power has been particularly acute amongst those on the political left and the political right who have dismissed the conventional notion of civil service neutrality. As pointed out above, Marxists have traditionally argued that class interests operate through the bureaucracy, tending, in particular, to dilute radical policy initiatives by socialist governments. The New Right insists that self-interested public officials foster state growth and are thus inclined to resist neoliberal or free-market policies. However, it is important to remember that the nature of bureaucratic power is, perhaps inevitably, shrouded in mystery and conjecture. This is both because, if civil servants exert power, they do so through private dealings with ministers that are not subject to public scrutiny, and because, in view of the myriad other pressures bearing on ministers, the influence of the civil service cannot be quantified. Nevertheless, three key sources of bureaucratic power can be identified:

- the strategic position of bureaucrats in the policy process
- the logistical relationship between bureaucrats and ministers
- the status and expertise of bureaucrats.

The policy process in all modern states is structured in a way that offers considerable scope for civil service influence. Most crucially, in their capacity as policy advisers, civil servants have access to information and are able to control its flow to their ministerial bosses. In government departments, knowledge is undoubtedly power, and it is officials who decide what ministers know and what they do not know. Policy options can thus be selected, evaluated and presented in such a way as to achieve a desired decision. This need not, of course, imply that bureaucrats are deliberately manipulative or openly political, but merely that their preferences – conscious or unconscious – significantly structure policy debate and so can influence the content of decisions made.

Links that develop between the bureaucracy and organized interests further strengthen their position. As the major interface between government and business, labour, professional and other groups, the bureaucracy can build up powerful alliances and play a crucial role in formulating and reviewing policy options. This has led to the emergence of 'policy networks' (see p. 432): that is, complex relationships between senior bureaucrats and representatives of interest groups that tend to be relatively impervious to influence from the public or elected politicians. Needless to say, bureaucratic power does not cease to play a role once policy decisions have been made. Whereas politicians can seek alternative sources of policy advice, they are compelled to leave policy implementation in the hands of the bureaucracy, whether organized as a unified entity or as a series of quasi-independent agencies. Control of implementation gives civil servants the opportunity to reinterpret the content of policy, as well as to delay or even thwart its introduction.

The second source of bureaucratic power is the operational relationship and distribution of advantage between ministers and civil servants. Ostensibly, ministers are political masters and appointed bureaucrats are loyal subordinates. However, there are reasons to believe that this relationship may be different, even reversed, in practice. The first of these is that politicians are heavily outnumbered by leading bureaucrats. For example, in the USA, even if only top-level political appointees (those who require Senate approval) are considered, US presidents, aided by a cabinet of fewer than 20 secretaries, confront more than 600 senior officials. In the UK, the ratio of ministers to civil servants of the rank of under-secretary and above is 2:13. Politicians' spans of control are therefore very limited, meaning that civil servants are necessarily allowed considerable discretion in carrying out their policy and administrative responsibilities.

A second factor is the different career structures of civil servants and elected politicians. Except where 'spoils systems' operate, as in the USA, civil servants are permanent in the sense that they remain in office while governments come and go. In contrast, ministers are only temporary, and in parliamentary systems like the UK's where reshuffles are frequent, may remain in office for only about two years on average. Incoming ministers may therefore be particularly susceptible to official influence while they acquire the administrative experience and specialist knowledge required to run their departments effectively, and they may well be moved to another department once this task has been accomplished. Civil servants, for their part, have the confidence of knowing that they are likely to outlive an unsympathetic political master.

The third advantage enjoyed by civil servants is that they are full-time policy advisers, while ministers are only part-time departmental bosses. At the same time as ministerial workloads have increased, owing to the growing scale and complexity of government business, ministers have also been faced by an expanding range of demands on their time and energy. These include cabinet and cabinet-committee duties, sometimes parliamentary responsibilities and constituency work, media appearances, attendance at ceremonial and public functions, and foreign visits and summitry. In short, however dedicated, tenacious and resourceful ministers may be, their role is restricted to the offering of strategic guidance, knowing that much of the detail of policy and operational matters must be left to appointed officials.

The final source of bureaucratic power is the status and respect that is often accorded to civil servants. This stems principally from their expertise and specialist knowledge. In many systems, senior bureaucrats are regarded as a meritocratic elite, and are invested with responsibility for the national interest. This is certainly reflected in an emphasis on merit and achievement in the recruitment and training of civil servants. Top German civil servants, for instance, are recruited by competitive examination from the ranks of university graduates, usually in law, and then endure a rigorous three-year training programme followed by a second state examination. In France, the École Nationale d'Administration was set up specifically to recruit and train the nation's top generalist civil servants, thus supplementing the work of schools like the École Polytechnique, which turn out technical experts. The elite status of Japanese bureaucrats is maintained by an examination system that recruits only one candidate in 40, and by the preponderance of Tokyo University entrants, who provide 70 per cent of senior civil servants, two-thirds of whom have law degrees. Their status was heightened by the responsibility that the relatively unpurged Japanese bureaucracy shouldered in the process of reconstruction after the Second World War, especially in the establishment of a planned market economy. Similarly, the status of the UK civil service has been linked with a traditional reliance on Oxbridge candidates and the rigours of the fast-stream entrance procedure.

In comparison, governments and ministers often come into office ill-prepared and in need of advice and support. Although governments are formed on the basis of party programmes and manifestos, they depend on civil servants to translate broad policy goals into practical and workable legislative programmes. This problem is particularly acute because of the mismatch between the skills and attributes required to win elective office and those needed to run an effective administration. In parliamentary systems in particular, ministers are appointed from an unusually small pool of talent (the members of the majority party or parties in the assembly), and it is rare for them to have either specialist knowledge of their departmental remit or previous experience of administering a large-scale organization.

How can bureaucrats be controlled?

The perceived need to control the bureaucracy reflects a wide range of concerns. Most importantly, unchecked bureaucratic power spells the demise of representative and responsible government. For political democracy to be meaningful, appointed officials must in some way be accountable to politicians who, in turn, are accountable to the general public. Indeed, one of the long-standing criticisms of liberal democracy is that behind the facade of party competition and public accountability lies the entrenched power of bureaucrats who are responsible to no one. Guarantees against corruption, **maladministration** and the arbitrary exercise of government power must therefore be established.

Political control is also required because of the need to promote efficiency in a bureaucracy that may be bent on maintaining its professional comforts and material security, and because of the need for administrative coordination to resist the centrifugal pressures of departmentalism. Bureaucrats themselves may argue that external control is unnecessary in view of the self-discipline imposed by strict professional standards and a deeply ingrained public-service ethos, especially in permanent civil services like those found in Germany, France, India and the UK. On the other hand, such a civil service culture may be part of the problem rather than part of the solution: it may entrench a lofty arrogance based on the belief that 'bureaucrats know best'. The principal forms of control over bureaucracies can be classified as follows:

- the creation of mechanisms of political accountability
- the politicization of the civil service
- the construction of counter-bureaucracies.

Political accountability

State bureaucracies can be made accountable (see p. 418) to the political executive, the assembly, the judiciary, or the public. The political executive is easily the most important of these bodies, because of its overall responsibility for government administration and its close working relationship with the civil service. The most elaborate system of executive control has been found in state socialist regimes such as those in China and the USSR, where a hierarchically structured network of party organs was constructed to run parallel to, and exercise supervision over, the state administration. However, so complex and extensive was the machinery of government in these regimes that even the pervasive influence of a 'leading' party failed to

Maladministration: Bad administration; the improper use of powers, biased application of rules, failure to follow procedures, or simple incompetence.

Concept

Ministerial responsibility

The doctrine of ministerial responsibility ('individual' responsibility) defines the relationship between ministers and their departments and ostensibly guarantees that the civil service is publicly accountable. This doctrine is observed in most parliamentary systems, most clearly in the UK, and has two key features. First, ministers are responsible for the acts and omissions of their departments, maintaining the fiction that ministers themselves make all the decisions taken in their name: 'the buck stops' with the minister. Second, ministers are accountable to the assembly, in the sense that they are answerable for anything that goes on in their departments, and are removable in the event of wrongdoing or incompetence by their civil servants. In theory, ministerial responsibility establishes a chain of accountability that links civil servants to the public via ministers and assemblies. In practice, it is often bent to the will of the government of the day.

prevent communist bureaucracies from developing interests of their own or acting as conduits through which economic, social and regional interests could be expressed.

In liberal democracies, especially ones with parliamentary executives, political control depends largely on respect for the doctrine of ministerial responsibility. This holds that ministers alone are responsible *to* the assembly *for* the actions of their officials and the policies pursued by their departments. Ministerial responsibility has been developed in its most extreme form in the UK, where it is taken to imply that civil servants have an exclusive responsibility to their minister and, therefore, to the government of the day. The ability of this doctrine to deliver political control is nevertheless hampered by three factors. First, as discussed above, the expertise, size and complexity of modern bureaucracies make effective ministerial oversight virtually impossible. Second, ministers have been unwilling to sacrifice their political careers by resigning as a result of blunders made by officials (or themselves), and prime ministers have been reluctant to encourage resignations that will attract adverse publicity. Third, assemblies usually lack the expertise and political will to subject either ministers or civil servants to effective scrutiny.

Legislative oversight may also help to ensure that bureaucrats are politically accountable. The decision in the UK in 1979 to allow the newly created departmental select committees to cross-examine senior civil servants as well as ministers was an implicit acknowledgement of the failings of the system of ministerial responsibility. Effective legislative control is tied up with the supply of money, however. The US Congress scrutinizes the presidential budget and has the constitutional authority to provide funds for the various executive departments and agencies. This gives congressional committees the opportunity to probe and investigate the workings of each department, scrutinize their estimates, and expose cases of maladministration and misappropriation. Congressional oversight may nevertheless allow powerful alliances to form, as in the so-called 'iron triangles': policy networks that comprise an executive agency, its relevant congressional committee and the interest groups with which both deal.

Judicial scrutiny of the bureaucracy is in particular found in systems in which administrative law, which defines the powers and functions of the executive organs of the state, is established as a separate branch of public law. In many continental European states this leads to the creation of a network of administrative courts and tribunals empowered to resolve disputes between the government bureaucracy and private citizens. In France the Conseil d'État is the supreme administrative court. It exercises general supervision over all forms of French administration, but may also weaken political control by protecting civil servants from unwarranted interference by their political masters.

Bureaucrats can be made accountable to the public in a number of ways, formal and informal. One method, Scandinavian in origin but later extended in different variations to countries such as New Zealand, Australia, the UK and France, is the ombudsman system. Although the ombudsman system offers a means through which individual grievances can be redressed, ombudsmen rarely operate with the force of law, and generally lack direct means of enforcing their decisions. The UK Parliamentary Commissioner for Administration is particularly ineffective, since complaints cannot be made directly by the public, but only on referral from an MP, and because there is widespread public ignorance about the office and its function.

Amongst the informal pressures on the bureaucracy are those exercised by the mass media and well-organized interest groups. Bureaucrats recognize that, regardless of the mechanisms of formal accountability, their status and public standing can be damaged by the exposure of scandals, corruption and administrative ineptitude. The publicity given to the Watergate affair in the USA in the 1970s thus led to tighter oversight of US government agencies such as the Central Intelligence Agency (CIA) and the Federal Bureau of Investigation (FBI). Similarly, the French newspaper *Le Monde* played a significant role in exposing the sinking in 1985 of the Greenpeace ship the *Rainbow Warrior*, thus contributing to the resignation of the defence minister. On the other hand, such investigations can be severely hampered by the culture of secrecy that usually pervades state administration, and by the absence of open government (see p. 436).

Politicization

One of the most common ways of exercising political control is to recruit the senior bureaucracy into the ideological enthusiasms of the government of the day. This effectively blurs the distinctions between politics and administration, and between politicians and public officials. Control is overtly accomplished through a system of political appointments. A spoils system, as it became known, was institutionalized in the USA by Andrew Jackson in the nineteenth century, when he replaced about 20 per cent of the federal civil service with his own men. When there is a new US president, the administration changes. Some 4000 top posts are filled by political appointees, mostly in a rush between the election in November and the inauguration of the new president in January. Fewer than 200 of these appointments are likely to be made by the president personally; the others are made by senior executive officers subject to presidential approval.

In Germany, although the formal scope for making ministerial appointments is limited, the *Berufsverbot* (literally, the 'denial of access to a profession') system allows incoming ministers and governments to discard unwanted officials by retiring them on full pay and appoint more sympathetic ones in their place. However, covert politicization is more widespread. In the UK, the abolition of the Civil Service Department in 1981 led to allegations that the senior personnel of the civil service were being 'Thatcherized'. Criticism stemmed from the close interest that Margaret Thatcher took in the new senior appointments system, and her well-publicized criteria for preferment: are they 'one of us'? Tony Blair was criticized for allowing senior Downing Street political advisers to exercise control over civil servants. Creeping politicization has also become a feature of French administration. Approximately 500 senior posts are now filled at the discretion of leading government figures, and, since the 1980s, those appointed have usually had a highly partisan profile or have been linked personally or politically with senior politicians. The French higher civil service therefore now resembles a patchwork of politicized clans, rather than a unified body standing above party politics.

The attraction of a politicized senior bureaucracy is plainly that it ensures that there is a higher level of loyalty and commitment in such a group than would be likely amongst politically impartial civil servants. Moreover, those observers who believe that neutrality is always a myth, arguing that some kind of political bias is inevitable in the state bureaucracy, generally hold that a system of overt politicization is preferable to one of covert politicization. However, political commitment also brings serious disadvantages. In the first place, politicization strikes at the very heart of the idea of a professional and permanent civil service. Once bureaucrats are selected on political grounds by the government of the day, or encouraged to share

Ombudsman

Ombudsman is a Scandinavian word that has no exact English equivalent. An ombudsman is an officer of the state who is appointed to safeguard citizens' rights in a particular sector and investigate allegations of maladministration, ranging from the improper use of powers to the failure to follow procedures and simple incompetence. The role of an ombudsman is to supplement, not replace, normal avenues of complaints such as administrative courts or elected representatives. However, as ombudsmen are concerned with wider administrative morality, their investigations and findings seldom have the force of law. While the ombudsman system may strengthen the exercise of oversight and redress, it has been criticized as tokenistic (ombudsmen lack executive power), and because it relies too heavily on the qualities of the incumbent (who is usually an 'insider').

their ideological sympathies, their appointments become as temporary as those of their political masters. This, in turn, means that knowledge and experience are not accumulated over a number of governments, and, as in the USA, that a change in administration brings about a major breach in the continuity of government.

Furthermore, it is difficult to have both political commitment and meritocracy within the civil service. In a politicized service, not only are appointments made on the basis of political affiliation and personal loyalty, rather than ability and training, but it may also be more difficult to attract high-calibre staff to work in temporary positions that offer no form of job security. A more insidious danger is that ideological enthusiasm may blind civil servants to the drawbacks and disadvantages of policy proposals. From this point of view, the virtue of neutrality is that it establishes an 'arm's length' relationship between bureaucrats and politicians, allowing the former to see the weaknesses, as well as the strengths, of the policy options they are required to examine. For instance, perhaps the ease with which the disastrous 'poll tax' was devised in the UK in the late 1980s bears witness to the degree to which civil servants under Margaret Thatcher had ceased to interject, 'But minister. . .'.

Counter-bureaucracies

The final mechanism of political control is through structures designed to support or assist politicians or to act as a counterweight to the official bureaucracy. The simplest such system is the use of political advisers or 'outsiders', which is now a feature of almost all modern states. More significantly, institutions of various kinds have been established to share ministers' workloads and provide them with personal advisory staff. In the UK, this has occurred on an *ad hoc* basis. Edward Heath set up the Central Policy Review Staff (CPRS) in 1970, and Harold Wilson created the Policy Unit in 1974. Margaret Thatcher in the 1980s expanded the role of the Private Office and also sought advice from right-wing 'think tanks' such as the Centre for Policy Studies and the Adam Smith Institute, while Blair strengthened the Cabinet Office and sought advice from bodies such as the Institute of Public Policy Research and Demos. Of more general application is the device of the *cabinet ministériel*. These have long been established in France and have been taken up in states like Italy and Austria, as well as by the EU. *Cabinets* are ministers' personal teams of advisers (in France, usually 15–20 strong) that help to formulate policy, assist in supervising departmental activities, and help ministers to carry out their various other responsibilities.

The idea of a counter-bureaucracy has been most elaborately developed in the USA, in the form of the Executive Office of the President (EOP). This was established by President Roosevelt following the Brownlow Committee's declaration that 'the President needs help'. The EOP is the president's personal bureaucracy. It consists of a growing number of councils and offices and employs about 1400 staff. Its key agencies are the White House Office, which comprises the president's closest political advisers, the Office of Management and Budget, which assists in the preparation of budgetary and legislative proposals, the National Security Council (NSC), which advises on defence and foreign-affairs issues, and the Council of Economic Advisers, which provides the president with professional advice on economic policy.

The purpose of counter-bureaucracies is to compensate for the imbalance in the relationship between amateur, temporary and outnumbered politicians and their expert, permanent and professional officials. However, this form of political control has its drawbacks. In the case of the EOP, it leads to the duplication of government agencies and so causes jurisdictional conflicts and a measure of bureaucratic in-fighting. This has been particularly evident in the often fraught relationship between the National Security Council and the State Department.

A further difficulty is that counter-bureaucracies may compound, rather than solve, the problem of political control. Margaret Thatcher, for instance, abolished the CPRS in 1983, believing it to be the source of damaging leaks during that year's election campaign. Similarly, NSC staff, including Lieutenant-Colonel Oliver North, were at the centre of the Iran–Contra affair that rocked the Reagan administration in the 1980s. Lastly, allowing politicians to surround themselves with hand-picked advisers creates the danger that they will cut themselves off from political reality and be told only what they want to hear. This problem was highlighted by both the Watergate and the Iran–Contra affairs, when the respective presidents, Nixon and Reagan, became overdependent on EOP advisers, partly because they believed that they could neither trust nor control an essentially hostile federal bureaucracy.

◼ Summary

◆ The term bureaucracy has been used in a number of ways. Originally, it meant rule by officials as opposed to elected politicians. In the social sciences, it is usually understood as a mode of organization. Modern political analysts, however, use the term bureaucracy to mean the administrative machinery of the state, bureaucrats being nonelected state officials or civil servants, who may or may not be subject to political control.

◆ Three major theories of bureaucracy have been advanced. The Weberian mode suggests that bureaucracy is a rational-administrative machine, the characteriztic form of organization in modern society. The conservative power-bloc model emphasizes the degree to which the bureaucracy reflects broader class interests and can resist political control. The bureaucratic oversupply model emphasizes a tendency towards 'big' government caused by the pursuit of career self-interest on the part of civil servants.

◆ The core function of the bureaucracy is to implement or execute law and policy through the administration of government business. However, civil servants also play a significant role in offering policy advice to ministers, in articulating and aggregating interests (especially through links to client groups), and in maintaining political stability and continuity when there is a change of government or administration.

◆ Bureaucracies have traditionally been organized on the basis of purpose or function: hence their division into departments, ministries and agencies. The degree of central-ization or decentralization within them varies considerably. Modern trends, however, are towards the divorce of policy-making from policy implementation, and the incorporation of private-sector management techniques, if not outright privatization.

◆ There is concern about bureaucratic power because of the threat it poses to democratic accountability. The principal sources of bureaucratic power include the ability of civil servants to control the flow of information and thus determine what their political masters know, the logistical advantages that they enjoy as permanent and full-time public officials, and their status as experts and custodians of the national interest.

◆ Control is exerted over bureaucracies in a number of ways. Mechanisms of public accountability to ministers, assemblies, the courts or ombudsmen can be established. The civil service can be politicized so that it shares the ideological enthusiasms of the government of the day. Counter-bureaucracies can be constructed to provide an alternative source of advice and to strengthen the hands of elected politicians.

▮ Questions for discussion

▶ Do bureaucrats really 'run' their countries?

▶ Can a clear distinction be drawn between making policy and offering policy advice?

▶ Can civil servants ever be politically neutral?

▶ Are public bureaucracies inherently inefficient?

▶ Do the benefits of a politically committed civil service outweigh the costs?

▶ What are the most effective mechanisms for controlling bureaucratic power?

▮ Further reading

Beetham, D., *Bureaucracy* (Milton Keynes: Open University Press, 1987). A clear and concise discussion of models of bureaucracy and theories of bureaucratic power.

Bekke, H., J. Perry and T. Toonen, *Civil Service Systems in Comparative Perspective* (Bloomington, Ind.: Indiana University Press, 1996). A wide-ranging and thorough study of civil services in different parts of the world.

Guy Peters, B., *The Politics of Bureaucracy* (White Plains, NY: Longman, 2001). An encyclopaedic exploration of the political and policy-making role of bureaucracies.

Self, P., *Government by the Market? The Politics of Public Choice* (Basingstoke: Palgrave Macmillan, 1994). A perceptive discussion of the remodelling of government according to the principles of market competition and efficiency.

Verheijen, T. and D. Coombes (eds), *Innovations in Public Management: Perspectives from East and West Europe* (Cheltenham and Northampton, MA: Edward Elgar, 1998). A comparative analysis of the ideas and impact of the new public management.

Militaries and Police Forces

'Political power grows out of the barrel of a gun.'

MAO ZEDONG, *Problems of War and Strategy* (1938)

No regime remains in power on the basis of political legitimacy or administrative efficiency alone. All systems of rule are underpinned, to a greater or lesser extent, by the exercise of coercive power through the institutions of the military and the police. However, the coercive power of the military and the police can be put to a wide variety of political uses. Militaries may function simply as instruments of foreign policy, or they may play a decisive domestic role, perhaps by quelling civil unrest or even propping up unpopular regimes. They may operate as powerful interest groups, or may, through the construction of military regimes, provide an alternative to civilian rule. In the same way, the police can act as a means of maintaining public order and civil liberty, or as a mechanism of political repression that may, in extreme cases, lead to the establishment of a police state. So great is the potential power of these institutions that questions about how they can be controlled or be made publicly accountable are of enduring political significance.

The central issues examined in this chapter are as follows:

Key issues

▶ What are the distinctive features of the military as a political institution?

▶ How, and in what ways, can the military intervene in politics?

▶ How can military power be brought under political control?

▶ In what ways does civil policing differ from political policing?

▶ What mechanisms are used to make police forces publicly accountable?

■ The military and politics

The development of modern armed forces can be traced back to the period following the Middle Ages when European powers started to develop a standardized form of military organization, usually based on a standing army. During the nineteenth century the military became a specialized institution with a professional leadership separate from the rest of society. European colonialism, in turn, ensured that this military model was adopted all over the world, turning the military into a near-universal component of state organization. Puerto Rico is sometimes identified as the classic exception to this rule, but its lack of armed forces is possible only because of the security provided by the US military.

The military is a political institution of a very particular kind. Four factors distinguish the military from other institutions and give it a distinct, and at times overwhelming, advantage over civilian organizations. First, as an instrument of war, the military enjoys a virtual monopoly of weaponry and substantial coercive power. As the military has the capacity to prop up or topple a regime, its loyalty is essential to state survival. Second, armed forces are tightly organized and highly disciplined bodies, characterized by a hierarchy of ranks and a culture of strict obedience. They are thus an extreme example of bureaucracy (see p. 383) in the Weberian sense. This gives the military an unusual degree of organizational effectiveness, although it can also breed inflexibility and discourage initiative and innovation. Third, the military is invariably characterized by a distinctive culture and set of values, and an *esprit de corps* that prepare its personnel to fight, kill and possibly die. Sometimes portrayed as implicitly right-wing and deeply authoritarian (by virtue of its traditional emphasis on leadership, duty and honour), military culture can also be grounded in creeds such as revolutionary socialism (as in China) or Islamic fundamentalism (as in Iran). Fourth, the armed forces are often seen, and generally regard themselves, as being 'above' politics, in the sense that, because they guarantee the security and integrity of the state, they are the repository of the national interest. This secures for most militaries a special status and respect, but it may also incline the military to intervene in politics, particularly when, in its view, vital national interests are under threat.

On the other hand, it is a mistake to view the military as a single, cohesive institution with common political features in all societies. Divisions within the military may stem from various sources. For example, conflicts may develop between broadly conservative senior officers, often recruited from elite backgrounds, and more junior officers, who may be either impatient for promotion or more open to progressive or radical ideas. Similarly, there is likely to be tension between an officer core that is privileged both socially and professionally, and conscripts or enlisted personnel, who are usually drawn from the working class or peasantry. Rivalry and competition for prestige and scarce resources may also divide the various services and units within the military, while regional or ethnic divisions can also be significant.

The character of particular armed forces is shaped by internal and external factors. These include the history and traditions of the military and specific regiments or units, and the nature of the broader political system, the political culture and the values of the regime itself. For example, the political orientation of the People's Liberation Army (PLA) in China is deeply influenced by the decisive role it played in establishing the communist regime in 1949 and by strict party control at every level of the Chinese military. In Israel, the military enjoys an unusual position of trust and respect, based on its role in absorbing and socializing immigrants, and on its record of safeguarding the security of the Israeli state. Finally, it is difficult to generalize about the nature and significance of the military because of the very different roles that the military can play in political life. The most important of these are the following:

- an instrument of war
- a guarantee of political order and stability
- an interest group
- an alternative to civilian rule.

Role of the military

Instrument of war

The central purpose of the military is to serve as an instrument of war that can be directed against other political societies if necessary. This is why the development of the military as a separate and permanent institution coincided with the emergence of the state system in early modern Europe. Crucially, however, the armed forces can be put to either defensive or offensive uses. It is the capacity of the military to defend a country against external aggression that ensures that practically all countries have armed forces, the military being seen as no less essential to the modern state than a police force, the courts or a postal service. However, this defensive role has conflicting implications for the size and nature of the military.

On the one hand, the armed forces must be powerful enough to at least match the might of likely aggressors and, preferably, deter aggression in the first place. Not uncommonly, such calculations have led to arms races and resulted in war, as defensive buildups have created international tension by appearing to neighbouring states to constitute an offensive threat. This certainly happened in the case of the naval race between the UK and imperial Germany in the years leading up to the outbreak of the First World War. However, an arms race that maintains an effective balance of power can also discourage military aggression, as was demonstrated by the Cold War. On the other hand, if the military has an exclusively defensive role, this can restrict it to long periods of inactivity, during which it must maintain a state of readiness that is never utilized. Moreover, success in deterring aggression may actually weaken public support for military spending, as such support is usually linked to the existence of a perceived threat.

When armed forces are used to pursue offensive or expansionist ends, the military becomes substantially more important. To wage war against other states requires both that the military is able and willing to act as an agent of aggression and that its offensive actions enjoy a significant measure of public support. Expansionist states are therefore usually characterized by a high level of military spending, the recruitment of military leaders into the process of policy-making, and the growth of militarism, in the sense that ideas and values usually associated with the military are spread throughout civilian society. The classic example of a militaristic regime was Hitler's Third Reich in Germany. Nazi totalitarianism (see p. 29) operated in part through the collapse of the distinction between military and civilian institutions, bringing about the militarization of political life. However, militarism (see p. 404)

(see p. 133)

Concept

War

War is a condition of open armed conflict between two or more parties (usually states). The term is also used metaphorically, as in 'class war', 'trade war' and 'cold war' (see p. 133). The emergence of war as an organized and goal-directed activity stems from the development of the European state system in the early modern period. War has a formal or quasi-legal character in that the declaration of a 'state of war' need not necessarily be accompanied by an outbreak of hostilities. The notion that war legitimizes unchecked barbarity is challenged by the sometimes controversial concept of war crimes. In the post-Cold-War era it has been common to refer to 'new' wars. These have been characterized, variously, as being linked to intra-state ethnic conflict, the use of advanced military technology, and the challenges of dealing with nonstate actors such as transnational terrorist organizations.

◆ **Concept**

Militarism

The term militarism can be used in two ways. First, it refers to the achievement of ends by the use of military force. Any attempt to solve problems by military means can be described as militarism in this sense. Second, and more commonly, militarism is a cultural or ideological phenomenon in which military priorities, ideals and values come to pervade the larger society. This typically includes a glorification of the armed forces, a heightened sense of national patriotism, the recognition of war as a legitimate instrument of policy, and an atavistic belief in heroism and self-sacrifice. In some cases, but not all, militarism is characterized by the abuse by the military of its legitimate functions, and its usurpation of responsibilities normally ascribed to civilian politicians.

should not be equated with the prioritization of military interests and the dominance of military leaders over civilian ones. To some extent, German militarism in the 1930s was a means of subordinating the army and turning it into an instrument for the achievement of Nazi ideological goals.

However, the role of the military has been redefined in the post-Cold-War period by the changing nature of war and warfare. The end of the Cold War led, initially, to a 'peace dividend' in the form of the transfer of resources, in both the former communist East and the capitalist West, from military to domestic purposes. This nevertheless concealed a significant shift, in that the reduction in tensions and wars between states was accompanied by an upsurge, from the 1990s onwards, in ethnic conflict and civil strife, sometimes manifest in **civil wars**. This has resulted, in some cases, in the use of military personnel and resources in humanitarian intervention (see p. 135) and to their wider involvement in peacekeeping operations, often carried out under the auspices of the United Nations. Another major influence on the nature of modern warfare is the advert of advanced military technology, such as the high-tech satellite guidance and surveillance systems that were used for the first time during the Gulf War of 1991. Advanced technology consolidated the move away from conscript armies based on, at best, semi-trained civilians, to fully professionalized armies, and appeared, at least at first, to reduce the need for land-based forces. Finally, the emergence of global terrorism (see p. 406) after 11 September, 2001 and the development of counter-insurgency wars fought against fiercely ideological foes in Afghanistan and Iraq as part of the 'war on terror' (see p. 137) have, in some cases, created an entirely new style of warfare. The task of dealing with nonstate actors, especially transnational terrorist groups, and of countering guerrilla fighters using tactics such as suicide bombing, present the armed forces of a growing number of states with challenges that are not only historically new but also profoundly difficult.

Guarantee of domestic order

Needless to say, the military's coercive power and operational efficiency are not only of significance in international politics. Although military force is usually directed against other political societies, it may also be a decisive factor in domestic politics. However, the circumstances in which militaries are deployed, and the uses to which they are put, vary from system to system and from state to state. One of the least controversial nonmilitary tasks that armed forces may be called upon to undertake is to act as an emergency service in the event of natural and other disasters. This type of involvement in domestic affairs is exceptional and is usually devoid of political significance. However, the same cannot be said of circumstances in which the armed forces are used to police domestic civil disturbances or disputes.

US troops, for instance, were deployed to implement federal racial desegregation orders during the civil rights struggles of the 1950s and 1960s. Similarly, in the UK in the 1970s and 1980s, the army was brought in during industrial disputes to provide emergency fire and ambulance services. Such actions provoke criticism, not only because the military is used in ways that encroach on responsibilities that usually belong to the police, but also because they compromise the traditional neutrality (see p. 329) of the armed forces. This highlights the difficulty of distinguishing between the domestic use of the military as a 'public' instrument serving the national interest and its use as a 'political' weapon furthering the partisan goals of the government of the day. This distinction becomes still more blurred when the military is used to quell civil unrest or counter popular insurrection.

Civil war: An armed conflict between politically organized groups within a state, usually fought to gain (or retain) control over the state or to establish a new state.

Certain states confront levels of political tension and unrest that are quite beyond the capacity of the civilian police to contain. This occurs particularly in the case of serious religious, ethnic or national conflict. In such circumstances the military can become the only guarantee of the integrity of the state, and may even be drawn into what may amount to a civil war to achieve this end. In 1969 UK troops were dispatched to Northern Ireland, initially to defend the beleaguered minority Catholic community, but increasingly to contain a campaign of sectarian terror waged by the Irish Republican Army (IRA) and opposing 'loyalist' groups such as the Ulster Defence Association (UDA) and the Ulster Defence Force (UDF). The Indian army has been used on a number of occasions to counter civil unrest and restore political order (see p. 413). These have included the eviction of Sikh separatists from the Golden Temple at Amritsar in 1984 at the cost of 1000 lives, and the seizure of Ayodhya from Hindu fundamentalists in 1992 following the destruction of the ancient Babri Masjid mosque. Russian troops were dispatched to the republic of Chechnya in 1994 to thwart its bid for independence in an operation that turned into a full-scale war, later developing into an ongoing guerilla struggle.

In cases in which political legitimacy has collapsed altogether, the military may become the only prop of the regime, safeguarding it from popular **rebellion** or revolution. When this occurs, however, all semblance of constitutionalism (see p. 321) and consent is abandoned as the government becomes an outright dictatorship. Thus, in May 1989, the survival of the Chinese communist regime was maintained only by the military assault on Tiananmen Square, which effectively neutralized the growing democracy movement. Such circumstances place a heavy strain on the loyalty of officers and the obedience of troops required to inflict violence on civilian demonstrators. Trouble was taken to deploy in Beijing only PLA divisions brought in from the countryside whose political loyalty could be counted on. In contrast, in Romania in December 1989, soldiers ordered to quell popular unrest went over to the demonstrators, effectively bringing about the collapse of the Ceauşescu regime.

Interest group

The military has been seen above largely as an instrument of policy: that is, as a device through which governments can achieve their foreign or domestic ends. However, armed forces are not neutral bodies that have no interest in the policy uses to which they are put. Rather, like bureaucracies, militaries can act as interest groups that seek to shape or influence the content of policy itself. In this respect, the military has a number of clear advantages. First, it possesses considerable technical knowledge and expertise. Although armed forces are usually constrained by formal subordination to civilian politicians and the requirements of political neutrality, it is difficult for governments not to listen to, and often heed, the advice of senior members of the military on strategic, defence and broader foreign policy matters.

Second, the military is an 'insider' group in the sense that it is represented on key policy-making bodies and so possesses an institutional power base. The US military, for instance, is able to exert influence through the Department of Defense ('the Pentagon') and the National Security Council, as well as through appearances before the congressional Armed Services Committees. Third, the military benefits from its status as the guarantor of national security and state integrity, and from the significance the public normally attaches to the issue of defence. Governments may thus calculate that there are votes in strengthening military capacity and increasing defence spending.

Concept

Dictatorship

A dictatorship is, strictly, a form of rule in which absolute power is vested in one individual; in this sense, dictatorship is synonymous with autocracy. Originally, the term was associated with the unrestricted emergency powers granted to a supreme magistrate in the early Roman Republic, which created a form of constitutional dictatorship. In the modern usage of the term, however, dictators are seen as being above the law and as acting beyond constitutional constraints. Early examples of dictators were Sulla, Julius Caesar and Augustus Caesar in Rome, more recent ones are Hitler, Mussolini and Saddam Hussein. More generally, dictatorship is characterized by the arbitrary and unchecked exercise of power, as in 'class dictatorship', 'party dictatorship', 'military dictatorship' and 'personal dictatorship'.

Rebellion: A popular uprising against the established order, usually (unlike a revolution) aimed at replacing rulers rather than the political system itself.

Concept

Terrorism

Terrorism, in its broadest sense, refers to the use of terror for furthering of political ends; it seeks to create a climate of fear, apprehension and uncertainty. The most common forms of terrorist action are assassinations, bombings, hostage seizures and plane hijacks, although the advent of terrorism with a global reach, as demonstrated by the September 11, 2001 attacks on the USA, threatened to redefine the phenomenon. The term is nevertheless highly controversial. First, the distinction between terrorism and other forms of violence or warfare is blurred by the fact that the latter may also aim to strike fear into the wider population. Second, as the term is highly pejorative, it tends to be used selectively and often subjectively (one person's 'terrorist' is another person's 'freedom fighter'). Third, although terrorism is usually conceived of as an anti-government activity, governments can employ terror against their own or other populations, as in the case of 'state terrorism'.

Military–industrial complex: A symbiotic relationship between the armed forces and defence industries, based on a common desire to increase military spending.

Just as public choice theorists (see p. 300) claim that civil servants are essentially concerned with career self-interest, it is possible to argue that the senior military is likely to 'push' policies that enhance the size and status of the armed forces, or guarantee their independence. This view sees the military as a lobby group that campaigns mainly for an increase in the military budget, or as a series of rival services or units that struggle for the largest possible cut of the defence cake. The armed forces are aided in this by a number of powerful allies in the form of what President Eisenhower, in his farewell address in 1961, referred to as the **military–industrial complex**. It is widely accepted, for example, that the Cold War was sustained partly by the vested interests of the US and Soviet military–industrial complexes, both of which had a strong incentive to exaggerate the strategic threat and offensive capabilities of the other. Some estimates of Soviet military and defence-related expenditure in the 1980s put it as high as 40 per cent of gross national product (GNP), Soviet military industry (in Khrushchev's words, 'the metal eaters') being the only efficient sector of a declining economy. While US defence spending in the same period accounted for only about 6 per cent of GNP, this represented, in real terms, an amount probably less than 10 per cent smaller than total Soviet defence spending.

Similarly, it has been suggested that one of the forces behind the outbreak of the 1991 Gulf War was the desire of the senior military and leading defence contractors in the USA to justify high levels of military investment by demonstrating the effectiveness of new technology such as the Stealth bomber and Cruise and Patriot missiles. On the other hand, it would be misleading always to characterize the military as warmongers. Following the humiliations of the Vietnam War, Colin Powell, President Bush's most senior military adviser, was amongst the most reluctant to support a military solution to the Gulf crisis, fearing the damage to the armed forces that would be caused by an operation that lacked clear and achievable political objectives. As Secretary of State under George W. Bush, Powell, together with leaders of the military, also argued that the 'war on terror' should be conducted against clearly defined and strategically specific targets in order to avoid drawing the USA into long-term involvements.

To some extent, the Russian military has played a greater role in Russian foreign policy and security policy since the collapse of communism in 1991. During the Soviet period, military interests, although always powerful, were generally constrained because of the leading role of the CPSU. However, a combination of political insecurity and strategic uncertainty in postcommunist Russia has created conditions that allow the armed forces greater influence and independence. The assault on the Russian parliament building by elite paratroops that ended the hardline rebellion in October 1993 merely emphasized that President Yeltsin had become, in a sense, a captive of the military. This was compounded by the electoral weakness of the reformers and Yeltsin's failure to gain support from a Duma (parliament) dominated by nationalists and communists. The Russian military, operating through the Defence Ministry, thus came to play a decisive role in shaping policy in relation to both the 'near abroad' and the 'far abroad'.

Although Russian military leaders were prepared to withdraw troops from the Baltic states, they succeeded in persuading Yeltsin to adopt a general policy of treating the borders of the Commonwealth of Independent States (CIS) as an extension of the Russian frontier. This led to a closer military association between Moscow and former Soviet republics such as Georgia and Tajikistan that border Islamic Central Asia. A shift in Russian policy towards the 'far' abroad was evident in 1995 in the adoption of a more assertively pro-Serbian stance in the Bosnian crisis, which effectively thwarted NATO moves to resolve the conflict through military pressure. The war in Chechnya, however, provided the clearest demonstration to date of the influence of the Russian military and its desire to maintain the integrity of the Russian Federation, following the abandonment of eastern Europe in 1989 and the breakaway of the non-Russian Soviet republics in 1991.

Alternative to civilian rule

Of course, the military is not always content to act as an interest group exerting pressure on and through civilian politicians. The control of weaponry and coercive power gives it the capacity to intervene directly in political life, leading in extreme cases to the establishment of military rule. Just as the military can prop up an unpopular government or regime, it can also remove and replace the governing elite or topple the regime itself. The precise circumstances in which armed forces seize power are examined later in this chapter; however, the form of rule they establish has a number of distinguishing characteristics. The defining feature of military rule is that members of the armed forces displace civilian politicians, meaning that the leading posts in government are filled on the basis of the person's position within the military chain of command.

One version of military rule is the military **junta**. Most commonly found in Latin America, the military junta is a form of collective military government centred on a command council of officers whose members usually represent the three services (the army, navy and air force). In its classic form, for example in Argentina in 1978–83, civilians are excluded from the governing elite, and trade union and broader political activity is banned. However, rivalry between the services and between leading figures usually ensures that formal positions of power change hands relatively frequently. In other cases a form of military dictatorship emerges as a single individual gains preeminence within the junta, as with Colonel Papadopoulos in Greece in 1974–80, General Pinochet in Chile after the 1973 coup, and General Abacha in Nigeria, 1993–98. In Africa especially, it has not been unknown for non-commissioned or junior officers to seize power. This occurred in Ghana in 1979, when power was seized by Flight Lieutenant Jerry Rawlings, and in Sergeant Samuel Doe's *coup d'état* in Liberia in 1980.

It is difficult, however, for military rule to exist in a stable and enduring political form. While military leaders may highlight the chronic weakness, intractable divisions and endemic corruption (see p. 389) of civilian government, it is unlikely that military rule will provide a solution to these problems or that it will be perceived as legitimate, except during temporary periods of national crisis or political emergency. This is why military regimes are typically characterized by the suspension of civil liberties and the suppression of all potential sources of popular involvement in politics. Protest and demonstrations are curtailed, opposition political parties and trade unions are banned, and the media are subjected to strict censorship. As a result, the military often prefers to rule behind the scenes and exercise power covertly through a civilianized leadership. This occurred in Zaire under Mobutu, who came to power in a military coup in 1965, but later allowed the army to withdraw progressively from active politics by ruling through the Popular Movement of the Revolution, founded in 1967. In the 1960s and 1970s, Egypt's transition from military government to authoritarian civilian rule was achieved under Gamal Nasser and Anwar Sadat, both military figures. The appointment of civilian cabinets and the

Junta: Literally, a council or board (Spanish); a group of military officers who hold political power.

emergence of parties and interest group politics not only strengthened the regime's legitimacy, but also gave Nasser and Sadat a greater measure of freedom from their own militaries.

Military regimes may come to a more dramatic end by collapsing or being overthrown when the authority of the armed forces is fatally compromised, usually by military defeat. This may also happen when military rulers are confronted by levels of popular opposition that can no longer be contained through repression (see p. 411) alone. Examples of the first situation include the fall of the Greek generals in 1974 following the Turkish seizure of northern Cyprus, and the collapse of the Argentine military junta in 1983, a year after its failure to win the Falklands (Malvinas) War. On the other hand, the overthrow in 1986 of the army-backed Marcos dictatorship in the Philippines resulted from a combination of internal pressures for democratic reform, articulated by Cory Aquino, and diplomatic pressure from the USA. However, once the military has had experience of direct intervention in politics, it may be reluctant to return to barracks permanently. This was demonstrated in the Philippines by three abortive coups in President Aquino's first 18 months in office.

Controlling the military

The undoubted power of the armed forces might suggest that the military is always a crucial, if not decisive, factor in politics. The reality is very different, however. Direct military intervention in politics, certainly when it is intended to displace civilian government, is in fact rare in many parts of the world, being largely confined to Latin America, Africa and parts of Asia. Both western liberal democracies and orthodox communist states have been comparatively free of military coups, attempted or successful. Since 1945 the only exceptions to this in western Europe have been in France in 1958 and 1961 (the first brought about the collapse of the Fourth Republic, and the latter was unsuccessful), in Portugal in 1974, when the army seized power to 'save the nation from government', and in Spain in 1981, when the army staged an abortive uprising. Exceptions in the communist world include the failed coup in China in 1971 associated with Lin Biao's leadership bid, General Jaruzelski's takeover in Poland in 1981, and the August 1991 hardline coup in Russia that briefly removed Gorbachev from power.

How is civilian control over the military achieved in other circumstances? The mechanisms and methods through which political control is exerted have been classified, broadly, into two types. Samuel Huntington (1957) described these as 'objective' and 'subjective' methods, while Eric Nordlinger (1977) used the terms 'liberal' and 'penetration'. The liberal, or objective, model of civil–military relations is best exemplified by western polyarchies. The chief feature of this form of control is that there is a clear division between political and military roles and responsibilities; quite simply, the military is kept out of politics. This is achieved in a number of ways.

First of all, the military is formally subordinate to civilian leaders, who are usually accountable to an assembly or the public. Second, policy-making, even in defence and military realms, is the responsibility of civilian politicians, the military being required merely to offer advice and to take charge of implementation. Although the military may be able to exert considerable policy influence in practice, it is only one interest group amongst many and is restricted by the recognition that it does not have the authority to *challenge* decisions made by civilian leaders. This, in turn, is underpinned by a third requirement: strict political neutrality within the armed forces, ensuring that they will remain loyal regardless of the party or government that is in power.

The USA offers a good example of the political subordination of the armed forces, although this is perhaps surprising in view of the role that military force played in the birth of the republic in the American War of Independence of 1775–83. This subordination was secured through the establishment of the US president as commander-in-chief of the armed forces, and the refusal of George Washington (first as the leader of the American troops fighting for independence, and later as the first president of the USA) to countenance military intervention in civilian affairs. This liberal pattern of civil–military relations later successfully withstood the pressures of the bloody American Civil War (1861–65), as well as the tests of the First World War and Second World War, despite the politically contentious nature of US involvement on both occasions. Even when the US president has been a former military leader and war hero, as in the case of President Eisenhower, 1953–61, the US armed forces have acknowledged the ascendancy of civilian politicians. However, civilian control does not mean that the military is politically impotent. While the US armed forces have never attempted to intervene directly in the political process, their routine interference as well-placed and influential lobbyists has had a significant impact on US defence and foreign policy.

A similar model of civil–military relations can be found in the UK. The UK armed forces are ultimately responsible to the Crown, which in practice means the prime minister and cabinet, via the Ministry of Defence. Not since the English Civil War of the seventeenth century and the rule of soldier–statesman Oliver Cromwell has the army exerted a direct influence on British political life. Indeed, in common with most other liberal democracies, the professionalism of the military in the UK is founded largely on its determination to keep out of politics. Only on very rare occasions has this self-restraint been tested. During the First World War, for instance, the soldier and administrator Lord Kitchener used his appointment as Secretary of State for War to instigate the raising of a vast volunteer army. Sir Douglas Haig, Commander-in-Chief of the British Expeditionary Force, had a crucial influence on the decision to use costly and exhausting trench-warfare tactics on the Western Front. He was able to exert this influence because the prime minister, H. H. Asquith, believed that it was the generals' job to run the war, and because King George V sometimes backed the military in its struggle against civilian politicians. No similar problems occurred under Churchill during the Second World War. Indeed, the general rule has been that developed western states with a history of constitutional stability and an entrenched democratic culture have experienced little difficulty in maintaining a liberal model of civil–military relations.

A very different form of civilian control has been employed in dictatorial or one-party states. Instead of relying on 'objective' mechanisms to establish the supremacy of civilian authority, the military is controlled by 'subjective' methods that bind it to the civilian leadership by imbuing it with the leadership's values and ideals. Whereas the liberal model operates through the exclusion of the armed forces from politics, the penetration model uses the opposite approach of systematic and thoroughgoing politicization. This has been achieved in various ways, and with differing degrees of success. Hitler attempted to turn the German army into 'political soldiers' through the personal oath of allegiance sworn to him as Führer in August 1934. At the same time he declared himself Head of the Armed Forces, and in 1941 he assumed the post of Supreme Commander. However, the army's loyalty was based more on the overlap between its authoritarian nationalism and the expansionist goals of the Hitler regime, than on its penetration by Nazi dogma. This was reflected in Hitler's growing reliance on the Waffen SS as a politically reliable elite army. Before committing suicide in April 1945, Hitler declared Admiral Dönitz the next Führer, because he believed that, of the various armed services, only the German navy had not abandoned him.

A substantially more brutal approach was adopted by Stalin in the USSR in the 1930s. Moves towards greater professionalisation in the Soviet armed forces, reflecting rising concern about the expansionist intentions of Nazi Germany, were abruptly ended in 1937 with the inauguration of a series of bloody purges. These led to the execution of three out of every five Soviet marshals and 13 out of 15 army commanders. In total, 90 per cent of all generals, 80 per cent of all colonels, and an estimated 30 000 officers of lower rank lost their posts, and often their lives. This effectively robbed the Red Army of its military expertise and threw it into almost total disarray, just at the time when it was being used to wage war against Finland, 1939–40, and was supposedly being prepared to defend the USSR against a possible German invasion.

In most instances, however, the penetration model entails not so much the culling of politically 'unreliable' members of the military as the promotion of politically 'correct' views and values through constant propaganda and agitation. For example, the Iraqi army, especially since Saddam Hussein assumed power in 1979, has been infused by the pan-Arab nationalism of the Ba'ath party. Ba'athism is committed to the unification of the Arab nation and to freeing it from western imperialism and **Zionism**. These goals provided an ideological justification for the invasion of Iran in 1980 and the annexation of Kuwait in 1990.

The institutional penetration of the armed forces has been developed in its highest form in communist states. In China, an elaborate network of party bodies parallels the structure of the military, offering leadership and guidance in areas of political and ideological significance. Civilian control is thus maintained through a level of interpenetration between the party and the armed forces that virtually obliterates any distinction between civil and military responsibilities. Party affiliation and a record of political commitment and loyalty to the communist regime are preconditions for the appointment and promotion of officers in the PLA. To the extent that the party operates in and through the military, however, the military also gains a voice in the policy process and is able to exert influence through an integrated party–state–military elite. In the USSR this approach sometimes allowed the senior military to play a decisive political role, as it did in 1957 in backing Khrushchev and helping him to foil an attempted coup by the so-called anti-party group, and again in 1964 when, in the aftermath of the Cuban Missile Crisis, it withdrew its support from Khrushchev, so contributing to his fall.

When does the military seize power?

Zionism: The movement for the establishment of a Jewish homeland, now linked to the defence of the interests and territorial integrity of Israel.

The most dramatic political manifestation of the power of the armed forces is, of course, the removal of a civilian government through a military *coup d'état*. The military can seize power either to displace the civilian leadership and establish a form of direct military rule, or to replace one set of civilian leaders by another through whom it is able to rule indirectly. In other cases, effective military government can be established without a formal bid for power on the part of the armed

Concept

Coup d'état

A *coup d'état* (from the French, a 'stroke of state') is a sudden and forcible seizure of government power through illegal and unconstitutional action. Coups are usually carried out by, or with the help of, the military; violence is often involved, although it may be limited and bloodless coups are not unheard of. *Coups d'état* differ from revolutions (see p. 224) in two respects. First, they are typically carried out by relatively small groups, usually from key institutions within the state (for example, the bureaucracy, the police or the armed forces), and thus do not involve mass political action. Second, they typically seek to replace the government or ruling group without necessarily changing the regime or bringing about broader social change.

forces, as occurred in the Philippines under President Marcos, especially after the declaration of martial law in 1972. In certain parts of the world, military intervention in politics has become a normal occurrence, and military regimes have achieved such a degree of stability that they can no longer be classified as exceptional or transitory phenomena. The military coup thus becomes the principal device for bringing about the transition of government power from one group of leaders to the next. This regularly happened in the nineteenth century in Latin America (particularly in Mexico, Peru and Chile), in Spain, and in the Balkan states. In the twentieth century, military intervention has been confined largely to developing states in Africa, Latin America and parts of Asia. Military coups appear to be associated with particular circumstances. The most significant of these are the following:

- economic backwardness
- loss of legitimacy by civilian rulers
- conflict between the military and the government
- a favourable international context.

There is a clear link between the incidence of military coups and economic underdevelopment. Pinkney (1990) pointed out that, of the 56 countries that have experienced military government since 1960, the vast majority are in the third world. Moreover, particular coups can be linked to economic downturns. The overthrow of four years of civilian rule in Nigeria in 1983, for example, occurred after a deterioration in the economy caused by falling oil prices. By the same token, growing prosperity appears to be an antidote to military intervention, as demonstrated by the tendency in Latin America since the 1970s for the military to return to the barracks. Widespread poverty and deep social inequality are clearly of significance in that they weaken support for the incumbent government and provide the military with a pretext for stepping in with a promise to deliver economic development. However, economic factors alone cannot explain military takeovers. India, for instance, suffers from serious levels of material deprivation, but its armed forces have maintained strict political neutrality and have never openly challenged the authority of civilian governments.

Part of the answer to the question why do military coups occur is surely that they occur because they *can* occur. In other words, the military is likely to intervene in politics only when it senses that the legitimacy (see p. 219) of existing institutions and the ruling elite is challenged, and when it calculates that its intervention is going to be successful. The armed forces thus rarely interfere directly in politics when a stable democratic culture has been successfully established. This is because military rule can only operate through a level of systematic repression, which, in turn, may be

Concept

Repression

Repression, in the political sense, is a state of subjugation brought about through systematic intimidation or open violence. Similar in kind to suppression, it differs in degree, being typically proactive rather than reactive (its aim is to 'root out' opposition rather than merely contain it). The purpose of repression is to uphold a regime or ruling elite by keeping the masses out of politics and depriving them of the means of expression. This is accomplished through both political and psychological means. Repressive regimes weaken or abolish the machinery of representative politics (elections, parties, trade unions, a free press and so on), and establish a climate of fear through routine surveillance and the exercise of force.

difficult to sustain because it strains the unity and discipline of the military itself. It is therefore not surprising that most of the successful military regimes have been established in parts of the world that have had a long history of colonial rule: Latin America, the Middle East, Africa and South East Asia. The political weakness and instability on which the military attempts to capitalize is certainly most acute in relatively new states. This not only stems from an unfamiliarity with democratic politics, but is also linked to the heightened expectations that independence brings, the poorly embedded nature of new political institutions and, sometimes, regional and ethnic tensions that have been inherited from the colonial past.

A good example is Nigeria, which has enjoyed only brief periods of civilian government since gaining independence from the UK in 1960. The colonial government had attempted to weaken and split the nationalist movement by politicizing national and ethnic divisions, particularly those between the Hausa in the north, the Yoruba in the west, and the Ibo in the east. This left Nigeria with a fractured and regionalized political elite and no ability to achieve the social consensus necessary for political stability. Growing civil disorder, a consequence of heightened ethnic tensions, led to an army takeover in 1966. However, intensified regional rivalry led to the outbreak of civil war the following year, as the eastern region, renamed Biafra, attempted to break away from the federal government. Rather than being the solution to Nigeria's problems, the military has merely perpetuated them. This is because the same ethnic, religious and regional conflicts that bedevil Nigerian society at large now permeate the military itself, and the army invariably exploits these conflicts in order to strengthen its hold on the country.

The third factor associated with military intervention is the degree to which the values, goals and interests of the armed forces differ from those of the broader regime. For example, despite widespread poverty and deep religious, linguistic and regional divisions, the Indian army has been prepared to leave politics to the politicians because of its engrained respect for the principles of liberal constitutionalism. When militaries move against governments, they do so either because they believe that their interests or values are threatened, or because they think that their actions are justified. In many newly independent developing states the military has taken over to 'save the nation', seeing itself as a 'westernizing' or 'modernizing' force confronting a traditionalist, rural, hierarchical and frequently divided political elite. This has occurred in Nigeria, Indonesia and Pakistan.

In other cases an authoritarian conservative military elite, often working in alliance with big business and enjoying support amongst the middle classes, has challenged the authority of reformist or socialist governments. The bloodless coup in Brazil in 1964 was largely a consequence of the army's suspicions about President Goulart's left-wing leanings. The Chilean president, Salvador Allende, the world's first democratically elected Marxist head of state, was overthrown and killed in 1973 by the army, which was led by General Pinochet. While the military is usually anxious to demonstrate that its intervention in politics is motivated by, for example, a desire to end corruption, heal divisions, or defend the nation, narrow selfish considerations are never entirely absent. Military coups are often an attempt to preserve the privileges, independence and prestige of the armed forces, or they may be a vehicle for the pursuit of political ambition.

Finally, the military's decision to seize power may also be affected by international considerations. There are few countries in which a military takeover does not have implications for neighbouring states, regional and international organizations, or the larger international community. In some cases, international pressures undoubtedly encourage military action. This was clearly the case with the Pinochet coup in Chile. The US Central Intelligence Agency (CIA) viewed Allende as a pro-Cuban communist whose economic reforms threatened the interests of US multinational corporations in Chile and elsewhere in Latin America. Not only did Pinochet receive covert advice and encouragement from the CIA, but he was also guaranteed US diplomatic support once his new military regime was established.

On other occasions, the prospect of an adverse diplomatic reaction has discouraged military plotters. In eastern Europe in 1989, for example, militaries remained largely passive as communist regimes collapsed in the face of mass demonstrations and popular pressure. In addition to a loss of political will on the part of communist leaderships, the armed forces recognized that military action would receive no support from President Gorbachev and the USSR, and that it would be fiercely condemned by the USA and the West. It would be wrong, however, to overstate the sensitivity of military regimes to diplomatic pressure. Saddam Hussein was little affected by international criticism of his military repression of the Kurds and the Shi'ite Moslems following the 1991 Gulf War. Similarly, General Abacha of Nigeria was unmoved by Commonwealth pressure in 1995 intended to prevent the execution of Ken Saro-Wiwa and other human rights protesters.

The police and politics

The police force, like the military, is part of the coercive state. However, whereas the principal function of the military is to uphold national defence, the central purpose of a police force is to maintain domestic order. Police forces came into existence in the nineteenth century, largely as a result of the higher levels of social unrest and political discontent that industrialization unleashed. For instance, in the UK, a paid, uniformed, full-time and specially trained police force was established by Robert Peel in London in 1829 following the Peterloo Massacre of 1819 in Manchester, when cavalry had been used to break up a large but peaceful working-class demonstration. This type of police system was introduced throughout the UK in 1856 and was later adopted by many other countries. Although police forces and militaries are similar in that they are both disciplined, uniformed, and (if to different degrees) armed bodies, important differences can be identified.

In the first place, whereas the military's essentially external orientation means that it is called into action only rarely, for example, in times of war, national emergency,

Concept

Order

The term order, in everyday language, refers to regular and tidy patterns, as when clothes are arranged in an 'orderly' fashion. As a political principle, order refers to stable and predictable forms of behaviour and, above all, to ones that safeguard personal security. *Disorder* therefore implies chaos and violence. Although order is universally valued, it has two very different political associations. Most commonly, it is linked with political authority and is thought to be achievable only if imposed 'from above' through a system of law. 'Law and order' thus become a single fused concept. The alternative view links order to equality and social justice, and emphasizes that stability and security may arise naturally 'from below', through cooperation and mutual respect.

Concept

Crime

A crime is a breach of criminal law, which is law that establishes the relationship between the state and the individual, and thus lays down the conditions for orderly and peaceful social interaction. Criminals (persons convicted of a crime) are usually seen as being motivated by self-gain of some kind, rather than broader political or moral considerations, as in the case of civil disobedience (see p. 307). Crime is often viewed as an indication of the general level of social disorder and personal insecurity. However, the causes of, and remedies for, crime are hotly contested. The general divide is between those who blame individual corruption and place their faith in punishment, and those who blame deprivation and thus look to reduce crime through social reform.

and national disaster, the police force's concern with domestic order means that it has a routine and everyday involvement in public life. The police force is also more closely integrated into society than is the military: its members and their families usually live in the communities in which they work, although, as discussed below, a distinctive police culture often develops. Furthermore, the police typically use nonmilitary tactics: because of their reliance on at least a measure of consent and legitimacy, they are either usually unarmed (as in the UK), or their arms are primarily a form of self-defence. To some extent, however, modern developments have tended to blur the distinction between the police and the military. Not only have armed forces been called in to deal with domestic disorder, as during the Los Angeles riots of 1992, but police forces have also tended to develop an increasingly paramilitary character. This is reflected in their access to progressively more sophisticated weaponry and, in many states, in their adoption of a quasi-military mode of operation.

Roles of the police

There are three contrasting approaches to the nature of policing and the role that it plays in society: the liberal, conservative and radical perspectives. The *liberal* perspective regards the police as an essentially neutral body, the purpose of which is to maintain domestic order through the protection of individual rights and liberties. In this view, police forces operate within a broad consensus and enjoy a high measure of legitimacy, based on the perception that policing promotes social stability and personal security. The police are essentially concerned with protecting citizens from each other. As policing is strictly concerned with upholding the rule of law (see p. 326), it has no broader political function.

The *conservative* perspective stresses the police's role in preserving the authority of the state and ensuring that its jurisdiction extends throughout the community. This view, which is rooted in a more pessimistic view of human nature, emphasizes the importance of the police as an enforcement agency capable of controlling social unrest and civil disorder. In this light, police forces are inevitably seen as mechanisms of political control.

The *radical* perspective advances a much more critical view of police power. This portrays police forces as tools of oppression that act in the interests of the state, rather than of the people, and serve elites rather than the masses. In the Marxist version of this theory the police are seen specifically as defenders of property and upholders of capitalist class interests.

The role of the police force is also shaped by the nature of the political system in which it operates and the ways in which the government uses the police. Civil policing tends to be distinguished from political policing, and divisions are usually identified between liberal states and so-called police states.

Civil policing

Civil policing refers to the role of the police in the enforcement of criminal law. This is the aspect of police work with which the general public is usually most familiar and which dominates the public image of the police force: the police force exists to 'fight crime'. This process increasingly has an international character, brought about by the advent of major transnational criminal organizations associated, in particular, with drug-trafficking and people-trafficking. However, the routine process of maintaining civil order is very different when undertaken in, say, rural India than in modern cities such as New York, Paris and St Petersburg. It is widely accepted that, while small and relatively homogeneous communities are characterized by a significant level of self-policing, this changes as societies become more fragmented (socially and culturally), and as large-scale organization depersonalizes relationships and interaction. The spread of industrialization in the twentieth century therefore brought about a measure of convergence in police organization and tactics in different parts of the world. Police forces everywhere tend to confront similar problems in the form of, for example, traffic infringements, car theft, burglary, street crime and organized crime.

However, various contrasting styles of civil policing have been adopted. On the one hand, there is the idea of community policing. This relies on a constant police presence within the community to ensure public cooperation and support in the investigation of crimes, and to encourage the development of values and attitudes that help to prevent law breaking in the first place. This system has traditionally been exemplified by the UK concept of policing – the 'bobby on the beat' – and has been particularly well developed in Japan. Japanese police officers are expected to know and visit the various families and workplaces that fall within their area of jurisdiction, operating either from police boxes (*koban*) or from residential police stations (*chuzaisho*). The success of this method, however, depends on the police being regarded as respected members of the local community and on citizens accepting that their lives will be closely monitored. Pressure for efficiency and cost cutting led to the phasing out of community policing in the UK in the 1960s and 1970s, although it was reintroduced in a limited fashion after the urban riots of the early 1980s.

On the other hand, there is what is called 'fire brigade' policing. This emphasizes the capacity of the police to react to breaches of law when they occur, in the hope that crime will be prevented by the effectiveness of the police response. Fire-brigade policing, or reactive policing, requires the adoption of harder, even paramilitary, tactics, and a greater emphasis on technology and arms. This type of approach has plainly been adopted in authoritarian and totalitarian states, but it is also found to some degree in liberal democracies. In an attempt to instil fear in potential offenders, the police in New York carry large-calibre revolvers and batons. Parisian police officers carry small-calibre semi-automatic pistols, batons and leaded capes, and the Cairo police carry submachine guns or automatic rifles.

Political policing

Policing can be 'political' in two senses. First, policing may be carried out in accordance with political biases or social prejudices that favour certain groups or interests over others. Second, policing may extend beyond civil matters and impact on specifically political disputes. The first concern has traditionally been raised by radicals and socialists, who dismiss the idea that police forces (or any other state body) act in a neutral and impartial fashion. From this perspective, the training and discipline of the police force and the nature of police work itself tend to breed a culture that is socially authoritarian and politically conservative. The working classes, strikers, protesters, women and racial minorities are therefore likely to be amongst the groups treated less sympathetically by the police.

Despite mechanisms of public accountability and protestations of impartiality, there is undoubtedly evidence to support these allegations, at least in particular circumstances. For instance, the US National Advisory Commission on Civil Disorders, set up by Lyndon Johnson to investigate the urban unrest that broke out in the USA during the 'long hot summer' of 1967, found that many of the disturbances were linked to the grievances of black ghetto dwellers about abusive or discriminatory police actions. The attack on Rodney King by four white Los Angeles police officers, whose acquittal in 1992 sparked two days of rioting, kept this image alive. Similarly, in the UK, the Macpherson Report (1999) into the murder of Stephen Lawrence concluded that the Metropolitan Police were guilty of **institutional racism**.

The level of political policing, meaning the use of the police as a political, rather than civil, instrument, has increased as societies have become more complex and fragmented. Some observers challenge the very distinction between civil and political areas of police work, arguing that all crime is 'political' in the sense that it springs from the distribution of wealth, power and other resources in society, all policing is 'political' because it defends the prevailing distribution of resources. The neutrality of the police force in the eyes of the public is particularly compromised when it is used to control strikes, demonstrations and civil unrest that stem from deep divisions in society. The threat of terrorism, especially since the events of 11 September, 2001, has drawn policing into some particularly difficult areas. Not only have many states strengthened national security legislation, and in the process extended the powers of the police, but in the USA, the UK and elsewhere policing strategies have been adapted so as to take better account of particular threats posed by terrorism. Most dramatically, this led to the killing by the Metropolitan Police of Jean de Menezes on the day after the 7 July 2005 terrorist attacks on London. Such incidents have led to the police bing criticized for being over-militarized and insensitive to the interests of minority ethnic (and usually Muslim) communities.

In many cases, specially trained paramilitary police units have been set up specifically to carry out politically sensitive operations. The classic example of this is the widely feared Compagnie Republicaine de Securité (CRS) in France, which is organized along military lines and whose members live in barracks. In the UK, the Special Patrol Group (SPG) was set up for similar purposes. In addition, virtually all states have intelligence or security agencies that are usually shrouded in secrecy. Their role is deeply political in that it includes the surveillance and sometimes destabilization

Fig. 19.1 The threat of terrorism means that paramilitary-style policing has become increasingly common in many states.

Institutional racism: A form of racism that operates through the culture or procedural rules of an organization, as distinct from personal prejudice.

of groups classified as a threat to the state or as opponents of the existing social system. These internal-security agencies include the Special Branch and MI5 in the UK, the FBI and the CIA in the USA, and the KGB in Russia.

Police states

The term 'police state' refers to a form of rule in which the liberal balance between police powers and civil liberties has been entirely abandoned, allowing a system of arbitrary and indiscriminate policing to develop. The police force therefore operates outside a legal framework and is accountable to neither the courts nor the general public. Police states have totalitarian features (see p. 29), in that the excessive and unregulated power that is vested in the police is designed to create a climate of fear and intimidation in which all aspects of social existence are brought under political control. However, a police state is not run by the police force in the same way as a military regime is controlled by the armed forces. Rather, the police force acts as a private army that is controlled by, and acts in the interests of, a ruling elite.

This was clearly the case in Nazi Germany, which spawned a vast apparatus of political intimidation and secret policing. The SA, or 'Brownshirts', operated as political bullies and street fighters, the Gestapo was a secret police force, the SD (Sicherheitsdienst) carried out intelligence and security operations, and the SS developed, under Himmler, into a state within a state. The USSR also relied heavily on the activities of the secret police. Lenin formed the Cheka in 1917 to undermine his political opponents, and this mutated into the OGPU (which was responsible for, amongst other things, forcible collectivization), then the NKVD (Stalin's personal instrument of terror), and eventually in 1953 the KGB. In addition to political policing, the KGB took control of frontier and general security and the forced-labour system. Other examples of communist secret police agencies were the Stasi in East Germany and the Securitate in Romania. Both of these operated tools of political repression, building up vast networks of civilian informers, infiltrating all areas of society, and, when required, 'neutralizing' opponents of the regime.

However, systems of security policing may operate alongside more 'orthodox' policing methods and machinery. For example, during the Nazi period in Germany, a conventional locally organized police force survived, albeit uncomfortably, and took responsibility for the more mundane and less political aspects of law enforcement. In the USSR the militia, which was separate from the KGB and ultimately responsible to the Ministry of Internal Affairs, was charged with the detection of crime, the apprehension of criminals, the supervision of the internal passport system, and the general maintenance of public order.

At the same time, some states usually classified as 'liberal' have also found a role for the secret police. The CIA in the USA has certainly engaged in a range of covert external operations, including the Pinochet coup in Chile, the attempted assassination of the Cuban leader Fidel Castro, and the supply of arms to the Contra rebels in El Salvador. It has also been subject to allegations of interference in domestic affairs, not least in the form of the still unsubstantiated claim that it played a role in the assassination of President Kennedy in 1962. Terroristic policing was used in Northern Ireland in the late 1960s in the form of the B-Specials. This was an auxiliary unit of the Royal Ulster Constabulary formed to control civilian demonstrations and fight the IRA. The B-Specials engaged in partisan and routine intimidation of the Catholic community and were disbanded in 1969, but only as the British army took on a more prominent role in policing 'the troubles'.

Political control and accountability

Accountability

Accountability means answerability: that is, a duty to explain one's conduct and be open to criticism by another. Accountability requires that the duties, powers and functions of bodies be defined in such a way that the performance of subordinate ones can be effectively monitored and evaluated. In this sense, accountability can operate only in a context of constitutionalism and respect for rules; being accountable does not mean being subject to arbitrary authority or capricious punishment. However, accountability may also amount to a weak form of responsibility (see p. 342), since it establishes a duty to answer and explain, but not necessarily to bear guilt and accept punishment.

The issue of the control of the police is often posed in terms of Aristotle's question '*quis custodiet ipsos custodes?*' ('who will guard the Guardians?'). The issue of political control is highly sensitive, and conjures up two contrasting images. In a positive sense, it suggests accountability, oversight and scrutiny, a police force constrained by and loyal to properly instituted authority. In a negative sense, however, it implies politicization and the possibility of police power being harnessed to the needs of the government of the day.

The key factor in determining where the balance lies between accountability and politicization in practice is whether the police force is organized on a centralized or decentralized basis. The attraction of decentralization is that a bottom-up structure allows the police a healthy independence from central government, whilst building in responsiveness to local needs and interests. This is why a decentralized, locally accountable police force is often considered to be the ideal. However, the pressures for centralization are considerable, even irresistible. Not only does centralization better meet the needs of national governments, it also holds out the prospect of greater administrative efficiency and increased political effectiveness.

Most continental European states have centrally controlled national police forces, the French police often being identified as the classic example of this model. France has two national police forces: the National Police, under the civilian control of the Ministry of the Interior, and the Gendarmerie, under the military control of the Ministry of Defence. Although the former is responsible for maintaining law and order in large towns and cities, and the latter is primarily responsible for policing rural areas, the jurisdiction of the two commonly overlaps, giving rise to a traditional 'police war'. Particular concern, however, has been expressed about the level of political control exercised over the National Police. Interior ministers are personally responsible for the appointment of senior officers; the prefects who head the forces in each of the 96 *départements* act simply as agents of the Ministry of the Interior, and police chiefs are allowed to exercise only limited operational autonomy.

These problems have been compounded by the relative weakness of the French Department of Justice, meaning that the accountability of the police to the judiciary has traditionally been weak. The National Police were therefore often seen as a mere instrument of government, insensitive to civil liberties and justice, with senior officers who were prepared publicly to express sympathy for right-wing parties such as the Rassemblement pour la République (RPR) and the Union pour la Démocratie Française (UDF). However, when a socialist government was formed in 1981 after the election of President Mitterrand, sweeping changes were made. These involved a shakeup of senior personnel, including the replacement of the Prefect of Police and the Director-General of the National Police, and the imposition of tighter restrictions on the power of the police to interfere with citizens' rights through practices such as unauthorized telephone tapping.

On the other hand, the experience in Scandinavian countries suggests that it is possible to combine a unified police service with a high level of public accountability. In Denmark the central government appoints the Commissioner of Police, a post that has broad strategic responsibilities, and the 72 local chief constables act as independent commanders of the personnel and resources placed at their disposal. In Sweden a nationally administered police force has existed since 1965, but a system of local police committees ensures that representatives of local government can review police budgets and discuss policy and operational issues with police chiefs.

Perhaps the most decentralized police system in the world is that in the USA. The multilayered US federal system results in no fewer than five major types of police agency. These include federal bodies attached to the Department of Justice (such as the FBI, the Bureau of Internal Revenue, and the Drug Enforcement Administration), the police forces of the 50 US states, sheriffs and deputy sheriffs at county level, city and township police forces, and, finally, a system of village and borough policing. The strength of this system is that it ensures that there is a high level of local responsiveness, the police being organized and operating according to the wishes of the communities they serve. The major drawbacks are that the system leads to considerable duplication and overlap amongst approximately 40 000 separate police agencies, and the balance between effective public accountability and unwarranted political interference is difficult to maintain.

In major US cities such as New York and Los Angeles political pressure on the operational decisions of police departments is almost unavoidable, in view of the fact that police commissioners, usually career police officers, are appointed by mayors for fixed terms, and are, in most circumstances, keen to be reappointed. In other cases, however, decentralized systems have been abandoned altogether. In both West Germany and Japan a shift towards decentralization in police organization was a major feature of democratic reconstruction after 1945. However, the resulting inefficiency and confusion soon led to a reversal of these policies. By 1950 West Germany had reestablished provincial (*Länder*) police forces, with national bodies, such as the Federal Criminal Police Bureau and the Frontier Police Force, being set up shortly afterwards. In Japan all the police forces were amalgamated into a single national service in 1954, responsible to the National Public Safety Commissioner, but it continues to be administered at the level of prefectural districts.

The UK is also usually considered to be an example of decentralized policing as it has never had a national police force. Apart from the Metropolitan Police in London, who are directly responsible to the Home Secretary, the police forces are locally organized and accountable, through their chief constables, to police committees that include magistrates and local councillors. However, this image of commendable decentralization is often not realized in practice. In the first place, the Home Secretary's powers extend well beyond responsibility for the Metropolitan police force and include all matters related to law enforcement. Through guidelines, directions and circulars, as well as legislation steered through Parliament, the Home Office exercises a continuing influence both on police authorities and on chief constables. In addition, there has been a trend towards increased centralization through the establishment of national data storage and retrieval systems, such as the National Police Computer, and the National Reporting Centre, used during the 1984–85 miners' strike to coordinate police operations across the country. Centralization was also fostered in the 1990s by the reduction of the influence of elected members of police authorities. Moreover, much politically sensitive policing is subject to little or inadequate democratic control. This is particularly true of MI5, whose remit was extended in 1996 to include intelligence related to crime and law enforcement as well as 'national security'. All MI5 operations are secret, its budget is not subject to parliamentary oversight, and alone amongst UK security agencies it is allowed to be 'self-tasking'. This means that, in theory, it can target who it likes, when it likes.

■ Summary

◆ The military is a political institution of a very particular kind. It is distinguished by its virtual monopoly of weaponry and substantial coercive power, its high level of internal discipline and strict hierarchical organization, a set of values and a culture separate from those of civilian society, and the perception that it embodies the national interest and so is 'above' politics.

◆ The central purpose of the military is to be an instrument of war that can be directed against other political societies. However, the military may also operate as a powerful interest group that influences defence and foreign policy in particular. In addition, it may help to maintain domestic order and stability when civilian mechanisms are unable or unwilling to act, and it may, in particular circumstances, displace civilian government with a form of military rule.

◆ Two contrasting mechanisms have been used to exert control over the military. Liberal, or 'objective', methods rely on keeping the military out of politics by ensuring that it is subordinate and accountable to civilian leaders. Penetration, or 'subjective', methods, on the other hand, attempt to bind the armed forces to the civilian leadership by imbuing them with the leadership's political values and ideological goals.

◆ Military coups have tended to be associated with particular circumstances. The most significant of these are economic backwardness (which weakens support for the incumbent government), a loss of legitimacy on the part of existing institutions and the ruling elite, a conflict of interests or political values between military and civilian leaderships, and an international context that favours, or at least tolerates, the advent of a military regime.

◆ The central role of the police is to enforce criminal law and maintain civil order. The police force may nevertheless have a political character if social or other biases operate within it, if it is deployed in the event of civil unrest or political disputes, and if there is a police state in which the police force is turned into a private army that serves only the interests of the ruling elite.

◆ The control of the police relies on an appropriate balance between accountability and politicization, which in turn depends on whether the police force is organized on a centralized or a decentralized basis. Decentralized police forces enjoy a healthy independence from central government and a high measure of local responsiveness. However, centralization better meets the needs of national governments, and also holds out the prospect of greater administrative efficiency and increased police effectiveness.

■ Questions for discussion

▶ If all states rest on coercive power, why do armed forces so rarely intervene directly in politics?

▶ When, if ever, is it justifiable to use the military as an instrument of domestic policy?

▶ Does the military–industrial complex pose a threat to the democratic process?

▶ Is it inevitable that the military will be wedded to right-wing or authoritarian values?

▶ Is all policing political?

▶ Is a decentralized police force always to be preferred to a centralized one?

Further reading

Brewer, J., A. Guelke, I. Hume, E. Moxon-Browne and R. Wilford, *The Police, Public Order and the State* (Basingstoke: Macmillan, 1988). A good comparative introduction to the role of the police in eight states.

Brooker, P., *Non-Democratic Regimes: Theory, Government and Politics* (Basingstoke and New York: Palgrave Macmillan, 2000). A comprehensive analysis of how military and party dictatorships emerge, operate and are sustained.

Holmes, J. S., *Terrorism and Democratic Stability* (Manchester: Manchester University Press, 2000). An examination of the effect of terrorism and state repression on democratic stability in Uruguay, Peru and Spain.

Nordlinger, E., *Soldiers in Politics: Military Coups and Governments* (Englewood Cliffs, NJ: Prentice Hall, 1977). An insightful introduction to the role of the military in politics and to means of achieving civilian control.

Pinkney, R., *Right-Wing Military Government* (London: Pinter, 1990). A useful study of military regimes in various parts of the world.

Policy and Performance

Policy Process and System Performance

'My policy is to have no policy.'

Remark made by ABRAHAM LINCOLN to his secretary (1861)

In a sense, policy is the aspect of politics that concerns most people. In crude terms, policy consists of the 'outputs' of the political process. It reflects the impact of government on society: that is, its ability to make things better or to make things worse. Indeed, during the 1960s and 1970s a distinctive area of study, policy analysis, was developed. This set out to examine how policy was initiated, formulated and implemented, and how the policy process could be improved. Policy analysis, however, is not concerned just with issues of efficiency and effectiveness, with the 'how' of policy-making. It also addresses the 'what' of policy-making: the nature of government 'outputs' and their 'outcomes' for the larger society. At the heart of policy analysis lie normative questions such as 'what is government *for*?' and 'what is the nature of the "good society"?'. Any attempt to evaluate the performance of government or the political system must therefore consider some of the deepest political and ideological divisions in the discipline itself.

The central issues examined in this chapter are as follows:

Key issues

▶ What is policy?

▶ How are decisions made? What theories have been developed to explain decision-making?

▶ What are the key stages in the policy process, and what is their significance?

▶ What are the desirable 'outcomes' of the policy process?

▶ How do particular states and political systems perform in relation to these 'outcomes'?

Policy

A policy, in a general sense, is a plan of action adopted by, for example, an individual, group, business or government. To designate something as a policy implies that a formal decision has been made, giving official sanction to a particular course of action. Public policy can therefore be seen as the formal or stated decisions of government bodies. However, policy is better understood as the linkage between intentions, actions and results. At the level of *intentions*, policy is reflected in the stance of government (what government says it will do). At the level of *actions*, policy is reflected in the behaviour of government (what government actually does). At the level of *results*, policy is reflected in the consequences of government action (the impact of government on the larger society).

◼ The policy process

The policy process relates to the mechanisms through which public (government) policy is made. Policy-making is a *process* in two senses. First, it involves a linked series of actions or events. These commence with the germination of ideas and the initiation of proposals, continue with some form of debate, analysis and evaluation, and conclude with the making of formal decisions and their implementation through designated actions. Policy-making is therefore similar to the process of digestion in the human body: it links certain 'inputs' to particular 'outputs'. Second, it is a process in the sense that it distinguishes the 'how' of government from the 'what' of government: that is, it focuses on the way in which policy is made (process), rather than on the substance of policy itself and its consequences (product). Ultimately, policy can be evaluated only in the light of its impact, according to 'what actually happens', for good or ill. The first section of this chapter considers how decisions are made, and examines the significance of the various stages in the policy process.

Theories of decision-making

The making of **decisions**, and specifically of bundles of decisions, is clearly central to the policy process. Although policy-making also relates to the acts of initiation and implementation, the making of decisions and reaching of conclusions is usually seen as its key feature. However, it may be difficult to establish how and why decisions are made. Decisions are undoubtedly made in different ways by individuals and by groups, within small bodies and within large organizations, and within democratic and authoritarian structures. Nevertheless, a number of general theories of political decision-making have been advanced. The most important of these are the following:

* rational actor models
* incremental models
* bureaucratic organization models
* belief system models.

Rational actor models

Decision-making models that emphasize human rationality have generally been constructed on the basis of economic theories that have themselves been derived from utilitarianism. Such ideas provide the basis for public-choice theories (see p. 300), developed by thinkers such as Anthony Downs (1957), and enthusiastically taken up by the New Right. At the heart of such theories lies the notion of so-called 'economic man', a model of human nature that stresses the self-interested pursuit of material satisfaction, calculated in terms of utility. In this light, decisions can be seen to be reached using the following procedures:

* The nature of the problem is identified.
* An objective or goal is selected on the basis of an ordering of individual preferences.
* The available means of achieving this objective are evaluated in terms of their effectiveness, reliability, costs and so on.
* A decision is made through the selection of the means most likely to secure the desired end.

Decision: An act of choice; a selection from a range of options.

This type of process assumes both that clear-cut objectives exist, and that human beings are able to pursue them in a rational and consistent manner. For this to occur, utility must be homogeneous: it must be possible to compare the amount of satisfaction (pleasure or happiness) that each action would bring with that which would result from any other action. The best example of such an approach to decision-making is found in the use of cost–benefit analysis in the making of business decisions.

The rational actor model is attractive, in part, because it reflects how most people believe decisions *should* be made. Certainly, politicians and others are strongly inclined to portray their actions as both goal-orientated and the product of careful thought and deliberation. When examined more closely, however, rational calculation may not appear to be a particularly convincing model of decision-making. In the first place, the model is more easily applied to individuals, who may have an ordered set of preferences, than it is to groups, within which there are likely to be a number of conflicting objectives. Organizations may therefore be said to make rational decisions only if they are highly centralized and possess a strict command structure.

A second problem is that, in practice, decisions are often made on the basis of inadequate and sometimes inaccurate information, and the benefits of various actions may in any case not be comparable. Is it possible, for instance, to compare the 'costs' of raising taxes with those of reducing healthcare provision? Such difficulties encouraged Herbert Simon (1983) to develop the notion of 'bounded rationality'. This acknowledges that, as it is impossible to analyse and select all possible courses of action, decision-making is essentially an act of compromising between differently valued and imprecisely calculated outcomes. Simon described this process as 'satisficing'. The final drawback of rational actor models is that they ignore the role of perception: that is, the degree to which actions are shaped by belief and assumptions about reality, rather than by reality itself. Little or no importance is thus attached to the values and ideological leanings of decision-makers.

Incremental models

Incrementalism is usually portrayed as the principal alternative to rational decision-making. David Braybrooke and Charles Lindblom (1963) termed this model 'disjointed incrementalism', neatly summed up by Lindblom (1959) as the 'science of muddling through'. This position holds that, in practice, decisions tend to be made on the basis of inadequate information and low levels of understanding, and this discourages decision-makers from pursuing bold and innovative courses of action. Policy-making is therefore a continuous, exploratory process: lacking overriding goals and clear-cut ends, policy-makers tend to operate within an existing pattern or framework, adjusting their position in the light of feedback in the form of information about the impact of earlier decisions. Indeed, incrementalism may suggest a strategy of avoidance or evasion, policy-makers being inclined to move away from problems, rather than trying to solve them.

Lindblom's case for incrementalism is normative as well as descriptive. In addition to providing a more accurate account of how decisions are made in the real world, he argued that this approach also has the merit of allowing for flexibility and the expression of divergent views. In this sense, it has a distinctly anti-utopian character and is well suited to policy-making in pluralist democracies: 'muddling through' at least implies responsiveness and flexibility, consultation and compromise. However, the model has also been criticized as profoundly conservative, in that it justifies a bias against innovation and in favour of inertia. Policy-makers

Concept

Utilitarianism

Utilitarianism is a moral philosophy that was developed by Jeremy Bentham (see p. 77) and James Mill (1773–1836). It claimed to propound a reliable, even scientific, ethical theory by equating 'good' with pleasure or happiness, and 'evil' with pain or unhappiness. Individuals are therefore assumed to act so as to maximize pleasure and minimize pain, these being calculated in terms of utility or use value, usually seen as satisfaction derived from material consumption. A principle of general or social utility can be used to evaluate laws, institutions and political systems in the form of 'the greatest happiness for the greatest number'. In political terms, utilitarianism has been linked to classical liberalism and free-market economics, providing, as it does, a theoretical and moral basis for egoistical individualism.

Incrementalism: The theory that decisions are made not in the light of clear-cut objectives, but through small adjustments dictated by changing circumstances.

who embrace incrementalism are more likely to be concerned with day-to-day problems than with indulging in long-term visionary thinking. Their energy is channelled into keeping the ship on course, not on reflecting on where that course is leading.

A further difficulty is that incrementalism sheds little light on those political decisions that are radical, even revolutionary, in character. For instance, Stalin's decision to launch the USSR's First Five Year Plan in 1928, Castro's decision to seize power in Cuba in 1959, and even Thatcher's decision to 'roll back the state' in the UK in the 1980s, can hardly be described as incremental adjustments. In view of such difficulties, Amitai Etzioni (1967) proposed the idea of 'mixed scanning', which attempts to bridge the gap between the rational approach and incrementalism. Mixed scanning allows for decision-making being carried out in two distinct phases. First, decision-makers broadly evaluate, or scan, all the available policy options in terms of their effectiveness in meeting pre-existing objectives. Then, a narrower and more incremental approach is adopted as the details of a selected policy option are reviewed. In this way, for example, a broad decision to cut public spending must be accompanied by a series of more narrowly focused decisions relating to the specific areas or programmes that may be affected.

Bureaucratic organization models

Both rational actor and incremental models are essentially 'black box' theories of decision-making; neither pays attention to the impact that the structure of the policy-making process has on the resulting decisions. Bureaucratic or organizational models, on the other hand, try to get inside the black box by highlighting the degree to which process influences product. This approach was pioneered by Graham Allison (1971) in his examination of US and USSR decision-making during the Cuban Missile Crisis of 1962. Two contrasting, but related, models emerged from this study. The first, usually called the 'organizational process' model, highlights the impact on decisions of the values, assumptions and regular patterns of behaviour that are found in any large organization. Rather than corresponding to rational analysis and objective evaluation, decisions are seen to reflect the entrenched culture of the government department or agency that makes them. The second theory, the 'bureaucratic politics' model, emphasizes the impact on decisions of bargaining between personnel and agencies each pursuing different perceived interests. This approach dismisses the idea of the state as a monolith united around a single view or a single interest, and suggests that decisions arise from an arena of contest in which the balance of advantage is constantly shifting.

Although these models undoubtedly draw attention to important aspects of decision-making, they also have their drawbacks. In the first place, the organizational process model allows little scope for political leadership (see p. 372) to be imposed from above. It would be foolish, for example, to suggest that all decisions are shaped by organizational pressures and perceptions, for this would be to ignore the personal role played by F. D. Roosevelt in initiating the New Deal, or Hitler's influence on Germany's decision to invade Poland. Second, it is simplistic to suggest, as the bureaucratic politics model does, that political actors simply hold views that are based on their own position and on the interests of the organizations in which they work. Although the aphorism 'where you stand depends on where you sit' may often be applicable, personal sympathies and individual goals cannot be altogether discounted. Finally, to explain decisions entirely in terms of black-box considerations is to fail to give any weight to the external pressures that emanate from the broader economic, political and ideological context.

Belief system models

Models of decision-making that place an emphasis on the role of beliefs and ideology (see p. 45) highlight the degree to which behaviour is structured by perception. What people see and understand is, to an extent, what their concepts and values allow them, or encourage them, to see and understand. This tendency is particularly entrenched because, in most cases, it is largely unconscious. Although decision-makers may believe that they are being rational, rigorous and strictly impartial, their social and political values may act as a powerful filter, defining for them what is thinkable, what is possible, and what is desirable. Certain information and particular options are therefore not appreciated or even considered, while other pieces of information and other courses of action feature prominently in the calculus of decision-making. Indeed, Kenneth Boulding (1956) underlined the vital importance of this process by pointing out that, without a mechanism to filter information, decision-makers would simply be overwhelmed by the sheer volume of data confronting them.

However, there are different views about the origin and nature of this filtering process. Robert Jervis (1968), for instance, drew attention to evidence of consistent misperception on the part of decision-makers in international affairs. In his view, this stemmed largely from ethnocentrism. The inclination of Anthony Eden and the UK government to view General Nasser as a 'second Hitler' during the 1956 Suez Crisis, and the tendency of the USA in 1959 to regard Fidel Castro as a Marxist revolutionary, may be examples of this phenomenon. Irving Janis (1972), on the other hand, suggested that many decisions in the field of international relations could be explained in terms of what he called 'groupthink'. This is the phenomenon in which psychological and professional pressures conspire to encourage a group of decision-makers to adopt a unified and coherent position, with contrary or inconvenient views being squeezed out of consideration.

An attempt to combine different approaches to decision-making that takes account of the impact of belief systems has been made by Paul Sabatier (1988). Sabatier's principal concern was to explain how policy changes occur. In particular, he drew attention to the role of 'policy subsystems': that is, collections of people who in some way contribute to influencing policy in a particular area. A policy system may include not only interlocking groups of politicians, civil servants and interest groups, but also researchers, academics and journalists concerned with that area. Sabatier maintained that, within these subsystems, 'advocacy coalitions' emerge that comprise collections of individuals who share broadly similar beliefs and values. These beliefs nevertheless operate on three different levels:

- deep core beliefs (fundamental moral or philosophical principles)
- near-core beliefs (policy preferences)
- secondary beliefs (views about implementation or application).

The importance of such beliefs is that they provide what Sabatier called the 'glue' of politics, binding people together on the basis of shared values and preferences. However, while core beliefs are highly resistant to change, a greater measure of disagreement and flexibility is usually found at the near-core and secondary levels. Using this framework, Sabatier proposed that policy change could be understood largely in

Concept

Ethnocentrism

Ethnocentrism has two related meanings. First, it refers to a personality type characterized by a rigid, implicitly authoritarian, belief in the superiority of his or her own group or people. Ethnocentrism in this sense overlaps with racism (see p. 120). Second, it refers to a mode of understanding in which the actions and intentions of other groups or peoples are understood through the application of values and theories drawn from the observer's own culture. In this sense, ethnocentrism is a (typically unconscious) bias that results from a failure to appreciate the significance of cultural differentiation. Ethnocentrism particularly bedevils comparative research, and perhaps makes it impossible to appreciate or understand other cultures fully, or to develop universal theories.

terms of the shifting balance of forces within a policy subsystem, in particular through the dominance of one advocacy coalition over others. This process may nevertheless be seen to be rational insofar as debate within a belief system, and rivalry between belief systems, promotes 'policy-orientated learning'.

In the hands of Marxists and feminists, however, such ideas can be used to draw very different conclusions (Hann, 1995). Marxists have argued that the core beliefs within any policy subsystem, or indeed amongst policy-makers and opinion formers at large, are structured by ruling-class ideology and so favour the interests of dominant economic interests. Feminists, for their part, may argue that a preponderance of men amongst policy-makers ensures that the 'glue' of politics is provided by patriarchal ideas and values. This results in policy biases that help to sustain a system of male power.

Stages in the policy process

Policy-making cannot be understood simply in terms of how decisions are made. Policy involves not only clusters of decisions, in the sense of a number of related decisions concerning a particular policy area, but also different *kinds* of decisions. For instance, in the first place, there is the 'decision to make a decision'. Such decisions arise from the perception that there are problems to solve and issues to address: in short, 'something must be done'. The policy process then moves on to a different set of decisions about exactly *what* should be done, *how* it should be done, and *when* it should be done. The matter does not stop there, however. Even when the 'doing' has been done and the decisions have been put into effect, other questions emerge and other decisions must be taken. These relate to whether policy outcomes match policy intentions, and whether the content of policy, as well as the process of decision-making, can be improved in the future. The policy process can thus be broken down into four distinct stages:

- policy initiation
- policy formulation
- policy implementation
- policy evaluation.

Initiation

Where does policy come from? How do policy proposals arise in the first place? Such questions are significant not only because policy must start somewhere (without initiation there can be no formulation, implementation, and so on), but also because this stage in the policy process structures all subsequent debate, discussion and decision-making. Policy initiation, then, is crucial in that it sets the political agenda both by defining certain problems as **issues** and by determining how those issues are to be addressed. Why, for example, did environmental protection, largely ignored up to that point, arise on the political agenda in the 1980s, and how did this occur? Also, why has unemployment, commonly understood in the 1950s and 1960s to imply a need to boost public spending, come to be linked with ideas such as labour flexibility and the weakening of trade union power? Why do other political options (for example, the extension of workers' self-management) fail to become issues at all?

The difficulty of studying policy initiation is that policy can originate in literally any part of the political system. Policy can stem 'from above' – that is, from political

Issue: A matter recognized as part of the policy agenda, over which there is public debate or disagreement.

leaders, cabinets, government agencies and so forth – and it can arise 'from below', through pressure from public opinion, the mass media (see p. 232), political parties (see p. 272), interest groups (see p. 296), 'think tanks' and the like. In the form of political leadership, policy initiation consists of mobilizing support for initiatives emanating from the personal vision of the leader or the ideological priorities of a ruling party or group. This is most clearly seen in cases of transformational leadership (exemplified by Lenin and the Bolsheviks in Russia, Hitler and the Nazis in Germany, and even Thatcher and the Conservatives in the UK), in which leaders set out to 'create a story' that has broad, popular resonance in order to carry through a major restructuring of society.

However, political leaders are rarely original thinkers and are seldom the source of genuine policy innovation. It is in this area that writers, academics and philosophers seemingly unconnected with the world of practical politics may play a vital role in the process of policy initiation by developing 'core' values and theories, later developed into specific policy proposals by leaders and parties. Much of the economic policy in developed western states during the early post-Second-World-War period emanated from the ideas of John Maynard Keynes (see p. 190). Similarly, New Right policies aimed at 'rolling back the state', reducing taxes, targeting welfare spending and so on, originally sprang from the writings of, for example, Friedrich von Hayek (see p. 52) and Milton Friedman (see p. 191).

Policy initiation 'from below' is significant in all political systems. As Harold Macmillan replied, when asked about the decisive factors in political life, 'Events, dear boy, events'. These events can range from strikes, riots and natural disasters to stock-market crashes in foreign states and investment decisions made by multinational corporations. As a general rule, however, the more democratic and pluralistic the political system, the more significant are bottom-up pressures on policy initiation. Indeed, democracy could be understood in this sense to imply that the political agenda is shaped 'from below' rather than 'from above'.

Public opinion clearly plays a significant role in this process insofar as regular and competitive elections force aspiring leaders to form policy proposals that take account of popular concerns and aspirations. However, these concerns and aspirations often remain shapeless and unformed until they are articulated by groups claiming to represent sections of the public. The mass media – newspapers, magazines, the radio and particularly television – undoubtedly make a major contribution to this process, both by selecting and prioritizing the information available to the public, and by digesting and interpreting it through the process of editorialization. Political corruption, for instance, became an issue in Italy and Japan largely through the publicity given to it by the print media.

Political parties and interest groups also play a key role in **agenda setting**. Opposition parties, for example, do not merely criticize government policy; they also develop alternative policies in an attempt to appear to be viable parties of government. Interest groups, for their part, highlight a broad array of grievances and concerns, promote causes and ideals, and give expression to the interests of diverse groups and sections of society. In the case of 'think tanks', interest groups have been formed specifically to develop policy proposals and to campaign for their acceptance amongst key players in the policy process.

Since the 1970s, researchers have tended to play down the role of formal, representative institutions, and to give greater prominence to the informal processes through which policy is initiated and developed. This highlights the importance of

Agenda setting: The ability to structure policy debate by controlling which issues are discussed or establishing a priority amongst them.

Concept

Policy network

A policy network (or policy community) is a systematic set of relationships between political actors who share a common interest or general orientation in a particular area. These relationships typically cut across formal institutional arrangements and the divide between government and nongovernmental bodies. A policy network may therefore embrace government officials, key legislators, well-placed lobbyists, sympathetic academics, leading journalists and others. The recognition of the existence of policy networks highlights the importance of informal processes and relationships in policy-making, and particularly in policy initiation. Policy networks have been criticized for being relatively impervious to external influence, and for reducing the impact of the public, via representative institutions, on the policy process.

policy networks: that is, communities of policy actors that crisscross the public and private sectors.

From a technical point of view – that is, taking account of the effectiveness of the policy process, not the quality of its outputs – policy initiation can suffer from two contrasting weaknesses. First, it can be stifled by a paucity of policy proposals and innovative ideas; in other words, there can be too few policy 'inputs'. This could be seen in the state socialist systems of the USSR and eastern Europe. In the absence of competitive elections, a free press, opposition parties and autonomous groups, policy initiation was left largely to networks of officials working within the party–state apparatus. The problem this caused was that, since those who initiated policy had a vested interest in maintaining the system of central planning, the issue of economic reform did not appear on the political agenda until the system itself was beyond salvation. The Gorbachev reforms in the late 1980s, for example, were simply 'too little, too late'.

The other weakness of policy initiation relates to the opposite problem. The policy process can, quite simply, be overwhelmed by the weight and diversity of policy 'inputs', bringing about stagnation and paralysis. This has been seen as the problem of government 'overload', a phenomenon associated with interventionist policies that heighten expectations of government. Expanding popular and interest group demands thus outstrip the capacity of government to respond. Samuel Beer (1982) termed this problem 'pluralistic stagnation'. As a consequence, in the 1980s and 1990s, New Right governments tried to reduce popular expectations of what the state can do, thus, to some extent, wresting back control of policy initiation.

Formulation

Once an issue, or set of issues, is on the political agenda, a process of detailed elaboration and analysis is required to develop systematic policy proposals. Conventionally seen as the most crucial stage in the policy process, policy formulation entails not only the translation of broad proposals into specific and detailed recommendations, but also the filtering out of proposals and perhaps even the fundamental recasting of the issue under consideration. In their analysis of the policy cycle, Hogwood and Gunn (1984) identified a number of stages in the formulation process, following the initiation of policy through to a 'decision to decide'. The first stage is the decision about how to decide: that is, a decision about which mechanisms or procedures and which political actors should be involved in the analysis and elaboration of policy. Should a particular policy be formulated by civil servants or by ministers? Should it be carried out through established processes, or should a special committee or commission be set up? Should interest groups and think tanks be consulted, and, if so, which ones? These decisions are clearly vital in that they determine the sympathies and interests that will be brought to bear on the policy as it is developed and discussed.

The second stage involves issue definition and forecasting. This stage allows considerable scope for reinterpretation, as those who formulate policy may view 'the problem' very differently from those who raised the issue in the first place. Third, there is the setting of objectives and priorities. Although public opinion and the concerns of bodies such as the media, political parties and interest groups are likely to influence objective setting, there is, of course, no guarantee that the priorities identified by priority formulators will be the same as those advanced by policy initiators.

Finally, there is the analysis and review of the policy options, leading to the selection of a preferred option. This, in effect, means that an authoritative decision is taken. Various factors are likely to be taken into account at this stage in policy formulation, the political and electoral ramifications of particular options being no less important than considerations of administrative efficiency and effectiveness. It is important to note, however, that the final decision, which brings the formulation process to an end, may be little more than a formality, decisive argument and debate having happened at a much earlier stage. Cabinets, legislatures and international summits thus often ratify or 'rubber stamp' decisions that have effectively been *made* elsewhere.

It would be foolish to imply that the task of formulation has the same character in different systems and different states. Richardson (1984) attempted to unravel different policy-formulation processes by identifying contrasting national 'policy styles'. In particular, he drew attention to two main dimensions: whether policy formulation is based on consultation or imposition, and whether governments engage in long-term planning or react to events on a more or less day-to-day basis. In this light, Sweden and Japan can perhaps be classified as states with policy styles that broadly favour both consultation and long-term planning. In both cases, there is an elaborate and formalized system of group consultation orientated around a widely agreed set of policy objectives and priorities. On the other hand, in the USA, although the fragmented nature of the federal government requires a high level of consensus for policy to be accepted, it also virtually rules out longer-term planning, and so entrenches a reactive, 'fire brigade' policy style.

The UK provides an example of how a policy style can shift over time. The style identified by Richardson highlighted both a British predilection for consultation, and a tendency to react to problems, rather than anticipate them. However, under Margaret Thatcher in the 1980s, a much clearer set of long-term policy goals was outlined in the form of a commitment to what Andrew Gamble (1988) described as 'the free economy and the strong state'. The pursuit of these goals was, in turn, accompanied by a shift from consultation to imposition, reflected in developments such as the growth of prime-ministerial power. However, John Major (1990–97) adopted a more collegiate and consensual leadership style in which cabinet consultation became once again a meaningful exercise. Tony Blair, on the other hand, reasserted centralized leadership by relying on special advisors and bilateral meetings with ministers rather than allowing the cabinet to play a major policy role.

A key feature of formulation, regardless of differences in national policy styles, is that it substantially reduces the range of actors involved in the policy process. While a broad variety of interests, groups and movements may play a role in policy initiation, policy formulation is the job of 'insiders' (government officials, key advisers, politicians and consulted groups), those who are either part of the machinery of government or have institutionalized access to it. This has left the formulation process open to a number of criticisms. One of these arises from the undue influence that civil servants supposedly exert by virtue of their role as policy advisers. Politicians, at best, set broad policy priorities and leave specific objectives and the review of policy options largely in the hands of government officials. Public choice theorists have argued that policy therefore tends to reflect the career interests of professional civil servants, while Marxists have pointed out that radical policy alternatives tend to be discounted because of the social and educational backgrounds of senior public officials.

Other criticisms relate to the growth in the level of consultation and thus in the number of groups and actors involved in policy formulation. New Right theorists in particular have argued that the drift towards corporatism has allowed policy to be shaped by powerful sectional interests rather than by the broader public good (Olson, 1982). From this perspective, corporatism can be seen to be a breach in the divide between initiation and formulation that allows groups that should be merely setting the political agenda to shape instead the content of government policy. A final set of criticisms are based on the general 'democratic deficit' in policy formulation. In democratic systems, although elected politicians oversee the policy process and make the final decisions, the process itself often guarantees that their contribution is marginal. Because it is time-consuming and exacting, policy formulation requires professionalism, specialist knowledge and a concern for detail, qualities that politicians, democratic or otherwise, rarely possess in abundance.

Implementation

One of the major advances made in the discipline of policy analysis has been to underline the importance of the implementation stage. Traditionally, implementation was taken for granted, being seen as an aspect of administration (see p. 387), not as a feature of politics. Analyses of the Great Society programme in the USA in the mid-1960s, however, destroyed illusions about the politics–administration divide, and graphically illustrated how far policy 'outputs' may differ from the intentions of policy-makers. For this reason, Wildavsky (1980) described policy analysis as 'speaking truth to power'. The conditions required to achieve 'perfect' implementation, in the sense of ensuring that policy is delivered exactly as intended, were outlined by Hood (1976) as follows:

- a unitary administrative system with a single line of authority to ensure central control
- uniform norms and rules that operate throughout the system
- perfect obedience or perfect control
- perfect information, perfect communication and perfect coordination
- sufficient time for administrative resources to be mobilized.

In view of the difficulty of achieving any of these conditions, let alone all of them, it is not surprising that the gap between decision and delivery is often a gulf. Indeed, not only may central control and strict obedience be unfeasible, they may also be undesirable. Although those who make policy may enjoy democratic legitimacy, those who implement it (civil servants, local government officers, teachers, doctors, police officers and so on) may have a better 'street level' understanding of what will work and what will not work. Such considerations have led to a 'bottom-up' tradition of policy analysis that stresses the need for flexibility as well as the value of leaving discretion in the hands of policy executors. This contrasts with the more conventional 'top-down' view of implementation that emphasizes uniformity and control. Most commentators, however, now recognize the tradeoff between central control and flexibility in application as the major dilemma in the area of policy implementation (Barrett and Fudge, 1981).

Although perfect implementation may be neither possible nor desirable, most of the concerns expressed about policy implementation have focused on the dangers of flexibility in application. This was underlined by Pressman and Wildavsky's (1973) pioneering study of implementation, subtitled *How Great Expectations in Washington Are Dashed in Oakland Or Why It's Amazing That Federal Programs Work At All....* Flexibility may arise for a number of reasons. One of these is that those who execute policy may not merely be anxious to use their experience and 'street-level' knowledge to ensure that implementation is effective, they may also, as public choice theorists point out, wish to protect their career and professional interests. Civil servants and public-sector professionals will then have an obvious incentive to filter out or reinterpret aspects of public policy that seem to be threatening or inconvenient.

Other concerns about policy implementation arise less from the inadequacy of political control from above and more from the absence of consumer pressure from below. From this perspective, poor implementation, especially in the delivery of public services, results from the fact that government typically operates outside the market mechanism and is usually a monopoly supplier of its 'goods'. Civil servants, local government officers and public-sector workers can in general afford to be sloppy and inefficient because, unlike in private businesses, they do not have to keep the customer satisfied.

An important response to this has been the emergence of the new public management (see p. 391). This allows private bodies to take greater responsibility for the delivery of service through privatization, 'contracting out' and 'market testing'. It has also led to the wider use of performance indicators that bind public services to a set of 'delivery standards' that effectively mimic market competition by penalizing substandard performance. These ideas have been taken up most enthusiastically in New Zealand, the UK and the USA, and in Scandinavia. While some argue that they have promoted efficiency and effectiveness, others warn that accountability and the public service ethos have been sacrificed to an overriding concern with cost cutting and lowering taxes.

Evaluation

The policy process culminates with the evaluation and review of policy, leading, in theory at least, to decisions being made about the maintenance, succession or termination of the policy in question. This stage completes the policy cycle in the sense that information acquired through evaluation can be fed back into the initiation and formulation stages. This process can throw up new policy proposals and help to refine and improve existing ones (see Figure 20.1).

As well as addressing substantive issues related to the appropriateness or effectiveness of public policy, evaluation may also shed light on procedural issues, such as how the formulation stage is organized, who is consulted and when, and how implementation is controlled. However, unfortunately, despite its manifest importance, governments have usually been reluctant to allocate funds for policy evaluation. In the USA in the late 1970s, President Carter's insistence that 1 per cent of the funds for any project should be devoted to evaluation may have been a bold innovation, but it generated an enormous amount of paperwork without bringing about a noticeable improvement in either the policy process or its products. The only states that take policy evaluation seriously are the few, usually consensual, democracies that are geared to long-term planning.

Academics have taken more interest in evaluation through policy output studies, widely undertaken, especially in the USA, since the late 1960s. Empirical

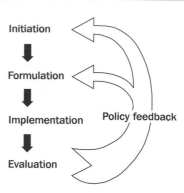

Fig. 20.1 Policy-feedback process

research is used to examine both what government does, in terms of laws, taxes, programmes and so on (outputs), and the consequences or impact of such policies (outcomes). As Dye (1995) put it, this form of policy analysis is concerned with 'who gets what'.

What is clear is that the outcomes of the policy process are often very different from what was intended by those who formulated or made policy decisions. There are many examples of this. Welfare policies designed to alleviate poverty and enable all citizens to participate in the life of the community have led, according to Le Grand (1982), to the cushioning of the middle classes, or, in the view of Murray (1984), to the growth of a welfare-dependent underclass. In their case study of the poll tax in the UK, Butler, Adonis and Travers (1994) highlighted a catalogue of

Focus on . . .

Open government: for and against

Open government is the principle that what happens in government should be open to public scrutiny and criticism on the basis of a free flow of information from public bodies to representative institutions, the mass media and the general public. As it is universally accepted that some information should be kept secret (on the grounds of national security, privacy and so on), open government is normally understood to imply a bias in favour of the public's 'right to know'. This is usually enshrined in a freedom of information act that forces the government to defend secrecy before the courts.

The advantages of open government include the following:

- It places a check on incompetence, corruption and tyranny.
- It promotes political argument and debate, and results in improved policy outcomes and a better-informed electorate.

Its drawbacks include the following:

- It hampers the efficiency of policy-making by exposing the formulation process to the glare of publicity.
- It discourages the consideration of unpopular, but nevertheless important, ideas and proposals.

failures and oversights in government, the cabinet and Parliament that allowed a policy primarily designed to control local government spending to result in widespread civil unrest. This contributed to the downfall of Margaret Thatcher and the swift reversal of the policy under her successor, John Major. Similarly, in the USA, the Bush administration's decision to invade Iraq in 2003 as part of the 'war on terror' led to an ongoing counter-insurgency war and, in some respects, strengthened militant Islam. For many, such policy failures highlight the pressing importance of open government and public accountability (see p. 418). For the policy process to work effectively in translating inputs into appropriate outputs, it must be open, at all times, to scrutiny and criticism. All too frequently, a culture of secrecy merely conceals incompetence and provides scope for arbitrary and self-serving behaviour.

System performance

The policy process has been analysed above in largely 'managerial' terms. How are decisions made? What stages are there in the policy process? How effective, efficient and economical (the 'three Es') is policy-making? However, a series of deeper 'political' issues underlie these questions. These are not so much concerned with what government *does* as with what government *should* do: that is, with what government is 'for'. The problem is that this uncovers those intractable normative questions that lie at the heart of politics. It is impossible to know what government is for without understanding such issues as the nature of justice and the desirable balance between freedom and authority – without, in other words, having a vision of the 'good society'.

Since views about such matters differ fundamentally, the standards against which governments and political systems can be judged also vary. Four widely held such standards can nevertheless be identified, each shedding a very particular light on system performance. These performance criteria are as follows:

- stability and order
- material prosperity
- citizenship
- democratic rule.

Stability performance

It can reasonably be claimed that the maintenance of stability and order (see p. 413) is the most basic function of government. With the exception of anarchists, who argue that social order will emerge from the spontaneous actions of free individuals, all political thinkers and philosophers have endorsed government as the only means of keeping chaos and instability at bay. In Thomas Hobbes's (see p. 327) words, in the absence of government, life would be 'solitary, poor, nasty, brutish and short'. From this perspective, the core purpose of government is to govern, to rule, to ensure stability through the exercise of authority. This, in turn, requires that government is able to perpetuate its own existence and ensure the survival of the broader political system. System performance can thus be judged on the basis of criteria such

◢ **Concept**

Relativism

Relativism is a position that denies the existence of objective or 'absolute' standards, and so holds that statements can be judged only in relation to their contexts. *Moral* relativism rejects the notion that there are, or can be, authoritative ethical principles, usually on the grounds that the individual is a morally autonomous being. *Cognitive*, or epistemological, relativism holds that different modes of knowing are equally valid, and thus dismisses the universalist pretensions of, say, science (see p. 16). Relativism has been criticized both for weakening the moral cement of society (creating a 'pathless desert'), and for being intellectually self-defeating (the denial of objective standards is itself relative). Relativism contrasts starkly with all forms of fundamentalism (see p. 66).

as longevity and endurance, as the simple fact of survival indicates a regime's ability to contain or reconcile conflict. However, there are differing views about how this goal can best be achieved.

These views fall into two broad categories. The first stems from the essentially liberal belief that stable government must be rooted in consensus and consent. In this view, what ensures the long-term survival of a regime is its responsiveness to popular demands and pressures. This is expressed in the language of systems theory as the ability to bring the 'outputs' of government into line with the various 'inputs'. This has often been identified as a particular strength of western liberal democracies. Advocates of liberal democracy (see p. 30) stress that, as it is based on consent, it embodies mechanisms that ensure that it is responsive, and so guarantees a high degree of systemic equilibrium. Government power is won through a competitive struggle for the popular vote, and can be lost when that support diminishes. A vigorous civil society allows citizens to exert influence through autonomous groups and associations.

To some extent, it has been the ability of liberal democracy to generate political stability that explains the wider adoption in the postcommunist and developing worlds of liberal-democratic practices such as electoral democracy and party competition. Nevertheless, liberal democracy also has its drawbacks in this respect. Chief amongst these is that responsiveness may generate instability, insofar as it heightens popular expectations of government and fosters the illusion that the political system can meet all demands and accommodate all 'inputs'. From this perspective, the central dilemma of stable government is that responsiveness must be balanced against effectiveness. Government must be sensitive to external pressures, but it must also be able to impose its will on society when those pressures threaten to generate irreconcilable conflict.

This latter fear underpins the alternative view of stability and order. Conservative thinkers have traditionally linked stability and order not to responsiveness but to authority. Thomas Hobbes presented this idea as a stark choice between absolutism and anarchy, between the acceptance of an unquestionable and sovereign power and a descent into the chaos and disorder of the state of nature. However, conservatives have been particularly concerned to stress the degree to which political authority is underpinned by shared values and a common culture. In this view, stability and order are largely the product of social and cultural cohesion, the capacity of society to generate respect for authority and maintain support for established institutions.

This position is clearly reflected in neoconservative fears about permissiveness and moral and cultural relativism, leading to calls for the restoration of 'traditional', 'family' or 'Christian' values. It is also possible, from this perspective, to suggest that East Asian states that subscribe to some form of Confucianism (see p. 36), as well as Islamic states, have a greater capacity to maintain political stability than do western liberal-democratic regimes. However, the weakness of this view of stability is that, since it relies on authority being exerted from above, it may not place effective constraints on the exercise of government power. If stability is seen as an end in itself, divorced from considerations such as democratic legitimacy, social justice and respect for human rights, the result may simply be tyranny and oppression. Saddam Hussein, after all, was able to perpetuate the existence of his Iraqi regime, despite economic sanctions, military attacks and opposition from Shi'ite Moslems and Kurds, largely through systematic terror and brutal repression.

Focus on . . .

The welfare debate

The most general meaning of the term welfare is happiness, prosperity and well-being: welfare implies not mere physical survival, but some measure of health and contentment as well. As a political principle, however, welfare has come to be associated with a particular means of achieving general well-being: collectively provided welfare, delivered by government through the mechanism of a so-called welfare state.

Supporters of welfare argue that its benefits include the following:

- It promotes national efficiency by creating a healthier and better educated workforce.
- It encourages personal development by safeguarding individuals from social deprivation.
- It fosters social cohesion by guaranteeing everyone a stake in society.

Critics of welfare have nevertheless opposed it for the following reasons:

- It breeds dependence by reducing the fear of poverty and thus the incentive to work.
- It undermines economic growth by adding to the tax burden.
- It ameliorates hardship and poverty without dealing with structural disadvantage and inequality.

Material performance

The idea that political systems can and should be judged by their material performance is a familiar one. Electoral politics, for example, is invariably dominated by economic issues and the so-called 'feel good' factor. Governments are usually reelected in periods of growth and widening prosperity, and defeated during recessions and economic crises. Similarly, there can be little doubt that the success of the broader political system is linked to its capacity to 'deliver the goods'. Widespread poverty and low levels of economic growth in developing states have deepened social and ethnic tensions, fuelled corruption, and undermined attempts to establish constitutional and representative government. The collapse of the state socialist regimes of eastern Europe and the USSR was also linked to the failure of central planning and, in particular, to its inability to deliver the levels of material prosperity and range of consumer goods that were available in the capitalist West. Moreover, it is no coincidence that advanced industrialized states have enjoyed both the greatest levels of political stability and the highest living standards in the world: hence their classification as first-world regimes.

Considerable debate has taken place about the most reliable means of generating wealth and achieving material prosperity. In some senses, this debate reflects the traditional ideological divide between capitalism and socialism; the former places its faith in the market (see p. 185) and competition, and the latter relies on nationalization and planning (see p. 192). However, the eastern European revolutions of 1989–91 dramatically changed the terms of this debate by (apparently) undermining the validity of any form of socialism qualitatively distinct from market capitalism. In

Concept

Equality

Equality is the principle of uniform apportionment, but does not imply identity, or sameness. The term equality has differing implications, depending on what is being apportioned. *Formal* equality means the equal distribution of legal and political rights, and is usually based on the assumption that human beings are 'born' equal. Equality of *opportunity* means that everyone has the same starting-point, or equal life chances, but may justify social inequality because talent and the capacity for hard work are unequally distributed. Equality of *outcome* (the most controversial manifestation of equality) means that there is an equal distribution of income, wealth and other social goods. Its supporters argue that it promotes justice and community (see p. 178); its detractors view it as 'levelling downwards' and a form of social engineering.

other words, even socialists came to accept that the market, or at least some form of market competition, is the only reliable mechanism for generating wealth. The 'capitalism or socialism?' debate has therefore developed into a 'what kind of capitalism?' debate. This issue is not merely about how wealth can be *generated*, but also about how it is *distributed*: that is, who gets what. This is closely linked to the balance between the market and the state, and the degree to which government can, and should, modify market outcomes through a system of welfare (see p. 439) and redistribution.

The central dilemma that arises from the use of material prosperity as a performance indicator is that growth must be balanced against fairness. This is the difficulty of being concerned both about the size of the cake and about how the cake is cut. Two contrasting views of this problem can be identified. The free-market view, advanced by theorists such as Hayek and Friedman, holds that general prosperity is best achieved by a system of unregulated capitalism. This is what Titmuss (1968) referred to as the 'industrial–achievement' performance model. From this perspective, economic growth is best promoted by material incentives that encourage enterprise and endeavour and penalize laziness. The welfare state should therefore act only as a safety net that protects individuals from absolute poverty in the sense that they lack the basic means of subsistence. Although this system is likely to increase social inequality, the theory holds that it benefits even the less well-off, who receive a smaller proportion of a much larger cake, so ending up better off. Free-market economists refer to this theory as the 'trickle down' effect. Such policy priorities have guided New Right governments since the 1970s in their attempts to break away from the 'fiscal crisis of the welfare state'. In this view, burgeoning social budgets led to a growing tax burden that, in turn, merely hampered the process of wealth generation.

The rival social-democratic view, which Titmuss called the 'institutional–redistributive' model, highlights the moral and economic benefits of equality. Not only is unregulated competition condemned for promoting greed and conflict, it is also seen as inefficient and unproductive. The virtue of social justice is that, by taking the distribution of wealth away from the vagaries of the market, it ensures that all citizens have a stake in society and that each of them has an incentive to contribute. In tolerating wide social inequality, free-market policies thus run the risk of promoting social exclusion, reflected in the growth of an underclass that is a breeding ground for crime and social unrest. Long-term and sustainable prosperity therefore requires that material incentives operate within a broader framework of fair distribution and effective welfare.

Citizenship performance

The idea that citizenship is the proper end of government can be traced back to the political thought of Ancient Greece. For instance, in 431 BCE, in his famous funeral oration, Pericles stated that:

An Athenian citizen does not neglect the state because he takes care of his own household; and even those of us who are engaged in business have a very fair idea of politics. We alone regard a man who takes no interest in public affairs, not as harmless, but as a useless character; and if few of us are originators, we are all sound judges of policy.

A citizen is a member of a political community or state, endowed with a set of rights and a set of obligations. Citizenship is therefore the 'public' face of individual existence. People are able to participate in the life of their communities to the extent that they possess entitlements and responsibilities. Civil participation is, in turn, linked to the advance of constitutional government, as reflected in the extension of political rights and civil liberties (see p. 407).

In his classic contribution to the study of citizenship rights, T. H. Marshall (1950) distinguished between three 'bundles of rights': civil rights, political rights and social rights. Civil rights were defined by Marshall as 'rights necessary for individual freedom'. These include freedom of speech, freedom of assembly, freedom of movement, freedom of conscience, the right to equality before the law, and the right to own property. Civil rights are therefore rights that are exercised within civil society; they are 'negative' rights in the sense that they limit or check the exercise of government power. Political rights provide the individual with the opportunity to participate in political life. The central political rights are thus the right to vote, the right to stand for election, and the right to hold public office. The provision of political rights clearly requires the development of universal suffrage, political equality (see p. 73), and democratic government. Finally, and most controversially, Marshall argued that citizenship implied social rights that guarantee the individual a minimum social status and therefore provide the basis for the exercise of both civil and political rights. Marshall defined these 'positive' rights, rather vaguely, as the right 'to live the life of a civilized being according to the standards prevailing in society'.

As the concept of citizenship is usually seen as a distinctively western invention, it is perhaps not surprising that liberal democracies perform particularly well in this respect. Civil and political rights clearly imply the form of constitutional and representative government commonly found in the industrialized West. The idea of social rights, however, has stimulated significant divisions, because it implies a level of welfare provision and redistribution that classical liberals and the New Right have regarded as both unjustifiable and economically damaging. Marxists and feminists have also criticized the idea of citizenship, the former on the grounds that it ignores unequal class power, and the latter because it takes no account of patriarchal oppression.

A major dilemma nevertheless confronts those who employ citizenship as a performance criterion: the need to balance rights against duties and thereby to apportion responsibilities between the individual and the community. Since the early 1980s, this issue has been taken up in the growing debate between liberalism and communitarianism. Communitarian theorists such as Alisdair MacIntyre (1981) and Michael Sandel (1982) have dismissed the idea of an unencumbered self, arguing that the 'politics of rights' should be replaced by a 'politics of the common good'. In this view, liberal individualism, in effect, eats itself. By investing individuals with rights and entitlements, it simply breeds atomism and alienation, weakening the communal bonds that hold society together. From this perspective, nonwestern societies that may appear to perform poorly in relation to citizenship indicators (with, for example, poor records on human rights) may nevertheless succeed in creating a stronger sense of community and social belonging.

Democracy performance

Whereas stability, material prosperity and citizenship are all outcomes or products of government, democracy is concerned essentially with the process itself, with *how* decisions are made, rather than with *what* decisions are made. Democracy means

Concept

Citizenship

Citizenship is a relationship between the individual and the state in which the two are bound together by reciprocal rights and duties. Citizens differ from subjects and aliens in that they are full members of their political community or state by virtue of their possession of basic rights. Citizenship is viewed differently depending on whether it is shaped by individualism (see p. 196) or communitarianism (see p. 179). The former, linked to liberalism, advances the principle of a 'citizenship of rights', and places particular stress on private entitlement and the status of the individual as an autonomous actor. There are socialist and conservative versions of communitarianism, but each advances the principle of a 'citizenship of duty'; they also highlight the role of the state as a moral agency and the importance of community or social existence.

Concept

Autonomy

The term autonomy (from the Greek, meaning 'law to oneself') literally means self-rule. States, institutions or groups can be said to be autonomous if they enjoy a substantial degree of independence, although autonomy in this connection is sometimes taken to imply a high measure of self-government, rather than sovereign independence. Applied to the individual, autonomy is closely linked with freedom (see p. 324). However, since it suggests not merely being 'left alone' but being rationally self-willed, autonomy is classified as a form of positive freedom. By responding to inner or 'genuine' drives, the autonomous individual is seen to achieve authenticity. Autonomy is often linked with democracy, but may nevertheless also limit the jurisdiction of democracy, as it emphasizes individuality rather than collective or majority rule.

popular rule – in crude terms, the widest possible dispersal of political power and influence. From the democratic perspective, the purpose of politics is to empower the individual and enlarge the scope of personal autonomy. Autonomy has been seen as both an end in itself and a means to an end. Classical theorists of democracy, such as J.-J. Rousseau (see p. 79) and J. S. Mill (see p. 48), portrayed political participation as a source of personal development and self-realization. Democracy is thus the stuff of freedom, or, as Rousseau put it, freedom means 'being one's own master'.

Taken to its logical extreme, the idea of popular self-government implies the abolition of the distinction between the state and civil society through the establishment of some form of direct democracy (see p. 74). For example, Athenian democracy, described in Chapter 4, amounted to a form of government by mass meeting, in which citizens were encouraged to participate directly and continuously in the life of their *polis*, or city-state. Modern notions of democracy, however, have shifted away from this utopian vision, and instead embrace democracy more as a means to an end. The more familiar machinery of representative democracy (see p. 74) – universal suffrage, the secret ballot, and competitive elections – has tended to be defended on the grounds, for example, that the existence of voting rights checks the abuse of government power and that party competition helps to generate social consensus. The ability of the people to 'kick the rascals out' therefore helps to ensure that government is limited and that there is at least a measure of public accountability.

However, most political systems fare poorly by the standards of personal autonomy and popular rule. What passes for democracy in the modern world tends to be a limited and indirect form of democracy: liberal democracy. This operates as little more than what Joseph Schumpeter (see p. 253) referred to as an 'institutional arrangement for arriving at political decisions in which individuals acquire the power to decide by means of a competitive struggle for the people's vote' (Schumpeter, 1942: 269). This 'institutional arrangement' has been criticized by radical democrats for reducing popular participation to a near meaningless ritual: casting a vote every few years for politicians who can be removed only by replacing them with another set of politicians. In short, the people never rule, and the growing gulf between government and the people is reflected in the spread of inertia, apathy and the breakdown of community.

This perspective is therefore linked to calls for radical, even revolutionary, political and social change. For example, government power should be decentralized so as to bring power 'closer' to the people. This could, for instance, require the breakup of the nation-state, as it is difficult, in practical terms, to see how a community the size of a modern nation could govern itself through direct and continuous participation. Similarly, insofar as the democratic principle is applied in modern societies, it is confined to a narrowly 'political' set of decisions. If democracy is understood as self-mastery, the ability to shape decisions that affect one's life, surely economic power must also be democratized, presumably through the machinery of workers' control and self-management.

As with the performance criteria examined above, democracy also poses its own set of dilemmas. The most important of these is the need for a balance between the twin goals of government *by* the people and government *for* the people. This highlights the tension between the competing virtues of popular participation and rule in the public interest. The most fundamental objection to participation, and thus to all forms of direct democracy, is simply that ordinary people lack the time, maturity and specialist knowledge to rule wisely on their own behalf. The earliest version of this argument was put by Plato (see p. 12), who advanced the idea of rule by the virtuous: that is, government by a class of philosopher kings. In this form, the case for government *for* the people amounts to an argument in favour of an enlightened despotism. The concern about the capabilities of ordinary people can, however, be dealt with more modestly, through the provision of representative processes that allow for a division of labour in political life. A further dilemma is that the empowerment of the individual must be balanced against the empowerment of the community. To give priority to personal autonomy is necessarily to place limits upon public authority. However, to extol the virtues of popular rule is to risk subordinating the individual to the will of the public or the majority. The tension between the individual and society not only raises major practical difficulties, but also highlights what some would argue has always been, and remains, the central issue in political theory.

◼ Summary

◆ Public policy consists of the formal and stated decisions of government bodies. Policy-making should be thought of as a process in two senses. First, it involves a linked series of actions through which policy intentions are translated into policy outputs. Second, policy-making relates primarily to how governments make decisions, rather than to the substance of the decisions they make.

◆ A decision is an act of choosing one of a range of options. Decisions have been explained in terms of the goal-directed behaviour of rational actors, incremental adjustments made in the light of changing circumstances, the bureaucratic or organizational factors that shape the decision-making process, and the beliefs and values held by decision-makers.

◆ The policy process can be broken down into four distinct stages. In the initiation stage, policy proposals are originated and the policy agenda is set. In the formulation stage, policy is developed in the sense that broad proposals are translated into specific and detailed recommendations. The implementation stage consists of the processes through which policy decisions are put into effect. The evaluation stage takes the form of critical reflection on policy outputs designed to improve the policy process in the future.

◆ Ultimately, policy can be judged only in terms of the impact it has on the larger society, for good or ill. However, as this raises normative questions, there is no consensus about the desirable 'outcomes' of government. The most commonly used indexes of a government's or system's performance include its ability to maintain stability and order, deliver material prosperity, promote citizenship, and foster democratic rule.

◆ Evaluating political systems is difficult because each performance indicator embodies complexities. Stability can be promoted through consent and popular responsiveness, or a shared culture and respect for authority. The generation of wealth may be hampered by policies designed to ensure that it is more equally distributed. The spread of citizenship rights may undermine civic duty and a sense of community. The extension of democratic rule may simply lead to restrictions on individual freedom or personal autonomy.

▪ Questions for discussion

▶ Do people generally make decisions in a rational and calculating fashion?

▶ What is the most important stage in the policy process, and why?

▶ Is there a moral or economic case for greater social equality?

▶ Can the 'politics of rights' threaten the 'politics of the common good'?

▶ Is there an inevitable tension between democracy and liberty?

▶ Are people the best judges of what is good for them?

▶ Which political system comes closest to achieving the 'good society'?

▪ Further reading

Bertsch, G., R. Clarke and D. Wood, *Comparing Political Systems: Power and Policy in Three Worlds* (4th edn.) (New York: Macmillan, 1992). A detailed analysis of the policy process in various parts of the world.

Hogwood, B. and L. Gunn, *Policy Analysis for the Real World* (Oxford: Oxford University Press, 1984) A very useful introduction to the concepts used in policy analysis.

Parsons, W., *Public Policy: Introduction to the Theory and Practice of Policy Analysis* (Aldershot: Edward Elgar, 1995). A wide-ranging and thorough analysis of policy and the policy makingprocess.

Pierson, C. (ed.), *The New Politics of the Welfare State* (Oxford and New York: Oxford University Press, 2000). An interesting examination of the political economy of welfare.

Roller, E., *The Performance of Democracies: Political Institutions and Public Policy* (Oxford and New York: Oxford University Press, 2005). A comprehensive analysis of 21 OECD states which considers performance across a wide range of domestic policy areas.

Glossary of Political Terms

When a term is discussed more fully in a box in the main text of the book, a page reference is given after the definition in the glossary.

Absolutism The theory or practice of absolute government, typically based on a claim to an unlimited right to rule (see p. 28).

Accountability Answerability; having a duty to explain one's conduct and being subject to monitoring and evaluation by a higher authority (see p. 418).

Administration The task of coordinating or executing policy; more narrowly, dealing with information and monetary control (see p. 387).

Administrative law Law that regulates the exercise of executive power and policy implementation.

Adversary politics A style of politics characterized by ideological antagonism and an ongoing electoral battle between major parties (see p. 350).

Affirmative action Reverse or 'positive' discrimination which accords preferential treatment to groups on the basis of their past disadvantage.

Agenda setting The ability to structure policy debate by controlling which issues are discussed or establishing a priority amongst them.

Alienation Separation from one's genuine or essential nature; for Marxists, the reduction of labour to a mere commodity.

Altruism A concern for the welfare of others, based on either enlightened self-interest or a recognition of a common humanity.

Anarchism An ideology committed to the abolition of the state and the outright rejection of political authority, based on an unqualified belief in liberty and equality.

Anarchy Literally, without rule; anarchy is often used pejoratively to suggest instability or even chaos.

Ancien régime (*French*) Literally, old order; usually linked with the absolutist structures that predated the French Revolution.

Anomie A weakening of values and normative rules, associated with feelings of isolation, loneliness and meaninglessness.

Anthropocentrism The belief that human needs and interests are of overriding moral and philosophical importance; the opposite of ecocentrism.

Antiparty parties Parties that set out to subvert traditional party politics by rejecting parliamentary compromise and emphasizing popular mobilization.

Anti-politics Disillusionment with formal and established political processes, reflected in nonparticipation, support for antisystem parties, or the use of direct action.

Anti-Semitism Prejudice or hatred towards Jews; anti-Semitism may take religious, economic or racial forms (see p. 000).

Asian values Values that supposedly reflect the history, culture and religious backgrounds of Asian societies; examples include social harmony, respect for authority and a belief in the family.

Assimilation The process through which immigrant communities lose their cultural distinctiveness by adjusting to the values, allegiances and lifestyles of the 'host' society.

Association A group formed by voluntary action, reflecting recognition of shared interests or common concerns.

Athenian democracy A form of direct democracy, based on government by mass meetings and the allocation of public offices through lot or rota.

Atomism The belief that society is made up of a collection of largely self-sufficient individuals; or a tendency towards social breakdown and isolation.

Autarky Literally, self-rule; usually associated with economic self-sufficiency brought about by either a withdrawal from intentional trade, or colonial expansion.

Authoritarianism The belief in or practice of government 'from above'; the exercise of authority regardless of the consent of the governed (see p. 38).

Authority The right to influence the behaviour of others on the basis of an acknowledged duty to obey; authority may be traditional, charismatic or legal–rational (see p. 5).

Autonomy Literally, self-rule; an autonomous person is rationally self-willed by virtue of his or her independence of external authority (see p. 442).

Balance of power A pattern of interaction amongst states that tends to curb aggression and expansionism by rendering them impracticable.

Balkanization The fragmentation of a political unit into a patchwork of antagonistic entities (as has often occurred in the Balkans).

Behaviouralism The belief that social theories should be constructed only on the basis of observable behaviour, providing quantifiable data for research.

Bias Sympathies or prejudices that (often unconsciously) affect human judgement; bias implies distortion (see p. 238).

Bicameralism The fragmentation of legislative power, established through the existence of two (co-equal) chambers in the assembly; a device of limited government (see p. 345).

Big government Interventionist government, usually understood to imply economic management and social regulation.

Bill Proposed legislation in the form of a draft statute; if passed, a bill becomes an act.

Bill of rights A constitutional document that specifies the rights and freedoms of the individual, and so defines the legal extent of civil liberty.

Bipolarity The tendency of the international system to revolve around two poles (major power blocs); bipolarity implies equilibrium and stability.

Bonapartism A style of government that fuses personal leadership with conservative nationalism; for Marxists, it reflects the relative autonomy of the state.

Bourgeois ideology A Marxist term, denoting ideas and theories that serve the interests of the bourgeoisie by disguising the contradictions of capitalist society.

Bourgeoisie A Marxist term, denoting the ruling class of a capitalist society, the owners of productive wealth.

Bureaucracy Literally, rule by officials; the administrative machinery of the state or, more broadly, a rational and rule-governed mode of organization (see p. 383).

Cabinet A group of senior ministers that meets formally and regularly, and is chaired by the chief executive; cabinets may make policy or be consultative.

Cabinet government A system of government in which executive power is vested in a cabinet, each member having (in theory) equal influence and being subject to collective responsibility (see p. 370).

Cadre A group of elite members of a party, distinguished by their ideological commitment and quasi-military discipline.

Capitalism A system of generalized commodity production in which wealth is owned privately and economic life is organized according to market principles.

Caucus A meeting of party members held to nominate election candidates or to discuss legislative proposals in advance of formal proceedings.

Censorship The control or suppression of publications, expressions of opinion, or other pubic acts; censorship may be formal or informal.

Centralization The concentration of political power or government authority at the national level.

Charisma Charm or personal power; the ability to inspire loyalty, emotional dependence, or even devotion, in others (see p. 221).

Chauvinism An irrational belief in the superiority or dominance of one's own group or cause.

Checks and balances Internal tensions within the governmental system that result from institutional fragmentation.

Christian democracy An ideological tradition within European conservatism, characterized by a commitment to the social market and qualified interventionism.

Citizenship Membership of a state; a relationship between the individual and state based on reciprocal rights and responsibilities (see p. 241).

Civic culture A culture that blends popular participation with effective government; supposedly, the basis for stable democratic rule.

Civic nationalism A form of nationalism that is based on common citizenship, rooted in support for an underlying set of political values, rather than a common culture.

Civil liberty The private sphere of existence, belonging to the citizen not to the state; freedom from government (see p. 407).

Civil society The realm of autonomous groups and associations; a private sphere independent from public authority (see p. 8).

Civil war An armed conflict between politically organized groups within a state, usually fought either for control of the state or to establish a new state.

Class consciousness A Marxist term, denoting an accurate awareness of class interests and a willingness to pursue them; a class-conscious class is a class for-itself (see p. 225).

Class dealignment A weakening of the relationship between social class and party support (see p. 267).

Clientelism A relationship through which government agencies come to serve the interests of the client groups they are responsible for regulating or supervising.

Coalition A grouping of rival political actors, brought together through the perception of a common threat or to harness collective energies (see p. 288).

Coalition government A government in which power is shared between two or more parties, based on the distribution among them of ministerial portfolios.

Cohabitation An arrangement in a semipresidential system in which the president works with a government and assembly controlled by a rival party or parties.

Cold War The period of rivalry between the USA-dominated West and the USSR-dominated East that extended from 1945 to the collapse of communism in the revolutions of 1989–91.

Collective responsibility The doctrine of cabinet government that holds that all ministers are obliged to give public support to government policies.

Collective security The theory or practice of resisting aggression through united action by a number of states (see p. 158).

Collectivization The abolition of private property in favour of a system of common or public ownership.

Collectivism A belief in the capacity of human beings for collective action, based on cooperation not self-striving; collectivism implies that social entities are meaningful (see p. 196).

Colonialism The theory or practice of establishing control over a foreign territory, usually by settlement and economic domination (see p. 122).

Committee A small workgroup composed of members drawn from a larger body and charged with specific responsibilities (see p. 346).

Common law Law based on custom and precedent; law that is supposedly 'common' to all.

Commune A small-scale collective organization based on the sharing of wealth and power, possibly also extending to personal and domestic arrangements.

Communism The principle of the common ownership of property; communism often refers to movements or regimes based on Marxist principles (see p. 35).

Communitarianism The belief that the self or person is constituted through the community in the sense that there are no 'unencumbered selves' (see p. 179).

Community A principle or sentiment based on the collective identity of a social group; bonds of comradeship, loyalty and duty (see p. 178).

Competition state A state which pursues strategies to ensure long-term competitiveness in a globalized economy.

Concept A general idea about something, usually expressed in a single word or short phrase.

Confederation A qualified union of states in which each state retains its independence, typically guaranteed by unanimous decision-making.

Conflict Competition between opposing forces, reflecting a diversity of opinions, preferences, needs or interests.

Confucianism A system of ethics derived from the philosophy of Confucius, which emphasizes respect and loyalty in human relationships and the cultivation of the self (see p. 36).

Consensus A broad agreement on fundamental principles, allowing for disagreement on matters of emphasis or detail (see p. 10).

Consensus politics A style of politics based on compromise and conciliation; or an overlap of policy and ideological priorities between parties.

Consent Assent or permission; in politics, usually an agreement to be governed or ruled.

Conservatism An ideology characterized by support for tradition, duty, authority and property, extending from Tory paternalism to the New Right.

Consociational democracy A form of democracy that operates through power-sharing and a close association amongst a number of parties or political formations.

Constitution A set of rules that establish the duties, powers and functions of the institutions of government and define the relationship between the state and the individual (see p. 316).

Constitutional government Government that operates within a set of legal and institutional constraints that both limit its power and protect individual liberty.

Constitutional law Law that regulates the relationship between branches of government and between the state and the individual.

Constitutionalism The theory or practice of limited government brought about by the existence of a constitution and the fragmentation of power (see p. 321).

Consumerism A psychic and social phenomenon whereby personal happiness is equated with the consumption of material possessions (see p. 241).

Contested concept A concept over which there is theoretical or political debate; concepts are 'essentially contested' when no settled definition can ever be developed.

Contract A voluntary agreement that is morally, and perhaps legally, binding.

Convention A rule of conduct or behaviour; a nonlegal constitutional rule (see p. 318).

Convergence thesis The theory that politicoeconomic factors dictate that capitalist and socialist states will become increasingly similar.

Cooperation Working together; achieving goals through collective action.

Core executive A network of institutions and actors who play key roles in the overall direction and coordination of government policy: 'the centre' (see p. 371).

Corporatism The incorporation of organized interests into the processes of government; corporatism may have a liberal or a fascist character (see p. 299).

Corruption A failure to carry out 'proper' responsibilities as a result of the pursuit of private (and usually material) gain (see p. 000).

Cosmopolitanism Literally, a belief in a world state; more usually, a commitment to fostering harmony and understanding amongst nations (see p. 217).

Coup d'état (*French*) A forcible seizure of power through illegal and unconstitutional action carried out (unlike in a revolution or rebellion) by a small group (see p. 411).

Cult of personality A propaganda device through which a political leader is portrayed as a heroic or God-like figure (see p. 375).

Cultural globalization The process whereby information, commodities and images produced in one part of the world enter into a global flow that tends to 'flatten out' cultural differences between nations and regions.

Cultural nationalism A form of nationalism that places primary emphasis on the regeneration of the nation as a distinctive civilization (see p. 112).

Culture A people's attitudes, beliefs, symbols and values; broadly, that which is acquired through learning, rather than through inheritance.

Decentralization The expansion of local autonomy through the transfer of powers and responsibilities away from national bodies.

Decision An act of choice; a selection from a range of options.

Deindustrialization A contraction of the economy's manufacturing base, reflected in the decline of 'heavy' industries.

Deliberative democracy A form of democracy that emphasizes the need for discourse and debate to help define the public interest.

Demagogue A political leader whose control over the masses is based on the ability to whip up hysterical enthusiasm.

Democracy Rule by the people; democracy implies both popular participation and government in the public interest, and can take a wide variety of forms (see Chapter 4).

Democratic centralism The Leninist principle of party organization, based on a supposed balance between freedom of discussion and strict unity of action.

Democratic deficit A lack of accountability of executive bodies to popular assemblies, or inadequate opportunities for popular participation.

Democratization The advance of liberal-democratic reform, implying, in particular, the granting of basic freedoms and the widening of popular participation and electoral choice.

Departmentalism The tendency for government agencies to pursue their own interests and resist political control or broader administrative disciplines (see p. 390).

Determinism The belief that human actions and choices are conditioned entirely by external factors; determinism implies that free will is a myth.

Devolution The transfer of power from central government to subordinate regional bodies, without (unlike federalism) leading to shared sovereignty (see p. 173).

Dialectic A process of interaction between two competing forces, giving rise to a higher stage of development.

Dialectical materialism The crude and deterministic form of Marxism that dominated intellectual life in orthodox communist states.

Dictatorship Rule by a single individual; the arbitrary and unchecked exercise of power (see p. 405).

Dictatorship of the proletariat A Marxist term, denoting the transitionary phase between the collapse of capitalism and the establishment of full communism.

Direct action Political action taken outside the constitutional and legal framework; direct action may range from passive resistance to terrorism.

Direct democracy Popular self-government, characterized by the direct and continuous participation of citizens in the tasks of government.

Discourse Human interaction, especially communication; discourse may disclose or illustrate power relationships.

Divine right The doctrine that earthly rulers are chosen by God and thus wield unchallengeable authority; a defence for monarchical absolutism.

Ecocentrism A theoretical orientation that gives priority to the maintenance of ecological balance rather than the satisfaction of human interests.

Ecologism An ideology based on the belief that there is an essential link between humankind and the natural world, and that the health of the ecosystem has priority over human interests.

Ecology The study of the relationship between living organisms and their environment; ecology highlights the interconnectedness of nature (see p. 64).

Economic globalization The absorption of national economies into a single global economy through the internationalization of production and transnational capital flows.

Economic liberalism A belief in the market as a self-regulating mechanism tending naturally to deliver general prosperity and opportunities for all.

Economic man A model of human nature that stresses the self-interested pursuit of material satisfaction, individuals being seen as utility maximizers.

Economic sovereignty The absolute authority which the state exercises over economic life conducted within its borders, involving independent control of fiscal and monetary policies and control over trade and capital flows.

Egalitarianism A theory or practice based on the desire to promote equality; or the belief that equality is the primary political value.

Election A device for filling an office or post through choices made by a designated body of people: the electorate.

Elective dictatorship A constitutional imbalance in which executive power is checked only by the need to win subsequent elections.

Electoral college An indirect electoral mechanism; a body of electors charged with responsibility for filling a party or public office.

Elite A minority in whose hands power, wealth or prestige is concentrated.

Elitism The belief in, or practice of, rule by an elite; the theory that political power is concentrated in the hands of the few (see p. 84).

Empire A structure of political domination comprising diverse cultures, ethnic groups and nationalities held together by force or the threat of force.

Empirical Based on observation and experiment; empirical knowledge is derived from sense data and experience.

Empiricism The belief that experience is the only basis for knowledge and that therefore all hypotheses and theories should be tested by observation and experiment.

Entrepreneurialism Values or practices associated with commercial risk-taking and profit-orientated business activity.

Environmentalism A concern with protecting or conserving nature, ultimately (unlike ecologism) for the benefit of humankind.

Equality The principle of uniform apportionment, rather than 'sameness'; equality may be applied to rights, opportunities or outcomes (see p. 440).

Ethnic cleansing The forcible expulsion or extermination of 'alien' peoples; often used as a euphemism for genocide.

Ethnic group A group of people who share a common cultural and historical identity, typically linked to a belief in common descent.

Ethnic nationalism A form of nationalism that is fuelled primarily by a keen sense of ethnic distinctiveness and the desire to preserve it.

Ethnicity A sentiment of loyalty towards a distinctive population, cultural group or territorial area; bonds that are cultural rather than racial (see p. 174).

Ethnocentrism The application of values and theories drawn from one's own culture to other groups and peoples; ethnocentrism implies bias or distortion (see p. 429).

Eurocommunism A form of deradicalized communism that attempted to blend Marxism with liberal-democratic principles.

Exceptionalism The features of a political system that are unique or particular to it, and thus restrict the application of broader categories.

Executive The branch of government that is responsible for implementing or carrying out law and policy (see p. 358).

Expansionism A policy of military aggression designed to secure territorial gains, a phenomenon closely linked to imperialism.

Fact A truth verified by experience or observation; something that is known to have happened or to be the case.

Faction A section or group within a larger formation, usually a party; a faction is distinguished by common policy commitments or ideological leanings (see p. 272).

Factionalism The proliferation of factions within a party or government; or the bitterness of factional rivalry or infighting.

False consciousness A Marxist term, denoting the delusion and mystification that prevents subordinate classes from recognizing the fact of their own exploitation.

Fascism An ideology characterized by a belief in anti-rationalism, struggle, charismatic leadership, elitism and extreme nationalism; Fascism (with a capital F) refers specifically to the Mussolini regime in Italy.

Federalism   A territorial distribution of power based on the sharing of sovereignty between central (usually national) bodies and peripheral ones (see p. 167).

Feminism   An ideology committed to promoting the social role of women and, in most cases, dedicated to the goal of gender equality.

Feudalism   A system of agrarian-based production characterized by fixed social hierarchies and a rigid pattern of obligations.

Fiscal crisis of the welfare state   The crisis in state finances that occurs when expanding social expenditure coincides with recession and declining tax revenues.

Fiscal policy   Government tax and spending policies, aimed primarily at influencing aggregate demand.

Franchise   The right to vote.

Fraternity   Literally, brotherhood; bonds of sympathy and comradeship between and amongst human beings.

Free market   The principle or policy of unfettered market competition, free from government interference.

Free press   Newspapers (and, by extension, other media outlets) that are free from censorship and political interference by government and, usually, are privately owned.

Free trade   A system of trading between states not restricted by tariffs or other forms of protectionism.

Freedom (or liberty)   The ability to think or act as one wishes; freedom implies either noninterference (negative freedom) or personal self-development (positive freedom) (see p. 324).

Functionalism   The theory that government is responsive primarily to human needs; as a theory of regional integration, it implies that the process is incremental and pragmatic.

Fundamentalism   A movement or style of thought that holds certain principles to be essential and unchallengeable 'truths' (see p. 66).

Gemeinschaft   (*German*) Community; social bonds based on organic ties and mutual respect.

Gender   A cultural distinction between females and males, based on their different social roles and positions (see p. 201).

General will   The genuine interests of a collective body, equivalent to the common good; the will of all provided each person acts selflessly.

Genocide   An attempt to eradicate a people, identified by their nationality, race, ethnicity or religion, through acts including mass murder, forced resettlement, deliberately induced starvation, and forced sterilization.

Gerrymandering   The manipulation of electoral boundaries so as to achieve political advantage for a party or candidate.

Gesellschaft   (*German*) Association; artificial and contractual social bonds based on a recognition of overlapping interests.

Glasnost   (*Russian*) Literally, openness; the relaxation of censorship and cultural repression.

Global consciousness   An awareness of global interconnectedness, reflected (usually) in the form of transnational moral responsibilities and universalist ethics.

Globalization   A complex web of interconnectedness through which life is increasingly shaped by decisions or events taken at a distance.

Governance   Broadly, the various ways in which social life is coordinated, of which government is merely one (see p. 6).

Government   The mechanism through which ordered rule is maintained; the machinery for making and enforcing collective decisions in society and elsewhere (see p. 26).

Government gridlock   Paralysis resulting from institutional rivalry within government or the attempt to respond to conflicting public demands.

Great power   A state deemed to rank amongst the most powerful in a hierarchical state system, reflected in its influence over minor states.

Gross domestic product   The total financial value of final goods and services produced in an economy over one year.

'Hard' power   The ability to influence others through the use of threats or rewards, typically involving military 'sticks' or economic 'carrots'.

Head of state   The leading representative of the state, usually either a president or monarch; a title of essentially symbolic significance (see p. 359).

Hegemony   The ascendency or domination of one element of a system over others; for Marxists, hegemony implies ideological domination (see p. 207).

Hierarchy   A gradation of social positions or status; hierarchy implies structural or fixed inequality in which position is unconnected with individual ability.

Historical materialism   A Marxist theory that holds that material or economic conditions ultimately structure law, politics, culture and other aspects of social existence.

Homogenization   The tendency for all parts or elements to become similar or identical, as in the case of cultural globalization.

Human nature   The essential and immutable character of all human beings; that which is innate to humankind rather than socially or culturally produced.

Human rights Rights to which people are entitled by virtue of being human; universal and fundamental rights (see p. 326).

Humanitarian intervention Military intervention that is carried out in pursuit of humanitarian rather than strategic objectives (see p. 135).

Hybridity A condition of social and cultural mixing; the term has been derived from cross-breeding between genetically unalike plants or animals.

Hyperglobalism The view that new, globalized economic and cultural patterns are inevitable, driven by advances in information and communications technology.

Hyperpower A power that commands much greater power than any of its potential rivals, and so dominates world politics.

Ideal type A mental construct designed to draw out meaning from a complex reality through the presentation of a logical extreme (see p. 18).

Idealism A view of politics that emphasizes the importance of morality and ideals; philosophically, idealism can imply that ideas are more 'real' than the material world.

Ideology A more or less coherent set of ideas that provides the basis for some kind of organized political action (see p. 45).

Immobilism Political paralysis stemming from the absence of a strong executive, caused by multiple divisions in the assembly and (probably) in society.

Impartiality The absence of bias; the capacity to prevent political sympathies from intruding into professional or public responsibilities.

Impeachment A formal process for the removal of a public official in the event of personal or professional wrongdoing.

Imperial overreach The tendency for imperial expansion to be unsustainable as wider military responsibilities outstrip the growth of the domestic economy.

Imperialism The policy or practice of extending the power or rule of a state beyond its borders; imperialism can be an ideology of expansionism (see p. 132).

Incrementalism The theory that decisions are made not in the light of clear-cut objectives, but through small adjustments dictated by changing circumstances.

Indigenization The process through which alien goods and practices are absorbed by being adapted to local needs and circumstances.

Individual responsibility See *ministerial responsibility*.

Individualism A belief in the supreme importance of the human individual rather than of any social group or collective body (see p. 196).

Industrialism An economic theory or system based on large-scale factory production and the relentless accumulation of capital.

Information society A society in which the creation, distribution and manipulation of information are core economic and cultural activities, underpinned by the 'new' media (see p. 237).

Initiative A type of referendum through which the public is able to raise legislative proposals.

Institutional racism A form of racism that operates through the culture or procedural rules of an organization, as distinct from personal prejudice.

Integral nationalism An intense, even hysterical, nationalist enthusiasm that absorbs individual identity into that of the nation.

Interest That which benefits an individual or group; interests (unlike wants or preferences) are usually understood to be objective, or 'real', as opposed to 'felt'.

Interest group (or pressure group) An organized association that aims to influence the policies or actions of government; interest groups may have a sectional or promotional character (see p. 296).

Intergovernmentalism Interaction between or amongst states that takes place on the basis of sovereign independence (see p. 153).

International law A system of rules that is binding on states, and thus defines the formal relationships between them (see p. 159).

Internationalism A theory or practice of politics based on transnational or global cooperation; the belief that nations are artificial and unwanted formations (see p. 130).

Interventionism Government policies designed to regulate or manage economic life; more broadly, a policy of engagement or involvement.

Iron triangle A policy network that comprises executive agencies, legislative committees and interest groups, typically found in the USA.

Isolationism The policy of withdrawal from international affairs and, in particular, avoiding political or military commitment to other states.

Issue A matter recognized as part of the policy agenda, over which there is public debate or disagreement.

Jingoism A mood of public enthusiasm and celebration provoked by military expansion or imperial conquest.

Judicial activism   The willingness of judges to arbitrate in political disputes, as opposed to merely saying what the law means.

Judicial independence   The constitutional principle that there should be a strict separation between the judiciary and other branches of government; an application of the separation of powers.

Judicial review   The power of the judiciary to review the laws, decrees and actions of other branches of government, and to declare them invalid (see p. 330).

Judiciary   The branch of government that is empowered to decide legal disputes and adjudicate on the meaning of the law.

Junta   Literally, a council or board (*Spanish*); a group of military officers who hold political power.

Justice   The morally justifiable apportionment of rewards or punishments, each person being given what he or she is 'due'.

Keynesianism   The theory (developed by John Maynard Keynes) or policy of economic management, usually associated with the goal of full employment.

Laissez-faire   (*French*) Literally, to leave to do; the principle of the noninterference of government in economic life (see p. 189).

Law   A set of public and enforceable rules that apply throughout a political community; law is usually recognized as binding.

Leadership   Influence exerted over a larger group or body, or personal qualities that foster willing obedience in others (see p. 372).

Left   A broad ideological disposition characterized by sympathy for principles such as liberty, equality, fraternity and progress (see p. 276).

Legislature   The branch of government that is empowered to make law through the formal enactment of legislation.

Legitimacy   Rightfulness; a quality that confers on a command an authoritative or binding character, implying a duty to obey (see p. 219).

Leninism   Lenin's theoretical contributions to Marxism, notably his belief in the need for a revolutionary or vanguard party.

Liberal democracy   A form of democracy that incorporates both limited government and a system of regular and competitive elections; liberal democracy is a regime type (see p. 30).

Liberalization   The introduction of internal and external checks on government power and/or shifts towards private enterprise and the market.

Liberalism   An ideology based on a commitment to individualism, freedom, toleration and consent; modern liberalism differs from classical liberalism.

Libertarianism   The belief that the realm of individual liberty should be maximized, usually associated with attempts to minimize the scope of public authority.

Liberty   See *freedom*.

Licence   Excessive liberty; the abuse of or disregard for others or the law.

Limited government   Government operating within constraints, usually imposed by law, a constitution or institutional checks and balances.

Lobby   *Verb*: to make representations to policy-makers; *noun*: an interest group that influences the policy process (see p. 305).

Local democracy   A principle that embodies both the idea of local autonomy and the goal of popular responsiveness.

Machiavellianism   Cunning and manipulative behaviour, usually aimed at personal or political advancement (after Niccolò Machiavelli) (see p. 6).

Machine politics   A style of politics in which party 'bosses' control a mass organization through patronage and the distribution of favours.

Majoritarianism   A theory or practice in which priority is accorded to the will of the majority; majoritarianism implies insensitivity towards minorities and individuals.

Maladministration   Bad administration; the improper use of powers, biased application of rules, failure to follow procedures, or simple incompetence.

Managerialism   The theory that in modern society class divisions have been replaced by ones based on managerial position and bureaucratic power; technocracy (rule by experts or specialists).

Mandate   An authoritative instruction or command; a mandate can be a legal order or a moral obligation (see p. 252).

Manifesto   A document outlining (in more or less detail) the policies or programme a party proposes to pursue if elected to power.

Market   A system of commercial exchange shaped by the forces of demand and supply, and regulated by the price mechanism (see p. 185).

Market socialism   An economic system based on self-managing cooperative enterprises operating in a context of market competition.

Marketization   The extension of market relationships, based on commercial exchange and material self-interest, across the economy and, possibly, society.

Marxism   The theoretical system devised by Karl Marx, characterized by a belief in historical materialism, dialectical change and the use of class analysis.

Mass media   Social institutions in print and electronic publishing and broadcasting that channel communication towards a large and undifferentiated audience (see p. 232).

Mass society   A society characterized by atomism and cultural and political rootlessness; the concept highlights pessimistic trends in modern societies.

Materialism   An emphasis on material needs and satisfaction; philosophically, either the belief that only matter is 'real' or that economic factors are fundamental to historical explanations.

McCarthyism   The use of witch hunts and unscrupulous investigations, as practised in the 1950s against 'communists' by US Senator Joseph McCarthy.

McDonaldization   The process whereby global commodities and commercial and marketing practices associated with the fast-food industry have come to dominate more and more economic sectors.

Mercantilism   A school of economic thought that emphasized the state's role in managing international trade and guaranteeing prosperity.

Meritocracy   Rule by the talented; the principle that rewards and positions should be distributed on the basis of ability.

Meta-ideology   A higher or second-order ideology that lays down the grounds on which ideological debate can take place.

Militarism   The achievement of ends by military means; or the spread of military ideas and values throughout civilian society (see p. 404).

Military–industrial complex   A symbiotic relationship between the armed forces and defence industries, based on a common desire to increase military spending.

Military regime   A regime in which political office is allocated on the basis of the holder's position in the military hierarchy.

Minimal state   A state whose functions are restricted to the maintenance of domestic order and the protection of property; a 'nightwatchman' state.

Ministerial (or individual) responsibility   The doctrine that ministers are responsible or accountable for the actions (and mistakes) of their civil servants (see p. 396).

Model   A theoretical representation of empirical data that aims to advance understanding by highlighting significant relationships and interactions.

Monarchy   An institution in which the post of head of state is filled through inheritance or by dynastic succession; monarchy may be absolute or constitutional (see p. 366).

Monetarism   The theory that inflation is caused by an increase in the supply of money; 'too much money chases too few goods'.

Monetary policy   A government's influence over the supply and value of money, exercised principally through the mechanism of interest rates.

Monism   A belief in only one theory or value; monism is reflected politically in enforced obedience to a unitary power and is thus implicitly totalitarian.

Multilateralism   A system of coordinated relations between three or more states based on principles of conduct laid down by treaties and international organizations.

Multilevel governance   A complex policy process in which authority is distributed horizontally and vertically across subnational, national and supranational levels of government.

Multiplier effect   The mechanism through which a change in aggregate demand has an increased effect on national income as it circulates through the economy.

Multipolarity   An international system in which there are three or more power centres, creating a bias in favour of fluidity and, perhaps, instability.

Nanny state   A state with extensive social responsibilities; the term implies that welfare programmes are unwarranted and demeaning to the individual.

Nation   A group of people who share a common cultural inheritance and regard themselves as a natural political community (see p. 110).

Nation-state   A sovereign political association within which citizenship and nationality overlap; one nation within a single state (see p. 123).

National self-determination   The principle that the nation is a sovereign entity; self-determination implies both national independence and democratic rule.

National Socialism (or Nazism)   A form of fascism practised in Hitler's Germany and characterized by totalitarian terror, genocidal anti-Semitism, and expansionist racism.

Nationalism   An ideology that takes the nation to be the central principle of political organization; nationalism can be associated with a wide range of ideals and goals (see Chapter 6).

Natural aristocracy The idea that talent and leadership are innate or inbred qualities that cannot be acquired through effort or self-advancement.

Natural law A moral system to which human laws do, or should, conform; natural law lays down universal standards of conduct.

Natural rights God-given rights that are fundamental to human beings and are therefore inalienable (they cannot be taken away).

Negative freedom Noninterference, the absence of external constraints on the individual; sometimes seen as freedom 'from'.

Negative rights Rights that mark out a realm of unconstrained action, and thus check the responsibilities of government.

Neocolonialism Control exercised over a foreign territory through economic (and sometimes cultural) domination rather than formal political direction.

Neoconservatism An updated version of social conservatism that emphasizes the need to restore authority and the return to traditional values (this term is also used to describe a distinctive approach to foreign policy).

Neocorporatism A tendency found in western polyarchies for organized interests to be granted privileged and institutionalized access to policy formulation.

Neofunctionalism A revision of functionalism that recognizes that regional integration in one area generates pressure for further integration in the form of 'spillover'.

Neo-idealism A perspective on international politics that emphasizes the practical value of morality and, in particular, respect for human rights and national independence.

Neoliberalism An updated version of classical political economy, dedicated to market individualism and minimal statism.

Neo-Marxism An updated and revised form of Marxism that rejects determinism, the primacy of economics, and the privileged status of the proletariat (see p. 96).

Neopluralism A revised form of pluralism that takes account of the imbalances of the market and the disproportionate power of private business (see p. 94).

Neo-realism A perspective on international politics that modifies the power-politics model by highlighting the structural constraints of the international system.

Neutrality The absence of partisanship or commitment; a refusal to 'take sides' (see p. 329).

New democracies Regimes in which the process of democratic consolidation is incomplete; democracy is not the 'only show in town'.

New Left An ideological movement that sought to revitalize socialist thought by developing a radical critique of advanced industrial society, stressing the need for decentralization, participation and personal liberation (see p. 308).

New public management The incorporation of private-sector management techniques into government and the transfer of public functions to private bodies (see p. 391).

New Right An ideological trend within conservatism that embraces a blend of market individualism and social authoritarianism.

Nightwatchman state A state with minimal responsibilities, linked primarily to the maintenance of domestic order and personal security.

Noblesse oblige (*French*) Literally, the obligations of the nobility; in general terms the responsibility to guide or protect those less fortunate or less privileged.

Nomenklatura (*Russian*) A system of vetted appointments that operates through a list of approved candidates.

Normative The prescription of values and standards of conduct; what 'should be' rather than what 'is'.

Objective External to the observer, demonstrable; untainted by feelings, values or bias.

Oligarchy Government or domination by the few (see p. 280).

Ombudsman An officer of the state appointed to safeguard citizens' rights and investigate allegations of maladministration (see p. 397).

One-nation conservatism A principle of conservative reformism, born out of a belief in paternal duty and a fear of social inequality.

Open government A free flow of information from government to representative bodies, the mass media and the electorate, based on the public's 'right to know' (see p. 436).

Order A stable and predictable pattern of behaviour associated, in particular, with personal security and public safety (see p. 413).

Organicism The belief that society operates like an organism or living entity, the whole being more than a collection of its individual parts.

Pacifism The principled rejection of war and all forms of violence as fundamentally evil.

Pan-nationalism A style of nationalism dedicated to unifying a disparate people through either expansionism or political solidarity ('pan' means all or every).

Paradigm An intellectual framework, comprising inter-related values, theories and assumptions, within which the search for knowledge is conducted (see p. 20).

Parliament A forum for debate and deliberation; parliament is equivalent to assembly or legislature.

Parliamentary democracy A form of democracy that operates through a popularly elected assembly and emphasizes the importance of deliberation (see p. 80).

Parliamentary government A system in which government governs in and through the assembly or parliament, thereby 'fusing' the legislature and executive (see p. 337).

Parliamentary sovereignty The absolute and unlimited authority of a parliament or assembly, reflected in its ability to make, repeal or amend any law (see p. 325).

Particularism The theory that identity is rooted in particular, rather than general, characteristics, highlighting the importance of factors such as locality, culture and ethnicity.

Partisan dealignment A weakening in the strength and extent of party identification, reflected in an increase in electoral volatility (see p. 266).

Party democracy The principle of the wide and even distribution of power within a party, or its concentration in the hands of its elected members (see p. 281).

Party government A system in which a party is able to govern alone and carry out a programme of policies (see p. 285).

Party system A relatively stable network of relationships between political parties that is structured by their number, size and ideological orientation.

Paternalism An attitude or policy that demonstrates care or concern for those unable to help themselves, as in the (supposed) relationship between a father and a child.

Patriarchy Literally, rule by the father; a system of male domination and female subordination in society at large (see p. 98).

Patriotism Literally, love of one's fatherland; a psychological attachment and loyalty to one's nation or country (see p. 119).

Peak association A group recognized by government as representing the general or collective interests of businesses or workers.

Perestroika (*Russian*) Literally, restructuring; a slogan that refers to the attempt to liberalize and democratize the Soviet system within a communist framework.

Permissiveness The willingness to allow people to make their own moral choices; permissiveness suggests that there are no authoritative values.

Planning A system of economic organization that relies on a rational allocation of resources in line with clearly defined goals; planning may be directive or indicative (see p. 192).

Plebiscitary democracy A form of democracy that operates through an unmediated link between rulers and the ruled, and is conducted through plebiscites (referendums) (see p. 75).

Pluralism A belief in, or commitment to, diversity or multiplicity; or the theory that power in modern societies is widely and evenly distributed (see p. 82).

Pluralist democracy A form of democracy that operates through the capacity of organized groups to articulate popular demands and ensure government responsiveness (see p. 83).

Plurality The largest of a collection of numbers; a 'relative' majority.

Police state A form of rule characterized by arbitrary and terroristic policing, in which the police act as a private army controlled by a ruling elite.

Policy Formal decisions made by public bodies; the 'outputs' of government (see p. 426).

Policy network A systematic set of relationships between political actors who share a common interest or general orientation in a particular area (see p. 432).

Polis (*Greek*) City-state; classically understood to imply the highest or most desirable form of social organization.

Political bias Political views that systematically favour the values or interests of one group over another (see p. 238).

Political culture A pattern of psychological orientations towards political objects; a people's political attitudes, beliefs, symbols and values (see p. 206).

Political equality The equal distribution of political power and influence, usually understood to imply 'one person, one vote; one vote, one value' (see p. 73).

Political globalization The growing importance of international bodies and organizations, which exercise jurisdiction within an international area comprising several states.

Political obligation The duty of the citizen towards the state; the basis of the state's right to rule.

Political party A group of people organized to gain formal representation or win government power; a party usually displays some measure of ideological cohesion (see p. 272).

Political philosophy The systematic analysis of the normative and methodological aspects of the study of politics.

Political pluralism The existence of a range of political values, philosophies and movements; in particular, a competitive party system.

Political science The study of government, the state and politics; more narrowly, the application of empirical theory and scientific methods to the analysis of political matters.

Political socialization The process through which individuals acquire political beliefs and values, and by which these are transmitted from generation to generation (see p. 233).

Political system A network of relationships through which government generates 'outputs' (policies) in response to 'inputs' (demands or support) from the general public.

Politics The activity through which people make, preserve and amend the general rules under which they live.

Polity A society organized through the exercise of political authority; for Aristotle, rule by the many in the interests of all.

Polyarchy Literally, rule by the many; an approximation of democracy based on the accountabiliy of power holders through regular and competitive elections (see p. 33).

Popular sovereignty The principle that there is no higher authority than the will of the people (the basis of the classical concept of democracy).

Populism The belief that the instincts of the masses are the only legitimate guide to political action; or a movement that appeals to popular instincts, resentments or aspirations (see p. 378).

Positive freedom Freedom as personal development, self-realization or self-mastery; sometimes seen as freedom 'to'.

Positive law A system of enforceable commands that operates irrespective of their moral content.

Positive rights Rights that make demands of government in terms of the provision of resources and support, and thus extend its responsibilities.

Positivism The theory that social and indeed all forms of enquiry should adhere strictly to the methods of the natural sciences.

Post-Fordism The transformation of modern society resulting from the shift away from large-scale, factory-based production methods (see p. 198).

Postindustrial society A society no longer dependent on manufacturing industry, but more reliant on knowledge and communication; an 'information society'.

Postmaterialism The theory that as material affluence spreads 'quality of life' issues and concerns tend to displace economic ones (see p. 211).

Postmodernism An intellectual movement that rejects the idea of absolute and universal truth, and usually emphasizes discourse, debate and democracy (see p. 67).

Power The ability to influence the behaviour of others, typically through the power to reward or punish (see p. 7).

Power politics An approach to politics based on the assumption that the pursuit of power is the principal human goal; the term is sometimes used descriptively.

Pragmatism A theory or practice that places primary emphasis on practical circumstances and goals; pragmatism implies a distrust of abstract ideas.

Preemptive attack Military action that is designed to forestall or prevent future aggression (see p. 139).

President A formal head of state, the republican equivalent of a monarch; executive presidents also serve as heads of government.

Presidential government A system of government in which executive authority is concentrated in the hands of a president, whose office is politically and constitutionally separate from the legislature (see p. 362).

Presidentialism Personalized leadership that is disengaged from parties or other government bodies, in the manner of an executive president.

Pressure group See *interest group*.

Primary election An intraparty election held to select a candidate to contest a subsequent 'official' election (see p. 278).

Prime minister A head of government whose power is derived from the leadership of the largest party (or coalition of parties) in the assembly.

Prime-ministerial government A system of government in which executive power is concentrated in the prime minister's hands through the suppression of collective cabinet government.

Privatization The transfer of state assets from the public to the private sector, reflecting a contraction of the state's responsibilities.

Progress Moving forwards; the belief that history is characterized by human advancement based on the accumulation of knowledge and wisdom.

Proletariat A Marxist term, denoting a class that subsists through the sale of its labour power; strictly speaking, the proletariat is not equivalent to the working class.

Propaganda Information disseminated in a deliberate attempt to shape opinions and, possibly, stimulate political action; communication as manipulation (see p. 242).

Proportional representation A principle or system in which parties are represented in an assembly in proportion to their overall electoral strength (see p. 258).

Protectionism Import restrictions such as quotas and tariffs, designed to protect domestic producers.

Public choice theory A subfield of rational-choice theory concerned with the provision of public goods (see p. 300).

Public goods Goods and benefits that individuals or groups who do not contribute to their provision cannot be prevented from enjoying.

Public interest The general or collective interests of a community; that which is good for society as a whole (see p. 264).

Qualified majority voting A system of voting used in the EU in which different majorities are needed in different policy areas and with states' votes weighted on the basis of population size.

Quango An acronym for quasi-autonomous nongovernmental organization: a public body staffed by appointees rather than by politicians or civil servants (see p. 392).

Race A group of people (supposedly) distinguished from other groups by physical or biological differences (see p. 200).

Racialism (or racism) The doctrine that political and social organization should be based on racial categories; racism may refer to prejudice or hostility towards members of other races (see p. 120).

Radical democracy A form of democracy that favours decentralization and participation, the widest possible dispersal of political power.

Radical feminism A form of feminism that holds gender divisions to be the most politically significant of social cleavages, and believes that they are rooted in the structure of domestic life.

Radicalism A commitment to thorough-going change that challenges basic or fundamental structures not merely superficial ones.

Rational choice An approach to politics based on the assumption that individuals are rationally self-interested actors; an 'economic' theory of politics.

Rationalism The belief that the world can be understood and explained through the exercise of human reason, based on assumptions about its rational structure.

Realism A view of politics that emphasizes the importance of power and self-interest, and disregards moral or normative considerations.

Rebellion A popular uprising against the established order, usually (unlike a revolution) aimed at replacing rulers rather than the political system itself.

Recall A process whereby the electorate can call unsatisfactory public officials to account and ultimately remove them.

Redistribution A narrowing of material inequalities brought about through a combination of progressive taxation and welfare provision.

Referendum A vote in which the electorate can express a view on a particular issue of public policy; referendums may be advisory or binding (see p. 250).

Reform Change brought about within a system, usually by peaceful and incremental measures; reform implies improvement.

Regime A system of rule; a political system.

Regionalization The tendency for patterns of economic and political co-operation to develop between states in the same region.

Representation Standing for, or acting on behalf of, a larger body of people; representation can involve trusteeship, delegation or resemblance (see p. 248).

Representative democracy A limited and indirect form of democracy based on the selection (usually by election) of those who will rule on behalf of the people.

Repression A state of subjugation brought about through systematic intimidation or open violence (see p. 411).

Republicanism The principle that political authority stems ultimately from the consent of the people; the rejection of monarchical and dynastic principles.

Reserve army of labour An available supply of labour easily shed in times of recession; the 'army' enjoys no security and exercises little market power.

Responsibility Sensible or morally correct behaviour; or accountability to a higher authority (see p. 342).

Responsible government A government that is answerable or accountable to an elected assembly and, through it, to the people.

Revisionism The modification of original or established beliefs; revisionism can imply the abandonment of principle or a loss of conviction.

Revolution A popular uprising that involves extralegal mass action aimed at changing the political system, not merely the ruling elite (see p. 224).

Rhetoric The art of using language to persuade or influence; rhetoric can imply high-sounding but essentially vacuous speech.

Right A broad ideological disposition characterized by sympathy for principles such as authority, order, hierarchy and duty (see p. 276).

Rights   Legal or moral entitlements to act or be treated in a particular way; civil rights differ from human rights.

Rogue state   A state whose foreign policy poses a threat to neighbouring or other states, through its aggressive intent, build-up of weapons, or association with terrorism.

Rule of law   The principle that law should 'rule' in the sense that it establishes a framework within which all conduct or behaviour takes place (see p. 326).

Ruling class   A Marxist term, denoting a class that dominates other classes and society at large by virtue of its ownership of productive wealth.

Science   The field of study that aims to develop reliable explanations of phenomena through repeatable experiments, observations and deductions (see p. 16).

Scientism   The belief that the scientific method is the only source of reliable knowledge, and is applicable to all fields of learning.

Secularism   The belief that religion should not intrude into secular (worldly) affairs, usually reflected in a desire to separate church from state.

Semi-democracy   A regime in which democratic and authoritarian features operate alongside one another in a stable combination.

Semipresidential system   A system of government in which a separately elected president presides over a government drawn from, and accountable to, the assembly.

Separation of powers   The principle that legislative, executive and judicial power should be separated through the construction of three independent branches of government (see p. 339).

Separatism   The quest to secede from a political formation with a view to establishing an independent state.

Shari'a   Islamic law, believed to be based on divine revelation, and derived from the Koran, the Hadith (the teachings of Muhammad), and other sources.

Social capital   Cultural and moral resources that help to promote social cohesion, political stability and prosperity (see p. 210).

Social class   A group of people who share a common social position and economic interests; classes can reflect unequal economic power or occupational status (see p. 197).

Social contract   A voluntary agreement through which an organized society or state is (supposedly) brought into existence; usually used as a theoretical device (see p. 93).

Social democracy   A moderate or reformist brand of socialism that favours a balance between the market and the state, rather than the abolition of capitalism.

Social justice   The morally justifiable distribution of material rewards; social justice is often seen to imply a bias in favour of equality.

Social market   An economy structured by market principles but underpinned by effective social provision designed to maintain cohesion (see p. 188).

Social movement   A collective body distinguished by a high level of commitment and political activism, but often lacking clear organization (see p. 308).

Social reflexivity   Interaction between people who enjoy a high level of autonomy within a context of reciprocity and interdependence.

Socialism   An ideology characterized by a belief in community, cooperation, equality and common ownership; socialist theories range from communism to social democracy.

'Soft' power   The ability to influence others by persuading them to follow or agree to norms and aspirations that produce the desired behaviour.

Sovereignty   Absolute and unlimited power; sovereignty can imply either supreme legal authority or unchallengeable political power (see p. 131).

Spin   The presentation of information so as to elicit a desired response, or being 'economical with the truth'.

Stalinism   Economic and political structures that resemble those constructed by Stalin in the USSR, particularly central planning and brutal political discipline.

State   A political association that establishes sovereign jurisdiction within defined territorial borders, characterized by its monopoly of legitimate violence (see p. 91).

State capitalism   A system of state ownership that replicates capitalist class relationships by concentrating economic power in the hands of a party–state elite.

State of nature   A society devoid of political authority and of formal (legal) checks on the individual; usually employed as a theoretical device.

State socialism   A form of socialism in which the state controls and directs economic life, acting, in theory, in the interests of the people.

Statism   The belief that the state is the most appropriate means of resolving problems and guaranteeing economic and social development (see p. 102).

Status   A position within a hierarchical order; a person's role, rights and duties in relation to others (see p. 197).

Subjective   Internal to the observer; related to or emanating from a person's feelings, values and opinions.

Subsidiarity   The transfer of decision-making from central to peripheral bodies; the principle that decisions should be taken at the lowest appropriate level (see p. 154).

Suffrage   The right to vote, or the exercising of that right.

Superpower   A state with preponderant nuclear military capacity and global territorial influence; a superpower is higher than a 'great' power.

Supranationalism   The ability of bodies with transnational or global jurisdiction to impose their will on nation-states (see p. 153).

Supraterritoriality   The reconfiguration of geography that has occurred through the declining importance of state borders, geographical distance and territorial location.

Sustainability   The ability of a system to maintain its health and continue to exist; the central principle of Green economics.

Systems theory   The theory that treats the political system as a self-regulating mechanism, responding to 'inputs' (demands and support) by issuing authoritative decisions or 'outputs' (policies).

Thatcherism   The free-market/strong-state ideological stance adopted by Margaret Thatcher; the UK version of the New Right political project.

Theocracy   Literally, rule by God; the principle that religious authority should prevail over political authority through the domination of church over state (see p. 37).

Theory   A systematic explanation of empirical data, usually (unlike a hypothesis) presented as reliable knowledge.

Think tank   An interest group specifically formed to develop policy proposals and campaign for their acceptance amongst opinion formers and policy-makers.

Tiger economies   Fast-growing and export-orientated economies modelled on Japan; for example, South Korea, Taiwan and Singapore.

Toleration   Forbearance; a willingness to allow people to think, speak and act in ways of which one disapproves.

Toryism   An ideological stance within conservatism characterized by a belief in hierarchy, an emphasis on tradition, and support for duty and organicism.

Totalitarian democracy   An absolute dictatorship that masquerades as a democracy, typically based on the leader's claim to a monopoly of ideological wisdom.

Totalitarianism   An all-encompassing system of political rule established through pervasive ideological manipulation and open brutality; the abolition of civil society (see p. 29).

Tradition   Continuity with the past, reflected in the transmission of institutions, values and practices from one generation to the next (see p. 221).

Transnational community   A community whose cultural identity, psychological orientation and political allegiances cut across or transcend national borders (see p. 214).

Tribalism   Group behaviour characterized by insularity and exclusivity, typically fuelled by hostility towards rival groups.

Tripartitism   The construction of bodies that represent government, business and the unions, designed to institutionalize group consultation.

Underclass   A classification of people who are socially and politically marginalised by virtue of a combination of material and cultural deprivation.

Unicameralism   The concentration of legislative power in a single-chamber assembly.

Unilateralism   One-sidedness; a policy determined by the interests and objectives of a single state, unconstrained by other states or bodies.

Unipolarity   An international system in which there is one predominant state; the existence of a single great power.

Universalism   The theory that there is a common core to human identity shared by people everywhere.

Utilitarianism   A moral philosophy that equates pleasure with 'good' and pain with 'evil', and aims to achieve the greatest happiness for the greatest number (see p. 427).

Utility   Use value; satisfaction derived from material consumption.

Utopia   Literally, nowhere or good place; an ideal or perfect society (see p. 27).

Utopianism   A style of political theorizing that develops a critique of the existing order by constructing a model of an ideal or perfect alternative (see p. 27).

Value   A moral principle that prescribes an accepted standard for individuals or groups.

Value pluralism   The theory that there is no single, overriding conception of the 'good life', but rather a number of competing and equally legitimate conceptions.

Vanguardism   The Leninist belief in the need for a party to lead and guide the proletariat towards the fulfilment of its revolutionary destiny.

Veto   The formal power to block a decision or action through the refusal of consent.

Volksgeist   (*German*) Literally, the spirit of the people; the organic identity of a people reflected in their culture and particularly their language.

War   A condition of open and violent conflict between two or more parties (usually states) (see p. 403).

Weak state   A state that lacks the capacity for effective action across a range of state functions (see p. 105).

Weapons of mass destruction   Weapons capable of destroying large areas or killing large segments of the population; nonconventional weapons, in particular nuclear, biological, chemical and radiological weapons.

Welfare   Well-being in general; politically, the term is usually associated with collectively provided welfare delivered through the mechanism of the welfare state (see p. 429).

Welfare state   A state that takes primary responsibility for the social welfare of its citizens, discharged through a range of social-security, health, education and other services (albeit different in different societies).

Westminster model   A system of government in which the executive is drawn from, and (in theory) accountable to, the assembly or parliament.

Written constitution   A single authoritative document that allocates duties, powers and functions amongst the institutions of government, and so constitutes 'higher' law.

Xenophobia   A fear or hatred of foreigners; pathological ethnocentrism.

Zionism   The movement for the establishment of a Jewish homeland, now linked to the defence of the interests and territorial integrity of Israel.

Bibliography

Abercrombie, W., S. Hill and B. Turner (1980) *The Dominant Ideology Thesis* (London: Allen & Unwin).

Albrow, M. (1970) *Bureaucracy* (London: Macmillan).

Alexander, L. (ed.) (1998) *Constitutionalism: Philosophical Foundations* (Cambridge and New York: Cambridge University Press).

Allison, G. (1971) *Essence of Decision* (Boston: Little, Brown).

Almond, G. (1989) *A Discipline Divided: Schools and Sects in Political Science* (Newbury Park, CA: Sage).

Almond, G. A. and S. Verba (1963) *The Civic Culture: Political Attitudes and Democracy in Five Nations* (Princeton: Princeton University Press).

Almond, G. A. and S. Verba (eds) (1980) *The Civic Culture Revisited* (Boston: Little, Brown).

Alter, P. (1989) *Nationalism* (London: Edward Arnold).

Anderson, B. (1983) *Imagined Communities: Reflections on the Origins and Spread of Nationalism* (London: Verso).

Anderson, J. (1984) *Public Policy-Making* (Orlando, FL: Holt, Rinehart & Winston).

Arblaster, A. (1984) *The Rise and Decline of Western Liberalism* (Oxford: Basil Blackwell).

Arblaster, A. (1994) *Democracy* (2nd edn) (Milton Keynes: Open University Press; Minneapolis: University of Minnesota Press).

Arendt, H. (1958) *The Human Condition* (Chicago: University of Chicago Press).

Aristotle (1948) *Politics* (Oxford: Clarendon Press) (ed. E. Baker).

Arrow, K. (1951) *Social Choice and Individual Values* (New York: Wiley).

Axford, B. and R. Huggins (eds) (2001) *The New Media and Politics* (London and Thousand Oaks, CA: Sage).

Babbington, A. (1990) *Military Intervention in Britain* (London: Routledge).

Bachrach, P. and M. Baratz (1962) 'The Two Faces of Power', in F. G. Castles, D. J. Murray and D. C. Potter (eds) *Decisions, Organisations and Society* (Harmondsworth: Penguin).

Bagehot, W. ([1867] 1963) *The English Constitution* (London: Fontana).

Balaam, D. N. and M. Veseth (2001) *International Political Economy* (London: Palgrave).

Ball, A. and F. Millward (1986) *Pressure Politics in Industrial Societies* (London: Macmillan).

Ball, A. and G. Peters (2005) *Modern Politics and Government* (Basingstoke and New York: Palgrave Macmillan).

Barber, B. (1995) *Jihad ve McWorld: How Globalism and Tribalism Are Reshaping the World* (New York: Ballantine Books).

Barber, J. (1988) *Politics by Humans: Research on American Leadership* (Durham, NC: Duke University Press).

Barrett, S. and C. Fudge (1981) *Policy and Action* (London: Methuen).

Barry, Brian (2002) *Culture and Equality* (Cambridge: Polity Press).

Barry, N. P. (1987) *The New Right* (London: Croom Helm).

Bartle, J. and D. Griffiths (eds) (2001) *Political Communications Transformed: From Morrison to Mandelson* (London: Palgrave).

Bauman, Z. (2004) *Identity* (Cambridge: Polity Press).

Baylis, J. and S. Smith (2005) *The Globalization of World Politics: An Introduction to International Relations* (Oxford and New York: Oxford University Press).

Beard, C. (1913) *Economic Interpretation of the Constitution of the United States* (New York: Macmillan).

Beck, U. (1992) *Risk Society: Towards New Modernity* (London: Sage).

Beer, S. (1982) *Britain Against Itself* (London: Faber).

Beetham, D. (1987) *Bureaucracy* (Milton Keynes: Open University Press).

Beetham, D. (1991) *The Legitimation of Power* (Basingstoke: Macmillan).

Bekke, H., J. Perry and T. Toonen (eds) (1996) *Civil Systems in Comparative Perspective* (Bloomington: Indiana University Press).

Bell, D. (1960) *The End of Ideology?: On the Exhaustion of Political Ideas in the 1950s* (New York: Free Press).

Bell, D. (1976) *The Cultural Contradictions of Capitalism* (London: Heinemann).

Bentham, J. ([1776] 1948) *Fragments on Government and an Introduction to the Principles of Law and Legislation* (Oxford: Blackwell) (ed. W. Harrison).

Bentley, A. ([1908] 1948) *The Process of Government* (Evanston, IL: Principia).

Berger, S. (ed.) (1981) *Organising Interests in Western Europe: Pluralism, Corporatism and the Transformation of Politics* (New York: Cambridge University Press).

Berlin, I. (1958) *Four Essays on Liberty* (Oxford: Oxford University Press).

Bernstein, E. ([1898] 1962) *Evolutionary Socialism* (New York: Schocken).

Bertsch, G., R. Clarke and D. Wood (1992) *Comparing Political Systems: Power and Policy in Three Worlds* (4th edn) (New York: Macmillan).

Birch, A. H. (1972) *Representation* (London: Macmillan; New York: Praeger).

Birch, A. H. (2000) *The Concepts and Theories of Democracy* (London: Routledge).

Blau, P. and M. Meyer (eds) (1987) *Bureaucracy in Modern Society* (3rd edn) (New York: Random House).

Blondel, J. (1973) *Comparative Legislatures* (Englewood Cliffs, NJ: Prentice Hall).

Bobbio, N. (1996) *Left and Right: The Significance of a Political Distinction* (Cambridge: Polity Press).

Bobbitt, P. (2002) *The Shield of Achilles: War, Peace and the Course of History* (London: Penguin).

Bodin, J. ([1576] 1962) *The Six Books of the Commonweal* (Cambridge, MA: Harvard University Press) (trans. R. Knolles).

Bogdanor, V. (1979) *Devolution* (Oxford: Oxford University Press).

Bogdanor, V. (ed.) (1988) *Constitutions in Democratic Politics* (Aldershot: Gower).

Bogdanor, V. and D. Butler (eds) (1983) *Democracy and Elections* (Cambridge: Cambridge University Press).

Bookchin, M. (1989) *Remaking Society* (Montreal: Black Rose).

Bottomore, T. (1991) *Classes in Modern Society* (London: Allen & Unwin).

Boulding, K. (1956) *The Image* (Ann Arbor: University of Michigan Press).

Boulding, K. (1989) *Three Faces of Power* (Newbury Park, CA: Sage).

Brandt Commission (1980) *North–South: A Programme for Survival* (Cambridge, MA: MIT Press).

Brandt Commission (1983) *Common Crisis: North–South Cooperation for World Recovery* (London: Pan).

Braybrooke, D. and C. Lindblom (1963) *A Strategy of Decision: Policy Evaluation as a Political Process* (New York: Collier Macmillan).

Breitenbach, H., T. Burden and D. Coates (1990) *Features of a Viable Socialism* (London and New York: Harvester Wheatsheaf).

Bretherton, C. and G. Ponton (eds) (1996) *Global Politics: An Introduction* (Oxford: Blackwell).

Brewer, J., A. Guelke, I. Hume, E. Moxon-Browne and R. Wilford (1988) *The Police, Public Order and the State* (Basingstoke: Macmillan).

Brittan, S. (1977) *The Economic Consequences of Democracy* (London: Temple Smith).

Brooker, P. (2000) *Non-Democratic Regimes: Theory, Government and Politics* (New York: St Martin's Press, and London: Macmillan).

Brown, D. (2000) *Contemporary Nationalism* (London and New York: Routledge).

Brown, M. B. (1995) *Models in Political Economy: A Guide to the Arguments* (2nd edn) (Harmondsworth: Penguin).

Bryson, V. (2003) *Feminist Political Theory: An Introduction* (Basingstoke: Macmillan).

Budge, I. and D. Mackie (eds) (1994) *Developing Democracy* (London: Sage).

Bull, H. (1977) *The Anarchical Society* (London: Macmillan).

Burchill, S. and A. Linklater (2005) *Theories of International Relations* (3rd edn) (Basingstoke: Palgrave Macmillan).

Burgess, M. and A.-G. Gagnon (eds) (1993) *Comparative Federalism and Federation* (London and New York: Harvester Wheatsheaf).

Burke, E. ([1790] 1968) *Reflections on the Revolution in France* (Harmondsworth: Penguin) (ed. C. C. O'Brien).

Burke, E. (1975) *On Government, Politics and Society* (London: Fontana) (ed. B. W. Hill).

Burnham, J. (1941) *The Managerial Revolution* (Harmondsworth: Penguin).

Burns, J. M. (1978) *Leadership* (New York: Harper & Row).

Burton, J. (1972) *World Society* (Cambridge: Cambridge University Press).

Butler, D. and D. Stokes (1969) *Political Change in Britain* (2nd edn) (London: Macmillan).

Butler, D., H. Penniman and A. Ranney (eds) (1981) *Democracy at the Polls* (Washington DC: American Enterprise Institute).

Butler, D., A. Adonis and T. Travers (1994) *Failure in British Government: The Politics of the Poll Tax* (Oxford: Oxford University Press).

Calvocoressi, P. (2001) *World Politics 1945–2000* (London and New York: Longman).

Campbell, A., P. Converse, W. E. Miller and D. Stokes (1960) *The American Voter* (New York: John Wiley).

Capra, F. (1983) *The Turning Point: Science, Society and the Rising Culture* (London: Fontana).

Carpenter, T. G. (2006) *America's Coming War with China: A Collision Course over Taiwan* (Basingstoke: Palgrave Macmillan).

Carr, E. H. (1939) *The Twenty Years' Crisis, 1919–1939* (London: Macmillan).

Castle, B. (1980) *The Castle Diaries 1974–1976* (London: Weidenfeld & Nicolson).

Castles, F. and R. Wildmann (eds) (1986) *The Future of Party Government – Vol. 1* (Berlin: Gruyter).

Chamberlain, H. S. ([1899] 1913) *The Foundations of the Nineteenth Century* (New York: John Lane).

Chomsky, N. (1994) *World Order, Old and New* (London: Pluto Press).

Chomsky, N. (2004) *Hegemony and Survival: America's Global Quest for Dominance (The American Empire Project)* (New York: Owl Books).

Chomsky, N. and E. Herman (1994) *Manufacturing Consent* (London: Vintage).

Chua, A. (2003) *World on Fire* (London: Heinemann).

Cigler, C. and B. Loomis (eds) (1998) *Interest Group Politics* (Washington DC: Congressional Quarterly Press).

Clarke, S. (ed.) (1991) *The State Debate* (London: Macmillan).

Cohen, A. (1975) *Theories of Revolution: An Introduction* (London: Nelson).

Connolly, W. (ed.) (1984) *Legitimacy and the State* (Oxford: Blackwell).

Cooper, R. (2004) *The Breaking of Nations: Order and Chaos in the Twenty-first Century* (London: Atlantic Books).

Cox, A. (1987) *The Court and the Constitution* (Boston: Houghton Mifflin).

Crewe, I. and D. Denver (eds) (1985) *Electoral Change in Western Democracies* (Beckenham: Croom Helm).

Crick, B. ([1962] 2000) *In Defence of Politics* (Harmondsworth and New York: Penguin).

Crosland, C. A. R. (1956) *The Future of Socialism* (London: Jonathan Cape).

Crossman, R. (1963) 'Introduction to W. Bagehot', in *The English Constitution* (London: Fontana).

Crossman, R. (1979) *The Crossman Diaries* (London: Methuen) (ed. A. Howard).

Curran, J. and J. Seaton (2003) *Power Without Responsibility* (London: Routledge).

Dahl, R. (1956) *A Preface to Democratic Theory* (Chicago: Chicago University Press).

Dahl, R. (1961) *Who Governs? Democracy and Power in an American City* (Newhaven, CT: Yale University Press).

Dahl, R. (1971) *Polyarchy: Participation and Opposition* (Newhaven, CT: Yale University Press).

Dahl, R. (1984) *Modern Political Analysis* (4th edn) (Englewood Cliffs, NJ: Prentice Hall).

Dahl, R. (1985) *A Preface to Economic Democracy* (Cambridge: Polity Press).

Dahl, R. (1989) *Democracy and its Critics* (New Haven, CT: Yale University Press).

Dahl, R. and C. Lindblom (1953) *Politics, Economics, and Welfare* (New York: Harper & Row).

Daly, M. (1978) *Gyn/Ecology: The Mathematics of Radical Feminism* (London: The Women's Press).

Davidson, R. and W. Oleszek (1999) *Congress and Its Members* (Washington DC: Congressional Quarterly).

Davidson, R. H. (ed.) (1992) *The Post-Reform Congress* (New York: St Martin's Press).

Davidson, R. H. and W. J. Oleszek (1993) *Congress and Its Members* (4th edn) (Washington DC: Congressional Quarterly Press).

Davies, J. (1971) *When Men Revolt and Why* (New York: Free Press).

Davis, R. (2005) *Electing Justice: Fixing the Supreme Court Nomination Process* (Oxford and New York: Oxford University Press).

Decalo, S. (1976) *Coups and Army Rule in Africa* (Newhaven, CT: Yale University Press).

Devlin, P. (1968) *The Enforcement of Morals* (Oxford: Oxford University Press).

Diamond, L., J. Linz and S. Lipset (eds) (1989) *Democracy in Developing Countries* (Boulder, CO: Lynne Rienner) (4 vols).

Dicey, A. V. ([1885] 1939) *Introduction to the Study of the Law of the Constitution* (London: Macmillan) (ed. E. C. S. Wade).

Djilas, M. (1957) *The New Class: An Analysis of the Communist System* (New York: Praeger).

Dobson, A. (1990) *Green Political Thought* (London: Routledge).

Downs, A. (1957) *An Economic Theory of Democracy* (New York: Harper & Row).

Drewry, G. (ed.) (1989) *The New Select Committees* (rev. edn) (Oxford: Oxford University Press).

Duchacek, I. (1973) *Power Maps: The Politics of Constitutions* (Santa Barbara, CA: ABC Clio).

Duncan, G. (ed.) (1983) *Democratic Theory and Practice* (Cambridge: Cambridge University Press).

Dunleavy, P. (1991) *Democracy, Bureaucracy and Public Choice: Economic Explanations in Political Science* (Hemel Hempstead: Harvester Wheatsheaf).

Dunleavy, P. and C. Husbands (1985) *British Democracy at the Crossroads* (London: Allen & Unwin).

Dunleavy, P. and B. O'Leary (1987) *Theories of the State* (London: Macmillan).

Dunn, J. (ed.) (1992) *Democracy: The Unfinished Journey 508 BC to AD 1993* (Oxford: Oxford University Press).

Duverger, M. (1954) *Political Parties* (London: Methuen).

Dworkin, R. (1986) *Law's Empire* (London: Fontana).

Dye, T. (1995) *Understanding Public Policy* (London: Prentice Hall).

Easton, D. (1979) *A Framework for Political Analysis* (2nd ed.) (Chicago: University of Chicago Press).

Easton, D. (1981) *The Political System* (3rd ed.) Chicago: University of Chicago Press).

Eccleston, B. (1989) *State and Society in Post-War Japan* (Cambridge: Polity Press).

Elgie, R. (1995) *Political Leadership in Liberal Democracies* (Basingstoke: Macmillan).

Etzioni, A. (1967) 'Mixed Scanning: A Third Approach to Decision Making', *Public Administration Review*, vol. 27, pp. 385–92.

Etzioni, A. (1995) *The Spirit of Community: Rights Responsibilities and the Communitarian Agenda* (London: Fontana).

Eysenck, H. (1964) *Sense and Nonsense in Psychology* (Harmondsworth: Penguin).

Fanon, F. (1968) *The Wretched of the Earth* (London: Penguin).

Farrell, D. M. (2001) *Electoral Systems: A Comparative Introduction* (London: Palgrave).

Fenton, S. (2003) *Ethnicity* (Cambridge: Polity Press).

Finer, S. (1975) *The Man on Horseback: The Role of the Military in Politics* (Harmondsworth: Penguin).

Finn, J. E. (1991) *Constitutions in Crisis: Political Violence and the Rule of Law* (New York: Oxford University Press).

Foley, M. (2000) *The British Presidency* (Manchester: Manchester University Press).

Forsyth, M. (1981) *Union of States: The Theory and Practice of Confederation* (London and New York: Leicester University Press).

Freud, S. and W. Bullitt (1967) *Thomas Woodrow Wilson: A Psychological Study* (Boston: Houghton Mifflin).

Friedan, B. (1963) *The Feminine Mystique* (Harmondsworth: Penguin).

Friedman, M. (1962) *Capitalism and Freedom* (Chicago: Chicago University Press).

Friedrich, C. J., M. Curtis and B. Barber (1960) *Totalitarianism in Perspective* (New York: Praeger).

Friedrich, C. J. and Z. Brzezinski (1963) *Totalitarian Dictatorships and Autocracy* (New York: Praeger).

Fromm, E. *The Fear of Freedom* (London: Ark).

Fukuyama, F. (1989) 'The End of History?', *National Interest*, Summer.

Fukuyama, F. (1992) *The End of History and the Last Man* (Harmondsworth: Penguin).

Fukuyama, F. (1996) *Trust* (Harmondsworth: Penguin).

Fukuyama, F. (2005) *State Building: Governance and World Order* (London: Profile Books).

Fukuyama, F. (2006) *After the Neocons: America at the Crossroads* (New York: Profile Books).

Galbraith, J. K. (1992) *The Culture of Contentment* (London: Sinclair Stevenson).

Gallagher, M. and P. Mitchell (2005) *The Politics of Electoral Systems* (Oxford and New York: Oxford University Press).

Gallie, W. B. (1955/56) 'Essentially Contested Concepts', *Proceedings of the Aristotelian Society*, vol. 56, pp. 167–97.

Gamble, A. (1981) *An Introduction to Modern Social and Political Thought* (London: Macmillan and New York: St Martin's Press).

Gamble, A. (1988) *The Free Market and the Strong State* (Basingstoke: Macmillan).

Gardner, H. (1996) *Leading Minds* (London: HarperCollins).

Gellner, E. (1983) *Nations and Nationalism* (Ithaca, NY: Cornell University Press).

Gibbins, J. (ed.) (1989) *Contemporary Political Culture: Politics in a Post-Modern Age* (London: Sage).

Giddens, A. (1994) *Beyond Left and Right: The Future of Radical Politics* (Cambridge: Polity Press).

Giddens, A. (ed.) (2001) *The Global Third Way Debate* (Cambridge: Polity Press).

Gill, S. and D. Law (1988) *The Global Political Economy: Perspectives, Problems and Policies* (Brighton: Harvester Wheatsheaf).

Ginsberg, B. (1982) *The Consequences of Consent* (Reading, MA: Addison–Wesley).

Glazer, N. and D. Moynihan (1975) *Ethnicity: Theory and Experience* (Cambridge, MA: Harvard University Press).

Gobineau, J.-A. ([1855] 1970) *Gobineau: Selected Political Writings* (New York: Harper & Row) (ed. M. D. Biddiss).

Graham, B. D. (1993) *Representation and Party Politics: A Comparative Perspective* (Oxford: Blackwell).

Graham, C. and T. Prosser (1988) *Waiving the Rules* (Milton Keynes: Open University Press).

Gramsci, A. (1971) *Selections from the Prison Notebooks* (Chicago: International Publishing Corporation) (ed. Q. Hoare and G. Nowell-Smith).

Grant, W. (1989) *Pressure Groups, Politics and Democracy in Britain* (Hemel Hempstead: Philip Allan).

Gray, J. (1993) *Post-Liberalism: Studies in Political Thought* (London: Routledge).

Griffen, R. (1991) *The Nature of Fascism* (London and New York: Pinter).

Griffiths, J. A. G. (1997) *The Politics of the Judiciary* (4th ed.) (London: Fontana).

Groz, A. (1982) *Farewell to the Working Class* (London: Pluto Press).

Gurr, T. (1970) *Why Men Rebel* (Princeton: Princeton University Press).

Habermas, J. (1973) *Legitimation Crisis* (Boston: Beacon).

Hague, R. and M. Harrop (2001) *Comparative Government and Politics: An Introduction* (5th edn) (Basingstoke: Macmillan) (US ed.: *Political Science: A Comparative Introduction* (New York: St Martin's Press)).

Hailsham, Lord (1976) *Elective Dictatorship* (BBC Publications).

Hall, P. and D. Soskice (eds) (2001) *Varieties of Capitalism: The Institutional Foundations of Comparative Advantage* (Oxford and New York: Oxford University Press).

Halliday, F. (1986) *The Making of the Second World War* (2nd edn) (London: Verso).

Halpern, D. (2005) *Social Capital* (Cambridge: Polity Press).

Hamilton, A., J. Jay and J. Madison ([1787–89] 1961) *The Federalist Papers* (New York: New American Library) (ed. C. Rossiter).

Hampden-Turner, C. and F. Trompenaars (1993) *The Seven Cultures of Capitalism* (New York: Doubleday).

Hann, A. (1995) 'Sharpening up Sabatier: Belief Systems and Public Policy', *Politics*, February.

Harrop, M. and W. L. Miller (1987) *Elections and Voters: A Comparative Introduction* (Basingstoke: Macmillan).

Hart, H. L. A. (1961) *The Concept of Law* (Oxford: Oxford University Press).

Hartz, L. (1955) *The Liberal Tradition in America* (New York: Harcourt Brace Jovanovich).

Hay, C., M. Lister and D. Marsh (2006) *The State: Theories and Issues* (Basingstoke and New York: Palgrave Macmillan).

Hayek, F. (1948) *The Road to Serfdom* (Chicago: University of Chicago Press).

Hazell, R. (ed.) (1999) *Constitutional Futures: A History of the Next Ten Years* (Oxford: Oxford University Press).

Heady, F. (1979) *Public Administration: A Comparative Perspective* (New York: Marcel Dekker).

Hearn, J. (2006) *Rethinking Nationalism: A Critical Introduction* (Basingstoke and New York: Palgrave Macmillan).

Hegel, G. W. F. ([1821] 1942) *The Philosophy of Right* (Oxford: Clarendon Press) (trans. T. M. Knox).

Heidenheimer, A., H. Heclo and C. T. Adams (1990) *Comparative Public Policy* (3rd edn) (New York: St Martin's Press).

Held, D. (1993) *Prospects for Democracy: North, South, East, West* (Oxford: Polity Press).

Held, D. (1995) *Democracy and the Global Order: From the Modern State to Global Governance* (Cambridge: Polity Press).

Held, D. (2006) *Models of Democracy* (3rd edn) (Oxford: Policy Press; Stanford: Stanford University Press).

Held, D. and A. McGrew (eds) (2000) *The Global Transformation: An Introduction to the Globalization Debate* (Cambridge and Malden MA: Polity Press).

Hennessy, P. (1986) *Cabinet* (Oxford: Blackwell).

Hennessy, P. (1990) *Whitehall* (rev. edn) (London: Fontana).

Herder, J. G. (1969) *J. G. Herder on Social and Political Culture* (Cambridge: Cambridge University Press) (ed. F. M. Barnard).

Hertz, N. (2001) *The Silent Take-over: Global Capitalism and the Death of Democracy* (London: Heinemann).

Hess, S. (1988) *Organising the Presidency* (Brookings Institution).

Heywood, A. (2007) *Political Ideologies: An Introduction* (4th edn) (Basingstoke and New York: Palgrave Macmillan).

Heywood, A. (2004) *Political Theory: An Introduction* (3rd edn) (Basingstoke and New York: Palgrave Macmillan).

Heywood, A. (2000) *Key Concepts in Politics* (Basingstoke: Macmillan).

Hill, R. and P. Frank (1983) *The Soviet Communist Party* (London: Allen & Unwin).

Himmelveit, H. T., P. Humphreys and M. Jaeger (1985) *How Voters Decide* (Milton Keynes: Open University Press).

Hirst, P. and G. Thompson (1999) *Globalization in Question: The International Economy and the Possibilities of Governance* (Cambridge: Polity Press).

Hitler, A. ([1925] 1969) *Mein Kampf* (London: Hutchinson) (trans. R. Mannheim).

Hobbes, T. ([1651] 1968) *Leviathan* (Harmondsworth: Penguin) (ed. C. B. Macpherson).

Hobsbawm, E. (1983) 'Inventing Traditions', in E. Hobsbawm and T. Ranger (eds) *The Invention of Tradition* (Cambridge: Cambridge University Press).

Hobsbawm, E. (1993) *Nations and Nationalism since 1780* (2nd edn) (Cambridge: Cambridge University Press).

Hocking, B. and M. Smith (1995) *World Politics: An Introduction to International Relations* (London: Harvester Wheatsheaf).

Hogwood, B. and L. Gunn (1984) *Policy Analysis for the Real World* (Oxford: Oxford University Press).

Holden, B. (1993) *Understanding Liberal Democracy)* (2nd edn) (London and New York: Harvester Wheatsheaf).

Holmes, J. S. (2000) *Terrorism and Democratic Stability* (Manchester: Manchester University Press).

Hondrich, T. (1992) *Conservatism* (Harmondsworth: Penguin).

Hood, C. C. (1976) *The Limits of Administration* (London: John Wiley).

Hough, J. (1977) *The Soviet Union and Social Science Theory* (Cambridge, MA: Harvard University Press).

Huntington, S. (1957) *The Soldier and the State: The Theory and Practice of Civil–Military Relations* (Cambridge, MA: Harvard University Press).

Huntington, S. (1991) *Third Wave: Democratization in the late Twentieth Century* (Norman, Okla. and London: University of Oklahoma Press).

Huntington, S. (1996) *The Clash of Civilizations and the Making of World Order* (New York: Simon & Schuster).

Hutchinson, J. and A. D. Smith (eds) (1994) *Nationalism* (Oxford and New York: Oxford University Press).

Hutton, W. (1995) *The State We're In* (London: Jonathan Cape).

Hyman, H. (1959) *Political Socialisation: A Study in the Psychology of Political Behaviour* (New York: Free Press).

Inglehart, R. (1977) *The Silent Revolution: Changing Values and Political Styles Amongst Western Publics* (Princeton: Princeton University Press).

Inglehart, R. (1990) *Cultural Shift in Advanced Industrial Society* (Princeton: Princeton University Press).

Inter-Parliamentary Union (1986) *Parliaments of the World* (Aldershot: Gower) (2 vols).

Janis, I. (1972) *Victims of Groupthink* (Boston: Houghton Mifflin).

Jenkins, S. (1995) *Accountable to None* (Harmondsworth: Penguin).

Jervis, R. (1968) 'Hypotheses on Misperception', *World Politics*, vol. 20, pp. 454–79.

Jessop, B. (1982) *The Capitalist State* (Oxford: Martin Robertson).

Jessop, B. (1990) *State Theory: Putting Capitalist States in Their Place* (Oxford: Polity Press).

Johnson, C. (1966) *Revolutionary Change* (Boston, MA: Little, Brown).

Jones, G. (ed.) (1991) *Western European Prime Ministers* (London: Frank Cass).

Jordan, J. (2006) *Interest Group Politics: Enhancing Participation?* (Basingstoke and New York: Palgrave Macmillan).

Kagan, R. (2004) *Paradise and Power: America and Europe in the New World Order* (London: Atlantic Books).

Kant, I. (1970) *Political Writings* (Cambridge: Cambridge University Press) (ed. H. Reiss).

Katz, R. (1997) *Democracy and Elections* (Oxford & New York: Oxford University Press).

Keating, M. (1988) *State and Regional Nationalism: Territorial Politics and the European State* (London and New York: Harvester Wheatsheaf).

Kegley, C. W. and E. R. Wittkopf (2001) *World Politics: Trend and Transformation* (Boston and New York: Bedford/St Martin's Press).

Keith, M. (1993) *Race Riots and Policing* (London: UCL Press).

Kellas, J. (1991) *The Politics of Nationalism and Ethnicity* (London: Macmillan).

Kellner, P. and Lord Crowther-Hunt (1980) *The Civil Servants* (London: Macdonald).

Kennedy, P. (1989) *The Rise and Fall of the Great Powers* (London: Fontana).

Key, V. O. (1966) *The Responsible Electorate* (New York: Vintage).

Keynes, J. M. ([1936] 1965) *The General Theory of Employment, Interest and Money* (San Diego: Harcourt Brace).

King, A. (1975) 'Overload: Problems of Governing in the 1970s', *Political Studies*, vol. 23, pp. 284–96.

King, A. (ed.) (1985) *The British Prime Minister* (2nd ed.) (London: Macmillan).

Kirchheimer, O. (1966) 'The Transformation of the Western European Party Systems', in J. la Palombara and M. Weiner (eds) *Political Parties and Political Development* (Princeton, NJ: Princeton University Press).

Klein, N. (2000) *No Logo* (London: Flamingo).

Knott, J. and G. Miller (1987) *Reforming Bureaucracy: The Politics of Institutional Choice* (Englewood Cliffs, NJ: Prentice Hall).

Koh, B. (1989) *Japan's Administrative Elite* (Berkeley, CA: University of California Press).

Kolko, G. (1968) *The Politics of War* (London: Weidenfeld and Nicolson).

Kolko, G. (1988) *Restructuring the World Economy* (New York: Pantheon Books).

Kressel, N. J. (ed.) (1993) *Political Psychology: Classic and Contemporary Readings* (New York: Paragon House).

Kristol, I. (1983) *Two Cheers for Capitalism* (New York: Basic Books).

Kristol, W. and R. Kagan (2004) 'National Interest and Global Responsibility', in I. Stelzer *Neoconservatism* (London: Atlantic Books).

Kropotkin, P. (1912) *Fields, Factories and Workshops* (London: Nelson).

Kuhn, T. (1962) *The Structure of Scientific Revolutions* (2nd ed.) (Chicago: Chicago University Press).

Kymlicka, William (1995) *Multicultural Citizenship* (Oxford: Oxford University Press).

Laclau, E. and C. Mouffe (1985) *Hegemony and Socialist Strategy: Towards a Radical Democratic Politics* (London: Verso).

Lafont, R. (1968) *Sur la France* (Paris: Gallimard).

Laqueur, W. (ed.) (1979) *Fascism: A Reader's Guide* (Harmondsworth: Penguin; Berkeley, CA: University of California Press).

Lane, J.-E. (1996) *Constitutions and Political Theory* (Manchester: Manchester University Press).

Lasswell, H. (1930) *Psychopathology and Politics* (New York: Viking).

Lasswell, H. (1936) *Politics: Who Gets What, When, How?* (New York: McGraw–Hill).

Le Bon, G. ([1895] 1960) *The Crowd* (New York: Viking Press).

Le Grand, J. (1982) *The Strategy of Equality: Redistribution and the Social Services* (London: Allen & Unwin).

LeDuc, L., R. G. Niemi and P. Norris (eds) (1996) *Comparing Democracies: Elections and Voting in Global Perspective* (London: Sage).

Lees, J. D. and M. Shaw (eds) (1979) *Committees in Legislatures: A Comparative Analysis* (Durham, NC: Duke University Press).

Leftwich, A. (ed.) (2004) *What is Politics? The Activity and Its Study* (Cambridge: Polity).

Lehmbruch, G. and P. C. Schmitter (1982) *Patterns of Corporatist Policy-Making* (London: Sage).

Leigh, D. and E. Vulliamy (1997) *Sleaze: The Corruption of Parliament* (London: Fourth Estate).

Lenin, V. I. ([1902] 1968) *What is to be Done?* (Harmondsworth and New York: Penguin).

Lenin, V. I. ([1916] 1970) *Imperialism: The Highest Stage of Capitalism* (Moscow: Progress).

Lichtheim, G. (1961) *Marxism* (London: Routledge & Kegan Paul).

Lijphart, A. (1990) 'Democratic Political Systems', in A. Bebler and J. Seroka (eds) *Contemporary Political Systems: Classifications and Typologies* (Boulder, CO: Lynne Reinner) pp. 71–87.

Lijphart, A. (ed.) (1992) *Parliamentary Versus Presidential Government* (Oxford: Oxford University Press).

Lijphart, A. (1999) *Democracies: Patterns of Majoritarian and Consensus Government in Thirty Six Countries* (New Haven, CT: Yale University Press).

Lijphart, A. and B. Grofman (eds) (1984) *Choosing an Electoral System* (New York: Praeger).

Lindblom, C. (1959) 'The Science of Muddling Through', *Public Administration Review*, vol. 19, pp. 79–88.

Lindblom, C. (1977) *Politics and Markets* (New York: Basic Books).

Lipset, S. and S. Rokkan (eds) (1967) *Party Systems and Voter Alignments* (New York: Free Press).

Little, R. and M. Smith (1991) *Perspective on World Politics* (London: Routledge).

Lively, J. (1975) *Democracy* (Oxford: Blackwell).

Lloyd, J. (2004) *What are the Media Doing to Our Politics?* (London: Constable).

Lloyd, J. and J. Seaton (eds) (2006) *What Can Be Done? Making the Media and Politics Better* (Oxford: Blackwell).

Locke, J. ([1690] 1965) *Two Treatises of Government* (New York: New American Library).

Loewenberg, F. and S. C. Patterson (1979) *Comparing Legislatures* (Boston, MA: Little, Brown).

Lovelock, J. (1979) *Gaia* (Oxford: Oxford University Press).

Lovelock, J. (2002) *Revenge of Gaia* (Santa Barbara, CA: Allen Lane).

Lukes, S. (2004) *Power: A Radical View* (Basingstoke and New York: Palgrave Macmillan).

Machiavelli, N. ([1531] 1961) *The Prince* (Harmondsworth: Penguin) (trans. G. Bau).

MacIntyre, A. (1981) *After Virtue* (Notre Dame, IL: University of Notre Dame Press).

Mackintosh, J. P. (1977) *The British Cabinet* (London: Stevens).

Macpherson, C. B. (1962) *The Theory of Possessive Individualism* (Oxford: Oxford University Press).

Macpherson, C. B. (1972) *The Real World of Democracy* (New York and Oxford: Oxford University Press).

Macpherson, C. B. (1977) *The Life and Times of Liberal Democracy* (Oxford: Oxford University Press).

Mair, P. (1990) *The West European Party System* (Oxford: Oxford University Press).

Mao, Z. (1971) *Selected Readings from the Works of Mao Zedong* (Peking: Foreign Languages Press).

Marcuse, H. (1964) *One-Dimensional Man: Studies in the Ideology of Advanced Industrial Society* (Boston: Beacon).

Marquand, D. (1988) *The Unprincipled Society* (London: Cape).

Marsh, D. and R. A. W. Rhodes (eds) (1992) *Policy Networks in British Government* (Oxford: Oxford University Press).

Marsh, D. and G. Stoker (eds) (1995) *Theory and Methods in Political Science* (Basingstoke: Macmillan).

Marshall, P. (1991) *Demanding the Impossible: A History of Anarchism* (London: HarperCollins).

Marshall, T. H. (1950) 'Citizenship and Social Class', in T. Marshall (ed.) *Sociology at the Crossroads* (London: Heinemann).

Marty, M. E. and R. S. Appleby (1993) *Fundamentalisms and the State: Remaking Polities, Economies, and Militance* (Chicago: University of Chicago Press).

Marx, K. ([1845] 1968) 'Theses on Feuerbach', in *Selected Works in One Volume* (London: Lawrence & Wishart), pp. 28–31.

Marx, K. ([1852] 1963) *The Eighteenth Brumaire of Louis Bonaparte* (New York: International Publishers).

Marx, K. ([1867, 1885, 1894] 1970) *Capital* (London: Lawrence and Wishart) (3 vols).

Marx, K. and Engels, F. ([1846] 1970) *The German Ideology* (London: Lawrence & Wishart) (ed. C. J. Arthur).

Marx, K. and Engels, F. ([1848] 1967) *The Communist Manifesto* (Harmondsworth: Penguin).

Mayes, P. (1986) *Gender* (London: Longman).

Mayo, H. (1960) *An Introduction to Democratic Theory* (New York: Oxford University Press).

McCarthy, J. D. and M. N. Zald (1973) *The Trend of Social Movements in America: Professionalisation and Resource Mobilisation* (Morristown, NJ: General Learning Press).

McCauley, M. (1983) *The Origins of War* (London: Longman).

McCormick, J. (2005) *Understanding the European Union: A Concise Introduction* (Basingstoke and New York: Palgrave Macmillan).

McDowell, L. and R. Pringle (eds) (1992) *Defining Women: Social Institutions and Gender Divisions* (Cambridge: Polity Press).

McGrew, A. G. *et al.* (eds) (1992) *Global Politics: Globalisation and the Nation-State* (Oxford: Policy Press).

McKenzie, R. T. (1955) *British Political Parties* (London: Heinemann).

McLellan, D. (1986) *Ideology* (Milton Keynes: Open University Press; Minneapolis: University of Minnesota Press).

McLennan, G., D. Held and S. Hall (eds) (1984) *The Idea of the Modern State* (Milton Keynes and Philadelphia, PA: Open University Press).

McQuail, D. (1992) *Media Performance* (London: Sage).

Meinecke, F. ([1907] 1970) *Cosmopolitanism and the National State* (Princeton: Princeton University Press).

Menon, A. and M. A. Schain (2006) *Comparative Federalism* (Oxford and New York: Oxford University Press).

Meny, Y. and V. Wright (eds) (1985) *Centre–Periphery Relations in Western Europe* (London: Croom Helm).

Mezey, M. (1979) *Comparative Legislatures* (Durham, NC: Duke University Press).

Michels, R. ([1911] 1962) *Political Parties: A Sociological Study of the Oligarchical Tendencies of Modern Democracy* (New York: Collier).

Miliband, R. (1969) *The State in Capitalist Society* (London: Weidenfeld and Nicolson).

Miliband, R. (1972) *Parliamentary Socialism* (London: Merlin).

Mill, J. S. ([1859] 1982) *On Liberty* (Harmondsworth: Penguin).

Mill, J. S. ([1861] 1951) *Considerations on Representative Government*, in H. B. Acton (ed.) *Utilitarianism, Liberty, and Representative Government* (London: Dent).

Millett, K. (1970) *Sexual Politics* (London: Granada).

Mills, C. W. (1956) *The Power Elite* (New York: Oxford University Press).

Monbiot, G. (2001) *Captive State: The Corporate Take-over of Britain* (London: Pan).

Montesquieu, C.-L. ([1748] 1949) *The Spirit of the Laws* (New York: Hafner) (trans. T. Nugent).

More, T. ([1516] 1965) *Utopia* (Harmondsworth: Penguin) (trans. P. Turner).

Morgenthau, H. (1948) *Politics Amongst Nations: The Struggle for Power and Peace* (New York: Knopf).

Mosca, G. ([1896] 1939) *The Ruling Class* (New York: McGraw–Hill) (trans. A. Livingstone).

Murray, C. (1984) *Losing Ground: American Social Policy (1950–80)* (New York: Basic Books).

Murray, C. and R. Herrnstein (1995) *The Bell Curve: Intelligence and Class Structure in American Life* (New York: Free Press).

Neumann, S. (1956) *Modern Political Parties* (Chicago: University of Chicago Press).

Neustadt, R. ([1964] 1980) *Presidential Power: The Politics of Leadership from FDR to Carter* (New York: John Wiley).

Nietzsche, F. (1982) *Thus Spoke Zarathustra* (New York: Random House) (trans. R. J. Hollingdale).

Niskanen, W. A. (1971) *Bureaucracy and Representative Government* (Chicago: Aldine–Atherton).

Nordlinger, E. (1977) *Soldiers in Politics: Military Coups and Governments* (Englewoods Cliffs, NJ: Prentice Hall).

Nordlinger, E. (1981) *On the Autonomy of the Democratic State* (Cambridge, MA: Harvard University Press).

Norton, A. (1994) *International Handbook of Local and Regional Government* (Aldershot and Brookfield, VT: Edward Elgar).

Norton, P. (ed.) (1990a) *Legislatures* (Oxford: Oxford University Press).

Norton, P. (ed.) (1990b) *Parliaments in Western Europe* (London: Frank Cass).

Norton, P. (1993) *Does Parliament Matter?* (London: Harvester Wheatsheaf).

Nove, A. (1983) *The Economics of Feasible Socialism* (London: Macmillan).

Nozick, R. (1974) *Anarchy, State and Utopia* (Oxford: Basil Blackwell).

Nugent, N. (1991) *The Government and Politics of the European Community* (2nd edn) (Basingstoke: Macmillan).

Oakeshott, M. (1962) *Rationalism in Politics and Other Essays* (London and New York: Methuen).

Oates, S. (2005) 'Media and Political Communication', in S. White, Z. Gitelman and R. Sakwa (eds) *Developments in Russian Politics 6* (Basingstoke and New York: Palgrave Macmillan).

O'Brien, D. (2000) *Storm Center: The Supreme Court in American Politics* (5th edn) (New York: Norton).

O'Brien, R. and M. Williams (2007) *Global Political Economy* (2nd edn) (Basingstoke and New York: Palgrave Macmillan).

OECD (1995) *Globalization: What Challenges and Opportunities for Governments?* (Paris: OECD)

Offe, C. (1984) *Contradictions of the Welfare State* (London: Hutchinson).

Ohmae, K. (1989) *Borderless World: Power and Strategy in the Interlinked Economy* (London: HarperCollins).

Olson, D. (1994) *Legislative Institutions: A Comparative View* (Armonk, NY: M. E. Sharpe).

Olson, M. (1968) *The Logic of Collective Action: Public Goods and the Theory of Groups* (Cambridge, MA: Harvard University Press).

Olson, M. (1982) *The Rise and Decline of Nations* (Newhaven, CT: Yale University Press).

Osborne, D. and T. Gaebler (1992) *Reinventing Government* (New York: Addison–Wesley).

Ostrogorski, M. (1902) *Democracy and the Organisation of Political Parties* (London: Macmillan).

O'Sullivan, N. (1976) *Conservatism* (London: Dent).

Paddison, R. (1983) *The Fragmented State: The Political Geography of Power* (New York: St Martin's Press).

Paine, T. ([1776] 1987) 'Common Sense', in M. Foot (ed.) *The Thomas Paine Reader* (Harmondsworth: Penguin).

Pakulski, J. (1990) *Social Movements: The Politics of Protest* (Melbourne: Longman).

Parekh, B. (2006) *Rethinking Multiculturalism in Cultural Diversity and Political Theory* (2nd edn) (Basingstoke and New York: Palgrave Macmillan).

Parry, G. and M. Moran (eds) (1994) *Democracy and Democratization* (London: Routledge).

Parsons, A. (1995) *From Cold War to Hot Peace: UN Interventions, 1945–1994* (London: Michael Joseph).

Parsons, W. (1995) *Public Policy: Introduction to the Theory and Practice of Policy Analysis* (Aldershot: Edward Elgar).

Pateman, C. (1970) *Participation and Democratic Theory* (Cambridge: Cambridge University Press).

Peele, G., C. Bailey, B. Cain and B. G. Peters (eds) (1994) *Developments in British Politics 2* (Basingstoke: Macmillan).

Philo, G. (ed.) (1999) *Message Received* (London: Longman).

Pierson, C. (2000) *The New Politics of Welfare* (Oxford and New York).

Pierre, J. and B. Guy Peters (2000) *Governance, Politics and the State* (London: Macmillan).

Pinkney, R. (1990) *Right-Wing Military Government* (London: Pinter).

Piore, M. J. and C. Sabel (1984) *The Second Industrial Divide: Possibilities for Prosperity* (New York: Basic Books).

Plant, R. (1991) *Modern Political Thought* (Oxford: Oxford University Press).

Plato (1955) *The Republic* (Harmondsworth: Penguin) (trans. H. D. Lee).

Poggi, G. (1990) *The State* (Cambridge: Polity Press).

Poguntke, T. and P. Webb (2005) *The Presidentialization of Politics: A Comparative Study of Modern Democracies* (Oxford and New York: Oxford University Press).

Polsby, N. (1963) *Community Power and Political Theory* Newhaven, CT: Yale University Press).

Poulantzas, N. (1968) *Political Power and Social Classes* (London: New Left Books).

Pressman, J. and A. Wildavsky (1973) *Implementation* (Berkeley, CA: University of California Press).

Proudhon, P.-J. ([1840] 1970) *What is Property?* (New York: Dover).

Przeworski, A. (1991) *Democracy and the Market: Political and Economic Reforms in Eastern Europe and Latin America* (Cambridge and New York: Cambridge University Press).

Pulzer, P. (1967) *Political Representation and Elections in Britain* (London: Allen & Unwin).

Putnam, R. (1993) *Making Democracy Work: Civic Traditions in Modern Italy* (Princeton, NJ: Princeton University Press).

Putnam, R. (1996) 'Who Killed Civic America?', *Prospect*, March, pp. 66–72.

Putnam, R. (2000) *Bowling Alone: The Collapse and Revival of American Community* (New York: Simon & Schuster).

Randall, V. (ed.) (1988) *Political Parties in the Third World* (London: Sage).

Rawls, J. (1971) *A Theory of Justice* (Oxford: Oxford University Press).

Reiner, R. (1993) *The Politics of the Police* (2nd ed.) (Hemel Hempstead: Harvester Wheatsheaf).

Rex, J. and D. Mason (eds) (1992) *Theories of Race and Ethnic Relations* (Cambridge: Cambridge University Press).

Rhodes, R. (1996) 'The New Governance: Governing without Government', *Political Studies*, vol. 44, pp. 652-67.

Rhodes, R. and P. Dunleavy (eds) (1995) *Prime Minister, Cabinet and Core Executive* (London: Macmillan).

Rhodes, R. A. W. (1988) *Beyond Westminster and Whitehall* (London: Unwin Hyman).

Richardson, J. (ed.) (1984) *Policy Styles in Western Europe* (London: Allen & Unwin).

Richardson, J. (ed.) (1993) *Pressure Groups* (Oxford and New York: Oxford University Press).

Ritzer, G. (2000) *The McDonaldization of Society* (Thousand Oaks, CA: Pine Forge Press).

Roach, J. and J. Thomaneck (1985) *Police and Public Order in Europe* (London: Croom Helm).

Robins, L., H. Blackmore and R. Pyper (eds) (1994) *Britain's Changing Party System* (London and New York: Leicester University Press).

Rokkan, S. (1970) *Citizens, Elections, Parties* (New York: McKay).

Roler, E. (2005) *The Performance of Democracies* (Oxford and New York: Oxford University Press).

Rose, R. (ed.) (1980) *Challenge to Governance: Studies in Overloaded Politics* (London: Sage).

Rose, R. (1987) *The Postmodern Presidency: The White House Meets the World* (New York: Chartham House).

Rousseau, J.-J. ([1762] 1913) *The Social Contract* (London: Dent) (trans. G. D. H. Cole).

Rowat, D. (ed.) (1988) *Public Administration in Developed Democracies: A Comparative Study* (New York: Marcel Dekker).

Rush, M. (1992) *Politics and Society: An Introduction to Political Sociology* (Hemel Hempstead: Harvester Wheatsheaf).

Russell, M. (2000) *Reforming the House of Lords: Lessons from Overseas* (Oxford and New York: Oxford University Press).

Sabatier, P. (1988) 'An Advocacy Coalition Model of Policy Making and Change and the Role of Policy Orientated Learning Therein', *Policy Sciences*, vol. 1, pp. 129–68.

Said, E. (1978) *Orientalism: Western Conceptions of the Orient* (New York: Vintage Books).

Said, E. (1978) *Orientalism: Western Conceptions of the Orient* (London: Penguin).

Sandel, M. (1982) *Liberalism and the Limits of Justice* (Cambridge: Cambridge University Press).

Sartori, G. (1976) *Parties and Party Systems: A Framework for Analysis* (Cambridge: Cambridge University Press).

Sartori, G. (1987) *The Theory of Democracy Revisited* (Chatham, NJ: Chatham House).

Saunders, P. (1990) *Social Class and Stratification* (London: Routledge).

Savage, S., R. Atkinson and L. Robins (1994) *Public Policy in Britain* (Basingstoke: Macmillan).

Scammel, M. (2000) 'New Media, New Politics' in Dunleavy, P., A. Gamble, I. Holliday and G. Peele (eds) *Developments in British Politics 6* (London: Macmillan).

Schlesinger, A. (1974) *The Imperial Presidency* (New York: Popular Library).

Scholte, J. A. (2005) *Globalization: A Critical Introduction* (Basingstoke and New York: Palgrave Macmillan).

Schumacher, E. F. (1973) *Small is Beautiful: A Study of Economics As If People Mattered* (London: Blond & Briggs).

Schumpeter, J. (1942) *Capitalism, Socialism and Democracy* (London: Allen & Unwin).

Schwarzmantel, J. (1991) *Socialism and the Idea of the Nation* (London: Harvester Wheatsheaf).

Schwarzmantel, J. (1994) *The State in Contemporary Society: An Introduction* (London and New York: Harvester Wheatsheaf).

Sedgemore, B. (1980) *The Secret Constitution* (London: Hodder & Stoughton).

Self, P. (1994) *Government by the Market? Politics of Public Choice* (Basingstoke: Macmillan).

Seliger, M. (1976) *Politics and Ideology* (London: Allen & Unwin).

Sen, Amartya (2006) *Identity and Violence* (New York: W. W. Norton).

Simon, H. (1983) *Models of Bounded Rationality – Vol. 2* (Cambridge, MA: MIT Press).

Skocpol, T. (1979) *States and Social Revolutions* (Cambridge: Cambridge University Press).

Smith, A. ([1776] 1930) *The Wealth of Nations* (London: Methuen).

Smith, A. D. (1986) *The Ethnic Origins of Nations* (Oxford: Basil Blackwell).

Smith, B. C. (1985) *Decentralisation: The Territorial Dimension of the State* (London: Allen & Unwin).

Smith, M. (1995) *Pressure Groups* (Manchester: Baseline Books).

Social Trends, 2005 (London: HMSO).

Sørenson, G. (2004) *The Transformation of the State: Beyond the Myth of Retreat* (Basingstoke and New York: Palgrave Macmillan).

Soros, G. (1998) *The Crisis of Global Capitalism: Open Society Endangered* (New York: BBS/Public Affairs).

Spencer, P. and H. Wollman (eds) (2005) *Nations and Nationalism* (Edinburgh: Edinburgh University Press).

Stoker, J. (2006) *Why Politics Matter: Making Democracy Work* (Basingstoke and New York: Palgrave Macmillan).

Strøm, K., W. Müller and T. Bergman (eds) (2006) *Delegation and Accountability in Parliamentary Democracies* (Oxford and New York: Oxford University Press).

Suleiman, E. (ed.) (1984) *Bureaucrats and Policy Making* (New York: Holmes & Meier).

Sun Tzu (1963) *The Art of War* (New York: Oxford University Press) (trans. S. B. Griffith).

Talmon, J. L. (1952) *The Origins of Totalitarian Democracy* (London: Secker & Warburg).

Tarrow, S. (1998) *Power in Movement: Social Movements and Contentious Politics* (Cambridge and New York: Cambridge University Press).

Thatcher, M. (1993) *The Downing Street Years* (London: HarperCollins).

Titmuss, R. M. (1968) *Essays on the Welfare State* (London: Allen & Unwin).

Tocqueville, A. de ([1856] 1947) *The Old Regime and the French Revolution* (Oxford: Blackwell) (trans. M. W. Patterson).

Trotsky, L. (1937) *The Revolution Betrayed* (London: Faber & Faber) (trans. M. Eastman).

Truman, D. (1951) *The Governmental Process* (New York: Knopf).

Verheijes, T. and D. Coombes (eds) (1998) *Innovations in Public Management: Perspectives from East and West Europe* (Cheltenham & Northampton, MA: Edward Elgar).

Wachendorfer-Schmidt, U. (ed.) (2000) *Federalism and Political Performance* (London & New York: Routledge).

Wallerstein, I. (1984) *The Politics of the World Economy* (Cambridge: Cambridge University Press).

Waltman, J. and K. Holland (eds) (1988) *The Political Role of Law Courts in Modern Democracies* (New York: St Martin's Press).

Waltz, K. N. (1979) *Theory of International Politics* (Reading, MA: Addison–Wesley).

Weber, M. (1948) *From Max Weber: Essays in Sociology* (London: Routledge & Kegan Paul).

Weller, P. (1985) *First Among Equals: Prime Ministers in Westminster Systems* (Sydney: Allen & Unwin).

White, S., J. Gardner, G. Schopflin and T. Saich (1990) *Communist and Postcommunist Political Systems* (Basingstoke: Macmillan).

Wildavsky, A. (1980) *Art and Craft of Policy Analysis* (Macmillan: London).

Wilson, G. (1990) *Interest Groups* (Oxford: Blackwell).

Wilson, W. ([1885] 1961) *Constitutional Government: A Study in American Politics* (New York: Meridian).

Wolinetz, S. (ed.) (1997) *Political Parties* (Aldershot and Brookfield, VT: Ashgate).

Wollstonecraft, M. ([1792] 1985) *A Vindication of the Rights of Women* (Harmondsworth: Penguin).

World Bank (1985) *World Development Report 1985* (Washington, DC: World Bank).

World Bank (1986) *World Development Report 1986* (Washington, DC: World Bank).

Wright, A. (1987) *Socialisms: Theories and Practices* (Oxford: Oxford University Press).

Wright, V., B. Guy Peters and R. Rhodes (eds) (2000) *Administering the Summit: Administration of the Core Executive in Developed Countries* (London: Macmillan).

Yergin, D. (1980) *Shattered Peace: The Origins of the Cold War and the National Security State* (Harmondsworth: Penguin).

Zimmerman, J. F. (1992) *Contemporary American Federalism* (London and New York: Leicester University Press).

Index

The
Working Horse
Manual

The Working Horse Manual

Edited by Diana Zeuner

FARMING PRESS

IN ASSOCIATION WITH

MAGAZINE

First published 1998
Copyright © Diana Zeuner

All rights reserved. No part of this publication may be reproduced, stored in a retrieval system, or transmitted, in any form or by any means, electronic, mechanical, photocopying, recording or otherwise, without prior permission of Farming Press.

ISBN 0 85236 401 6

A catalogue record for this book is available from the British Library

Published by Farming Press, Miller Freeman UK Ltd, 2, Wharfedale Road, Ipswich IP1 4LG, United Kingdom

In association with Heavy Horse World Magazine, Park Cottage, West Dean, Chichester, West Sussex, PO18 0RX

Distributed in North America by Diamond Farm Enterprises, Box 537, Alexandria Bay, NY 13607, USA

Cover design by Mark Dunningham
Printed and bound in Great Britain by The Bath Press, Bath

Acknowledgements

I am indebted to countless people from the world of the working horse with whom conversations were held as this manual progressed, and especially to all the authors and practitioners whose contributions form this book. In addition special help was given by Keith Chivers, Nick Rayner, Terry and Mary Keegan, Richard and Angela Gifford, Beatrice Potter, Sara Roberts, Jim Waterson, Charlie Coffen, Rob Dash, John and Betty Peacock, Tom and Cate Brewster, Audrey Hart, Roy Fox and John Rotheroe.

Finally, I am most grateful to Chris Zeuner for moral support and useful bits of advice, and to Francesca and Anna Zeuner for their tolerance in putting up with an even busier work schedule than usual.

Acknowledgements for photographs and drawings

The Modern Draught Horse in the UK
1.1   Countryside Audio and Visual
1.2   Richard Gifford
1.3   Chris Wadsworth
1.8   David Bakewell
1.9   Sam Smith's Brewery
1.10 Bracknell Forest Borough Council
1.11 Reg Wilcox
1.12 John Zawadzki
1.13 Roy Fox
1.14 George Ladds
1.15 Jo Hewitt
1.16 Romany Gypsy Photograph Collection – Barrie
      Law/Edward Hart
1.17 Charlie and Gina Parker
1.18 and 1.19 Audrey Hart
1.20 redrawn by Carole Vincer

Choosing and Keeping a Working Horse
2.1   Roy Fox
2.2 – 2.15 courtesy of Bob Mouland

Veterinary Care of the Draught Horse
3.6 RSPCA

Farriery for the Working Horse
All illustrations courtesy of Roger Clark
4.2   redrawn by Graham Butler

Harness for the Working Horse
All illustrations except 7.8 and 7.10, including drawings –
      Terry Keegan

Working Draught Horses as Singles and Pairs
8.1, 8.6, 8.8, 8.15 courtesy of Terry Keegan, *The Heavy Horse, its Harness and Harness Decoration*
8.2   courtesy of Nick Rayner/Keith Chivers, *The Heavy Horse Manual*
8.4   Graham Butler after Angela Gifford
8.32 A Massey Harris instruction book for assembly of corn drill, circa 1940
All other illustrations by Angela and Richard Gifford
8.1, 8.6, 8.8, 8.9, 8.15, 8.17c redrawn by Carole Vincer

Ploughing
9.1   *Heavy Horse Handbook* (Southern Counties Heavy Horse
      Association). Redrawn by Terry Keegan
9.2   redrawn by Terry Keegan
9.5   Terry Keegan
9.3a Angela Gifford
9.3b and 9.4 Roy Fox
9.5   *Horse Ploughing*, Terry Keegan
9.6   redrawn by Carole Vincer
9.7   Jeff Smith
9.8   Mike Flood
9.10 Graham Butler after Mike Flood
9.11 Mike Flood
Common Horse Ploughing Terms – *Heavy Horse Handbook*
      (Southern Counties Heavy Horse Association), plus
      additions specially for this book

Horse-drawn Machinery and Equipment
10.2 Mrs V. Brake
10.3, 10.5 Angela and Richard Gifford
10.7 Linda Chapman
10.9 Charlie Pinney

Multiple Hitches
All figures except Figure 11.5 Geoff Morton
11.10 redrawn by Carole Vincer

Working Horses in Forestry
Figures 12.1, 12.2 Graham Butler after Hans Sidbäck, *The Horse
      in the Forest,* Swedish University of Agricultural Science
      Research Information Centre
All other illustrations Angela and Richard Gifford
12.7a, b and c, 12.14 redrawn by Carole Vincer

Selecting a Show Horse
13.1 John Peacock

Preparation of a Show Horse
14.1, 14.3, 14.6a, 14.10 Roy Fox
14.4, 14.7, 14.8 14.9 Reg Wilcox

Plaiting a Heavy Horse for Showing
The Clydesdale – Graham Butler after Cate Brewster
The Shire: plaiting – John Peacock
15.1.6 Roy Fox
15.4.2 – 15.4.6 redrawn by Carole Vincer
The Suffolk: plaiting – Norma Bradley;
      photographs – Roy Fox
The Percheron: plaiting – Matthew Bradley;
      photographs – Roy Fox

Road Driving
John Peacock

Caring for Horse-drawn Vehicles
17.2, 17.5b Carole Vincer after Mike Horler

All other photographs by Diana Zeuner

Contents

Appendices

Foreword

Keith Chivers

The sudden collapse of the horse age after the Second World War left just a very few people obstinately continuing to breed animals of a type which appeared to be of no use or value to anyone else. In the eye of any member of the general public who was aware of such a man, he was like the folk who in 1922 'did not believe in the wireless'.

Illogically, new breeders and owners began to join the old faithfuls in the 1960s, chiefly as a hobby. They were now applauded, rather than pitied, by those who increasingly relished nostalgia or, at a higher level, the preservation of heritage.

When in 1983 the Shire Horse Society initiated the project 'History with a Future', in order to investigate the future of the heavy horse, it heralded a revolution in thinking. It posed many questions. Were there tasks to which the draught horse could be economically and efficiently harnessed in modern times, bearing in mind that it is environmentally and ecologically friendly and more acceptable socially than the motor engine? Could there be forms of competition more interesting to spectators and testing for horses and their handlers than the esoteric mystery of in-hand and turnout judging? How could new or potential owners learn how to manage and work horses? Were there any new ideas on other matters and so on?

In 10 study groups 76 different people spent 3 years debating and even experimenting by means of demonstrations and trials. Most were members of one or other of the breed societies, though none was a delegate or had a sectarian axe to grind. Others brought a variety of knowledge and abilities from outside. All contributed only their own individual ideas.

In 1987 – more than a year before the project report was published – one of these, Christopher Zeuner, and his wife Diana, launched the *Heavy Horse World* magazine, with Diana as editor, advertising and business manager. Terry Keegan, also a project man, was the magazine's representative "in the field" so to speak, often literally. I hate to think how slowly history would have progressed into the future without that quarterly magazine, which keeps everyone in touch with everything that is going on. It is therefore entirely appropriate that this book is the brain-child of Diana and has been assembled and edited by her. I believe that, historically, it will prove the most important manual since William Youatt and I.K. Brunel collaborated in 1831. That's really something.

Having been privileged to read the text in advance, I cannot resist a brief verdict of my own. All contributions are remarkable in four special respects – comprehensiveness, attention to detail, terseness (every word counts) and clarity. However self-confident one may be, would it not be good to have, as neighbours at your beck and call, a bevy of experts whose abilities covered the whole range of expertise? Of course, but in this book you have the next best thing. Incidentally, 11 of the 24 contributors were among those who travelled and toiled so selflessly, and at their own expense, to debate the possibility of a future for history.

Contributors

Mike Bingham Head of School, Rother Valley College; heavy horse representative of the National Horse Education and Training Company; BHS (British Horse Society) accredited NVQ assessor and verifier

Carl Boyde MRCVS Veterinary surgeon with specialist interest in draught and working horses; President, Southern Counties Heavy Horse Association; panel judge of the Shire and Percheron Horse Societies; past President, British Percheron Horse Society

Matthew Bradley Suffolk and British Percheron exhibitor

Norma Bradley Suffolk and British Percheron exhibitor; braiding judge for Suffolk Horse Society

Cate Brewster Clydesdale exhibitor

Tom Brewster Clydesdale exhibitor; past President of Clydesdale Horse Society; panel judge of the Shire, Percheron and Clydesdale Horse Societies; BHS (British Horse Society) NVQ accredited assessor; BHS Road Driving Assessment examiner

Roger Clark FWCF (Hons) Specialist heavy horse farrier and farmer; Fellow of the Worshipful Company of Farriers and member of their examination board; past President of the Suffolk Horse Society; panel judge of the Shire, British Percheron and Suffolk Horse Societies

Mike Flood Ploughing competitor and judge; past Chairman of the Eastern Counties Heavy Horse Association

Roy Fox Specialist photographer of heavy horses

Angela Gifford BEd Farmer; qualified teacher; ATB (Agricultural Training Board) instructor; professional trainer in horsemanship; BHS (British Horse Society) NVQ accredited assessor

Edward Hart Agricultural journalist, author and bookseller with specialist interest in heavy horses and rural life

Mike Horler Wheelwright; BHS (British Horse Society) NVQ accredited assessor; Shire exhibitor; panel judge of the Shire Horse Society

Terry Keegan Specialist supplier of heavy horse harness and decorations; author on heavy horse subjects; past President of the Western Counties Heavy Horse Society and of the Wessex Shire Horse Hiring Society

Rowena McDermott British Percheron exhibitor; panel judge of the British Percheron Horse Society; joint founder of British Heavy Horse Driving Trials Club

Geoff Morton MBE Farmer; past President of the British Percheron Horse Society

John Peacock Shire exhibitor; panel judge of the Shire, British Percheron and Suffolk Horse Societies; Shire Horse Society Council member; Road Driving Assessment standard co-author and examiner; BHS (British Driving Society) NVQ accredited assessor

Charlie Pinney Farmer; inventor of modern horse-drawn machinery and joint proprietor of Cart Horse Machinery Ltd

Nick Rayner Farmer; past Chairman of Southern Counties Heavy Horse Association; ploughing judge

Sara Roberts Field Officer for the South of England, Forestry Contracting Association

Philip Ryder-Davies MB, BS, BVsc, MRCVS Secretary of the Suffolk Horse Society; veterinary surgeon

John Ward Field Officer of the Shire Horse Society

Nigel Westacott Formerly with the enforcement branch of the Department of Transport; former heavy horse event organiser

John Zawadzki Editor, *The Clydesdale International*

Diana Zeuner Publisher/Editor *Heavy Horse World* magazine

Introduction

For 15 years, *The Heavy Horse Manual* by Nick Rayner and Keith Chivers was a bible to all those determined to keep the working horse and the skills of horsemanship alive in modern times. Despite the revival of interest in the heavy horse throughout the UK in the 1970s and 1980s, the working horse could still appear incongruous in a world where industrialization, mechanization and most recently the information technology revolution seem to render the draught horse a relic of a past age.

Yet the 1990s is also a period when people are increasingly conscious of their natural environment and the importance of applying low-technology solutions to modern problems. At the same time, great emphasis is placed on leisure activities and marketing and promotion of products and services. These are two different sides of the same coin, yet suddenly the draught horse finds a place for its future in both.

To capitalize on these needs and demands, draught horses must be well bred, well cared for and well trained. Equally, the men and women who work them need to have access to information and training of high quality. New owners of draught horses and those determined to work their animals in field, forest and town are very far from the experienced horsemen who once characterized the draught horse scene. Men who worked as carters and horsemen in the heyday of the horse are fewer and fewer. The gap of knowledge and experience is widening.

It is also true that although many of the traditional ways of horsemanship are as relevant today as they ever were, there are other methods and techniques of the modern age which can play their part in fashioning the working horse and the horsemen and women of the future.

This manual is therefore designed to do two things — to fill a perceived gap in the information currently available and to bring together traditional ways and modern techniques to suit today's circumstances. These are the most pressing needs which constantly recur in contacts and discussions with all those with an interest in *Heavy Horse World* magazine, the only magazine in the British Isles devoted solely to the draught horse and working horsemanship.

We hope the manual will be a worthy successor to *The Heavy Horse Manual*. Although our objectives are very similar, we have taken a different approach. As with any sector of society, the heavy horse world has attracted some distinguished individuals, who have played a significant role in furthering its fortunes. Many of these people have been asked to contribute to the manual. They also reflect the geographical spread of interest in working horses in the UK, and the different aspects of work in which we find heavy horses playing a part.

Inevitably some sections will contain material which overlaps with other sections, but we have striven to keep this to a minimum. Where contributors differ on the best way to achieve something, we hope readers will appreciate that this simply reflects life. There is usually more than one way to reach the same end result. Often both, or all, have equal merit — the difference is in style, not substance. Practitioners will decide which way suits them best in their own circumstances.

Safety runs as an undercurrent through all the sections, reflecting an increasing preoccupation with care in all aspects of horsemanship, especially in public situations. Political correctness, another current preoccupation, is less easy to adhere to in a world which accepts that many of the traditional ways are still the best. When the word 'horseman' is used, therefore, it should be taken to mean 'horsewoman' also. Equally, the word 'him' used to describe a horse could just as well read 'her'.

In the text there is no beating about the bush. The sections are designed to be practical, easy to refer to, and therefore, we hope, of the greatest use to those seeking information about horsemanship. Alongside the sections are appendices and sources directing readers to further information about a wide variety of aspects of working horses and their tasks. Inevitably there will be some omissions. There will also be those who disagree with the advice offered. We hope, however, that this manual contains the essentials needed by anyone resolved to follow the advice of the contributors and others, whose determination and activity have ensured the survival of the working horse thus far.

Diana Zeuner
Editor, Heavy Horse World

CHAPTER 1

The Modern Draught Horse in the UK

Diana Zeuner

Introduction

The 20th century has seen wild swings in the fortunes of the working horse. From its heyday in the first quarter, when it was the engine of industry in a way which is generally unappreciated, to its decline during the war years, its near disappearance in the 1950s and 1960s and its revival in the 1970s and 1980s, the future of working horses has been at the impulse of man and his inventions.

The 1990s can probably be seen as a period of consolidation of those revival years.

Despite recession and the dramatic effects on agriculture of various public health scares affecting the finances of many heavy horse owners, the numbers and activities of draught horses appear to have been maintained. As at other times during the century, the tenacity of individuals and a few organisations have been responsible for the survival of this draught animal in roles which may appear incongruous in the modern age.

As we reach the end of the century men who worked daily with horses on farms and fields, in towns and cities, in docks and on railways, in factories and yards are passing on – and with them their intimate knowledge of the skills and techniques of horsemanship at its best.

Yet they are being replaced, by younger men and women keen to work with horses whose temperament and usefulness is both endearing and challenging. The most forward-thinking of the traditional carters and experienced horsemen are prepared to pass on their knowledge, and there now exists a national training framework through which they can do so. For others, chats over the fence are preferred, and many of today's younger horsemen and women are pleased to acknowledge older mentors.

There are fewer modern horsemen than there were of course, and the tasks for which they use their horses are often different to those of the past. The role of the working horse, whether a Shire, a native pony or a working cross, is evolving and changing in response to a changing world.

Great interest is now being shown in developing modern machinery suitable for horse-drawn use. The indomitable machines of the horse age remain in use on smallholdings throughout the UK, but new equipment has been developed for today's agricultural situations. Some modern machinery has been imported from the USA, Scandinavia and Eastern European countries where horse-drawn equipment continued to evolve during the low point of the draught horse in the UK.

Today's world of the working horse is a kaleidoscope of activity, albeit specialist and small-scale. From breeding draught horses, through shows, parades, matches and workings, leisure activities, marketing and promotion, to agriculture, horticulture and forestry, each aspect has an important part to play and contributes to a new role for the working horse.

Breeding

The breeding of pedigree draught horses remains predominantly in the hands of

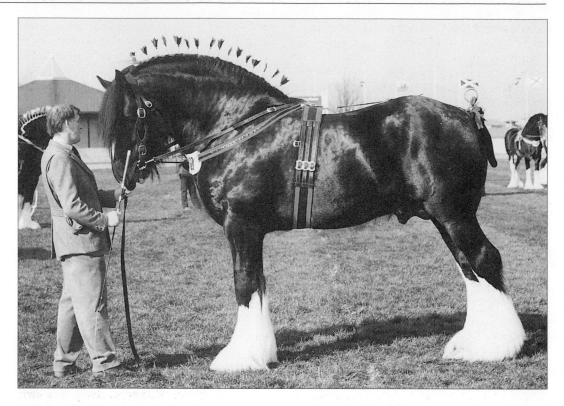

1.1 'Trelow Father Abraham', owned by Terry and Vicky Sandling of the Shires Family Adventure Park, Wadebridge, Cornwall. Abraham was the first Shire stallion from whom semen was taken for freezing and export to Australia in 1996.

those who saved them during the 1950s and 1960s and their successors, very often sons or daughters. Yet the traditional ways, which are still important, are giving ground to modern techniques. Greater mobility within the UK means that mare owners are prepared to travel many miles to a suitable, or fashionable, stallion. Stallions, once 'walked' to mares at local farms, but now they stand at stud either with their owner or with a society which hires them for a season. Other stallions, not of championship quality but sound in all other respects, are probably just as good a sire for most mares, and worth some research before they are rejected. Appropriate stallions can best be found through the secretaries of the various breed societies, which receive financial assistance towards breeding programmes from the Horserace Betting Levy Board.

However, breeding horizons are widening rapidly and AI (artificial insemination) coupled with chilled or frozen semen means that a stallion in eastern Lincolnshire can father a colt or filly in the USA or Australia (1.1). The skills and techniques involved in collecting the semen, storing it and transporting it are being refined all the time, and increasing numbers of people in the draught horse world internationally are prepared to pay the comparatively high costs of this new breeding system. For a Shire owner in Australia it is vital to encourage diversity in breed lines. For a British stallion owner it can be useful income. Exporting genes overseas in this way can sustain a line which has become rare, or even extinct, in its home country. Others point out that it can have the effect of encouraging widespread use of genes from a very few popular stallions, thereby reducing the gene pool rather than widening it.

Breeding pedigree draught horses has its limitations. Demand for them is not high, prices are sometimes low and a future as a meat animal is all that some youngstock can expect. Yet committed new breeders are important, particularly to those breeds with small numbers, such as the Suffolk. Breeding strategies are complex, and anyone contemplating serious breeding is well advised to contact the appropriate breed society.

Cross-breeding is also an important element for the breeders of both stallions and mares to bear in mind. A cross-bred animal can be useful to a wider sector of the population, perhaps as a heavy hunter, a driving horse for leisure use, or for general hacking. Crossing can be an important source of income for the breeder.

In the show ring judges of all pedigree breeds are looking for certain conformation characteristics. In some breeds this has changed considerably in recent years. The modern Shire is taller, less feathered on the leg, has a narrower chest and less bone than its predecessor, partly through cross-breeding with the Clydesdale, and partly as a result of greater demand as a driven draught horse in dray teams and for promotional purposes. Height and silky feathers have given both these breeds a majesty which is attractive, not least to the new European enthusiasts. Some would claim the Suffolk has been bred too tall, compared with its sometimes shorter draught ancestors. Whilst a tall animal is dramatic in shows, parades and promotions, a shorter, compact, more heavily built animal with a broad chest is necessary for 'real' agricultural draught work or in timber extraction. Both types have their place in the modern draught horse world, and breeders need to provide both sorts for the market. Judges at shows should acknowledge the qualities of both. In practice, breeders tend to concentrate on one type or another. Judging tends to favour those being produced for promotional purposes.

Exports of pedigree draught horses increased in the 1970s and 1980s. Clydesdale breeders were very successful at selling to Canada, the USA and Australasia in particular. Some concern is expressed that many of the best animals go overseas. The Shire found a new market in Europe –

in Germany, France and the Netherlands especially. In these countries new societies have been established which are affiliated to the mother society in Britain. The USA continues to import Shires, including some notable champion stallions.

The fortunes of the breeds are monitored by the Rare Breeds Survival Trust (RBST). The Suffolk is on the priority list in category 1 (critical), and has some 80 breeding females. The Clydesdale is in category 4 (at risk). The Shire remains the most numerous of the heavy breeds, staying off the priority list, but included among minority breeds being constantly monitored. Economic factors could easily shift it into the priority category however, and some, especially its American supporters, believe that its numbers are sufficiently low to cause concern. Other horses and ponies on the RBST priority or minority lists are the Cleveland Bay, Eriskay, Exmoor, Dales, Irish Draught and Fell, all of which were traditionally used for draught work in their native regions. The British Percheron, while not a native breed, is given financial help towards breeding programmes by the Horserace Betting Levy Board on the basis that its breeding statistics are comparable to those on the RBST list. Fortunately its relationship with its relatively numerous French cousins gives it stability.

Agriculture and Horticulture

It is always surprising to those unfamiliar with heavy horses to discover that they can still be found working the land on farms, smallholdings and in market gardens. No middle to large-scale commercial farmer is going to reintroduce horses onto his land, but for smaller farms and those who care for the natural power and quiet friendship which working with a horse can bring, there is still a place for draught animals. In practice, such a farmer will probably also have a tractor in the yard, but for some tasks a working horse is ideal. Harrowing, rolling, cultivating and carting are all jobs for which the horse is suited on small farms. Horses can carry winter feed out to cattle and sheep, keep pasture in good

1.2 John Dodd, of Haydon Bridge, Northumberland, loading mangolds on his farm, where he uses horses for all agricultural tasks.

heart, hoe between vegetable or vine rows and move endless objects about the farm, whether gate posts and fencing wire, or pig arks and troughs (1.2).

Such a farmer who 'thinks horse' will have no difficulty in running his business substantially, or even completely, by horse, comforted in the knowledge that increasing interest in our natural environment and its protection, particularly among the younger generation, may actually lead to an increase in people like him in the future.

Forestry

Timber extraction by horse has been the surprising growth area in the use of working horses in the UK over the last 20 years. From a handful of people in the early 1970s, this activity has grown until the new British Horse Loggers Assocation was subsumed into the larger, professional Forestry Contractors Assocation in the mid-1990s – the clearest indication that horses were accepted by the forestry industry. Prior to that, the Forestry Authority had carried out technical research surveys into the production levels of horse-drawn extraction operations and found in their favour. Where environmentally sensitive ground, conservation areas or steep slopes were involved, horses were economically sound. Their production levels were less than those of modern machines, but not drastically so. While machinery could still do the job, the damage to the forest floor was unacceptable – the imprint of hooves and dragged timber was negligible in comparison.

In addition to the Forestry Authority, the National Trust, Countryside Commission and individual landowners took a serious interest in the use of horses in forestry, sealing its acceptance and putting it on a commercially viable footing.

A number of horsemen used to agricultural

1.3 Chris Wadsworth, a professional horse logger, working his Clydesdale gelding in Guisborough Forest, near Cleveland.

work began extracting timber as part of their living, a few eventually turning to the work full-time. Some foresters were prepared to turn away from machines to horses – an important factor, since a knowledge of forestry is vital to horse operations in woodland. Courses encouraged the safe efficient practice of horse extraction using horses. There are now some 70 professional or part-professional horse loggers working throughout Britain (1.3).

Shows, Parades, Ploughing Matches and Workings

Agricultural and specialist heavy horse shows, town parades, ploughing matches and workings present the public face of working horses. Here, those newly interested in working horses can collect much information, both visual and verbal, by watching proceedings and chatting with horse owners. Heavy horses can be seen at some 250 shows and events annually all over the country. The smaller local shows make an excellent introduction for anyone wanting to show their horse in hand or with a vehicle, while the parades, such as those at Battersea, Portsmouth and Burton-on-Trent,

are enormous fun and offer the opportunity of turning out your horse and vehicle to the best of your ability (1.4).

Ploughing matches had virtually ceased by the 1950s and 1960s, but were revived by horsemen determined to keep the skills of the ploughman alive. The leader in the field was the Southern Counties Heavy Horse Association (SCHHA), which began as a ploughing association in the early 1970s, and whose rules form the basis of many matches all over England today (see appendix A). The Association's Great All England Ploughing Match is the largest horses-only ploughing match in the country. Classes for novices are also held.

Workings have also increased in number, especially since the growth of working horse associations. These exist now in the southern, western, eastern, midland and northern counties, all brought together under the umbrella of a newly formed Federation. Their aim is to encourage the working of draught horses and to enable members to meet together for

1.4 Taking part in the annual parade on Portsmouth seafront.

camaraderie and practical horsemanship. Their less competitive nature, the fact that they allow the cultivation of suitable fields in the company of like-minded people and the variety of activities which they have encouraged have made them a great success (1.5).

Skills Tests, Obstacle Driving, Timber Snigging and Cross-country Trials

At shows, matches and workings several new activities have been introduced over the last 20 years designed to demonstrate the versatility and usefulness of the working horse and to enable their owners to have fun.

An added impetus was the Shire Horse Society project History with a Future (1985–1988), which was designed to highlight ways in which the draught horse could be used in the future. Obstacle driving and timber snigging, in particular, developed from ideas explored during the project.

Obstacle driving involves a single horse or pair of horses driving through a course of cones accurately against the clock. Heats of a national competition take place at different shows during the year, culminating in a championship. Competitors tend to be drawn from show turnout enthusiasts (see appendix B).

Timber snigging is more likely to be found at a working and involves a horse being driven through a course of cones dragging a log, without touching the cones and against the clock. Considerable skill is necessary to achieve a competent round, but it is a highly suitable activity for people relatively new to heavy horses (see appendix C).

Skills tests involve a course of varied hazards and are designed to show the horse's versatility. Horses pull a two- or four-wheeled vehicle through the course, which can involve such skills as accurate backing, loading and unloading, standing and turning ability, steadiness and ability to drive past noisy or distracting obstacles. Such tests can be set up anywhere, usually in a field at a working (1.6). The only skills tests to take place regularly in an industrial environment are run at Chatham Historic Dockyard.

The cross-country trial is the newest of these activities and aims to demonstrate that draught horses can follow a course imilar to those for light horse driving marathons, involving skill and endurance. Such relay races are very popular in France, where they have played a significant part in increasing the profile of the draught breeds. In the UK pairs of horses working together in teams tackle the course, typically a UK Chasers Course, involving stretches of trotting and walking, hazards involving water, hill climbs, chicanes and slaloms. Competitors have to finish the course in an optimum time and with as few penalties as possible. Introduced to the UK by Rowena and John McDermott of Hampshire, these trials are now held in that county, in Warwickshire and Sussex, and are fast gaining in popularity. The British Heavy Horse Driving Trials Club has been established. This particular 'sport' is exciting to watch, fun to take part in and has much potential for growth (see appendix D and 1.7).

Leisure

Draught horses in leisure has probably been the fastest growing new use during the revival period. Quite apart from the fact that horse owners are often showing and working them in their own leisure time, the interest in heavy horses has led to the opening of several heavy horse centres all over the country. The National Shire Horse Centre in Devon was the market leader. Others mushroomed, until nearly every county had its own heavy horse centre, working farm or rare breeds farm centre. Museums of rural life, such as those at Beamish, Co Durham; Acton Scott in Shropshire, the Norfolk Rural Life Museum at Gressenhall and the Weald and Downland Museum in West Sussex also bought heavy horses. At most of these the horses can be seen at work regularly, demonstrating agricultural tasks to their visitors (1.8).

Working horses are also in use on the inland waterway system, where they pull barges along canals, on quiet country lanes where they draw 'gypsy' caravans for holidaymakers and in attractive countryside where heavy horse owners give rides to paying passengers, perhaps with a pub lunch as part of the experience.

Marketing and Promotion

A vital aspect of the heavy horse's revival

1.5 Horsemen gathered at a Southern Counties Heavy Horse Association working to enjoy their animals in the company of like-minded people.

1.6 Eddie Dore drives a Shire horse through a typical skills test, designed to show the horse's versatility.

was the part the horses themselves played in marketing and promotion. The breweries, which had continued to use them for beer deliveries in towns, led the way, with their heavy horse operations becoming part of their public relations departments. Their appearance in their smart drays in London and other towns where breweries were found publicized the brewery's products and drew attention to the majestic nature of

1.7 Ann Williams' Shires from Devon tackling the water hazard during a heavy horse cross-country driving trials event.

the animals themselves. Whitbreads, Youngs, Ind Coope, Fullers, Joshua Tetley, Vaux, Thwaites, Samuel Smith's, to name only a few, have also set the standard by which heavy horse turnouts are to be judged (1.9). Sadly, economics have forced a reduction of heavy horse operations, and their activity has been curtailed.

Other companies joined the breweries in making use of heavy horses for marketing and promotion, appearing at shows, in parades and in towns where they were perceived to be beneficial to the sales of their product or service. Rather than run their own teams they have contracted-out the heavy horse operation, a factor which has helped the few professional heavy horse businesses which exist.

Public Authorities

Far-sighted local authorities saw the potential of heavy horses on their streets as the revival gathered pace. The City of Aberdeen led the way, with other authorities joining them in running teams of horses in a variety of tasks, such as park maintenance, rubbish clearance, plant watering in town centres and promotion. The public preferred them to polluting lorries and felt their local

1.8 David Bakewell giving a cultivation demonstration for visitors at his Norfolk Shire Horse Centre.

1.9 Samuel Smith's turnout visiting one of the brewery's pubs near Tadcaster, West Yorkshire.

1.10 Bracknell Forest Borough Council uses horses in its parks and the town centre for a variety of tasks, from watering hanging baskets to hauling rubbish and gang mowing.

authority was being environmentally conscious while at the same time helping the cause of heavy horses (1.10). Local authorities also introduced heavy horses at city farms.

Other public authorities such as the Royal Parks also took on heavy horses for tasks such as timber and grounds clearance, harrowing rides and general promotion.

Other Activities

Heavy horse owners have become adept at finding all sorts of uses for their animals and their own enjoyment. Many provide their horse and waggon for weddings, join in with local carnivals and appear at village fetes. Some have provided horse power to harrow sports grounds, where this natural alternative to the tractor does much less damage. Others are engaged in harrowing river beds for their local water and environment agencies to refresh stale fish breeding grounds. Many of these 'new uses' are adaptations of what used to happen, and no doubt fresh activities will continue to be found.

Putting the Horse Before the Cart

A potential working horseman will usually have some idea of what he would like to achieve with his equine companion. As it is best to put the horse before the cart, this manual starts by considering the breeds of horse which might be best suited to work. The heavy breeds dominate, but native ponies or cross-bred horses can be considered. In the next sections and chapters it is hoped those who are new to the world of working horses will find the essentials to lead them into a contented and rewarding life in partnership with these remarkable draught animals.

The Shire Horse

John Ward

History

The most familiar and most numerous of the heavy draught breeds in Britain, the Shire horse is a descendant of the Great Horse, used in medieval warfare and bred from crossing a large native horse with heavy horses imported from Flanders and Holland. Henry VIII introduced laws imposing penalties on anyone breeding 'little horses and nags of small stature' in an attempt to increase the size of horses needed to carry heavily armoured knights into battle.

When heavy plate armour disappeared, lighter horses were required for battle and the heavy horse became a valuable draught animal in agriculture. In the mid-17th century, references speak of the Black Horse, a type of Great Horse based in the Midlands. Not until the end of that century is the term 'Shire horse' used, and it was the late 18th century before records, albeit incomplete, first appeared. The best-known animal from this period is the 'Packington Blind Horse', whose direct descendants are recorded from 1770 to 1832, and who came from Leicestershire. Others were bred in Derbyshire and Staffordshire.

In the mid 1800s the Shire breed was blooming and great stallions were being bred. Many people regard 'Lincolnshire Lad', foaled in 1865 and bred in Norfolk, as the greatest sire until that time. This reputation was superseded by that of his son, 'Lincolnshire Lad II', foaled in 1872, who sired many winners in the show ring, including the famous 'Harold', foaled in 1881 and champion in London in 1887.

To rationalize breeding activities and improve the qualities of the Shire, the English Cart Horse Society was formed in 1878, when the horse was found predominantly from the Humber to the Cam and westwards to Cheshire and parts of Lancashire and adjoining counties. Later the society changed its name to the Shire Horse Society. The first volume of the stud book contained the records of 2,381 stallions, dating back to 1770.

The new-found popularity of the Shire soon spread to the US. Between 1900 and 1918 almost 4,000 Shires were imported into the USA. Most of the well-known British stud names are to be found in the early American stud books.

With increasing mechanization at the time of the Second World War, thousands of Shires were slaughtered. Strict regulations restricting the purchase of fodder from other holdings also dramatically reduced the number of animals farmers could keep. Some of the largest studs, including the Forshaws at Carlton-on-Trent and Cumbers at Yatesbury, closed completely.

In the late 1950s and 1960s there was a danger that the breed would disappear. At the Spring Show in 1955 there were only 26 stallions, 28 mares and 14 geldings. The Society finances were at an all-time low. Fortunately, a small dedicated group of breeders, with financial support from a few leading brewers, kept the Society, and the breed, alive.

1.11 A typical Shire gelding, Mr T. J. Yates' 'Springbank Pride', champion gelding at the National Shire Horse Show, 1997.

The Modern Shire

In the 1970s numbers increased and there was a renewed interest in the breed from the public. In the early part of the decade, blood typing was introduced by the Society, enabling it to determine the correct parentage of progeny entering the stud book.

The revival of the breed has now been consolidated, especially with the renewed demand from all over the world. Active societies have become established in Germany, France and the Netherlands, as well as the USA and Canada. The first World Shire Horse Congress was held at Peterborough in March 1996. Delegates from 10 countries met to discuss veterinary, husbandry and welfare topics, and a committee was set up to investigate the use of frozen semen for export. In January 1997 mares in Australia were the first to be scanned and found to be in foal as a result of AI with frozen semen, a first for the breed.

The modern Shire differs greatly from the traditional horse used in the heyday of the breed, the 1920s–1930s. During the late 1950s and early 1960s, the influence of the Clydesdale in cross-breeding was evident in changed conformation. The mass of coarse leg hair and its associated problems largely became a characteristic of the past, being replaced by the silky feathering now seen in a modern Shire.

Today, the nature of the breed is being influenced to some extent by the export market. Overseas buyers are looking for animals which are black in colour, preferably with four white legs. This is causing a shortage of good black horses, although most breeders are striving to produce such animals. Greys and well-marked bays are also in demand.

Modern uses for the breed include forestry work, recreational riding (especially in Europe) and promotional work.

Conformation, Colour and Characteristics

One of the most favoured characteristics of the breed is its equable temperament, strong character and courageous nature. A Shire stallion should be black, brown, bay or grey. The tallest of Britain's draught horses, he should stand from 17.2 hh and weigh 2,000–2,464 lb when mature, without being overdone in condition. He should possess a masculine head and a good crest with sloping, not upright, shoulders running well into the back, which should be well set up and not 'goose-rumped'. Both head and tail should be carried erect. The ribs should be well sprung, not flat-sided, with a good middle, which generally denotes a good constitution. A stallion should have good feet and joints; the feet should be wide and big around the top of the coronets with sufficient length in the pasterns. When in motion he should go with force using both knees and hocks, with hocks kept close together. He should go straight and true before and behind.

The mare should be long and deep with a free action, of a feminine and matronly appearance, standing from 16 hh on short legs. She should have plenty of room to carry her foal. Roan is acceptable as a colour in mares but not in stallions.

The gelding should be upstanding, thick, well-balanced, very active and a good mover. He should be courageous and should look and be capable of a full day's work. Geldings should weigh 1,905–2,464 lb (1.11).

As a working horse, the smaller type of Shire is preferred – up to 17 hh. For new owners a smaller horse, weighing 1,570–2,020 lb, will be cheaper to buy and keep and easier to manage. There will, however, always be a strong market for the horse of 18.2 hh and over for promotional and show purposes, so long as the horse meets the breed's conformation and colour criteria (see the end of this chapter for conformation diagram 1.20).

The Clydesdale

John Zawadzki

History

The Clydesdale is Scotland's indigenous breed of heavy draught horse. It takes its name from the district of Scotland through which the upper reaches of the River Clyde flow. It is from this area, now known as South Lanarkshire, that the breed originated in c. 1700.

The farmers of the Clyde Valley prided themselves on developing a breed of horse capable of drawing 20–30 cwt, in a single cart, at a pace of from 3.5 to 5 miles an hour at a walking gait. To do this with ease for any length of time, a certain springiness of stride was needed and was obtained through breeding for well-sloped pasterns and sound, big feet.

For almost two centuries the Clydesdale has been recognised as a distinct breed, but it was not until 1877 that the Clydesdale Horse Society of Great Britain and Ireland was established to promote the breed and maintain its purity.

The two most successful stallions of the late 19th century were 'Darnley' and his contemporary, 'Prince of Wales'. Celebrated stallions that followed them include 'Hiawatha' and 'Baron's Pride'. The latter was owned by A & W Montgomery, proprietors of the Netherhall Stud, which until 1918 was considered to be the biggest and most influential Clydesdale stud in the world. They played a significant role in the establishment of the breed in North America.

The popularity of 'the soundest horse in the world' peaked immediately after the First World War. In 1920 the Society's stud book held a record number of entries – 6,870. The most important of the 300 stallions listed in that year was 'Fyvie Sensation', a Cawdor Cup winner for Netherhall in 1922, and sire of the 1926 Cawdor Cup winner, 'Benefactor', arguably one of the greatest stallions in the history of the breed. His reputation is eclipsed only by those of the legendary 'Baron of Buchlyvie', the most expensive Clydesdale of all time, and Baron's most famous son, the prolific 'Dunure Footprint' (1908–1930). Winner of every trophy available to a stallion, 'Footprint' is reputed to have sired more foals than any other Clydesdale stallion. In one year, 146 foals were registered in the stud book as sired by him. His fee at the height of his fame was a record 60 guineas for service and a further 60 guineas when the mare proved to be in foal (a guinea was one pound one shilling in old money, which is £1.05 today).

The outstanding personality in the history of the Clydesdale is undoubtedly James Kilpatrick, owner of the Craigie Mains Stud, Ayrshire, and winner of more trophies than any other showyard exhibitor. His first Cawdor Cup win was in 1893, and he recorded his final Cawdor victory some 57 years later with 'Craigie Commodore' in 1950. He won the Cawdor Cup 16 times in all.

Interest in the breed slumped dramatically after the Second World War. By the early 1970s the Clydesdale was considered to be a rare breed, forsaken by all but a small band of dedicated enthusiasts, many of whom continue to be actively involved with the breed.

Today the Clydesdale Society has around 900 members and the breed enjoys particular popularity not only in Scotland, northern England and Northern Ireland, but also in North America, Australia and New Zealand, where 'sister' breed societies are thriving.

In Britain today there are around 350 registered breeders, registering on average a total of around 150 foals per year. Modern uses of the Clydesdale mirror those of other draught breeds.

Breed Description

General Appearance

(See the end of this chapter for conformation diagram 1.20.)

The ideal is neither grossness nor bulk but quality and weight, giving it the general appearance of strength, power and activity (1.12).

Weight – Mature stallions and geldings should weigh 2,000–2,250 lb and mares proportionally less.

Height – Females: 16.3–18 hh; Males: 17.1–18.2 hh.

Symmetry – There should be a broad, clear outline, well proportioned with the body depth balanced for height.

Quality – Fine, clean bone, silky feather, well-defined tendons and fine silky hair.

Temperament – Alert, docile disposition and tractable.

Colour – Traditionally, the preferred colours are dark brown or bay with a white stripe on the face and white legs to just over the knees and hocks. However, chestnuts, blacks, light bays and roans, are not uncommon. Strawberry roans and blue roans are quite popular in many quarters and can be attractive. Greys are acceptable, but very rare.

Head and Neck

The head should be of moderate size, carried erect and possessing an open forehead, broad between the eyes. The front of the face should be flat rather than 1dished or roman. The eyes should be full, round, bright, clear, placid and intelligent-looking.

The ears should be fairly large and smartly set, and the muzzle wide and rather square. Nostrils should be large and open, and the lower jaw deep and broad with wide angles.

The neck should be strong, muscular and of medium length. Well arched and showing more crest than other breeds, it should be springing out of an oblique shoulder with high withers and complemented by a large windpipe and fine throat latch.

Forequarters

Strong, muscular and moderately sloped shoulders should have a broad bearing surface and be close topped. The arm should be short and strongly muscled with a long, broad and muscular forearm. Large, broad, flat and straight knees should have no openness and no inclination to knock together. The cannon bones should not only be flat and flinty, but also long to place the knee well up the leg. Tendons should be hard, clean and distinct.

The fetlocks should be well defined and the ankles fine, of medium length and set at an angle of 45 degrees from the hoof head to the fetlock joint. A good strong ankle is one with enough slope to cushion the shock of hitting the ground. The feet should be symmetrical, open, wide, round and squarely placed with wide heels, dense horn and elastic frogs. The coronets should be wide and round, and the hoofs should spread as they descend from the coronet.

Forelegs should be planted well under the shoulders and hang plumb from the shoulder to the fetlock joint. There should be a fine growth of soft, silky, straight hair, forming a feather from the back of the knee down the leg to the pastern joint. The front of the leg and fetlock joint must be clean and smooth.

Body

The chest should be well developed, capacious and deep, with a large girth and high withers. The fore-ribs should be well sprung and deep; the back ribs should be deep, round and well let down, forming a round barrel and short coupling. A good

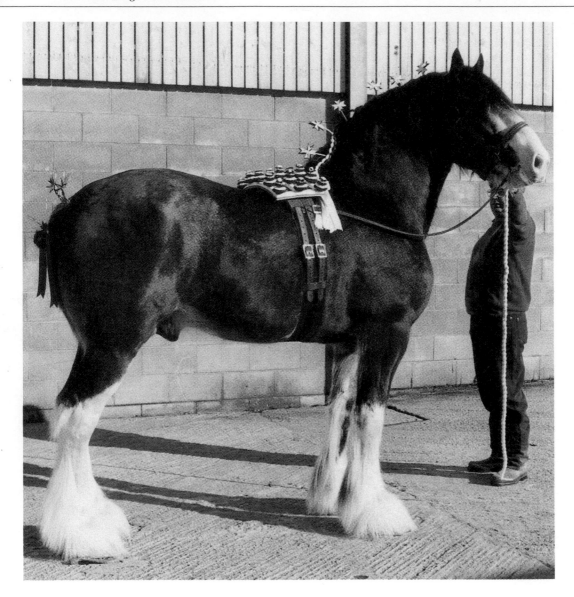

1.12 'Hillhouse General Elect' foaled 1992, sire: 'Doura Expectation', owned by the executors of the late D. Weir, Hillhouse, Lanark.

Hindquarters

The bones of the hips should be well apart, symmetrical and smooth. The croup should be level, with strongly developed muscles. The tail should be set well up. The thighs should be strong, muscular, deep and broad, the quarters well-turned, broad, deep and heavily muscled, and the gaskins prominent, wide and muscular.

The hocks, turned inwards, should be flat, wide, deep and correctly set, and with the points well defined. They should be placed well up and the points of the hock

middle generally denotes a good constitution. The back should be short, level, broad and muscular, and the loin wide, level, short and muscular. The underline should be fairly horizontal with the flanks low and full.

must be carried together, somewhat inclined inwards. Lower hocks give a more sickled look. Sickle hocks are a bad fault as they lead to loss of leverage.

As in the fore quarters, cannons should be of flat, flinty bone, and tendons hard, clean and distinct. Fetlocks should be well defined and the pasterns oblique, long and strong. The feet, which should slant less than the fore feet, should be open, large and of even size with dense horns, elastic frogs and wide heels. The hind legs should be set tight, not open, at the thighs and close at the hocks.

Action

The Clydesdale is an active horse and at every step the foot should be lifted clean off the ground, showing the full sole, and then placed squarely on the ground. He should go straight and true both fore and aft. When walking, the strides should be light, springy, smooth, quick and long. The hind leg should be lifted smartly and placed on the spot that the front foot has just left. When trotting there should be a clean lift of the feet using the knees and hocks well, giving a smart, gay bearing.

The Suffolk

Philip Ryder-Davies MB, BS, BVSc, MRCVS

History

The Suffolk horse is the oldest breed of horse to exist in a form which we can recognize today. It has the oldest breed society in England and the longest unbroken written pedigree of any breed of horse.

The long history of the Suffolk breed has enabled man to produce in it a perfect working horse. In the 15th century, John Campden wrote in his 'Britannica' of the native breed of working carthorse in the Eastern Counties, a description which can easily be recognized as our present-day Suffolk. The creation of the breed will have taken a minimum of 200 years. The first secretary of the Suffolk Horse Society, Herman Biddell, undertook an immense amount of research to produce the first volume of the stud book. With illustrations by John Duvall, this book is considered to be one of the finest ever written on livestock history. Biddell's researches produced written pedigrees back to a stallion called 'Crisp's Horse of Ufford', foaled in 1768. This horse was not, of course, the first Suffolk, as is frequently, but mistakenly, thought. The reality is that at that date all other male lines had died out. Another genetic bottleneck occurred at the end of the 18th century.

These factors, together with the popularity of in-breeding by breeders throughout the breed's history, mean that the Suffolk is probably homozygous for a large number of its characteristics. Early breeders have therefore bequeathed to today's breeders a situation in which the in-breeding forced on us by the current rarity of the Suffolk has no obvious disadvantages. In-breeding concentrates genes, and this is equally important for useful characteristics as it is for damaging ones.

Management Regimes

Before the First World War there were tens of thousands of Suffolk horses in East Anglia. Harness was characterized by wooden hames and saddles with exposed wooden trees, and the plough harness was of extremely light construction. Larger farms had many working horses, housed at night in straw yards with shelters like bullock yards. The stable was a long building with a manger running the length of it, used for tying up horses in the morning and at the end of the day's work for grooming, feeding and harnessing. There were no stall divisions; the excellent temperament of the breed allowed horses to be loose-housed in this way. The Suffolk is capable of working for a very long period without a break. The standard working day in East Anglia in the winter was from 6.30 a.m. to 2.30 p.m. Regular journeys by commercial horses at work on the roads were of astounding lengths. Agricultural work practices were carried out to exact routines and the head horseman on a large Suffolk farm was a master of his craft.

Decline

Mechanization had a dramatic effect on the Suffolk breed. The large arable and level farms of East Anglia were admirably suited to early tractors and the larger farms had the necessary capital. The Second World War stimulated a major increase in food production, and these factors together virtually eliminated the Suffolk horse. Many large farms sold perhaps 30–40 Suffolks in a single day, and the glut on the market meant that there was no sale for them other than to the slaughterman. By 1966, only nine foals were registered. At this lowest point in their fortunes, half a dozen breeders preserved the breed from extinction. The revival of interest of Suffolks began in the late 1960s, and numbers have risen continuously since then. However, the breed remains extremely rare, with only 80 breeding females producing some 40 foals a year. This figure is similar to the efficiency of foal production of all breeds of horse in the UK; horses as a species are inefficient reproducers.

The Modern Suffolk

The Suffolk Horse Society, with the aid of a grant from the Horserace Betting Levy Board, does all it can to stimulate interest in the breed. Today Suffolks are being used commercially in forestry operations, on farms and for advertising purposes. An important new use is in the tourist industry; a number of establishments open to the public keep Suffolks. An encouraging recent development has been an explosion of interest in breaking these horses to work. The breed's excellent temperament is an important factor; many people leading busy lives are still able to work their Suffolks in a modern situation with safety.

Conformation, Colour and Characteristics

The Suffolk is always chesnut (spelt without the 't') in colour, although the shade can vary from lemon through to a very dark liver. The only white allowed is on the face. Its conformation is easily recognizable as the overall appearance is of a very large body on relatively short legs, which gives the Suffolk its tremendous strength. There is no superfluous hair on the legs, which is an advantage in a working horse as excessive hair can cause skin infections. This breed is alone in having foot

competitions as a regular feature at major shows, a factor which has contributed to the unrivalled standard of foot conformation in the Suffolk horse. Its temperament is outstanding.

Longevity is a noted feature of the breed, with horses working or producing foals, or both, well into their teens. Hardiness is another strength of the breed. The breed standard has never stipulated a height, but the preferred heights are in the region of 17.2 hh for a stallion and 16.2 hh for a mare (1.13).

The Suffolk makes extremely good use of his food. A maintenance ration of a third of a bucket of wet sugar beet pulp, 2 lb cooked, flaked barley, 1 lb soya flakes and a bucket filled with chaff, fed twice daily with grass or hay ad lib, will keep a Suffolk in excellent condition. Hay can be replaced with good clean barley straw. This is an extremely cheap ration for a large horse. Teeth must be rasped annually and worming carried out at 3-monthly intervals for food to be utilised to best advantage. For a horse in work, the quantity of barley (or oats as an alternative) should be increased. (See the end of this chapter for conformation diagram 1.20.)

1.13 The influential modern Suffolk stallion, 'Honingbeck Henry', bred by P. Adams and Sons (Farms) Ltd.

The British Percheron

Rowena McDermott

History

The Percheron is one of the oldest draught breeds in the world. The ancient French chroniclers trace it back to AD 732, when Charles Martel defeated Abdul Rahman, the Saracen leader, at Poitiers. As the victor he claimed the horses as spoils of war, and these animals were dispersed throughout France and particularly in the Perche district of Normandy. Rotrou, Count of Perche, also brought home several Eastern

1.14 A characteristic British Percheron, R. and S. A. Fuller's 'Park Lincoln', champion gelding in 1995, bred by J. and M. L. Henfrey.

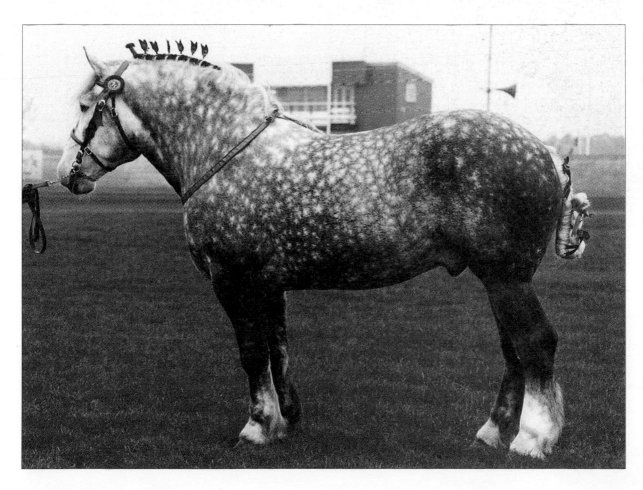

stallions from the Crusades, and these were crossed with the local mares to improve the Norman war horses.

The first Norman horses in the British Isles are thought to have been brought by William, Duke of Normandy, in 1066, and among these there may well have been some from the Perche region. In his book *The Shire Horse*, Keith Chivers states that in 1188, Giraldus Cambrensis mentioned 'many excellent studs set apart for breeding in Powys, all originating from Robert de Belleme's Percheron stallions,' which he imported when he inherited the Welsh estates in 1098. The name Percheron here applies to horses originating from that area, but these were not necessarily a type or breed.

The breed's origins are lost in legend, and although the modern Percheron may well owe some characteristics to the warhorse of the Middle Ages, it has changed considerably since then.

The Percheron came to the fore in Britain when it was used to pull buses in the big cities in the latter quarter of Victoria's reign. Thomas Tilling, the London Jobmaster, imported grade (part-bred) Percherons from the USA. Americans had been importing quality French stock since the 1830s. The stallions were used to improve local draught mares, resulting in the cross-breds which were exported in their thousands. According to the 'Livestock Journal' of 30 November 1917, many of these imported horses were sold to farmers when they finished work on the city streets. The British Army also bought horses from Tilling. In 1900 he sold them 325 horses which were shipped out to South Africa and used in the Boer War.

Role in the First World War

During the First World War the qualities of the Percheron as a heavy draught horse were appreciated by the British Army. In autumn 1916, the Ministry of Agriculture obtained leave from its French equivalent for the export of two pure-bred stallions and 12 mares. In 1917, a British Commission was sent out under Sir William Birkbeck, Director of Remounts, and they purchased 12 stallions and 33 mares. Between 1918 and 1922, 36 stallions and 321 mares were imported from France.

The absence of feather meant that the Percherons were more easily cared for in the mud and poor conditions of the war than were the hairier breeds. Once out of the heavy mud and onto paved roads, the Percheron was a fast trotter, making it more versatile than a motorized vehicle. Their calm nature fitted them for use on the guns and forward transports; their constitution enabled them to withstand the privations of the war well. Under the circumstances they were well cared for, often better than the men.

In November 1916 the 'Livestock Journal' stated ' … the Percheron type has made many friends in England … mostly represented … by "grade" horses as yet, and is firmly established in the hearts and minds of the responsible officers of the British Army … there is nothing but praise for a horse that has proved his sterling worth in artillery … the half-bred Percheron has filled many wants and has proved himself a gentleman of a horse, as well as a willing and never failing worker.' Many of the horses returned to Britain after the war to work on the farms.

The Modern British Percheron

Two years after the first horses were imported into this country (1916), the British Percheron Horse Society was formed for the purpose of registering and promoting the breeding of the Percheron horse. Today the Society continues this work, as well as seeking to promote the breed by obtaining greater public recognition and awareness. Its main aim is to secure its future in the 21st century by ensuring that new outlets are found for it. The British society works closely with other Percheron horse societies particularly in France.

In the UK today there are probably about 300 pure-bred Percherons (in France the figure is around 5,000). British Percheron enthusiasts are still importing Percherons from France (between 4 and 10 a year) and, very rarely in view of the costs involved, from Canada.

Percherons are in use in the UK for farm and forestry work, and for advertising and publicity. In turnout showing they compete well with the more numerous Shire and Clydesdale breeds. They excel in competitions using draught skills and marathons. appealing to younger people as well as to those coming new into the modern draught horse world. Percherons are increasingly sought by breeders of heavy hunters and other light equines for cross-breeding to increase and improve substance and temperament.

Today there are larger numbers of Percheron horses throughout the world than any other draught breed. More than 760 foals a year are registered in France, and the figures for the USA and Canada exceed 1,000 registrations annually. No other draught breed has colonized the new and old worlds in the same way.

Conformation, Colour and Characteristics

Most Percherons in this country are born black but the marjority will turn grey eventually. These normally show a few grey hairs around the eyes and muzzle when they lose their foal coat and then go grey progressively with each coat change. A black Percheron is born a dark dun and with the loss of its foal coat is black for the rest of its life. Those with no white hairs remain black. However, a number of foals each year are born dun; these invariably become black on losing their foal coats and remain that colour (1.14).

In France, the Percheron varies enormously in height as two types are recognized, the Petit, under 16 hh, and the Grand, over this height. This height variation is typical. Two tall parents will not necessarily produce a tall offspring. In the USA and Canada, the horses are bred to be black and over 18 hh. Short blacks and some greys are still produced, but do not rate in the show ring, where hitch-driving

classes exist for pairs and teams of four, six or eight.

In Britain, mares should exceed 16.1 hh and stallions 16.3 hh. They should have great muscular development but with style and activity, and possess ample bone of good quality to give a general impression of balance and power. The head should be broad across the eyes, which should be wide and docile. The cheek should be deep curved on the lower side and not long from eye to nose. The ears should be medium and erect. The horse should have an intelligent expression. The neck should be strong, not short but full and arched, with a crest in stallions. The shoulders should be deep and well laid, the chest wide and deep, the ribs open and the flank deep.

The hindquarters should be wide and long from hips to tail, but not goose-rumped. The limbs should have strong arms and full second thighs, with big knees and broad hocks, heavy flat bone, quality cannon bones and medium-length pasterns. Feet should be a reasonable size, with good-quality hard blue horn. The legs should be clean and free of hair. The action should be straight, bold and with a long free stride; the hocks should be well flexed. The Percheron is known worldwide for the quality of its bone and hooves probably because of the influence of the rich grasslands of the Le Perche region of Normandy.

A Percheron can weigh anything from 1,790 lb to well over a ton. In temperament they should be docile and good natured, but never dull and sluggish. They are very accommodating, quickly accepting changes in work or environment. As a work horse they are willing and genuine, capable of working hard without undue strain and maintaining good body weight at the same time. This ability comes from a very strong constitution and an almost complete lack of nervous tension. This makes them easy to train and work, and ideal for the hobby enthusiast as well as the experienced horseman.

The Ardennes

Charlie Pinney

A triangle of rolling wooded hills in eastern France, southern Belgium and Luxembourg known as the Ardennes region is the home of this small, stocky draught horse, which has a long history and is highly valued today.

History

Julius Caesar praised the quality of the Ardennes horse and used the breed for heavy cavalry work. In 1096, led by Geoffrey of Boullion from the Ardennes region, crusaders rode many stallions 2,500 miles to battle in the Holy Land. Napoleon employed them as artillery horses; indeed their hardiness enabled them to survive his disastrous Russian campaign. The French and especially the Belgian armies used them to haul artillery until after the First World War.

The breed has changed considerably over time. Pictures taken at the turn of the century show a much lighter, finer-legged animal than exists today. However, the Ardennes region has long been a horse breeding area and the general form of its draught horses retains some of the characteristics of the feral horse of northern Europe which existed in prehistoric times. Some of these characteristics – such as a very thick winter coat, a mealy coloured muzzle and an ability to thrive on poor quality fodder – the Ardennes shares with some of the most ancient native northern pony races, showing little evidence of the influence of warm blood crossings which characterize the Percheron or Boulonnais breeds, for example.

The Ardennes has been used extensively to found or improve other local breeds – its close cousin the Auxois for example – and its influence can be seen in the Comtois when it was used in the 1920s to put more substance in the breed. It has been exported throughout the world for the same reason. A version of the breed is well established in Sweden where it is in demand as a forestry horse. There is much interchange of blood lines between the French, Belgian and Luxembourg stud books, although the modern Ardennes is very much the end product of crossing the old, lighter type with the heavier Brabant horses from northern Belgium. This was initially to provide a weightier animal for very heavy farm draught after motorization diminished the role of the Ardennes in the armies. This increase in size and weight from around 1,210 lb as an artillery horse to 1,760–2,200 lb today has been very much the result of its demand as a meat animal, its most important role at present, although it is seen in increasing numbers at work in the farms, forests and leisure industries of its native region and elsewhere.

The Modern Ardennes

The Ardennes breed offers much to the professional or leisure user today. It is a powerful, active draught horse with the ideal conformation for efficient power production and utilisation. Add to this its thriftiness, its ability to withstand inclement weather and to survive on poor pastures, its longevity and good hoof quality and its superb temperament, and it is not surprising that it has long been a popular choice for farmer, forester or army general!

These characteristics are responsible for the interest shown in the breed in the UK, and several horses have been imported from Europe, over the last 20 years in particular. Owners can now belong to the newly formed Ardennes Horse Society of Great Britain.

All over Europe the breed is increasingly used for competitive driving where its surprisingly nimble action and tremendous stamina and good temper is proving highly suitable. A number of Ardennes are used in the UK by the Riding for the Disabled Association and several are in use as sturdy riding horses.

Conformation and Characteristics

It is claimed that the breed, which has always been early maturing, has a faster growth rate than the best of the beef bulls and it retains its reputation as a thrifty animal, needing little supplementary food unless in regular hard work. It should be remembered that meat is muscle, and it is muscle that pulls the plough. The Ardennes has never lost its working abilities, neither structurally nor psychologically. It has never been a tall breed, averaging 14.2–16.3 hh high, and this, coupled with its short back, deep round rib cage and massive bone – 10–12 inches below the knee – and joints makes it an ideal height for a draught animal, particularly in conjunction with its heavily muscled forearms and hindquarters. It is, above all, a real pulling machine. It uses weight very well, leaning low into its collar when moving a heavy load, and its ample girth means there is plenty of room for heart and lungs to work efficiently, giving stamina and endurance (1.15).

It is a comparatively clean-legged horse, although it does carry some feather. Its small feet have hard blue horn of high quality, a legacy of generations at work on the hard paved roads as artillery horses.

Despite its blocky appearance, the Ardennes is a free-moving horse, with a deceptively long stride and a willingness to trot which might be unexpected in such a heavily built breed, leading it to cover the ground at a surprising speed. Its small pricked ears, fine head and calm eye give a clue to its other outstanding characteristic – its remarkable temperament. Very few other draught horses are as easy to break in and handle as an Ardennes. The breed has long been recognised as having an exceptionally quiet and calm character, and this feature has been retained. Its phlegmatic and unflustered nature is one of the reasons why it made such a successful artillery horse, being active and flexible, yet remarkably unflappable.

The two most common colours are bays of various shades, usually with black manes, tails and lower limbs, or a quite startling variety of roans from sandy pinks to dark greys. Pure blacks are rare and whites unacceptable. White markings are usually restricted to a star or blaze.

1.15 'Fayard', an Ardennes stallion belonging to Jo Hewitt of Sissinghurst, Kent.

Natives and Working Crosses: Lighter Working Types

Edward Hart

Introduction

It is worth remembering that while the UK now relies heavily on mechanization for power in both town and country, it is not so everywhere. Worldwide over 50 per cent of draught power is still provided by animals, mainly equine or bovine.

The slogan 'weight is needed to move weight' harks back to selection of the powerful shunting horses used a hundred years ago in railways and dock yards. A pair of substantial animals weighing in the region of 2,000 lb was needed for the heavy loads which could be up to 3 tons in weight.

Today it is likely that you will only need to move half a ton at a time, and plough and harrow a few fields without too tight a schedule, and for this kind of work there is no need to keep a 2,000lb animal. For lighter jobs, a lighter horse or pony suffices, and it is worth considering native ponies and working crosses. They will probably cost less to buy, certainly less to house and feed and, vitally important, considerably less to harness and shoe.

In some areas there is a shortage of farriers willing to shoe heavy horses. A farrier who concentrates on light horses will seldom baulk at a cob. Also harness is lighter and cheaper. It must still be up to its job, but the really large collar or saddle is where the high costs come in. Travelling people seldom go for a horse much above 14.3 hh; they consider economy in all these points, plus greater 'wearability'.

Sir Alfred Pease neatly summed up the position in *Horse Breeding for Farmers*, (Macmillan and Co., 1894): 'There are many jobs on the farm for which a light horse is better suited, being handier and quicker, such as the market cart, the milk cart, the hoe, the scuffler, moving feeding racks and light loading; whilst a mare of this sort will be always ready to take her place when necessary in hay or corn harvest, in the plough, in the harrow, or as leader of a team.'

In considering the most suitable lighter animals here, we deal with types rather than breeds, although most pure native breeds are assessed.

The Vanner

This most useful animal suffered early and badly when the working horse declined. It is essentially a light cart-horse; strong, quick-stepping, and able and willing to trot on command, especially with an empty vehicle. If it is a mare, it also makes an admirable brood animal. The Vanner is out of a heavy-breed mare by a lighter stallion, or by a cart stallion out of one of the bigger pony breeds, especially Dales, Fell or Highland. It usually has some hair on the legs.

The return of the Vanner was advocated for certain tasks as recently as the early 1990s by Syd Emmerson, the recently retired first Head of Equine Services, ADAS (Agricultural Development and Advisory Service). He had been involved with national breeding policies for the Ministry of Agriculture, and he praised this 'half-legged' type. It had strong bone and some hair, but less of both than the Shire or Clydesdale from which it was often derived. It was performance-tested by virtue of its hours on hard roads. Feet and temperament had to be sound (1.16).

1.16 Typical Vanners or half-legged horses, bred out of a heavy mare and a lighter stallion, seen here drawing a caravan driven by holidaymakers – an increasing market.

The Vanner was employed in the lighter delivery trades by the milkman or greengrocer. It was too light to be ideal for a coal merchant, yet not swift or smart enough for a cab. Such a horse would be about 14.1–15.1 hh. There are no recognized sales where Vanners can be purchased, but a suitable one might be found at fairs frequented by the travelling people, such as Stow-on-the-Wold, Lee Fair, Wakefield, or Appleby, in Cumbria. It is worth trying sales at Wigton, Cumbria, or indeed at any non-specialist event.

Thoroughbred

During the Second World War Thoroughbreds were tried on the land. In most cases they were unsuccessful. They were too quick, and given to short bursts of speed rather than the steady pull which was required.

Cleveland Bay

Bays and other 'coaching' horses are generally unsuitable for the novice, being inclined to 'rive', and being difficult to match for pace and willingness. Sir Alfred Pease praised the Cleveland, which needed a 'real horseman', whereas 'anyone could drive the slower heavies'. Today's position is the complete reverse. Most people who work horses today are amateurs in the true sense of the word; they do not wish to spend their time mastering an unruly animal.

Gypsy Cob

Ivan Armitage, a 'settled traveller', described the ideal physique of the Gypsy

1.17 Registered Dales pony 'Escowbeck Star', working with owner Charlie Parker in timber hauling.

Cob, bearing in mind that he was dealing with a road horse rather than a land horse. The neck should be short and strong and the shoulder straight. The back may be broad and the animal should be short-coupled and deep-bodied. Forearms should be strong, knees large and flat, and the cannon short and strong. A springing pastern and a well set-up heel are desired. A broad and round foot is essential.

Hindquarters should be strong, powerful and 'apple cheeked'. The tail should be set higher than a cart-horse's, but lower than an Arab's. The tail on a Gypsy Cob sweeps the ground and is of great width and density. When the owner of a 'full tail' turns its back to the wind, it is sheltered by the equivalent of half a topcoat and can not only winter out, but do so on only a little hay. The ideal height for a gypsy pony is 14.1–14.2 hh.

Welsh

The Welsh is a varied breed, ranging from the small mountain pony to the cob.

Originally all worked. The Welsh breeds cover almost the entire range of weights and heights possible for riding and driving, divided by size, weight and type into four categories. The Welsh Pony and Cob Society differentiates them as follows: Welsh Mountain Pony (Section A) not exceeding 12 hh. Welsh Pony (Section B) up to 13.2 hh. Sections A and B are often too fine for draught work. Welsh Pony of Cob Type (Section C) up to 13.2 hh. This is the stronger counterpart of the Welsh Pony, but with Cob blood. It is dual purpose and excels in harness. Welsh Cob (Section D) exceeding 13.2 hh. Most are around 15–15.2 hh, though can be 16 hh.

Of all native pony breeds, none needs greater care than the Welsh Cob when selecting an individual animal for draught. A steady one is unbeatable, but the buyer must remember that there are fiery Cobs that require '10 days work a week' to keep them easily manageable.

Highland

The Highland combines size with placidity. For decades it provided the motive power in its native glens, and Andrew F. Fraser in *The Native Horses of Scotland*, (John Donald, 1987) describes it as 'particularly suitable for endurance riding and draught work'. For pack and pannier work in steep, rugged country, the Highland is ideal. More recently it has proved itself in the Scottish forests for timber hauling.

Greys and various shades of dun are found, but there are also cream duns and yellow duns. Most specimens of the breed may be turned away for a few weeks, then caught and put straight into harness without a skirmish. Height is 13–14.2 hh, although some grow bigger.

The Fell and Dales

The Fell and the Dales are north-country ponies whose territory is roughly divided by the Pennines. The Fell is the smaller, not over 14 hh, and shines in inter-breed classes. Registered females are expensive. However, a gelding bought for a reasonable sum will be up to most jobs and make a quick and sure-footed draught animal.

The Dales and its crosses may often top the 14.2 hh stipulated pony size, and make admirable draught animals. Earlier this century some Dales mares were crossed with Clydesdales to power the grass reapers designed for low-country farms and bigger horses. Such was the agricultural depression that no implement makers catered specifically for dales farmers working on hillsides. 'Steady, quiet and sensible' describes the average Dales (1.17).

Dartmoor

The Dartmoor is a splendid native pony, which once ran wild in herds on its native moors. Some were caught and used by the moormen for sledging, carrying packs or carrying the owners. Today's emphasis is more on showing and children's pony work than on draught. The height is up to 12.2 hh.

Exmoor

The Exmoor is much used in its own locality, but is generally smaller than the average teamster wants. It has a thick, woolly undercoat and a topcoat of thick, harsh, waterproofing hairs. Height is 12.3 hh for males and 12.2 hh for females.

New Forest

New Forests are docile and friendly and used to outdoor life. Of mixed ancestry, they are now being carefully selected and are often good in traffic and harness. The height limit is 14.2 hh.

Connemara

In 1900, leading equine authority Professor J. Cosser Ewart visited Ireland to study the Connemara. He found the ponies as strong and hardy as mules, and capable of living where all except wild ponies would starve. Enthusiastic breeders have raised standards in recent years and the breed is a fine ride-and-drive. It makes up to 14.2 hh. Some strong types capable of any job on a small-holding can still be found.

Irish Draught

The Irish Draught is ideal for any work requiring less than a very powerful heavy. It is, however, in such demand for breeding performance horses and show-jumpers that the females are inordinately expensive. If a gelding can be picked up cheaply enough, one need look no further.

The Irish Draught official breed standard describes an active, short-shinned, powerful horse with substance and quality, proud of bearing, with deep girth, strong back, loins and quarters. Known for its intelligent and gentle nature and good sense, its height at three years is as follows: stallions 16 hh and over; mares from 15.2 hh, with 9 in. or more of clean flat bone. Any strong whole colour is accepted including grey.

Shetland

Although the Shetland is regarded as a children's pony it can carry a man mile after mile, is the strongest equine for its size (that is, strongest in proportion to its height) and was used in thousands to draw coal mine

1.18 A Shire cross, in this case a coloured animal, being used in a pair at a ploughing match.

loads. Shetland ponies are very popular, and have the attraction of a range of coat colours. Piebalds and skewbalds are encouraged. Shetlands and their crosses are used in scurry-driving competitions, proving their worth as harness ponies, although driven at a lower speed on the land! Registered Shetlands must not exceed 40 in. (102 cm) at three years old, nor 42 in. (107 cm) at four years old.

Haflinger

The Haflinger came to Britain from Austria and the Tyrol after the Second World War. It is a small but thickset mountain horse, formerly much used for pack work. The art of packing has been largely lost in Britain, but has many virtues in difficult terrain, and the Haflinger is an ideal pony on which to practise.

Its height is about 14 hh, colour chestnut, with full flaxen or lighter mane and tail. Short-legged, it has strong quarters, broad back, hard joints and hooves. The breed's strength and sure-footedness make it excellent in harness, with cart or sleigh.

Donkey

The donkey has served man since biblical times and although it is usually associated with small children and beaches today, it has played a full part in agriculture. In the UK, donkeys met a special need in supplying the power to raise water from deep wells – a fact recorded by Stella Walker in *Enamoured of an Ass* (Angus & Robertson, 1977). The animals worked wooden treadwheels in the chalk hills of south-east England, raising water from up to 300 ft with ease.

Early this century, donkey teams were used widely in North Western Australia, taking over from bullock teams. Huge teams of over 20 donkeys were led by intelligent leaders; none was bitted, and the whole team was controlled by verbal command. Stella Walker quotes older teamsters on how donkey teams would pull slowly, inch by inch, in situations where horses would have given up.

Donkeys were an important draught animal in Ireland until relatively recently. Enthusiasts drive their animals successfully and they would certainly be capable of work on a smallholding.

Mule

Another use of the donkey is, of course, to breed the mule. Britain lags behind most other countries in its use. Draught mules are bred by using large donkey jacks on heavy breed mares. Height varies, but individuals can be as tall as average draught horses. Such animals hauled American combines in teams of 40, and have both advantages and disadvantages compared with horses.

Their devotees claim that mules will live longer, require less attention and feed, and are less liable to digestive upsets, lameness and disease. In 1930, almost five and a half million mules were found on USA farms, the bulk of them in the hotter southern states. The US Department of Agriculture stated in the 1920s that 'a very desirable "mule mare"' is one having about one-fourth draft blood. A smart, alert mule, with a long, free stride at the walk and a snappy balanced trot is highly desired.' Experiments in 1962 showed that the mule's pulse and respiration rates after ploughing rose far less than those of horses, and they returned to normal more rapidly.

Crosses

A number of people using draught horse power on their land today are content to use a working cross, typically a Shire or Clydesdale, Percheron or Suffolk crossed with a smaller, lighter animal, perhaps one of the native ponies described above, giving a lower point of draught and being quite adequate for most tasks. These can be obtained privately or at sales and their heavy horse genes are usually obvious in their conformation (1.18 and 1.19).

1.19 An ideal forestry horse: a Shire, but of lighter conformation than those to be seen in pure-bred in-hand show classes.

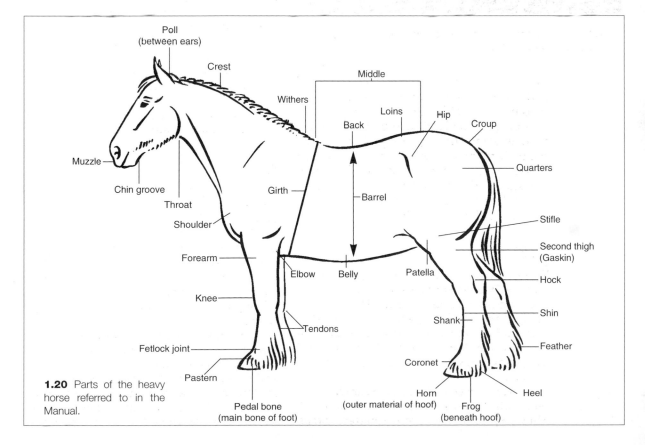

1.20 Parts of the heavy horse referred to in the Manual.

CHAPTER 2

Choosing and Keeping a Working Horse

Nick Rayner

Introduction

Finding the right working horse for your particular needs is not likely to be an easy task. There are many ways of buying horses and many pitfalls to avoid. If you are a novice, the first step to take is to find someone who can advise you, someone who really knows heavy horses well, perhaps a retired horseman, who you can make friends with, and who will accompany you to look at the animals.

If you want a horse suitable for ordinary work you need to find one with a good temperament. You can generally tell by a horse's nature when you first meet him if he is going to be quiet to handle and work, and whether he is broken or unbroken. Another indicator of temperament is the horse's breeding. If you can find out which stallion and mare the horse is from you can research the breeding back from there, which will tell you more about his probable behaviour characteristics. There are always one or two rogue stallions about which you would want to avoid. Your adviser will certainly be able to help here.

If you are a novice you ought to start with a middle-aged well-broken horse – it will save you a lot of grief at the beginning of the process. You can learn from that horse for a time before moving on to the next stage and buying yourself a younger horse or horses, and setting yourself the challenge of starting from scratch.

Buying at Auction or Farm Sales

People are sometimes frightened of buying from auctions or at farm sales. Nevertheless you are in control of the amount you spend. In addition to farm sales held at the owner's retirement or death, where there may be a few horses forward among the other items, there are regularly held horse auctions at markets in certain parts of the country where you may find heavy breeds or heavy types, as well as specialist heavy horse sales. These occur annually at either end of the summer season, sometimes run by local heavy horse breed associations.

With your advisor by your side, you will set your price and follow his advice on the quality of the horses put forward. Make sure you arrive in time to look at them carefully. Hopefully the animals will be run out, but if not you can ask to see a horse you are interested in run out before the sale (2.1). However, beware that this request could cause your interest in the horse to be noted, thereby raising the price.

You will be bidding in guineas, following a long-standing tradition in horse-buying, and there may be VAT to add as well as the cost of transport home. There may be a warranty, which is the vendor's legally binding guarantee, printed in the catalogue or announced by the auctioneer (2.22 See end of chapter). Some phrases are accepted as implying a warranty, such as the statement that a particular horse is a good worker, or 'quiet in all gears'. A young horse will not come with a warranty as there has been no time to assess his qualities. Descriptions of age, height or general 'qualities' do not constitute warranties.

If a horse does not fulfil the warranty you will only have a short time, perhaps a day, to advise the auctioneer. It is therefore

2.1. A horse being run out at a sale to show his conformation and paces.

important to test your new purchase as soon as you get him home. In the event of a dispute, a third party will be called in to test the horse. Should you discover evidence of disease or disability, a veterinary inspection will have to be carried out. Expenses will be paid by the losing party.

Fortunately the likelihood of a problem is small, but you will certainly be wise to attend several auctions before attempting to buy at one. An alternative may be to get your advisor, or someone else experienced with heavy horses, to buy for you. Some experienced horsemen are prepared to buy on a commission basis.

Buying from Dealers, Breeders or Private Individuals

There is no doubt that this can also be risky. Again an adviser is essential. You need to avoid the situation where the vendor has you in for lunch or a drink and before you know where you are you feel obliged to buy their horse even though you know it to be unwise.

Your decision should be entirely dependent on your view of what the horse can do and how he behaves. You will certainly want to see him carrying out ordinary work tasks, for example harrowing or carting. You and your adviser will know the amount you want to spend. Do not give this away in conversation; if you decide to buy the horse then you can begin bargaining. Vendors will sometimes be prepared to take the horse back if it does not suit you, but be sure to ring him or her promptly, rather than leaving it weeks or months.

If you are responding to an advertisement, be cautious. Why is the horse being sold? Make sure you study the advertisement carefully to see if a warranty is implied. If it is breached, you will only be entitled to damages if it is a condition of sale (as at auctions). The Trade Descriptions Act 1968 or the Misrepresentation Act 1967 may be of help. Details of various acts can be found in local libraries; guidance is also given by Trading Standards offices of local authorities.

When you arrive to see the horse, explore

the reasons for sale with the vendor, and reassure yourself that he or she is genuine. Again try the horse out when you get him home. If there is any doubt, be prompt in contacting the vendor. If he refuses to admit an error, you will be forced to contact your solicitor, which could be expensive.

Despite their reputation, not all dealers are rogues. A reputable dealer, or a heavy horse breeder, has a living to make and needs you to return next time you are looking for a horse. He will certainly be prepared to show you what the horse can do, and will be quite content with a veterinary inspection.

Unless you are familiar with horses, a veterinary inspection is useful, but remember that it is only legal on the day. One day a horse may be fine in wind and limb and eye, the next day it could drop dead with heart failure. Such an inspection is not an MOT which is valid for 12 months.

Characteristics to Look for in a Working Horse

If you want a horse with which to do a few parades, a little bit of showing and some work, you want a nice upstanding horse.

It is not necessary to buy a horse of 18 or 19 hh – the current popularity of this height is producing horses with spindly legs and narrow chests. It is impossible to put harness on them without a step-ladder, and your implements and vehicles will be too small. Also, you will pay for size. A horse which is 16.3–17.2 hh is quite big enough. Such a horse, if well bred, will be deep-bodied, with a nice wide chest giving plenty of room for the heart and lungs. He will be capable and willing to work for you.

Types of Working Horse

There is very little to choose between geldings and mares when it comes to working. Sometimes mares can be a little temperamental, while a really honest gelding will pull his heart out for you. One or two stallions are worked in the UK, but not many, unlike the situation in France and elsewhere in Europe where stallions are worked just as much as geldings and

mares. Working stallions which are quiet and have a good temperament would be good to breed from.

Whether he be black, grey or strawberry roan makes little difference. It is nicer if he is well marked; he looks smarter, but as the saying goes, no good horse is a bad colour. Colour is really a matter of personal preference – if you want a black Shire with four white legs, that is top of the range and you will pay for it. If you are content with a horse with three white legs and one brown, he will be a lot cheaper, be just as attractive with his harness on, and equally effective. Illustrations 2.2–2.15 show the points of a working horse, and what to look for to find a sound, useful animal.

Current prices (1998) are hardly buoyant. It barely pays to breed heavy horses at the moment, and you ought to be able to pick up a reasonable working horse for £1,000 or perhaps less, depending on the circumstances. Some unbroken mares have recently been making only £450, whereas a few years ago they would have made over £1,000. Run-of-the-mill foals will make about £250–£350. These prices are similar for all pure-bred heavy breeds, but of course the market can change.

Cross-bred horses should not be ignored. They have many characteristics which may suit someone wanting to work a smallholding, for instance. A one-off cross from a stouter horse and a full pedigree well-bred mare can be a very useful animal. They seem to be tougher, and they very often have better joints than pure-breds; they may not be so handsome, but they may last longer and they can put up with rough work on the farm.

Keeping a Working Horse

Unless your horse is to be a town horse with sufficient outside work to keep him fit, you should not house him indoors constantly, and you will need some grazing. If you do not have suitable land adjoining your house, you will probably need to buy or rent a field nearby. Two or three acres is sufficient for one horse; six acres will enable you to expand to two horses if you want to.

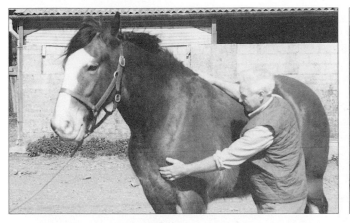

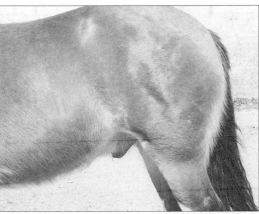

2.2 Head: lean, nose slightly roman. Eyes: large and docile. Forehead: broad. Nostrils: fine and wide. Ears: long, lean and sensitive. Shoulders: obliquely set, good length from withers to point, and wide enough for a collar to rest on.

2.5 Loin: short and strongly coupled.

2.3 Girth: Deep, with ribs well sprung, giving plenty of heart room.

2.4 Hindquarters: long, level and sweeping, great length from hip to hock, with well-developed second thighs. Tail set high.

2.6 Back: broad, short and strong.

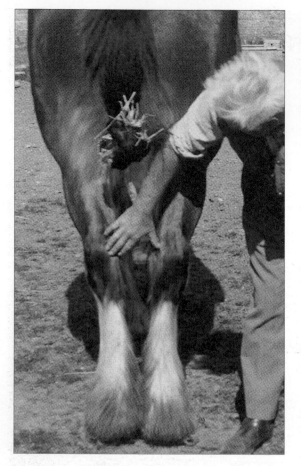 

2.7 and **2.8** Hocks: wide, flat and clean cut, set at the correct angle for leverage. Close together with points slightly inwards. Breech: deep, wide and well rounded.

The paddock needs to be divided into two or three plots to allow fresh grazing and time for tired land to recover. Grazing rotation also assists in eliminating parasites. Horses are gregarious creatures and some company will be welcome, whether it is your child's pony or an arrangement with someone else to keep their horse with yours.

The quality of the grazing is important. It should contain mixed grasses and no noxious weeds. It is particularly important to remove yew, deadly nightshade, bracken, foxglove and ragwort. Acorns or chestnuts from overhead trees could be a problem.

When the grass gets short, the horse should be moved to another paddock. Cattle or sheep introduced to clean up areas the horse has spurned will do the land good. Try to rest every paddock for two-thirds of the year, which will help control worms and other parasites. To keep it in good condition, chain harrow in the spring and roll after winter grazing has poached the ground. During the summer, try to harrow when you can to spread droppings. A dose of fertiliser may be appropriate during rest periods. If you can, plough up each paddock every few years and re-seed.

Beware of spraying done by your neighbour as this can be poisonous for horses,

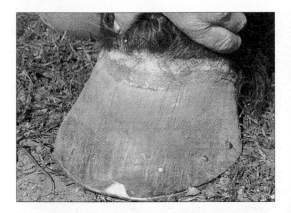

2.9 Feet: deep, solid and tough; broad at top (i.e. open coronets).

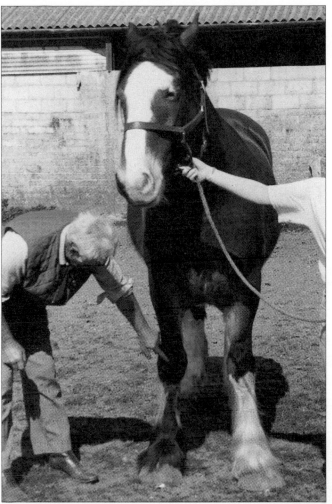

2.11 Knee: bold. Chest: wide and deep.

2.10 Forearm: long and muscular.

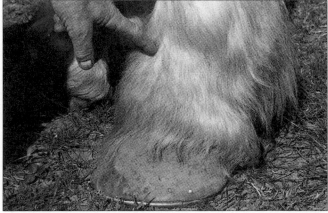

2.12 Ankle joint (fetlock): clean cut and set at the correct angle. Hair: moderate quantity, fine, straight and silky.

2.13 General: active and powerful; deep and symmetrical body with a leg at each corner; strong neck of medium length and moderately arched; average height at about 17 hh.

2.15 Cannon bone: perpendicular and short; good width of flat flinty bone.

2.14 Action: straight and level with a good stride, knees and hocks well flexed, and hocks kept close together.

and watch out for well-wishers feeding your horse tit-bits over the fence, especially in suburban situations.

Make sure you have a fresh supply of water to all the paddocks. A stream may be appropriate if it is really clean and does not have a sandy bottom. Shelter is important to protect the horse from sun, wind and rain. A field shelter can be built to serve more than one paddock. Even a suitable-sized unroofed shelter can afford your horse comfort in extremes of weather.

Fencing

It is an advantage if the field has a good hedge, but more often than not you will need to erect some fencing. A heavy horse weighs nearly a ton, and when he leans or rubs on something it will give easily! Post and rail looks nice, but it is expensive and can splinter. Plain wire can be dangerous: if a horse gets his foot caught it can cut like cheese wire. Barbed wire, whilst unsightly, can be effective because horses develop a respect for it. Kept really taut, it should consist of four strands, with the top wire at least as high as the top of the horse's legs and preferably half-way up his chest, i.e. about 4 ft 6 in. high.

Electric fencing has the advantage of being flexible should you want to change the size or shape of the paddocks. It is run off the mains, and will keep a stallion in, even with mares about. It is important to keep it taut, and new developments in fencing wire are helping with this.

Gates are expensive items and frequently inadequate! Ignore them at your peril, since the consequences of an escaped heavy horse on today's busy roads is awful to contemplate. (2.16).

Stabling

Stable buildings and fittings need to be adequate for a heavy horse. If your stable is

2.16 A well-fenced paddock. This example includes post and rail with taut barbed wire between rails; electric fence to sub-divide the paddock; solid gate; a shelter and water provision.

suitable only for a pony, you will find it disintegrating in quite a short space of time. Stables should be dry, well ventilated and free from draughts (2.17). Suitable space is also needed for bedding, hay and feed, harness, grooming kit and medicines, which should be kept in a locked cupboard.

You may be able to adapt a suitable existing building rather than erect purpose-built new stabling. Make sure you check whether you need planning permission. Stalls are suitable for horses in regular work. Otherwise a loose-box is advisable, measuring not less than 14ft by 12ft for one animal (2.18 and 2.19).

Concrete is a suitable flooring material in many ways, but where heavy horses stamp, holes will eventually appear. Blue bricks are ideal since they will take considerable pressure. It is also important to ensure that the doorway is sufficiently wide, at least 4ft, and the stable has adequate headroom.

Overhead hay racks are more suitable than hay nets. They are less time-consuming to fill and in practice falling seeds rarely cause eye problems. Hay on the ground is another possibility, but it can be wasteful if quantities are dropped on the floor and then trodden into the bedding.

Security is an important consideration, especially with the growth in equine-related theft. Suitable systems to protect buildings and paddocks, and methods of identifying items of harness are vital. Several commercial companies offer solu-

tions to these problems. Plainly, the nearer your equipment is to your house, the better its security is likely to be.

Feeding

The average working heavy horse should do well on ad lib hay and some 6lb rolled barley with chaff in two meals a day. There is a huge variety of horse feeds on the market today, some low energy, some high energy. Feeding 'up', giving oats or giving too much commercial feed is not necessary and might even be harmful to a heavy horse. The best thing to do is to chat to your local feed merchant and experienced horsemen to get some advice on what is the best feed to use in your circumstances.

2.17 A roomy loose box with overhead hay racks, salt licks, mangers and water provision. Note the open window.

2.18 A simple method of dividing a loose box into two for use as stalls.

2.19 An ideal stall arrangement for horses in regular work.

2.20a and **b** Training a horse to load and unload.

Travelling

It is important to make sure that your horse is used to travelling, since he will have to make journeys at some stage in his life.

A properly designed horse box is vital. Trailers are not suitable for a big horse. A livestock transport lorry with a rear gate is essential, so that when the horse is loaded he does not put his leg over the tailboard. There should be double thickness floors, 7ft 1in. (inside measurement) head-room, and divisions between each horse. Some people carry horses crossways, but this can be dangerous because every time the lorry sways towards the kerb the horse hits his head on the side of the lorry. Carrying them lengthways is advisable.

Steady driving is vital for the comfort of the horse; take care round roundabouts and over cambers, and watch for low branches whose noise might terrify horses inside the lorry. On the other hand, there is no need to creep around in second gear.

It should not be necessary to put leg bandages on your horse, although a tail bandage may be helpful to prevent the tail rubbing.

There is nothing worse than a horse which will not load at the end of a show. Give the horse plenty of practice at home.

When he loads give him something to eat and let him stand there for half an hour. Repeat this frequently until the horse feels that loading is part of life. Make sure the tailboard is not too steep, and if necessary put a rug or old carpet on it so that it does not rattle too much when he walks up it (2.20a and b and 2.21).

Finally, make sure you are familiar with the regulations about travelling horses and journey plans. Legislation is increasing at the moment, and it is important to have the correct completed forms with you if you are stopped on the highway. Information on these can be obtained from your local Animal Health Inspector. See also chapter 18 – Transport and the Law.

2.21 Leading a horse calmly out of his box on arrival at a show.

CHAPTER 3

Veterinary Care of the Draught Horse

Carl Boyde MRCVS

Introduction

Good quality general health care and management of draught horses is essential for their well-being and usefulness at work, whether it be in the fields or forests or on the showground. Some common ailments and diseases are mentioned below, but the intention of this chapter is to steer owners on a sound course as far as their animal's welfare is concerned.

Stabling

Stabling is all-important for the welfare of a horse. You can put a perfectly good horse into the wrong stabling and it will become a perfectly bad horse, for psychological or physical reasons, or both. A relaxed horse will digest its food properly and be much less prone to colic than one which is stressed for any reason.

Stable Size

Modern heavy horses are larger than their predecessors. The average working horse used to be 15.2–16 hh. Today, they can be as tall as 19 hh, especially showhorses. The original stalls and loose-boxes in old stables are frequently not big enough. The traditional concept of housing a working horse in stalls where they were fed, groomed, harnessed and kept is now changing. Large loose-boxes are much more satisfactory from the point of view of the horse. He can get up and down easily and avoid two of the problems he faced previously – capped elbow and capped hock. Self-inflicted injuries caused by the

difficulty of disposing of his shod feet when getting up or down are much reduced.

Water

It is vital for a horse to have adequate and permanent supplies of fresh drinking water in a large water-container. Small buckets are not sufficient for a large horse and are apt to get knocked over. Either a drum, or better still a water-trough with a ball-valve, is a suitable solution.

Bedding

Bedding should be generous. Use a peat base or straw. Many people object to horses eating their straw bed, but in my experience they come to no harm if properly fed otherwise. Using plenty of clean bedding will also assist the horse to get up and down without injury.

Doors and Windows

Doorways should be free of obstruction. In the old days, horses often injured their heads going in and out of stables. Many had poll evil as a result of repeated blows to the top of the head. Hip injuries as a result of going through narrow doorways with projections were also common (3.1).

There should not be glazed windows in the front of a heavy-horse box. Air should be able to circulate freely. A top door needs to be fitted in one or two boxes only in a larger stable: these are only needed very occasionally, for instance to examine a

3.1 A doorway of an adequate size for a heavy horse – 4 ft wide x 7 ft 6 in. high.

horse's eyes in the dark. Otherwise there is no need for a top door at all.

Mites can live in stable woodwork, and some horses can get an allergic reaction to these. Keeping stables clean is vital – there was a very good reason for the traditional whitewashing which used to be done regularly on farms.

Air

A horse breathes in and out an amazingly large volume of air. On a cold frosty morning, a horse can fill the stable with water vapour in three or four breaths. Generally, owners do not take nearly enough notice of the need for air changes. Old contractors' stables often had elaborate ventilation arrangements and were built with high ceilings – I would commend lofty stabling for heavy horses. Given adequate ventilation, coughs or colds will not necessarily be transmitted to all other horses as you might expect.

Owners should be very conscious of the risks to the horse of dust and mould spores.

3.2 Good grazing showing well tended pasture with no toxic plants.

These can lead to allergic problems in the horse's lung, which were commonly known as broken wind or heaves, but are now known to be chronic obstructive pulmonary disease (COPD). This can be avoided by making sure that stables are clean, and dust-free feed is vital.

Social Life

Ideally, stabled horses ought to be able to see each other. Some sort of grille or other device so that the horse can know who is in the next box is ideal. It is completely against the nature of a gregarious animal to be separated from its fellows. Modern stables with a verandah, allowing horses to put their heads out and look about in all weathers, are very suitable. However, at feeding times horses do need to be kept separate because the arrival of food will encourage bad behaviour. A mare will fight her foal for food, and vice versa. Smell is enormously important too.

Grazing

The grazing regime you adopt for your horses will make a great deal of difference to how well they digest their food, and consequently to their health and well-being.

Digestion

The principle thing to remember about the horse's digestive tract is that the stomach is small, and so the horse must eat almost continuously. The stomach of a Shire will hold, at best, 3 gallons. The hind gut will hold 30 gallons. Think about those proportions! The normal habit of the horse is to eat – left by itself it will eat for 16 hours a day out of 24. It will also lie down for 2 or 3 hours. This is why fields are particularly suitable, as a horse can relax so much better lying flat out on a good field.

Correct Grazing

Ideal grazing pasture consists of a mixture of grasses on well-limed, ragwort-free land, preferably with sheep and/or cattle to assist in natural parasite control (3.2 and 3.3). Two acres would be appropriate for a single heavy horse. Grazing must be adequate otherwise various veterinary problems can occur. For example, if the grass provided is not long enough and a horse is made to crop too close on light and sandy ground it will pull up sandy soil with the grass and consume it, resulting in a very good chance of developing sand colic. Horses will bark trees, which may not do the horse much harm, but will certainly harm the trees. Occasionally horses will eat acorns and oak leaves; a few will not hurt but too many will cause impactive colic. It is important not to allow horses to graze on fattening pastures. This can cause laminitis. Horses will not commit digestive suicide if they can possibly avoid it – if the correct food is available they will take that.

Toxic Plants

Great care should be taken to ensure that a horse does not have access to toxic plants. Yew (3.4) should be removed from horse pasture, although a horse will not eat it unless he is a foal lacking experience or desperate for food. Yew is instantly poisonous. Ragwort (3.5) (often preserved by local authorities!) is another plant about which owners must be vigilant. Seeds will blow into your field from verges. Do not let this plant get a hold. It can be difficult to exterminate, but can be pulled out quite easily (pulling is the best method of eradication). Ragwort is a common cause of hepatopathy, in which the liver cannot function properly. The effect of this on a horse can be tested by examining the liver enzymes in a blood sample. It is possible for all types of horse, including heavy horses, to get ragwort poisoning, and ultimately the liver damage is compounded by nerve damage. Symptoms include headaches and sight and balance difficulties. Putting the horse down is the only solution to this problem. The Government has ordered the extinction of ragwort, but it is ignored.

Worms

Parasitic worms can cause damage both on pasture and in the stable, but there are methods of controlling them from spreading. Horses dung in particular areas within a field, and these can usually be recognized by a strong growth of nettles. Worm larvae are passed onto these dunged areas, either already hatched or in egg form, and if the horse does not eat too close to the dunging areas the larvae have difficulty getting back into the horse again. Horses are selective grazers and they are more likely to eat close to such areas if the grazing is poor.

One problem in stables is a very small worm called a cyathostome, which can

3.3 Poor grazing showing poor pasture with sparse grass and nettles taking nourishment away from the grass.

complete its life-cycle inside a stable. There is also the red worm, which causes damage to blood vessels, and the large round worm, which can be up to a foot long. The eggs of these worms have to be out on the pasture for some time before they can 'hatch' and become infective larvae. Larvae accumulate during spring, summer and autumn, and tend to die out during winter. By using restricted dunging areas, as described above, the horse can largely avoid reinfection.

Many good worming remedies are available. It is important to use certain ones at the correct times of the year. Equalan, for instance, is very good at dealing with migratory phases of the red worm through the gut, and is best used four times a year. This is very important to a horse's health because its use can discourage an embolism (blockage of blood vessels) in the mesentery, and consequential colic and then possibly twist.

Grass Sickness

Grass sickness is a particular problem in the northern part of the country and in some localized conditions. There is much that is unknown about this disease and research

3.4 Yew

3.5 Ragwort

continues. If diagnosed, it is, regrettably, almost always fatal. In its acute form it appears much like colic, and can produce acute diarrhoea, fluid from the stomach running down the nose and severe constipation. A horse that survives it never regains its previous form.

Photosensitization

Owners are often unaware of the problems of sunburn on the white parts of horses. Use a factor 15–20 sun cream on the muzzle.

Size and Fencing of Pasture

It is essential to have adequate fencing for the welfare of the horse. Post and rail, wire or electric fencing are the choices available.

If a field is fenced with barbed wire it is vital that it is as tight as a violin string. Loops of barbed wire can be dangerous. Horses will paw their feet, get them tied up in the wire and damage themselves. Rails or electric tape are more appropriate and much respected by horses. This type of fencing will save the owner unnecessary veterinary bills.

Water

It is vital for horses to have an adequate supply of clean water in their pasture, ideally in a ball-valve tank. Access to the tank must be maintained. There should be no mud, and the tank should stand very firmly. Where a river adjoins the pasture it is preferable to have a separate water supply, because horses can get stuck in bank mud.

Shelter

Horses need shelter in summer. There is no need for a shelter in winter. In bad weather they seem perfectly happy with their rears to the wind and rain or covered in frost. In summer, however, when flies are at their worst, they must have a place to which to retreat. Horse flies, stable flies and *Stomoxys calicitrans*, which lives in the ear, are a very great nuisance. Head-shy horses are often suffering from such flies. Ear caps are a useful protection, and ought to be compulsory in summer. Fly fringes can also be very valuable. Generally, owners do not provide nearly enough suitable field shelter. Flies are active morning and evening, never at midday or at night. Grazing times need to take account of this (3.6).

Feed

Feed and health go hand in glove. Remember the great disparity between the horse's front stomach and hind gut. They are hind-gut digesters and need to eat continuously. In stables, there must always be an adequate supply of hay. It is preferable for the horse to feed 'downwards'. The length of the head and neck are designed to meet the ground, the horse's natural position for eating (3.7). They eat and digest much better if they eat and swallow downwards, and no dust gets in their eyes. Hay nets are a mixed blessing – although they control the rate of eating and stay tidy, horses can get hooked up and eat part of the net. Also, dust gets in their eyes. Place the hay on the ground and always in plentiful supplies. If left hungry, a horse will eat ferociously when it is fed and is likely to contract colic.

It is not necessary to chop hay into chaff unless horses are working. Traditionally, this was done to halve the job of chewing. Heavy horses should not be fed a heating ration. Oats need only be fed if a horse is working. For a heavy horse hauling timber all day, oats and chaff is the best feed – a high intake of fuel enables the horse to digest quickly and efficiently and convert the food into energy.

Horses which stand about all day need only good quality hay, and if they need a feed at all you can make your own out of bran and horse nuts. An average horse, which has finished growing and is not working, will do very well on minimal short feeds and hay. As a food, hay will be as good as the grass it came from. Much also depends on the way the hay has been harvested. Bad hay should not be fed. Good hay is wonderful for horses; their digestive system is completely adapted to it – they have been living on it for five million years.

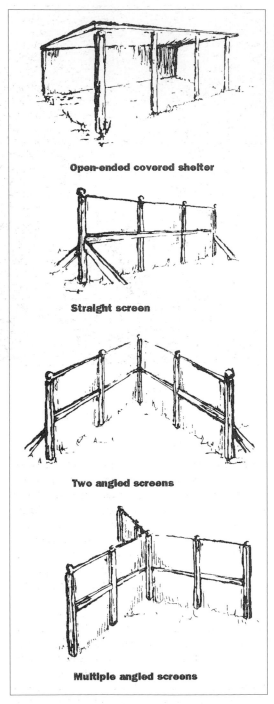

Open-ended covered shelter

Straight screen

Two angled screens

Multiple angled screens

3.6 Four shelter styles approved by the RSPCA

3.7 A horse eating 'downwards': its natural position.

What about the various composite feeds on the market? Adapt your feeding regime to the work you expect from the horse. Small amounts of highly concentrated amino acids will give you good results in a short space of time. There is no shortage of good advice and no shortage of good horse feeds. What you must not do is feed high-energy rations to a horse which is not exercised. See also chapter two – Choosing and Keeping a Working Horse, and chapter 14 – Preparation of a Show Horse.

Mineral and Vitamin Supplements

Mineral and vitamin supplements are a good idea, and a salt lick is always appreciated by animals. In some areas where there are mineral deficiencies feeding appropriate supplements will be very important. In copper-deficient areas, watch out for pale rings around the eyes. Limestone and chalk pastures are ideal, owing to their richness in calcium. Mineral supplements are a must for growing or pregnant animals.

Teeth

Just as we say 'No foot, no horse', we can equally say 'No teeth, no horse', since it is important that a horse's teeth should meet properly. Overshot or undershot jaws can be coped with, but do not buy a horse with such a condition. Molars must be lined up so that top and bottom sets are the same length. If there is irregularity it is possible that a hook will form at one end or the other when the unworn molar grows down (3.8).

Owners must check that the horse is eating well and managing to get his food down properly. An imperfection in the teeth will lead to food being balled up in the cheeks or dropped onto the floor again, i.e. quidding. This is a dental matter and can be dealt with. Pre-molar or wolf teeth can get in the way of the bit, in which case they need to be removed. Horses start with an amazing head-full of teeth; the sinuses are some 5 in. long in a big horse. As the teeth come down, the sinus almost empties of teeth. I have never found a horse which has run out of tooth – at the age of 40 years there is still a bit of tooth left to come! Incisors need a certain amount of watching as they can get injured, and may need to be removed. As horses get older, their teeth can get longer and longer, and the expression 'long in the tooth' applies literally to some horses.

Ageing a horse by its teeth involves making an informed guess, and one is usually 2 or 3 years wide of the mark, depending on the individual horse and its feed. Horses' teeth wear better if they are fed on feeds containing a good deal of silica with a lot of chew in it rather than on grass all the time.

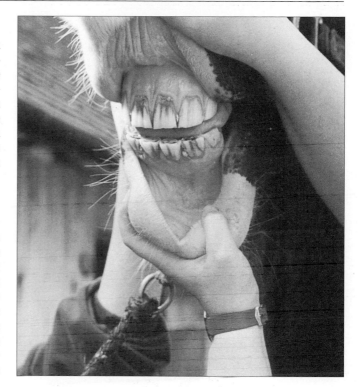

3.8 A good set of teeth.

Feet and Legs

Special attention must be paid to the feet of heavy horses. This need is greater in heavy horses than in other horses because of the sheer weight placed on the feet. A large heavy horse weighs nearly a ton. Five hundredweight is transmitted down to each foot. Keep the hooves well trimmed; do not allow them to crack and spread. Regular visits from the farrier are essential (3.9).

Whether heavy horses need to wear shoes at all times is debatable. If the feet are properly trimmed and the horse is working on soft ground, it is not always necessary to shoe the hind feet. However, it is probably a good idea to shoe the front feet. Horses working on roads must be shod all round. The essential element to good shoeing is to get the balance of the foot right. There should be plenty of heel and a vertical drop through the centre of the hoof. Fifty per cent of the shoe should be behind the centre and fifty per cent in front. Very often, too much of the shoe protrudes in front. In northern England the provision of caulkins for extra grip has been traditional, but caulkins on the hooves of horses kept in stalls was a major cause of capped elbow. See also chapter 4 — Farriery for the Working Horse.

Shoeing for Shows

It is complete nonsense to shoe a horse to make his feet appear as big as possible for showing. However, in North America the so-called Scotch shoe results in an almost square foot and no judge will look at a horse without these shoes. It is not unknown for car body filler to be applied. This type of shoeing produces an exaggerated action in the horse, and can also be used to correct an action. However, horses are not worked in these shoes. The equivalent in the UK is the big bevel shoe of our show Shires.

It is uncommon to find a horse spoilt by shoeing in the UK today since most shoeing is sensible. It is important, however, not to forget about the horse's hooves and shoes once he is turned out. Left on too long they can become loose, damaging the hoof and causing infection where nail holes are left.

Foot Care

If horses stand for any length of time in bad conditions, infection of the frog and frog area can occur. It is rare to see true thrush, where puss is oozing out of the frog, but usual to see and smell decay. It is not at all uncommon to find flyblow. Blow flies lay their eggs in the frog area and a nest of maggots is found in the foot. Maggots eat dead tissue, so in effect they are carrying out a useful clean-up job! In horses, they do not do much harm. See chapter 4 on farriery for a diagram of foot structure.

Feather Care

This is largely a question of hygiene – feathers must be kept clean and any sign of infection must be dealt with, whether caused by parasitic mites or moulds. The *Dermatophilus* mould, called rainscald on

top of the body and mud fever on the legs, is one of the most usual conditions.

Care of Legs

An important element in the care of horses' legs is parasite control. Many heavily feathered horses get small chorioptic mange mites in the skin, leading to irritation and discomfort. Grease is a secondary infection due to failure to maintain healthy skin. Mud fever is also a secondary infection of chapped skin, caused by a fungal parasite called *Dermatophilus congolense*. Avoid infection in the first place through good management and prompt treatment. Nowadays we can use a number of traditional parasite controls such as flowers of sulphur and oil, but active compounds such as Gammexane have been withdrawn due to potential harmful effects to others in the food chain. However, newer compounds are available, for example, Aludex, Ivermectin (the active ingredient in Equalan) and its associated compounds such as Dectomax.

A great many leg problems stem from irritation of the skin. A horse will start stamping and kicking, predisposing him to arthritic conditions of the foot and limb, colloquially known as ringbone and sidebone. Sidebone is ossification of the lateral cartilages in the foot. Whether it is a disease or a normal occurrence is arguable – personally I regard it as a normal change in an ageing horse: the consequence of the horse's weight transmitted to hard ground over a period of time. Providing the horse is sound, I do not think it matters how much extra bone he has. Ringbone can have a bad effect on joint articulations, but having extra bone round the pedal bone does not matter if it does not actually make the horse lame. Relate that problem to the usefulness of the horse and the working tasks he is doing. It is conventional for vets making a veterinary examination for a prospective owner to turn down horses with these conditions. I would judge them entirely on whether there was interference with the soundness of the horse for the job it was doing.

Further up the limb, a badly managed

3.9 A regularly trimmed and well-shod hoof.

heavy horse can fall down in front and break his knees. This is very much a matter of the way in which he is driven. If he goes down in front it is the fault of the driver; if he goes down behind it might be bad luck, but it ought not to happen.

Nowadays there is a growing incidence of OCD (osteo chondritis dessicans) – a degenerative disease in the hocks of large horses. This is often associated with tendon problems. Growing too rapidly can give rise to chronic lameness and uselessness if the owner is not careful. This can be controlled by management, especially by lowering the rate of nutrition. There should be, as we would say with cattle, a 'store' period, where the horse is allowed to get a bit plain and not 'do' very well, until nature has sorted the matter out.

Occasionally we meet classic lamenesses – the luxating patella (the kneecap which comes off) – very often in a youngish horse. This is a question of growth and development, and given time and exercise in straight lines, it sorts itself out. We still see odd cases of disorders like string halt – a snatch of the leg, which is a nerve disorder. If it happens it is an unsoundness, but it might not interfere with the usefulness of the horse. There is nothing that can be done about it.

Percussion

Modern heavy horses do not work in the way they used to. Most arthritic problems suffered by working horses have disappeared. Forty to fifty years ago, thousands of working horses in towns pulled loads of 1–2.5 tons across cobbles and between tram lines with considerable camber. Their feet were always turning. Today the incidence of osteo-arthritic conditions of the foot or hock are much lower. Neither do horses get spavin like they did. Changed circumstances have removed a complete range of problems.

Laminitis

Laminitis is nutrition-associated. Some people producing horses for show are prone to over-feed their animals, and I have seen several horses with a foot which has collapsed with chronic low-grade laminitis. Laminitis can also be caused by grazing a horse on grass which is too rich in nutrients, say after the first flush of growth in spring. In this disease there is a separation of the bony and soft laminae in the foot. The pedal bone comes away and is in great danger of poking through the sole of the foot. Another tragic but typical laminitis situation relates to foaling problems. A retained afterbirth can lead to toxic laminitis. This has the same effect, with the mare being unable to stand. This is a severe problem in a big animal.

Harness Fitting

The fit of a collar to a horse is very important, and will affect the ability of the horse to work. Where a collar fits badly, shoulder injuries will result, and the only treatment is to stop working the horse and let the injury mend. In addition, it is vital that the collar does not sit on the windpipe. Also, a collar which fitted last year may not fit now – horses may get fat, or change shape on the shoulder due to increased work. In earlier days the police would stop horsemen if a horse looked uncomfortable and perhaps find a sore beneath the collar. Carefully fitted bits and bridles are also vital. If badly fitted, they can cause lip injuries and sore faces. Blinkers have to be arranged so that the horse can see things properly, and bridles must not pinch the head. Properly fitting harness is all a matter of good management. There is no necessity for injuries from harness. See chapter 7 – Harness for the Working Horse.

Diseases and Immunization

Working heavy horses must be immunized. It is important to immunize against tetanus, which in country life is everywhere. Vaccinating against influenza should be related to where the horse is travelling. Shows expect owners to have protected their horses from this disease, but equine influenza is not everywhere and there is no special need to keep them perfectly immunized. Nowadays, we can also vaccinate against the equine herpes virus.

Take veterinary advice on this: so much depends on the individual situation. The Shire Horse Society now insists on blood testing for equine viral arteritis for Shire stallions, but this, again, is very rare.

Breeding

If you are considering breeding working horses it is worth remembering that not every mare is worth breeding from. It is pointless to take a poor mare on a long journey to a premium stallion, which will cost you a lot of money and time, if you are unlikely to get a decent foal. If you have a good mare, it might also be worth considering crossing her with a thoroughbred to produce a heavyweight hunter, for which there is currently a steady demand. If your mare has bad conformation or is not very good-tempered, it is best not to breed from her, but to use her for work.

A mare should be prepared for breeding by ensuring that she is in good condition but not too fat. Start breeding at age four. A mare which is not in the habit of breeding is unlikely to be a successful candidate. The owner of a mare and the stud to which she is taken should agree whether to swab before service. Consult your vet in individual cases. The birth of a foal is a management matter. It is preferable for a mare to foal in a large box or a field depending on whether it is night or day, and adequate help should be on hand. The chances of losing a foal go up in proportion to its size. If you find that the foal has a leg back, help is needed instantly. Repositioning everything can be very difficult. After the birth, the first essential is to get the foal onto its feet and to dress the navel. If there is any worry, use antibiotics. The main concern with the mare is to prevent post-partum metritis (inflammation of the uterus): this is more likely with a retained afterbirth or following a difficult birth. This is also the time when you may be faced with post-partum laminitis. Mastitis must also be avoided. To help prevent this, the udder should be handled before the birth. Also make sure that the foal suckles quickly (3.10); again this is a matter of management. You may need help with the mare – if she is

3.10 A foal suckling

squealing and kicking and because of her sheer weight and size, it is advisable to call your vet. Nowadays adequate sedation is available, as well as substitute milk.

Foal Rearing

Foal rearing is best done in small numbers rather than large. Cross-infection is far less likely when there are fewer animals. Treatment for colic in foals has altered dramatically, and nowadays injections will usually solve the problem.

Older Horses

Getting cast, going down and being unable to get up is a particular difficulty with older, large heavy horses. Older horses also get more diseases. Bute is a splendid drug which enables many horses to live much longer by reducing excess inflammation. An old horse with osteo-arthritis can continue living for a number of years if bute is used under proper conditions. Unfortunately bute is currently being considered for withdrawal as some humans can be sensitive to it through the food chain. In the UK, where horses are not eaten, it seems unnecessary to ban it, however. Euthanasia is sometimes necessary, and is often the kindest approach if an old or ill horse is simply going to get cold and miserable in a field. It is totally unfair to keep crippled horses who cannot breathe because of wind problems or cannot move because of limb problems.

This is a subject which must be faced up to. Conventional shooting is instantaneous.

Conformation and General Points

Modern heavy horses are being bred with the showing scene or public relations in mind. Tall rangy animals are required for big teams. This trend is developing an animal which is over-straight on the pasterns, and therefore too upright. A

3.11 A mare using her tail to flick away flies in the summer.

certain degree of angle to the pastern, the fetlock joint, is associated with better movement and therefore better health. See chapter 1 – The Modern Draught Horse in the UK for a diagram showing the basic conformation of the heavy horse (1.20).

Eyes

A horse with cataracts may become blind, but can sometimes carry on with some work. Arthur Young, the rural historian rode on one, and I know of a performance horse with only one eye.

Tumours

Sarcoids are tumours brought on as a result of a virus. A variety of treatments are now available, and this should be discussed with the vet.

Heart

Heavy horses seem to have remarkably sound hearts and heart attacks are very rare.

Tails

Please leave tails on, as nature intended. They are very useful as a fly switch. If they are in the way for work or show, braid them up (3.11 and 3.12).

Genetics and Temperament

Many diseases contracted by lighter horses are avoided by heavy horses. Often this is because particular characteristics have been bred out. Many characteristics are genetically conditioned. A tendency to laminitis and broken wind, for instance, can be inherited, and affected animals should not be used for breeding. It is vital to choose good healthy stock from which to breed. Temperament is inherited, and a good temperament is worth its weight in gold. Don't breed from the barmy – eat 'em!

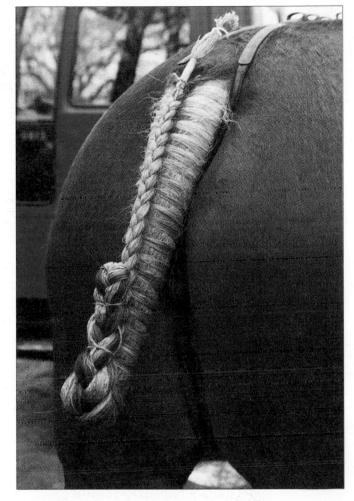

3.12 A Suffolk tail (always left long) plaited (braided up) for working.

CHAPTER 4

Farriery for the Working Horse

Roger Clark

Introduction

The successful use of the horse, bearing its welfare and comfort in mind, depends on the correctness of the principles and practices on which shoeing is based. The horse would be almost useless for heavy draught on the artificial road surfaces we have today without shoes. By studying the anatomy and function of the foot, we can see how it serves the purposes of locomotion and weight bearing, and how it must be shod on sound principles if the function of the foot is not to be impaired.

The horse's foot has always been looked upon by horsemen as the principal region to which care should be given, because without a good sound foot the horse's uses are diminished or lost, hence the old adage, 'no foot, no horse'.

The amount of injury done to a foot by incorrect shoeing is much greater than a cursory examination would lead one to believe, especially over a period of time. So good shoeing principles are of immense benefit, not only to the horse but to the user as well (4.1).

Anatomy

It is important to understand the fundamental aspects of hoof anatomy. The hoof contains two and a half bones, the pedal bone, the navicular bone and half the short pastern.

The pedal bone resembles the hoof in shape and is the foundation on which the foot is built. The navicular bone lies behind the pedal bone and forms a fulcrum over which the deep flexor tendon glides to its insertion on the solar surface of the pedal bone, thus providing flexion to the foot. The extensor tendon is attached on the apex of the pedal bone, thus providing extension to the foot. Half the short pastern is within the hoof capsule and forms the pedal joint.

The two lateral cartilages are attached to the wings of the pedal bone and form the flexible foundation to the heels, thus allowing the foot to expand. The fibrous coronary cushion, in conjunction with the horny frog and digital cushion, helps dissipate concussion. The horny sole protects the solar surface of the hoof and the bars keep the foot strong and the heels open. The white line forms a flexible bond between the wall and the sole, which it allows to flatten slightly under the body weight. It also indicates the thickness of the wall and shows the farrier how much wall there is to nail to.

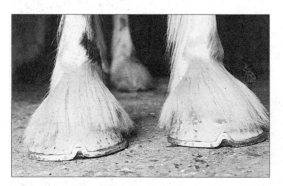

4.1 A pair of well-shod Shire front feet, with bevelled shoes and hand-drawn clips.

The shoeing nail may enter the white line but must not go beyond it, as this may cause 'pricking' or 'nail binding' to the sensitive circulatory tissue (4.2).

Although this is a very brief description of the structures which make up the hoof, it is enough to appreciate the necessity of understanding the anatomy of the foot, which is vital if the horse is to be shod on sound principles (4.3).

Shoeing a Heavy Horse

In order to shoe the heavy horse appropriately, we need to consider its role in the 1990s. There are still some horses working on the land, some are in town work, and a few are engaged in the forestry industry. Many are used for promotional work and advertising, showing in harness. The majority, however, are used for breeding and showing in-hand.

Horses that were worked hard and regularly were seldom difficult to shoe, as they were, in the main, handled by people who knew their job and were probably not influenced by the 'gentle giant' syndrome we are familiar with today. Shoeing cart horses is hard work, and can be made much harder by horses that have never been taught to

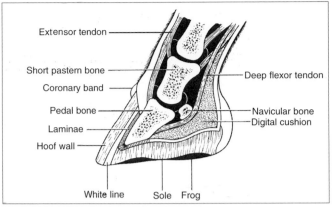

4.2 Vertical cross-section of the hoof showing the main bone structure.

4.3 A good deep heel with the foot the same angle as the pastern.

4.4 Shoeing a difficult Shire 'two-handed'.

stand still while their feet are handled and shod. If a young farrier's first introduction to cart horses is to be leant upon or thrown about, then there is no wonder that some farriers refuse to shoe them (4.4).

Some horses, particularly those with an abundance of hair and inclined to be 'itchy', are made difficult by using the feather hair to pull up the hind feet. It is far better to pull up the hind foot with the claw of the hammer and then take hold of the toe. Remember it is not the fault of the horse that it is 'itchy'. It is advisable not to get too far underneath the horse whilst 'clenching up'. Unclenching can be made easier by taking the foot forward on a stool and knocking a few nails back with a buffer, before proceeding to pull the shoes off. Of course using pincers with large jaws makes the task much easier. This is a useful tip for an owner or attendant of a horse with a twisted shoe or one that is half off and needs urgent attention. Reshoeing is usually necessary every 6 weeks or before if the shoe is loose or worn.

Shoeing an Agricultural Horse

Agricultural horses are often shod with shoes which are too long and heavy. We need to understand the type of work they do. The major benefit of cart horses is that they can be used when it would not be practical to use a tractor: for instance, in wet sticky conditions for feeding stock living out during the winter. These horses are best shod with a light shoe, which should last for about 6 weeks. The foot can be shod slightly longer than the last bearing point of the heel, and any protruding shoe boxed to the foot. We not only have to safeguard the horse from standing on its own shoes, but because farm horses often work in pairs, we must safeguard his work mate also. The inside branch of the hind shoe should be narrowed about one-third of the width of material and well rounded off on the ground surface. If a horse is used in the furrow, he is apt to 'brush' or 'cut' if this precaution is not taken.

In parts of the eastern counties it was customary to forge twisted wedge heels on the hind shoes for grip and support (4.5). It was not often done to forge caulkins for farm horses, because it is potentially damaging to the opposite foot when turning tight in heavy ground.

The main problem with farm horses, as they do not often wear out their shoes, is the amount of time owners leave shoes on between shoeings. If shoes are left on too long it can cause excessive strain on the tendons and throw the feet into a state of imbalance. In some cases, horses doing land work can be shod in front only, or even not at all. As an unshod horse loses a lot of traction, shoeing is essential if heavy work is undertaken. It is preferable to shoe a horse before it becomes foot-sore. This applies especially to young horses when they are first put to work. If their feet are sore it can make them troublesome at their first shoeing, which is not their fault.

Shoeing a Commercial Horse

A commercial horse requires another style of shoeing, since their work differs from that of the farm horse. Again, it is beneficial to the wear and tear on the horse's feet if the shoes will withstand at least 1 month on the roads without being too heavy. These horses can be shod much longer and wider than the farm horse, but such shoes must be well rounded on the protruding edges for safety and to prevent them being trodden off. Capped elbows can be caused by the prominent heel of a shoe rubbing when the horse is lying down.

4.5 Cart horse with twisted wedge heels and rolled toe behind.

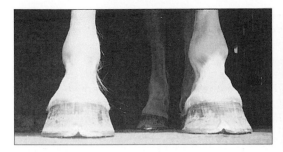

4.6 Suffolk horse shod with bevelled shoes. Clips are positioned in order to make the horse appear to stand square.

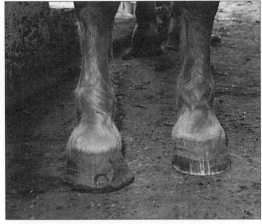

4.7 Suffolk horse trimmed (left) before and (right) after a run at grass.

The fore shoe should have a wide bold toe, which can be rolled slightly to assist the horse with the 'break over': the point at which the horse's foot rolls over the toe. As most cart horses are pigeon-toed, the clip can be fitted slightly to the outside; this will give the appearance that the horse is standing straighter (4.6).

As most wear in the hind shoe is taken on the outside toe quarter, plenty of width in this area will help withstand wear. If the shoe is driven across the foot, then a strong quarter clip will help prevent this. With regard to non-slip devices, a plug stud in each heel quarter will suffice; large prominent studs are often too traumatic for the joints. Double caulkins or caulk and wedge seem to have fallen into disuse for road horses, and on modern road surfaces there is no advantage in having them.

Shoeing a Heavy Horse for the Show Ring

For showing, a horse should be shod in such a way as to show it off to its best advantage to the judge. This is often a very controversial subject, with many theories on the correct way to do it, often from self-appointed experts! This causes a problem, because the farrier is not willing to compromise. It is often the farrier who is blamed by the owner if the horse 'dishes' whilst giving its show in front of the judge. In many cases it is because the groom has not learned to show a horse properly. Many horses can be made to appear to move straight if correctly paced and shown. Some horses move straight when in a 'natural' condition, but once brought up to show condition, faults in stance and gait are often exaggerated. Having a horse in tiptop condition and keeping the feet and legs in good condition is another element in the art of showing heavy horses. See also chapter 14 – Preparation of a Show Horse.

Ensuring that the horse has good sound feet and is well prepared in advance is a matter of good management. At the end of the showing season, the shoes should be removed and the feet trimmed prior to a run at grass. Too often shoes are left on, and after a time they become loose. Then they fall off, in many cases breaking large pieces out of the hoof wall and leaving the feet in a state of imbalance. The horse's feet should be trimmed again during the rest period and a light set of shoes put on as soon as the horse is brought back to be prepared for the next show season (4.7). This should be done in plenty of time. It should be remembered that because the horse has run 'barefooted' it will be at least a month before any sign of growth will be perceived, and therefore shoeing early is important if the feet are to be strong for the coming season. A strong sound foot should be deep in the heel, short in the toe and wide in the quarters, with the bars left intact. A very long foot is not necessarily a big foot. It is not possible to get length and breadth in a foot at the same time.

4.8 Hind feet shod with bevelled shoes showing the exaggeration of the bevel on the outside quarters.

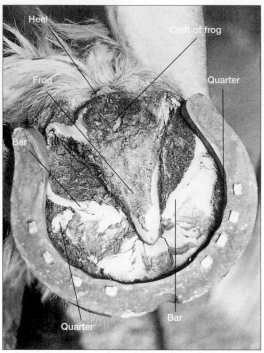

4.9 A fore foot bold in the quarters with a slightly donkey heel to give the appearance of width, and the bars of the foot left strong.

Shoeing a Shire Horse

The main purpose of bevelled shoes is to enhance a good foot and improve the appearance of a poor one (4.8). The bevel should be at the same angle as the hoof wall and exaggerated at the heels. It is important to shoe with a good length, especially on the outside heels, which can be 'donkeyed out' if required to give the appearance of more width at the heels (4.9). Again the clips should be positioned to make the horse stand square. It is important to have the feet trimmed and balanced before the shoe is fitted. If a horse is shod light before fitting the heavier bevels, this will exaggerate the action. It is unfortunate that some judges of in-hand Shire classes continue to place horses with long, over-sized feet at the top of the line, which perpetuates this practice. There must be some compromise.

Hind shoes need to be narrowed up slightly on the inside branch, which should be hot-rasped to give an almost rounded effect. If the horse is used on the road, it is advisable to take the rough edge off with an old rasp. This will help a Shire keep his feather. It is surprising how they will shave themselves when the inner edge of the shoe is sharp. The outside branch of the hind shoe can be thickened to encourage the horse to keep his hocks together. If they turn their toes out, then fit the clip to the inside of the middle line. If a horse is sluggish in its hock action then shoe with plenty of length behind; this will certainly help.

Nail holes should be stamped very coarse, thus utilizing the full thickness of the wall. This will keep the feet strong and sound. The hoof wall will chip and break if the shoe is made with fine nail holes.

Shoeing a Suffolk Horse

The shoeing of Suffolk horses requires a different style to that of Shire horses. Suffolk horses compete regularly in best-foot classes at major shows where the prize money is divided between the groom and the farrier. The reasoning behind the foot classes is that historically, the main criticism of Suffolk horses was their weak shelly feet. The Suffolk Horse Society Council promoted best-foot classes, and this had three major effects. It encouraged breeders to use stallions with good feet, it gave an incentive to the groom to look after the feet and it gave an incentive to the farrier to make an extra effort (4.10a and b). Nowadays, it is not often that Suffolk horses are seen with poor feet. However, foot classes remain as popular as ever.

The Suffolk horse should be shod as light as possible, with the same amount of bevelling on the inside and outside borders of the shoe, exaggerated at the heels, which gives the appearance of a wider foot. The position of the clips is most important because Suffolk horses are more prone than most to being pigeon-toed (4.11). Great care is needed in the fitting of the shoes if they are to appear straight. The feet should not be left long. If they are, they will soon become weak and start to chip and break.

Shoeing a Percheron and an Ardennes

The Percheron is noted for its hard blue feet, a trait which found favour with British officers in France during the First World War. Percheron feet are strong and able to withstand much wear without shoes. The Ardennes, now much more numerous in this country, have very similar feet. The toughness of the feet in these breeds often leads owners to leave the shoes on for far too long. This is not beneficial to the horse: it does nothing but harm to the joints and throws excessive strain on the flexor tendons.

Percherons can be shod 'heavier' than Suffolk horses, and as they are also inclined to be pigeon-toed, they should be shod accordingly.

Shoeing a Clydesdale Horse

Those who favour this breed, especially in the north of the UK, prefer a much squarer toe on the fore foot, the theory being that it helps the fore foot 'break over' better, thus improving the horse's action.

The hind feet are encouraged to grow with a flared outside quarter. This is brought about by lowering the inner-heel quarter and letting the outside grow. Often a three-quarter hind shoe is fitted, sometimes with a caulkin on the outside heel to

encourage the hocks to be kept together (4.12). As this will make the toes turn outwards, the clip must be placed well to the inside of the middle line, to give the appearance of being straight.

Shoeing a Working Cob

Cross-bred horses, light vanners and cobs are suitable for light draught work, both on the streets and in agriculture, as well as the heavy draught horse. A Fell or Dales pony is an ideal 'workhorse' for the smallholder or hill farmer, and can often perform light tasks without shoes. A light, plain stamped or three-quarter fullered shoe will suffice for this type of horse, but the principles of shoeing are still as important as for any other horse.

4.10a and b Horses shod by the late Les Finch of Martlesham, Suffolk. Above, the feet of 3-year-old Suffolk stallion 'Beau Boy' 6079, and below, the feet of 6-year-old Suffolk mare 'Orwell Dame' 13251, both awarded first prize for best feet at the Suffolk County Show, 1930.

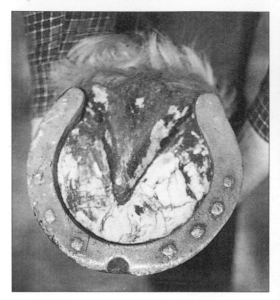

4.11 A pigeon-toed Suffolk with offset clip

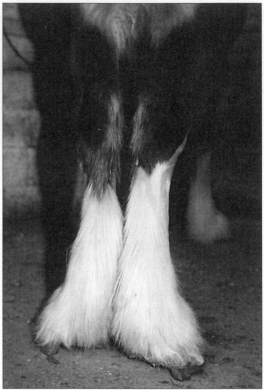

4.12 A horse shod with a single caulkin to encourage the hocks together.

If this type of horse is used for riding as well as draught work, then a hind shoe with quarter clips is preferable, as this lessens the tendency to 'over-reach' in wet ground. A small plug stud or non-slip nail with a tungsten pin will normally be sufficient to stop too much slipping on the road.

Shoeing in Winter

If a horse is to be used all the year round, it is often a good plan in the winter to have each shoe drilled and threaded in each heel and outside toe for the reception of studs should it become necessary. In the event of a heavy fall of snow, the stud holes can then be cleared with a 'tap' designed for the purpose, and either a sharp jumping stud or the correct chisel-shaped frost stud screwed in. Remember these studs must be taken out at night to prevent the horse damaging itself. This will enable the horse to keep on its feet when travelling over packed snow or ice. Filling the soles with grease will stop snow balling in the hooves in the short term.

Conclusion

Looking forward it is doubtful whether any major change will be introduced in the principles or techniques of shoeing heavy horses. No shoe the farrier can buy will ever equal the very best hand-made shoes, especially for Shire horses. Very good shoes for heavy horses have been produced in the Netherlands, and now appear to have over-taken the British equivalent.

Bevelled shoeing will always remain a specialized practice. Often these and other techniques related to shoeing heavy horses do not meet with the approval of the new generation of farriers and theorists.

Possibly the most difficult problem for a heavy-horse owner is finding a farrier who is willing to shoe his horse. It is a great pity that whilst many heavy-horse shoeing competitions are over-subscribed, very few of the competitors would consider shoeing a heavy horse in a day's work.

Farriery and the Law

By law, only registered farriers can shoe a horse. Any heavy-horse owner who prepares his horses' feet for shoeing or who goes as far as shoeing them himself is breaking the law. The only exception is for emergency first aid to a horse's foot.

The 1975 Farriers Registration Act recognized that many owners had in fact been preparing and shoeing their horses' feet themselves, and included provision for anyone who had been doing this for at least 2 years before 1980 to apply for registration. This provision is still in operation. It does not apply to anyone who has been doing such work since 1980. There is, of course, nothing to prevent an owner from removing a horse's shoe.

A number of people working regularly with heavy horses have trained and registered as a farrier to enable them to attend to their own horses. Information about training and registering can be obtained from the Farriers Registration Council, Sefton House, Adam Court, Newark Road, Peterborough PE1 5PP.

CHAPTER 5

Training for Horsemen

Mike Bingham and Sara Roberts

Introduction

Historically, many of those from the different horse disciplines have been concerned about the training of horsemen and the assessment of competence. The British Horse Society, the British Driving Society and others have been involved over many years in developing a qualification structure with levels of competence which are measurable. The structure covers all aspects of horse management and horse usage from a very basic level up to the highest levels of horsemanship.

In the draught horse world, very little attention was paid to the training of horsemen until the early 1980s, when Keith Chivers collected groups of individuals together to produce the Shire Horse Society report 'History with a Future'. This report recommended that careful thought should be given to the training of those working with heavy horses. Since that time dramatic progress has been made in the development of a qualification structure and training programmes for people working with, or wishing to work with, heavy horses.

The qualifications available in the heavy horse sector are accredited by both the Scottish Vocational Education Council (SCOTVEC) and the National Council for Vocational Qualifications (NCVQ), and fit into the national framework of vocational qualifications. The current qualifications available are at S/NVQ Levels 1–3, with Level 4, to include specialized showing skills and preparation, nearing completion.

In addition to these qualifications, the Heavy Horse Training Committee, now renamed the Draught Horse Training Committee, has produced free-standing Road Driving Assessments, which are administered by the British Horse Society at single, pairs and team levels. For more information on this see chapter 16 – Road Driving.

There has never been a better time for newcomers to the heavy horse sector. There are plenty of good horses for sale at reasonable prices, and it is important for the sector's survival that people wishing to become involved with working or showing heavy horses are encouraged. Throughout the British Isles there are many very experienced, competent horsemen who have devoted their lives to heavy horses. Not all are willing or prepared to become involved in teaching skills to those individuals who are entering their industry, but fortunately there is a group of people who are determined to pass on their knowledge through properly organized training programmes.

An important aspect of training is the updating of skills to take account of the modern environment, with its greater emphasis on health and safety and new legislation affecting horse ownership. Traditional techniques are not always appropriate, and new skills have sometimes to be mastered. It is imperative that anyone entering the heavy horse world receives the most up-to-date information, advice and instruction available to cope with today's ever changing demands. It is also essential that people carrying out this instruction have themselves undertaken the updating processes and are familiar with modern instructional techniques.

When someone learns to drive a car they receive instruction from a qualified instructor who then submits them for testing to ensure they have achieved the standard of competence necessary to pass the road driving test. An almost identical situation exists in the case of training and qualifications for horse people. Some breed societies issue certificates of competence, but these are not nationally recognized. The S/NVQ structure is a nationally recognised qualification which in the future will almost certainly become recognized within the international, and especially the European, community also.

The Department of Transport has recently published a *Code of Practice for Horse Drawn Vehicles* which offers guidance to people taking horses and vehicles out onto the roads in modern traffic situations. The Code is advisory, and aimed primarily at people carrying paying passengers 'for hire and reward'. It recommends that such people should be trained and tested taking the Road Driving Assessment and receiving S/NVQ accreditation. Local authorities and other public bodies are increasingly expecting this official proof of competence for anyone operating on their behalf. Others regularly taking their horses out onto the road or operating in a public place are also urged to take notice of the new Code.

It is essential, regardless of whether or not a training programme leads to a national qualification, for all trainers to deliver a quality product. A candidate should have access to a structured, negotiated and reviewed training programme. The client should be assessed at the preliminary stage, an action plan produced, individual lesson plans drawn up and records of the candidate's achievements kept. It is totally unacceptable for trainers within the heavy horse world to give scant consideration to the preparation and outcome of their programmes.

S/NVQ Qualifications and Sources of Training

Level 1 – Horse care, plus a working horse specialist unit.

Level 2 – Horse care, plus a working horse specialist unit.
Level 3 – Horse care, plus a working horse specialist unit, and including road driving and woodland maintenance.
Level 4 – Horse care, plus showing and show preparation specialist unit.

Training towards these qualifications is offered at certain colleges of further education and agricultural colleges, and by private training individuals or organizations.

Two other training awards are available which are not full S/NVQs but can be credited towards an S/NVQ.

Road Driving Assessment – single horse (S/NVQ Level 2).
Road Driving Assessment – pair of horses (S/NVQ Level 3).
Road Driving Assessment – team of horses.

As an indication of the costs and time involved, in 1998 the full S/NVQ Level 2 costs £140, Level 3, £160 and the specialist units on their own, £45. The time involved can be anything from 6 months to 3 years, depending on the candidate's experience and the presentation of evidence. The Road Driving Assessment costs £50 plus examiner's expenses and takes about 2 hours.

Information about all qualifications can be obtained from: British Horse Society, Training and Examinations Department, Stoneleigh Deer Park, Kenilworth, Warwickshire, CV8 2XZ.

A training manual for people undergoing training towards S/NVQ Level 2, giving information specific to work with heavy horses, has been prepared by Andrew Morton and Mike Bingham with support from the Department of Employment via the Horse Education and Training Council. It can be obtained from: Horse Education and Training Company, The Burgess Building, The Green, Stafford ST17 4BL.

Training for Timber Extraction by Horse

The Forestry Contracting Association is the body which coordinates training for timber extraction by horse. The FCA, in conjunction with their British Horse Loggers group, has

5.1 Training a pupil to back a horse and cart at Holme Lacy College.

written and piloted the relevant Forestry NVQs and runs a range of training courses providing the basic skills needed. The courses, which are practical and involve husbandry and operational skills, are listed below.

Basic Draught Horse Handling – This course includes health and safety, grooming and feeding, horse health, harness and harnessing, working horses with chain equipment, shafted equipment and four-wheeled waggons (5.1).

Draught Horses in Woodlands and Forestry – Previous experience with working draught horses or attendance on the basic course is an entry requirement. The course includes health and safety, care and feeding of draught horses at work, care, maintenance and selection of harness and equipment, work study and systems analysis, extraction of short-wood material and extraction of pole-length material.

These courses lead towards the S/NVQ in Forestry – Extracting Wood Products by Horse. Candidates can use this as performance evidence towards the final qualification. Information about these qualifications can be obtained from: The Forestry Contracting Association, Dalfling, Blairdaff, Inverurie, Aberdeenshire AB51 5LA.

FCA training packages are available throughout the UK, but their courses are also offered at some colleges, currently including Coleg Llysfasi, Ruthin, Clywd LL15 2LB. Other colleges, including Kirkley Hall and The Barony College in Dumfries, hope to develop courses in the future. Also a number of Woodland Initiatives (e.g. Cumbria Broadleaves) run FCA Horse Logging courses.

CHAPTER 6

Training Your Horse

Nick Rayner

Introduction

Before you start training a young horse there are some basic disciplines you need to adopt for your own safety. Lead a horse decisively, with your right hand close to his mouth and your left hand on the other end of the lead rein (6.1). If he is young and inexperienced, make sure you are never too far away to take hold of the reins.

If using a cart, do not stand close to a shaft which is pointing towards you, and take care not to stand close to the wheels. When getting into a cart, do not stand on a spoke of a wheel since any sudden movement will throw you off balance. Get into a cart, with the reins held in your hand, by stepping on the shaft close to its juncture with the cart and swinging yourself on (6.2a and b). Never ride sitting on a shaft, or on any part of a cart which is not intended for riding on.

Do not leave a horse facing an open gate; he may regard this as an invitation to go home. If you need the horse to stand for a while on a hill or incline, position the horse and the vehicle along the contours of the hill, rather than expecting him to hold a heavy cart in place against gravity. Some vehicles will have drag shoes or brakes which you can use.

Make sure your harness is in good condition; this means regular oiling and frequent checks. Always carry a penknife for the quick release of harness in case of an accident. A first-aid kit of baler twine is also useful to have with you.

Starting Training

A young horse intended for work should be regularly handled from birth, encouraging

6.1 The correct way to lead a horse.

him to be calm and quiet. He should gradually be got used to being led and having his legs picked up.

You should begin breaking in or training a young horse at the age of two and a half or three years. A good method is to bring him into the stable and tie him up for 3 or 4

6.2 Getting into, or onto, a cart **a** the correct way; **b** the incorrect way.

Bridle

Side reins

Roller

6.3 A horse wearing breaking harness and a roller, ready for his first proper lesson.

days, thus letting you get used to each other. Talk to the horse and build up a relationship: you will be the best thing he knows, as you are now the only source of food! During this process pay plenty of attention to the horse, including 'sacking out', rubbing an old sack or cloth all over his body. This will encourage him to accept the harness for the first time.

The next step is to put breaking harness, or stallion harness and a roller with side reins and a bridle, on the horse and take him outside (6.3). See chapter 7 for more information on harness. Do everything quietly and do not hurry. A straight bit is the best one to use for a young horse being prepared for work as it is gentle on the mouth. Sometimes a jointed one is used, but more usually on older horses. The straight bit should be adequate for most of your work. Keep the halter on under the bridle for safety or for tying up.

For these first lessons, and every time you start something new, it is important to have someone to help you. Your helper should lead the horse by standing back behind his shoulder, so that the horse thinks he is achieving everything himself. Do the driving with the reins from behind, keeping the horse going forward and using a whip if necessary (6.4).

Drive him anywhere, doing figures of eight, and going in and out of places around your farm or field, introducing him to different sights. Carry on doing this for a week or 10 days until he is absolutely perfect. All the time teach him the basic commands, 'come here' to go left, 'walk off' to go right, 'whoa' to stop and 'get back' to go backwards. These commands will vary slightly in different parts of the country.

Getting a Horse used to Draught

The next stage is to introduce full cart harness and traces, which bang round the horse's legs. This process takes another few days. If all goes well you may then be ready to go out on a quiet road, but make sure you take a helper with you. Back in the yard, attach a whipple tree to the traces, and ask your helper to pull tight on a long rope

6.4 Driving a young horse, with a helper holding a long lead rein and on hand in case of need.

attached to the whipple. This demonstrates to the horse how the collar feels when it goes tight, and what it feels like having chains touching the sides of his legs.

When he has got used to that, attach him to a sledge or light log – a railway sleeper is suitable – and drive him round the field for about half an hour (6.5). Do not go on for longer than three-quarters of an hour because his interest only lasts for short periods, and once he is bored you will not make headway. Even if you have all day free, divide the lesson into two chunks to ensure his attention.

If things go wrong, or the horse is alarmed by an unusual noise or sight and takes off, try to turn him to one side and keep him going round in a circle, rather than allowing him to go straight. With the assistance of your helper at his head, you may be able to prevent a disaster. If you succeed, you will have the satisfaction of knowing that he did not get away from you.

Once you have perfected this stage, you can introduce some noise. A 40-gallon drum with a brick inside it placed on the sledge is ideal for this purpose; if the horse puts up with that he will put up with most things! A single-horse chain-harrow can be introduced next. Alternate the sledge and the chain-harrow for several sessions before introducing the horse to pulling something along on gravel or tarmac. All the time your commands must be repeated, so that it becomes second nature for the horse to listen to you and do what you ask. The best horsemen are capable of controlling their horses by voice alone.

Shafted Vehicles and Implements

Next introduce the horse to shafted vehicles; a light hitch cart with rubber-tyred wheels is ideal. While the training is proceeding always use second-best harness, vehicles and equipment in case of disaster. Start off on grass, and graduate to gravel or concrete and an iron-tyred vehicle, which makes a considerable amount of noise. Never let the horse trot, because a farm horse should walk and only be allowed to trot if he has to pull up a hill.

When introducing a horse to shafts, it is a good idea to get him used to being backed between two long pieces of wood, angled

6.5 Attaching the horse to a light weight.

like shafts, perhaps using a gate to hold them (6.6). Make sure he sometimes touches them with his feet. Another approach is to make him a bit tired by pulling the chain-harrow, and then put him straight into shafts before he has time to think about it. Nine times out of ten he will be alright.

Once in the shafts, do not let him move off straight away. He should first stand for a while: learning to stand is one of the most essential lessons for the young horse. Take every procedure quietly and steadily. You can gradually increase the weight of the load in the cart, and you must teach him to back it. If you need to stop and there is a danger that he might walk off, tie him to a nearby immovable object; this will teach him to stand still.

Let him meet all manner of situations at this stage – tractors at work, lorries coming into the yard, walking through puddles and streams, road signs, plastic bags and sacks on the ground which he must walk over and through, etc. (6.7). You will soon have an idea of the things he copes with well and the things he hates. This will show you where further concentrated training is needed.

6.6 Using two pieces of wood, angled with the help of a gate, to help the horse get used to shafts.

6.7 Let the horse meet all manner of situations ... and discover the circumstances for which further training is needed.

Introducing a Horse to Pair Work

When the horse has reached this stage in his training, it is time to introduce him to another horse if you want to do pair work with him. Some people advocate putting a young horse together with an older horse to start with, but young animals can become reliant on others and misbehave when the older horse is not present.

Tie the horses side by side in a stall for a day or two so they can get to know each other first, especially if one is a mare. The best first companion is a quiet experienced horse. Then hitch them to a chain-harrow which is not too heavy. Drive them around, and present an opportunity for the chains to become entangled in the young horse's legs. It is a good idea to cover the chains with a bit of heavy-duty hosepipe, so that they do not pull the tender skin off his legs.

Novice horses have to get used to the idea that, when turning, one horse has to go faster, or slower, than the other. Always remember to praise your horse when he has done well. Some people advocate training horses by putting them straight onto the plough. In this case, the best position for him is in the furrow. This helps to guide him: he will very likely become a good plough horse as a result.

The young horse is then ready to go on the pole. He knows shafts well by now, but the pole comes lower down his legs. Put him on the nearside, where you can reach him, and the more experienced horse on the offside. Very likely he will be drawing a new type of vehicle for the first time, so there will be a lot for him to get used to.

The Training Schedule

The essential thing to remember when training a young horse is to continue regularly and frequently once you have started. It is no use choosing odd weekends and nice fine evenings, because the horse will forget what he has been taught in between.

If you are a complete novice you may prefer to take your horse to an experienced horseman for breaking-in. He would probably keep the horse for 6 weeks, at the end of which time he should take a day to show you what the horse can do, and what, if anything, needs further work. If the horse seems unsuitable for work (and there are a few which come into this category) it is helpful for the trainer to contact the owner within about 10 days to let him know the bad news! It is important for the owner to continue with the training when the horse is back home. If it is left, the training will all have been a waste of time and money.

It is essential to realize that a horse cannot be brought out every few months to drive down to the pub on a nice day, and be expected to cooperate. A working horse needs regular attention and regular tasks.

CHAPTER 7

Harness for the Working Horse

Terry Keegan

Introduction

To describe in detail all the regional variations once found in the working-horse harness of the UK would take a book in itself. The description of traditional harness here is limited to those types of harness currently in use and which can still be made by today's harness makers, using fittings which are available from the few remaining saddlers' ironmongers. Some horsemen prefer the modern webbing harness and other recent introductions from overseas, which are practical and effective in some circumstances, and these are also described.

7.1 A set of shaft harness of mixed origin, including a trade-type bridle with full noseband.

Traditional Harness

Although there is harness still in use which is over 60 years old, most of that which has yet to be unearthed from dusty lofts is now well past its use-by date. Those seeking harness with which to put their horses to work now find it necessary to start from scratch and order a new set of harness from one of the many very competent harness makers still to be found up and down the country.

There are four basic types of harness in use today which cover the needs of 99 per cent of those putting their horses to work — each designed for a different type of work situation. These are known as shaft (or cart) harness, trace harness, plough harness and pairs (or pole) harness.

Shaft Harness

For a full set of shaft harness designed for horses working with two-wheeled vehicles or double-shafted waggons, the following items are required: bridle, collar and hames, cart saddle or pad, and a set of breechings (7.1).

The bridle provides the horseman with a means of guiding the horse. Its main function is to hold a bit in the horse's mouth, and through the use of reins attached to the bit the horseman is able to communicate with the horse, not only which way he wants it to turn but also when he wants it to stop or to back up. To most horsemen these signals to the horse through the bit are supplementary to the voice commands which usually go with them. Most well-trained horses will react to the voice without too much use of the reins.

Most working-horse bridles in use today also have a secondary function – to restrict the sight-lines of the horse to a narrow forward and downward range. The arguments for and against the use of blinkers are numerous. It is sufficient to say here that horses can work in blinkerless bridles as well as blinkered ones, and many were trained to do so (7.2).

In the past, hundreds of different designs of bit have been used to fit onto bridles. Each one had its own champions, and although many of the old ones do still exist, for all practical purposes there are now only two basic designs made in the full range of sizes suitable for heavy horses. These are the straight bar, with one face smooth and the other ribbed to give differing degrees of control when pulled against the bars of the horse's jaw, and the Liverpool bit, a curbed driving bit which gives greater control over horses when they are being driven on the roads or in confined spaces, such as the show ring.

Whichever bit is chosen, it is essential that the bridle used can be adjusted so that the bit fits correctly and comfortably into the horse's mouth. On the simple bridle in the illustration (7.2), this can only be done effectively by altering the length of the headstrap, as the ring of the bit is permanently attached to the ring of the bridle by a

7.2 A traditional draught horse blinkered bridle.

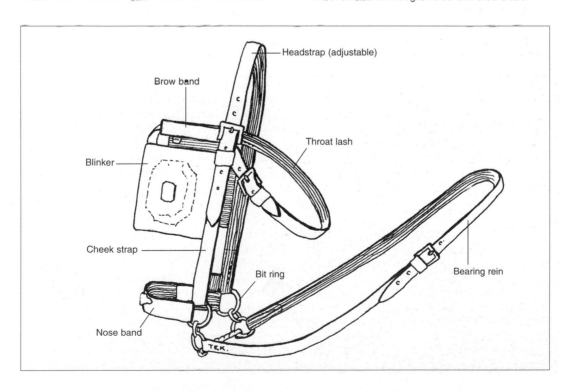

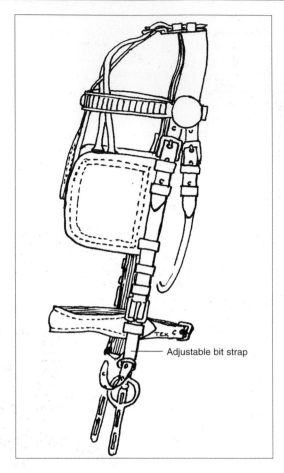

7.3 The London or Trade bridle.

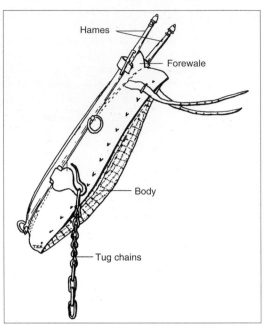

7.4 English padded collar with hames and tug chains, ready to attach to the shafts of a vehicle.

small non-adjustable link. On most Scottish bridles, the bit is attached to the bridle by small straps which can be used to adjust the height. On the London, or trade, bridle, a strap is fixed to the cheek of the bridle which drops down through the loop of the bit and buckles back up to the side of the cheek, giving plenty of scope for adjustment (7.3).

The next item required for a set of shaft harness is a well-fitting padded collar complete with a pair of hames. The hames form a rigid frame around the neck collar and provide a means of attaching a horse to its load. In the example shown (7.4), this would be to the staples on the shafts of the vehicle by means of a pair of short tug or shoulder chains. In Scotland and on the south-west peninsula of England 36 in. tug

chains are used, which are attached to the shafts further back, nearer to the body of the vehicle.

Although many attempts have been made to find a substitute for the English-type collar which has a forewale solidly stuffed with ryestraw and an equally firm body similarly stuffed, each time the customers have returned to the well-tried but laboriously constructed English neck collar. Good collar makers are few and far between, but after many years of decline, the art of collar making is again being taught in an effort to fulfil the growing demand for good English-style collars.

Split or open collars, designed to part sufficiently at the top to slip onto a horse's neck without having to pass it over his head, are still being made in south-west England where they have always been popular. At the other end of the country, the Scottish peaked show collars continue to be in demand for those who can afford them — although it is a growing problem to find a collar maker willing to produce them.

Cheap wooden hames are still being produced for working harness, but the manufacture of the traditional cased hames

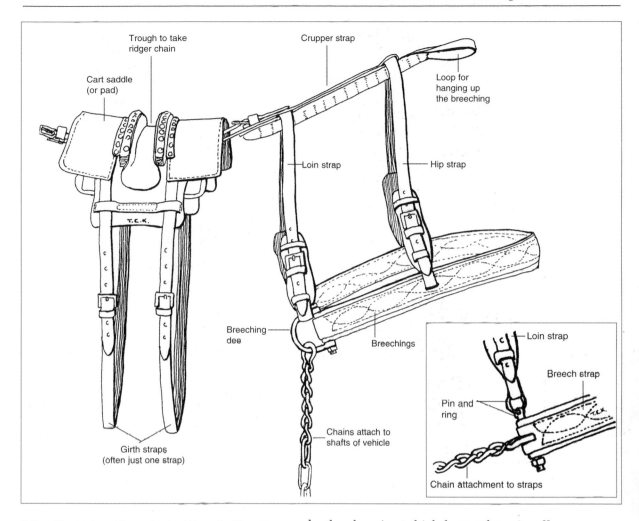

Trough to take
ridger chain

Cart saddle
(or pad)

Crupper strap

Loop for
hanging up
the breeching

Loin strap

Hip strap

T.C.K.

Breeching
dee

Breechings

Girth straps
(often just one strap)

Chains attach to
shafts of vehicle

Loin strap

Breech strap

Pin and
ring

T.C.K.

Chain attachment to straps

7.5a The cart saddle and breechings. **b** Alternative method of attaching the breeching chain by using a pin and ring in place of the breeching dees.

(a wooden core cased in iron and then sheet brass) ceased a few years ago. The alternatives being produced today are either a solid aluminium-bronze casting or a half-round steel tubing which can be tailored to individual collars and even lengthened at the top to resemble the long showy hames which went with the Scottish peaked collars.

The cart saddle or pad is designed to take a small part of the weight of a shafted vehicle on the horse's back. The saddle consists of a pair of pads which lie either side of the horse's spine and are attached to a wooden frame or 'tree'. This, in turn, is covered with

a leather housing which keeps the rain off the pads. The bridge of the tree has a metal channel or trough and into this fits the back-chain or ridger, the purpose of which is to hold up the shafts of the vehicle. Ridger chains can be either single – or double-linked chain, but the latter is said to move more freely in the channel. There are also numerous regional designs of cart saddle, the most unusual being the Scottish saddle with its high chine in the front. Over most of the rest of the UK designs are being standardized to fit the patterns of the one or two suppliers of the wooden trees on which the saddle is built. The cart saddle is held firmly in position by one or two girth straps which pass under the belly of the horse and buckle to the saddle on the other side (7.5a and b).

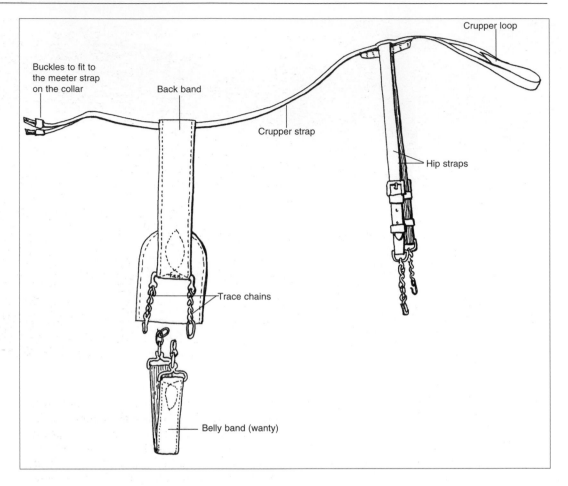

Cart harness is finished off with a set of breechings. This provides the horse with a means of reversing the vehicle by 'sitting' into the breech strap. The breech strap is attached to the shafts by short chains, so the whole cart and its load can be reversed (7.5b). The breeching also acts as part of the braking system when a horse is going downhill and prevents the cart from overtaking the horse. The breech band is held up by hip and loin straps attached to a broad top strap called a crupper strap. In cart harness there is a small loop at the rear end of the crupper strap, not to put the horse's tail through, but as a means of hanging the full breeching on a peg. The front of the crupper strap is attached to the cart saddle by one, or sometimes two, straps and as the front of the cart saddle is similarly attached to the collar, the full set of harness becomes one.

7.6 Trace harness

There remains one small, but very important piece of harness to complete the cart set – the 'wanty' or belly band. This is attached to the shafts of the vehicle, passes under the belly of the horse, and prevents the shafts tipping up when too much of the load in a two-wheeled cart is behind the axle.

Trace Harness

Trace harness, sometimes known as long gears, is used when horses are coupled in line, one in front of the other. This can be to assist a horse in shafts to pull a loaded vehicle, or when the horses are ploughing heavy land so that the plough team can walk in line down the furrow. The bridle, collar and hames are the same as for the cart harness.

7.7 A pair of horses harnessed to a plough. The simple plough harness has had a crupper strap added, with hip straps to hold up the chains, towards the rear of the horses. Brass decorations can be attached to the crupper strap.

The special trace harness consists of a backband, which is a broad strip of leather with fittings to hold up the 12 ft trace chains, and a crupper strap with buckles at the front end to fix to the meeter straps of the collar. The crupper strap runs the length of the horse's back and ends in a crupper loop through which the horse's tail is drawn. This strap also keeps the back-band in position, and from a point near to the crupper loop, a pair of hip straps drop down on either side of the horse to hook into the trace chains, keeping the traces well clear of the horse's feet when they are slack. A belly-band hooks into the traces forward of the back-band to help to keep the collar below the horse's windpipe when in a strong pull (7.6).

Plough Harness

Plough harness, usually used when working a pair of horses side by side, requires the bridle, collar and hames as before and, in its simplest form, a plough-band or backband to hold up the plough traces at a point between the hame hooks and the swingle trees, which are attached to the plough or similar implement. Many southern ploughmen prefer to use harness similar to the trace horse harness described above, but with plough-bands with hooks replacing the back-band with hook and ring used on trace harness.

Those ploughmen who like to put on a display of brass decorations use the trace harness, since the crupper strap provides a useful platform for attaching bell terrets and plumes on top, and through the provision of brass dees attached to the side of the crupper strap, they can buckle on various decorated side-straps, both in front of and behind the plough-band. No belly-band is needed as the downward pull of the traces keeps the collar off the horse's windpipe (7.7).

Cotton plough lines are used to drive and control the horses when ploughing, and either rope, leather or chain couplers are used to keep the horses together.

Pole chains

Meeter strap

Curl hook

Ring terrets

Reins

Pole

Belly band

Trace chains

Trace carrier

Pairs (or Pole) Harness

7.8   Pairs show harness seen from the side.

A pair of horses harnessed to a vehicle with a pole between them instead of shafts use special pairs harness. The four elements making up this harness are basically the same as shaft harness: bridle, collar and hames, saddle pad and breechings. However, only the collar and hames are of a similar pattern to those worn on most shaft harness. As pole vehicles are mainly used in a town situation, the bridle is usually of the London or trade type, with a full noseband and a Liverpool bit attached to the extended cheek straps (7.8).

The pad is of lightweight construction as it is not employed to carry any weight. Its main functions are to hold up the trace chains and to act as a platform for a pair of ring terrets through which the leather reins are threaded, and a centre curl hook to which the meeter strap from the collar is attached (7.9).

The breechings on pairs harness are of lightweight construction as they do not perform the same function as in shaft harness.

In pole harness, the braking action and reversing which necessitate breeching in shaft harness is taken over by a pair of pole chains from the front of the pole to the bottom chain of the hames. The actual braking action is controlled by the driver of the vehicle, who is provided with a foot brake acting on the rear wheels of the vehicle. The breeching is provided with a dock at the end of the crupper strap to go comfortably under the horse's tail. The forward end of the crupper strap is attached to the pad, so that collar, hames, pad and breeching are all connected to each other.

A further function of the breeching in pole harness is to hold up the trace chains towards the rear of the horses. A pair of looped straps, known as trace carriers, extend below the seat of the breeching strap immediately under the back pair of hip straps which connect the crupper to the breeching strap. Note that the decorated panels on pairs harness breeching are only

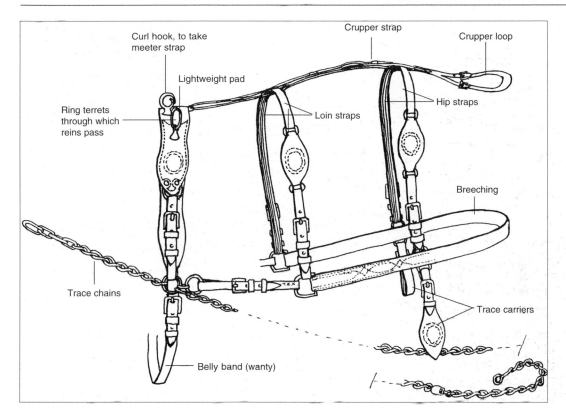

Curl hook, to take meeter strap

Crupper strap

Crupper loop

Lightweight pad

Hip straps

Ring terrets through which reins pass

Loin straps

Breeching

Trace chains

Trace carriers

Belly band (wanty)

7.9 Pairs (or pole) harness.

seen on one side of each horse, and the inside straps are not usually decorated. Thus, each set of pairs harness has a near-side and an offside set of breeching.

The trace chains of pole harness, usually referred to as wheeler traces (to distinguish them from the leader traces worn by leader horses coupled in front of a pair attached to a pole), are provided with a large ring about one-fifth of their length from the hame hook. The pad is strapped to the top of this ring and the belly-band is buckled to the bottom. A second ring, attached to the first one by a connecting link, is used to couple the breeching to the traces by another length of strap. The ends of the wheeler traces traditionally have pigtail hooks so that a loop can be formed in the chain end to fit over the mushroom bolts on the splinter bar of the vehicle.

The use of belly-bands may seem superfluous on pole harness and trace harness, but most turnouts use them as a safety measure.

Leader harness for pairs horses coupled

in front of a pair of wheelers differs slightly from the trace horse harness already described. The bridles, collars and hames are the same as for the wheeler horses, and although a lighter form of saddle pad was traditionally used in the working situation, nowadays, where the teams are only shown in the ring and on parades, it is customary to match the leaders' pads with those of the wheelers to give uniformity to the turnout.

There are no breechings on leader harness. A crupper strap, ending in a crupper loop to go under the horse's tail, supports straps either side of the horse's rump to hold up the leader traces. Leader traces have a ring at the end to couple onto the hook on the swingle tree. As there is no breeching strap, only a single ring is needed where the pad and belly-band are attached to the traces.

Leather driving reins are used on all town harness. For a single horse in shafts, a pair of reins would be about 12 ft long. For pairs harness the reins divide at a point about 3 ft behind the pad. The main outside rein goes to the outside of each horse's bit by way of the rein terrets on the pad, and the coupling reins, similarly threaded through a rein terret on the pad, then cross over each other to the inside of the bit of the opposite horse. These are adjustable, so that a pull on the left-hand rein will pull on the left-hand side of the bit of each horse equally, and similarly a pull on the right-hand rein should pull equally on the right-hand sides of both horse's bits.

Modern Harness Developments

Over the past 10–15 years, items of overseas harness have been imported into the UK, particularly from North America, where the production of harness has always been on a very large scale. The Amish and Mennonite communities still use horse power on their farms, and practising harness makers flourish. In particular, a growing number of horsemen who work their horses in this country are turning to the American collar, which has the double advantage of being adjustable and cheaper than its English equivalent. These are usually worn with washable pads between the collar and the horse's shoulders.

Another recent introduction to Britain is the Scandinavian system of harnessing for horse logging. This is needed for hitching a horse into the Scandinavian logging equipment which is increasingly being imported

from Norway and Sweden: a specialized type of harness designed for use with specialized equipment. See chapter 8 pages 93–96 for more information and illustrations of Scandinavian harness.

For practical work some horsemen prefer harness made from nylon webbing; this is strong, lightweight, easily cleaned and cheap. The use of breast collars is common in eastern Europe and some nylon webbing breast collars are in use here, particularly when the horse is harnessed to a lightweight four-wheeled vehicle, for cross-country trials, for instance. However, the preference in the British Isles has always been for padded neck collars, so those who use webbing harness often combine it with a leather neck collar (7.10).

Conclusion

Horsemen must therefore consider which type of harness is best for their needs. For practical work at home, webbing harness, or a hybrid set, may be adequate or even preferable. However, traditional harness will no doubt continue to be used for shows and parades, and even ploughing matches. The future for traditional heavy horse harness manufacture in Britain, if there is one, must therefore surely be a gradual standardization of the still numerous local styles to two or three basic designs using standardized fittings.

7.10 Simple, but effective, webbing harness used for working a pair to a hitch cart.

CHAPTER 8

Working Draught Horses as Singles and Pairs

Angela Gifford

Introduction

Throughout history man has needed some form of draught power to till the land and harvest crops. Man himself provided this power in areas not suitable for supporting animals. It was not until William the Conqueror invaded Britain that the large heavy breeds of horses were introduced here. Their breeding and geographical spread remained in the hands of the barons on their large estates until the gradual introduction of enclosures, which made the controlled breeding of agricultural animals easier. Oxen were the dominant draught animals in Britain until the 18th century when more sophisticated implements began to be invented and faster draught power was required.

The horse became the mainstay of British agriculture until the invention of fossil-fuelled engines. Once Harry Ferguson had developed the hydraulic system for tractors the days of the draught horse in British agriculture were numbered. However, despite technological advances here varied sources of power are still in common use overseas today: worldwide oxen still outnumber any other animal as a source of draught power. In Europe, with the increasing awareness of conservation issues, there is once again a place for the draught horse in certain agricultural and forestry situations, backed increasingly by public authorities as well as private individuals.

Training and Safety

The historical links in skill and experience in draught horsemanship were broken with the advent of mechanization, so training for man and horse is essential. Ideally horsemen should undertake training with one of the colleges offering appropriate courses, or with experienced individuals, before working draught horses (see chapter 5 – Training for Horsemen). Horsemen need to develop horse sense and be able to read the body language of the horse as it reacts to external circumstances. Well-trained animals are a joy to work with, but their instincts are very near the surface. Their handler needs to be aware of their mood at all times. Safety is paramount – an accident caused by carelessness can have severe, even fatal, effects on the horseman, animals and others in the vicinity. Third-party and employers liability insurance is advisable, and in many cases essential. It is normal to work alone in most regular work with horses, but for safety reasons it is essential that at least one other horseman should be present when working in public. In such a situation, horses should not be left unattended.

Harness

Harness design varies throughout the world, but the basic principles are governed by the point of draught, two-thirds of the way down the shoulder blade of the horse, and the job in hand. A strong, heavyweight head collar with a lead rope is used to catch and lead the horse. When leading, always hold the lead rope near the horse's head, but never wind it round the hand or hold the metal clip. Fold any excess rope, and lead from the nearside. When handling, be aware of the proximity of your feet to the

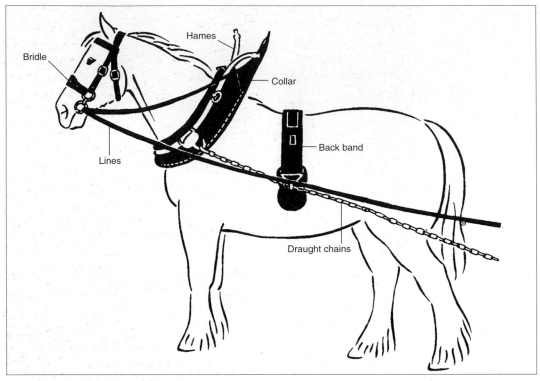

8.1   Plough harness, here with a Scottish collar.

horse, and always enter a building or narrow place ahead of the animal. Never walk backwards leading a horse.

Plough Harness and Harnessing

In Britain and across much of Europe, the basic harness for chain work with ground-engaging implements requires collar, hames, back-band, draught chains, bridle and lines (8.1). The horseman should work from the nearside (the left) when harnessing a horse. It is most important that the collar fits well, as this takes the strain of the load. It is generally put over the horse's head upside down, with care being taken to miss the eyes. It should then be turned at the narrowest point of the neck, behind the ears, and pushed down the neck the right way up. Excess mane can be moved out of the way when the collar is sitting well back on the shoulders. There should be sufficient room to slide a finger down the side of the collar and slip an adult hand in between the collar and the throat of the horse (8.2). Too

big a collar will 'wring' a horse's shoulders, and a collar that is too tight will choke him. Work around the horse in a quiet, efficient manner. Some young horses are nervous of the collar, so it is a good idea to reverse them into a stall or up against a wall in the stable. When harnessing in the open, it is advisable to pass the lead rope through the collar before putting it on. The horse can then be tied up.

Hames should fit snugly into the groove on the collar. Most hames have a choice of two slots for the hame-strap, and can be adjusted at the top and bottom; there are regional differences for securing them. In the eastern counties a thong of leather is used at the top and bottom; in the western counties a dog-leg hook and chain is used at the bottom, secured by a ring which should be tied to prevent it unfastening (8.3). A plain hook and chain is used in other regions. The last two use a leather hame-strap at the top of the hames. This should be inspected regularly and kept well oiled. If it broke while the horse was in draught, the hames would fall off.

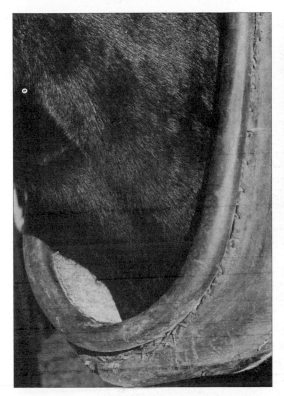

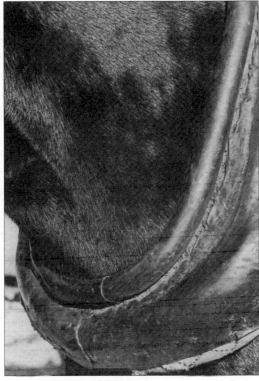

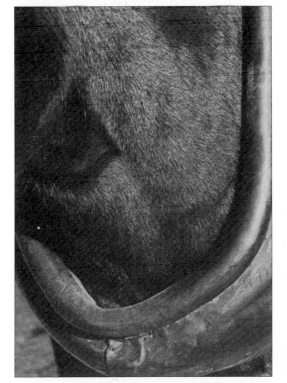

8.2 Ensuring that a collar fits properly. **a** (left) A collar which is too large. **b** (above) A collar which is too tight. **c** (below) A collar which fits perfectly.

When rethreading the hame-strap on the hames for a single or nearside pair horse, it is first threaded from the back of the offside hame to the front, through the keeper at the back of the buckle, through from the front of the nearside hame and then through the buckle and keeper on top. This allows quick release, should it be necessary. Care should be taken that the hames do not pinch the collar on the side of the neck. The hame strap on an offside horse of a pair should be threaded the opposite way, with the buckle still at the rear (8.4).

Next place the back-band in position across the horse's back. The horse is less likely to get a leg over the chains while working if a crupper with hip straps is used. First the crupper is laid along the middle of the horse's back and the tail is fed through the crupper loop. The other end is threaded through the back-band and attached to the hame strap or rings on either

8.3   Securing the hames: in this western counties example they are fixed into position with a dog-leg hook and chain secured by a ring, and tied to prevent it unfastening.

Back view
near side hame

Back view
offside hame

Step 2

Step 1

Step 3

Step 4

8.4   How to do up a hame strap
Step 1   Pass tongue through staple from rear of offside hame
Step 2   Pass tongue through keeper behind buckle
Step 3   Pass tongue through staple on nearside hame from the front
Step 4   Secure tongue in buckle and keeper

side of the collar according to the design. The length of the hip straps is adjusted to the task in hand. Then the draught chains are attached to the hame hooks. The hooks or rings on the back-band vary regionally, but all are attached to the draught chains, while holding them taut. These chains should be approximately 8 ft 6 in. long (8.5a). If hip straps are used, the chains are attached to them. The crook on the end of the chains can be hung on the hames or on the dee at the top of the hip straps.

If a martingale is used, a belly-band (or wanty) should be added to the harness and fixed to the draught chains in line with the back-band. Ensure that it cannot slide backwards. The belly-band is a must for timber and trace work. When fitted, it must be loose under the belly with a gap of about 5 in. between the horse's belly and the band. The belly-band stops the collar riding up and choking the horse. If a horse was extracting timber down a steep slope, the line of the draught would be above it and the harness could be pulled over its back. The belly-band prevents this. When extracting timber, the hip straps should be shortened so that more weight is on the horse's rump. This gives lift to the load and gives the horse better traction.

A whipple tree is used to keep the draught chains apart for ploughing, using a chain-harrow etc. It is also possible to use one for timber work, as it can be hooked to the choke-chain which is round the tree. To prevent it snagging on stumps when it is not being used release and tie up one draught chain so that the whipple tree drags in a straight line until the next load is ready (8.5b).

For agricultural work it is normal for the horse to wear an under halter so that he can be tied up if necessary. A horse should *never* be tied up by the bit. The bridle should be put on just before leaving the stable. It should be fitted with a hame rein, which prevents the horse putting his head

Crupper Back-band Hame strap

Hip straps

Crook

Draught chain

8.5a Horse working in plough harness with crupper, hip straps and belly-band. **b** Whipple tree dragging in a straight line to prevent snagging when it is being pulled with nothing attached to it.

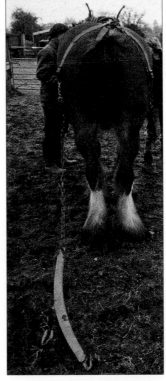

down to eat when left to stand. This lessens the likelihood of the horse moving. Some bits are detachable on one side. In this case first place the bridle over the horse's ears, do up the throat lash, feed the bit into the horse's mouth and secure. With fixed bitted bridles, stand facing forward on the near-side holding the head strap of the bridle, and place the hame rein over the horse's head. Hold the bridle over the horse's face and gently slide the bit into the mouth. If the horse resists this, insert the thumb of the hand supporting the bit into the corner of the mouth where there are no teeth. Then secure the throat lash, which should be loose enough not to restrict the horse in any way.

The hame rein should not be hung over the hame until the horse is out of the stable. When turning in a confined space a horse can lose its footing and it could not get to its

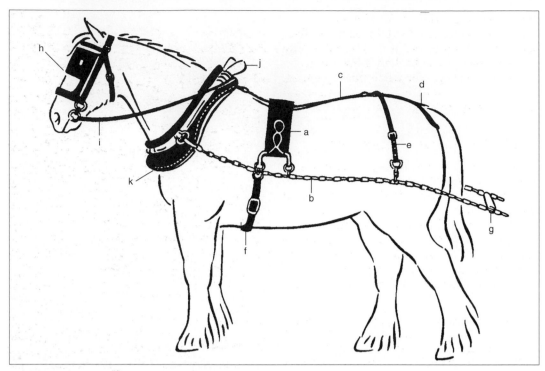

8.6 Modern trace harness of the Norfolk pattern. a, back band; b, trace chain; c, crupper strap; d, dock or crupper; e, hip strap; f, belly band; g, spreader bar; h, bridle; i, hame or bearing rein; j, hame; k, collar

feet with the hame rein hooked up, because its mouth would, in effect, be tied to its tail. There is some controversy about which hame this rein should be hung over. The southern tradition was to hang it over the offside hame so that the nearside hame could be used to carry the nosebag for both man and horse. Certainly the hame rein should not be trapped underneath anything in case there is a need to release it quickly. With an offside horse the rein goes on the opposite hame. When a horse is working on steep ground or in very wet conditions, the hame rein should be released to allow him to lower his head and put extra effort into his work.

Reins should be of sufficient length for whatever work is undertaken. It is dangerous to work with short reins. Before leaving the stable, the reins are fed through either a dropped link on the front of the draught chains, or a ring that can be clipped into the

same position before the reins are attached to the bit. Make sure that a safe knot is used, as some horses fiddle with the ends of the reins. When working on the ground, the reins should be in a straight line from the horse's mouth to the horseman's hands.

This harness is also used for pole work with mowers, etc., with the addition of pole straps which attach the horses to each end of the breast pole. When using a pair or multiple hitches of horses for work abreast, they are coupled together with coupling and tie-back chains (see section on hitching and working horses for chain work).

To unharness, reverse the procedure for harnessing.

Trace Harness

Trace harness can be used for team work or forestry chain work (8.6). Trace chains should be heavier than those used for plough harness and are approximately 12 ft long. They are used with a spreader bar to keep them apart. Heavier chains are necessary when there is extra horse-power involved. The bar is fixed in position so that it does not chafe the horse or interfere with its walking action (8.7). The chains are hung up when no load is being pulled, leaving nothing to catch on obstacles. The same system is used when a trace horse is added for extra power when pulling a load. It is usual to fix reins to the lead horse, and a lead rein on the wheel, or rear, horse.

Shaft Harness and Harnessing

This harness is used for any shafted implement such as a single-horse roller, hay turner, mower, cart or single/double-shafted waggon (8.8).

The collar and hames remain the same as for chain work. Note that some hames have tug/shoulder chains attached to them (8.9). A meeter strap with a buckle is attached to a ring on either side of the collar or a strap

8.8 Modern shaft harness of the London pattern. Bridle: a, blinker; b, brow-band; c, nose-band; d, cheek-strap; e, head-strap; f, throat-lash; g, bit; h, bearing rein. Collar: i, forewale; j, side-piece; k, body (padding); l, hames; m, housen. Saddle: n, saddle housing; o, bridge; p, pad; q, girth-strap; r, belly-band. Breechings: s loin-strap; t, hip-strap; u, breech-band; v, tug chain.

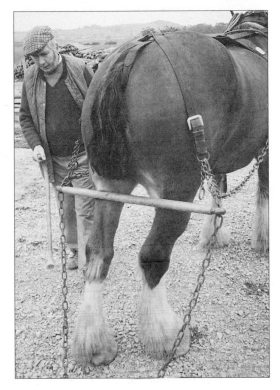

8.7 Position of the spreader bar attached to trace harness.

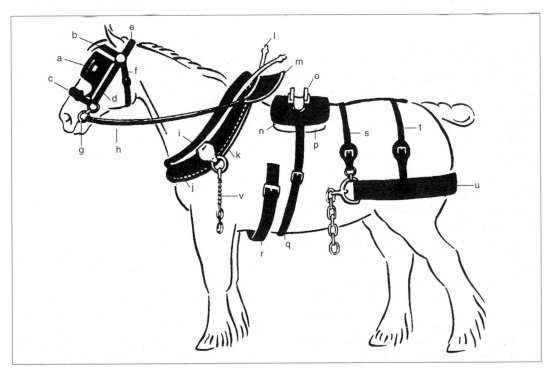

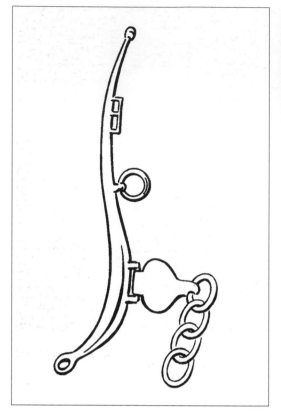

8.9 Hames with tug chains attached.

8.10 Harness (pad and breeching) stored to avoid damage.

round the middle of the hame strap. The pad/saddle carries the weight of the shafts and the breeching acts as the braking system. These parts are normally stored coupled together. A curved bracket attached to the stable wall carries the breeching, and the pad hangs from the hook at the end of the back strap, or is rested on a saddle horse (8.10).

The collar and hames are put on first. Pass the right arm through the breeching, which then rests on the right shoulder. This releases the two hands to pick up the pad, making sure the girth does not drag on the floor. Working from the nearside, the pad is rested in position on the horse's back behind the withers, and the meeter strap is attached (8.11). The pad will now be secure and the hands are free to place the girth-strap and breeching in position. Secure the girth, taking care not to pinch the horse. Many will nap or blow out at this moment, so

adjustment will be necessary before hitching up. The breeching can now be checked to see if it is the correct height. The hip-straps should be of equal length, because they are fixed at the back strap. The loin-strap is a running one and need not be secured in equal holes on both sides. The breeching should sit level. It must not be so low that the horse's legs are forced under him while backing or braking a load. If it is too high, it could ride over the horse's rump in extreme circumstances.

If the tug chains are not a permanent fixture on the implement/vehicle they should be safely stowed on the hames to avoid them flapping and catching on the door frame when moving away from the stable area (8.12).

Finally the bridle and reins are fitted. Thread the ends of the reins through the rings on the pad, then through the hame rings and secure to the bit. As safety must be paramount, it is advisable to use a trade bridle with a Liverpool bit when working in public.

Scandinavian Harness

This harness design is universal for single horses, pairs and teams for all vehicles and implements fitted with the Scandinavian shaft-fitting system (8.13). It cannot be used in conjunction with English shaft fittings. It can, however, be adapted for pole and chain work. Its main application in Britain is in the forestry sector.

The inner surfaces of the wooden hames are lined with leather padding which is attached by straps at the top and sides. The hames are joined by a leather hame strap at the top. They are longer than the English design to give greater clearance to the

8.11 Putting on pad and breeching together and securing the meeter strap.

8.12 Tug chains safely stowed when not in use.

Hame strap

Hames

Pad

Meeter strap

Girth strap

Breeching

Tug ring

Tug strap

8.13 Scandinavian logging harness.

8.14 Detail of the ring attachment which is crucial to the Scandinavian harness system.

horse's throat. The wide leather tug-strap is fitted round the hames, and the tug ring, crucial to the system, is fixed to the other end of the tug-strap.

To harness, hold the top of each hame and swing the offside one over the horse's withers. Settle the hames in position, with even contact on the horse's shoulder. Secure the two sides with the leather strap at the bottom. To check for a good fit it should be possible to slide the fingers between the horse's neck and collar from the front, with a little resistance. It is worse for it to be too loose than too tight, as chafing can occur when in work.

The simple pad/saddle holds the back support strap which carries the ring attachment to which the tugs and breeching are hooked (8.14). The ring also carries the belly-band strap and the shaft attachment. The back-strap, fixed to the back of the pad, carries the breeching or crupper and is similar to the English system. The pad is placed just behind the withers and the meeter straps are attached to the collar just above

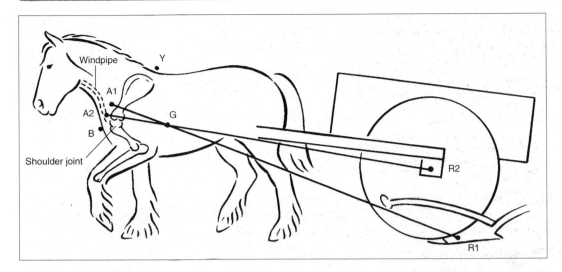

8.15 Diagram of correct line of draught for shafted vehicles or ground-driven implements from the tug point on hames. A1, A2, ideal point of draught and tug point on harness; R1, R2, centre of resistance; G, centre of gravity of the horse; Y, point of draught of the yoke; B, point of draught of the breast collar.

the tug leather. The breeching is positioned and hooked to the ring. It should be adjusted so that it is horizontal, allows for freedom of movement when the horse is working, and yet brakes the load when required. The girth-strap is then secured. The reins and correct fitting adjustments are the same as for English harness.

Hitching to Scandinavian-design Shafts

The horse should be backed into the shafts and the tug pins on the tug rings put through the shaft fittings and secured with a wooden or plastic peg. The draught line should be straight from the tug point on the hames, through the tug ring and back to the rear end of the shafts (8.15). Note that plough chains can be fixed to the tug rings if the task requires chain work instead of a shafted implement as long as the adjustments on the harness produce a straight draught.

American Pair Harness

There are many designs of harness throughout North America (8.16). This section concentrates mainly on the pairs harness being imported into Britain. It is available in leather or nylon and is ideal in the work situation. Although mass-produced, it stands the test of time and heavy work. The basic design difference from the British

system is with the breeching. This is far more efficient and kinder on the horse, especially for hard work. A drop-pole is preferable to the usual English-style pole and a breast-yoke advisable, as these give the most efficient braking line. The breeching and drop pole are both designed to be flexible on rough ground and so reduce the strain on the horses.

The split collars are adjustable for size within 3 in. (for example 25/26/27 in). Straps on either side can be let out or tightened, and there is a firm cap holding the split collar together. For heavy work it is important for the horse to wear a sweat pad, which clips inside the collar. This absorbs the shock and sweat and can easily be cleaned (8.17).

The hames are fitted with leather traces and rings above and below the trace fittings. When these are in place a V-shaped breast-yoke fitted with a breast-strap clips to the lower rings on the hames. A lightweight pad and breeching, with or without a crupper, is placed on the horse's back. A split meeter-strap passes through rings on either side of the pad and clips to the ring above

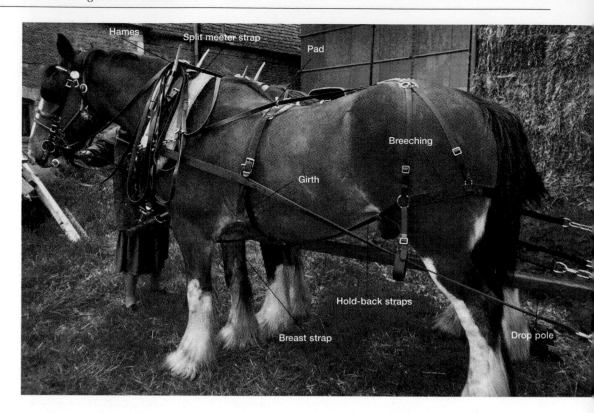

8.16 American pairs harness. See also Figure 8.30 which shows the American pairs harness from the front.

the trace fitting on the hames. The breeching is coupled to hold-back straps which are passed in front of the back legs, under the stomach and are clipped to the breast-strap which is between the horse's front legs. The girth should be buckled loosely. When in draught, as a rough guide, the hold-back strap should be approximately 6 in. below the horse's stomach at the lowest point. As this harness is so light it is poss-ible to keep the hames, traces, pad and breeching coupled together so that it is put on the horse as one unit.

Hitching and Working Horses for Chain Work

Working a single horse in chains is appropriate for light agricultural tasks such as chain-harrowing in light soils, hoeing crops and driving the gearing which works barn machinery. There are increasing demands for the use of horses in forestry in either plough/long gears or trace harness, and this is covered in the forestry chapter. A trace horse can be used in line to add extra power when pulling heavy loads.

Much of what follows describes the process for a working pair, and can be adapted or omitted quite easily for those working with a single horse. It is advisable to set up the implements before taking the horse(s) out of the stable. A single horse uses one whipple tree, and the chain harrow should not be larger than 8 ft by 4 ft. A pair can work a harrow of 8 ft by 8ft comfortably all day, and a set of three whipple trees are used (8.18). There are often three settings on the back whipple tree, and by placing the crook in the middle, the two horses do equal work. If the crook is adjusted to the left, the left-hand horse will do more work and vice versa. This is a valuable adjustment if one horse is keener than the other, or if a young horse needs more or less work. Teams of horses can be used abreast following the same principle.

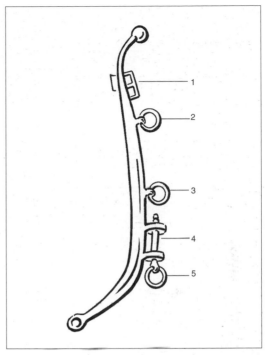

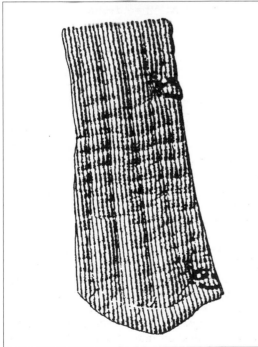

8.17 a American split collar. **b** Sweat pad (it is advisable to order a size larger than the collar). **c** American hame. 1, hame strap fitting; 2, rein ring; 3, meeter strap fitting ring; 4, trace fitting; 5, breast-yoke fitting ring.

For a pair, the reins should be attached to the outside ends of the bits. The coupling chain/rope should be about 45 in. long and fixed to the inside ends of the bits of a pair

(8.19). It can be adjusted according to the job in hand. If the horses need to work wider apart, the coupling chain can be extended. Tie-back chains of the same length are a big advantage for keeping the pair level. These can either be fixed to the inside bit of one horse and then over to the trace chain of the other, or from the head collar ring under the horse's throat onto the hame ring of the other horse. The latter is more suitable if the horse has a particularly soft mouth. If hemp halters are used, the lead rope can be tied back instead.

The reins are then taken to the back of the horses ready to drive them to the implement. It is inadvisable to wind the reins round the hands as this can cause a burn if the horses take fright. Adjust the reins by folding for travelling short distances. It is essential to drive at a safe distance away from the rear ends of the horses.

Approach the whipple trees at a right-

8.18 A pair hitched to a chain harrow.

angle until the horses' heads are level with the middle of the implement. Then command them to come round into position. There will be little need for backing if the horses are driven accurately. The use of the voice when working horses is invaluable, since well-trained horses are capable of all manoeuvres on command. There are countless different colloquial terms in use throughout the country. When buying a horse, check the language it is used to and introduce any new commands gradually in conjunction with the old.

There are two schools of thought about hitching horses to implements, and discretion should be used in both cases. The reins should be held and contact with the horse's mouth maintained at all times. The chains should be in easy reach of the horseman, hooked up on the dee on the crupper. With a pair or team of horses, the most experienced one should be hitched first. In the first method the chains are taken from the dee and attached to the whipple tree one by one. In the second method both chains are taken back down at once and then attached. In this method it is possible for the loose

chain to hit the horse if he moves, but at the same time it has the advantage of making the chains more accessible for quicker hitching. This might help with an inexperienced horse, which can be fidgety. The quicker he can get to work, the less likelihood there is of a problem developing. Once the chains are attached to the whipple trees, the crooks should face upwards or inwards according to the design of the trees.

Accurate driving is a must in any field work. The carter should walk 3–4 ft behind but to the side of the implement to give him good vision once a line is established across the field. Horses have a natural tendency to wander, and there is no point in covering ground twice. As with driving a vehicle, it is easier to maintain a straight line if the eyes can focus well ahead. When pausing during work or unhitching, always face away from gates and ease the horses back to take the weight off the draught chains and thus also off the horses. The length and frequency of rest periods should be related to the fitness of the horses and the severity of the work.

If anything goes wrong, the horses should be brought round in a wide circle until they can be brought under control. In an emergency, shouting can only make matters worse. Never end a day's work on a bad note; carry on until the horses are working well. To unhitch, gather the reins up shorter, unhitch the chains and hang them on the dee on the crupper. Drive the horses back to the stable and uncouple them outside.

Using a Trace Horse

If more power is required to pull a heavy load, trace horses can be added in line in front of the rear horse (8.20). If they are all working in chains, the draught chains of the additional horses should be attached to the draught chains behind the hame hooks of the horse behind. If a cart or waggon is being pulled there is a fitting on the shafts to hook on to the trace horse. Sufficient space should be allowed between the horses, and this can vary from horse to horse.

The horseman walks beside the head of the rear horse holding him with a lead rein, and drives the lead horse with a continuous rein which is threaded through the hame rings; the offside rein comes over the back of the horse to the nearside. This is held in the left hand, and by tilting and moving the hand to the left and right it should be possible to drive accurately. Remember that the lead horse should take a wider turning circle than the shaft horse to allow for the extra length of load. Traditionally the shaft horse was always the larger animal. Nowadays, if more than two horses are used, an extra helper is usually required.

Horse Gearing

Portable single-horse gearings were once in common use for driving elevators and static barn machinery (8.21). Chain harness fitted with hip straps should be used. The horse is hitched to a whipple tree attached to the drive pole, and kept in position by a thin metal rod attached to the centre of the gearing and to the horse's inside bit. This keeps the horse travelling in an even circle. The drive shaft is often let into the ground on a static engine, but is proud of the ground on a portable one. The horse soon learns to step over it.

8.19 A pair of horses coupled together with rope (in this case) or chains.

Working Horses in Shafts

All these procedures refer to any shafted implement or vehicle. All moving parts of vehicles and implements should be oiled regularly and the blades sharpened. Wheels should be removed periodically and

8.20 Trace horse being used on a shafted timber waggon.

greased. Work with one horse is appropriate for general carting, rolling, hay turning with a swathe-turner/side-rake, fertiliser spreading and spraying. Mowing is very hard work for a single horse unless an engine is fitted to the machine. If farm implements are fitted with seats, these should be used. If there is no seat the horseman should walk behind the implement, either in the middle or at the side according to the task in hand (8.22).

If a machine is fitted with wheel-driven gears, e.g. mowers and binders, they should be disengaged whenever the machine is stopped. Before starting, re-engage the gears and allow the machine to reach full speed before beginning to work.

Generally a cart is defined as a two-wheeled vehicle and a waggon as a four-wheeled vehicle. Low-slung carts are parked with their shafts on the ground.

Higher carts are left with their shafts in the air. The heavier type of tip carts can be parked with their shafts on the ground if the body of the cart is partially tipped. This takes the weight off the shafts when hitching in.

Check that the ridger chain is in position with the swivel on the offside (the right). The chain is secured on both sides in the case of raised shafts, and the horse is backed into position (8.23). Care should be taken that the cart does not hit the horse when the shafts are lowered. The ridger chain is fed into the channel on the pad as the shafts are brought down.

The ridger chain is attached to the offside of the shafts if they are on the ground. The horse is backed into position with the horseman facing the cart, allowing for maximum vision. Backing commands should be given, as clicking or forward commands only confuse the horse. From the offside, lift the shaft and support it by hooking the offside tug chain to the tug hook in the shortest

Metal rod

Drive pole

Whipple tree

Drive shaft

position. This keeps the shafts suspended high enough to allow the ridger chain to be thrown over the pad. Check that it is lying flat (8.24) then move to the nearside, place the left forearm under the end of the shaft to lift it, and secure the ridger chain to the appropriate shaft fitting.

The position of the shafts is critical, and their height is adjusted on the ridger chain. If they are too low, the weight of the cart is taken on the neck instead of the back. If they are too high the horse would pull the shafts down onto his back making the work harder. The ends of the shafts should be below the hame hooks (8.25). After the height has been adjusted, the nearside tug chain can be attached, followed by the off-side one. It is critical that these are of equal length to avoid an uneven pull and sore shoulders. Check that they lie flat and are of sufficient length to allow the shaft to be in front of the back of the collar. There is a danger that the end of the shaft could be trapped behind the collar when the horse turns a corner. Should this happen, the

8.21 Horse gearing at Acton Scott Working Farm.

8.22 Correct walking position for a horseman using a roller.

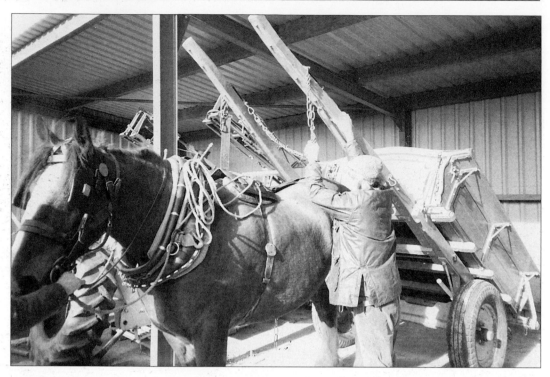

8.23 Hitching a horse to a cart with the shafts raised.

harness would be tightened and this would result in an accident. Some shafts used to be bow-shaped so that they could not get trapped. When the draught chains are tight the ridger should be vertical. The draught line of the tug chains should be the same as the draught line of the vehicle.

When these points have been checked, the offside breeching is secured to the breeching hook on the shaft fitting, followed by the nearside breeching. The breeching should be adjusted so that the horse has free movement and yet it brakes the vehicle on a downward slope, or comes into play when the horse is backing. When the horse takes the strain on the tugs there should be clearance at the back of the breeching when it is pulled back. It must be tight enough to stop the vehicle touching the rear of the horse, and the hocks of the horse must not touch the shafts when working.

The belly-band is then secured in position, either around the shafts in the middle of the shaft fitting or on a hook provided. The purpose of this is to stop the shafts rising if the load becomes tail heavy. In the case of a waggon, it stops the shafts lifting when descending a steep hill or backing.

The unhitching procedure for shafts stowed in the air is the reverse of hitching in. For shafts on the ground, the same procedure is followed until it is time to lower the shafts. The ridger chain is then unhooked on the nearside and the shafts are lowered to the ground, allowing the chain to slide over onto the ground. Check that all hooks, belly-band and ridger chain are clear of the inside of the shafts before moving the horse forward. It is prudent to keep the horse waiting a short time before moving off, for some horses have a tendency to move directly they feel free of the vehicle. This is a bad habit and can lead to problems, especially when unhitching pairs and teams.

Farm vehicles are generally difficult to mount. Care must be taken, as many horses have a tendency to move when contact with the reins or vehicle is felt. Until the horse-man has developed a good balance to stand and drive, it is advisable to sit on a made-up seat rather than pull the horse's mouth.

8.24 Hitching a horse to a cart after the shafts have been lifted from the ground.

The reins should be of adequate length and thought of as a continuous thread that goes from the horseman's hands, through the bit in the horse's mouth and back to the horseman. As a horse naturally looks from side to side, contact should be kept on both sides of the mouth, compensating the offside with the nearside at all times. In the show ring, leather reins are smarter and are usually held in the left hand in classical English style, freeing the right hand to hold the whip and make adjustments. In Scotland and in many other parts of the world the reins are held in both hands, as are the rope reins (or lines) normally used for agricultural work. Certainly the novice will find it easier to keep contact with both sides of the mouth using both hands.

If passengers are being transported, the golden rule is that the horseman mounts the vehicle first and leaves last. All passengers should be safely seated, with no limbs protruding over the sides of the vehicle. If children are being carried there should be sides on the vehicle. The horseman should check that the way is clear in front and behind before moving off, and give clear signals to any traffic with the whip. Give verbal commands to the horse fractionally before using the reins when changing direction. Remember, horses are unaware of the length of the load and will tend to cut corners.

In agricultural work the horseman must not ride on a loaded vehicle unless there is a fixed seat as on trade vehicles. A loaded cart should *never* be tail-heavy, but be balanced so that there is slightly more weight on the horse's back. Either lead, holding the rein near the bit, or drive from the nearside, level with the horse's flank. More skill is required when driving from the ground as the vision is restricted. If leading, stow the reins safely. Reins should not be tied to a four-wheeled vehicle as a serious accident can occur if the horse jack-knifes (8.26).

When turning to the offside, check that the road is clear, give the verbal command,

Hame hook

Shafts (positioned just below the hame hooks)

8.25 A horse correctly hitched to a cart.

guide the head to the offside and quietly execute the turn. On slippery surfaces the horse can slip if rushed, and with a heavy load he can be thrown off balance. For a wide nearside turn the reverse applies. For a tight nearside turn, the horseman needs to position himself on the offside/front if leading the horse, so that the load is moving away from him (8.27). This cuts down the risk of the horse being pulled on top of the horseman. If driving from the ground, keep well away from the vehicle.

Backing a load is best done from the horse's head. It used to be a sackable offence to do it from the waggon in many of the top trade yards! The horseman should face the vehicle and stand on whichever side needs the greatest care and therefore the best line of vision. On the nearside, the left hand should guide the horse; on the offside it should be the right hand

(8.28). It is dangerous for a horseman to walk backwards when working a horse. Quiet backing commands and slow movements are advisable to avoid the horse becoming confused. Again, never click or give forward commands when backing. Occasionally horses get stuck in reverse, and then all pressure on the mouth should be released. In the case of a two-wheeled cart, the horse is an extension of the vehicle. If the head is guided to the offside, the hind-quarters will push the cart to the nearside, and *vice versa*. A waggon has a fifth wheel or turntable so if the horse's head is guided to the offside, the waggon will be pushed to the offside. Only small movements are necessary. Once the vehicle is moving the horse must be straightened to avoid over-running the desired position.

Care should be taken to allow for the lock on the vehicle. Some traditional waggons have only a quarter lock, and these require a wider turning circle. Those with a full lock can become unstable when turning sharply with a full load.

8.26 The correct walking position for a horseman when driving from the ground.

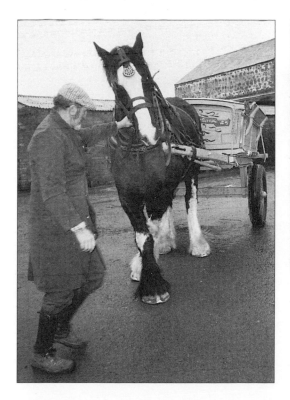

8.28 (above) The correct position of the horseman when backing a waggon to the nearside.

8.27 The correct position of the horseman when turning short to the nearside.

8.29 Drag shoe and chain in operation

Working on Steep Ground

The first thing to consider when working on steep ground is the size of the load. It should be light enough for the horse to cope with on the steepest ground, or other horses should be used to add extra power. The hame rein should be released when ascending steep hills. Stopping on hills should be avoided if possible, but if it cannot be avoided, the curb or verge can be used to hold the load. If a roller is fitted to the waggon, it can be lowered to run behind the back wheel to hold it in the event of stopping. If baulked on a hill, it will probably be necessary to guide the horse at an angle across the hill to make it easier for him to start moving. When descending hills, verges will provide extra resistance to the wheels and so help the horses hold the load.

Drag shoes and a chain to tie to the back

8.30 Front view of the fixing to the breast pole using American harness.

wheel can be used for descending steep hills. On approaching a steep slope on the road, place the drag shoe in front of the back wheel and secure the chain around the rim and next to the appropriate spoke of the wheel to allow it to tighten when the wheel mounts the shoe (8.29). In fields, it is sufficient to tie the back near-side wheel of an iron-tyred waggon with a chain. When descending any hill great care should be taken to keep good contact with the horse's mouth in case he should miss his footing. Studs should be fitted to horse shoes for road work, as tarmac is very slippery.

Hitching and Working Pairs and Teams

Using multiple hitches for agricultural work opens up the possibilities of achieving a much higher output. See also chapter 11 – Multiple Hitches. The level of the horseman's ability is very important, and knowledgeable help may be necessary at first. Generally, most horses are happier working with other horses once they have been trained to do so.

Double Shafts

Horses in double shafts are hitched in exactly the same way as for single shafts. The ridger chain on the offside horse has to be reversed so that the swivel end is in the middle, and adjustments for length can be made on the offside. The quietest horse is hitched in first. To attach the inside end of the breeching chain of the second horse, the horseman should stand between the front of the shafts. A hook can be used to reach the chain to attach it to the crook on the shaft fitting. The horseman is in a vulnerable position here, and great care should be taken. It is worth pointing out that many horses find this hitch difficult to get used to. They are usually much happier working as a pair on a pole, where they have more freedom.

Pole Work

Pole straps should be fitted to the breast pole, which can vary in design. With a few exceptions, such as the two-horse hay sweep, breeching is not essential for agricultural implements and plough harness is used. However, if using American harness, the breeching is part of the harness design and the yoke strap hooks directly onto the breast pole (8.30).

All implements carry compensating whipple trees which enable each horse to do a fair share of the work. Lead or back the horses into position on either side of the pole. The inside bits of both horses should be coupled together (see section on chain-work). Both reins are stored on the hames of the nearside horse. If the horses cannot be trusted, or if the work is being carried out in public, someone should hold the horses' heads while they are hitched to the implement. Once horses have learned to run away, they tend not to forget! Always hitch the quietest horse first. Attach the pole straps round the base of the collars from back to front, and through the ring at the end of the breast pole, buckling in the front with the point of the buckle facing downwards. It is helpful to rest the weight of the pole on the horseman's knee when attaching the first horse. Hitch the outside trace to the whipple tree first. This keeps the horse parallel to the pole and prevents him swinging outwards. Then hitch the inside trace and repeat with the other horse. Take up the reins and mount the implement where appropriate, or walk behind in a position where the line of work is visible. These procedures are reversed for unhitching.

Three- or Four-horse Hitches

Larger corn drills often require three horses abreast when working heavy land. Three-horse whipple trees are attached to the pole and the additional horse is worked in chains alongside the two on the pole. They are all coupled together in the normal way at all the bits. Heavy work on a binder also usually requires three or even four horses (8.31). Sometimes two trace horses are added to the two on the pole and someone rides postillion on one of the lead horses.

8.31 Three-horse hitch on a binder.

Yorkshire Wolds Waggon

The Yorkshire Wolds Waggon is the only traditional farm waggon to be fitted with a pole. The whipple trees are attached to a splinter bar and chained together in the middle allowing limited compensation. Breeching is worn and long breeching chains are attached forward to the hame crook. Bellybands are attached to the trace chains to prevent the traces riding up over the horse's back in the event of trouble. The pole chains are fixed to the eyelet on a bolt through the pole head. It was traditional for the horseman to ride the nearside horse using the short hame reins to guide the hitch.

Once the horses are in position and coupled together with the coupling rein, the pole chains are attached to a fitting below the inside hame crooks. Then the same procedure as for hitching to a poled implement should be followed. When working on level ground, it is essential to have the horses fairly tightly hitched to prevent the waggon running into them. In deep muddy conditions the chains can be looser, to allow them more freedom to get the load started. If driving from the vehicle and working in public, it is advisable to use double reins (see chapter 16 – Road Driving) as these provide greater control.

Hay Sweeps

Plough harness with extra long trace chains is used for the single-horse hay sweep. The longer chains allow the sweep to operate. They are hooked to swivel links at each end of the beam carrying the tines. The horseman tips the handles when the sweep is full so that it somersaults, leaving the load in the desired place (8.32)

There are various designs of two-horse sweeps on the market, with the more sophisticated ones having lifting mechanisms (8.33). To avoid all the weight being put on the top of the horse's neck when backing, a light breeching should be worn. American pairs harness is ideal. Two horses are hitched to fixed poles and whipple trees on either side of the sweep. Plough lines are attached to the outside bits and a long coupling rein joins the inside bits. The carter sits on a seat at the rear and drives the horses either side of the windrows to collect the hay. To unload, the tines are lowered and the outfit is backed, leaving the load in the desired postion.

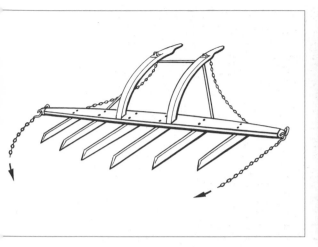

8.32 a Diagram of a single-horse hay sweep.

8.32 b Implement in action.

8.33 Two-horse hay sweep.

CHAPTER 9

Ploughing

Mike Flood

Introduction

Ploughing is the skill of cultivating land for the growing of crops. Early ploughs were forked sticks or stag's antlers which scratched the surface of the soil, but by Roman times animal power was being used to pull shaped pieces of wood to turn the soil. By the time of William the Conqueror the basic parts of the plough had evolved – a coulter to cut a vertical slice through the soil, a share to undercut the slice horizontally, and a mould-board to turn the slice over and bury any vegetation. In the 11th century wheels were developed to regulate the depth of the furrow.

Medieval ploughs were very heavy and pulled by teams of oxen, controlled by whip or pole. The oxen ploughed steadily and did a good job. Farms were small and the land would have been ploughed more often than today to control weeds.

The early ploughs had wooden beams and handles and wooden mould-boards shaped in different ways to suit the land in the area. Later mould-boards had small pieces of metal attached to improve their wearing qualities. The point was made of iron or steel, sometimes cast. Many of the parts were blacksmith-made, including the bolts and nuts.

In the 18th century – a time of much agricultural progress – a lightweight plough

9.1 The parts of a single-furrow horse plough. a, Beam; b, Body; c, Mould-board; d, Share; e, Coulter; f, Skimmer ; g, Furrow wheel; h, Land wheel; i, Hake; j, Sole or Frog.

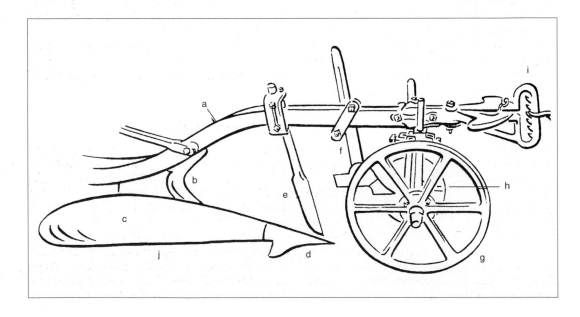

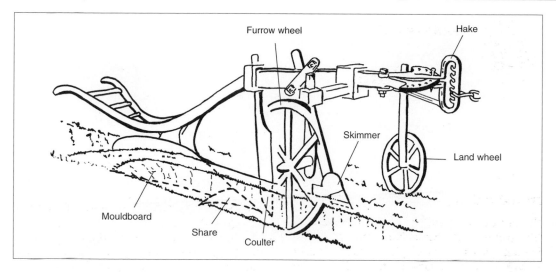

Furrow wheel   Hake

Skimmer

Land wheel

Mouldboard

Share

Coulter

9.2   The action of the plough.

was produced which could be pulled by a pair of horses, which were faster than oxen. In the 19th century manufacturers took over production from the village blacksmith, and development was rapid. In East Anglia, especially, many competitive companies designed and produced a wide range of types of plough. Many of these traditional implements survive and are sought after by those wishing to plough with horses.

How a Plough Works

The parts of a wheeled single-furrow horse plough and its action are shown in 9.1 and 9.2. As a plough cuts through the soil the coulter makes a vertical cut. The share makes a horizontal cut at the same depth as the coulter, perhaps 6 in. The mould-board is shaped to turn over the slice cut by the coulter and the share and lay it alongside and parallel to the ploughing line to the right.

The ploughman sets his plough so that the depth of the furrows is consistent. Adjustments can be made to this setting according to conditions. On a wheel plough, the depth of the furrow can be determined by adjusting the smaller land wheel and the larger furrow wheel vertically. The width of the furrow can be determined by adjusting the furrow wheel horizontally. If the horses pull the plough to one side, the line of ploughing can be corrected by horizontal adjustment on the hake.

To ensure that the furrow slice is rectangular, the plough must rest flat on its sole plate. If it is set to lean over to the left, the horses' work is easier but the furrows will not lie flat against each other.

When correctly adjusted, the plough will produce furrow slices which are straight, parallel and all the same height. The form and angle of the crests should be similar and they should lie flat upon each other. The crowns, also known as ridges or tops, should be level with the rest of the ploughing and the last furrow slice should be the same width as the rest.

Please consult the glossary at the end of the chapter for further explanation of the technical terms given in the following sections.

Working Ploughing

Traditionally the fields were ploughed on rig work in which the width of each rig is 10 – 18 yds, with the rigs set out across the field. The headland furrow would be marked out about 8 yds from the hedge at each end to give a mark for the start of ploughing. The headland was ploughed by turning the land towards the hedge one year and the opposite way the next year. When ploughing was started the second year, the top or crown was set in the furrow that was

9.3a An excellent example of high-cut work at the British National Ploughing Championships, Ross-on-Wye, 1959. The ploughman is Austin Rivett.

left the previous year; this helped to keep the land fairly level and made working easier for drills, binders and other machines that followed the plough. Half the value of the crop comes from good ploughing.

Match Ploughing

Ploughing matches became very popular among country folk in the 19th century. They started as a result of challenges between ploughmen to see who could draw the straightest furrow, and developed into the complex competitions demanding great skill which we know today. The modern horse ploughing match is a sport, and ploughmen will travel long distances to compete (9.3 a and b).

The judging and point systems vary slightly between different ploughing societies, but the Society of Ploughmen's rules will suffice to give an idea of how the match works. Out of 200 points awarded, 45 go to completing the crown (the first three furrows either side of the opening), 30 to the burying of grass and stubble, 35 for the uniformity of ploughing, 30 for the firmness of the furrow, 10 for straightness, 10 for the 'ins and outs' of the plough at the end of the furrows, and 40 for the finish (the last three furrows either side of the mould furrow) (9.4).

Classes

The two classes of horse ploughing mostly seen at today's matches are general purpose and high-cut, also known as oat seed furrow. General purpose ploughing produces a more broken furrow which can easily be harrowed down to form a seed bed. High-cut ploughing produces a furrow suitable for sowing seed by broadcasting over the furrows. When it is done properly,

the pressed and 'polished' sides of the furrows allow the seed to fall to the bottom and achieve an even distribution. Nowadays, this style of ploughing is used very little in practical situations, but it attracts competitors because of the skill required to produce this very eye-catching style.

The plough used for high-cut work has an extra long mould-board which turns the furrow slowly to ensure that the soil remains unbroken. For the polish, the ploughman uses two attachments, a press wheel shaped to the profile of the furrow which runs in the previously ploughed furrow, and a boat-shaped weight to polish the sides of the next furrow (9.5).

Basic Ploughing Procedure

A typical plough plot is 8 yards by 80 yards, and a common ploughing pattern is shown in 9.6. Before starting to plough, the ploughman should make sure that the plot

has been measured out correctly by width and length and clear any excess straw out of the way. Then a maximum of three sighting poles must be positioned. Most ploughmen prefer to plough with one horse in the furrow and the other on the land, but some ploughmen like both horses to walk on the unploughed land. To do this it is necessary to have a much longer draw chain (9.7), and to make sure that it does not interfere with turning on the headland where the horses go past the adjacent plot. This would restrict the adjacent competitor from coming out of his own work, should both teams arrive at the same end at the same time.

General Purpose

In general purpose classes all land has to be moved. The first operation is opening up. The land wheel is raised to increase the

9.4   A typical pair of plough horses at a match, with the offside horse walking in the furrow and the nearside horse on the land.

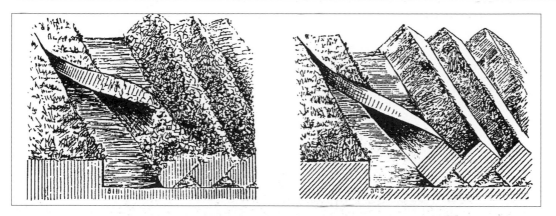

9.5   The appearance of the furrows in **a** (left) general purpose work and **b** (right) high-cut work.

angle of the plough and allow the plough-man to make the first shallow furrow 3 in. deep. This is ploughed following the sight poles which have been set up on the head-land opposite the planned first furrow of the opening, and half-way down the proposed first furrow if wished. After a second furrow the return is made parallel to it, leaving the opening clean and wide enough to allow you to set the crown level and clean.

This completes the opening, which is then judged. The crown can now be formed and is the same as in high-cut ploughing. After ploughing five furrows each side of the opening move over to the highest numbered neighbouring plot. If this furrow is not straight, bring it to the steward's attention and allowances will be made. Continue ploughing, keeping the work level and with furrows 5 in. deep and 9–9.5 in. wide. Depending on the land and conditions and the plot measurements, some 32 furrows will be ploughed.

The finish is produced as in high-cut work (see next paragraph). The ideal is to have a small ledge at the bottom of the furrow towards your neighbour's work, and the mould, or earth, taken from this furrow should be two-thirds up the normal work. It will be necessary to alter the hake when ploughing to make the plough pull in line. This is also important at the start and finish of the work. In all these cases the horses are working in an offset position (to the left), thus the need for adjustment (9.8).

High Cut

The first job in high-cut work is to set the plough (9.9), and a match ploughman should not forget the use of the skimmer, which pushes the weeds to the bottom of the furrow, burying them and so helping with the finished result. Often good work is spoilt at matches because the skimmer has not been used. It is important to get the knife coulter set right, just outside the shear or point, so that it gives a nice clean edge to the furrow wall. The bottom must also be level. The landslide should make a slight mark on the bottom of the furrow (see 9.1 for parts of the plough).

To form the opening, a scratch furrow should be created with a chipping share (a special share shaped like a small mould-board) following the line of the sight poles, with the return down the right side 23 in. from the first mark. The land wheel should be adjusted so that the first furrow is thrown halfway between the scratch marks at a depth of 4–5 in. The return is in the opposite direction to form the crown or ridge. The next step is to go round the crown again pushing these first two furrows

9.6 (over page) A competition ploughing plot. The ploughman has opened, ploughed the gather, split in the direction of his neighbour's plot and finished. The drawing at the bottom of the page shows the shape of the furrows. A typical 8-yd plot x 9 in. furrow size equals 32 furrows in total.

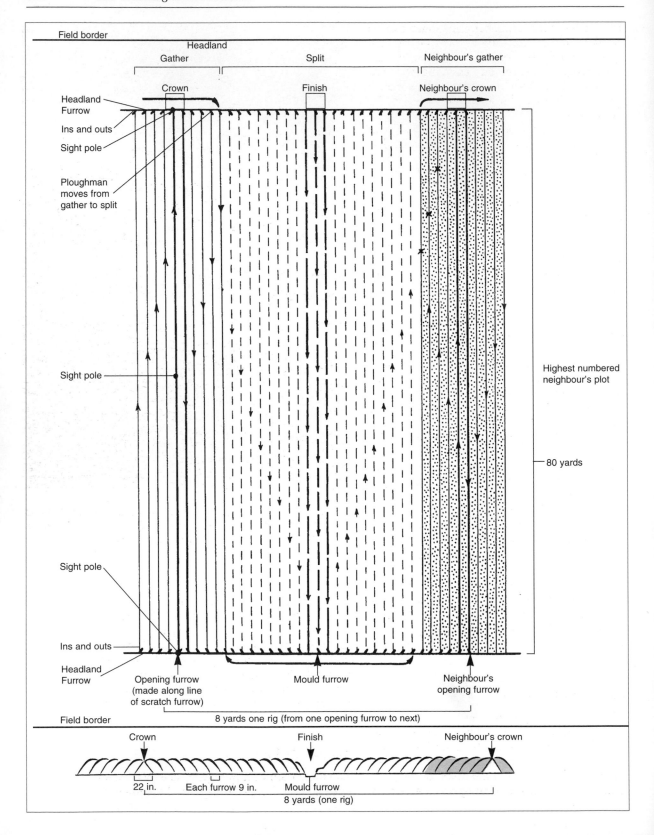

Field border

Headland

Gather | Split | Neighbour's gather

Crown | Finish | Neighbour's crown

Headland
Furrow

Ins and outs

Sight pole

Ploughman
moves from
gather to split

Sight pole

Highest numbered
neighbour's plot

80 yards

Sight pole

Ins and outs

Headland
Furrow

Opening furrow
(made along line
of scratch furrow)

Mould furrow

Neighbour's
opening furrow

Field border

8 yards one rig (from one opening furrow to next)

Crown | Finish | Neighbour's crown

22 in. | Each furrow 9 in. | Mould furrow

8 yards (one rig)

tighter together. The chipping share can be used to make the crown, but the normal type should be used for the rest of the ploughing. A wider bar carrying the two plough wheels can be used, and this makes marks which can be followed to make the start easier.

There should be a nice V in the centre of the crown, so that when the press wheel is used it will press down in the V giving a nicer finish. The boat, which follows the press wheel, will finish this off to a high standard (9.10). The furrows must be kept exactly uniform for the press wheel to run down the middle of the work. The point or shear for high-cut work should have a slightly raised front edge, so that when the slice of soil is turned over it will be slightly concave; then the work will pack together giving a smart finish. The straighter you can keep this work, the better it looks.

The furrows in high-cut work are generally 8 in. wide and 5 in. deep. Five furrows should be shown each side of the crown before casting onto a neighbour's plot, again always choosing the neighbour with the highest numbered plot. The rest of the plot, known as the split, is ploughed in until an even 8-inch strip is left. This has to be turned towards your crown, leaving an open trench. The final path is made in the same direction along the trench putting up a mould furrow which is 1–2 in. lower than the previous furrows.

When finishing off high-cut work, the offside horse must walk in the furrow so that he does not tread the work. Many older ploughmen finish off with both horses in line in the furrow so that no footmarks at all are made on the ploughed land. High-cut work at ploughing matches is usually allowed additional time as it is a much more precise job than general purpose work.

Learning to Plough

The skill of ploughing is learned over many years. You cannot buy experience, but you may be fortunate enough to find an older ploughman who worked during the heyday of the horse on the land. Not all experienced horsemen are willing or able to pass

9.7 Champion ploughman Jim Elliott chooses to work both his Clydesdales on unploughed land at the British National Ploughing Championships; hence the very long draw chain.

on their knowledge, but many are. If you can interest them in your efforts to become a good ploughman, they will certainly repay you with help and advice. Think out your questions carefully: the best approach is to tell the ploughman that you are interested in horses and ploughing and would like to invite him to come and have a look at your work.

Types of Plough

The most common plough in use by farmers with heavy horses today is the wheeled,

9.8 Mike Flood demonstrating the finish in general purpose work. Finishing with two horses side by side is usual in the southern part of the country. The finish can also be made with two horses in line, or by a single horse only.

single-furrow plough, as described above. Many types of plough are used in modern ploughing matches, and all kinds of adaptations are available to suit the ploughman's taste. A Ransomes YL general purpose plough is a good tool to start with, since the short mould-board gives a good class of work (9.11). The chief difficulty on modern fields is the tram lines made by tractors during spraying operations. If your land wheel drops into the rut it can alter the angle of the plough and make it difficult to achieve a good piece of work. One way round this is to have a long skid in place of the land wheel or, if you do not have a skid, put a little pressure on the right-hand handle of the plough when you reach the tram lines. By using the short-turn mould-board the soil is

more broken up, which helps to cover up the variations in the land. For general purpose work the YL skimmer is one of the best for burying the stubble and weeds if it is not set too deep.

A plough which is now more widely used in ploughing matches is the long mould-board type, although more skill is needed in setting it up to get a good result in general purpose work. A longer draw chain from the hake to the whipple trees will help. This will allow the horses to move out of line and not affect the ploughing. A wider cross-shaft can also be of help in keeping the plough level. The wider the shaft the less the plough will roll about; a narrow wheel base is less stable. Also, weight on the land wheel side of the plough keeps it on the ground, giving a better class of work.

Other types of plough which may be seen at matches and demonstrated at working days include the swing plough and the reversible plough. Once common in Wales

9.9 A match ploughman, like Jack House, has to make constant adjustments to the plough to achieve the desired result.

and Scotland, the swing plough has no wheels, but longer handles and a shorter beam than average, giving the ploughman more leverage. A swing plough needs a lot of muscle to keep it under control.

The reversible plough throws the furrow slice to the left or the right, so there is only one ridge and no open furrows or finishes. The ploughman reverses the throw of the furrow when he turns at the headland, laying each furrow in the same direction over the whole field. There are three types of reversible plough. The balance plough has two complete sets of handles, beam, mould-board, coulter and share, fixed at 90 degrees to each other. On reaching the headland the ploughman tips the plough up to bring the other set into use. The horses walk back down the furrow previously ploughed. The turnover plough also has two sets of parts. To reverse the action it is turned over sideways with the beam as axis. This is most popular in the west of England. The turnwrest plough has one mould-board with two faces. To reverse the

9.10 The position of the press wheel and boat in high-cut (or oat seed furrow) work.

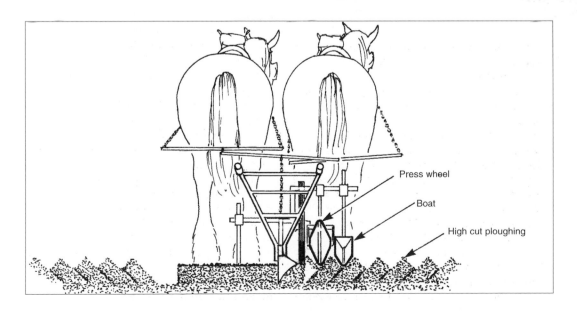

Press wheel

Boat

High cut ploughing

9.11   The author's Ransomes YL general purpose plough.

action, the plough is tilted through 90 degrees.

A few ride-on American sulky ploughs have been imported into the UK and may be seen at demonstrations. The chief advantages of these are that they plough a wider furrow and the ploughman sits above the plough achieving more in a given time-period. This plough needs three or four horses.

Conclusion

Ploughing matches have attracted a great deal of interest among the general public, and they keep ploughing skills alive as well as acting as a gathering place for keen ploughmen. Experience gained at matches assists those people who are carrying out horse ploughing on their own farms, and vice versa.

Glossary of Common Horse Ploughing Terms

Balance plough – plough with two sets of handles, *beam*, *mould-board*, *coulter* and *share,* fixed at 90 degrees to each other. At the *headland* the plough is tipped up to bring the other set into use.

Beam – the spine or main section of the plough, to which the handles are attached.

Blind pass – the ploughman steers horses and ploughs alongside the ploughed land but without ploughing a further furrow in order to position himself to plough the next furrow alongside the last one.

Boat – boat-shaped weight dragged alongside the *mould-board* to press and smooth the *furrow-slice* previously cut; particularly used to put a 'polish' on *high-cut* ploughing.

Breast – another name for *mould-board.*

Broken work – ploughing so that the *furrow-slice* is broken as it is turned, using a sharply curving *mould-board*, sometimes with fins or blades attached to divide the slice as it passes.

Butts – short furrows taking up odd areas beyond, or linking, the main ploughed areas.

Cant – a *land* or *plot:* area marked out for ploughing.

Casting off – also known as *splitting* or *throwing off.*

Chipping share – a special share shaped like a small mould-board used to make the scratch furrows in an opening in high-cut ploughing.

Coulter – the blade attached to the plough beam that makes the vertical cut in the soil. See *share, mould-board* and *skim coulter.*

Cross-shaft – metal shaft at right angles to line of plough, which holds the two wheels.

Crown – the first three furrows each side of the *opening*. In some places it represents a larger number of furrows each side. Also known as the *ridge*.

Finish – the last part of the area to be ploughed, consisting of three *rounds* and the *sole furrow.*

Furrow wheel – the larger of the two wheels which travels within the furrow.

Furrow-slice – the long strip of soil cut, lifted and turned by the plough. Also called the *sod.*

Gather – ploughing around the *opening* or first furrows by continuously turning right at the *headlands.* This always turns the furrow-slice towards the opening. See *splitting.*

General purpose ploughing – type of ploughing which produces a broken furrow which can be easily harrowed to form a seed bed.

Grit furrow – see *mould furrow, sole furrow*

Hake – device on the front end of the plough *beam* which allows vertical and horizontal adjustment at the point of attachment of the draught chains.

Headland – the area at the end of the furrow between the ploughed area and the edge of the field, allowing space for the horse team and plough to be turned. It is usually ploughed last by going round and round the field.

High-cut – ploughing which turns a *furrow-slice* that stands as high as its width, and gives a relatively narrow furrow, between 5 and 7 in. wide. These close-packed, sharp-angled furrows best accept seed sown broadcast (by hand), and weather best through the winter on soil prone to puddling. Also called an *oat seed furrow.*

Ins and outs – the points where the plough share enters and leaves the ground at the headland. They should be well in line with the *headland furrow* so that the headland ploughing neatly completes the job.

Journey – one day's ploughing.

Knife coulter – another name for *coulter*.

Land – the area beside the furrow not yet ploughed; hence *land-side,* furrow-side etc. The land horse is the one that walks on the unploughed ground; the furrow horse actually walks in the furrow.

Land-side – the side towards the unploughed land. The side of the furrow against which the vertical part of the *slade* presses.

Landslide – the vertical part of the *slade.*

Land wheel – the smaller of the two wheels which travels on the unploughed land.

Mould – the section of earth turned over by the plough.

Mould-board – the conspicuously curving plate on the plough that turns the cut *furrow-slice* over. Also called the *breast, wing* or *turn-furrow.*

Mould furrow – the last furrow to be turned in a finish (two-thirds the way up the normal ploughing). See also *sole furrow, grit furrow.*

Oat seed furrow – another name for *high-cut* ploughing.

Opening – the first operation in ploughing, consisting of two *scratch* furrows which support the first full furrow-slices at the correct angle. Also called a *veering.*

Packing – a term describing how well the turned furrow-slices press against each other to make good *seams.* Bad packing would let broadcast seeds fall through the seam; it would also encourage growth of weeds turned in.

Plot – the area in a ploughing match which the contestant has to plough.

Point – another name for *share, shear* or *sock.*

Press wheel – solid profiled wheel which follows the plough to press the *seams* tight in *high-cut* ploughing, ready to take broadcast seed.

Reversible plough – throws the furrow slice to the left or the right, so there is only one *ridge* and no open furrows or *finishes.* The ploughman reverses the throw of the furrow when he turns at the *headland,* laying each furrow in the same direction over the whole field.

Ridge – three *rounds* around the *opening,* also called a backing or *crown.*

Rig/rig work – sections of ploughing within a field, measuring 8-18 yds each, set out across the field to break it up into efficient-sized pieces for the ploughman to plough without having to walk too far to make the next furrow.

Round – a single pass in the direction of the ploughing. Thus three rounds around the *opening* forms the *ridge.*

Rubbish – particularly stubble, weeds, grass and other surface material that, in good ploughing, should be properly buried so that it will rot.

Scratch furrow – the first shallow furrows turned which support the first full furrows.

Seam – the trough between the laid *furrow-slices.* Good seams are pressed close so that broadcast seeds will not fall through. See *packing.*

Setting out – measuring the area to be ploughed, and marking it with sighting poles placed in the *headland* furrows.

Share – the blade attached to the frame of the plough which makes the horizontal cut in the soil. Often it is attached to a lever so that the point may be raised or lowered. Also called a *sock, point* or *shear.*

Shear – another name for *share, point* or *shear.*

Skid – a piece of metal to take the place of the land wheel where tramlines or uneven ground cause the small wheel to leap out of place.

Skimmer – device in front of the coulter to collect weeds and push them into the bottom of the furrow. Also known as *skim coulter*.

Slade – a right-angled metal section consisting of the *sole* and *landslide* of the plough, fastened to the bottom of the frame.

Sock – another word for *share*, *point* or *shear*.

Sod – the long strip of soil cut, lifted and turned by the plough. Also called *furrow-slice*.

Sole furrow – see *mould furrow, grit furrow*.

Sole (plate) – the base of the plough which slides along the bottom of the furrow.

Splitting – ploughing land so that the *furrow-slice* is turned away each side of the *finish* by turning left at the *headland* and going around the diminishing area of land to be ploughed. Also called *throwing out* or *casting off*. The usual way of ploughing is to complete a *gather* round the *opening* and then *split* the rest of the *land* or *cant*.

Swing plough – plough with no wheels but longer handles and a shorter *beam*, giving more leverage. Once common in Wales and Scotland.

Throwing out – also known as *splitting*, or *casting off*.

Top – Another name for *crown*. 'Tops' of the furrow should be evenly matched.

Turn furrow – another name for the *mould-board*.

Turnover plough – another type of plough with two sets of parts. To reverse the action it is turned over sideways with the *beam* as axis. Most popular in the west of England.

Turnwrest plough – this plough has one *mould-board* with two faces. To reverse the action the plough is tilted through 90 degrees.

Veering – another name for *opening*.

Wing – device on digger ploughs positioned in front of the *mould-board* on the *land-side* of the *share* which carries out the slicing motion in the furrow bottom.

CHAPTER 10

Horse-drawn Machinery and Equipment

Charlie Pinney

Introduction

Like much in the world of heavy horses, the subject of machinery for them to work with is composed of a mixture of individual preference, local prejudice, regional obsession, national tradition and a sprinkling of objective facts. The study of past and present solutions to the universal problems of soil cultivation, the planting and harvesting of crops and their transport is worth a complete book in itself. Here we confine ourselves to reviewing what realistic options are available for today's working horseman, and what they can offer in a commercial context. By this I mean machinery capable of performing useful work in a realistic duty cycle. Except where production prices for machines or components are available, I will not give values for old ploughs or antique hay turners – these machines are worth exactly what you are prepared to pay for them, and that will depend on how badly you want them, and how much you can save by using them instead of using a contractor to cut your hay or by setting off to dig your potatoes with a spade.

Choices of Machinery

The choice of machinery falls broadly into three categories – old, new and what you can adapt yourself or persuade someone to adapt for you. In the earliest days of farm mechanization, machinery was made by local blacksmiths or inventors to suit local requirements, and only when the Industrial Revolution spawned mass-production techniques did some of those designs become widely available, to emerge as standard work items throughout the country. Even then, internationally recognized firms such as Ransomes, Simms and Jefferies of Ipswich made a bewildering range of horse ploughs to suit a variety of soil conditions, field sizes and work requirements. So there remains, in museums, barns, hedgerows and pub gardens, a staggering variety of old horse machinery, some very much a local product, perhaps only sold within its county of origin, and others more easily recognized. Herein lies one of the snags of old machinery – finding the parts to keep it going. It is clear that the chances of finding a supply of plough shares for a blacksmith-made product are nil. However, if you can find a good Ransomes plough, then enough were made, and enough components such as wheels were common to enough models, for it to be a realistic possibility to keep the plough going for a few acres more.

If you cannot weld, cut threads, drill a hole in the right place and generally carry out adequate machinery maintenance, then consider the idea of a short training course at an agricultural college, or night classes in basic workshop practice, at a technical college. If you opt for reviving old machinery, you will need all these skills as well as a well-equipped workshop; without them you will not achieve the quality of work necessary to get old machines to perform adequately, you will break irreplaceable components, or you will end up paying a fortune to get someone else to sort out the mess you have made. Restoration can be fun and rewarding, but it has to be done well or it is a waste of money. Night classes are available for people restoring vintage cars and motorcycles, and it would be worth enquiring about these as the disciplines involved are exactly the same.

It is impossible to give a complete list of all parts which are interchangeable between models. Sometimes a little research and a lot of luck can yield a solution and keep a machine viable, but beware – fascinating though it is, this sort of activity will take up much time and possibly a small fortune in wasted journeys to rumoured sources of spares.

Ploughs

Probably only Howards of Bedford (alas, like so many of the horse-machinery firms, no longer in existence) made as wide a range of horse ploughs as Ransomes, and you might be lucky and find a Howard plough with a reasonable mould-board and some shares. However, I would recommend a Ransomes as a first choice, and preferably a YL model because you can still buy new shares for this model. Fortunately, the YL (Yorkshire Loam) uses the same shares as a very popular tractor plough with the same model designation. At the time of writing,

Spaldings of Lincolnshire still produce pattern plough shares for the tractor plough, and these will fit a horse version. The same applies to the mould-board.

However, it would not be safe to assume that this happy state of affairs will apply to many other old horse machines. Equally, it is not easy to get a foundry to cast up some new shares for the locally made antique you have rescued from the scrap man. I was recently quoted a price of £650 to make the mould for a share; after that, each share taken from the mould would only be about £10. They would have to sell a lot of shares to get a reasonable return on investment, and bitter experience has taught me that every horse ploughman had his own idea of the best share!

When contemplating purchasing a plough, make sure that the beam is straight – in other words, check that the main frame of the plough has not been twisted by being used behind a tractor for ploughing round headlands, where it will have encountered

10.1 An American ride-on sulky plough in use in Hampshire.

rocks and tree roots; this is an all too common fate for old horse ploughs and one from which they do not recover easily. A small distortion in the narrow, weak part of the beam over the wheel axle will throw the alignment, and therefore the accuracy, of the whole implement, and you will find it very hard to set the plough properly so that it runs, as it should, hands off, in good soil. It is not easy to straighten bent beams without a lot of very painstaking work, so if the choice is available, find a plough where there is a true right angle (measured with a set square) between the transverse axle which carries the wheel stems and the centre line of the beam. See chapter 9 – Ploughing – for parts of the plough.

The rest of the components are relatively unimportant – handles can be made by anyone with a wood lathe, stilts (the bits that the handles bolt to and steer the plough) can be straightened, landslides can be copied in flat steel plate, coulters fabricated from a round bar and a leaf of a lorry spring, and wheels re-used from almost any make of plough, potato baulker or lifting plough, but a straight beam, an unpitted mould-board and a ready supply of shares are the absolute basic essentials.

For a new horse plough you will currently have to go to America, Italy or Poland. A trip to any of these countries is a valuable and enjoyable experience since, if you are lucky, you will meet a number of fascinating horse farmers and get a lot of useful ideas. It is not difficult, but it is expensive, to import their machinery, and I would give this advice to the inexperienced: remember Ransomes' vast range of ploughs. It was vast because of the wide variety of soil types and cultivating techniques for which they catered. This is where you can have problems with imported ploughs unless you know exactly what work and soil they are designed for. For example, several American two-furrow ride-on ploughs have been imported into this country, and they work fine if you have large, flattish fields and enough horses to pull them (10.1). Much of the American horse agriculture that still flourishes takes place on what we would consider prairie land and on a comparatively large scale. For them it is no problem to put together a large team of horses, four, six, eight or more, and set off to plough with an implement that cuts a 14 or 16 in. furrow just like a tractor, instead of the 10 or 12 in. furrow that is usual for horse work in this country. Although you could get a terrific work output per day, you may find that on our sometimes heavier soils you will have a real problem working down a seed bed.

By contrast, the opposite is true of the Italian and Polish single-furrow ploughs. These are simply too small and light for anything much more taxing than market garden work on light soils – they would be struggling to plough a field of ley or turn stubble on a clay farm. New single-furrow walking ploughs are also available in America, and these may be suitable for a two-horse farm in this country. I do not know anyone who has tried one here, but it might be worth investigating.

Cultivation Equipment

Cultivation equipment is not such a problem – chain harrows and zig-zag harrows are made by several manufacturers, and are usually available in sectional form, so you can buy the width you want (10.2). These items are also easily found at farm or machinery sales. Heavier cultivation equipment such as spring-tine harrows or ride-on cultivators are not normally considered to be as collectable as horse ploughs, and thus tend to fetch scrap price. If the wearing parts are worn badly, they can be built up with weld, or tips from modern tractor cultivators can be adapted to suit – suppliers' pattern part catalogues are recommended reading. However, it is essential to ensure that wheels and chassis components are sound and not worn dangerously thin on critically loaded parts such as seats, bearings and drawbars. It is uncomfortable to find oneself sitting amongst rusty tines and bent wheels while your team gallops off across the fields.

Horse rollers are usually easy to find, but be careful to inspect and renew the axle and bearings as wear here greatly increases the draught requirement, and make sure that the shafts or poles are really sound (10.3).

10.2 Randy Hiscock using chain harrows behind three Suffolks.

Alternatively, a tractor roller with a jockey wheel in place of the drawbar pin, or pulled by a hitch cart, is a practical modern option. Disc harrows specifically constructed for horses are a rarity in this country, and you may have to adapt a light tractor set. Fortunately, the Italian firm that makes the plough mentioned above has also produced a very nice set of ride-on disc harrows, and perhaps some of the makers of small implements for lightweight tractors could be persuaded to adapt their products for horse use. Single-horse hoes and inter-row crop tools can be revived with modern hoe feet, and generally their much lighter construction allows a bent beam or chassis member to be straightened with far greater success than in the case of a plough.

Drills

Corn drills made for horses are getting scarcer, and at present I cannot tell you where to buy new ones (10.3). Old machines can be revived with care, time, new woodwork, and attention to the bearings and the correct meshings of the gear wheels. Although heavy wear does not affect their performance too much, it is comparatively simple to refurbish gear wheels with brass or Oilite bushes – any small engineering firm could do this for you. I would try to find a drill with all-steel ground wheels rather than the half steel, half wood variety as these are more difficult to repair. A lot of old horse machinery is made from cast iron, which was cheap to produce in volume, easy to machine and largely self-lubricating, but it is horrible to mend by welding as any unevenness in heating the component results in distortion and instant disintegration. Therefore, it is necessary to be very careful, even when warming up a casting to free a seized bolt.

10.3 A corn drill and roller being demonstrated at the Great Dorset Steam Fair.

Often it may be easier to fabricate and machine a new component than try to mend an old one if spares are unobtainable.

Haymaking Equipment

Haymaking equipment presents another set of problems, one of design, the other historic (10.4 and 10.5). To deal with the latter first: a very high proportion of old horse equipment was adapted for tractor use by cutting off the shafts, bolting on a drawbar and then thrashing around the field at a far higher speed than was ever intended. The result was that everything wore rapidly and got bent or broken, or all three. When you try to revive such equipment, at best 50 and often 80 years after it left the factory, you will usually find you have a major rebuild on your hands. Spares will be virtually   non-existent, especially castings and gearwheels. Any model of any

make will always wear at its weakest point, so buying another machine for spares is often not the panacea it seems. To add to the problems, the old finger-bar mowers and associated hay turners were designed to work in much lighter crops than are the norm today. Frustration at the limitations of the condition and design performance of old haymaking equipment is likely to add to the difficulties of an already stressed season.

In the absence of an ideal tool I would recommend a Nicholson hay turner, a clever machine that is more advanced than many of today's multipurpose machines as it can turn, ted and windrow a crop, and has sufficient adjustments built in to cope with a thickish shear without problems. However, these are not easy to find. Mowing machines need very careful adjustment and maintenance if they are to work without risking over-tiring the horses — pointed, polished fingers; razor-sharp sections and ledger plates; correct knife back-clearances and perfect Pitman pivots are a prerequisite. Anything less will be

10.4 A traditional horse-drawn mowing machine at work. This example is a Massey Harris 33.

10.5 A hay turner in use.

10.6 Two Shires drawing an Albion binder harvesting a crop of wheat.

very hard to pull, will block at every mouse's nest in the grass, and will generally send you off to borrow the neighbour's tractor. Opinions vary, but most people opt for Bamlett (which are lighter than the Bamford, with an all-important higher knife speed) or International mowers. It is just possible that you will find sections and fingers for these, as I believe the last International horse mowers had the same knife bed as their early mounted tractor mowers. A few dealers who have not computerized their stock control systems may have a sack of rusty bits in a cupboard in the workshop.

Do not forget that most two-horse mowers took a 4 ft 6 in. cut and the turners were of the same width. If you cut your grass with a 5 or 6 ft tractor mower, your horse turner will not follow the swath width correctly and you will find that you take a row and a half, leaving grass unturned and an awful mess. A few single-horse mowers with engines to drive the knife were produced. These are fine in principle, but you will have difficulty in finding knife parts. Theoretically you can (and I have done it) make a mower with a modern light and quiet stationary engine and a new cutter bar, but it is still a noisy, vibratory device, defeating the pleasure of animal traction. I believe that an Austrian firm has produced a prototype of a modern version of this, but it is expensive. I have imported Polish horse mowers, but I found that the antiquated design and poor quality control meant that they were not a significant advance on rebuilt old native machines: it is also difficult to ascertain production levels and availability on these at present.

Binders

Many of the above remarks also apply to binders (10.6). It is not possible to give an in-depth review of makes and problems,

10.7 Using a modern horse-drawn manure spreader imported into the UK from its Amish maker in Ontario, Canada.

but try to get a well-known make such as Albion, take great care in setting it up with sharp knives, correctly set knotters and sound canvasses, oil it well, store it in the dry and have the telephone number of a friend with a combine in your pocket. With such a heavy and complex machine, it is vital to ensure that the pole and its fittings and draught bars are 100 per cent sound or a very nasty accident could occur.

Modern Machinery

For the beginner wishing to work his horses seriously, commercially and professionally, as opposed to only taking part in traction engine rallies or horse workings using old machinery is not an easy scenario. The point is that the best team of horses cannot work efficiently with worn-out or badly adjusted machinery. With a tractor you can cope with a rusty mould-board or a blunt mower by opening up the throttle, but a horse has a very limited power output in comparison, and every stride he takes should do useful work.

Therefore it is absolutely essential that what he is pulling is the most efficient, light and well-maintained machine possible. I believe that this must mean modern machinery. Apart from the obvious truth in that last sentence, it seems nonsense to spend a lot of money on a new team of horses, new harness and comfortable stabling, and then try to make use of collapsing relics from a previous age.

We have already seen that a limited amount of new machinery is available which is proper specialized horse equipment. There is one other item being imported from America and Canada that works really well – the muck-spreader (10.7). These ground-drive machines are correctly geared for the forward speed of the horse and are a big improvement over pulling tractor ground-drive spreaders with a hitch-cart because the beaters revolve fast enough to be efficient at a walk. Most

10.8   A typical modern hitch cart.

tractor spreaders were designed to operate at 6 m.p.h. – below that speed they clog up and 6 m.p.h. is a fair trot for the horses. Prices on these items, as on all imports, will vary according to the current exchange rate and the quantity ordered, as this drastically affects shipping costs, but budget for about £2,000 if you can find some other people willing to place a joint order, and you will not be too far out at current prices.

For all other purposes there seems to be only one realistic solution at present – the hitch cart (10.8). This device has been around in a simple form for a number of years. Being just a wheeled axle with a drawbar, seat and pole or shafts, it allows a range of tractor implements to be pulled by horses – trailers, harrows, rollers, cultivators, drills and so on. If fitted with brakes it

10.9a

10.9   The Pintow range, made by Cart Horse Machinery. **a** Single-horse cart: this comes in larger versions for use with a pair of horses. **b** Basic hitchcart. **c** Three-horse/team hitchcart. **d** Three-horse/team hitchcart used with standard tractor mowing machine. **e** Two-horse hitchcart with standard tractor fertiliser spreader. This unit is making use of Cart Horse Machinery's new springs, fitted where the traces join the whipple tree, which take the strain and reduce damage to the horses' shoulders and harness.

works on steep ground, and it is also a very useful breaking and exercise vehicle. The bonus is that you do not have to alter the tractor implement to use it with horses – drop in the drawbar pin and away you go.

The snag with the simple hitch cart is that you are limited in the choice of modern implements by its lack of a power take-off shaft and a lifting system as a lot of new machinery requires either or both of these facilities. The company Cart Horse Machinery produces a range of single, pair and team hitch-carts which get around this problem by incorporating both a multi-speed p.t.o. and a 3-point lifting system (10.9a – e). See the list of useful addresses at the back of the book for further details about where to obtain heavy horse machinery. The net result is that you can use new or second-hand tractor implements with your horses, with all that that implies in terms of modern, efficient design, spare parts and service back-up, and, most importantly, a choice of power source that is appropriate for the job in hand. Because these hitch carts replicate the rear end of a tractor, you do not have to alter the implement at all when it is used either with horses or with a tractor. If you have a large acreage to cover quickly and one of your horses is lame, you can use the modern hay turner with your tractor instead of behind your hitch cart. The selection of new and

10.9b▲

10.9c▼

10.9d▼

10.9e▼

10.10   A farm waggon. This 1929 boat waggon is relatively versatile for modern use as well as for showing.

second-hand tractor implements that are potentially horse-drawn under this system is limited only by the size of your wallet and the number of horses at your disposal.

Carts, Waggons and Drays

Old carts and waggons were even more of a regionalized product than the plough, and were usually designed with local geographical considerations in mind, a point that should be remembered. For example, the tiny Dorset spring waggon was made to suit the steep narrow lanes of that county, and came equipped with brakes. Try driving a vast Yorkshire Wolds waggon down a leafy Dorset road – it probably would not fit between the hedgerows, let alone safely descend the hills (10.10).

The basic principles of selection and care apply to all wooden vehicles. First and foremost, everything must be sound – be ruthless in avoiding any vehicle with

evidence of rotten shafts, poles, chassis members or wheels unless you can repair, or afford to have the offending parts repaired. Do not forget that paintwork can hide all sorts of problems, and car body filler covering a collapsing joint is a favourite trick. Judicious use of a penknife will reveal soft and rotting woodwork. Examine every stressed point very closely, as a collapsing wheel or snapped splinter bar can cause nasty accidents on the farm, let alone on the public highway.

On two-wheeled carts pay special attention to the shafts where they attach to the chassis, as this joint is often hidden under bodywork. Similarly, on waggons the pivot pin on the forecarriage can wear unnoticed to pencil thinness. Lift up the front corner of the waggon and inspect the pin and its retaining clip, the bearing plates or turntable rings and the condition of the whole forecarriage and chassis combination.

Springs and their shackles, axle-retaining bolts and other structural fixings must be examined closely. Also look out for rotten boards and worn shaft pins, crooks and chains. Brakes operated via rusty iron

10.11 Fuller's Brewery rides vehicle on pneumatic tyres, with robust steps, seating and a safety rail.

linkage to press wooden blocks onto the wheel rims are marginally more efficient than the drag shoe and safety chain on a spoke alternative, and certainly quicker to apply, but they must move freely on and off.

Wooden wheels can have loose bonds, collapsing spokes and rims, cracked hubs, loose and worn axle boxes and axle arms, worn or missing retaining pins and many other problems usually beyond the scope of the amateur. More modern carts and waggons fitted with pneumatic tyres can cause problems if they need the special sizes of balloon tyres which are no longer obtainable. If you are lucky, though, the specialist suppliers of obscure tyres for vintage cars may be able to help.

However, modern technology has made it possible to make carts and waggons which are stronger and lighter, and which run more easily than the older types. Ball-race turntables, roller-bearing axles and efficient drum or disc brakes have increased safety and reduced specialist maintenance tasks. Although strictly speaking a steel-tyred wheel has a lower rolling resistance than one with a pneumatic tyre because it does not distort and thus absorb energy when under load, in practical terms

I would advise the use of modern wheels because of their silence, shock absorbence and vastly superior braking ability on tarmac. Choose a vehicle with as large a wheel diameter as possible, as this will be lighter in draught than a small-wheeled equivalent and will not tumble into every pothole, as well as proving easier to pull in muddy fields.

If you are contemplating giving waggon rides to the public, then obviously you must be even more rigorous in the selection and care of your vehicle, and other considerations also become important (10.11). To ensure that you conform to regulations, you should consult your local safety officer or licencing authority if you will be operating on the public highway.

Things such as the provision of steps and hand-rails for access, adequately high safety bars or sides to enclose passengers, firmly secured seating, fully operative brakes, rear reflectors and a driving position with a commanding view of the vehicle as well as the road are self-evident necessities. Incidently, you can run into trouble with iron-tyred wheels in the summer if they begin to cause ruts in heat-softened road surfaces on regular routes. The local council will often not tolerate this, even if they are not aware that by law only farmers transporting their goods are allowed to use iron wheels on the public roads! See also, chapter 16 – Road Driving.

10.12 A modern trials vehicle suitable for a pair of heavy horses. This example is owned by John and Rowena McDermott, prime movers behind the sport, which is new to this country for heavy horses.

You will not gain many prizes in a turnout class at a show if your vehicle is immaculately clean, but has cracked or bulging tyre walls, ungreased turntable rings and frayed brake cables. The standard of presentation is generally very high, and judges are beginning to scrutinize the total condition of the vehicle beyond the gloss of the paintwork and the provision of full nosebags. A number of waggon-wrights will construct new show drays or restore old ones for you, and in any case I would strongly advise asking one to assess the condition of any vehicle you are about to buy and give a guide to the probable repair costs.

Trials Vehicles

The use of lightweight exercise vehicles and FEI-type marathon trials waggons is increasing rapidly among heavy horse enthusiasts (10.12). In most cases these are of recent construction, so many of the wear and tear problems outlined above will not apply for a few years. However, be aware that some of the cheaper examples are often of very light and flimsy construction, with poorly welded thin-wall tubing which will distort or break if you hit a gatepost.

Check that wheels are in line (and round!), solid rubber tyres are firmly bonded in place, hydraulic brakes and their fluid reservoirs are up to scratch and all wheel bearings and turntable pivots are correctly lubricated and adjusted. Leaf springs crack and their shackles wear rapidly unless greased, giving a poor ride, and rubber suspension units deteriorate in time, giving the vehicle a pronounced list to one side – replacement is then the only answer. Swingle-tree pivots may not be bushed properly and will wear their pins to the point of shearing under load. As always, inspect everything very closely, both before buying and as a regular routine.

A well-maintained vehicle is not only safer, but it also runs much better and is easier for the horse and more pleasurable for you.

CHAPTER 11

Multiple Hitches

Geoff Morton

Introduction

Most present-day horsemen and women will be using a single horse or a pair for everyday work, but there are occasions when a greater number of horses is appropriate. There can be considerably increased efficiency if the size of the team is adjusted to suit the size of the load and/or the soil conditions. When driving a pair of horses there are only two methods of yoking in common use: tandem, with the front horse harnessed with long traces and a stretcher, or two horses side by side in double shafts, traces and a pole, or plough traces. However, when a three-horse team is used, various methods are available.

11.1 Three horses in line at work. These three Percherons are drawing a harvest cart in Mayenne, France.

11.2 Close-up of the eveners and chains for the three abreast hitch.

Three in Line

Probably the oldest method is three horses in line, and this is still widely used in Europe (11.1). The chief weakness of the system is that it is not possible to equalize the draught of horses yoked in this way, but with willing horses and a skilled horseman it is possible for each animal to exert its full power.

In ploughing with three in line the rear horse is often fitted with a cart saddle, instead of a normal plough back-band, to carry the considerable pressure of the traces on his back in this position. The pressure can be lessened by attaching the second horse's traces well behind the collar of the horse nearest to the plough, as this considerably lowers the line of draught of the second set of traces. The second place in line is a good position for yoking young horses for the first time.

This is not the easiest hitch to drive, so anyone proposing to use three horses in this way and who has not done so before should do so with a light load and in good conditions the first time. It is often convenient for the horseman to walk alongside the shaft horse and drive the trace horses by long reins. When making sharp turns it will be necessary to bring the two leading horses back out of draught and let the shaft horse handle the load round the actual point of the corner. Similarly, when ploughing, the horse nearest to the plough has to finish the last few feet of the furrow alone as the other horses begin to turn. Because of this, it is prudent to use one of the strongest horses in the shafts or nearest to the plough.

The leader of a three-horse team needs to be an active and willing horse who will keep his traces tight with little urging from the horseman. It is often helpful if the leader trots round long turns to cover the extra distance it travels compared with the shaft horse.

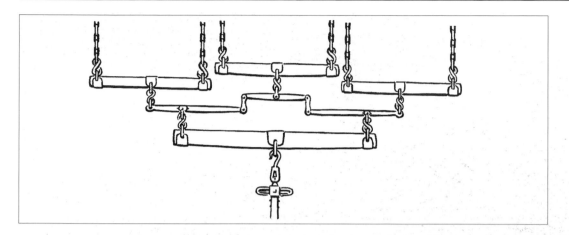

11.3 Scottish-pattern three-horse yoke which through a system of levers enables a fairer apportionment of the work to each horse.

11.4 (below) A unicorn of Shires working three-row potato happers, showing details of the reins and eveners.

Three Abreast

For deep ploughing, cultivating, etc. three horses abreast are often used, and this is an easy hitch to drive (11.2). It is often worth yoking three horses in this way for loads or implements which two horses can move, as time is saved by not having to stop and rest the horses so often. This type of hitch can be used with an ordinary set of three-horse eveners, or with a Scottish-pattern three-horse yoke (11.3).

11.5   A unicorn of Shires competing in a trade turnout class.

Unicorn

Occasionally three horses are driven in a 'unicorn', that is with wheelers abreast of the pole, or in double shafts with the third horse in traces in front (11.4). This is considered difficult to drive and is not an equalized hitch. Nevertheless, it can sometimes provide the extra power needed in a particular situation. This is especially true when using a three-row 'happer' to split the rows and cover potato setts. In this case a wide-neck yoke equal to the width of two potato rows is used between the pole horses, and the leader is attached by a light chain which runs through a ring under the pole and hooks onto the implement. Each of the three horses walks on the row tops and does not tread on the potatoes. Careful judgement and well-worked horses are called for to achieve this!

The unicorn is also a very attractive formation for showing trade turnouts in the show ring, and has been used to great effect by experienced drivers (11.5).

11.6 Three horses being driven pickaxe fashion to a cart hauling mangolds.

Pickaxe

Another possibility when driving three horses in a cart or waggon is to use a pickaxe formation, which consists of two horses abreast in the lead and one in the shafts (11.6). This is easier to drive than a unicorn, and if the draught of the leaders is equalized by using a Lincolnshire-pattern stretcher and two horse eveners, it is a very efficient hitch. Pickaxes were often used in the big shaft waggons in north Lincolnshire, where the roads were dry and free from ruts (11.7). In wet conditions the horsemen changed to three horses in line.

A modified pickaxe, which is effective when carting along deeply rutted roads, can be achieved by attaching the leader's eveners to one shaft only, using a chain of suitable length. This places one leader ahead of the shaft horse in the centre of the

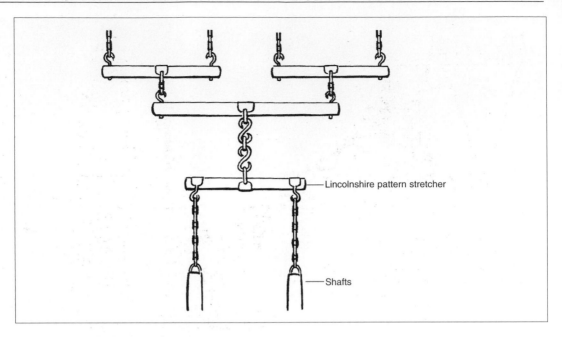

Lincolnshire pattern stretcher

Shafts

11.7   Pickaxe arrangement using a stretcher connected to the shafts by chains which are just long enough to place the stretcher just in front of the shaft horse's nose when the team is in draught.

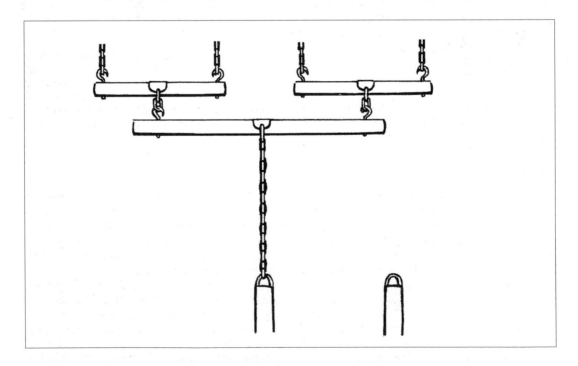

11.8   Modified pickaxe, which is suitable for use instead of the special stretcher in 11.7 or if the leaders need to walk clear of deep ruts. The chief disadvantage is the offset position of one of the leaders, which can cause difficulties when approaching narrow gateways or roadside obstructions.

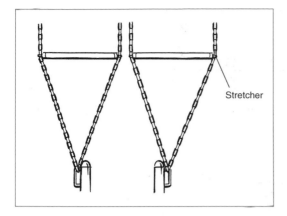

11.9 Alternative pickaxe, using long traces and stretchers. This arrangement, which is often used with timber waggons, is useful when bigger teams are called for, as more than one horse could be attached to each shaft in this way.

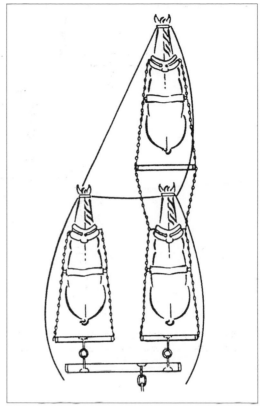

11.10 Bodkin fashion. The horses are often driven with plough cords running from bit to bit. These must be adjusted to allow the leader to tighten his traces on the one hand and to retain bit pressure on the other. Good farm horsemen will be able to control their horses largely by voice command.

road and the other leader walks to one side clear of the ruts (11.8). This works well and does not cause side draught. The position of the offset horse must be borne in mind when approaching gateways.

An alternative pickaxe, which is often used with timber waggons, uses long traces and stretchers to attach the leaders. When bigger teams are called for, more than one horse could be attached to each shaft in this way (11.9).

Bodkin

The strong land of Holderness and some other parts of Yorkshire sometimes needed three horses for single-furrow ploughing, and this was often done in Bodkin fashion, that is two horses in the furrow, the front horse being yoked with long traces and a stretcher, and one on the land (11.10). The advantage of this hitch – essentially a compromise between three in line and three abreast – is its relative ease of driving and having only one horse walking on the land, thus minimizing the damage caused by treading the surface of the unploughed soil. Also, there is less side draught on the plough than with three abreast.

When starting a fresh horse as leader in this hitch, it may be necessary to have a helper for a time, driving the new leader with long reins rather than leading him. This will accustom the animal to being driven by the ploughman.

There are many other forms of eveners and arrangements for driving three horses, e.g. the double-pole arrangement seen on some town vehicles, and large North American corn drills. For practical purposes in Britain, however, the hitches detailed above will be the most useful.

CHAPTER 12

Working Horses in Forestry

Angela Gifford

Introduction

In Europe horses were used extensively to extract timber until the 1960s–70s. The size and weight of the timber governed the number of horses used. They wore trace harness and were hitched to choker chains round the butt of a tree. The timber was simply dragged (snigged, tushed) to remove it from the forest. Any exceptionally large piece of timber was slung under a pole arch which raised the tree off the ground, allowing the horses to extract greater weights. In the snowy and icy conditions of Scandinavia, horses wore light shaft harness to pull sledges and timber arches.

The introduction of machines saw the demise of the horse as a source of draught power in forestry. Inevitably this led to a loss of horsemanship skills among forestry workers, and less awareness of the horse as a working system among foresters and managers.

Since 1980 environmental considerations have put a different complexion on some parts of the forestry industry. The Scandinavians have led the way in developing modern equipment for extraction with horses. A variety of implements is being produced, and some are well suited to the very different British forestry conditions. In some circumstances the traditional method of ground-skidding used in the UK remains highly effective. There is an urgent need for a remarriage of the disciplines of horsemanship and forestry skills.

Basic Systems of Timber Extraction

Mechanised Extraction

In this system the majority of the work is done using mechanised equipment such as the following:

Agricultural or forestry tractors with winches – Produce is skidded to the stacking area (landing) or to the ride side, using tractors with winches. From the ride side it is ready for forwarding to the landing on trailers.

Skylines/cable cranes – Used on steep upland or difficult sites. Wide racks are necessary in order to maximize operating efficiency. Skylines and cable cranes can only operate in straight lines, and require extensive set-up and take-down time. Generally they are only used in large-scale operations.

Horse Extraction

In this system some of the processes involved are done using horse power – mechanised methods are often used for parts of the work such as forwarding produce from the rack side to the road side.

Horse extraction uses horses with either chains or specialist equipment (sledges, arches or trailers) to extract timber to the rack side or landing.

The following processes take place within both systems:

Snigging or tushing – Extracting timber by dragging it along the ground, usually from stump to ride (compartment) side, where it can be converted and forwarded to the road side.

Skidding – Extracting timber by lifting one end and dragging it along the ground, usually from stump to ride (compartment) side, where it can be converted and forwarded to the road side.

Forwarding – Extracting the felled produce and taking it to the road side/landing.

Specialised equipment such as the following can be used for forwarding.

Forwarding trailers – Carry bulk loads of timber clear of the ground on wheeled trailer units, usually incorporating a hydraulic grapple for self-load.

Purpose-built forwarder – Combined tractor and trailer unit with loader/grab which can operate in the stand if the racks are wide enough and extract to the landing. They are very expensive.

Situations for Working a Horse

Situations which are particularly suitable for working with horses are listed below.

1. Horses can be used economically for short hauls (generally around 100 m) to extract timber to the rack side or landing. They can complement machinery on certain sites.
2. The horse can work selectively in a stand of trees and reduce the need to line-thin in order to make room for mechanised extraction equipment. This factor can reduce wind-blow in certain stands of trees.
3. First and second thinnings, often extracted in full pole length (using chain harness), or in bunches cross-cut to 3 – 6 m size (using a shafted implement).
4. Sites of Special Scientific Interest (SSSI) and other environmentally sensitive sites where the impact on flora and fauna must be kept to a minimum.
5. Publicly sensitive sites such as way-marked walks, recreational areas etc.
6. Where minimal ground disturbance is essential, where large machinery and skylines are environmentally intrusive, where noise must be kept to a minimum, or for appearance.
7. In small parcels of woodland where the transportation of heavy machinery to and from the site is uneconomic.
8. For wind-blow sites or timber which is difficult to reach.

Selection and Training of Horses for Forest Work

Consideration of the general terrain in the district to be worked should be the deciding factor as to the size of the horse chosen, bearing in mind that weight is needed to pull weight. In very steep conditions a Cob is more agile than a heavyweight cart horse.

Temperament is of prime importance. A mature, well-trained horse, quiet in all gears, is essential for forestry work. It should not have erratic behaviour or snatch at loads. A good mouth makes the task so much easier, for frequent precise maneouvres are vital to position the horse. The training should work towards the horse being capable of working to voice command.

An agricultural work background is ideal for teaching a horse to stand still for long periods. However, even an experienced draught horse will need to be introduced gradually to the woodland environment. It should be driven and manoeuvred in the stand of trees in tight limited spaces and on steep slopes. At first, horses are often nervous of backing in these situations. The noise of chain saws should be introduced carefully. Given patience this should not present a problem, but care should be taken that sawdust does not hit the horse.

Always be aware that the horse is an instinctive animal. Care should be taken when trees are being felled. As a minimum, horse and operator must be at least two tree lengths away from any tree being felled.

Care of the Horse

Grooming – Normal grooming and foot care procedures should be followed.
Foot care – Shoes should be well studded

for additional traction in slippery conditions. Caulkins should be fitted for extreme conditions. See also chapter 4 – Farriery for the Working Horse.

Fitness – Work up the fitness of the horse before embarking on hard work. This can be achieved gradually by walking and pulling light loads over a period of 4 – 6 weeks. At the start of a working day, loads should be lighter.

Transportation – If the work is away from the horse's home base suitable transportation for horse and equipment is necessary. Vehicles should be suitable for rough off-road conditions and for carriage of all the equipment needed for the task and for the welfare of the horse. Weight and load legislation should be adhered to. See also chapter 18 – Transport and the Law.

Overnight accommodation – Either grazing or stabling near to the work site should be arranged. Electric fencing is useful to define an area for grazing. Temporary shelter strung between trees or fixed to the trailer is often suitable.

Rests and breaks – 2 - 3 hour stints of work should be interspersed with 1-hour breaks for feeding and drinking. Care should be taken to rug-up a hot horse in cold/windy conditions while at rest. A normal working day is 6–7 hours. It is worth noting that steep conditions demand more effort in getting up banks without a load than in extracting timber downhill.

Feeding – Each horse has a different metabolism. He should be fed according to the work expected. This can be adjusted to suit the behaviour of the horse. See also chapter 2 – Choosing a Working Horse, and chapter 6 – Training for the Horse.

Equipment

Harness – This needs to be appropriate for the work to be undertaken.

Long gears – This is either plough harness with a whipple tree, or trace harness with a spreader bar. The heavier trace chains are essential for larger timber.

Scandinavian-design harness – This is used with shafted equipment. In a forestry situation, it is essential for the horse to have the freedom of movement which is allowed

with this harness. Variations of this design can be used as long as the principles of freedom of movement and the horse's welfare are adhered to. See also chapter 7 – Harness for the Working Horse.

Implements – All implements should be light but strong for easy manoeuvrability, and to enable maximum loads to be carried. A choker chain should be used with long gears.

Training and experience – The chain-saw operator must have the relevant NPTC (National Proficiency Test Council) certificate and have completed the appropriate NVQ in forestry. See also chapter 5 – Training for Horsemen. All necessary protective equipment should be worn.

Considerations when Planning a Timber-harvesting Operation

When planning a timber-harvesting operation the physical impact on a site of using various extraction systems must always be considered, as well as the following details: weather; soil conditions; the stability of the ground; ground compaction; damage to standing trees; the width of the racks; terrain; rocks and boulders; stumps; steepness; extraction routes; extraction distance; landings; the size of the timber; volume plus weight; felling and presentation of the timber; owners/managers' objectives; timescale.

Planning and Basic Work Practices

Using your working knowledge of harvesting systems, work out the felling plan, the layout of the racks, and the landings and extraction routes to ensure the maximum efficiency in the use of the horse (12.1a and b).

It is necessary to work closely with the cutters to achieve optimum efficiency. Cutters must keep stumps low, and it is vital to have good-quality snedding (debranching) to avoid sprags that will hinder extraction. Felled timber should be at 45 degrees to the extraction rack to avoid tight corners when extracting. Different types of produce can be marked with different sprays to help the logger place it in

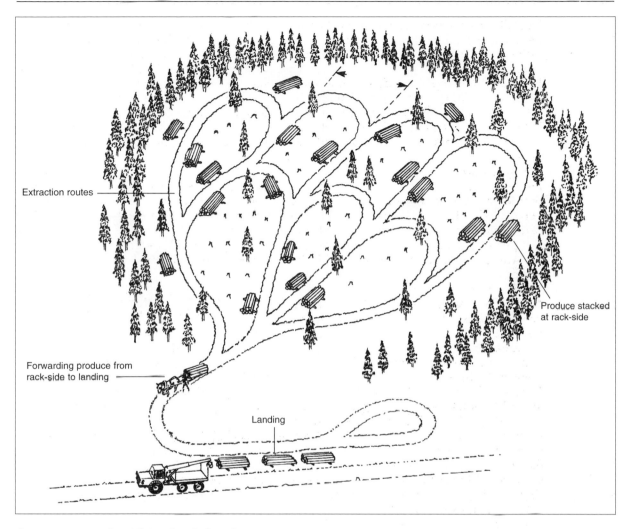

Extraction routes

Produce stacked
at rack-side

Forwarding produce from
rack-side to landing

Landing

12.1a A network of extraction routes suitable for efficient forwarding of produce to rack-side and ride-side (or landing) ready for collection by vehicle.

the correct stacks. This also helps loggers identify valuable produce which must be treated carefully. Serious economic loss can result if different specifications become mixed. Butts should face out towards the rack unless the extraction method will be skidding on a steep downhill track using long gears.

The site should be thoroughly surveyed and the extraction racks planned preferably before felling starts. Protective bunks should be placed on corners to prevent scarring of standing trees. Wet patches, ditches and holes should be avoided or made negotiable by filling them with wood and branches or stone, as applicable.

Safety ropes should be used in areas of public access. Always warm up the horse

by extracting light loads at the beginning of the day's work. It is important for the horse to take up any slack before moving off. In really soft conditions, take the horse out of draught and allow him to move off at an angle to help start the load. The initial movement is the most difficult. If the horse cannot cope, reduce the load. Once a horse has a full load it will need to work with greater effort, and care must be exercised for both horse and man.

12.1b Skidding timber to ride-side.

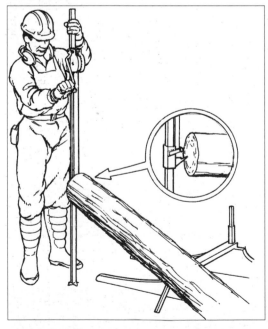

12.2 Using a jack for pivoting logs onto equipment.

Safe Lifting and Handling Techniques

It is when lifting and handling that the logger is at most risk of injury. Top-quality equipment must be used, in particular forestry boots. If using a chain saw, safety trousers, chains, helmet and gloves must be used. The logger will also need a pulp hook, bill hook, tongs, breaking bar and loading aids, for all of which there are several designs.

It is important to warm up when starting work. Never use brute force to handle wood. Either move equipment or roll/pivot produce rather than lifting it. The following rules should be remembered at all times:

Correct stance – legs hip-width apart, one foot forward.

Correct position – get down to work, bend your knees, not your back.

Correct grip – with the palms of the hands, draw the object towards the body.

12.3a Stacking produce. **12.3b and c** Using two stakes set at right angles to the stack to aid stacking.

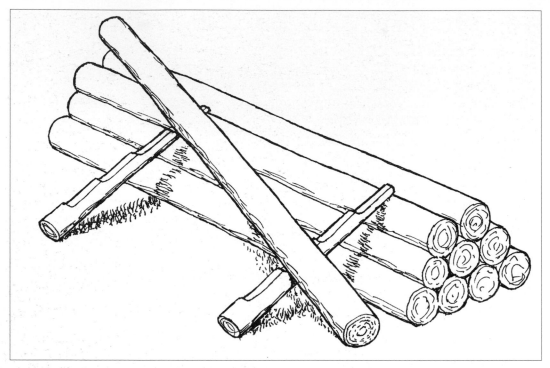

12.3c

Correct lift – back straight, lift with your leg muscles, do not jerk but lift smoothly, use your knee as an aid when stacking.

Use stacking tools – to avoid bending your back. Check that all tools are sharp and capable of holding produce to avoid stretching and jarring injuries.

Use a simple yoke or jack for pivoting logs onto equipment (12.2). A breaking bar and tongs can be used in conjunction with the jack for loading onto forwarders. Use a levering technique on the stanchions that hold the loads, or use side-skids to load. Always chock the wheels of a forwarder when loading/unloading.

Good handling skills avoid accidents.

Procedures and Use of Equipment

Stacking at Landing

Stack produce on clean ground on bearers with their ends flush, either parallel to or at right angles to the road (12.3a). Ditches can be used if bearers are placed across them to support the timber out of the water. Mechanical grapple loaders must be able to pick up produce without hassle, so it must be within easy reach and have a level face. Use both sides of the track if it is possible to load from both sides without the truck moving. Accurate driving can help with unloading at the landing bay. Drive close to the stack so that smaller produce can be off-loaded on top of the stack. Roll larger logs off to form the base. Sufficient room should be left between stacks of differing specifications. If unloading parallel to the road use several stacks in order to avoid one pile becoming too high and thus making it difficult to reach the other stacks. To help stack, it is possible to roll the produce up two stakes set at right angles against the stack (12.3b and c). If necessary to help pull the produce into place, the horse can be used at right angles on the other side of the stack, using a chain to draw the produce up onto the stack.

Long Gears (Skidding and Tushing)

12.4 Position for driving when timber-skidding.

The maximum load size depends on the size of the horse and the optimum type of terrain for extraction. As a benchmark, a Shire-type horse can skid half a ton on the level. Shorten the hip straps to give the horse more traction and help lift the front of the load. Check that the produce has been well snedded to facilitate a smooth pull.

Attach the choker chain round the tree about 10–15 in. from the end, with the ring or hook near the ground so that maximum tightening of the choker is achieved when the horse is in draught. The placing of the choker ring/hook can help to turn poles trapped behind stumps. When extracting downhill, attach the chain to the top end of the log as the butt acts as a brake. On the level, the butt end can face forward since it is the heaviest end and is thus lifted slightly by the traction of the horse. (There is some controversy on this point.)

From the position shown in illustration 12.4 you can drive the horse on either side depending on the lie of the land and obstacles to be encountered en route. Always drive uphill of the load or corner, and watch the log for any unexpected movements in transit. When leading, the horse logger should be on the outside of any corners and should never bring the horse towards themselves. When a horse can be trusted to work to voice command, it can extract the timber to the rack side without driving if the route is clear of obstacles such as people or stumps. The logger should be in full view of the horse at all times.

Always make sure the horse has taken up the strain of the load before allowing it to extract timber to avoid snatching. Clear timber from the front of the felled area first, then work back into the stand. If skidding full-length poles, beware of the ends becoming trapped against standing trees or other felled trees. They can act as a catapult when released.

Skid Tongs

Skid tongs are used for pulling single logs using long gear harness. Depending on

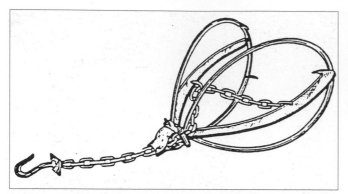

12.5a Skid tongs used for pulling single logs using long gear harness **b** Skid tongs in use.

the design, either the tong jaws grab the load directly, or a choker chain passes through the tongs and tightens as the horse moves forward. Loads are deflected off obstacles, resulting in less jarring (12.5a and b). Follow the driving procedure for long gears.

Shafted Implements

Scandinavian-design harness must be used with shafted implements to allow maximum freedom of movement for the horse. Loads are partially raised off the ground – this allows one horse to pull greater loads owing to the reduced drag. Shafted systems also allow the load to be braked via the use of breeching. Smaller produce can be bunched with a single choker chain. Drive from the position shown in 12.6, changing sides as necessary for safety.

Shaft Skidder

Several designs of shaft skidder are available (12.7a, b and c). Note that these can have considerable side draught on sidling ground (working across a bank). Some bunkheads drop down for ease of loading if the produce has been stacked on bearers. The skidder is backed under the raised end of the produce stack and then secured; the bunkhead then rises as the horse moves forward. These are ideal for small-specification timber on level ground. For mixed-size timber, load the largest timber onto the bunkhead first, with the smaller timber on top. Secure the load with a chain which tightens when driving forward, or with a chain/belt strap with a bear trap. Readjust the load after 10 m as the initial movements will loosen the load. One shaft skidder is designed so that the horse tightens the chains when in draught.

Skid Arch

Various designs of skid arch are available. Simple arches with flanges to carry the timber chains are restricted to produce that can be lifted manually (12.8). Others are fitted with ratchets to lift one end of the timber clear of the ground. The loading must be carefully planned with regard to cornering maneouvres. Arches are suitable for use in a variety of terrains, such as extracting down fairly steep slopes, on the level and uphill, although uphill work should be approached with care. It is usually more efficient to cross-cut produce at the stump to 11 ft, 12 ft 4 in. or 15 ft depending on the produce specification required. This results in less drag and facilitates greater loads, allowing for more mobility in thinning work.

The Ulvins arch is fitted with ratchets to raise the timber, and is designed to carry two tons. Choker the produce individually or in bunches, and thread the chain under the ratchet and over the top and ratchet handle. Travel with the handles facing backwards (12.9a and b), and push the handles sharply forward to release the load. In the event of getting stuck, release the load, dismantle the arch from the shafts, move the horse and shafts forward, reassemble the arch and reload. The wheels can be removed in snow, but they help manoeuvrability and alleviate side draught in steep conditions. Choker chains can be joined together to reach awkward timber, and dragged into position using the flanges on the arch.

▼ **12.7a**, **b** and **c** Diagram of shaft skidder.

12.6 Shafted implement, showing driving position.

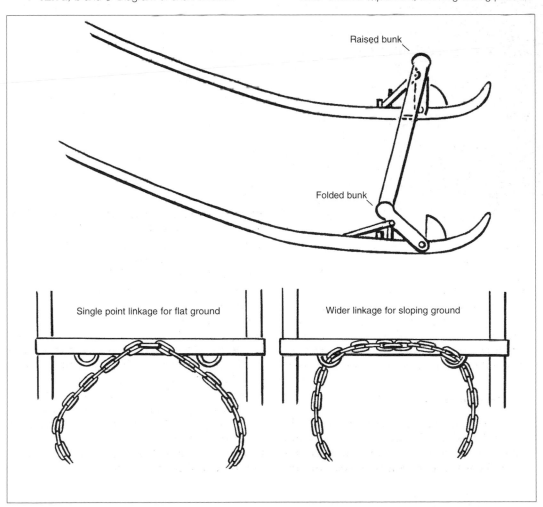

Raised bunk

Folded bunk

Single point linkage for flat ground

Wider linkage for sloping ground

12.8 Skid arch with simple flanges to hold chains.

Drive from the side or behind the arch according to the space available when empty or loaded. The logger should be on the upper side on sidling ground and on the outside of any bends. Arches are designed to travel over rough terrain and allow the horse to remain stable.

For economic reasons aim to emerge from the rack with a full load and with one produce specification to assist with unloading onto the correct stacks. The Ulvins arch has an adaptation kit to replace the arch component with a bunkhead, so that it can be converted into a forwarder to carry 30-cwt loads over greater distances on flatter terrain (12.10).

Sledges

Sledges are ideal for use in snow and ice on reasonably flat terrain. Check that the produce is not frozen to the ground, and if it is, release it with a bar. The horse needs caulkins and wedges on its shoes when working in these conditions. An adequate braking system must be adopted, such as reinforced shaft ends designed to dig into the ground when the load overruns. Brake chains can be attached to the runner

12.9a (top) The Ulvins arch being used to extract small timber, and **b** (above) Ulvins arch in use with larger timber.

12.10 The Ulvins arch converted into a forwarder.

12.11a (below left) Fore-end of a traditional goat and rain sledge showing the braking system at the end of reinforced shafts. **b** (below) Modern sledge showing the addition of brake chains, from the implement to the shafts, which aid breaking efficiency.

12.12 Bogie wagon/trailer – many designs are available.

tips and allowed to run under the runners, but then the load cannot be backed satisfactorily. A maximum 15–20 degree slide articulation is advised (12.11a and b).

Care in loading is essential, and the heaviest produce should be on the base of the sledge. Secure the load with chains which bite into the timber and a bear trap or belt strap, and adjust after moving 10 m. Using a mat, it is possible to sit on top of the load to drive the horse when extracting. In snowy conditions, loads of up to 3 tons can be extracted on gentle downhill gradients by one large horse.

Bogie Waggons/Trailers

Various designs of bogie waggons/trailers are available. Timber can be loaded by hand using loading aids, by a cable crane, or with a small engine driving a grab. Stanchions and chains secure the load. For use in normal weather conditions, the wheels must be blocked when loading and unloading (12.12).

12.13a Pole arch being placed in position.

Pole Arch

Use long gears harness with a pole arch, which is designed for extracting large single trees. Raise the pole in the air, place the chain round the tree approximately half-way along the trunk and attach it to the arch. Pull the pole down with the chain attached to the spreader bar. Check that the tree is balanced. Extract with horse/horses in line. In good level ground conditions it is possible for one fit cart horse of considerable weight to pull 3 tons if the tree is balanced. The disadvantage is the lack of a braking system (12.13a and b).

Working and Marketing Systems

A basic working knowledge of how timber is bought and sold, and how conventional contractors operate is essential. Forestry managers usually require a complete package, i.e. felling and extraction. The owner or forester/forest manager may require a fell and extract operation or a simple extraction job.

Different types of timber are bought and sold in different ways. Valuable hard and softwood thinnings are often sold standing,

12.13b Pole arch in use.

to be felled and extracted by the purchaser or his contractors. This allows the quality to be assessed. The horse-logging contractor should be very clear about what he is contracting to do. It may be difficult to arrange effective felling if he is new to the business and does not have reliable contacts. No felling should be attempted unless the logger is suitably trained and experienced. He should be adequately equipped, and will usually be required to have substantial insurance cover.

Before beginning work, all parties should understand who is responsible for the various stages of the operation (i.e. felling, extraction, conversion and stacking). Contracts should be negotiated and signed. The logger should establish how payment is to be made (i.e. by the cubic metre or by the ton). A system of measurement should be agreed (e.g. stack measure at the road-side or waggon tickets from a weighbridge.)

Shortwood is felled, snedded, converted and stacked in the wood. It is extracted to the stacking bay using forwarding equipment. The advantages are clean produce, waste left in eco-piles in the wood, and produce which is presented well for easy extraction. The disadvantage is a more demanding specification for the cutters.

Pole lengths are felled, snedded and extracted along the ground to the conversion bay. The advantages are that it is a quick and simple method. The disadvantages are 'dirty' timber (which can damage the saws at the mill), brash piles up in front of the timber and snags on rocks and stumps, and the load is much smaller.

Measurement of Timber

A working knowledge of timber measurements and specifications is an insurance for the horse logger (12.14). Some basic terms are explained below.

Stack volume – For low-value timber. Reasonably accurate and very quick. Length x width x average height = stack volume in cubic metres.

Solid volume – Multiply stack volume by 70 per cent for conifers and by 55–65 per cent for hardwood (i.e. the volume of the stack excluding air spaces between pieces).

Saw-log volume, for high-value logs – Very accurate, but takes time. Measure length from butt end and round down using established conventions (under 10 m round down to the nearest 0.1 m; over 10 m, round down to the nearest whole metre). Measure the mid-diameter of the rounded-down length. Consult round-wood tables in Forestry Commission Booklet No. 39 (see Further Reading). Mid-diameter/ rounded down length gives the volume in cubic metres.

Saw-log volume, for many medium-value, uniform logs – Reasonably accurate and fairly quick. Either: measure length, measure TDUB (top diameter under bark) using a saw-log scale, record the volume directly from the scale; or: measure length, measure TDUB using a tape or ruler, consult saw-log tables in booklet 39. The top diameter class/length gives the volume in cubic metres.

Some Basic Timber Specifications

Firewood – Hardwood or softwood logs. Cords of 4 ft or 2 m lengths.

Softwood for paper *and hardwood* for pulp – Check preferred length specification with intended purchaser or forest manager.

Bars – small sawlogs. 1.86 m x minimum 15 cm TDUB (6 ft 2 in. x 6 in.). For garden panels and fencing material, e.g. cleft chestnut, treated softwood.

Stakes – 1.7 m x 5–12 cm TDUB (5 ft 6 in. x 2–5 in.).

Straining posts – 2.3 m x 12–20 cm TDUB (7 ft 6 in. x 5+ in.).

Rails (fencing) – 12 ft 2 in. x 3–4 in. TDUB, straight and clean.

Sawlogs – 6 ft 2 in.–12 ft or 24 ft x 6 in. TDUB and above. Softwood or hardwood for construction.

12.14 Average width x average height = stack volume in cubic metres.

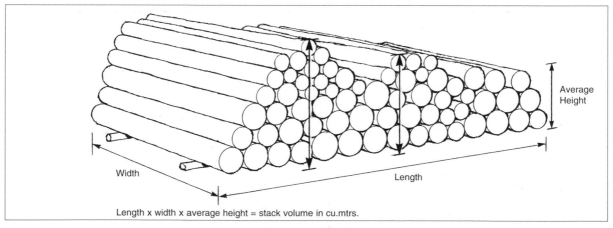

Length x width x average height = stack volume in cu.mtrs.

Summary

The horse can be regarded as an economically viable alternative system for extracting timber on a wide range of site types. A sound knowledge of the following elements of forestry procedures is necessary: presentation of timber; planning and preparation; drawing up an agreement covering prices, work details etc.; choice of systems; economics; horsemanship; care of the horse; the capabilities of the horse; working in partnership with the horse. Training is advisable in the two disciplines of forestry and horsemanship.

Glossary of Common Forestry Terms

Bearer – pole laid on the ground before stacking to keep timber off the ground and assist drying out.

Brash – waste branches from poles and timber trees (also *lop and top*).

Bunkhead – crosspiece of metal on top of implement on which timber is placed for extraction. Used in conjuction with chains to tighten the load.

Butt – the stump end rather than top end of the stem of a tree.

Cutter – a timber-cutting contractor or feller.

Landing – timber stacking area (*bing* in Scotland).

Line-thin – straight line of trees felled to enable machines to enter and exit for extraction purposes.

Lop and top – waste branches from poles and timber trees (also *brash*).

Rack – a route for extraction in a stand of trees, which is formed by cutting out a line of trees.

Ride – unmetalled woodland road/track, suitable for extraction at certain times of the year if soft, or all year round if well drained.

Saw-log – timber which is to be converted into planks.

Snedding – debranching a tree by cutting branches off flush with the main stem (also *dressing out*).

Snigging/tushing – pulling timber along the ground with long gears.

Stand – a compartment or parcel of trees between rides.

Wind-blow – area where strong wind has blown down trees, usually a funnel into a *stand* and circular area where whirlwind has occurred.

CHAPTER 13

Selecting a Show Horse

John Peacock

All heavy horses are *draught* horses and it is important to bear in mind when selecting one suitable for showing that it should not only look as though it could do a day's work, but actually be able to do so. The basic principles of conformation are identical for a work or show horse – for showing we should choose the best of our working horses. See also chapter 2 – Choosing a Working Horse.

First, decide on the type of showing you wish to compete in, i.e. breed classes, gelding or turnout. If you intend to show breeding stock it is advisable to look into the pedigrees of both the sire and dam of any horse you may wish to buy, as many characteristics are passed on.

The ideal source of show horses is the breeders themselves and the various breed societies can provide you with appropriate names and addresses. You may be able to obtain such a horse form the auctions and sales which exist, or you may visit a horse you have heard of by word of mouth. Great care should be exercised in the choice to avoid disappointment.

Colour

Colour should not be a big issue as long as you keep within the breed society's guidelines. If in doubt check with the particular society – many people new to heavy horses have rushed in with great enthusiasm and been sorry for their decision later on. With the Shire or Clydesdale it is very fashionable to have four white legs, particularly for turnout classes. Horses with this colouring are also more valuable at sale.

Conformation

Size is more important for a show horse than for a work horse. Generally speaking, 'A good big 'un will usually beat a good little 'un'. When selecting a show horse I do not go as far as putting a measuring stick to them, but I believe size is important in any breed. A lot of people believe that, 'you need weight to move weight,' but that said, I think 17.2 hh–18 hh is big enough for any horse. Many very good horses are much smaller, particularly in the Suffolk and British Percheron breeds.

Try to avoid wall eyes (where the eye has a pronounced amount of white) and look for a 'kind' eye. A long neck in proportion to the body, with plenty of neck through the collar, is appropriate. The throat should be clean-cut and lean, leading to deep and oblique shoulders to support the collar. The back needs to be short-coupled for stallions and geldings, and slightly longer for females. It should not be dipped or 'roached' and should have prominent loins leading to long sweeping hind quarters with plenty of muscle and a tail set well up.

Hocks should be set at the correct angle for leverage. They should be not too far back but in line wth the hind quarters. Avoid 'sickle' hocks, which come too far under the horse, and puffiness in the hock area. The front legs need to be as straight as possible down to the pastern, which should slope at some 45 degrees down to the feet. There is a lot of truth in the old saying, 'no foot, no horse,' so a good sound foot with no cracks and plenty of depth at the heel is needed. As with the hind legs, the fore limbs need to

13.1 'Earl', owned by John Peacock, an ideal draught show horse, combining good conformation and ability to work.

be sound with no blemishes such as sidebone, ringbone or splints.

Next check for movement – have the horse walked and trotted towards and away from you. See also chapter 14 – Preparation of a Show Horse. If you are intending to show the horse in turnout classes it is appropriate to see the horse drawing a vehicle or implement before making your decision.

If you are still interested and it is a valuable horse I would recommend you call in a veterinary surgeon to examine the horse for soundness of wind, limbs, eyes, heart and movement and also the suitability for the job you require it to do. It is also advisable to have blood samples taken for further reference. A few pounds spent at this stage could save you a lot of disappointment and money later on (13.1).

Care of the Show Horse

Having purchased your potential show horse, its care will be all-important. You will only get out what you put in. People who prefer Shires or Clydesdales with a lot of feather will need to spend time looking after them to prevent staining. These breeds are also prone to sores on their legs. Manes and tails need to be given attention as it becomes very difficult to plait them if too much rubbing occurs. Excessive rubbing can sometimes be caused by wrong feeding, especially with some of the highly mollassed straw feeds. Your feeding programme needs to start in the early part of the year for the coming show season.

Schooling the Show Horse

The other important factor is the work you will put in at home in schooling your horse, be it for in-hand showing or harness, because a class can be won or lost in the way your horse goes in the show ring.

To get your horse to a show you will probably need to transport it in a box and practice is needed to make sure it will load and unload without problems. General handling of your horse, such as picking up and picking out feet, will not only help to prevent thrush and other problems developing unseen, but will help the farrier when he comes to shoe your horse.

If you intend to show a mare and foals, plenty of practice is needed with the foal. Teach it to walk, trot and stand still. This will apply to all young stock – the more they are handled the better they will go when you get them to a show. With harness horses never ever take them out to any public event until they are absolutely ready. Do not attempt to take horses to shows to break them in.

The more care and attention to detail you put in, the more you will get from your horse or horses.

For more detail on training horses see chapter 6 – Training for the Horse.

CHAPTER 14

Preparing and Showing Heavy Horses

Tom Brewster

Preparing a Show Horse

The preparation of a show horse starts months before the date of the first show. Some say that a horse should be ready to show at any time. However, it is very costly to keep a horse 'show-fit' at all times, and the best thing to do is to decide when you need your horse to be at '12 o'clock'. You should aim to get your horse ready gradually, as there will then be time to sort out any difficulties before the big day. Feeding is an important element. If this is correct, your horse will bloom when you need to have him ready, making the show day easy and enjoyable (14.1).

To show your horse to best advantage in front of the judge, you must have done your homework. It should be remembered that show conditions are totally different from working with your horse at home. Anything you can do at home to prepare your horse for this unusual occasion will help on the day. It is a good idea to get him used to sudden noise: if your horse can get used to loud voices and music on the radio, it will usually not flinch at anything.

Make sure your horse can walk and trot when asked and that he can move correctly. It is most helpful to invite someone with experience to your home to watch your horse and help you decide at which speed he goes best. Some perform best at a slower pace and others at a faster pace. The judge will ask to see your horse move at a walk and a trot: this is called the stand show. It is his chance to see how well your animal moves. As a general rule, if a horse cannot move correctly it will not stand a good chance of winning a class. It is also important to make sure your horse can back (go backwards) correctly.

The judge will be looking for straight movement, with feet picked up clearly, showing the sole of the feet when viewed from behind, with a well-flexing ankle and a length of stride. If judging a turnout he will be watching to see that the feet of one horse are not catching on its neighbour. Generally good conformation, according to the different breed standards, is important. So is the carriage of the horse's head. A horse which carries its head well from the moment it enters the ring will catch the judge's eye.

Feeding

Feeding the heavy horse for the show ring is a complex subject as each horse has different needs. Most important of all is the quality of the feed you use. Good quality hay is vital because the fibre will be more digestible and the feed value higher than poor quality hay. Hay actually has the potential to provide all a horse needs to keep it healthy.

Hay aside, your feeding regime will be dependent on a wide variety of different factors—the horse's age, the amount of work it is to do, what work is expected of it, plus its own individual characteristics.

Horses that are stabled need a variation in their diet to prevent them getting bored. Hay should be fed 'to appetite' but give less if the horse is wasting it. Chop (chopped hay) fed with bran, oats and/or pellets,

14.1 A 'show fit' Suffolk, standing perfectly: Roger Clark with 'Laurel Keepsake'.

cubes or coarse mix will reduce the amount of hay the horse will eat. It is advisable to dampen dry food. Sugar beet pulp, steeped in water, should not be overfed. It makes feed palatable and moist but may increase grease in the legs, which needs to be avoided at all costs. A general mineral preparation made for horses should be fed to keep a nutritional balance. It is very important to worm your horse regularly.

It cannot be stressed enough that each horse is different. Feeding regimes are largely a matter of trial and error until you get to know how your horse behaves. The essential point to remember is not to feed your horse an over-abundance of any one type of feed.

Legs, Feet and Body

Long-term Preparation

The horse's legs and feet should be oiled regularly with clear oil (pig oil or pale cooking oil is suitable) and sulphur powder. Weekly is about right, depending on the weather. This treatment keeps the hair growing and the legs free from grease. It also keeps the legs clean, and the white parts snow white. For care and preparation of the hooves see chapter 4 – Farriery for the Working Horse. General regular grooming of the body is important to ensure a healthy-looking coat.

On the Show Day

On the day of the show, different breeds of draught horse are made ready for their classes in recognized different ways, but the beginning is the same – you must get your animal spotlessly clean. If this means shampooing it all over, then do so, making sure it is done in time to allow the body to dry properly.

It may be appropriate to wash him a week beforehand and again once or twice just before show day. This will depend on whether he is kept largely outdoors or indoors and on the other activities he may be involved in. Sometimes you may get away with just washing out the mane and tail, but always shampoo the legs. It is important to use good-quality soap as cheap washing-up liquid or soap flakes do not achieve the lather required to remove the dirt completely. Make sure you wash well underneath the heel hair and get right into the roots, or your horse will not take on the bloom required to get noticed by the judge. After the soap has been rinsed out well it is always best to dry the legs with woodflour or white sawdust. The legs will stay clea-ner if they are dried immediately before showing because if the horse is put into a stall, or even out in the field, he can pick up dye from the bedding or the grass if they are wet (14.2).

When you have finished cleaning your horse decide what you need to do to improve the way he looks. All too often oil is applied to the legs, hoof-head hair is soaped up and so on, more because people feel it is expected than through real necessity. Stand back and look at your horse. Does it need its bones oiled? Does it need its hoof-heads soaped up? If you are unsure or need advice there are always experienced people at the show who will help you. Don't be afraid to ask.

Plaiting Tails and Manes

Plaiting tails and manes is a traditional part of showing a heavy horse (14.3). It takes a little time to learn the skills involved and it is essential to have some help from someone already experienced if you want to produce a competently plaited horse. Methods vary from breed to breed and even within breeds. For guidance on plaiting see chapter 15 – Plaiting a Heavy Horse for Showing.

Preparing for Turnout and Harness Classes

Presentation of a turnout (the name given to a horse harnessed to a vehicle) requires

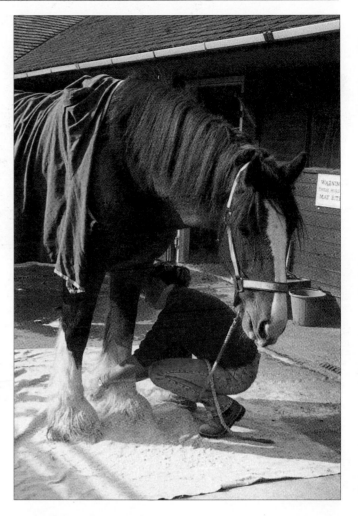

14.2 Preparing the feathered legs of a Shire. After thorough washing, treat the legs with woodflour or white sawdust to dry them and keep them white.

attention to detail, particularly to cleanliness. The horse, harness and vehicle must be as spotless as possible. The top turnouts exhibiting today all reach a very similar standard in this respect, and often the deciding factor is the way in which the horse or horses perform, so to be placed among the top teams in the country you must at least be equal to them in the inspection section of turnout judging. The stand show then becomes a very important element of the judging process (14.4).

Turnout harness must be immaculately clean, not just on the outer surface, but

14.3 The advantages of competent plaiting to the appearance of the horse are plain in this photograph of champion Shire stallion 'Deighton Commodore', owned by P. and W. Bedford.

14.4 A champion single turnout from Bass Museum and Shire Horse Stables.

14.5 A dray, properly dressed with feed bags and water bucket.

most importantly underneath, and this applies to metal work as well as to leather. Whether the metal is brass, nickel or chrome, it still needs to be properly cleaned. Start cleaning your harness as soon as it comes off the horse. This is the easiest time to remove sweat and grime. Then when you are ready to prepare it for a show, the cleaning process is easier. Everyone has their own way of cleaning leather, and you will know whether your finished result is good enough. Be honest with yourself. If it is not up to scratch, try different products or methods.

Harness must be black. If it has a silvery appearance, it needs to be dyed. The leather can be cleaned and fed with black saddle soap or glycerine and a sponge. A good quality black polish should be applied, but not so much as to come off on the horse, and then buffed up severely. Good quality brass cleaner or metal cleaner should be

applied to the brass and chrome fittings. Brass tarnishes very easily and a good showman always touches up his brass just before going into the show ring.

Remember that the harness is made dirty by the horse. If the horse is clean, while you may still have sweat to wipe off, there will be no grime or grease on the harness at all.

Your vehicle, whether a farm waggon, an agricultural implement or a dray, needs to be scrupulously cleaned. Most of the work will have been done in advance of the show day, but there is always dust and dirt to wipe off after the journey to the show-ground. It is important to check that the moving parts are well greased. Small bumps and marks, especially on the wheels, may have to be touched up between shows. When you dress a dray for the show ring, make sure that everything you hang, hook or clip on is securely attached (14.5). Do not give the judge a reason to drop you down a place or two. A dray will require a whip, safety belt and a seat cushion for the driver. You are also required to have a bucket and one nose bag per horse hanging on the back, and three lamps, two on the front of the vehicle and one on the back. If the lamps have wax candles in them, these should have been lit (so that, theoretically, they are easy to relight if necessary).

Types of Class

A wide variety of showing opportunities is available to the potential heavy horse show-man, from local events to major agricultural shows lasting several days. A good starting point is your local show which is ideally suited to helping you find your feet. Here the in-hand classes may incude 'class for heavy horse, any breed', and different types of turnouts may be merged into one class. The atmosphere will generally be one of friendliness and informality.

At a county show, especially those which have developed a reputation for heavy horse classes, it is a rather different world. Here you will be competing against some of the top breeders and top drivers in the country. You should not be daunted however. Everyone has to start somewhere! Generally you will find most of your competitors approachable and, if you demonstrate your willingness to learn, helpful. At these shows typical in-hand classes are held for geldings; mares; mares with foal at foot; barren (called yeld or gast in Scotland) mares; colts; fillies and stallions. Some of these will be sub-divided into different age groups.

There may also be harness and decorated classes for those who want to show their horses off wearing harness but without a vehicle. Harness classes require an immaculate set of harness, but without too much decoration. Decorated harness classes offer a similar opportunity to those who have built up a collection of horse brasses and who enjoy showing their skills at floral or woollen decorations.

At some shows there may be 'best foot'

classes, designed to reward good farriery practice; and classes for young handlers, designed to encourage young people to take an interest in showing heavy horses.

Then there are the turnout classes, divided into trade and agricultural. Trade includes single, pair, and team classes and at some shows the highly specialist unicorn or tandem classes. Agricultural classes are usually divided into single and pair, although some tandems are shown within the pair classes.

To enter classes you must obtain a schedule from the show organiser and there will usually be a small fee. It is important to abide by the closing date for entries. Nothing annoys a show organiser more than someone who expects to be included in a class after this date has passed.

Arrival at the Showground

On the night before the show make sure you have everything you need packed and ready to go. A check list is a good idea until you are well practised. The essentials for a horse and vehicle are: equipment for watering and feeding your horse; grooming kit; plaiting equipment; harness and spares; polishing equipment; spares for the vehicle and appropriate clothing for yourself and your groom in the show ring. Do not forget to consider anything you may need in the event of a horsebox breakdown and any paperwork relating to the show itself.

In the horsebox allow enough ventilation so that the horse does not break into a sweat, as you want him to be in tip-top condition for the show ring. Some people prefer to travel their horse diagonally, with his back facing the cab of the vehicle; others travel them forward facing or backward facing. This enables the horse to use his rump rather than his neck and front legs when the horsebox brakes. This is usually a matter of personal preference. It is not necessary to allow him access to a hay-net during the journey: he can be given some hay half way through a long journey. Again this is a matter of personal preference.

On arrival at the showground you will usually be directed to a designated parking area. The first job is to get your horse out of

the horsebox and give him a hay-net or a feed and take him for a short walk to get him used to the new environment. When he is settled, leaving someone at the horsebox with him, visit the steward on the horsebox lines or the secretary's tent to collect your number ticket and discover the time of your class or classes. The ticket should be attached around your horse's neck or at the base of the collar if he is wearing harness, or alternatively around your arm. On turnouts the ticket should be placed on the nearside of the seat or the vehicle itself.

You should allow two hours preparation time for an in-hand horse, and another hour for cleaning and preparing a vehicle. It may take you half an hour to finally buff up your harness and brasses.

Dress

It is important, no matter what type of horse you are showing, to be tidy and correctly dressed in the show ring. If you are not sure what to wear, speak to the secretary of your breed society, who will be able to tell you what is correct. Some breeds are not as strict as others. Whatever is acceptable to your breed, always be clean, neat and tidy. This definitely helps the overall picture you present when you walk into the show ring with your horse. In trade turnout classes personal livery depends on the type of vehicle you have. Long before you are ready to show, look at turnouts at other shows. It will be easy to see the correct apparel for your particular vehicle. The best time to change is after all your preparation work is over and before you hitch in (14.6 a and b).

Entering the ring

It is essential for the smooth running of the show and for your own peace of mind to find out in good time when you will be required in the ring and where you should go. At larger shows there will be a collecting ring in which you gather while awaiting your class and before the previous class has finished. Keep in touch with the timing of the show as the day proceeds. Sometimes the classes run late. You do not want to have your horses ready too early.

14.6 Immaculately turned out handlers with **a** a Percheron mare and foal, and **b** an agricultural turnout.

14.7 A Shire making its stand show, trotting steadily towards the judge.

Alternatively, you may even find classes are running early! You do not want to have to face a last-minute rush. A calm entry into the ring will prevent the horse becoming unsettled at the vital moment.

For in-hand classes you are allowed a helper in the ring in the north of the country and in Scotland. In the south the handler only enters with the horse. In turnout showing the driver should be accompanied by a groom for each pair of horses. For a single horse one groom is expected.

Once you enter the ring, do as the ring steward asks you. It is always a good idea to watch someone who has been showing for a long time and then you will not go far wrong. Make sure you look closely at the procedure being followed in your class. This can vary from show to show and in different parts of the country.

During the Class

The judging of in-hand and turnout classes varies slightly between the north and south of Britain and sometimes varies according to the methods of different judges. But the essential elements are common to all classes.

The Inspection

In in-hand judging the judge will inspect the horse for good conformation according to breed standards paying special attention to the legs and feet. In harness and turnout classes he will inspect the harness for cleanliness and neatness and in turnout classes he will inspect the vehicle for readiness and cleanliness. In harness and turnout classes the conformation of the animal is less important. In turnout judging if the competitors are very close in their standards the judge may take the appearance and presentation of the horse into greater consideration to assist him in the final decision.

The Stand Show

In in-hand classes each competitor will be expected to perform their individual stand show. The horse is first walked and then trotted in a line away from the judge and then back. Usually he will also expect the horse to be backed a few paces. The horse and owner then return to their place in the line. The same procedure is followed for turnout classes. In harness classes the horses are not expected to trot or back (14.7).

In-hand

In the north, especially in Scotland and Northern Ireland, competitors enter the show ring and either walk round several times and then line up in any order, or line up straight away. The judge watches as each handler carries out his stand show, at the walk and at the trot (14.8). Each animal is closely inspected at this time. After all have been shown and inspected, the judge usually takes a second look at each exhibit while they stand in line. It is at this time that he is making his final decision (14.9). The judge will then pick out the horses in descending order, and then walk them round. This gives him the chance to see them next to each other and compare them to see if his placements are correct. If he feels they are not, he will change the order at this time. The animals are then pulled into line and the places are awarded.

In the south, the exhibits enter the ring, walk round and are then pulled into line in

14.8 American judge Brit McLin judging a class at the National Shire Horse Show.

provisional order. They are inspected individually while standing in the ring, before being pulled in or after each show. After they have completed their individual shows, the animals are walked round in a circle before being pulled into line in the final order.

Turnouts

In trade turnout classes the competitors enter and compete at a trot. In agricultural turnout classes competitors compete at a walk. When preparing to enter the ring, try to follow someone who goes at the same pace as yourself. Do not do anything you do not need to do thinking that you will impress the judge. More often than not, it can work in reverse. When the turnouts are going round the ring waiting to be pulled into line, make sure your groom watches for the steward's nod. It may be your turn next. Never ever pass anyone; this is the height of bad manners. If the person in front is having difficulties, stop. You can always ask them if you can proceed. Safety must always take priority.

In both in-hand and turnout showing first impressions matter. You must be as ready when first entering the ring as you are when doing your stand show later in the class. Try to keep an eye on the judge and

14.9 Concentration, as a judge weighs up the qualities of the animal.

his movements and interest, and react accordingly. If you have turned out yourself, the horse, and if appropriate, the harness and the vehicle to the best of your ability, you can ask for no more. Remember, you are only as good as the next time you turn out, not the last time (14.10).

General Conventions and Etiquette

The traditional methods of showing are tried and tested over many years, and act as a standard to be followed by all those entering the world of showing heavy horses. For each breed there is a different set of conventions to follow and this can cause difficulties when judges are asked to judge different breeds of horse against each other and also when new practices (perhaps from abroad) are in the process of being introduced but are not widely accepted. For example, in the Clydesdale breed, most people turn the horse around themselves,

i.e. to the left (this is most easily seen during the stand show). However, nowadays there are a growing number of Clydesdale owners turning the other way (as in the Shire, Suffolk and Percheron breeds), partly because this is the way it is done in the United States and Canada, where there are many Clydesdales. There are arguments for and against – some maintain it is safer and easier to turn a horse to the left – but generally the Clydesdale 'rule' is simply a matter of tradition. I would not condemn either way. It certainly makes no difference to the quality of the horse, and as such should not come into any decision about where a horse will be placed in a class. However, one should be aware that some judges might expect the traditional conventions to be followed and you should find out what the fixed requirements are in advance and practice at home.

I would like to see more shows recognizing the different breeds in all their variety, to avoid the conventions of one breed being mistakenly applied to others by judges. For

14.10 The highest standards are important in turnout classes. Here Tom Brewster is competing at the East of England Show.

example sometimes entrants are penalized for using the 'wrong' method of plaiting or for turning horses the 'wrong' way. There are also physical distinctions between the breeds which are often not taken into account. For example, Suffolks are often faulted for 'daisy cutting' or not lifting the feet high enough (mainly by Shire or Clydesdale enthusiasts) when in fact they are not expected to pick up their feet in the same way as a high-stepping Clydesdale or Shire would do. It is important for all those interested in the heavy breeds, in and out of the show ring, to take a close look at the qualities of each of the breeds and develop an understanding of the value of different characteristics.

At the end of the day the judge's opinion is final, and how he arrives at that opinion does not come into question. However, do not be afraid to ask a judge where he faulted your horse, and how you could improve your own chances should you meet that judge again in the future.

Looking to the Future

Keep your eyes and ears open. Learn by what you see and hear. Ask around among experienced showmen to find out who would be willing to help you long before your arrival in the show ring. A good horse person is prepared to go on learning until the day they give up.

CHAPTER 15

Plaiting a Heavy Horse for Showing

Whether you plan to show your horse in-hand or in turnout, it is essential to be able to produce a good plait, or braid. Each breed has specific requirements for the plaiting of manes and tails and some breeds share the same methods. There are many variations on the basic theme, with owners adapting the patterns to suit their own situation or experience. This is what makes plaiting-up daunting for the newcomer. The main methods are shown here, and will assist the novice to get started. However, there is no substitute for practice, and the best advice is to find someone experienced to show you the process. After that, practice will make perfect.

Plaiting-up draught horses for the show ring is essentially for decoration. Traditionally tails were put up in a 'working plait' to ensure they did not get caught up in machinery. At parades horsemen all over Britain took pleasure in more decorative plaits for both tails and manes as they competed against each other for best decorated animals.

Today decorating your heavy horse is an integral part of correct presentation at shows (in-hand and turnout), parades and special occasions. It is usual for ploughing matches, although some ploughmen leave manes unplaited for matches.

Different traditions in types of plaiting have grown up for different breeds.

Manes

In Shires, Clydesdales and Percherons the majority of the mane hangs loose while a small proportion of the hair is used within the plait. In Suffolks the whole mane is always included in the plait.

In Clydesdale showing, mares and young stock are not required to be plaited, but it is necessary for colts of 2 years old and upwards. In no other section should manes be plaited, although geldings can be if their owners wish. Plaiting Clydesdale geldings has increased recently, mainly as a result of the increase in turnouts in Scotland. Shires, Suffolks and Percherons all require young stock, mares, geldings and stallions to have their manes plaited.

Tails

Tail decoration is much more varied. It varies from area to area as well as between breeds. There is probably more discussion about what is right and wrong in this field than any other! Deriving from practical necessity, tail preparation has depended on what type of work the horse was doing as well as the type of implement or vehicle he was pulling. Nowadays, however, discussion revolves around whether to clip the dock or not, whether to leave hair hanging naturally, whether to plait the whole tail and whether to use segg plaits (two small raffia plaits standing up at the top) in Clydesdales or a jug handle in Shires.

Clydesdale tails are normally put up in seggs. For horses less than 2 years old tails are left natural, with or without a ribbon. Three-year olds and upwards can have their tails tied up in a bun, although breeding mares can be left natural. Shires should have a 'jug handle' (a ring of plaited raffia) inserted in the tail bun, and their tails are often shown short, even in young stock. Suffolks and Percherons have their tails left long and all the hair plaited in.

In this manual we have restricted ourselves to describing the most usual forms of tail plait.

Materials

Essential equipment for plaiting is -

- A plaiting stool, tall enough to enable you to reach over the horse's mane, and long enough to enable you to 'walk' along it as the mane plait grows longer. Many people make their own; a standard portable workbench from a DIY store can work well
- Grooming brush and comb to prepare the mane and tail hair before starting plaiting
- A three-strand plait (two-strand roller for Clydesdales) for each horse. This can be of raffia alone, raffia enclosed in ribbon, raffia with three ribbons running alongside, or multiple strands of wool, separated into three. A plait should be about 61 cm long for showing a horse in turnout and a little longer for a horse to be shown in-hand (plaits are shorter for turnout horses to allow space for the collar). There should be enough to hang down at the end of the plait and lie against the horse's neck.
- A set of flights (also known as standards or flags) for each horse. A full set can vary between 16 and 20 flights: most of them will be used on a horse shown in-hand (depending on the length of the horse's neck and mane) while some 10-13 flights will be used for a horse shown in turnout (stopping just before the collar). Standards in Clydesdales are normally two colours crossed with raffia between the crosses. Flights are normally tulip-shaped and can be of two or three colours. These can be home-made or obtained from suppliers.

Clydesdale

Cate Brewster

Clydesdale stallions of 2 years or over are plaited for in-hand showing. Geldings may or may not be plaited. Traditionally raffia was used as the roller, and the standards were usually royal blue and white. Nowadays, coloured wool or tape is quite acceptable. Certain colours show off different coloured horses better than others, e.g. blue and white on a grey, or red and white on a bay.

Mane

Foursome Plait

Clydesdale owners use a traditional 'foursome' plait, with a roller divided into two sections and two further sections of mane hair. The plait sits alongside the ridge of the mane, not on top of the ridge as in the Shire.

A foursome plait for a Clydesdale is carried out as follows:

Stage 1. Tie up the horse with his head held high. Comb the mane to the offside. Take up about an inch of hair at the top of the mane, place one half of the roller next to it and take up another inch of hair on the bottom side. N.B. The hair nearest the ears is the 'top', and hair on the other side of the roller is the bottom. The roller on the opposite side from the mane is the top roller, and the roller over the mane is the bottom roller (**15.1.1**).

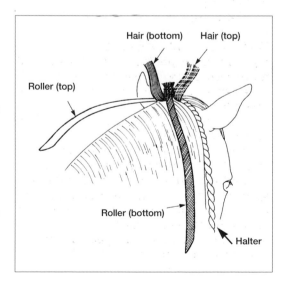

Stage 2. Cross the top hair away from you and the bottom hair towards you, pull tight and hold in one hand (**15.1.2**).

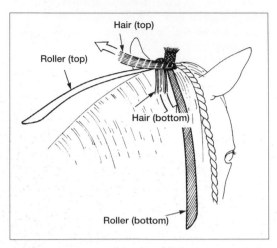

Stage 3. Cross over the bottom roller to the top and the top roller to the bottom, pull tight. Repeat for the required length, remembering that for in-hand showing the plait is taken the full length of the mane, and for harness and turnout showing the plait stops in front of the collar position (**15.1.3**).

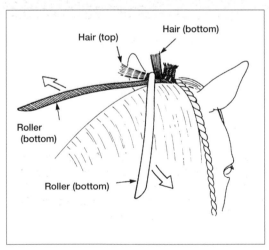

Stage 4. To finish off the plait at the end of the mane continue the method, but without picking up any more hair, then take one section of the roller and wrap the whole plait round and through itself, pulling tight (**15.1.4 and 15.1.5**).

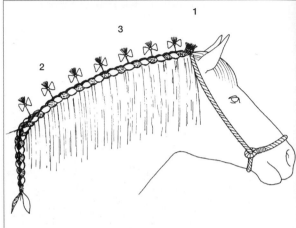

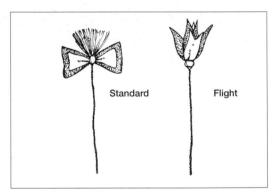

Always use an odd number of standards or flights. Push the wire of the standard or flight through under the plait and wrap it around itself. Put the first flight at the top of the mane, place the second at the bottom of the plait, centre the third, and thereafter divide the rest of the space evenly between the remaining flights (**15.1.6**).

15.1.6 Foursome plait, final stage.

Tail

Clydesdale tails can be decorated using seggs. These are two small raffia plaits worked into the top of the tail, and decorated with small bows. Young stock, mares and stallions with long tails can be decorated with a ribbon tied in a bow round the upper part of the tail. If the tail has been shortened and the dock shaved, the hair can be put up in a bun and decorated with a bow.

Seggs for the tail

Plaiting seggs into the tail can be done by one person, but two people make the job much easier. The second person can hold the plait tight while the first continues with the action of plaiting. The materials required are raffia, about 61 cm long and almost the thickness of a cigarette, small bows and scissors. The procedure is described on the next page.

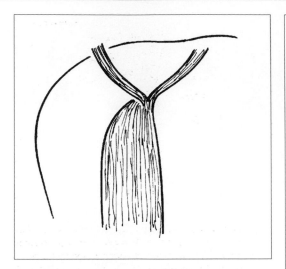

Stage 1. Take up about an inch square of hair at the top right-hand side of the tail. Split this in half, holding half in each hand (**15.2.1**). The rest of the tail hair is not included in the plait.

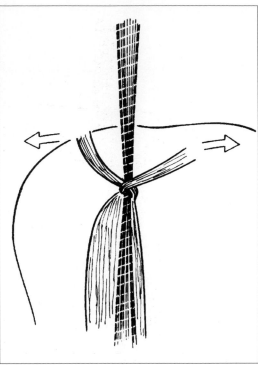

Stage 3. Cross the hair over (horizontally) and pull tight (**15.2.3**). Cross the raffia over (vertically) and pull tight.

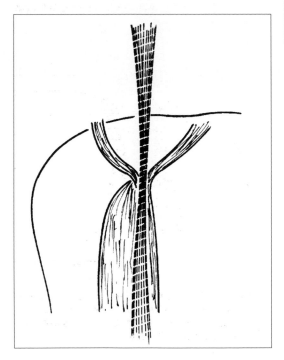

Stage 2. The second person puts the raffia between the divided hair (**15.2.2**).

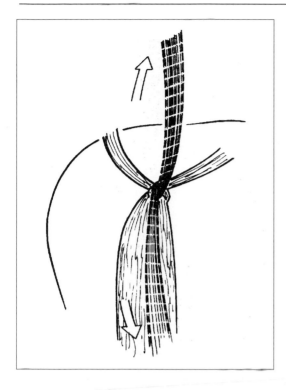

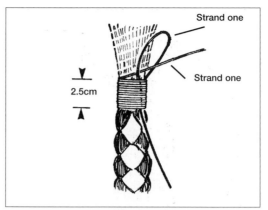

Strand one

2.5cm

Strand one

Stage 4. For the next stage the second person holds both hair and raffia firmly in one hand. The first person selects a strand of raffia and loops it around their little finger. They then take another strand and wrap it round the plait several times, about 2.5 cm in length, finishing at the top. Put the strand through the loop and pull the bottom strand tight (**15.2.5**).

Stage 5. Repeat stages 1-4 to form the left-hand plait.

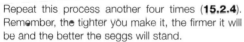

Repeat this process another four times (**15.2.4**). Remember, the tighter you make it, the firmer it will be and the better the seggs will stand.

Remaining tail hair

Stage 6. Trim the top of the raffia. Do not have it too long – level with the rump of the horse is acceptable, but no higher. Decorate by pinning small bows to the wound raffia (**15.2.6**).

Tail bun

A tail bun for a Clydesdale is made as follows:

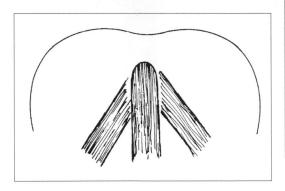

Stage 1. Divide the tail hair into three equal parts (**15.3.1**).

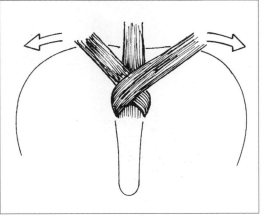

Stage 3. Take the right-hand strand and cross it over the centre strand. Do the same with the left-hand strand (**15.3.3**).

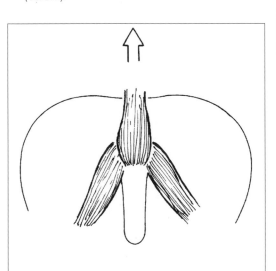

Stage 2. Smooth the centre strand firmly up the tail and over the rump (**15.3.2**).

Stage 4. Do a threesome plait (continuing as above) in an upwards direction, keeping the plait tight at all times. Plait to the end of the tail hair (**15.3.4**).

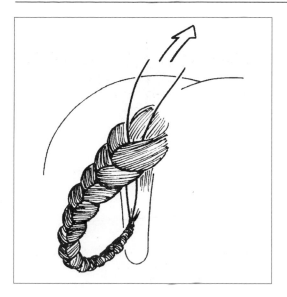

Stage 5. Tie a length of strong string near the end of the plait. Then pass the string and the end of the plait up through the centre base of the plait to form the bun (**15.3.5**).

Stage 6. Hold the bun firmly with one hand, and with the other wind the remainder of the plait and string tightly around the bun. Tie in a triple knot and decorate with a ribbon around the bun tied at the top (**15.3.6**).

Shire

John Peacock

Manes and tails of all Shires shown in-hand and turnout – young stock, mares, geldings and stallions – are plaited up. The most usual Shire tail plait is the bun with jug handle, although others can be seen in the show ring. Shire owners who have left their horse's tails long sometimes prefer to plait the whole tail, as in the Percheron and Suffolk. Here we show the tail bun and jug handle. The full tail plait can be followed in the section for the Percheron later in this chapter.

Mane

The Shire's mane is plaited along the ridge. Small amounts of mane are taken up to anchor the plait in place leaving the majority of the mane hair flowing. The aim is to make the plait as tight as possible with no daylight showing between plait and mane. Flights (also known as flags or standards) are plaited in as you proceed along the plait, not inserted afterwards. There is always an odd number of these. The plait for a horse shown in-hand continues along the full length of the mane, while the plait for a horse shown in turnout stops before the collar. Judicious placing of the flights can enhance the arch of the neck in stallions.

Stage 1. The equipment you will need is a plaiting stool, mane brush and comb, a three-strand plait, in this case raffia with coloured ribbon, although some people use wool, and the flights, which can be bought from suppliers or home-made (**15.4.1**).

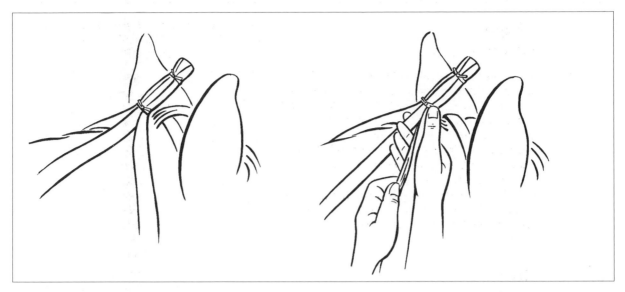

Stage 2. Separate the plait into three and hold it firmly behind the horse's ears. With this first part of the plait it is essential to keep it tight against the horse – a loose start can never be overcome! (**15.4.2**)

With the left hand pick up a small amount of hair and place it In the right hand with and underneath the right-hand section of the plait. Anchor it firmly under the right thumb and tightly against the horse's neck, using the index finger to support it. It is essential to hide the hair beneath the plait, as no hair should be seen in the finished plait (**15.4.3**).

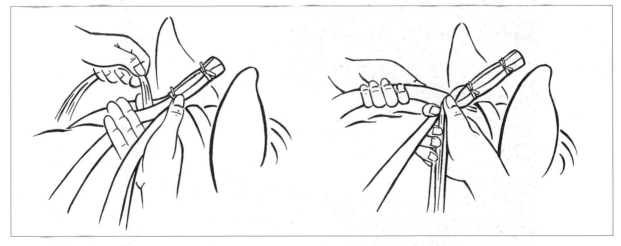

Take another small amount of hair from the ridge of the mane with the left hand and the second section of the plait above it and hold it between the right thumb and index finger (the right-hand section is now supported by the remaining three fingers still held tightly against the horse's neck). This second section becomes the 'centre' strand of the plait (**15.4.4**).

With the left hand take a third amount of hair and the third (left-hand) section of the plait and hold it beneath the left thumb.
Then bring the left-hand section over the centre strand and the right-hand (and first) section over the left-hand section. All three are now crossed in together to make the first part of the plait (**15.4.5**).

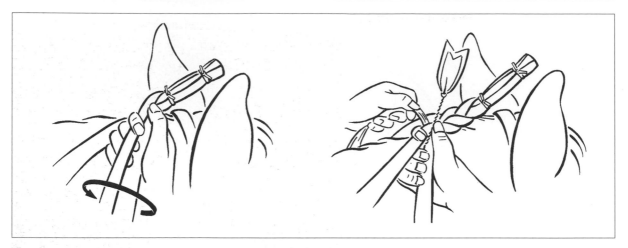

Hold this in the left hand and begin the second part of the plait by taking up a small amount of hair and folding it beneath the plait closest to it. Holding the plait in the right hand take a further amount of hair and fold it under the plait closest to it and so on, along the length of the plait (**15.4.6**).

At all times keep the plait and your hand as close to the neck as possible keeping a firm hold with the left or right hand and thumbs whilst working with the other hand.

Stage 3. Every third, or if you prefer second, plait insert a flight, laying the wire along the section of plait you have just completed with the end of the wire in the palm of your right hand. Hold it in position with your thumb along with the plait. The length of wire gets plaited in as you continue the plaiting. Leave about one and a half inches of wire and the ribbon top showing above the plait (**15.4.7** – **15.4.9**).

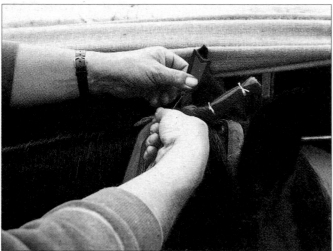

15.4.7

15.4.8

Stage 3 contd. **15.4.9**

Stage 4. Continue in this way along the ridge of the mane (**15.4.10**).

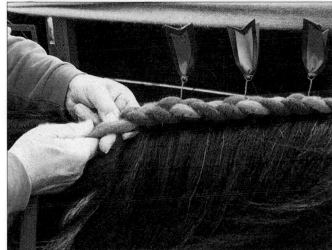

Stage 5. At the end of the plait, fold one piece of ribbon through the other two to tie off (**15.4.11**).

Stage 6. When complete, the plait should lie along the ridge in a straight line, just tailing off at the end. Make sure the flights are all standing up (**15.4.12** and **15.4.13**).

15.4.12

15.4.13 ▼

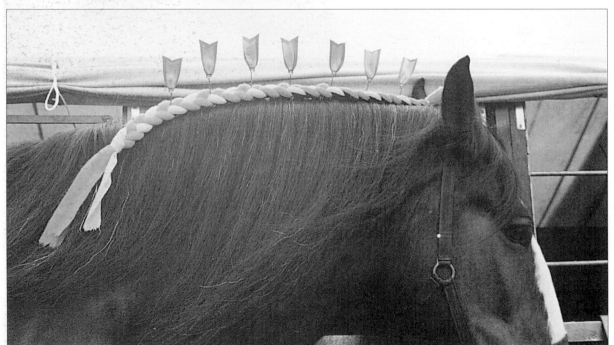

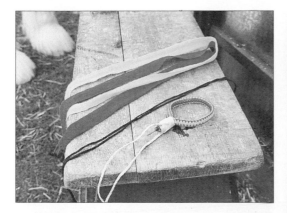

15.5.1 ▲

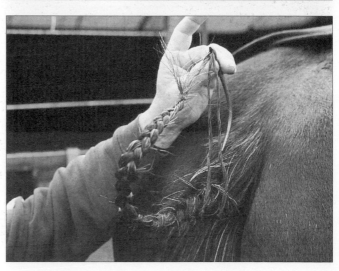

15.5.2 ▶

Tail

The equipment you will need for a tail bun is two pieces of coloured ribbon, a bootlace and a 'jug handle' (**15.5.1**).

Stage 1. Separate the top section of the tail into three strands (**15.5.2**).

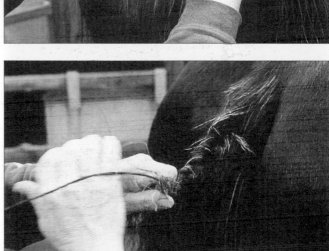

15.5.3 ▶

Stage 2. Plait the strands together (using a simple threesome plait), inserting the boot lace after about 4 inches of plaiting: the boot lace should be laid across the plait with the two ends dangling either side and plaited in from that point (**15.5.3**).

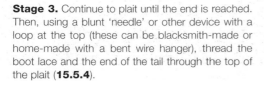

15.5.4 ▶

Stage 3. Continue to plait until the end is reached. Then, using a blunt 'needle' or other device with a loop at the top (these can be blacksmith-made or home-made with a bent wire hanger), thread the boot lace and the end of the tail through the top of the plait (**15.5.4**).

15.5.5 ▶

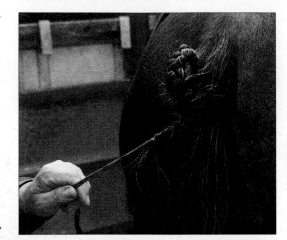

Stage 4. Pull tight and wind the end of the plait round the bun that has formed until you can use the boot lace to tie it off (**15.5.5** and **15.5.6**).

Stage 5. Insert the jug handle and tie it around the bun (**15.5.7** and **15.5.8**).

15.5.8 ▼

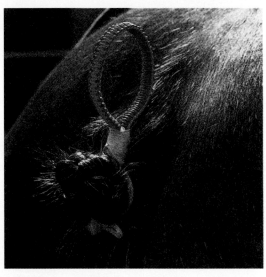

15.5.6 ▼

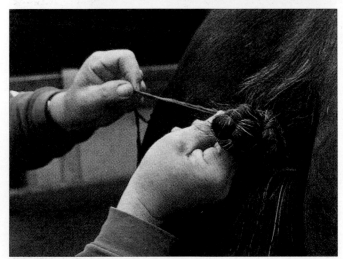

Stage 6. Tie a ribbon around the bun and the jug handle to finish (**15.5.9**). ▼

15.5.7 ▼

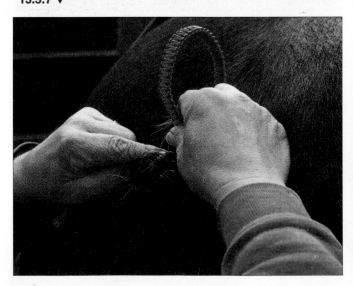

Suffolk

Norma Bradley

When braiding up a Suffolk all the hair is included in both mane and tail plait, with none left free when the plait is finished. This enhances the natural flowing lines of this breed. Naturally coloured raffia (also known as bass) is traditionally used. In the mane plait bows are inserted between the mane hair and the raffia plait using a piece of wire with a loop for decoration. Some owners use flights, as with the Shire and Percheron. The tail plait is the same as with the Percheron and the Shire if a full plait is used.

Mane

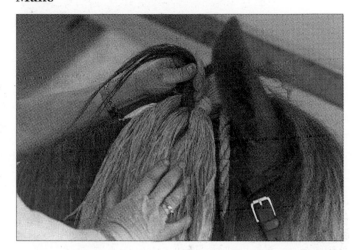

Stage 1. Separate the raffia into three, and holding it firmly just behind the ears and at the side of the ridge of the mane, take two pieces of mane hair and tie them around the centre section of raffia to anchor it. Start the plait, a simple threesome plait, plaiting the mane hair in beneath each section of raffia (**15.6.1**).

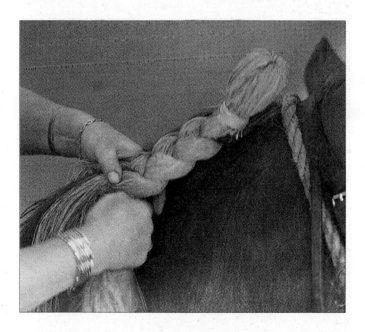

Stage 2. Continue down the neck. No mane hair should be visible along the length of the raffia plait (**15.6.2**).

Stage 3. Continue the plait all down the neck for in-hand showing, and to the collar position for turnout showing. Tie off at the end, leaving a short piece of raffia which will need to be trimmed (**15.6.3**).

Stage 4. When the plait is finished the raffia should lie just below the ridge of the mane at eye level. Flights or bows are used to decorate the plait. Flights are always incorporated into the plait as you go, as with the Shire. Bows are inserted after the plait is completed, as seen here. Thread coloured ribbons through the hair within the plait using a piece of folded wire with a loop at the head, like a needle. The ribbons are tied around the sections of mane where they enter the raffia plait (**15.6.4**).

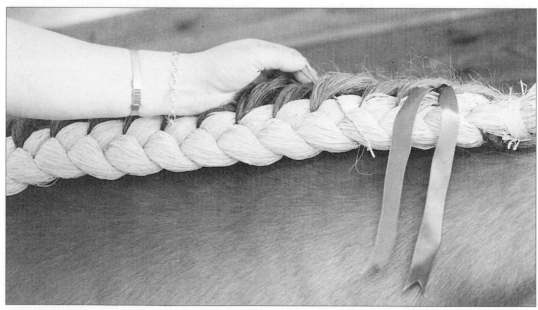

Stage 5. The finished plait (**15.6.5**). A small section of hair is sometimes left to lie along the ridge at the very end. This enables the end of the plait with its bow of raffia to sit neatly against the offside of the horse's neck.

Tail

The same method is used as for the British Percheron – see below.

British Percheron
Matthew Bradley

The mane of the Percheron is plaited in the same way as that of the Shire in this country (see the Shire section for instructions). However, the tail is plaited in full, as it is for the Suffolk. Some Shire owners who prefer to leave their horse with a full tail also use this plait. To plait a Percheron tail, follow the procedures listed over the page.

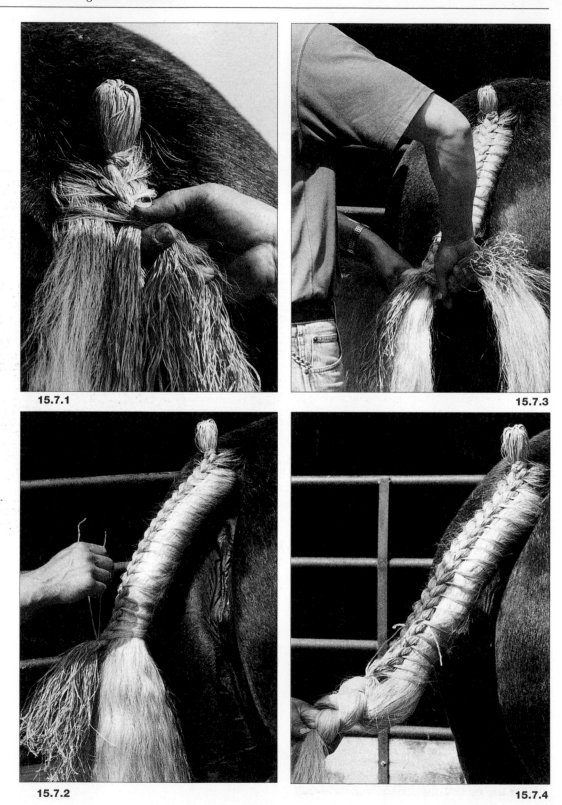

15.7.1

15.7.3

15.7.2

15.7.4

Tail

Stage 1. Divide the raffia into three, and holding it firmly at the base of the tail, start plaiting in small sections of the tail hair drawn from either side of the tail. In the same way as with the Shire mane plait, keep the hair beneath the raffia. Make sure that the hair comes from the junction of the hair with the skin of the tail dock. This will ensure a tight neat plait (**15.7.1**).

Stage 2 and 3. Continue in this way down the tail to 6 inches below the end of the dock, keeping the plait as tight as possible. Tie off the raffia plait at the end of the dock (**15.7.2**).

Stage 4. Separate the remaining raffia and the rest of the tail hair into three sections (**15.7.3**).

Stage 5. Plait the rest of the tail, folding the raffia into the hair so that it is not seen (**15.7.4**).

Stage 6. Continue to the end of the tail and tie off. Then roll up the plaited tail as tightly as possible and fold against the first section of the plait by the dock (**15.7.5**).

Stage 7. Thread coloured ribbons into the plait for decoration, perhaps two or three, and tie in bows (**15.7.6** and **15.7.7**).

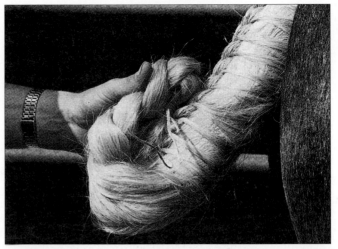

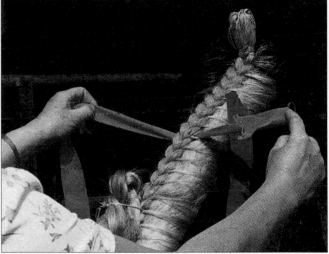

15.7.5

15.7.6

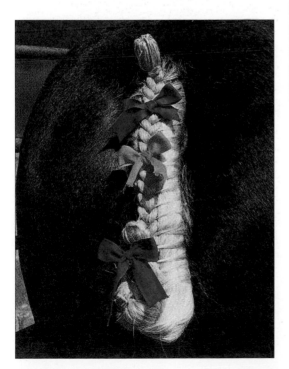

Glossary

Braid/braiding up – another term for plait/plaiting up.

Flights – also known as flags or standards, two or sometimes three small coloured shapes of ribbon bound together and attached to wire to be inserted into the horse's mane or tail plait for decoration. Experienced showmen can enhance the quality of the horse through their positioning of the flights.

Jug handle – a ring of plaited raffia stiffened by wire, pre-prepared or ready-bought and inserted into the top of a Shire tail bun.

Plait – the mane plait itself (called **roller** in Scotland), bound together tightly at one end, the rest to be divided into two. The plait can be made of raffia alone, raffia enclosed in ribbon, raffia with three ribbons running alongside, or multiple strands of wool, separated into three. It should be 61 cm long for a horse shown in turnout, and a little longer for a horse shown in-hand. There should be enough to hang down at the end of the plait and lie against the horse's neck. The word plait is used to describe the raffia/wool used to plait into the mane and also the finished plait incorporating the mane hair.

Seggs – in plaiting Clydesdale tails, two small raffia plaits standing up at the base (top) of the tail. Is sometimes used on Shires.

Foursome – word used to describe the traditional Clydesdale mane plait in which two strands of the roller and two sections of hair are used along the length of the plait.

CHAPTER 16

Road Driving

John Peacock

If you own a heavy horse or horses, whether for driving or for working on the land it is essential that you are fully competent to take them out on the road in a vehicle. This chapter takes you through the various procedures and methods you need to adopt to make driving on the roads enjoyable and safe.

There are more people driving horse-drawn vehicles on the road today than there have been for very many years. It is therefore essential to prepare carefully, follow certain safety procedures and be aware of other road users. Many motorists have no experience of horse-drawn vehicles. However, there is no reason why horse-drawn vehicles should not be used safely on our busy roads (16.1).

There is a wide range of horse-drawn vehicles suitable for road use, from farm carts and waggons, to four-wheel trolleys and drays, to driving trials vehicles and exercise carts. Essentially they fall into two categories – two-wheeled vehicles and four-wheeled vehicles.

General Safety

Anyone driving horses on the public roads should know and observe the Highway Code. The golden rule is always be aware of other road users and make sure they know exactly what your intentions are by giving clear and precise signals. It is not sufficient to just put out your arm; you must look and make sure that all pedestrians, cyclists and motorists have seen and know what your intentions are.

It is important that your vehicle is in good condition. If you have a four-wheeled vehicle make sure that the fifth wheel, or turntable, is always kept well greased. Brakes, if fitted, should be in good working order. Make sure that the shafts or pole and splinter bar are sound. If you have a two-wheeled vehicle it should be well balanced.

Regardless of your type of vehicle, it is essential that you can be seen by other road users at all times. Red reflectors should be fitted to the rear of the vehicle, and for any night work it is of course necessary by law to have lamps or lights that you know are operational. The requirement is for two lamps on the front and one on the offside rear of the vehicle. Anyone doing a lot of night driving is strongly recommended to have two rear lamps (16.2).

Before even attempting to go out on busy roads or to any event attended by the public, it is very important to have your horse or horses well prepared. Firstly, I would suggest many hours of work long-reining, and schooling them to follow basic commands and, more importantly, to be patient. A horse that has to stand for a long time at any event should not get impatient or fidgety. Secondly, always have good experienced help when working young horses, particularly when putting in inexperienced horses for the first time: someone who does not flap, knows the horses well and can handle any difficult situation that may arise competently and safely. For further details about training horses and horsemen see chapter 5 – Training for Horsemen, and chapter 6 – Training for the Horse.

16.1 Driving a pair of horses on today's busy roads.

Vehicle Checks

There are a number of basic checks that should be carried out on a regular basis before any vehicle or carriage is taken onto the public highway. All vehicles must be in sound condition. This applies to old traditional vehicles as well as more modern ones. Regular maintenance will ensure that your vehicle is safe. For further details and illustrations see chapter 17 – Caring for Horse-drawn Vehicles and the useful information section at the end of the book.

Wheels

Wooden wheels need to have tight joints into the hubs and felloes. Never let any wooden component dry out. Iron tyres should be tight, as should any steel rims or clinchers on felloes with tight-fitting rubbers. Pneumatic tyres should have no deep cuts and a reasonable amount of tread on them, spread evenly over the tyre. With new modern steel vehicles, check the welding on all the joints. For help with any of these problems contact your local wheelwright.

Balance

With two-wheeled vehicles, whether tumbril carts or those for private carriage, balance is essential, and on most load-carrying carts it is important to be accurate with the loading, ensuring that it is well distributed. Always start your loading pattern from the front end of a vehicle. If anything your load should be front-end heavy, with the weight taken firmly on the horse's back. With any private driving vehicles you must check that the sliding balance on the seats is working. With four-wheeled carts, waggons or passenger-carrying vehicles, you need to know the extent of the lock on the turntable. This is necessary because too sharp a turn with a restricted lock could lead to the vehicle turning over. Ensure that the turntable and centre pin are regularly inspected and kept well greased.

16.2 One of the two front lamps required by law for driving after dark. A lamp is also required on the back of the vehicle – having two is an even safer option.

Brakes

With traditional braking systems (a block with a rubber or leather lining which is forced against the tyre when the driver operates the brake handle) check regularly for worn or damaged blocks and any excessive play or wear to the linkage. With vehicles using hydraulic brakes, checks for low fluid levels and leaks and any worn pads must be undertaken regularly. Remember that whatever braking system you have it should only be used for slowing or stopping the vehicle, and certainly not to stop the horses.

Poles, Shafts and Seat Belts

On single-horse vehicles the shafts need to be checked for thickness and strength for the intended job. Working shafts must be strong and sound; they can wear at the point where the breeching chains may rub. Some vehicles have a brass covering over the shafts at this point. Shaft hooks and staples should be in good condition and the hooks should be able to slide on the staples. On lighter vehicles, tug stops and breeching staples need to be well fixed and sound. With pair or team vehicles, the pole and splinter bar or the double shafts should be checked for any splits, cracks or wear, as a lot of strain is taken on these parts, especially when the vehicle is being used on rough or uneven ground. Seat belts must be in good order. Sometimes known as 'dicky straps' they are highly recommended for a vehicle driven from a high seat. They should be fixed at one side of the seat and do up with a buckle at the front or a clip onto the other side of the seat.

Harness

The type of harness used depends on the type of work you are intending to do. It is important for all harness to be well maintained and in a strong and sound condition. Never neglect harness; always put it away clean and make regular checks to the stitching and leather to satisfy yourself that it is in the best condition possible. This way, any repairs can be carried out in good time, rather than just before you need to harness up. For more information and illustrations of different types of harness see chapter 7 – Harness for the Working

Horse and the useful information section at the end of the book.

Bridle

Starting from the front, the bridle should be adjusted so that the horse's eye comes half way up the blinker to prevent the horse being able to see over, under or behind it.

Bits

The most popular bit for road driving is the Liverpool, which gives the option of a rough or smooth side; curb chain, to give greater control; and a choice of rein position from plain cheek to bar or bottom bar, although the latter should only be used with extreme caution. These three alternatives enable you to have increasing control, depending on the nature of the horse. Plain cheek is ideal for use on a horse with a 'soft mouth' and a willing disposition. Many drivers use the bar to give slightly more control. The bottom bar is for use with a potentially difficult horse (16.3).There are many other types of bits, and if your horse or horses are used to one of the more severe agricultural bits, then these are also acceptable for driving on the roads.

Collar

As all the pulling of the load is done through the collar, it is very important to have one which fits well. One of the most common causes of sore shoulders is collars that are too big rather than (as many people think) too small. The collar should lay at the same angle as the shoulder, with just enough room for a flat hand between the collar and the horse at the bottom, and for the finger tips at the sides. This is to prevent the horse's airway being restricted when working. The hames need to lay as deep as possible into the collar forewale. For pair and team driving, it is advisable to have safety straps fitted round the bottom of the collars to prevent the hames being pulled out of position. This guards against problems associated with sideways pull when driving any pair or team. It is not necessary with a single horse.

Remaining Harness

With the rest of the harness, be it for singles or pairs, remember that its prime function is either to hold up the shafts for single work, or to hold up the traces for pair work. Therefore it is important that the adjustments of the tug chains keep the ridger chain in a vertical position. Likewise, the carrying straps on the pair pads should be in an absolutely vertical position when the horses are in draught.

Breeching

Care needs to be taken when fitting breeching. If fitted too high, it could ride up under the horse's tail, and not only will it not function properly, it could set the horse kicking. If it is set too low, it could take the horse's legs from under him when descending a steep hill with a load. The position of the horse in the shafts or on the pole is all-important to prevent the vehicle hitting the horse on the hocks, but the horse should not be so far out that the shafts could get behind the collar when the vehicle is turning.

Preparation for Hitching In

Before hitching in horses, you must always make sure that they have been well groomed, their feet and shoes have been checked for wear and tightness and the harness fitted correctly. You also need to ensure that all ridger chains, pole chains or straps are on the vehicle, along with seat cushions, whip and dicky (box) seat strap or chain. Have any hat, coat, gloves and driving apron that will be needed on the vehicle or close to hand ready to put on. In short, all equipment needed has to be ready and at hand, so that the last thing you think about is putting the horses to the vehicle. This way the horses are not left for a long while whilst hitched to the vehicle. When taking the horse or horses to the vehicle, it is always advisable to have an assistant if possible.

16.3   Adjusting a bridle, complete with Liverpool bit.

Hitching In

Single

With a single horse, the safest method of putting the horse into the shafts (hitching in) is as follows. Position the horse (this will depend upon the type of vehicle or yard practice). The important thing is to have control of the horse at all times. A helper to hold the horse can be useful. It is important also to ensure that the horse does

16.4 A pair of horses correctly hitched to a dray.

not tread on the shafts as this will damage them. The sequence of hitching will be appropriate to the type of harness used, but whether the shafts are on the ground or in the air it is very important to attach the tug chains before the breeching chains. The sequence is: nearside tug chain first, then offside tug chain, offside breeching chain, belly band. The ridger chain will be in position if the shafts were in the air, as it is always attached to both shafts first in that situation. If the shafts were on the ground the ridger should be attached to the nearside shaft before lifting the shaft and after fitting the nearside tug chain (always first). The ridger is laid across the cart saddle or pad and fitted to the other shaft on the offside after the offside tug chain has been secured. The ridger chain needs to be

checked and adjusted. If it is too long it will drop the shafts too low, putting too much weight on the horse's back, or worse still, carry the shafts by the tug chains. If the ridger chain is too short, everything will be unbalanced and the shafts could foul the tug hooks. It is also absolutely necessary to have a wanty (belly-band) to prevent the shafts lifting up with an unbalanced load. The reins are always attached to the bit and secured over the hame before hitching in. Before mounting or moving off always stand the horse up into his collar and check the harness is correctly secured and fitted.

Pairs

The sequence for hitching a pair of horses is as follows. Position the horses to the pole and attach pole chains or straps first. Then attach the coupling reins. Next attach the outside trace of the nearside horse, followed by the inside trace. Then walk round to the

16.5a and **b** Hame safety straps and quick-release locks on the pole.

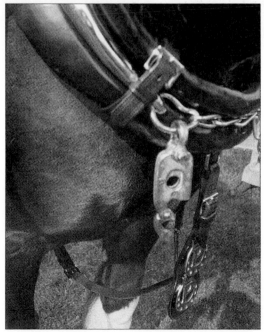

other side and attach the outside trace of the offside horse, followed by the inside trace. Then throw the offside driving rein over to the nearside. Make sure they are not twisted and buckle both reins together. Be careful to check that all the traces are of appropriate length by standing the horses up into the collar – moving the horses forward a pace or two to allow the harness to 'settle' into the correct driving position (16.4).

The type of pole lock also needs careful thought, because should one of a pair be unfortunate enough to go down, it is necessary to be able to free that horse from the pole head quickly. I would recommend whenever possible the use of quick-release locks, e.g. Shepherd's locks (16.5a and b).

16.6 The correct way to mount a road vehicle.

Driving

Correct Mounting

Take the reins from the nearside hame where they were stored during hitching in. Keeping the reins in your hands during mounting ensure that you have contact with the horse(s) and can take action if they suddenly move. If the vehicle has steps use these to climb into the vehicle or up into the seat if there is one. Always use steps in preference to climbing in via the wheel itself. In some vehicles there is no alternative however. Either way it is essential not to get between the horse(s) and the front of the vehicle (16.6).

Holding the Reins

It is essential to be able to signal to other road users, and to do this you need to be able to drive with the reins in one hand. The correct way is to hold the reins in your left hand, leaving the right hand to hold the whip and to signal (16.7).

Turning

When turning check that the road is clear of vehicles and pedestrians in front and behind; make sure you have adequate turning space and complete the manoeuvre positively (16.8).

Reversing

When it comes to backing or reversing into a confined space, e.g. a loading bay, dung heap, shed or gateway, I believe the best and safest way is to dismount from the vehicle, make sure that the reins are stored appropriately, check that the pathway behind is clear, go to the horse's head and face the way you wish to reverse, and then push the horse(s) back. From this position it is easier to see and steer into a confined space, and it is much kinder on the horses' mouths than pulling them back from the vehicle (16.9).

Tackling Steep Hills

If they are being used, bearing reins (used to prevent the horse lowering his head) should be slackened off before attempting to take a load up a steep hill. This enables the horse to put the required effort into the pull: he needs his head, neck and chest muscles to be unfettered for this action.

After Your Drive

After your drive it is important to park your vehicle and unhitch your horses correctly. Use almost the reverse procedure as for hitching in. Unbuckle the reins, throw the offside rein over, secure first the nearside rein and then the offside rein. Take the inside trace off the offside horse and secure; then take off the outside trace and secure.

Repeat the procedure with the nearside horse. Uncouple the reins. Lastly, undo the pole chains or straps. When both horses are free from the vehicle, take care not to snag any chains or harness when leading them away from the pole.

When unharnessed the horses should be returned to their stables or stalls and checked for any harness rubs. If they are hot or sweaty they should be cooled or sponged off and lightly rugged. This is also a good time to make sure they have not picked up anything in their feet. A few moments spent caring for the horses now could prevent bigger problems later on.

Driving Assessment

For anyone driving or intending to drive on the highway, it is strongly recommended that they take the Road Driving Assessment. This has been developed by the Heavy Horse Training Committee under the administration of the British Horse Society. It is approved by the British Driving Society, and more importantly by the Department of Transport, which has recently issued a Code of Practice for Horse-Drawn Vehicles.

The Road Driving Assessment is a free-standing part of the National Vocational Qualification (NVQ) for employment at level 2 for a single horse, at level 3 for a pair of horses, and at level 4 for a team of horses. The test can be carried out in a rural or urban environment, and certificates are worded accordingly.

The following tasks are included in the practical part of the Road Driving Assessment: preparing horses before harnessing, harnessing, hitching in, picking up the reins and mounting the vehicle, keeping the horses under control with the reins and voice commands. You will be expected to carry out the following standard operations:

1. Drive along the road for approximately a quarter of a mile, start and stop and change pace when appropriate. Check that the road is clear of vehicles and pedestrians. Be in control of the horse(s) at all times (no slack reins). There must

16.7 The correct way to hold the reins.

be a smooth start at walk, and reins must be handled appropriately.
2. Turn at junctions (a) with the traffic and (b) against the traffic. Check that the road is clear of vehicles and pedestrians both in front and behind. Ensure that you have adequate turning space, and then take up a nearside position on the road after the turn.
3. Pass a stationary vehicle. Check that the road in front and behind is clear of vehicles and pedestrians. Signal with the hand or whip. Stop or slow down as required. Proceed smoothly. Take up a nearside position on the road after the manoeuvre.

16.8 Preparing to make a right turn.

16.9 Reversing your horses and vehicle from the ground.

4. Operations at roundabouts. Signal with the hand or whip both when entering and when leaving the roundabout. Take up position in the appropriate lane, and proceed smoothly. Use the reins and voice commands as required.

5. Tight turns. Should you need to make a very tight turn or turn through a semi-circle, check that the road is clear. Also observe the limitations of lock on four-wheeled vehicles.

As part of the Road Driving Assessment, the candidate will also be required to answer questions specifically relating to driving horses. There are six to eight mandatory questions (depending on the assessment being taken) which must be answered correctly. The candidate will also be asked 10 other questions from a list of 60–80 possibilities.

A sample of these questions is given below.

Q. Why do you always attach pole chains or straps before traces when putting to, or vice versa when unhitching?

A. To prevent the horse moving away from the pole when attaching the traces, and to prevent the vehicle running forward and hitting the horse.

Q. Why do you never drive a horse with a slack rein?

A. Because then you would not have proper control of the horse. This is a prosecutable offence.

Q. When a horse is holding the vehicle back, what should one check?

A. That his hocks are clear of the vehicle.

Q. Why is it unwise to trot a horse and cart downhill?

A. A heavy vehicle can quickly gain momentum and start pushing the horse, causing it to slip and lose its footing.

Q. When should you allow a horse to speed up?

A. At the foot of a hill, so it can gain momentum to crest the brow.

Q. What precautions should you take when carrying passengers in carts and waggons or any other passenger-carrying vehicle?

A. The driver should get on first and get off last. Do not let passengers ride on loads of bales or any loose materials when travelling up, down or across steep ground, or where they are liable to be struck by tree branches etc.

Q. Does the Highway Code apply to horse-drawn vehicles?

A. Yes, it applies to all road users.

Anyone applying to take the Road Driving Assessment will be given a full list of practical tasks to be undertaken, and also a list of questions and answers which the examiner may ask. The entire test takes about 2 hours.

More information can be obtained by contacting one of the assessors direct, or the training department of the British Horse Society at Stoneleigh, Warwickshire. See the useful addresses section at the back of the book.

Glossary

Blinker – squarish piece of leather attached to the bridle at the position of the horse's eye to prevent him from distraction from vehicles and other activities around him. Not considered necessary by all horsemen, the blinker is nonetheless a traditional part of English harness.

Clincher – metal sections used to clamp *felloes* of wheels to their tight-fitting rubber tyres.

Long-reining – a common way of exercising and training all horses, this involves a horse on a very long single rein being put through his paces in a circle around the horseman.

Hitching in – the act of harnessing a draught horse to a vehicle or implement: also known as *putting to*, although this term is usually used in connection with *private driving*.

Pole lock – lock used to attach pole straps to the pole in pair or team driving. Quick-release locks, such as Sheherd's locks are recommended.

Private driving – driving a horse for pleasure, this is a term usually applied to light horses driven in gigs and carriages.

Standing – as in 'standing a horse up' into his collar and harness: the horse is told to step forward a pace or two to allow the harness to settle and the horseman to check that all is correctly adjusted in relation to the vehicle.

Tumbril – a two-wheeled cart, usually of the tipping variety.

Turntable – or fifth wheel: the mechanism which allows the front axle of a horse-drawn vehicle to turn.

CHAPTER 17

Caring for Horse-drawn Vehicles

Mike Horler

Introduction

Traditionally made horse-drawn vehicles need to be cared for and maintained with thought to ensure their longevity and keep repair and restoration costs to a minimum. If you can spot potential problems before they threaten your purse, or even the future of the vehicle, it is an enormous help.

Wooden wheels

Illustration 17.1 shows the main problems which can occur with wooden wheels; in particular watch out for loose bonds (the steel rims around the outside of the wheel). Other things to look for are: cracks in the paintwork over the joints between the felloes (the wooden section around the edge of the wheel); cracks in the paint where the spokes meet the stocks or hubs (the centre of the wheel); decayed timber immediately under the bond; loose felloes. With your hand on top of the wheel and with the wheel on the axle, rock the wheel and look for movement where the spokes meet the stocks.

Look for woodworm or decayed timber in the spokes, in particular at the top where the spokes meet the felloes. Look out for splits in the stocks. If they run from front to back the vehicle may be structurally unsound; these splits are called shakes. They occur when the timber dries out. The stock bonds prevent the stock from splitting right through. However, beware of large splits as these retain moisture and can cause rotting later.

If your wheel is a Warner type, i.e. all the spokes are fitted into the stock in line rather than staggered, the spokes are fitted through a metal bond, which is fitted around the stock (17.2). This is called a cage. If the stock shrinks this cage becomes loose. A sign of this is paint cracking around the edge of the cage, about three-quarters of an inch either side of the spokes.

Some people are of the opinion that if your wheel bonds are loose, they can be tightened by soaking with water and this will cure the problem. I am afraid that this is not the case – soaking will only expand the wooden felloes to tighten the bond, and after a few days they will be as loose as ever. Also, continued soaking will result in timber decay.

The only cure for loose bonds is to remove the bonds, cut out a section of the bond, reweld and refit. This is best undertaken by a wheelwright or blacksmith who has a bonding plate and the necessary knowledge. When the bond is fitted, if the heat from the hot bond causes the timber felloes to catch fire, ash will build up under the bond when it cools. Then when the wheel trundles along the road, this ash will fall out and the bond will come loose again. Experience is also required to judge how much metal to take out of the bond, as this determines the amount of dish on the wheel. The smaller the bond the greater the dish. The purpose of the dish is to take the strain.

If the spokes move in the stock, but there is no sign of movement in the joints of the felloes, this means that either the stock has

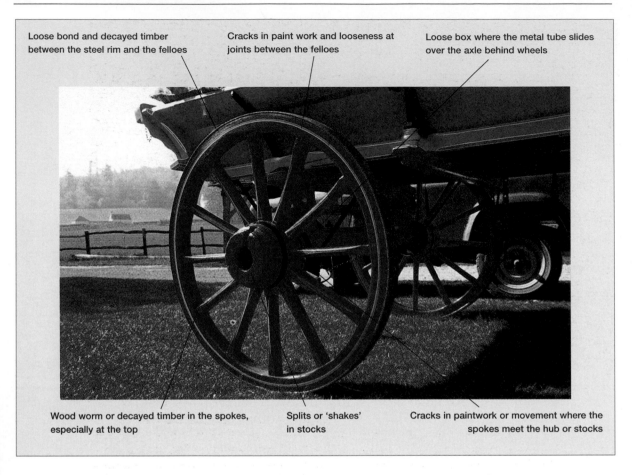

Loose bond and decayed timber between the steel rim and the felloes

Cracks in paint work and looseness at joints between the felloes

Loose box where the metal tube slides over the axle behind wheels

Wood worm or decayed timber in the spokes, especially at the top

Splits or 'shakes' in stocks

Cracks in paintwork or movement where the spokes meet the hub or stocks

17.1 (above) Signs of wear and tear on a wooden wheel.

17.2 (below) Two types of wheel stock, left the English type, and right, the continental or Warner type.

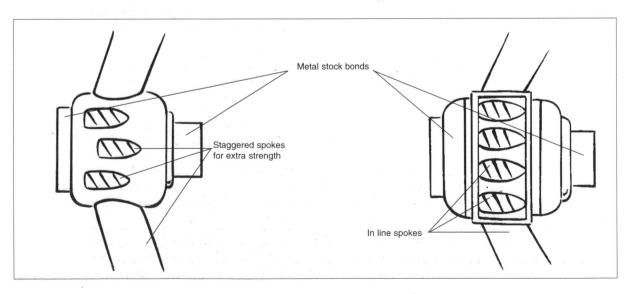

Metal stock bonds

Staggered spokes for extra strength

In line spokes

17.3   Shaft connecting bar on a Sussex waggon.

shrunk, i.e. the timber was not seasoned enough when the stock was fitted, or there was not enough joint between the felloes when the bond was fitted. Again this is a job for an experienced wheelwright. If a new stock is required, then the whole wheel will have to be dismantled to allow it to be fitted.

While inspecting the stock, look at the box (the metal tube that runs through the stock that slides over the axle, acting as a bearing). This box is held into the stock with wooden wedges at the inside and outside. Make sure these are not loose.

Shafts

Waggons are often found without shafts because when the waggons were stored after being used for the last time, the shafts were often stored above the roof purlins of the barn for safe keeping and to prevent them being driven over. Unfortunately, woodworm (*Anobium punctatum*) in the softwood roof timbers very often attacked

the shafts, so that they were of no further use.

Make sure the shafts are the right size as well as the correct design to fit the waggon. Often the wrong design of shafts has been fitted to waggons. I have even seen elevator shafts fitted. This is dangerous, because this design is not strong enough for a waggon, being built of much smaller-section timber.

There are two basic designs for the connection between the shaft and the waggon.

1. The type which allows the two main shaft side-members to run past the outside of the turntable of the waggon with holes bored through them to line up with holes bored through the outside members of the turntable. The holes are for the shaft connecting bar to be threaded through to connect the shafts to the waggon. This is a very vulnerable point, and care should be taken to look out for rot or splits in the timber and enlargement of the holes. Also, inspect the iron connecting bar for rust where it fits through the holes in the timber, as I have often found that rust attacks at this

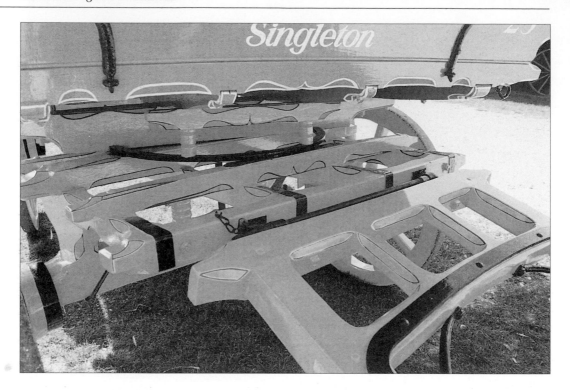

17.4 Eyelet-type connection between the shafts and the front of the turntable of the waggon.

point causing the bar to become thin and therefore dangerous. Make sure that the bar is the correct diameter and length to fit the shafts (17.3).

2. The more common type has metal eyelets fitted to the shafts and eyelets fitted to the front of the turntable. Again, look for movement of the eyelets where they are bolted through the shafts and turntable. Also make sure that the eyelets line up. There should be no more than half an inch gap between the eyelets on the shafts and the eyelets on the turntable. I have seen pieces of pipe as much as 6 inches long used as 'spacing', and slid over the connecting pin. This is dangerous because the pressure on the connecting bar when the vehicle is turning could bend the pipe, resulting in difficulty in removing it if the horse went down and the shafts had to be disconnected from the waggon in a hurry (17.4).

Waggons

The most vulnerable part of the waggon is the floor. These are often of softwood as this was cheaper to replace, but ideally it should be hardwood, preferably elm.

Many waggons have floorboards running from front to back (rather than across) and set down between the floor runners. They rest on timbers morticed through runners along the body. These are called 'keys', and allow the top of the boards to be level with the top of the runners. This construction allowed loads of roots, etc., to be shovelled from front to back through the open tailboard without the carter's shovel fouling on the edge of the floorboards (17.5a and b).

Waggons often have double floors. Secondary flooring is often fitted across the body on top of the runners because the keys, if defective, are difficult to replace. This was often done leaving the rotted floor in position, which resulted in water being trapped between the floor and the waggon sides, causing rot to occur in the outside body members. To replace these members is a major job and is very expensive. So when inspecting a waggon with a view to buying,

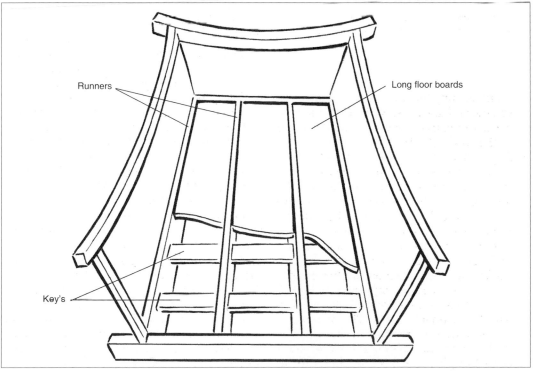

17.5a and **b** Floorboards of waggon running from front to back between the floor runners and resting on keys. This design allowed loads to be shovelled without fouling on the edge of floorboards.

Spring hanger

Leaves

Bolts

17.6 Springs should be checked for rust before a vehicle is purchased

17.7 Breeching, ridger chain and tug hooks on the shaft of a cart.

beware of rot or of fibreglass body filler at this point, which is no answer to structural defects.

The top body side members are also liable to rot or to attack by woodworm. If the attack is slight, then treatment with a proprietary brand woodworm killer is sufficient to prevent further attack. However, if the attack is extensive, causing the timber to be defective or cracked, especially at the front and back where the body members overhang the waggon, then replacement is the only answer. To replace these members is a long and expensive job, made more difficult because in order to remove the body members, the outside rave also has to be removed and these are riveted together. The top member is also riveted to the bottom body member. The tell-tale signs of active

17.8 A good decorating job

woodworm are small holes in the wood and piles of fine wood dust beneath the waggon, where the woodworm grub has bored its way out, usually in May or June.

The undercarriage of waggons usually remains fairly sound, but attention should be given to the turntable, especially at the place where the shafts are fitted.

Delivery Vans, Rulleys and Drays

All the points mentioned above also apply to delivery vans, rulleys and drays. An extra problem to look out for with these

vehicles is the condition of the springs – look out for a build-up of flakes of rust between the leaves. Also check the bolts through the spring eyelets and the spring hangers, as these often become badly rusted and need replacing. If this is the case, use high-tensile steel bolts (17.6).

Carts

When inspecting two-wheel carts and putts look out for the same points on the body as described for waggons. Carefully inspect the shafts for decay. Watch out for pieces which have been spliced onto defective or short shafts, as these can be a potential danger. Carts often had their shafts cut off and an 'A' bar fitted to convert them into tractor trailers. When, at a later date, the carts were converted back to horse-drawn use, new short shafts were bolted on top of the existing stub ends of the original shafts instead of replacing the whole shaft. This not only creates a point of weakness, but also alters the point of balance.

Pay particular attention to the tug, ridger and breeching hooks on the shafts, as carts were used more frequently than waggons and quite often these hooks show signs of a great deal of wear, to the point where the metal can be seriously worn away and present a danger (17.7).

Painting Vehicles

The most important part of achieving a professional finish on paintwork is the preparation. Many of the old vehicles were painted with lead-based paints, so great care should be taken when rubbing down. Always use a mask and try where possible to do it outside, or at least have the doors of the building open.

When you have sanded down the vehicle in preparation for painting, the first coat should be a very thin coat of primer paint. This will seal the absorbent areas of the surface of the vehicle as well as exposing any areas that require filler. The filler used should be a proprietary brand that complements the type of paint you plan to use. Your paint supplier will recommend a type.

When the filler is dry, usually within 12 hours, rub down using a fairly coarse wet and dry paper. If this shows up any other defects, then further filler should be applied. Next a brush filler (a paint-consistency material) should be applied. A smooth mirror finish should be achieved with the filler coats before attempting to apply an undercoat.

Use a very fine wet and dry paper to rub down the undercoats lightly until you are satisfied with the finish you have achieved. You are then ready to apply the top gloss coat. If your preparations have been correct, two undercoats and one gloss coat should be sufficient to achieve a satisfactory professional finish. The quality of the modern proprietary brands of coach paints does not require a varnish coat to achieve a satisfactory high-gloss finish.

Paint lining a vehicle is a specialist trade and it is best to employ a professional signwriter. However, it is possible to obtain lining wheels, lining tape, etc. to help anyone who wants to carry out their own lining. I still favour the lining 'fitches' or brushes.

The main thing to avoid is over-lining. Too much lining spoils a good decorating job. Remember, lining should only be used to highlight the chamfers and the edges of the panels etc. (17.8).

Finally, when cleaning your newly painted vehicle do not be tempted to use spray polish on the paintwork as this will leave smears. To prepare your vehicle for exhibition, simply wash with clean water and wipe with a chamois leather.

Glossary

Bond – the iron tyre around the outside of the wheel.
Cage – the metal bond which fits around the stock or hub of a wheel, through which the spokes are fitted to the hub.
Chamfer – moulding made by a chisel on edges of timber used in wooden vehicles.
Felloes – curved wooden sections used to form the outside of a wheel.

Hub – or *stock*, the centre section of a wheel which holds the spokes and joins onto the axle of a horse-drawn vehicle.
Lining fitch – extra-long brush used to put decorative lines on horse-drawn vehicles.
Raves – front, back and sometimes side ladders used to support a large load on a cart or waggon.
Rulley – four-wheel flat-bed horse-drawn trolley.
Stock – see *hub*.

CHAPTER 18

Transport and the Law

Nigel Westacott

This chapter is not intended for those who use their vehicles for hire or reward*, or in connection with a trade or business, for which there are more stringent rules which can be obtained from the Department of Transport and the traffic police.

This is a simple guide to those whose heavy horses are kept as a hobby, are not sponsored and do not use the show ring as an advertising medium for their breeding and sales activities. In other words, this is designed for people whose motor vehicles are for private use – 'private driving' as the regulations describe it.

Goods Vehicles Operators Licence

A Goods Vehicles Operators Licence is not required providing the vehicle is used for private driving, but one does need to be careful. For example, a market gardener keeping heavy horses as a hobby could carry a load of straw to bed his horses, but would need an operators licence to carry straw to bed his strawberries. A nursery owner who used his daughter's horse-box to deliver a load of tall shrubs was prosecuted for not having an operators licence.

Vehicle Excise Licence (i.e. road tax)

Provided the use is private driving the vehicle can be taxed as Private Light Goods, a considerable cash saving! The old 'Farmer's Goods' taxation concession ceased in 1995, so for farming use, as

opposed to private use, the vehicle should now be taxed at the appropriate 'Goods' rate.

Tachograph or Drivers Record Books

Again, provided the use is private, there is no requirement to use a tachograph or record book to record the driver's hours.

Should the vehicle be fitted with a tachograph it would indicate a responsible attitude by the driver if he were to use it. Nevertheless the tachograph would need to be up to date with its calibration check and/or its 2-year test for it to be a legal record.

If no separate speedometer is fitted and the tachograph is being used as a speedometer, then it would need to have been calibrated at some time to ensure that it is accurate enough to use as a speedometer.

Driver's Hours

Driving which is purely private is not subject to the Driver's Hours rules. However, it would be well to remember that the maximum total hours of driving (at the wheel) under the less-stringent Domestic Rules is 10 hours in any 24-hour period. Should an accident occur and it could be proved (i.e. by distance travelled and average speed or other evidence) that the driver had been driving in excess of 10 hours, it would be a strong factor leading to a charge of 'dangerous driving'.

* Reward means payment with goods or services and includes payment for fuel.

MOT Plate

This document, which is covered in plastic and is approximately 5 in. x 6 in., is normally held in a metal frame in a prominent place in the driver's cab. The plate shows the maximum permitted weights (in kilograms) of axle 1 (the front axle) and axle 2 (the back axle), and the maximum gross weight (of the vehicle as a whole) and train weight (of the vehicle including any trailer towed). This plate and its details are very important.

Overweight!

Should you be stopped by the police or Department of Transport or Trading Standards officials and be directed to a weighbridge, and any of the axle, gross or train weights exceed those shown on the MOT plate, you will be warned or prosecuted and probably prohibited. Prohibited means that you will be prevented from driving on until the offending weight is reduced to that shown on the MOT plate – the responsibility for guarding and subsequent removal from the weighbridge site of whatever is taken off to reduce weight is entirely yours. Normally you will be warned if you are up to 10 per cent overweight, unless the excess weight is more than 500 kg on an axle or 1,000 kg on the gross, when you will be prosecuted and prohibited, as you will be in any case for an overweight load of more than 10 per cent.

If you think the vehicle may be overweight, but wish to check, you may legally drive to the nearest available weighbridge for a check weigh without being prosecuted. Do not try to use this excuse when stopped unless you are on the direct road from your point of loading to the weighbridge – they have heard this one before!

Be warned – fines for being overweight can be very high, as also can the cost of 'clearing' the prohibition. If in doubt, check in advance.

Trailers

The driving licence requirements for trailers are given in the Driving Licence section which follows. The overall weight of a loaded towing vehicle and the loaded trailer must not exceed the permitted train weight shown on the MOT plate of the towing vehicle. All trailers over 1,020 kg (approximately one ton) unladen weight need to have:

1. A manufacturer's plate showing the maximum axle and gross weights and year of manufacture. (Home-built trailers will need a plate made to show what weights it is designed to carry.)
2. If it is being used one year or more after the date of manufacture, it will need its own MOT plate. It will need to be 'plated' at the Department of Transport Goods Vehicle Test Station and it will need an annual MOT test.

Trailers under 1,020 kg ULW (unladen weight) are not subject to these rules, but need to comply with other rules regarding brakes, lights and mudguards, etc. This information can be obtained from your local police traffic department. Most heavy horses will need to be travelled in larger trailers than these, however.

MOT Annual Test Certificate

Vehicles over 3,500 kg gross plated weight will need to be tested at a Department of Transport Goods Vehicle Testing Station, where someone will explain the procedure to you. However, it is probably cheaper and less trouble in the end to have your favourite local goods vehicle repairer prepare the vehicle and take it through the test. Be warned – the standards expected are very high.

Speed Limiters

These devices must be installed, and set as required, on the categories of goods vehicles set out below whether they are being used for private driving or commercial activities.

1. Goods vehicles exceeding 7.5 tonnes, but not exceeding 12 tonnes gross weight, first used on or after 1.8.1992. The limiter should be set at 60 m.p.h./97 k.p.h. (max.)

2. Goods vehicles exceeding 12 tonnes gross weight, first used on or after 1.1.1988. The limiter should be set at 56 m.p.h./90 k.p.h. (max.)

Note: The speed limiter must be sealed and maintained in good and efficient working order.

Goods vehicles used before the dates shown above are exempt from the requirements.

Driving Licence

At the moment some people hold the old-style green licence and some have the new red one.

'Old' Licence

Drivers holding Group A licences may drive goods vehicles up to 7,500 kg gross weight and with trailers up to 8,250 kg train weight. For any vehicles over this weight an additional old HGV licence would have been required, but the holder is now issued with a new-style licence.

'New' Licence

For drivers who passed the appropriate test prior to 1 January 1997, the following rules apply.

1. Lorries between 3,500 and 7,500 kg gross weight without a trailer will need a Class C1 licence (old licence group A).
2. Lorries between 3,500 and 7,500 kg gross weight with a trailer over 750 kg (i.e. combined, or train, weight not exceeding 8,250 kg) will need a Class C1 + E licence (old licence group A).
3. Large lorries over 3,500 kg gross weight, any number of axles, and towing a trailer up to 750 kg gross weight will need a Class C licence (the old HGV groups II and III).
4. Articulated lorries and rigid vehicles over 3,500 kg with trailers over 750 kg will need a Class C + E licence (the old HGV Group I).

For drivers who passed the appropriate test on or after 1 January 1997, the following rules apply.

1. Vehicles between 3,500 and 7,500 kg with or without a trailer up to 750 kg will need a Class CI licence (driver over 18).
2. Vehicles between 3,500 kg and 7,500 kg with a trailer over 750 kg with a combined, or train, weight of not more than 12,000 kg will need a Class C1 + E licence (driver over 18).
3. Vehicles over 3,500 kg with a trailer up to 750 kg will need a Class C licence (driver over 21). Although this class may seem similar to No.2 above, there is no restriction of combined, or train, weight to under 12,000 kg.
4. Vehicles over 3,500 kg with a trailer over 750 kg will need a Class C + E licence.

Since 1 January 1997 a test pass in a car must precede a test in most other categories. (Before this date a test passed in a lorry could also be counted as having passed in a car.) Also, any driver wishing to tow a heavy trailer (over 750 kg) must first pass a test in the associated rigid vehicle. Learner drivers in categories B, C1 and C cannot draw a trailer of any size. Should they wish to tow large trailers, they must pass further tests. If in doubt, check with the Department of Transport or the Traffic Police.

Do not forget, most Certificates of Insurance state that the driver 'must hold or have held' (i.e. expired) 'a licence to drive *that class of vehicle*' (or *the vehicle*, which means the same thing). For a "no insurance offence" you face certain *disqualification* in addition to the fine.

Livestock Vehicle Construction

The regulations regarding the construction of livestock vehicles are specific and detailed. The main points are given below.

General – The vehicle must be of substantial design, and able to withstand the action of the weather and the weight of any animal that may be thrown against it (18.1).

Partitions – The maximum length of a pen for horses is 3.7 m. Too long a pen can cause the horse unnecessary extra movement and discomfort on the journey.

18.1 A purpose-built horsebox, suitable for heavy horses.

Barriers – These are to prevent animals falling out when the ramp is lowered (straps may be used for horses).

Foot battens – Battens, or some other means of preventing animals slipping, are required e.g. sand or some other substance allowing a proper foothold.

External ramps – Ramps must be provided with foot battens. They should not be steeper than four in seven; the top step should not exceed 21 cm; there must be no gaps of more than 6 cm; there must be gates each side of the ramp at least 1.3 m in height, with no dangerous gaps (18.2).

Adequate ventilation – Ventilation must be adequate for the animal's health and comfort.

Suitable for cleaning and disinfecting – It must be possible to clean and disinfect the vehicle easily and efficiently.

Inspection facilities – From outside, e.g. apertures, footholds, doors.

Lighting – This can be fixed or portable, but must be capable of illuminating the whole interior.

Roofing – Vehicles must have rigid sides and a weatherproof roof.

Hazard-free interior – Vehicles must have fully covered wheel arches, be free of sharp edges or projections, and all electrical fittings must be covered.

Height – The minimum height for horses is 1.98 m, but this must be increased if necessary to allow the animal to stand in a natural position. The height should also be sufficient to allow free circulation of air.

If you buy a livestock or horsebox body, you would probably assume that it conforms to the above requirements, but you should always check. Those who contemplate building their own livestock body should take specialist advice.

Animal Welfare Requirements

To those who have a good feel for handling animals, these requirements make sense. However, it is sometimes helpful to be aware of the actual rules – you never know

18.2   A well-maintained ramp with non-slip surface and battens to help the horses' grip.

who is watching you and your antics in public! The main requirements are listed below.

Loading/unloading Animals

If the floor of the vehicle is over 31 cm from the ground, animals must be assisted by a loading ramp or loading bank. Do not goad the animals excessively, suspend the animals by mechanical means, or lift or drag the animals by their head or tail.

During Carriage

During carriage, do not subject any animals to severe jolting or shaking. Do not transport secured and unsecured animals in the same vehicle (except unweaned young with the mother). Do not carry horses in the same vehicle as pigs. Do not transport carcases with live animals. Horses carried together in unpartitioned vehicles should be unshod on their hind feet.

Litter

On journeys of over 50 km, the floor should be covered with sufficient litter to absorb droppings, unless these are cleared out regularly.

Feeding and Watering

Animals must be provided with food and water before a journey. The maximum permitted interval between feeds on a journey is 15 hours.

The private user is not required to keep records of animal movements.

The National Farmers Union (NFU) produces a useful specialist guide entitled *The Transport of Livestock*.

Appendices

Appendix A: Southern Counties Heavy Horse Association Official Rules of Horse Ploughing for Use at all Association Matches

Competitors may open out in two or three furrows at their discretion, but in every case *all ground* must be moved. This rule shall *not* apply to ley ground.

Three sticks only may be used. There shall be no other mark except the plot mark.

Each competitor must show *ten furrows* before starting to split out to the neighbour's work. Before starting to split out, competitors must check that their neighbour has completed at least *five furrows*.

Any competitor who, *60 minutes* after ploughing commences, is still preventing their neighbour from splitting out shall lose *all* points awarded for the crown.

The competitor thus held up by their neighbour's slow progress may, at the end of that 60 minutes, commence to split out into their neighbour's work and will be allowed an extra 5 minutes only for each additional turn thus involved. Such splitting out is only to be done with agreement from the Chief Steward or Plot Steward.

Competitors should continue to turn to the plot with the next highest number until their own is completed. The last furrow must be thrown towards the competitor's crown.

All ploughing must be a minimum depth of *5 inches* except for the first two furrows, i.e. one each side of the crown and the last two furrows at the finish: these shall be a minimum depth of *2 inches*.

In classes 1, 5 and 6, each competitor shall be allowed *one assistant only* on the plot to lead the horses. In Class 1, horses can be led only for the crown (the first two shown furrows). Points are lost in this class if the horses are led after this. In Classes 3 and 7, no competitor shall be allowed *any assistance* on the plot. In Class 2, *one assistant* will be allowed if four or more horses are used. Only competitors' ploughing *unassisted* shall be eligible for the Championship. The competitor alone must set and/or adjust the plough.

At 2.30 p.m., competitors shall be allowed to finish the turn being worked. *No further work will be allowed.*

Handling: there must be *no* handling or shaping of the work after the veering has been completed.

Provided that the Stewards are alerted immediately, an allowance will be made for time lost due to a genuine breakdown. Such allowance is at the discretion of the Chief Steward.

Competitors must use *all horses* of their team throughout the entire competition except for the *last three turns only*, when the horses may be driven in tandem. *Only in Class 7* may a single horse be used.

Boats, presses and seamers may only be used in Class 1.

Marking shall be out of a total of 200 points as follows:

Split	10 points	Crown	35 points
Skimmers	30 points	Uniformity	25 points
Firmness	30 points	Straightness	20 points
Ins and outs	10 points	Finish	40 points

The plot sizes will be as follows: 4 hours work, 8 yards x 80 yards (or equivalent, i.e. 640 square yards); 3 hours work, 7 yards x 80 yards (or equivalent, i.e. 560 square yards); Class 7 plot size, 7 yards x 50 yards.

Only work finished by 2.30 p.m. will be judged. Competitors will be disqualified for infringement of these rules. They will also forfeit any prize and/or money won in the horse or harness classes of the ploughing competition.

Bad treatment of horses will not be tolerated. Those doing so will be asked to refrain, or if necessary, to leave the site.

Ploughing Classes

Class 1 – High-cut work: no opening; width of furrow to competitor's choice; one assistant allowed on the plot during work.

Class 2 – Two-furrow ploughs: any length turn furrow with three or more horses; any competitor using four or more horses is allowed one assistant to drive the front horses.

Class 3 – Long turn furrow plough: turn furrow exceeding 43 in; no assistance allowed after setting sight ploughs.

Class 4 – Short turn furrow plough: turn furrow less than 43 in; no assistance allowed after setting sight poles.

Class 5 – Ploughman needing an assistant on plot: any length turn furrow; one assistant allowed on the plot all the time.

Class 6 —Les Stokes novice ploughman: any length turn furrow; one assistant allowed on the plot all the time; competitor not to have won more than two first prizes.

Class 7 – Single heavy horse and plough: plough to be suitable and the right weight for a single horse.

Best crown

Best finish

Class 8 – Best working team: sound horses judged solely on their working ability; no horses that have been led are eligible.

Class 9 – Best pair: judged on conformation as a matching pair.

Class 10 – Best team from regular work.

Class 11 – Best turned out plough team.

Class 12 – Best mare.

Class 13 – Best gelding.

Note: Many ploughing associations and matches use Southern Counties Heavy Horse Association rules. However, there are some regional differences in the rules for ploughing competitions. The chief variation is in the number of horses which competitors are allowed to use to finish their work. Many matches allow the use of one horse only for this, whereas others stipulate that both horses must finish. In Scotland and some regions of England, competitors are allowed to 'handle' the work, e.g. shaping the furrows etc. In other areas this practice is not allowed.

Appendix B: **Horse Driving Trials Association Heavy Horse Obstacle Driving Rules (1997)**

These rules are in addition to The British Horse Driving Trials Association National Rules, which apply for any points not covered in the Heavy Horse Obstacle Driving Rules. These rules cannot provide for every eventuality but should be interpreted with intelligence and in the spirit of the sport.

Heavy Horse Obstacle Driving is designed to show the versatility of the heavy horse using traditional harness and vehicles.

1. Fault competition for singles and pairs of heavy horses. Horses must be at least 16.0 hh, and cobs and vanners are not allowed. Drivers must be members of the Heavy Horse Obstacle Driving Club.

2. Horses must be 4 years old or over.

3. Vehicles must be recognized four-wheeled heavy horse type vehicles – no customized vehicles are allowed.

4. Harness must be in good condition, clean and safe, uniform in appearance and of an appropriate style.

5. Competitors and grooms must be properly dressed for the competition in the arena – jeans are not allowed – this includes for the inspection of the course and presentation of awards. They must be suitably dressed to drive or groom. Whips may be carried at the discretion of the driver.

6. A groom must accompany the driver and must remain on the vehicle at all times

during the competition. He must not give directions to the driver. Grooms must be 14 years or over. Drivers must remain seated – on a bale of straw or a plank if necessary – at all times.

7. Any competitor deliberately breaking pace out of a trot at any time whilst in the ring or during the competition or prize giving will be eliminated and forfeit his prize money.

8. Exhibitors may make as many entries as they wish in each class, but each entry must have a different driver, horse(s) and vehicle. No horse(s) may compete more than once in any one class, but a horse that competes as a single may also compete as a pair. No horse, driver or vehicle may go more than once in any class.

NB In all cases it is the driver, not the horse, that qualifies, but this does not nullify the above rule and, should more than one driver qualify the same horse, it will be necessary for all but one of the drivers concerned to find another horse to drive in the Championship.

9. One of a pair of horses may be substituted prior to the competition, but this may not be one of a pair who have already competed or intend to compete.

10. Drivers may be substituted, but the judge must be informed prior to the start of the competition and a doctor's note must be produced for the substitution.

11. Any persons receiving an invitation for the Heavy Horse Obstacle Driving competitions must notify the Heavy Horse Obstacle Driving Club, stating details of the competition(s) and any financial implications for the competitors.

Any preference by sponsors and/or organizers as far as competitors and/or horses are concerned would be looked upon favourably.

Unaffiliated events

Members and registered horses of the four breed Societies (Shire, Clydesdale, Suffolk, Percheron) or any other breed affiliated to the BHDTA (British Horse Driving Trials Association), may not take part in unaffiliated shows, except minor shows.

Panel Judges and Course Builders may not officiate in competitions at an event/show which is not affiliated, except a minor show/event.

Minor events/shows are those at which the aggregate value of any prize and/or the proceeds of any sweepstake, whether in cash or kind, given to a competitor or competitors in each and every competition at the event/show does not exceed £20.

12. The course to consist of up to a minimum of 8 obstacles and a maximum of 12 obstacles depending on the size of arena, and may include one multiple obstacle in addition to a serpentine.

    The distance between the markers will be a minimum of 30 cm and a maximum of 40 cm wider than the track width of the vehicle.

    The distance between the markers in a serpentine, which must not consist of more than four posts in a straight line, must be at least 12 m.

    Multiples in the form of a U or L must have a minimum track width of 5 m and may not consist of more than three lettered gates.

    No water obstacles or bridges are allowed.

    All obstacles must be clearly numbered.

    The starting line may not be more that 30 m or less than 15 m from the first obstacle. The finishing line may not be less than 20 m or more than 40 m from the last obstacle.

13. The maximum length allowed for the course is 500 m and the time allowed will be calculated from the speed of 150 m per minute. The time limit is twice the time allowed. Competitors will be timed by electronic timing or stop-watch from the moment the nose of the horse(s) crosses the starting line to the moment it crosses the finishing line.

14. The order of going will be drawn, and competitors must enter the ring within one minute of the bell being rung and must start the competition within one minute of the bell being rung after entering the arena. Failure to comply will result in elimination.

15. Circling before an obstacle or stopping will be a disobedience. If a competitor has

a disobedience and knocks over the obstacle without completing it correctly the bell will be rung and the clock stopped for the obstacle to be rebuilt, and 5 penalty points will be added. When the obstacle has been rebuilt, the bell will be rung, the clock started and the competitor will retake the obstacle.

If a competitor takes the wrong course but corrects himself before passing through another obstacle, he will not be penalized unless he crosses his original track. In the event of a competitor taking the wrong course and not rectifying his mistake, the Judge will ring the bell after he passes through another obstacle and the competitor will be eliminated.

Penalties for disobediences are cumulative, whether they are incurred at the same obstacle or throughout the same course.

16. Faults will be penalised as follows:
17. In the event of equality of faults, time will decide.
18. Competitors will drive the course as presented, i.e. if an obstacle has not been rebuilt from a previous round and the competitor has started, he will not be penalized.
19. Any contravention of paragraphs 2–9 inclusive will be penalized with elimination or disqualification. Repeated contravention of these rules by a competitor will result in a report to The British Horse Driving Trials Association Council. The discipline of The British Horse Driving Trials National Rules also applies for the Heavy Horse Obstacle Driving competitors and competitions.
20. It is strongly recommended that drivers should have Third Party Liability Insurance.

For exceeding the time allowed, every commenced period of one second	**0.5 penalty points**
For knocking over or displacing an obstacle or if the ball on top is dislodged (whether it is on one or both of the above)	**5 penalty points**
For knocking over or displacing an element of a multiple obstacle	**5 penalty points**
For knocking down any part of a multiple obstacle other than a cone, the bell will be rung, and the clock stopped. The obstacle will be rebuilt and at the sound of the second bell, the clock will be re-started and the competitor will retake the whole of the obstacle	**5 penalty points**
For knocking over or displacing an obstacle other than the one being driven	**5 penalty points**
If it is an obstacle in advance of the one being driven, the bell will be rung, the clock stopped and the obstacle rebuilt	**5 penalty points**
If it is an obstacle that has already been driven, the bell will not be rung	**5 penalty points**
For knocking over a start or finishing flag	**5 penalty points**
For knocking over the automatic timing equipment	**5 penalty points**
For first disobedience	**5 penalty points**
For second disobedience	**5 penalty points**
For third disobedience	**Elimination**
For groom dismounting the first time	**5 penalty points**
For groom dismounting the second time	**10 penalty points**
For groom dismounting the third time	**Elimination**
For taking the wrong course	**Elimination**
For exceeding the time limit	**Elimination**
For starting before the bell	**Elimination**
For failing to pass through the start or finish flags	**Elimination**
For receiving outside assistance (including from groom)	**Elimination**

Appendix C: **Course for Timber Snigging**

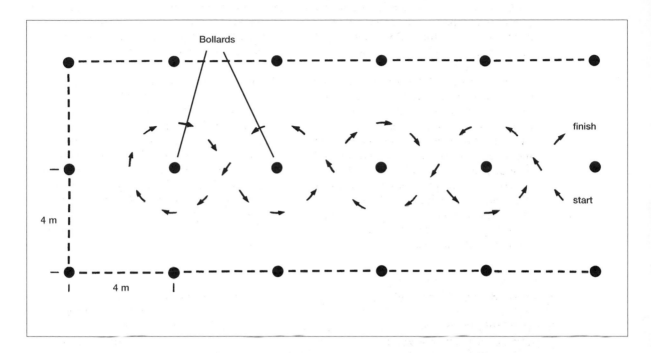

This course layout is taken from the report 'History With a Future' by Keith Chivers, published by the Shire Horse Society.

C1 Course for timber snigging. Bollards are set out to define the edges of the course and in the centre. The horseman enters with his horse and log and proceeds to do figures of eight around the course. The aim is to finish without knocking down any bollards and against time. (This can vary according to conditions/level of skill of competitors).

Appendix D: **British Heavy Horse Driving Trials Club Competition Rules**

Horses should be four years old and over.

All competitors (i.e. drivers or grooms) must be over 12 years of age and those under 18 must be accompanied by a capable adult.

It is the responsibility of the driver to ensure that the horses are safe and reliable when driven.

Vehicles must be in sound condition, two or four wheeled and capable of carrying a groom.

Horses do not have to be turned out to show standard, harness must be correctly fitting and in good condition, breeching must be used if the vehicle does not have an independent braking system.

Horses, harness and vehicles may be inspected by the Safety Officer.

Competitors should make sure that they are ready to start, there will be a 10 minute rest period after the completion of your dressage test before you will be expected to start the cross country. Your time will be started then; lateness will result in a shortened time for the cross-country.

Each pair to complete one course of the cross-country, the obstacle driving, and the dressage test. The dressage test is optional but only pairs who complete all three disciplines will be eligible for the overall prize. Failure to report to the ring at the correct time will incur penalties for the pair.

It is strongly advised that hard hats should be worn for the cross-country phase.

It is the duty of all competitors and their team members to be aware of Health and Safety at all times.

All drivers taking part must be members of BHHDTC to be covered by third party insurance.

Cross Country Rules

The competition is for pairs or single (separate class) heavy horses of any recognised heavy type.

The course will be marked in kilometres and calculated at approximately 11 k per hour.

A shortened course will be available to novices which will include obstacles: this will count as a separate course.

The competitor nearest the optimum time with the least penalties on the course will be the winner. However penalties will be incurred for completing the course under or over the set time.

Each pair will be responsible for timing themselves.

Competitors will not be allowed to deviate (or circle) from the track, and stopping is only permitted for emergencies.

Overtaking will only be allowed where there is sufficient room to do so in safety and without running onto crops.

All obstacles will be marked with red and white flags and must be driven with the white flag on the left and the red on the right. Failure to observe this rule will result in penalties.

In all circumstances the judge's decision is final.

The Committee retains the right to amend the rules.

Complaints will only be considered if accompanied by a £20 deposit returnable if the complaint is upheld.

Penalties will be incurred for –
Failing to complete the various obstacles.
Hesitation – a pause followed by obedience to the driver.
Refusal – stopping and stepping back.
Putting a groom down in an obstacle.
Omitting an obstacle.
Breaking out of a walk on compulsory walk section.

Cones Rules

Timed competition for pairs or singles to drive a set course of cones at any pace.

The competitor with the fastest round will be the winner. Knocking over or displacing a marker or any part of an obstacle will incur a 10 second penalty.

The course time is calculated at 300m per minute and the total time before time penalties are incurred will be declared on the day.

Time penalties incurred will be scored as a complete second for every commenced second over the time allowed. Should a competitor take twice the allowed time to complete the course they will be eliminated. The course will include a serpentine and a multiple obstacle.

Competitors will be able to walk the course before the competition starts. An error of course which is not corrected will result in a zero score for the competitor.

Dressage Competition

This is based on the BHDTA (British Horse Driving Trials Association) Novice tests and may be included in the competition to further emphasise the all-round abilities of the heavy horse. This will not be judged on turnout presentation but on the driving skills i.e. rein handling and use of aids, obedience and suppleness of the horses, and obviously the accuracy of the figures and paces. A whip is to be carried at all times.

Appendix E: **Shire Horse Society Guide Notes for Judging**

Horse judging

1. Judging Appointments

All judges are bound by the Society's Memorandum and Articles of Association, By-Laws and Regulations and the Guide Lines for Judges, and all judges must judge in accordance with these guidelines and in accordance with the Society's Standard of Points and Conformation for Shire Horses.

If a judge is invited to officiate at more than one show in his/her locality, before accepting the second or third invitation, he/she should always let the inviting society know of his/her appointments. It is not in the best interests of the breed for the judge to officiate at several shows throughout the year, particularly if they are within the same region, which could well mean that the same horses would be appearing.

2. Judges Nominations

The Society is responsible for nominating the judges for the Royal Show, the National Shire Horse Show and the Horse of the Year Show. It can only provide an official list of judges for affiliated societies, and nominations of individual names cannot be submitted.

3. Judge's Accommodation

If a judge requires overnight accommodation he should either ask the secretary of the show concerned to provide this, or if accommodation is being provided by a friend, this should not be a person who is exhibiting at the Show the following day.

4. Arrival on Showground

A judge should never look at animals he/she has been asked to adjudicate on, either in the horse lines or anywhere else on the showground before judging.

5. Discussions During Judging

Judges are asked to follow the accepted rule that they do not hold discussions whilst the class is in the ring, either with their stewards or with exhibitors, unless it is to ask direct questions.

During the break, whilst classes enter and leave the ring, judges should not hold conversations with spectators around the ringside. At that time, the judge is fully entitled to talk to his/her steward, but not to spectators.

6. Reasons

If, on completion of judging, an exhibitor asks, in the correct way, for the judge's opinion on the animal which they had exhibited, the judge, at his discretion, is perfectly entitled to give a reason for his placing. *This is entirely a matter for the discretion of the judge.* Quite often exhibitors find judge's comments helpful.

7. Judge's Interest in a Horse

If a horse appears in front of a judge and he/she finds that because he/she owned or bred the animal, or has now or has had an interest in the animal, then he/she should *not under any circumstances* place that animal. The judge must inform the steward and invite a referee or another nominated judge to place the animal in question. The judge should place the remainder of the class and the proposed referee should watch the judging of the class. On completion, the judge should ask the steward to ask the referee to place the horse in question. *The Society relies entirely on the integrity of its judges.*

8. Basis of Judging

Exhibitors always enter shows in the rightful belief that their animals will be fairly judged, and there are very few cases of proven judging irregularities. However, it is important for all judges not only to act properly, but also to 'be seen to be acting in this way'. *An adequate amount of time should be spent with each exhibit and all exhibits should be seen to have equal attention. Judges should never unnecessarily give exhibitors a chance to be critical.*

9. Guidelines

These notes have in no way been prepared to reflect the way in which judges either behave or carry out their work, but merely as guidelines, particularly for younger judges in answer to questions raised with the Society.

10. Horse's Tails

Horses with unclipped tails should not be penalized.

11. Horse's Feet

If a judge is of the opinion that a horse's feet and shoes are not in accordance with the published guidelines, *then the horse should be placed down the line*. Equally, if a judge is of the opinion that the shoes fitted to a horse affect its movement, then this fact will be taken into consideration when placing horses in their respective classes. Horses shown without bevelled shoes should not be penalized.

12. Artificial Appearance

Soap and resin. The use of soap and resin or any other substance on coats is prohibited. Damping of coats with clean water only will be allowed. This ruling does not apply to foals.

13. Exhibitors' Behaviour in the Ring

If for any reason an exhibitor wishes to leave the ring before the final completion of the class judging, then that exhibitor should ask the steward's permission to do so, and the steward in turn should seek the judge's permission.

Exhibitors must not powder horses once they have entered the ring for judging. Horses remaining in the ring for the Championship may be dusted and cleaned at the back of the ring or in the collecting ring. Under no circumstances are horses to be dusted or cleaned when standing in the line during judging.

Only one person is allowed into the ring with each entry unless special permission is sought from the class steward. This will be granted only in exceptional circumstances, e.g. where someone is needed to trot the horse.

If in the opinion of a judge an exhibitor conducts himself in an improper way during judging, this should immediately be reported to the Society.

14. Steward's Responsibilities

It is the responsibility of the steward to present the animals in the ring for the judge to place in order of merit according to the Society's published Standards of Points and Conformation.

It is not the responsibility of the judge to decide which animals are eligible for the class (in any case judges are not allowed to see a catalogue of entries until all classes have been judged).

It is the steward's responsibility to let the judge know how much time there is for each class, or at least to give some indication. If the stewards do not indicate to the judge the time allowed for the class, then the judge should ask that question.

Stewards should not stand with judges whilst the class is actually being judged. They should be available as and when required to convey the judge's wishes to exhibitors. If a steward persists in talking to, or standing near to, the judge, then he/she should be asked to stand away.

If the system or quality of stewarding at a Show presents problems, then judges are asked to notify the Secretary who can, in a diplomatic way, take matters up with the affiliated society.

16. Judge's Dress

When judging, judges should at all times wear a hard hat, a suit (dark if possible) and a suitable coat (which might be a Barbour-type oil skin coat), but should not wear an anorak; it is essential that judges can be distinguished by their dress.

Turnout Judging

1. Horses

The horse or horses must be working well on the day. Their manners must be good. They must be able to do a day's work. Conformation for harness horses need not necessarily be as perfect as for in-hand classes.

2. Description of Class

It is suggested that all heavy horse turnout classes should be worded 'of Shire type'.

3. Driving

Importance should be placed on the standard of driving and the overall smartness of driver and attendant.

4. Harness

Harness should be fitted correctly and be a matching set, neatly and cleanly presented.

5 General Appraisal

Emphasis is to be placed on the appearance of the turnout as a whole. Pairs and teams must be balanced and work as a pair or a team. Judges should not climb or stand on any part of the turnout except the steps. Judges may ask for turnouts to walk, trot, stand or back. Judges should avoid asking a driver to continue to take a horse round the ring for long periods. Judges are also requested to ensure that horses are not trotted unnecessarily.

Note: Judges should not insist that horses should back.

5.1 Judges' Examination of Horses in Turnouts

Judges should be asked to make a close inspection of horse, harness and wagon, but have due regard to the overall appearance of the turnout and the attendants in deciding the final placing.

6 Preliminary and Final Judging

Where a judge is asked to undertake preliminary judging prior to final judging, the following guide notes should apply:

6.1 Preliminary Judging

The judge should decide in which order he/she will place *all entries* in the final judging. However, he/she would not draw them up in that order in the preliminary judging. He/she would leave them in the order in which they had entered the ring.

6.2 Final Judging

Unless something had happened between the preliminary judging and the final judging, e.g. the horse had gone lame or it could not be handled or driven, then there should not be any alteration in the judge's preliminary placings. However, if a horse came in lame, could not be handled or could not be driven, then the judge would have no option but either to place that horse at the bottom of the class or to ask the exhibitor if he/she would like to retire.

7 Agricultural/Farmer's Turnout

The committee agree that the following guidelines should be given to Affiliated Societies for turnouts:

7.1 Definition of an Agricultural Turnout

An agricultural turnout should be a vehicle built specifically for an agricultural purpose and still in its original state except for maintenance. Vehicles should not have any of the following: high seats; commercial advertising (other than the name of the owner or exhibitor); patent leather harness.

7.2 Definition of a Farmer's Turnout

A farmer's turnout should be a turnout which is the property of a farmer who is mainly dependant on farming for a livelihood.

Useful Addresses and Further Reading

Publications

Heavy Horse World Magazine
Editor: Diana Zeuner
Park Cottage
West Dean
Chichester
West Sussex PO18 0RX
Tel/Fax: 01243 811364.
e-mail: zeuner@BTInternet.com
Includes annual directories for harness makers (spring issue) and wheelwrights (winter issue), and regular directories for shows and events (spring/summer issue), breeders and breed societies, and working associations.

Draught Horse Journal
PO Box 670
Waverly
IA 50677
USA
Tel: (001) 319 352 4046
Fax: (001) 319 352 2232

Rural Heritage Magazine
281-R Dean Ridge Lane
Gainesboro
TN 38562 5039
USA
Tel: (001) 625 268 0655
e-mail: editor@ruralheritage.com
web site: www.ruralheritage.com

Breed Societies and Working Associations

Shire Horse Society
Secretary: Tonie Gibson OBE
East of England Showground
Peterborough
PE2 6XE
Tel: 01733 234451
Fax: 01733 370038

Clydesdale Horse Society
Secretary: Kate Stephen
3 Grosvenor Gardens
Edinburgh
EH12 5JU
Tel: 0131 337 0923
Fax: 0131 337 7678

Suffolk Horse Society
Secretary: Philip Ryder-Davies MB, BS, BVSc, MRCVS
The Market Hill
Woodbridge
Suffolk IP12 4LU
Tel: 01394 380643

British Percheron Horse Society
Secretary: Beatrice Potter
The White House
South Harting
Petersfield
Hampshire GU31 5PZ
Tel: 01730 814636
Fax: 01730 825061

Ardennes Horse Society of Great Britain
Secretary: Jo Hewitt
White Ash Farm
Starvenden Lane
Sissinghurst
Kent TN17 2AN
Tel: 01580 715001
Fax: 01730 825061

Federation of Working Horse Associations
Secretary: Bryan Green
43 The Moor
Melbourn
Royston
Hertfordshire SG8 6ED
Tel: 01763 261456

Forestry Contracting Association
(including the British Horse Loggers'
Association)
Dalfling
Blairdaff
Inverurie
Aberdeenshire AB51 5LA
Tel: 01467 651368
Fax: 01467 651595

British Heavy Horse Driving Trials Club
Rowena McDermott
3 Field Barn Cottages
North Charford
Braemore
Fordingbridge
Hampshire SP6 2DW
Tel: 01725 511951

British Horse Society
Stoneleigh Deer Park
Kenilworth
Warwickshire CV8 2XZ
Tel: 01926 707700
Fax: 01926 707800

Training

*S/NVQ Qualifications/Road Driving
Assessment*
British Horse Society Training and
Examinations Department
Stoneleigh Deer Park
Kenilworth
Warwickshire CV8 2XZ
Tel: 01926 707700
Fax: 01926 707800

S/NVQ Heavy Horse Training Manual, Level 2
Horse Education and Training Company
The Burgess Building
The Green
Stafford
ST17 4BL

Forestry Contracting Association (see above)

National Proficiency Test Council
(chainsaw certification)
Stoneleigh
Kenilworth
CV8 2LR

*Code of Practice for Horse Drawn Vehicles
and other matters concerning horses on
public roads*
Department of Transport
Great Minster House
76 Marsham Street
London SW1P 4DR
Tel: 0171 271 4633

Vehicles, Machinery, Harness, Decoration

The Heavy Horse Enthusiast
Terry and Mary Keegan
The Oxleys
Clows Top
Kidderminster
Worcestershire DY14 9HE
Tel: 01299 832358

National Horse Brass Society
Jim Elworthy
2 Blue Barn Cottage
Blue Barn Lane
Weybridge
KT13 0NH
Tel: 01932 354193

Cart Horse Machinery Ltd
Egremont Farm
Payhembury
Honiton
Devon EX14 0JA
Tel/fax: 01404 841233

Agent for Canadian muck-spreaders
Jonathan Waterer
Higher Biddacott Farm
Chittlehampton
Nr. Umberleigh
Devon
Tel: 01769 540222

Italian horse-drawn machinery
Mipe Viviani snc
Officine meccaniche
Loc. Plan del Casone
53035 Monteriggioni: (SI)
Italy
Tel: (0039) 577 304069/304070
Fax: (0039) 577 304070

Plaits, Flights and Standards

Wendy Slade
Sladbrook Stud
15 Bull Lane
Little Ickford
Aylesbury
Buckinghamshire HP18 9HR
Tel: 01844 339319

Elaine Ramsay
Millisle Farm
Garlieston
Newton Stewart
Wigtownshire
Tel: 01988 600622

Heavy Horse World Magazine publishes directories of harness makers, wheelwrights and trials vehicle manufacturers covering the whole of the UK. Information on suppliers of modern horse-drawn machinery made in the US and Canada can be obtained from *Draft Horse Journal and Rural Heritage Magazine* – see under publications section.

Farriery

Farriers' Registration Council
Sefton House
Adam Court
Newark Road
Peterborough
PE1 5PP
Tel: 01733 319911

Forestry

See Forestry Contracting Association under **Breed Societies and Working Associations**

Robert Sampson
Bergan Horse Logging Equipment
Harbridge Farm House
Ringwood
Hampshire BH24 3PW
Tel: 01425 470273

Transport

The NFU Transport of Livestock guide
The National Farmers' Union
Agriculture House
164 Shaftesbury Avenue
London WC2H 8HL

Further Reading

The Heavy Horse Manual, Nick Rayner and Keith Chivers.
History With A Future, Keith Chivers/The Shire Horse Society.
The Shire Horse, Keith Chivers.
The Clydesdale Horse, Eric Baird.
Le Cheval Percheron (with English translation by Beatrice Potter), Jean-Leo Dugast.
Training Workhorses/Training Teamsters, L. R. Miller (USA).
The Draft Horse Primer, Maurice Telleen (USA).
Horse Ploughing, Terry Keegan.
The Heavy Horse, its Harness and Harness Decoration, Terry Keegan.
Discovering Horse-drawn Farm Machinery, D. J. Smith.
Discovering Horse-drawn Vehicles, D. J. Smith.
The Care and Showing of The Heavy Horse, Edward Hart.
The Complete Book of In-Hand Showing, Alex Fell.
Heavy Horse Handbook, Southern Counties Heavy Horse Association.
The Horse in the Forest, Hans Sidbäck. Swedish University of Agricultural Sciences/Research Information Centre/Forestry. Available from Sara Roberts, FCA, Upper Cwm, Little Dewchurch, Hereford HR2 6PS.
Forestry Authority Work Study on Horse Extraction, Jim Dewar. Forestry Authority, Ae Village, Dumfriesshire DG1 1QB.
Forestry Commission Booklet No. 39, *Timber Measurement;* Booklet No. 15, *Conifers*; Booklet No. 20, *Broadleaves;* Handbook No. 6 *Forestry Practice*. Forestry Commission Publications, Forest Research Station, Alice Holt Lodge, Wrecclesham, Farnham, Surrey GU10 4LH. Tel: 01420 22255.
The Silviculture of Trees used in British Forestry, Peter S. Savill, CAB International, 1991, ISBN 0851 987397. Landsmans Bookshop Ltd, Buckenhill, Bromyard, Herefordshire. Tel: 01885 483420.
Forestry Tools and Aids. Stanton Hope Ltd, 11 Seax Court, Southfield, Laidon, Basildon, Essex SS15 6LY. Tel: 01268 419141.

Videos covering training heavy horses to work and for show, Farming Press, 2 Wharfedale Road, Ipswich, Suffolk, IP1 4LG. Tel: 01473 241122 for a catalogue.

First Steps to the Furrow: *Training the Heavy Horse for Work*, Roger and Cheryl Clark with Paul Heiney.

Harnessed to the Plough: *a Year Farming with Horses*, Roger and Cheryl Clark with Paul Heiney.

Training a Gentle Giant: Preparing Scotland's Native Heavy Horse for Show, Tom and Cate Brewster.

Holding the Reins: John Parker's Introduction to Carriage Driving with Paul Heiney.

Videos covering plaiting, team driving and showing, Countryside Audio and Visual, Firs Court Farm House, Ramsdell, Nr. Basingstoke, Hampshire, RG26 5SJ. Tel: 01256 850142.

Plaiting a Shire Horse for Showing, John Peacock.

'Come on Together': Showing the Lingwood Shires, John Peacock.

National Shire Horse Show video filmed annually.

The British Horse Society publishes a range of booklets covering a wide variety of matters concerning general equine care, veterinary matters and equine activities. These generally emphasise the light horse rather than the heavy horse, but frequently such matters are common to both types. See page 232 for address.

Many of the publications and videos listed above are available from *Heavy Horse World Magazine, The Heavy Horse Enthusiast* or Edward Hart, The Manor House, Birdsall, Malton, North Yorkshire YO17 9NS (especially out-of-print books).

Glossary

Arms – forearms of the horse. See illustration 1.20.

Back-band – in plough harness, broad leather strap which goes over the horse's back to support chains from the *hames* to the implement.
Back-chain – see *ridger chain*.
Balance plough – plough with two sets of handles, *beam*, *mould-board*, *coulter* and *share*, fixed at 90 degrees to each other. At the *headland* the plough is tipped up to bring the other set into use.
Bass – also known as *raffia*, used to *plait* or *braid* up a horse's mane and tail. Also excellent beer, brewed in Burton on Trent and supporter of heavy horses!
Beam – the spine or main section of the plough, to which the handles are attached.
Bearer – in forestry, pole laid on ground before stacking to keep timber off the ground and assist drying out or subsequent loading.
Bear trap – in forestry, a metal bar with a curved hook at one end inserted through chains to tighten and secure a load of timber.
Belly-band – see *wanty*.
Bevel – in farriery, method of forging a shoe to give outer border of shoe the same angle as the wall of the hoof.
Blind pass – the ploughman steers horses and plough alongside the ploughed land but without ploughing a further furrow in order to position himself to plough the next furrow alongside the last one ploughed. A blind pass is needed to execute the *finish*.
Blinker – squarish piece of leather attached to the bridle at the position of the horse's eye to prevent him from distraction from vehicles and other activities around him. Not considered necessary by all horsemen, the blinker is nonetheless a traditional part of English harness.
Blow out – expression used to describe the condition of a horse which has been overfed.
Blue – used to describe the hardness of a horse's hoof: a bueish tinge indicates a particularly hard hoof, appropriate especially in the case of the Percheron breed. See also *flinty*.
Boat – boat-shaped weight dragged alongside the *mould-board* to press and smooth the furrow-slice previously cut: particularly used to put a 'polish' on *high-cut* ploughing.
Bond – in wheelwrighting, the iron tyre around the outside of a wheel.
Box – box seat, dicky seat: the seat on a dray or other horse-drawn vehicle on which the driver sits.
Braid – see *plait*.
Brash – in forestry, waste branches from poles and timber trees. Also *lop and top*.
Breaking harness – used in the initial stages of breaking a horse to harness.
Breakover – the point at which the horse's toe takes over from the heel to enable the foot to lift away. The way in which a horse's shoe is forged can correct poor action at this point.
Breast – another name for *mould-board* on a plough.
Breast-yoke – in pair driving, cross-bar at the front end of the *pole* to which the *pole straps* are attached to support the pole at the bottom of the horse's collar.
Breeching(s) – breech, breech band. Broad leather strap which sits around the horse's rear; allows the horse to brake or reverse the vehicle or implement he is pulling.
Broken work – ploughing so that the furrow-slice is broken as it is turned using a sharply curving *mould-board*, sometimes with fins or blades attached to divide the slice as it passes.
Brush – where a horse's hooves touch each other in progression. Can result in worn hair or cut *fetlocks*, or even broken skin. Also *cut*.
Bunkhead – in forestry, crosspiece of metal on top of implement on which timber is placed for extraction. Used in conjunction with chains to tighten and secure load.
Butt/s – in forestry, the stump end rather than

the top end of the stem of a tree. In ploughing, short furrows taking up odd areas beyond, or linking, the main ploughed areas.

Cage – in wheelwrighting, the metal bond, which fits around the *stock* or *hub* of a wheel, through which the spokes are fitted to the hub.

Cannon – see illustration 1.20.

Cant – see *land* or *plot*.

Cast, to get – when a horse finds it difficult or impossible to get up after lying down or rolling because it cannot straighten its front legs out: usually occurs in a loose box or stall where space is confined.

Casting off – see *splitting*, *throwing out*.

Canvasses – canvas sheets used on a binder to propel the cut crop to the *knotter* mechanism to form a sheaf.

Capped elbow – where a horse injures its elbow with a shod hoof, leading to enlargement of the joint: usually occurs in a loose box or stall where space is confined.

Capped hock – where a horse injures its *hock* through strain or injury usually through lack of straw in a loose box.

Caulkins – forged upright projections on the heels of the hind shoes to enable the horse to grip when going downhill or backing a load.

Chamfer – moulding made by a chisel on edges of timber used in wooden vehicles.

Chine – the raised ridge on a Scottish saddle, higher than that on an English saddle.

Chipping share – a special *share* shaped like a small *mould-board* used to make the *scratch furrows* in an opening in *high-cut ploughing*.

Choke chain (or choker) – chain which tightens firmly against load (i.e. of timber) when horse moves off.

Clenching up – in farriery, hammering projecting nail from shoe over and into the upper face of the hoof.

Clincher – on some horse-drawn vehicles, metal sections used to clamp *felloes* of wheels to their tight-fitting rubber tyres.

Close-coupled – see *short-coupled*.

Cobbletree – a three-horse *whipple tree* or *swingle tree* used to even out draught. Term used mainly in Yorkshire.

Colic – the symptoms of abdominal pain brought on by a variety of factors from eating too fast to twisted gut.

Conformation – the way the horse is formed physically.

Coronet – See illustration 1.20.

Coulter – see *knife coulter*.

Crest – the top line of a horse's neck.

Crook – see *hame crook*.

Cross-shaft – metal shaft at right angle to line of plough which holds the two wheels.

Croup – The area between the horse's tail and the loin. See illustration 1.20.

Crown – the first 3-5 furrows each side of the *opening*. See also *top*.

Crupper strap – a leather strap which runs down the centre of a horse's back from the collar to the top of his rump, ending in a crupper loop through which the tail or dock is threaded.

Cut – see *brush*.

Cutter – a timber-cutting contractor or feller.

Dee – the 'D' shaped ring on harness to which leather straps or chains are attached.

Dish (ed) – the saucer-shape of some wheels. Also the angle at which a horse throws his front feet outwards as he moves. Careful shoeing can assist a horse with bad dishing.

Dock – the base of the horse's tail. See illustration 1.20.

Donkeyed out – where a horse's heel is set out at an angle. Careful shoeing can correct poor action.

Drag shoe – a heavy channel-shaped piece of metal attached to a chain on a waggon used to wedge a back wheel to prevent the vehicle from moving on slopes. Used in conjunction with a tie chain attached to a waggon to tie the wheel.

Draught chains – long chains either side of the horse, attached to *hame* hooks and to implement to be used.

Drawbar – metal bar which allows a tractor implement to be pulled by a hitchcart.

Dray – horse-drawn vehicle used for delivering beer. Most modern heavy horse turnouts are shown with a dray.

Dressing out – see *snedding*.

Drop-pole – an unsupported pole attached to the front of a horse-drawn vehicle, the weight of which is carried on the horse's collar. Generally used with American-design pair harness.

Eveners – American word also used in this country for the system of evening out draught pull of horses in multiple hitches using *swingle trees* in different formations.

Feather – the silky hair around the *cannon* of Shires and Clydesdales.

FEI – Fédération Equestre Internationale, the governing body of international equestrian sport.

Felloes – curved wooden sections used to form the outside of a wheel.

Fenders – in forestry, poles placed along extraction route to prevent damage to remaining crop.

Fetlock – see illustration 1.20.

Fingers – pointed metal fixtures to support cutting knives on mowing machines and binders.

Finish – in ploughing, the last part of the area to be ploughed, consisting of three *rounds* and the *sole furrow*.

Flags – shaped (usually tulip-shaped) ribbons attached to wire used to decorate a plaited mane or tail. See also *flights*, *standards*.

Flange – metal bar on some timber arches round which chains can be wound, attached to felled timber to be extracted.

Flights – see *flags, standards.*

Flinty – see *blue.*

Forearms – See illustration 1.20.

Forewale – part of the collar; hard leather strip filled with rye straw with rounded profile attached to the front of the collar giving it rigidity. The *hames* sit between it and the body of the collar.

Forwarder – in forestry, implement used for extracting felled produce which is loaded onto a trailer and carried out of the wood.

Foursome – word used to describe the traditional Clydesdale mane plait in which two strands of the *roller* and two sections of hair are used along the length of the *plait.*

Frog – rubbery triangular pad of horn on the underside of the hoof which acts as a support and shock absorber.

Fullered – a shoe which has had a fuller or groove cut into the metal to receive nails to achieve better grip. Used mostly in Scotland.

Furrow wheel – the larger of the two wheels on a plough, which travels within the furrow.

Gaskin – see illustration 1.20.

Gather – ploughing around the *opening* or first furrows by continuously turning right at the *headlands.* This always turns the furrow-slice towards the opening. See *splitting.*

Gearing – arrangement of cog wheels and shafts used for driving agricultural machinery.

General purpose ploughing – type of ploughing which produces a broken furrow which can be easily harrowed to form a seed bed.

Girth strap – leather strap on cart saddle or pad secured by a buckle, which goes around the horse's belly just behind the front legs.

Goose rumped – a horse with a sloping rump; where he 'slopes off the back'.

Grease – common ailment of horse's lower leg, but usually applies only to feathered breeds; sore patches exuding pus appear among the silky hair, exacerbated by rich food.

Grit furrow – see *sole furrow, mould furrow.*

Ground-drive – where an implement is driven by a mechanism deriving its power from the wheels in contact with the ground.

Ground-skidding – dragging felled timber along the ground with a chain attached to the *whipple tree* behind the horse.

Hake – device on the front end of the plough *beam* which allows vertical and horizontal adjustment at the point of attachment of the *draught chains.*

Hames – curved lengths of wood, metal or a combination of the two which sit between the *forewale* and the body of the collar, fixed tightly top and bottom and which hold the chains or *traces* to attach to vehicles or implements.

Hame crook – hook or dog-leg shaped piece of metal which links into a short piece of chain to adjust fitting of the *hames* at the base of the collar.

Hand – unit of measurement to describe a horse's height. One hand is 4 in. (10 cm).

Happers – implement used in planting potatoes.

Headland – the area at either end of the furrows between the ploughed area and the edge of the field, allowing space for the horse team and plough to be turned. It is usually ploughed by going round and round the field after the rest of the field has been ploughed.

Hepatopathy – liver damage produced by toxins, e.g. ragwort poisoning.

High-cut ploughing – ploughing which turns a *furrow-slice* that stands as high as its width and gives a relatively narrow furrow, between 5 and 7 in. wide. These close-packed, sharp-angled furrows best accept seed sown broadcast (by hand) and weather best through winter on soil prone to puddling. Also called an *oat seed furrow.*

Hitch/hitching in – the act of harnessing a draught horse to a vehicle or implement: see also *putting to.*

Hocks – See illustration 1.20.

Hold-back strap – strap used in American pair harness which is buckled to the breeching, passing in front of the back legs and under the stomach, and clipped to the breast strap between the horse's front legs.

Homozygous – where genes leading to a particular characteristic have been drawn from both parents.

Hoof head – the very top of the hoof where the *coronet* band meets the hair roots. Thickening the hair here with soap is sometimes done by showmen to give the feather a thicker appearance.

Housen – a rectangular piece of leather attached above the collar used to flatten against horse's shoulders in bad weather to prevent rain penetrating behind the collar.

Hub – or *stock*, the centre section of a wheel which holds the spokes and joins onto the axle of a horse-drawn vehicle.

In-hand – method of showing a horse for his conformation where the animal is led round the show ring by his handler.

Ins and outs – the point where the plough share enters and leaves the ground at the *headland.* Should be well in line with the *headland furrow* so that the headland ploughing neatly completes the job.

Journey – one day's ploughing.
Jug handle – a ring of plaited raffia stiffened by wire, pre-prepared or ready-bought and inserted into the top of a Shire tail bun.

Keeper – a small piece of leather around straps used in conjunction with the buckle to secure the ends of leather straps.
Keys – specialised bit, with metal keys on it used to accustom a young horse to wearing bits (known as mouthing).
Knife coulter – part of a plough, which makes the vertical cut in the soil when ploughing.
Knotters – mechanism on a binder used to knot bundles of crops during harvesting.

Laminitis – inflammation of the sensitive laminae in the foot, most frequently associated with rapidly growing grass.
Land – in ploughing, the area beside the furrow not yet ploughed, hence *land-side, furrow-side* etc. The land horse is the one that walks on the unploughed land; the furrow horse walks in the furrow.
Landing – in forestry, timber stacking area ('bing' in Scotland).
Land-side – the side of the furrow towards the unploughed land, against which the vertical part of the *slade* presses.
Landslide – the vertical part of the *slade.*
Land wheel – the smaller of the two wheels on a plough which travels on the unploughed land and determines the depth of ploughing.
Leader – the lead horse when two or more are used in line.
Ledger plates – the plates (surfaces) against which a mower knife cuts: they must be kept sharp.
Lines – ropes used as reins to drive horses.
Line-thin – in forestry, straight line of trees felled to enable machines to enter and exit for extraction purposes.
Lining fitch – extra-long brush used to put decorative lines on horse-drawn vehicles.
Long gears – another name for trace harness.
Long-reining – a common way of exercising and training all horses, this involves a horse on a very long single rein being put through his paces in a circle around the horseman.
Lop and top – see *brash.*
Martingale – leather strap attached to the bottom joint of the *hames* at one end and to the *girth strap* at the other on which decorative brasses can be hung.
Match ploughing – ploughing according to specific rules drawn up for competitive matches
Mastitis – inflammation of the mammary glands brought on by infection, usually at foaling time

Meeter strap – short leather stap from top of *hames* to the cart saddle or pad which keeps the pad from slipping back and the collar from slipping forward.
Mesentery – the membrane which suspends the intestine inside the abdomen.
Mollassed – Where liquid sugar or mollasses has been added. This provides a lot of energy to the feed and also helps digestion.
Mould – the section of earth turned over by the plough.
Mould-board – the conspicuously curving plate on the plough that turns the cut *furrow-slice* over. Also called the *breast, wing* or *turn-furrow.*
Mould furrow – the last furrow to be turned in a *finish* (two-thirds the way up normal ploughing). See also *sole furrow, grit furrow.*

Nap, (to) – when a horse will not obey commands.
Nearside – on the left.
Nosebag – hessian bag strengthened with leather and a strap to tie around horse's neck filled with feed for the horse during a break in work. Little used in modern times but essential part of dressing *turnout* vehicles in showing.

Offside – on the right.
Opening – the first operation in ploughing, consisting of two *scratch* furrows which support the first full furrow-slices at the correct angle. Also called a *veering.*
Overdone – a horse which has been fed excessively.
Over-reach – an action fault where a horse's back feet reach beyond the imprint of the front feet.
Oat seed furrow – another name for *high-cut* ploughing.

Packing – describes how well the turned furrow-slices press against each other to make good *seams.* Bad packing would let broadcast seeds fall through the seam; it would also encourage growth of weeds turned in.
Pasterns – see illustration 1.20.
Pedal bone – see illustration 1.20.
Piebald – colour of a horse, where the coat is patched in black and white.
Pigeon-toed – where toes of a horse turn inwards.
Pitman pivots – connecting rod from gearbox to knife in a mowing machine or binder.
Plait (plaiting up) – decorating a horse's mane. Bound tightly at one end, the plait is divided into three to be plaited with sections of the horse's hair to decorate the mane. Made of

raffia, raffia and ribbon or wool and about 61 cm long. See also *braid* and *roller*.

Plot – the area, in a ploughing match, which the competitor has to plough.

Plug stud – tungsten pin recessed into a soft metal stud in the horse's shoe. Used to prevent slipping.

Point – another name for *share*, *shear* or *sock*.

Point of draught – the point on its body at which the horse takes the strain of drawing an implement or vehicle.

Pole – long single timber pole attached to the centre front of a horse-drawn vehicle which is to be pulled by a pair of horses.

Pole arch – see *timber arch*.

Pole lock – lock used to attach pole straps to the pole in pair or team driving. Quick-release locks, such as Shepherd's locks are recommended.

Pole strap – strap wrapped around the base of the collar and *hames* and attached to either end of the *breast yoke* holding the pole up.

Poll evil – infection of the back of the head, most frequently caused by banging head on entering low stable; like tennis elbow.

Postilion – where a horseman rides on the near-side horse of a pair, or on one of the nearside horses in a team to drive or work them.

Post partum merritis – disease of the uterus after mare has given birth.

Press wheel – solid discus-shaped wheel which follows the plough to press the *seams* tight in *high-cut* ploughing, ready to take broadcast seed.

Private driving – driving a horse for pleasure, this is a term usually applied to light horses driven to gigs and carriages. In transport law, it refers specifically to motor vehicles driven for private, not commercial, use.

Pulp hook – in forestry, timber lifting aid.

Putting to – see *hitch/hitching in*.

Putt – two-wheeled dung cart.

Quarters – see illustration 1.20.

Quidding – where a horse with dental problems cannot chew its food properly and balls of food drop from its mouth.

Rack – in forestry, a route for extraction in a stand of trees, formed by felling a line of trees.

Raffia – see *bass*.

Ratchet – bar with set of teeth in which metal lug engages to ensure motion in one direction only.

Raves – front, back and sometimes side ladders used to support a large load on a cart or waggon.

Reversible plough – throws the furrow slice to the left or the right, so there is only one *ridge* and no open furrows or *finishes*. The plough-

man reverses the throw of the furrow when he turns at the *headland*, laying each furrow in the same direction over the whole field.

Ride – in forestry, unmetalled woodland road or track, often separating stands of timber, suitable for extraction at certain times of the year if soft, or all year round if well drained.

Ridge – in ploughing , a number of *rounds* (usually 5 – 10 furrows) around the *opening*, also called a backing.

Ridger chain – chain which sits across the top of a cart saddle or pad and is attached either side to metal furniture on *shafts* to support it. See also *back chain*.

Rig/rig work – sections of ploughing within a field, measuring 8-18 yds each, set out across the field to break it up into efficiently sized pieces for the ploughman to plough without having to walk too far to make the next furrow.

Roan – often strawberry or blue roan, a horse's colour, found in Clydesdales or Ardennes in which the coat is flecked with white hairs interspersed.

Roller – name given to the mane *plait* in Scotland. Bound tightly at one end, the rest is divided into two to be plaited with sections of horse's hair to decorate the mane. Also leather strap fixed round the horse's belly as part of stallion harness. Also canvas surcingle used to hold a protective rug in position.

Round – a single pass in the direction of the ploughing. Thus 3-5 rounds around the *opening* forms the *ridge*.

Rulley – see *trolley*.

Sacking out – rubbing an old sack or cloth over the body of a young horse to familiarise him with being touched.

Saw-log – quality high-value timber (minimum 15 cm TDUB) for construction, fencing etc.

Scratch-furrow – the first shallow furrows turned which support the first full furrows.

Scuffler – implement to remove weeds and rubbish prior to ploughing.

Seam – the trough between the laid furrow slices. Good seams are pressed close so that broadcast seeds will not fall through. See *packing*.

Seamer – boat-shaped metal attachment which follows in the *seam* behind the press wheel in *high-cut* ploughing

Second thighs – See illustration 1.20.

Segg plaits – two small upstanding plaits at the top of the tail applied especially to Clydesdales.

Setting out – measuring the area to be ploughed, and marking it with sight poles placed in the headland furrows and, optionally, half way up the plot.

Shafts – pair of wooden poles attached to the front of horse-drawn vehicles or implements between which the horse is hitched for draught.

Shaft hooks – metal furniture on shafts to which the *tug chains*, *ridger* and *breeching chains* are attached.

Shaft skidder – items of forestry equipment, used to remove small specification timber from wood.

Shakes – narrow cracks which appear in wooden vehicles, especially wheels, and indicate fragility.

Share – the blade attached to the frame of the plough which makes the horizontal cut in the soil. Often it is attached to a lever so that the plough may be raised or lowered. Also called a *sock*, *shear* or *point*.

Shear – another name for *share*, *point* or *sock*.

Shelly – when a horse's hoof is inclined to crack and peel.

Short-coupled – where a horse's back is not over long, but 'short' and therefore, strong: usually an advantageous characteristic. See also *close-coupled*.

Shortwood – in forestry, name given to timber felled, prepared, converted and stacked within wood ready for forwarding to the stacking bay.

Sickled – viewed from the side, the angle of the *hock* causes the hind legs to be shaped like a sickle tool underneath the body and denotes weakness.

Sidling ground – in forestry, steep sloping ground.

Skid – in ploughing, a piece of metal to take the place of the land wheel where tramlines or uneven ground cause the small wheel to leap out of place.

Skidding – in forestry, extracting felled produce by lifting one end and dragging it out to be converted.

Skimmer – device in front of the *coulter* to collect weeds and push them into the bottom of the furrow.

Skim coulter – see *skimmer*.

Skylines – mechanised non-horse power method of extracting timber from steep slopes, using pulleys and levers anchored at either end of the slope.

Slade – a right-angled metal section consisting of the *sole* and *land-side* of the plough, fastened to the bottom of the frame.

Snedding – in forestry, taking branches off a felled tree flush with the main stem. Also dressing out.

Snigging – pulling timber along the ground, with long gears. Also *tushing*.

Sock – another word for *share, shear* or *point*.

Sod – the long strip of soil cut, lifted and turned by the plough. Also called furrow-slice.

Sole furrow – see *mould furrow, grit furrow*.

Sole (plate) – the base of the plough which slides along the bottom of the furrow.

Spavin – osteo-arthritis of the hock joint; where the strain of ligaments forces the joint together and extra bone is formed.

Splinter bar – cross-bar at the rear of a fixed pole on a waggon to which the *traces* are hitched.

Splitting – ploughing land so that the furrow-slice is turned away each side of the *finish* by turning left at the *headland* and going around the diminishing area of land to be ploughed. Also called *throwing out* or *casting off*. The usual way of ploughing is to complete a *gather* around the *opening* and then split the rest of the *land* or *cant*.

Sprags – jagged branch ends still attached to a tree after felling which must be removed before extraction for safety and efficiency.

Spreader bar – another name for *stretcher*. Used to keep draught chains apart at the back of a horse in *traces*.

Stanchions – upright pillars at four corners of some forestry equipment to keep load of timber in place.

Stand – a compartment or parcel of trees between *rides*.

Standing – as in 'standing a horse up' into his collar and harness: the horse is told to step forward a pace or two to allow the harness to settle and the horseman to check that all is correctly adjusted in relation to the vehicle.

Standard – see *flag* and *flight*.

Stand show – in showing, individual competitors walk and trot their horse before the judge, in front of the stand where spectators sit.

Staples – metal fittings on *hames* through which the hame strap is threaded.

Stilts – metal arms on a plough to which the wooden handles bolt and are used to steer the plough.

Stock – see *hub*.

Stretcher – see *spreader bar*.

Swing plough – plough with no wheels but longer handles and a shorter *beam*, giving more leverage. Once common in Wales and Scotland.

Swingle tree – shaped length of wood or metal bar used to keep chains apart at the back of a horse and to attach implements. Can be used in various formations for multiple hitches. Also known as *whipple tree*.

TDUB – 'top diameter under bark' – a method of timber measurement in forestry.

Ted – in haymaking, the fluffing up of hay to allow it to dry.

Terret – the ring on the *hames*, saddle or pad through which the rein passes.

Throat latch – see illustration 1.20.

Timber arch – in forestry, equipment with an arch above the axle from which felled timber is suspended ready for extraction out of the wood. Also *pole arch*.

Throwing out/off – also known as *splitting*, or *casting off*.

Top – another name for *crown*. 'Tops' of the furrow should be evenly matched. Also, in forestry, the top of a tree.

Traces – draught chains, varying in length, according to which vehicle or implement is being used.

Train weight – the weight allowed by law on a trailer.

Trolley – four-wheel, flat-bed, horse-drawn vehicle.

Tug chains – short draught chains which come in pairs to attach *hames* to *shafts* of vehicle or implement.

Tumbril – a two-wheeled cart, usually of the tipping variety.

Turner – implement used in hay-making to turn the hay crop.

Turn furrow – another name for the *mould-board*.

Turnover plough – another type of plough with two sets of parts. To reverse the action it is turned over sideways with the *beam* as axis. Most popular in the west of England.

Turnout – in showing, the name given to the combination of a horse and horse-drawn vehicle such as a dray or waggon. Turnout classes include: single turnout, pairs turnout etc.

Turntable – or fifth wheel: the mechanism which allows the front axle of a horse-drawn vehicle to turn.

Turnwrest plough – this plough has one *mould-board* with two faces. To reverse the action the plough is tilted through 90 degrees.

Tushing – see *snigging*.

Twist – a twisted bunch of hay or straw used to rub down a sweating horse. Also *wisp*.

Underline – the line of the horse beneath its belly.

Unicorn – formation of horses drawing a vehicle in which two horses are harnessed as a pair to the vehicle and a single horse is attached in front of them by chains and whipple tree.

Veering – another name for *opening*.

Webbing harness – harness made of strong woven fabric, rather than the more traditional leather.

Wanty – or *belly band*, wide leather strap attached to the shafts to prevent them lifting when backing or carrying a tail-heavy load.

Also used to keep draught chains from lifting and causing the horse to choke when working in trace harness.

Wheeler – horse(s) nearest to the vehicle in team driving.

Whipple tree – see *swingle tree*.

Windrow – row of hay gathered together by hay-making implements ready for turning or baling.

Wind-blow – an area where whole or parts of trees have been blown down by strong wind.

Wing – device on digger ploughs in front of the *mould-board* on the *land-side* of the *share* which carves out the slicing motion in the furrow bottom.

Wisp – see *twist*.

Withers – see illustration 1.20.

Workings – events at which horsemen and their supporters gather together to display and enjoy traditional and modern horse-drawn activity.

Yoke strap – v-shaped strap attached to the *hames* which hitches the horse to the *breast-yoke*. Mostly used in American harness.

Index

Note: pages on which diagrams (of equipment etc.) occur are indicated in the text by **bold** type